HALSBURY'S
Laws of England

FIFTH EDITION
2013

Volume 38

This is volume 38 of the Fifth Edition of Halsbury's Laws of England, containing the second part of the title ELECTIONS AND REFERENDUMS.

The title ELECTIONS AND REFERENDUMS replaces the Fourth Edition title ELECTIONS AND REFERENDUMS, contained in vol 15(3) (2007 Reissue) and vol 15(4) (2007 Reissue). Both of those Fourth Edition volumes have been completely replaced and may now be archived.

For a full list of volumes comprised in a current set of Halsbury's Laws of England please see overleaf.

Fifth Edition volumes:

1 (2008), 2 (2008), 3 (2011), 4 (2011), 5 (2013), 6 (2011), 7 (2008), 8 (2010), 9 (2012), 10 (2012), 11 (2009), 12 (2009), 13 (2009), 14 (2009), 15 (2009), 16 (2011), 17 (2011), 18 (2009), 19 (2011), 21 (2011), 22 (2012), 23 (2013), 24 (2010), 25 (2010), 26 (2010), 27 (2010), 28 (2010), 30 (2012), 31 (2012), 32 (2012), 33 (2013), 34 (2011), 35 (2011), 36 (2011), 37 (2013), 38 (2013), 38A (2013), 39 (2009), 40 (2009), 41 (2009), 42 (2011), 43 (2011), 44 (2011), 45 (2010), 46 (2010), 48 (2008), 49 (2008), 50 (2008), 51 (2013), 52 (2009), 53 (2009), 54 (2008), 55 (2012), 56 (2011), 57 (2012), 60 (2011), 61 (2010), 62 (2012), 63 (2012), 64 (2012), 65 (2008), 66 (2009), 67 (2008), 68 (2008), 69 (2009), 70 (2012), 71 (2013), 72 (2009), 73 (2009), 74 (2011), 75 (2013), 76 (2013), 77 (2010), 78 (2010), 79 (2008), 80 (2013), 81 (2010), 82 (2010), 83 (2010), 84 (2013), 84A (2013), 85 (2012), 86 (2013), 87 (2012), 88 (2012), 88A (2013), 89 (2011), 90 (2011), 91 (2012), 92 (2010), 93 (2008), 94 (2008), 95 (2013), 96 (2012), 97 (2010), 98 (2013), 99 (2012), 100 (2009), 101 (2009), 102 (2010), 103 (2010)

Fourth Edition volumes (bold figures represent reissues):

1(1) (2001 Reissue), **8(1)** (2003 Reissue), 8(2), **12(1)**, 16(2), 17(2), 23(1), 23(2), 24, 39(1B), **48** (2007 Reissue), 51, 52

Additional Materials:

Housing (*Housing Benefit*) containing vol **22** (2006 Reissue) paras 140–186; *Sentencing and Disposition of Offenders* (*Release and Recall of Prisoners*) containing vol **92** (2010) paras 761–820; *Tort* (*Conversion and Wrongful Interference with Goods*) containing vol **45(2)** (Reissue) paras 542–686

Fourth and Fifth Edition volumes:

2013 Consolidated Index (A–E), 2013 Consolidated Index (F–O), 2013 Consolidated Index (P–Z), 2014 Consolidated Table of Statutes, 2014 Consolidated Table of Statutory Instruments, etc, 2014 Consolidated Table of Cases (A–G), 2014 Consolidated Table of Cases (H–Q), 2014 Consolidated Table of Cases (R–Z, ECJ Cases)

Updating and ancillary materials:

2013 Annual Cumulative Supplement; Monthly Current Service; Annual Abridgments 1974–2012

December 2013

HALSBURY'S
Laws of England

FIFTH EDITION

LORD MACKAY OF CLASHFERN

Lord High Chancellor of Great Britain
1987–97

Volume 38

2013

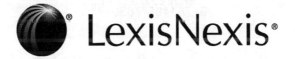

Members of the LexisNexis Group worldwide

United Kingdom	LexisNexis, a Division of Reed Elsevier (UK) Ltd, Lexis House, 30 Farringdon Street, LONDON, EC4A 4HH, and London House, 20–22 East London Street, EDINBURGH, EH7 4BQ
Australia	LexisNexis Butterworths, Chatswood, New South Wales
Austria	LexisNexis Verlag ARD Orac GmbH & Co KG, Vienna
Benelux	LexisNexis Benelux, Amsterdam
Canada	LexisNexis Canada, Markham, Ontario
China	LexisNexis China, Beijing and Shanghai
France	LexisNexis SA, Paris
Germany	LexisNexis GmbH, Dusseldorf
Hong Kong	LexisNexis Hong Kong, Hong Kong
India	LexisNexis India, New Delhi
Italy	Giuffrè Editore, Milan
Japan	LexisNexis Japan, Tokyo
Malaysia	Malayan Law Journal Sdn Bhd, Kuala Lumpur
New Zealand	LexisNexis NZ Ltd, Wellington
Poland	Wydawnictwo Prawnicze LexisNexis Sp, Warsaw
Singapore	LexisNexis Singapore, Singapore
South Africa	LexisNexis Butterworths, Durban
USA	LexisNexis, Dayton, Ohio

FIRST EDITION	*Published in 31 volumes between 1907 and 1917*
SECOND EDITION	*Published in 37 volumes between 1931 and 1942*
THIRD EDITION	*Published in 43 volumes between 1952 and 1964*
FOURTH EDITION	*Published in 56 volumes between 1973 and 1987, with reissues between 1988 and 2008*
FIFTH EDITION	*Commenced in 2008*

A CIP Catalogue record for this book is available from the British Library.

ISBN 13 (complete set, standard binding): 9781405734394

ISBN 13: 9781405763677

ISBN 978-1-4057-6367-7

Typeset by Letterpart Limited, Caterham on the Hill, Surrey CR3 5XL
Printed and bound by CPI Group (UK) Ltd, Croydon, CR0 4YY
Visit LexisNexis at www.lexisnexis.co.uk

Editor in Chief

THE RIGHT HONOURABLE

LORD MACKAY OF CLASHFERN

LORD HIGH CHANCELLOR OF GREAT BRITAIN

1987–97

ELECTIONS AND REFERENDUMS

Consultant Editor

RICHARD PRICE, LLB, OBE, QC,

Bencher of the Honourable Society of Gray's Inn

The law stated in this volume is in general that in force on 1 November 2013, although subsequent changes have been included wherever possible.

Any future updating material will be found in the Current Service and annual Cumulative Supplement to Halsbury's Laws of England.

TABLE OF CONTENTS

HOW TO USE HALSBURY'S LAWS OF ENGLAND

Volumes

Each text volume of Halsbury's Laws of England contains the law on the titles contained in it as at a date stated at the front of the volume (the operative date).

Information contained in Halsbury's Laws of England may be accessed in several ways.

First, by using the tables of contents.

Each volume contains both a general Table of Contents, and a specific Table of Contents for each title contained in it. From these tables you will be directed to the relevant part of the work.

Readers should note that the current arrangement of titles can be found in the Current Service.

Secondly, by using tables of statutes, statutory instruments, cases or other materials.

If you know the name of the Act, statutory instrument or case with which your research is concerned, you should consult the Consolidated Tables of statutes, cases and so on (published as separate volumes) which will direct you to the relevant volume and paragraph. The Consolidated Tables will indicate if the volume referred to is a Fifth Edition volume.

(Each individual text volume also includes tables of those materials used as authority in that volume.)

Thirdly, by using the indexes.

If you are uncertain of the general subject area of your research, you should go to the Consolidated Index (published as separate volumes) for reference to the relevant volume(s) and paragraph(s). The Consolidated Index will indicate if the volume referred to is a Fifth Edition volume.

(Each individual text volume also includes an index to the material contained therein.)

Additional Materials

The reorganisation of the title scheme of Halsbury's Laws for the Fifth Edition means that from time to time Fourth Edition volumes will be *partially* replaced by Fifth Edition volumes.

In certain instances an Additional Materials softbound book will be issued, in which will be reproduced material which has not yet been replaced by a Fifth Edition title. This will enable users to remove specific Fourth Edition volumes from the shelf and save valuable space pending the replacement of that material in the Fifth Edition. These softbound books are supplied to volumes subscribers free of charge. They continue to form part of the set of Halsbury's Laws Fourth Edition Reissue, and will be updated by the annual Cumulative Supplement and monthly Noter-Up in the usual way.

Updating publications

The text volumes of Halsbury's Laws should be used in conjunction with the annual Cumulative Supplement and the monthly Noter-Up.

The annual Cumulative Supplement

The Supplement gives details of all changes between the operative date of the text volume and the operative date of the Supplement. It is arranged in the same volume, title and paragraph order as the text volumes. Developments affecting particular points of law are noted to the relevant paragraph(s) of the text volumes. As from the commencement of the Fifth Edition, the Supplement will clearly distinguish between Fourth and Fifth Edition titles.

For narrative treatment of material noted in the Cumulative Supplement, go to the Annual Abridgment volume for the relevant year.

Destination Tables

In certain titles in the annual *Cumulative Supplement,* reference is made to Destination Tables showing the destination of consolidated legislation. Those Destination Tables are to be found either at the end of the titles within the annual *Cumulative Supplement,* or in a separate *Destination Tables* booklet provided from time to time with the *Cumulative Supplement.*

The Noter-Up

The Noter-Up is contained in the Current Service Noter-Up booklet, issued monthly and noting changes since the publication of the annual Cumulative Supplement. Also arranged in the same volume, title and paragraph order as the text volumes, the Noter-Up follows the style of the Cumulative Supplement. As from the commencement of the Fifth Edition, the Noter-Up will clearly distinguish between Fourth and Fifth Edition titles.

For narrative treatment of material noted in the Noter-Up, go to the relevant Monthly Review.

REFERENCES AND ABBREVIATIONS

ACT	Australian Capital Territory
A-G	Attorney General
Admin	Administrative Court
Admlty	Admiralty Court
Adv-Gen	Advocate General
affd	affirmed
affg	affirming
Alta	Alberta
App	Appendix
art	article
Aust	Australia
B	Baron
BC	British Columbia
C	Command Paper (of a series published before 1900)
c	chapter number of an Act
CA	Court of Appeal
CAC	Central Arbitration Committee
CA in Ch	Court of Appeal in Chancery
CB	Chief Baron
CCA	Court of Criminal Appeal
CCR	County Court Rules 1981 (SI 1981/1687) as subsequently amended
CCR	Court for Crown Cases Reserved
C-MAC	Courts-Martial Appeal Court
CO	Crown Office
COD	Crown Office Digest
CPR	Civil Procedure Rules 1998 (SI 1998/3132) as subsequently amended (see the Civil Court Practice)
Can	Canada
Cd	Command Paper (of the series published 1900–18)
Cf	compare
Ch	Chancery Division
ch	chapter
cl	clause

Cm	Command Paper (of the series published 1986 to date)
Cmd	Command Paper (of the series published 1919–56)
Cmnd	Command Paper (of the series published 1956–86)
Comm	Commercial Court
Comr	Commissioner
Court Forms (2nd Edn)..........	Atkin's Encyclopaedia of Court Forms in Civil Proceedings, 2nd Edn. See note 2 post.
Court Funds Rules 1987	Court Funds Rules 1987 (SI 1987/821) as subsequently amended
CrimPR	Criminal Procedure Rules 2010 (SI 2010/60) as subsequently amended
DC..	Divisional Court
DPP	Director of Public Prosecutions
EAT	Employment Appeal Tribunal
EC	European Community
ECJ..	Court of Justice of the European Community
EComHR..............................	European Commission of Human Rights
ECSC..	European Coal and Steel Community
ECtHR Rules of Court..........	Rules of Court of the European Court of Human Rights
EEC..	European Economic Community
EFTA	European Free Trade Association
EWCA Civ	Official neutral citation for judgments of the Court of Appeal (Civil Division)
EWCA Crim..........................	Official neutral citation for judgments of the Court of Appeal (Criminal Division)
EWHC..............................	Official neutral citation for judgments of the High Court
Edn..	Edition
Euratom	European Atomic Energy Community
Ex Ch..	Court of Exchequer Chamber
ex p	ex parte
Fam	Family Division
Fed	Federal
Forms & Precedents (5th Edn)..	Encyclopaedia of Forms and Precedents other than Court Forms, 5th Edn. See note 2 post.
GLC	Greater London Council
HC	High Court
HC	House of Commons
HK	Hong Kong
HL..	House of Lords

IAT	Immigration Appeal Tribunal
ILM	International Legal Materials
INLR	Immigration and Nationality Law Reports
IRC	Inland Revenue Commissioners
Ind	India
Int Rels	International Relations
Ir	Ireland
J	Justice
JA	Judge of Appeal
Kan	Kansas
LA	Lord Advocate
LC	Lord Chancellor
LCC	London County Council
LCJ	Lord Chief Justice
LJ	Lord Justice of Appeal
LoN	League of Nations
MR	Master of the Rolls
Man	Manitoba
n	note
NB	New Brunswick
NI	Northern Ireland
NS	Nova Scotia
NSW	New South Wales
NY	New York
NZ	New Zealand
OHIM	Office for Harmonisation in the Internal Market
OJ	The Official Journal of the European Community published by the Office for Official Publications of the European Community
Ont	Ontario
P	President
PC	Judicial Committee of the Privy Council
PEI	Prince Edward Island
Pat	Patents Court
q	question
QB	Queen's Bench Division
QBD	Queen's Bench Division of the High Court
Qld	Queensland
Que	Quebec
r	rule
RDC	Rural District Council
RPC	Restrictive Practices Court

RSC	Rules of the Supreme Court 1965 (SI 1965/1776) as subsequently amended
reg	regulation
Res	Resolution
revsd	reversed
Rly	Railway
s	section
SA	South Africa
S Aust	South Australia
SC	Supreme Court
SI	Statutory Instruments published by authority
SR & O	Statutory Rules and Orders published by authority
SR & O Rev 1904	Revised Edition comprising all Public and General Statutory Rules and Orders in force on 31 December 1903
SR & O Rev 1948	Revised Edition comprising all Public and General Statutory Rules and Orders and Statutory Instruments in force on 31 December 1948
SRNI	Statutory Rules of Northern Ireland
STI	Simon's Tax Intelligence (1973–1995); Simon's Weekly Tax Intelligence (1996-current)
Sask	Saskatchewan
Sch	Schedule
Sess	Session
Sing	Singapore
TCC	Technology and Construction Court
TS	Treaty Series
Tanz	Tanzania
Tas	Tasmania
UDC	Urban District Council
UKHL	Official neutral citation for judgments of the House of Lords
UKPC	Official neutral citation for judgments of the Privy Council
UN	United Nations
V-C	Vice-Chancellor
Vict	Victoria
W Aust	Western Australia
Zimb	Zimbabwe

NOTE 1. A general list of the abbreviations of law reports and other sources used in this work can be found at the beginning of the Consolidated Table of Cases.

NOTE 2. Where references are made to other publications, the volume number precedes and the page number follows the name of the publication; eg the reference '12 Forms & Precedents (5th Edn) 44' refers to volume 12 of the Encyclopaedia of Forms and Precedents, page 44.

NOTE 3. An English statute is cited by short title or, where there is no short title, by regnal year and chapter number together with the name by which it is commonly known or a description of its subject matter and date. In the case of a foreign statute, the mode of citation generally follows the style of citation in use in the country concerned with the addition, where necessary, of the name of the country in parentheses.

NOTE 4. A statutory instrument is cited by short title, if any, followed by the year and number, or, if unnumbered, the date.

TABLE OF STATUTES

TABLE OF STATUTORY INSTRUMENTS

TABLE OF CIVIL PROCEDURE

Practice Directions supplementing Civil Procedure Rules 1998, SI 1998/3132 (CPR)

TABLE OF EUROPEAN UNION LEGISLATION

TABLE OF CONVENTIONS ETC

TABLE OF CASES

Decisions of the European Court of Justice are listed below numerically. These decisions
are also included in the preceding alphabetical list.

ELECTIONS AND REFERENDUMS

VOLUME 37

5. PROCEDURE FOR CONDUCTING ELECTIONS

(4) THE BALLOT

(i) The Voting Systems

339. Elections taking place in a constituency or electoral area. Contested elections for the return of a member to represent a parliamentary constituency[1], a local government electoral area[2] (including a London Assembly constituency[3]) or a Welsh Assembly constituency[4] take place under a voting system where the result is ascertained by counting the votes given to each candidate[5] and the candidate to whom the majority of votes has been given is declared to have been elected[6]. Where, after the counting of the votes (including any recount) is completed, an equality of votes is found to exist between any candidates, and the addition of a vote would entitle any of those candidates to be declared elected, the returning officer must forthwith decide between those candidates by lot, and proceed as if the candidate on whom the lot falls had received an additional vote[7].

1   As to the meaning of 'parliamentary election', and as to the meaning of 'constituency' in the context of a parliamentary election, see PARA 9.
2   As to the meaning of 'local government election', and as to the meaning of 'electoral area' in the context of a local government election, see PARA 11.
3   As to the meaning of 'Assembly constituency' in the context of elections to the London Assembly see PARA 11. As to elections for the return of constituency members of the London Assembly see PARA 199 et seq.
4   As to the meanings of 'constituency election' and 'Assembly constituency' in the context of a Welsh Assembly election see PARA 3 note 2.
5   As to the meaning of 'candidate' generally see PARA 230. Note also the use of the term 'individual candidate' as it is used in the context of regional elections, where party lists operate, to indicate a person standing for election who is not included in the list of candidates of a registered party: see PARA 340. As to the counting of votes at a parliamentary or local government election (except a London Authority election) see PARA 425; in relation to a London Authority election see PARA 444; and in relation to a Welsh Assembly election see PARA 458.
    In the case of a Welsh Assembly constituency election, the result is ascertained under the simple majority system in accordance with the Government of Wales Act 2006 s 6(2), (4) (see PARA 364); and, in the case of the election of an Assembly member for an Assembly constituency, the member is returned under the simple majority system in accordance with the Greater London Authority Act 1999 s 4(1)(b), (4) (see PARA 363).
6   Representation of the People Act 1983 Sch 1 r 18; Local Elections (Principal Areas) (England and Wales) Rules 2006, SI 2006/3304, Sch 2 r 15; Local Elections (Parishes and Communities) (England and Wales) Rules 2006, SI 2006/3305, Sch 2 r 15; National Assembly for Wales (Representation of the People) Order 2007, SI 2007/236, Sch 5 para 23(1), (3); Greater London Authority Elections Rules 2007, SI 2007/3541, Sch 1 r 16. In the case of a local government election, the candidate or candidates to whom more votes have been given than to the other candidates, up to the number of councillors to be elected, is or are declared to have been elected: see the Local Elections (Principal Areas) (England and Wales) Rules 2006, SI 2006/3304, Sch 2 r 15; and the Local Elections (Parishes and Communities) (England and Wales) Rules 2006, SI 2006/3305, Sch 2 r 15.
    This voting system is known variously as the 'simple majority', 'relative majority' or 'first past the post' system: see eg the Government of Wales Act 2006 s 6(2), (4); and CONSTITUTIONAL LAW AND HUMAN RIGHTS. In none of these terms is it to be implied that the successful candidate has to receive more than a certain number (or more than 50%) of the votes cast before he can be declared to be elected.
7   As to parliamentary elections see the Representation of the People Act 1983 Sch 1 r 49 (cited in PARA 434). As to local government elections see the Local Elections (Principal Areas) (England and Wales) Rules 2006, SI 2006/3304, Sch 2 r 49; and the Local Elections (Parishes and Communities) (England and Wales) Rules 2006, SI 2006/3305, Sch 2 r 49 (cited in PARA 434). As to London Assembly constituency elections see the Greater London Authority Elections

Rules 2007, SI 2007/3541, Sch 1 r 53 (cited in PARA 448). As to Welsh Assembly constituency elections see the National Assembly for Wales (Representation of the People) Order 2007, SI 2007/236, Sch 5 para 60 (cited in PARA 463); and CONSTITUTIONAL LAW AND HUMAN RIGHTS.

340. Elections taking place in an electoral region. Where contested elections take place to return London members of the London Assembly[1], or members to represent Welsh Assembly electoral regions[2], or members to represent European parliamentary electoral regions[3], votes are given for the candidates[4] by ballot and the results are ascertained, after counting the votes given to each individual candidate or registered political party, using a 'corrective' system of calculation[5] as follows:

(1) in the case of an 'additional member' system:

    (a) a figure (the 'electoral region figure')[6] for each registered political party[7] is arrived at[8] by adding together the number of electoral region votes[9] given for the party in the constituencies included in the electoral region[10] and dividing the number thereby arrived at by the aggregate of one plus the number of candidates of the party returned as constituency members for any of those constituencies[11]; and

    (b) the electoral region figure for each individual candidate is arrived at[12] by adding together the number of electoral region votes given for that candidate in the constituencies included in the electoral region[13],

    but, in the case of a 'regional list' system, the 'electoral region figure' is simply the number of votes cast for each registered party or candidate;

(2) the first of the seats for the electoral region is allocated to the party or individual candidate with the highest electoral region figure[14];

(3) the second and subsequent seats for the electoral region are allocated to the party or individual candidate with the highest electoral region figure after any required recalculation[15] has been carried out[16].

An individual candidate already returned as a regional member (or, in the case of an election for the return of London members of the London Assembly, as the Mayor of London) is disregarded for the purposes of allocating any but the first seat to regional members[17]. Electoral region seats allocated to a party are filled by the persons on the party's list in the order in which they appear on the list[18], and once a party's list has been exhausted[19] the party is disregarded[20]. However, in the case of the last seat to be allocated, where two or more registered parties or individual candidates have an equal number of votes, and that number is greater than the number of votes of any other party or candidate, one vote must be added to the votes of each party or individual candidate having such an equal number and the operation in head (3) above is reapplied[21]. If, after that, the highest electoral region figure is still the electoral region figure of two or more parties or individual candidates, the appropriate returning officer[22] must forthwith decide between the parties and individual candidates having such an equal number by lot, and allocate the seat to the party or candidate on whom the lot falls[23].

1   As to the meaning of 'London member' see PARA 11 note 5. As to elections for the return of the London members of the London Assembly see PARA 199 et seq; and see LONDON GOVERNMENT vol 71 (2013) PARA 76 et seq.

2   As to the meanings of 'regional election' and 'Assembly electoral region' in the context of a Welsh Assembly election see PARA 3 note 2.

3   As to the establishment of electoral regions (including the 'combined region') for the purpose of elections to the European Parliament see PARA 77. As to European parliamentary elections see PARA 217 et seq.

4   In an election of London members of the London Assembly, of members of the European Parliament ('MEPs'), or of Welsh Assembly regional members, electors may give a vote for:

       (1)   a registered party which has submitted a list of candidates (see the Greater London Authority Act 1999 s 4(1)(c), (5)(a) (cited in PARA 363; and see LONDON GOVERNMENT vol 71 (2013) PARA 78); the European Parliamentary Elections Act 2002 s 2(3), (4) (see PARA 365); and the Government of Wales Act 2006 s 6(3)(a) (see PARA 364; and CONSTITUTIONAL LAW AND HUMAN RIGHTS)); or

       (2)   an individual who is named on the ballot paper as a candidate (see the Greater London Authority Act 1999 s 4(1)(c), (5)(b) (cited in PARA 363; and see LONDON GOVERNMENT vol 71 (2013) PARA 78); the European Parliamentary Elections Act 2002 s 2(3), (4) (cited in PARA 365); and the Government of Wales Act 2006 s 6(3)(b) (see PARA 364; and CONSTITUTIONAL LAW AND HUMAN RIGHTS)).

     As to individual candidates and the submission of lists of candidates to be London members of the London Assembly see PARA 226; and as to references to party lists in elections for the return of London members of the London Assembly see PARA 255 note 23. As to the meaning of 'registered political party' in this context see PARA 226 note 16.

     As to the submission of lists of candidates to be MEPs see PARA 228. As to the meaning of 'list', in the context of a European parliamentary election, see PARA 230 note 29; and as to the meaning of 'individual candidate' see PARA 230 note 32. As to the meaning of 'registered party' for these purposes see PARA 365 note 10.

     As to the meanings of 'constituency candidate' at an Assembly constituency election and 'individual candidate' at a Welsh Assembly regional election see PARA 230 note 19; and as to the meanings of 'party list' and 'party list candidate' see PARA 230 note 23. As to individual candidates and the submission of lists of candidates to be members for a Welsh Assembly region see PARA 227.

5   European Parliamentary Elections Regulations 2004, SI 2004/293, Sch 1 para 21 (Sch 1 substituted by SI 2009/186); National Assembly for Wales (Representation of the People) Order 2007, SI 2007/236, Sch 5 para 23(2), (3); Greater London Authority Elections Rules 2007, SI 2007/3541, Sch 2 r 17. At a Welsh Assembly general election, both constituency and electoral region votes must be given in an Assembly constituency: see the National Assembly for Wales (Representation of the People) Order 2007, SI 2007/236, art 3; and PARA 364. As to the counting of votes at a London Authority election see PARA 444; in relation to a Welsh Assembly election see PARA 458; and as to the counting of votes at a European parliamentary election see PARA 465 et seq.

     The system is known as the 'additional member' system of proportional representation for the election of Welsh Assembly regional members (see the Government of Wales Act 2006 s 6(5)) and as a 'regional list' system for the election of MEPs in a European parliamentary electoral region (see the European Parliamentary Elections Act 2002 s 2(1) (amended by SI 2004/366)). The 'regional list' system is similar to the 'additional member' system but the members elected from a European parliamentary electoral region are not 'additional' to constituency members because that element is absent in such elections. A form of the 'additional member' system is used for the election of London members of the London Assembly. The aim of the 'corrective' system of calculation is to allocate seats in proportion to the overall share of the vote of each party or each candidate in the electoral region. The return of Welsh Assembly regional members for an electoral region at a general election is governed by the Government of Wales Act 2006 ss 8, 9 (see the text and notes 6–23): see s 8(1).

6   See the Government of Wales Act 2006 s 8(5); and the Greater London Authority Act 1999 s 4(6), Sch 2 para 6(3). In the context of an election for the return of London members of the London Assembly, this figure is referred to as the 'London figure': see Sch 2 para 6(3). To apply the prevailing terminology, London constitutes the 'electoral region' for a regional election in which there is only one region, so it can be named specifically.

7   Ie each registered political party by which a list of candidates has been submitted (see note 4).

8   Greater London Authority Act 1999 Sch 2 para 6(3)(a); Government of Wales Act 2006 s 8(5)(a).

9   In the context of an election for the return of London members of the London Assembly, these votes are referred to as 'London votes': see the Greater London Authority Act 1999 ss 4(1)(c), 29; and notes 6–8.

10   Greater London Authority Act 1999 Sch 2 para 6(1)(a); Government of Wales Act 2006 s 8(3)(a).

11 Greater London Authority Act 1999 Sch 2 para 6(1)(b); Government of Wales Act 2006
s 8(3)(b). Accordingly, the persons who are to be returned as the constituency members for each
constituency included in the electoral region (and, in the case of an election for the return of
London members of the London Assembly, the person who is returned as the Mayor of London)
must be determined before it is determined who are to be returned as the regional members for
the electoral region: Greater London Authority Act 1999 s 4(7); Government of Wales Act 2006
s 8(2). As to elections for the return of a Mayor of London see PARA 199.

However, in the context of an election for the return of London members of the London
Assembly, if the poll at the election of an Assembly member for an Assembly constituency is
countermanded or abandoned for any reason, the persons who are to be returned as the London
members must be determined without regard to the determination of the Assembly member for
that Assembly constituency: Greater London Authority Act 1999 s 4(8). If a person who is a
candidate of a registered political party in a London Assembly constituency is returned as the
Assembly member for the constituency and is also returned as the Mayor of London, that
person counts for the purposes of calculating the aggregate number in head (1)(a) in the text as
a candidate of the party returned as a constituency member, notwithstanding that a vacancy
arises in the Assembly constituency by virtue of s 4(10) (person returned as Mayor of London
also returned as Assembly constituency member: see PARA 341): see Sch 2 para 6(4). Also, if the
number of London votes for each registered political party arrived at in head (1)(a) in the text
(ie in the case of a registered political party) is not more than 5% of the total number of London
votes polled by all the registered political parties and all the individual candidates at the election,
none of the seats for London members is allocated to that party (Sch 2 para 7(1)(a)), and that
party is accordingly left out of account for the purposes of heads (2) and (3) in the text (Sch 2
para 7(1)(a), (2)).

12 Greater London Authority Act 1999 Sch 2 para 6(3)(b); Government of Wales Act 2006
s 8(5)(b).

13 Greater London Authority Act 1999 Sch 2 para 6(2); Government of Wales Act 2006 s 8(4).

In the context of an election for the return of London members of the London Assembly, if
the number of London votes for an individual candidate arrived at under head (1)(b) in the text
(ie in the case of an individual candidate) is not more than 5% of the total number of London
votes polled by all the registered political parties and all the individual candidates at the election,
none of the seats for London members is allocated to that individual candidate (Greater London
Authority Act 1999 Sch 2 para 7(1)(b)), and that candidate is accordingly left out of account for
the purposes of heads (2) and (3) in the text (Greater London Authority Act 1999 Sch 2
para 7(1)(b), (2)).

14 Greater London Authority Act 1999 Sch 2 para 8(1); European Parliamentary Elections
Act 2002 s 2(5); Government of Wales Act 2006 s 9(1).

In the case of an 'additional member' system, where the application of head (2) in the text
results in two or more registered parties or individual candidates having an equal number of
votes, and that number is greater than the number of votes of any other party or candidate,
head (2) in the text applies to each of them: Greater London Authority Act 1999 Sch 2
para 8(7); Government of Wales Act 2006 s 9(7).

15 Ie the number of votes given to a party to which one or more seats have already been allocated
are to be divided by the number of seats allocated plus one: Greater London Authority Act 1999
Sch 2 para 8(3); European Parliamentary Elections Act 2002 s 2(6); Government of Wales
Act 2006 s 9(3).

16 Greater London Authority Act 1999 Sch 2 para 8(2); European Parliamentary Elections
Act 2002 s 2(6); Government of Wales Act 2006 s 9(2).

In the case of a European parliamentary election, it is specified that fractions are to be taken
into account for this purpose: see the European Parliamentary Elections Act 2002 s 2(9).

In the case of an 'additional member' system, where the application of head (3) in the text
results in two or more registered parties or individual candidates having an equal number of
votes, and that number is greater than the number of votes of any other party or candidate, head
(3) in the text applies to each of them: Greater London Authority Act 1999 Sch 2 para 8(7);
Government of Wales Act 2006 s 9(7).

17 Greater London Authority Act 1999 Sch 2 para 8(4); European Parliamentary Elections
Act 2002 s 2(7)(b); Government of Wales Act 2006 s 9(4).

18 Greater London Authority Act 1999 Sch 2 para 8(5); European Parliamentary Elections
Act 2002 s 2(8); Government of Wales Act 2006 s 9(5).

In the case of an election for the return of London members of the London Assembly
(including for the purpose of filling a vacancy: see PARA 204), a person included on a list
submitted by a registered political party who is returned as the Mayor of London or as a

London Assembly member is treated as ceasing to be on the list (even if his return is void): Greater London Authority Act 1999 Sch 2 para 8(10).

19 Ie by the return of persons included on it as constituency members or by the previous application of head (2) or head (3) in the text.

20 Greater London Authority Act 1999 Sch 2 para 8(6); European Parliamentary Elections Act 2002 s 2(7)(a); Government of Wales Act 2006 s 9(6).

21 Greater London Authority Act 1999 Sch 2 para 8(8); Government of Wales Act 2006 s 9(8); European Parliamentary Elections Regulations 2004, SI 2004/293, Sch 1 para 60(1) (as substituted: see note 5).

It is possible that the operation in head (2) in the text would result in more candidates having the same highest electoral region figure than there are seats to be allocated, in which case the same principle applies, with the operation in head (2) in the text being reapplied after a recalculation as mentioned in the text: see the Greater London Authority Act 1999 Sch 2 para 8(8); and the Government of Wales Act 2006 s 9(8).

22 In the case of an election for the return of London members of the London Assembly, the reference is to the Greater London returning officer (as to the meaning of which see PARA 211 note 8).

In relation to a Welsh Assembly regional election, the reference is to a regional returning officer (as to the meaning of which see PARA 18 note 2).

As to returning officers for European parliamentary elections see PARA 360 et seq.

23 Greater London Authority Act 1999 Sch 2 para 8(9); Government of Wales Act 2006 s 9(9); European Parliamentary Elections Regulations 2004, SI 2004/293, Sch 1 para 60(2) (as substituted: see note 5).

In the case of a European parliamentary election, it is specified that, where the lot falls on a party, the returning officer must allocate the seat according to the order in which the persons named on the party's list of candidates appear on that list: European Parliamentary Elections Act 2002 s 2(8); European Parliamentary Elections Regulations 2004, SI 2004/293, Sch 1 para 60(3) (as so substituted).

341.   Elections to the office of mayor.   An elected local authority mayor[1] or the Mayor of London ('an elected mayor') is returned[2] under the simple majority system, unless there are three or more candidates[3], in which case the mayor must be returned under the supplementary vote system[4] and a voter's mayoral vote[5] will be a vote capable of being given to indicate the voter's first and second preferences from among the candidates[6].

Where the supplementary vote system is applied, if one of the candidates to be the elected mayor receives more than half of all the first preference votes[7] given in the election[8], that candidate is returned as the elected mayor[9]. If none of the candidates receives more than half of all the first preference votes given in the election[10], the two candidates who received the greatest number of such votes remain in the contest[11] (the other candidates being eliminated[12]), and the number of second preference votes[13] given in the election for each of the remaining candidates by voters who did not give their first preference vote to any of those candidates is ascertained[14] and added to the number of first preference votes given for that candidate, to give his total number of preference votes[15]. The person who is to be returned as the elected mayor is that one of the remaining candidates who has the greatest total number of preference votes[16].

If the person who is returned at an election as the elected mayor of a local authority is also returned as (or was already) a councillor of the authority, a vacancy arises in the office of councillor[17]. If the person who is returned as the Mayor of London is also returned as (or was already) a London Assembly member for an Assembly constituency[18], a vacancy arises in the Assembly constituency[19].

1   As to an election for the return of an elected local authority mayor see PARA 198. See also LOCAL GOVERNMENT vol 69 (2009) PARA 320 et seq.
2   As to elections for the return of a Mayor of London see PARA 199.

3 Greater London Authority Act 1999 s 4(2); Local Government Act 2000 s 9HC(2) (s 9HC added by the Localism Act 2011 s 21, Sch 2 para 1); Local Government Act 2000 s 42(2).
   The provision made by Pt II (ss 10–48A) (local authorities in Wales: arrangements with respect to executives etc) (see LOCAL GOVERNMENT vol 69 (2009) PARA 303 et seq), has been amended by the Localism Act 2011 s 22, Sch 3 so that it confers powers on the Welsh Ministers only: see LOCAL GOVERNMENT vol 69 (2009) PARA 320.
4 Ie in accordance with the Greater London Authority Act 1999 s 4(3)(a), Sch 2 Pt I (paras 1–4) or the Local Government Act 2000 ss 9HC(3), 42(3), Sch 2 (see the text and notes 5–16).
5 Ie the vote which each elector may give for a candidate to be an elected mayor: Greater London Authority Act 1999 s 4(1)(a); Local Government Act 2000 ss 9HC(1), 42(1) (s 9HC as added: see note 3). See further PARA 363.
6 Greater London Authority Act 1999 s 4(3)(b); Local Government Act 2000 ss 9HC(3), 42(3) (s 9HC as added: see note 3). In such circumstances a voter's mayoral vote is known as a 'supplementary vote'.
7 For these purposes, 'first preference vote' means a mayoral vote to the extent that it is given so as to indicate a voter's first preference from among the candidates to be the elected mayor: Greater London Authority Act 1999 Sch 2 para 2; Local Government Act 2000 ss 9HC(1)(a), 42(1)(a) (s 9HC as added: see note 3).
8 In the case of an election for the return of a Mayor of London, the votes are given in the London Assembly constituencies. As to the meaning of 'Assembly constituency' in the context of elections to the London Assembly see PARA 11.
9 Greater London Authority Act 1999 Sch 2 para 3; Local Government Act 2000 Sch 2 para 2.
10 Greater London Authority Act 1999 Sch 2 para 4(1); Local Government Act 2000 Sch 2 para 3(1).
11 Greater London Authority Act 1999 Sch 2 para 4(2); Local Government Act 2000 Sch 2 para 3(2). If, by reason of an equality of first preference votes, three or more candidates are qualified to remain in the contest, all of them remain in the contest: Greater London Authority Act 1999 Sch 2 para 4(3); Local Government Act 2000 Sch 2 para 3(3).
12 Greater London Authority Act 1999 Sch 2 para 4(4); Local Government Act 2000 Sch 2 para 3(4).
13 For these purposes, 'second preference vote' means a mayoral vote to the extent that it is given so as to indicate a voter's second preference from among the candidates to be the elected mayor: Greater London Authority Act 1999 Sch 2 para 2; Local Government Act 2000 ss 9HC(1)(b), 42(1)(b) (s 9HC as added: see note 3).
14 Greater London Authority Act 1999 Sch 2 para 4(5); Local Government Act 2000 Sch 2 para 3(5).
15 Greater London Authority Act 1999 Sch 2 para 4(6); Local Government Act 2000 Sch 2 para 3(6).
16 Greater London Authority Act 1999 Sch 2 para 4(7); Local Government Act 2000 Sch 2 para 3(7).
   If, by reason of an equality of total number of preference votes, two or more of the remaining candidates each have the greatest total number of preference votes, the returning officer must decide by lots which of them is returned as the elected mayor: Greater London Authority Act 1999 Sch 2 para 4(8); Local Government Act 2000 Sch 2 para 3(8). In the case of an election for the return of the Mayor of London, the reference is to the Greater London returning officer (as to the meaning of which see PARA 211 note 8). As to returning officers for the election of a local authority elected mayor see PARA 354.
17 See the Local Government Act 2000 ss 9HA, 40; and LOCAL GOVERNMENT vol 69 (2009) PARA 323.
18 See PARA 339.
19 Greater London Authority Act 1999 s 4(10). See LONDON GOVERNMENT vol 71 (2013) PARA 106.

342. Polls consequent on a parish meeting taken on the question of appointment to any office. In the case of a contested poll consequent on a parish meeting taken on the question of appointment to any office[1], the candidate or candidates to whom more votes have been given than to other candidates, up to the number of appointments to be made, are declared to be elected[2].

Where, after the counting of the votes (including any recount) is completed, an equality of votes is found to exist between any candidates and the addition of a vote would entitle any of those candidates to be declared elected or would decide the question, the returning officer must forthwith decide between those candidates or that question by lot, and proceed as if the candidate on whom or answer in favour of or against the question on which the lot falls had received an additional vote[3].

1   As to polls consequent on a parish meeting taken on the question of appointment to any office see PARA 200 et seq.
2   See the Parish and Community Meetings (Polls) Rules 1987, SI 1987/1, Schedule r 32(a); and PARA 483.
3   See the Parish and Community Meetings (Polls) Rules 1987, SI 1987/1, Schedule r 31; and PARA 434.

(ii) Polling Districts and Polling Places

343. Polling districts at parliamentary elections. Every parliamentary constituency[1] is to be divided into polling districts[2]. A relevant authority[3] must:

(1)   divide its area into polling districts for the purpose of parliamentary elections for so much of any constituency as is situated in its area[4]; and

(2)   keep the polling districts under review[5].

The authority must seek to ensure that all electors in a constituency in its area have such reasonable facilities for voting as are practicable in the circumstances[6]; and, unless there are special circumstances[7], in England each parish is to be a separate polling district[8], and in Wales each community is to be a separate polling district[9].

If an alteration of polling districts in an area is made:

(a)   the registration officer who acts for the area[10] must make such adaptations of his register of parliamentary electors[11] as are necessary to take account of the alteration[12]; and

(b)   the alteration is effective on the date on which the registration officer publishes a notice stating that any such adaptations have been made by him[13].

No election is to be questioned by reason of any non-compliance with the rules relating to the designation of parliamentary polling districts (including provision made for their review)[14], or by reason of any informality relative to polling districts[15].

1   As to the meaning of 'constituency' in the context of a parliamentary election see PARA 9.
2   Representation of the People Act 1983 s 18A(1) (ss 18A, 18E added by the Electoral Administration Act 2006 s 16(1)).
3   In relation to England, the council of a district or London borough is a relevant authority (Representation of the People Act 1983 s 18E(1), (3)(a) (as added: see note 2)); and, in relation to Wales, the council of a county or county borough is a relevant authority (s 18E(1), (3)(c) (as so added)). As to the meanings of 'England' and 'Wales' see PARA 1 note 1. As to districts in England, and their councils, see LOCAL GOVERNMENT vol 69 (2009) PARA 24 et seq; as to counties and county boroughs in Wales, and their councils, see LOCAL GOVERNMENT vol 69 (2009) PARA 37 et seq; and as to London boroughs and their councils see LOCAL GOVERNMENT vol 69 (2009) PARA 35; LONDON GOVERNMENT vol 71 (2013) PARA 15 et seq.
4   Representation of the People Act 1983 s 18A(2)(a) (as added: see note 2).
5   Representation of the People Act 1983 s 18A(2)(b) (as added: see note 2). As to the review of parliamentary polling districts see PARA 345.
6   Representation of the People Act 1983 s 18A(3)(a) (as added: see note 2). As to the meaning of 'elector', in relation to a parliamentary election, see PARA 95 note 2.
7   Representation of the People Act 1983 s 18A(4) (as added: see note 2).
8   Representation of the People Act 1983 s 18A(3)(b) (as added: see note 2). As to parishes generally see LOCAL GOVERNMENT vol 69 (2009) PARA 27 et seq.

9 Representation of the People Act 1983 s 18A(3)(c) (as added: see note 2). As to communities generally see LOCAL GOVERNMENT vol 69 (2009) PARA 41 et seq.
10 As to electoral registration officers and the areas for which they act see PARA 139 et seq.
11 As to the duty of each registration officer to maintain the registers of electors see PARA 143 et seq.
12 Representation of the People Act 1983 s 18A(5)(a) (as added: see note 2).
13 Representation of the People Act 1983 s 18A(5)(b) (as added: see note 2).
14 Representation of the People Act 1983 s 18E(1), (2)(a) (as added: see note 2). As to the questioning of parliamentary elections see PARA 761 et seq.
15 Representation of the People Act 1983 s 18E(1), (2)(b) (as added: see note 2).

344. Polling places at parliamentary elections. A polling place is to be designated for each polling district in a constituency[1], unless the size or other circumstances of a polling district are such that the situation of the polling stations does not materially affect the convenience of the electors or any body of them[2]. A relevant authority[3] must:

(1) designate the polling places for the polling districts in its area[4]; and
(2) keep the polling places in its area under review[5],

in relation to which the following rules apply[6]:

(a) the authority must seek to ensure that all electors in a constituency in its area have such reasonable facilities for voting as are practicable in the circumstances[7];
(b) the authority must seek to ensure that so far as is reasonable and practicable every polling place for which it is responsible is accessible to electors who are disabled[8];
(c) the authority must have regard to the accessibility to disabled persons of potential polling stations in any place which it is considering designating as a polling place or the designation of which as a polling place it is reviewing[9];
(d) the polling place for a polling district must be an area in the district, unless special circumstances make it desirable to designate an area wholly or partly outside the district[10];
(e) the polling place for a polling district must be small enough to indicate to electors in different parts of the district how they will be able to reach the polling station[11].

If no polling place is designated for a polling district, the polling district is to be taken to be the polling place[12].

No election is to be questioned by reason of any non-compliance with the rules relating to the designation of parliamentary polling places (including provision made for their review)[13], or by reason of any informality relative to polling places[14].

1 Representation of the People Act 1983 s 18B(1) (ss 18B, 18E added by the Electoral Administration Act 2006 s 16(1)). As to the meaning of 'constituency' in the context of a parliamentary election see PARA 9. As to the designation of polling districts at parliamentary elections see PARA 343.
2 Representation of the People Act 1983 s 18B(2) (as added: see note 1). As to the meaning of 'elector', in relation to a parliamentary election, see PARA 95 note 2.
3 As to the relevant authorities for these purposes see PARA 343 note 3.
4 Representation of the People Act 1983 s 18B(3)(a) (as added: see note 1).
5 Representation of the People Act 1983 s 18B(3)(b) (as added: see note 1).
6 Representation of the People Act 1983 s 18B(4) (as added: see note 1).
7 Representation of the People Act 1983 s 18B(4)(a) (as added: see note 1).
8 Representation of the People Act 1983 s 18B(4)(b) (as added: see note 1).
9 Representation of the People Act 1983 s 18B(4)(c) (as added: see note 1).
10 Representation of the People Act 1983 s 18B(4)(d) (as added: see note 1).

11 Representation of the People Act 1983 s 18B(4)(e) (as added: see note 1).
12 Representation of the People Act 1983 s 18B(5) (as added: see note 1).
13 Representation of the People Act 1983 s 18E(1), (2)(a) (as added: see note 1). As to the
    questioning of parliamentary elections see PARA 761 et seq.
14 Representation of the People Act 1983 s 18E(1), (2)(b) (as added: see note 1).

345.   Review of parliamentary polling districts and polling places.   A relevant
authority[1] must during each compulsory review period[2] carry out and complete[3]:
    (1)   a review[4] of all the polling districts in its area[5]; and
    (2)   a review[6] of all the polling places in its area[7],
although this requirement[8] does not prevent a relevant authority carrying out a
review of some or all of the polling districts or polling places in its area at other
times[9].

The relevant authority must publish notice of the holding of a review[10]. The
authority must consult the returning officer for every parliamentary election[11]
held in a constituency[12] that is wholly or partly in its area[13]; and every such
returning officer must make to the authority representations[14], which must
include information as to the location of polling stations (existing or proposed)
within polling places (existing or proposed)[15], and which must be published in
such manner as is prescribed[16]. The authority must seek representations also
from such persons as it thinks have particular expertise in relation to access to
premises or facilities for persons who have different forms of disability[17]; and
such persons must have an opportunity both to make representations[18], and to
comment on the returning officer's representations[19]. Any elector in a
constituency situated in whole or in part in the authority's area may make
representations[20]. Representations made by any person in connection with a
review of polling places may include proposals for specified alternative polling
places[21]. On completion of a review, the authority must give reasons for its
decisions in the review[22], and it must publish such other information as is
prescribed[23].

No election is to be questioned by reason of any non-compliance with the
rules relating to the review of parliamentary polling districts and polling places[24],
or by reason of any informality relative to polling districts or polling places[25].

1   As to the relevant authorities for these purposes see PARA 343 note 3.
2   The compulsory review periods are:
        (1)   the period of 16 months beginning with 1 October 2013 (Representation of the People
               Act 1983 s 18C(2)(a) (ss 18C, 18E, Sch A1 added by the Electoral Administration
               Act 2006 s 16(1), (2); the Representation of the People Act 1983 s 18C(1)–(3)
               substituted, s 18C(4), (5) repealed, by the Electoral Registration and Administration
               Act 2013 s 17)); and
        (2)   the period of 16 months beginning with 1 October of every fifth year after that
               (Representation of the People Act 1983 s 18C(2)(b) (as so added and substituted)).
3   See the Representation of the People Act 1983 s 18C(1) (as added and substituted: see note 2).
4   Ie under the Representation of the People Act 1983 s 18A (see PARA 343): see s 18C(1)(a) (as
    added and substituted: see note 2).
5   Representation of the People Act 1983 s 18C(1)(a) (as added and substituted: see note 2).
6   Ie under the Representation of the People Act 1983 s 18B (see PARA 344): see s 18C(1)(b) (as
    added and substituted: see note 2).
7   Representation of the People Act 1983 s 18C(1)(b) (as added and substituted: see note 2).
8   Ie the Representation of the People Act 1983 s 18C(1) (see the text and notes 1–7): see s 18C(3)
    (as added and substituted: see note 2).
9   Representation of the People Act 1983 s 18C(3) (as added and substituted: see note 2).
10 Representation of the People Act 1983 Sch A1 para 1 (as added: see note 2). The provision made
    by Sch A1 has effect in relation to a review: s 18C(6) (as so added).
11 As to returning officers for parliamentary elections see PARA 350 et seq.
12 As to the meaning of 'constituency' in the context of a parliamentary election see PARA 9.

13 Representation of the People Act 1983 Sch A1 para 2 (as added: see note 2).

14 Representation of the People Act 1983 Sch A1 para 3(1) (as added: see note 2).

15 Representation of the People Act 1983 Sch A1 para 3(2) (as added: see note 2).

16 Representation of the People Act 1983 Sch A1 para 3(3) (as added: see note 2). 'Prescribed' means prescribed by regulations: see s 202(1). As to the making of regulations under the Representation of the People Act 1983 generally see PARA 28 note 16. Accordingly, a relevant authority must, within 30 days of receipt, publish representations made by a returning officer for the purposes of the review of polling districts or polling places:

  (1)   by posting a copy of them at its office and in at least one conspicuous place in its area (Review of Polling Districts and Polling Places (Parliamentary Elections) Regulations 2006, SI 2006/2965, reg 3(a)); and

  (2)   if the authority maintains a website, by placing a copy on the authority's website (reg 3(b)).

17 Representation of the People Act 1983 Sch A1 para 4(1) (as added: see note 2).

18 Representation of the People Act 1983 Sch A1 para 4(2)(a) (as added: see note 2).

19 Representation of the People Act 1983 Sch A1 para 4(2)(b) (as added: see note 2).

20 Representation of the People Act 1983 Sch A1 para 5 (as added: see note 2). As to the meaning of 'elector', in relation to a parliamentary election, see PARA 95 note 2.

21 Representation of the People Act 1983 Sch A1 para 6 (as added: see note 2).

22 Representation of the People Act 1983 Sch A1 para 7(a) (as added: see note 2).

23 Representation of the People Act 1983 Sch A1 para 7(b) (as added: see note 2). 'Prescribed' means prescribed by regulations: see s 202(1). See also note 16. Accordingly, on completion of a review the authority must publish the following:

  (1)   all correspondence sent to a returning officer in connection with the review (Polling Districts and Polling Places (Parliamentary Elections) Regulations 2006, SI 2006/2965, reg 4(a));

  (2)   all correspondence sent to any person whom the authority thinks has particular expertise in relation to access to premises or facilities for persons who have different forms of disability (reg 4(b));

  (3)   all representations made by any person in connection with the review (reg 4(c));

  (4)   the minutes of any meeting held by the authority to consider any revision to the designation of polling districts or polling places within its area as a result of the review (reg 4(d));

  (5)   details of the designation of polling districts or polling places within its area as a result of the review (reg 4(e));

  (6)   details of the places where the results of the review have been published (reg 4(f)).

24 Representation of the People Act 1983 s 18E(1), (2)(a) (as added: see note 2). As to the questioning of parliamentary elections see PARA 761 et seq.

25 Representation of the People Act 1983 s 18E(1), (2)(b) (as added: see note 2).

346. Representations made to the Electoral Commission regarding review of parliamentary polling districts and places. If, in relation to a constituency[1] in the area of a relevant authority[2], a relevant representation[3] is made to the Electoral Commission[4]:

  (1)   by an interested authority in England and Wales[5];

  (2)   by not less than 30 electors in the constituency[6];

  (3)   by a person (other than the returning officer) who has made representations in connection with a review of parliamentary polling districts and polling places[7];

  (4)   by a person who is not an elector in a constituency in the authority's area, but who the Commission thinks has sufficient interest in the accessibility of disabled persons to polling places in the area, or has particular expertise in relation to the access to premises or facilities of disabled persons[8],

the Commission must consider such representations (including any observations on the representations which may be made by the returning officer for the constituency) and may, if it thinks fit[9], direct the relevant authority to make any alterations to the polling places designated by the review which the Commission thinks necessary in the circumstances[10]. If the authority fails to make those alterations before the end of the period of two months starting on the day the direction is given, the Commission may, if it thinks fit, itself make the alterations[11]; and any alterations so made by the Commission have effect as if they had been made by the relevant authority[12].

No election is to be questioned by reason of any non-compliance with the rules relating to the review of parliamentary polling districts and polling places[13], or by reason of any informality relative to polling districts or polling places[14].

1　As to the meaning of 'constituency' in the context of a parliamentary election see PARA 9.
2　As to the relevant authorities for these purposes see PARA 343 note 3.
3　A relevant representation is a representation that a review under the Representation of the People Act 1983 s 18A (see PARA 343) or s 18B (see PARA 344) has not been conducted by a relevant authority so as (see s 18D(2) (ss 18D, 18E added by the Electoral Administration Act 2006 s 16(1))):
　　(1)　to meet the reasonable requirements of the electors in the constituency or any body of those electors (Representation of the People Act 1983 s 18D(2)(a) (as so added)); or
　　(2)　to take sufficient account of the accessibility to disabled persons of polling stations within a designated polling place (s 18D(2)(b) (as so added)).
4　Representation of the People Act 1983 s 18D(1) (as added: see note 3). As to the Electoral Commission see PARA 34 et seq.
5　Representation of the People Act 1983 s 18D(1)(a) (as added: see note 3). For these purposes, an interested authority means:
　　(1)　in relation to a constituency in England, the council of a parish (or, where there is no such council, the parish meeting of a parish which is wholly or partly situated within the constituency) (s 18D(6)(a) (as so added)); and
　　(2)　in relation to a constituency in Wales, the council of a community which is wholly or partly situated within the constituency (see s 18D(6)(b) (as so added)).
　　As to the meanings of 'England' and 'Wales' see PARA 1 note 1. As to parishes generally see LOCAL GOVERNMENT vol 69 (2009) PARA 27 et seq; and as to communities generally see LOCAL GOVERNMENT vol 69 (2009) PARA 41 et seq.
6　Representation of the People Act 1983 s 18D(1)(b) (as added: see note 3). The reference in s 18D(1)(b) to electors does not include persons who have an anonymous entry in the register of parliamentary electors or local government electors: s 18D(7) (as so added). As to the meaning of 'elector', in relation to a parliamentary election, see PARA 95 note 2; and as to the meaning of 'anonymous entry', in relation to a register of electors, see PARA 148.
7　Representation of the People Act 1983 s 18D(1)(c) (as added: see note 3). The text refers to representations made under s 18C(6), Sch A1 (see PARA 345): see s 18D(1)(c) (as so added).
8　Representation of the People Act 1983 s 18D(1)(d) (as added: see note 3).
9　See the Representation of the People Act 1983 s 18D(3), (4) (as added: see note 3).
10　Representation of the People Act 1983 s 18D(4)(a) (as added: see note 3).
11　Representation of the People Act 1983 s 18D(4)(b) (as added: see note 3).
12　Representation of the People Act 1983 s 18D(5) (as added: see note 3).
13　Representation of the People Act 1983 s 18E(1), (2)(a) (as added: see note 3). As to the questioning of parliamentary elections see PARA 761 et seq.
14　Representation of the People Act 1983 s 18E(1), (2)(b) (as added: see note 3).

347.　Polling districts and polling stations at local government elections. For elections of county councillors in England[1], and of county or county borough councillors in Wales[2], the appropriate county or county borough council may divide an electoral division[3] into polling districts, and may alter any polling district[4].

For elections of London borough or district councillors[5], the London borough or district council may divide the London borough or district or any ward thereof into polling districts, and may alter any polling district[6]. For any London Authority elections[7], a London borough council or the Common Council of the City of London[8] may divide its area into polling districts and may alter any polling district[9].

Any power to constitute polling districts for the purpose of local government elections[10] must be exercised so that electors from any parliamentary polling district wholly or partly within the electoral area[11] can, in the absence of special circumstances, be allotted to a polling station within the parliamentary polling place for that district unless the parliamentary polling place is outside the electoral area[12].

1   As to the meaning of 'England' see PARA 1 note 1. As to the election of councillors for local government principal areas see PARA 197. As to counties in England, and their councils, see LOCAL GOVERNMENT vol 69 (2009) PARA 24 et seq.
2   As to the meaning of 'Wales' see PARA 1 note 1. As to counties and county boroughs in Wales, and their councils, see LOCAL GOVERNMENT vol 69 (2009) PARA 37 et seq.
3   As to electoral divisions established for the purpose of local government elections in England and Wales see PARA 74.
4   See the Representation of the People Act 1983 s 31(1) (amended by the Local Government Act 1985 s 102(2), Sch 17; and the Local Government (Wales) Act 1994 s 66(6), Sch 16 para 68(6)); Representation of the People Act 1983 s 31(1A) (added by the Local Government (Wales) Act 1994 Sch 16 para 68(6)).
    The Representation of the People Act 1983 s 31 is applied and modified for the purpose of local authority mayoral elections in England and Wales by the Local Authorities (Mayoral Elections) (England and Wales) Regulations 2007, SI 2007/1024, reg 3(2)–(5), Sch 2 Table 1 (see PARA 11 note 14); and the Representation of the People Act 1983 s 31 has effect also for the purposes of local authority referendums, subject to the modifications specified, in relation to Wales, by the Local Authorities (Conduct of Referendums) (Wales) Regulations 2008, SI 2008/1848, reg 8(2), Sch 4 Table 1, and, in relation to England, by the Local Authorities (Conduct of Referendums) (England) Regulations 2012, SI 2012/323, regs 8(2), 11–13, Sch 4 Table 1 (see PARA 15 note 2).
5   As to the London boroughs and their councils see LOCAL GOVERNMENT vol 69 (2009) PARA 35; LONDON GOVERNMENT vol 71 (2013) PARA 15 et seq.
6   See the Representation of the People Act 1983 s 31(1) (as amended: see note 4).
7   As to the meaning of 'Authority election' see PARA 11.
8   As to the Common Council of the City of London see LONDON GOVERNMENT vol 71 (2013) PARA 34 et seq.
9   Representation of the People Act 1983 s 31(1B) (added by the Greater London Authority Act 1999 s 17, Sch 3 paras 1, 2). For these purposes, the Inner Temple and the Middle Temple are treated as forming part of the City of London: see the Representation of the People Act 1983 s 31(1B) (as so added). As to elections in the City of London see PARA 33. As to the Temples see LONDON GOVERNMENT vol 71 (2013) PARA 17.
10 As to the meaning of 'local government election' see PARA 11.
11 In this context, 'electoral area' means an electoral division of a county or a ward of a district or London borough: see PARA 11. As to the meaning of 'elector', in relation to a local government election, see PARA 95 note 2. As to parliamentary polling districts see PARA 343 et seq.
12 Representation of the People Act 1983 s 31(3).

348.   Polling districts and polling places at Welsh Assembly elections.   For the purpose of Welsh Assembly elections[1], every Assembly constituency[2] must be divided into polling districts, and there must be a polling place for each polling district[3], unless the size or other circumstances of a polling district are such that the situation of the polling stations does not materially affect the convenience of the electors or any body of them[4]. The polling districts and polling places so designated for the purposes of Assembly elections must generally be the districts and places designated for parliamentary elections[5].

A Welsh Assembly election cannot be questioned by reason of any non-compliance with these rules[6], or by reason of any irregularity relating to polling districts or polling places[7].

1   As to the meaning of 'Assembly election' see PARA 3 note 2.
2   As to the meaning of 'Assembly constituency' in the context of a Welsh Assembly election see PARA 3 note 2.

3 As to parliamentary polling districts and polling places see PARA 343 et seq.
4 National Assembly for Wales (Representation of the People) Order 2007, SI 2007/236, art 6(1). As to the meaning of 'elector', in relation to an Assembly election, see PARA 110 note 6.
5 National Assembly for Wales (Representation of the People) Order 2007, SI 2007/236, art 6(2). See, however, PARA 76 note 5.
6 National Assembly for Wales (Representation of the People) Order 2007, SI 2007/236, art 6(3)(a). As to the questioning of Welsh Assembly elections see PARA 764 et seq.
7 National Assembly for Wales (Representation of the People) Order 2007, SI 2007/236, art 6(3)(b).

349. Polling districts and polling places for European parliamentary elections. Every European parliamentary electoral region[1] must be divided into polling districts, and a polling place must be designated for each polling district[2]. The polling district and polling places so designated must be the same as those used or designated for parliamentary elections[3], except where it appears to those responsible for the designation of parliamentary polling districts and polling places that special circumstances make it desirable for some other polling district or polling place to be designated[4].

A European parliamentary election cannot be questioned by reason of any non-compliance with these rules[5], or by reason of any informality relative to polling districts or polling places[6].

1 As to the establishment of electoral regions (including the 'combined region') for the purpose of elections to the European Parliament see PARA 77; and as to European parliamentary elections see PARA 217 et seq.
2 European Parliamentary Elections Regulations 2004, SI 2004/293, reg 8(1).
3 As to parliamentary polling districts and polling places see PARA 343 et seq.
4 European Parliamentary Elections Regulations 2004, SI 2004/293, reg 8(2). In Gibraltar, for the purposes of a European parliamentary election held in the combined region, the polling districts and polling places designated for each district are the same as those used or designated for elections to the Gibraltar Parliament: see reg 8(4) (amended by SI 2009/186). As to elections to the European Parliament held in the combined region see PARA 77.
5 European Parliamentary Elections Regulations 2004, SI 2004/293, reg 8(3)(a). As to the questioning of European parliamentary elections see PARA 765 et seq.
6 European Parliamentary Elections Regulations 2004, SI 2004/293, reg 8(3)(b).

(iii) Returning Officers

A. PARLIAMENTARY ELECTIONS

350. Returning officers for parliamentary elections. In England and Wales[1], the returning officer for a parliamentary election is[2]:

(1)   in the case of a county constituency[3] in England which is coterminous with or wholly contained in a county[4], the sheriff of the county[5];

(2)   in the case of a county constituency in Wales which is coterminous with or wholly contained in a preserved county[6], the sheriff of the county[7];

(3)   in the case of a borough constituency in England which is coterminous with or wholly contained in a district[8], the chairman of the district council[9];

(4)   in the case of a borough constituency in Wales which is coterminous with or wholly contained in a county or county borough[10], the chairman of the county or county borough council[11];

(5)   in the case of any other constituency in England wholly outside Greater London[12], such sheriff or chairman of a district council as the Secretary of State[13] may designate in an order made by statutory instrument[14];

(6)   in the case of any other constituency in Wales, such sheriff or chairman

of a county or county borough council as the Secretary of State may designate in an order made by statutory instrument[15];

(7)   in the case of a constituency which is coterminous with or wholly contained in a London borough[16], the mayor of the borough[17];

(8)   in the case of a council of a London borough operating executive arrangements which involve a mayor and cabinet executive[18], the chairman of the borough[19];

(9)   in the case of a constituency wholly or partly in Greater London which is situated partly in one London borough[20] and partly in a district or any other London borough, the mayor or the chairman of such London borough or the chairman of such district council as the Secretary of State may designate in an order made by statutory instrument[21].

It is the general duty of the returning officer at a parliamentary election to do all such acts and things as may be necessary for effectively conducting the election in the manner provided by the parliamentary election rules[22]. The execution of the writ for a parliamentary election[23] belongs to the returning officer as such, the office of returning officer being a distinct office from that by virtue of which he becomes returning officer[24]; and where a person enters on an office by virtue of which he becomes returning officer, it belongs to him and not to the outgoing holder of that office to complete the execution of a writ for a parliamentary election previously issued and not yet returned[25].

No parliamentary election may be declared invalid by reason of any act or omission by the returning officer or any other person in breach of his official duty in connection with the election or otherwise of the parliamentary elections rules[26] if it appears to the tribunal having cognisance of the question[27]:

(a)   that the election was so conducted as to be substantially in accordance with the law as to elections[28]; and

(b)   that the act or omission did not affect its result[29].

Nor is a parliamentary election liable to be questioned by reason of a defect in the title, or want of title, of the person presiding at or conducting the election, if that person was then in actual possession of, or acting in, the office giving the right to preside at or conduct the election[30].

A public notice which is required by or under the Representation of the People Act 1983 to be given by a returning officer for a parliamentary election must be given by posting the notice in some conspicuous place or places in the constituency and may also be given in such other manner as he thinks desirable for publicising it[31].

A returning officer for a parliamentary election must take such steps as he thinks appropriate to encourage the participation by electors in the electoral process in the area for which he acts[32]. In so doing, he must have regard to any guidance issued by the Electoral Commission[33].

1   As to the meanings of 'England' and 'Wales' see PARA 1 note 1.
2   See the Representation of the People Act 1983 s 24(1). A person is not subject to any incapacity to vote at a parliamentary election by reason of being or acting as returning officer at that election: s 27(3). Returning officers were formerly unable to vote at the election for which they acted as returning officers because they were called upon to decide in the event of an equality of votes (a question which is now to be determined by lot: see PARA 434). As to the meaning of 'parliamentary election' see PARA 9.
      Any reference in any Act (whenever passed) to the returning officer for a parliamentary election or constituency must be taken as a reference to the returning officer appointed under the Representation of the People Act 1983: see s 206, Sch 7 para 11. As to the meaning of 'constituency' in the context of a parliamentary election see PARA 9. As to the discharge of the returning officer's functions for parliamentary elections see PARA 351; and as to the returning

officer's general duty at a parliamentary election to effectively conduct the election in the manner provided by the appropriate rules see PARA 383.

3   As to county constituencies and borough constituencies see PARA 73.

4   Ie as defined by the Sheriffs Act 1887 s 38 (see SHERIFFS vol 42 (Reissue) PARA 1101): see the Representation of the People Act 1983 s 24(1)(a) (amended by the Local Government (Wales) Act 1994 s 66(6), Sch 16 para 68(3); and SI 1995/1748).

5   Representation of the People Act 1983 s 24(1)(a) (as amended: see note 4). In the event of the death of a sheriff, the acting returning officer discharges all the duties of sheriff as returning officer at a parliamentary election until another sheriff is appointed and has made the declaration of office: s 28(6). The Sheriffs Act 1887 s 25 (duty of under-sheriff to act as high sheriff in certain cases: see SHERIFFS vol 42 (Reissue) PARA 1115) does not authorise the under-sheriff to discharge the duties of returning officer at a parliamentary election: see the Representation of the People Act 1983 s 28(6). As to the acting returning officer at a parliamentary election see PARA 351.

6   Ie as defined by the Local Government (Wales) Act 1994 s 64 (see LOCAL GOVERNMENT vol 69 (2009) PARA 1): see the Representation of the People Act 1983 s 24(1)(aa) (s 24(1)(aa), (bb), (cc) added by the Local Government (Wales) Act 1994 Sch 16 para 68(3)).

7   Representation of the People Act 1983 s 24(1)(aa) (as added: see note 6).

8   As to districts in England see LOCAL GOVERNMENT vol 69 (2009) PARA 24 et seq.

9   Representation of the People Act 1983 s 24(1)(b) (amended by the Local Government (Wales) Act 1994 Sch 16 para 68(3)).

10 As to counties and county boroughs in Wales, and their councils, see LOCAL GOVERNMENT vol 69 (2009) PARA 37 et seq.

11 Representation of the People Act 1983 s 24(1)(bb) (as added: see note 6).

12 As to Greater London see LONDON GOVERNMENT vol 71 (2013) PARA 14.

13 As to the Secretary of State see PARA 2.

14 Representation of the People Act 1983 s 24(1)(c) (amended by the Local Government (Wales) Act 1994 Sch 16 para 68(3)). As to the making of orders under the Representation of the People Act 1983 generally see PARA 28 note 16. Before making an order designating returning officers, the authority making the instrument must consult the Electoral Commission: see the Political Parties, Elections and Referendums Act 2000 ss 7(1), (2)(c), 160(1); and PARA 54. As to the Electoral Commission see PARA 34 et seq. As to the order made see the Returning Officers (Parliamentary Constituencies) (England) Order 2007, SI 2007/2878, arts 3, 6, Schs 1, 3.

15 Representation of the People Act 1983 s 24(1)(cc) (as added: see note 6). Before making an order designating returning officers, the authority making the instrument must consult the Electoral Commission: see the Political Parties, Elections and Referendums Act 2000 ss 7(1), (2)(c), 160(1); and PARA 54. As to the order made see the Returning Officers (Parliamentary Constituencies) (Wales) Order 2007, SI 2007/171, arts 3–4.

16 As to the London boroughs and their councils see LOCAL GOVERNMENT vol 69 (2009) PARA 35; LONDON GOVERNMENT vol 71 (2013) PARA 15 et seq.

17 Representation of the People Act 1983 s 24(1)(d).

18 For these purposes, 'executive arrangements' and 'mayor and cabinet executive' have the same meanings as in the Local Government Act 2000 Pt 1A (ss 9B–9R) (arrangements with respect to local governance in England: see LOCAL GOVERNMENT): Representation of the People Act 1983 s 24(1A) (added, in relation to England, by SI 2002/1057); Interpretation Act 1978 s 17(2)(b).

19 Representation of the People Act 1983 s 24(1)(d); applied by s 24(1)(dd) (added, in relation to England, by SI 2002/1057; and amended by the Local Government and Public Involvement in Health Act 2007 ss 74(1), 241, Sch 3 paras 16, 17, Sch 18 Pt 3).

20 The City of London, the Inner Temple and the Middle Temple are, for the purposes of the Representation of the People Act 1983 s 24, treated as if together they formed a London borough: see s 24(1). As to the Temples see LONDON GOVERNMENT vol 71 (2013) PARA 17 et seq. As to elections in the City of London see PARA 33.

21 Representation of the People Act 1983 s 24(1)(e) (amended, in relation to England, by SI 2002/1057). Before making an order designating returning officers, the authority making the instrument must consult the Electoral Commission: see the Political Parties, Elections and Referendums Act 2000 ss 7(1), (2)(c), 160(1); and PARA 54. As to the order made see the Returning Officers (Parliamentary Constituencies) (England) Order 2007, SI 2007/2878, arts 4, 5, Sch 2.

22 Representation of the People Act 1983 s 23(2). As to the meaning of 'parliamentary election rules' see PARA 383 note 2.

23 As to the issue and execution of writs for a parliamentary election see PARA 192 et seq.

24 Representation of the People Act 1983 s 27(1). Since the only duty in connection with the execution of the writ which is to be performed by the returning officer rather than the acting

returning officer is the declaration of the result of the poll, and then only if the returning officer by notice reserves that duty to himself (see PARA 351), this provision needs to be read with s 28(4), so that references to the returning officer include, as respects England and Wales, the acting returning officer (see PARA 351). On this interpretation the reference to execution of the writ means doing all the things that are required to elect a member of Parliament. An alternative construction would be to limit the meaning of the reference to the execution of the writ to the declaration of the result of the poll. But this construction presents difficulties when applied to the words 'execution of the writ' in s 27(2): see note 25. The former construction is therefore to be preferred.

25 Representation of the People Act 1983 s 27(2). If this provision is applied, as respects England and Wales, to the returning officer, the reference to the completion of the execution of the writ for a parliamentary election can refer only to the declaration of the result of the poll since all other remaining duties are discharged by the acting returning officer: see PARA 351. However, those duties can only be discharged by the person who for the time being holds the office of returning officer (see s 28(2)(b); and PARA 351) if he has given the notice required by s 28(3) (see PARA 351), not later than the day following that on which the writ is received. Accordingly, if s 27(2) is construed as applying to the returning officer, it would produce a conflict with s 28(2)(b), (3) by purporting to allow a person who came into the office of returning officer and who had not given such a notice to make the declaration of the result of the poll. It is submitted therefore that, as respects England and Wales, the provision applies to the acting returning officer. Thus, where a person comes into the office of registration officer and the holder of that office is required by the provisions referred to in PARA 351 to be the acting returning officer, it falls to that person and not the previous holder to complete the proceedings on the election. See also note 24.

26 As to the meaning of 'parliamentary elections rules' see PARA 383 note 2. A returning officer for a parliamentary election may take such steps as he thinks appropriate to remedy any act or omission on his part, or on the part of a relevant person, which arises in connection with any function the returning officer or relevant person has in relation to the election, and which is not in accordance with the rules or any other requirements applicable to the election: Electoral Administration Act 2006 s 46(1), (3)(a). However, a returning officer may not in exercise of this power recount the votes given at an election after the result has been declared: s 46(2). For these purposes, a 'relevant person' is an electoral registration officer, a presiding officer, a person providing goods or services to the returning officer or a deputy of any such person or a person appointed to assist, or in the course of his employment assisting, such a person in connection with any function he has in relation to the election: see s 46(4). Section 46(1)–(4) must be construed as part of the Representation of the People Acts: Electoral Administration Act 2006 s 46(5). As to the meaning of the 'Representation of the People Acts' see PARA 3 note 1.

27 Representation of the People Act 1983 s 23(3). As to the questioning of parliamentary elections see PARA 761 et seq.

28 Representation of the People Act 1983 s 23(3)(a).

29 Representation of the People Act 1983 s 23(3)(b).

30 Representation of the People Act 1983 s 24(2).

31 Representation of the People Act 1983 s 200(1) (substituted by the Representation of the People Act 1985 s 24, Sch 4 para 68).

32 Electoral Administration Act 2006 s 69(1), (8)(b), (9)(a). As to the meaning of 'elector', in relation to a parliamentary election, see PARA 95 note 2.

33 Electoral Administration Act 2006 s 69(2).

351. Discharge of returning officer's functions for parliamentary elections. With certain exceptions[1], the duties of the returning officer at a parliamentary election[2] are discharged, as acting returning officer, by[3]:

(1) in the case of a constituency in England[4] for which the chairman of a district council or the mayor or the chairman of a London borough is returning officer[5], the registration officer[6] appointed by that council[7];

(2) in the case of a constituency in Wales[8] for which the chairman of a county or county borough council is returning officer[9], the registration officer appointed by that council[10];

(3) in the case of any other constituency, such registration officer as may be designated in an order made by statutory instrument by the Secretary of State[11].

The exceptions are:
  (a)   any duty imposed on a returning officer in connection with the delivery of the writ of election[12]; and
  (b)   any duty imposed in connection with the declaration of the result of the poll[13] which the person, if any, who for the time being holds the office of returning officer reserves to himself and undertakes to perform in person[14].

The returning officer must give to the acting returning officer written notice of any duties which he reserves to himself under head (b) above; and, in the case of any election, head (b) above applies to the duties, if any, of which such a notice is given not later than the day following that on which the writ is received, and to no others[15].

An acting returning officer at a parliamentary election in the discharge of his duties has all the powers, obligations, rights and liabilities of the returning officer under the Representation of the People Act 1983[16], and the Representation of the People Act 1983 has effect accordingly[17]. An acting returning officer has power to appoint deputies to discharge all or any of those duties[18]; and an English district council, London borough council, Welsh county council or county borough council may assign officers to assist in carrying out all or any of those duties[19]. On the death of a sheriff, the acting returning officer discharges all the duties of sheriff as returning officer at a parliamentary election until another sheriff is appointed and has made the declaration of office[20].

1   Ie subject to the exceptions mentioned in the Representation of the People Act 1983 s 28(2) (the text and notes 12–14): see s 28(1).
2   As to the appointment of returning officers for a parliamentary election see PARA 350. As to the meaning of 'parliamentary election' see PARA 9. As to the transferred functions of returning officers where polls are combined see PARA 18.
3   See the Representation of the People Act 1983 s 28(1).
4   As to the meaning of 'constituency' in the context of a parliamentary election see PARA 9; and as to the meaning of 'England' see PARA 1 note 1.
5   Ie by virtue of the Representation of the People Act 1983 s 24(1) (see PARA 350): see s 28(1)(a) (amended by the Local Government (Wales) Act 1994 s 66(6), Sch 16 para 68(4); and in relation to England by SI 2002/1057). A chairman may be designated in the case of a London borough council which is operating executive arrangements involving a mayor and cabinet executive or a mayor (see LOCAL GOVERNMENT vol 69 (2009) PARA 327 et seq). As to districts in England, and their councils, see LOCAL GOVERNMENT vol 69 (2009) PARA 24 et seq; and as to the London boroughs and their councils see LOCAL GOVERNMENT vol 69 (2009) PARA 35; LONDON GOVERNMENT vol 71 (2013) PARA 15 et seq.
6   As to the electoral registration officer see PARA 139.
7   Representation of the People Act 1983 s 28(1)(a) (as amended: see note 5).
8   As to the meaning of 'Wales' see PARA 1 note 1.
9   Ie by virtue of the Representation of the People Act 1983 s 24(1) (see PARA 350): see s 28(1)(aa) (added by the Local Government (Wales) Act 1994 Sch 16 para 68(4)). As to counties and county boroughs in Wales, and their councils, see LOCAL GOVERNMENT vol 69 (2009) PARA 37 et seq.
10   Representation of the People Act 1983 s 28(1)(aa) (as added: see note 9).
11   Representation of the People Act 1983 s 28(1)(b) (amended by the Representation of the People Act 1985 s 24, Sch 4 para 6(a)). As to the Secretary of State see PARA 2. As to the making of orders under the Representation of the People Act 1983 generally see PARA 28 note 16. Before making an order designating returning officers, the authority making the instrument must consult the Electoral Commission: see the Political Parties, Elections and Referendums Act 2000 ss 7(1), (2)(c), 160(1); and PARA 54. As to the Electoral Commission see PARA 34 et seq. As to the orders that have been made see the Returning Officers (Parliamentary Constituencies) (Wales) Order 2007, SI 2007/171, art 5, Schedule; and the Returning Officers (Parliamentary Constituencies) (England) Order 2007, SI 2007/2878, art 7, Sch 4.
12   Representation of the People Act 1983 s 28(2)(a). The text refers to any duty imposed by Sch 1 r 3 (see PARA 192): see s 28(2)(a).

13 Ie the duty imposed on a returning officer by the Representation of the People Act 1983 Sch 1 r 50 (see PARA 479): see s 28(2)(b).

14 Representation of the People Act 1983 s 28(2)(b).

15 Representation of the People Act 1983 s 28(3).

16 See the Representation of the People Act 1983 s 28(4).

17 See the Representation of the People Act 1983 s 28(4). It is by virtue of this provision that references in the Representation of the People Act 1983 to the returning officer, except in relation to Sch 1 rr 3, 50 (see heads (a), (b) in the text), are, as respects England and Wales, to be read as references to the acting returning officer.

18 See the Representation of the People Act 1983 s 28(5).

19 See the Representation of the People Act 1983 s 28(5) (amended by the Representation of the People Act 1985 s 24, Sch 4 para 6(b); and the Local Government (Wales) Act 1994 Sch 16 para 68(5)).

20 See the Representation of the People Act 1983 s 28(6); and PARA 350 note 5.

352. Payments by and to returning officer for parliamentary elections. No consideration is to be given by or to a returning officer at a parliamentary election[1] for the making out, receipt, delivery or return of the writ for a parliamentary election[2] or otherwise[3] in connection with its execution[4]. This prohibition does not apply, however, to any inclusive salary payable to a returning officer at a parliamentary election in respect of the office by virtue of which he becomes returning officer[5].

A returning officer is entitled to recover his charges in respect of services properly rendered, or expenses properly incurred, for or in connection with a parliamentary election[6]:

(1) if the services were necessarily rendered, or the expenses were necessarily incurred, for the efficient and effective conduct of the election[7]; and

(2) if the total of his charges does not exceed the amount (the 'overall maximum recoverable amount') specified in, or determined in accordance with, an order made by the Secretary of State for these purposes[8].

In any order so made, the Secretary of State may specify, or make provision for determining in accordance with the order, a maximum recoverable amount for services or expenses of any specified description and the returning officer may not recover more than that amount in respect of any such services or expenses[9]. However, the Secretary of State may, in a particular case, authorise the payment of:

(a) more than the overall maximum recoverable amount[10]; or

(b) more than the specified maximum amount for any specified services or expenses[11],

if satisfied that[12]:

(i) it was reasonable for the returning officer concerned to render the services or incur the expenses[13]; and

(ii) the charges in question are reasonable[14].

On the returning officer's request for an advance on account of his charges, the Secretary of State may, on such terms as he thinks fit, make such an advance[15]. The amount of any charges recoverable in accordance with these provisions must be charged on and paid out of the Consolidated Fund[16] on an account being submitted to the Secretary of State, but he may if he thinks fit before payment, apply for a detailed assessment to be made of the account[17]. Where the superannuation contributions required to be paid by a local authority in respect of any person are increased by any fee paid under these provisions as part of a returning officer's charges at a parliamentary election, then on an account being submitted to the Secretary of State a sum equal to the increase will be charged on and paid out of the Consolidated Fund to the authority[18]. Regulations may make provision as to the time when and the manner and form in which accounts are to be rendered to the Secretary of State for the purposes of the payment of a returning officer's charges[19].

The Secretary of State may also reimburse a returning officer for a parliamentary election in respect of any expenditure incurred by the officer for the purposes of encouraging electoral participation[20]. However, the amount so paid must not in any year exceed such amount as is determined in accordance with regulations made by the Secretary of State[21].

1   As to the meaning of 'parliamentary election' see PARA 9. As to the designation of returning officers for a parliamentary election see PARA 350.

     The Representation of the People Act 1983 s 29 is applied with modifications for the purposes of combined polls: see the Representation of the People (Combination of Polls) (England and Wales) Regulations 2004, SI 2004/294, reg 6; and PARA 18.

2   As to the issue and execution of a writ for a parliamentary election see PARA 192 et seq.

3   Ie subject to the Representation of the People Act 1983 s 29(2)–(9) (see the text and notes 5–19): see s 29(1).

4   Representation of the People Act 1983 s 29(1).

5   Representation of the People Act 1983 s 29(2). In practice, this provision applies to the acting returning officer since it is that officer who executes the writ at a parliamentary election. Such an officer is a registration officer and a salary is paid to him by the relevant local authority in respect of that office: see PARAS 139, 351.

6   Representation of the People Act 1983 s 29(3) (s 29(3) substituted, s 29(3A)–(3C) added, by the Electoral Administration Act 2006 s 68(1), (2)). As from a day to be appointed under the Electoral Registration and Administration Act 2013 s 27(1), the Representation of the People Act 1983 s 29(3) is amended so that it is subject to s 29A: see s 29(3) (as so substituted; prospectively amended by the Electoral Registration and Administration Act 2013 s 18(1)). The Representation of the People Act 1983 s 29A is prospectively added by the Electoral Registration and Administration Act 2013 s 18(2), as from a day to be appointed under s 27(1), and applies to a service rendered by a returning officer for or in connection with a parliamentary election in Great Britain which, in the opinion of the Electoral Commission, was inadequately performed: see the Representation of the People Act 1983 s 29A(1) (prospectively added). The Commission may recommend to the Secretary of State that the returning officer is entitled under s 29(3) to no more than a specified amount (which may be nil) in respect of that service: s 29A(2) (prospectively added). In making such a recommendation, the Commission must have regard to:

     (1)   any report prepared under the Political Parties, Elections and Referendums Act 2000 s 5 (see PARA 51) on the administration of the parliamentary election concerned (Representation of the People Act 1983 s 29A(3)(a) (prospectively added));

     (2)   any assessments of the level of performance of the returning officer in relation to that election prepared under the Political Parties, Elections and Referendums Act 2000 s 9B(4) (see PARA 57) (Representation of the People Act 1983 s 29A(3)(b) (prospectively added));

     (3)   any representations made to the Commission by the returning officer in respect of the performance of the service (s 29A(3)(c) (prospectively added)); and

     (4)   any other information relating to the performance of the service by the returning officer that has been provided to the Commission (s 29A(3)(d) (prospectively added)).

     Where the Commission makes a recommendation under s 29A(2), the returning officer is entitled under s 29(3) to no more than the amount (which may be nil) determined by the Secretary of State, having regard to the recommendation by the Commission: s 29A(4) (prospectively added). As to the Secretary of State see PARA 2. As to the Electoral Commission see PARA 34 et seq. At the date at which this volumes states the law, no such day had been appointed in relation to the Electoral Registration and Administration Act 2013 s 18.

     The commencement of the Electoral Administration Act 2006 s 68 has the effect that prospective amendments made to the Representation of the People Act 1983 s 29 by the Political Parties, Elections and Referendums Act 2000 s 158(1), Sch 21 para 6(1), (3) (ie the Representation of the People Act 1983 s 29(3)–(9) prospectively substituted, s 29(1), (11) prospectively added), and by the Electoral Administration Act 2006 s 74(1), Sch 1 paras 104, 107(1), (2) (ie the Representation of the People Act 1983 s 29(3)–(6) prospectively further substituted), will not take effect: see the Electoral Administration Act 2006 s 68(4). Notwithstanding this provision, the Electoral Administration Act 2006 Sch 1 Pt 7 para 107(2) is prospectively amended by the Electoral Registration and Administration Act 2013 s 18(3), as from a day to be appointed under s 27(1), so that it amends the Representation of the People Act 1983 s 29(3) (prospectively substituted by the Electoral Administration Act 2006 Sch 1 paras 104, 107(1), (2)), making it subject to the Representation of the People Act 1983 s 29A: see s 29(3) (as so substituted; prospectively amended). At the date at which this volumes states the law, however, no such day had been appointed.

7 Representation of the People Act 1983 s 29(3)(a) (as substituted: see note 6).
8 Representation of the People Act 1983 s 29(3)(b) (as substituted: see note 6). The power to make orders under s 29(3) must be exercised by statutory instrument; and any such order may make different provision for different cases, circumstances or areas and may contain such incidental, supplemental, saving or transitional provisions as the Secretary of State thinks fit: s 29(4C) (added by the Representation of the People Act 1991 s 1(2); and amended by the Representation of the People Act 2000 s 15(1), Sch 6 paras 3, 4). Any exercise by the Secretary of State of his functions under the Representation of the People Act 1983 s 29(3) requires the consent of the Treasury: s 29(9) (added by the Representation of the People Act 1991 s 1(4); substituted by SI 1991/1728; and amended by the Electoral Administration Act 2006 s 68(1), (3)). As to the Treasury see CONSTITUTIONAL LAW AND HUMAN RIGHTS vol 8(2) (Reissue) PARAS 512–517. As to the order made under these provisions see the Parliamentary Elections (Returning Officers' Charges) Order 2010, SI 2010/830, art 3, Sch 1. At an uncontested election, however, arts 3–7 (see also note 9) do not apply, and the overall maximum recoverable amount for each constituency is £1,750: see art 8.

   As to where the poll at an election is taken together with the poll at another election see PARAS 21–30.

9 Representation of the People Act 1983 s 29(3A) (as added: see note 6). As to the order made under these provisions see the Parliamentary Elections (Returning Officers' Charges) Order 2010, SI 2010/830, arts 4, 6, Sch 1. The specified services are:
   (1)   conducting the election (art 5(a));
   (2)   discharging the returning officer's duties at the election (art 5(b)); and
   (3)   making arrangements for the election (art 5(c)).
   The specified expenses are:
   (a)   the appointment and payment of persons to assist the returning officer (art 7(a));
   (b)   travel and overnight subsistence for the returning officer and any person appointed to assist the returning officer (art 7(b));
   (c)   the costs of the nomination process (art 7(c));
   (d)   printing or otherwise producing the ballot papers (art 7(d));
   (e)   printing, producing or purchasing postal vote stationery (art 7(e));
   (f)   printing or otherwise producing and arranging for the delivery of poll cards (art 7(f));
   (g)   printing or otherwise producing and, where appropriate, publishing notices and any other documents required by any enactment for or in connection with a parliamentary election (art 7(g));
   (h)   renting, heating, lighting, cleaning, adapting or restoring any building or room (art 7(h));
   (i)   providing and transporting equipment (art 7(i));
   (j)   providing information and communications technology equipment and software and associated costs (art 7(j));
   (k)   providing security, including any necessary secure storage of ballot boxes, ballot papers and verification documents (art 7(k));
   (l)   conducting the verification and the count (art 7(l));
   (m)   providing and receiving training (art 7(m)); and
   (n)   providing stationery and meeting postage, telephone, printing, translation and banking costs and the costs of other miscellaneous items (art 7(n)).
   As to uncontested elections, however, see art 8; and note 8.

10 Representation of the People Act 1983 s 29(3B)(a) (as added: see note 6).
11 Representation of the People Act 1983 s 29(3B)(b) (as added: see note 6).
12 See the Representation of the People Act 1983 s 29(3B), (3C) (s 29(3B), (3C) as added: see note 6).
13 Representation of the People Act 1983 s 29(3C)(a) (as added: see note 6).
14 Representation of the People Act 1983 s 29(3C)(b) (as added: see note 6).
15 Representation of the People Act 1983 s 29(7) (amended by SI 1991/1728).
16 As to the Consolidated Fund see CONSTITUTIONAL LAW AND HUMAN RIGHTS vol 8(2) (Reissue) PARA 711 et seq; PARLIAMENT vol 78 (2010) PARAS 1028–1031.

17 Representation of the People Act 1983 s 29(5) (amended by the Representation of the People Act 1991 s 1(3); and SI 1991/1728). The text refers to the detailed assessment of a returning officer's account under the Representation of the People Act 1983 s 30 (see PARA 353): see s 29(5) (as so amended).

18 Representation of the People Act 1983 s 29(6) (amended by SI 1991/1728).

19 Representation of the People Act 1983 s 29(8) (substituted by SI 1991/1728). The regulations are not made by statutory instrument and are not recorded in this work.

20 Electoral Administration Act 2006 s 69(4), (8)(b), (9)(a). As to a returning officer's duty to encourage electoral participation at parliamentary elections see s 69(1), (2); and PARA 350.

21 Electoral Administration Act 2006 s 69(5). The power to make such regulations is exercisable by statutory instrument subject to annulment in pursuance of a resolution of either House of Parliament: s 69(6). Such regulations may make different provision for different purposes: s 69(7). The Encouraging Electoral Participation (Reimbursement of Expenses) (England and Wales) Regulations 2006, SI 2006/2972, which came into force on 1 April 2007 (see reg 1(1)), provide that the total amount that may be paid to local electoral officers in England and Wales in pursuance of the Electoral Administration Act 2006 s 69(4) in the year ending on 31 March 2008 and each successive year is £2,500,000: Encouraging Electoral Participation (Reimbursement of Expenses) (England and Wales) Regulations 2006, SI 2006/2972, reg 2. For these purposes, 'year' means a period of 12 months ending on 31 March (see reg 1(2)); and 'local electoral officer' means a returning officer for parliamentary elections (see the Electoral Administration Act 2006 s 69(8)(b), (9)(a)).

353. Detailed assessment and examination of returning officer's account at parliamentary elections. On a returning officer's account being submitted to the Secretary of State[1], the Secretary of State may, if he thinks fit, before payment, apply for a detailed assessment to be made of the account[2]. An application for a returning officer's account to be assessed in this way (a 'detailed assessment') must be made, where the account relates to a constituency in England or Wales[3], to the county court[4]. On any such application, the county court has jurisdiction:

(1)   to assess the account in such manner and at such time and place as the court thinks fit[5]; and

(2)   finally to determine the amount payable to the returning officer[6].

On any such application, the returning officer also may apply to the county court to examine any claim made by any person against him in respect of matters charged in the account (an 'examination')[7]; and the court:

(a)   after notice given to the claimant, must give him an opportunity to be heard and to tender any evidence[8]; and

(b)   may allow, disallow or reduce the claim objected to with or without costs[9].

The court's determination on the examination is final for all purposes and as against all persons[10].

The examination and detailed assessment may take place on the same day, provided that the examination is determined before the detailed assessment is concluded[11].

1 Ie under the Representation of the People Act 1983 s 29: see PARA 352. As to the Secretary of State see PARA 2. As to payments made by and to returning officer for parliamentary elections see PARA 352.

2 See the Representation of the People Act 1983 s 29(5); and PARA 352. The text refers to the detailed assessment of a returning officer's account under s 30 (see the text and notes 3–11): see s 29(5); and PARA 352.

     The Representation of the People Act 1983 ss 29–30 are applied with modifications for the purposes of combined polls: see the Representation of the People (Combination of Polls) (England and Wales) Regulations 2004, SI 2004/294, reg 6; and PARA 18.

3 As to the meanings of 'England' and 'Wales' see PARA 1 note 1. As to the meaning of 'constituency' in the context of a parliamentary election see PARA 9. As to the discharge of the returning officer's functions for parliamentary elections see PARA 351.

4   Representation of the People Act 1983 30(1)(a). An application by the Secretary of State under
    s 30 for the detailed assessment of a returning officer's account must be made by claim form:
    CPR PD 8A—*Alternative Procedure for Claims* para 17.1.
5   See the Representation of the People Act 1983 s 30(2). When it issues the claim form, the court
    will fix a date for the hearing of the detailed assessment to be dealt with if the application is
    granted: CPR PD 8A—*Alternative Procedure for Claims* para 17.2. An application for detailed
    assessment may be heard and determined by the district judge: see CPR PD 8A—*Alternative
    Procedure for Claims* para 17.7(a).
6   See the Representation of the People Act 1983 s 30(2). The court must serve a copy of the order
    made in the application on the Secretary of State and on the returning officer: see
    CPR PD 8A—*Alternative Procedure for Claims* para 17.8.
7   See the Representation of the People Act 1983 s 30(3); and CPR PD 8A—*Alternative Procedure
    for Claims* para 17.3. To make an application under para 17.3, the returning officer must file an
    application within seven days of being served with a copy of the application for detailed
    assessment: CPR PD 8A—*Alternative Procedure for Claims* para 17.4. When an application is
    filed under para 17.3, the court will fix a date for the hearing, give notice of the hearing date to
    the returning officer, and serve a copy of the application and notice of hearing on the claimant:
    see CPR PD 8A—*Alternative Procedure for Claims* para 17.5. Any application under para 17.3
    may be heard and determined by the district judge: see CPR PD 8A—*Alternative Procedure for
    Claims* para 17.7(b).
8   See the Representation of the People Act 1983 s 30(3).
9   See the Representation of the People Act 1983 s 30(3).
10 See the Representation of the People Act 1983 s 30(3). The court must serve a copy of the order
    made in the application on the Secretary of State, on the returning officer, and (in an application
    under CPR PD 8A—*Alternative Procedure for Claims* para 17.3) (see note 7), the claimant: see
    CPR PD 8A—*Alternative Procedure for Claims* para 17.8.
11 CPR PD 8A—*Alternative Procedure for Claims* para 17.6.

B. LOCAL GOVERNMENT ELECTIONS

354.   Designation of returning officer at local government elections.   In
England[1], every non-metropolitan county[2] council must appoint an officer of the
council to be the returning officer for elections of councillors of the county[3]; and
every district council[4] must appoint an officer of the council to be the returning
officer for the elections of councillors of the district, and an officer of the council
to be the returning officer for elections of councillors of parishes within the
district[5]. The returning officer at an election of London borough councillors[6] is
the proper officer of the borough[7]. The returning officer at an election of a
constituency member of the London Assembly[8] is such a person, or a person of
such a description, as may be designated by the Secretary of State[9] in an order
made by statutory instrument[10]. The returning officer at any election of the
Mayor of London[11], at the election of the London members of the London
Assembly at an ordinary election[12], and for the purposes of the return of London
members of the London Assembly otherwise than at an election[13], is the proper
officer of the Greater London Authority[14]. The council for any London borough
must place the services of its officers at the disposal of any person acting as the
returning officer at an Authority election[15] for an electoral area[16] situated wholly
or partly in the borough[17]; and, at an ordinary election, it is the duty of returning
officers for London Authority elections (both the Constituency returning officers
and the Greater London returning officers) to co-operate with each other in the
discharge of their functions[18].

In Wales[19], the council of every county or county borough[20] must appoint an
officer of the council to be the returning officer for elections of councillors of the
county or county borough[21], and an officer of the council to be the returning
officer for elections of councillors of communities within the county or county
borough[22].

A returning officer at any such election in England and Wales may by writing under his hand appoint one or more persons to discharge all or any of his functions[23]. No local government election[24] may be declared invalid by reason of any act or omission by the returning officer or any other person in breach of his official duty in connection with the election or otherwise of the elections rules[25] if it appears to the tribunal having cognisance of the question[26]:

(1)   that the election was so conducted as to be substantially in accordance with the law as to elections[27]; and

(2)   that the act or omission did not affect its result[28].

Nor is a local government election in England and Wales liable to be questioned[29] by reason of a defect in the title, or want of title, of the person presiding at or conducting the election, if that person was then in actual possession of, or acting in, the office giving the right to preside at or conduct the election[30].

A person is not subject to any incapacity to vote at a local government election by reason of being or acting as returning officer at that election[31].

A public notice which is required by or under the Representation of the People Act 1983 to be given by the proper officer of a local authority at a local government election must be given by posting the notice in some conspicuous place or places in the local government area[32] and may also be given in such other manner as he thinks desirable for publicising it[33].

A returning officer for local government elections in England and Wales must take such steps as he thinks appropriate to encourage the participation by electors in the electoral process in the area for which he acts[34]. In so doing, he must have regard to any guidance issued by the Electoral Commission[35].

1   As to the meaning of 'England' see PARA 1 note 1.

2   As to the meaning of 'non-metropolitan county' see LOCAL GOVERNMENT vol 69 (2009) PARA 24.

3   See the Representation of the People Act 1983 s 35(1) (amended by the Local Government Act 1985 s 102, Sch 16 para 11; and the Local Government (Wales) Act 1994 s 66(6), (8), Sch 16 para 68(7), Sch 18).

      The Representation of the People Act 1983 s 35 is applied and modified for the purpose of local authority mayoral elections in England and Wales by the Local Authorities (Mayoral Elections) (England and Wales) Regulations 2007, SI 2007/1024, reg 3(2)–(5), Sch 2 Table 1 (see PARA 11 note 14). Accordingly, in relation to a local authority mayoral election in England and Wales, the returning officer is either the proper officer of the London borough concerned (see the text and notes 6–7) or, as the case may be, the person appointed as the returning officer in accordance with the Representation of the People Act 1983 s 35(1) (see also the text and notes 1–2, 4–5) or s 35(1A) (see the text and notes 19–22), as those provisions are so applied, and any person appointed under the Representation of the People Act 1983 s 35(4) (see the text and note 23) by such a person: see the Local Authorities (Mayoral Elections) (England and Wales) Regulations 2007, SI 2007/1024, reg 2(1). As to an election for the return of an elected local authority mayor see PARA 198. See also LOCAL GOVERNMENT vol 69 (2009) PARA 320 et seq.

4   As to districts in England see LOCAL GOVERNMENT vol 69 (2009) PARA 24 et seq.

5   See the Representation of the People Act 1983 s 35(1) (as amended: see note 3). As to parishes generally see LOCAL GOVERNMENT vol 69 (2009) PARA 27 et seq.

6   As to the London boroughs and their councils see LOCAL GOVERNMENT vol 69 (2009) PARA 35; LONDON GOVERNMENT vol 71 (2013) PARA 15 et seq.

7   Representation of the People Act 1983 s 35(3). As to the meaning of 'proper officer' see PARA 140 note 2.

8   As to the meanings of 'constituency member' (of the London Assembly) and 'election of a constituency member of the London Assembly' see PARA 11. As to ordinary elections of constituency members of the London Assembly see PARA 199 et seq. As to the London Assembly see LONDON GOVERNMENT vol 71 (2013) PARA 70; and as to constituency members of the London Assembly see further LONDON GOVERNMENT vol 71 (2013) PARA 80.

9   As to the Secretary of State see PARA 2.

10 Representation of the People Act 1983 s 35(2A), (2B) (s 35(2A)–(2C) added by the Greater London Authority Act 1999 s 17, Sch 3 paras 1, 3(1), (2)). As to the order so made see the Greater London Authority (Assembly Constituencies and Returning Officers) Order 1999, SI 1999/3380, art 2.

11 Representation of the People Act 1983 s 35(2A), (2C)(a) (as added: see note 10). As to the meaning of 'election of the Mayor of London' see PARA 11. As to elections for the return of a Mayor of London see PARA 199. See also LONDON GOVERNMENT vol 71 (2013) PARA 76 et seq.

12 Representation of the People Act 1983 s 35(2A), (2C)(b) (as added: see note 10). As to the meaning of 'London member' see PARA 11 note 5. As to ordinary elections for the return of the London members of the London Assembly see PARA 199 et seq.

13 Representation of the People Act 1983 s 35(2A), (2C)(c) (as added: see note 10). The text refers to the returning officer for the purposes of the Greater London Authority Act 1999 s 11 (see PARA 204; and LONDON GOVERNMENT vol 71 (2013) PARA 112): see the Representation of the People Act 1983 s 35(2A), (2C)(c) (as so added).

14 Representation of the People Act 1983 s 35(2A), (2C) (as added: see note 10). As to the meaning of 'proper officer of the Greater London Authority' see LONDON GOVERNMENT vol 71 (2013) PARA 71.

15 As to the meaning of 'Authority election' see PARA 11.

16 As to the meaning of 'electoral area' see PARA 11.

17 Representation of the People Act 1983 s 35(6) (added by the Greater London Authority Act 1999 Sch 3 paras 1, 3(1), (3)).

18 Greater London Authority Elections Rules 2007, SI 2007/3541, r 10(1). As to the meaning of the 'Greater London returning officer' ('GLRO') see PARA 211 note 8; and as to the meaning of the 'constituency returning officer' ('CRO') in this context see PARA 211 note 9.

Where a poll is to be taken for the return of the London members, or for the return of the London Mayor, it is the duty of CROs to perform any of the functions they are required to perform by the rules applying to those elections (ie the rules in the Greater London Authority Elections Rules 2007, SI 2007/3541, Sch 2, Sch 3), including verifying the ballot papers at the poll (or each poll if both are to be taken), and counting the votes cast in that poll (or each poll, if both are to be taken): see r 10(2). The GLRO may give to any CRO a direction:

(1)   as to the manner in which he must discharge any of his functions set out in the Greater London Authority Elections Rules 2007, SI 2007/3541 (see r 11(1)(a)); or

(2)   requiring him to provide the GLRO with any information which the CRO has or is entitled to have in accordance with those rules (r 11(1)(b)),

relating to election (see r 11(1)); and it is the duty of each CRO to whom a direction is given under r 11(1) to discharge his functions in accordance with that direction (r 11(2)). Without prejudice to the generality of r 11(1), (2), a GLRO may exercise the power conferred by r 11(1) to give the directions set out in heads (a) to (c) below, subject to the requirements in r 11(5), (6): see r 11(3). Accordingly, the GLRO may direct the CRO to:

(a)   include alternative information in the appropriate form of postal voting statement, in place of the paragraphs beneath the heading 'Instructions to the voter' (r 11(4)(a));

(b)   issue additional information to those entitled to vote by post (r 11(4)(b)); or

(c)   exercise his discretion to include additional information in poll cards (r 11(4)(c)).

Where the GLRO has decided to direct the CRO in accordance with r 11(4), he must:

(i)   supply the alternative or additional information which the CRO is to issue to voters either electronically or in a printed form (r 11(5)(a)); and

(ii)   direct the CRO in writing as to how the information is to be used (r 11(5)(b)),

by no later than the date of the notice of election (r 11(5)). As to notice of a local government election see PARA 211. The alternative or additional information supplied under head (i) above must comply with r 9, Sch 9 para 4 (ie the requirement that all notices provided for the guidance of voters must be of the same description and appearance or in a form to like effect for use at polling stations in all Assembly constituencies: see PARA 391 note 18), as though that information were to be included in a notice (see r 11(7)(a)); and the information so supplied must relate to the system of voting at the Authority election, to how many votes a voter has at each Authority election, and to the marks to be used, and the manner in which they should be used, in order to ensure that a vote is counted for any candidate (see r 11(7)(b)). For these purposes, 'postal voting statement' and 'poll card' mean the documents issued under the relevant rules in Sch 2, Sch 3 pertaining to the election, and set out in r 9, Sch 10 (see PARAS 389, 406 note 5): see r 11(8). The Queen's Printers copy of r 11(7) refers to the 'alternative or additional information supplied under r 11(5)(b)' (see head (ii) above) rather than under r 11(5)(a) (see head (i) above) but it is submitted that a reference to the latter provision is to be preferred in the context.

Where the CRO does not discharge the functions specified in the Representation of the People (Combination of Polls) (England and Wales) Regulations 2004, SI 2004/294, reg 5 (functions at combined polls: see PARA 18), the GLRO may give a direction under the Greater London Authority Elections Rules 2007, SI 2007/3541, r 11(4) to the returning officer who does discharge those functions: see r 11(6).

19   As to the meaning of 'Wales' see PARA 1 note 1.

20   As to counties and county boroughs in Wales, and their councils, see LOCAL GOVERNMENT vol 69 (2009) PARA 37 et seq.

21   Representation of the People Act 1983 s 35(1A)(a) (s 35(1A) added by the Local Government (Wales) Act 1994 Sch 16 para 68(7)).

22   Representation of the People Act 1983 s 35(1A)(b) (as added: see note 21). As to communities generally see LOCAL GOVERNMENT vol 69 (2009) PARA 41 et seq.

23   Representation of the People Act 1983 s 35(4) (amended by the Education Reform Act 1988 s 237, Sch 12 para 50).

The Representation of the People Act 1983 s 35(4) has effect for the purposes of local authority referendums, subject to the modifications specified, in relation to Wales, by the Local Authorities (Conduct of Referendums) (Wales) Regulations 2008, SI 2008/1848, reg 8(2), Sch 4 Table 1, and, in relation to England, by the Local Authorities (Conduct of Referendums) (England) Regulations 2012, SI 2012/323, regs 8(2), 11–13, Sch 4 Table 1 (see PARA 15 note 2).

24   As to the meaning of 'local government election' see PARA 11.

25   Ie the rules under the Representation of the People Act 1983 s 36 (see PARA 383): see s 48(1). A returning officer for a local government election in England and Wales (within the meaning of the Representation of the People Act 1983: see PARA 11) may take such steps as he thinks appropriate to remedy any act or omission on his part, or on the part of a relevant person, which arises in connection with any function the returning officer or relevant person has in relation to the election, and which is not in accordance with the rules or any other requirements applicable to the election: Electoral Administration Act 2006 s 46(1), (3)(b). However, a returning officer may not in exercise of this power recount the votes given at an election after the result has been declared: s 46(2). For these purposes, a 'relevant person' is an electoral registration officer, a presiding officer, a person providing goods or services to the returning officer, or a deputy of any such person or a person appointed to assist, or in the course of his employment assisting, such a person in connection with any function he has in relation to the election: see s 46(4). Section 46(1)–(4) must be construed as part of the Representation of the People Acts: see the Electoral Administration Act 2006 s 46(5). As to the meaning of the 'Representation of the People Acts' see PARA 3 note 1.

The Electoral Administration Act 2006 s 46 has effect for the purposes of local authority referendums, subject to the modifications specified, in relation to Wales, by the Local Authorities (Conduct of Referendums) (Wales) Regulations 2008, SI 2008/1848, reg 8(2), Sch 4 Table 4, and, in relation to England, by the Local Authorities (Conduct of Referendums) (England) Regulations 2012, SI 2012/323, regs 8(2), 11–13, Sch 4 Table 5 (see PARA 15 note 2).

26   see the Representation of the People Act 1983 s 48(1).

27   Representation of the People Act 1983 s 48(1)(a).

28   Representation of the People Act 1983 s 48(1)(b).

29   As to the questioning of local government elections see PARA 762 et seq.

30   Representation of the People Act 1983 s 35(5)

31   Representation of the People Act 1983 s 46(2). The provision is necessary because returning officers were formerly unable to vote at the election for which they acted as returning officers because they decided any equality of votes (which question is now determined by lot: see PARA 434).

The Representation of the People Act 1983 s 46 is applied and modified for the purpose of local authority mayoral elections in England and Wales by the Local Authorities (Mayoral Elections) (England and Wales) Regulations 2007, SI 2007/1024, reg 3(2)–(5), Sch 2 Table 1 (see PARA 11 note 14).

32   As to the meaning of 'local government area' see PARA 33 note 7.

33   Representation of the People Act 1983 s 200(1A) (substituted by the Representation of the People Act 1985 s 24, Sch 4 para 68).

34   Electoral Administration Act 2006 s 69(1), (8)(b), (9)(b). As to the meaning of 'elector', in relation to a local government election, see PARA 95 note 2.

The Electoral Administration Act 2006 s 69 has effect for the purposes of local authority referendums, subject to the modifications specified, in relation to Wales, by the Local Authorities (Conduct of Referendums) (Wales) Regulations 2008, SI 2008/1848, reg 8(2), Sch 4 Table 4, and, in relation to England, by the Local Authorities (Conduct of Referendums) (England) Regulations 2012, SI 2012/323, regs 8(2), 11–13, Sch 4 Table 5 (see PARA 15 note 2).

35 Electoral Administration Act 2006 s 69(2). See note 34. As to the Electoral Commission see PARA 34 et seq.

355. Returning officer's expenses for local elections. All expenditure properly incurred by a returning officer[1]:

(1) in relation to the holding of an election of a councillor for a principal area[2], must be paid by that council in so far as such expenditure does not, in cases where there is a scale fixed for the purpose[4] by the council for that area, exceed that scale[4];

(2) in relation to the holding of an Authority election[5], in so far as it does not, in cases where there is a scale fixed for the purpose[6] by the Greater London Authority[7], exceed that scale, must be paid by the Greater London Authority[8];

(3) in relation to the holding of an election of a parish councillor in England[9], in so far as it does not, in cases where there is a scale fixed for the purpose[10] by the council of the district in which the parish is situated, exceed that scale, must be paid by the district council, but any expenditure so incurred must, if the district council so requires, be repaid to that council by the council of the parish for which the election is held[11];

(4) in relation to the holding of an election of a community councillor in Wales[12], in so far as it does not, in cases where there is a scale fixed for this purpose[13] by the council of the county or county borough in which the community is situated (the 'principal council'), exceed that scale, must be paid by the principal council, but any expenditure so incurred must, if the principal council so requires, be repaid to that council by the community council[14].

Before a poll is taken at an election for any local government area in England and Wales[15], the council of that area (or, in the case of an election of a parish or community councillor, the council which appointed the returning officer) must, at the request of the returning officer or of any person acting as returning officer, advance to him such reasonable sum in respect of his expenses at the election as he may require[16]; and before a poll is taken at an Authority election, the Greater London Authority must, at the request of the returning officer or of any person acting as returning officer, advance to him such reasonable sum in respect of his expenses at the election as he may require[17].

The council which is required to pay the expenses properly incurred by a returning officer in relation to any local government election[18] may treat those expenses as including all costs properly incurred by the returning officer in connection with or in contemplation of any legal proceedings arising out of the election (including any criminal proceedings against the returning officer), whether or not the proceedings are in fact instituted[19].

The Secretary of State[20] may reimburse a returning officer for a local government election in England and Wales in respect of any expenditure incurred by the officer for the purposes of encouraging electoral participation[21]. However, the amount so paid must not in any year exceed such amount as is determined in accordance with regulations made by the Secretary of State[22].

1 As to the designation of returning officers at local government elections see PARA 354.
2 Ie a county, a county borough, a district or a London borough: see the Representation of the People Act 1983 s 36(4) (amended by the Local Government Act 1985 s 102, Sch 17; and the Local Government (Wales) Act 1994 s 66(6), Sch 16 para 68(9)). As to the election of councillors for local government principal areas see PARA 197. As to counties and districts in

England, and their councils, see LOCAL GOVERNMENT vol 69 (2009) PARA 24 et seq; as to counties and county boroughs in Wales, and their councils, see LOCAL GOVERNMENT vol 69 (2009) PARA 37 et seq; and as to the London boroughs and their councils see LOCAL GOVERNMENT vol 69 (2009) PARA 35; LONDON GOVERNMENT vol 71 (2013) PARA 15 et seq.

     The Representation of the People Act 1983 s 36 is applied and modified for the purpose of local authority mayoral elections in England and Wales by the Local Authorities (Mayoral Elections) (England and Wales) Regulations 2007, SI 2007/1024, reg 3(2)–(5), Sch 2 Table 1 (see PARA 11 note 14). As to elections for the return of an elected mayor for a local authority see PARA 198 et seq.

3   Ie fixed for the purposes of the Representation of the People Act 1983 s 36: see s 36(4) (as amended: see note 2).

4   Representation of the People Act 1983 s 36(4) (as amended: see note 2). As to expenditure incurred for the purposes of combined polls see PARA 17.

5   As to the meaning of 'Authority election' see PARA 11.

6   Ie fixed for the purposes of the Representation of the People Act 1983 s 36: see s 36(4B) (added by the Greater London Authority Act 1999 s 17, Sch 3 paras 1, 4(1), (3)).

7   As to the Greater London Authority see LONDON GOVERNMENT vol 71 (2013) PARA 67 et seq.

8   Representation of the People Act 1983 s 36(4B) (as added: see note 6).

9   As to the meaning of 'England' see PARA 1 note 1. As to the election of councillors for parish councils see PARA 200.

10   Ie fixed for the purposes of the Representation of the People Act 1983 s 36: see s 36(5) (amended by the Local Government (Wales) Act 1994 s 66(8), Sch 16 para 68(10), Sch 18; and SI 1991/1730).

11   Representation of the People Act 1983 s 36(5) (as amended: see note 10).

12   As to the meaning of 'Wales' see PARA 1 note 1. As to the election of councillors for community councils see PARA 200.

13   Ie fixed for the purposes of the Representation of the People Act 1983 s 36: see s 36(5A) (added by the Local Government (Wales) Act 1994 Sch 16 para 68(10)).

14   Representation of the People Act 1983 s 36(5A) (as added: see note 13).

15   Ie at an election of a councillor for any local government area, or at an election of an elected mayor of the council of any such area (see note 2). As to the meaning of 'local government area' see PARA 33 note 7.

16   Representation of the People Act 1983 s 36(6).

17   Representation of the People Act 1983 s 36(6); applied by s 36(6A) (added by the Greater London Authority Act 1999 Sch 3 paras 1, 4(1), (4)).

18   In relation to an Authority election, the Greater London Authority is treated as the council which is required to pay the expenses properly incurred by the returning officer: Representation of the People Act 1983 s 48(3A) (added by the Greater London Authority Act 1999 Sch 3 paras 1, 9). As to the meaning of 'local government election' see PARA 11.

     The Representation of the People Act 1983 s 48 is applied and modified for the purpose of local authority mayoral elections in England and Wales by the Local Authorities (Mayoral Elections) (England and Wales) Regulations 2007, SI 2007/1024, reg 3(2)–(5), Sch 2 Table 1 (see PARA 11 note 14).

19   Representation of the People Act 1983 s 48(3).

20   As to the Secretary of State see PARA 2.

21   Electoral Administration Act 2006 s 69(4), (8)(b), (9)(b). For these purposes, references to a local government election are to be construed in accordance with the Representation of the People Act 1983: see the Electoral Administration Act 2006 s 69(10). As to a returning officer's duty to encourage electoral participation at local government elections see s 69(1), (2); and PARA 354.

     The Electoral Administration Act 2006 s 69 is applied and modified for the purpose of local authority mayoral elections in England and Wales by the Local Authorities (Mayoral Elections) (England and Wales) Regulations 2007, SI 2007/1024, reg 3(2)–(5), Sch 2 Table 5 (see PARA 11 note 14); and has effect for the purposes of local authority referendums, subject to the modifications specified, in relation to Wales, by the Local Authorities (Conduct of Referendums) (Wales) Regulations 2008, SI 2008/1848, reg 8(2), Sch 4 Table 4, and, in relation to England, by the Local Authorities (Conduct of Referendums) (England) Regulations 2012, SI 2012/323, regs 8(2), 11–13, Sch 4 Table 5 (see PARA 15 note 2).

22   Electoral Administration Act 2006 s 69(5). The power to make such regulations is exercisable by statutory instrument subject to annulment in pursuance of a resolution of either House of Parliament: s 69(6). Such regulations may make different provision for different purposes: s 69(7). See note 21. The Encouraging Electoral Participation (Reimbursement of Expenses) (England and Wales) Regulations 2006, SI 2006/2972, which came into force on 1 April 2007

(see reg 1(1)), provide that the total amount that may be paid to local electoral officers in England and Wales in pursuance of the Electoral Administration Act 2006 s 69(4) in the year ending on 31 March 2008 and each successive year is £2,500,000: Encouraging Electoral Participation (Reimbursement of Expenses) (England and Wales) Regulations 2006, SI 2006/2972, reg 2. For these purposes, 'year' means a period of 12 months ending on 31 March (reg 1(2)); and 'local electoral officer' means a returning officer for local government elections in England and Wales (Electoral Administration Act 2006 s 69(8)(b), (9)(b)).

356. Returning officer and appointment of office at a poll consequent on parish meeting. If a poll consequent on a parish meeting is required to be taken in respect of any appointment to office[1], the chairman of the meeting must notify the district council[2] in which the parish is situated[3], and the council must appoint an officer of the council to be returning officer[4]. The returning officer must appoint an office for the purpose of the poll[5].

Any public notice required to be given by a returning officer for these purposes must be given by the notice being posted in some conspicuous place or places in the parish, and may also be given in such other manner as the returning officer thinks desirable for publicising it[6].

1   As to when such a poll is required to be taken see PARA 200.
2   As to districts, and their councils, see LOCAL GOVERNMENT vol 69 (2009) PARA 24 et seq.
3   See the Parish and Community Meetings (Polls) Rules 1987, SI 1987/1, r 4(1); and PARA 212. As to parishes generally see LOCAL GOVERNMENT vol 69 (2009) PARA 27 et seq.
4   See the Parish and Community Meetings (Polls) Rules 1987, SI 1987/1, r 4(1). The chairman of the meeting must give the returning officer such particulars as will enable him to give notice of the poll: see r 4(2); and PARA 212.
5   Parish and Community Meetings (Polls) Rules 1987, SI 1987/1, r 4(3).
6   Parish and Community Meetings (Polls) Rules 1987, SI 1987/1, Schedule r 38(2). Where the poll is held in part only of a parish, any reference to a parish in the rules is to be construed as a reference to part of the parish: Schedule r 38(1).

C. WELSH ASSEMBLY ELECTIONS

357. Designation of returning officers for Welsh Assembly elections. For the purpose of Welsh Assembly elections[1], there must be:
(1)   a constituency returning officer[2] for each Assembly constituency[3]; and
(2)   a regional returning officer[4] for each Assembly electoral region[5].

A constituency returning officer is the person who is appointed under the Representation of the People Act 1983[6] to be the returning officer for elections of councillors of a county or county borough[7] situated wholly or partly in the Assembly constituency[8], and (in the case where there is more than one such person) who is for the time being designated by the National Assembly for Wales as returning officer for the constituency[9].

A regional returning officer is the person who is appointed under the Representation of the People Act 1983[10] to be the returning officer for elections of councillors of a county or county borough situated wholly or partly in the Assembly electoral region[11], and (in the case where there is more than one such person) who is for the time being designated by the Assembly as returning officer for the electoral region[12].

The office of returning officer is a distinct office from that by virtue of which the person becomes returning officer[13].

The council of each county or county borough must place the services of its officers at the disposal of any constituency returning officer for an Assembly constituency wholly or partly situated in its area[14]; and the services so placed at the disposal of such an officer may relate to the exercise of that officer's functions in connection with a constituency election, a regional election or to both such elections[15]. The council of each county or county borough must also place the services of its officers at the disposal of any regional returning officer for an Assembly electoral region partly situated in its area[16].

Either a constituency returning officer (whether at a constituency or regional Assembly election) or a regional returning officer (at a regional Assembly election) may, in writing, appoint one or more persons to discharge all or any of his functions[17]. Except in the case of an election to fill a casual vacancy[18], it is the duty of each regional returning officer, and each constituency returning officer for an Assembly constituency in the Assembly electoral region, to co-operate with each other in the discharge of their functions[19]; and this duty applies as between constituency returning officers in an Assembly electoral region as well as between such officers and the regional returning officer for the electoral region[20].

In addition to the functions otherwise conferred or imposed on a constituency or regional returning officer at an Assembly election, it is the general duty of such an officer to do all such acts as may be necessary for effectively conducting the election[21]. No Assembly election may be declared invalid by reason of any act or omission by such a returning officer or any other person in breach of his official duty in connection with the election or otherwise in breach of the Assembly election rules[22], if it appears to the election court having cognisance of the question[23]:

(a)   that the election was so conducted as to be substantially in accordance with the law as to Assembly elections[24]; and

(b)   that the act or omission did not affect the result[25].

Nor is an Assembly election liable to be questioned[26] by reason of a defect in the title, or want of title, of the person presiding at or conducting the election, if that person was then in actual possession of, or acting in, the office giving the right to preside at, or conduct, the election[27]. A person is not subject to any incapacity to vote at an Assembly election by reason of being returning officer at that election[28].

A returning officer for elections to the National Assembly for Wales must take such steps as he thinks appropriate to encourage the participation by electors in the electoral process in the area for which he acts[29]. In so doing, he must have regard to any guidance issued by the Electoral Commission[30].

1   As to the meaning of 'Assembly election' see PARA 3 note 2.
2   As to the meaning of 'constituency returning officer' see PARA 18 note 2.
3   National Assembly for Wales (Representation of the People) Order 2007, SI 2007/236, art 18(1)(a). Such a person holds office in accordance with art 18(2)–(6) (see the text and notes 6–13): see art 18(1). As to the meaning of 'Assembly constituency' see PARA 3 note 2.
4   As to the meaning of 'regional returning officer' see PARA 18 note 2.
5   National Assembly for Wales (Representation of the People) Order 2007, SI 2007/236, art 18(1)(b). Such a person holds office in accordance with art 18(2)–(6) (see the text and notes 6–13): see art 18(1). As to the meaning of 'Assembly electoral region' see PARA 3 note 2.
6   Ie under the Representation of the People Act 1983 s 35(1A)(a) (see PARA 354): see the National Assembly for Wales (Representation of the People) Order 2007, SI 2007/236, art 18(2)(a).
7   As to counties and county boroughs in Wales, and their councils, see LOCAL GOVERNMENT vol 69 (2009) PARA 37 et seq.
8   National Assembly for Wales (Representation of the People) Order 2007, SI 2007/236, art 18(2)(a).
9   National Assembly for Wales (Representation of the People) Order 2007, SI 2007/236, art 18(2)(b). The designation of a constituency returning officer under art 18 must be in writing: see art 18(4). As to the National Assembly for Wales see CONSTITUTIONAL LAW AND HUMAN RIGHTS.

10 Ie under the Representation of the People Act 1983 s 35(1A)(a) (see PARA 354): see the National Assembly for Wales (Representation of the People) Order 2007, SI 2007/236, art 18(3)(a).

11 National Assembly for Wales (Representation of the People) Order 2007, SI 2007/236, art 18(3)(a).

12 National Assembly for Wales (Representation of the People) Order 2007, SI 2007/236, art 18(3)(b). The designation of a regional returning officer under art 18 must be in writing: see art 18(4).

13 National Assembly for Wales (Representation of the People) Order 2007, SI 2007/236, art 18(5). Where a person takers any office by virtue of which he becomes a returning officer. he (and not the outgoing holder of the office) must complete the conduct of any outstanding election in accordance with the Assembly election rules: see art 18(6). 'Assembly election rules' means the rules for the conduct of Assembly elections set out in Sch 5 (see PARA 383): see art 2(1).

14 National Assembly for Wales (Representation of the People) Order 2007, SI 2007/236, art 19(1).

15 National Assembly for Wales (Representation of the People) Order 2007, SI 2007/236, art 19(2). In the National Assembly for Wales (Representation of the People) Order 2007, SI 2007/236, a reference to a constituency returning officer in relation to the discharge of functions at a regional election is a reference to the discharge of such functions in relation to the Assembly constituency for which he is the returning officer: see art 20(5).

16 National Assembly for Wales (Representation of the People) Order 2007, SI 2007/236, art 19(3).

17 See the National Assembly for Wales (Representation of the People) Order 2007, SI 2007/236, art 20(1), (2).

18 As to Welsh Assembly elections to fill a casual vacancy see PARAS 214, 215.

19 National Assembly for Wales (Representation of the People) Order 2007, SI 2007/236, art 20(3).

20 National Assembly for Wales (Representation of the People) Order 2007, SI 2007/236, art 20(4).

21 National Assembly for Wales (Representation of the People) Order 2007, SI 2007/236, art 17(2). The text refers to effectively conducting the election in the manner provided by the Assembly election rules (see note 13): see art 17(2).

22 A constituency or regional returning officer at an Assembly election may take such steps as he thinks appropriate to remedy any act or omission on his part, or on the part of a relevant person, which arises in connection with any function the returning officer or relevant person has in relation to the election, and which is not in accordance with the rules or any other requirements applicable to the election: see art 21(1). However, a returning officer may not in exercise of this power recount the votes given at an election after the result has been declared: art 21(2). For these purposes, a 'relevant person' is:

    (1)   an electoral registration officer (art 21(3)(a));

    (2)   (in relation to a regional Assembly election) a relevant returning officer at that election (art 21(3)(b));

    (3)   a presiding officer (art 21(3)(c));

    (4)   a person providing goods or services to the returning officer (art 21(3)(d)); and

    (5)   a deputy of any such person mentioned in heads (1) to (3) above, or a person appointed to assist, or in the course of his employment assisting, such a person in connection with any function he has in relation to the election (art 21(3)(e)).

For the purposes of head (2) above, a 'relevant returning officer' means:

    (a)   in the case of a regional returning officer taking steps under art 21(1), a constituency returning officer at that regional election (art 21(4)(a));

    (b)   in the case of a constituency returning officer taking steps under art 21(1), the regional returning officer at that regional election (art 21(4)(b)).

Where the act or omission to be remedied is that of a relevant returning officer, then, before taking steps under art 21(1), the regional returning officer must consult the constituency returning officer whose act or omission is to be remedied, and a constituency returning officer must consult the regional returning officer: see art 21(5).

23 National Assembly for Wales (Representation of the People) Order 2007, SI 2007/236, art 17(3).

24 National Assembly for Wales (Representation of the People) Order 2007, SI 2007/236, art 17(3)(a).

25 National Assembly for Wales (Representation of the People) Order 2007, SI 2007/236, art 17(3)(b).

26 As to the questioning of Welsh Assembly elections see PARA 764 et seq.

27 National Assembly for Wales (Representation of the People) Order 2007, SI 2007/236, art 22(1).
28 National Assembly for Wales (Representation of the People) Order 2007, SI 2007/236, art 22(2).
29 Electoral Administration Act 2006 s 69(1), (8)(b), (9)(f). As to the meaning of 'elector', in relation to a Welsh Assembly election, see PARA 110 note 6.
30 Electoral Administration Act 2006 s 69(2). As to the Electoral Commission see PARA 34 et seq.

358. Payments by and to returning officer for Welsh Assembly elections. A constituency[1] or a regional returning officer[2] is entitled to recover his charges in respect of services rendered, or expenses incurred, for, or in connection with, a Welsh Assembly election, if[3]:

(1) the services were necessarily rendered, or the expenses were necessarily incurred, for the efficient and effective conduct of the election[4]; and

(2) the total of his charges does not exceed the amount (the 'overall maximum recoverable amount') specified in, or determined in accordance with, an order made by the National Assembly for Wales for these purposes[5].

Any order made under head (2) above may specify, or make provision for determining in accordance with the order, a maximum recoverable amount for services or expenses of any specified description, and the returning officer may not recover more than that amount in respect of any such services or expenses[6], except that the Assembly may, in a particular case, authorise the payment of[7]:

(a) more than the overall maximum recoverable amount[8]; or

(b) more than the specified maximum recoverable amount for any specified services or expenses[9],

if the Assembly is satisfied that[10]:

(i) it was reasonable for the returning officer concerned to render the services or incur the expenses[11]; and

(ii) the charges in question are reasonable[12].

The Assembly must pay the amount of any charges so recoverable on an account being submitted to it, but the Assembly may, if it thinks fit, before payment, apply for a detailed assessment of the account[13]. Where the superannuation contributions required to be paid by a local authority in respect of any person are increased by any fee so paid as part of a returning officer's charges at an Assembly election, then, on an account being submitted to the Assembly, a sum equal to the increase must be paid by the Assembly to the authority[14]. On a returning officer's request for an advance on account of his charges, the Assembly may, on such terms as it thinks fit, make such an advance[15]. The Assembly by regulations may make provision as to the time when and the manner and form in which accounts are to be rendered to the Assembly for the purpose of the payment of a returning officer's charges; and such regulations may make different provision for different purposes[16]. Any sums so payable by the Assembly or Welsh Ministers must be charged to the Welsh Consolidated Fund[17].

The Secretary of State may reimburse a returning officer for a Welsh Assembly election in respect of any expenditure incurred by the officer for the purposes of encouraging electoral participation[18]. However, the amount so paid must not in any year exceed such amount as is determined in accordance with regulations made by the Secretary of State[19].

1 As to the meaning of 'constituency returning officer' see PARA 18 note 2. As to the designation of returning officers for Welsh Assembly elections see PARA 357.
2 As to the meaning of 'regional returning officer' see PARA 18 note 2.

3   See the National Assembly for Wales (Representation of the People) Order 2007, SI 2007/236, art 23(1). As to the meaning of 'Assembly election' see PARA 3 note 2.

4   National Assembly for Wales (Representation of the People) Order 2007, SI 2007/236, art 23(1)(a). In the case of a constituency returning officer, art 23(1) applies to services rendered or expenses incurred for, or in connection with, a constituency or a regional election: see art 23(1). As to the meanings of 'constituency election' and 'regional election' see PARA 3 note 2.

5   National Assembly for Wales (Representation of the People) Order 2007, SI 2007/236, art 23(1)(b). See note 4. As to the National Assembly for Wales see CONSTITUTIONAL LAW AND HUMAN RIGHTS.

The power to make orders under art 23(1) must be exercised by statutory instrument and, for the purpose of the Statutory Instruments Act 1946 s 1 (see STATUTES AND LEGISLATIVE PROCESS vol 96 (2012) PARA 1045), the National Assembly for Wales (Representation of the People) Order 2007, SI 2007/236, art 23 has effect as if contained in an Act of Parliament: art 23(5). Any order under art 23(1) also may make different provision for different purposes, and may contain such incidental supplemental saving or transitional provision as the Assembly thinks fit: art 23(6). As to the order so made see the National Assembly for Wales (Returning Officers' Charges) Order 2011, SI 2011/632, arts 4, 7, Sch 1 (arts 4, 7 amended, Sch 1 substituted, by SI 2012/2478). However, at an uncontested Assembly constituency election, the National Assembly for Wales (Returning Officers' Charges) Order 2011, SI 2011/632, arts 4–6 do not apply (see art 10(a)); and, at an uncontested Assembly regional election, arts 7–9 do not apply (see art 11(a)). Accordingly, at an uncontested Assembly constituency election, the overall maximum recoverable amount for services and expenses for each constituency is £1,750 (one thousand seven hundred and fifty pounds) (see art 10(b)); and, at an uncontested Assembly regional election, the overall maximum recoverable amount for services and expenses for each region is £350 (three hundred and fifty pounds) (see art 11(b)).

6   National Assembly for Wales (Representation of the People) Order 2007, SI 2007/236, art 23(2). As to the order made under these provisions see the National Assembly for Wales (Returning Officers' Charges) Order 2011, SI 2011/632, arts 5(1), 6(1), 8(1), 9(1), Schs 1, 2 (arts 5(1), 6(1), 8(1), 9(1) amended, Sch 1 substituted, by SI 2012/2478). The specified services, in relation to either a constituency or regional election, are:
  (1)   making arrangements for the election (National Assembly for Wales (Returning Officers' Charges) Order 2011, SI 2011/632, arts 5(2)(a), 8(2)(a));
  (2)   conducting the election (arts 5(2)(b), 8(2)(b)); and
  (3)   discharging the returning officer's duties at the election (arts 5(2)(c), 8(2)(c)).
The specified expenses, in relation to a constituency election, are:
  (a)   the appointment and payment of persons to assist the returning officer (art 6(2)(a));
  (b)   reimbursement of travel and subsistence expenses incurred by any person appointed to assist the returning officer and the returning officer (art 6(2)(b));
  (c)   printing or production of ballot papers (art 6(2)(c));
  (d)   printing and delivery of postal voting documents (art 6(2)(d));
  (e)   printing and delivery of poll cards (art 6(2)(e));
  (f)   printing and publishing of all election notices and documents (art 6(2)(f));
  (g)   renting and adaptation of premises for use as polling stations or count centres, including heating, lighting, cleaning and restoring building or room to original condition (art 6(2)(g));
  (h)   providing and transporting all equipment necessary for the conduct of the election and count (art 6(2)(h));
  (i)   providing all information and communications technology equipment and software and associated costs (art 6(2)(i));
  (j)   providing security and secure storage of electoral documents during the period of the election (art 6(2)(j));
  (k)   conducting the verification and the count (art 6(2)(k));
  (l)   providing and receiving training (art 6(2)(l)); and
  (m)   the costs of miscellaneous items not accounted for elsewhere such as stationery, postage, telephone, printing and translation (art 6(2)(m)).
The specified expenses, in relation to a regional election, are:
  (i)   appointment and payment of fees to persons who assist the regional returning officer (art 9(2)(2)(a));
  (ii)   reimbursement of travel and subsistence expenses incurred by any person appointed to assist the regional returning officer and the regional returning officer (art 9(2)(2)(b));
  (iii)   printing and publishing of notices (art 9(2)(2)(c));
  (iv)   preparing the ballot paper (art 9(2)(2)(d)); and

    (v)   the costs of miscellaneous items not accounted for elsewhere such as stationery, postage, telephone, printing and translation (art 9(2)(2)(e)).

As to uncontested Assembly elections see note 5.

7   National Assembly for Wales (Representation of the People) Order 2007, SI 2007/236, art 23(3).

8   National Assembly for Wales (Representation of the People) Order 2007, SI 2007/236, art 23(3)(a).

9   National Assembly for Wales (Representation of the People) Order 2007, SI 2007/236, art 23(3)(b).

10 See the National Assembly for Wales (Representation of the People) Order 2007, SI 2007/236, art 23(3), (4).

11 National Assembly for Wales (Representation of the People) Order 2007, SI 2007/236, art 23(4)(a).

12 National Assembly for Wales (Representation of the People) Order 2007, SI 2007/236, art 23(4)(b).

13 National Assembly for Wales (Representation of the People) Order 2007, SI 2007/236, art 23(7). The text refers to a detailed assessment conducted under art 24 (see PARA 359): see art 23(7).

14 National Assembly for Wales (Representation of the People) Order 2007, SI 2007/236, art 23(8).

15 National Assembly for Wales (Representation of the People) Order 2007, SI 2007/236, art 23(9).

16 National Assembly for Wales (Representation of the People) Order 2007, SI 2007/236, art 23(10). In exercise of the powers so conferred on the National Assembly for Wales, the Welsh Ministers have made the National Assembly for Wales (Returning Officers' Accounts) Regulations 2011, SI 2011/676. Accordingly, an account submitted under the National Assembly for Wales (Representation of the People) Order 2007, SI 2007/236, art 23(7) (see the text and note 13), for the payment of a constituency or a regional returning officer's charges for, or in connection with, an Assembly election, must be submitted within the period of eight months commencing with the day of the Assembly election to which the account relates: see the National Assembly for Wales (Returning Officers' Accounts) Regulations 2011, SI 2011/676, reg 3(1). Such an account must be accompanied: (1) by a receipt in respect of each charge for an expense incurred by the constituency or regional returning officer to whom the account relates (see reg 3(4)(a)); and (2) by a certificate, either in English or in Welsh, signed by that returning officer, declaring that the account submitted is correct to the best of that officer's knowledge and belief (see reg 3(4)(b)). An account may be submitted in respect of some of the charges which a constituency or a regional returning officer is entitled to recover (an 'incomplete account'): reg 3(2). However, where a further account is likely to be submitted, the incomplete account must include a statement to this effect, plus the reason for the submission of an incomplete account and the proposed date (agreed with the Principal Accounting Officer) by which the complete accounts will be submitted: see reg 3(2), (3). The form in which an account is submitted must be such that the charges in respect of each listed item are shown separately, where 'listed item' ('eitem a restrir') refers to a kind of service rendered or expense incurred by a constituency or a regional returning officer for, or in connection with, the Assembly election to which the account relates: see reg 4(1), (2). As to the Welsh Ministers see PARA 2. As to the principal accounting officer for the Welsh Ministers see CONSTITUTIONAL LAW AND HUMAN RIGHTS.

17 National Assembly for Wales (Representation of the People) Order 2007, SI 2007/236, art 23(11). As to the Welsh Consolidated Fund see CONSTITUTIONAL LAW AND HUMAN RIGHTS.

18 Electoral Administration Act 2006 s 69(4), (8)(b), (9)(f). As to the duty of a returning officer for a Welsh Assembly election to encourage electoral participation see s 69(1), (2); and PARA 357. As to the Secretary of State see PARA 2.

19 Electoral Administration Act 2006 s 69(5). The power to make such regulations is exercisable by statutory instrument subject to annulment in pursuance of a resolution of either House of Parliament: s 69(6). Such regulations may make different provision for different purposes: s 69(7). The Encouraging Electoral Participation (Reimbursement of Expenses) (England and Wales) Regulations 2006, SI 2006/2972, which came into force on 1 April 2007 (see reg 1(1)), provide that the total amount that may be paid to local electoral officers in England and Wales in pursuance of the Electoral Administration Act 2006 s 69(4) in the year ending on 31 March 2008 and each successive year is £2,500,000: Encouraging Electoral Participation (Reimbursement of Expenses) (England and Wales) Regulations 2006, SI 2006/2972, reg 2. For

these purposes, 'year' means a period of 12 months ending on 31 March (reg 1(2)); and 'local electoral officer' means a returning officer for Welsh Assembly elections (Electoral Administration Act 2006 s 69(8)(b), (9)(f)).

359. Detailed assessment and examination of returning officer's account at Welsh Assembly elections. On a returning officer's account being submitted to the National Assembly for Wales[1], the Assembly may, if it thinks fit, before payment, apply for a detailed assessment to be made of the account[2]. An application for a returning officer's account to be assessed in this way (a 'detailed assessment') must be made to the county court[3]. On any such application, the county court has jurisdiction:

(1) to assess the account in such manner and at such time and place as the court thinks fit[4]; and

(2) finally to determine the amount payable to the returning officer[5].

On any such application, the returning officer also may apply to the county court to examine any claim made by any person against him in respect of matters charged in the account (an 'examination')[6]; and the court:

(a) after notice given to the claimant, must give him an opportunity to be heard and to tender any evidence[7]; and

(b) may allow, disallow or reduce the claim objected to with or without costs[8].

The court's determination on the examination is final for all purposes and as against all persons[9].

The examination and detailed assessment may take place on the same day, provided that the examination is determined before the detailed assessment is concluded[10].

1 Ie under the National Assembly for Wales (Representation of the People) Order 2007, SI 2007/236, art 23: see PARA 358. As to the National Assembly for Wales see CONSTITUTIONAL LAW AND HUMAN RIGHTS.

2 See the National Assembly for Wales (Representation of the People) Order 2007, SI 2007/236, art 23(7); and PARA 358. The text refers to the detailed assessment of a returning officer's account under the provisions of art 24 (see the text and notes 3–10): see art 23(7); and PARA 358.

3 National Assembly for Wales (Representation of the People) Order 2007, SI 2007/236, art 24(1). CPR Sch 2 CCR Ord 45 r 1 has effect, with modifications, in relation to applications made under the National Assembly for Wales (Representation of the People) Order 2007, SI 2007/236, art 24: see art 24(4). However, CPR Sch 2 CCR Ord 45 r 1 has been repealed and the reference should be to CPR PD 8A—*Alternative Procedure for Claims* para 17: see the Interpretation Act 1978 s 17(2). Accordingly, an application by the Assembly under the National Assembly for Wales (Representation of the People) Order 2007, SI 2007/236, art 24 for the detailed assessment of a returning officer's account must be made by claim form: CPR PD 8A—*Alternative Procedure for Claims* para 17.1. For these purposes, references to returning officers must be construed as references to:

(1) constituency returning officers in relation to a constituency election (see the National Assembly for Wales (Representation of the People) Order 2007, SI 2007/236, art 24(4)(b)(i)); and

(2) constituency and regional returning officers in relation to a regional election (art 24(4)(b)(ii)).

As to the meanings of 'constituency election' and 'regional election' in the context of Welsh Assembly elections see PARA 3 note 2; and as to the meanings of 'constituency returning officer' and 'regional returning officer' in this context see PARA 18 note 2.

4 See the National Assembly for Wales (Representation of the People) Order 2007, SI 2007/236, art 24(2). When it issues the claim form, the court will fix a date for the hearing of the detailed assessment to be dealt with if the application is granted: CPR PD 8A—*Alternative Procedure for Claims* para 17.2. An application for detailed assessment may be heard and determined by the district judge: see CPR PD 8A—*Alternative Procedure for Claims* para 17.7(a).

5   See the National Assembly for Wales (Representation of the People) Order 2007, SI 2007/236, art 24(2). The court must serve a copy of the order made in the application on the Assembly and on the returning officer: see CPR PD 8A—*Alternative Procedure for Claims* para 17.8.
6   See the National Assembly for Wales (Representation of the People) Order 2007, SI 2007/236, art 24(3); and CPR PD 8A—*Alternative Procedure for Claims* para 17.3. To make an application under para 17.3, the returning officer must file an application within seven days of being served with a copy of the application for detailed assessment: CPR PD 8A—*Alternative Procedure for Claims* para 17.4. When an application is filed under para 17.3, the court will fix a date for the hearing, give notice of the hearing date to the returning officer, and serve a copy of the application and notice of hearing on the claimant: see CPR PD 8A—*Alternative Procedure for Claims* para 17.5. Any application under para 17.3 may be heard and determined by the district judge: see CPR PD 8A—*Alternative Procedure for Claims* para 17.7(b).
7   See the National Assembly for Wales (Representation of the People) Order 2007, SI 2007/236, art 24(3).
8   See the National Assembly for Wales (Representation of the People) Order 2007, SI 2007/236, art 24(3).
9   See the National Assembly for Wales (Representation of the People) Order 2007, SI 2007/236, art 24(3). The court must serve a copy of the order made in the application on the Assembly, on the returning officer, and (in an application under CPR PD 8A—*Alternative Procedure for Claims* para 17.3) (see note 6), the claimant: see CPR PD 8A—*Alternative Procedure for Claims* para 17.8.
10 CPR PD 8A—*Alternative Procedure for Claims* para 17.6.

D. EUROPEAN PARLIAMENTARY ELECTIONS

360.   Designation of returning officers and local returning officers for European parliamentary elections.   There must be a returning officer for each European parliamentary electoral region[1].

For a region in England[2] and Wales[3], the returning officer is to be a person who[4]:

(1)   is an acting returning officer by virtue of the Representation of the People Act 1983[5], in relation to a parliamentary election, or is the proper officer of the Greater London Authority for the purposes of the Representation of the People Act 1983[6], in relation to an Authority election[7]; and

(2)   is designated for these purposes by order of the Secretary of State[8];

and the local returning officer for a local counting area[9] is the person who, in relation to a parliamentary election, is the acting returning officer for the parliamentary constituency which is coterminous with the local counting area[10].

The Secretary of State may by regulations confer functions on the returning officers for the electoral regions and on local returning officers[11]. Accordingly, the local returning officer for each local counting area wholly or partly comprised in an electoral region is responsible for[12]:

(a)   the conduct of the poll in that area[13];

(b)   unless the returning officer otherwise directs, the printing of the ballot papers[14];

(c)   the issue and receipt of postal ballot papers for electors in that area and their proxies[15];

(d)   the verification of the ballot paper accounts[16]; and

(e)   the counting of the votes given in that area[17].

Where such regulations confer functions on a person in relation to an electoral region other than the combined region[18], the council of a district or London borough in England, or the council of a county or county borough in Wales, falling wholly or partly within that region[19], must place the services of their officers at his disposal for the purpose of assisting him in the discharge of those functions[20]. Similarly, where functions are conferred on the proper officer of the Greater London Authority in relation to the London electoral region, the Authority must place the services of its employees at his disposal for the purpose of assisting him in the discharge of those functions[21].

A returning officer and a local returning officer may, in writing, appoint deputies to discharge all or any of the functions imposed on them[22]; and a returning officer may appoint such clerks as may be necessary to assist him in his functions in relation to an election[23]. The returning officer may give to any local returning officer for a local counting area in the electoral region for which he acts directions relating to the discharge of his functions, including directions requiring the provision to him of any information which that person has or is entitled to have[24]; and it is the duty of any local returning officer to whom directions are so given to discharge his functions in accordance with the directions[25].

It is the general duty of a returning officer and the local returning officer at a European parliamentary election to do all such acts and things as may be necessary for effectively conducting the election in accordance with the European parliamentary elections rules[26]. No European parliamentary election may be declared invalid by reason of any act or omission by the returning officer, local returning officer, or any other person in breach of his official duty in connection with the election, or otherwise in breach of the European parliamentary election rules, if it appears to the tribunal having cognisance of the question that[27]:

(i)   the election was so conducted as to be substantially in accordance with the law as to elections[28]; and

(ii)   the act or omission did not affect the result[29].

Nor is a European parliamentary election liable to be questioned[30] by reason of a defect in the title, or want of title, of the person presiding at or conducting the election, if that person was then in actual possession of, or acting in, the office giving the right to preside at or conduct the election[31].

A returning officer or local returning officer for a European parliamentary election must take such steps as he thinks appropriate to encourage the participation by electors in the electoral process in the area or region for which he acts[32]. In so doing, he must have regard to any guidance issued by the Electoral Commission[33].

1   European Parliamentary Elections Act 2002 s 6(1). As to the establishment of electoral regions for the purpose of elections to the European Parliament see PARA 77; and as to European parliamentary elections see PARA 217 et seq.

2   Ie and including the combined region: see the European Parliamentary Elections Act 2002 s 6(2) (amended by the European Parliament (Representation) Act 2003 s 20(1), (2)). As to elections to the European Parliament held in the combined region see PARA 77. As to the meaning of 'England' see PARA 1 note 1.

3   As to the meaning of 'Wales' see PARA 1 note 1.

4   See the European Parliamentary Elections Act 2002 s 6(2) (as amended: see note 2).

5   Ie by virtue of the Representation of the People Act 1983 s 28(1) (see PARA 351): see the European Parliamentary Elections Act 2002 s 6(2)(a) (amended by the Political Parties and Elections Act 2009 s 27(1), (2)).

6   Ie by virtue of the Representation of the People Act 1983 s 35(2C) (see PARA 354): see the European Parliamentary Elections Act 2002 s 6(2)(a) (as amended: see note 5). As to the meaning of 'proper officer of the Greater London Authority' see LONDON GOVERNMENT vol 71 (2013) PARA 71. As to the Greater London Authority see LONDON GOVERNMENT vol 71 (2013) PARA 67 et seq.

7   European Parliamentary Elections Act 2002 s 6(2)(a) (as amended: see note 5). As to the meaning of 'Authority election' see PARA 11.

8   European Parliamentary Elections Act 2002 s 6(2)(b). As to the Secretary of State see PARA 2; and as to the making of orders under the European Parliamentary Elections Act 2002 generally

see PARA 13 note 12. As to the order so made see the European Parliamentary Elections (Returning Officers) Order 2013, SI 2013/2064, arts 3, 4, Schedule.
9   As to the meaning of 'local counting area' see PARA 139 note 1.
10 European Parliamentary Elections Regulations 2004, SI 2004/293, reg 6(2) (reg 6(2) amended, reg 6(2A), Sch A1 added, by SI 2009/186). The local returning officers for each local counting area are as specified: see the European Parliamentary Elections Regulations 2004, SI 2004/293, reg 6(2A), Sch A1 (as so added). Cf note 11. With effect from 1 January 2014, reg 6, Sch A1 are amended to harmonise with the European Parliamentary Elections Act 2002 s 6(5A): see the European Parliamentary Elections (Amendment) Regulations 2013, SI 2013/2876, reg 8.
11 European Parliamentary Elections Act 2002 s 6(5) (s 6(5) substituted, s 6(5A) added, by the European Parliament (Representation) Act 2003 s 20(1), (3)). Charges to which persons on whom functions are conferred under the European Parliamentary Elections Act 2002 s 6(5) are entitled under regulations made under the European Parliamentary Elections Act 2002, and any sums required by the Secretary of State for expenditure on the provision of training relating to functions conferred under s 6(5), are to be charged on, and paid out of, the Consolidated Fund: see s 6(6). As to the Consolidated Fund see CONSTITUTIONAL LAW AND HUMAN RIGHTS vol 8(2) (Reissue) PARA 711 et seq; PARLIAMENT vol 78 (2010) PARAS 1028–1031.
    For these purposes, 'local returning officer' means a person who, by virtue of the Representation of the People Act 1983 s 35 (see PARA 354), is a returning officer for:
    (1)   elections of councillors of a district or London borough (European Parliamentary Elections Act 2002 s 6(5A)(a)(i) (s 6(5A) as so added; s 6(5A)(a) substituted by the Political Parties and Elections Act 2009 s 27(1), (3)));
    (2)   elections of councillors of a county in which there are no district councils (European Parliamentary Elections Act 2002 s 6(5A)(a)(ii) (s 6(5A) as so added; s 6(5A)(a) as so substituted));
    (3)   elections to the Council of the Isles of Scilly (s 6(5A)(a)(iii) (s 6(5A) as so added; s 6(5A)(a) as so substituted)); or
    (4)   elections of councillors of a county or county borough in Wales (s 6(5A)(a)(iv) (s 6(5A) as so added; s 6(5A)(a) as so substituted)).
    As to the meaning of 'local returning officer' in relation to elections to the European Parliament held in the combined region see the European Parliamentary Elections Act 2002 s 6(5A)(b) (as so added); and the European Parliamentary Elections Regulations 2004, SI 2004/293, reg 6(3). As to counties and districts in England, and their councils, see LOCAL GOVERNMENT vol 69 (2009) PARA 24 et seq; as to the Council of the Isles of Scilly see LOCAL GOVERNMENT vol 69 (2009) PARA 36; and as to counties and county boroughs in Wales see LOCAL GOVERNMENT vol 69 (2009) PARA 37 et seq. As to the London boroughs and their councils see LOCAL GOVERNMENT vol 69 (2009) PARA 35; LONDON GOVERNMENT vol 71 (2013) PARA 15 et seq.
12 See the European Parliamentary Elections Regulations 2004, SI 2004/293, reg 6(1).
13 European Parliamentary Elections Regulations 2004, SI 2004/293, reg 6(1)(a). As to the conduct of the poll see PARA 383 et seq.
14 European Parliamentary Elections Regulations 2004, SI 2004/293, reg 6(1)(b). As to the form and printing of ballot papers see PARA 386.
15 European Parliamentary Elections Regulations 2004, SI 2004/293, reg 6(1)(c). As to the issue and receipt of postal ballot papers see PARA 406 et seq.
16 European Parliamentary Elections Regulations 2004, SI 2004/293, reg 6(1)(d). As to the verification of ballot paper accounts at a European parliamentary election see PARAS 465–466.
17 European Parliamentary Elections Regulations 2004, SI 2004/293, reg 6(1)(e). As to the counting of votes at a European parliamentary election see PARA 466 et seq.
18 As to the combined region itself see the European Parliamentary Elections Act 2002 s 6(7)(b) (s 6(7) amended by the European Parliament (Representation) Act 2003 s 20(1), (4)).
19 See the European Parliamentary Elections Act 2002 s 6(7)(a), (8) (s 6(7) as amended: see note 18).
20 See the European Parliamentary Elections Act 2002 s 6(7) (as amended: see note 18).
21 European Parliamentary Elections Act 2002 s 6(9) (added by the Political Parties and Elections Act 2009 s 27(1), (4)).
22 European Parliamentary Elections Regulations 2004, SI 2004/293, reg 7(1). The text refers to functions imposed both under the European Parliamentary Elections Regulations 2004, SI 2004/293 and under the provisions applied by those regulations: see reg 7(1).
23 European Parliamentary Elections Regulations 2004, SI 2004/293, reg 7(2).
24 European Parliamentary Elections Regulations 2004, SI 2004/293, reg 9(3).
25 European Parliamentary Elections Regulations 2004, SI 2004/293, reg 9(4).
26 European Parliamentary Elections Regulations 2004, SI 2004/293, reg 9(2). As to the meaning of 'European parliamentary elections rules' see PARA 383 note 16.

A returning officer or a local returning officer for a European parliamentary election may take such steps as he thinks appropriate to remedy any act or omission on his part, or on the part of a relevant person, which arises in connection with any function the returning officer or relevant person has in relation to the election, and which is not in accordance with the European parliamentary elections rules, or any other requirements applicable to the election: see reg 9(4A) (9(4A)–(4E) added by SI 2009/186). However, a returning officer may not in exercise of this power recount the votes given at an election after the result has been declared: European Parliamentary Elections Regulations 2004, SI 2004/293, reg 9(4B) (as so added). For these purposes, a 'relevant person' is:

(1)   an electoral registration officer (reg 9(4C)(a) (as so added));
(2)   a presiding officer (reg 9(4C)(b) (as so added));
(3)   a person providing goods or services to the returning officer or local returning officer (reg 9(4C)(c) (as so added)); and
(4)   a deputy of any such person mentioned in heads (1) to (3) above, or a person appointed to assist, or in the course of his employment assisting, such a person in connection with any function he has in relation to the European parliamentary election (reg 9(4C)(d) (as so added)).

27 European Parliamentary Elections Regulations 2004, SI 2004/293, reg 9(5).
28 European Parliamentary Elections Regulations 2004, SI 2004/293, reg 9(5)(a).
29 European Parliamentary Elections Regulations 2004, SI 2004/293, reg 9(5)(b).
30 As to the questioning of European parliamentary elections see PARA 765 et seq.
31 European Parliamentary Elections Regulations 2004, SI 2004/293, reg 14.
32 Electoral Administration Act 2006 s 69(1), (8)(b), (9)(c); European Parliamentary Elections Regulations 2004, SI 2004/293, reg 9(4D) (as added: see note 26). As to the meaning of 'elector', in relation to a European parliamentary election, see PARA 111 note 4.
33 Electoral Administration Act 2006 s 69(2); European Parliamentary Elections Regulations 2004, SI 2004/293, reg 9(4E) (as added: see note 26). As to the Electoral Commission see PARA 34 et seq.

361.   Payments by and to returning officer for European parliamentary elections.   A returning officer or local returning officer at a European parliamentary election[1] is entitled to recover his charges in respect of services rendered, or expenses incurred, for, or in connection with such an election, if[2]:

(1)   the services were necessarily rendered, or the expenses were necessarily incurred, for the efficient and effective conduct of the election[3]; and

(2)   the total of his charges does not exceed the amount (the 'overall maximum recoverable amount') specified in, or determined in accordance with, an order made by the Secretary of State for these purposes[4].

Any order made under head (2) above may specify, or make provision for determining in accordance with the order, a maximum recoverable amount for services or expenses of any specified description, and the returning officer or local returning officer may not recover more than that amount in respect of any such services or expenses[5], except that the Secretary of State may, in a particular case, authorise the payment of[6]:

(a)   more than the overall maximum recoverable amount[7]; or

(b)   more than the specified maximum recoverable amount for any specified services or expenses[8],

if the Secretary of State is satisfied that[9]:

(i)   it was reasonable for the returning officer concerned to render the services or incur the expenses[10]; and

(ii)   the charges in question are reasonable[11].

On the returning officer's or local returning officer's request for an advance on account of his charges, the Secretary of State may, on such terms as he thinks fit, make such an advance[12].

The amount of any charges so recoverable must be charged on and paid out of the Consolidated Fund[13] on an account being submitted to the Secretary of State, but the Secretary of State may, if he thinks fit, before payment apply for a detailed assessment of the account[14]. Where the superannuation contributions required to be paid by a local authority in respect of any person are increased by any fee paid as part of a returning officer's or local returning officer's charges at a European parliamentary election, then on an account being submitted to the Secretary of State a sum equal to the increase may be charged on and paid out of the Consolidated Fund to the authority[15]. Regulations by the Secretary of State may make provision as to the time when and the manner and form in which accounts are to be rendered to the Secretary of State for the purposes of the payment of a returning officer's or local returning officer's charges, and may include different provision for different cases, circumstances or areas[16].

The Secretary of State may also reimburse a returning officer for a European parliamentary election in respect of any expenditure incurred by the officer for the purposes of encouraging electoral participation[17]. However, the amount so paid must not in any year exceed such amount as is determined in accordance with regulations made by the Secretary of State[18].

1   As to European parliamentary elections see PARA 217 et seq; and as to the designation of returning officers and local returning officers at a European parliamentary election see PARA 360.

2   See the European Parliamentary Elections Regulations 2004, SI 2004/293, reg 15(1) (reg 15(1)–(4) substituted, reg 15(10) amended, by SI 2009/186).

3   European Parliamentary Elections Regulations 2004, SI 2004/293, reg 15(1)(a) (as substituted: see note 2).

4   European Parliamentary Elections Regulations 2004, SI 2004/293, reg 15(1)(b) (as substituted: see note 2). The power to make orders under reg 15(1) must be exercised by statutory instrument, and the Statutory Instruments Act 1946 s 1 (definition of statutory instrument: see STATUTES AND LEGISLATIVE PROCESS vol 96 (2012) PARA 1045) applies accordingly: see the European Parliamentary Elections Regulations 2004, SI 2004/293, reg 15(5). Any such order may make different provision for different cases, circumstances or areas and may contain such incidental, supplemental, saving or transitional provisions as the Secretary of State thinks fit: see reg 15(5). Any exercise by the Secretary of State of his functions under reg 15(1) requires the consent of the Treasury: reg 15(10) (as amended: see note 2). As to the Secretary of State see PARA 2. As to the Treasury see CONSTITUTIONAL LAW AND HUMAN RIGHTS vol 8(2) (Reissue) PARAS 512–517.
    As to the orders so made see the European Parliamentary Elections (Returning Officers' Charges) (Great Britain and Gibraltar) Order 2009, SI 2009/1069, art 4, Schedule; and the European Parliamentary Elections (Local Returning Officers' Charges) (England, Wales and Gibraltar) Order 2009, SI 2009/1077, art 3, Schedule. However, at an uncontested election, the European Parliamentary Elections (Returning Officers' Charges) (Great Britain and Gibraltar) Order 2009, SI 2009/1069, arts 4–8 do not apply (see art 9(a)); and the European Parliamentary Elections (Local Returning Officers' Charges) (England, Wales and Gibraltar) Order 2009, SI 2009/1077, arts 3–7 do not apply (see art 8(a)). In such circumstances, the overall maximum recoverable amount for each electoral region is £350 (European Parliamentary Elections (Returning Officers' Charges) (Great Britain and Gibraltar) Order 2009, SI 2009/1069, art 9(b)); and the overall maximum recoverable amount for each local counting area is £1,750 (European Parliamentary Elections (Local Returning Officers' Charges) (England, Wales and Gibraltar) Order 2009, SI 2009/1077, art 8(b)).

5   European Parliamentary Elections Regulations 2004, SI 2004/293, reg 15(2) (as substituted: see note 2).
    As to the orders so made see the European Parliamentary Elections (Returning Officers' Charges) (Great Britain and Gibraltar) Order 2009, SI 2009/1069, arts 5, 7, Schedule; and the European Parliamentary Elections (Local Returning Officers' Charges) (England, Wales and Gibraltar) Order 2009, SI 2009/1077, arts 4, 6, Schedule. The specified services are:
    (1)   discharging the returning officer's duties at the election (European Parliamentary Elections (Returning Officers' Charges) (Great Britain and Gibraltar) Order 2009,

SI 2009/1069, art 6(a); European Parliamentary Elections (Local Returning Officers' Charges) (England, Wales and Gibraltar) Order 2009, SI 2009/1077, art 5(b)); and

(2)   making arrangements for the election (European Parliamentary Elections (Returning Officers' Charges) (Great Britain and Gibraltar) Order 2009, SI 2009/1069, art 6(b); European Parliamentary Elections (Local Returning Officers' Charges) (England, Wales and Gibraltar) Order 2009, SI 2009/1077, art 5(c)).

In relation to a local returning officers' charges, conducting the election is also a specified service: see art 5(a).

In relation to a returning officers' charges, the specified expenses are:

(a)   the appointment and payment of persons to assist the returning officer (European Parliamentary Elections (Returning Officers' Charges) (Great Britain and Gibraltar) Order 2009, SI 2009/1069, art 8(a));

(b)   travel and overnight subsistence for the returning officer and any person appointed to assist the returning officer (art 8(b));

(c)   the costs of the nomination process (art 8(c));

(d)   printing or otherwise producing ballot papers (art 8(d));

(e)   printing or otherwise producing and, where appropriate, publishing notices required by the European Parliamentary Elections Regulations 2004, SI 2004/293 (European Parliamentary Elections (Returning Officers' Charges) (Great Britain and Gibraltar) Order 2009, SI 2009/1069, art 8(e));

(f)   renting, heating, lighting, cleaning, adapting or restoring any building or room (art 8(f));

(g)   providing and transporting equipment (art 8(g));

(h)   providing security (art 8(h));

(i)   conducting the count (art 8(i));

(j)   providing training (art 8(j)); and

(k)   providing stationery and meeting postage, telephone, printing and banking costs and costs of other miscellaneous items (art 8(k)).

In relation to a local returning officers' charges, the specified expenses are:

(i)   the appointment and payment of persons to assist the local returning officer (European Parliamentary Elections (Local Returning Officers' Charges) (England, Wales and Gibraltar) Order 2009, SI 2009/1077, art 7(a));

(ii)   travel and overnight subsistence for the local returning officer and any person appointed to assist the local returning officer (art 7(b));

(iii)   printing or otherwise producing the ballot papers (art 7(c));

(iv)   printing, producing or purchasing postal vote stationery (art 7(d));

(v)   printing or otherwise producing and arranging for the delivery of poll cards (art 7(e));

(vi)   printing or otherwise producing and, where appropriate, publishing notices and any other documents required by the European Parliamentary Elections Regulations 2004, SI 2004/293 (European Parliamentary Elections (Local Returning Officers' Charges) (England, Wales and Gibraltar) Order 2009, SI 2009/1077, art 7(f));

(vii)   renting, heating, lighting, cleaning, adapting or restoring any building or room (art 7(g));

(viii)   providing and transporting equipment (art 7(h));

(ix)   providing security, including secure storage of ballot boxes, ballot papers and verification documents between polling day and the count (art 7(i));

(x)   conducting the verification and the count (art 7(j));

(xi)   providing training (art 7(k)); and

(xii)   providing stationery and meeting postage, telephone, printing, translation and banking costs and the costs of other miscellaneous items (art 7(l)).

As to uncontested European parliamentary elections see note 4.

6   See the European Parliamentary Elections Regulations 2004, SI 2004/293, reg 15(3) (as substituted: see note 2).

7   European Parliamentary Elections Regulations 2004, SI 2004/293, reg 15(3)(a) (as substituted: see note 2).

8   European Parliamentary Elections Regulations 2004, SI 2004/293, reg 15(3)(b) (as substituted: see note 2).

9   See the European Parliamentary Elections Regulations 2004, SI 2004/293, reg 15(3), (4) (as substituted: see note 2).

10   European Parliamentary Elections Regulations 2004, SI 2004/293, reg 15(4)(a) (as substituted: see note 2).

11   European Parliamentary Elections Regulations 2004, SI 2004/293, reg 15(4)(b) (as substituted: see note 2).

12 European Parliamentary Elections Regulations 2004, SI 2004/293, reg 15(8).

13 As to the Consolidated Fund see CONSTITUTIONAL LAW AND HUMAN RIGHTS vol 8(2) (Reissue) PARA 711 et seq; PARLIAMENT vol 78 (2010) PARA 1028–1031.

14 European Parliamentary Elections Regulations 2004, SI 2004/293, reg 15(6). The text refers to a detailed assessment under reg 16 (see PARA 362): see reg 15(6).

15 European Parliamentary Elections Regulations 2004, SI 2004/293, reg 15(7).

16 European Parliamentary Elections Regulations 2004, SI 2004/293, reg 15(9). The regulations so made are not made by statutory instrument and are not recorded in this work.

17 Electoral Administration Act 2006 s 69(4), (8)(b), (9)(c). As to the duty of a returning officer for a European parliamentary election to encourage electoral participation see s 69(1), (2); and PARA 360.

18 Electoral Administration Act 2006 s 69(5). The power to make such regulations is exercisable by statutory instrument subject to annulment in pursuance of a resolution of either House of Parliament: s 69(6). Such regulations may make different provision for different purposes: s 69(7). The Encouraging Electoral Participation (Reimbursement of Expenses) (England and Wales) Regulations 2006, SI 2006/2972, which came into force on 1 April 2007 (see reg 1(1)), provide that the total amount that may be paid to local electoral officers in England and Wales in pursuance of the Electoral Administration Act 2006 s 69(4) in the year ending on 31 March 2008 and each successive year is £2,500,000: Encouraging Electoral Participation (Reimbursement of Expenses) (England and Wales) Regulations 2006, SI 2006/2972, reg 2. For these purposes, 'year' means a period of 12 months ending on 31 March (reg 1(2)); and 'local electoral officer' means a returning officer for European parliamentary elections (Electoral Administration Act 2006 s 69(8)(b), (9)(c)).

362. Detailed assessment of returning officer or local returning officer's account at European parliamentary elections. On an account of a returning officer or a local returning officer at a European parliamentary election being submitted[1] to the Secretary of State[2], he may if he thinks fit before payment, apply for a detailed assessment to be made of the account[3]. An application for a returning officer's account to be assessed in this way (a 'detailed assessment') must be made, where the account relates to an election in an electoral region in England or Wales[4], to the county court[5]. On any such application, the county court has jurisdiction:

(1)   to assess the account in such manner and at such time and place as the court thinks fit[6]; and

(2)   finally to determine the amount payable to the returning officer[7].

On any such application, the returning officer or local returning officer also may apply to the county court to examine any claim made by any person against him in respect of matters charged in the account (an 'examination')[8]; and the court:

(a)   after notice given to the claimant, must give him an opportunity to be heard and to tender any evidence[9]; and

(b)   may allow, disallow or reduce the claim objected to with or without costs[10].

The court's determination on the examination is final for all purposes and as against all persons[11].

1 Ie under the European Parliamentary Elections Regulations 2004, SI 2004/293, reg 15(6): see PARA 361. As to returning officers and local returning officers appointed for the purposes of elections to the European Parliament see PARA 360.

2 As to the Secretary of State see PARA 2.

3 See the European Parliamentary Elections Regulations 2004, SI 2004/293, reg 15(6); and PARA 361. The text refers to the detailed assessment of a returning officer's account under the provisions of reg 16 (see the text and notes 4–11): see reg 15(6); and PARA 361.

4 As to the meanings of 'England' and 'Wales' see PARA 1 note 1. Where the account is that of the local returning officer for the Gibraltar local counting area, the account must be read as an account that relates to the whole of the combined region: European Parliamentary Elections

Regulations 2004, SI 2004/293, reg 16(4). As to the establishment of electoral regions (including the 'combined region') for the purpose of elections to the European Parliament see PARA 77.

5   European Parliamentary Elections Regulations 2004, SI 2004/293, reg 16(1)(a). Where the account is that of the local returning officer for the Gibraltar local counting area, the county court must be read as a reference to the Gibraltar court: see reg 16(1)(c).

6   European Parliamentary Elections Regulations 2004, SI 2004/293, reg 16(2).
     An application to assess or examine a returning officer's account that is made in relation to a parliamentary or Welsh Assembly election is explicitly made in accordance with the Civil Procedure Rules (ie CPR PD 8A—*Alternative Procedure for Claims* para 17: see PARAS 353, 359), but no such provision is made in relation to an application made pursuant to the European Parliamentary Elections Regulations 2004, SI 2004/293.

7   European Parliamentary Elections Regulations 2004, SI 2004/293, reg 16(2).
8   European Parliamentary Elections Regulations 2004, SI 2004/293, reg 16(3).
9   European Parliamentary Elections Regulations 2004, SI 2004/293, reg 16(3).
10 European Parliamentary Elections Regulations 2004, SI 2004/293, reg 16(3).
11 European Parliamentary Elections Regulations 2004, SI 2004/293, reg 16(3).

(iv) Manner of Voting at Elections

A. VOTING OPTIONS

363.   Manner of voting at a parliamentary or local government election. A person entitled to vote as an elector at a parliamentary or local government election[1] may vote in person at the polling station allotted to him[2], unless he is entitled as an elector to an absent vote at the election[3], in which case:

(1)   if he is entitled as an elector to vote by post at the election, he may vote by post[4]; or

(2)   if he is entitled to vote by proxy at the election, he may vote in this way unless, before a ballot paper has been issued for him to vote by proxy, he applies at the polling station allotted to him under the appropriate rules for a ballot paper for the purpose of voting in person, in which case he may vote in person there[5].

If:

(a)   he is not entitled as an elector to an absent vote at the election[6]; but

(b)   he cannot reasonably be expected to go in person to the polling station allotted to him under the appropriate rules by reason of the particular circumstances of his employment (either as a constable[7] or by the returning officer) on the date of the poll for a purpose connected with the election[8],

he may vote in person at any polling station in the constituency or, as the case may be, electoral area[9].

Subject to these provisions:

(i)   a person is not entitled to vote as an elector more than once in the same constituency at any parliamentary election, or in more than one constituency at a general election[10];

(ii)   at a local government election for any electoral area (except in relation to Authority elections[11]), no person as an elector, and no person as proxy for any one elector[12], may: (A) give more than one vote for any one candidate[13]; or (B) give more votes in all than the total number of councillors to be elected for the electoral area[14];

(iii) each person entitled to vote as an elector at a London Authority ordinary election has[15]: (A) one vote (a 'mayoral vote') which may be given for a candidate to be the Mayor of London[16]; (B) one vote (a 'constituency vote') which may be given for a candidate to be the

Assembly member for the Assembly constituency[17]; and (C) one vote (a 'London vote') which may be given for either a registered political party[18] which has submitted a list of candidates to be London members[19], or an individual who is a candidate to be a London member[20]; and

(iv) at an election for an elected local authority mayor[21], each person entitled to vote as an elector has one vote which may be given for the voter's first preference from among the candidates to be the elected mayor[22] but a person is not entitled as an elector to cast more than one first preference vote (or, where it applies, more than one second preference vote) at an election for the return of an elected mayor[23].

1 See the Representation of the People Act 2000 s 12, Sch 4 para 2(1). As to the meaning of 'parliamentary election' see PARA 9. 'Local government election' means a local government election in England or Wales: see Sch 4 para 1(1). As to the meaning of 'local government election' see PARA 11; definition applied by virtue of Sch 4 para 1(2). As to the meanings of 'England' and 'Wales' see PARA 1 note 1. As to the meaning of 'elector' in relation to a parliamentary or local government election see PARA 95 note 2.
   Nothing in Sch 4 para 2(1)–(5) (see the text and notes 2–9) applies to a person to whom the Representation of the People Act 1983 s 7 (deemed residence for persons in mental hospitals who are not detained offenders or on remand: see PARA 119) applies and who is liable, by virtue of any enactment, to be detained in the mental hospital in question, whether he is registered by virtue of s 7 or not: Representation of the People Act 2000 Sch 4 para 2(5A) (added by the Electoral Administration Act 2006 s 35(1), (2), (4)). Such a person may vote:
   (1) in person (where he is granted permission to be absent from the hospital and voting in person does not breach any condition attached to that permission) (Representation of the People Act 2000 Sch 4 para 2(5A)(a) (as so added)); or
   (2) by post or by proxy (where he is entitled as an elector to vote by post or, as the case may be, by proxy at the election) (Sch 4 para 2(5A)(b) (as so added)).
   Nor does anything in Sch 4 para 2(1)–(5), (5A) apply to a person to whom the Representation of the People Act 1983 s 7A (deemed residence for persons on remand: see PARA 120) applies (Representation of the People Act 2000 Sch 4 para 2(6)(b)), whether he is registered by virtue of the Representation of the People Act 1983 s 7A or not (see the Representation of the People Act 2000 Sch 4 para 2(6)). Such a person may only vote by post or by proxy (where he is entitled as an elector to vote by post or, as the case may be, by proxy at the election): see Sch 4 para 2(6). As to voting by proxy see PARA 374 et seq.
   The Representation of the People Act 2000 s 12, Sch 4 are applied and modified for the purpose of local authority mayoral elections in England and Wales by the Local Authorities (Mayoral Elections) (England and Wales) Regulations 2007, SI 2007/1024, reg 3(2)–(5), Sch 2 Table 3 (see PARA 11 note 14); and they have effect for the purposes of local authority referendums, subject to the modifications specified, in relation to Wales, by the Local Authorities (Conduct of Referendums) (Wales) Regulations 2008, SI 2008/1848, reg 8(2), Sch 4 Table 2, and, in relation to England, by the Local Authorities (Conduct of Referendums) (England) Regulations 2012, SI 2012/323, regs 8(2), 11–13, Sch 4 Table 3 (see PARA 15 note 2).
2 Ie under the appropriate rules: see the Representation of the People Act 2000 Sch 4 para 2(2). As to the provision and allotment of polling stations see PARA 390. For these purposes, the 'appropriate rules' means:
   (1) in the case of a parliamentary election, the parliamentary elections rules (Sch 4 para 1(1)(a)); and
   (2) in the case of a local government election, rules made (or having effect as if made) under the Representation of the People Act 1983 s 36 (see PARA 383) (Representation of the People Act 2000 Sch 4 para 1(1)(b)).
   As to the meaning of 'parliamentary elections rules' see PARA 383 note 2.; definition applied by virtue of Sch 4 para 1(2).
3 See the Representation of the People Act 2000 Sch 4 para 2(1), (2). This provision does not prevent a person, at the polling station allotted to him, marking a tendered ballot paper in pursuance of the Representation of the People Act 1983 Sch 1 r 40(1ZC), (1ZE) (see PARA 403): Representation of the People Act 2000 Sch 4 para 2(6A) (added by the Electoral Administration Act 2006 s 38(6)(a)). For the purposes of the provisions of the Representation of the People Act 1983 (so far as it has effect in relation to England and Wales), and for the purposes of the provisions of the Representation of the People Act 2000 Sch 4, a person entitled to vote as an

elector at a parliamentary or local government election is entitled as an elector to vote by post, or is entitled to vote by proxy at the election, if Sch 4 para 2(8) or Sch 4 para 2(9), as the case may be, applies to him in relation to the election: see Sch 4 para 2(7) (Sch 4 para 2(7) amended, Sch 4 para 2(8), (9), added, by the Electoral Administration Act 2006 s 74(1), Sch 1 Pt 7 para 137(1), (3)). The Representation of the People Act 2000 Sch 4 para 2(8) applies to a person who is shown in the postal voters list mentioned in Sch 4 para 5(2) (see PARA 373) as entitled to vote by post at an election (Sch 4 para 2(8) (as so added)); and Sch 4 para 2(9) applies to a person who is shown in the list of proxies mentioned in Sch 4 para 5(3) (see PARA 373) as entitled to vote by proxy at an election (Sch 4 para 2(9) (as so added)). As to the postal voters list and the list of proxies see PARA 373.

4   See the Representation of the People Act 2000 Sch 4 para 2(1), (3).

5   See the Representation of the People Act 2000 Sch 4 para 2(1), (4).

6   See the Representation of the People Act 2000 Sch 4 para 2(1), (5)(a).

7   As from a day to be appointed under the Electoral Registration and Administration Act 2013 s 27(1), the Representation of the People Act 2000 Sch 4 para 2(5ZA) is added by the Electoral Registration and Administration Act 2013 s 21(3). Accordingly, as from such a day, in the application of the Representation of the People Act 2000 Sch 4 para 2(5) to an election in England or Wales, a reference to a constable includes a person designated as a community support officer under the Police Reform Act 2002 s 38 (police powers for employees: see POLICE AND INVESTIGATORY POWERS vol 84 (2013) PARA 366): see the Representation of the People Act 2000 Sch 4 para 2(5ZA) (prospectively added by the Electoral Registration and Administration Act 2013 s 21(3)). At the date at which this volume states the law, no such day had been appointed.

8   See the Representation of the People Act 2000 Sch 4 para 2(1), (5)(b). As to the date of the poll at a parliamentary general election or by-election see PARA 195; and as to the date of the poll at local government elections (including elections to fill vacancies) see PARAS 206–209.

9   See the Representation of the People Act 2000 Sch 4 para 2(1), (5). As to the meaning of 'constituency' in the context of a parliamentary election see PARA 9; and as to the meaning of 'electoral area' see PARA 11.

10 See the Representation of the People Act 1983 s 1(2); and PARA 95.

11 In relation to Authority elections, the votes allowed to be given are as specified in the applicable provisions of the Greater London Authority Act 1999 s 4 (see the text and notes 15–20), s 10 (vacancy arising as constituency member of the London Assembly: see LONDON GOVERNMENT vol 71 (2013) PARA 111), or s 16 (vacancy arising in the office of Mayor of London: see LONDON GOVERNMENT vol 71 (2013) PARA 99): see the Representation of the People Act 1983 s 46(1) (amended by the Greater London Authority Act 1999 s 17, Sch 3 paras 1, 8). As to the meaning of 'Authority election' see PARA 11. As to filling vacancies arising in the office of Mayor of London or in membership of the London Assembly see also PARA 204.

12 Representation of the People Act 1983 s 46(1) (as amended: see note 11).
    The Representation of the People Act 1983 s 46 is applied and modified for the purpose of local authority mayoral elections in England and Wales by the Local Authorities (Mayoral Elections) (England and Wales) Regulations 2007, SI 2007/1024, reg 3(2)–(5), Sch 2 Table 1 (see PARA 11 note 14).

13 Representation of the People Act 1983 s 46(1)(a).

14 Representation of the People Act 1983 s 46(1)(b).

15 See the Greater London Authority Act 1999 s 4(1). As to London Assembly ordinary elections see PARA 199 et seq.

16 Greater London Authority Act 1999 s 4(1)(a). However, if there are three or more candidates to be Mayor of London, a supplementary vote system operates and a voter's mayoral vote will be a vote capable of being given to indicate the voter's first and second preferences from among the candidates: see further PARA 341. As to elections for the return of a Mayor of London see PARA 199. See also LONDON GOVERNMENT vol 71 (2013) PARA 78.

17 Greater London Authority Act 1999 s 4(1)(b). An Assembly member for an Assembly constituency is returned under the simple majority system (see PARA 339): s 4(4). As to the meanings of 'Assembly constituency' and 'constituency member' in the context of elections to the London Assembly see PARA 11. As to elections for the return of constituency members of the London Assembly see PARA 199 et seq.

18 As to the meaning of 'registered political party' in this context see PARA 226 note 16.

19 Greater London Authority Act 1999 s 4(1)(c), (5)(a). As to the meaning of 'London member' (of the London Assembly) see PARA 11 note 5. As to the submission of lists of candidates to be London members of the London Assembly see PARA 226; and as to references to party lists in elections for the return of London members of the London Assembly see PARA 255 note 23. See also PARA 340.

20 Greater London Authority Act 1999 s 4(1)(c), (5)(b). As to elections for the return of the London members of the London Assembly see PARA 199 et seq; and as to individual candidates to be London members of the London Assembly see PARA 226.

21 As to elections for the return of an elected local authority mayor see PARA 198.

22 However, if there are three or more candidates to be the elected mayor, a supplementary vote system operates and another vote (in addition to the first preference vote) is capable of being given to indicate the voter's second preference from among the candidates: see further PARA 341.

23 See the Local Government Act 2000 ss 9HC(1), 9HD(2), 42(1), 43(2), Sch 2 paras 2, 3; and LOCAL GOVERNMENT vol 69 (2009) PARA 321.

364.   Manner of voting at a Welsh Assembly election.   A person entitled to vote as an elector at a Welsh Assembly election[1] may vote in person at the polling station allotted to him[2], unless he is entitled as an elector to an absent vote at the Assembly election[3], in which case:

(1)   if he is entitled as an elector to vote by post at the Assembly election, he may vote by post[4]; or

(2)   if he is entitled to vote by proxy at the Assembly election, he may vote in this way unless, before a ballot paper has been issued for him to vote by proxy, he applies at the polling station allotted to him for a ballot paper for the purposes of voting in person, in which case he may vote in person there[5].

If he is not entitled as an elector to an absent vote at an Assembly election, but cannot reasonably be expected to go in person to the polling station allotted to him[6], by reason of the particular circumstances of his employment[7]: (a) as a constable[8]; (b) by a constituency returning officer (in the case of a constituency election)[9]; (c) by a regional returning officer (in the case of a regional election)[10]; or (d) by a constituency returning officer (in the case of a regional election where that officer is exercising functions in relation to the election)[11], on the date of the poll for a purpose connected with the election, he may vote in person at any polling station in an Assembly constituency[12] for which the election is being held (in the case of a constituency election)[13], or in which he is entitled to give his vote (in the case of a regional election)[14]. But where the polls at a constituency election and a regional election are to be taken together, and if a person is employed at those elections for a purpose connected with only one of those two elections at which he is entitled to give a vote, he is treated for these purposes as employed for a purpose connected with both elections, provided that, if a person is so treated, in exercising the right so conferred to vote in person at any polling station, those votes will be given at the same polling station[15].

Each person entitled to vote at a general election in an Assembly constituency[16] has two votes[17], as follows:

(i)   one (a 'constituency vote') is a vote which may be given for a candidate to be the Assembly constituency member for the Assembly constituency[18];

(ii)   the other (an 'electoral region vote') is a vote which may be given for either: (A) a registered political party[19] which has submitted a list of candidates to be Assembly regional members for the Assembly electoral region[20] in which the Assembly constituency is included[21]; or (B) an individual who is a candidate to be an Assembly regional member[22] for that Assembly electoral region[23].

At a Welsh Assembly general election, both the constituency vote and the electoral region vote must be given in an Assembly constituency[24]. A person is not entitled as an elector to cast more than one constituency vote or more than one electoral region vote in the same Assembly constituency at any general election[25], or to vote in more than one Assembly constituency at any general election[26], or to cast more than one vote in any election held to fill a vacancy in a constituency seat[27].

The Assembly constituency member for the Assembly constituency is to be returned under the simple majority system[28]; and the Assembly regional members for the Assembly electoral region are to be returned under the additional member system of proportional representation[29].

1   See the National Assembly for Wales (Representation of the People) Order 2007, SI 2007/236, art 7(1). As to the meaning of 'Assembly election' see PARA 3 note 2.

    For these purposes, a person entitled to vote as an elector at an Assembly election is entitled as an elector to vote by post, or is entitled to vote by proxy, at the election if art 7(11) or art 7(12), as the case may be, applies to him in relation to the election: art 7(10). Article 7(11) applies to a person who is shown in the postal voters list mentioned in art 10(2) (see PARA 373) as entitled to vote by post at an election (art 7(11)); and art 7(12) applies to a person who is shown in the list of proxies mentioned in art 10(3) (see PARA 373) as entitled to vote by proxy at an election (art 7(12)). As to the postal voters list and the list of proxies see PARA 373.

    Nothing in art 7(1)–(7) (see the text and notes 2–15) applies to a person to whom the Representation of the People Act 1983 s 7 (deemed residence for persons in mental hospitals who are not detained offenders or on remand: see PARA 119) applies and who is liable, by virtue of any enactment, to be detained in the mental hospital in question, whether he is registered by virtue of s 7 or not: National Assembly for Wales (Representation of the People) Order 2007, SI 2007/236, art 7(8). Such a person may vote:

(1)   in person (where he is granted permission to be absent from the hospital and voting in person does not breach any condition attached to that permission) (art 7(8)(a)); or

(2)   by post or by proxy (where he is entitled as an elector to vote by post or, as the case may be, by proxy at the election) (art 7(8)(b)).

    Nor does anything in art 7(1)–(7) apply to a person to whom the Representation of the People Act 1983 s 7A (deemed residence for persons on remand: see PARA 120) applies, whether he is registered by virtue of s 7A or not: see the National Assembly for Wales (Representation of the People) Order 2007, SI 2007/236, art 7(9). Such a person may only vote by post or by proxy (where he is entitled as an elector to vote by post or, as the case may be, by proxy at the election): see art 7(9). As to voting by post or by proxy see note 3.

2   Ie allotted to him under the National Assembly for Wales (Representation of the People) Order 2007, SI 2007/236 (the 'appropriate rules'): see art 7(2). As to the provision and allotment of polling stations see PARA 390.

3   See the National Assembly for Wales (Representation of the People) Order 2007, SI 2007/236, art 7(1), (2). This provision does not prevent a person, at the polling station allotted to him, marking a tendered ballot paper in pursuance of Sch 5 para 49(4), (6) (see PARA 403): art 7(13).

4   National Assembly for Wales (Representation of the People) Order 2007, SI 2007/236, art 7(1), (3). As to voting by post see note 3.

5   National Assembly for Wales (Representation of the People) Order 2007, SI 2007/236, art 7(1), (4). As to voting by proxy see note 3.

6   Ie allotted to him under the National Assembly for Wales (Representation of the People) Order 2007, SI 2007/236: see art 7(5).

7   See the National Assembly for Wales (Representation of the People) Order 2007, SI 2007/236, art 7(5).

8   National Assembly for Wales (Representation of the People) Order 2007, SI 2007/236, art 7(5)(a).

9   National Assembly for Wales (Representation of the People) Order 2007, SI 2007/236, art 7(5)(b). As to the meaning of 'constituency election' in the context of Welsh Assembly elections see PARA 3 note 2. As to the meaning of 'constituency returning officer' see PARA 18 note 2. As to the designation of returning officers for Welsh Assembly elections see PARA 357.

10   National Assembly for Wales (Representation of the People) Order 2007, SI 2007/236, art 7(5)(c). As to the meaning of 'regional election' in the context of Welsh Assembly elections see PARA 3 note 2. As to the meaning of 'regional returning officer' see PARA 18 note 2.

11   National Assembly for Wales (Representation of the People) Order 2007, SI 2007/236, art 7(5)(d). A constituency returning officer may exercise or discharge functions at a constituency or regional Assembly election: see PARA 357.

12   See the National Assembly for Wales (Representation of the People) Order 2007, SI 2007/236, art 7(5), (6). As to the date of the poll at Welsh Assembly elections (including elections to fill vacancies in an Assembly constituency) see PARAS 213, 214.

13 National Assembly for Wales (Representation of the People) Order 2007, SI 2007/236, art 7(6)(a).
14 National Assembly for Wales (Representation of the People) Order 2007, SI 2007/236, art 7(6)(b).
15 National Assembly for Wales (Representation of the People) Order 2007, SI 2007/236, art 7(7).
16 As to the establishment of constituencies for the purpose of Welsh Assembly elections see PARA 76 et seq. As to ordinary Assembly elections see PARA 213 et seq.
17 Government of Wales Act 2006 s 6(1).
18 Government of Wales Act 2006 s 6(2). As to the meaning of 'Assembly constituency member' see PARA 12.
19 As to the meaning of 'registered political party' in this context see PARA 227 note 4.
20 As to the establishment of electoral regions for the purpose of Welsh Assembly elections see PARA 76 et seq. As to the meaning of 'Assembly regional member' in the context of a Welsh Assembly regional election see PARA 12; and as to the meaning of 'party list candidate' see PARA 230 note 23. As to the submission of lists of candidates to be members for a Welsh Assembly region see PARA 227.
21 Government of Wales Act 2006 s 6(3)(a).
22 As to the meaning of 'individual candidate' in the context of a Welsh Assembly regional election see PARA 230 note 19. As to individual candidates to be members for a Welsh Assembly region see also PARA 227.
23 Government of Wales Act 2006 s 6(3)(b).
24 National Assembly for Wales (Representation of the People) Order 2007, SI 2007/236, art 3.
25 See the Government of Wales Act 2006 s 12(2)(a); and PARA 99.
26 See the Government of Wales Act 2006 s 12(2)(b); and PARA 99.
27 See the Government of Wales Act 2006 s 12(2)(c); and PARA 99. As to elections held to fill a vacancy in a constituency seat see s 10; and PARA 214.
28 Government of Wales Act 2006 s 6(4).
29 Government of Wales Act 2006 s 6(5). As to the additional member system of proportional representation see PARA 340.

365. Manner of voting at a European parliamentary election. A person entitled to vote as an elector at a European parliamentary election[1] may vote in person at his allotted polling station[2], unless he is entitled as an elector to an absent vote at the election[3], in which case:

(1) if he is entitled as an elector to vote by post at the election, he may vote by post[4]; or

(2) if he is entitled to vote by proxy at the election, he may vote in this way unless, before a ballot paper has been issued for him to vote by proxy, he applies at the polling station allotted to him under the European parliamentary elections rules for a ballot paper for the purpose of voting in person, in which case he may vote in person there[5].

If:

(a) he is not entitled as an elector to an absent vote at the election[6]; but

(b) he cannot reasonably be expected to go in person to the allotted polling station by reason of the particular circumstances of his employment (either as a constable or by the local returning officer[7]), on the date of the poll for a purpose connected with the election[8],

he may vote in person at any polling station in the local counting area[9].

The system of election at a European parliamentary election requires a vote to be cast either for a registered party[10] or for an individual candidate named on the ballot paper[11]. If, on any occasion when elections to the European Parliament are held in all the member states, a person votes as an elector more than once in those elections, whether in the United Kingdom or elsewhere, he is guilty of an offence[12].

1 See the European Parliamentary Elections Regulations 2004, SI 2004/293, reg 10, Sch 2 para 2(1) (Sch 2 substituted by SI 2009/186). For the purposes of the provisions of the European

Parliamentary Elections Regulations 2004, SI 2004/293 (the 'appropriate rules'), and the Representation of the People Act 1983, the European Parliamentary Elections Act 2002 and the European Parliament (Representation) Act 2003, a person entitled to vote as an elector at a European parliamentary election is entitled as an elector to vote by post, or is entitled to vote by proxy, at the election if the European Parliamentary Elections Regulations 2004, SI 2004/293, Sch 2 para 2(10) or Sch 2 para 2(11), as the case may be, applies to him in relation to the election: Sch 2 para 2(9) (as so substituted). Schedule 2 para 2(10) applies to a person who is shown in the postal voters list mentioned in Sch 2 para 5(2) (see PARA 373) as entitled to vote by post at an election (Sch 2 para 2(10) (as so substituted)); and Sch 2 para 2(11) applies to a person who is shown in the list of proxies mentioned in Sch 2 para 5(3) (see PARA 373) as entitled to vote by proxy at an election (Sch 2 para 2(11) (as so substituted)). As to the postal voters list and the list of proxies see PARA 373.

However, nothing in Sch 2 para 2(1)–(5) (see the text and notes 2–9) applies to a person to whom the Representation of the People Act 1983 s 7 (deemed residence for persons in mental hospitals who are not detained offenders or on remand: see PARA 119) applies and who is liable, by virtue of any enactment, to be detained in the mental hospital in question, whether he is registered by virtue of s 7 or not: European Parliamentary Elections Regulations 2004, SI 2004/293, Sch 2 para 2(6) (as so substituted). Such a person may vote:

(1)   in person (where he is granted permission to be absent from the hospital and voting in person does not breach any condition attached to that permission) (Sch 2 para 2(6)(a) (as so substituted)); or

(2)   by post or by proxy (where he is entitled as an elector to vote by post or, as the case may be, by proxy at the election) (Sch 2 para 2(6)(b) (as so substituted)).

Nor does anything in Sch 2 para 2(1)–(6) apply to a person to whom the Representation of the People Act 1983 s 7A (deemed residence for persons on remand: see PARA 120) applies, whether he is registered by virtue of s 7A or not: see the European Parliamentary Elections Regulations 2004, SI 2004/293, Sch 2 para 2(7) (as so substituted). Such a person may only vote by post or by proxy (where he is entitled as an elector to vote by post or, as the case may be, by proxy at the election): see Sch 2 para 2(7) (as so substituted).

2   For these purposes, 'allotted polling station' has the meaning set out in the European Parliamentary Elections Regulations 2004, SI 2004/293, Sch 2 para 23(8) (see PARA 368 note 32): see Sch 2 para 1(1) (as substituted: see note 1).

3   European Parliamentary Elections Regulations 2004, SI 2004/293, Sch 2 para 2(1), (2) (as substituted: see note 1). This provision does not prevent a person, at his allotted polling station, marking a tendered ballot paper in pursuance of reg 44(4), (6) (see PARA 403): Sch 2 para 2(8) (as so substituted).

4   European Parliamentary Elections Regulations 2004, SI 2004/293, Sch 2 para 2(1), (3) (as substituted: see note 1).

5   European Parliamentary Elections Regulations 2004, SI 2004/293, Sch 2 para 2(1), (4) (as substituted: see note 1). As to the meaning of 'European parliamentary elections rules' see PARA 383 note 16.

6   European Parliamentary Elections Regulations 2004, SI 2004/293, Sch 2 para 2(1), (5)(a) (as substituted: see note 1).

7   As to local returning officers appointed for the purposes of elections to the European Parliament see PARA 360.

8   European Parliamentary Elections Regulations 2004, SI 2004/293, Sch 2 para 2(1), (5)(b) (as substituted: see note 1). As to the date of the poll at a European parliamentary election see PARA 222.

9   European Parliamentary Elections Regulations 2004, SI 2004/293, Sch 2 para 2(1), (5) (as substituted: see note 1). As to the meaning of 'local counting area' see PARA 139 note 1.

10   For these purposes, 'registered party' means a party which was registered under the Political Parties, Elections and Referendums Act 2000 Pt II (ss 22–40) (registration of political parties: see PARA 253): see the European Parliamentary Elections Act 2002 s 2(10). As to the submission by a registered party of lists of candidates to be members of the European Parliament ('MEPs') see PARA 228.

11   See the European Parliamentary Elections Act 2002 s 2(3), (4). As to the meaning of 'individual candidate' in the context of a European parliamentary election see PARA 230 note 32.

12   See the European Parliamentary Elections Act 2002 s 9; and PARA 700 note 12. As to the meaning of 'United Kingdom' see PARA 1 note 1.

366.   Absent voting.   A person may vote by post if he is either an elector entitled to vote by post or a person who is entitled to vote by post as proxy on behalf of an elector[1]. Alternatively, a person entitled to vote as proxy for an elector at an election may do so in person at the polling station allotted to the elector under the appropriate rules[2]. Where a person is entitled to vote by post as proxy for the elector at any election, the elector may not apply for a ballot paper for the purpose of voting in person at the election[3]. Provision is made for the procedure by which a person may apply to make an absent vote (for voting by post or by proxy either for a specified or indefinite period[4] or at a particular election only[5]), and for the procedure by which a person is appointed to vote as proxy for an elector[6]. The Secretary of State[7] may by regulations[8] make provision[9]:

(1) enabling the registration officer[10] to require an existing absent voter[11] to provide the registration officer with a signature and date of birth[12]; and

(2) as to the consequences of an existing absent voter refusing or failing in such circumstances as are prescribed to provide a signature and date of birth[13].

Accordingly, the registration officer must, every year by 31 January, send every person who remains an absent voter[14] (and whose signature held on the personal identifiers record[15] is more than five years old) a notice in writing[16], requiring him to provide a fresh signature[17], and informing him of the date (six weeks from the date of sending the notice) on which he would cease to be entitled to vote by post or by proxy in the event of a failure or refusal to provide a fresh signature[18]. The notice must be sent by the registration officer to the current or last known address of the absent voter[19]. The registration officer must, if the absent voter has not responded to the notice within three weeks from the date on which the notice was sent, as soon as practicable send a copy of the notice to him[20]. Upon the expiration of the period specified in the notice sent to the absent voter, the registration officer must determine whether the absent voter has failed or refused to provide a fresh signature[21]. Where the registration officer determines that the absent voter has refused or failed to provide a fresh signature within the specified period, he must remove that person's entry from the records kept of those entitled to an absent vote at elections (either for a particular period or for an indefinite period)[22] or of those entitled to vote by post as proxy at elections[23] and from the postal voters list[24], the list of proxies[25] or the proxy postal voters list[26], as the case may be[27]. Where a registration officer removes an absent voter's entry in such circumstances[28]:

(a) the registration officer must inform the absent voter, where appropriate, of the location of the polling station allotted or likely to be allotted[29] to him[30];

(b) the provisions governing the refusal of an application for absent voting[31] and notice of appeal[32] apply as if the registration officer were refusing an application for absent voting[33]; and

(c) in the case of an entry removed from the proxy postal voters list, the registration officer must also notify the elector who appointed the proxy whose entry has been removed[34].

The registration officer must maintain a record (the 'personal identifiers record'), apart from the other records and lists which he is required to keep in relation to applications made for absent voting[35], of the signatures and dates of birth provided by persons whose applications[36] were granted, until the expiry of 12 months from[37]:

(i) the date on which a person is removed from the record kept of those entitled to an absent vote at elections either for a particular period or for an indefinite period[38], or from the record kept of those entitled to vote by post as proxy at elections[39]; or

(ii)   the date of the poll for the purposes of which the person's application for an absent vote was granted[40].

The personal identifiers record must contain, in respect of each absent voter on the postal voters list, list of proxies or proxy postal voters list, his name[41], his date of birth[42], and his signature (or a record of the waiver by the registration officer of the requirement for a signature)[43]. The registration officer may disclose information held in the personal identifiers records either: (A) to any candidate or agent attending proceedings[44] on receipt of postal ballot papers[45]; or (B) to any person attending proceedings on receipt of postal ballot papers who is entitled to do so by virtue of the Political Parties, Elections and Referendums Act 2000[46], but only to the extent required to permit them to observe the proceedings[47].

1   See PARA 378 et seq. As to the mechanism by which postal ballots are issued and counted see PARA 406 et seq.
2   See PARA 377.
3   See PARA 377.
4   See PARA 367 et seq.
5   See PARA 371 et seq.
6   See PARA 374 et seq.
7   As to the Secretary of State see PARA 2.
8   The regulations may make different provision for different purposes and must be made by statutory instrument subject to annulment in pursuance of a resolution of either House of Parliament: see the Electoral Administration Act 2006 s 14(7).
9   Electoral Administration Act 2006 s 14(5).
10 As to the meaning of 'registration officer' see PARA 139.
11 For these purposes, an existing absent voter is a person whose application under the Representation of the People Act 2000 s 12, Sch 4 para 3(1) or Sch 4 para 3(2) (absent vote at elections for definite or indefinite period: see PARA 367) or under Sch 4 para 4(1) or Sch 4 para 4(2) (absent vote at particular election: see PARA 371) or under Sch 4 para 7(4) (voting as proxy for an indefinite period or for a particular period or at a particular election: see PARA 378) has been granted before 1 January 2007 (ie the date at which the Electoral Administration Act 2006 s 14 came into force): see s 14(6). As to the transitional provisions made for the capture of the personal identifiers of those who were existing absent voters under the Representation of the People Act 2000 at 1 January 2007 see the Absent Voting (Transitional Provisions) (England and Wales) Regulations 2006, SI 2006/2973, regs 2–5 (which reflect the force of the provisions set out in the text and notes 14–34). In relation to those who had an entry as existing absent voters or postal proxies in the absent voting records used for Welsh Assembly elections, as at 1 February 2007, see the National Assembly for Wales (Representation of the People) Order 2007, SI 2007/236, arts 13(2), 15(2), Sch 2 para 1–5; and, in relation to those who were existing absent voters for European parliamentary elections at 28 February 2009, see the European Parliamentary Elections Regulations 2004, SI 2004/293, reg 10, Sch 2 Pt 3 (paras 35–39) (Sch 2 substituted by SI 2009/186; the European Parliamentary Elections Regulations 2004, SI 2004/293, Sch 2 paras 36, 39 amended by SI 2009/848).
12 Electoral Administration Act 2006 s 14(5)(a).
13 Electoral Administration Act 2006 s 14(5)(b).
14 For the purposes of the Representation of the People (England and Wales) Regulations 2001, SI 2001/341, Pt IV (regs 50–63A), the European Parliamentary Elections Regulations 2004, SI 2004/293, Sch 2, and in relation to the National Assembly for Wales (Representation of the People) Order 2007, SI 2007/236, 'absent voter' means an elector who is entitled to vote by proxy or an elector or proxy who is entitled to vote by post: see the Representation of the People (England and Wales) Regulations 2001, SI 2001/341, reg 50 (definition added by SI 2006/2910); the European Parliamentary Elections Regulations 2004, SI 2004/293, Sch 2 para 1(1) (as substituted: see note 11); and the National Assembly for Wales (Representation of the People) Order 2007, SI 2007/236, art 2(1).
15 As to the personal identifiers record see the text and notes 35–47.
16 Representation of the People (England and Wales) Regulations 2001, SI 2001/341, reg 60A(1) (reg 60A added by SI 2006/2910); European Parliamentary Elections Regulations 2004,

SI 2004/293, Sch 2 para 31(1) (as substituted: see note 11); National Assembly for Wales (Representation of the People) Order 2007, SI 2007/236, Sch 1 para 12(1).

Where a notice is sent by post, the registration officer may use either a universal postal service provider, or a commercial delivery firm, and postage must be pre-paid: Representation of the People (England and Wales) Regulations 2001, SI 2001/341, reg 60A(4) (as so added); European Parliamentary Elections Regulations 2004, SI 2004/293, Sch 2 para 31(4) (as so substituted); National Assembly for Wales (Representation of the People) Order 2007, SI 2007/236, Sch 1 para 12(4). A notice sent to an absent voter in accordance with the Representation of the People (England and Wales) Regulations 2001, SI 2001/341, reg 60A(1), the European Parliamentary Elections Regulations 2004, SI 2004/293, Sch 2 para 31(1), or the National Assembly for Wales (Representation of the People) Order 2007, SI 2007/236, Sch 1 para 12(1), as the case may be, must be accompanied by a pre-addressed reply envelope and, in the case of any notice sent to an address in the United Kingdom, return postage must be pre-paid: Representation of the People (England and Wales) Regulations 2001, SI 2001/341, reg 60A(5) (as so added); European Parliamentary Elections Regulations 2004, SI 2004/293, Sch 2 para 31(5) (as so substituted); National Assembly for Wales (Representation of the People) Order 2007, SI 2007/236, Sch 1 para 12(5). As to the meaning of 'United Kingdom' see PARA 1 note 1. As to the meaning of 'universal postal service provider' for the purposes of the National Assembly for Wales (Representation of the People) Order 2007, SI 2007/236, see PARA 330 note 1.

In relation to European parliamentary elections, return postage must be paid also in the case of any notice sent to an address in Gibraltar: see the European Parliamentary Elections Regulations 2004, SI 2004/293, Sch 2 para 31(5) (as so substituted). For these purposes, 'universal postal service provider' means a universal service provider within the meaning of the Postal Services Act 2011 Pt 3 (ss 27–67) (see POSTAL SERVICES vol 85 (2012) PARA 252) and, in relation to Gibraltar, such person or persons with the right to exercise the functions of a universal service provider within the meaning of European Parliament and European Council Directive (EC) 97/67 of 15 December 1997 (OJ L15, 21.01.1998, p 14) on common rules for the development of the internal market of Community postal services and the improvement of quality of service ('the Postal Services Directive') (see POSTAL SERVICES vol 85 (2012) PARA 205): European Parliamentary Elections Regulations 2004, SI 2004/293, reg 2(1) (reg 2(1) substituted by SI 2009/186; definition of 'universal postal service provider' amended by SI 2011/2085). As to the establishment of electoral regions (including the 'combined region', which incorporates Gibraltar) for the purpose of elections to the European Parliament see PARA 77.

In the period beginning on 31 July 2013 and ending on 31 December 2014, the Representation of the People (England and Wales) Regulations 2001, SI 2001/341, reg 60A(1), and the European Parliamentary Elections Regulations 2004, SI 2004/293, Sch 2 para 31(1), were modified by the Elections (Fresh Signatures for Absent Voters) Regulations 2013, SI 2013/1599, regs 2, 4, and the National Assembly for Wales (Representation of the People) Order 2007, SI 2007/236, Sch 1 para 12, was modified by the National Assembly for Wales (Representation of the People) (Fresh Signatures for Absent Voters) Order 2013, SI 2013/1514, art 2, in line with the transitional arrangements for the implementation of individual electoral registration under the Electoral Registration and Administration Act 2013 (see PARA 152).

17　Representation of the People (England and Wales) Regulations 2001, SI 2001/341, reg 60A(1)(a) (as added: see note 16); European Parliamentary Elections Regulations 2004, SI 2004/293, Sch 2 para 31(1)(a) (as substituted: see note 11); National Assembly for Wales (Representation of the People) Order 2007, SI 2007/236, Sch 1 para 12(1)(a).

18　Representation of the People (England and Wales) Regulations 2001, SI 2001/341, reg 60A(1)(b) (as added: see note 16); European Parliamentary Elections Regulations 2004, SI 2004/293, Sch 2 para 31(1)(b) (as substituted: see note 11); National Assembly for Wales (Representation of the People) Order 2007, SI 2007/236, Sch 1 para 12(1)(b).

Where a person to whom the European Parliamentary Elections Regulations 2004, SI 2004/293, Sch 2 para 31(1) applies has provided a registration officer with the required personal identifiers under the Representation of the People Act 2000 s 12, Sch 4 para 3 (absent vote at elections for definite or indefinite period: see PARA 367), or under Sch 4 para 4 (absent vote at particular election: see PARA 371), or under Sch 4 para 7 (voting as proxy for an indefinite period or for a particular period or at a particular election: see PARA 378), or under the Representation of the People (England and Wales) Regulations 2001, SI 2001/341, or the National Assembly for Wales (Representation of the People) Order 2007, SI 2007/236, before the date specified in the notice sent to the absent voter in accordance with the European Parliamentary Elections Regulations 2004, SI 2004/293, Sch 2 para 31(1)(b), the registration officer may use them, or enter them in his records, in accordance with Sch 2 para 3(9) (record of those entitled to an absent vote at elections for a definite period or for an indefinite period see

PARA 370), Sch 2 para 4(7) (record of persons entitled to absent vote at a particular election: see PARA 373), Sch 2 para 7(13) (voting as proxy: see PARA 379) and Sch 2 para 18 (personal identifiers record: see the text and notes 35–47): Sch 2 para 31(10) (as so substituted).

19 Representation of the People (England and Wales) Regulations 2001, SI 2001/341, reg 60A(2) (as added: see note 16); European Parliamentary Elections Regulations 2004, SI 2004/293, Sch 2 para 31(2) (as substituted: see note 11); National Assembly for Wales (Representation of the People) Order 2007, SI 2007/236, Sch 1 para 12(2).

20 Representation of the People (England and Wales) Regulations 2001, SI 2001/341, reg 60A(3) (as added: see note 16); European Parliamentary Elections Regulations 2004, SI 2004/293, Sch 2 para 31(3) (as substituted: see note 11); National Assembly for Wales (Representation of the People) Order 2007, SI 2007/236, Sch 1 para 12(3).

Where a copy of a notice is sent by post, the registration officer may use either a universal postal service provider, or a commercial delivery firm, and postage must be pre-paid: Representation of the People (England and Wales) Regulations 2001, SI 2001/341, reg 60A(4) (as so added); European Parliamentary Elections Regulations 2004, SI 2004/293, Sch 2 para 31(4) (as so substituted); National Assembly for Wales (Representation of the People) Order 2007, SI 2007/236, Sch 1 para 12(4). A copy of a notice sent to an absent voter in accordance with the Representation of the People (England and Wales) Regulations 2001, SI 2001/341, reg 60A(3), the European Parliamentary Elections Regulations 2004, SI 2004/293, Sch 2 para 31(3), or the National Assembly for Wales (Representation of the People) Order 2007, SI 2007/236, Sch 1 para 12(3), as the case may be, must be accompanied by a pre-addressed reply envelope and, in the case of any copy of a notice sent to an address in the United Kingdom, return postage must be pre-paid: Representation of the People (England and Wales) Regulations 2001, SI 2001/341, reg 60A(5) (as so added); European Parliamentary Elections Regulations 2004, SI 2004/293, Sch 2 para 31(5) (as so substituted); National Assembly for Wales (Representation of the People) Order 2007, SI 2007/236, Sch 1 para 12(5). In relation to European parliamentary elections, return postage must be paid also in the case of any copy of a notice sent to an address in Gibraltar: see the European Parliamentary Elections Regulations 2004, SI 2004/293, Sch 2 para 31(5) (as so substituted).

21 Representation of the People (England and Wales) Regulations 2001, SI 2001/341, reg 60A(6) (as added: see note 16); European Parliamentary Elections Regulations 2004, SI 2004/293, Sch 2 para 31(6) (as substituted: see note 11); National Assembly for Wales (Representation of the People) Order 2007, SI 2007/236, Sch 1 para 12(6).

22 Ie the record kept pursuant to the Representation of the People Act 2000 Sch 4 para 3(4), the European Parliamentary Elections Regulations 2004, SI 2004/293, Sch 2 para 3(4), the National Assembly for Wales (Representation of the People) Order 2007, SI 2007/236, art 8(3), as the case may be (see PARA 370): see the Representation of the People (England and Wales) Regulations 2001, SI 2001/341, reg 60A(7) (as added: see note 16); the European Parliamentary . Elections Regulations 2004, SI 2004/293, Sch 2 para 31(7) (as substituted: see note 11); and the National Assembly for Wales (Representation of the People) Order 2007, SI 2007/236, Sch 1 para 12(7).

23 Ie the record kept pursuant to the Representation of the People Act 2000 Sch 4 para 7(6), the European Parliamentary Elections Regulations 2004, SI 2004/293, Sch 2 para 7(6), or the National Assembly for Wales (Representation of the People) Order 2007, SI 2007/236, art 12(6), as the case may be (see PARA 379): see the Representation of the People (England and Wales) Regulations 2001, SI 2001/341, reg 60A(7) (as added: see note 16); the European Parliamentary Elections Regulations 2004, SI 2004/293, Sch 2 para 31(7) (as substituted: see note 11); and the National Assembly for Wales (Representation of the People) Order 2007, SI 2007/236, Sch 1 para 12(7).

24 Ie the list kept under the Representation of the People Act 2000 Sch 4 para 5(2), the European Parliamentary Elections Regulations 2004, SI 2004/293, Sch 2 para 5(2), or the National Assembly for Wales (Representation of the People) Order 2007, SI 2007/236, art 10(2), as the case may be (see PARA 373): see the Representation of the People (England and Wales) Regulations 2001, SI 2001/341, reg 60A(7) (as added: see note 16); the European Parliamentary Elections Regulations 2004, SI 2004/293, Sch 2 para 31(7) (as substituted: see note 11); and the National Assembly for Wales (Representation of the People) Order 2007, SI 2007/236, Sch 1 para 12(7).

25 Ie the list kept under the Representation of the People Act 2000 Sch 4 para 5(3), the European Parliamentary Elections Regulations 2004, SI 2004/293, Sch 2 para 5(3), or the National Assembly for Wales (Representation of the People) Order 2007, SI 2007/236, art 10(3), as the case may be (see PARA 373): see the Representation of the People (England and Wales) Regulations 2001, SI 2001/341, reg 60A(7) (as added: see note 16); the European Parliamentary

Elections Regulations 2004, SI 2004/293, Sch 2 para 31(7) (as substituted: see note 11); and the National Assembly for Wales (Representation of the People) Order 2007, SI 2007/236, Sch 1 para 12(7).

26 Ie the list kept under the Representation of the People Act 2000 Sch 4 para 7(8), the European Parliamentary Elections Regulations 2004, SI 2004/293, Sch 2 para 7(8), or the National Assembly for Wales (Representation of the People) Order 2007, SI 2007/236, art 12(8), as the case may be (see PARA 381): see the Representation of the People (England and Wales) Regulations 2001, SI 2001/341, reg 60A(7) (as added: see note 16); the European Parliamentary Elections Regulations 2004, SI 2004/293, Sch 2 para 31(7) (as substituted: see note 11); and the National Assembly for Wales (Representation of the People) Order 2007, SI 2007/236, Sch 1 para 12(7).

27 Representation of the People (England and Wales) Regulations 2001, SI 2001/341, reg 60A(7) (as added: see note 16); European Parliamentary Elections Regulations 2004, SI 2004/293, Sch 2 para 31(7) (as substituted: see note 11); National Assembly for Wales (Representation of the People) Order 2007, SI 2007/236, Sch 1 para 12(7).

28 Representation of the People (England and Wales) Regulations 2001, SI 2001/341, reg 60A(8) (as added: see note 16); European Parliamentary Elections Regulations 2004, SI 2004/293, Sch 2 para 31(8) (as substituted: see note 11); National Assembly for Wales (Representation of the People) Order 2007, SI 2007/236, Sch 1 para 12(8) (amended by SI 2010/2931). The registration officer must include in the notice to be sent to an absent voter regarding removal from:

(1) the record kept pursuant to the Representation of the People Act 2000 Sch 4 para 3(4), the European Parliamentary Elections Regulations 2004, SI 2004/293, Sch 2 para 3(4), or the National Assembly for Wales (Representation of the People) Order 2007, SI 2007/236, art 8(3), as the case may be (see PARA 370); or

(2) the record kept pursuant to the Representation of the People Act 2000 Sch 4 para 7(6), the European Parliamentary Elections Regulations 2004, SI 2004/293, Sch 2 para 7(6), or the National Assembly for Wales (Representation of the People) Order 2007, SI 2007/236, art 12(6), as the case may be (see PARA 379); and

(3) the postal voters list kept under the Representation of the People Act 2000 Sch 4 para 5(2), the European Parliamentary Elections Regulations 2004, SI 2004/293, Sch 2 para 5(2), or the National Assembly for Wales (Representation of the People) Order 2007, SI 2007/236, art 10(2), as the case may be (see PARA 373);

(4) the list of proxies list kept under the Representation of the People Act 2000 Sch 4 para 5(3), the European Parliamentary Elections Regulations 2004, SI 2004/293, Sch 2 para 5(3), or the National Assembly for Wales (Representation of the People) Order 2007, SI 2007/236, art 10(3), as the case may be (see PARA 373);

(5) the proxy postal voters list kept under the Representation of the People Act 2000 Sch 4 para 7(8), the European Parliamentary Elections Regulations 2004, SI 2004/293, Sch 2 para 7(8), or the National Assembly for Wales (Representation of the People) Order 2007, SI 2007/236, art 12(8), as the case may be (see PARA 381),

information (see the Representation of the People (England and Wales) Regulations 2001, SI 2001/341, reg 60A(9) (as so added); the European Parliamentary Elections Regulations 2004, SI 2004/293, Sch 2 para 31(9) (as so substituted); and the National Assembly for Wales (Representation of the People) Order 2007, SI 2007/236, Sch 1 para 12(9)):

(a) explaining the effect of such removal (Representation of the People (England and Wales) Regulations 2001, SI 2001/341, reg 60A(9)(a) (as so added); European Parliamentary Elections Regulations 2004, SI 2004/293, Sch 2 para 31(9)(a) (as so substituted); National Assembly for Wales (Representation of the People) Order 2007, SI 2007/236, Sch 1 para 12(9)(a)); and

(b) reminding the absent voter that he may make a fresh application under the Representation of the People Act 2000 Sch 4, the European Parliamentary Elections Regulations 2004, SI 2004/293, Sch 2 Pt 2 (paras 12–34), or the National Assembly for Wales (Representation of the People) Order 2007, SI 2007/236, art 8(1), art 9(1), or art 12(4), as the case may be, to vote by post or by proxy (see PARA 367 et seq) (Representation of the People (England and Wales) Regulations 2001, SI 2001/341, reg 60A(9)(b) (as so added); European Parliamentary Elections Regulations 2004, SI 2004/293, Sch 2 para 31(9)(b) (as so substituted); National Assembly for Wales (Representation of the People) Order 2007, SI 2007/236, Sch 1 para 12(9)(b)).

29 Ie under the appropriate rules, as defined in the Representation of the People Act 2000 Sch 4 para 1 (see PARA 363 note 2), in accordance with the European parliamentary elections rules, or under the National Assembly for Wales (Representation of the People) Order 2007, SI 2007/236, as the case may be: see the Representation of the People (England and Wales)

Regulations 2001, SI 2001/341, reg 60A(8)(a) (as added: see note 16); the European Parliamentary Elections Regulations 2004, SI 2004/293, Sch 2 para 31(8)(a) (as substituted: see note 11); and the National Assembly for Wales (Representation of the People) Order 2007, SI 2007/236, Sch 1 para 12(8)(a). As to the meaning of 'European parliamentary elections rules' see PARA 383 note 16.

30 Representation of the People (England and Wales) Regulations 2001, SI 2001/341, reg 60A(8)(a) (as added: see note 16); European Parliamentary Elections Regulations 2004, SI 2004/293, Sch 2 para 31(8)(a) (as substituted: see note 11); National Assembly for Wales (Representation of the People) Order 2007, SI 2007/236, Sch 1 para 12(8)(a).

31 Ie under the Representation of the People (England and Wales) Regulations 2001, SI 2001/341, reg 57(4), the European Parliamentary Elections Regulations 2004, SI 2004/293, Sch 2 para 27(3), or the National Assembly for Wales (Representation of the People) Order 2007, SI 2007/236, Sch 1 para 8(4), as the case may be: see the Representation of the People (England and Wales) Regulations 2001, SI 2001/341, reg 60A(8)(b) (as added: see note 16); the European Parliamentary Elections Regulations 2004, SI 2004/293, Sch 2 para 31(8)(b) (as substituted: see note 11); and the National Assembly for Wales (Representation of the People) Order 2007, SI 2007/236, Sch 1 para 12(8)(b). In the case of a Welsh Assembly election, the National Assembly for Wales (Representation of the People) Order 2007, SI 2007/236, Sch 1 para 8(6), (7), are also specified (see PARA 370): see Sch 1 para 12(8)(b).

Where the registration officer refuses an application for an absent vote, he must notify the applicant of his decision and of the reason for it: Representation of the People (England and Wales) Regulations 2001, SI 2001/341, reg 57(4); European Parliamentary Elections Regulations 2004, SI 2004/293, Sch 2 para 27(3) (as so substituted); National Assembly for Wales (Representation of the People) Order 2007, SI 2007/236, Sch 1 para 8(4).

32 Ie the Representation of the People (England and Wales) Regulations 2001, SI 2001/341, reg 58, under the European Parliamentary Elections Regulations 2004, SI 2004/293, Sch 2 para 28, or under the National Assembly for Wales (Representation of the People) Order 2007, SI 2007/236, Sch 1 para 9, as the case may be (see PARAS 173–174): see the Representation of the People (England and Wales) Regulations 2001, SI 2001/341, reg 60A(8)(b) (as added: see note 16); the European Parliamentary Elections Regulations 2004, SI 2004/293, Sch 2 para 31(8)(b) (as substituted: see note 11); and the National Assembly for Wales (Representation of the People) Order 2007, SI 2007/236, Sch 1 para 12(8)(b).

33 Representation of the People (England and Wales) Regulations 2001, SI 2001/341, reg 60A(8)(b) (as added: see note 16); European Parliamentary Elections Regulations 2004, SI 2004/293, Sch 2 para 31(8)(b) (as substituted: see note 11); National Assembly for Wales (Representation of the People) Order 2007, SI 2007/236, Sch 1 para 12(8)(b).

34 Representation of the People (England and Wales) Regulations 2001, SI 2001/341, reg 60A(8)(c) (as added: see note 16); European Parliamentary Elections Regulations 2004, SI 2004/293, Sch 2 para 31(8)(c) (as substituted: see note 11); National Assembly for Wales (Representation of the People) Order 2007, SI 2007/236, Sch 1 para 12(8)(c).

35 Ie under the Representation of the People Act 2000 Sch 4, under the European Parliamentary Elections Regulations 2004, SI 2004/293, Sch 2, or under the National Assembly for Wales (Representation of the People) Order 2007, SI 2007/236, as the case may be (see PARA 367 et seq): see the Representation of the People (England and Wales) Regulations 2001, SI 2001/341, reg 61B(1) (reg 61B added by SI 2006/2910); the European Parliamentary Elections Regulations 2004, SI 2004/293, Sch 2 para 18(1) (as substituted: see note 11); and the National Assembly for Wales (Representation of the People) Order 2007, SI 2007/236, Sch 1 para 2(1). An application for an absent vote or postal proxy made in accordance with the National Assembly for Wales (Representation of the People) Order 2007, SI 2007/236, art 8 (see PARA 367 et seq), art 9 (see PARA 371 et seq), art 11 (see PARA 374 et seq), or art 12, must comply with Sch 1 para 2: see art 13(1).

The Representation of the People (England and Wales) Regulations 2001, SI 2001/341, reg 61B has effect for the purposes of local authority referendums, subject to the modifications specified, in relation to Wales, by the Local Authorities (Conduct of Referendums) (Wales) Regulations 2008, SI 2008/1848, reg 8(2), Sch 4 Table 5, and, in relation to England, by the Local Authorities (Conduct of Referendums) (England) Regulations 2012, SI 2012/323, regs 8(2), 11–13, Sch 4 Table 6 (see PARA 15 note 2).

36 Ie under the Representation of the People Act 2000 Sch 4 para 3(1), (2) (absent vote at elections for definite or indefinite period: see PARA 367), Sch 4 para 4(1), (2) (absent vote at particular election: see PARA 371) or Sch 4 para 7(4)(a), (b) (voting as proxy for an indefinite period or for a particular period or at a particular election: see PARA 378), under the European Parliamentary Elections Regulations 2004, SI 2004/293, Sch 2 para 3(1), (2) (absent vote at elections for definite or indefinite period: see PARA 367), Sch 2 para 4(1), (2) (absent vote at particular

election: see PARA 371) or Sch 2 para 7(4)(a), (b) (voting as proxy for an indefinite period or for a particular period or at a particular election: see PARA 378), or under the National Assembly for Wales (Representation of the People) Order 2007, SI 2007/236, art 8(1) (absent vote at elections for definite or indefinite period: see PARA 367), art 9(1) (absent vote at particular election: see PARA 371) or art 12(4)(a), (b) (voting as proxy for an indefinite period or for a particular period or at a particular election: see PARA 378), as the case may be: see the Representation of the People (England and Wales) Regulations 2001, SI 2001/341, reg 61B(1) (as added: see note 35); the European Parliamentary Elections Regulations 2004, SI 2004/293, Sch 2 para 18(1) (as substituted: see note 11); and the National Assembly for Wales (Representation of the People) Order 2007, SI 2007/236, Sch 1 para 2(1).

37 Representation of the People (England and Wales) Regulations 2001, SI 2001/341, reg 61B(1) (as added: see note 35); European Parliamentary Elections Regulations 2004, SI 2004/293, Sch 2 para 18(1) (as substituted: see note 11); National Assembly for Wales (Representation of the People) Order 2007, SI 2007/236, Sch 1 para 2(1).

38 Ie the record kept pursuant to the Representation of the People Act 2000 Sch 4 para 3(4), the European Parliamentary Elections Regulations 2004, SI 2004/293, Sch 2 para 3(4), or the National Assembly for Wales (Representation of the People) Order 2007, SI 2007/236, art 8(3), as the case may be (see PARA 370): see the Representation of the People (England and Wales) Regulations 2001, SI 2001/341, reg 61B(1)(a) (as added: see note 35); the European Parliamentary Elections Regulations 2004, SI 2004/293, Sch 2 para 18(1)(a) (as substituted: see note 11); and the National Assembly for Wales (Representation of the People) Order 2007, SI 2007/236, Sch 1 para 2(1)(a) (amended by SI 2010/2931).

39 Representation of the People (England and Wales) Regulations 2001, SI 2001/341, reg 61B(1)(a) (as added: see note 35); European Parliamentary Elections Regulations 2004, SI 2004/293, Sch 2 para 18(1)(a) (as substituted: see note 11); National Assembly for Wales (Representation of the People) Order 2007, SI 2007/236, Sch 1 para 2(1)(a) (as amended: see note 38). The text refers to the record kept pursuant to the Representation of the People Act 2000 Sch 4 para 7(6), the European Parliamentary Elections Regulations 2004, SI 2004/293, Sch 2 para 7(6), or the National Assembly for Wales (Representation of the People) Order 2007, SI 2007/236, art 12(6), as the case may be (see PARA 379): see the Representation of the People (England and Wales) Regulations 2001, SI 2001/341, reg 61B(1)(a) (as so added); the European Parliamentary Elections Regulations 2004, SI 2004/293, Sch 2 para 18(1)(a) (as so substituted); and the National Assembly for Wales (Representation of the People) Order 2007, SI 2007/236, Sch 1 para 2(1)(a) (as so amended).

40 Representation of the People (England and Wales) Regulations 2001, SI 2001/341, reg 61B(1)(b) (as added: see note 35); European Parliamentary Elections Regulations 2004, SI 2004/293, Sch 2 para 18(1)(b) (as substituted: see note 11); National Assembly for Wales (Representation of the People) Order 2007, SI 2007/236, Sch 1 para 2(1)(b). The text refers to the date of the poll for the purposes of which the person's application for an absent vote was granted under the Representation of the People Act 2000 Sch 4 para 4(1), (2) (absent vote at particular election: see PARA 371) or Sch 4 para 7(4)(b) (voting as proxy at a particular election: see PARA 378), under the European Parliamentary Elections Regulations 2004, SI 2004/293, Sch 2 para 4(1), (2) (absent vote at particular election: see PARA 371) or Sch 2 para 7(4)(b) (voting as proxy at a particular election: see PARA 378), or under the National Assembly for Wales (Representation of the People) Order 2007, SI 2007/236, art 9(1) (absent vote at particular election: see PARA 371) or art 12(4)(b) (voting as proxy at a particular election: see PARA 378): see the Representation of the People (England and Wales) Regulations 2001, SI 2001/341, reg 61B(1)(b) (as so added); the European Parliamentary Elections Regulations 2004, SI 2004/293, Sch 2 para 18(1)(b) (as so substituted); and the National Assembly for Wales (Representation of the People) Order 2007, SI 2007/236, Sch 1 para 2(1)(b).

41 Representation of the People (England and Wales) Regulations 2001, SI 2001/341, reg 61B(2)(a) (as added: see note 35); European Parliamentary Elections Regulations 2004, SI 2004/293, Sch 2 para 18(2)(a) (as substituted: see note 11); National Assembly for Wales (Representation of the People) Order 2007, SI 2007/236, Sch 1 para 2(2)(a).

42 Representation of the People (England and Wales) Regulations 2001, SI 2001/341, reg 61B(2)(b) (as added: see note 35); European Parliamentary Elections Regulations 2004, SI 2004/293, Sch 2 para 18(2)(b) (as substituted: see note 11); National Assembly for Wales (Representation of the People) Order 2007, SI 2007/236, Sch 1 para 2(2)(b).

43 Representation of the People (England and Wales) Regulations 2001, SI 2001/341, reg 61B(2)(c) (as added: see note 35); European Parliamentary Elections Regulations 2004, SI 2004/293, Sch 2 para 18(2)(c) (as substituted: see note 11); National Assembly for Wales (Representation of the People) Order 2007, SI 2007/236, Sch 1 para 2(2)(c).

44 Ie in accordance with and for the purposes referred to in the Representation of the People (England and Wales) Regulations 2001, SI 2001/341, reg 85, in the European Parliamentary Elections Regulations 2004, SI 2004/293, regs 62, 63, or in the National Assembly for Wales (Representation of the People) Order 2007, SI 2007/236, Sch 3 paras 22, 23 (see PARA 421): see the Representation of the People (England and Wales) Regulations 2001, SI 2001/341, reg 61B(3)(a) (as added: see note 35); the European Parliamentary Elections Regulations 2004, SI 2004/293, Sch 2 para 18(3)(a) (as substituted: see note 11); and the National Assembly for Wales (Representation of the People) Order 2007, SI 2007/236, Sch 1 para 2(3)(a).

45 Representation of the People (England and Wales) Regulations 2001, SI 2001/341, reg 61B(3)(a) (as added: see note 35); European Parliamentary Elections Regulations 2004, SI 2004/293, Sch 2 para 18(3)(a) (as substituted: see note 11); National Assembly for Wales (Representation of the People) Order 2007, SI 2007/236, Sch 1 para 2(3)(a).

46 Ie by virtue of any of the Political Parties, Elections and Referendums Act 2000 ss 6A–6D (see PARA 53): see the Representation of the People (England and Wales) Regulations 2001, SI 2001/341, reg 61B(3)(b) (as added: see note 35); the European Parliamentary Elections Regulations 2004, SI 2004/293, Sch 2 para 18(3)(b) (as substituted: see note 11); and the National Assembly for Wales (Representation of the People) Order 2007, SI 2007/236, Sch 1 para 2(3)(b).

47 Representation of the People (England and Wales) Regulations 2001, SI 2001/341, reg 61B(3)(b) (as added: see note 35); European Parliamentary Elections Regulations 2004, SI 2004/293, Sch 2 para 18(3)(b) (as substituted: see note 11); National Assembly for Wales (Representation of the People) Order 2007, SI 2007/236, Sch 1 para 2(3)(b).

B. ABSENT VOTING

(A) Applications relating to a Particular Period or an Indefinite Period

367. Application for absent vote at elections whether for a particular period or for an indefinite period. Where a person applies to the registration officer[1] to vote by post at parliamentary[2] or local government elections[3] (or at both), or at Welsh Assembly elections[4], or at European parliamentary elections[5], whether for an indefinite period or for a particular period specified in his application, the registration officer must grant the application[6]:

(1) if he is satisfied that the applicant is or will be registered in the register of electors for the election[7]; and

(2) if the application contains the applicant's signature and date of birth and meets the statutory requirements[8].

Where a person applies to the registration officer to vote by proxy[9] at such an election, whether for an indefinite period or for a particular period specified in his application, the registration officer must grant the application[10]:

(a) if he is satisfied that the applicant is eligible to vote by proxy at elections to which the application relates[11];

(b) if he is satisfied that the applicant is or will be registered in the relevant register of electors[12]; and

(c) if the application contains the applicant's signature and date of birth and meets the statutory requirements[13].

For these purposes, a person is eligible to vote by proxy at such elections:

(i) if he is or will be registered as a service voter[14];

(ii) if he has an anonymous entry in the register of electors[15] for the election[16];

(iii) if he cannot reasonably be expected either to go in person to the polling station allotted or likely to be allotted to him under the appropriate rules[17], or to vote unaided there[18], by reason of blindness or other disability[19];

(iv) if he cannot reasonably be expected to go in person to that polling station by reason of the general nature of his occupation, service or employment (or that of his spouse or civil partner), or by reason of his (or his spouse's or his civil partner's) attendance on a course provided by an educational institution[20]; or

(v)   if he cannot go in person from his qualifying address to that polling station without making a journey by air or sea[21].

A person is also eligible to vote by proxy at parliamentary elections, or at European parliamentary elections, if he is or will be registered in pursuance of an overseas elector's declaration (or, further, in the case of a European parliamentary election, in pursuance of a European parliamentary overseas elector's declaration)[22].

Any such application for an absent vote[23] must state:

(A)   the full name of the applicant[24];

(B)   the address in respect of which the applicant is registered or has applied to be (or is treated as having applied to be) registered in the register[25];

(C)   in the case of a person applying to vote by post, the address to which the ballot paper should be sent[26];

(D)   in the case of an application to vote by proxy, the grounds on which the elector claims to be entitled to an absent vote[27]; and

(E)   in the case of a person who is unable to provide a signature, the reasons for his request for waiver of any such requirement[28] to provide a signature, and the name and address of any person who has assisted him to complete his application[29]; and

(F)   where the applicant has, or has applied for, an anonymous entry, that fact[30].

The application must be made in writing and dated[31], and, where it is made for an indefinite period or for the period specified in the application, it must state that it is so made[32], and (except in relation to a Welsh Assembly election) must specify the election (or elections) in respect of which it is made[33]. Where an application is made by an elector to vote by proxy, it must include an application for the appointment of a proxy which meets the statutory requirements[34].

Where the registration officer grants an application to vote by post, he must notify the applicant of his decision[35]; and where he refuses such an application, he must notify the applicant of his decision and of the reason for it[36]. An appeal lies to the county court from any decision of the registration officer disallowing a person's application to vote by proxy or by post as elector in any case where the application is not made for a particular election only[37].

1   The registration officer must supply free of charge as many forms for use in connection with applications made under the Representation of the People Act 2000 s 12, Sch 4, the Representation of the People (England and Wales) Regulations 2001, SI 2001/341, Pt IV (regs 50–63A), or the European Parliamentary Elections Regulations 2004, SI 2004/293, reg 10, Sch 2, as appear to that officer reasonable in the circumstances to any person who satisfies that officer of his intention to use the forms in connection with an election: Representation of the People (England and Wales) Regulations 2001, SI 2001/341, reg 4(1)(b); European Parliamentary Elections Regulations 2004, SI 2004/293, Sch 2 para 12(1) (Sch 2 substituted by SI 2009/186). As to electoral registration officers and the areas for which they act see PARA 139 et seq.

    The Representation of the People Act 2000 s 12, Sch 4 are applied and modified for the purpose of local authority mayoral elections in England and Wales by the Local Authorities (Mayoral Elections) (England and Wales) Regulations 2007, SI 2007/1024, reg 3(2)–(5), Sch 2 Table 3 (see PARA 11 note 14); and they have effect for the purposes of local authority referendums, subject to the modifications specified, in relation to Wales, by the Local Authorities (Conduct of Referendums) (Wales) Regulations 2008, SI 2008/1848, reg 8(2), Sch 4 Table 2, and, in relation to England, by the Local Authorities (Conduct of Referendums)

(England) Regulations 2012, SI 2012/323, regs 8(2), 11–13, Sch 4 Table 3 (see PARA 15 note 2). The Representation of the People (England and Wales) Regulations 2001, SI 2001/341, regs 4, 50, 51, 51A, 51AA, 56, 57 also have effect for the purposes of local authority referendums, subject to the modifications specified, in relation to Wales, by the Local Authorities (Conduct of Referendums) (Wales) Regulations 2008, SI 2008/1848, reg 8(2), Sch 4 Table 5, and, in relation to England, by the Local Authorities (Conduct of Referendums) (England) Regulations 2012, SI 2012/323, regs 8(2), 11–13, Sch 4 Table 6 (see PARA 15 note 2).

2   As to the meaning of 'parliamentary election' see PARA 9.

3   As to the meaning of 'local government election' see PARA 11; definition applied by virtue of the Representation of the People Act 2000 s 12, Sch 4 para 1(2). See also PARA 363 note 1.

4   As to the meaning of 'Assembly election' in the context of Welsh Assembly elections see PARA 3 note 2.

5   As to European parliamentary elections see PARA 217 et seq.

6   Representation of the People Act 2000 Sch 4 para 3(1); European Parliamentary Elections Regulations 2004, SI 2004/293, Sch 2 para 3(1) (as substituted: see note 1); National Assembly for Wales (Representation of the People) Order 2007, SI 2007/236, art 8(1). Such an application must be disregarded for the purposes of any particular election mentioned in the text if it is received by the registration officer after 5 pm on the eleventh day before the date of the poll at that election: Representation of the People (England and Wales) Regulations 2001, SI 2001/341, reg 56(1) (amended by SI 2006/752); European Parliamentary Elections Regulations 2004, SI 2004/293, Sch 2 para 26(1) (as so substituted); National Assembly for Wales (Representation of the People) Order 2007, SI 2007/236, art 15(2), Sch 1 para 7(1). Where a registration officer disregards such an application for the purposes of any particular election, he must notify the applicant of this: Representation of the People (England and Wales) Regulations 2001, SI 2001/341, reg 57(5) (amended by SI 2006/752); European Parliamentary Elections Regulations 2004, SI 2004/293, Sch 2 para 27(7) (as so substituted); National Assembly for Wales (Representation of the People) Order 2007, SI 2007/236, Sch 1 para 8(8). As to the date of the poll at a parliamentary general election or by-election see PARA 195; as to the date of the poll at local government elections (including elections to fill vacancies) see PARAS 206–209; as to the date of the poll at Welsh Assembly elections (including elections to fill vacancies in an Assembly constituency) see PARAS 213–214; and as to the date of the poll at a European parliamentary election see PARA 222.

    In computing a period of days for these purposes, Saturday, Sunday, Christmas Eve, Christmas Day, Good Friday or a bank holiday is to be disregarded: Representation of the People (England and Wales) Regulations 2001, SI 2001/341, reg 56(6) (amended by SI 2006/2910); European Parliamentary Elections Regulations 2004, SI 2004/293, Sch 2 para 26(7) (as so substituted); National Assembly for Wales (Representation of the People) Order 2007, SI 2007/236, Sch 1 para 7(6). 'Bank holiday' means a day which is a bank holiday under the Banking and Financial Dealings Act 1971 (see TIME vol 97 (2010) PARA 321) in any part of the United Kingdom, except in relation to a by-election (parliamentary or European parliamentary), or local government election, or Welsh Assembly election (or where, at a parliamentary general election, any proceedings are commenced afresh by reason of a candidate's death) where 'bank holiday' means a day which is a bank holiday under the Banking and Financial Dealings Act 1971 in the area in which the election is to take place: Representation of the People (England and Wales) Regulations 2001, SI 2001/341, reg 56(7); European Parliamentary Elections Regulations 2004, SI 2004/293, Sch 2 para 26(8) (as so substituted); National Assembly for Wales (Representation of the People) Order 2007, SI 2007/236, Sch 1 para 7(7). As to the meaning of 'United Kingdom' see PARA 1 note 1.

7   Representation of the People Act 2000 Sch 4 para 3(1)(a); European Parliamentary Elections Regulations 2004, SI 2004/293, Sch 2 para 3(1)(a) (as substituted: see note 1); National Assembly for Wales (Representation of the People) Order 2007, SI 2007/236, art 8(1)(b). In the case of a parliamentary election, the register referred to in the text is the register of parliamentary electors and, in the case of a local government election, it is the register of local government electors (although an application under the Representation of the People Act 2000 Sch 4 may relate to both types of election, in which case the requirement is for the applicant to be registered in both): see the Representation of the People Act 2000 Sch 4 para 3(1)(a). For the purposes of a Welsh Assembly election, 'register' means the register of local government electors: see the National Assembly for Wales (Representation of the People) Order 2007, SI 2007/236, art 2(1). As to the meaning of the 'register of electors', in relation to a European parliamentary election, see PARA 111 note 4. As to registration as an elector see PARA 113 et seq; and as to the registers of electors maintained by registration officers see PARA 143 et seq.

8   Representation of the People Act 2000 Sch 4 para 3(1)(b) (amended by the Electoral Administration Act 2006 s 14(1)(a), (8)); European Parliamentary Elections Regulations 2004,

SI 2004/293, Sch 2 para 3(1)(b) (as substituted: see note 1); National Assembly for Wales (Representation of the People) Order 2007, SI 2007/236, art 8(1)(c). In the case of a parliamentary or local government election, the application referred to in the text must meet the prescribed requirements: see the Representation of the People Act 2000 Sch 4 para 3(1)(b) (as so amended). For the purposes of Sch 4, 'prescribed' means prescribed by regulations (see the Representation of the People Act 1983 s 202(1); definition applied by virtue of the Representation of the People Act 2000 Sch 4 para 1(2)); and, accordingly, the text refers to the requirements set out in the Representation of the People (England and Wales) Regulations 2001, SI 2001/341, Pt IV (regs 50–63A). In the case of a European parliamentary election, the application referred to in the text must meet the requirements of the European Parliamentary Elections Regulations 2004, SI 2004/293, Sch 2: see Sch 2 para 3(1)(b) (as so substituted). In the case of a Welsh Assembly election, the application referred to in the text must meet the requirements of the National Assembly for Wales (Representation of the People) Order 2007, SI 2007/236, Sch 1: see art 8(1)(c).

Where an application is required to contain a signature and date of birth, the information must be set out in a manner that is sufficiently clear and unambiguous as to be capable of electronic scanning into his record: Representation of the People (England and Wales) Regulations 2001, SI 2001/341, reg 51(3A) (reg 51(3A), (3B) added, by SI 2006/2910); European Parliamentary Elections Regulations 2004, SI 2004/293, Sch 2 para 17(4) (as so substituted); National Assembly for Wales (Representation of the People) Order 2007, SI 2007/236, Sch 1 para 1(3). This requirement is met by configuring the information as follows:

(1)   the signature must appear against a background of white unlined paper of at least five centimetres long and two centimetres high (Representation of the People (England and Wales) Regulations 2001, SI 2001/341, reg 51(3A)(a) (as so added); European Parliamentary Elections Regulations 2004, SI 2004/293, Sch 2 para 17(4)(a) (as so substituted); National Assembly for Wales (Representation of the People) Order 2007, SI 2007/236, Sch 1 para 1(3)(a)); and

(2)   the applicant's date of birth must be set out numerically configured in the sequence of date, month and year, namely [d][d][m][m][y][y][y][y] (Representation of the People (England and Wales) Regulations 2001, SI 2001/341, reg 51(3A)(b) (as so added); European Parliamentary Elections Regulations 2004, SI 2004/293, Sch 2 para 17(4)(b) (as so substituted); National Assembly for Wales (Representation of the People) Order 2007, SI 2007/236, Sch 1 para 1(3)(b)).

The registration officer may dispense with the requirement under the Representation of the People Act 2000 Sch 4 para 3(1)(b), the European Parliamentary Elections Regulations 2004, SI 2004/293, Sch 2 para 3(1)(b), or the National Assembly for Wales (Representation of the People) Order 2007, SI 2007/236, art 8(1)(c), as the case may be, for the applicant to provide a signature, if he is satisfied that the applicant is unable to provide a signature because of any disability the applicant has, or is unable to provide a signature because the applicant is unable to read or write, or is unable to sign in a consistent and distinctive way because of any such disability or inability: Representation of the People Act 2000 Sch 4 para 3(8) (added by the Electoral Administration Act 2006 s 14(1)(c), (8)); European Parliamentary Elections Regulations 2004, SI 2004/293, Sch 2 para 3(8) (as so substituted); National Assembly for Wales (Representation of the People) Order 2007, SI 2007/236, art 8(8). Where the application contains a request that the registration officer waive the requirement for a signature, head (1) above does not apply: Representation of the People (England and Wales) Regulations 2001, SI 2001/341, reg 51(3B) (as so added); European Parliamentary Elections Regulations 2004, SI 2004/293, Sch 2 para 17(5) (as so substituted); National Assembly for Wales (Representation of the People) Order 2007, SI 2007/236, Sch 1 para 1(4). For these purposes, 'disability', in relation to doing a thing, includes a short term inability to do it: see the Representation of the People Act 1983 s 202(1) (definition added by the Electoral Administration Act 2006 s 47, Sch 1 paras 69, 76; definition applied by virtue of the Representation of the People Act 2000 Sch 4 para 1(2)); European Parliamentary Elections Regulations 2004, SI 2004/293, reg 2(1) (substituted by SI 2009/186); National Assembly for Wales (Representation of the People) Order 2007, SI 2007/236, art 2(1).

The registration officer may satisfy himself:

(a)   that an application under the Representation of the People Act 2000 Sch 4, or the European Parliamentary Elections Regulations 2004, SI 2004/293, Sch 2, or the National Assembly for Wales (Representation of the People) Order 2007, SI 2007/236, art 8(1) (see also the text and notes 1–7), as the case may be, meets any requirements that it has been signed by the applicant and states his date of birth by referring to any signature and date of birth either previously provided by the applicant to the registration officer or to the returning officer or previously provided by the applicant to the authority referred to in the Representation of the People (England and Wales) Regulations 2001, SI 2001/341, reg 35(2)(a) (ie the council which appointed him: see PARA 142), which the registration officer is authorised to inspect for the purposes of his registration duties (Representation of the People (England and Wales) Regulations 2001, SI 2001/341, reg 51A(a) (reg 51A added by SI 2006/752; and substituted by SI 2006/2910); European Parliamentary Elections Regulations 2004, SI 2004/293, Sch 2 para 19(a) (as so substituted); National Assembly for Wales (Representation of the People) Order 2007, SI 2007/236, Sch 1 para 1(6)(a)); and

(b)   as to whether the applicant is unable to provide a signature or a consistent signature due to any disability or inability to read or write (Representation of the People (England and Wales) Regulations 2001, SI 2001/341, reg 51A(b) (reg 51A as so added and substituted); European Parliamentary Elections Regulations 2004, SI 2004/293, Sch 2 para 19(b) (as so substituted); National Assembly for Wales (Representation of the People) Order 2007, SI 2007/236, Sch 1 para 1(6)(b)).

As to the provisions made for the initial and continuing capture of the personal identifiers of those who are existing absent voters see PARA 366.

9   As to applications made to vote by proxy see PARA 374 et seq.

10   Representation of the People Act 2000 Sch 4 para 3(2); European Parliamentary Elections Regulations 2004, SI 2004/293, Sch 2 para 3(2) (as substituted: see note 1); National Assembly for Wales (Representation of the People) Order 2007, SI 2007/236, art 8(1). Such an application must be disregarded for the purposes of a particular election if it is received by the registration officer after 5 pm on the sixth day before the date of the poll at that election: Representation of the People (England and Wales) Regulations 2001, SI 2001/341, reg 56(2) (amended by SI 2006/752); European Parliamentary Elections Regulations 2004, SI 2004/293, Sch 2 para 26(2) (as so substituted); National Assembly for Wales (Representation of the People) Order 2007, SI 2007/236, Sch 1 para 7(2). Where a registration officer disregards an application for the purposes of any particular election, he must notify the applicant of this: Representation of the People (England and Wales) Regulations 2001, SI 2001/341, reg 57(5) (as amended: see note 6); European Parliamentary Elections Regulations 2004, SI 2004/293, Sch 2 para 27(7) (as so substituted); National Assembly for Wales (Representation of the People) Order 2007, SI 2007/236, Sch 1 para 8(8). As to the computation of time for these purposes see note 6.

11   Representation of the People Act 2000 Sch 4 para 3(2)(a); European Parliamentary Elections Regulations 2004, SI 2004/293, Sch 2 para 3(2)(a) (as substituted: see note 1); National Assembly for Wales (Representation of the People) Order 2007, SI 2007/236, art 8(1)(a).

12   Representation of the People Act 2000 Sch 4 para 3(2)(b); European Parliamentary Elections Regulations 2004, SI 2004/293, Sch 2 para 3(2)(b) (as substituted: see note 1); National Assembly for Wales (Representation of the People) Order 2007, SI 2007/236, art 8(1)(b). As to the relevant register of electors for each election see note 7.

13   Representation of the People Act 2000 Sch 4 para 3(2)(c) (amended by the Electoral Administration Act 2006 s 14(1)(b), (8)); European Parliamentary Elections Regulations 2004, SI 2004/293, Sch 2 para 3(2)(c) (as substituted: see note 1); National Assembly for Wales (Representation of the People) Order 2007, SI 2007/236, art 8(1)(c). The registration officer may dispense with the requirement under the Representation of the People Act 2000 Sch 4 para 3(2)(c), the European Parliamentary Elections Regulations 2004, SI 2004/293, Sch 2 para 3(2)(c), or the National Assembly for Wales (Representation of the People) Order 2007, SI 2007/236, art 8(1)(c), as the case may be, for the applicant to provide a signature, if he is satisfied that the applicant is unable to provide a signature because of any disability the applicant has, or is unable to provide a signature because the applicant is unable to read or write, or is unable to sign in a consistent and distinctive way because of any such disability or inability: Representation of the People Act 2000 Sch 4 para 3(8) (as added: see note 8); European Parliamentary Elections Regulations 2004, SI 2004/293, Sch 2 para 3(8) (as so substituted); National Assembly for Wales (Representation of the People) Order 2007, SI 2007/236, art 8(8).

In the case of a parliamentary or local government election, the application referred to in the text must meet the prescribed requirements (see note 8): see the Representation of the People Act 2000 Sch 4 para 3(2)(c) (as so amended).

In the case of a European parliamentary election, the application referred to in the text must meet the requirements of the European Parliamentary Elections Regulations 2004, SI 2004/293, Sch 2: see Sch 2 para 3(2)(c) (as so substituted).

In the case of a Welsh Assembly election, the application referred to in the text must meet the requirements of the National Assembly for Wales (Representation of the People) Order 2007, SI 2007/236, Sch 1: see art 8(1)(c).

14 Representation of the People Act 2000 Sch 4 para 3(3)(a); European Parliamentary Elections Regulations 2004, SI 2004/293, Sch 2 para 3(3)(a) (as substituted: see note 1); National Assembly for Wales (Representation of the People) Order 2007, SI 2007/236, art 8(2)(a). As to registration as a service voter see PARA 125 et seq.

15 As to the meaning of 'anonymous entry' in relation to a register of electors see PARA 148.

16 Representation of the People Act 2000 Sch 4 para 3(3)(aa) (added by the Electoral Administration Act 2006 s 10(2), Sch 1 paras 19, 20(1)–(3)); European Parliamentary Elections Regulations 2004, SI 2004/293, Sch 2 para 3(3)(b) (as substituted: see note 1); National Assembly for Wales (Representation of the People) Order 2007, SI 2007/236, art 8(2)(b).

17 Representation of the People Act 2000 Sch 4 para 3(3)(b)(i); European Parliamentary Elections Regulations 2004, SI 2004/293, Sch 2 para 3(3)(c)(i) (as substituted: see note 1); National Assembly for Wales (Representation of the People) Order 2007, SI 2007/236, art 8(2)(c)(i). As to the appropriate rules, in relation to a parliamentary or local government election, see PARA 363 note 2; in relation to a Welsh Assembly election, see PARA 364 note 2; and, in relation to a European parliamentary election, see PARA 365 note 1.

18 Representation of the People Act 2000 Sch 4 para 3(3)(b)(ii); European Parliamentary Elections Regulations 2004, SI 2004/293, Sch 2 para 3(3)(c)(ii) (as substituted: see note 1); National Assembly for Wales (Representation of the People) Order 2007, SI 2007/236, art 8(2)(c)(ii).

19 Representation of the People Act 2000 Sch 4 para 3(3)(b) (amended by the Electoral Administration Act 2006 s 74(1), Sch 1 Pt 7 para 137(1), (4)); European Parliamentary Elections Regulations 2004, SI 2004/293, Sch 2 para 3(3)(c) (as substituted: see note 1); National Assembly for Wales (Representation of the People) Order 2007, SI 2007/236, art 8(2)(c). As to additional requirements see the text and note 34.

20 Representation of the People Act 2000 Sch 4 para 3(3)(c) (amended by the Civil Partnership Act 2004 s 261(1), Sch 27 para 164(1), (2)); European Parliamentary Elections Regulations 2004, SI 2004/293, Sch 2 para 3(3)(d) (as substituted: see note 1); National Assembly for Wales (Representation of the People) Order 2007, SI 2007/236, art 8(2)(d). It is suggested that the test would be satisfied where the duties of a person's employment frequently required him to be away from home at night. Where, however, a person was away on rare occasions only, the 'general nature' test would appear not to be satisfied, but the person would be eligible for an absent vote for a particular election if his employment duties required him to be away from his qualifying address on polling day (see PARA 371). In order for a person's spouse or partner to qualify under this category it would be necessary to show that the general nature of the person's occupation, service or employment required him to be frequently away from home at night with the other spouse or partner in accompaniment.

21 Representation of the People Act 2000 Sch 4 para 3(3)(d); European Parliamentary Elections Regulations 2004, SI 2004/293, Sch 2 para 3(3)(e) (as substituted: see note 1); National Assembly for Wales (Representation of the People) Order 2007, SI 2007/236, art 8(2)(e).

22 Representation of the People Act 2000 Sch 4 para 3(3); European Parliamentary Elections Regulations 2004, SI 2004/293, Sch 2 para 3(3) (as substituted: see note 1). As to registration in pursuance of an overseas elector's declaration see PARA 114; and as to peers entitled to be registered in pursuance of a European parliamentary overseas elector's declaration see PARA 115.

23 Applications made under the Representation of the People Act 2000 Sch 4, or the European Parliamentary Elections Regulations 2004, SI 2004/293, Sch 2 Pt 2 (Sch 2 paras 12–34), or the National Assembly for Wales (Representation of the People) Order 2007, SI 2007/236, art 8, must comply with the requirements, in relation to a parliamentary or local government election, of the Representation of the People (England and Wales) Regulations 2001, SI 2001/341, reg 51, or, in relation to a European parliamentary election, of the European Parliamentary Elections Regulations 2004, SI 2004/293, Sch 2 para 17, or, in relation to a Welsh Assembly election, of the National Assembly for Wales (Representation of the People) Order 2007, SI 2007/236, Sch 1 para 1, as well as such further requirements in the Representation of the People (England and Wales) Regulations 2001, SI 2001/341, Pt IV, or the European Parliamentary Elections Regulations 2004, SI 2004/293, Sch 2 Pt 2, as are relevant to the application: Representation of the People (England and Wales) Regulations 2001, SI 2001/341, reg 51(1); European Parliamentary Elections Regulations 2004, SI 2004/293, Sch 2 para 17(1) (as substituted: see note 1); National Assembly for Wales (Representation of the People) Order 2007, SI 2007/236, art 13(1). As to additional requirements for applications to vote by proxy for a definite or indefinite period see PARAS 368–369.

24 Representation of the People (England and Wales) Regulations 2001, SI 2001/341, reg 51(2)(a); European Parliamentary Elections Regulations 2004, SI 2004/293, Sch 2 para 17(2)(a) (as substituted: see note 1); National Assembly for Wales (Representation of the People) Order 2007, SI 2007/236, Sch 1 para 1(1)(a).

25 Representation of the People (England and Wales) Regulations 2001, SI 2001/341, reg 51(2)(b) (amended by SI 2006/752); European Parliamentary Elections Regulations 2004, SI 2004/293, Sch 2 para 17(2)(b) (as substituted: see note 1); National Assembly for Wales (Representation of the People) Order 2007, SI 2007/236, Sch 1 para 1(1)(b). See note 26. Head (B) in the text does not apply in the case of an application under the Representation of the People Act 2000 Sch 4 para 7(4), (7), or the European Parliamentary Elections Regulations 2004, SI 2004/293, Sch 2 para 7(4), (7), or the National Assembly for Wales (Representation of the People) Order 2007, SI 2007/236, art 12(4), (7) (voting as proxy for an indefinite period or for a particular period or at a particular election: see PARA 378).

For the purposes of the National Assembly for Wales (Representation of the People) Order 2007, SI 2007/236, Sch 1 para 1(1)(b), the address in respect of which the applicant is registered or has applied to be (or is treated as having applied to be) registered includes:

(1)   in the case of a service voter, the address given in the service declaration in accordance with the Representation of the People Act 1983 s 16(d) (see PARA 127) (National Assembly for Wales (Representation of the People) Order 2007, SI 2007/236, Sch 1 para 1(9)(a));

(2)   in the case of a person to whom the Representation of the People Act 1983 s 7 (deemed residence for persons in mental hospitals who are not detained offenders or on remand: see PARA 119) applies, the address of the mental hospital or the address shown on the declaration of local connection in accordance with s 7B(3)(d) (see PARA 122) (National Assembly for Wales (Representation of the People) Order 2007, SI 2007/236, Sch 1 para 1(9)(b));

(3)   in the case of a person to whom the Representation of the People Act 1983 s 7A (deemed residence for persons on remand: see PARA 120) applies, the address of the place at which he is detained or the address shown on the declaration of local connection in accordance with s 7B(3)(d) (National Assembly for Wales (Representation of the People) Order 2007, SI 2007/236, Sch 1 para 1(9)(c)); and

(4)   in the case of a homeless person, the address shown on the declaration of local connection in accordance with the Representation of the People Act 1983 s 7B(3)(d) (National Assembly for Wales (Representation of the People) Order 2007, SI 2007/236, Sch 1 para 1(9)(d)).

26 Representation of the People (England and Wales) Regulations 2001, SI 2001/341, reg 51(2)(d) (reg 51(2)(d) amended, reg 51AA added, by SI 2006/2910); European Parliamentary Elections Regulations 2004, SI 2004/293, Sch 2 para 17(2)(d) (as substituted: see note 1); National Assembly for Wales (Representation of the People) Order 2007, SI 2007/236, Sch 1 para 1(1)(d).

In the case of an application to vote by post made under the Representation of the People Act 2000 Sch 4 para 3(1), the European Parliamentary Elections Regulations 2004, SI 2004/293, Sch 2 para 3(1), or the National Assembly for Wales (Representation of the People) Order 2007, SI 2007/236, art 8(1) (see the text and notes 1–8), as the case may be, where the addresses stated in accordance with head (B) in the text, and head (C) in the text, are different, except where an applicant has, or has applied for, an anonymous entry, the application must set out why the applicant's circumstances will be or are likely to be such that he requires the ballot paper to be sent to the address stated in accordance with head (C) in the text: see the Representation of the People (England and Wales) Regulations 2001, SI 2001/341, reg 51AA(1)–(3) (as so added); the European Parliamentary Elections Regulations 2004, SI 2004/293, Sch 2 para 20(1)–(3) (as so substituted); and the National Assembly for Wales (Representation of the People) Order 2007, SI 2007/236, Sch 1 para 1(7)(a)(i), (b). This provision also applies in the case of an application to vote by post made under the Representation of the People Act 2000 Sch 4 para 3(7), the European Parliamentary Elections Regulations 2004, SI 2004/293, Sch 2 para 3(7), or the National Assembly for Wales (Representation of the People) Order 2007, SI 2007/236, art 8(7): see PARA 370.

27 Representation of the People (England and Wales) Regulations 2001, SI 2001/341, reg 51(2)(e); European Parliamentary Elections Regulations 2004, SI 2004/293, Sch 2 para 17(2)(e) (as substituted: see note 1); National Assembly for Wales (Representation of the People) Order 2007, SI 2007/236, Sch 1 para 1(1)(e).

28 Ie under the Representation of the People Act 2000 Sch 4 para 3, the European Parliamentary Elections Regulations 2004, SI 2004/293, Sch 2 para 3, or the National Assembly for Wales (Representation of the People) Order 2007, SI 2007/236, art 8 (see the text and notes 1–21), as the case may be: see the Representation of the People (England and Wales) Regulations 2001, SI 2001/341, reg 51(2)(f) (reg 51(2)(f), (g) added by SI 2006/2910); the European Parliamentary Elections Regulations 2004, SI 2004/293, Sch 2 para 17(2)(f) (as substituted: see note 1); and the National Assembly for Wales (Representation of the People) Order 2007, SI 2007/236, Sch 1 para 1(1)(f).

29 Representation of the People (England and Wales) Regulations 2001, SI 2001/341, reg 51(2)(f) (as added: see note 28); European Parliamentary Elections Regulations 2004, SI 2004/293, Sch 2 para 17(2)(f) (as substituted: see note 1); National Assembly for Wales (Representation of the People) Order 2007, SI 2007/236, Sch 1 para 1(1)(f).

30 Representation of the People (England and Wales) Regulations 2001, SI 2001/341, reg 51(2)(g) (as added: see note 28); European Parliamentary Elections Regulations 2004, SI 2004/293, Sch 2 para 17(2)(g) (as substituted: see note 1); National Assembly for Wales (Representation of the People) Order 2007, SI 2007/236, Sch 1 para 1(1)(g).

31 Representation of the People (England and Wales) Regulations 2001, SI 2001/341, reg 51(3) (reg 51(3) substituted, reg 51(3A), (3B) added, by SI 2006/2910); European Parliamentary Elections Regulations 2004, SI 2004/293, Sch 2 para 17(3) (as substituted: see note 1); National Assembly for Wales (Representation of the People) Order 2007, SI 2007/236, Sch 1 para 1(2).

32 Representation of the People (England and Wales) Regulations 2001, SI 2001/341, reg 51(4)(a); European Parliamentary Elections Regulations 2004, SI 2004/293, Sch 2 para 17(6)(a) (as substituted: see note 1); National Assembly for Wales (Representation of the People) Order 2007, SI 2007/236, Sch 1 para 1(5)(a). Where, however, the poll for an Assembly election falls on the same day as the poll at another election, the same application may be used for both elections: Sch 1 para 1(5).

33 Representation of the People (England and Wales) Regulations 2001, SI 2001/341, reg 51(4)(b); European Parliamentary Elections Regulations 2004, SI 2004/293, Sch 2 para 17(6)(b) (as substituted: see note 1).

34 See the Representation of the People (England and Wales) Regulations 2001, SI 2001/341, regs 51(6), 52; the European Parliamentary Elections Regulations 2004, SI 2004/293, Sch 2 paras 17(8), 22; the National Assembly for Wales (Representation of the People) Order 2007, SI 2007/236, Sch 1 paras 1, 3; and PARA 375.

35 Representation of the People (England and Wales) Regulations 2001, SI 2001/341, reg 57(1) (amended by SI 2006/752); European Parliamentary Elections Regulations 2004, SI 2004/293, Sch 2 para 27(1) (as substituted: see note 1); National Assembly for Wales (Representation of the People) Order 2007, SI 2007/236, Sch 1 para 8(1). Where the registration officer at a parliamentary or Welsh Assembly election is not the acting returning officer for any constituency (or part of such a constituency), or where the registration officer at a European parliamentary election is not the local returning officer for any local counting area (or part of such an area), in the area for which he is the registration officer, he must send to that officer details of any application to vote by post which he has granted as soon as practicable after doing so: Representation of the People (England and Wales) Regulations 2001, SI 2001/341, reg 57(6); European Parliamentary Elections Regulations 2004, SI 2004/293, Sch 2 para 27(8) (as so substituted); National Assembly for Wales (Representation of the People) Order 2007, SI 2007/236, Sch 1 para 8(9). As to the meaning of 'local counting area' see PARA 139 note 1. As to local returning officers appointed for the purposes of elections to the European Parliament see PARA 360.

　　Where a registration officer is required by the National Assembly for Wales (Representation of the People) Order 2007, SI 2007/236, Sch 1 to notify any person, such notification must be in writing and may be sent by post: Sch 1 para 17. In the case of a person other than a service voter, the notification may be sent to the address provided by that person for the purpose of such notification or of any record or, if there is no such address, to the last known place of abode of that person: Sch 1 para 17(a). In the case of a service voter, the notification may be sent to any address provided by him for the purpose of such notification or of any record or to the address provided for the purpose by the appropriate government department (as defined by the Representation of the People Act 1983 s 59(3B) (see PARA 131 note 1)) or, as the case may be, the British Council: National Assembly for Wales (Representation of the People) Order 2007, SI 2007/236, Sch 1 para 17(b). As to the persons who have a service qualification see PARA 125. As to the British Council see NATIONAL CULTURAL HERITAGE vol 77 (2010) PARA 966.

36 Representation of the People (England and Wales) Regulations 2001, SI 2001/341, reg 57(4); European Parliamentary Elections Regulations 2004, SI 2004/293, Sch 2 para 27(3) (as substituted: see note 1); National Assembly for Wales (Representation of the People) Order 2007, SI 2007/236, Sch 1 para 8(4).

37 See PARA 172 et seq.

368. Additional requirements for applications for a proxy vote for a definite or indefinite period by reason of physical incapacity. An application to vote by proxy for a particular or indefinite period by reason of blindness or other disability[1] must specify the disability by reason of which it is made[2]. Such an application must be attested and signed[3] by:

(1)   a registered medical practitioner[4];

(2)   a registered nurse[5];

(3)   a registered dentist[6], a registered dispensing optician or registered optometrist[7], a registered pharmacist[8], a registered osteopath[9], or a registered chiropractor[10];

(4)   a Christian Science practitioner[11];

(5)   a person registered as a member of a profession to which the Health and Social Work Professions Order 2001[12] for the time being extends[13];

(6)   the person carrying on a care home registered under Part II of the Care Standards Act 2000[14];

(7)   the warden of premises forming one of a group of premises provided for persons of pensionable age or disabled persons for which there is a resident warden, where the applicant states that he resides in such premises[15];

(8)   a manager within the meaning of the Mental Health Act 1983[16], or a person authorised to act on behalf of such a manager for these purposes[17]; or

(9)   a person registered in the register for social workers maintained by the Care Council for Wales ('Cyngor Gofal Cymru')[18].

A person who qualifies:

(a)   by virtue of any of heads (1) to (5) above may not attest an application for these purposes, however, unless he is treating the applicant for the disability specified in the application[19], or unless the applicant is receiving care from him in respect of that disability[20], or unless the person is a social worker who qualifies by virtue of head (5) above, and has arranged care or assistance for the applicant in respect of that disability[21];

(b)   by virtue of head (9) above may not attest an application for these purposes unless he is treating the applicant for the disability specified in the application[22], or unless the applicant is receiving care from him in respect of that disability[23], or unless he has arranged care or assistance for the person in respect of his disability[24].

The person attesting the application must state:

(i)   his name and address and the qualification by virtue of which he attests the application[25], unless he qualifies by virtue of head (8) in the text[26];

(ii) where the person who attests the application is a person who qualifies by virtue of head (a) above, that he is treating the applicant for the disability specified in the application[27], or that the applicant is receiving care from him in respect of that disability[28];

(iii) where the person who attests the application is a person who qualifies by virtue of head (b) above, that he is treating the applicant for the disability specified in the application[29], or that the applicant is receiving care from him in respect of that disability[30], or that he has arranged care or assistance for the applicant in respect of that disability[31];

(iv) that, to the best of his knowledge and belief, the applicant has the disability specified in the application, and that he cannot reasonably be expected to go in person to his allotted polling station[32] or to vote unaided there by reason of that disability[33]; and

(v)   that, to the best of his knowledge and belief, the disability specified in the application is likely to continue either indefinitely or for a period specified by the person attesting the application[34].

However, the provisions as to attestation[35] do not apply where:

(A) the application is based on the applicant's blindness and the applicant is registered as a blind person by the local authority[36] which is specified in the application[37]; or

(B) the application states that the applicant is in receipt of the higher rate of the mobility component of a disability living allowance[38] because of the disability specified in the application[39].

For the purpose of determining whether there has been a material change of circumstances, the registration officer may, at such times as he thinks fit, make inquiries of a person[40] who is shown as voting by proxy[41] in the record kept of those entitled to an absent vote at elections either for a particular period or for an indefinite period[42]. The registration officer may treat the failure by a person of whom inquiries have been made to respond to such inquiries within one month of the date on which they were made as sufficient evidence of a material change in circumstances[43].

1   Ie, at a parliamentary or local government election, under the Representation of the People Act 2000 s 12, Sch 4 para 3(3)(b), or, at a European parliamentary election, under the European Parliamentary Elections Regulations 2004, SI 2004/293, reg 10, Sch 2 para 3(3)(c), or, at a Welsh Assembly election, under the National Assembly for Wales (Representation of the People) Order 2007, SI 2007/236, art 8(2)(c), as the case may be (see PARA 367): see the Representation of the People (England and Wales) Regulations 2001, SI 2001/341, reg 53(1) (amended by SI 2001/1700; SI 2006/2910); the European Parliamentary Elections Regulations 2004, SI 2004/293, Sch 2 para 23(1) (Sch 2 substituted by SI 2009/186); and the National Assembly for Wales (Representation of the People) Order 2007, SI 2007/236, art 15(2), Sch 1 para 4(1). As to the meaning of 'Assembly election' in the context of Welsh Assembly elections see PARA 3 note 2. As to the meaning of 'parliamentary election' see PARA 9. As to the meaning of 'local government election' see PARA 11; definition applied by virtue of the Representation of the People Act 2000 Sch 4 para 1(2). See also PARA 363 note 1. As to European parliamentary elections see PARA 217 et seq.

2   Representation of the People (England and Wales) Regulations 2001, SI 2001/341, reg 53(1) (as amended: see note 1); European Parliamentary Elections Regulations 2004, SI 2004/293, Sch 2 para 23(1) (as substituted: see note 1); National Assembly for Wales (Representation of the People) Order 2007, SI 2007/236, Sch 1 para 4(1). The application must also satisfy the general requirements of absent voting applications: see PARA 367. As to the offence in respect of false statements made in any declaration or form used in connection with absent voting see PARA 735.

3   Representation of the People (England and Wales) Regulations 2001, SI 2001/341, reg 53(2) (reg 53(2)–(4) substituted by SI 2006/2910); European Parliamentary Elections Regulations 2004, SI 2004/293, Sch 2 para 23(2) (as substituted: see note 1); National Assembly for Wales (Representation of the People) Order 2007, SI 2007/236, Sch 1 para 4(2). As to attesting such an application in Gibraltar see the European Parliamentary Elections Regulations 2004, SI 2004/293, Sch 2 para 23(2)(o), (p) (as so substituted). The European Parliamentary Elections Regulations 2004, SI 2004/293, also allow for an application to be attested and signed by a person for the time being listed in the British Psychological Society's Register of Chartered Psychologists (see Sch 2 para 23(2)(i) (as so substituted)), but the Health Care and Associated Professions (Miscellaneous Amendments and Practitioner Psychologists) Order 2009, SI 2009/1182, art 4(1), Sch 4 Pt 1, revoked this head from both the Representation of the People (England and Wales) Regulations 2001, SI 2001/341 (see reg 53(2)(i) (as so revoked)), and the National Assembly for Wales (Representation of the People) Order 2007, SI 2007/236 (see Sch 1 para 4(2)(i) (as so revoked)), and it is submitted that the European Parliamentary Elections Regulations 2004, SI 2004/293, Sch 2 para 23(2)(i) should no longer be regarded as forming part of the scheme either. As to the offence of attesting an application when not authorised to do so see PARA 735.

4   Representation of the People (England and Wales) Regulations 2001, SI 2001/341, reg 53(2)(a) (as substituted: see note 3); European Parliamentary Elections Regulations 2004, SI 2004/293, Sch 2 para 23(2)(a) (as substituted: see note 1); National Assembly for Wales (Representation of the People) Order 2007, SI 2007/236, Sch 1 para 4(2)(a).

5 Representation of the People (England and Wales) Regulations 2001, SI 2001/341, reg 53(2)(b) (as substituted: see note 3); European Parliamentary Elections Regulations 2004, SI 2004/293, Sch 2 para 23(2)(b) (as substituted: see note 1); National Assembly for Wales (Representation of the People) Order 2007, SI 2007/236, Sch 1 para 4(2)(b).

Except in relation to a European parliamentary election, the reference in head (2) in the text specifically is to a nurse registered on the register maintained by the Nursery and Midwifery Council under the Nursing and Midwifery Order 2001, SI 2002/253, art 5 (see MEDICAL PROFESSIONS vol 74 (2011) PARA 713), by virtue of qualifications in nursing: see the Representation of the People (England and Wales) Regulations 2001, SI 2001/341, reg 53(2)(b) (as so substituted); and the National Assembly for Wales (Representation of the People) Order 2007, SI 2007/236, Sch 1 para 4(2)(b).

6 Representation of the People (England and Wales) Regulations 2001, SI 2001/341, reg 53(2)(c) (as substituted: see note 3); European Parliamentary Elections Regulations 2004, SI 2004/293, Sch 2 para 23(2)(c) (as substituted: see note 1); National Assembly for Wales (Representation of the People) Order 2007, SI 2007/236, Sch 1 para 4(2)(c). The text refers to a registered dentist as defined by the Dentists Act 1984 s 53(1) (see MEDICAL PROFESSIONS vol 74 (2011) PARA 442): see the Representation of the People (England and Wales) Regulations 2001, SI 2001/341, reg 53(2)(c) (as so substituted); the European Parliamentary Elections Regulations 2004, SI 2004/293, Sch 2 para 23(2)(c) (as so substituted); and the National Assembly for Wales (Representation of the People) Order 2007, SI 2007/236, Sch 1 para 4(2)(c).

7 Representation of the People (England and Wales) Regulations 2001, SI 2001/341, reg 53(2)(d) (as substituted: see note 3); European Parliamentary Elections Regulations 2004, SI 2004/293, Sch 2 para 23(2)(d) (as substituted: see note 1); National Assembly for Wales (Representation of the People) Order 2007, SI 2007/236, Sch 1 para 4(2)(d). The text refers to a registered dispensing optician or a registered optometrist within the meaning of the Opticians Act 1989 (see MEDICAL PROFESSIONS vol 74 (2011) PARA 343 et seq): see the Representation of the People (England and Wales) Regulations 2001, SI 2001/341, reg 53(2)(d) (as so substituted); the European Parliamentary Elections Regulations 2004, SI 2004/293, Sch 2 para 23(2)(d) (as so substituted); and the National Assembly for Wales (Representation of the People) Order 2007, SI 2007/236, Sch 1 para 4(2)(d).

8 Representation of the People (England and Wales) Regulations 2001, SI 2001/341, reg 53(2)(e) (reg 53(2) as substituted (see note 3); reg 53(2)(e) further substituted by SI 2010/231); European Parliamentary Elections Regulations 2004, SI 2004/293, Sch 2 para 23(2)(e) (as substituted: see note 1); National Assembly for Wales (Representation of the People) Order 2007, SI 2007/236, Sch 1 para 4(2)(e) (substituted by SI 2010/231). The text refers to a registered pharmacist as defined by the Pharmacy Order 2010, SI 2010/231, art 3(1) (see MEDICAL PROFESSIONS vol 74 (2011) PARA 784): see the Representation of the People (England and Wales) Regulations 2001, SI 2001/341, reg 53(2)(e) (as so further substituted); the European Parliamentary Elections Regulations 2004, SI 2004/293, Sch 2 para 23(2)(e) (as so substituted); Interpretation Act 1978 s 17(2); and the National Assembly for Wales (Representation of the People) Order 2007, SI 2007/236, Sch 1 para 4(2)(e) (as so substituted).

9 Representation of the People (England and Wales) Regulations 2001, SI 2001/341, reg 53(2)(f) (as substituted: see note 3); European Parliamentary Elections Regulations 2004, SI 2004/293, Sch 2 para 23(2)(f) (as substituted: see note 1); National Assembly for Wales (Representation of the People) Order 2007, SI 2007/236, Sch 1 para 4(2)(f). The text refers to a registered osteopath as defined by the Osteopaths Act 1993 s 41 (see MEDICAL PROFESSIONS vol 74 (2011) PARA 525 et seq): see the Representation of the People (England and Wales) Regulations 2001, SI 2001/341, reg 53(2)(f) (as so substituted); the European Parliamentary Elections Regulations 2004, SI 2004/293, Sch 2 para 23(2)(f) (as so substituted); and the National Assembly for Wales (Representation of the People) Order 2007, SI 2007/236, Sch 1 para 4(2)(f).

10 Representation of the People (England and Wales) Regulations 2001, SI 2001/341, reg 53(2)(g) (as substituted: see note 3); European Parliamentary Elections Regulations 2004, SI 2004/293, Sch 2 para 23(2)(g) (as substituted: see note 1); National Assembly for Wales (Representation of the People) Order 2007, SI 2007/236, Sch 1 para 4(2)(g). The text refers to a registered chiropractor as defined by the Chiropractors Act 1994 s 43 (see MEDICAL PROFESSIONS vol 74 (2011) PARA 603 et seq): see the Representation of the People (England and Wales) Regulations 2001, SI 2001/341, reg 53(2)(g) (as so substituted); the European Parliamentary Elections Regulations 2004, SI 2004/293, Sch 2 para 23(2)(g) (as so substituted); and the National Assembly for Wales (Representation of the People) Order 2007, SI 2007/236, Sch 1 para 4(2)(g).

11 Representation of the People (England and Wales) Regulations 2001, SI 2001/341, reg 53(2)(h) (as substituted: see note 3); European Parliamentary Elections Regulations 2004, SI 2004/293,

Sch 2 para 23(2)(h) (as substituted: see note 1); National Assembly for Wales (Representation of the People) Order 2007, SI 2007/236, Sch 1 para 4(2)(h).

12 Ie the Health and Social Work Professions Order 2001, SI 2002/254 (see MEDICAL PROFESSIONS vol 74 (2011) PARA 916 et seq): see the Representation of the People (England and Wales) Regulations 2001, SI 2001/341, reg 53(2)(j) (reg 53(2) as substituted (see note 3); reg 53(2)(j) amended by SI 2012/1479); the European Parliamentary Elections Regulations 2004, SI 2004/293, Sch 2 para 23(2)(j) (Sch 2 as substituted (see note 1); Sch 2 para 23(2)(j) amended by SI 2012/1479); and the National Assembly for Wales (Representation of the People) Order 2007, SI 2007/236, Sch 1 para 4(2)(j) (amended by SI 2012/1479).

13 Representation of the People (England and Wales) Regulations 2001, SI 2001/341, reg 53(2)(j) (as substituted and amended: see note 12); European Parliamentary Elections Regulations 2004, SI 2004/293, Sch 2 para 23(2)(j) (as substituted and amended: see note 12); National Assembly for Wales (Representation of the People) Order 2007, SI 2007/236, Sch 1 para 4(2)(j) (as amended: see note 12).

14 Representation of the People (England and Wales) Regulations 2001, SI 2001/341, reg 53(2)(k) (as substituted: see note 3); European Parliamentary Elections Regulations 2004, SI 2004/293, Sch 2 para 23(2)(k) (as substituted: see note 1); National Assembly for Wales (Representation of the People) Order 2007, SI 2007/236, Sch 1 para 4(2)(k). The text refers to a care home registered under the Care Standards Act 2000 Pt II (ss 11–42) (see SOCIAL SERVICES AND COMMUNITY CARE vol 44(2) (Reissue) PARA 1042 et seq): see the Representation of the People (England and Wales) Regulations 2001, SI 2001/341, reg 53(2)(k) (as so substituted); the European Parliamentary Elections Regulations 2004, SI 2004/293, Sch 2 para 23(2)(k) (as so substituted); and the National Assembly for Wales (Representation of the People) Order 2007, SI 2007/236, Sch 1 para 4(2)(k). The European Parliamentary Elections Regulations 2004, SI 2004/293, requires the applicant to state that he resides in such premises before head (6) in the text applies: see Sch 2 para 23(2)(k) (as so substituted); cf head (7) in the text.

15 Representation of the People (England and Wales) Regulations 2001, SI 2001/341, reg 53(2)(l) (as substituted: see note 3); European Parliamentary Elections Regulations 2004, SI 2004/293, Sch 2 para 23(2)(l) (as substituted: see note 1); National Assembly for Wales (Representation of the People) Order 2007, SI 2007/236, Sch 1 para 4(2)(l).

16 Ie within the meaning of the Mental Health Act 1983 s 145(1) (see MENTAL HEALTH AND CAPACITY vol 75 (2013) PARA 778): see the Representation of the People (England and Wales) Regulations 2001, SI 2001/341, reg 53(2)(m) (as substituted: see note 3); the European Parliamentary Elections Regulations 2004, SI 2004/293, Sch 2 para 23(2)(m) (as substituted: see note 1); and the National Assembly for Wales (Representation of the People) Order 2007, SI 2007/236, Sch 1 para 4(2)(m).

17 Representation of the People (England and Wales) Regulations 2001, SI 2001/341, reg 53(2)(m) (as substituted: see note 3); European Parliamentary Elections Regulations 2004, SI 2004/293, Sch 2 para 23(2)(m) (as substituted: see note 1); National Assembly for Wales (Representation of the People) Order 2007, SI 2007/236, Sch 1 para 4(2)(m).

18 Representation of the People (England and Wales) Regulations 2001, SI 2001/341, reg 53(2)(n) (as substituted: see note 3); European Parliamentary Elections Regulations 2004, SI 2004/293, Sch 2 para 23(2)(n)(i) (Sch 2 as substituted (see note 1); Sch 2 para 23(2)(n) amended by SI 2012/1479); National Assembly for Wales (Representation of the People) Order 2007, SI 2007/236, Sch 1 para 4(2)(n). The text refers to the register for social workers maintained in accordance with the Care Standards Act 2000 s 56 (see SOCIAL SERVICES AND COMMUNITY CARE): see the Representation of the People (England and Wales) Regulations 2001, SI 2001/341, reg 53(2)(n) (as so substituted); the European Parliamentary Elections Regulations 2004, SI 2004/293, Sch 2 para 23(2)(n)(i) (as so substituted and amended); and the National Assembly for Wales (Representation of the People) Order 2007, SI 2007/236, Sch 1 para 4(2)(n).

19 Representation of the People (England and Wales) Regulations 2001, SI 2001/341, reg 53(3)(a)(i) (as substituted: see note 3); European Parliamentary Elections Regulations 2004, SI 2004/293, Sch 2 para 23(3)(a)(i) (as substituted: see note 1); National Assembly for Wales (Representation of the People) Order 2007, SI 2007/236, Sch 1 para 4(3)(a)(i).

20 Representation of the People (England and Wales) Regulations 2001, SI 2001/341, reg 53(3)(a)(ii) (as substituted: see note 3); European Parliamentary Elections Regulations 2004, SI 2004/293, Sch 2 para 23(3)(a)(ii) (as substituted: see note 1); National Assembly for Wales (Representation of the People) Order 2007, SI 2007/236, Sch 1 para 4(3)(a)(ii).

21 Representation of the People (England and Wales) Regulations 2001, SI 2001/341, reg 53(3)(a)(iii) (reg 53(3) as substituted (see note 3); reg 53(3)(a)(iii) added by SI 2012/1479); European Parliamentary Elections Regulations 2004, SI 2004/293, Sch 2 para 23(3)(a)(iii)

(Sch 2 as substituted (see note 1); Sch 2 para 23(3)(a)(iii) added by SI 2012/1479); National Assembly for Wales (Representation of the People) Order 2007, SI 2007/236, Sch 1 para 4(3)(a)(iii) (added by SI 2012/1479).

22 Representation of the People (England and Wales) Regulations 2001, SI 2001/341, reg 53(3)(b)(i) (as substituted: see note 3); European Parliamentary Elections Regulations 2004, SI 2004/293, Sch 2 para 23(3)(b)(i) (as substituted: see note 1); National Assembly for Wales (Representation of the People) Order 2007, SI 2007/236, Sch 1 para 4(3)(b)(i).

23 Representation of the People (England and Wales) Regulations 2001, SI 2001/341, reg 53(3)(b)(ii) (as substituted: see note 3); European Parliamentary Elections Regulations 2004, SI 2004/293, Sch 2 para 23(3)(b)(ii) (as substituted: see note 1); National Assembly for Wales (Representation of the People) Order 2007, SI 2007/236, Sch 1 para 4(3)(b)(ii).

24 Representation of the People (England and Wales) Regulations 2001, SI 2001/341, reg 53(3)(b)(iii) (as substituted: see note 3); European Parliamentary Elections Regulations 2004, SI 2004/293, Sch 2 para 23(3)(b)(iii) (as substituted: see note 1); National Assembly for Wales (Representation of the People) Order 2007, SI 2007/236, Sch 1 para 4(3)(b)(iii).

25 Representation of the People (England and Wales) Regulations 2001, SI 2001/341, reg 53(4)(a) (as substituted: see note 3); European Parliamentary Elections Regulations 2004, SI 2004/293, Sch 2 para 23(4)(a) (as substituted: see note 1); National Assembly for Wales (Representation of the People) Order 2007, SI 2007/236, Sch 1 para 4(4)(a).

26 Instead of the matters specified in head (i) in the text, a person who qualifies by virtue of head (8) in the text must state in the attestation:

(1) his name (Representation of the People (England and Wales) Regulations 2001, SI 2001/341, reg 53(5A)(i) (reg 53(5A) added by SI 2006/2910); European Parliamentary Elections Regulations 2004, SI 2004/293, Sch 2 para 23(5)(a) (as substituted: see note 1); National Assembly for Wales (Representation of the People) Order 2007, SI 2007/236, Sch 1 para 4(6)(a));

(2) his position in the hospital at which the applicant is liable to be detained or at which he is receiving treatment (Representation of the People (England and Wales) Regulations 2001, SI 2001/341, reg 53(5A)(ii) (as so added); European Parliamentary Elections Regulations 2004, SI 2004/293, Sch 2 para 23(5)(c) (as so substituted); National Assembly for Wales (Representation of the People) Order 2007, SI 2007/236, Sch 1 para 4(6)(b));

(3) that he is a person authorised to make the attestation (Representation of the People (England and Wales) Regulations 2001, SI 2001/341, reg 53(5A)(iii) (as so added); European Parliamentary Elections Regulations 2004, SI 2004/293, Sch 2 para 23(5)(b) (as so substituted); National Assembly for Wales (Representation of the People) Order 2007, SI 2007/236, Sch 1 para 4(6)(c)); and

(4) in the case of an applicant who is liable to be detained in hospital, the statutory provision under which the applicant is liable to be so detained (Representation of the People (England and Wales) Regulations 2001, SI 2001/341, reg 53(5A)(iv) (as so added); European Parliamentary Elections Regulations 2004, SI 2004/293, Sch 2 para 23(5)(d) (as so substituted); National Assembly for Wales (Representation of the People) Order 2007, SI 2007/236, Sch 1 para 4(6)(d)).

27 Representation of the People (England and Wales) Regulations 2001, SI 2001/341, reg 53(4)(b)(i) (as substituted: see note 3); European Parliamentary Elections Regulations 2004, SI 2004/293, Sch 2 para 23(4)(b)(i) (as substituted: see note 1); National Assembly for Wales (Representation of the People) Order 2007, SI 2007/236, Sch 1 para 4(4)(b)(i).

28 Representation of the People (England and Wales) Regulations 2001, SI 2001/341, reg 53(4)(b)(ii) (as substituted: see note 3); European Parliamentary Elections Regulations 2004, SI 2004/293, Sch 2 para 23(4)(b)(ii) (as substituted: see note 1); National Assembly for Wales (Representation of the People) Order 2007, SI 2007/236, Sch 1 para 4(4)(b)(ii).

29 Representation of the People (England and Wales) Regulations 2001, SI 2001/341, reg 53(4)(c)(i) (as substituted: see note 3); European Parliamentary Elections Regulations 2004, SI 2004/293, Sch 2 para 23(4)(c)(i) (as substituted: see note 1); National Assembly for Wales (Representation of the People) Order 2007, SI 2007/236, Sch 1 para 4(4)(c)(i).

30 Representation of the People (England and Wales) Regulations 2001, SI 2001/341, reg 53(4)(c)(ii) (as substituted: see note 3); European Parliamentary Elections Regulations 2004, SI 2004/293, Sch 2 para 23(4)(c)(ii) (as substituted: see note 1); National Assembly for Wales (Representation of the People) Order 2007, SI 2007/236, Sch 1 para 4(4)(c)(ii).

31 Representation of the People (England and Wales) Regulations 2001, SI 2001/341, reg 53(4)(c)(iii) (as substituted: see note 3); European Parliamentary Elections Regulations 2004,

SI 2004/293, Sch 2 para 23(4)(c)(iii) (as substituted: see note 1); National Assembly for Wales (Representation of the People) Order 2007, SI 2007/236, Sch 1 para 4(4)(c)(iii).

32 For these purposes, 'his allotted polling station', in relation to an elector, means the polling station allotted or likely to be allotted to him under the appropriate rules: Representation of the People (England and Wales) Regulations 2001, SI 2001/341, reg 53(7); European Parliamentary Elections Regulations 2004, SI 2004/293, Sch 2 paras 1(2), 23(8); National Assembly for Wales (Representation of the People) Order 2007, SI 2007/236, Sch 1 para 4(8) (amended by SI 2010/2931). As to the appropriate rules, in relation to a parliamentary or local government election, see PARA 363 note 2; in relation to a Welsh Assembly election, see PARA 364 note 2; and, in relation to a European parliamentary election, see PARA 365 note 1.

33 Representation of the People (England and Wales) Regulations 2001, SI 2001/341, reg 53(4)(d) (as substituted: see note 3); European Parliamentary Elections Regulations 2004, SI 2004/293, Sch 2 para 23(4)(d) (as substituted: see note 1); National Assembly for Wales (Representation of the People) Order 2007, SI 2007/236, Sch 1 para 4(4)(d).

34 Representation of the People (England and Wales) Regulations 2001, SI 2001/341, reg 53(4)(e) (as substituted: see note 3); European Parliamentary Elections Regulations 2004, SI 2004/293, Sch 2 para 23(4)(e) (as substituted: see note 1); National Assembly for Wales (Representation of the People) Order 2007, SI 2007/236, Sch 1 para 4(4)(e).

35 Ie the Representation of the People (England and Wales) Regulations 2001, SI 2001/341, reg 53(2)–(4), or the European Parliamentary Elections Regulations 2004, SI 2004/293, Sch 2 para 23(2), (4), (5), or the National Assembly for Wales (Representation of the People) Order 2007, SI 2007/236, Sch 1 para 4(2)–(4), as the case may be (see the text and notes 3–34): see the Representation of the People (England and Wales) Regulations 2001, SI 2001/341, reg 53(5); the European Parliamentary Elections Regulations 2004, SI 2004/293, Sch 2 para 23(6) (as substituted: see note 1); and the National Assembly for Wales (Representation of the People) Order 2007, SI 2007/236, Sch 1 para 4(5).

36 Ie the local authority which has made arrangements for compiling and maintaining classified registers of persons who are blind, etc under the National Assistance Act 1948 s 29(4)(g) (see SOCIAL SERVICES AND COMMUNITY CARE vol 44(2) (Reissue) PARA 1021): see the Representation of the People (England and Wales) Regulations 2001, SI 2001/341, reg 53(5)(a); the European Parliamentary Elections Regulations 2004, SI 2004/293, Sch 2 para 23(6)(a) (as substituted: see note 1); and the National Assembly for Wales (Representation of the People) Order 2007, SI 2007/236, Sch 1 para 4(5)(a).

37 Representation of the People (England and Wales) Regulations 2001, SI 2001/341, reg 53(5)(a); European Parliamentary Elections Regulations 2004, SI 2004/293, Sch 2 para 23(6)(a) (as substituted: see note 1); National Assembly for Wales (Representation of the People) Order 2007, SI 2007/236, Sch 1 para 4(5)(a). The fact that an applicant is registered with a local authority under the National Assistance Act 1948 s 29(4)(g) (see SOCIAL SERVICES AND COMMUNITY CARE vol 44(2) (Reissue) PARA 1021) is deemed sufficient evidence that he is eligible to vote by proxy on the grounds set out in the Representation of the People Act 2000 Sch 4 para 3(3)(b), or the European Parliamentary Elections Regulations 2004, SI 2004/293, Sch 2 para 3(3)(c), or the National Assembly for Wales (Representation of the People) Order 2007, SI 2007/236, art 8(2)(c) (see PARA 367), as the case may be: Representation of the People (England and Wales) Regulations 2001, SI 2001/341, reg 53(6); European Parliamentary Elections Regulations 2004, SI 2004/293, Sch 2 para 23(7) (as so substituted); National Assembly for Wales (Representation of the People) Order 2007, SI 2007/236, Sch 1 para 4(7). As to Gibraltar see the European Parliamentary Elections Regulations 2004, SI 2004/293, Sch 2 para 23(6)(b), (7) (as so substituted).

38 Ie payable under the Social Security Contributions and Benefits Act 1992 s 73 (see SOCIAL SECURITY AND PENSIONS vol 44(2) (Reissue) PARA 106): see the Representation of the People (England and Wales) Regulations 2001, SI 2001/341, reg 53(5)(b) (amended by SI 2006/2910); the European Parliamentary Elections Regulations 2004, SI 2004/293, Sch 2 para 23(6)(d) (as substituted: see note 1); and the National Assembly for Wales (Representation of the People) Order 2007, SI 2007/236, Sch 1 para 4(5)(b).

39 Representation of the People (England and Wales) Regulations 2001, SI 2001/341, reg 53(5)(b) (as amended: see note 38); European Parliamentary Elections Regulations 2004, SI 2004/293, Sch 2 para 23(6)(d) (as substituted: see note 1); National Assembly for Wales (Representation of the People) Order 2007, SI 2007/236, Sch 1 para 4(5)(b).

40 Representation of the People (England and Wales) Regulations 2001, SI 2001/341, reg 60(1); European Parliamentary Elections Regulations 2004, SI 2004/293, Sch 2 para 30(1) (as substituted: see note 1); National Assembly for Wales (Representation of the People) Order 2007, SI 2007/236, Sch 1 para 11(1).

41 Ie where applications have been granted on the grounds set out, at a parliamentary or local government election, in the Representation of the People Act 2000 Sch 4 para 3(3)(b), or, at a European parliamentary election, in the European Parliamentary Elections Regulations 2004, SI 2004/293, Sch 2 para 3(3)(c), or, at a Welsh Assembly election, in the National Assembly for Wales (Representation of the People) Order 2007, SI 2007/236, art 8(2)(c) (see PARA 367): see the Representation of the People (England and Wales) Regulations 2001, SI 2001/341, reg 60(1)(a); the European Parliamentary Elections Regulations 2004, SI 2004/293, Sch 2 para 30(1) (as substituted: see note 1); and the National Assembly for Wales (Representation of the People) Order 2007, SI 2007/236, Sch 1 para 11(1)(a).

Except in the case of European parliamentary elections, this includes applications granted under predecessor provisions: see the Representation of the People (England and Wales) Regulations 2001, SI 2001/341, reg 60(1)(b); and the National Assembly for Wales (Representation of the People) Order 2007, SI 2007/236, Sch 1 para 11(1)(b).

42 Representation of the People (England and Wales) Regulations 2001, SI 2001/341, reg 60(1)(a); European Parliamentary Elections Regulations 2004, SI 2004/293, Sch 2 para 30(1) (as substituted: see note 1); National Assembly for Wales (Representation of the People) Order 2007, SI 2007/236, Sch 1 para 11(1)(a). The text refers to the record kept, in relation to a parliamentary or local government election, under the Representation of the People Act 2000 Sch 4 para 3(4), or, in relation to a European parliamentary election, under the European Parliamentary Elections Regulations 2004, SI 2004/293, Sch 2 para 3(4), or, in relation to a Welsh Assembly election, under the National Assembly for Wales (Representation of the People) Order 2007, SI 2007/236, art 8(3), as the case may be (see PARA 370): see the Representation of the People (England and Wales) Regulations 2001, SI 2001/341, reg 60(1)(a); the European Parliamentary Elections Regulations 2004, SI 2004/293, Sch 2 para 30(1) (as so substituted); and the National Assembly for Wales (Representation of the People) Order 2007, SI 2007/236, Sch 1 para 11(1)(a).

43 Representation of the People (England and Wales) Regulations 2001, SI 2001/341, reg 60(3); European Parliamentary Elections Regulations 2004, SI 2004/293, Sch 2 para 30(3) (as substituted: see note 1); National Assembly for Wales (Representation of the People) Order 2007, SI 2007/236, Sch 1 para 11(3).

369. Additional requirements for applications for a proxy vote for a definite or indefinite period by reason of occupation, service or employment or attendance on a course. An application to vote by proxy for a particular or indefinite period by reason of occupation, service or employment or attendance on a course[1] must state[2]:

(1)   whether the occupation, service or employment in respect of which it is made is that of the applicant or his spouse or civil partner or, as the case may be, whether it is the applicant or his spouse or civil partner who is attending the course provided by an educational institution in respect of which the application is made[3];

(2)   the nature of the occupation, service or employment or course provided by an educational institution giving rise to the application[4];

(3)   where the person in respect of whose occupation, service or employment it is made (the 'employed person') is self-employed, that fact and, in any other case, the name of that person's employer[5];

(4)   the reason, relevant to the general nature of the employment, service or occupation in question or the course provided by an educational institution, why the applicant cannot reasonably be expected to go in person to his allotted polling station[6].

Such an application must be attested and signed:

(a)   where the person is self-employed, by a person who is aged 18 years or over[7], knows the self-employed person[8], and is not related to him[9]; or

(b)   by the employer of the employed person, or by another employee to whom this function is delegated by the employer[10]; or

(c)   in the case of a course provided by an educational institution, by the director or tutor of that course, or by the principal or head of that institution, or an employee to whom this function is delegated by the head or principal[11].

The person attesting an application so made must (where the applicant is the employed person, self-employed person, or the person attending the course) certify that the statements required by heads (1) to (4) above to be included in the application are true[12], or (where the applicant is the spouse or civil partner of the employed person, self-employed person, or the person attending the course) certify that the statements included in the application in accordance with the requirements of heads (1) to (3) above are true[13]. The person so attesting an application must also state:

(i)   if he is attesting pursuant to head (a) above, his name and address, that he is aged 18 years or over, that he knows the employed person, self-employed person or person attending a course provided by an educational institution, but is not related to him[14]; and

(ii)   if he is attesting pursuant to head (b) above, that he is the employer, or the position he holds in the employment of that employer[15]; or

(iii)   if he is attesting pursuant to head (c) above, the post he holds at that institution[16].

For the purpose of determining whether there has been a material change of circumstances, the registration officer may, at such times as he thinks fit, make inquiries of a person[17] who is shown as voting by proxy, in the record kept of those entitled to an absent vote at elections either for a particular period or for an indefinite period[18], by reason of occupation, service or employment or attendance on a course[19]; and where the grant of such an application was based on such grounds[20], the registration officer must make the inquiries referred to not later than three years after the granting of the application or the last such inquiries, as the case may be[21]. The registration officer may treat the failure by a person of whom inquiries have been made to respond to such inquiries within one month of the date on which they were made as sufficient evidence of a material change in circumstances[22].

1   Ie, at a parliamentary or local government election, under the Representation of the People Act 2000 s 12, Sch 4 para 3(3)(c), or, at a European parliamentary election, under the European Parliamentary Elections Regulations 2004, SI 2004/293, reg 10, Sch 2 para 3(3)(d), or, at a Welsh Assembly election, under the National Assembly for Wales (Representation of the People) Order 2007, SI 2007/236, art 8(2)(d), as the case may be (see PARA 367): see the Representation of the People (England and Wales) Regulations 2001, SI 2001/341, reg 54(1) (amended by SI 2001/1700); the European Parliamentary Elections Regulations 2004, SI 2004/293, Sch 2 para 24(1) (Sch 2 substituted by SI 2009/186); and the National Assembly for Wales (Representation of the People) Order 2007, SI 2007/236, art 15(2), Sch 1 para 5(1). As to the meaning of 'parliamentary election' see PARA 9. As to the meaning of 'local government election' see PARA 11; definition applied by virtue of the Representation of the People Act 2000 Sch 4 para 1(2). See also PARA 363 note 1. As to the meaning of 'Assembly election' in the context of Welsh Assembly elections see PARA 3 note 2. As to European parliamentary elections see PARA 217 et seq.

2   Representation of the People (England and Wales) Regulations 2001, SI 2001/341, reg 54(1) (as amended: see note 1); European Parliamentary Elections Regulations 2004, SI 2004/293, Sch 2 para 24(1) (as substituted: see note 1); National Assembly for Wales (Representation of the People) Order 2007, SI 2007/236, Sch 1 para 5(1). The application must also satisfy the general requirements of absent voting applications (see PARA 367). As to the offence in respect of false statements made in any declaration or form used in connection with absent voting see PARA 735.

3   Representation of the People (England and Wales) Regulations 2001, SI 2001/341, reg 54(1)(a) (amended by SI 2005/2114); European Parliamentary Elections Regulations 2004, SI 2004/293, Sch 2 para 24(1)(a) (as substituted: see note 1); National Assembly for Wales (Representation of the People) Order 2007, SI 2007/236, Sch 1 para 5(1)(a).

4   Representation of the People (England and Wales) Regulations 2001, SI 2001/341, reg 54(1)(b);
    European Parliamentary Elections Regulations 2004, SI 2004/293, Sch 2 para 24(1)(b) (as
    substituted: see note 1); National Assembly for Wales (Representation of the People)
    Order 2007, SI 2007/236, Sch 1 para 5(1)(b).

5   Representation of the People (England and Wales) Regulations 2001, SI 2001/341, reg 54(1)(c);
    European Parliamentary Elections Regulations 2004, SI 2004/293, Sch 2 para 24(1)(c) (as
    substituted: see note 1); National Assembly for Wales (Representation of the People)
    Order 2007, SI 2007/236, Sch 1 para 5(1)(c).

6   Representation of the People (England and Wales) Regulations 2001, SI 2001/341, reg 54(1)(d);
    European Parliamentary Elections Regulations 2004, SI 2004/293, Sch 2 para 24(1)(d) (as
    substituted: see note 1); National Assembly for Wales (Representation of the People)
    Order 2007, SI 2007/236, Sch 1 para 5(1)(d). As to the meaning of 'his allotted polling station',
    in relation to an elector, see PARA 368 note 32.

7   Representation of the People (England and Wales) Regulations 2001, SI 2001/341,
    reg 54(2)(a)(i); European Parliamentary Elections Regulations 2004, SI 2004/293, Sch 2
    para 24(2)(a)(i) (as substituted: see note 1); National Assembly for Wales (Representation of the
    People) Order 2007, SI 2007/236, Sch 1 para 5(2)(a)(i).

8   Representation of the People (England and Wales) Regulations 2001, SI 2001/341,
    reg 54(2)(a)(ii); European Parliamentary Elections Regulations 2004, SI 2004/293, Sch 2
    para 24(2)(a)(ii) (as substituted: see note 1); National Assembly for Wales (Representation of the
    People) Order 2007, SI 2007/236, Sch 1 para 5(2)(a)(ii).

9   Representation of the People (England and Wales) Regulations 2001, SI 2001/341,
    reg 54(2)(a)(iii); European Parliamentary Elections Regulations 2004, SI 2004/293, Sch 2
    para 24(2)(a)(iii) (as substituted: see note 1); National Assembly for Wales (Representation of
    the People) Order 2007, SI 2007/236, Sch 1 para 5(2)(a)(iii). For these purposes, one person is
    related to another if he is the spouse, civil partner, parent, grandparent, brother, sister, child or
    grandchild of the other: Representation of the People (England and Wales) Regulations 2001,
    SI 2001/341, reg 54(5) (amended by SI 2005/2114); European Parliamentary Elections
    Regulations 2004, SI 2004/293, Sch 2 para 24(5) (as so substituted); National Assembly for
    Wales (Representation of the People) Order 2007, SI 2007/236, Sch 1 para 5(5).

10 Representation of the People (England and Wales) Regulations 2001, SI 2001/341, reg 54(2)(b);
    European Parliamentary Elections Regulations 2004, SI 2004/293, Sch 2 para 24(2)(b) (as
    substituted: see note 1); National Assembly for Wales (Representation of the People)
    Order 2007, SI 2007/236, Sch 1 para 5(2)(b).

11 Representation of the People (England and Wales) Regulations 2001, SI 2001/341, reg 54(2)(c);
    European Parliamentary Elections Regulations 2004, SI 2004/293, Sch 2 para 24(2)(c) (as
    substituted: see note 1); National Assembly for Wales (Representation of the People)
    Order 2007, SI 2007/236, Sch 1 para 5(2)(c).

12 Representation of the People (England and Wales) Regulations 2001, SI 2001/341, reg 54(3)(a);
    European Parliamentary Elections Regulations 2004, SI 2004/293, Sch 2 para 24(3)(a) (as
    substituted: see note 1); National Assembly for Wales (Representation of the People)
    Order 2007, SI 2007/236, Sch 1 para 5(3)(a).

13 Representation of the People (England and Wales) Regulations 2001, SI 2001/341, reg 54(3)(b)
    (amended by SI 2005/2114); European Parliamentary Elections Regulations 2004, SI 2004/293,
    Sch 2 para 24(3)(b) (as substituted: see note 1); National Assembly for Wales (Representation of
    the People) Order 2007, SI 2007/236, Sch 1 para 5(3)(b). The reason why the applicant cannot
    reasonably be expected to go in person to the allotted polling station is not included in the
    statements that the person attesting the application has to certify as true in the case of the spouse
    or civil partner of an employed person or person attending a course.

14 Representation of the People (England and Wales) Regulations 2001, SI 2001/341, reg 54(4)(a);
    European Parliamentary Elections Regulations 2004, SI 2004/293, Sch 2 para 24(4)(a) (as
    substituted: see note 1); National Assembly for Wales (Representation of the People)
    Order 2007, SI 2007/236, Sch 1 para 5(4)(a).

15 Representation of the People (England and Wales) Regulations 2001, SI 2001/341, reg 54(4)(b);
    European Parliamentary Elections Regulations 2004, SI 2004/293, Sch 2 para 24(4)(b) (as
    substituted: see note 1); National Assembly for Wales (Representation of the People)
    Order 2007, SI 2007/236, Sch 1 para 5(4)(b).

16 Representation of the People (England and Wales) Regulations 2001, SI 2001/341, reg 54(4)(c);
    European Parliamentary Elections Regulations 2004, SI 2004/293, Sch 2 para 24(4)(c) (as
    substituted: see note 1); National Assembly for Wales (Representation of the People)
    Order 2007, SI 2007/236, Sch 1 para 5(4)(c).

17 Representation of the People (England and Wales) Regulations 2001, SI 2001/341, reg 60(1); European Parliamentary Elections Regulations 2004, SI 2004/293, Sch 2 para 30(1) (as substituted: see note 1); National Assembly for Wales (Representation of the People) Order 2007, SI 2007/236, Sch 1 para 11(1).

18 Ie in the record kept, in relation to a parliamentary or local government election, under the Representation of the People Act 2000 Sch 4 para 3(4), or, in relation to a European parliamentary election, under the European Parliamentary Elections Regulations 2004, SI 2004/293, Sch 2 para 3(4), or, in relation to a Welsh Assembly election, under the National Assembly for Wales (Representation of the People) Order 2007, SI 2007/236, art 8(3), as the case may be (see PARA 370): see the Representation of the People (England and Wales) Regulations 2001, SI 2001/341, reg 60(1)(a); the European Parliamentary Elections Regulations 2004, SI 2004/293, Sch 2 para 30(1) (as so substituted); and the National Assembly for Wales (Representation of the People) Order 2007, SI 2007/236, Sch 1 para 11(1)(a).

19 Representation of the People (England and Wales) Regulations 2001, SI 2001/341, reg 60(1)(a); European Parliamentary Elections Regulations 2004, SI 2004/293, Sch 2 para 30(1) (as substituted: see note 1); National Assembly for Wales (Representation of the People) Order 2007, SI 2007/236, Sch 1 para 11(1)(a). The text refers to applications that have been granted on the grounds set out, at a parliamentary or local government election, in the Representation of the People Act 2000 Sch 4 para 3(3)(c), or, at a European parliamentary election, in the European Parliamentary Elections Regulations 2004, SI 2004/293, Sch 1 para 3(3)(d), or, at a Welsh Assembly election, in the National Assembly for Wales (Representation of the People) Order 2007, SI 2007/236, art 8(2)(d), as the case may be (see PARA 367): see the Representation of the People (England and Wales) Regulations 2001, SI 2001/341, reg 60(1)(a); the European Parliamentary Elections Regulations 2004, SI 2004/293, Sch 2 para 30(1) (as so substituted); and the National Assembly for Wales (Representation of the People) Order 2007, SI 2007/236, Sch 1 para 11(1)(a).

Except in the case of European parliamentary elections, this includes applications granted under predecessor provisions: see the Representation of the People (England and Wales) Regulations 2001, SI 2001/341, reg 60(1)(b); and the National Assembly for Wales (Representation of the People) Order 2007, SI 2007/236, Sch 1 para 11(1)(b).

20 Ie on the grounds set out, at a parliamentary or local government election, in the Representation of the People Act 2000 Sch 4 para 3(3)(c) (or grounds corresponding to those grounds set out in Sch 4 para 3(3)(c), under predecessor legislation), or, at a European parliamentary election, in the European Parliamentary Elections Regulations 2004, SI 2004/293, Sch 1 para 3(3)(d), or, at a Welsh Assembly election, in the National Assembly for Wales (Representation of the People) Order 2007, SI 2007/236, art 8(2)(d) (or grounds corresponding to those grounds set out in art 8(2)(d), under predecessor legislation), as the case may be (see PARA 367): see the Representation of the People (England and Wales) Regulations 2001, SI 2001/341, reg 60(2) (amended by SI 2001/1700); the European Parliamentary Elections Regulations 2004, SI 2004/293, Sch 2 para 30(2) (as substituted: see note 1); and the National Assembly for Wales (Representation of the People) Order 2007, SI 2007/236, Sch 1 para 11(2).

21 Representation of the People (England and Wales) Regulations 2001, SI 2001/341, reg 60(2) (as amended: see note 20); European Parliamentary Elections Regulations 2004, SI 2004/293, Sch 2 para 30(2); National Assembly for Wales (Representation of the People) Order 2007, SI 2007/236, Sch 1 para 11(2).

22 Representation of the People (England and Wales) Regulations 2001, SI 2001/341, reg 60(3); European Parliamentary Elections Regulations 2004, SI 2004/293, Sch 2 para 30(3); National Assembly for Wales (Representation of the People) Order 2007, SI 2007/236, Sch 1 para 11(3).

370. Record of those entitled to an absent vote at elections for a definite period or for an indefinite period. The registration officer[1] must keep a record of those whose applications for an absent vote at elections for a definite period or for an indefinite period[2] have been granted showing[3]:

   (1)   whether their applications were to vote by post or proxy for an indefinite or a particular period (specifying that period)[4];

   (2)   in the case of those who may vote by post, the addresses provided by them in their applications as the addresses to which their ballot papers are to be sent[5]; and

   (3)   in the case of those who may vote by proxy, the names and addresses of those appointed as their proxies[6]; and

(4)　(in the case of applications made in respect of parliamentary or local government elections) whether their applications were in respect of parliamentary elections, local government elections or both[7].

The registration officer must remove a person from the record[8]:

(a)　if he applies to the registration officer to be removed[9];

(b)　in the case of a person who is eligible to vote by proxy by virtue of having an anonymous entry[10], if he ceases to have an anonymous entry[11];

(c)　in the case of any registered person, if he ceases to be registered or registered at the same qualifying address or ceases to be, or becomes, registered in pursuance of[12] a service declaration[13], or a declaration of local connection[14], or (except in the case of a Welsh Assembly election) an overseas elector's declaration[15];

(d)　in the case of any person shown in the record as voting by proxy, if the registration officer gives notice that he has reason to believe there has been a material change of circumstances[16]; or

(e)　in the case of a person who applied to vote by post or proxy for a particular period, once that period has expired[17].

Where a person is removed from the record under any of heads (a) to (e) above, the registration officer must, where practicable, notify him of this and the reason for it[18].

A person shown in the record as voting by post may subsequently alter his choice by applying to the registration officer to vote by proxy instead (whether for an indefinite period or for a particular period specified in his application); and, if the registration officer would be required to grant that application to vote by proxy[19], the registration officer must amend the record accordingly[20]. Equally, a person shown in the record as voting by proxy may subsequently alter his choice by applying to the registration officer to vote by post instead (whether for an indefinite period or for a particular period specified in his application); and, if the application meets the statutory requirements, the registration officer must amend the record accordingly[21].

The registration officer must also keep a record in relation to those whose applications for an absent vote at elections for a particular period or for an indefinite period have been granted showing[22]:

(i)　their dates of birth[23]; and

(ii)　except in cases where the registration officer[24] has dispensed with the requirement to provide a signature, their signatures[25].

This record must be retained by the registration officer for the prescribed period[26]. The registration officer must either provide a copy of the information contained in records so kept by him[27] to the returning officer for an election in relation to electors at the election[28], or give the returning officer access to such information[29]. Information contained in such records may be disclosed by a registration officer (subject to any prescribed conditions) to any other registration officer if he thinks that to do so will assist the other registration officer in the performance of his duties[30], or to any person exercising functions in relation to the preparation or conduct of legal proceedings under the relevant election provisions[31], or (except in relation to a European parliamentary election) to such other persons for such other purposes relating to elections as may be prescribed[32].

A person who remains on the record of those entitled to an absent vote at parliamentary or local government elections for a particular period or for an indefinite period[33] may, at any time, provide the registration officer with a fresh signature[34]; and anything required or authorised to be done for the purposes of any enactment in relation to a signature required to be provided in pursuance of absent voting in Great Britain[35] must be done in relation to a signature so provided instead of in relation to a signature provided on any earlier occasion[36].

1   As to electoral registration officers and the areas for which they act see PARA 139 et seq.
2   Ie whose applications, for the purposes of a parliamentary or local government election, under the Representation of the People Act 2000 Sch 4 para 3, or, for the purposes of a European parliamentary election, under the European Parliamentary Elections Regulations 2004, SI 2004/293, reg 10, Sch 2 para 3, or, for the purposes of a Welsh Assembly election, under the National Assembly for Wales (Representation of the People) Order 2007, SI 2007/236, art 8, as the case may be (see PARA 367): see the Representation of the People Act 2000 Sch 4 para 3(4); the European Parliamentary Elections Regulations 2004, SI 2004/293, Sch 2 para 3(4) (Sch 2 substituted by SI 2009/186); and the National Assembly for Wales (Representation of the People) Order 2007, SI 2007/236, art 8(3). As to the meaning of 'parliamentary election' see PARA 9. As to the meaning of 'local government election' see PARA 11; definition applied by virtue of the Representation of the People Act 2000 s 12, Sch 4 para 1(2). See also PARA 363 note 1. As to the meaning of 'Assembly election' in the context of Welsh Assembly elections see PARA 3 note 2. As to European parliamentary elections see PARA 217 et seq.
        The Representation of the People Act 2000 s 12, Sch 4 are applied and modified for the purpose of local authority mayoral elections in England and Wales by the Local Authorities (Mayoral Elections) (England and Wales) Regulations 2007, SI 2007/1024, reg 3(2)–(5), Sch 2 Table 3 (see PARA 11 note 14); and they have effect for the purposes of local authority referendums, subject to the modifications specified, in relation to Wales, by the Local Authorities (Conduct of Referendums) (Wales) Regulations 2008, SI 2008/1848, reg 8(2), Sch 4 Table 2, and, in relation to England, by the Local Authorities (Conduct of Referendums) (England) Regulations 2012, SI 2012/323, regs 8(2), 11–13, Sch 4 Table 3 (see PARA 15 note 2). The Representation of the People (England and Wales) Regulations 2001, SI 2001/341, regs 4, 50, 51, 51A, 51AA, 56, 57 also have effect for the purposes of local authority referendums, subject to the modifications specified, in relation to Wales, by the Local Authorities (Conduct of Referendums) (Wales) Regulations 2008, SI 2008/1848, reg 8(2), Sch 4 Table 5, and, in relation to England, by the Local Authorities (Conduct of Referendums) (England) Regulations 2012, SI 2012/323, regs 8(2), 11–13, Sch 4 Table 6 (see PARA 15 note 2).
3   Representation of the People Act 2000 Sch 4 para 3(4); European Parliamentary Elections Regulations 2004, SI 2004/293, Sch 2 para 3(4) (as substituted: see note 2); National Assembly for Wales (Representation of the People) Order 2007, SI 2007/236, art 8(3).
4   Representation of the People Act 2000 Sch 4 para 3(4)(a)(ii); European Parliamentary Elections Regulations 2004, SI 2004/293, Sch 2 para 3(4)(a) (as substituted: see note 2); National Assembly for Wales (Representation of the People) Order 2007, SI 2007/236, art 8(3).
5   Representation of the People Act 2000 Sch 4 para 3(4)(b); European Parliamentary Elections Regulations 2004, SI 2004/293, Sch 2 para 3(4)(b) (as substituted: see note 2); National Assembly for Wales (Representation of the People) Order 2007, SI 2007/236, art 8(4)(a).
6   Representation of the People Act 2000 Sch 4 para 3(4)(c); European Parliamentary Elections Regulations 2004, SI 2004/293, Sch 2 para 3(4)(c) (as substituted: see note 2); National Assembly for Wales (Representation of the People) Order 2007, SI 2007/236, art 8(4)(b). As to the appointment of proxies to vote see PARA 374 et seq.
7   Representation of the People Act 2000 Sch 4 para 3(4)(a)(i).
8   Representation of the People Act 2000 Sch 4 para 3(5); European Parliamentary Elections Regulations 2004, SI 2004/293, Sch 2 para 3(5) (as substituted: see note 2); National Assembly for Wales (Representation of the People) Order 2007, SI 2007/236, art 8(5).
9   Representation of the People Act 2000 Sch 4 para 3(5)(a); European Parliamentary Elections Regulations 2004, SI 2004/293, Sch 2 para 3(5)(a) (as substituted: see note 2); National Assembly for Wales (Representation of the People) Order 2007, SI 2007/236, art 8(5)(a).
        Such an application made under the Representation of the People Act 2000 Sch 4 para 3(5)(a), or the European Parliamentary Elections Regulations 2004, SI 2004/293, Sch 2 para 3(5)(a), or the National Assembly for Wales (Representation of the People) Order 2007, SI 2007/236, art 8(5)(a), as the case may be, must be disregarded for the purposes of a particular election if it is received by the registration officer after 5 pm on the eleventh day before the date of the poll at that election: Representation of the People (England and Wales) Regulations 2001, SI 2001/341, reg 56(5) (amended by SI 2001/1700); European Parliamentary Elections Regulations 2004, SI 2004/293, Sch 2 para 26(6)(a) (as so substituted); National Assembly for

Wales (Representation of the People) Order 2007, SI 2007/236, Sch 1 para 7(5)(a). Where a registration officer disregards an application for the purposes of any particular election, he must notify the applicant of this: Representation of the People (England and Wales) Regulations 2001, SI 2001/341, reg 57(5) (amended by SI 2006/752); European Parliamentary Elections Regulations 2004, SI 2004/293, Sch 2 para 27(7) (as so substituted); National Assembly for Wales (Representation of the People) Order 2007, SI 2007/236, Sch 1 para 8(8). As to the computation of time for these purposes see PARA 367 note 6. As to the date of the poll at a parliamentary general election or by-election see PARA 195; as to the date of the poll at local government elections (including elections to fill vacancies) see PARAS 206–209; as to the date of the poll at Welsh Assembly elections (including elections to fill vacancies in an Assembly constituency) see PARAS 213–214; and as to the date of the poll at a European parliamentary election see PARA 222.

10 Ie an anonymous entry in relation to a register of electors (see PARA 148); and see also PARA 367.

11 Representation of the People Act 2000 Sch 4 para 3(5)(aa) (added by the Electoral Administration Act 2006 s 10(2), Sch 1 paras 19, 20(1), (4)); European Parliamentary Elections Regulations 2004, SI 2004/293, Sch 2 para 3(5)(b) (as substituted: see note 2); National Assembly for Wales (Representation of the People) Order 2007, SI 2007/236, art 8(5)(b).

12 Representation of the People Act 2000 Sch 4 para 3(5)(b); European Parliamentary Elections Regulations 2004, SI 2004/293, Sch 2 para 3(5)(c) (as substituted: see note 2); National Assembly for Wales (Representation of the People) Order 2007, SI 2007/236, art 8(5)(c).

13 Representation of the People Act 2000 Sch 4 para 3(5)(b)(i); European Parliamentary Elections Regulations 2004, SI 2004/293, Sch 2 para 3(5)(c)(i) (as substituted: see note 2); National Assembly for Wales (Representation of the People) Order 2007, SI 2007/236, art 8(5)(c)(i). As to registration in pursuance of a service declaration see PARA 125 et seq.

14 Representation of the People Act 2000 Sch 4 para 3(5)(b)(ii); European Parliamentary Elections Regulations 2004, SI 2004/293, Sch 2 para 3(5)(c)(ii) (as substituted: see note 2); National Assembly for Wales (Representation of the People) Order 2007, SI 2007/236, art 8(5)(c)(ii). As to registration in pursuance of a declaration of local connection see PARA 121 et seq.

15 Representation of the People Act 2000 Sch 4 para 3(5)(b)(iii); European Parliamentary Elections Regulations 2004, SI 2004/293, Sch 2 para 3(5)(c)(iii) (as substituted: see note 2). As to registration in pursuance of an overseas elector's declaration see PARA 114 et seq.

16 Representation of the People Act 2000 Sch 4 para 3(5)(c); European Parliamentary Elections Regulations 2004, SI 2004/293, Sch 2 para 3(5)(d) (as substituted: see note 2); National Assembly for Wales (Representation of the People) Order 2007, SI 2007/236, art 8(5)(d). As to the registration officer's powers and duties to make inquiries of persons included in this record see PARAS 368–369.

17 Representation of the People Act 2000 Sch 4 para 3(5)(d); European Parliamentary Elections Regulations 2004, SI 2004/293, Sch 2 para 3(5)(e) (as substituted: see note 2); National Assembly for Wales (Representation of the People) Order 2007, SI 2007/236, art 8(5)(e).

18 Representation of the People (England and Wales) Regulations 2001, SI 2001/341, reg 57(4B) (added by SI 2006/752; and amended by SI 2006/2910); European Parliamentary Elections Regulations 2004, SI 2004/293, Sch 2 para 27(5) (as substituted: see note 2); National Assembly for Wales (Representation of the People) Order 2007, SI 2007/236, Sch 1 para 8(6). As to notification see PARA 367 note 35.

19 Ie as if it were an application that had been made, for the purposes of a parliamentary or local government election, under the Representation of the People Act 2000 Sch 4 para 3(2), or, for the purposes of a European parliamentary election, under the European Parliamentary Elections Regulations 2004, SI 2004/293, Sch 2 para 3(2), or if, for the purposes of a Welsh Assembly election, it meets the requirements of the National Assembly for Wales (Representation of the People) Order 2007, SI 2007/236, Sch 1 (see PARA 367), as the case may be: see the Representation of the People Act 2000 Sch 4 para 3(6); the European Parliamentary Elections Regulations 2004, SI 2004/293, Sch 2 para 3(6); and the National Assembly for Wales (Representation of the People) Order 2007, SI 2007/236, art 8(6).

20 Representation of the People Act 2000 Sch 4 para 3(6); European Parliamentary Elections Regulations 2004, SI 2004/293, Sch 2 para 3(6) (as substituted: see note 2); National Assembly for Wales (Representation of the People) Order 2007, SI 2007/236, art 8(6).

Such an application must be disregarded for the purposes of a particular election if it is received by the registration officer after 5 pm on the eleventh day before the date of the poll at that election: Representation of the People (England and Wales) Regulations 2001, SI 2001/341, reg 56(1) (amended by SI 2006/752); European Parliamentary Elections Regulations 2004, SI 2004/293, Sch 2 para 26(1) (as so substituted); National Assembly for Wales (Representation of the People) Order 2007, SI 2007/236, Sch 1 para 7(4) (amended by SI 2010/2931). Where a registration officer disregards an application for the purposes of any particular election, he must notify the applicant of this: Representation of the People (England and Wales) Regulations 2001, SI 2001/341, reg 57(5) (as amended: see note 9); European Parliamentary Elections Regulations 2004, SI 2004/293, Sch 2 para 27(7) (as so substituted); National Assembly for Wales (Representation of the People) Order 2007, SI 2007/236, Sch 2 para 8(8). As to the computation of time for these purposes see PARA 367 note 6.

21 Representation of the People Act 2000 Sch 4 para 3(7); European Parliamentary Elections Regulations 2004, SI 2004/293, Sch 2 para 3(7) (as substituted: see note 2); National Assembly for Wales (Representation of the People) Order 2007, SI 2007/236, art 8(7). For the purposes of the Representation of the People Act 2000 Sch 4, the requirements are as prescribed; and 'prescribed' means prescribed by regulations (see the Representation of the People Act 1983 s 202(1); applied by virtue of the Representation of the People Act 2000 Sch 4 para 1(2)). Accordingly, the text refers to the requirements set out, in the case of a parliamentary or local government election, in the Representation of the People (England and Wales) Regulations 2001, SI 2001/341, Pt IV (regs 50–63A), or, in the case of a European parliamentary election, the European Parliamentary Elections Regulations 2004, SI 2004/293, Sch 2, or, in the case of a Welsh Assembly election, in the National Assembly for Wales (Representation of the People) Order 2007, SI 2007/236, Sch 1, as the case may be (see PARAS 367–369): see the Representation of the People Act 2000 Sch 4 para 3(7); the European Parliamentary Elections Regulations 2004, SI 2004/293, Sch 2 para 3(7); and the National Assembly for Wales (Representation of the People) Order 2007, SI 2007/236, art 8(7).

An application of the kind referred to in the text must be disregarded for the purposes of a particular election if it is received by the registration officer after 5 pm on the eleventh day before the date of the poll at that election: Representation of the People (England and Wales) Regulations 2001, SI 2001/341, reg 56(1) (as amended: see note 20); European Parliamentary Elections Regulations 2004, SI 2004/293, Sch 2 para 26(1) (as so substituted); National Assembly for Wales (Representation of the People) Order 2007, SI 2007/236, Sch 1 para 7(4) (as amended: see note 20). Where a registration officer disregards an application for the purposes of any particular election, he must notify the applicant of this: Representation of the People (England and Wales) Regulations 2001, SI 2001/341, reg 57(5) (as amended: see note 9); European Parliamentary Elections Regulations 2004, SI 2004/293, Sch 2 para 27(7) (as so substituted); National Assembly for Wales (Representation of the People) Order 2007, SI 2007/236, Sch 2 para 8(8).

22 Representation of the People Act 1983 Sch 4 para 3(9) (Sch 4 para 3(9)–(10) added by the Electoral Administration Act 2006 s 14(1)(c), (8)); European Parliamentary Elections Regulations 2004, SI 2004/293, Sch 2 para 3(9) (as substituted: see note 2); National Assembly for Wales (Representation of the People) Order 2007, SI 2007/236, art 8(9).

Where a person to whom the European Parliamentary Elections Regulations 2004, SI 2004/293, Sch 2 para 31(1) applies (see PARA 366) has provided a registration officer with the required personal identifiers under the Representation of the People Act 2000 s 12, Sch 4 para 3 (absent vote at elections for definite or indefinite period: see PARA 367) or under Sch 4 para 4 (absent vote at particular election: see PARA 371) or under Sch 4 para 7 (voting as proxy for an indefinite period or for a particular period or at a particular election: see PARA 378), or under the Representation of the People (England and Wales) Regulations 2001, SI 2001/341, or the National Assembly for Wales (Representation of the People) Order 2007, SI 2007/236, before the date specified in the notice sent to the absent voter in accordance with the European Parliamentary Elections Regulations 2004, SI 2004/293, Sch 2 para 31(1)(b), the registration officer may use them, or enter them in his records, in accordance with Sch 2 para 3(9): see Sch 2 para 31(10) (as so substituted); and PARA 366.

23 Representation of the People Act 2000 Sch 4 para 3(9)(a) (as added: see note 22); European Parliamentary Elections Regulations 2004, SI 2004/293, Sch 2 para 3(9)(a) (as substituted: see note 2); National Assembly for Wales (Representation of the People) Order 2007, SI 2007/236, art 8(9)(a).

24 Ie in pursuance of the Representation of the People Act 2000 Sch 4 para 3(8), or the European Parliamentary Elections Regulations 2004, SI 2004/293, Sch 2 para 3(8), or the National or the National Assembly for Wales (Representation of the People) Order 2007, SI 2007/236, art 8(8) (see PARA 367), as the case may be: see the Representation of the People Act 2000 Sch 4 para 3(9)(b) (as added: see note 22); the European Parliamentary Elections Regulations 2004, SI 2004/293, Sch 2 para 3(9)(b) (as substituted: see note 2); and the National Assembly for Wales (Representation of the People) Order 2007, SI 2007/236, art 8(9)(b).

25 Representation of the People Act 2000 Sch 4 para 3(9)(b) (as added: see note 22); European Parliamentary Elections Regulations 2004, SI 2004/293, Sch 2 para 3(9)(b) (as substituted: see note 2); National Assembly for Wales (Representation of the People) Order 2007, SI 2007/236, art 8(9)(b).

26 Representation of the People Act 2000 Sch 4 para 3(10) (as added: see note 22); European
Parliamentary Elections Regulations 2004, SI 2004/293, Sch 2 para 3(10) (as substituted: see
note 2); National Assembly for Wales (Representation of the People) Order 2007, SI 2007/236,
art 8(10). As to the retention of the records referred to in the text see PARA 503 et seq.

27 Ie in pursuance of the Representation of the People Act 2000 Sch 4 para 3(9), or the European
Parliamentary Elections Regulations 2004, SI 2004/293, Sch 2 para 3(9), or the National
Assembly for Wales (Representation of the People) Order 2007, SI 2007/236, art 8(9) (see the
text and notes 22–25): see the Representation of the People Act 2000 Sch 4 para 7C(a) (Sch 4
paras 7A–7D added by the Electoral Administration Act 2006 s 14(4), (8)); the European
Parliamentary Elections Regulations 2004, SI 2004/293, Sch 2 para 9(1)(a); and the National
Assembly for Wales (Representation of the People) Order 2007, SI 2007/236, art 13(5)(a).

28 Representation of the People Act 2000 Sch 4 para 7C(a) (as added: see note 27); European
Parliamentary Elections Regulations 2004, SI 2004/293, Sch 2 para 9(1)(a) (as substituted: see
note 2); National Assembly for Wales (Representation of the People) Order 2007, SI 2007/236,
art 13(5)(a).
    At a European parliamentary election, the local returning officer is the returning officer
referred to in the text: see the European Parliamentary Elections Regulations 2004, SI 2004/293,
Sch 2 para 9(1)(a) (as so substituted). As to local returning officers appointed for the purposes of
elections to the European Parliament see PARA 360.
    At a Welsh Assembly election, the constituency returning officer is the returning officer
referred to in the text: see the National Assembly for Wales (Representation of the People)
Order 2007, SI 2007/236, art 13(5)(a). As to the meanings of 'constituency returning officer'
and 'regional returning officer' for the purposes of Welsh Assembly elections see PARA 18 note 2.

29 Representation of the People Act 2000 Sch 4 para 7C(b) (as added: see note 27); European
Parliamentary Elections Regulations 2004, SI 2004/293, Sch 2 para 9(1)(b) (as substituted: see
note 2); National Assembly for Wales (Representation of the People) Order 2007, SI 2007/236,
art 13(5)(b). As to the returning officer referred to in the text see note 28.

30 Representation of the People Act 2000 Sch 4 para 7D(a) (as added: see note 27); European
Parliamentary Elections Regulations 2004, SI 2004/293, Sch 2 para 9(2)(a) (as substituted: see
note 2); National Assembly for Wales (Representation of the People) Order 2007, SI 2007/236,
art 13(6)(a). As to the prescribed conditions see PARA 179 et seq.

31 Representation of the People Act 2000 Sch 4 para 7D(b) (as added: see note 27); European
Parliamentary Elections Regulations 2004, SI 2004/293, Sch 2 para 9(2)(b) (as substituted: see
note 2); National Assembly for Wales (Representation of the People) Order 2007, SI 2007/236,
art 13(6)(b). As to the meaning of 'the Representation of the People Acts' see PARA 3 note 1.
    At a parliamentary or local government election, the functions referred to in the text are
those under the Representation of the People Acts: see the Representation of the People
Act 2000 Sch 4 para 7D(b) (as so added).
    At a European parliamentary election, the functions referred to in the text are those under
the European Parliamentary Elections Regulations 2004, SI 2004/293: see Sch 2 para 9(2)(b) (as
so substituted).
    At a Welsh Assembly election, the functions referred to in the text are those under the
Representation of the People Acts or the National Assembly for Wales (Representation of the
People) Order 2007, SI 2007/236: see art 13(6)(b).

32 Representation of the People Act 1983 Sch 4 para 7D(c) (as added: see note 27); National
Assembly for Wales (Representation of the People) Order 2007, SI 2007/236, art 13(6)(c). As to
the prescribed conditions see PARA 179 et seq.

33 Ie who remains on the record kept, in relation to a parliamentary or local government election,
under the Representation of the People Act 2000 Sch 4 para 3(4), or, in relation to a European
parliamentary election, under the European Parliamentary Elections Regulations 2004,
SI 2004/293, Sch 2 para 3(4), or, in relation to a Welsh Assembly election, under the National
Assembly for Wales (Representation of the People) Order 2007, SI 2007/236, art 8(3) (see the
text and notes 1–7), as the case may be: see the Representation of the People Act 2000 Sch 4
para 7A(1) (as added: see note 27); the European Parliamentary Elections Regulations 2004,
SI 2004/293, Sch 2 para 8(1) (as substituted: see note 2); and the National Assembly for Wales
(Representation of the People) Order 2007, SI 2007/236, art 13(3).

34 Representation of the People Act 2000 Sch 4 para 7A(1) (as added: see note 27); European
Parliamentary Elections Regulations 2004, SI 2004/293, Sch 2 para 8(1) (as substituted: see
note 2); National Assembly for Wales (Representation of the People) Order 2007, SI 2007/236,
art 13(3).
    Regulations under the Representation of the People Act 1983 may make provision as to
circumstances in which a registration officer may require a person who remains on the record
kept under the Representation of the People Act 2000 Sch 4 para 3(4) (see the text and

notes 1–7) to provide a fresh signature (see Sch 4 para 7B(a) (as so added)), and as to the consequences of a person refusing or failing to comply with a requirement to provide a fresh signature (see Sch 4 para 7B(b) (as so added)). As to the regulations so made see the Elections (Fresh Signatures for Absent Voters) Regulations 2013, SI 2013/1599; the National Assembly for Wales (Representation of the People) (Fresh Signatures for Absent Voters) Order 2013, SI 2013/1514 (made under the Government of Wales Act 2006 s 13(1), (4)); and PARA 366 note 16.

35 Ie in pursuance of, in relation to a parliamentary or local government election, the Representation of the People Act 2000 Sch 4, or, in relation to a European parliamentary election, under the European Parliamentary Elections Regulations 2004, SI 2004/293, Sch 2, or, in relation to a Welsh Assembly election, under the National Assembly for Wales (Representation of the People) Order 2007, SI 2007/236: see the Representation of the People Act 2000 Sch 4 para 7A(2) (as added: see note 27); the European Parliamentary Elections Regulations 2004, SI 2004/293, Sch 2 para 8(2) (as substituted: see note 2); and the National Assembly for Wales (Representation of the People) Order 2007, SI 2007/236, art 13(4).

36 Representation of the People Act 2000 Sch 4 para 7A(2) (as added: see note 27); European Parliamentary Elections Regulations 2004, SI 2004/293, Sch 2 para 8(2) (as substituted: see note 2); National Assembly for Wales (Representation of the People) Order 2007, SI 2007/236, art 13(4).

(B) Applications relating to a Particular Election

371. Applications for an absent vote at a particular election. Where a person applies to the registration officer[1] to vote by post at a particular parliamentary[2], local government[3], Welsh Assembly[4] or European parliamentary election[5], the registration officer must grant the application[6]:

(1)   if he is satisfied that the applicant is or will be registered in the register of electors for the election[7]; and

(2)   if the application contains the applicant's signature and date of birth and meets the statutory requirements[8].

Where a person applies to the registration officer to vote by proxy[9] at a particular such election, the registration officer must grant the application[10]:

(a)   if he is satisfied that the applicant's circumstances on the date of the poll will be or are likely to be such that he cannot reasonably be expected to vote in person at the polling station allotted or likely to be allotted to him under the appropriate rules[11];

(b)   if he is satisfied that the applicant is or will be registered in the register of electors for the election[12]; and

(c)   if the application contains the applicant's signature and date of birth and meets the statutory requirements[13].

Where a person who has an anonymous entry in the register of electors for the election[14] applies to the registration officer to vote by proxy at a particular such election, the registration officer must grant the application if it meets the prescribed requirements[15].

A person who is included in the record kept of those entitled to an absent vote in respect of such elections either for a particular period or for an indefinite period[16] may, in respect of a particular election of the kind in question, apply to the registration officer[17], either for his ballot paper to be sent to a different address from that shown in the record[18], or to vote by proxy[19], if he is shown in the record so kept as voting by post at elections of the kind in question[20]; and the registration officer must grant such an application if[21] (in the case of any application) it meets the statutory requirements[22], and (in the case of an application to vote by proxy) the registration officer is satisfied that the applicant's circumstances on the date of the poll will be or are likely to be such that he cannot reasonably be expected to vote in person at the polling station allotted or likely to be allotted to him under the appropriate rules[23].

Such an application[24] must state:

(i) the full name of the applicant[25];

(ii) the address in respect of which the applicant is registered or has applied to be (or is treated as having applied to be) registered in the register[26];

(iii) in the case of a person applying to vote by post, the address to which the ballot paper should be sent[27];

(iv) in the case of an application to vote by proxy, the grounds on which the elector claims to be entitled to an absent vote[28];

(v) in the case of a person who is unable to provide a signature, the reasons for his request for waiver of any requirement[29] to provide a signature and the name and address of any person who has assisted him to complete his application[30]; and

(vi) where the applicant has, or has applied for, an anonymous entry, that fact[31].

An application made for a particular election must identify the election in question (except in the case of a Welsh Assembly election)[32], and such an application must state that it is made for a particular election[33]. Such an application may be combined where polls fall on the same day[34]. The application must be made in writing and dated[35]. Where an application is made by an elector to vote by proxy, it must include an application for the appointment of a proxy which meets the statutory requirements[36].

Where the registration officer grants an application to vote by post, he must notify the applicant of his decision[37]; and where he refuses an application, he must notify the applicant of his decision and of the reason for it[38]. An appeal does not lie from any decision of the registration officer disallowing a person's application to vote by proxy or by post as elector made for a particular election only[39].

1 The registration officer must supply free of charge as many forms for use in connection with applications made under the Representation of the People Act 2000 s 12, Sch 4, the Representation of the People (England and Wales) Regulations 2001, SI 2001/341, Pt IV (regs 50–63A), or the European Parliamentary Elections Regulations 2004, SI 2004/293, reg 10, Sch 2, as appear to that officer reasonable in the circumstances to any person who satisfies that officer of his intention to use the forms in connection with an election: Representation of the People (England and Wales) Regulations 2001, SI 2001/341, reg 4(1)(b); European Parliamentary Elections Regulations 2004, SI 2004/293, Sch 2 para 12(1) (Sch 2 substituted by SI 2009/186). As to electoral registration officers and the areas for which they act see PARA 139 et seq.
   The Representation of the People Act 2000 s 12, Sch 4 are applied and modified for the purpose of local authority mayoral elections in England and Wales by the Local Authorities (Mayoral Elections) (England and Wales) Regulations 2007, SI 2007/1024, reg 3(2)–(5), Sch 2 Table 3 (see PARA 11 note 14); and they have effect for the purposes of local authority referendums, subject to the modifications specified, in relation to Wales, by the Local Authorities (Conduct of Referendums) (Wales) Regulations 2008, SI 2008/1848, reg 8(2), Sch 4 Table 2, and, in relation to England, by the Local Authorities (Conduct of Referendums) (England) Regulations 2012, SI 2012/323, regs 8(2), 11–13, Sch 4 Table 3 (see PARA 15 note 2). The Representation of the People (England and Wales) Regulations 2001, SI 2001/341, regs 4, 51, 51A, 51AA, 51B, 56, 57 also have effect for the purposes of local authority referendums, subject to the modifications specified, in relation to Wales, by the Local Authorities (Conduct of Referendums) (Wales) Regulations 2008, SI 2008/1848, reg 8(2), Sch 4 Table 5, and, in relation to England, by the Local Authorities (Conduct of Referendums) (England) Regulations 2012, SI 2012/323, regs 8(2), 11–13, Sch 4 Table 6 (see PARA 15 note 2).
2 As to the meaning of 'parliamentary election' see PARA 9.
3 As to the meaning of 'local government election' see PARA 11; definition applied by virtue of the Representation of the People Act 2000 s 12, Sch 4 para 1(2). See also PARA 363 note 1.

4   As to the meaning of 'Assembly election' in the context of Welsh Assembly elections see PARA 3 note 2. For these purposes, 'particular election', where a person (whether as elector or as proxy) is entitled to give two votes at an ordinary election, refers to both elections at which he is entitled to so vote; and references to an absent vote at a particular Assembly election must be construed accordingly: see the National Assembly for Wales (Representation of the People) Order 2007, SI 2007/236, art 9(8). As to ordinary general Welsh Assembly elections see PARA 12 et seq.

5   As to European parliamentary elections see PARA 217 et seq.

6   Representation of the People Act 2000 Sch 4 para 4(1); European Parliamentary Elections Regulations 2004, SI 2004/293, Sch 2 para 4(1) (as substituted: see note 1); National Assembly for Wales (Representation of the People) Order 2007, SI 2007/236, art 9(1).

    Such an application must be refused if it is received by the registration officer after 5 pm on the eleventh day before the date of the poll at the election for which it is made: Representation of the People (England and Wales) Regulations 2001, SI 2001/341, reg 56(4) (amended by SI 2006/752); European Parliamentary Elections Regulations 2004, SI 2004/293, Sch 2 para 26(5) (as so substituted); National Assembly for Wales (Representation of the People) Order 2007, SI 2007/236, art 15(2), Sch 1 para 7(1). Where a registration officer refuses such an application, he must notify the applicant of his decision and the reason for it: Representation of the People (England and Wales) Regulations 2001, SI 2001/341, reg 57(4); European Parliamentary Elections Regulations 2004, SI 2004/293, Sch 2 para 27(3) (as so substituted); National Assembly for Wales (Representation of the People) Order 2007, SI 2007/236, Sch 1 para 8(4). As to the computation of time for these purposes see PARA 367 note 6. As to the date of the poll at a parliamentary general election or by-election see PARA 195; as to the date of the poll at local government elections (including elections to fill vacancies) see PARAS 206–209; as to the date of the poll at Welsh Assembly elections (including elections to fill vacancies in an Assembly constituency) see PARAS 213–214; and as to the date of the poll at a European parliamentary election see PARA 222.

7   Representation of the People Act 2000 Sch 4 para 4(1)(a); European Parliamentary Elections Regulations 2004, SI 2004/293, Sch 2 para 4(1)(a) (as substituted: see note 1); National Assembly for Wales (Representation of the People) Order 2007, SI 2007/236, art 9(1)(b).

    In the case of a parliamentary election, the register referred to in the text is the register of parliamentary electors and, in the case of a local government election, it is the register of local government electors (although an application under the Representation of the People Act 2000 Sch 4 may relate to both types of election, in which case the requirement is for the applicant to be registered in both): see the Representation of the People Act 2000 Sch 4 para 4(1)(a). As to the meaning of the 'register of electors', in relation to a European parliamentary election, see PARA 111 note 4. As to the meaning of 'register', for the purposes of a Welsh Assembly election, see PARA 367 note 7. As to registration as an elector see PARA 113 et seq; and as to the registers of electors maintained by registration officers see PARA 143 et seq.

8   Representation of the People Act 2000 Sch 4 para 4(1)(b) (amended by the Electoral Administration Act 2006 s 14(2)(a), (8)); European Parliamentary Elections Regulations 2004, SI 2004/293, Sch 2 para 4(1)(b) (as substituted: see note 1); National Assembly for Wales (Representation of the People) Order 2007, SI 2007/236, art 9(1)(c). In the case of a parliamentary or local government election, the application referred to in the text must meet the prescribed requirements: see the Representation of the People Act 2000 Sch 4 para 4(1)(b) (as so amended). For the purposes of Sch 4, 'prescribed' means prescribed by regulations (see the Representation of the People Act 1983 s 202(1); definition applied by virtue of the Representation of the People Act 2000 Sch 4 para 1(2)); and, accordingly, the text refers to the requirements set out in the Representation of the People (England and Wales) Regulations 2001, SI 2001/341, Pt IV (regs 50–63A). In the case of a European parliamentary election, the application referred to in the text must meet the requirements of the European Parliamentary Elections Regulations 2004, SI 2004/293, Sch 2: see Sch 2 para 4(1)(b) (as so substituted). In the case of a Welsh Assembly election, the application referred to in the text must meet the requirements of the National Assembly for Wales (Representation of the People) Order 2007, SI 2007/236, Sch 1: see art 9(1)(c).

    Where an application is required to contain a signature and date of birth, the information must be set out in a manner that is sufficiently clear and unambiguous as to be capable of electronic scanning into his record: Representation of the People (England and Wales) Regulations 2001, SI 2001/341, reg 51(3A) (reg 51(3A), (3B) added, by SI 2006/2910); European Parliamentary Elections Regulations 2004, SI 2004/293, Sch 2 para 17(4) (as so substituted); National Assembly for Wales (Representation of the People) Order 2007, SI 2007/236, Sch 1 para 1(3). This requirement is met by configuring the information as follows:

    (1)   the signature must appear against a background of white unlined paper of at least five

centimetres long and two centimetres high (Representation of the People (England and Wales) Regulations 2001, SI 2001/341, reg 51(3A)(a) (as so added); European Parliamentary Elections Regulations 2004, SI 2004/293, Sch 2 para 17(4)(a) (as so substituted); National Assembly for Wales (Representation of the People) Order 2007, SI 2007/236, Sch 1 para 1(3)(a)); and

(2) the applicant's date of birth must be set out numerically configured in the sequence of date, month and year, namely [d][d][m][m][y][y][y][y] (Representation of the People (England and Wales) Regulations 2001, SI 2001/341, reg 51(3A)(b) (as so added); European Parliamentary Elections Regulations 2004, SI 2004/293, Sch 2 para 17(4)(b) (as so substituted); National Assembly for Wales (Representation of the People) Order 2007, SI 2007/236, Sch 1 para 1(3)(b)).

The registration officer may dispense with the requirement under the Representation of the People Act 2000 Sch 4 para 4(1)(b), the European Parliamentary Elections Regulations 2004, SI 2004/293, Sch 2 para 4(1)(b), or the National Assembly for Wales (Representation of the People) Order 2007, SI 2007/236, art 9(1)(c), as the case may be, for the applicant to provide a signature, if he is satisfied that the applicant is unable to provide a signature because of any disability the applicant has, or is unable to provide a signature because the applicant is unable to read or write, or is unable to sign in a consistent and distinctive way because of any such disability or inability: Representation of the People Act 2000 Sch 4 para 4(5) (added by the Electoral Administration Act 2006 s 14(2)(c), (8)); European Parliamentary Elections Regulations 2004, SI 2004/293, Sch 2 para 4(6) (as so substituted); National Assembly for Wales (Representation of the People) Order 2007, SI 2007/236, art 9(5). Where the application contains a request that the registration officer waive the requirement for a signature, head (1) above does not apply: Representation of the People (England and Wales) Regulations 2001, SI 2001/341, reg 51(3B) (as so added); European Parliamentary Elections Regulations 2004, SI 2004/293, Sch 2 para 17(5) (as so substituted); National Assembly for Wales (Representation of the People) Order 2007, SI 2007/236, Sch 1 para 1(4). As to the meaning of 'disability' for these purposes see PARA 367 note 8.

The registration officer may satisfy himself:

(a) that an application under the Representation of the People Act 2000 Sch 4, or the European Parliamentary Elections Regulations 2004, SI 2004/293, Sch 2, or the National Assembly for Wales (Representation of the People) Order 2007, SI 2007/236, art 9, as the case may be, meets any requirements that it has been signed by the applicant and states his date of birth by referring to any signature and date of birth either previously provided by the applicant to the registration officer or to the returning officer or previously provided by the applicant to the council which appointed him (see PARA 142), which the registration officer is authorised to inspect for the purposes of his registration duties (Representation of the People (England and Wales) Regulations 2001, SI 2001/341, reg 51A(a) (reg 51A added by SI 2006/752; and substituted by SI 2006/2910); European Parliamentary Elections Regulations 2004, SI 2004/293, Sch 2 para 19(a) (as so substituted); National Assembly for Wales (Representation of the People) Order 2007, SI 2007/236, Sch 1 para 1(6)(a)); and

(b) as to whether the applicant is unable to provide a signature or a consistent signature due to any disability or inability to read or write (Representation of the People (England and Wales) Regulations 2001, SI 2001/341, reg 51A(b) (reg 51A as so added and substituted); European Parliamentary Elections Regulations 2004, SI 2004/293, Sch 2 para 19(b) (as so substituted); National Assembly for Wales (Representation of the People) Order 2007, SI 2007/236, Sch 1 para 1(6)(b)).

As to the provisions made for the initial and continuing capture of the personal identifiers of those who are existing absent voters see PARA 366.

9 As to voting by proxy see PARA 374 et seq.

10 Representation of the People Act 2000 Sch 4 para 4(2); European Parliamentary Elections Regulations 2004, SI 2004/293, Sch 2 para 4(2) (as substituted: see note 1); National Assembly for Wales (Representation of the People) Order 2007, SI 2007/236, art 9(1).

Such an application must be refused if it is received by the registration officer after 5 pm on the sixth day before the date of the poll at the election for which it is made: Representation of the People (England and Wales) Regulations 2001, SI 2001/341, reg 56(3) (reg 56(3) substituted by SI 2006/752); European Parliamentary Elections Regulations 2004, SI 2004/293, Sch 2 para 26(3) (as so substituted); National Assembly for Wales (Representation of the People) Order 2007, SI 2007/236, Sch 1 para 7(2). Where a registration officer refuses such an application, he must notify the applicant of his decision and the reason for it: Representation of the People (England and Wales) Regulations 2001, SI 2001/341, reg 57(4); European

Parliamentary Elections Regulations 2004, SI 2004/293, Sch 2 para 27(3) (as so substituted); National Assembly for Wales (Representation of the People) Order 2007, SI 2007/236, Sch 1 para 8(4).

Where an application is made under the Representation of the People Act 2000 Sch 4 para 4(2), under the European Parliamentary Elections Regulations 2004, SI 2004/293, Sch 2 para 4(2), or under the National Assembly for Wales (Representation of the People) Order 2007, SI 2007/236, art 9(1), as the case may be, on the grounds of the applicant's disability, and where the applicant became disabled after 5 pm on the sixth day before the date of the poll at the election for which it is made, or where such an application is made by a person to whom the Representation of the People Act 2000 Sch 4 para 2(5A), the European Parliamentary Elections Regulations 2004, SI 2004/293, Sch 2 para 2(6), or the National Assembly for Wales (Representation of the People) Order 2007, SI 2007/236, art 7(8) applies (ie a person in a mental hospital who is not a detained offender or on remand but who is liable to be detained in the mental hospital in question: see PARAS 363 note 1, 364 note 1, 365 note 1), the application must be refused if it is received after 5 pm on the day of the poll at the election for which it is made: Representation of the People (England and Wales) Regulations 2001, SI 2001/341, reg 56(3A) (reg 56(3A) added by SI 2006/752; and substituted by SI 2006/2910); European Parliamentary Elections Regulations 2004, SI 2004/293, Sch 2 para 26(4) (as so substituted); National Assembly for Wales (Representation of the People) Order 2007, SI 2007/236, Sch 1 para 7(3) (amended by SI 2010/2931). This restriction applies also to applications for the appointment of a proxy to vote at a particular election under the Representation of the People Act 2000 Sch 4 para 6(8) (made by virtue of an application under Sch 4 para 4(2)), to applications under the European Parliamentary Elections Regulations 2004, SI 2004/293, Sch 2 para 6(7) (made by virtue of an application under Sch 2 para 4(2)), and to applications under the National Assembly for Wales (Representation of the People) Order 2007, SI 2007/236, art 11(7) (made by virtue of an application under art 9(1)): see PARA 375.

11 Representation of the People Act 2000 Sch 4 para 4(2)(a); European Parliamentary Elections Regulations 2004, SI 2004/293, Sch 2 para 4(2)(a) (as substituted: see note 1); National Assembly for Wales (Representation of the People) Order 2007, SI 2007/236, art 9(1)(a). As to the appropriate rules referred to in the text, in relation to a parliamentary or local government election, see PARA 363 note 2; in relation to a Welsh Assembly election, see PARA 364 note 2; and, in relation to a European parliamentary election, see PARA 365 note 1.

12 Representation of the People Act 2000 Sch 4 para 4(2)(b); European Parliamentary Elections Regulations 2004, SI 2004/293, Sch 2 para 4(2)(b) (as substituted: see note 1); National Assembly for Wales (Representation of the People) Order 2007, SI 2007/236, art 9(1)(b). As to the registers mentioned in the text see note 7.

13 Representation of the People Act 2000 Sch 4 para 4(2)(c) (amended by the Electoral Administration Act 2006 s 14(2)(b), (8)); European Parliamentary Elections Regulations 2004, SI 2004/293, Sch 2 para 4(2)(c) (as substituted: see note 1); National Assembly for Wales (Representation of the People) Order 2007, SI 2007/236, art 9(1)(c). As to the requirements so prescribed, in the case of a parliamentary or local government election, see note 8. In the case of a European parliamentary election, the application referred to in the text must meet the requirements of the European Parliamentary Elections Regulations 2004, SI 2004/293, Sch 2: see Sch 2 para 4(2)(c) (as so substituted). In the case of a Welsh Assembly election, the application referred to in the text must meet the requirements of the National Assembly for Wales (Representation of the People) Order 2007, SI 2007/236, Sch 1: see art 9(1)(c). The registration officer may dispense with the requirement under the Representation of the People Act 2000 Sch 4 para 4(2)(c), the European Parliamentary Elections Regulations 2004, SI 2004/293, Sch 2 para 4(2)(c), or the National Assembly for Wales (Representation of the People) Order 2007, SI 2007/236, art 9(1)(c), as the case may be, for the applicant to provide a signature, if he is satisfied that the applicant is unable to provide a signature because of any disability the applicant has, or is unable to provide a signature because the applicant is unable to read or write, or is unable to sign in a consistent and distinctive way because of any such disability or inability: Representation of the People Act 2000 Sch 4 para 4(5) (as added: see note 8); European Parliamentary Elections Regulations 2004, SI 2004/293, Sch 2 para 4(6) (as so substituted); National Assembly for Wales (Representation of the People) Order 2007, SI 2007/236, art 9(5). As to additional requirements to be included in applications to vote by proxy at a particular election see PARA 372.

14 As to the meaning of 'anonymous entry' in relation to a register of electors see PARA 148.

15 Representation of the People Act 2000 Sch 4 para 4(2A) (added by the Electoral Administration Act 2006 s 10(2), Sch 1 paras 19, 21); European Parliamentary Elections Regulations 2004, SI 2004/293, Sch 2 para 4(3) (as substituted: see note 1); National Assembly for Wales (Representation of the People) Order 2007, SI 2007/236, art 9(2). As to the requirements so

prescribed, in the case of a parliamentary or local government election, see note 8. In the case of a European parliamentary election, the application referred to in the text must meet the requirements of the European Parliamentary Elections Regulations 2004, SI 2004/293, Sch 2: see Sch 2 para 4(3) (as so substituted). In the case of a Welsh Assembly election, the application referred to in the text must meet the requirements of the National Assembly for Wales (Representation of the People) Order 2007, SI 2007/236, Sch 1: see art 9(2).

16 Ie the record kept, in relation to a parliamentary or local government election, under the Representation of the People Act 2000 Sch 4 para 3, or, in relation to a European parliamentary election, under the European Parliamentary Elections Regulations 2004, SI 2004/293, Sch 2 para 3, or, in relation to a Welsh Assembly election, under the National Assembly for Wales (Representation of the People) Order 2007, SI 2007/236, art 8 (see PARA 370), as the case may be: see the Representation of the People Act 2000 Sch 4 para 4(3); the European Parliamentary Elections Regulations 2004, SI 2004/293, Sch 2 para 4(4) (as substituted: see note 1); and the National Assembly for Wales (Representation of the People) Order 2007, SI 2007/236, art 9(3).

17 Representation of the People Act 2000 Sch 4 para 4(3); European Parliamentary Elections Regulations 2004, SI 2004/293, Sch 2 para 4(4) (as substituted: see note 1); National Assembly for Wales (Representation of the People) Order 2007, SI 2007/236, art 9(3).

18 Representation of the People Act 2000 Sch 4 para 4(3)(a); European Parliamentary Elections Regulations 2004, SI 2004/293, Sch 2 para 4(4)(a) (as substituted: see note 1); National Assembly for Wales (Representation of the People) Order 2007, SI 2007/236, art 9(3)(a). Except where an applicant has, or has applied for, an anonymous entry, an application for a ballot paper to be sent to a different address from that shown in the record must set out why the applicant's circumstances will be or are likely to be such that he requires his ballot paper to be sent to that address: Representation of the People (England and Wales) Regulations 2001, SI 2001/341, reg 51B(1)(a), (2) (reg 51B added by SI 2006/752; and renumbered by SI 2006/2910); European Parliamentary Elections Regulations 2004, SI 2004/293, Sch 2 para 21(1)(a), (2) (as so substituted); National Assembly for Wales (Representation of the People) Order 2007, SI 2007/236, Sch 1 para 1(8)(a)(i), (b).

Where the registration officer grants such an application made by a person shown in the record as voting by post, he must notify the applicant of this: Representation of the People (England and Wales) Regulations 2001, SI 2001/341, reg 57(4A)(a) (added by SI 2006/752); European Parliamentary Elections Regulations 2004, SI 2004/293, Sch 2 para 27(4)(a) (as so substituted); National Assembly for Wales (Representation of the People) Order 2007, SI 2007/236, Sch 1 para 8(5)(a).

19 Representation of the People Act 2000 Sch 4 para 4(3)(b); European Parliamentary Elections Regulations 2004, SI 2004/293, Sch 2 para 4(4)(b) (as substituted: see note 1); National Assembly for Wales (Representation of the People) Order 2007, SI 2007/236, art 9(3)(b).

20 Representation of the People Act 2000 Sch 4 para 4(3); European Parliamentary Elections Regulations 2004, SI 2004/293, Sch 2 para 4(4) (as substituted: see note 1); National Assembly for Wales (Representation of the People) Order 2007, SI 2007/236, art 9(3). Such an application must be refused for the purposes of any particular election if it is received by the registration officer after 5 pm on the eleventh day before the date of the poll at that election: Representation of the People (England and Wales) Regulations 2001, SI 2001/341, reg 56(1) (amended by SI 2006/752); European Parliamentary Elections Regulations 2004, SI 2004/293, Sch 2 para 26(1) (as so substituted); National Assembly for Wales (Representation of the People) Order 2007, SI 2007/236, art 15(2), Sch 1 para 7(4) (amended by SI 2010/2931). Where the registration officer refuses an application for an absent vote, he must notify the applicant of his decision and of the reason for it: Representation of the People (England and Wales) Regulations 2001, SI 2001/341, reg 57(4); European Parliamentary Elections Regulations 2004, SI 2004/293, Sch 2 para 27(3) (as so substituted); National Assembly for Wales (Representation of the People) Order 2007, SI 2007/236, Sch 1 para 8(8).

21 Representation of the People Act 2000 Sch 4 para 4(4); European Parliamentary Elections Regulations 2004, SI 2004/293, Sch 2 para 4(5) (as substituted: see note 1); National Assembly for Wales (Representation of the People) Order 2007, SI 2007/236, art 9(4).

22 Representation of the People Act 2000 Sch 4 para 4(4)(a); European Parliamentary Elections Regulations 2004, SI 2004/293, Sch 2 para 4(5)(a) (as substituted: see note 1); National Assembly for Wales (Representation of the People) Order 2007, SI 2007/236, art 9(4)(a). As to the requirements so prescribed, in the case of a parliamentary or local government election, see note 8. In the case of a European parliamentary election, the application referred to in the text must meet the requirements of the European Parliamentary Elections Regulations 2004, SI 2004/293, Sch 2: see Sch 2 para 4(5)(a) (as so substituted). In the case of a Welsh Assembly

election, the application referred to in the text must meet the requirements of the National Assembly for Wales (Representation of the People) Order 2007, SI 2007/236, Sch 1: see art 9(4)(a).

23 Representation of the People Act 2000 Sch 4 para 4(4)(b); European Parliamentary Elections Regulations 2004, SI 2004/293, Sch 2 para 4(5)(b) (as substituted: see note 1); National Assembly for Wales (Representation of the People) Order 2007, SI 2007/236, art 9(4)(b).

24 Applications made under the Representation of the People Act 2000 Sch 4, or the European Parliamentary Elections Regulations 2004, SI 2004/293, Sch 2 Pt 2 (Sch 2 paras 12–34), or the National Assembly for Wales (Representation of the People) Order 2007, SI 2007/236, art 9, must comply with the requirements, in relation to a parliamentary or local government election, of the Representation of the People (England and Wales) Regulations 2001, SI 2001/341, reg 51, or, in relation to a European parliamentary election, of the European Parliamentary Elections Regulations 2004, SI 2004/293, Sch 2 para 17, or, in relation to a Welsh Assembly election, of the National Assembly for Wales (Representation of the People) Order 2007, SI 2007/236, Sch 1 para 1, as well as such further requirements in the Representation of the People (England and Wales) Regulations 2001, SI 2001/341, Pt IV, or the European Parliamentary Elections Regulations 2004, SI 2004/293, Sch 2 Pt 2, as are relevant to the application: Representation of the People (England and Wales) Regulations 2001, SI 2001/341, reg 51(1); European Parliamentary Elections Regulations 2004, SI 2004/293, Sch 2 para 17(1) (as substituted: see note 1); National Assembly for Wales (Representation of the People) Order 2007, SI 2007/236, art 13(1). As to additional requirements for applications to vote by proxy for a definite or indefinite period see PARAS 368–369.

25 Representation of the People (England and Wales) Regulations 2001, SI 2001/341, reg 51(2)(a); European Parliamentary Elections Regulations 2004, SI 2004/293, Sch 2 para 17(2)(a) (as substituted: see note 1); National Assembly for Wales (Representation of the People) Order 2007, SI 2007/236, Sch 1 para 1(1)(a).

26 Representation of the People (England and Wales) Regulations 2001, SI 2001/341, reg 51(2)(b) (amended by SI 2006/752); European Parliamentary Elections Regulations 2004, SI 2004/293, Sch 2 para 17(2)(b) (as substituted: see note 1); National Assembly for Wales (Representation of the People) Order 2007, SI 2007/236, Sch 1 para 1(1)(b). Head (ii) in the text does not apply in the case of an application under the Representation of the People Act 2000 Sch 4 para 7(4), (7), or the European Parliamentary Elections Regulations 2004, SI 2004/293, Sch 2 para 7(4), (7), or the National Assembly for Wales (Representation of the People) Order 2007, SI 2007/236, art 12(4), (7) (voting as proxy for an indefinite period or for a particular period or at a particular election: see PARA 378).

For the purposes of the National Assembly for Wales (Representation of the People) Order 2007, SI 2007/236, Sch 1 para 1(1)(b), the address in respect of which the applicant is registered or has applied to be (or is treated as having applied to be) registered includes:

(1)   in the case of a service voter, the address given in the service declaration in accordance with the Representation of the People Act 1983 s 16(d) (see PARA 127) (National Assembly for Wales (Representation of the People) Order 2007, SI 2007/236, Sch 1 para 1(9)(a));

(2)   in the case of a person to whom the Representation of the People Act 1983 s 7 (deemed residence for persons in mental hospitals who are not detained offenders or on remand: see PARA 119) applies, the address of the mental hospital or the address shown on the declaration of local connection in accordance with s 7B(3)(d) (see PARA 122) (National Assembly for Wales (Representation of the People) Order 2007, SI 2007/236, Sch 1 para 1(9)(b));

(3)   in the case of a person to whom the Representation of the People Act 1983 s 7A (deemed residence for persons on remand: see PARA 120) applies, the address of the place at which he is detained or the address shown on the declaration of local connection in accordance with s 7B(3)(d) (National Assembly for Wales (Representation of the People) Order 2007, SI 2007/236, Sch 1 para 1(9)(c)); and

(4)   in the case of a homeless person, the address shown on the declaration of local connection in accordance with the Representation of the People Act 1983 s 7B(3)(d) (National Assembly for Wales (Representation of the People) Order 2007, SI 2007/236, Sch 1 para 1(9)(d)).

27 Representation of the People (England and Wales) Regulations 2001, SI 2001/341, reg 51(2)(d) (reg 51(2)(d) amended, reg 51AA added, by SI 2006/2910); European Parliamentary Elections Regulations 2004, SI 2004/293, Sch 2 para 17(2)(d) (as substituted: see note 1); National Assembly for Wales (Representation of the People) Order 2007, SI 2007/236, Sch 1 para 1(1)(d).

In the case of an application to vote by post made under the Representation of the People Act 2000 Sch 4 para 4(1), the European Parliamentary Elections Regulations 2004, SI 2004/293,

Sch 2 para 4(1), or the National Assembly for Wales (Representation of the People) Order 2007, SI 2007/236, art 9(1) (see the text and notes 1–13), as the case may be, where the addresses stated in accordance with head (ii) in the text, and head (iii) in the text, are different, except where an applicant has, or has applied for, an anonymous entry, the application must set out why the applicant's circumstances will be or are likely to be such that he requires the ballot paper to be sent to the address stated in accordance with head (iii) in the text: see the Representation of the People (England and Wales) Regulations 2001, SI 2001/341, reg 51AA(1)–(3) (as so added); the European Parliamentary Elections Regulations 2004, SI 2004/293, Sch 2 para 20(1)–(3) (as so substituted); and the National Assembly for Wales (Representation of the People) Order 2007, SI 2007/236, Sch 1 para 1(7)(a)(i), (b).

28   Representation of the People (England and Wales) Regulations 2001, SI 2001/341, reg 51(2)(e); European Parliamentary Elections Regulations 2004, SI 2004/293, Sch 2 para 17(2)(e) (as substituted: see note 1); National Assembly for Wales (Representation of the People) Order 2007, SI 2007/236, Sch 1 para 1(1)(e).

29   Ie under the Representation of the People Act 2000 Sch 4 para 4, the European Parliamentary Elections Regulations 2004, SI 2004/293, Sch 2 para 4, or the National Assembly for Wales (Representation of the People) Order 2007, SI 2007/236, art 9 (see the text and notes 1–23), as the case may be: see the Representation of the People (England and Wales) Regulations 2001, SI 2001/341, reg 51(2)(f) (reg 51(2)(f), (g) added by SI 2006/2910); the European Parliamentary Elections Regulations 2004, SI 2004/293, Sch 2 para 17(2)(f) (as substituted: see note 1); and the National Assembly for Wales (Representation of the People) Order 2007, SI 2007/236, Sch 1 para 1(1)(f).

30   Representation of the People (England and Wales) Regulations 2001, SI 2001/341, reg 51(2)(f) (as added: see note 29); European Parliamentary Elections Regulations 2004, SI 2004/293, Sch 2 para 17(2)(f) (as substituted: see note 1); National Assembly for Wales (Representation of the People) Order 2007, SI 2007/236, Sch 1 para 1(1)(f).

31   Representation of the People (England and Wales) Regulations 2001, SI 2001/341, reg 51(2)(g) (as added: see note 29); European Parliamentary Elections Regulations 2004, SI 2004/293, Sch 2 para 17(2)(g) (as substituted: see note 1); National Assembly for Wales (Representation of the People) Order 2007, SI 2007/236, Sch 1 para 1(1)(g).

32   Representation of the People (England and Wales) Regulations 2001, SI 2001/341, reg 51(5)(b); European Parliamentary Elections Regulations 2004, SI 2004/293, Sch 2 para 17(7)(b) (as substituted: see note 1).

33   Representation of the People (England and Wales) Regulations 2001, SI 2001/341, reg 51(5)(a); European Parliamentary Elections Regulations 2004, SI 2004/293, Sch 2 para 17(7)(a) (as substituted: see note 1); National Assembly for Wales (Representation of the People) Order 2007, SI 2007/236, Sch 1 para 1(5)(b).

34   See the Representation of the People (England and Wales) Regulations 2001, SI 2001/341, reg 51(5); the European Parliamentary Elections Regulations 2004, SI 2004/293, Sch 2 para 17(9) (as substituted: see note 1); and the National Assembly for Wales (Representation of the People) Order 2007, SI 2007/236, Sch 1 para 1(5).

35   Representation of the People (England and Wales) Regulations 2001, SI 2001/341, reg 51(3) (substituted by SI 2006/2910); European Parliamentary Elections Regulations 2004, SI 2004/293, Sch 2 para 17(3) (as substituted: see note 1); National Assembly for Wales (Representation of the People) Order 2007, SI 2007/236, Sch 1 para 1(2).

36   See the Representation of the People (England and Wales) Regulations 2001, SI 2001/341, regs 51(6), 52; the European Parliamentary Elections Regulations 2004, SI 2004/293, Sch 2 paras 17(8), 22; the National Assembly for Wales (Representation of the People) Order 2007, SI 2007/236, Sch 1 paras 1, 3; and PARA 375.

37   Representation of the People (England and Wales) Regulations 2001, SI 2001/341, reg 57(1) (amended by SI 2006/752); European Parliamentary Elections Regulations 2004, SI 2004/293, Sch 2 para 27(1) (as substituted: see note 1); National Assembly for Wales (Representation of the People) Order 2007, SI 2007/236, Sch 1 para 8(1). Where the registration officer at a parliamentary or Welsh Assembly election is not the acting returning officer for any constituency (or part of such a constituency), or where the registration officer at a European parliamentary election is not the local returning officer for any local counting area (or part of such an area), in the area for which he is the registration officer, he must send to that officer details of any application to vote by post which he has granted as soon as practicable after doing so: Representation of the People (England and Wales) Regulations 2001, SI 2001/341, reg 57(6); European Parliamentary Elections Regulations 2004, SI 2004/293, Sch 2 para 27(8) (as so substituted); National Assembly for Wales (Representation of the People) Order 2007, SI 2007/236, Sch 1 para 8(9). As to the meaning of 'local counting area' see PARA 139 note 1. As

to local returning officers appointed for the purposes of elections to the European Parliament see PARA 360. As to notification by the registration officer at a Welsh Assembly election see PARA 367 note 35.

38 Representation of the People (England and Wales) Regulations 2001, SI 2001/341, reg 57(4); European Parliamentary Elections Regulations 2004, SI 2004/293, Sch 2 para 27(3) (as substituted: see note 1); National Assembly for Wales (Representation of the People) Order 2007, SI 2007/236, Sch 1 para 8(4).

39 See PARA 172 et seq.

372. Additional requirements for applications for a proxy vote at a particular election. An application to vote by proxy at a particular election[1] must set out why the applicant's circumstances on the date of the poll for that election in respect of which it is made will be or are likely to be such that he cannot reasonably be expected to vote in person at his allotted polling station[2]. Where such an application is made on the grounds of the applicant's disability[3], and where it is made after 5 pm on the sixth day before the date of the poll at the election for which it is made[4], such an application must be attested and signed by[5]:

(1)   a registered medical practitioner[6];

(2)   a registered nurse[7];

(3)   a registered dentist[8], a registered dispensing optician or registered optometrist[9], a registered pharmacist[10], a registered osteopath[11], or a registered chiropractor[12];

(4)   a Christian Science practitioner[13];

(5)   a person registered as a member of a profession to which the Health and Social Work Professions Order 2001[14] for the time being extends[15];

(6)   the person carrying on a care home registered under Part II of the Care Standards Act 2000[16];

(7)   the warden of premises forming one of a group of premises provided for persons of pensionable age or disabled persons for which there is a resident warden, where the applicant states that he resides in such premises[17];

(8)   a manager within the meaning of the Mental Health Act 1983[18], or a person authorised to act on behalf of such a manager for these purposes[19]; or

(9)   a person registered in the register for social workers maintained by the Care Council for Wales ('Cyngor Gofal Cymru')[20].

A person who qualifies:

(a)   by virtue of any of heads (1) to (5) above may not attest an application for these purposes, however, unless he is treating the applicant for the disability specified in the application[21], or unless the applicant is receiving care from him in respect of that disability[22], or unless the person is a social worker who qualifies by virtue of head (5) above, and has arranged care or assistance for the applicant in respect of that disability[23];

(b)   by virtue of head (9) above may not attest an application for these purposes unless he is treating the applicant for the disability specified in the application[24], or unless the applicant is receiving care from him in respect of that disability[25], or unless he has arranged care or assistance for the person in respect of his disability[26].

The person attesting the application must state:

(i)   his name and address and the qualification by virtue of which he attests the application[27], unless he qualifies by virtue of head (8) above[28];

(ii)   where the person who attests the application is a person who qualifies by virtue of head (a) above, that he is treating the applicant for the disability specified in the application[29], or that the applicant is receiving care from him in respect of that disability[30];

(iii)   where the person who attests the application is a person who qualifies by virtue of head (b) above, that he is treating the applicant for the disability specified in the application[31], or that the applicant is receiving care from him in respect of that disability[32], or that he has arranged care or assistance for the applicant in respect of that disability[33];

(iv)   that, to the best of his knowledge and belief, the applicant has the disability specified in the application, and that he cannot reasonably be expected to go in person to his allotted polling station, or to vote unaided there by reason of that disability[34]; and

(v)   that, to the best of his knowledge and belief, the disability specified in the application is likely to continue either indefinitely or for a period specified by the person attesting the application[35].

In addition[36], the person who attests the application must state, to the best of his knowledge and belief, the date upon which the applicant became disabled[37].

However, the provisions as to attestation[38] do not apply where: (A) the application is based on the applicant's blindness and the applicant is registered as a blind person by the local authority[39] which is specified in the application[40]; or (B) where the application states that the applicant is in receipt of the higher rate of the mobility component of a disability living allowance[41] because of the disability specified in the application[42].

1   Ie an application, at a particular parliamentary or local government election, under the Representation of the People Act 2000 s 12, Sch 4 para 4(2), or, at a particular European parliamentary election, under the European Parliamentary Elections Regulations 2004, SI 2004/293, reg 10, Sch 2 para 4(2), or, at a particular Welsh Assembly election, under the National Assembly for Wales (Representation of the People) Order 2007, SI 2007/236, art 9(1) (see PARA 371): see the Representation of the People (England and Wales) Regulations 2001, SI 2001/341, reg 55(1) (reg 55 substituted by SI 2006/752); the European Parliamentary Elections Regulations 2004, SI 2004/293, Sch 2 para 25(1) (Sch 2 substituted by SI 2009/186); and the National Assembly for Wales (Representation of the People) Order 2007, SI 2007/236, art 15(2), Sch 1 para 6(1). As to the meaning of 'parliamentary election' see PARA 9. As to the meaning of 'local government election' see PARA 11; definition applied by virtue of the Representation of the People Act 2000 Sch 4 para 1(2). See also PARA 363 note 1. As to the meaning of 'Assembly election' in the context of Welsh Assembly elections see PARA 3 note 2; but in relation to a particular Welsh Assembly election see PARA 371 note 4. As to European parliamentary elections see PARA 217 et seq.
    The Representation of the People Act 2000 s 12, Sch 4 are applied and modified for the purpose of local authority mayoral elections in England and Wales by the Local Authorities (Mayoral Elections) (England and Wales) Regulations 2007, SI 2007/1024, reg 3(2)–(5), Sch 2 Table 3 (see PARA 11 note 14); and they have effect for the purposes of local authority referendums, subject to the modifications specified, in relation to Wales, by the Local Authorities (Conduct of Referendums) (Wales) Regulations 2008, SI 2008/1848, reg 8(2), Sch 4 Table 2, and, in relation to England, by the Local Authorities (Conduct of Referendums) (England) Regulations 2012, SI 2012/323, regs 8(2), 11–13, Sch 4 Table 3 (see PARA 15 note 2). The Representation of the People (England and Wales) Regulations 2001, SI 2001/341, reg 55 also has effect for the purposes of local authority referendums, subject to the modifications specified, in relation to Wales, by the Local Authorities (Conduct of Referendums) (Wales) Regulations 2008, SI 2008/1848, reg 8(2), Sch 4 Table 5, and, in relation to England, by the Local Authorities (Conduct of Referendums) (England) Regulations 2012, SI 2012/323, regs 8(2), 11–13, Sch 4 Table 6 (see PARA 15 note 2).

2   Representation of the People (England and Wales) Regulations 2001, SI 2001/341, reg 55(1) (as substituted: see note 1); European Parliamentary Elections Regulations 2004, SI 2004/293, Sch 2 para 25(1) (as substituted: see note 1); National Assembly for Wales (Representation of the People) Order 2007, SI 2007/236, art 15(2), Sch 1 para 6(1). As to the meaning of 'his

allotted polling station', in relation to an elector, see PARA 368 note 32. As to the date of the poll at a parliamentary general election or by-election see PARA 195; as to the date of the poll at local government elections (including elections to fill vacancies) see PARAS 206–209; as to the date of the poll at Welsh Assembly elections (including elections to fill vacancies in an Assembly constituency) see PARAS 213–214; and as to the date of the poll at a European parliamentary election see PARA 222. Any application for absent voting must also satisfy the general requirements: see PARA 371. As to the offence in respect of false statements made in any declaration or form used in connection with absent voting see PARA 735.

The Representation of the People (England and Wales) Regulations 2001, SI 2001/341, reg 55, the European Parliamentary Elections Regulations 2004, SI 2004/293, Sch 2 para 25, and the National Assembly for Wales (Representation of the People) Order 2007, SI 2007/236, Sch 1 para 6, do not apply where the applicant has an anonymous entry: Representation of the People (England and Wales) Regulations 2001, SI 2001/341, reg 55(1A), (6) (reg 55 as so substituted; reg 55(1A), (4)–(6) added by SI 2006/2910); European Parliamentary Elections Regulations 2004, SI 2004/293, Sch 2 para 25(6) (as so substituted); National Assembly for Wales (Representation of the People) Order 2007, SI 2007/236, Sch 1 para 6(6). As to the meaning of 'anonymous entry', in relation to a register of electors, see PARA 148.

3   Representation of the People (England and Wales) Regulations 2001, SI 2001/341, reg 55(2)(a) (reg 55 as substituted (see note 1); reg 55(2)(a) amended by SI 2006/2910); European Parliamentary Elections Regulations 2004, SI 2004/293, Sch 2 para 25(2)(a) (as substituted: see note 1); National Assembly for Wales (Representation of the People) Order 2007, SI 2007/236, Sch 1 para 6(2)(a). As to the meaning of 'disability' for these purposes see PARA 367 note 8.

4   Representation of the People (England and Wales) Regulations 2001, SI 2001/341, reg 55(2)(b) (as substituted: see note 1); European Parliamentary Elections Regulations 2004, SI 2004/293, Sch 2 para 25(2)(b) (as substituted: see note 1); National Assembly for Wales (Representation of the People) Order 2007, SI 2007/236, Sch 1 para 6(2)(b).

Where an application under the Representation of the People Act 2000 Sch 4 para 4(2) is made by a person to whom Sch 4 para 2(5A) applies, or where an application under the European Parliamentary Elections Regulations 2004, SI 2004/293, Sch 2 para 4(2) is made by a person to whom Sch 2 para 2(6) applies, or where an application under the National Assembly for Wales (Representation of the People) Order 2007, SI 2007/236, art 9(1) is made by a person to whom art 7(7) applies (ie persons in mental hospitals who are not detained offenders or on remand but who are liable to be detained in the mental hospital in question: see PARAS 363 note 1, 364 note 1, 365 note 1, 371 note 10), after 5 pm on the sixth day before the date of the poll at the election for which it is made, then (Representation of the People (England and Wales) Regulations 2001, SI 2001/341, reg 55(4) (reg 55 as so substituted; reg 55(4) as added (see note 2); European Parliamentary Elections Regulations 2004, SI 2004/293, Sch 2 para 25(4) (as so substituted); National Assembly for Wales (Representation of the People) Order 2007, SI 2007/236, Sch 1 para 6(4)):

(1)   the application must additionally state the name and address of the hospital at which the applicant is liable to be detained (Representation of the People (England and Wales) Regulations 2001, SI 2001/341, reg 55(5)(a) (reg 55 as so substituted; reg 55(5) as so added); European Parliamentary Elections Regulations 2004, SI 2004/293, Sch 2 para 25(5)(a) (as so substituted); National Assembly for Wales (Representation of the People) Order 2007, SI 2007/236, Sch 1 para 6(5)(a)); and

(2)   the application must be attested by or on behalf of a manager, within the meaning of the Mental Health Act 1983 s 145(1) (see MENTAL HEALTH AND CAPACITY vol 75 (2013) PARA 778), of the hospital at which the applicant is liable to be detained (Representation of the People (England and Wales) Regulations 2001, SI 2001/341, reg 55(5)(b) (reg 55 as so substituted; reg 55(5) as so added); European Parliamentary Elections Regulations 2004, SI 2004/293, Sch 2 para 25(5)(b) (as so substituted); National Assembly for Wales (Representation of the People) Order 2007, SI 2007/236, Sch 1 para 6(5)(b)); and the attestation must state:

(a)   the name of the person attesting the application (Representation of the People (England and Wales) Regulations 2001, SI 2001/341, reg 55(5)(b)(i) (reg 55 as so substituted; reg 55(5) as so added); European Parliamentary Elections Regulations 2004, SI 2004/293, Sch 2 para 25(5)(b)(i) (as so substituted); National Assembly for Wales (Representation of the People) Order 2007, SI 2007/236, Sch 1 para 6(5)(b)(i));

(b)   his position in the hospital at which the applicant is liable to be detained (Representation of the People (England and Wales) Regulations 2001, SI 2001/341, reg 55(5)(b)(ii) (reg 55 as so substituted; reg 55(5) as so added); European Parliamentary Elections Regulations 2004, SI 2004/293, Sch 2

> para 25(5)(b)(iii) (as so substituted); National Assembly for Wales (Representation of the People) Order 2007, SI 2007/236, Sch 1 para 6(5)(b)(ii));
>
> (c) that he is a person authorised to make the attestation (Representation of the People (England and Wales) Regulations 2001, SI 2001/341, reg 55(5)(b)(iii) (reg 55 as so substituted; reg 55(5) as so added); European Parliamentary Elections Regulations 2004, SI 2004/293, Sch 2 para 25(5)(b)(iii) (as so substituted); National Assembly for Wales (Representation of the People) Order 2007, SI 2007/236, Sch 1 para 6(5)(b)(iii)); and
>
> (d) the statutory provision under which the applicant is liable to be detained in the hospital (Representation of the People (England and Wales) Regulations 2001, SI 2001/341, reg 55(5)(b)(iv) (reg 55 as so substituted; reg 55(5) as so added); European Parliamentary Elections Regulations 2004, SI 2004/293, Sch 2 para 25(5)(b)(iv) (as so substituted); National Assembly for Wales (Representation of the People) Order 2007, SI 2007/236, Sch 1 para 6(5)(b)(iv)).

5 Representation of the People (England and Wales) Regulations 2001, SI 2001/341, reg 53(2) (reg 53(2)–(4) substituted by SI 2006/2910); European Parliamentary Elections Regulations 2004, SI 2004/293, Sch 2 para 23(2) (as substituted: see note 1); National Assembly for Wales (Representation of the People) Order 2007, SI 2007/236, Sch 1 para 4(2). Where the circumstances that are set out in the text and notes 3–4 apply, the requirements of the Representation of the People (England and Wales) Regulations 2001, SI 2001/341, reg 53, or of the European Parliamentary Elections Regulations 2004, SI 2004/293, Sch 2 para 23, or of the National Assembly for Wales (Representation of the People) Order 2007, SI 2007/236, Sch 1 paras 1, 4, as the case may be, apply as to the matters to be specified and as to the attestation itself (subject to the exception set out in note 4): Representation of the People (England and Wales) Regulations 2001, SI 2001/341, reg 55(2) (as substituted: see note 1); European Parliamentary Elections Regulations 2004, SI 2004/293, Sch 2 para 25(2) (as so substituted); National Assembly for Wales (Representation of the People) Order 2007, SI 2007/236, Sch 1 para 6(2) (amended by SI 2010/2931). As to the offence of attesting an application when not authorised to do so see PARA 735. See also PARA 368 note 3.

   An application to vote by proxy at a particular election by reason of the applicant's disability must specify the disability by reason of which it is made: Representation of the People (England and Wales) Regulations 2001, SI 2001/341, reg 53(1) (reg 53 as so applied; reg 53(1) amended by SI 2001/1700; SI 2006/2910); European Parliamentary Elections Regulations 2004, SI 2004/293, Sch 2 para 23(1) (Sch 2 as substituted (see note 1); Sch 2 para 23 as so applied); National Assembly for Wales (Representation of the People) Order 2007, SI 2007/236, Sch 1 para 4(1) (as so applied).

6 Representation of the People (England and Wales) Regulations 2001, SI 2001/341, reg 53(2)(a) (as substituted and applied: see note 5); European Parliamentary Elections Regulations 2004, SI 2004/293, Sch 2 para 23(2)(a) (Sch 2 as substituted (see note 1); Sch 2 para 23 as applied (see note 5)); National Assembly for Wales (Representation of the People) Order 2007, SI 2007/236, Sch 1 para 4(2)(a) (as applied: see note 5).

7 Representation of the People (England and Wales) Regulations 2001, SI 2001/341, reg 53(2)(b) (as substituted and applied: see note 5); European Parliamentary Elections Regulations 2004, SI 2004/293, Sch 2 para 23(2)(b) (Sch 2 as substituted (see note 1); Sch 2 para 23 as applied (see note 5)); National Assembly for Wales (Representation of the People) Order 2007, SI 2007/236, Sch 1 para 4(2)(b) (as applied: see note 5).

   Except in relation to a European parliamentary election, the reference in head (2) in the text specifically is to a nurse registered on the register maintained by the Nursery and Midwifery Council under the Nursing and Midwifery Order 2001, SI 2002/253, art 5 (see MEDICAL PROFESSIONS vol 74 (2011) PARA 713), by virtue of qualifications in nursing: see the Representation of the People (England and Wales) Regulations 2001, SI 2001/341, reg 53(2)(b) (as so substituted and applied); and the National Assembly for Wales (Representation of the People) Order 2007, SI 2007/236, Sch 1 para 4(2)(b) (as so applied).

8 Representation of the People (England and Wales) Regulations 2001, SI 2001/341, reg 53(2)(c) (as substituted and applied: see note 5); European Parliamentary Elections Regulations 2004, SI 2004/293, Sch 2 para 23(2)(c) (Sch 2 as substituted (see note 1); Sch 2 para 23 as applied (see note 5)); National Assembly for Wales (Representation of the People) Order 2007, SI 2007/236, Sch 1 para 4(2)(c) (as applied: see note 5). The text refers to a registered dentist as defined by the Dentists Act 1984 s 53(1) (see MEDICAL PROFESSIONS vol 74 (2011) PARA 442): see the Representation of the People (England and Wales) Regulations 2001, SI 2001/341, reg 53(2)(c) (as so substituted and applied); the European Parliamentary Elections Regulations 2004,

SI 2004/293, Sch 2 para 23(2)(c) (as so substituted and applied); and the National Assembly for Wales (Representation of the People) Order 2007, SI 2007/236, Sch 1 para 4(2)(c) (as so applied).

9 Representation of the People (England and Wales) Regulations 2001, SI 2001/341, reg 53(2)(d) (as substituted and applied: see note 5); European Parliamentary Elections Regulations 2004, SI 2004/293, Sch 2 para 23(2)(d) (Sch 2 as substituted (see note 1); Sch 2 para 23 as applied (see note 5)); National Assembly for Wales (Representation of the People) Order 2007, SI 2007/236, Sch 1 para 4(2)(d) (as applied: see note 5). The text refers to a registered dispensing optician or a registered optometrist within the meaning of the Opticians Act 1989 (see MEDICAL PROFESSIONS vol 74 (2011) PARA 343 et seq): see the Representation of the People (England and Wales) Regulations 2001, SI 2001/341, reg 53(2)(d) (as so substituted and applied); the European Parliamentary Elections Regulations 2004, SI 2004/293, Sch 2 para 23(2)(d) (as so substituted and applied); and the National Assembly for Wales (Representation of the People) Order 2007, SI 2007/236, Sch 1 para 4(2)(d) (as so applied).

10 Representation of the People (England and Wales) Regulations 2001, SI 2001/341, reg 53(2)(e) (reg 53(2) as substituted and applied (see note 5); reg 53(2)(e) further substituted by SI 2010/231); European Parliamentary Elections Regulations 2004, SI 2004/293, Sch 2 para 23(2)(e) (Sch 2 as substituted (see note 1); Sch 2 para 23 as applied (see note 5)); National Assembly for Wales (Representation of the People) Order 2007, SI 2007/236, Sch 1 para 4(2)(e) (Sch 1 para 4 as applied (see note 5); Sch 1 para 4(2)(e) substituted by SI 2010/231). The text refers to a registered pharmacist as defined by the Pharmacy Order 2010, SI 2010/231, art 3(1) (see MEDICAL PROFESSIONS vol 74 (2011) PARA 784): see the Representation of the People (England and Wales) Regulations 2001, SI 2001/341, reg 53(2)(e) (as so substituted and applied); the European Parliamentary Elections Regulations 2004, SI 2004/293, Sch 2 para 23(2)(e) (as so substituted and applied); Interpretation Act 1978 s 17(2); and the National Assembly for Wales (Representation of the People) Order 2007, SI 2007/236, Sch 1 para 4(2)(e) (as so substituted and applied).

11 Representation of the People (England and Wales) Regulations 2001, SI 2001/341, reg 53(2)(f) (as substituted and applied: see note 5); European Parliamentary Elections Regulations 2004, SI 2004/293, Sch 2 para 23(2)(f) (Sch 2 as substituted (see note 1); Sch 2 para 23 as applied (see note 5)); National Assembly for Wales (Representation of the People) Order 2007, SI 2007/236, Sch 1 para 4(2)(f) (as applied: see note 5). The text refers to a registered osteopath as defined by the Osteopaths Act 1993 s 41 (see MEDICAL PROFESSIONS vol 74 (2011) PARA 525 et seq): see the Representation of the People (England and Wales) Regulations 2001, SI 2001/341, reg 53(2)(f) (as so substituted and applied); the European Parliamentary Elections Regulations 2004, SI 2004/293, Sch 2 para 23(2)(f) (as so substituted and applied); and the National Assembly for Wales (Representation of the People) Order 2007, SI 2007/236, Sch 1 para 4(2)(f) (as so applied).

12 Representation of the People (England and Wales) Regulations 2001, SI 2001/341, reg 53(2)(g) (as substituted and applied: see note 5); European Parliamentary Elections Regulations 2004, SI 2004/293, Sch 2 para 23(2)(g) (Sch 2 as substituted (see note 1); Sch 2 para 23 as applied (see note 5)); National Assembly for Wales (Representation of the People) Order 2007, SI 2007/236, Sch 1 para 4(2)(g) (as applied: see note 5). The text refers to a registered chiropractor as defined by the Chiropractors Act 1994 s 43 (see MEDICAL PROFESSIONS vol 74 (2011) PARA 603 et seq): see the Representation of the People (England and Wales) Regulations 2001, SI 2001/341, reg 53(2)(g) (as so substituted and applied); the European Parliamentary Elections Regulations 2004, SI 2004/293, Sch 2 para 23(2)(g) (as so substituted and applied); and the National Assembly for Wales (Representation of the People) Order 2007, SI 2007/236, Sch 1 para 4(2)(g) (as so applied).

13 Representation of the People (England and Wales) Regulations 2001, SI 2001/341, reg 53(2)(h) (as substituted and applied: see note 5); European Parliamentary Elections Regulations 2004, SI 2004/293, Sch 2 para 23(2)(h) (Sch 2 as substituted (see note 1); Sch 2 para 23 as applied (see note 5)); National Assembly for Wales (Representation of the People) Order 2007, SI 2007/236, Sch 1 para 4(2)(h) (as applied: see note 5).

14 Ie the Health and Social Work Professions Order 2001, SI 2002/254 (see MEDICAL PROFESSIONS vol 74 (2011) PARA 916 et seq): see the Representation of the People (England and Wales) Regulations 2001, SI 2001/341, reg 53(2)(j) (reg 53(2) as substituted and applied (see note 5); reg 53(2)(j) amended by SI 2012/1479); the European Parliamentary Elections Regulations 2004, SI 2004/293, Sch 2 para 23(2)(j) (Sch 2 as substituted (see note 1); Sch 2 para 23 as applied (see note 5); Sch 2 para 23(2)(j) amended by SI 2012/1479); and the National Assembly for Wales (Representation of the People) Order 2007, SI 2007/236, Sch 1 para 4(2)(j) (Sch 1 para 4 as applied (see note 5); Sch 1 para 4(2)(j) amended by SI 2012/1479).

15 Representation of the People (England and Wales) Regulations 2001, SI 2001/341, reg 53(2)(j) (as substituted, amended and applied: see note 14); European Parliamentary Elections Regulations 2004, SI 2004/293, Sch 2 para 23(2)(j) (as substituted, amended and applied: see note 14); National Assembly for Wales (Representation of the People) Order 2007, SI 2007/236, Sch 1 para 4(2)(j) (as amended and applied: see note 14).

16 Representation of the People (England and Wales) Regulations 2001, SI 2001/341, reg 53(2)(k) (as substituted and applied: see note 5); European Parliamentary Elections Regulations 2004, SI 2004/293, Sch 2 para 23(2)(k) (Sch 2 as substituted (see note 1); Sch 2 para 23 as applied (see note 5)); National Assembly for Wales (Representation of the People) Order 2007, SI 2007/236, Sch 1 para 4(2)(k) (as applied: see note 5). The text refers to a care home registered under the Care Standards Act 2000 Pt II (ss 11–42) (see SOCIAL SERVICES AND COMMUNITY CARE vol 44(2) (Reissue) PARA 1042 et seq): see the Representation of the People (England and Wales) Regulations 2001, SI 2001/341, reg 53(2)(k) (as so substituted and applied); the European Parliamentary Elections Regulations 2004, SI 2004/293, Sch 2 para 23(2)(k) (as so substituted and applied); and the National Assembly for Wales (Representation of the People) Order 2007, SI 2007/236, Sch 1 para 4(2)(k) (as so applied). The European Parliamentary Elections Regulations 2004, SI 2004/293, requires the applicant to state that he resides in such premises before head (6) in the text applies: see Sch 2 para 23(2)(k) (as so substituted and applied); cf head (7) in the text.

17 Representation of the People (England and Wales) Regulations 2001, SI 2001/341, reg 53(2)(l) (as substituted and applied: see note 5); European Parliamentary Elections Regulations 2004, SI 2004/293, Sch 2 para 23(2)(l) (Sch 2 as substituted (see note 1); Sch 2 para 23 as applied (see note 5)); National Assembly for Wales (Representation of the People) Order 2007, SI 2007/236, Sch 1 para 4(2)(l) (as applied: see note 5).

18 Ie within the meaning of the Mental Health Act 1983 s 145(1) (see MENTAL HEALTH AND CAPACITY vol 75 (2013) PARA 778): see the Representation of the People (England and Wales) Regulations 2001, SI 2001/341, reg 53(2)(m) (as substituted and applied: see note 5); the European Parliamentary Elections Regulations 2004, SI 2004/293, Sch 2 para 23(2)(m) (Sch 2 as substituted (see note 1); Sch 2 para 23 as applied (see note 5)); and the National Assembly for Wales (Representation of the People) Order 2007, SI 2007/236, Sch 1 para 4(2)(m) (as applied: see note 5).

19 Representation of the People (England and Wales) Regulations 2001, SI 2001/341, reg 53(2)(m) (as substituted and applied: see note 5); European Parliamentary Elections Regulations 2004, SI 2004/293, Sch 2 para 23(2)(m) (Sch 2 as substituted (see note 1); Sch 2 para 23 as applied (see note 5)); National Assembly for Wales (Representation of the People) Order 2007, SI 2007/236, Sch 1 para 4(2)(m) (as applied: see note 5).

20 Representation of the People (England and Wales) Regulations 2001, SI 2001/341, reg 53(2)(n) (as substituted and applied: see note 5); European Parliamentary Elections Regulations 2004, SI 2004/293, Sch 2 para 23(2)(n)(i) (Sch 2 as substituted (see note 1); Sch 2 para 23 as applied (see note 5); Sch 2 para 23(2)(n) amended by SI 2012/1479); National Assembly for Wales (Representation of the People) Order 2007, SI 2007/236, Sch 1 para 4(2)(n) (as applied: see note 5). The text refers to the register for social workers maintained in accordance with the Care Standards Act 2000 s 56 (see SOCIAL SERVICES AND COMMUNITY CARE): see the Representation of the People (England and Wales) Regulations 2001, SI 2001/341, reg 53(2)(n) (as so substituted and applied); the European Parliamentary Elections Regulations 2004, SI 2004/293, Sch 2 para 23(2)(n)(i) (as so substituted, amended and applied); and the National Assembly for Wales (Representation of the People) Order 2007, SI 2007/236, Sch 1 para 4(2)(n) (as so applied).

21 Representation of the People (England and Wales) Regulations 2001, SI 2001/341, reg 53(3)(a)(i) (as substituted and applied: see note 5); European Parliamentary Elections Regulations 2004, SI 2004/293, Sch 2 para 23(3)(a)(i) (Sch 2 as substituted (see note 1); Sch 2 para 23 as applied (see note 5)); National Assembly for Wales (Representation of the People) Order 2007, SI 2007/236, Sch 1 para 4(3)(a)(i) (as applied: see note 5).

22 Representation of the People (England and Wales) Regulations 2001, SI 2001/341, reg 53(3)(a)(ii) (as substituted and applied: see note 5); European Parliamentary Elections Regulations 2004, SI 2004/293, Sch 2 para 23(3)(a)(ii) (Sch 2 as substituted (see note 1); Sch 2 para 23 as applied (see note 5)); National Assembly for Wales (Representation of the People) Order 2007, SI 2007/236, Sch 1 para 4(3)(a)(ii) (as applied: see note 5).

23 Representation of the People (England and Wales) Regulations 2001, SI 2001/341, reg 53(3)(a)(iii) (reg 53(3) as substituted and applied (see note 5); reg 53(3)(a)(iii) added by SI 2012/1479); European Parliamentary Elections Regulations 2004, SI 2004/293, Sch 2 para 23(3)(a)(iii) (Sch 2 as substituted (see note 1); Sch 2 para 23 as applied (see note 5); Sch 2

para 23(3)(a)(iii) added by SI 2012/1479); National Assembly for Wales (Representation of the People) Order 2007, SI 2007/236, Sch 1 para 4(3)(a)(iii) (Sch 1 para 4 as applied (see note 5); Sch 1 para 4(3)(a)(iii) added by SI 2012/1479).

24 Representation of the People (England and Wales) Regulations 2001, SI 2001/341, reg 53(3)(b)(i) (as substituted and applied: see note 5); European Parliamentary Elections Regulations 2004, SI 2004/293, Sch 2 para 23(3)(b)(i) (Sch 2 as substituted (see note 1); Sch 2 para 23 as applied (see note 5)); National Assembly for Wales (Representation of the People) Order 2007, SI 2007/236, Sch 1 para 4(3)(b)(i) (as applied: see note 5).

25 Representation of the People (England and Wales) Regulations 2001, SI 2001/341, reg 53(3)(b)(ii) (as substituted and applied: see note 5); European Parliamentary Elections Regulations 2004, SI 2004/293, Sch 2 para 23(3)(b)(ii) (Sch 2 as substituted (see note 1); Sch 2 para 23 as applied (see note 5)); National Assembly for Wales (Representation of the People) Order 2007, SI 2007/236, Sch 1 para 4(3)(b)(ii) (as applied: see note 5).

26 Representation of the People (England and Wales) Regulations 2001, SI 2001/341, reg 53(3)(b)(iii) (as substituted and applied: see note 5); European Parliamentary Elections Regulations 2004, SI 2004/293, Sch 2 para 23(3)(b)(iii) (Sch 2 as substituted (see note 1); Sch 2 para 23 as applied (see note 5)); National Assembly for Wales (Representation of the People) Order 2007, SI 2007/236, Sch 1 para 4(3)(b)(iii) (as applied: see note 5).

27 Representation of the People (England and Wales) Regulations 2001, SI 2001/341, reg 53(4)(a) (as substituted and applied: see note 5); European Parliamentary Elections Regulations 2004, SI 2004/293, Sch 2 para 23(4)(a) (Sch 2 as substituted (see note 1); Sch 2 para 23 as applied (see note 5)); National Assembly for Wales (Representation of the People) Order 2007, SI 2007/236, Sch 1 para 4(4)(a) (as applied: see note 5).

28 Instead of the matters specified in head (i) in the text, a person who qualifies by virtue of head (8) in the text must state in the attestation:

(1) his name (Representation of the People (England and Wales) Regulations 2001, SI 2001/341, reg 53(5A)(i) (reg 53 as applied (see note 5); reg 53(5A) added by SI 2006/2910); European Parliamentary Elections Regulations 2004, SI 2004/293, Sch 2 para 23(5)(a) (Sch 2 as substituted (see note 1); Sch 2 para 23 as applied (see note 5)); National Assembly for Wales (Representation of the People) Order 2007, SI 2007/236, Sch 1 para 4(6)(a) (as applied: see note 5));

(2) his position in the hospital at which the applicant is liable to be detained or at which he is receiving treatment (Representation of the People (England and Wales) Regulations 2001, SI 2001/341, reg 53(5A)(ii) (as so added and applied); European Parliamentary Elections Regulations 2004, SI 2004/293, Sch 2 para 23(5)(c) (as so substituted and applied); National Assembly for Wales (Representation of the People) Order 2007, SI 2007/236, Sch 1 para 4(6)(b) (as so applied));

(3) that he is a person authorised to make the attestation (Representation of the People (England and Wales) Regulations 2001, SI 2001/341, reg 53(5A)(iii) (as so added and applied); European Parliamentary Elections Regulations 2004, SI 2004/293, Sch 2 para 23(5)(b) (as so substituted and applied); National Assembly for Wales (Representation of the People) Order 2007, SI 2007/236, Sch 1 para 4(6)(c) (as so applied)); and

(4) in the case of an applicant who is liable to be detained in hospital, the statutory provision under which the applicant is liable to be so detained (Representation of the People (England and Wales) Regulations 2001, SI 2001/341, reg 53(5A)(iv) (as so added and applied); European Parliamentary Elections Regulations 2004, SI 2004/293, Sch 2 para 23(5)(d) (as so substituted and applied); National Assembly for Wales (Representation of the People) Order 2007, SI 2007/236, Sch 1 para 4(6)(d) (as so applied)).

29 Representation of the People (England and Wales) Regulations 2001, SI 2001/341, reg 53(4)(b)(i) (as substituted and applied: see note 5); European Parliamentary Elections Regulations 2004, SI 2004/293, Sch 2 para 23(4)(b)(i) (Sch 2 as substituted (see note 1); Sch 2 para 23 as applied (see note 5)); National Assembly for Wales (Representation of the People) Order 2007, SI 2007/236, Sch 1 para 4(4)(b)(i) (as applied: see note 5).

30 Representation of the People (England and Wales) Regulations 2001, SI 2001/341, reg 53(4)(b)(ii) (as substituted and applied: see note 5); European Parliamentary Elections Regulations 2004, SI 2004/293, Sch 2 para 23(4)(b)(ii) (Sch 2 as substituted (see note 1); Sch 2 para 23 as applied (see note 5)); National Assembly for Wales (Representation of the People) Order 2007, SI 2007/236, Sch 1 para 4(4)(b)(ii) (as applied: see note 5).

31 Representation of the People (England and Wales) Regulations 2001, SI 2001/341, reg 53(4)(c)(i) (as substituted and applied: see note 5); European Parliamentary Elections Regulations 2004, SI 2004/293, Sch 2 para 23(4)(c)(i) (Sch 2 as substituted (see note 1); Sch 2

para 23 as applied (see note 5)); National Assembly for Wales (Representation of the People) Order 2007, SI 2007/236, Sch 1 para 4(4)(c)(i) (as applied: see note 5).

32 Representation of the People (England and Wales) Regulations 2001, SI 2001/341, reg 53(4)(c)(ii) (as substituted and applied: see note 5); European Parliamentary Elections Regulations 2004, SI 2004/293, Sch 2 para 23(4)(c)(ii) (Sch 2 as substituted (see note 1); Sch 2 para 23 as applied (see note 5)); National Assembly for Wales (Representation of the People) Order 2007, SI 2007/236, Sch 1 para 4(4)(c)(ii) (as applied: see note 5).

33 Representation of the People (England and Wales) Regulations 2001, SI 2001/341, reg 53(4)(c)(iii) (as substituted and applied: see note 5); European Parliamentary Elections Regulations 2004, SI 2004/293, Sch 2 para 23(4)(c)(iii) (Sch 2 as substituted (see note 1); Sch 2 para 23 as applied (see note 5)); National Assembly for Wales (Representation of the People) Order 2007, SI 2007/236, Sch 1 para 4(4)(c)(iii) (as applied: see note 5).

34 Representation of the People (England and Wales) Regulations 2001, SI 2001/341, reg 53(4)(d) (as substituted and applied: see note 5); European Parliamentary Elections Regulations 2004, SI 2004/293, Sch 2 para 23(4)(d) (Sch 2 as substituted (see note 1); Sch 2 para 23 as applied (see note 5)); National Assembly for Wales (Representation of the People) Order 2007, SI 2007/236, Sch 1 para 4(4)(d) (as applied: see note 5).

35 Representation of the People (England and Wales) Regulations 2001, SI 2001/341, reg 53(4)(e) (as substituted and applied: see note 5); European Parliamentary Elections Regulations 2004, SI 2004/293, Sch 2 para 23(4)(e) (Sch 2 as substituted (see note 1); Sch 2 para 23 as applied (see note 5)); National Assembly for Wales (Representation of the People) Order 2007, SI 2007/236, Sch 1 para 4(4)(e) (as applied: see note 5).

36 Ie in addition to those matters specified, in relation to a particular parliamentary or local government election, in the Representation of the People (England and Wales) Regulations 2001, SI 2001/341, reg 53, or, in relation to a particular European parliamentary election, in the European Parliamentary Elections Regulations 2004, SI 2004/293, Sch 2 para 23, or, in relation to a particular Welsh Assembly election, in the National Assembly for Wales (Representation of the People) Order 2007, SI 2007/236, Sch 1 para 4, as the case may be, and as those provisions are applied for the purpose (see the text and notes 5–35): Representation of the People (England and Wales) Regulations 2001, SI 2001/341, reg 55(3) (reg 55 as substituted (see note 1); reg 55(3) amended by SI 2006/2910); European Parliamentary Elections Regulations 2004, SI 2004/293, Sch 2 para 25(3) (as substituted: see note 1); National Assembly for Wales (Representation of the People) Order 2007, SI 2007/236, Sch 1 para 6(3) (as applied: see note 5).

37 Representation of the People (England and Wales) Regulations 2001, SI 2001/341, reg 55(3) (reg 55 as substituted (see note 1); reg 55(3) as amended (see note 36)); European Parliamentary Elections Regulations 2004, SI 2004/293, Sch 2 para 25(3) (as substituted: see note 1); National Assembly for Wales (Representation of the People) Order 2007, SI 2007/236, Sch 1 para 6(3) (as applied: see note 5).

38 Ie the Representation of the People (England and Wales) Regulations 2001, SI 2001/341, reg 53(2)–(4), or the European Parliamentary Elections Regulations 2004, SI 2004/293, Sch 2 para 23(2), (4), (5), or the National Assembly for Wales (Representation of the People) Order 2007, SI 2007/236, Sch 1 para 4(2)–(4), as the case may be, and as those provisions are applied for the purpose (see the text and notes 3–35): see the Representation of the People (England and Wales) Regulations 2001, SI 2001/341, reg 53(5) (as applied: see note 5); the European Parliamentary Elections Regulations 2004, SI 2004/293, Sch 2 para 23(6) (Sch 2 as substituted (see note 1); Sch 2 para 23 as applied (see note 5)); and the National Assembly for Wales (Representation of the People) Order 2007, SI 2007/236, Sch 1 para 4(5) (as applied: see note 5).

39 Ie the local authority which has made arrangements for compiling and maintaining classified registers of persons who are blind, etc under the National Assistance Act 1948 s 29(4)(g) (see SOCIAL SERVICES AND COMMUNITY CARE vol 44(2) (Reissue) PARA 1021): see the Representation of the People (England and Wales) Regulations 2001, SI 2001/341, reg 53(5)(a) (as applied: see note 5); the European Parliamentary Elections Regulations 2004, SI 2004/293, Sch 2 para 23(6)(a) (Sch 2 as substituted (see note 1); Sch 2 para 23 as applied (see note 5)); and the National Assembly for Wales (Representation of the People) Order 2007, SI 2007/236, Sch 1 para 4(5)(a) (as applied: see note 5).

40 Representation of the People (England and Wales) Regulations 2001, SI 2001/341, reg 53(5)(a) (as applied: see note 5); European Parliamentary Elections Regulations 2004, SI 2004/293, Sch 2 para 23(6)(a) (Sch 2 as substituted (see note 1); Sch 2 para 23 as applied (see note 5)); National Assembly for Wales (Representation of the People) Order 2007, SI 2007/236, Sch 1 para 4(5)(a) (as applied: see note 5). The fact that an applicant is registered with a local authority under the National Assistance Act 1948 s 29(4)(g) (see SOCIAL SERVICES AND COMMUNITY CARE vol 44(2)

(Reissue) PARA 1021) is deemed sufficient evidence that he is eligible to vote by proxy on the grounds set out in the Representation of the People Act 2000 Sch 4 para 3(3)(b), or the European Parliamentary Elections Regulations 2004, SI 2004/293, Sch 2 para 3(3)(c), or the National Assembly for Wales (Representation of the People) Order 2007, SI 2007/236, art 8(2)(c) (see PARA 367), as the case may be: Representation of the People (England and Wales) Regulations 2001, SI 2001/341, reg 53(6) (as so applied); European Parliamentary Elections Regulations 2004, SI 2004/293, Sch 2 para 23(7) (as so substituted and applied); National Assembly for Wales (Representation of the People) Order 2007, SI 2007/236, Sch 1 para 4(7) (as so applied). As to Gibraltar see PARA 368 note 3.

41 Ie payable under the Social Security Contributions and Benefits Act 1992 s 73 (see SOCIAL SECURITY AND PENSIONS vol 44(2) (Reissue) PARA 106): see the Representation of the People (England and Wales) Regulations 2001, SI 2001/341, reg 53(5)(b) (reg 53 as applied (see note 5); reg 53(5)(b) amended by SI 2006/2910); the European Parliamentary Elections Regulations 2004, SI 2004/293, Sch 2 para 23(6)(d) (Sch 2 as substituted (see note 1); Sch 2 para 23 as applied (see note 5)); and the National Assembly for Wales (Representation of the People) Order 2007, SI 2007/236, Sch 1 para 4(5)(b) (as applied: see note 5).

42 Representation of the People (England and Wales) Regulations 2001, SI 2001/341, reg 53(5)(b) (as amended and applied: see note 41); European Parliamentary Elections Regulations 2004, SI 2004/293, Sch 2 para 23(6)(d) (Sch 2 as substituted (see note 1); Sch 2 para 23 as applied (see note 5)); National Assembly for Wales (Representation of the People) Order 2007, SI 2007/236, Sch 1 para 4(5)(b) (as applied: see note 5).

373. Lists of absent voters. In respect of each parliamentary[1], local government[2], Welsh Assembly[3] or European parliamentary election[4], the registration officer[5] must keep two special lists in respect of absent voters[6].

The first of those lists is a list (the 'postal voters list')[7]:

(1)   of those whose applications to vote by post at that particular election have been granted[8], together with the addresses provided by them in their applications as the addresses to which their ballot papers are to be sent[9]; and

(2)   of those who are for the time being shown in the record kept of those entitled to an absent vote at elections either for a particular period or for an indefinite period[10] as voting by post at particular elections of the kind in question[11], together with the addresses provided by them in their applications[12] as the addresses to which their ballot papers are to be sent[13].

The second of those lists is a list (the 'list of proxies')[14]:

(a)   of those whose applications to vote by proxy at that particular election[15] have been granted[16]; or

(b)   of those who are for the time being shown in the record kept of those entitled to an absent vote at elections either for a particular period or for an indefinite period[17] as voting by proxy at particular elections of the kind in question[18],

together with (in each case) the names and addresses of those appointed as their proxies[19].

The registration officer must also keep a record in relation to those whose applications for an absent vote at a particular election[20] have been granted showing[21]:

(i)   their dates of birth[22]; and

(ii)   except in cases where the registration officer[23] has dispensed with the requirement to provide a signature, their signatures[24].

This record must be retained by the registration officer for the prescribed period[25]. The registration officer must either provide a copy of the information contained in records so kept by him[26] to the returning officer for an election in relation to electors at the election[27], or give the returning officer access to such information[28]. Information contained in such records may be disclosed by a registration officer (subject to any prescribed conditions) to any other registration officer if he thinks that to do so will assist the other registration officer in the performance of his duties[29], or to any person exercising functions in relation to the preparation or conduct of legal proceedings under the relevant election provisions[30], or (except in relation to a European parliamentary election) to such other persons for such other purposes relating to elections as may be prescribed[31].

Any person entitled to be supplied with copies of the full register is also a person entitled to request that the registration officer supply free of charge a copy of current information which he keeps for the purposes of maintaining the postal voters lists or the list of proxies[32].

1   As to the meaning of 'parliamentary election' see PARA 9.
2   As to the meaning of 'local government election' see PARA 11; definition applied by virtue of the Representation of the People Act 2000 s 12, Sch 4 para 1(2). See also PARA 363 note 1.
     The Representation of the People Act 2000 s 12, Sch 4 are applied and modified for the purpose of local authority mayoral elections in England and Wales by the Local Authorities (Mayoral Elections) (England and Wales) Regulations 2007, SI 2007/1024, reg 3(2)–(5), Sch 2 Table 3 (see PARA 11 note 14).
3   As to the meaning of 'Assembly election' in the context of Welsh Assembly elections see PARA 3 note 2.
4   As to European parliamentary elections see PARA 217 et seq.
5   As to electoral registration officers and the areas for which they act see PARA 139 et seq.
6   Representation of the People Act 2000 Sch 4 para 5(1) (amended by the Electoral Administration Act 2006 s 74(1), Sch 1 para 137(1), (5)); European Parliamentary Elections Regulations 2004, SI 2004/293, Sch 2 para 5(1) (Sch 2 substituted by SI 2009/186); National Assembly for Wales (Representation of the People) Order 2007, SI 2007/236, art 10(1). In the case of a person who has an anonymous entry in a register, the postal voters list or list of proxies (as the case may be) must show in relation to the person only his electoral number, and the period for which the anonymous entry has effect: Representation of the People Act 2000 Sch 4 para 5(4) (Sch 4 para 5(4) added by the Electoral Administration Act 2006 s 10(2), Sch 1 paras 19, 22); European Parliamentary Elections Regulations 2004, SI 2004/293, Sch 2 para 5(4) (as so substituted); National Assembly for Wales (Representation of the People) Order 2007, SI 2007/236, art 10(4). As to the meaning of 'electoral number' see PARA 145; and as to the meaning of 'anonymous entry' in relation to a register of electors see PARA 148.
     At a European parliamentary election, the registration officer must, forthwith on completion of the compilation of the special list, supply to the local returning officer for any local counting area wholly or partly within the area for which he acts so much of that list as relates to that constituency: European Parliamentary Elections Regulations 2004, SI 2004/293, Sch 2 para 5(5) (as so substituted). As to the meaning of 'local counting area' see PARA 139 note 1. As to local returning officers appointed for the purposes of elections to the European Parliament see PARA 360.
     Where electors at a Welsh Assembly election are entitled to give two votes in an Assembly constituency, only one list is to be kept under each of the National Assembly for Wales (Representation of the People) Order 2007, SI 2007/236, art 10(2) (the 'postal voters list': see the text and notes 7–13) and art 10(3) (the 'list of proxies': see the text and notes 14–19), and those lists have effect in relation to both elections: art 10(5). Where a Welsh Assembly constituency is not coterminous with, or wholly situated in, a county or county borough:
     (1)   the registration officer for any part of the Assembly constituency must, if he is not the returning officer for the constituency, consult him concerning the form of so much of the postal voters list and the list of proxies, as relates to the constituency, in order to ensure that, so far as practicable, it is in a form similar to that in use elsewhere in the constituency (art 140(a)(iii)); and
     (2)   if the registration officer for any part of the Assembly constituency at an Assembly election is not the returning officer for the constituency, he must forthwith supply to the constituency returning officer a copy of the lists compiled under art 10 on completion of the compilation of them (art 140(b)).
     As to the meaning of 'Assembly constituency' see PARA 3 note 2; and as to the meaning of 'constituency returning officer' for these purposes see PARA 18 note 2. As to the duty of

registration officers to maintain, prepare and publish registers of electors see PARA 143. As to counties and county boroughs in Wales see LOCAL GOVERNMENT vol 69 (2009) PARA 37 et seq.

7   Representation of the People Act 2000 Sch 4 para 5(2) (amended by the Electoral Administration Act 2006 Sch 1 para 137(1), (6)); European Parliamentary Elections Regulations 2004, SI 2004/293, Sch 2 para 5(2) (as substituted: see note 6); National Assembly for Wales (Representation of the People) Order 2007, SI 2007/236, art 10(2).
     The list referred to in the text, which is known as the 'postal voters list', refers to the list kept, in relation to a parliamentary or local government election, pursuant to the Representation of the People Act 2000 Sch 4 para 5(2), in relation to a European parliamentary election, pursuant to the European Parliamentary Elections Regulations 2004, SI 2004/293, Sch 2 para 5(2), and, in relation to a Welsh Assembly election, pursuant to the National Assembly for Wales (Representation of the People) Order 2007, SI 2007/236, art 10(2) (ie the list of persons whose applications to vote by post have been granted): see the Representation of the People Act 1983 s 202(1) (definition added by the Electoral Administration Act 2006 Sch 1 paras 104, 128(1), (3)); the Representation of the People Act 2000 Sch 4 para 5(2) (as so amended); the European Parliamentary Elections Regulations 2004, SI 2004/293, reg 2(1) (substituted by SI 2009/186); the European Parliamentary Elections Regulations 2004, SI 2004/293, Sch 2 para 5(2) (as substituted: see note 6); the National Assembly for Wales (Representation of the People) Order 2007, SI 2007/236, art 2(1); art 10(2).

8   Ie those whose applications, in relation to a particular parliamentary or local government election, under the Representation of the People Act 2000 Sch 4 para 4(1) have been granted, or those whose applications, in relation to a particular European parliamentary election, under the European Parliamentary Elections Regulations 2004, SI 2004/293, Sch 2 para 4(1) have been granted, or those whose applications, in relation to a particular Welsh Assembly election, under the National Assembly for Wales (Representation of the People) Order 2007, SI 2007/236, art 9(1) have been granted (see PARA 371), as the case may be: see the Representation of the People Act 2000 Sch 4 para 5(2)(a); the European Parliamentary Elections Regulations 2004, SI 2004/293, Sch 2 para 5(2)(a) (as substituted: see note 6); and the National Assembly for Wales (Representation of the People) Order 2007, SI 2007/236, art 10(2)(b).

9   Representation of the People Act 2000 Sch 4 para 5(2)(a); European Parliamentary Elections Regulations 2004, SI 2004/293, Sch 2 para 5(2)(a) (as substituted: see note 6); National Assembly for Wales (Representation of the People) Order 2007, SI 2007/236, art 10(2)(b).

10   Ie the record kept, for the purposes of a parliamentary or local government election, under the Representation of the People Act 2000 Sch 4 para 3, or, for the purposes of a European parliamentary election, under the European Parliamentary Elections Regulations 2004, SI 2004/293, Sch 2 para 3, or, for the purposes of a Welsh Assembly election, under the National Assembly for Wales (Representation of the People) Order 2007, SI 2007/236, art 8 (see PARA 370), as the case may be: see the Representation of the People Act 2000 Sch 4 para 5(2)(b); the European Parliamentary Elections Regulations 2004, SI 2004/293, Sch 2 para 5(2)(b) (as substituted: see note 6); and the National Assembly for Wales (Representation of the People) Order 2007, SI 2007/236, art 10(2)(a).

11   Ie excluding those so shown whose applications to vote by proxy at the election, in relation to a parliamentary or local government election, under the Representation of the People Act 2000 Sch 4 para 4(3)(b), or, in relation to a European parliamentary election, under the European Parliamentary Elections Regulations 2004, SI 2004/293, Sch 2 para 4(4)(b), or, in relation to a Welsh Assembly election, under the National Assembly for Wales (Representation of the People) Order 2007, SI 2007/236, art 9(3)(b), as the case may be, have been granted (see PARA 371): see the Representation of the People Act 2000 Sch 4 para 5(2)(b); the European Parliamentary Elections Regulations 2004, SI 2004/293, Sch 2 para 5(2)(b) (as substituted: see note 6); and the National Assembly for Wales (Representation of the People) Order 2007, SI 2007/236, art 10(2)(a).

12   Ie the applications made, in relation to a parliamentary or local government election, under the Representation of the People Act 2000 Sch 4 para 3 or Sch 4 para 4(3)(a), or, in relation to a European parliamentary election, under the European Parliamentary Elections Regulations 2004, SI 2004/293, Sch 2 para 3 or Sch 2 para 4(4)(a), or, in relation to a Welsh Assembly election, under the National Assembly for Wales (Representation of the People) Order 2007, SI 2007/236, art 8 or art 9(3)(a) (see PARAS 370, 371), as the case may be: see the Representation of the People Act 2000 Sch 4 para 5(2)(b); the European Parliamentary Elections Regulations 2004, SI 2004/293, Sch 2 para 5(2)(b) (as substituted: see note 6); and the National Assembly for Wales (Representation of the People) Order 2007, SI 2007/236, art 10(2)(a).

13   Representation of the People Act 2000 Sch 4 para 5(2)(b); European Parliamentary Elections Regulations 2004, SI 2004/293, Sch 2 para 5(2)(b) (as substituted: see note 6); National Assembly for Wales (Representation of the People) Order 2007, SI 2007/236, art 10(2)(a).

14 Representation of the People Act 2000 Sch 4 para 5(3); European Parliamentary Elections Regulations 2004, SI 2004/293, Sch 2 para 5(3) (as substituted: see note 6); National Assembly for Wales (Representation of the People) Order 2007, SI 2007/236, art 10(3).

The list referred to in the text, which is known as the 'list of proxies', refers to the list kept, in relation to a parliamentary or local government election, pursuant to the Representation of the People Act 2000 Sch 4 para 5(3), in relation to a European parliamentary election, pursuant to the European Parliamentary Elections Regulations 2004, SI 2004/293, Sch 2 para 5(3), and, in relation to a Welsh Assembly election, pursuant to the National Assembly for Wales (Representation of the People) Order 2007, SI 2007/236, 10(3): see the Representation of the People Act 1983 s 202(1) (definition added by the Representation of the People Act 1985 ss 4(5), 11, Sch 2 Pt I; and amended by the Representation of the People Act 2000 s 15, Sch 6 paras 3, 9(b)); the Representation of the People Act 2000 Sch 4 para 5(3); the European Parliamentary Elections Regulations 2004, SI 2004/293, reg 2(1) (as substituted: see note 7); Sch 2 para 5(3) (as so substituted); the National Assembly for Wales (Representation of the People) Order 2007, SI 2007/236, art 2(1); art 10(3).

15 Ie the applications made, in relation to a parliamentary or local government election, under the Representation of the People Act 2000 Sch 4 para 4(2), (3), or, in relation to a European parliamentary election, under the European Parliamentary Elections Regulations 2004, SI 2004/293, Sch 2 para 4(2), (4), or, in relation to a Welsh Assembly election, under the National Assembly for Wales (Representation of the People) Order 2007, SI 2007/236, art 9 (see PARA 371), as the case may be: see the Representation of the People Act 2000 Sch 4 para 5(3)(a); the European Parliamentary Elections Regulations 2004, SI 2004/293, Sch 2 para 5(3)(a) (as substituted: see note 6); and the National Assembly for Wales (Representation of the People) Order 2007, SI 2007/236, art 10(3).

16 Representation of the People Act 2000 Sch 4 para 5(3)(a); European Parliamentary Elections Regulations 2004, SI 2004/293, Sch 2 para 5(3)(a) (as substituted: see note 6); National Assembly for Wales (Representation of the People) Order 2007, SI 2007/236, art 10(3).

17 Ie the record kept, for the purposes of a parliamentary or local government election, under the Representation of the People Act 2000 Sch 4 para 3, or, for the purposes of a European parliamentary election, under the European Parliamentary Elections Regulations 2004, SI 2004/293, Sch 2 para 3, or, for the purposes of a Welsh Assembly election, under the National Assembly for Wales (Representation of the People) Order 2007, SI 2007/236, art 8 (see PARA 370), as the case may be: see the Representation of the People Act 2000 Sch 4 para 5(3)(b); the European Parliamentary Elections Regulations 2004, SI 2004/293, Sch 2 para 5(3)(b) (as substituted: see note 6); and the National Assembly for Wales (Representation of the People) Order 2007, SI 2007/236, art 10(3).

18 Representation of the People Act 2000 Sch 4 para 5(3)(b); European Parliamentary Elections Regulations 2004, SI 2004/293, Sch 2 para 5(3)(b) (as substituted: see note 6); National Assembly for Wales (Representation of the People) Order 2007, SI 2007/236, art 10(3).

19 Representation of the People Act 2000 Sch 4 para 5(3); European Parliamentary Elections Regulations 2004, SI 2004/293, Sch 2 para 5(3) (as substituted: see note 6); National Assembly for Wales (Representation of the People) Order 2007, SI 2007/236, art 10(3). As to the appointment of proxies see PARA 374 et seq.

20 Ie applications, in relation to a parliamentary or local government election, under the Representation of the People Act 2000 Sch 4 para 4, or, in relation to a European parliamentary election, under the European Parliamentary Elections Regulations 2004, SI 2004/293, Sch 2 para 4, or, in relation to a Welsh Assembly election, under the National Assembly for Wales (Representation of the People) Order 2007, SI 2007/236, art 9 (see PARA 371), as the case may be: see the Representation of the People Act 2000 Sch 4 para 4(6) (Sch 4 para 4(6), (7) added by the Electoral Administration Act 2006 s 14(2)(c), (8)); the European Parliamentary Elections Regulations 2004, SI 2004/293, Sch 2 para 4(7) (as substituted: see note 6); and the National Assembly for Wales (Representation of the People) Order 2007, SI 2007/236, art 9(6).

21 Representation of the People Act 2000 Sch 4 para 4(6) (as added: see note 20); European Parliamentary Elections Regulations 2004, SI 2004/293, Sch 2 para 4(7) (as substituted: see note 6); National Assembly for Wales (Representation of the People) Order 2007, SI 2007/236, art 9(6).

22 Representation of the People Act 2000 Sch 4 para 4(6)(a) (as added: see note 20); European Parliamentary Elections Regulations 2004, SI 2004/293, Sch 2 para 4(7)(a) (as substituted: see note 6); National Assembly for Wales (Representation of the People) Order 2007, SI 2007/236, art 9(6)(a).

23 Ie in pursuance of the Representation of the People Act 2000 Sch 4 para 4(5), or the European Parliamentary Elections Regulations 2004, SI 2004/293, Sch 2 para 4(6), or the National Assembly for Wales (Representation of the People) Order 2007, SI 2007/236, art 9(5) (see PARA

371 note 8), as the case may be: see the Representation of the People Act 2000 Sch 4 para 4(6)(b) (as added: see note 20); the European Parliamentary Elections Regulations 2004, SI 2004/293, Sch 2 para 4(7)(b) (as substituted: see note 6); and the National Assembly for Wales (Representation of the People) Order 2007, SI 2007/236, art 9(6)(b).

24   Representation of the People Act 2000 Sch 4 para 4(6)(b) (as added: see note 20); European Parliamentary Elections Regulations 2004, SI 2004/293, Sch 2 para 4(7)(b) (as substituted: see note 6); National Assembly for Wales (Representation of the People) Order 2007, SI 2007/236, art 9(6)(b).

25   Representation of the People Act 2000 Sch 4 para 4(7) (as added: see note 20); European Parliamentary Elections Regulations 2004, SI 2004/293, Sch 2 para 4(8) (as substituted: see note 6); National Assembly for Wales (Representation of the People) Order 2007, SI 2007/236, art 9(7).
     For the purposes of the Representation of the People Act 2000 Sch 4, the requirements are as prescribed; and 'prescribed' means prescribed by regulations (see the Representation of the People Act 1983 s 202(1); applied by virtue of the Representation of the People Act 2000 Sch 4 para 1(2)). Accordingly, the text refers to the requirements set out, in the case of a parliamentary or local government election, in the Representation of the People (England and Wales) Regulations 2001, SI 2001/341, Pt IV (regs 50–63A), or, in the case of a European parliamentary election, the European Parliamentary Elections Regulations 2004, SI 2004/293, Sch 2 para 18(1), or, in the case of a Welsh Assembly election, in the National Assembly for Wales (Representation of the People) Order 2007, SI 2007/236, Sch 1 para 2, as the case may be (see PARA 366): see the Representation of the People Act 2000 Sch 4 para 4(7); the European Parliamentary Elections Regulations 2004, SI 2004/293, Sch 2 para 4(8) (as so substituted); and the National Assembly for Wales (Representation of the People) Order 2007, SI 2007/236, art 9(7). As to the conditions relating to the retention of the records referred to in the text see PARA 503 et seq.

26   Ie in pursuance of the Representation of the People Act 2000 Sch 4 para 4(6), or the European Parliamentary Elections Regulations 2004, SI 2004/293, Sch 2 para 4(7), or the National Assembly for Wales (Representation of the People) Order 2007, SI 2007/236, art 9(6) (see the text and notes 20–24): see the Representation of the People Act 2000 Sch 4 para 7C(a) (Sch 4 paras 7A–7D added by the Electoral Administration Act 2006 s 14(4), (8)); the European Parliamentary Elections Regulations 2004, SI 2004/293, Sch 2 para 9(1)(a) (as substituted: see note 6); and the National Assembly for Wales (Representation of the People) Order 2007, SI 2007/236, art 13(5)(a).

27   Representation of the People Act 2000 Sch 4 para 7C(a) (as added: see note 26); European Parliamentary Elections Regulations 2004, SI 2004/293, Sch 2 para 9(1)(a) (as substituted: see note 6); National Assembly for Wales (Representation of the People) Order 2007, SI 2007/236, art 13(5)(a).
     At a European parliamentary election, the local returning officer is the returning officer referred to in the text: see the European Parliamentary Elections Regulations 2004, SI 2004/293, Sch 2 para 9(1)(a) (as so substituted). As to local returning officers appointed for the purposes of elections to the European Parliament see PARA 360.
     At a Welsh Assembly election, the constituency returning officer is the returning officer referred to in the text: see the National Assembly for Wales (Representation of the People) Order 2007, SI 2007/236, art 13(5)(a). As to the meaning of 'regional returning officer' for the purposes of Welsh Assembly elections see PARA 18 note 2.

28   Representation of the People Act 2000 Sch 4 para 7C(b) (as added: see note 26); European Parliamentary Elections Regulations 2004, SI 2004/293, Sch 2 para 9(1)(b) (as substituted: see note 6); National Assembly for Wales (Representation of the People) Order 2007, SI 2007/236, art 13(5)(b). As to the returning officer referred to in the text see note 27.

29   Representation of the People Act 2000 Sch 4 para 7D(a) (as added: see note 26); European Parliamentary Elections Regulations 2004, SI 2004/293, Sch 2 para 9(2)(a) (as substituted: see note 6); National Assembly for Wales (Representation of the People) Order 2007, SI 2007/236, art 13(6)(a). As to the prescribed conditions see PARA 179 et seq.

30   Representation of the People Act 2000 Sch 4 para 7D(b) (as added: see note 26); European Parliamentary Elections Regulations 2004, SI 2004/293, Sch 2 para 9(2)(b) (as substituted: see note 6); National Assembly for Wales (Representation of the People) Order 2007, SI 2007/236, art 13(6)(b). As to the meaning of 'the Representation of the People Acts' see PARA 3 note 1.
     At a parliamentary or local government election, the functions referred to in the text are those under the Representation of the People Acts: see the Representation of the People Act 2000 Sch 4 para 7D(b) (as so added).

At a European parliamentary election, the functions referred to in the text are those under the European Parliamentary Elections Regulations 2004, SI 2004/293: see Sch 2 para 9(2)(b) (as so substituted).

At a Welsh Assembly election, the functions referred to in the text are those under the Representation of the People Acts or the National Assembly for Wales (Representation of the People) Order 2007, SI 2007/236: see art 13(6)(b).

31 Representation of the People Act 1983 Sch 4 para 7D(c) (as added: see note 26); National Assembly for Wales (Representation of the People) Order 2007, SI 2007/236, art 13(6)(c). As to the prescribed conditions see PARA 179 et seq.

32 See the Representation of the People (England and Wales) Regulations 2001, SI 2001/341, reg 61; the European Parliamentary Elections Regulations 2004, SI 2004/293, Sch 2 para 32; the National Assembly for Wales (Representation of the People) Order 2007, SI 2007/236, Sch 1 para 13; and PARA 185. As to restrictions on use of the data so supplied see the Representation of the People (England and Wales) Regulations 2001, SI 2001/341, reg 61A; the European Parliamentary Elections Regulations 2004, SI 2004/293, Sch 2 para 33; the National Assembly for Wales (Representation of the People) Order 2007, SI 2007/236, Sch 1 para 14; and PARA 179 note 18.

(C) *Applications by Persons to Vote as Proxy for an Elector*

(a) Appointment as Proxy

374. Capacity of person to act as proxy for an elector. Any person is capable of being appointed proxy to vote for another[1] at any parliamentary[2], local government[3], Welsh Assembly[4] or European parliamentary election[5], and he may vote in pursuance of the appointment[6]. However, the elector[7] cannot have more than one person at a time appointed as proxy to vote for him:

(1)   at parliamentary elections (whether in the same constituency or elsewhere)[8]; or

(2)   at the local government elections in the same electoral area[9]; or

(3)   at a Welsh Assembly election (whether in the same Assembly constituency or elsewhere)[10]; or

(4)   at European parliamentary elections (whether in the same electoral region or elsewhere)[11].

A person is not capable of being appointed to vote, or voting, as proxy at any such election if he is subject to any legal incapacity[12] (age apart[13]) to vote at that election as elector[14], or:

(a)   at a parliamentary election, if he is neither a Commonwealth citizen[15] nor a citizen of the Republic of Ireland[16];

(b)   at a local government election or at a Welsh Assembly election, if he is neither a Commonwealth citizen nor a citizen of the Republic of Ireland nor a relevant citizen of the Union[17]; or

(c)   at a European parliamentary election, if he is neither a Commonwealth citizen nor a citizen of the Union[18].

A person is not capable of voting as proxy at any such election unless on the date of the poll he has attained the age of 18[19]. A person is not entitled to vote as proxy:

(i)   at the same parliamentary election in any constituency[20]; or

(ii)   at the same local government election in any electoral area[21]; or

(iii)   at the same Welsh Assembly constituency or regional elections, as specified[22]; or

(iv)   at the same European parliamentary election in any electoral region[23],

on behalf of more than two electors of whom that person is not the spouse, civil partner, parent, grandparent, brother, sister, child or grandchild[24].

1 Ie subject to the restrictions contained, in relation to a parliamentary or local government election, in the Representation of the People Act 2000 s 12, Sch 4 para 6, or, in relation to a European parliamentary election, in the European Parliamentary Elections Regulations 2004, SI 2004/293, reg 10, Sch 2 para 6, or, in relation to a Welsh Assembly election, in the National Assembly for Wales (Representation of the People) Order 2007, SI 2007/236, art 11 (see the text and notes 2–24; and see PARA 375), as the case may be: see the Representation of the People Act 2000 Sch 4 para 6(1); the European Parliamentary Elections Regulations 2004, SI 2004/293, Sch 2 para 6(1) (Sch 2 substituted by SI 2009/186); and the National Assembly for Wales (Representation of the People) Order 2007, SI 2007/236, art 11(1). As to applications made by an elector to vote by proxy at elections for a particular period or for an indefinite period see PARA 367 et seq; and as to such applications made in relation to a particular election see PARA 371 et seq.

The Representation of the People Act 2000 s 12, Sch 4 are applied and modified for the purpose of local authority mayoral elections in England and Wales by the Local Authorities (Mayoral Elections) (England and Wales) Regulations 2007, SI 2007/1024, reg 3(2)–(5), Sch 2 Table 3 (see PARA 11 note 14).

2 As to the meaning of 'parliamentary election' see PARA 9.

3 As to the meaning of 'local government election' see PARA 11; definition applied by virtue of the Representation of the People Act 2000 Sch 4 para 1(2). See also PARA 363 note 1.

4 As to the meaning of 'Assembly election' in the context of Welsh Assembly elections see PARA 3 note 2.

5 As to European parliamentary elections see PARA 217 et seq.

6 Representation of the People Act 2000 Sch 4 para 6(1); European Parliamentary Elections Regulations 2004, SI 2004/293, Sch 2 para 6(1) (as substituted: see note 1); National Assembly for Wales (Representation of the People) Order 2007, SI 2007/236, art 11(1).

7 For these purposes, the term 'elector' refers to a person for whom a proxy is appointed: see the Representation of the People Act 2000 Sch 4 para 6(1); the European Parliamentary Elections Regulations 2004, SI 2004/293, Sch 2 para 6(1) (as substituted: see note 1); and the National Assembly for Wales (Representation of the People) Order 2007, SI 2007/236, art 11(1). Under the general definition of that term (in relation to a parliamentary or local government election, see PARA 95 note 2; in relation to European parliamentary election, see PARA 111 note 4; and in relation to a Welsh Assembly election, see PARA 110 note 6), an elector is required to be registered in the register of electors to be used at an election; however, a person may be appointed as proxy for another person notwithstanding that the latter is not at the time registered as an elector if the registration officer is satisfied that he will be registered: see PARA 375. Cf notes 15–17.

8 Representation of the People Act 2000 Sch 4 para 6(2)(a). As to the meaning of 'constituency', in relation to a parliamentary election, see PARA 9.

9 Representation of the People Act 2000 Sch 4 para 6(2)(b). As to the meaning of 'electoral area' see PARA 11; definition applied by virtue of Sch 4 para 1(2).

10 National Assembly for Wales (Representation of the People) Order 2007, SI 2007/236, art 11(2). As to the meaning of 'Assembly constituency' see PARA 3 note 2.

11 European Parliamentary Elections Regulations 2004, SI 2004/293, Sch 2 para 6(2) (as substituted: see note 1). As to electoral regions constituted for the purposes of European parliamentary elections see PARA 77.

12 As to the meaning of 'legal incapacity (to vote)' see PARAS 95 note 8, 102 note 7.

13 'Voting age' is currently 18 years for all purposes: see PARAS 95 note 2, 97 note 14, 102 note 10.

14 Representation of the People Act 2000 Sch 4 para 6(3)(a), (4)(a); European Parliamentary Elections Regulations 2004, SI 2004/293, Sch 2 para 6(3)(a) (as substituted: see note 1); National Assembly for Wales (Representation of the People) Order 2007, SI 2007/236, art 11(3)(a).

As from a day to be appointed under the Electoral Registration and Administration Act 2013 s 27(1), the Representation of the People Act 2000 Sch 4 para 6(3), (4) is prospectively substituted by the Electoral Registration and Administration Act 2013 s 3. Accordingly, as from such a day, a person is not capable of being appointed to vote, or voting, as proxy at a parliamentary or local government election if the person is subject to any legal incapacity (age apart) to vote at that election as an elector: see the Representation of the People Act 2000 Sch 4 para 6(4) (prospectively substituted). However, at the date at which this volume states the law, no such day had been appointed.

15 As to who are Commonwealth citizens see BRITISH NATIONALITY vol 4 (2011) PARA 409.

16 Representation of the People Act 2000 Sch 4 para 6(3)(b). As to who are citizens of the Republic of Ireland see BRITISH NATIONALITY vol 4 (2011) PARA 410.

As from a day to be appointed under the Electoral Registration and Administration Act 2013 s 27(1), the Representation of the People Act 2000 Sch 4 para 6(3), (4) is prospectively substituted by the Electoral Registration and Administration Act 2013 s 3. Accordingly, as from such a day, a person is not capable of being appointed to vote, or voting, as proxy at a parliamentary election unless the person is or will be registered in a register of parliamentary electors in Great Britain or Northern Ireland: see the Representation of the People Act 2000 Sch 4 para 6(3) (prospectively substituted). However, at the date at which this volume states the law, no such day had been appointed.

17 Representation of the People Act 2000 Sch 4 para 6(4)(b); National Assembly for Wales (Representation of the People) Order 2007, SI 2007/236, art 11(3)(b). At a Welsh Assembly election, the reference is to a 'qualifying Commonwealth citizen' (see PARA 149 note 17): see art 11(3)(b). As to the meaning of 'relevant citizen of the Union' see PARAS 97 note 13, 149 note 17.

As from a day to be appointed under the Electoral Registration and Administration Act 2013 s 27(1), the Representation of the People Act 2000 Sch 4 para 6(3A) is prospectively added by the Electoral Registration and Administration Act 2013 s 3. Accordingly, as from such a day, a person is not capable of being appointed to vote, or voting, as proxy at a local government election unless the person is or will be registered in a register of local government electors in Great Britain or Northern Ireland: see the Representation of the People Act 2000 Sch 4 para 6(3A) (prospectively added). However, at the date at which this volume states the law, no such day had been appointed.

18 European Parliamentary Elections Regulations 2004, SI 2004/293, Sch 2 para 6(3)(b) (as substituted: see note 1).

19 Representation of the People Act 2000 Sch 4 para 6(5); European Parliamentary Elections Regulations 2004, SI 2004/293, Sch 2 para 6(4) (as substituted: see note 1); National Assembly for Wales (Representation of the People) Order 2007, SI 2007/236, art 11(4). As to the date of the poll at a parliamentary general election or by-election see PARA 195; as to the date of the poll at local government elections (including elections to fill vacancies) see PARAS 206–209; as to the date of the poll at Welsh Assembly elections (including elections to fill vacancies in an Assembly constituency) see PARAS 213–214; and as to the date of the poll at a European parliamentary election see PARA 222.

20 Representation of the People Act 2000 Sch 4 para 6(6)(a).

21 Representation of the People Act 2000 Sch 4 para 6(6)(b).

22 Ie:

   (1) in the case of an Assembly general election, in the same Assembly constituency, or constituencies in the same electoral region (National Assembly for Wales (Representation of the People) Order 2007, SI 2007/236, art 11(5)(a));

   (2) in the case of a constituency election other than at an Assembly general election, in the same constituency election (art 11(5)(b)); or

   (3) in a regional election (art 11(5)(c)).

   As to the meanings of 'Assembly region', 'constituency election' and 'regional election' see PARA 3 note 2. As to Welsh Assembly general elections see PARA 12 et seq.

23 European Parliamentary Elections Regulations 2004, SI 2004/293, Sch 2 para 6(5) (Sch 2 as substituted (see note 1); Sch 2 para 6(5) amended by SI 2005/2114).

24 Representation of the People Act 2000 Sch 4 para 6(6) (amended by the Civil Partnership Act 2004 s 261(1), Sch 27 para 164(1), (3)); European Parliamentary Elections Regulations 2004, SI 2004/293, Sch 2 para 6(5) (Sch 2 as substituted (see note 1); Sch 2 para 6(5) as amended (see note 23)); National Assembly for Wales (Representation of the People) Order 2007, SI 2007/236, art 11(5).

375. Applications for appointment to vote as proxy for an elector. Where the elector[1] applies to the registration officer[2] for the appointment of a proxy to vote for him at parliamentary[3] or local government elections[4] (or at both) or at Welsh Assembly[5] or European parliamentary elections[6] (whether for an indefinite period or for a particular period specified in his application[7]), the registration officer must make the appointment if:

   (1) the application meets the statutory requirements[8]; and

   (2) he is satisfied that[9]: (a) the elector is or will be registered in the register of electors for the election in question[10]; and (b) the elector is or will be shown in the record kept of those entitled to an absent vote at elections

either for a particular period or for an indefinite period[11] as voting by proxy at such elections[12]; and (c) the proxy is capable of being, and willing to be, appointed to vote as proxy at such elections[13].

Where the elector applies to the registration officer for the appointment of a proxy to vote for him at a particular such election[14], the registration officer must make the appointment if:

(i)   the application meets the statutory requirements[15]; and

(ii)   he is satisfied that: (A) the elector is or will be registered in the register of electors relevant to that election[16]; and (B) the elector is or will be entitled to vote by proxy at that election by virtue of that application[17]; and (C) the proxy is capable of being, and willing to be, appointed[18].

Such an application[19] must state:

(aa)   the full name of the applicant[20]; and

(bb)   the address in respect of which the applicant is registered or has applied to be (or is treated as having applied to be) registered in the register[21].

The application must be made in writing and dated[22]. Where it is made for an indefinite period or for the period specified in the application, it must state that it is so made[23], and (except in relation to a Welsh Assembly election) must specify the election (or elections) in respect of which it is made[24]; where it is made for a particular such election, it must identify the election in question (except in the case of a Welsh Assembly election)[25], and must state that it is made for a particular election[26]; and such an application may be combined where polls at different elections fall on the same day[27].

An application made by an elector to vote by proxy must include an application for the appointment of a proxy which states the full name and address of the person whom the applicant wishes to appoint, together with his family relationship (if any) with the applicant[28]. If an application for appointment to vote as proxy is signed only by the applicant, it must contain a statement by him that he has consulted the person named as proxy and that the person is capable of being and willing to be appointed to vote as his proxy[29]; or, if the application is signed also by the person to be appointed, it must contain a statement by that person that he is capable of being and willing to be appointed to vote as the applicant's proxy[30]. The appointment of a proxy must be made by means of a proxy paper in the prescribed form issued by the registration officer[31].

Where the registration officer grants an application for the appointment of a proxy, he must confirm in writing to the elector that the proxy has been appointed, his name and address, and the duration of the appointment[32]. Where he refuses an application, he must notify the applicant of his decision and of the reason for it[33].

1   As to the meaning of 'elector' for these purposes see PARA 374 note 7.

2   The registration officer must supply free of charge as many forms for use in connection with applications made under the Representation of the People Act 2000 s 12, Sch 4, the Representation of the People (England and Wales) Regulations 2001, SI 2001/341, Pt IV (regs 50–63A), or the European Parliamentary Elections Regulations 2004, SI 2004/293, reg 10, Sch 2, as appear to that officer reasonable in the circumstances to any person who satisfies that officer of his intention to use the forms in connection with an election: Representation of the People (England and Wales) Regulations 2001, SI 2001/341, reg 4(1)(b); European Parliamentary Elections Regulations 2004, SI 2004/293, Sch 2 para 12(1) (Sch 2 substituted by SI 2009/186). As to electoral registration officers and the areas for which they act see PARA 139 et seq.

The Representation of the People Act 2000 s 12, Sch 4 are applied and modified for the purpose of local authority mayoral elections in England and Wales by the Local Authorities

(Mayoral Elections) (England and Wales) Regulations 2007, SI 2007/1024, reg 3(2)–(5), Sch 2 Table 3 (see PARA 11 note 14); and the Representation of the People (England and Wales) Regulations 2001, SI 2001/341, regs 51, 52, 56, 57, Sch 3, also have effect for the purposes of local authority referendums, subject to the modifications specified, in relation to Wales, by the Local Authorities (Conduct of Referendums) (Wales) Regulations 2008, SI 2008/1848, reg 8(2), Sch 4 Table 5, and, in relation to England, by the Local Authorities (Conduct of Referendums) (England) Regulations 2012, SI 2012/323, regs 8(2), 11–13, Sch 4 Table 6 (see PARA 15 note 2).

3   As to the meaning of 'parliamentary election' see PARA 9.
4   As to the meaning of 'local government election' see PARA 11; definition applied by virtue of the Representation of the People Act 2000 s 12, Sch 4 para 1(2). See also PARA 363 note 1.
5   As to the meaning of 'Assembly election' in the context of Welsh Assembly elections see PARA 3 note 2.
6   As to European parliamentary elections see PARA 217 et seq.
7   As to such applications see PARA 367.
8   Representation of the People Act 2000 Sch 4 para 6(7); European Parliamentary Elections Regulations 2004, SI 2004/293, Sch 2 para 6(6) (as substituted: see note 2); National Assembly for Wales (Representation of the People) Order 2007, SI 2007/236, art 11(6). For the purposes of the Representation of the People Act 2000 Sch 4, the requirements are as prescribed; and 'prescribed' means prescribed by regulations (see the Representation of the People Act 1983 s 202(1); applied by virtue of the Representation of the People Act 2000 Sch 4 para 1(2)). Accordingly, the text refers to the requirements set out, in the case of a parliamentary or local government election, in the Representation of the People (England and Wales) Regulations 2001, SI 2001/341, Pt IV (regs 50–63A), or, in the case of a European parliamentary election, the European Parliamentary Elections Regulations 2004, SI 2004/293, Sch 2 Pt 2 (Sch 2 paras 12–34), or, in the case of a Welsh Assembly election, in the National Assembly for Wales (Representation of the People) Order 2007, SI 2007/236, Sch 1, as the case may be (see PARA 366): see the Representation of the People Act 2000 Sch 4 para 6(7); European Parliamentary Elections Regulations 2004, SI 2004/293, Sch 2 para 6(6) (as so substituted); and the National Assembly for Wales (Representation of the People) Order 2007, SI 2007/236, art 11(6). As to the conditions relating to the retention of the records referred to in the text see PARA 503 et seq.

    Such an application must be disregarded for the purposes of a particular election if it is received by the registration officer after 5 pm on the sixth day before the date of the poll at that election: Representation of the People (England and Wales) Regulations 2001, SI 2001/341, reg 56(2) (amended by SI 2006/752); European Parliamentary Elections Regulations 2004, SI 2004/293, Sch 2 para 26(2) (as so substituted); National Assembly for Wales (Representation of the People) Order 2007, SI 2007/236, Sch 1 para 7(2). Where a registration officer disregards such an application for the purposes of any particular election, he must notify the applicant of this: Representation of the People (England and Wales) Regulations 2001, SI 2001/341, reg 57(5) (amended by SI 2006/752); European Parliamentary Elections Regulations 2004, SI 2004/293, Sch 2 para 27(7) (as so substituted); National Assembly for Wales (Representation of the People) Order 2007, SI 2007/236, Sch 1 para 8(8). As to the date of the poll at a parliamentary general election or by-election see PARA 195; as to the date of the poll at local government elections (including elections to fill vacancies) see PARAS 206–209; as to the date of the poll at Welsh Assembly elections (including elections to fill vacancies in an Assembly constituency) see PARAS 213–214; and as to the date of the poll at a European parliamentary election see PARA 222. As to the computation of time for these purposes see PARA 367 note 6.

9   See the Representation of the People Act 2000 Sch 4 para 6(7); the European Parliamentary Elections Regulations 2004, SI 2004/293, Sch 2 para 6(6) (as substituted: see note 2); and the National Assembly for Wales (Representation of the People) Order 2007, SI 2007/236, art 11(6).

10   Representation of the People Act 2000 Sch 4 para 6(7)(a); European Parliamentary Elections Regulations 2004, SI 2004/293, Sch 2 para 6(6)(a) (as substituted: see note 2); National Assembly for Wales (Representation of the People) Order 2007, SI 2007/236, art 11(6)(a).

    In the case of a parliamentary election, the register referred to in the text is the register of parliamentary electors and, in the case of a local government election, it is the register of local government electors (although an application under the Representation of the People Act 2000 Sch 4 may relate to both types of election, in which case the requirement is for the applicant to be registered in both): see the Representation of the People Act 2000 Sch 4 para 6(7)(a). As to the meaning of the 'register of electors', in relation to a European parliamentary election, see PARA 111 note 4. As to the meaning of 'register', for the purposes of a Welsh Assembly election, see PARA 367 note 7. As to registration as an elector see PARA 113 et seq; and as to the registers of electors maintained by registration officers see PARA 143 et seq.

11 Ie the record kept for the purposes of a parliamentary or local government election under the Representation of the People Act 2000 Sch 4 para 3, or for the purposes of a European parliamentary election under the European Parliamentary Elections Regulations 2004, SI 2004/293, Sch 2 para 3, or for the purposes of a Welsh Assembly election under the National Assembly for Wales (Representation of the People) Order 2007, SI 2007/236, art 8 (see PARA 370), as the case may be: see the Representation of the People Act 2000 Sch 4 para 6(7)(b); the European Parliamentary Elections Regulations 2004, SI 2004/293, Sch 2 para 6(6)(b) (as substituted: see note 2); and the National Assembly for Wales (Representation of the People) Order 2007, SI 2007/236, art 11(6)(b).

12 Representation of the People Act 2000 Sch 4 para 6(7)(b); European Parliamentary Elections Regulations 2004, SI 2004/293, Sch 2 para 6(6)(b) (as substituted: see note 2); National Assembly for Wales (Representation of the People) Order 2007, SI 2007/236, art 11(6)(b).

13 Representation of the People Act 2000 Sch 4 para 6(7); European Parliamentary Elections Regulations 2004, SI 2004/293, Sch 2 para 6(6) (as substituted: see note 2); National Assembly for Wales (Representation of the People) Order 2007, SI 2007/236, art 11(6).

14 As to such applications see PARA 371.

15 Representation of the People Act 2000 Sch 4 para 6(8); European Parliamentary Elections Regulations 2004, SI 2004/293, Sch 2 para 6(7) (as substituted: see note 2); National Assembly for Wales (Representation of the People) Order 2007, SI 2007/236, art 11(7). The text refers to the requirements set out, in the case of a parliamentary or local government election, in the Representation of the People (England and Wales) Regulations 2001, SI 2001/341, Pt IV (see note 8), or, in the case of a European parliamentary election, the European Parliamentary Elections Regulations 2004, SI 2004/293, Sch 2 Pt 2, or, in the case of a Welsh Assembly election, in the National Assembly for Wales (Representation of the People) Order 2007, SI 2007/236, Sch 1 para 2, as the case may be (see PARA 366): see the Representation of the People Act 2000 Sch 4 para 6(8); the European Parliamentary Elections Regulations 2004, SI 2004/293, Sch 2 para 6(7) (as so substituted); and the National Assembly for Wales (Representation of the People) Order 2007, SI 2007/236, art 11(7). In the case of an application made in relation to a Welsh Assembly election, it is specified that the application must also contain the signature and date of birth of the applicant: see art 11(7). Where such an application is required to contain a signature and date of birth see Sch 1 para 1(3); and PARA 378 note 12.

Such an application must be refused if it is received by the registration officer after 5 pm on the sixth day before the date of the poll at the election for which it is made: Representation of the People (England and Wales) Regulations 2001, SI 2001/341, reg 56(3) (reg 56(3) substituted by SI 2006/752); European Parliamentary Elections Regulations 2004, SI 2004/293, Sch 2 para 26(3) (as so substituted); National Assembly for Wales (Representation of the People) Order 2007, SI 2007/236, Sch 1 para 7(2). Where a registration officer refuses such an application, he must notify the applicant of his decision and the reason for it: Representation of the People (England and Wales) Regulations 2001, SI 2001/341, reg 57(4); European Parliamentary Elections Regulations 2004, SI 2004/293, Sch 2 para 27(3) (as so substituted); National Assembly for Wales (Representation of the People) Order 2007, SI 2007/236, Sch 1 para 8(4).

Where an application is made under the Representation of the People Act 2000 Sch 4 para 4(2), the European Parliamentary Elections Regulations 2004, SI 2004/293, Sch 2 para 4(2), or the National Assembly for Wales (Representation of the People) Order 2007, SI 2007/236, art 9(1), as the case may be, on the grounds of the applicant's disability, and where the applicant became disabled after 5 pm on the sixth day before the date of the poll at the election for which it is made, or where such an application is made by a person to whom the Representation of the People Act 2000 Sch 4 para 2(5A), the European Parliamentary Elections Regulations 2004, SI 2004/293, Sch 2 para 2(6), or the National Assembly for Wales (Representation of the People) Order 2007, SI 2007/236, art 7(8) applies (ie a person in a mental hospital who is not a detained offender or on remand but who is liable to be detained in the mental hospital in question: see PARAS 363 note 1, 364 note 1, 365 note 1), the application, or applications for the appointment of a proxy to vote at a particular election under the Representation of the People Act 2000 Sch 4 para 6(8) (made by virtue of an application under Sch 4 para 4(2)), or under the European Parliamentary Elections Regulations 2004, SI 2004/293, Sch 2 para 6(7) (made by virtue of an application under Sch 2 para 4(2)), or under the National Assembly for Wales (Representation of the People) Order 2007, SI 2007/236, art 11(7) (made by virtue of an application under art 9(1)) (see PARA 371 note 10), must be refused if it is received after 5 pm on the day of the poll at the election for which it is made: Representation of the People (England and Wales) Regulations 2001, SI 2001/341, reg 56(3A) (reg 56(3A) added by SI 2006/752; and substituted by SI 2006/2910); European Parliamentary Elections Regulations 2004, SI 2004/293, Sch 2 para 26(4) (as so substituted); National

Assembly for Wales (Representation of the People) Order 2007, SI 2007/236, Sch 1 para 7(3) (amended by SI 2010/2931). Where a registration officer disregards such an application for the purposes of any particular election, he must notify the applicant of this: Representation of the People (England and Wales) Regulations 2001, SI 2001/341, reg 57(5) (as amended: see note 8); European Parliamentary Elections Regulations 2004, SI 2004/293, Sch 2 para 27(7) (as so substituted); National Assembly for Wales (Representation of the People) Order 2007, SI 2007/236, Sch 1 para 8(8).

16 Representation of the People Act 2000 Sch 4 para 6(8)(a); European Parliamentary Elections Regulations 2004, SI 2004/293, Sch 2 para 6(7); (as substituted: see note 2) National Assembly for Wales (Representation of the People) Order 2007, SI 2007/236, art 11(7)(a). As to the registers in use for each election see note 10.

17 Representation of the People Act 2000 Sch 4 para 6(8)(b); European Parliamentary Elections Regulations 2004, SI 2004/293, Sch 2 para 6(7) (as substituted: see note 2); National Assembly for Wales (Representation of the People) Order 2007, SI 2007/236, art 11(7)(b). The text refers to applications made under the Representation of the People Act 2000 Sch 4 para 4(2), (3), the European Parliamentary Elections Regulations 2004, SI 2004/293, Sch 2 para 4(2) (4), or the National Assembly for Wales (Representation of the People) Order 2007, SI 2007/236, art 9 (see PARA 371), as the case may be: see the Representation of the People Act 2000 Sch 4 para 6(8)(b); the European Parliamentary Elections Regulations 2004, SI 2004/293, Sch 2 para 6(7) (as so substituted); and the National Assembly for Wales (Representation of the People) Order 2007, SI 2007/236, art 11(7)(b).

18 Representation of the People Act 2000 Sch 4 para 6(8); European Parliamentary Elections Regulations 2004, SI 2004/293, Sch 2 para 6(7) (as substituted: see note 2); National Assembly for Wales (Representation of the People) Order 2007, SI 2007/236, art 11(7).

19 Applications made under the Representation of the People Act 2000 Sch 4, or the European Parliamentary Elections Regulations 2004, SI 2004/293, Sch 2 Pt 2 (Sch 2 paras 12–34), or the National Assembly for Wales (Representation of the People) Order 2007, SI 2007/236, art 11, must comply with the requirements, in relation to a parliamentary or local government election, of the Representation of the People (England and Wales) Regulations 2001, SI 2001/341, reg 51, or, in relation to a European parliamentary election, of the European Parliamentary Elections Regulations 2004, SI 2004/293, Sch 2 para 17, or, in relation to a Welsh Assembly election, of the National Assembly for Wales (Representation of the People) Order 2007, SI 2007/236, Sch 1 para 1, as well as such further requirements in the Representation of the People (England and Wales) Regulations 2001, SI 2001/341, Pt IV, or the European Parliamentary Elections Regulations 2004, SI 2004/293, Sch 2 Pt 2, as are relevant to the application: Representation of the People (England and Wales) Regulations 2001, SI 2001/341, reg 51(1); European Parliamentary Elections Regulations 2004, SI 2004/293, Sch 2 para 17(1) (as substituted: see note 6); National Assembly for Wales (Representation of the People) Order 2007, SI 2007/236, art 13(1). As to additional requirements for applications to vote by proxy for a definite or indefinite period see PARAS 368–369.

20 Representation of the People (England and Wales) Regulations 2001, SI 2001/341, reg 51(2)(a); European Parliamentary Elections Regulations 2004, SI 2004/293, Sch 2 para 17(2)(a) (as substituted: see note 2); National Assembly for Wales (Representation of the People) Order 2007, SI 2007/236, Sch 1 para 1(1)(a).

21 Representation of the People (England and Wales) Regulations 2001, SI 2001/341, reg 51(2)(b) (amended by SI 2006/752); European Parliamentary Elections Regulations 2004, SI 2004/293, Sch 2 para 17(2)(b) (as substituted: see note 2); National Assembly for Wales (Representation of the People) Order 2007, SI 2007/236, Sch 1 para 1(1)(b). As to the address to be specified for the purposes of Sch 1 para 1(1)(b) see PARA 367 note 25. Head (bb) in the text does not apply in the case of an application under the Representation of the People Act 2000 Sch 4 para 7(4), (7), or the European Parliamentary Elections Regulations 2004, SI 2004/293, Sch 2 para 7(4), (7), or the National Assembly for Wales (Representation of the People) Order 2007, SI 2007/236, art 12(4), (7) (voting as proxy for an indefinite period or for a particular period or at a particular election: see PARA 378).

22 Representation of the People (England and Wales) Regulations 2001, SI 2001/341, reg 51(3) (reg 51(3) substituted, reg 51(3A), (3B) added, by SI 2006/2910); European Parliamentary Elections Regulations 2004, SI 2004/293, Sch 2 para 17(3) (as substituted: see note 2); National Assembly for Wales (Representation of the People) Order 2007, SI 2007/236, Sch 1 para 1(2).

23 Representation of the People (England and Wales) Regulations 2001, SI 2001/341, reg 51(4)(a); European Parliamentary Elections Regulations 2004, SI 2004/293, Sch 2 para 17(6)(a) (as substituted: see note 2); National Assembly for Wales (Representation of the People) Order 2007, SI 2007/236, Sch 1 para 1(5)(a).

24 Representation of the People (England and Wales) Regulations 2001, SI 2001/341, reg 51(4)(b); European Parliamentary Elections Regulations 2004, SI 2004/293, Sch 2 para 17(6)(b) (as substituted: see note 2).

25 Representation of the People (England and Wales) Regulations 2001, SI 2001/341, reg 51(5)(b); European Parliamentary Elections Regulations 2004, SI 2004/293, Sch 2 para 17(7)(b) (as substituted: see note 2).

26 Representation of the People (England and Wales) Regulations 2001, SI 2001/341, reg 51(5)(a); European Parliamentary Elections Regulations 2004, SI 2004/293, Sch 2 para 17(7)(a) (as substituted: see note 2); National Assembly for Wales (Representation of the People) Order 2007, SI 2007/236, Sch 1 para 1(5)(b).

27 See the Representation of the People (England and Wales) Regulations 2001, SI 2001/341, reg 51(5); the European Parliamentary Elections Regulations 2004, SI 2004/293, Sch 2 para 17(9) (as substituted: see note 2); and the National Assembly for Wales (Representation of the People) Order 2007, SI 2007/236, Sch 1 para 1(5).

28 Representation of the People (England and Wales) Regulations 2001, SI 2001/341, regs 51(6), 52; European Parliamentary Elections Regulations 2004, SI 2004/293, Sch 2 paras 17(8), 22 (as substituted: see note 2); National Assembly for Wales (Representation of the People) Order 2007, SI 2007/236, Sch 1 para 3.

29 Representation of the People (England and Wales) Regulations 2001, SI 2001/341, reg 52(a); European Parliamentary Elections Regulations 2004, SI 2004/293, Sch 2 para 22(a) (as substituted: see note 2); National Assembly for Wales (Representation of the People) Order 2007, SI 2007/236, Sch 1 para 3(a). As to capacity to act as proxy see PARA 374.

30 Representation of the People (England and Wales) Regulations 2001, SI 2001/341, reg 52(b); European Parliamentary Elections Regulations 2004, SI 2004/293, Sch 2 para 22(b) (as substituted: see note 2); National Assembly for Wales (Representation of the People) Order 2007, SI 2007/236, Sch 1 para 3(b).

31 Representation of the People Act 2000 Sch 4 para 6(9); European Parliamentary Elections Regulations 2004, SI 2004/293, Sch 2 para 6(8) (as substituted: see note 2); National Assembly for Wales (Representation of the People) Order 2007, SI 2007/236, art 11(8). As to the prescribed form of proxy paper, by means of which the appointment of a proxy is to be made:

    (1)   for the purposes of a parliamentary or local government election, see the Representation of the People (England and Wales) Regulations 2001, SI 2001/341, reg 57(3), Sch 3 (Form E: proxy paper) (amended by SI 2005/2114);

    (2)   for the purposes of a European parliamentary election, see the form set out in the European Parliamentary Elections Regulations 2004, SI 2004/293, Sch 2 paras 1(2), 6(8), Pt 5 (Appendix of Forms) (Form N: form of proxy paper) (as so substituted);

    (3)   for the purposes of a Welsh Assembly election, see the form set out in English and Welsh in the National Assembly for Wales (Representation of the People) Order 2007, SI 2007/236, Sch 1 para 8(3), Sch 10 Appendix of Forms (Form CA: form of proxy paper), but this may be combined with another form of proxy paper if the registration officer is issuing a proxy paper appointing that person as proxy for the same elector in respect of another election or other elections (see Sch 1 para 8(3)).

A version of the form cited in head (1) above partly in Welsh and partly in English must be used in Wales: see the Parliamentary Elections (Welsh Forms) Order 2007, SI 2007/1014, art 6(k), Sch 2 (Form 11: proxy paper; papur dirprwyo). A version of the form cited in head (2) above partly in Welsh and partly in English must be used in Wales: see the European Parliamentary Elections (Welsh Forms) Order 2009, SI 2009/781, art 6(1)(l), Sch 2 (Form 12: proxy paper, papur dirprwy). The forms cited further to heads (1) to (3) above may be used with such adaptations or variations as the circumstances may require: see the Representation of the People (England and Wales) Regulations 2001, SI 2001/341, reg 4(2); the Parliamentary Elections (Welsh Forms) Order 2007, SI 2007/1014, art 7; the European Parliamentary Elections Regulations 2004, SI 2004/293, Sch 2 para 12(2), Pt 5 (Appendix of Forms: note) (as so substituted); and the National Assembly for Wales (Representation of the People) Order 2007, SI 2007/236, Sch 10 Appendix of Forms (note). As to forms generally see note 2.

32 Representation of the People (England and Wales) Regulations 2001, SI 2001/341, reg 57(2); European Parliamentary Elections Regulations 2004, SI 2004/293, Sch 2 para 27(2) (as substituted: see note 2); National Assembly for Wales (Representation of the People) Order 2007, SI 2007/236, Sch 1 para 8(2).

33 Representation of the People (England and Wales) Regulations 2001, SI 2001/341, reg 57(4); European Parliamentary Elections Regulations 2004, SI 2004/293, Sch 2 para 27(3) (as substituted: see note 2); National Assembly for Wales (Representation of the People) Order 2007, SI 2007/236, Sch 1 para 8(4). An appeal does not lie from any such decision of the registration officer: see PARA 172 et seq.

376. Duration of appointment to vote as proxy for an elector. The appointment of a proxy[1] may be cancelled by the elector[2] giving notice to the registration officer[3]. An appointment also ceases to be in force[4]:

(1) where it related to a parliamentary election[5] or parliamentary elections, on the issue of a proxy paper[6] appointing a different person to vote for him at a parliamentary election or parliamentary elections (whether in the same constituency[7] or elsewhere)[8];

(2) where it related to a local government election[9] or local government elections, on the issue of a proxy paper appointing a different person to vote for him at a local government election or local government elections in the same electoral area[10];

(3) where it related to a particular European parliamentary election or elections[11], on the issue of a proxy paper appointing a different person to vote for him at a European parliamentary election or elections (whether in the same electoral region[12] or elsewhere)[13];

(4) where it related to a Welsh Assembly election[14], on the issue of a proxy paper appointing a different person to vote for him at an Assembly election or Assembly elections (whether in the same Assembly constituency[15] or elsewhere)[16];

(5) in relation to any such election, where the appointment was for a particular period, once that period expires[17].

The appointment otherwise remains in force for the particular election for which the appointment was made[18], or, where the appointment was made for a particular period or for an indefinite period, while the elector is shown as voting by proxy in the record kept of those entitled to an absent vote at elections either for a particular period or for an indefinite period[19], in pursuance of the same application[20] in respect of which he was included in that record[21].

Where the appointment of a proxy is cancelled by the elector or otherwise ceases to be in force, the registration officer must, where practicable, notify the elector that the appointment has been cancelled or, as the case may be, notify him that the appointment has ceased and the reason for it[22]. Where the appointment of a proxy is cancelled by notice given to the registration officer or so ceases to be in force[23] or is no longer in force for a particular period or for an indefinite period[24], the registration officer must[25]: (a) notify the person whose appointment as proxy has been cancelled, expired, ceases to be or is no longer in force (unless the registration officer has previously been notified by that person that he no longer wishes to act as proxy)[26]; and (b) remove his name from the record of names and addresses of those appointed as proxies[27].

1 As to applications for the appointment of a proxy see PARA 375.
2 As to the meaning of 'elector' for these purposes see PARA 374 note 7.
3 Representation of the People Act 2000 s 12, Sch 4 para 6(10); European Parliamentary Elections Regulations 2004, SI 2004/293, reg 10, Sch 2 para 6(9) (Sch 2 substituted by SI 2009/186); National Assembly for Wales (Representation of the People) Order 2007, SI 2007/236, art 11(9). Such a notice cancelling a proxy's appointment must be disregarded for the purposes of a particular election if it is received by the registration officer after 5 pm on the eleventh day before the date of the poll at that election: Representation of the People (England and Wales) Regulations 2001, SI 2001/341, reg 56(5) (amended by SI 2001/1700); European Parliamentary Elections Regulations 2004, SI 2004/293, Sch 2 para 26(6) (as so substituted); National Assembly for Wales (Representation of the People) Order 2007, SI 2007/236, art 15(2), Sch 1 para 7(5)(c). Where a registration officer disregards an application for the purposes of any particular election, he must notify the applicant of this: Representation of the People (England and Wales) Regulations 2001, SI 2001/341, reg 57(5) (amended by SI 2006/752); European Parliamentary Elections Regulations 2004, SI 2004/293, Sch 2 para 27(7) (as so substituted); National Assembly for Wales (Representation of the People) Order 2007, SI 2007/236, Sch 1

para 8(8). As to the computation of time for these purposes see PARA 367 note 6. As to electoral registration officers and the areas for which they act see PARA 139 et seq. As to the date of the poll at a parliamentary general election or by-election see PARA 195; as to the date of the poll at local government elections (including elections to fill vacancies) see PARAS 206–209; as to the date of the poll at Welsh Assembly elections (including elections to fill vacancies in an Assembly constituency) see PARAS 213–214; and as to the date of the poll at a European parliamentary election see PARA 222.

The Representation of the People Act 2000 s 12, Sch 4 are applied and modified for the purpose of local authority mayoral elections in England and Wales by the Local Authorities (Mayoral Elections) (England and Wales) Regulations 2007, SI 2007/1024, reg 3(2)–(5), Sch 2 Table 3 (see PARA 11 note 14); and the Representation of the People (England and Wales) Regulations 2001, SI 2001/341, regs 56, 57, 59, also have effect for the purposes of local authority referendums, subject to the modifications specified, in relation to Wales, by the Local Authorities (Conduct of Referendums) (Wales) Regulations 2008, SI 2008/1848, reg 8(2), Sch 4 Table 5, and, in relation to England, by the Local Authorities (Conduct of Referendums) (England) Regulations 2012, SI 2012/323, regs 8(2), 11–13, Sch 4 Table 6 (see PARA 15 note 2).

4   Representation of the People Act 2000 Sch 4 para 6(10); European Parliamentary Elections Regulations 2004, SI 2004/293, Sch 2 para 6(9) (as substituted: see note 3); National Assembly for Wales (Representation of the People) Order 2007, SI 2007/236, art 11(9).

5   As to the meaning of 'parliamentary election' see PARA 9.

6   As to the issue of a proxy paper by the registration officer see PARA 375.

7   As to the meaning of 'constituency' in the context of a parliamentary election see PARA 9.

8   Representation of the People Act 2000 Sch 4 para 6(10)(a).

9   As to the meaning of 'local government election' see PARA 11; definition applied by virtue of the Representation of the People Act 2000 Sch 4 para 1(2). See also PARA 363 note 1.

10 Representation of the People Act 2000 Sch 4 para 6(10)(b). As to the meaning of 'electoral area' see PARA 11; definition applied by virtue of Sch 4 para 1(2).

11 As to European parliamentary elections see PARA 217 et seq.

12 As to electoral regions constituted for the purposes of European parliamentary elections see PARA 77.

13 European Parliamentary Elections Regulations 2004, SI 2004/293, Sch 2 para 6(9)(a) (as substituted: see note 3).

14 As to the meaning of 'Assembly election' in the context of Welsh Assembly elections see PARA 3 note 2.

15 As to the meaning of 'Assembly constituency' in relation to a Welsh Assembly election see PARA 3 note 2.

16 National Assembly for Wales (Representation of the People) Order 2007, SI 2007/236, art 11(9).

17 Representation of the People Act 2000 Sch 4 para 6(10)(c); European Parliamentary Elections Regulations 2004, SI 2004/293, Sch 2 para 6(9)(b) (as substituted: see note 3); National Assembly for Wales (Representation of the People) Order 2007, SI 2007/236, art 11(9).

18 Representation of the People Act 2000 Sch 4 para 6(11)(a); European Parliamentary Elections Regulations 2004, SI 2004/293, Sch 2 para 6(10)(a) (as substituted: see note 3); National Assembly for Wales (Representation of the People) Order 2007, SI 2007/236, art 11(10)(a).

19 Ie the record kept for the purposes of a parliamentary or local government election under the Representation of the People Act 2000 Sch 4 para 3, or for the purposes of a European parliamentary election under the European Parliamentary Elections Regulations 2004, SI 2004/293, Sch 2 para 3, or for the purposes of a Welsh Assembly election under the National Assembly for Wales (Representation of the People) Order 2007, SI 2007/236, art 8 (see PARA 370), as the case may be: see the Representation of the People Act 2000 Sch 4 para 6(11)(b); the European Parliamentary Elections Regulations 2004, SI 2004/293, Sch 2 para 6(10)(b) (as substituted: see note 3); and the National Assembly for Wales (Representation of the People) Order 2007, SI 2007/236, art 11(10)(b).

20 Ie, in relation to a parliamentary or local government election, under the Representation of the People Act 2000 Sch 4 para 3, or, in relation to a European parliamentary election, under the European Parliamentary Elections Regulations 2004, SI 2004/293, Sch 2 para 3, or, in relation to a Welsh Assembly election, under the National Assembly for Wales (Representation of the People) Order 2007, SI 2007/236, art 8 (see PARA 370), as the case may be: see the Representation of the People Act 2000 Sch 4 para 6(11)(b); the European Parliamentary Elections Regulations 2004, SI 2004/293, Sch 2 para 6(10)(b) (as substituted: see note 3); and the National Assembly for Wales (Representation of the People) Order 2007, SI 2007/236, art 11(10)(b).

21	Representation of the People Act 2000 Sch 4 para 6(11)(b); European Parliamentary Elections Regulations 2004, SI 2004/293, Sch 2 para 6(10)(b) (as substituted: see note 3); National Assembly for Wales (Representation of the People) Order 2007, SI 2007/236, art 11(10)(b).

22	Representation of the People (England and Wales) Regulations 2001, SI 2001/341, reg 57(4C) (added by SI 2006/752; and amended by SI 2006/2910); European Parliamentary Elections Regulations 2004, SI 2004/293, Sch 2 para 27(6) (as substituted: see note 3); National Assembly for Wales (Representation of the People) Order 2007, SI 2007/236, Sch 1 para 8(7). As to notification see PARA 367 note 35.

23	Ie, in relation to a parliamentary or local government election, under the Representation of the People Act 2000 Sch 4 para 6(10), or, in relation to a European parliamentary election, under the European Parliamentary Elections Regulations 2004, SI 2004/293, Sch 2 para 6(9), or, in relation to a Welsh Assembly election, under the National Assembly for Wales (Representation of the People) Order 2007, SI 2007/236, art 11(9) (see the text and notes 1–3), as the case may be: see the Representation of the People (England and Wales) Regulations 2001, SI 2001/341, reg 59; the European Parliamentary Elections Regulations 2004, SI 2004/293, Sch 2 para 29 (as substituted: see note 3); and the National Assembly for Wales (Representation of the People) Order 2007, SI 2007/236, Sch 1 para 10.

24	Ie, in relation to a parliamentary or local government election, under the Representation of the People Act 2000 Sch 4 para 6(11)(b), or, in relation to a European parliamentary election, under the European Parliamentary Elections Regulations 2004, SI 2004/293, Sch 2 para 6(10)(b), or, in relation to a Welsh Assembly election, under the National Assembly for Wales (Representation of the People) Order 2007, SI 2007/236, art 11(10)(b) (see the text and notes 19–21), as the case may be: see the Representation of the People (England and Wales) Regulations 2001, SI 2001/341, reg 59; the European Parliamentary Elections Regulations 2004, SI 2004/293, Sch 2 para 29 (as substituted: see note 3); and the National Assembly for Wales (Representation of the People) Order 2007, SI 2007/236, Sch 1 para 10.

25	Representation of the People (England and Wales) Regulations 2001, SI 2001/341, reg 59; European Parliamentary Elections Regulations 2004, SI 2004/293, Sch 2 para 29 (as substituted: see note 3); National Assembly for Wales (Representation of the People) Order 2007, SI 2007/236, Sch 1 para 10.

26	Representation of the People (England and Wales) Regulations 2001, SI 2001/341, reg 59(a); European Parliamentary Elections Regulations 2004, SI 2004/293, Sch 2 para 29(a) (as substituted: see note 3); National Assembly for Wales (Representation of the People) Order 2007, SI 2007/236, Sch 1 para 10(a).

27	Representation of the People (England and Wales) Regulations 2001, SI 2001/341, reg 59(b); European Parliamentary Elections Regulations 2004, SI 2004/293, Sch 2 para 29(b) (as substituted: see note 3); National Assembly for Wales (Representation of the People) Order 2007, SI 2007/236, Sch 1 para 10(b). The text refers to the record kept for the purposes of a parliamentary or local government election under the Representation of the People Act 2000 Sch 4 para 3(4)(c), or for the purposes of a European parliamentary election under the European Parliamentary Elections Regulations 2004, SI 2004/293, Sch 2 para 3(4)(c), or for the purposes of a Welsh Assembly election under the National Assembly for Wales (Representation of the People) Order 2007, SI 2007/236, art 8(3) (see PARA 370), as the case may be: see the Representation of the People (England and Wales) Regulations 2001, SI 2001/341, reg 59(b); the European Parliamentary Elections Regulations 2004, SI 2004/293, Sch 2 para 29(b) (as so substituted); and the National Assembly for Wales (Representation of the People) Order 2007, SI 2007/236, Sch 1 para 10(b).

(b) Voting in Person as Proxy for an Elector

377. Voting in person where a proxy has been appointed. A person entitled to vote as proxy for an elector[1] at a parliamentary[2], local government[3], Welsh Assembly[4] or European parliamentary[5], election may do so in person at the polling station allotted to the elector under the appropriate rules[6]. However, the elector may not apply for a ballot paper for the purpose of voting in person at the election, where a person is entitled instead to vote by post as proxy for the elector at any such election[7].

In order to indicate that an elector or his proxy is entitled to vote by post, and is for that reason not entitled to vote in person, the letter 'A' is placed against the entry of that elector in any copy of the register, or part of it, provided for a polling station[8].

1   As to the meaning of 'elector' for these purposes see PARA 374 note 7. As to applications for the appointment of a proxy see PARA 375.
2   As to the meaning of 'parliamentary election' see PARA 9.
3   As to the meaning of 'local government election' see PARA 11; definition applied by virtue of the Representation of the People Act 2000 s 12, Sch 4 para 1(2). See also PARA 363 note 1.
4   As to the meaning of 'Assembly election' in the context of Welsh Assembly elections see PARA 3 note 2.
5   As to European parliamentary elections see PARA 217 et seq.
6   Representation of the People Act 2000 Sch 4 para 7(1); European Parliamentary Elections Regulations 2004, SI 2004/293, reg 10, Sch 2 para 7(1) (Sch 2 substituted by SI 2009/186); National Assembly for Wales (Representation of the People) Order 2007, SI 2007/236, art 12(1). As to the appropriate rules referred to in the text, in relation to a parliamentary or local government election, see PARA 363 note 2; in relation to a Welsh Assembly election, see PARA 364 note 2; and, in relation to a European parliamentary election, see PARA 365 note 1.
    The Representation of the People Act 2000 s 12, Sch 4 are applied and modified for the purpose of local authority mayoral elections in England and Wales by the Local Authorities (Mayoral Elections) (England and Wales) Regulations 2007, SI 2007/1024, reg 3(2)–(5), Sch 2 Table 3 (see PARA 11 note 14); and the Representation of the People (England and Wales) Regulations 2001, SI 2001/341, reg 62, also has effect for the purposes of local authority referendums, subject to the modifications specified, in relation to Wales, by the Local Authorities (Conduct of Referendums) (Wales) Regulations 2008, SI 2008/1848, reg 8(2), Sch 4 Table 5, and, in relation to England, by the Local Authorities (Conduct of Referendums) (England) Regulations 2012, SI 2012/323, regs 8(2), 11–13, Sch 4 Table 6 (see PARA 15 note 2).
7   Representation of the People Act 2000 Sch 4 para 7(2); European Parliamentary Elections Regulations 2004, SI 2004/293, Sch 2 para 7(2) (as substituted: see note 6); National Assembly for Wales (Representation of the People) Order 2007, SI 2007/236, art 12(2). As to voting by post as proxy for an elector see PARA 378 et seq.
    The Representation of the People Act 2000 Sch 4 para 7(2), or the European Parliamentary Elections Regulations 2004, SI 2004/293, Sch 2 para 7(2), or the National Assembly for Wales (Representation of the People) Order 2007, SI 2007/236, art 12(2), as the case may be, does not prevent a person, at the polling station allotted to him, marking a tendered ballot paper in pursuance of the Representation of the People Act 1983 Sch 1 r 40(1ZC), (1ZE), or the European Parliamentary Elections Regulations 2004, SI 2004/293, Sch 1 para 44(4), (6), or the National Assembly for Wales (Representation of the People) Order 2007, SI 2007/236, Sch 5 para 49(4), (6) (see PARA 403), as the case may be: Representation of the People Act 2000 Sch 4 para 7(10) (added by the Electoral Administration Act 2006 s 38(6)(b)); European Parliamentary Elections Regulations 2004, SI 2004/293, Sch 2 para 7(11) (as so substituted); National Assembly for Wales (Representation of the People) Order 2007, SI 2007/236, art 12(11).
8   Representation of the People (England and Wales) Regulations 2001, SI 2001/341, reg 62 (amended by SI 2006/2910); European Parliamentary Elections Regulations 2004, SI 2004/293, Sch 2 para 34 (as substituted: see note 6); National Assembly for Wales (Representation of the People) Order 2007, SI 2007/236, art 15(2), Sch 1 para 15.

(c) Voting by Post as Proxy for an Elector

378. Application by person to vote by post as proxy. Where a person applies to the registration officer[1] to vote by post:

(1)   as proxy at parliamentary[2] or local government elections[3] (or at both) or at Welsh Assembly[4], or European parliamentary[5], elections (whether for an indefinite period or for a particular period specified in his application)[6]; or

(2)   as proxy at a particular such election[7],

the registration officer must grant the application if[8]:

(a)   the registration officer is satisfied that the elector[9] is or will be registered in the register of electors relevant to the election[10]; and

(b)   there is in force an appointment of the applicant as the elector's proxy to vote for him at elections of the kind in question or, as the case may be, the election concerned[11]; and

(c)   the application contains the applicant's signature and date of birth and meets the statutory requirements[12].

Such an application[13] must state:

(i)   the full name of the applicant[14];

(ii)   the proxy's address, together with the name of the elector for whom he will act as proxy and the elector's address in respect of which the elector is registered or has applied to be (or is treated as having applied to be) registered in the register[15];

(iii) the address to which the ballot paper should be sent[16];

(iv)   the grounds on which the elector claims to be entitled to an absent vote[17];

(v)   in the case of a person who is unable to provide a signature, the reasons for his request for waiver of any requirement[18] to provide a signature and the name and address of any person who has assisted him to complete his application[19]; and

(vi)   where the applicant has, or has applied for, an anonymous entry, that fact[20].

An application made for a particular election (except in the case of a Welsh Assembly election) must identify the election in question[21], and such an application must state that it is made for a particular election[22]. Such an application may be combined where polls for different elections fall on the same day[23]. The application must be made in writing and dated[24]. Where an application is made by an elector to vote by proxy, it must include an application for the appointment of a proxy which meets the statutory requirements[25].

Where the registration officer grants an application to vote by post, he must notify the applicant of his decision[26]; and where he refuses an application, he must notify the applicant of his decision and give the reason for it[27]. An appeal lies to the county court from any decision of the registration officer disallowing a person's application to vote by post as proxy in any case where the application is not made for a particular election only[28].

1   As to electoral registration officers and the areas for which they act see PARA 139 et seq.
2   As to the meaning of 'parliamentary election' see PARA 9.
3   As to the meaning of 'local government election' see PARA 11; definition applied by virtue of the Representation of the People Act 2000 s 12, Sch 4 para 1(2). See also PARA 363 note 1.
4   As to the meaning of 'Assembly election' in the context of Welsh Assembly elections see PARA 3 note 2.
5   As to European parliamentary elections see PARA 217 et seq.
6   Representation of the People Act 2000 Sch 4 para 7(4)(a); European Parliamentary Elections Regulations 2004, SI 2004/293, reg 10, Sch 2 para 7(4)(a) (Sch 2 substituted by SI 2009/186); National Assembly for Wales (Representation of the People) Order 2007, SI 2007/236, art 12(4)(a). As to applications so made see PARA 367.
    The Representation of the People Act 2000 s 12, Sch 4 are applied and modified for the purpose of local authority mayoral elections in England and Wales by the Local Authorities (Mayoral Elections) (England and Wales) Regulations 2007, SI 2007/1024, reg 3(2)–(5), Sch 2 Table 3 (see PARA 11 note 14); and the Representation of the People (England and Wales) Regulations 2001, SI 2001/341, regs 51, 51A, 51AA, 56, 57, also have effect for the purposes of local authority referendums, subject to the modifications specified, in relation to Wales, by the Local Authorities (Conduct of Referendums) (Wales) Regulations 2008, SI 2008/1848, reg 8(2),

Sch 4 Table 5, and, in relation to England, by the Local Authorities (Conduct of Referendums) (England) Regulations 2012, SI 2012/323, regs 8(2), 11–13, Sch 4 Table 6 (see PARA 15 note 2).

7   Representation of the People Act 2000 Sch 4 para 7(4)(b); European Parliamentary Elections Regulations 2004, SI 2004/293, Sch 2 para 7(4)(b) (as substituted: see note 6); National Assembly for Wales (Representation of the People) Order 2007, SI 2007/236, art 12(4)(b). As to applications so made see PARA 371.

8   Representation of the People Act 2000 Sch 4 para 7(4), (5); European Parliamentary Elections Regulations 2004, SI 2004/293, Sch 2 para 7(4), (5) (as substituted: see note 6); National Assembly for Wales (Representation of the People) Order 2007, SI 2007/236, art 12(4), (5).

Such an application from a proxy to vote by post must be disregarded for the purposes of any particular election if it is received by the registration officer after 5 pm on the eleventh day before the date of the poll at that election: Representation of the People (England and Wales) Regulations 2001, SI 2001/341, reg 56(1) (amended by SI 2006/752); European Parliamentary Elections Regulations 2004, SI 2004/293, Sch 2 para 26(1) (as so substituted); National Assembly for Wales (Representation of the People) Order 2007, SI 2007/236, art 15(2), Sch 1 para 7(1). Where a registration officer disregards such an application for the purposes of any particular election, he must notify the applicant of this: Representation of the People (England and Wales) Regulations 2001, SI 2001/341, reg 57(5) (amended by SI 2006/752); European Parliamentary Elections Regulations 2004, SI 2004/293, Sch 2 para 27(7) (as so substituted); National Assembly for Wales (Representation of the People) Order 2007, SI 2007/236, Sch 1 para 8(8). As to the computation of time for these purposes see PARA 367 note 6. As to the date of the poll at a parliamentary general election or by-election see PARA 195; as to the date of the poll at local government elections (including elections to fill vacancies) see PARAS 206–209; as to the date of the poll at Welsh Assembly elections (including elections to fill vacancies in an Assembly constituency) see PARAS 213–214; and as to the date of the poll at a European parliamentary election see PARA 222.

9   As to the meaning of 'elector' for these purposes see PARA 374 note 7.

10   Representation of the People Act 2000 Sch 4 para 7(5)(a); European Parliamentary Elections Regulations 2004, SI 2004/293, Sch 2 para 7(5)(a) (as substituted: see note 6); National Assembly for Wales (Representation of the People) Order 2007, SI 2007/236, art 12(5)(a). In the case of a parliamentary election, the register referred to in the text is the register of parliamentary electors and, in the case of a local government election, it is the register of local government electors (although an application under the Representation of the People Act 2000 Sch 4 may relate to both types of election, in which case the requirement is for the applicant to be registered in both): see the Representation of the People Act 2000 Sch 4 para 7(5)(a). As to the meaning of the 'register of electors', in relation to a European parliamentary election, see PARA 111 note 4. As to the meaning of 'register', for the purposes of a Welsh Assembly election, see PARA 367 note 7. As to registration as an elector see PARA 113 et seq; and as to the registers of electors maintained by registration officers see PARA 143 et seq.

11   Representation of the People Act 2000 Sch 4 para 7(5)(b); European Parliamentary Elections Regulations 2004, SI 2004/293, Sch 2 para 7(5)(b) (as substituted: see note 6); National Assembly for Wales (Representation of the People) Order 2007, SI 2007/236, art 12(5)(b). As to the appointment of a proxy see PARA 375 et seq.

12   Representation of the People Act 2000 Sch 4 para 7(5)(c) (amended by the Electoral Administration Act 2006 s 14(3)(a), (8)); European Parliamentary Elections Regulations 2004, SI 2004/293, Sch 2 para 7(5)(c) (as substituted: see note 6); National Assembly for Wales (Representation of the People) Order 2007, SI 2007/236, art 12(5)(c). For the purposes of the Representation of the People Act 2000 Sch 4, the requirements are as prescribed; and 'prescribed' means prescribed by regulations (see the Representation of the People Act 1983 s 202(1); applied by virtue of the Representation of the People Act 2000 Sch 4 para 1(2)). Accordingly, the text refers to the requirements set out, in the case of a parliamentary or local government election, in the Representation of the People (England and Wales) Regulations 2001, SI 2001/341, Pt IV (regs 50–63A), or, in the case of a European parliamentary election, the European Parliamentary Elections Regulations 2004, SI 2004/293, Sch 2 Pt 2 (Sch 2 paras 12–34), or, in the case of a Welsh Assembly election, in the National Assembly for Wales (Representation of the People) Order 2007, SI 2007/236, Sch 1, as the case may be (see PARA 366): see the Representation of the People Act 2000 Sch 4 para 7(5)(c) (as so amended); the European Parliamentary Elections Regulations 2004, SI 2004/293, Sch 2 para 7(5)(c) (as so substituted); and the National Assembly for Wales (Representation of the People) Order 2007, SI 2007/236, art 12(5)(c). As to the conditions relating to the retention of the records referred to in the text see PARA 503 et seq.

Where an application is required to contain a signature and date of birth, the information must be set out in a manner that is sufficiently clear and unambiguous as to be capable of electronic scanning into his record: Representation of the People (England and Wales) Regulations 2001, SI 2001/341, reg 51(3A) (reg 51(3A), (3B) added, by SI 2006/2910); European Parliamentary Elections Regulations 2004, SI 2004/293, Sch 2 para 17(4) (as so substituted); National Assembly for Wales (Representation of the People) Order 2007, SI 2007/236, Sch 1 para 1(3). This requirement is met by configuring the information as follows:

(1) the signature must appear against a background of white unlined paper of at least five centimetres long and two centimetres high (Representation of the People (England and Wales) Regulations 2001, SI 2001/341, reg 51(3A)(a) (as so added); European Parliamentary Elections Regulations 2004, SI 2004/293, Sch 2 para 17(4)(a) (as so substituted); National Assembly for Wales (Representation of the People) Order 2007, SI 2007/236, Sch 1 para 1(3)(a)); and

(2) the applicant's date of birth must be set out numerically configured in the sequence of date, month and year, namely [d][d][m][m][y][y][y][y] (Representation of the People (England and Wales) Regulations 2001, SI 2001/341, reg 51(3A)(b) (as so added); European Parliamentary Elections Regulations 2004, SI 2004/293, Sch 2 para 17(4)(b) (as so substituted); National Assembly for Wales (Representation of the People) Order 2007, SI 2007/236, Sch 1 para 1(3)(b)).

The registration officer may dispense with the requirement under the Representation of the People Act 2000 Sch 4 para 7(5)(c), the European Parliamentary Elections Regulations 2004, SI 2004/293, Sch 2 para 7(5)(c), or the National Assembly for Wales (Representation of the People) Order 2007, SI 2007/236, art 12(5)(c), as the case may be, for the applicant to provide a signature, if he is satisfied that the applicant is unable to provide a signature because of any disability the applicant has, or is unable to provide a signature because the applicant is unable to read or write, or is unable to sign in a consistent and distinctive way because of any such disability or inability: Representation of the People Act 2000 Sch 4 para 7(11) (added by the Electoral Administration Act 2006 s 14(3)(b), (8)); European Parliamentary Elections Regulations 2004, SI 2004/293, Sch 2 para 7(12) (as so substituted); National Assembly for Wales (Representation of the People) Order 2007, SI 2007/236, art 12(12). Where the application contains a request that the registration officer waive the requirement for a signature, head (1) above does not apply: Representation of the People (England and Wales) Regulations 2001, SI 2001/341, reg 51(3B) (as so added); European Parliamentary Elections Regulations 2004, SI 2004/293, Sch 2 para 17(5) (as so substituted); National Assembly for Wales (Representation of the People) Order 2007, SI 2007/236, Sch 1 para 1(4). As to the meaning of 'disability' for these purposes see PARA 367 note 8.

The registration officer may satisfy himself:

(a) that an application under the Representation of the People Act 2000 Sch 4, or the European Parliamentary Elections Regulations 2004, SI 2004/293, Sch 2, or the National Assembly for Wales (Representation of the People) Order 2007, SI 2007/236, art 12 (see also the text and notes 1–11), as the case may be, meets any requirements that it has been signed by the applicant and states his date of birth by referring to any signature and date of birth either previously provided by the applicant to the registration officer or to the returning officer or previously provided by the applicant to the authority referred to in the Representation of the People (England and Wales) Regulations 2001, SI 2001/341, reg 35(2)(a) (ie the council which appointed him: see PARA 142), which the registration officer is authorised to inspect for the purposes of his registration duties (Representation of the People (England and Wales) Regulations 2001, SI 2001/341, reg 51A(a) (reg 51A added by SI 2006/752; and substituted by SI 2006/2910); European Parliamentary Elections Regulations 2004, SI 2004/293, Sch 2 para 19(a) (as so substituted); National Assembly for Wales (Representation of the People) Order 2007, SI 2007/236, Sch 1 para 1(6)(a)); and

(b) as to whether the applicant is unable to provide a signature or a consistent signature due to any disability or inability to read or write (Representation of the People (England and Wales) Regulations 2001, SI 2001/341, reg 51A(b) (reg 51A as so added and substituted); European Parliamentary Elections Regulations 2004, SI 2004/293, Sch 2 para 19(b) (as so substituted); National Assembly for Wales (Representation of the People) Order 2007, SI 2007/236, Sch 1 para 1(6)(b)).

As to the provisions made for the initial and continuing capture of the personal identifiers of those who are existing absent voters see PARA 366.

13 Applications made under the Representation of the People Act 2000 Sch 4, or the European Parliamentary Elections Regulations 2004, SI 2004/293, Sch 2 Pt 2, or the National Assembly for Wales (Representation of the People) Order 2007, SI 2007/236, art 12, must comply with the requirements, in relation to a parliamentary or local government election, of the Representation of the People (England and Wales) Regulations 2001, SI 2001/341, reg 51, or, in relation to a

European parliamentary election, of the European Parliamentary Elections Regulations 2004, SI 2004/293, Sch 2 para 17, or, in relation to a Welsh Assembly election, of the National Assembly for Wales (Representation of the People) Order 2007, SI 2007/236, Sch 1 para 1, as well as such further requirements in the Representation of the People (England and Wales) Regulations 2001, SI 2001/341, Pt IV, or the European Parliamentary Elections Regulations 2004, SI 2004/293, Sch 2 Pt 2, as are relevant to the application: Representation of the People (England and Wales) Regulations 2001, SI 2001/341, reg 51(1); European Parliamentary Elections Regulations 2004, SI 2004/293, Sch 2 para 17(1) (as substituted: see note 6); National Assembly for Wales (Representation of the People) Order 2007, SI 2007/236, art 13(1). As to additional requirements for applications to vote by proxy for a definite or indefinite period see PARAS 368–369.

14 Representation of the People (England and Wales) Regulations 2001, SI 2001/341, reg 51(2)(a); European Parliamentary Elections Regulations 2004, SI 2004/293, Sch 2 para 17(2)(a) (as substituted: see note 6); National Assembly for Wales (Representation of the People) Order 2007, SI 2007/236, Sch 1 para 1(1)(a).

15 Representation of the People (England and Wales) Regulations 2001, SI 2001/341, reg 51(2)(b), (c) (reg 51(2)(b) amended by SI 2006/752); European Parliamentary Elections Regulations 2004, SI 2004/293, Sch 2 para 17(2)(b), (c) (as substituted: see note 6); National Assembly for Wales (Representation of the People) Order 2007, SI 2007/236, Sch 1 para 1(1)(b), (c). As to the address to be specified for the purposes of Sch 1 para 1(1)(b) see PARA 367 note 25.

16 Representation of the People (England and Wales) Regulations 2001, SI 2001/341, reg 51(2)(d) (reg 51(2)(d) amended, reg 51AA added, by SI 2006/2910); European Parliamentary Elections Regulations 2004, SI 2004/293, Sch 2 para 17(2)(d) (as substituted: see note 6); National Assembly for Wales (Representation of the People) Order 2007, SI 2007/236, Sch 1 para 1(1)(d).
    In the case of an application to vote by a proxy to vote by post made under the Representation of the People Act 2000 Sch 4 para 7(4), the European Parliamentary Elections Regulations 2004, SI 2004/293, Sch 2 para 7(4), or the National Assembly for Wales (Representation of the People) Order 2007, SI 2007/236, art 12(4) (see the text and notes 1–8), as the case may be, where the addresses stated in accordance with head (ii) in the text, and head (iii) in the text, are different, except where an applicant has, or has applied for, an anonymous entry, the application must set out why the applicant's circumstances will be or are likely to be such that he requires the ballot paper to be sent to the address stated in accordance with head (iii) in the text: see the Representation of the People (England and Wales) Regulations 2001, SI 2001/341, reg 51AA(1)–(3) (as so added); the European Parliamentary Elections Regulations 2004, SI 2004/293, Sch 2 para 20(1)–(3) (as so substituted); and the National Assembly for Wales (Representation of the People) Order 2007, SI 2007/236, Sch 1 para 1(7)(a)(ii), (b).

17 Representation of the People (England and Wales) Regulations 2001, SI 2001/341, reg 51(2)(e); European Parliamentary Elections Regulations 2004, SI 2004/293, Sch 2 para 17(2)(e) (as substituted: see note 6); National Assembly for Wales (Representation of the People) Order 2007, SI 2007/236, Sch 1 para 1(1)(e).

18 Ie under the Representation of the People Act 2000 Sch 4 para 7, the European Parliamentary Elections Regulations 2004, SI 2004/293, Sch 2 para 7, or the National Assembly for Wales (Representation of the People) Order 2007, SI 2007/236, art 12 (see the text and notes 1–12), as the case may be: see the Representation of the People (England and Wales) Regulations 2001, SI 2001/341, reg 51(2)(f) (reg 51(2)(f), (g) added by SI 2006/2910); the European Parliamentary Elections Regulations 2004, SI 2004/293, Sch 2 para 17(2)(f) (as substituted: see note 6); and the National Assembly for Wales (Representation of the People) Order 2007, SI 2007/236, Sch 1 para 1(1)(f).

19 Representation of the People (England and Wales) Regulations 2001, SI 2001/341, reg 51(2)(f) (as added: see note 18); European Parliamentary Elections Regulations 2004, SI 2004/293, Sch 2 para 17(2)(f) (as substituted: see note 6); National Assembly for Wales (Representation of the People) Order 2007, SI 2007/236, Sch 1 para 1(1)(f).

20 Representation of the People (England and Wales) Regulations 2001, SI 2001/341, reg 51(2)(g) (as added: see note 18); European Parliamentary Elections Regulations 2004, SI 2004/293, Sch 2 para 17(2)(g) (as substituted: see note 6); National Assembly for Wales (Representation of the People) Order 2007, SI 2007/236, Sch 1 para 1(1)(g).

21 Representation of the People (England and Wales) Regulations 2001, SI 2001/341, reg 51(5)(b); European Parliamentary Elections Regulations 2004, SI 2004/293, Sch 2 para 17(7)(b) (as substituted: see note 6).

22 Representation of the People (England and Wales) Regulations 2001, SI 2001/341, reg 51(5)(a); European Parliamentary Elections Regulations 2004, SI 2004/293, Sch 2 para 17(7)(a) (as substituted: see note 6).

23 See the Representation of the People (England and Wales) Regulations 2001, SI 2001/341, reg 51(5); the European Parliamentary Elections Regulations 2004, SI 2004/293, Sch 2 para 17(9) (as substituted: see note 6); and the National Assembly for Wales (Representation of the People) Order 2007, SI 2007/236, Sch 1 para 1(5).

24 Representation of the People (England and Wales) Regulations 2001, SI 2001/341, reg 51(3) (substituted by SI 2006/2910); European Parliamentary Elections Regulations 2004, SI 2004/293, Sch 2 para 17(3) (as substituted: see note 6); National Assembly for Wales (Representation of the People) Order 2007, SI 2007/236, Sch 1 para 1(2).

25 See the Representation of the People (England and Wales) Regulations 2001, SI 2001/341, regs 51(6), 52; the European Parliamentary Elections Regulations 2004, SI 2004/293, Sch 2 paras 17(8), 22; the National Assembly for Wales (Representation of the People) Order 2007, SI 2007/236, Sch 1 paras 1, 3; and PARA 375.

26 Representation of the People (England and Wales) Regulations 2001, SI 2001/341, reg 57(1) (amended by SI 2006/752); European Parliamentary Elections Regulations 2004, SI 2004/293, Sch 2 para 27(1) (as substituted: see note 6); National Assembly for Wales (Representation of the People) Order 2007, SI 2007/236, Sch 1 para 8(1). Where the registration officer at a parliamentary or Welsh Assembly election is not the acting returning officer for any constituency (or part of such a constituency), or where the registration officer at a European parliamentary election is not the local returning officer for any local counting area (or part of such an area), in the area for which he is the registration officer, he must send to that officer details of any application to vote by post which he has granted as soon as practicable after doing so: Representation of the People (England and Wales) Regulations 2001, SI 2001/341, reg 57(6); European Parliamentary Elections Regulations 2004, SI 2004/293, Sch 2 para 27(8) (as so substituted); National Assembly for Wales (Representation of the People) Order 2007, SI 2007/236, Sch 1 para 8(9). As to the meaning of 'local counting area' see PARA 139 note 1. As to local returning officers appointed for the purposes of elections to the European Parliament see PARA 360. As to notification by the registration officer at a Welsh Assembly election see PARA 367 note 35.

27 Representation of the People (England and Wales) Regulations 2001, SI 2001/341, reg 57(4); European Parliamentary Elections Regulations 2004, SI 2004/293, Sch 2 para 27(3) (as substituted: see note 6); National Assembly for Wales (Representation of the People) Order 2007, SI 2007/236, Sch 1 para 8(4).

28 See PARA 172 et seq.

379. Record of persons entitled to vote by post as proxy. The registration officer[1] must keep a record of those whose applications to vote by post as proxy at parliamentary[2] or local government elections[3] (or at both) or at Welsh Assembly[4] or European parliamentary elections[5] (whether for an indefinite period or for a particular period specified in the application) have been granted[6] showing[7]:

(1) whether their applications were to vote by post as proxy for an indefinite or a particular period (specifying that period)[8];

(2) the addresses provided by them in their applications as the addresses to which their ballot papers are to be sent[9]; and

(3) where the applications were in respect of parliamentary or local government elections, whether they were in respect of parliamentary elections or local government elections (or both)[10].

A person who remains on the record of those entitled to vote by post as proxy at such elections (whether for an indefinite period or for a particular period specified in the application)[11] may, at any time, provide the registration officer with a fresh signature[12]; and anything required or authorised to be done for the purposes of any enactment in relation to a signature required to be provided in pursuance of absent voting in Great Britain[13] must be done in relation to a signature so provided instead of in relation to a signature provided on any earlier occasion[14].

The registration officer must remove a person from the record so kept of those whose applications to vote by post as proxy at elections (whether for an indefinite period or for a particular period specified in the application) have been granted[15]:

(a)   if he applies to the registration officer to be removed[16],

(b)   if the elector[17] ceases to be registered in the register of electors relevant to the election[18];

(c)   if the appointment of the person concerned as the elector's proxy ceases to be in force (whether or not he is re-appointed)[19]; or

(d)   in the case of a person who applied to vote by post as proxy for a particular period, once that period expires[20].

Where a person is removed from the record under any of heads (a) to (d) above, the registration officer must, where practicable, notify him of this and the reason for it[21].

The registration officer must also keep a record in relation to those whose applications to vote by post either as proxy at such elections (whether for an indefinite period or for a particular period specified in the application)[22], or at a particular such election[23], have been granted showing:

(i)   their dates of birth[24]; and

(ii)   except in cases where the registration officer[25] has dispensed with the requirement to provide a signature, their signatures[26].

The record so kept must be retained by the registration officer for the prescribed period[27]. The registration officer must either provide a copy of the information contained in records so kept by him[28] to the returning officer for an election in relation to electors at the election[29], or give the returning officer access to such information[30]. Information contained in such records may be disclosed by a registration officer (subject to any prescribed conditions) to any other registration officer if he thinks that to do so will assist the other registration officer in the performance of his duties[31], or to any person exercising functions in relation to the preparation or conduct of legal proceedings under the relevant election provisions[32], or (except in relation to a European parliamentary election) to such other persons for such other purposes relating to elections as may be prescribed[33].

1   As to electoral registration officers and the areas for which they act see PARA 139 et seq.
2   As to the meaning of 'parliamentary election' see PARA 9.
3   As to the meaning of 'local government election' see PARA 11; definition applied by virtue of the Representation of the People Act 2000 s 12, Sch 4 para 1(2). See also PARA 363 note 1.
        The Representation of the People Act 2000 s 12, Sch 4 are applied and modified for the purpose of local authority mayoral elections in England and Wales by the Local Authorities (Mayoral Elections) (England and Wales) Regulations 2007, SI 2007/1024, reg 3(2)–(5), Sch 2 Table 3 (see PARA 11 note 14); and the Representation of the People (England and Wales) Regulations 2001, SI 2001/341, regs 56, 57, also have effect for the purposes of local authority referendums, subject to the modifications specified, in relation to Wales, by the Local Authorities (Conduct of Referendums) (Wales) Regulations 2008, SI 2008/1848, reg 8(2), Sch 4 Table 5, and, in relation to England, by the Local Authorities (Conduct of Referendums) (England) Regulations 2012, SI 2012/323, regs 8(2), 11–13, Sch 4 Table 6 (see PARA 15 note 2).
4   As to the meaning of 'Assembly election' in the context of Welsh Assembly elections see PARA 3 note 2.
5   As to European parliamentary elections see PARA 217 et seq.
6   Ie a record of those whose applications have been granted, in relation to a parliamentary or local government election, under the Representation of the People Act 2000 Sch 4 para 7(4)(a), or, in relation to a European parliamentary election, under the European Parliamentary Elections Regulations 2004, SI 2004/293, Sch 2 para 7(4)(a), or, in relation to a Welsh Assembly election, under the National Assembly for Wales (Representation of the People) Order 2007, SI 2007/236, art 12(4)(a) (see PARA 378), as the case may be: see the Representation of the

People Act 2000 Sch 4 para 7(6); the European Parliamentary Elections Regulations 2004, SI 2004/293, Sch 2 para 7(6) (Sch 2 substituted by SI 2009/186); and the National Assembly for Wales (Representation of the People) Order 2007, SI 2007/236, art 12(6).

7 Representation of the People Act 2000 Sch 4 para 7(6); European Parliamentary Elections Regulations 2004, SI 2004/293, Sch 2 para 7(6) (as substituted: see note 6); National Assembly for Wales (Representation of the People) Order 2007, SI 2007/236, art 12(6).

8 Representation of the People Act 2000 Sch 4 para 7(6)(a)(ii); European Parliamentary Elections Regulations 2004, SI 2004/293, Sch 2 para 7(6)(a) (as substituted: see note 6); National Assembly for Wales (Representation of the People) Order 2007, SI 2007/236, art 12(6)(a).

9 Representation of the People Act 2000 Sch 4 para 7(6)(b); European Parliamentary Elections Regulations 2004, SI 2004/293, Sch 2 para 7(6)(b) (as substituted: see note 6); National Assembly for Wales (Representation of the People) Order 2007, SI 2007/236, art 12(6)(b).

10 Representation of the People Act 2000 Sch 4 para 7(6)(a)(i).

11 Ie who remains on the record kept, in relation to a parliamentary or local government election, under the Representation of the People Act 2000 Sch 4 para 7(6), or, in relation to a European parliamentary election, under the European Parliamentary Elections Regulations 2004, SI 2004/293, Sch 2 para 7(6), or, in relation to a Welsh Assembly election, under the National Assembly for Wales (Representation of the People) Order 2007, SI 2007/236, art 12(6) (see the text and notes 1–10), as the case may be: see the Representation of the People Act 2000 Sch 4 para 7A(1) (Sch 4 paras 7A–7D added by the Electoral Administration Act 2006 s 14(4), (8)); the European Parliamentary Elections Regulations 2004, SI 2004/293, Sch 2 para 8(1) (as substituted: see note 6); and the National Assembly for Wales (Representation of the People) Order 2007, SI 2007/236, art 13(3).

12 Representation of the People Act 2000 Sch 4 para 7A(1) (as added: see note 11); European Parliamentary Elections Regulations 2004, SI 2004/293, Sch 2 para 8(1) (as substituted: see note 6); National Assembly for Wales (Representation of the People) Order 2007, SI 2007/236, art 13(3).

Regulations under the Representation of the People Act 1983 may make provision as to circumstances in which a registration officer may require a person who remains on the record kept under the Representation of the People Act 2000 Sch 4 para 7(6) (see the text and notes 1–10) to provide a fresh signature (see Sch 4 para 7B(a) (as so added)), and as to the consequences of a person refusing or failing to comply with a requirement to provide a fresh signature (see Sch 4 para 7B(b) (as so added)). As to the regulations so made see the Elections (Fresh Signatures for Absent Voters) Regulations 2013, SI 2013/1599; the National Assembly for Wales (Representation of the People) (Fresh Signatures for Absent Voters) Order 2013, SI 2013/1514 (made under the Government of Wales Act 2006 s 13(1), (4)); and PARA 366 note 16.

13 Ie in pursuance of, in relation to a parliamentary or local government election, the Representation of the People Act 2000 Sch 4, or, in relation to a European parliamentary election, under the European Parliamentary Elections Regulations 2004, SI 2004/293, Sch 2, or, in relation to a Welsh Assembly election, under the National Assembly for Wales (Representation of the People) Order 2007, SI 2007/236: see the Representation of the People Act 2000 Sch 4 para 7A(2) (as added: see note 11); the European Parliamentary Elections Regulations 2004, SI 2004/293, Sch 2 para 8(2) (as substituted: see note 6); and the National Assembly for Wales (Representation of the People) Order 2007, SI 2007/236, art 13(4).

14 Representation of the People Act 2000 Sch 4 para 7A(2) (as added: see note 11); European Parliamentary Elections Regulations 2004, SI 2004/293, Sch 2 para 8(2) (as substituted: see note 6); National Assembly for Wales (Representation of the People) Order 2007, SI 2007/236, art 13(4).

15 Representation of the People Act 2000 Sch 4 para 7(9); European Parliamentary Elections Regulations 2004, SI 2004/293, Sch 2 para 7(10) (as substituted: see note 6); National Assembly for Wales (Representation of the People) Order 2007, SI 2007/236, art 12(10).

16 Representation of the People Act 2000 Sch 4 para 7(9)(a); European Parliamentary Elections Regulations 2004, SI 2004/293, Sch 2 para 7(10)(a) (as substituted: see note 6); National Assembly for Wales (Representation of the People) Order 2007, SI 2007/236, art 12(10)(a).

Such an application, made by a proxy to be removed from the record, under the Representation of the People Act 2000 Sch 4 para 7(9)(a), or the European Parliamentary Elections Regulations 2004, SI 2004/293, Sch 2 para 7(10)(a), or the National Assembly for Wales (Representation of the People) Order 2007, SI 2007/236, art 12(10)(a), as the case may be, must be disregarded for the purposes of a particular election if it is received by the registration officer after 5 pm on the eleventh day before the date of the poll at that election: Representation of the People (England and Wales) Regulations 2001, SI 2001/341, reg 56(5) (amended by SI 2001/1700); European Parliamentary Elections Regulations 2004, SI 2004/293,

Sch 2 para 26(6)(b) (as so substituted); National Assembly for Wales (Representation of the People) Order 2007, SI 2007/236, Sch 1 para 7(5)(b). Where a registration officer disregards an application for the purposes of any particular election, he must notify the applicant of this: Representation of the People (England and Wales) Regulations 2001, SI 2001/341, reg 57(5) (amended by SI 2006/752); European Parliamentary Elections Regulations 2004, SI 2004/293, Sch 2 para 27(7) (as so substituted); National Assembly for Wales (Representation of the People) Order 2007, SI 2007/236, Sch 1 para 8(8). As to the computation of time for these purposes see PARA 367 note 6. As to the date of the poll at a parliamentary general election or by-election see PARA 195; as to the date of the poll at local government elections (including elections to fill vacancies) see PARAS 206–209; as to the date of the poll at Welsh Assembly elections (including elections to fill vacancies in an Assembly constituency) see PARAS 213–214; and as to the date of the poll at a European parliamentary election see PARA 222.

17 As to the meaning of 'elector' for these purposes see PARA 374 note 7.

18 Representation of the People Act 2000 Sch 4 para 7(9)(b); European Parliamentary Elections Regulations 2004, SI 2004/293, Sch 2 para 7(10)(b) (as substituted: see note 6); National Assembly for Wales (Representation of the People) Order 2007, SI 2007/236, art 12(10)(c).

19 Representation of the People Act 2000 Sch 4 para 7(9)(c); European Parliamentary Elections Regulations 2004, SI 2004/293, Sch 2 para 7(10)(c) (as substituted: see note 6); National Assembly for Wales (Representation of the People) Order 2007, SI 2007/236, art 12(10)(d).

20 Representation of the People Act 2000 Sch 4 para 7(9)(d); European Parliamentary Elections Regulations 2004, SI 2004/293, Sch 2 para 7(10)(d) (as substituted: see note 6); National Assembly for Wales (Representation of the People) Order 2007, SI 2007/236, art 12(10)(b).

21 Representation of the People (England and Wales) Regulations 2001, SI 2001/341, reg 57(4B) (added by SI 2006/752; and amended by SI 2006/2910); European Parliamentary Elections Regulations 2004, SI 2004/293, Sch 2 para 27(5) (as substituted: see note 6); National Assembly for Wales (Representation of the People) Order 2007, SI 2007/236, Sch 1 para 8(6). As to notification see PARA 367 note 35.

22 Ie a record of those whose applications have been granted, in relation to a parliamentary or local government election, under the Representation of the People Act 2000 Sch 4 para 7(4)(a), or, in relation to a European parliamentary election, under the European Parliamentary Elections Regulations 2004, SI 2004/293, Sch 2 para 7(4)(a), or, in relation to a Welsh Assembly election, under the National Assembly for Wales (Representation of the People) Order 2007, SI 2007/236, art 12(4)(a) (see PARA 378): see the Representation of the People Act 2000 Sch 4 para 7(12) (Sch 4 paras 7(12), (13) added by the Electoral Administration Act 2006 s 14(3)(b), (8)); the European Parliamentary Elections Regulations 2004, SI 2004/293, Sch 2 para 7(13) (as substituted: see note 6); and the National Assembly for Wales (Representation of the People) Order 2007, SI 2007/236, art 12(13).

23 Ie a record of those whose applications have been granted, in relation to a parliamentary or local government election, under the Representation of the People Act 2000 Sch 4 para 7(4)(b), or, in relation to a European parliamentary election, under the European Parliamentary Elections Regulations 2004, SI 2004/293, Sch 2 para 7(4)(b), or, in relation to a Welsh Assembly election, under the National Assembly for Wales (Representation of the People) Order 2007, SI 2007/236, art 12(4)(b) (see PARA 378), as the case may be: see the Representation of the People Act 2000 Sch 4 para 7(12) (as added: see note 22); the European Parliamentary Elections Regulations 2004, SI 2004/293, Sch 2 para 7(13) (as substituted: see note 6); and the National Assembly for Wales (Representation of the People) Order 2007, SI 2007/236, art 12(13).

24 Representation of the People Act 2000 Sch 4 para 7(12)(a) (as added: see note 22); European Parliamentary Elections Regulations 2004, SI 2004/293, Sch 2 para 7(13)(a) (as substituted: see note 6); National Assembly for Wales (Representation of the People) Order 2007, SI 2007/236, art 12(13)(a).

Where a person to whom the European Parliamentary Elections Regulations 2004, SI 2004/293, Sch 2 para 31(1) applies (see PARA 366) has provided a registration officer with the required personal identifiers under the Representation of the People Act 2000 Sch 4 para 3 (absent vote at elections for definite or indefinite period: see PARA 367) or under Sch 4 para 4 (absent vote at particular election: see PARA 371) or under Sch 4 para 7 (voting as proxy for an indefinite period or for a particular period or at a particular election: see PARA 378), or under the Representation of the People (England and Wales) Regulations 2001, SI 2001/341, or the National Assembly for Wales (Representation of the People) Order 2007, SI 2007/236, before the date specified in the notice sent to the absent voter in accordance with the European Parliamentary Elections Regulations 2004, SI 2004/293, Sch 2 para 31(1)(b), the registration officer may use them, or enter them in his records, in accordance with Sch 2 para 7(13): see Sch 2 para 31(10) (as so substituted); and PARA 366.

25 Ie in pursuance of the Representation of the People Act 2000 Sch 4 para 7(11), or the European
   Parliamentary Elections Regulations 2004, SI 2004/293, Sch 2 para 7(12), or the National
   Assembly for Wales (Representation of the People) Order 2007, SI 2007/236, art 12(12) (see
   PARA 378), as the case may be: see the Representation of the People Act 2000 Sch 4
   para 7(12)(b) (as added: see note 22); the European Parliamentary Elections Regulations 2004,
   SI 2004/293, Sch 2 para 7(13)(b) (as substituted: see note 6); and the National Assembly for
   Wales (Representation of the People) Order 2007, SI 2007/236, art 12(13)(b).
26 Representation of the People Act 2000 Sch 4 para 7(12)(b) (as added: see note 22); European
   Parliamentary Elections Regulations 2004, SI 2004/293, Sch 2 para 7(13)(b) (as substituted: see
   note 6); National Assembly for Wales (Representation of the People) Order 2007, SI 2007/236,
   art 12(13)(b). See note 24.
27 Representation of the People Act 2000 Sch 4 para 7(13) (as added: see note 22); European
   Parliamentary Elections Regulations 2004, SI 2004/293, Sch 2 para 7(14) (as substituted: see
   note 6); National Assembly for Wales (Representation of the People) Order 2007, SI 2007/236,
   art 12(14). For the purposes of the Representation of the People Act 2000 Sch 4, the
   requirements are as prescribed; and 'prescribed' means prescribed by regulations (see the
   Representation of the People Act 1983 s 202(1); applied by virtue of the Representation of the
   People Act 2000 Sch 4 para 1(2)). Accordingly, the text refers to the requirements set out, in the
   case of a parliamentary or local government election, in the Representation of the People
   (England and Wales) Regulations 2001, SI 2001/341, Pt IV (regs 50–63A), or, in the case of a
   European parliamentary election, the European Parliamentary Elections Regulations 2004,
   SI 2004/293, Sch 2 para 18(1), or, in the case of a Welsh Assembly election, in the National
   Assembly for Wales (Representation of the People) Order 2007, SI 2007/236, Sch 1 para 2, as
   the case may be (see PARA 366): see the Representation of the People Act 2000 Sch 4 para 7(13);
   the European Parliamentary Elections Regulations 2004, SI 2004/293, Sch 2 para 7(14) (as so
   substituted); and the National Assembly for Wales (Representation of the People) Order 2007,
   SI 2007/236, art 12(14).
28 Ie in pursuance of the Representation of the People Act 2000 Sch 4 para 7(12), or the European
   Parliamentary Elections Regulations 2004, SI 2004/293, Sch 2 para 7(13), or the National
   Assembly for Wales (Representation of the People) Order 2007, SI 2007/236, art 12(13) (see the
   text and notes 22–26): see the Representation of the People Act 2000 Sch 4 para 7C(a) (as
   added: see note 11); the European Parliamentary Elections Regulations 2004, SI 2004/293,
   Sch 2 para 9(1)(a); and the National Assembly for Wales (Representation of the People)
   Order 2007, SI 2007/236, art 13(5)(a).
29 Representation of the People Act 2000 Sch 4 para 7C(a) (as added: see note 11); European
   Parliamentary Elections Regulations 2004, SI 2004/293, Sch 2 para 9(1)(a) (as substituted: see
   note 2); National Assembly for Wales (Representation of the People) Order 2007, SI 2007/236,
   art 13(5)(a). At a European parliamentary election, the local returning officer is the returning
   officer referred to in the text: see the European Parliamentary Elections Regulations 2004,
   SI 2004/293, Sch 2 para 9(1)(a) (as so substituted). As to local returning officers appointed for
   the purposes of elections to the European Parliament see PARA 360. At a Welsh Assembly
   election, the constituency returning officer is the returning officer referred to in the text: see the
   National Assembly for Wales (Representation of the People) Order 2007, SI 2007/236,
   art 13(5)(a). As to the meanings of 'constituency returning officer' and 'regional returning
   officer' for the purposes of Welsh Assembly elections see PARA 18 note 2.
30 Representation of the People Act 2000 Sch 4 para 7C(b) (as added: see note 11); European
   Parliamentary Elections Regulations 2004, SI 2004/293, Sch 2 para 9(1)(b) (as substituted: see
   note 2); National Assembly for Wales (Representation of the People) Order 2007, SI 2007/236,
   art 13(5)(b). As to the returning officer referred to in the text see note 29.
31 Representation of the People Act 2000 Sch 4 para 7D(a) (as added: see note 11); European
   Parliamentary Elections Regulations 2004, SI 2004/293, Sch 2 para 9(2)(a) (as substituted: see
   note 2); National Assembly for Wales (Representation of the People) Order 2007, SI 2007/236,
   art 13(6)(a). As to the prescribed conditions see PARA 179 et seq.
32 Representation of the People Act 2000 Sch 4 para 7D(b) (as added: see note 11); European
   Parliamentary Elections Regulations 2004, SI 2004/293, Sch 2 para 9(2)(b) (as substituted: see
   note 2); National Assembly for Wales (Representation of the People) Order 2007, SI 2007/236,
   art 13(6)(b). As to the meaning of 'the Representation of the People Acts' see PARA 3 note 1.
        At a parliamentary or local government election, the functions referred to in the text are
   those under the Representation of the People Acts: see the Representation of the People
   Act 2000 Sch 4 para 7D(b) (as so added).
        At a European parliamentary election, the functions referred to in the text are those under
   the European Parliamentary Elections Regulations 2004, SI 2004/293: see Sch 2 para 9(2)(b) (as
   so substituted).

At a Welsh Assembly election, the functions referred to in the text are those under the Representation of the People Acts or the National Assembly for Wales (Representation of the People) Order 2007, SI 2007/236: see art 13(6)(b).

33 Representation of the People Act 1983 Sch 4 para 7D(c) (as added: see note 11); National Assembly for Wales (Representation of the People) Order 2007, SI 2007/236, art 13(6)(c). As to the prescribed conditions see PARA 179 et seq.

380. Application by person entitled to vote by post as proxy in respect of a particular election to send ballot paper to different address. Where a person who is included in the record kept of those entitled to vote by post as proxy[1] in respect of a particular parliamentary[2], local government[3], Welsh Assembly[4] or European parliamentary[5], election, applies to the registration officer[6] for his ballot paper, in relation to a particular election of the kind in question, to be sent to a different address from that shown in the record, the registration officer must grant the application if it meets the statutory requirements[7]. Such an application[8] must state:

(1)   the full name of the applicant[9]; and

(2)   the proxy's address, together with the name of the elector for whom he will act as proxy and the elector's address in respect of which the elector is registered or has applied to be (or is treated as having applied to be) registered in the register[10].

Such an application also must set out why the applicant's circumstances will be or are likely to be such that he requires his ballot paper to be sent to a different address from that shown in the record[11]. An application made for a particular election must state that it is so made[12]; and must identify the election in question (except where the election in question is a Welsh Assembly election)[13]. The application must be made in writing and dated[14]; and such an application may be combined where the polls fall on the same day[15].

Where the registration officer grants an application to vote by post as proxy, he must notify the applicant of his decision[16]; and where he refuses an application, he must notify the applicant of his decision and give the reason for it[17]. An appeal lies to the county court from any decision of the registration officer disallowing a person's application to vote by post as proxy in any case where the application is made for a particular election only[18].

1   Ie a record kept, in relation to a parliamentary or local government election, under the Representation of the People Act 2000 s 12, Sch 4 para 7(6), or, in relation to a European parliamentary election, under the European Parliamentary Elections Regulations 2004, SI 2004/293, reg 10, Sch 2 para 7(6), or, in relation to a Welsh Assembly election, under the National Assembly for Wales (Representation of the People) Order 2007, SI 2007/236, art 12(6) (see PARA 379), as the case may be: see the Representation of the People Act 2000 Sch 4 para 7(7); the European Parliamentary Elections Regulations 2004, SI 2004/293, Sch 2 para 7(7) (Sch 2 substituted by SI 2009/186); and the National Assembly for Wales (Representation of the People) Order 2007, SI 2007/236, art 12(7).

The Representation of the People Act 2000 Sch 4 are applied and modified for the purpose of local authority mayoral elections in England and Wales by the Local Authorities (Mayoral Elections) (England and Wales) Regulations 2007, SI 2007/1024, reg 3(2)–(5), Sch 2 Table 3 (see PARA 11 note 14); and the Representation of the People (England and Wales) Regulations 2001, SI 2001/341, regs 51, 51B, 56, 57, also have effect for the purposes of local authority referendums, subject to the modifications specified, in relation to Wales, by the Local Authorities (Conduct of Referendums) (Wales) Regulations 2008, SI 2008/1848, reg 8(2), Sch 4 Table 5, and, in relation to England, by the Local Authorities (Conduct of Referendums) (England) Regulations 2012, SI 2012/323, regs 8(2), 11–13, Sch 4 Table 6 (see PARA 15 note 2).

2   As to the meaning of 'parliamentary election' see PARA 9.

3   As to the meaning of 'local government election' see PARA 11; definition applied by virtue of the Representation of the People Act 2000 Sch 4 para 1(2). See also PARA 363 note 1.

4   As to the meaning of 'Assembly election' in the context of Welsh Assembly elections see PARA 3 note 2.
5   As to European parliamentary elections see PARA 217 et seq.
6   As to electoral registration officers and the areas for which they act see PARA 139 et seq.
7   Representation of the People Act 2000 Sch 4 para 7(7); European Parliamentary Elections Regulations 2004, SI 2004/293, Sch 2 para 7(7) (as substituted: see note 1); National Assembly for Wales (Representation of the People) Order 2007, SI 2007/236, art 12(7). For the purposes of the Representation of the People Act 2000 Sch 4, the requirements are as prescribed; and 'prescribed' means prescribed by regulations (see the Representation of the People Act 1983 s 202(1); applied by virtue of the Representation of the People Act 2000 Sch 4 para 1(2)). Accordingly, the text refers to the requirements set out, in the case of a parliamentary or local government election, in the Representation of the People (England and Wales) Regulations 2001, SI 2001/341, Pt IV (regs 50–63A), or, in the case of a European parliamentary election, the European Parliamentary Elections Regulations 2004, SI 2004/293, Sch 2 Pt 2 (Sch 2 paras 12–34), or, in the case of a Welsh Assembly election, in the National Assembly for Wales (Representation of the People) Order 2007, SI 2007/236, Sch 1, as the case may be (see PARA 366): see the Representation of the People Act 2000 Sch 4 para 7(7); the European Parliamentary Elections Regulations 2004, SI 2004/293, Sch 2 para 7(7) (as so substituted); and the National Assembly for Wales (Representation of the People) Order 2007, SI 2007/236, art 12(7).
    Such an application must be refused if it is received by the registration officer after 5 pm on the eleventh day before the date of the poll at the election for which it is made: Representation of the People (England and Wales) Regulations 2001, SI 2001/341, reg 56(4) (amended by SI 2006/752); European Parliamentary Elections Regulations 2004, SI 2004/293, Sch 2 para 26(5) (as so substituted); National Assembly for Wales (Representation of the People) Order 2007, SI 2007/236, art 15(2), Sch 1 para 7(4) (amended by SI 2010/2931). Where a registration officer refuses such an application, he must notify the applicant of his decision and the reason for it: Representation of the People (England and Wales) Regulations 2001, SI 2001/341, reg 57(4); European Parliamentary Elections Regulations 2004, SI 2004/293, Sch 2 para 27(3) (as so substituted); National Assembly for Wales (Representation of the People) Order 2007, SI 2007/236, Sch 1 para 8(4). As to the computation of time for these purposes see PARA 367 note 6. As to the date of the poll at a parliamentary general election or by-election see PARA 195; as to the date of the poll at local government elections (including elections to fill vacancies) see PARAS 206–209; as to the date of the poll at Welsh Assembly elections (including elections to fill vacancies in an Assembly constituency) see PARAS 213–214; and as to the date of the poll at a European parliamentary election see PARA 222.
8   Applications made under the Representation of the People Act 2000 Sch 4, or the European Parliamentary Elections Regulations 2004, SI 2004/293, Sch 2 Pt 2, or the National Assembly for Wales (Representation of the People) Order 2007, SI 2007/236, art 12, must comply with the requirements, in relation to a parliamentary or local government election, of the Representation of the People (England and Wales) Regulations 2001, SI 2001/341, reg 51, or, in relation to a European parliamentary election, of the European Parliamentary Elections Regulations 2004, SI 2004/293, Sch 2 para 17, or, in relation to a Welsh Assembly election, of the National Assembly for Wales (Representation of the People) Order 2007, SI 2007/236, Sch 1 para 1, as well as such further requirements in the Representation of the People (England and Wales) Regulations 2001, SI 2001/341, Pt IV, or the European Parliamentary Elections Regulations 2004, SI 2004/293, Sch 2 Pt 2, as are relevant to the application: Representation of the People (England and Wales) Regulations 2001, SI 2001/341, reg 51(1); European Parliamentary Elections Regulations 2004, SI 2004/293, Sch 2 para 17(1) (as substituted: see note 1); National Assembly for Wales (Representation of the People) Order 2007, SI 2007/236, art 13(1). As to additional requirements for applications to vote by proxy for a definite or indefinite period see PARAS 368–369.
9   Representation of the People (England and Wales) Regulations 2001, SI 2001/341, reg 51(2)(a); European Parliamentary Elections Regulations 2004, SI 2004/293, Sch 2 para 17(2)(a) (as substituted: see note 1); National Assembly for Wales (Representation of the People) Order 2007, SI 2007/236, Sch 1 para 1(1)(a).
10 Representation of the People (England and Wales) Regulations 2001, SI 2001/341, reg 51(2)(b), (c) (reg 51(2)(b) amended by SI 2006/752); European Parliamentary Elections Regulations 2004, SI 2004/293, Sch 2 para 17(2)(b), (c) (as substituted: see note 1); National Assembly for Wales (Representation of the People) Order 2007, SI 2007/236, Sch 1 para 1(1)(b), (c). As to the address to be specified for the purposes of Sch 1 para 1(1)(b) see PARA 367 note 25.
11 Representation of the People (England and Wales) Regulations 2001, SI 2001/341, reg 51B(1)(b) (reg 51B added by SI 2006/752; reg 51B(1) renumbered by SI 2006/2910); European

Parliamentary Elections Regulations 2004, SI 2004/293, Sch 2 para 21(1)(b) (as substituted: see note 1); National Assembly for Wales (Representation of the People) Order 2007, SI 2007/236, Sch 1 para 1(8)(a)(ii). This requirement does not apply, however, where an applicant has, or has applied for, an anonymous entry: Representation of the People (England and Wales) Regulations 2001, SI 2001/341, reg 51B(2) (as so added); European Parliamentary Elections Regulations 2004, SI 2004/293, Sch 2 para 21(2) (as so substituted); National Assembly for Wales (Representation of the People) Order 2007, SI 2007/236, Sch 1 para 1(8)(b). As to the meaning of 'anonymous entry' in relation to a register of electors see PARA 148.

12 Representation of the People (England and Wales) Regulations 2001, SI 2001/341, reg 51(5)(a); European Parliamentary Elections Regulations 2004, SI 2004/293, Sch 2 para 17(7)(a) (as substituted: see note 1); National Assembly for Wales (Representation of the People) Order 2007, SI 2007/236, Sch 1 para 1(5)(b).

13 Representation of the People (England and Wales) Regulations 2001, SI 2001/341, reg 51(5)(b); European Parliamentary Elections Regulations 2004, SI 2004/293, Sch 2 para 17(7)(b) (as substituted: see note 1)

14 Representation of the People (England and Wales) Regulations 2001, SI 2001/341, reg 51(3) (substituted by SI 2006/2910); European Parliamentary Elections Regulations 2004, SI 2004/293, Sch 2 para 17(3) (as substituted: see note 1); National Assembly for Wales (Representation of the People) Order 2007, SI 2007/236, Sch 1 para 1(2).

15 See the Representation of the People (England and Wales) Regulations 2001, SI 2001/341, reg 51(5); the European Parliamentary Elections Regulations 2004, SI 2004/293, Sch 2 para 17(9) (as substituted: see note 1); and the National Assembly for Wales (Representation of the People) Order 2007, SI 2007/236, Sch 1 para 1(5).

16 Representation of the People (England and Wales) Regulations 2001, SI 2001/341, reg 57(4A)(b) (added by SI 2006/752); European Parliamentary Elections Regulations 2004, SI 2004/293, Sch 2 para 27(4)(b) (as substituted: see note 1); National Assembly for Wales (Representation of the People) Order 2007, SI 2007/236, Sch 1 para 8(1).
    Where the registration officer at a parliamentary or Welsh Assembly election is not the acting returning officer for any constituency (or part of such a constituency), or where the registration officer at a European parliamentary election is not the local returning officer for any local counting area (or part of such an area), in the area for which he is the registration officer, he must send to that officer details of any application to vote by post which he has granted as soon as practicable after doing so: Representation of the People (England and Wales) Regulations 2001, SI 2001/341, reg 57(6); European Parliamentary Elections Regulations 2004, SI 2004/293, Sch 2 para 27(8) (as so substituted); National Assembly for Wales (Representation of the People) Order 2007, SI 2007/236, Sch 1 para 8(9). As to the meaning of 'local counting area' see PARA 139 note 1. As to local returning officers appointed for the purposes of elections to the European Parliament see PARA 360. As to notification by the registration officer at a Welsh Assembly election see PARA 367 note 35.

17 Representation of the People (England and Wales) Regulations 2001, SI 2001/341, reg 57(4); European Parliamentary Elections Regulations 2004, SI 2004/293, Sch 2 para 27(3) (as substituted: see note 1); National Assembly for Wales (Representation of the People) Order 2007, SI 2007/236, Sch 1 para 8(5).
18 See PARA 172 et seq.

381. Proxy postal voters list. The registration officer[1] must, in respect of each parliamentary[2], local government[3], Welsh Assembly[4] or European parliamentary[5] election, keep a special list (the 'proxy postal voters list')[6]:

(1) of those who are for the time being included in the record kept of persons entitled to vote by post as proxy (whether for an indefinite period or for a particular period that is specified)[7], together with the addresses provided by them in their applications[8] as the addresses to which their ballot papers are to be sent[9]; and

(2) of those whose applications to vote by post as proxy at a particular election[10] have been granted in respect of the election concerned, together with the addresses provided by them in their applications as the addresses to which their ballot papers are to be sent[11].

Any person entitled to be supplied with copies of the full register is also a person entitled to request that the registration officer supply free of charge a copy of current information which he keeps for the purposes of maintaining the proxy postal voters list[12].

1　As to electoral registration officers and the areas for which they act see PARA 139 et seq.

2　As to the meaning of 'parliamentary election' see PARA 9.

3　As to the meaning of 'local government election' see PARA 11; definition applied by virtue of the Representation of the People Act 2000 s 12, Sch 4 para 1(2). See also PARA 363 note 1.

　　The Representation of the People Act 2000 Sch 4 are applied and modified for the purpose of local authority mayoral elections in England and Wales by the Local Authorities (Mayoral Elections) (England and Wales) Regulations 2007, SI 2007/1024, reg 3(2)–(5), Sch 2 Table 3 (see PARA 11 note 14).

4　As to the meaning of 'Assembly election' in the context of Welsh Assembly elections see PARA 3 note 2.

5　As to European parliamentary elections see PARA 217 et seq.

6　Representation of the People Act 2000 Sch 4 para 7(8) (amended by the Electoral Administration Act 2006 s 74(1), Sch 1 Pt 7 para 137(1), (7)); European Parliamentary Elections Regulations 2004, SI 2004/293, Sch 2 para 7(8) (Sch 2 substituted by SI 2009/186); National Assembly for Wales (Representation of the People) Order 2007, SI 2007/236, art 12(8). The list referred to in the text, which is known as the 'proxy postal voters list', refers to the list kept, in relation to a parliamentary or local government election, pursuant to the Representation of the People Act 2000 Sch 4 para 7(8), in relation to a European parliamentary election, pursuant to the European Parliamentary Elections Regulations 2004, SI 2004/293, Sch 2 para 7(8), and, in relation to a Welsh Assembly election, pursuant to the National Assembly for Wales (Representation of the People) Order 2007, SI 2007/236, art 12(8) (ie the list of persons whose applications to vote by post as proxy have been granted): see the Representation of the People Act 1983 s 202(1) (definition added by the Electoral Administration Act 2006 Sch 1 Pt 7 paras 104, 128(1), (3)); the Representation of the People Act 2000 Sch 4 para 7(8) (as so amended); the European Parliamentary Elections Regulations 2004, SI 2004/293, reg 2(1) (substituted by SI 2009/186); the European Parliamentary Elections Regulations 2004, SI 2004/293, Sch 2 para 7(8) (as so substituted); the National Assembly for Wales (Representation of the People) Order 2007, SI 2007/236, art 2(1); art 12(8).

　　In the case of a person who has an anonymous entry in a register, the list referred to in the text must contain only the person's electoral number, and the period for which the anonymous entry has effect: Representation of the People Act 2000 Sch 4 para 7(8A) (added by the Electoral Administration Act 2006 s 10(2), Sch 1 paras 19, 23); European Parliamentary Elections Regulations 2004, SI 2004/293, Sch 2 para 7(9) (as so substituted); National Assembly for Wales (Representation of the People) Order 2007, SI 2007/236, art 12(9). As to the meaning of 'electoral number' see PARA 145; and as to the meaning of 'anonymous entry' in relation to a register of electors see PARA 148. Where a Welsh Assembly constituency is not coterminous with, or wholly situated in, a county or county borough:

　(1)　the registration officer for any part of the Assembly constituency must, if he is not the returning officer for the constituency, consult him concerning the form of so much of the proxy postal voters list, as relates to the constituency, in order to ensure that, so far as practicable, it is in a form similar to that in use elsewhere in the constituency (art 140(a)(iii)); and

　(2)　if the registration officer for any part of the Assembly constituency at an Assembly election is not the returning officer for the constituency, he must forthwith supply to the constituency returning officer a copy of the list compiled under art 12(8) on completion of the compilation of them (art 140(b)).

　　As to the meaning of 'Assembly constituency' see PARA 3 note 2; and as to the meaning of 'constituency returning officer' for these purposes see PARA 18 note 2. As to the duty of registration officers to maintain, prepare and publish registers of electors see PARA 143. As to counties and county boroughs in Wales see LOCAL GOVERNMENT vol 69 (2009) PARA 37 et seq.

7　Ie a record kept, in relation to a parliamentary or local government election, under the Representation of the People Act 2000 Sch 4 para 7(6), or, in relation to a European parliamentary election, under the European Parliamentary Elections Regulations 2004, SI 2004/293, Sch 2 para 7(6), or, in relation to a Welsh Assembly election, under the National Assembly for Wales (Representation of the People) Order 2007, SI 2007/236, art 12(6) (see PARA 379), as, the case may be: see the Representation of the People Act 2000 Sch 4 para 7(8)(a); the European Parliamentary Elections Regulations 2004, SI 2004/293, Sch 2 para 7(8)(a) (as substituted: see note 6); and the National Assembly for Wales (Representation of the People) Order 2007, SI 2007/236, art 12(8)(a).

8   Ie applications made, in relation to a parliamentary or local government election, under the Representation of the People Act 2000 Sch 4 para 7(4)(a) (or, as the case may be, under Sch 4 para 7(7)), or applications made, in relation to a European parliamentary election, under the European Parliamentary Elections Regulations 2004, SI 2004/293, Sch 2 para 7(4)(a) (or, as the case may be, under Sch 2 para 7(7)), or applications made, in relation to a Welsh Assembly election, under the National Assembly for Wales (Representation of the People) Order 2007, SI 2007/236, art 12(4)(a) (or, as the case may be, under art 12(7)) (see PARAS 378, 380), as the case may be: see the Representation of the People Act 2000 Sch 4 para 7(8)(a); the European Parliamentary Elections Regulations 2004, SI 2004/293, Sch 2 para 7(8)(a) (as substituted: see note 6); and the National Assembly for Wales (Representation of the People) Order 2007, SI 2007/236, art 12(8)(a).

9   Representation of the People Act 2000 Sch 4 para 7(8)(a); European Parliamentary Elections Regulations 2004, SI 2004/293, Sch 2 para 7(8)(a) (as substituted: see note 6); National Assembly for Wales (Representation of the People) Order 2007, SI 2007/236, art 12(8)(a). Where the polls at a Welsh Assembly constituency election and at a Welsh Assembly regional election are to be taken together, only one list is to be kept under art 12(8) and that list is to have effect in relation to both elections: see art 12(8). As to the meanings of 'constituency election' and 'regional election' for these purposes see PARA 3 note 2.

10 Ie a record of those whose applications have been granted, in relation to a parliamentary or local government election, under the Representation of the People Act 2000 Sch 4 para 7(4)(b), or, in relation to a European parliamentary election, under the European Parliamentary Elections Regulations 2004, SI 2004/293, Sch 2 para 7(4)(b), or, in relation to a Welsh Assembly election, under the National Assembly for Wales (Representation of the People) Order 2007, SI 2007/236, art 12(4)(b) (see PARA 378), as the case may be: see the Representation of the People Act 2000 Sch 4 para 7(8)(b); the European Parliamentary Elections Regulations 2004, SI 2004/293, Sch 2 para 7(8)(b) (as substituted: see note 6); and the National Assembly for Wales (Representation of the People) Order 2007, SI 2007/236, art 12(8)(b).

11 Representation of the People Act 2000 Sch 4 para 7(8)(b); European Parliamentary Elections Regulations 2004, SI 2004/293, Sch 2 para 7(8)(b) (as substituted: see note 6); National Assembly for Wales (Representation of the People) Order 2007, SI 2007/236, art 12(8)(b). In relation to a Welsh Assembly election see note 9.

12 See the Representation of the People (England and Wales) Regulations 2001, SI 2001/341, reg 61; the European Parliamentary Elections Regulations 2004, SI 2004/293, Sch 2 para 32; the National Assembly for Wales (Representation of the People) Order 2007, SI 2007/236, Sch 1 para 13; and PARA 185. As to restrictions on use of the data so supplied see the Representation of the People (England and Wales) Regulations 2001, SI 2001/341, reg 61A; the European Parliamentary Elections Regulations 2004, SI 2004/293, Sch 2 para 33; the National Assembly for Wales (Representation of the People) Order 2007, SI 2007/236, Sch 1 para 14; and PARA 179 note 18.

    At a European parliamentary election, the registration officer must, forthwith on completion of the compilation of the proxy postal voters list, supply to the local returning officer for any local counting area wholly or partly within the area for which he acts so much of that list as relates to any such area: European Parliamentary Elections Regulations 2004, SI 2004/293, Sch 2 para 7(8). As to the meaning of 'local counting area' see PARA 139 note 1. As to local returning officers appointed for the purposes of elections to the European Parliament see PARA 360.

382. Voting by post as proxy. If a person is entitled to vote as proxy for an elector[1] at a parliamentary[2], local government[3], Welsh Assembly[4] or European parliamentary[5] election (that is, by virtue of being included in the relevant list[6] in respect of that election) he may vote by post[7]. Where a person is entitled to vote by post as proxy for an elector at such an election[8], the elector may not apply for a ballot paper for the purpose of voting in person at the election[9].

1   As to the meaning of 'elector' for these purposes see PARA 374 note 7. As to applications to vote by post as a proxy see PARA 378 et seq.
2   As to the meaning of 'parliamentary election' see PARA 9.
3   As to the meaning of 'local government election' see PARA 11; definition applied by virtue of the Representation of the People Act 2000 s 12, Sch 4 para 1(2). See also PARA 363 note 1.

The Representation of the People Act 2000 Sch 4 are applied and modified for the purpose of local authority mayoral elections in England and Wales by the Local Authorities (Mayoral Elections) (England and Wales) Regulations 2007, SI 2007/1024, reg 3(2)–(5), Sch 2 Table 3 (see PARA 11 note 14).

4   As to the meaning of 'Assembly election' in the context of Welsh Assembly elections see PARA 3 note 2.

5   As to European parliamentary elections see PARA 217 et seq.

6   Ie the list kept, in relation to a parliamentary or local government election, under the Representation of the People Act 2000 Sch 4 para 7(8), or, in relation to a European parliamentary election, under the European Parliamentary Elections Regulations 2004, SI 2004/293, Sch 2 para 7(8), or, in relation to a Welsh Assembly election, under the National Assembly for Wales (Representation of the People) Order 2007, SI 2007/236, art 12(8) (see PARA 381), as, the case may be: see the Representation of the People Act 2000 Sch 4 para 7(1), (3); the European Parliamentary Elections Regulations 2004, SI 2004/293, Sch 2 para 7(1), (3) (Sch 2 substituted by SI 2009/186); and the National Assembly for Wales (Representation of the People) Order 2007, SI 2007/236, art 12(1), (3).

7   Representation of the People Act 2000 Sch 4 para 7(1), (3); European Parliamentary Elections Regulations 2004, SI 2004/293, Sch 2 para 7(1), (3) (as substituted: see note 6); National Assembly for Wales (Representation of the People) Order 2007, SI 2007/236, art 12(1), (3).

8   To indicate that an elector or his proxy is entitled to vote by post, and is for that reason not entitled to vote in person, the letter 'A' is placed against the name of that elector in any copy of the register, or part of it, provided for a polling station: see the Representation of the People (England and Wales) Regulations 2001, SI 2001/341, reg 62; the European Parliamentary Elections Regulations 2004, SI 2004/293, Sch 2 para 34; the National Assembly for Wales (Representation of the People) Order 2007, SI 2007/236, art 15(2), Sch 1 para 15; and PARA 377.

9   Representation of the People Act 2000 Sch 4 para 7(2); European Parliamentary Elections Regulations 2004, SI 2004/293, Sch 2 para 7(2) (as substituted: see note 6); National Assembly for Wales (Representation of the People) Order 2007, SI 2007/236, art 12(2). The Representation of the People Act 2000 Sch 4 para 7(2), or the European Parliamentary Elections Regulations 2004, SI 2004/293, Sch 2 para 7(2), or the National Assembly for Wales (Representation of the People) Order 2007, SI 2007/236, art 12(2), as the case may be, does not prevent a person, at the polling station allotted to him, marking a tendered ballot paper in pursuance of the Representation of the People Act 1983 Sch 1 r 40(1ZC), (1ZE), or the European Parliamentary Elections Regulations 2004, SI 2004/293, Sch 1 para 44(4), (6), or the National Assembly for Wales (Representation of the People) Order 2007, SI 2007/236, Sch 5 para 49(4), (6) (see PARA 403), as the case may be: Representation of the People Act 2000 Sch 4 para 7(10) (added by the Electoral Administration Act 2006 s 38(6)(b)); European Parliamentary Elections Regulations 2004, SI 2004/293, Sch 2 para 7(11) (as so substituted); National Assembly for Wales (Representation of the People) Order 2007, SI 2007/236, art 12(11).

(v) Rules for Conduct of Elections

383.   Rules for the conduct of elections.   The proceedings at a parliamentary election[1] must be conducted in accordance with the parliamentary elections rules[2]. The parliamentary elections rules are applied[3] for the purpose of elections of councillors for local government areas[4] in England and Wales[5], which must be conducted in accordance with rules made by the Secretary of State[6]. As regards the Greater London Authority[7], Authority elections[8], and the return of London members of the London Assembly otherwise than at an election[9], must be conducted in accordance with rules made under the Representation of the People Act 1983 by the Secretary of State, which need not comply with the rules made for the purpose of the election of councillors for local government areas generally[10]. The Secretary of State or the Lord President of the Council may by regulations under the Local Government Act 2000[11] make provision as to the conduct of elections for the return of elected mayors (that is, individuals elected as mayor of a local authority)[12]; and such regulations may apply or incorporate, with or without modifications or exceptions, any provision of, or made under, the Representation of the People Acts or any provision of any other enactment (whenever passed or made) relating to parliamentary elections or local government elections[13]. An election for the return of an elected local authority mayor must be conducted in accordance with the mayoral elections rules so made[14].

The Secretary of State may by regulations make provision as to the conduct of elections to the European Parliament[15]; and proceedings at a European parliamentary election must be conducted in accordance with the European parliamentary elections rules so made[16].

The Secretary of State may by order make provision as to the conduct of Welsh Assembly elections[17] for the return of Assembly members[18]; and the proceedings at Assembly elections[19], including the return of Assembly members, must be conducted in accordance with the Assembly election rules so made[20].

The Secretary of State or the Lord President of the Council may by regulations under the Local Government Act 2000 also make provision for the combination of polls at local authority referendums with polls at any elections[21].

It is the general duty of returning officers at an election to do all such acts and things as may be necessary for effectively conducting the election in accordance with these rules[22]; but no parliamentary election may be declared invalid by reason of any act or omission by the returning officer or any other person in breach of his official duty in connection with the election or otherwise of the elections rules if the election was so conducted as to be substantially in accordance with the law as to elections and the act or omission did not affect its result[23].

1　As to the meaning of 'parliamentary election' see PARA 9. As to parliamentary elections see PARA 189 et seq.
2　Representation of the People Act 1983 s 23(1). For these purposes, 'parliamentary elections rules' means the parliamentary elections rules in s 23(1), Sch 1: see ss 23(1), 202(1).
3　Representation of the People Act 1983 s 36(2). The parliamentary elections rules in Sch 1 must be applied subject to such adaptations, alterations and exceptions as seem appropriate to the Secretary of State (see note 6): see s 36(2). As to the Secretary of State see PARA 2. As to the rules for combining the poll at such an election with that at another election or referendum see PARA 21 et seq.
4　As to the meaning of 'local government area' see PARA 33 note 7. As to the election of councillors for local government principal areas see PARA 197 et seq; as to the election of councillors for parish or community councils see PARA 200 et seq.
5　As to the meanings of 'England' and 'Wales' see PARA 1 note 1.
6　Representation of the People Act 1983 s 36(1). Rules made under s 36 must be made by statutory instrument and are subject to annulment in pursuance of a resolution of either House of Parliament: s 36(7). In the application of the parliamentary elections rules to the election of councillors of the council of a principal area, parish or community, where the poll at such an election is not taken together with the poll at another election, under the Representation of the People Act 1983 s 36(3), (3AB), (3AC) (see PARAS 28, 29), or under the Representation of the People Act 1985 s 15(1) (see PARAS 21–22, 24, 26–27) or s 15(2) (see PARAS 30, 31), adaptations, alterations and exceptions must be made to the parliamentary elections rules so that the election is conducted in accordance with the rules set out in the Local Elections (Principal Areas) (England and Wales) Rules 2006, SI 2006/3304, Sch 2, or the Local Elections (Parishes and Communities) (England and Wales) Rules 2006, SI 2006/3305, Sch 2 (see PARAS 211 et seq, 384 et seq), as the case may: Local Elections (Principal Areas) (England and Wales) Rules 2006, SI 2006/3304, r 3; Local Elections (Parishes and Communities) (England and Wales) Rules 2006, SI 2006/3305, r 3. For these purposes, 'principal area' means, in England, a county, district or London borough and, in Wales, a county or county borough: Local Elections (Principal Areas) (England and Wales) Rules 2006, SI 2006/3304, r 2(1); Local Elections (Parishes and Communities) (England and Wales) Rules 2006, SI 2006/3305, r 2(1). As to districts in England, and their councils, see LOCAL GOVERNMENT vol 69 (2009) PARA 24 et seq; and as to parishes and their councils see LOCAL GOVERNMENT vol 69 (2009) PARA 27 et seq. As to counties and county boroughs in Wales, and their councils, see LOCAL GOVERNMENT

vol 69 (2009) PARA 37 et seq; and as to communities and their councils see LOCAL GOVERNMENT vol 69 (2009) PARA 41 et seq. As to London boroughs and their councils see LOCAL GOVERNMENT vol 69 (2009) PARA 35; LONDON GOVERNMENT vol 71 (2013) PARA 15 et seq.

A poll consequent on a parish meeting is taken by ballot in accordance with rules made by the Secretary of State; and the provisions of the rules with respect to the elections of parish councillors under the Representation of the People Act 1983 s 36 and of the enactments mentioned in s 187(1) (ie s 60, s 62A and s 66, Pt II (ss 67–119), Pt III (ss 120–186), and s 189), subject to any adaptations, alterations or exceptions made by the first-mentioned rules, apply in the case of a poll so taken as if it were a poll for the election of parish councillors: see the Local Government Act 1972 s 99, Sch 12 para 18(5), Sch 12 para 34(5); and LOCAL GOVERNMENT vol 69 (2009) PARA 638. In the application of the Local Elections (Parishes and Communities) (England and Wales) Rules 2006, SI 2006/3305, by virtue of the Interpretation Act 1978 s 17(2)(b), to a poll consequent on a parish or community meeting, adaptations, alterations and exceptions must be made to those rules so that the poll is conducted in accordance with the Parish and Community Meetings (Polls) Rules 1987, SI 1987/1, Schedule (see PARA 200 et seq): r 5. In the application of those provisions of the Representation of the People Act 1983 mentioned in s 187(1), references to the proper officer of the authority for which the election was held must be taken as references to the returning officer (Parish and Community Meetings (Polls) Rules 1987, SI 1987/1, r 6(b)); and references to an election under the local government Act are deemed to include a reference to a poll consequent on a parish or community meeting (r 6(g)). As to other modifications that apply for these purposes see r 6(c)–(f). As to the meaning of 'election under the local government Act' see PARA 11 note 2. As to a poll consequent on a parish or community meeting taken on a question other than any appointment to office see PARA 556 et seq.

7 As to the Greater London Authority see LONDON GOVERNMENT vol 71 (2013) PARA 67 et seq.

8 Representation of the People Act 1983 s 36(2A)(a) (s 36(2A), (2B) added by the Greater London Authority Act 1999 s 17, Sch 3 paras 1, 4(1), (2)). As to the meaning of 'Authority election' see PARA 11. See also LONDON GOVERNMENT vol 71 (2013) PARA 86.

9 Representation of the People Act 1983 s 36(2A)(b) (as added: see note 8). As to the meaning of 'London member' of the London Assembly see PARA 11 note 5. As to filling vacancies in the offices of London members of the London Assembly see PARA 204 et seq. As to London members of the London Assembly see further LONDON GOVERNMENT vol 71 (2013) PARA 70.

10 Representation of the People Act 1983 s 36(2A) (as added: see note 8). The text refers to the provision that rules made under s 36(2A) need not comply with the requirements of s 36(2) (see the text and note 3): see s 36(2A) (as so added). The provision that may be made by rules under s 36(2A) as regards lists of candidates submitted under the Greater London Authority Act 1999 s 4(6), Sch 2 para 5(2) (election of London members of the London Assembly: see PARA 226) includes provision for or in connection with the inclusion, withdrawal, addition or removal of persons, and cases where a person included in such a list is or becomes, or seeks to become, an individual candidate to be a London member of the London Assembly: see the Representation of the People Act 1983 s 36(2B) (as so added). As to individual candidates and the submission of lists of candidates to be London members of the London Assembly see PARA 226; and as to references to party lists in elections for the return of London members of the London Assembly see PARA 255 note 23. In exercise of the powers conferred by s 36(2) and s 36(2A), (2B), the Secretary of State has made the Greater London Authority Elections Rules 2007, SI 2007/3541. For these purposes, the 'constituency members election rules' means the rules set out in rr 3(2), 5(3), Sch 1, Sch 5 (where r 5(3), Sch 5 applies to an Authority election that is taken together with the poll at another election or referendum: see PARA 22 note 11); the 'London members election rules' means the rules in rr 3(3), 5(4), Sch 2, Sch 6 (where r 5(4), Sch 6 applies to an Authority election that is taken together with the poll at another election or referendum: see PARA 22 note 11); and the 'mayoral election rules' means the rules in rr 3(4), 5(5), Sch 3, Sch 7 (where r 5(5), Sch 7 applies to an Authority election that is taken together with the poll at another election or referendum: see PARA 22 note 11): r 2(1). An election held under the constituency members election rules, the London members election rules, or the mayoral election rules is known as a an 'Authority election': r 2(1). To avoid confusion, in this work the mayoral elections rules are referred to as the 'London mayoral elections rules': cf the 'local authority mayoral elections rules'; and note 14. The constituency members election rules in Sch 1 have effect for the purposes of the election of constituency members of the London Assembly, whether at an ordinary election or in the circumstances mentioned in the Greater London Authority Act 1999 s 10 (filling a vacancy in an Assembly constituency: see PARA 204): Greater London Authority Elections Rules 2007, SI 2007/3541, r 3(1), (2). The London members election rules in Sch 2 with the exception of Pt 7 (Sch 2 rr 63–67) (list candidates and the filling

of vacancies: see PARA 204), have effect for the purposes of any election of London members of the London Assembly; and Pt 7 has effect for the purposes of the Greater London Authority Act 1999 s 11 (filling a vacancy among the London members: see PARA 204): Greater London Authority Elections Rules 2007, SI 2007/3541, r 3(1), (3). The mayoral election rules in Sch 3 have effect for the purposes of any election of the Mayor of London at an ordinary election, and any election under the Greater London Authority Act 1999 s 16(2) (filling a vacancy in the office of Mayor: see PARA 204): Greater London Authority Elections Rules 2007, SI 2007/3541, r 3(1), (4). Where some or all of the votes cast at an Authority election to which r 3 applies are to be counted without the use of an electronic counting system, the constituency members election rules, the London members election rules and the mayoral election rules have effect, in respect of those votes counted manually, subject to the modifications set out in the manual counts rules in r 4, Sch 4: rr 2(1), 4. As to the modification of the combined poll rules contained in Schs 5–7 where votes are counted without the use of an electronic counting system see r 6, Sch 8 (the 'combined manual count rules': see r 2(1)); and PARA 22 note 11. As to the meaning of 'constituency member' (of the London Assembly) see PARA 11 note 6. As to the meaning of 'electronic counting system' see PARA 443 note 18. As to ordinary elections of the Mayor of London and constituency members of the London Assembly see PARA 199 et seq. As to verifying and counting the ballot papers at elections of London Assembly members see PARA 444; and as to verifying and counting the ballot papers at a London mayoral election see PARA 451.

11　Ie by regulations made, in relation to England, under the Local Government Act 2000 ss 9HE, 105, and, in relation to Wales, under ss 44, 105 (see LOCAL GOVERNMENT vol 69 (2009) PARA 303 et seq): see s 9HE(1) (ss 9B–9R added by the Localism Act 2011 s 21, Sch 2 Pt 1 para 1; Local Government Act 2000 s 9HE(1) amended by SI 2013/2597); and the Local Government Act 2000 s 44(1). At the date at which this volume states the law, no such regulations had been made under ss 9HE, 105, and the Local Authorities (Mayoral Elections) (England and Wales) Regulations 2007, SI 2007/1024, which were made under the Local Government Act 2000 ss 44, 105, continue to apply to England as well as to Wales. Regulations made under the Local Government Act 2000 ss 9HE, 44 may:

(1)　modify any form contained in, or in regulations or rules made under, the Representation of the People Acts so far as may be necessary to enable it to be used both for the original purpose and in relation to elections for the return of elected mayors (Local Government Act 2000 ss 9HE(3)(b), 44(3)(b) (s 9HE as so added)); and

(2)　so far as may be necessary in consequence of any such regulations or any provision made by or under the Local Government Act 2000 Pt 1A (ss 9B–9R) (arrangements with respect to local governance in England) or Pt II (ss 10–48A) (Local authorities in Wales: arrangements with respect to executives etc) (see LOCAL GOVERNMENT vol 69 (2009) PARA 303 et seq), as the case may be, amend any provision of any enactment (whenever passed or made) relating to the registration of parliamentary electors or local government electors (ss 9HE(3)(c), 44(3)(c) (s 9HE as so added)).

As to the forms so modified see the Local Authorities (Mayoral Elections) (England and Wales) Regulations 2007, SI 2007/1024, Sch 1 Appendix of Forms (amended by SI 2011/1043). As to the meaning of 'the Representation of the People Acts' see PARA 3 note 1. As to the making of regulations under the Local Government Act 2000 generally see LOCAL GOVERNMENT vol 69 (2009) PARA 98.

12　Local Government Act 2000 s 9HE(1)(a) (s 9HE as added: see note 11); s 44(1)(a). Such regulations may include provision for the combination of polls at elections for the return of elected mayors and other elections: see ss 9HE(2)(d), 44(2)(d) (s 9HE as so added). As to the rules for combining polls at such an election with that at another election or referendum see PARA 26. As to elections for the return of elected mayors see PARA 198 et seq. As to the meaning of 'elected mayor' see LOCAL GOVERNMENT vol 69 (2009) PARA 320.

13　Local Government Act 2000 ss 9HE(3)(a), 44(3)(a) (s 9HE as added: see note 11). The provisions in the Representation of the People Act 1983, the Representation of the People Act 1985, the Representation of the People Act 2000, the Electoral Administration Act 2006, and the Representation of the People (England and Wales) Regulations 2001, SI 2001/341, which have effect in relation to the conduct of the election of councillors for any county electoral division or district or London borough ward (in England) or any county electoral division or county borough ward (in Wales) have effect, in relation to the conduct of a mayoral election in England, as they have effect in relation to the conduct of an election of councillors for any county electoral division or district or London borough ward, and, in relation to the conduct of a mayoral election in Wales, as they have effect in relation to the conduct of an election of councillors for any county electoral division or county borough ward, subject to the modifications set out in the Local Authorities (Mayoral Elections) (England and Wales)

Regulations 2007, SI 2007/1024, reg 3(4), Sch 2: see reg 3; and PARA 11 note 14. As to the establishment of electoral areas for the purpose of local government elections in England and Wales see PARA 74.

14 Local Authorities (Mayoral Elections) (England and Wales) Regulations 2007, SI 2007/1024, reg 3(1). For these purposes, 'mayoral election' means an election for the return of an elected mayor; and 'mayoral elections rules' means the rules that are set out in Sch 1: see reg 2(1). To avoid confusion, in this work, these rules are referred to as the 'local authority mayoral elections rules': cf the 'London mayoral elections rules'; and note 10.

15 See the European Parliamentary Elections Act 2002 s 7(1); and PARA 13. As to the rules for combining polls at such an election with that at another election or referendum see PARA 21 et seq. As to European parliamentary elections see PARA 217 et seq.

16 European Parliamentary Elections Regulations 2004, SI 2004/293, reg 9(1). For these purposes, 'European parliamentary elections rules' means the rules in Sch 1: reg 2(1) (substituted by SI 2009/186).

17 As to Welsh Assembly elections see PARA 213 et seq.

18 See the Government of Wales Act 2006 s 13(1); and PARA 12. As to the meaning of 'Assembly member' in the context of Welsh Assembly elections see PARA 12. As to the rules for combining polls at such an election with that at another election or referendum see PARA 23 et seq.

19 As to the meaning of 'Assembly election' in the context of Welsh Assembly elections see PARA 3 note 2.

20 National Assembly for Wales (Representation of the People) Order 2007, SI 2007/236, art 17(1). The text refers to the rules set out in Sch 5 (ie the 'Assembly election rules': see art 2(1)): see art 17(1).

21 See the Local Government Act 2000 ss 9MG, 105 (conduct of local authority referendums in England: see PARA 555), ss 45, 105 (conduct of local authority referendums in Wales: see PARA 555). The regulations referred to in the text are those made under the Local Government Act 2000 s 9MG (ie, the Local Authorities (Conduct of Referendums) (England) Regulations 2012, SI 2012/323): see PARA 27. At the date at which this volume states the law, the Local Authorities (Conduct of Referendums) (Wales) Regulations 2008, SI 2008/1848, which were made under the Local Government Act 2000 ss 45, 105, make no provision for polls at local authority referendums in Wales to be taken together with polls at another election or referendum.

22 As to the designation and appointment of returning officers generally see PARA 350 et seq.

23 See PARA 350 et seq.

(vi) Contested Elections

A. IN GENERAL

384. Method of election. If the statement of persons nominated[1] at:

(1) a parliamentary election[2]; or

(2) a Welsh Assembly constituency election[3],

shows more than one person standing nominated, a poll must be taken in accordance with the rules that govern contested elections[4]; and a poll must be taken in accordance with the rules that govern contested London Assembly constituency elections[5] if, after any withdrawals under the constituency members election rules[6], the number of persons remaining validly nominated for the London Assembly constituency exceeds one[7].

A poll must be taken in accordance with the rules that govern contested elections at a local government election for a principal area, parish or community[8], if, after any withdrawals under the appropriate electoral rules, the number of persons remaining validly nominated for the electoral area[9] exceeds the number of councillors to be elected[10]. If the number of candidates remaining at a poll consequent on a parish meeting on a question involving appointment to office, after any withdrawals, exceeds the number of persons to be elected, then a poll must be taken[11].

If, after any withdrawals under the appropriate rules[12],the number of persons remaining validly nominated at:

(a)   an election for the return of London members of the London Assembly[13]; or

(b)   a Welsh Assembly regional election[14]; or

(c)   a European parliamentary election[15],

exceeds the number of seats available for allocation[16], then, unless all of those persons are named on the same party list[17], a poll must be taken in accordance with the rules that govern contested elections[18].

If, after any withdrawals under the appropriate rules that govern a local authority mayoral, or London mayoral, election[19], two or more candidates remain validly nominated, a poll must be taken in accordance with the rules that govern contested mayoral elections[20].

If the number of persons remaining validly nominated after any withdrawals under the appropriate rules does not exceed the number of offices available to be filled in the election, such person or persons must be declared to be elected in accordance with the appropriate rules[21].

1   As to the statement of persons nominated see PARA 267.
2   As to the meaning of 'parliamentary election' see PARA 9. As to parliamentary elections see PARA 189 et seq.
3   As to the meanings of 'Assembly election' and 'constituency election' see PARA 3 note 2.
4   Representation of the People Act 1983 Sch 1 r 17(1); National Assembly for Wales (Representation of the People) Order 2007, SI 2007/236, Sch 5 para 21(a). The text refers to the rules set out, in relation to a parliamentary election, in the Representation of the People Act 1983 Sch 1 Pt III (Sch 1 rr 18–49), or, in relation to a Welsh Assembly election, in the National Assembly for Wales (Representation of the People) Order 2007, SI 2007/236, Sch 5 Pt 3 (Sch 5 paras 23–61) (see PARA 385 et seq), as, the case may be: see the Representation of the People Act 1983 Sch 1 r 17(1); and the National Assembly for Wales (Representation of the People) Order 2007, SI 2007/236, Sch 5 para 21(a). As to the rules that govern the conduct of parliamentary and Welsh Assembly constituency elections see PARA 383. As to the manner of voting (including absent voting) see PARA 363 et seq; and as to uncontested elections see PARA 474 et seq.
5   Ie in accordance with the Greater London Authority Elections Rules 2007, SI 2007/3541, Sch 1 Pt 4 (Sch 1 rr 16–53): see Sch 1 r 15(1). As to the meaning of 'Assembly constituency' in the context of elections to the London Assembly see PARA 11 note 6. As to constituency members of the London Assembly see further LONDON GOVERNMENT vol 71 (2013) PARA 80. As to contested elections for the return of London members of the London Assembly see the text and notes 12–18; and as to contested elections for the return of the Mayor of London see the text and notes 19–20.
6   As to the meaning of 'constituency members election rules' see PARA 383 note 10. As to the meaning of 'constituency member', in relation to the London Assembly, see PARA 11 note 6; definition applied by virtue of the Greater London Authority Elections Rules 2007, SI 2007/3541, r 2(3).
7   Greater London Authority Elections Rules 2007, SI 2007/3541, Sch 1 r 15(1). As to ordinary elections of constituency members of the London Assembly see PARA 199 et seq.
8   Ie, in relation to local government elections for principal areas, in accordance with the rules in the Local Elections (Principal Areas) (England and Wales) Rules 2006, SI 2006/3304, Sch 2 Pt 3 (Sch 2 rr 15–49), or, in relation to local government elections for parishes and communities, in accordance with the rules in the Local Elections (Parishes and Communities) (England and Wales) Rules 2006, SI 2006/3305, Sch 2 Pt 3 (Sch 2 rr 15–49) (see PARA 385 et seq): see the Local Elections (Principal Areas) (England and Wales) Rules 2006, SI 2006/3304, Sch 2 r 14(1); and the Local Elections (Parishes and Communities) (England and Wales) Rules 2006, SI 2006/3305, Sch 2 r 14(1). As to the meaning of 'local government election' see PARA 11. As to the election of councillors for local government principal areas see PARA 197 et seq; and as to the election of councillors for parish or community councils see PARA 200 et seq. As to the rules that govern the conduct of local government elections see PARA 383.
9   As to the meaning of 'electoral area' see PARA 11.
10   Local Elections (Principal Areas) (England and Wales) Rules 2006, SI 2006/3304, Sch 2 r 14(1); Local Elections (Parishes and Communities) (England and Wales) Rules 2006, SI 2006/3305, Sch 2 r 14(1).

11 This is the sense of the Parish and Community Meetings (Polls) Rules 1987, SI 1987/1, Schedule r 3(2): see PARA 478. As to polls consequent on a parish meeting generally see PARA 200 et seq.

12 As to the rules that govern the conduct of Welsh Assembly regional elections, elections for the return of London members of the London Assembly, and European parliamentary elections, see PARA 383.

13 As to the meaning of 'London member' of the London Assembly see PARA 11 note 5. As to elections for the return of the members of the London Assembly see PARA 199 et seq. As to London members of the London Assembly see further LONDON GOVERNMENT vol 71 (2013) PARA 70.

14 As to the meaning of 'regional election', in relation to a Welsh Assembly election, see PARA 3 note 2.

15 As to European parliamentary elections see PARA 217 et seq.

16 Ie, if the statement of persons standing nominated at a Welsh Assembly regional election shows more persons nominated (whether as individual candidates or party list candidates) than the number of seats for that Welsh Assembly electoral region (see the National Assembly for Wales (Representation of the People) Order 2007, SI 2007/236, Sch 5 para 22(1)); or if the statement of parties and individual candidates nominated at a European parliamentary election shows more candidates than there are seats to be filled (see the European Parliamentary Elections Regulations 2004, SI 2004/293, Sch 1 para 20(1) (Sch 1 substituted by SI 2009/186)). As to the meaning of 'Assembly electoral region' see PARA 3 note 2. As to the meaning of 'individual candidate' at a Welsh Assembly regional election see PARA 230 note 19; and as to the meanings of 'party list' and 'party list candidate' for these purposes see PARA 230 note 23. As to the meaning of 'individual candidate' at a European parliamentary election see PARA 230 note 32; and as to the meaning of 'statement of parties and individual candidates nominated' see PARA 267 note 3.

17 See PARA 475 et seq. As to references to party lists in elections for the return of London members of the London Assembly see PARA 255 note 23. As to the meaning of 'list' in the context of a European parliamentary election see PARA 230 note 29.

18 European Parliamentary Elections Regulations 2004, SI 2004/293, Sch 1 para 20(1) (as substituted: see note 16); National Assembly for Wales (Representation of the People) Order 2007, SI 2007/236, Sch 5 para 22(1); Greater London Authority Elections Rules 2007, SI 2007/3541, Sch 2 r 16. The text refers to the rules, in relation to a European parliamentary election, in the European Parliamentary Elections Regulations 2004, SI 2004/293, Sch 1 Pt 3 (Sch 1 paras 21–60), or, in relation to a Welsh Assembly election, in the National Assembly for Wales (Representation of the People) Order 2007, SI 2007/236, Sch 5 Pt 3 (Sch 5 paras 23–61), or, in relation to an election for the return of London members of the London Assembly, in the Greater London Authority Elections Rules 2007, SI 2007/3541, Sch 2 Pt 4 (Sch 2 rr 17–56) (see PARA 385 et seq): see the European Parliamentary Elections Regulations 2004, SI 2004/293, Sch 1 para 20(1) (as so substituted); the National Assembly for Wales (Representation of the People) Order 2007, SI 2007/236, Sch 5 para 22(1); and the Greater London Authority Elections Rules 2007, SI 2007/3541, Sch 2 r 16.

19 Ie, in relation to a local authority mayoral election, under the local authority mayoral election rules (see PARA 383 note 14) or, in relation to the election for the Mayor of London, under the London mayoral election rules (see PARA 383 note 10). As to elections for the return of elected local authority mayors see PARA 198 et seq; and as to ordinary elections for the return of the Mayor of London see PARA 199 et seq.

20 Local Authorities (Mayoral Elections) (England and Wales) Regulations 2007, SI 2007/1024, Sch 1 r 16(a), (b); Greater London Authority Elections Rules 2007, SI 2007/3541, Sch 3 r 15(a), (b). If exactly two candidates remain validly nominated as referred to in the text, the poll, in relation to a local authority mayoral election, must be taken in accordance with the Local Authorities (Mayoral Elections) (England and Wales) Regulations 2007, SI 2007/1024, Sch 1 Pt 4 (Sch 1 rr 17–51), and, in relation to the election of the Mayor of London, the poll must be taken in accordance with the Greater London Authority Elections Rules 2007, SI 2007/3541, Sch 3 Pt 4 (Sch 3 rr 16–55) (see PARA 385 et seq): see the Local Authorities (Mayoral Elections) (England and Wales) Regulations 2007, SI 2007/1024, Sch 1 r 16(b); and the Greater London Authority Elections Rules 2007, SI 2007/3541, Sch 3 r 15(b). However, if more than two candidates remain validly nominated, the poll, in relation to a local authority mayoral election, must be taken in accordance with the Local Authorities (Mayoral Elections) (England and Wales) Regulations 2007, SI 2007/1024, Sch 1 Pt 4 and Pt 5 (Sch 1 rr 52, 53) (see PARA 441), and, in relation to the election of the Mayor of London, the poll must be taken in accordance with the Greater London Authority Elections Rules 2007, SI 2007/3541, Sch 3 Pt 4 and Pt 5 (Sch 3 r 56) (see PARA 457): see the Local Authorities (Mayoral Elections) (England and

Wales) Regulations 2007, SI 2007/1024, Sch 1 r 16(a); and the Greater London Authority Elections Rules 2007, SI 2007/3541, Sch 3 r 15(a).

21 See PARA 474 et seq.

385. Poll to be taken by secret ballot. Polling takes place between the hours of seven in the morning and ten at night on the day of election[1] (except where a poll is taken consequent on a parish meeting on a question which involves appointment to office, in which case polling takes place between the hours of four in the afternoon and nine at night on the day fixed for the poll)[2]. The votes at the poll at any such election (or where such a poll is taken) must be given by ballot[3].

The returning officer[4] must make such arrangements as he thinks fit to ensure that:

(1)   every person attending at a polling station (otherwise than for the purpose of voting or assisting a voter with disabilities to vote[5] or as a constable on duty there)[6]; and

(2)   every person attending at the counting of the votes (including those attending at the verification of ballot paper accounts at a European parliamentary election) otherwise than as a constable on duty at the counting (or at any such verification)[7],

has been given a copy in writing of the statutory provisions that require the secrecy of the vote to be preserved by persons attending under head (1) or head (2) above[8]. No person who has voted at such an election (or at such a poll) must, in any legal proceeding to question the election (or poll), be required to state for whom he has voted[9]. It is an offence to obtain or attempt to obtain in a polling station information as to the candidate for whom a voter votes, or to communicate information so obtained[10].

No inquiry is permitted as to the right of any person to vote, except so far as the voter may be asked the prescribed questions[11]. The register of electors is conclusive as to certain questions in connection with a person's entitlement to vote[12]; and a person entitled to vote as an elector is entitled to vote by post or by proxy at the election if he is shown in the absent voters list for the election as so entitled[13]. A person registered as an elector or entered in the list of proxies must not be excluded from voting on the ground of legal incapacity[14]; if, however, an entry in the register shows that the person named will attain voting age on a given date and the date fixed for the poll falls before the date, the entry is conclusive that he is not entitled to be treated as an elector until the date given, and accordingly a ballot paper must not be delivered to him[15]. No misnomer or inaccurate description of any person or place named in the register affects the full operation of it with respect to that person or place in any case where the description of the person or place is such as to be commonly understood[16].

1   Representation of the People Act 1983 Sch 1 r 1; European Parliamentary Elections Regulations 2004, SI 2004/293, Sch 1 para 1 (Sch 1 substituted by SI 2009/186); Local Elections (Principal Areas) (England and Wales) Rules 2006, SI 2006/3304, Sch 2 r 1; Local Elections (Parishes and Communities) (England and Wales) Rules 2006, SI 2006/3305, Sch 2 r 1; National Assembly for Wales (Representation of the People) Order 2007, SI 2007/236, Sch 5 para 1(1); Local Authorities (Mayoral Elections) (England and Wales) Regulations 2007, SI 2007/1024, Sch 1 r 3; Greater London Authority Elections Rules 2007, SI 2007/3541, Sch 1 r 3; Sch 2 r 3; Sch 3 r 3. Votes which are given by post must also reach either the returning officer or the polling station by the close of poll: see PARA 418.

     The provision set out in the text applies to a parliamentary election (whether a general election or by-election), a local government election (which includes an Authority election and a local authority mayoral election), a Welsh Assembly constituency or regional election and a European parliamentary election. As to the meanings of 'Assembly election', 'constituency election' and 'regional election' see PARA 3 note 2. As to the meaning of 'parliamentary election' see PARA 9. As to the meanings of 'Authority election' and 'local government election' see PARA 11. As to elections in the City of London see PARA 33. As to the date of the poll at a parliamentary general election or by-election see PARA 195; as to the date of the poll at elections for the return of a local authority mayor see PARA 198; as to the date of the poll at local government elections (including elections to fill vacancies) see PARAS 206–209; as to the date of the poll at Welsh Assembly elections (including elections to fill vacancies in an Assembly constituency) see PARAS 213–214; and as to the date of the poll at a European parliamentary election see PARA 222.

2   Parish and Community Meetings (Polls) Rules 1987, SI 1987/1, Schedule r 1. As to polls consequent on a parish meeting see PARA 200 et seq; and as to the date of the poll consequent on a parish meeting on a question involving appointment to office see PARA 207.

3   Representation of the People Act 1983 Sch 1 r 18; European Parliamentary Elections Regulations 2004, SI 2004/293, Sch 1 para 21 (as substituted: see note 1); Local Elections (Principal Areas) (England and Wales) Rules 2006, SI 2006/3304, Sch 2 r 15; Local Elections (Parishes and Communities) (England and Wales) Rules 2006, SI 2006/3305, Sch 2 r 15; National Assembly for Wales (Representation of the People) Order 2007, SI 2007/236, Sch 5 para 23(1), (2); Local Authorities (Mayoral Elections) (England and Wales) Regulations 2007, SI 2007/1024, Sch 1 r 17; Greater London Authority Elections Rules 2007, SI 2007/3541, Sch 1 r 16, Sch 2 r 17, Sch 3 r 16. As to polls consequent on a parish meeting see the Local Government Act 1972 s 99, Sch 12 Pt III para 18(5), Pt V para 34(5); and LOCAL GOVERNMENT vol 69 (2009) PARA 638. It is not illegal for an employer to permit electors or their proxies to absent themselves from his employment for a reasonable time for the purpose of voting at the poll at an election without having any deduction from their salaries or wage on account of their absence but the permission must adhere to certain conditions if it is not to be taken as a form of bribery: see PARA 712. As to the manner of voting at elections see PARAS 363–366.

4   As to returning officers for elections generally see PARA 350 et seq. In London Authority and Welsh Assembly elections, the reference is to the constituency returning officer (see PARAS 18 note 2, 211 note 9); and in a European parliamentary election, the reference is to the local returning officer (see PARA 360).

5   As to companions assisting voters with incapacities see PARA 402. At a European parliamentary election, it is further provided that a person under the age of 18 accompanying a voter may attend: see the European Parliamentary Elections Regulations 2004, SI 2004/293, Sch 1 para 34(a) (as substituted: see note 1).

6   Representation of the People Act 1983 Sch 1 r 31(a) (Sch 1 r 31 substituted by the Representation of the People Act 1985 s 24, Sch 4 para 80); Parish and Community Meetings (Polls) Rules 1987, SI 1987/1, Schedule r 13(a); European Parliamentary Elections Regulations 2004, SI 2004/293, Sch 1 para 34(a) (as substituted: see note 1); Local Elections (Principal Areas) (England and Wales) Rules 2006, SI 2006/3304, Sch 2 r 28(a); Local Elections (Parishes and Communities) (England and Wales) Rules 2006, SI 2006/3305, Sch 2 r 28(a); National Assembly for Wales (Representation of the People) Order 2007, SI 2007/236, Sch 5 para 39(a); Local Authorities (Mayoral Elections) (England and Wales) Regulations 2007, SI 2007/1024, Sch 1 r 30(a); Greater London Authority Elections Rules 2007, SI 2007/3541, Sch 1 r 31(a), Sch 2 r 32(a), Sch 3 r 31(a). As to the attendance of constables on duty see PARA 395.

As from a day to be appointed under the Electoral Registration and Administration Act 2013 s 27(1), the Representation of the People Act 1983 Sch 1 r 31 is numbered as Sch 1 r 31(1), and Sch 1 r 31(2) is prospectively added, by the Electoral Registration and Administration Act 2013 s 21(1). Accordingly, as from such a day, the Representation of the People Act 1983 Sch 1 r 31(a) becomes Sch 1 r 31(1)(a) (Sch 1 r 31 as so substituted; Sch 1 r 31(1) prospectively renumbered); and, in the application of Sch 1 r 31 to an election in England or Wales, a reference to a constable includes a person designated as a community support officer under the Police Reform Act 2002 s 38 (police powers for employees: see POLICE AND INVESTIGATORY POWERS vol 84 (2013) PARA 366) (see the Representation of the People Act 1983 Sch 1 r 31(2) (Sch 1 r 31 as so substituted; Sch 1 r 31(2) prospectively added by the Electoral Registration and Administration Act 2013 s 21(1))). However, at the date at which this volume states the law, no such day had been appointed.

7   Representation of the People Act 1983 Sch 1 r 31(b) (as substituted: see note 6); Parish and Community Meetings (Polls) Rules 1987, SI 1987/1, Schedule r 13(b); European Parliamentary Elections Regulations 2004, SI 2004/293, Sch 1 para 34(b) (as substituted: see note 1); Local Elections (Principal Areas) (England and Wales) Rules 2006, SI 2006/3304, Sch 2 r 28(b); Local Elections (Parishes and Communities) (England and Wales) Rules 2006, SI 2006/3305, Sch 2 r 28(b); National Assembly for Wales (Representation of the People) Order 2007, SI 2007/236,

Sch 5 para 39(b); Local Authorities (Mayoral Elections) (England and Wales) Regulations 2007, SI 2007/1024, Sch 1 r 30(b); Greater London Authority Elections Rules 2007, SI 2007/3541, Sch 1 r 31(b), Sch 2 r 32(b), Sch 3 r 31(b). As to the counting of votes at a local government election (except a London Authority election) see PARA 425; in relation to a local authority mayoral election see PARA 436; in relation to a London Authority election see PARA 444; in relation to a London mayoral election see PARA 451; in relation to a Welsh Assembly election see PARA 458; and as to the counting of votes at a European parliamentary election see PARA 466 et seq.

As from a day to be appointed under the Electoral Registration and Administration Act 2013 s 27(1), the Representation of the People Act 1983 Sch 1 r 31(b) is renumbered as Sch 1 r 31(1)(b), and Sch 1 r 31(2) is prospectively added, by the Electoral Registration and Administration Act 2013 s 21(1): see note 6. However, at the date at which this volume states the law, no such day had been appointed.

8   Representation of the People Act 1983 Sch 1 r 31(a), (b) (as substituted: see note 6); Parish and Community Meetings (Polls) Rules 1987, SI 1987/1, Schedule r 13(a), (b); European Parliamentary Elections Regulations 2004, SI 2004/293, Sch 1 para 34(a), (b) (as substituted: see note 1); Local Elections (Principal Areas) (England and Wales) Rules 2006, SI 2006/3304, Sch 2 r 28(a), (b); Local Elections (Parishes and Communities) (England and Wales) Rules 2006, SI 2006/3305, Sch 2 r 28(a), (b); National Assembly for Wales (Representation of the People) Order 2007, SI 2007/236, Sch 5 para 39(a), (b); Local Authorities (Mayoral Elections) (England and Wales) Regulations 2007, SI 2007/1024, Sch 1 r 30(a), (b); Greater London Authority Elections Rules 2007, SI 2007/3541, Sch 1 r 31(a), (b), Sch 2 r 32(a), (b), Sch 3 r 31(a), (b). The text refers:
   (1)   for the purposes of those attending at a polling station (see head (1) in the text), to the requirement of secrecy set out, in relation to a parliamentary of local government election, in the Representation of the People Act 1983 s 66(1), (3), (6), or, in relation to a European parliamentary election, in the European Parliamentary Elections Regulations 2004, SI 2004/293, reg 29(1), (4), (7), or, in relation to a Welsh Assembly election, in the National Assembly for Wales (Representation of the People) Order 2007, SI 2007/236, art 35(1), (3), (6) (see PARAS 739, 741); and
   (2)   for the purposes of those attending the counting of the votes (including the verification of ballot paper accounts at a European parliamentary election) (see head (2) in the text), to the requirement of secrecy set out, in relation to a parliamentary of local government election, in the Representation of the People Act 1983 s 66(2), (6), or, in relation to a European parliamentary election, in the European Parliamentary Elections Regulations 2004, SI 2004/293, reg 29(2), (3), (7), or, in relation to a Welsh Assembly election, in the National Assembly for Wales (Representation of the People) Order 2007, SI 2007/236, art 35(2), (6) (see PARA 740).
At a poll consequent on a parish or community meeting, the provisions relating to the requirement of secrecy referred to in heads (1) and (2) above are subject to the adaptations, alterations and exceptions set out in the Parish and Community Meetings (Polls) Rules 1987, SI 1987/1, r 6(e) (as to which see PARA 383 note 6): Schedule r 13(a), (b).

As from a day to be appointed under the Electoral Registration and Administration Act 2013 s 27(1), the Representation of the People Act 1983 Sch 1 r 31 is renumbered as Sch 1 r 31(1), and Sch 1 r 31(2) is prospectively added, by the Electoral Registration and Administration Act 2013 s 21(1): see note 6. However, at the date at which this volume states the law, no such day had been appointed.

9   Representation of the People Act 1983 Sch 1 r 21; Parish and Community Meetings (Polls) Rules 1987, SI 1987/1, Schedule r 6; European Parliamentary Elections Regulations 2004, SI 2004/293, Sch 1 para 25 (as substituted: see note 1); Local Elections (Principal Areas) (England and Wales) Rules 2006, SI 2006/3304, Sch 2 r 19; Local Elections (Parishes and Communities) (England and Wales) Rules 2006, SI 2006/3305, Sch 2 r 19; National Assembly for Wales (Representation of the People) Order 2007, SI 2007/236, Sch 5 para 30; Local Authorities (Mayoral Elections) (England and Wales) Regulations 2007, SI 2007/1024, Sch 1 r 21; Greater London Authority Elections Rules 2007, SI 2007/3541, Sch 1 r 20, Sch 2 r 21, Sch 3 r 20. At a parliamentary or Welsh Assembly election, the legal proceedings referred to in the text might also include questioning the return (ie rather than the election): see the Representation of the People Act 1983 Sch 1 r 21; and the National Assembly for Wales (Representation of the People) Order 2007, SI 2007/236, Sch 5 para 30.
10 See PARA 739 et seq.
11 See PARA 398.
12 See PARA 149.

13 See PARA 366. For the purposes of the statutory provisions governing elections, a voter is defined
     as a person voting at an election and includes a person voting as proxy (but not necessarily a
     person voting by proxy): in relation to parliamentary and local government elections, see
     PARA 95 note 2; in relation to Welsh Assembly elections, see PARA 110 note 7; and in relation to
     European parliamentary elections, see PARA 111 note 5. To indicate that an elector or his proxy
     is entitled to vote by post and is for that reason not entitled to vote in person, the letter 'A' is
     placed against the name of that elector in any copy of the register, or part of it, provided for a
     polling station: see PARA 377.
14 See PARA 149.
15 See PARA 149.
16 See PARA 150.

386. Form and printing of ballot papers. The ballot of every voter[1] consists of
a ballot paper[2], which must be in the prescribed form and must be printed in
accordance with the prescribed directions[3].

Those entitled to have their names inserted in the ballot paper are:

(1)   at a parliamentary or Welsh Assembly constituency election, those
       persons shown in the statement of persons nominated as standing
       nominated for the constituency, and no others[4];

(2)   at a local government election (including a London Assembly
       constituency members election), those persons remaining validly
       nominated for the electoral area, after any withdrawals, and no others[5];

(3)   at an election for the return of the Mayor of London, or a local
       authority mayor, those persons remaining validly nominated for election
       to the office, after any withdrawals, and no other[6];

(4)   at a London members election, each registered party that remains
       validly nominated and whose party list includes a person who remains
       validly nominated as a list candidate after any withdrawals, and no
       other[7], as well as each person remaining validly nominated as an
       individual candidate at that election, after any withdrawals, and no
       other[8];

(5)   at a European parliamentary election, the registered parties, together
       with their candidates shown in the statement of parties and individual
       candidates nominated, and the individual candidates shown as standing
       nominated, and no others[9]; and

(6)   at a Welsh Assembly regional election, those persons (including their
       descriptions) shown in the statement of persons nominated as standing
       nominated as individual candidates, and no others[10]; and the registered
       political parties (including their descriptions) which have submitted a
       party list and are shown in the statement of persons nominated as
       standing nominated, together with the party list candidates appearing
       on the party list of each such party and as standing nominated, and no
       others[11].

There is authority to the effect that where the name of a candidate who had
withdrawn was retained on a ballot paper, the election was avoided[12].

The ballot paper at such an election[13] must contain:

(a)   the names and other particulars[14] of the candidates as shown in the
       statement of persons nominated, with the names in the order as shown
       in that statement[15]; and

(b)   in the case of a London members election, the authorised descriptions of
       the registered parties, in the same order as in the statement of parties
       and persons nominated[16]; or

(c)   in the case of a European parliamentary election, the names followed by the descriptions, if any, of the registered parties shown in the statement of parties and individual candidates nominated, together with the names of the candidates of those parties, in the same order as in that statement[17]; or

(d)   in the case of a Welsh Assembly regional election, the names or, as the case may be, the descriptions of the registered political parties shown in the statement of persons nominated, together with the names of the candidates included on those parties' lists, in the same order as in that statement[18].

At a poll consequent on a parish meeting taken on a question of appointment to any office, the ballot paper must contain the full names, home addresses and, if required, descriptions of the candidates arranged alphabetically in the order of their surnames (and, if there are two or more of them with the same surname, of their other names)[19].

1   Ie at an election, or at a poll taken consequent on a parish meeting on a question which involves appointment to office. As to polls consequent on a parish meeting on a question involving appointment to office see PARA 200 et seq. The text applies to a parliamentary election, a local government election (which includes any London Authority election and a local authority mayoral election), a Welsh Assembly constituency or regional election and a European parliamentary election. As to the meanings of 'Assembly election', 'constituency election' and 'regional election' see PARA 3 note 2. As to the meaning of 'parliamentary election' see PARA 9. As to the meanings of 'Authority election' and 'local government election' see PARA 11. As to elections in the City of London see PARA 33. As to elections for the return of a local authority mayor see PARA 198; and as to European parliamentary elections see PARA 217 et seq.

2   Representation of the People Act 1983 Sch 1 r 19(1); Parish and Community Meetings (Polls) Rules 1987, SI 1987/1, Schedule r 4(1); European Parliamentary Elections Regulations 2004, SI 2004/293, Sch 1 para 22(1) (Sch 1 substituted by SI 2009/186); Local Elections (Principal Areas) (England and Wales) Rules 2006, SI 2006/3304, Sch 2 r 16(1); Local Elections (Parishes and Communities) (England and Wales) Rules 2006, SI 2006/3305, Sch 2 r 16(1); National Assembly for Wales (Representation of the People) Order 2007, SI 2007/236, Sch 5 paras 24(1), 25(1); Local Authorities (Mayoral Elections) (England and Wales) Regulations 2007, SI 2007/1024, Sch 1 r 18(1); Greater London Authority Elections Rules 2007, SI 2007/3541, Sch 1 r 17(1), Sch 2 r 18(1), Sch 3 r 17(1).

3   Representation of the People Act 1983 Sch 1 r 19(2); Parish and Community Meetings (Polls) Rules 1987, SI 1987/1, Schedule r 4(2); European Parliamentary Elections Regulations 2004, SI 2004/293, Sch 1 para 22(2) (as substituted: see note 2); Local Elections (Principal Areas) (England and Wales) Rules 2006, SI 2006/3304, Sch 2 r 16(2); Local Elections (Parishes and Communities) (England and Wales) Rules 2006, SI 2006/3305, Sch 2 r 16(2); National Assembly for Wales (Representation of the People) Order 2007, SI 2007/236, Sch 5 paras 24(3), 25(3); Local Authorities (Mayoral Elections) (England and Wales) Regulations 2007, SI 2007/1024, Sch 1 r 18(3); Greater London Authority Elections Rules 2007, SI 2007/3541, Sch 1 r 17(1), (3)(a), Sch 2 r 18(1), (4)(a), Sch 3 r 17(1), (3)(a). As to the prescribed forms of ballot paper:
    (1)   in relation to a parliamentary election, see the Representation of the People Act 1983 Sch 1 Appendix (Form of ballot paper (form of front of ballot paper; form of back of ballot paper); Directions as to printing the ballot paper) (amended by the Representation of the People Act 1985 s 24, Sch 4 paras 84, 85; the Welsh Language Act 1993 s 35(4); the Registration of Political Parties Act 1998 s 13, Sch 2 paras 5, 6, Appendix; the Electoral Administration Act 2006 ss 30(1), (3), 31(1), (9), 47, 74(2), Sch 1 paras 69, 93(1), (2), Sch 2; and the Political Parties and Elections Act 2009 s 39, Sch 6 para 8(1), (6));
    (2)   in relation to a poll taken consequent on a parish meeting on a question which involves appointment to office, see the Parish and Community Meetings (Polls) Rules 1987, SI 1987/1, Schedule Appendix of Forms (Form of ballot paper on a question of appointment to an office and directions as to printing the ballot paper) (amended by SI 1987/262);
    (3)   in relation to a European parliamentary election, see the European Parliamentary

Elections Regulations 2004, SI 2004/293, Sch 1 Appendix of Forms (Form A: Form of front of ballot paper; Form of back of ballot paper; Directions for printing the ballot paper) (as so substituted);

(4)   in relation to an election of councillors for a principal area, parish or community, see the Local Elections (Principal Areas) (England and Wales) Rules 2006, SI 2006/3304, Sch 2 Appendix of Forms (Form of front of ballot paper; Form of back of ballot paper; Directions as to printing the ballot paper); and the Local Elections (Parishes and Communities) (England and Wales) Rules 2006, SI 2006/3305, Sch 2 Appendix of Forms (Form of front of ballot paper; Form of back of ballot paper; Directions as to printing the ballot paper);

(5)   in relation to a local authority mayoral election, see the Local Authorities (Mayoral Elections) (England and Wales) Regulations 2007, SI 2007/1024, Sch 1 Appendix of Forms (Form 3: ballot paper (two candidates) (Form of front of ballot paper; Form of back of ballot paper; Directions for printing the ballot paper); Form 4: ballot paper (three or more candidates) (Form of front of ballot paper; Form of back of ballot paper; Directions for printing the ballot paper)) (Forms 3, 4 substituted by SI 2012/2059);

(6)   in relation to London Authority elections, see the Greater London Authority Elections Rules 2007, SI 2007/3541, Sch 10 r 2 (Form 5: Ballot paper for constituency members elections; Directions as to printing the ballot paper; Form 6: Ballot paper for London members elections; Directions as to printing the ballot paper; Form 7: Ballot paper for mayoral elections; Directions as to printing the ballot paper);

(7)   in relation to a Welsh Assembly election, see the National Assembly for Wales (Representation of the People) Order 2007, SI 2007/236, Sch 10 Appendix of Forms (Form CK: Form of ballot paper (constituency election); Form CK1: Directions as to printing the ballot paper (constituency election): constituency election; Form CL: Form of ballot paper (regional election); Form CL1: Directions as to printing the ballot paper (regional election)).

The usual provisions that require any document which, by virtue of the European Parliamentary Elections Regulations 2004, SI 2004/293, is required or authorised to be displayed in public, to be made readily accessible (ie reg 122A(1)–(3): see PARA 239 note 23) do not apply to the ballot paper: see reg 122A(4)(b) (reg 122A added by SI 2009/186).

Where elections take place in Wales see also the forms issued partly in English and partly in Welsh in:

(a)   the Parliamentary Elections (Welsh Forms) Order 2007, SI 2007/1014, arts 4(1), (2), 6(a), Sch 2 (Form 1 (Ffurflen 1): Form of Back of Ballot Paper; Ffurf ar gyfer Cefn y Papur Pleidleisio) (art 4(1) substituted, art 4(2) amended, by SI 2010/1078);

(b)   the Local Elections (Principal Areas) (Welsh Forms) Order 2007, SI 2007/1015, arts 4(1), (2), 5, Sch 1 (Form of Back of Ballot Paper; Ffurf ar gyfer Cefn y Papur Pleidleisio);

(c)   the Local Elections (Communities) (Welsh Forms) Order 2007, SI 2007/1013, arts 4(1), (2), 5, Sch 1 (Form of Back of Ballot Paper; Ffurf ar gyfer Cefn y Papur Pleidleisio); and

(d)   the European Parliamentary Elections (Welsh Forms) Order 2009, SI 2009/781, arts 4(1), (2), 6(1)(a), Sch 2 (Form 1 (Ffurflen 1): Form of Back of Ballot Paper; Ffurf ar gyfer Cefn y Papur Pleidleisio).

In the case of a parliamentary election, the Secretary of State may in regulations prescribe a different form of ballot paper from that in the Representation of the People Act 1983 Sch 1 Appendix, amend or replace the directions as to printing the ballot paper in the Appendix and, in consequence of anything done for either of those purposes, amend or replace in the Appendix the form of directions for the guidance of the voters in voting: see Sch 1 r 19(4) (added by the Electoral Administration Act 2006 s 30(1), (2)). As to the making of regulations under the Representation of the People Act 1983 generally see PARA 28 note 16. Provision is made also for the Secretary of State to make a pilot order for the purposes of enabling ballot papers issued at such local government elections as are specified in the order to contain photographs of the candidates and for any such scheme to be evaluated and to be applied on a permanent basis in relation to specified elections: see the Electoral Administration Act 2006 ss 32–34; and PARAS 524–526. As to the Secretary of State see PARA 2.

4   Representation of the People Act 1983 Sch 1 r 19(1); National Assembly for Wales (Representation of the People) Order 2007, SI 2007/236, Sch 5 para 24(2). Head (1) in the text applies to a constituency candidate at a Welsh Assembly constituency election: see Sch 5 para 24(2). As to the meaning of 'constituency candidate' for these purposes see PARA 230 note 19. As to the statement of persons nominated see PARA 267.

5   Local Elections (Principal Areas) (England and Wales) Rules 2006, SI 2006/3304, Sch 2 r 16(1); Local Elections (Parishes and Communities) (England and Wales) Rules 2006, SI 2006/3305, Sch 2 r 16(1); Greater London Authority Elections Rules 2007, SI 2007/3541, Sch 1 r 17(2). As to the meaning of 'constituency member', in relation to the London Assembly, see PARA 11 note 6; definition applied by virtue of r 2(2).

6   Local Authorities (Mayoral Elections) (England and Wales) Regulations 2007, SI 2007/1024, Sch 1 r 18(2); Greater London Authority Elections Rules 2007, SI 2007/3541, Sch 3 r 17(2).

7   Greater London Authority Elections Rules 2007, SI 2007/3541, Sch 2 r 18(2). As to the meaning of 'London member', in relation to the London Assembly, see PARA 11 note 5; definition applied by virtue of r 2(2). As to the meaning of 'registered political party' for these purposes see PARA 256 note 27. As to references to party lists in elections for the return of London members of the London Assembly see PARA 255 note 23.

8   Greater London Authority Elections Rules 2007, SI 2007/3541, Sch 2 r 18(3). As to individual candidates to be London members of the London Assembly see further LONDON GOVERNMENT vol 71 (2013) PARA 81.

9   European Parliamentary Elections Regulations 2004, SI 2004/293, Sch 1 para 22(1) (as substituted: see note 2). As to the meaning of 'registered political party' for these purposes see PARA 230 note 29; as to the meaning of 'individual candidate' at a European parliamentary election see PARA 230 note 32; and as to the meaning of 'statement of parties and individual candidates nominated' see PARA 267 note 3.

10 National Assembly for Wales (Representation of the People) Order 2007, SI 2007/236, Sch 5 para 25(2)(a). Head (6) in the text applies to an individual candidate at a Welsh Assembly regional election: see Sch 5 para 25(2)(a). As to the meaning of 'individual candidate' for these purposes see PARA 230 note 19.

11 National Assembly for Wales (Representation of the People) Order 2007, SI 2007/236, Sch 5 para 25(2)(b). As to the meaning of 'registered political party' for these purposes see PARA 215 note 19. As to the meanings of 'party list' and 'party list candidate' for these purposes see PARA 230 note 23. As to a registered party's description see PARA 256.

12 *Wilson v Ingham* (1895) 64 LJ QB 775, DC.

13 As to a poll consequent on a parish meeting taken on a question of appointment to any office see the text and note 19.

14 If a candidate who is the subject of a party's authorisation (see PARA 256) so requests, the ballot paper must contain, against the particulars of that candidate, the party's registered emblem (or, as the case may be, one of the party's registered emblems): Representation of the People Act 1983 Sch 1 r 19(2A) (Sch 1 r 19(2A), (2B) added by the Registration of Political Parties Act 1998 s 13, Sch 2 para 4); Local Elections (Principal Areas) (England and Wales) Rules 2006, SI 2006/3304, Sch 2 r 16(3); Local Elections (Parishes and Communities) (England and Wales) Rules 2006, SI 2006/3305, Sch 2 r 16(3); National Assembly for Wales (Representation of the People) Order 2007, SI 2007/236, Sch 5 para 24(5); Local Authorities (Mayoral Elections) (England and Wales) Regulations 2007, SI 2007/1024, Sch 1 r 18(4); Greater London Authority Elections Rules 2007, SI 2007/3541, Sch 1 r 17(4), Sch 3 r 17(4). Except in the case of a Welsh Assembly election, if a candidate who is the subject of an authorisation by two or more parties (see PARA 256) so requests, the ballot paper must contain, against the candidate's particulars, the registered emblem (or one of the registered emblems) of one of those parties: Local Elections (Principal Areas) (England and Wales) Rules 2006, SI 2006/3304, Sch 2 r 16(3A) (added by SI 2011/563); Local Elections (Parishes and Communities) (England and Wales) Rules 2006, SI 2006/3305, Sch 2 r 16(3A) (added by SI 2011/562); Local Authorities (Mayoral Elections) (England and Wales) Regulations 2007, SI 2007/1024, Sch 1 r 18(4A) (added by SI 2011/926); Greater London Authority Elections Rules 2007, SI 2007/3541, Sch 1 r 17(4A), Sch 3 r 17(4A) (Sch 1 r 17(4A), Sch 3 r 17(4A), added by SI 2012/198). Except in the case of a Welsh Assembly election, any such request must be made in writing to the returning officer and be received by him during the period for delivery of nomination papers (as to which see PARA 260): Representation of the People Act 1983 Sch 1 r 19(2B) (as so added); Local Elections (Principal Areas) (England and Wales) Rules 2006, SI 2006/3304, Sch 2 r 16(4) (amended by SI 2011/563); Local Elections (Parishes and Communities) (England and Wales) Rules 2006, SI 2006/3305, Sch 2 r 16(4) (amended by SI 2011/562); Local Authorities (Mayoral Elections) (England and Wales) Regulations 2007, SI 2007/1024, Sch 1 r 18(5) (amended by SI 2011/926); Greater London Authority Elections Rules 2007, SI 2007/3541, Sch 1 r 17(5), Sch 3 r 17(5) (Sch 1 r 17(5), Sch 3 r 17(5), amended by SI 2012/198). In the case of a London Assembly constituency members election, the returning officer specified is the constituency returning officer ('CRO') (see the Greater London Authority Elections Rules 2007, SI 2007/3541, Sch 1 r 17(5) (as so amended)); and, in the case of any other London Authority election (see also note 16), the returning officer specified is the Greater London returning officer ('GLRO') (see Sch 2 r 18(6),

Sch 3 r 17(5) (as so amended)). As to the meaning of the 'Greater London returning officer' see PARA 211 note 8; and as to the meaning of the 'constituency returning officer' in this context see PARA 211 note 9. In the case of a Welsh Assembly constituency election, the returning officer specified is the constituency returning officer: see the National Assembly for Wales (Representation of the People) Order 2007, SI 2007/236, Sch 5 para 24(5). As to the meaning of 'constituency returning officer' see PARA 18 note 2.

As from a day to be appointed under the Electoral Registration and Administration Act 2013 s 27(1), the Representation of the People Act 1983 Sch 1 r 19(2B) is amended, and Sch 1 r 19(2AA) is prospectively added, so that, if a candidate who is the subject of an authorisation by two or more parties (see PARA 256) so requests, the ballot paper at a parliamentary election must contain, against the candidate's particulars, the registered emblem (or one of the registered emblems) of one of those parties (see the Representation of the People Act 1983 Sch 1 r 19(2AA) (prospectively added by the Electoral Registration and Administration Act 2013 s 20(1), (2))); and the Representation of the People Act 1983 Sch 1 r 19(2B) applies accordingly to Sch 1 r 19(2AA) also (see Sch 1 r 19(2B) (prospectively amended by the Electoral Registration and Administration Act 2013 s 20(1), (3))). However, at the date at which this volume states the law, no such day had been appointed.

15 Representation of the People Act 1983 Sch 1 r 19(2)(a), (3); European Parliamentary Elections Regulations 2004, SI 2004/293, Sch 1 para 22(2)(a), (5) (as substituted: see note 2); Local Elections (Principal Areas) (England and Wales) Rules 2006, SI 2006/3304, Sch 2 r 16(2)(a), (5); Local Elections (Parishes and Communities) (England and Wales) Rules 2006, SI 2006/3305, Sch 2 r 16(2)(a), (5); National Assembly for Wales (Representation of the People) Order 2007, SI 2007/236, Sch 5 paras 24(3)(a), (4), 25(3)(a), (4)(a); Local Authorities (Mayoral Elections) (England and Wales) Regulations 2007, SI 2007/1024, Sch 1 r 18(3)(a), (6); Greater London Authority Elections Rules 2007, SI 2007/3541, Sch 1 r 17(3)(b), (6), Sch 2 r 18(4)(b), (7), Sch 3 r 17(3)(b), (6). In the case of an election of the Mayor of London, it is specified further that, if there are two or more candidates with the same surname, the names of those candidates must be arranged alphabetically in order of their other names: see Sch 2 r 17(6). In the case of a European parliamentary election, head (a) in the text refers to the names, followed by the descriptions (if any) of any individual candidate shown in the statement of parties and individual candidates nominated: see the European Parliamentary Elections Regulations 2004, SI 2004/293, Sch 1 para 22(2)(a) (as so substituted). In the case of a Welsh Assembly regional election, head (a) in the text refers to the names and descriptions of the individual candidate shown in the statement of persons nominated: see the National Assembly for Wales (Representation of the People) Order 2007, SI 2007/236, Sch 5 para 25(3)(a).

16 Greater London Authority Elections Rules 2007, SI 2007/3541, Sch 2 r 18(4)(b), (7). If a request is made by or on behalf of a registered party's nominating officer (see PARA 256), the ballot paper must contain, against the party's authorised description, the party's registered emblem (or, as the case may be, one of the party's registered emblems): Sch 2 r 18(5). Such a request must be made in writing to the GLRO (see note 14), and be received by him during the period for delivery of nomination papers (as to which see PARA 260): see Sch 2 r 18(6). As to a registered party's nominating officer see PARA 253.

17 European Parliamentary Elections Regulations 2004, SI 2004/293, Sch 1 para 22(2)(a), (5) (as substituted: see note 2). If a request is made by or on behalf of a registered party's nominating officer (see PARA 256), the ballot paper must contain, adjacent to the party's name, the registered party's registered emblem (or, as the case may be, one of the party's registered emblems): Sch 1 para 22(3) (as so substituted). Such a request must be made in writing to the returning officer, and be received by him before the last time for the delivery of nomination papers (as to which see PARA 260): see Sch 1 para 22(4) (as so substituted).

18 National Assembly for Wales (Representation of the People) Order 2007, SI 2007/236, Sch 5 para 25(3)(b), (4)(b). Head (d) in the text refers to the order set out in the statement of persons nominated of the names or, as the case may be, descriptions of the registered political parties, together with (in respect of each such name or names or, as the case may be, description of a registered political party) the names of its party list candidates: see Sch 5 para 25(4)(b). If a certificate received by the regional returning officer under Sch 5 para 8(1) (see PARA 256) has requested that the registered political party's registered emblem (or, as the case may be, one of the party's registered emblems) is to be shown on the ballot paper against the party's description, the ballot paper must contain that emblem in that way: Sch 5 para 25(5). As to the meaning of 'regional returning officer' see PARA 18 note 2.

19 Parish and Community Meetings (Polls) Rules 1987, SI 1987/1, Schedule r 4(2)(a). See also Appendix of Forms (Form of Directions for the Guidance of the Voters in Voting where the poll is on a question of appointment to an office).

387. Security measures associated with the ballot paper. The ballot paper to be used at an election[1] must have a number and other unique identifying mark printed on the back[2], and the returning officer[3] must prepare a list (the 'corresponding number list')[4] containing the numbers and other unique identifying marks of all of the ballot papers which either are to be issued by him to those entitled to vote by post[5] or are to be provided by him to each presiding officer for use at polling stations[6]. The ballot paper to be used at polls consequent on a parish meeting on a question involving appointment to office[7] must have a number printed on the back[8] and must have attached a counterfoil with the same number printed on it[9]. At elections or polls where voters may cast more than one vote, the ballot paper must have such other distinguishing features as may be specified[10].

The ballot paper to be used at any such election (or any such poll) must be capable of being folded up[11].

Every ballot paper to be used at an election must contain an appropriate security marking (the 'official mark')[12]. At a poll consequent on a parish meeting taken on a question of appointment to any office, the official mark must both mark and perforate every ballot paper[13]. The official mark must be kept secret and any re-use of the same official mark is subject to the following constraints[14]:

(1)　at a parliamentary election, an interval of not less than seven years must intervene between the use of the same official mark at elections for the same constituency[15];

(2)　at a local government election, an interval of not less than five years must intervene between the use of the same official mark for elections in the same county, county borough, district, London borough, parish or community (or between the use of the same official mark at any Authority election, as the case may be)[16];

(3)　at a poll consequent on a parish meeting taken on a question of appointment to any office, the same official mark must not be used at consecutive polls in the same parish[17];

(4)　at a Welsh Assembly election, an interval of not less than seven years must intervene between the use of the same official mark at elections for the same Assembly constituency or, in relation to the same Assembly constituency, at elections in the same Assembly electoral region[18]; and

(5)　at a European parliamentary election, an interval of not less than five years must intervene between the use of the same official mark at elections for the same local counting area[19].

The returning officer may use a different official mark for different purposes at the same election[20].

1　Ie at an election, but not at a poll taken consequent on a parish meeting on a question which involves appointment to office (see the text and notes 7–9). The text applies to a parliamentary election, a local government election (which includes any London Authority election and a local authority mayoral election), a Welsh Assembly constituency or regional election and a European parliamentary election. As to the meanings of 'Assembly election', 'constituency election' and 'regional election' see PARA 3 note 2. As to the meaning of 'parliamentary election' see PARA 9. As to the meanings of 'Authority election' and 'local government election' see PARA 11. As to elections in the City of London see PARA 33. As to elections for the return of a local authority mayor see PARA 198; and as to European parliamentary elections see PARA 217 et seq. As to the form and printing of ballot papers see PARA 386.

2　Representation of the People Act 1983 Sch 1 r 19(2)(c) (amended by the Electoral Administration Act 2006 s 47, Sch 1 paras 69, 87); European Parliamentary Elections Regulations 2004, SI 2004/293, Sch 1 para 22(2)(c) (Sch 1 substituted by SI 2009/186); Local Elections (Principal Areas) (England and Wales) Rules 2006, SI 2006/3304, Sch 2 r 16(2)(c);

Local Elections (Parishes and Communities) (England and Wales) Rules 2006, SI 2006/3305, Sch 2 r 16(2)(c); Local Authorities (Mayoral Elections) (England and Wales) Regulations 2007, SI 2007/1024, Sch 1 r 18(3)(c); National Assembly for Wales (Representation of the People) Order 2007, SI 2007/236, Sch 5 paras 24(3)(c), 25(3)(d); Greater London Authority Elections Rules 2007, SI 2007/3541, Sch 1 r 17(3)(c), Sch 2 r 18(4)(c), Sch 3 r 17(3)(c). At a Welsh Assembly regional election, it is specified further that the number and other unique identifying mark printed on the back of the ballot paper must be accompanied by a mark or other distinguishing feature by which the Assembly constituency can be identified in which the vote is to be given in relation to the ballot paper: see the National Assembly for Wales (Representation of the People) Order 2007, SI 2007/236, Sch 5 para 25(3)(d). Where the poll at a Welsh Assembly regional election is to be taken together with the poll at a constituency election for a constituency which is situated in the region in respect of which the regional election is being held (a 'relevant constituency'), the constituency returning officer must ensure that the number on the back of a constituency ballot paper is the same as the number on the back of one (but not more than one) regional ballot paper: see Sch 5 para 26(1), (2). As to the meanings of 'Assembly constituency' and 'Assembly electoral region' see PARA 3 note 2; and as to the meaning of 'constituency returning officer' see PARA 18 note 2.

3   As to returning officers see PARA 350 et seq. In the case of a London Assembly election, the returning officer specified for these purposes is the constituency returning officer ('CRO'): see the Greater London Authority Elections Rules 2007, SI 2007/3541, Sch 1 r 18(1), Sch 2 r 19(1), Sch 3 r 18(1). As to the meaning of the 'constituency returning officer' in this context see PARA 211 note 9. In the case of a European parliamentary election, the local returning officer is specified: see the European Parliamentary Elections Regulations 2004, SI 2004/293, Sch 1 para 23(1) (as substituted: see note 2). As to local returning officers appointed for the purposes of elections to the European Parliament see PARA 360. In the case of a Welsh Assembly election, the returning officer specified for these purposes is the constituency returning officer: see the National Assembly for Wales (Representation of the People) Order 2007, SI 2007/236, Sch 5 para 27(1).

4   For the purposes of a parliamentary election, the list must be in such form as the Secretary of State in regulations prescribes: Representation of the People Act 1983 Sch 1 r 19A(2) (Sch 1 r 19A added by the Electoral Administration Act 2006 s 31(1), (2)). Accordingly, the form of the corresponding number list to be prepared by a returning officer under the Representation of the People Act 1983 Sch 1 r 19A must be in the form set out in the Representation of the People (England and Wales) Regulations 2001, SI 2001/341, Sch 3 (Form L1: corresponding number list to be used at parliamentary election taken alone) (added by SI 2006/2910): Representation of the People (England and Wales) Regulations 2001, SI 2001/341, reg 63A(1) (reg 63A added by SI 2006/2910). As to the Secretary of State see PARA 2. When a parliamentary election is combined with another poll under the Representation of the People Act 1985 s 15 (see PARAS 21–22) or under the Local Government Act 2000 s 44 (provision for the combination of polls at elections for the return of elected mayors: see PARA 26) or under s 45 (provision for the combination of polls at referendums with polls at any elections: see PARA 27), the corresponding number list to be prepared by a returning officer under the Representation of the People Act 1983 Sch 1 r 19A must be in the form set out in the Representation of the People (England and Wales) Regulations 2001, SI 2001/341, Sch 3 (Form M1: corresponding number list to be used when a parliamentary election is combined with another election/referendum) (added by SI 2006/2910): Representation of the People (England and Wales) Regulations 2001, SI 2001/341, reg 63A(3) (reg 63A as so added; reg 63A(3) amended by SI 2007/1025).

For the purposes of local government elections mentioned in the text:

(1)   for principal areas, the corresponding number list must be in the appropriate form, or a form to like effect in the Local Elections (Principal Areas) (England and Wales) Rules 2006, SI 2006/3304, Sch 2 r 17(2), Appendix of Forms (Form L1: corresponding number list to be used at a local government election taken alone); and Sch 3 r 17(2), Appendix of Forms (Form M1: corresponding number list to be used when a local government election is combined with another election/referendum);

(2)   for parishes and communities, the corresponding number list must be in the appropriate form, or a form to like effect in the Local Elections (Parishes and Communities) (England and Wales) Rules 2006, SI 2006/3305, Sch 2 r 17(2), Sch 2 Appendix of Forms (Form L1: corresponding number list to be used at a parish or community election taken alone); and Sch 3 r 17(2), Appendix of Forms (Form M1: corresponding number list to be used when a parish or community election is combined with another election/referendum);

(3)   for a local authority mayoral election, the corresponding number list must be in the appropriate form, or a form to like effect in the Local Authorities (Mayoral Elections)

(England and Wales) Regulations 2007, SI 2007/1024, Sch 1 r 19(2), Appendix of Forms (Form 5: corresponding number list L1), Sch 3 r 19(2), Appendix of Forms (Form 5: corresponding number list M1); and

(4) for an Authority election, the corresponding number list must be in the appropriate form, or a form to like effect in the Greater London Authority Elections Rules 2007, SI 2007/3541, Sch 1 r 18(2), Sch 2 r 19(2), Sch 3 r 18(2), Sch 10 r 2 (Form 8: corresponding number list L1).

At an ordinary election under head (4) above, the same corresponding number list may be used for each of the Authority elections which are combined: Sch 1 r 18(3), Sch 2 r 19(3), Sch 3 r 18(3).

For the purposes of a European parliamentary election, the form of corresponding number list to be prepared by a local returning officer for the purpose of the European Parliamentary Elections Regulations 2004, SI 2004/293, Sch 1 para 28(1) (procedure on issue to those entitled to vote by post of a ballot paper and postal voting statement: see PARA 406) and Sch 2 para 48(1) (procedure on issue of postal ballot paper: see PARA 408) must be in Sch 1 Pt 7 Appendix of Forms (Form B: Corresponding Number List for issue of postal ballot papers at a European Parliamentary election): see Sch 1 para 23(2) (as substituted: see note 2). The form of corresponding number list to be prepared by the local returning officer for the purposes of Sch 1 para 32(3)(d) (form to be provided by local returning officer to each polling station: see PARA 391 note 23) and Sch 1 para 41(1)(b) (voting procedure (elector's number to be marked on the list): see PARA 399) must be in Sch 1 Pt 7 Appendix of Forms (Form C: Corresponding Number List for use in polling station at a European Parliamentary election) (as so substituted): Sch 1 para 23(3) (as so substituted). As to combined elections see Sch 1 para 23(4,) (5), Sch 1 Pt 7 Appendix of Forms (Form D: Corresponding Number List for issue of postal ballot papers to be used when a European Parliamentary election is combined with another election or referendum; Form E: Corresponding Number List for use in polling station when a European Parliamentary election is combined with another election or referendum) (as so substituted).

For the purposes of a Welsh Assembly election, the corresponding number list must be as set out in English and Welsh in the National Assembly for Wales (Representation of the People) Order 2007, SI 2007/236, Sch 10 Appendix of Forms (Form CM: Form of Corresponding Number List): Sch 5 para 27(2).

Where elections take place in Wales see also the forms issued partly in English and partly in Welsh in the Parliamentary Elections (Welsh Forms) Order 2007, SI 2007/1014, art 6(p), (r), Sch 2 (Forms 16, 18).

Where elections take place in Wales see also the forms issued partly in English and partly in Welsh in the Parliamentary Elections (Welsh Forms) Order 2007, SI 2007/1014, art 6(q), (s), Sch 2 (Forms 17, 19); the Local Elections (Principal Areas) (Welsh Forms) Order 2007, SI 2007/1015, art 7(1)(a), Sch 3 (Form 1 (Ffurflen 1) (Corresponding Number List—L1/Rhestr Rhif Cyfatebol—L1)); the Local Elections (Communities) (Welsh Forms) Order 2007, SI 2007/1013, art 7(1)(a), Sch 3 (Form 1 (Ffurflen 1) (Corresponding Number List—L1/Rhestr Rhif Cyfatebol—L1)); and the European Parliamentary Elections (Welsh Forms) Order 2009, SI 2009/781, art 6(1)(b), (d), Sch 2 (Forms 2, 4).

5   Ie, in relation to a parliamentary election, in pursuance of the Representation of the People Act 1983 Sch 1 r 24(1), or, in relation to a European parliamentary election, in pursuance of the European Parliamentary Elections Regulations 2004, SI 2004/293, Sch 1 para 28(1), or, in relation to a local government election for a principal area, in pursuance of the Local Elections (Principal Areas) (England and Wales) Rules 2006, SI 2006/3304, Sch 2 r 22(1) or, in relation to a local government election for a parish or community council, in pursuance of the Local Elections (Parishes and Communities) (England and Wales) Rules 2006, SI 2006/3305, Sch 2 r 22(1), or, in relation to a Welsh Assembly election, in pursuance of the National Assembly for Wales (Representation of the People) Order 2007, SI 2007/236, Sch 5 para 33(1), or, in relation to a local authority mayoral election, in pursuance of the Local Authorities (Mayoral Elections) (England and Wales) Regulations 2007, SI 2007/1024, Sch 1 r 24, or, in relation to an Authority election, in pursuance of the Greater London Authority Elections Rules 2007, SI 2007/3541, Sch 1 r 23(1), Sch 2 r 24(1), Sch 3 r 23(1) (see PARA 406): see the Representation of the People Act 1983 Sch 1 r 19A(1) (as added: see note 4); the European Parliamentary Elections Regulations 2004, SI 2004/293, Sch 1 para 23(1) (as substituted: see note 2); the Local Elections (Principal Areas) (England and Wales) Rules 2006, SI 2006/3304, Sch 2 r 17(1); the Local Elections (Parishes and Communities) (England and Wales) Rules 2006, SI 2006/3305, Sch 2 r 17(1); the National Assembly for Wales (Representation of the People) Order 2007, SI 2007/236, Sch 5 para 27(1); the Local Authorities (Mayoral Elections) (England and Wales)

Regulations 2007, SI 2007/1024, Sch 1 r 19(1); and the Greater London Authority Elections Rules 2007, SI 2007/3541, Sch 1 r 18(1), Sch 2 r 19(1), Sch 3 r 18(1). As to voting by post see PARA 406 et seq.

6   Representation of the People Act 1983 Sch 1 r 19A(1) (as added: see note 4); European Parliamentary Elections Regulations 2004, SI 2004/293, Sch 1 para 23(1) (as substituted: see note 2); Local Elections (Principal Areas) (England and Wales) Rules 2006, SI 2006/3304, Sch 2 r 17(1); Local Elections (Parishes and Communities) (England and Wales) Rules 2006, SI 2006/3305, Sch 2 r 17(1); National Assembly for Wales (Representation of the People) Order 2007, SI 2007/236, Sch 5 para 27(1); Local Authorities (Mayoral Elections) (England and Wales) Regulations 2007, SI 2007/1024, Sch 1 r 19(1); Greater London Authority Elections Rules 2007, SI 2007/3541, Sch 1 r 18(1), Sch 2 r 19(1), Sch 3 r 18(1). The text refers to ballot papers to be provided by the returning officer to each presiding officer, in relation to a parliamentary election, in pursuance of the Representation of the People Act 1983 Sch 1 r 29(1), or, in relation to a European parliamentary election, in pursuance of the European Parliamentary Elections Regulations 2004, SI 2004/293, Sch 1 para 32(1), or, in relation to a local government election for a principal area, in pursuance of the Local Elections (Principal Areas) (England and Wales) Rules 2006, SI 2006/3304, Sch 2 r 26(1) or, in relation to a local government election for a parish or community council, in pursuance of the Local Elections (Parishes and Communities) (England and Wales) Rules 2006, SI 2006/3305, Sch 2 r 26(1), or, in relation to a Welsh Assembly election, in pursuance of the National Assembly for Wales (Representation of the People) Order 2007, SI 2007/236, Sch 5 para 37(1), or, in relation to a local authority mayoral election, in pursuance of the Local Authorities (Mayoral Elections) (England and Wales) Regulations 2007, SI 2007/1024, Sch 1 r 28, or, in relation to an Authority election, in pursuance of the Greater London Authority Elections Rules 2007, SI 2007/3541, Sch 1 r 28(1), Sch 2 r 29(1), Sch 3 r 28(1) (see PARA 391): see the Representation of the People Act 1983 Sch 1 r 19A(1) (as so added); the European Parliamentary Elections Regulations 2004, SI 2004/293, Sch 1 para 23(1) (as so substituted); the Local Elections (Principal Areas) (England and Wales) Rules 2006, SI 2006/3304, Sch 2 r 17(1); the Local Elections (Parishes and Communities) (England and Wales) Rules 2006, SI 2006/3305, Sch 2 r 17(1); the National Assembly for Wales (Representation of the People) Order 2007, SI 2007/236, Sch 5 para 27(1); the Local Authorities (Mayoral Elections) (England and Wales) Regulations 2007, SI 2007/1024, Sch 1 r 19(1); and the Greater London Authority Elections Rules 2007, SI 2007/3541, Sch 1 r 18(1), Sch 2 r 19(1), Sch 3 r 18(1). As to presiding officers at an election see PARA 393.

7   As to polls consequent on a parish meeting on a question involving appointment to office see PARA 200 et seq. No provision is made for postal voting at a poll consequent on a parish meeting taken on a question of appointment to any office.

8   Parish and Community Meetings (Polls) Rules 1987, SI 1987/1, Schedule r 4(2)(d).

9   Parish and Community Meetings (Polls) Rules 1987, SI 1987/1, Schedule r 4(2)(e).

10   Generally, where the polls at elections are taken together, the ballot papers must be of a different colour for each election: see the rules cited at PARA 16 et seq.

The ballot papers for use at an ordinary London Authority election must be supplied by the Greater London returning officer ('GLRO') to the CRO by such date as may be agreed between them; and the ballot papers so supplied must be of a different colour from those used at any other Authority election with which the election to be held under the constituency member election rules, the London member election rules or the mayoral election rules, as the case may be, is taken: Greater London Authority Elections Rules 2007, SI 2007/3541, Sch 1 r 17(7), (8), Sch 2 r 18(8), (9), Sch 3 r 17(7), (8). As to the meaning of the 'Greater London returning officer' see PARA 211 note 8; and as to the meanings of 'constituency member election rules', 'London member election rules' and 'London mayoral elections rules' see PARA 383 note 10.

In the case of a Welsh Assembly election, where a voter is entitled to give two votes, the ballot paper for each vote must be of a different colour: National Assembly for Wales (Representation of the People) Order 2007, SI 2007/236, Sch 5 para 28.

Where a poll consequent on a parish or community meeting on the question of appointment to any office and a poll on any other question (as to which see PARA 556 et seq) are taken together, ballot papers of a different colour must be used for each poll: Parish and Community Meetings (Polls) Rules 1987, SI 1987/1, Schedule r 4(3).

11   Representation of the People Act 1983 Sch 1 r 19(2)(b); Parish and Community Meetings (Polls) Rules 1987, SI 1987/1, Schedule r 4(2)(c); European Parliamentary Elections Regulations 2004, SI 2004/293, Sch 1 para 22(2)(b) (as substituted: see note 2); Local Elections (Principal Areas) (England and Wales) Rules 2006, SI 2006/3304, Sch 2 r 16(2)(b); Local Elections (Parishes and Communities) (England and Wales) Rules 2006, SI 2006/3305, Sch 2 r 16(2)(b); National Assembly for Wales (Representation of the People) Order 2007, SI 2007/236, Sch 5 paras 24(3)(b), 25(3)(c); Local Authorities (Mayoral Elections) (England and Wales)

Regulations 2007, SI 2007/1024, Sch 1 r 18(3)(b); Greater London Authority Elections Rules 2007, SI 2007/3541, Sch 1 r 17(3)(d), Sch 2 r 18(4)(d), Sch 3 r 17(3)(d). In the case of an Authority election, the specific wording of the provision allows that the ballot papers for use at the polling station may be marked with the words 'do not fold': see Sch 1 r 17(3)(d), Sch 2 r 18(4)(d), Sch 3 r 17(3)(d).

12 Representation of the People Act 1983 Sch 1 r 20(1) (substituted by the Electoral Administration Act 2006 Sch 1 paras 69, 88(1), (2)); European Parliamentary Elections Regulations 2004, SI 2004/293, Sch 1 para 24(1) (as substituted: see note 2); Local Elections (Principal Areas) (England and Wales) Rules 2006, SI 2006/3304, Sch 2 r 18(1); Local Elections (Parishes and Communities) (England and Wales) Rules 2006, SI 2006/3305, Sch 2 r 18(1); National Assembly for Wales (Representation of the People) Order 2007, SI 2007/236, Sch 5 para 29(1); Local Authorities (Mayoral Elections) (England and Wales) Regulations 2007, SI 2007/1024, Sch 1 r 20(1); Greater London Authority Elections Rules 2007, SI 2007/3541, Sch 1 r 19(1), Sch 2 r 20(1), Sch 3 r 19(1). Absence of the official mark invalidates the vote: see PARA 427 et seq.

13 Parish and Community Meetings (Polls) Rules 1987, SI 1987/1, Schedule r 5(1).

14 Representation of the People Act 1983 Sch 1 r 20(2); Parish and Community Meetings (Polls) Rules 1987, SI 1987/1, Schedule r 5(2); European Parliamentary Elections Regulations 2004, SI 2004/293, Sch 1 para 24(2) (as substituted: see note 2); Local Elections (Principal Areas) (England and Wales) Rules 2006, SI 2006/3304, Sch 2 r 18(2); Local Elections (Parishes and Communities) (England and Wales) Rules 2006, SI 2006/3305, Sch 2 r 18(2); National Assembly for Wales (Representation of the People) Order 2007, SI 2007/236, Sch 5 para 29(2); Local Authorities (Mayoral Elections) (England and Wales) Regulations 2007, SI 2007/1024, Sch 1 r 20(2); Greater London Authority Elections Rules 2007, SI 2007/3541, Sch 1 r 19(2), Sch 2 r 20(2), Sch 3 r 19(2). As to the offence of disclosing an official mark see PARA 739.

15 Representation of the People Act 1983 Sch 1 r 20(2). As to the meaning of 'constituency' for the purposes of parliamentary elections see PARA 9.

16 Local Elections (Principal Areas) (England and Wales) Rules 2006, SI 2006/3304, Sch 2 r 18(2); Local Elections (Parishes and Communities) (England and Wales) Rules 2006, SI 2006/3305, Sch 2 r 18(2); Local Authorities (Mayoral Elections) (England and Wales) Regulations 2007, SI 2007/1024, Sch 1 r 20(2); Greater London Authority Elections Rules 2007, SI 2007/3541, Sch 1 r 19(2), Sch 2 r 20(2), Sch 3 r 19(2). As to districts in England, and their councils, see LOCAL GOVERNMENT vol 69 (2009) PARA 24 et seq; and as to parishes and their councils see LOCAL GOVERNMENT vol 69 (2009) PARA 27 et seq. As to counties and county boroughs in Wales, and their councils, see LOCAL GOVERNMENT vol 69 (2009) PARA 37 et seq; and as to communities and their councils see LOCAL GOVERNMENT vol 69 (2009) PARA 41 et seq. As to London boroughs and their councils see LOCAL GOVERNMENT vol 69 (2009) PARA 35; LONDON GOVERNMENT vol 71 (2013) PARA 15 et seq.

17 Parish and Community Meetings (Polls) Rules 1987, SI 1987/1, Schedule r 5(2).

18 National Assembly for Wales (Representation of the People) Order 2007, SI 2007/236, Sch 5 para 29(2).

19 European Parliamentary Elections Regulations 2004, SI 2004/293, Sch 1 para 24(2) (as substituted: see note 2). As to the meaning of 'local counting area' see PARA 139 note 1.

20 Representation of the People Act 1983 Sch 1 r 20(3) (substituted by the Electoral Administration Act 2006 Sch 1 paras 69, 88(1), (3)); European Parliamentary Elections Regulations 2004, SI 2004/293, Sch 1 para 24(3) (as substituted: see note 2); Local Elections (Principal Areas) (England and Wales) Rules 2006, SI 2006/3304, Sch 2 r 18(3); Local Elections (Parishes and Communities) (England and Wales) Rules 2006, SI 2006/3305, Sch 2 r 18(3); National Assembly for Wales (Representation of the People) Order 2007, SI 2007/236, Sch 5 para 29(3); Local Authorities (Mayoral Elections) (England and Wales) Regulations 2007, SI 2007/1024, Sch 1 r 20(3); Greater London Authority Elections Rules 2007, SI 2007/3541, Sch 1 r 19(3), Sch 2 r 20(3), Sch 3 r 19(3). At a London Authority election, the reference to the returning officer is to the GLRO, except at a constituency members election which is not an ordinary election, when the reference must be understood as a reference to the CRO: see Sch 1 r 19(3), Sch 2 r 20(3), Sch 3 r 19(3). In the case of a Welsh Assembly election, the 'appropriate returning officer' (see PARA 18 note 2) is specified: see the National Assembly for Wales (Representation of the People) Order 2007, SI 2007/236, Sch 5 para 29(3).

388. Notice of poll. In the statement of persons nominated[1] at an election[2], except a local government election[3], the returning officer[4] must include a notice of the poll, stating the day on which and hours during which the poll will be taken[5].

At a local government election (but including, of the Authority elections, only a London Assembly constituency election), the returning officer must publish the notice of poll not later than the sixth day before the day of election[6]; and this notice must state:

(1) the day and hours fixed for the poll[7];

(2) the particulars of each candidate remaining validly nominated (the names and other particulars of the candidates, and the order of the names of the candidates, being the same as in the statement of persons nominated)[8]; and

(3) (excluding for this purpose a London Assembly constituency election) the names of all persons signing a candidate's nomination paper[9].

The notice at a local government election for a principal area, parish or community must also state the number of councillors to be elected[10].

In the case of a London members election, the Greater London returning officer must publish the notice of poll not later than the sixth day before the day of election[11]; and such notice must state:

(a) the day and hours fixed for the poll[12];

(b) the number of seats for London members available for allocation at that election[13];

(c) the authorised description of each registered party whose party list includes persons who remain validly nominated as list candidates[14]; and

(d) the name and description (if any) of each individual candidate remaining validly nominated[15],

with the names of the registered parties arranged alphabetically according to the authorised descriptions given in their nomination papers, followed by the names of the list candidates arranged as they are in those lists, and then the individual candidates arranged alphabetically in order of their surnames (and, if there are two or more of them with the same surname, of their other names)[16].

At a London mayoral election, the Greater London returning officer must publish notice of the poll not later than the sixth day before the day of election[17], stating the day and hours fixed for the poll and the particulars of each candidate remaining validly nominated[18], with the names of the candidates arranged alphabetically in the order of their surnames (and, if there are two or more of them with the same surname, of their other names)[19].

The returning officer at a poll consequent on a parish meeting taken on a question of appointment to any office must, not later than the fifth day before the day of the poll[20], give public notice of the poll which refers to the parish or meeting at which a poll was demanded[21]; and which states: (i) the day and hours fixed for the poll[22]; and (ii) the name of the office, the number of vacancies, the particulars of each candidate who has not withdrawn (the order of the names of the candidates and particulars being the same as in the ballot papers) and the name of the proposer of each candidate[23].

At any election, the returning officer must also give public notice of the situation of each polling station, and the description of voters entitled to vote at that station[24], and (at elections where election agents are appointed) he must as soon as practicable after giving such a notice give a copy of it to each of the election agents[25].

Where the poll at an election is taken together with the poll at another election or referendum, special provision is made for giving the notice of poll[26].

1   As to the statement of persons nominated see PARA 267. At a European parliamentary election, the reference is to a 'statement of parties and individual candidates nominated' (see PARA 267 note 3): see the European Parliamentary Elections Regulations 2004, SI 2004/293, Sch 1 para 27(1) (Sch 1 substituted by SI 2009/186).

2   Ie at a parliamentary election, a Welsh Assembly constituency or regional election or a European parliamentary election. As to the meaning of 'parliamentary election' see PARA 9; As to the meanings of 'constituency election' and 'regional election' in the context of Welsh Assembly elections see PARA 3 note 2. As to European parliamentary elections see PARA 217 et seq.

3   As to the meanings of 'local government election' (which includes an Authority election and a local authority mayoral election) and 'Authority election' see PARA 11. As to elections in the City of London see PARA 33.

4   As to returning officers for parliamentary elections see PARA 350 et seq; and as to returning officers for European parliamentary elections see PARA 360 et seq. In the case of a Welsh Assembly election, the 'appropriate returning officer' (see PARA 18 note 2) is specified: see the National Assembly for Wales (Representation of the People) Order 2007, SI 2007/236, Sch 5 para 32(1).

5   Representation of the People Act 1983 Sch 1 r 23(1); European Parliamentary Elections Regulations 2004, SI 2004/293, Sch 1 para 27(1) (as substituted: see note 1); National Assembly for Wales (Representation of the People) Order 2007, SI 2007/236, Sch 5 para 32(1). As to the date of the poll at a parliamentary general election or by-election see PARA 195; as to the date of the poll at Welsh Assembly elections (including elections to fill vacancies in an Assembly constituency) see PARAS 213–214; and as to the date of the poll at a European parliamentary election see PARA 222. As to the hours of polling at an election see PARA 385.

   As to the requirements applying to any document which is required or authorised to be given to voters or displayed in any place for the purposes of a European Parliamentary election, see the European Parliamentary Elections Regulations 2004, SI 2004/293 reg 122A; and PARA 239 note 23.

6   Local Elections (Principal Areas) (England and Wales) Rules 2006, SI 2006/3304, Sch 2 r 1; Local Elections (Parishes and Communities) (England and Wales) Rules 2006, SI 2006/3305, Sch 2 r 1; Local Authorities (Mayoral Elections) (England and Wales) Regulations 2007, SI 2007/1024, Sch 1 r 3; Greater London Authority Elections Rules 2007, SI 2007/3541, Sch 1 r 3. The notice of poll at an ordinary London Authority election must include the heading 'GREATER LONDON AUTHORITY ELECTION': Sch 1 r 22(3). The appropriate returning officer at a London constituency members election is the constituency returning officer (see PARA 211 note 9): see Sch 1 r 22(1). As to returning officers for local government elections generally see PARA 354 et seq. As to the date of the poll at an election for the return of a local authority mayor see PARA 198; and as to the date of the poll at other local government elections (including elections to fill vacancies) see PARAS 206–209.

7   Local Elections (Principal Areas) (England and Wales) Rules 2006, SI 2006/3304, Sch 2 r 21(1)(a); Local Elections (Parishes and Communities) (England and Wales) Rules 2006, SI 2006/3305, Sch 2 r 21(1)(a); Local Authorities (Mayoral Elections) (England and Wales) Regulations 2007, SI 2007/1024, Sch 1 r 23(1)(a); Greater London Authority Elections Rules 2007, SI 2007/3541, Sch 1 r 22(1)(a).

8   Local Elections (Principal Areas) (England and Wales) Rules 2006, SI 2006/3304, Sch 2 r 21(1)(c); Local Elections (Parishes and Communities) (England and Wales) Rules 2006, SI 2006/3305, Sch 2 r 21(1)(c); Local Authorities (Mayoral Elections) (England and Wales) Regulations 2007, SI 2007/1024, Sch 1 r 23(1)(b); Greater London Authority Elections Rules 2007, SI 2007/3541, Sch 1 r 22(1)(b).

9   Local Elections (Principal Areas) (England and Wales) Rules 2006, SI 2006/3304, Sch 2 r 21(1)(d); Local Elections (Parishes and Communities) (England and Wales) Rules 2006, SI 2006/3305, Sch 2 r 21(1)(d); Local Authorities (Mayoral Elections) (England and Wales) Regulations 2007, SI 2007/1024, Sch 1 r 23(1)(c). Where a candidate is nominated by more than one nomination paper, the nomination paper referred to in the text must be that from which the names and other particulars of the candidate shown in the statement of persons nominated are taken: Local Elections (Principal Areas) (England and Wales) Rules 2006, SI 2006/3304, Sch 2 r 21(2); Local Elections (Parishes and Communities) (England and Wales) Rules 2006, SI 2006/3305, Sch 2 r 21(2); Local Authorities (Mayoral Elections) (England and Wales) Regulations 2007, SI 2007/1024, Sch 1 r 23(2). At a parish or community council election, the nomination paper is signed only by a proposer and seconder; at other local government elections, eight electors must also sign as assenting to the nomination: see PARA 257.

10 Local Elections (Principal Areas) (England and Wales) Rules 2006, SI 2006/3304, Sch 2 r 21(1)(b); Local Elections (Parishes and Communities) (England and Wales) Rules 2006, SI 2006/3305, Sch 2 r 21(1)(b). This provision does not, of course, apply to a local authority mayoral election.

11 Greater London Authority Elections Rules 2007, SI 2007/3541, Sch 2 r 3. As to the meaning of 'London member', in relation to the London Assembly, see PARA 11 note 5; definition applied by virtue of r 2(2). The notice of poll at such a London Authority election must include the heading 'GREATER LONDON AUTHORITY ELECTION': Sch 2 r 23(3). As to the Greater London returning officer ('GLRO') see PARA 211 note 8.

12 Greater London Authority Elections Rules 2007, SI 2007/3541, Sch 2 r 23(1)(a).

13 Greater London Authority Elections Rules 2007, SI 2007/3541, Sch 2 r 23(1)(b).

14 Greater London Authority Elections Rules 2007, SI 2007/3541, Sch 2 r 23(1)(c). As to the meaning of 'registered political party' for these purposes see PARA 256 note 27. As to references to party lists in elections for the return of London members of the London Assembly see PARA 255 note 23. As to party list candidates who are subject to a party's authorisation see PARA 256.

15 Greater London Authority Elections Rules 2007, SI 2007/3541, Sch 2 r 23(1)(d). As to individual candidates to be London members of the London Assembly see further LONDON GOVERNMENT vol 71 (2013) PARA 81.

16 Greater London Authority Elections Rules 2007, SI 2007/3541, Sch 2 rr 12(5), 23(1).

17 Greater London Authority Elections Rules 2007, SI 2007/3541, Sch 3 r 3. The notice of poll at such a London Authority election must include the heading 'GREATER LONDON AUTHORITY ELECTION': Sch 3 r 22(3).

18 Greater London Authority Elections Rules 2007, SI 2007/3541, Sch 3 r 22(1).

19 Greater London Authority Elections Rules 2007, SI 2007/3541, Sch 3 rr 11(6), 22(1).

20 Parish and Community Meetings (Polls) Rules 1987, SI 1987/1, Schedule r 1. As to the computation of any period of time for these purposes see PARA 212 note 5. As to polls consequent on a parish meeting on a question involving appointment to office see PARA 200 et seq; and as to the date of such a poll see PARA 207. As to returning officers appointed for such a poll see PARA 356.

21 Parish and Community Meetings (Polls) Rules 1987, SI 1987/1, Schedule r 8.

22 Parish and Community Meetings (Polls) Rules 1987, SI 1987/1, Schedule r 8(a).

23 Parish and Community Meetings (Polls) Rules 1987, SI 1987/1, Schedule r 8(b).

24 Representation of the People Act 1983 Sch 1 r 23(2); Parish and Community Meetings (Polls) Rules 1987, SI 1987/1, Schedule r 8(d); European Parliamentary Elections Regulations 2004, SI 2004/293, Sch 1 para 27(2) (as substituted: see note 1); Local Elections (Principal Areas) (England and Wales) Rules 2006, SI 2006/3304, Sch 2 r 21(3); Local Elections (Parishes and Communities) (England and Wales) Rules 2006, SI 2006/3305, Sch 2 r 21(3); National Assembly for Wales (Representation of the People) Order 2007, SI 2007/236, Sch 5 para 32(2), (3); Local Authorities (Mayoral Elections) (England and Wales) Regulations 2007, SI 2007/1024, Sch 1 r 23(3); Greater London Authority Elections Rules 2007, SI 2007/3541, Sch 1 r 22(2), Sch 2 r 23(2), Sch 3 r 22(2). The appropriate returning officer for giving the notice referred to in the text at any London Authority election is the constituency returning officer: see Sch 1 r 22(2), Sch 2 r 23(2), Sch 3 r 22(2). As to public notice by a returning officer for a European Parliamentary election that is required to be given by or under the European Parliamentary Elections Regulations 2004, SI 2004/293, see PARA 239 note 23. As to the giving of public notices by a returning officer generally see PARA 350 et seq. As to the provision and allotment of polling stations see PARA 390.

At a parliamentary election, the notice referred to in the text may be combined with the statement of persons nominated: see the Representation of the People Act 1983 Sch 1 r 23(2).

At any local government election, the notice must be given not later than the time of the publication of the notice of the poll: Local Elections (Principal Areas) (England and Wales) Rules 2006, SI 2006/3304, Sch 2 r 21(3); Local Elections (Parishes and Communities) (England and Wales) Rules 2006, SI 2006/3305, Sch 2 r 21(3); Local Authorities (Mayoral Elections) (England and Wales) Regulations 2007, SI 2007/1024, Sch 1 r 23(3); Greater London Authority Elections Rules 2007, SI 2007/3541, Sch 1 r 22(2), Sch 2 r 23(2), Sch 3 r 22(2).

At a European parliamentary election, the notice referred to in the text is given by the local returning officer and in respect of each local counting area or part of an area contained in the electoral region: see the European Parliamentary Elections Regulations 2004, SI 2004/293, Sch 1 para 27(2) (as so substituted). As to the meaning of 'local counting area' see PARA 139 note 1. As to local returning officers appointed for the purposes of elections to the European Parliament see PARA 360. As to electoral regions constituted for the purposes of European parliamentary elections see PARA 77.

In the case of a Welsh Assembly constituency election, the constituency returning officer must prepare and publish the notice of poll (which may be combined with the statement of persons nominated): see the National Assembly for Wales (Representation of the People) Order 2007, SI 2007/236, Sch 5 para 32(2). In the case of a Welsh Assembly regional election, the constituency returning officer for each Assembly constituency in the Assembly electoral region must prepare and publish the notice of poll (which may be combined with the statement of persons nominated) setting out the situation of each polling station in the Assembly constituency for which he is returning officer and the description of voters entitled to vote there: see Sch 5 para 32(3). At an ordinary Welsh Assembly election, the notices so prepared by a constituency returning officer for the purposes of a constituency election and a regional election may be combined: Sch 5 para 32(4). As to the meanings of 'Assembly constituency' and 'Assembly electoral region' see PARA 3 note 2; and as to the meaning of 'constituency returning officer' see PARA 18 note 2.

25 Representation of the People Act 1983 Sch 1 r 23(2) (amended by the Representation of the People Act 1985 ss 24, 28, Sch 4 para 77, Sch 5); European Parliamentary Elections Regulations 2004, SI 2004/293, Sch 1 para 27(2) (as substituted: see note 1); Local Elections (Principal Areas) (England and Wales) Rules 2006, SI 2006/3304, Sch 2 r 21(3); Local Elections (Parishes and Communities) (England and Wales) Rules 2006, SI 2006/3305, Sch 2 r 21(3); National Assembly for Wales (Representation of the People) Order 2007, SI 2007/236, Sch 5 para 32(3); Local Authorities (Mayoral Elections) (England and Wales) Regulations 2007, SI 2007/1024, Sch 1 r 23(3); Greater London Authority Elections Rules 2007, SI 2007/3541, Sch 1 r 22(2), Sch 2 r 23(2), Sch 3 r 22(2). In the case of a Welsh Assembly regional election, the constituency returning officer for each Assembly constituency in the Assembly electoral region must, as soon as practicable after publishing the notice of poll, give a copy of it to each of the election agents and deliver, or cause to be delivered, a copy of it to the regional returning officer: see the National Assembly for Wales (Representation of the People) Order 2007, SI 2007/236, Sch 5 para 32(3). As to the meaning of 'regional returning officer' see PARA 18 note 2.

26 As to polls at elections or referendums which are taken together see PARA 16 et seq.

389. Issue of official poll cards at elections. The returning officer at an election[1] must, as soon as practicable[2], send an official poll card to electors and their proxies[3]. Such a card must not be sent, however, to a person registered, or to be registered, in pursuance of an overseas elector's declaration for the purposes of a parliamentary or European parliamentary election[4]. An elector's official poll card must be sent or delivered to his qualifying address[5], and a proxy's card to his address as shown in the list of proxies[6].

The official poll card must be in the prescribed form or a form to the like effect[7]; and it must set out:

(1)   the name of the electoral division to which it relates (or, at a London members ordinary election, or at an election for the return of a local authority or London Mayor, the election to which it relates)[8];

(2)   the elector's name, qualifying address and number on the register[9];

(3)   the date and hours of the poll and situation of the elector's polling station[10]; and

(4)   such other information as the returning officer thinks appropriate[11];

and different information may be provided in pursuance of head (4) above to different electors, or to different descriptions of elector[12]. The official poll card to be used for a parliamentary election must set out such other additional information as is prescribed[13].

In circumstances when the polls at elections or referendums are taken together, the official poll card may be combined[14].

The issue of any poll card, or any document so closely resembling an official poll card as to be calculated to deceive, is an offence at certain elections and an illegal practice[15].

1   Ie at an election, but not at a poll taken consequent on a parish meeting on a question which involves appointment to office (where no provision is made for poll cards to be issued: see

PARA 200 et seq). The text applies to a parliamentary election, a local government election (which includes any London Authority election and a local authority mayoral election), a Welsh Assembly constituency or regional election and a European parliamentary election. As to the meanings of 'Assembly election', 'constituency election' and 'regional election' see PARA 3 note 2. As to the meaning of 'parliamentary election' see PARA 9. As to the meanings of 'Authority election' and 'local government election' see PARA 11. As to elections in the City of London see PARA 33. As to elections for the return of a local authority mayor see PARA 198; and as to European parliamentary elections see PARA 217 et seq.

As to returning officers generally see PARA 350 et seq. The constituency returning officer (see PARA 211 note 9) is specified for the purposes of a London Authority election: see the Greater London Authority Elections Rules 2007, SI 2007/3541, Sch 1 r 26(1), (3), (5), Sch 2 r 27(1), (3), (5), Sch 3 r 26(1), (3), (5). At a European parliamentary election, the reference is to a local returning officer (see PARA 360 et seq): see the European Parliamentary Elections Regulations 2004, SI 2004/293, Sch 1 para 31(1) (Sch 1 substituted by SI 2009/186). At a Welsh Assembly election, the constituency returning officer (see PARA 18 note 2) is specified for the purposes of a Welsh Assembly election: see the National Assembly for Wales (Representation of the People) Order 2007, SI 2007/236, Sch 5 para 36(1).

2   Ie as soon as practicable after the publication of notice of the election (except at a parish or community election): Representation of the People Act 1983 Sch 1 r 28(1) (Sch 1 r 28(1) substituted, Sch 1 r 28(1A) added, by the Electoral Administration Act 2006 s 47, Sch 1 paras 69, 70(1), (2)); European Parliamentary Elections Regulations 2004, SI 2004/293, Sch 1 para 31(1) (as substituted: see note 1); Local Elections (Principal Areas) (England and Wales) Rules 2006, SI 2006/3304, Sch 2 r 25(1); National Assembly for Wales (Representation of the People) Order 2007, SI 2007/236, Sch 5 para 36(1); Local Authorities (Mayoral Elections) (England and Wales) Regulations 2007, SI 2007/1024, Sch 1 r 27(1); Greater London Authority Elections Rules 2007, SI 2007/3541, Sch 1 r 26(1), Sch 2 r 27(1), Sch 3 r 26(1). As to the meaning of 'anonymous entry' in relation to a register of electors see PARA 148. As to publication of the notice of election, in relation to a parliamentary election, see PARA 196; in relation to a local government election, see PARA 211; in relation to a Welsh Assembly election, see PARA 216; and, in relation to a European parliamentary election, see PARA 223.

    Where the poll at a parish or community election is not to be taken together with the poll at some other election, the returning officer acts only after receiving a request to issue official poll cards for that election from the council of the parish or community, such a request having to be made not later than noon on the nineteenth day before the day of election: Local Elections (Parishes and Communities) (England and Wales) Rules 2006, SI 2006/3305, Sch 2 r 25(1).

3   Representation of the People Act 1983 Sch 1 r 28(1) (as substituted: see note 2); European Parliamentary Elections Regulations 2004, SI 2004/293, Sch 1 para 31(1) (as substituted: see note 1); Local Elections (Principal Areas) (England and Wales) Rules 2006, SI 2006/3304, Sch 2 r 25(1); Local Elections (Parishes and Communities) (England and Wales) Rules 2006, SI 2006/3305, Sch 2 r 25(2); National Assembly for Wales (Representation of the People) Order 2007, SI 2007/236, Sch 5 para 36(1); Local Authorities (Mayoral Elections) (England and Wales) Regulations 2007, SI 2007/1024, Sch 1 r 27(1); Greater London Authority Elections Rules 2007, SI 2007/3541, Sch 1 r 26(1), Sch 2 r 27(1), Sch 3 r 26(1). As to the meaning of 'elector': by virtue of the Representation of the People Act 1983 Sch 1 r 28(4), see PARA 255 note 5; and, by virtue of the Local Elections (Principal Areas) (England and Wales) Rules 2006, SI 2006/3304, Sch 2 r 25(5), the Local Elections (Parishes and Communities) (England and Wales) Rules 2006, SI 2006/3305, Sch 2 r 25(6), and the Local Authorities (Mayoral Elections) (England and Wales) Regulations 2007, SI 2007/1024, Sch 1 r 27(5), see PARA 255 note 13. In relation to a London Authority election, for these purposes, 'elector' means an elector with an entry on the register to be used at the election on the last day for the publication of the notice of the election; and the definition includes a person shown in the register as being below voting age if (but only if) it appears from the register that he will be of voting age on the day fixed for the poll: see the Greater London Authority Elections Rules 2007, SI 2007/3541, Sch 1 r 26(6), Sch 2 r 27(6), Sch 3 r 26(6). In relation to a Welsh Assembly election, for these purposes, 'elector' means a person who is registered in the register for the Assembly constituency or the Assembly electoral region (as the case may be) on the last day for publication of notice of the election in question; and the definition includes a person that is shown in that register as being below voting age if (but only if) it appears from the register that he will be of voting age on the day fixed for the poll: see the National Assembly for Wales (Representation of the People) Order 2007, SI 2007/236, Sch 5 r 36(9). 'Voting age' is currently 18 years for all purposes: see PARAS 95 note 2, 97 note 14, 102 note 10. As to entitlement to registration as an elector see PARA 113 et seq; and as to the registers of electors see PARA 145 et seq. As to the meaning of

'elector', in relation to a European parliamentary election generally, see PARA 111 note 4. As to voting by proxy at elections see PARA 367 et seq.

4   Representation of the People Act 1983 Sch 1 r 28(1A) (as added: see note 2); European Parliamentary Elections Regulations 2004, SI 2004/293, Sch 1 para 31(1) (as substituted: see note 1). As to registration in pursuance of an overseas elector's declaration and a European parliamentary overseas elector's declaration see PARA 114 et seq.

5   As to the meaning of 'qualifying address' see PARA 145 note 5.

6   Representation of the People Act 1983 Sch 1 r 28(2); European Parliamentary Elections Regulations 2004, SI 2004/293, Sch 1 para 31(2) (as substituted: see note 1); Local Elections (Principal Areas) (England and Wales) Rules 2006, SI 2006/3304, Sch 2 r 25(2); Local Elections (Parishes and Communities) (England and Wales) Rules 2006, SI 2006/3305, Sch 2 r 25(3); National Assembly for Wales (Representation of the People) Order 2007, SI 2007/236, Sch 5 para 36(2); Local Authorities (Mayoral Elections) (England and Wales) Regulations 2007, SI 2007/1024, Sch 1 r 27(2); Greater London Authority Elections Rules 2007, SI 2007/3541, Sch 1 r 26(2), Sch 2 r 27(2), Sch 3 r 26(2). As to the meaning of 'list of proxies' see PARA 373 note 14.

7   Representation of the People Act 1983 Sch 1 r 28(3); European Parliamentary Elections Regulations 2004, SI 2004/293, Sch 1 para 31(3)–(6) (as substituted: see note 1); Local Elections (Principal Areas) (England and Wales) Rules 2006, SI 2006/3304, Sch 2 r 25(3); Local Elections (Parishes and Communities) (England and Wales) Rules 2006, SI 2006/3305, Sch 2 r 25(4); National Assembly for Wales (Representation of the People) Order 2007, SI 2007/236, Sch 5 para 36(3); Local Authorities (Mayoral Elections) (England and Wales) Regulations 2007, SI 2007/1024, Sch 1 r 27(3); Greater London Authority Elections Rules 2007, SI 2007/3541, Sch 1 r 26(3), Sch 2 r 27(3), Sch 3 r 26(3).

     For the purposes of the Representation of the People Act 1983, 'prescribed' means prescribed by regulations: see s 202(1). As to the prescribed forms of official poll card:

(1)   in relation to a parliamentary election, see the Representation of the People (England and Wales) Regulations 2001, SI 2001/341, reg 9(1), (2), Sch 3 (Form A: official poll card (to be sent to an elector voting in person)) (reg 9(1)–(3), substituted, reg 9(4), (5), Sch 3 (Forms A1, B1) added, by SI 2006/2910; Representation of the People (England and Wales) Regulations 2001, SI 2001/341, Sch 3 (Forms A, B) substituted by SI 2007/1025); the Representation of the People (England and Wales) Regulations 2001, SI 2001/341, reg 9(1), (3), Sch 3 (Form A1: official postal poll card (to be sent to an elector voting by post)) (reg 9(1), (3) as so substituted; Sch 3 (Form A1) as so added); reg 9(1), (4), Sch 3 (Form B: official proxy poll card (to be sent to an appointed proxy voting in person)) (reg 9(1), Sch 3 (Form B) as so substituted, reg 9(4) as so added); and reg 9(1), (5), Sch 3 (Form B1: official proxy postal poll card (to be sent to an appointed proxy voting by post)) (reg 9(1) as so substituted; reg 9(5), Sch 3 (Form B1) as so added);

(2)   in relation to a European parliamentary election, see the European Parliamentary Elections Regulations 2004, SI 2004/293, Sch 1 Pt 7 Appendix of Forms (Form F: official poll card issued to an elector voting at a polling station; Form G: official poll card issued to a postal elector; Form H: official poll card issued to a proxy voting at a polling station; Form J: official poll card issued to a postal proxy);

(3)   in relation to an election of councillors for a principal area, parish or community, see the Local Elections (Principal Areas) (England and Wales) Rules 2006, SI 2006/3304, Sch 2 Appendix of Forms (official poll card; official postal poll card; official proxy poll card; official proxy postal poll card), and Sch 3 Appendix of Forms (official poll card; official postal poll card; official proxy poll card; official proxy postal poll card) (where such a poll is taken together with another relevant election or referendum); and the Local Elections (Parishes and Communities) (England and Wales) Rules 2006, SI 2006/3305, Sch 2 Appendix of Forms (official poll card; official postal poll card; official proxy poll card; official proxy postal poll card), and Sch 3 Appendix of Forms (official poll card; official postal poll card; official proxy poll card; official proxy postal poll card) (where such a poll is taken together with another relevant election or referendum);

(4)   in relation to a local authority mayoral election, see the Local Authorities (Mayoral Elections) (England and Wales) Regulations 2007, SI 2007/1024, Sch 1 Appendix of Forms (Form 8: official poll card; Form 9: official postal poll card; Form 10: official proxy poll card; Form 11: official proxy postal poll card) (Forms 8, 9, 10, 11 substituted by SI 2012/2059);

(5)   in relation to any London Authority election, see the Greater London Authority

Elections Rules 2007, SI 2007/3541, Sch 10 r 2 (Form 12: official poll card; Form 13: official postal poll card; Form 14: official proxy poll card; Form 15: official proxy postal poll card);

(6)   in relation to a Welsh Assembly election, see the forms set out in English and Welsh in the National Assembly for Wales (Representation of the People) Order 2007, SI 2007/236, Sch 10 Appendix of Forms (Form CN1: elector's form of poll card; Form CN2: proxy's form of poll card; Form CN3: postal voter's form of poll card; Form CN4: postal proxy voter's form of poll card) (Sch 5 para 36(5)–(8)).

In the case of an elector at a parish or community election with an anonymous entry, the returning officer must issue an official poll card in the appropriate form (see head (3) above) to every such elector or to his proxy (if appointed) whether or not the local council of the parish or community makes a request under the Local Elections (Parishes and Communities) (England and Wales) Rules 2006, SI 2006/3305, Sch 2 r 25(1) (see note 2): Sch 2 r 25(5)(a). In the case of such an elector with an anonymous entry, the official poll card must be sent in an envelope or other form of covering so as not to disclose that the elector has an anonymous entry in the register: Sch 2 r 25(5)(c). As to the meaning of 'anonymous entry' in relation to a register of electors see PARA 148. In relation to a London Authority ordinary election, or where ordinary elections for constituency members and the Mayor are contested, the CRO must issue a combined poll card in the appropriate form: Greater London Authority Elections Rules 2007, SI 2007/3541, Sch 1 r 26(5), Sch 2 r 27(5), Sch 3 r 26(5).

Where elections take place in Wales see also the forms issued partly in English and partly in Welsh in:

(a)   the Parliamentary Elections (Welsh Forms) Order 2007, SI 2007/1014, art 6(e)–(h), Sch 2 (Form 5 (Ffurflen 5): official poll card, cerdyn pleidleisio swyddogol; Form 6 (Ffurflen 6): official postal poll card; cerdyn pleidleisio swyddogol drwy'r post; Form 7 (Ffurflen 7): official proxy poll card, cerdyn pleidleisio swyddogol dirprwy; Form 8 (Ffurflen 8): official proxy postal poll card, cerdyn pleidleisio swyddogol dirprwy drwy'r post);

(b)   the Local Elections (Principal Areas) (Welsh Forms) Order 2007, SI 2007/1015, arts 7(1)(d)–(g), 9(1)(e)–(h), Sch 3 (Form 4 (Ffurflen 4): official poll card, cerdyn pleidleisio swyddogol; Form 5 (Ffurflen 5): official postal poll card; cerdyn pleidleisio swyddogol drwy'r post; Form 6 (Ffurflen 6): official proxy poll card, cerdyn pleidleisio swyddogol dirprwy; Form 7 (Ffurflen 7): official proxy postal poll card, cerdyn pleidleisio swyddogol dirprwy drwy'r post), Sch 5 (Form 5 (Ffurflen 5): official poll card, cerdyn pleidleisio swyddogol; Form 6 (Ffurflen 6): official postal poll card; cerdyn pleidleisio swyddogol drwy'r post; Form 7 (Ffurflen 7): official proxy poll card, cerdyn pleidleisio swyddogol dirprwy; Form 8 (Ffurflen 8): official proxy postal poll card, cerdyn pleidleisio swyddogol dirprwy drwy'r post);

(c)   the Local Elections (Communities) (Welsh Forms) Order 2007, SI 2007/1013, arts 7(1)(d)–(g), 9(1)(e)–(h), Sch 3 (Form 4 (Ffurflen 4): official poll card, cerdyn pleidleisio swyddogol; Form 5 (Ffurflen 5): official postal poll card; cerdyn pleidleisio swyddogol drwy'r post; Form 6 (Ffurflen 6): official proxy poll card, cerdyn pleidleisio swyddogol dirprwy; Form 7 (Ffurflen 7): official proxy postal poll card, cerdyn pleidleisio swyddogol dirprwy drwy'r post), Sch 5 (Form 5 (Ffurflen 5): official poll card, cerdyn pleidleisio swyddogol; Form 6 (Ffurflen 6): official postal poll card; cerdyn pleidleisio swyddogol drwy'r post; Form 7 (Ffurflen 7): official proxy poll card, cerdyn pleidleisio swyddogol dirprwy; Form 8 (Ffurflen 8): official proxy postal poll card, cerdyn pleidleisio swyddogol dirprwy drwy'r post); and

(d)   the European Parliamentary Elections (Welsh Forms) Order 2009, SI 2009/781, art 6(1)(f)–(i), Sch 2 (Form 6 (Ffurflen 6): cerdyn pleidleisio swyddogol, official poll card; Form 7 (Ffurflen 7): cerdyn pleidleisio swyddogol drwy'r post, official postal poll card; Form 8 (Ffurflen 8): cerdyn pleidleisio swyddogol dirprwy, official proxy poll card; Form 9 (Ffurflen 9): cerdyn pleidleisio swyddogol dirprwy drwy'r post, official proxy postal poll card).

8   Representation of the People Act 1983 Sch 1 r 28(3)(a); European Parliamentary Elections Regulations 2004, SI 2004/293, Sch 1 para 31(7)(a) (as substituted: see note 1); Local Elections (Principal Areas) (England and Wales) Rules 2006, SI 2006/3304, Sch 2 r 25(3)(a); Local Elections (Parishes and Communities) (England and Wales) Rules 2006, SI 2006/3305, Sch 2 r 25(4)(a); National Assembly for Wales (Representation of the People) Order 2007, SI 2007/236, Sch 5 para 36(3)(a); Local Authorities (Mayoral Elections) (England and Wales) Regulations 2007, SI 2007/1024, Sch 1 r 27(3)(a), (b); Greater London Authority Elections Rules 2007, SI 2007/3541, Sch 1 r 26(3)(a), Sch 2 r 27(3)(a), Sch 3 r 26(3)(a). An official poll card must set out:

(1)   at a parliamentary election, the name of the constituency (Representation of the People Act 1983 Sch 1 r 28(3)(a));

(2)   at an election of councillors for a principal area, parish or community, the name of the council and (where appropriate) the name of the electoral division or ward to which councillors are to be elected (see the Local Elections (Principal Areas) (England and Wales) Rules 2006, SI 2006/3304, Sch 2 r 25(3)(a); and the Local Elections (Parishes and Communities) (England and Wales) Rules 2006, SI 2006/3305, Sch 2 r 25(4)(a));

(3)   at a local authority mayoral election, the name of the local authority to which the election relates, together with the fact that the election is a mayoral election (Local Authorities (Mayoral Elections) (England and Wales) Regulations 2007, SI 2007/1024, Sch 1 r 27(3)(a), (b));

(4)   at a London Assembly constituency election, the name of the Assembly constituency for which a constituency member is to be elected (Greater London Authority Elections Rules 2007, SI 2007/3541, Sch 1 r 26(3)(a));

(5)   at an election of London members, that the election is of the London members of the London Assembly at an ordinary election (Sch 2 r 27(3)(a));

(6)   at an election for the return of the London Mayor, that the election is a mayoral election (Sch 3 r 26(3)(a));

(7)   at a European parliamentary election, the name of the electoral region and electoral area (European Parliamentary Elections Regulations 2004, SI 2004/293, Sch 1 para 31(7)(a) (as so substituted));

(8)   at a Welsh Assembly election, the name of the Assembly constituency or Assembly electoral region for which the election is to be held, or, where the polls at a constituency election and a regional election are to be taken together, both such areas (National Assembly for Wales (Representation of the People) Order 2007, SI 2007/236, Sch 5 para 36(3)(a)).

As to the meanings of 'Assembly constituency' and 'Assembly electoral region' at a Welsh Assembly election see PARA 3 note 2; as to the meaning of 'constituency' for the purposes of parliamentary elections see PARA 9; and as to the meaning of 'Assembly constituency' in the context of London Authority elections see PARA 11 note 6.

As to the establishment of electoral areas for the purpose of local government elections in England see PARA 74; and as to electoral regions constituted for the purposes of European parliamentary elections see PARA 77.

9   Representation of the People Act 1983 Sch 1 r 28(3)(b); European Parliamentary Elections Regulations 2004, SI 2004/293, Sch 1 para 31(7)(b) (as substituted: see note 1); Local Elections (Principal Areas) (England and Wales) Rules 2006, SI 2006/3304, Sch 2 r 25(3)(b); Local Elections (Parishes and Communities) (England and Wales) Rules 2006, SI 2006/3305, Sch 2 r 25(4)(b); National Assembly for Wales (Representation of the People) Order 2007, SI 2007/236, Sch 5 para 36(3)(b); Local Authorities (Mayoral Elections) (England and Wales) Regulations 2007, SI 2007/1024, Sch 1 r 27(3)(c); Greater London Authority Elections Rules 2007, SI 2007/3541, Sch 1 r 26(3)(b), Sch 2 r 27(3)(b), Sch 3 r 26(3)(b).

In the case of an elector with an anonymous entry, instead of containing the information mentioned in head (2) in the text, the polling card must contain:

(1)   in the case of a parliamentary election, such matter as is prescribed (Representation of the People Act 1983 Sch 1 r 28(3A) (added by the Electoral Administration Act 2006 s 10(2), Sch 1 paras 2, 14(1), (3))).

(2)   in the case of a local government election (except for a parish or community council), such matter as is specified in the appropriate form (see note 7) (Local Elections (Principal Areas) (England and Wales) Rules 2006, SI 2006/3304, Sch 2 r 25(4); Local Authorities (Mayoral Elections) (England and Wales) Regulations 2007, SI 2007/1024, Sch 1 r 27(4); Greater London Authority Elections Rules 2007, SI 2007/3541, Sch 1 r 26(4), Sch 2 r 27(4), Sch 3 r 26(4));

(3)   in the case of a local government election for a parish or community council, the elector's number on the register, and such other matter as is specified in the appropriate form (see note 7) (Local Elections (Parishes and Communities) (England and Wales) Rules 2006, SI 2006/3305, Sch 2 r 25(5)(b));

(4)   in the case of a European parliamentary election, such matter as is specified in the European Parliamentary Elections Regulations 2004, SI 2004/293, Sch 1 Pt 7 Appendix of Forms (Forms F–J) (see note 7) (Sch 1 para 31(8) (as so substituted));

(5)   in the case of a Welsh Assembly election, such matter as is specified in the National Assembly for Wales (Representation of the People) Order 2007, SI 2007/236, Sch 10 Appendix of Forms (Forms CN1, CN2, CN3, CN4) (see note 7) (Sch 5 para 36(4)).

For the purposes of head (1) above, 'prescribed' means prescribed by regulations: see the Representation of the People Act 1983 s 202(1). As to regulations made for the purposes of head (1) above see note 7.

10   Representation of the People Act 1983 Sch 1 r 28(3)(c); European Parliamentary Elections Regulations 2004, SI 2004/293, Sch 1 para 31(7)(c) (as substituted: see note 1); Local Elections (Principal Areas) (England and Wales) Rules 2006, SI 2006/3304, Sch 2 r 25(3)(c); Local Elections (Parishes and Communities) (England and Wales) Rules 2006, SI 2006/3305, Sch 2 r 25(4)(c); National Assembly for Wales (Representation of the People) Order 2007, SI 2007/236, Sch 5 para 36(3)(c); Local Authorities (Mayoral Elections) (England and Wales) Regulations 2007, SI 2007/1024, Sch 1 r 27(3)(d); Greater London Authority Elections Rules 2007, SI 2007/3541, Sch 1 r 26(3)(c), Sch 2 r 27(3)(c), Sch 3 r 26(3)(c). As to the provision and allotment of polling stations see PARA 390.

11   Representation of the People Act 1983 Sch 1 r 28(3)(e) (Sch 1 r 28(3) amended, Sch 1 r 28(3)(d), (e) added, by the Electoral Administration Act 2006 Sch 1 paras 69, 70(1), (3)); European Parliamentary Elections Regulations 2004, SI 2004/293, Sch 1 para 31(7)(e) (as substituted: see note 1); Local Elections (Principal Areas) (England and Wales) Rules 2006, SI 2006/3304, Sch 2 r 25(3)(d); Local Elections (Parishes and Communities) (England and Wales) Rules 2006, SI 2006/3305, Sch 2 r 25(4)(d); National Assembly for Wales (Representation of the People) Order 2007, SI 2007/236, Sch 5 para 36(3)(d); Local Authorities (Mayoral Elections) (England and Wales) Regulations 2007, SI 2007/1024, Sch 1 r 27(3)(e); Greater London Authority Elections Rules 2007, SI 2007/3541, Sch 1 r 26(3)(d), Sch 2 r 27(3)(d), Sch 3 r 26(3)(d). The information set out under head (4) in the text for the purposes of a Welsh Assembly election must not relate to any candidate or registered political party: see the National Assembly for Wales (Representation of the People) Order 2007, SI 2007/236, Sch 5 para 36(3)(d). As to the meaning of 'registered political party' for these purposes see PARA 215 note 19.

12   Representation of the People Act 1983 Sch 1 r 28(3) (as amended: see note 11); European Parliamentary Elections Regulations 2004, SI 2004/293, Sch 1 para 31(7) (as substituted: see note 1); Local Elections (Principal Areas) (England and Wales) Rules 2006, SI 2006/3304, Sch 2 r 25(3); Local Elections (Parishes and Communities) (England and Wales) Rules 2006, SI 2006/3305, Sch 2 r 25(4); National Assembly for Wales (Representation of the People) Order 2007, SI 2007/236, Sch 5 para 36(3); Local Authorities (Mayoral Elections) (England and Wales) Regulations 2007, SI 2007/1024, Sch 1 r 27(3); Greater London Authority Elections Rules 2007, SI 2007/3541, Sch 1 r 26(3), Sch 2 r 27(3), Sch 3 r 26(3).

13   Representation of the People Act 1983 Sch 1 r 28(3)(d) (as added: see note 11). For these purposes, 'prescribed' means prescribed by regulations: see s 202(1). At the date at which this volume states the law, no such regulations had been made.

14   As to polls at elections or referendums which are taken together see PARA 16 et seq. See also note 7.

15   See PARA 702.

B.   VOTES GIVEN AT A POLLING STATION

390.   Provision and allotment of polling stations. At any election[1], or at a poll taken consequent on a parish meeting on a question which involves appointment to office[2], the returning officer[3] must provide a sufficient number of polling stations, and allot the electors[4] to the polling stations in such manner as he thinks most convenient, subject to the following requirements[5]. The polling station allotted to the electors from any polling district must be in the polling place for that district[6], except that:

(1)   at a local government election, the polling station allotted to electors from any parliamentary polling district wholly or partly within the electoral area[7] (or within the London Assembly constituency[8], as the case may be) must, in the absence of special circumstances, be in the parliamentary polling place for that district, unless the polling place is outside that electoral area (or outside that constituency)[9]; and

(2)   at a poll consequent on a parish meeting taken on a question of appointment to any office, the polling station allotted to electors from any parliamentary polling district wholly or partly within the parish

must, in the absence of special circumstances, be in the parliamentary polling place for that district, unless the polling place is outside the parish[10].

One or more polling stations may be provided in the same room[11]. The returning officer must provide each polling station with such number of compartments as may be necessary in which the voters can mark their votes screened from observation[12].

The returning officer may use free of charge, for the purpose of taking the poll[13]:

(a)   a room in a school maintained or assisted by a local authority[14], or in a school in respect of which grants are made out of money provided by Parliament (or by the National Assembly for Wales, as the case may be) to the person or body of persons responsible for the management of the school[15]; or

(b)   a room the expense of maintaining which is payable out of any rate[16], or (at a local authority mayoral or London Authority election) which is met by any local authority[17], or (at a Welsh Assembly election) which is payable wholly or mainly out of public funds[18].

At a local government election, or at a poll consequent on a parish meeting taken on a question of appointment to any office, such a room may also be used for the purpose of counting the votes[19]. The returning officer must make good any damage done to, and defray any expense incurred by the persons having control over, any such room as is mentioned in head (a) or head (b) above by reason of its being used for the purpose of taking the poll (or counting the votes, as the case may be)[20].

Where the poll at an election is taken together with the poll at another election or referendum, special provision is made as to which polling stations are to be used[21].

1   Ie a parliamentary election, a local government election (which includes any London Authority election and a local authority mayoral election), a Welsh Assembly constituency or regional election or a European parliamentary election. As to the meanings of 'Assembly election', 'constituency election' and 'regional election' see PARA 3 note 2. As to the meaning of 'parliamentary election' see PARA 9. As to the meanings of 'Authority election' and 'local government election' see PARA 11. As to elections in the City of London see PARA 33. As to elections for the return of a local authority mayor see PARA 198; and as to European parliamentary elections see PARA 217 et seq.

2   As to polls consequent on a parish meeting on a question involving appointment to office see PARA 200 et seq.

3   As to returning officers generally see PARA 350 et seq. The constituency returning officer (see PARA 211 note 9) is specified for the purposes of any London Authority election: see the Greater London Authority Elections Rules 2007, SI 2007/3541, Sch 1 r 24(1), (4), Sch 2 r 25(1), (4), Sch 3 r 24(1), (4). At a European parliamentary election, the reference is to a local returning officer (see PARA 360 et seq): see the European Parliamentary Elections Regulations 2004, SI 2004/293, Sch 1 paras 26, 29(1), (4) (Sch 1 substituted by SI 2009/186). At a Welsh Assembly election, the constituency returning officer (see PARA 18 note 2) is specified: see the National Assembly for Wales (Representation of the People) Order 2007, SI 2007/236, Sch 5 paras 31, 34(1), (4).

4   As to the meaning of 'elector', in relation to a parliamentary or local government election, see PARA 95 note 2; in relation to a Welsh Assembly election, see PARA 110 note 6; and, in relation to European parliamentary election, see PARA 111 note 4.

5   Representation of the People Act 1983 Sch 1 r 25(1); Parish and Community Meetings (Polls) Rules 1987, SI 1987/1, Schedule r 9(1); European Parliamentary Elections Regulations 2004, SI 2004/293, Sch 1 para 29(1) (as substituted: see note 3); Local Elections (Principal Areas) (England and Wales) Rules 2006, SI 2006/3304, Sch 2 r 23(1); Local Elections (Parishes and Communities) (England and Wales) Rules 2006, SI 2006/3305, Sch 2 r 23(1); National Assembly for Wales (Representation of the People) Order 2007, SI 2007/236, Sch 5 para 34(1);

Local Authorities (Mayoral Elections) (England and Wales) Regulations 2007, SI 2007/1024, Sch 1 r 25(1); Greater London Authority Elections Rules 2007, SI 2007/3541, Sch 1 r 24(1), Sch 2 r 25(1), Sch 3 r 24(1). At a poll consequent on a parish meeting taken on a question of appointment to any office, it is specified that the returning officer's duty to allot electors to a particular polling station applies only where more than one polling station is provided: see the Parish and Community Meetings (Polls) Rules 1987, SI 1987/1, Schedule r 9(1). As to polling districts and polling places see PARA 343 et seq.

6   Representation of the People Act 1983 Sch 1 r 25(3); European Parliamentary Elections Regulations 2004, SI 2004/293, Sch 1 para 29(3) (as substituted: see note 3); National Assembly for Wales (Representation of the People) Order 2007, SI 2007/236, Sch 5 para 34(3).

7   As to the meaning of 'electoral area' see PARA 11.

8   As to the meaning of 'Assembly constituency' in the context of London Authority elections see PARA 11 note 6.

9   Local Elections (Principal Areas) (England and Wales) Rules 2006, SI 2006/3304, Sch 2 r 23(3); Local Elections (Parishes and Communities) (England and Wales) Rules 2006, SI 2006/3305, Sch 2 r 23(3); Local Authorities (Mayoral Elections) (England and Wales) Regulations 2007, SI 2007/1024, Sch 1 r 25(3); Greater London Authority Elections Rules 2007, SI 2007/3541, Sch 1 r 24(3), Sch 2 r 25(3), Sch 3 r 24(3).

10   Parish and Community Meetings (Polls) Rules 1987, SI 1987/1, Schedule r 9(3).

11   Representation of the People Act 1983 Sch 1 r 25(2); Parish and Community Meetings (Polls) Rules 1987, SI 1987/1, Schedule r 9(2); European Parliamentary Elections Regulations 2004, SI 2004/293, Sch 1 para 29(2) (as substituted: see note 3); Local Elections (Principal Areas) (England and Wales) Rules 2006, SI 2006/3304, Sch 2 r 23(2); Local Elections (Parishes and Communities) (England and Wales) Rules 2006, SI 2006/3305, Sch 2 r 23(2); National Assembly for Wales (Representation of the People) Order 2007, SI 2007/236, Sch 5 para 34(2); Local Authorities (Mayoral Elections) (England and Wales) Regulations 2007, SI 2007/1024, Sch 1 r 25(2); Greater London Authority Elections Rules 2007, SI 2007/3541, Sch 1 r 24(2), Sch 2 r 25(2), Sch 3 r 24(2).

12   Representation of the People Act 1983 Sch 1 r 25(5); Parish and Community Meetings (Polls) Rules 1987, SI 1987/1, Schedule r 9(4); European Parliamentary Elections Regulations 2004, SI 2004/293, Sch 1 para 29(4) (as substituted: see note 3); Local Elections (Principal Areas) (England and Wales) Rules 2006, SI 2006/3304, Sch 2 r 23(4); Local Elections (Parishes and Communities) (England and Wales) Rules 2006, SI 2006/3305, Sch 2 r 23(4); National Assembly for Wales (Representation of the People) Order 2007, SI 2007/236, Sch 5 para 34(4); Local Authorities (Mayoral Elections) (England and Wales) Regulations 2007, SI 2007/1024, Sch 1 r 25(4); Greater London Authority Elections Rules 2007, SI 2007/3541, Sch 1 r 24(4), Sch 2 r 25(4), Sch 3 r 24(4). See note 3. The compartments provided need, however, only afford voters, if careful, reasonable facilities for secrecy: *Nicholson v Wick Magistrates* 1922 SC 374, Ct of Sess. As to the requirement for secrecy in the taking of a poll see PARA 385; and as to the consequences of contravening this requirement see PARA 739 et seq.

13   Representation of the People Act 1983 Sch 1 r 22(1); Parish and Community Meetings (Polls) Rules 1987, SI 1987/1, Schedule r 7(1); European Parliamentary Elections Regulations 2004, SI 2004/293, Sch 1 para 26(1) (as substituted: see note 3); Local Elections (Principal Areas) (England and Wales) Rules 2006, SI 2006/3304, Sch 2 r 20(1); Local Elections (Parishes and Communities) (England and Wales) Rules 2006, SI 2006/3305, Sch 2 r 20(1); National Assembly for Wales (Representation of the People) Order 2007, SI 2007/236, Sch 5 para 31(1); Local Authorities (Mayoral Elections) (England and Wales) Regulations 2007, SI 2007/1024, Sch 1 r 22(1); Greater London Authority Elections Rules 2007, SI 2007/3541, Sch 1 r 21(1), Sch 2 r 22(1), Sch 3 r 21(1). The returning officer referred to in the text at any London Authority election is the constituency returning officer for these purposes: see Sch 1 r 21(1), Sch 2 r 22(1), Sch 3 r 21(1). See also note 3. As to such schools as are mentioned in the text see EDUCATION vol 35 (2011) PARA 106 et seq.

14   As to the general education duties and functions of local authorities (within the meaning of the Education Act 1996) see EDUCATION vol 35 (2011) PARA 24 et seq.

15   Representation of the People Act 1983 Sch 1 r 22(1)(a), (i) (Sch 1 r 22(1)(i) amended by the School Standards and Framework Act 1998 s 140(3), Sch 31; and by SI 2010/1158); Parish and Community Meetings (Polls) Rules 1987, SI 1987/1, Schedule r 7(1)(a) (amended by SI 2010/1172); European Parliamentary Elections Regulations 2004, SI 2004/293, Sch 1 para 26(1)(a), (2)(a) (Sch 1 as substituted (see note 3); Sch 1 para 26(2)(a) amended by SI 2010/1172); Local Elections (Principal Areas) (England and Wales) Rules 2006, SI 2006/3304, Sch 2 r 20(1)(a) (amended by SI 2010/1172); Local Elections (Parishes and Communities) (England and Wales) Rules 2006, SI 2006/3305, Sch 2 r 20(1)(a) (amended by SI 2010/1172); National Assembly for Wales (Representation of the People) Order 2007,

SI 2007/236, Sch 5 para 31(1)(a), (2) (Sch 5 para 31(2) amended by SI 2010/1142); Local Authorities (Mayoral Elections) (England and Wales) Regulations 2007, SI 2007/1024, Sch 1 r 22(1)(a) (amended by SI 2010/1172); Greater London Authority Elections Rules 2007, SI 2007/3541, Sch 1 r 21(1)(a), Sch 2 r 22(1)(a), Sch 3 r 21(1)(a) (Sch 1 r 21(1)(a), Sch 2 r 22(1)(a), Sch 3 r 21(1)(a) amended by SI 2010/1172). As to such schools as are mentioned in the text see EDUCATION vol 35 (2011) PARA 106 et seq. As to the schools in Gibraltar to which the European Parliamentary Elections Regulations 2004, SI 2004/293, Sch 1 para 26 applies see Sch 1 para 26(2)(c). As to the 'combined' electoral region constituted for the purposes of European parliamentary elections, which includes Gibraltar, see PARA 77.

16 Representation of the People Act 1983 Sch 1 r 22(1)(b); Parish and Community Meetings (Polls) Rules 1987, SI 1987/1, Schedule r 7(1)(b); European Parliamentary Elections Regulations 2004, SI 2004/293, Sch 1 para 26(1)(b) (as substituted: see note 3); Local Elections (Principal Areas) (England and Wales) Rules 2006, SI 2006/3304, Sch 2 r 20(1)(b); Local Elections (Parishes and Communities) (England and Wales) Rules 2006, SI 2006/3305, Sch 2 r 20(1)(b). At a poll consequent on a parish meeting taken on a question of appointment to any office, the use of a room in an unoccupied house for the purpose of taking the poll (or counting the votes, as the case may be: see the text and note 19) does not render a person liable to be rated or to pay any rate for the house: Parish and Community Meetings (Polls) Rules 1987, SI 1987/1, Schedule r 7(3). For the purposes of determining rateable occupation, a hereditament is to be treated as unoccupied if it would otherwise be treated as occupied by reason only, if it is a house, of the use of a room in it by a returning officer for the purpose of taking the poll in a parliamentary or local government election: see the Local Government Finance Act 1988 s 65(6); and LOCAL GOVERNMENT FINANCE vol 70 (2012) PARA 62. As to the meaning of 'hereditament' in this context see LOCAL GOVERNMENT FINANCE vol 70 (2012) PARA 82 et seq. As to the application (with slight modifications) of s 65(6) for the purposes of a European parliamentary election see PARA 334.

17 Local Authorities (Mayoral Elections) (England and Wales) Regulations 2007, SI 2007/1024, Sch 1 r 22(1)(b); Greater London Authority Elections Rules 2007, SI 2007/3541, Sch 1 r 21(1)(b), Sch 2 r 22(1)(b), Sch 3 r 21(1)(b). The use of a room in an unoccupied heridament for the purpose of taking the poll (or counting the votes, as the case may be: see the text and note 17) at a local authority mayoral election does not render a person liable to any payment by way of council tax or non-domestic rate in respect of that heridament and any day on which it is so used: Local Authorities (Mayoral Elections) (England and Wales) Regulations 2007, SI 2007/1024, Sch 1 r 22(2). See also note 16.

18 National Assembly for Wales (Representation of the People) Order 2007, SI 2007/236, Sch 5 para 31(1)(b). As to the application (with slight modifications) of the Local Government Finance Act 1988 s 65(6) (see note 16) for the purposes of a Welsh Assembly election see PARA 334.

19 See the Parish and Community Meetings (Polls) Rules 1987, SI 1987/1, Schedule r 7(1); the Local Elections (Principal Areas) (England and Wales) Rules 2006, SI 2006/3304, Sch 2 r 20(1); the Local Elections (Parishes and Communities) (England and Wales) Rules 2006, SI 2006/3305, Sch 2 r 20(1); the Local Authorities (Mayoral Elections) (England and Wales) Regulations 2007, SI 2007/1024, Sch 1 r 22(1); and the Greater London Authority Elections Rules 2007, SI 2007/3541, Sch 1 r 21(1), Sch 2 r 22(1), Sch 3 r 21(1). As to the counting of votes at a local government election (except a London Authority election) see PARA 425; in relation to a local authority mayoral election see PARA 436; in relation to a London Authority election see PARA 444; and in relation to a London mayoral election see PARA 451.

20 Representation of the People Act 1983 Sch 1 r 22(2); Parish and Community Meetings (Polls) Rules 1987, SI 1987/1, Schedule r 7(2); European Parliamentary Elections Regulations 2004, SI 2004/293, Sch 1 para 26(3) (as substituted: see note 3); Local Elections (Principal Areas) (England and Wales) Rules 2006, SI 2006/3304, Sch 2 r 20(2); Local Elections (Parishes and Communities) (England and Wales) Rules 2006, SI 2006/3305, Sch 2 r 20(2); National Assembly for Wales (Representation of the People) Order 2007, SI 2007/236, Sch 5 para 31(3); Local Authorities (Mayoral Elections) (England and Wales) Regulations 2007, SI 2007/1024, Sch 1 r 22(3); Greater London Authority Elections Rules 2007, SI 2007/3541, Sch 1 r 21(2), Sch 2 r 22(2), Sch 3 r 21(2). In the case of an election for the return of the London Mayor, the CRO's duty to make good etc applies only where the election is required to fill a vacancy in the office of the Mayor: see Sch 3 r 21(2). As to elections to fill vacancies arising in the office of Mayor of London see PARA 204.

21 As to the polling stations to be used where polls at elections or referendums are taken together see PARA 19.

391. Equipment of polling stations. At an election[1], or at a poll taken consequent on a parish meeting on a question which involves appointment to office[2], the returning officer[3] must provide each presiding officer[4] with such number of ballot boxes and ballot papers as in the returning officer's opinion may be necessary[5]; and the returning officer at an election (but not at a poll) must also provide each polling station with a device[6] for enabling voters who are blind or partially-sighted to vote without any need for assistance from the presiding officer or any companion[7].

Every ballot box at such an election or poll must be so constructed that the ballot papers can be put in it, but cannot be withdrawn from it, without the box being unlocked[8] (or, as the case may be, without the seal being broken)[9]. The returning officer also must provide each polling station with[10]:

(1)   materials to enable voters at the election or poll in question to mark the ballot papers[11];

(2)   copies of the register of electors that is appropriate to the election or poll in question (or such part of it as contains the entries relating to the electors allotted to the station)[12];

(3)   the parts of any special lists prepared for the election in question corresponding to the register of electors or the part of it provided under head (2) above[13];

(4)   a list consisting of that part of the corresponding number list[14] prepared for the election in question which contains the numbers (but not the other unique identifying marks) corresponding to those on the ballot papers provided to the presiding officer of the polling station[15].

The following notices must be displayed or exhibited[16]:

(a)   a notice in the specified form, giving directions for the guidance of the voters in voting[17], which must be printed in conspicuous characters and exhibited inside and outside every polling station[18];

(b)   in every compartment of every polling station[19], the statutory notice which instructs voters how many votes they may give at the election[20]; and

(c)   at least one large version of the ballot paper, provided to each polling station by the returning officer, which must be displayed inside the polling station for the assistance of voters at any election (but not at a poll) who are partially-sighted[21].

The statement of persons nominated at a Welsh Assembly constituency election, and at a Welsh Assembly regional election, must be printed in conspicuous characters and exhibited inside and outside every polling station at such an election[22]. Notice of the death of an individual candidate standing at a London members or European parliamentary election, or of a candidate who appears on a registered party's list for such an election, must also be provided by the returning officer to each polling station and displayed there[23].

Where the poll at an election is taken together with the poll at another election or referendum, special provision is made as to the equipment of polling stations[24].

1   Ie a parliamentary election, a local government election (which includes any London Authority election and a local authority mayoral election), a Welsh Assembly constituency or regional election or a European parliamentary election. As to the meanings of 'Assembly election', 'constituency election' and 'regional election' see PARA 3 note 2. As to the meaning of 'parliamentary election' see PARA 9. As to the meanings of 'Authority election' and 'local

government election' see PARA 11. As to elections in the City of London see PARA 33. As to elections for the return of a local authority mayor see PARA 198; and as to European parliamentary elections see PARA 217 et seq.

2   As to polls consequent on a parish meeting on a question involving appointment to office see PARA 200 et seq.

3   As to returning officers generally see PARA 350 et seq. At a London Authority election, the duties mentioned in the text are undertaken by the constituency returning officer ('CRO'): see the Greater London Authority Elections Rules 2007, SI 2007/3541, Sch 1 r 28(1), (3), (5), (7), (8), Sch 2 r 29(1), (3), (5), (8), Sch 3 r 28(1), (3), (5), (8). However, the Greater London returning officer ('GLRO') may direct the CRO to use joint ballot boxes (see Sch 1 r 28(9), Sch 2 r 29(9), Sch 3 r 28(9); and note 5), and the GLRO must prepare the notices to be exhibited under Sch 1 r 28(8) at an ordinary election, and under Sch 2 r 29(8), Sch 3 r 28(8) (see Sch 1 r 29(3), (5), Sch 2 r 30(1)–(3), Sch 3 r 29(1)–(3); and note 18). As to the meaning of the 'constituency returning officer' ('CRO') see PARA 211 note 9; and as to the meaning of the 'Greater London returning officer' ('GLRO') see PARA 211 note 8. At a European parliamentary election, the reference is to a local returning officer (see PARA 360 et seq): see the European Parliamentary Elections Regulations 2004, SI 2004/293, Sch 1 para 32(1), (3), (5) (Sch 1 substituted by SI 2009/186). At a Welsh Assembly election, the constituency returning officer (see PARA 18 note 2) is specified: see the National Assembly for Wales (Representation of the People) Order 2007, SI 2007/236, Sch 5 para 37(1), (5), (7).

4   As to the appointment of presiding officers and their clerks see PARA 393.

5   Representation of the People Act 1983 Sch 1 r 29(1); Parish and Community Meetings (Polls) Rules 1987, SI 1987/1, Schedule r 11(1); European Parliamentary Elections Regulations 2004, SI 2004/293, Sch 1 para 32(1) (as substituted: see note 3); Local Elections (Principal Areas) (England and Wales) Rules 2006, SI 2006/3304, Sch 2 r 26(1); Local Elections (Parishes and Communities) (England and Wales) Rules 2006, SI 2006/3305, Sch 2 r 26(1); National Assembly for Wales (Representation of the People) Order 2007, SI 2007/236, Sch 5 para 37(1); Local Authorities (Mayoral Elections) (England and Wales) Regulations 2007, SI 2007/1024, Sch 1 r 28(1); Greater London Authority Elections Rules 2007, SI 2007/3541, Sch 1 r 28(1)(a), (b), Sch 2 r 29(1)(a), (b), Sch 3 r 28(1)(a), (b). As to the form and printing of ballot papers see PARA 386.

At a London Authority election, the CRO must take account of any direction made by the GLRO in accordance with Sch 1 r 28(9), Sch 2 r 29(9), Sch 3 r 28(9) before providing ballot boxes to each presiding officer: see Sch 1 r 28(1)(b), Sch 2 r 29(1)(b), Sch 3 r 28(1)(b). Accordingly, if the GLRO thinks fit he may, not later than the date of the notice of election, direct the CRO that joint ballot boxes must be used for the ballot papers at the election and any or all Authority elections with which the election is taken: Sch 1 r 28(9), Sch 2 r 29(9), Sch 3 r 28(9). As to notice of a local government election see PARA 211.

Where the polls at an Assembly constituency election and an Assembly regional election are to be taken together, the same ballot box may be used for the receipt of ballot papers at the regional election and at the constituency election if the constituency returning officer so determines; and such a determination may make different provision for different polling stations: National Assembly for Wales (Representation of the People) Order 2007, SI 2007/236, Sch 5 para 37(2). Where separate ballot boxes are to be used for the receipt of ballot papers at a constituency election and at a regional election, however, each ballot box must be clearly marked with the Assembly election to which it relates, and the words: 'Place the [*specify the colour of the ballot papers in question*] ballot paper here/Rhowch y papur pleidleisio [*nodwch liw'r papurau pleidleisio dan sylw*] yma': see Sch 5 para 37(3).

6   Ie a device of such description as may be prescribed, for the purposes of a parliamentary election: see the Representation of the People Act 1983 Sch 1 r 29(3A)(b) (r 29(3A) added by the Representation of the People Act 2000 s 13(1), (2)). Under the Representation of the People Act 1983, 'prescribed' means prescribed by regulations: see s 202(1). As to the making of regulations under the Representation of the People Act 1983 generally see PARA 28 note 16. As to the regulations so prescribed see the Representation of the People (England and Wales) Regulations 2001, SI 2001/341; and note 7. In all other cases, the device must conform to the description that is set out (as the case may be) in the European Parliamentary Elections Regulations 2004, SI 2004/293, Sch 1 para 32(8); the Local Elections (Principal Areas) (England and Wales) Rules 2006, SI 2006/3304, Sch 2 r 26(9); the Local Elections (Parishes and Communities) (England and Wales) Rules 2006, SI 2006/3305, Sch 2 r 26(9); the National Assembly for Wales (Representation of the People) Order 2007, SI 2007/236, Sch 5 para 37(8), (9); the Local Authorities (Mayoral Elections) (England and Wales) Regulations 2007, SI 2007/1024, Sch 1 r 28(8); and the Greater London Authority Elections Rules 2007, SI 2007/3541, Sch 1 r 28(6), Sch 2 r 29(6), Sch 3 r 28(6): see note 7.

7   Representation of the People Act 1983 Sch 1 r 29(3A)(b) (as added: see note 6); European
     Parliamentary Elections Regulations 2004, SI 2004/293, Sch 1 para 32(5)(b) (as substituted: see
     note 3); Local Elections (Principal Areas) (England and Wales) Rules 2006, SI 2006/3304, Sch 2
     r 26(5)(b); Local Elections (Parishes and Communities) (England and Wales) Rules 2006,
     SI 2006/3305, Sch 2 r 26(5)(b); National Assembly for Wales (Representation of the People)
     Order 2007, SI 2007/236, Sch 5 para 37(7)(c); Local Authorities (Mayoral Elections) (England
     and Wales) Regulations 2007, SI 2007/1024, Sch 1 r 28(5)(b); Greater London Authority
     Elections Rules 2007, SI 2007/3541, Sch 1 r 28(5), Sch 2 r 29(5), Sch 3 r 28(5). As to the
     provision and allotment of polling stations see PARA 390. As to companions assisting voters with
     incapacities see PARA 402. The device referred to in the text:
     (1)   must be capable of allowing a ballot paper to be inserted into and removed from it (or
           capable of allowing a ballot paper to be attached firmly to and detached from the
           device after use) easily and without damage to the paper (Representation of the People
           (England and Wales) Regulations 2001, SI 2001/341, reg 12(1), (2); European
           Parliamentary Elections Regulations 2004, SI 2004/293, Sch 1 para 32(8)(a) (as so
           substituted); Local Elections (Principal Areas) (England and Wales) Rules 2006,
           SI 2006/3304, Sch 2 r 26(9)(a); Local Elections (Parishes and Communities) (England
           and Wales) Rules 2006, SI 2006/3305, Sch 2 r 26(9)(a); National Assembly for Wales
           (Representation of the People) Order 2007, SI 2007/236, Sch 5 para 37(8); Local
           Authorities (Mayoral Elections) (England and Wales) Regulations 2007, SI 2007/1024,
           Sch 1 r 28(8)(a); Greater London Authority Elections Rules 2007, SI 2007/3541, Sch 1
           r 28(6)(a), Sch 2 r 29(6)(a), Sch 3 r 28(6)(a));
     (2)   must have, for use at a parliamentary or Welsh Assembly election, on its right-hand
           side, tabs of equal size which:
           (a)   are capable of being positioned on the ballot paper so that each one is above one
                 of the spaces to the right of the particulars of the candidates on which the vote is
                 to be marked (the 'relevant space') (Representation of the People (England and
                 Wales) Regulations 2001, SI 2001/341, reg 12(1), (3), (4); National Assembly for
                 Wales (Representation of the People) Order 2007, SI 2007/236, Sch 5
                 para 37(9), (10));
           (b)   are numbered, with each number on a tab being in raised form and capable of
                 being clearly identified by touch, so that, when the device is positioned over a
                 ballot paper, the number of each tab corresponds to that of the candidate (ie at a
                 Welsh Assembly election, the registered political party or the candidate) whose
                 particulars are to the left of the relevant space covered by the tab in question
                 (Representation of the People (England and Wales) Regulations 2001,
                 SI 2001/341, reg 12(1), (3), (5), (6); National Assembly for Wales
                 (Representation of the People) Order 2007, SI 2007/236, Sch 5
                 para 37(9), (11), (12)); and
           (c)   are capable of being lifted so as to reveal the relevant space and so that there is
                 sufficient room to allow a voter to mark a cross on that space (Representation of
                 the People (England and Wales) Regulations 2001, SI 2001/341, reg 12(1), (3),
                 (7); National Assembly for Wales (Representation of the People) Order 2007,
                 SI 2007/236, Sch 5 para 37(9), (13)).
     (3)   must, for use at a local government or European parliamentary election, keep the ballot
           paper firmly in place during use (European Parliamentary Elections Regulations 2004,
           SI 2004/293, Sch 1 para 32(8)(b) (as so substituted); Local Elections (Principal Areas)
           (England and Wales) Rules 2006, SI 2006/3304, Sch 2 r 26(9)(b); Local Elections
           (Parishes and Communities) (England and Wales) Rules 2006, SI 2006/3305, Sch 2
           r 26(9)(b); Local Authorities (Mayoral Elections) (England and Wales)
           Regulations 2007, SI 2007/1024, Sch 1 r 28(8)(b); Greater London Authority Elections
           Rules 2007, SI 2007/3541, Sch 1 r 28(6)(b), Sch 2 r 29(6)(b), Sch 3 r 28(6)(b)); and
           provide suitable means for the voter to:
           (a)   identify the spaces on the ballot paper on which he may mark his vote (European
                 Parliamentary Elections Regulations 2004, SI 2004/293, Sch 1 para 32(8)(c)(i) (as
                 so substituted); Local Elections (Principal Areas) (England and Wales)
                 Rules 2006, SI 2006/3304, Sch 2 r 26(9)(c)(i); Local Elections (Parishes and
                 Communities) (England and Wales) Rules 2006, SI 2006/3305, Sch 2
                 r 26(9)(c)(i); Local Authorities (Mayoral Elections) (England and Wales)
                 Regulations 2007, SI 2007/1024, Sch 1 r 28(8)(c)(i); Greater London Authority
                 Elections Rules 2007, SI 2007/3541, Sch 1 r 28(6)(c)(i), Sch 2 r 29(6)(c)(i), Sch 3
                 r 28(6)(c)(i));

    (b)   identify the candidate (ie at a European parliamentary election, the registered party or individual candidate) to which each such space refers (European Parliamentary Elections Regulations 2004, SI 2004/293, Sch 1 para 32(8)(c)(ii) (as so substituted); Local Elections (Principal Areas) (England and Wales) Rules 2006, SI 2006/3304, Sch 2 r 26(9)(c)(ii); Local Elections (Parishes and Communities) (England and Wales) Rules 2006, SI 2006/3305, Sch 2 r 26(9)(c)(ii); Local Authorities (Mayoral Elections) (England and Wales) Regulations 2007, SI 2007/1024, Sch 1 r 28(8)(c)(ii); Greater London Authority Elections Rules 2007, SI 2007/3541, Sch 1 r 28(6)(c)(ii), Sch 2 r 29(6)(c)(ii), Sch 3 r 28(6)(c)(ii)); and

    (c)   mark his vote on the space he has chosen (European Parliamentary Elections Regulations 2004, SI 2004/293, Sch 1 para 32(8)(c)(iii) (as so substituted); Local Elections (Principal Areas) (England and Wales) Rules 2006, SI 2006/3304, Sch 2 r 26(9)(c)(iii); Local Elections (Parishes and Communities) (England and Wales) Rules 2006, SI 2006/3305, Sch 2 r 26(9)(c)(iii); Local Authorities (Mayoral Elections) (England and Wales) Regulations 2007, SI 2007/1024, Sch 1 r 28(8)(c)(iii); Greater London Authority Elections Rules 2007, SI 2007/3541, Sch 1 r 28(6)(c)(iii), Sch 2 r 29(6)(c)(iii), Sch 3 r 28(6)(c)(iii)).

Under head (2)(a) above, as it applies to a Welsh Assembly election, the tabs must be capable of being positioned on the ballot paper so that each one is above one of the spaces to the right of:

    (i)   in the case of a constituency election, the particulars of a constituency candidate (National Assembly for Wales (Representation of the People) Order 2007, SI 2007/236, Sch 5 para 37(10)(a)); or

    (ii)   in the case of a regional election, the name or names or, as the case may be, description of a registered political party, or the particulars of an individual candidate (Sch 5 para 37(10)(b)),

on which the vote is to be marked (the 'relevant space') (see Sch 5 para 37(10)). As to the meanings of 'candidate', 'constituency candidate' and 'individual candidate' for these purposes see PARA 230 note 19; and as to the meaning of 'registered political party' see PARA 215 note 19. As to the meaning of 'registered party' for the purposes of a European parliamentary election see PARA 230 note 29; and as to the meaning of 'individual candidate' at a European parliamentary election see PARA 230 note 32.

8   Representation of the People Act 1983 Sch 1 r 29(2); Parish and Community Meetings (Polls) Rules 1987, SI 1987/1, Schedule r 11(2); European Parliamentary Elections Regulations 2004, SI 2004/293, Sch 1 para 32(2) (as substituted: see note 3); Local Elections (Principal Areas) (England and Wales) Rules 2006, SI 2006/3304, Sch 2 r 26(2); Local Elections (Parishes and Communities) (England and Wales) Rules 2006, SI 2006/3305, Sch 2 r 26(2); National Assembly for Wales (Representation of the People) Order 2007, SI 2007/236, Sch 5 para 37(4); Local Authorities (Mayoral Elections) (England and Wales) Regulations 2007, SI 2007/1024, Sch 1 r 28(2); Greater London Authority Elections Rules 2007, SI 2007/3541, Sch 1 r 28(2), Sch 2 r 29(2), Sch 3 r 28(2).

9   Only the rules that apply at a local government or European parliamentary election include specific additional wording that provides for a ballot box, where the box has no lock, to be so constructed that the ballot papers can be put in it, but cannot be withdrawn from it, without the seal being broken: see the European Parliamentary Elections Regulations 2004, SI 2004/293, Sch 1 para 32(2) (as so substituted); the Local Elections (Principal Areas) (England and Wales) Rules 2006, SI 2006/3304, Sch 2 r 26(2); the Local Elections (Parishes and Communities) (England and Wales) Rules 2006, SI 2006/3305, Sch 2 r 26(2); the Local Authorities (Mayoral Elections) (England and Wales) Regulations 2007, SI 2007/1024, Sch 1 r 28(2); and the Greater London Authority Elections Rules 2007, SI 2007/3541, Sch 1 r 28(2), Sch 2 r 29(2), Sch 3 r 28(2). At a Welsh Assembly election, no mention is made of a ballot box with a lock and the wording provides only for a ballot box to have a seal: see the National Assembly for Wales (Representation of the People) Order 2007, SI 2007/236, Sch 5 para 37(4). Ballot boxes must have seals applied to them by the presiding officer regardless of whether they have a lock or not: see PARA 397.

10   Representation of the People Act 1983 Sch 1 r 29(3); Parish and Community Meetings (Polls) Rules 1987, SI 1987/1, Schedule r 11(3); European Parliamentary Elections Regulations 2004, SI 2004/293, Sch 1 para 32(3) (as substituted: see note 3); Local Elections (Principal Areas) (England and Wales) Rules 2006, SI 2006/3304, Sch 2 r 26(3); Local Elections (Parishes and Communities) (England and Wales) Rules 2006, SI 2006/3305, Sch 2 r 26(3); National Assembly for Wales (Representation of the People) Order 2007, SI 2007/236, Sch 5 para 37(5);

Local Authorities (Mayoral Elections) (England and Wales) Regulations 2007, SI 2007/1024, Sch 1 r 28(3); Greater London Authority Elections Rules 2007, SI 2007/3541, Sch 1 r 28(3), Sch 2 r 29(3), Sch 3 r 28(3).

11 Representation of the People Act 1983 Sch 1 r 29(3)(a); Parish and Community Meetings (Polls) Rules 1987, SI 1987/1, Schedule r 11(3)(a); European Parliamentary Elections Regulations 2004, SI 2004/293, Sch 1 para 32(3)(a) (as substituted: see note 3); Local Elections (Principal Areas) (England and Wales) Rules 2006, SI 2006/3304, Sch 2 r 26(3)(a); Local Elections (Parishes and Communities) (England and Wales) Rules 2006, SI 2006/3305, Sch 2 r 26(3)(a); National Assembly for Wales (Representation of the People) Order 2007, SI 2007/236, Sch 5 para 37(5)(a); Local Authorities (Mayoral Elections) (England and Wales) Regulations 2007, SI 2007/1024, Sch 1 r 28(3)(a); Greater London Authority Elections Rules 2007, SI 2007/3541, Sch 1 r 28(3)(a), Sch 2 r 29(3)(a), Sch 3 r 28(3)(a). At a poll taken consequent on a parish meeting on a question which involves appointment to office, the returning officer must also provide instruments for stamping the official mark on the ballot papers: see the Parish and Community Meetings (Polls) Rules 1987, SI 1987/1, Schedule r 11(3)(b). As to the official mark see PARA 387.

12 Representation of the People Act 1983 Sch 1 r 29(3)(c) (amended by the Electoral Administration Act 2006 s 10(2), Sch 1 paras 2, 14(1), (4)); Parish and Community Meetings (Polls) Rules 1987, SI 1987/1, Schedule r 11(3)(c); European Parliamentary Elections Regulations 2004, SI 2004/293, Sch 1 para 32(3)(b) (as substituted: see note 3); Local Elections (Principal Areas) (England and Wales) Rules 2006, SI 2006/3304, Sch 2 r 26(3)(b); Local Elections (Parishes and Communities) (England and Wales) Rules 2006, SI 2006/3305, Sch 2 r 26(3)(b); National Assembly for Wales (Representation of the People) Order 2007, SI 2007/236, Sch 5 para 37(5)(b); Local Authorities (Mayoral Elections) (England and Wales) Regulations 2007, SI 2007/1024, Sch 1 r 28(3)(b); Greater London Authority Elections Rules 2007, SI 2007/3541, Sch 1 r 28(3)(b), Sch 2 r 29(3)(b), Sch 3 r 28(3)(b).

The reference in head (2) in the text to the copies of the registers of electors includes a reference to copies of any notices issued under the Representation of the People Act 1983 s 13B(3B) or s 13B(3D) (see PARA 168), specifying appropriate alterations to the register: Sch 1 r 29(6) (added by the Electoral Administration Act 2006 s 11(6), Sch 1 paras 31, 33, 34); European Parliamentary Elections Regulations 2004, SI 2004/293, Sch 1 para 32(4) (as so substituted); Local Elections (Principal Areas) (England and Wales) Rules 2006, SI 2006/3304, Sch 2 r 26(4); Local Elections (Parishes and Communities) (England and Wales) Rules 2006, SI 2006/3305, Sch 2 r 26(4); National Assembly for Wales (Representation of the People) Order 2007, SI 2007/236, Sch 5 para 37(6); Local Authorities (Mayoral Elections) (England and Wales) Regulations 2007, SI 2007/1024, Sch 1 r 28(4); Greater London Authority Elections Rules 2007, SI 2007/3541, Sch 1 r 28(4), Sch 2 r 29(4), Sch 3 r 28(4).

13 Representation of the People Act 1983 Sch 1 r 29(3)(d); European Parliamentary Elections Regulations 2004, SI 2004/293, Sch 1 para 32(3)(c) (as substituted: see note 3); Local Elections (Principal Areas) (England and Wales) Rules 2006, SI 2006/3304, Sch 2 r 26(3)(c); Local Elections (Parishes and Communities) (England and Wales) Rules 2006, SI 2006/3305, Sch 2 r 26(3)(c); National Assembly for Wales (Representation of the People) Order 2007, SI 2007/236, Sch 5 para 37(5)(c); Local Authorities (Mayoral Elections) (England and Wales) Regulations 2007, SI 2007/1024, Sch 1 r 28(3)(c); Greater London Authority Elections Rules 2007, SI 2007/3541, Sch 1 r 28(3)(c), Sch 2 r 29(3)(c), Sch 3 r 28(3)(c). The provision set out in head (3) in the text does not apply to polls consequent on a parish meeting on a question involving appointment to office. As to the preparation of special lists as mentioned in the text see PARAS 373, 381.

14 Ie the list prepared, in relation to a parliamentary election, under the Representation of the People Act 1983 Sch 1 r 19A, or, in relation to a local government election, under the Local Elections (Principal Areas) (England and Wales) Rules 2006, SI 2006/3304, Sch 2 r 17, the Local Elections (Parishes and Communities) (England and Wales) Rules 2006, SI 2006/3305, Sch 2 r 17, the Local Authorities (Mayoral Elections) (England and Wales) Regulations 2007, SI 2007/1024, Sch 1 r 19, or the Greater London Authority Elections Rules 2007, SI 2007/3541, Sch 1 r 18, Sch 2 r 19, Sch 3 r 18, or, in relation to a European parliamentary election, under the European Parliamentary Elections Regulations 2004, SI 2004/293, Sch 1 para 23, or, in relation to a Welsh Assembly election, under the National Assembly for Wales (Representation of the People) Order 2007, SI 2007/236, Sch 5 para 27 (see PARA 387): see the Representation of the People Act 1983 Sch 1 r 29(3)(e) (added by the Electoral Administration Act 2006 s 31(1), (3)); the European Parliamentary Elections Regulations 2004, SI 2004/293, Sch 1 para 32(3)(d) (as substituted: see note 3); the Local Elections (Principal Areas) (England and Wales) Rules 2006, SI 2006/3304, Sch 2 r 26(3)(d); the Local Elections (Parishes and Communities) (England and Wales) Rules 2006, SI 2006/3305, Sch 2 r 26(3)(d); the National Assembly for Wales

(Representation of the People) Order 2007, SI 2007/236, Sch 5 para 37(5)(d); the Local Authorities (Mayoral Elections) (England and Wales) Regulations 2007, SI 2007/1024, Sch 1 r 28(3)(d); and the Greater London Authority Elections Rules 2007, SI 2007/3541, Sch 1 r 28(3)(d), Sch 2 r 29(3)(e), Sch 3 r 28(3)(d).

The form of the corresponding number list to be prepared for these purposes by a returning officer at a parliamentary election must be in the form set out in the Representation of the People (England and Wales) Regulations 2001, SI 2001/341, Sch 3 (Form L2: corresponding number list to be used in polling stations at parliamentary election taken alone) (reg 63A, Forms L2, M2, added by SI 2006/2910; Representation of the People (England and Wales) Regulations 2001, SI 2001/341, Sch 3 Forms L2, M2 substituted by SI 2007/1025): Representation of the People (England and Wales) Regulations 2001, SI 2001/341, reg 63A(2) (reg 63A as so added; reg 63A(2), (4), amended by SI 2007/1025). When a parliamentary election is combined with another poll under the Representation of the People Act 1985 s 15 (see PARAS 21–22) or under the Local Government Act 2000 s 44 (provision for the combination of polls at elections for the return of elected mayors: see PARA 26) or under s 45 (provision for the combination of polls at referendums with polls at any elections: see PARA 27), the corresponding number list to be prepared by a returning officer for the purposes of the Representation of the People Act 1983 Sch 1 r 29(3)(e) must be in the form set out in the Representation of the People (England and Wales) Regulations 2001, SI 2001/341, Sch 3 (Form M2: corresponding number list to be used in polling stations when a parliamentary election is combined with another election/referendum) (as so added): Representation of the People (England and Wales) Regulations 2001, SI 2001/341, reg 63A(4) (reg 63A as so added; reg 63A(4) as so amended).

For the purposes of local government elections mentioned in the text:

(1)   for principal areas, the corresponding number list must be in the appropriate form, or a form to like effect, in the Local Elections (Principal Areas) (England and Wales) Rules 2006, SI 2006/3304, Sch 2 r 17(2), Appendix of Forms (Form L2: corresponding number list to be used in polling stations at a local government election taken alone); and Sch 3 r 17(2), Appendix of Forms (Form M2: corresponding number list to be used in polling stations when a local government election is combined with another election/referendum);

(2)   for parishes and communities, the corresponding number list must be in the appropriate form, or a form to like effect, in the Local Elections (Parishes and Communities) (England and Wales) Rules 2006, SI 2006/3305, Sch 2 r 17(2), Sch 2 Appendix of Forms (Form L2: corresponding number list to be used in polling stations at a parish or community election taken alone); and Sch 3 r 17(2), Appendix of Forms (Form M2: corresponding number list to be used in polling stations when a parish or community election is combined with another election/referendum);

(3)   for a local authority mayoral election, the corresponding number list must be in the appropriate form, or a form to like effect, in the Local Authorities (Mayoral Elections) (England and Wales) Regulations 2007, SI 2007/1024, Sch 1 r 19(2), Appendix of Forms (Form 6: corresponding number list L2 to be used in polling stations in a mayoral election taken alone); and Sch 3 r 19(2), Appendix of Forms (Form 6: corresponding number list M2 to be used in polling stations when a mayoral election is combined with another election/referendum); and

(4)   for an Authority election, the corresponding number list must be in the appropriate form, or a form to like effect, in the Greater London Authority Elections Rules 2007, SI 2007/3541, Sch 1 r 18(2), Sch 2 r 19(2), Sch 3 r 18(2), Sch 10 r 2 (Form 9: corresponding number list L2).

At an ordinary election under head (4) above, the same corresponding number list may be used for each of the Authority elections which are combined: Sch 1 r 18(3), Sch 2 r 19(3), Sch 3 r 18(3).

The form of corresponding number list to be prepared by the local returning officer for the purposes of the European Parliamentary Elections Regulations 2004, SI 2004/293, Sch 1 para 32(3)(d) (form to be provided by local returning officer to each polling station) must be in Sch 1 Pt 7 Appendix of Forms (Form C: Corresponding Number List for use in polling station at a European Parliamentary election) (as so substituted): see Sch 1 para 23(3) (as so substituted); and PARA 387 note 4. As to combined elections see Sch 1 para 23(5), Sch 1 Pt 7 Appendix of Forms (Form E: Corresponding Number List for use in polling station when a European Parliamentary election is combined with another election or referendum) (as so substituted).

For the purposes of a Welsh Assembly election, the corresponding number list must be as set out in English and Welsh in the National Assembly for Wales (Representation of the People)

Order 2007, SI 2007/236, Sch 10 Appendix of Forms (Form CO: Form of corresponding number list for use by presiding officers in polling stations): see Sch 5 para 37(5)(d).

Where elections take place in Wales see also the forms issued partly in English and partly in Welsh in the Parliamentary Elections (Welsh Forms) Order 2007, SI 2007/1014, art 6(q), (s), Sch 2 (Forms 17, 19); the Local Elections (Principal Areas) (Welsh Forms) Order 2007, SI 2007/1015, art 7(1)(b), Sch 3 (Form 2 (Ffurflen 2) (Corresponding Number List—L2/Rhestr Rhif Cyfatebol—L2)); the Local Elections (Communities) (Welsh Forms) Order 2007, SI 2007/1013, art 7(1)(b), Sch 3 (Form 2 (Ffurflen 2) (Corresponding Number List—L2/Rhestr Rhif Cyfatebol—L2)); and the European Parliamentary Elections (Welsh Forms) Order 2009, SI 2009/781, art 6(1)(c), (e), Sch 2 (Forms 3, 5).

15 Representation of the People Act 1983 Sch 1 r 29(3)(e) (as added: see note 14); European Parliamentary Elections Regulations 2004, SI 2004/293, Sch 1 para 32(3)(d) (as substituted: see note 3); Local Elections (Principal Areas) (England and Wales) Rules 2006, SI 2006/3304, Sch 2 r 26(3)(d); Local Elections (Parishes and Communities) (England and Wales) Rules 2006, SI 2006/3305, Sch 2 r 26(3)(d); National Assembly for Wales (Representation of the People) Order 2007, SI 2007/236, Sch 5 para 37(5)(d); Local Authorities (Mayoral Elections) (England and Wales) Regulations 2007, SI 2007/1024, Sch 1 r 28(3)(d); Greater London Authority Elections Rules 2007, SI 2007/3541, Sch 1 r 28(3)(d), Sch 2 r 29(3)(e), Sch 3 r 28(3)(d). The provision set out in head (4) in the text does not apply to polls consequent on a parish meeting on a question involving appointment to office. As to security measures associated with the ballot paper see PARA 387.

16 As to the giving of public notices by a returning officer generally see PARA 350 et seq. See also note 18.

17 As to the form giving directions for the guidance of the voters in voting see:
    (1) in the case of a parliamentary election, the Representation of the People Act 1983 Sch 1 Appendix of Forms (Form of directions for the guidance of the voters in voting) (Form substituted by the Electoral Administration Act 2006 s 47, Sch 1 paras 69, 93(1), (3));
    (2) at a European parliamentary election, the notice must in the form specified in the European Parliamentary Elections Regulations 2004, SI 2004/293, Sch 1 Appendix of Forms (Form K: Form of directions for the guidance of the voters in voting) (as substituted: see note 3);
    (3) in the case of a local government election:
        (a) Local Elections (Principal Areas) (England and Wales) Rules 2006, SI 2006/3304, Sch 2 Appendix of Forms (Form of directions for the guidance of the voters in voting); and Sch 3 Appendix of Forms (Form of directions for the guidance of the voters in voting) (guidance for voters at combined polls);
        (b) Local Elections (Parishes and Communities) (England and Wales) Rules 2006, SI 2006/3305, Sch 2 Appendix of Forms (Form of directions for the guidance of the voters in voting); and Sch 3 Appendix of Forms (Form of directions for the guidance of the voters in voting) (guidance for voters at combined polls);
        (c) Local Authorities (Mayoral Elections) (England and Wales) Regulations 2007, SI 2007/1024, Sch 1 Appendix of Forms (Form 12: Directions for the guidance of voters) (Form 12 substituted by SI 2012/2059); and Local Authorities (Mayoral Elections) (England and Wales) Regulations 2007, SI 2007/1024, Sch 3 Appendix of Forms (Form 12: Directions for the guidance of voters);
        (d) Greater London Authority Elections Rules 2007, SI 2007/3541, Sch 10 r 2 (Form 16: Notices for guidance of voters at ordinary day elections (or for filling of a vacancy in an Assembly constituency or filling of vacancy in the office of Mayor) (Notice A–Notice for guidance of voters for display inside and outside polling stations; Notice B–Notice for guidance of voters for display inside polling stations; Notice C–Notice for guidance of voters for display inside polling stations (election of London members of the London Assembly only); Notice D1–Notice for guidance of voters for display inside polling booths (different coloured ballot papers); Notice D2–Notice for guidance of voters for display inside polling stations (different coloured ballot papers)); Form 17: Notices for guidance of voters at GLA elections combined with another election or referendum (Notice A1–Notice for guidance of voters for display inside and outside polling stations; Notice B1–Notice for guidance of voters for display inside polling stations; Notice D3–Notice for guidance of voters for display inside polling booths (different coloured ballot papers)));
        (4) at a Welsh Assembly election, the form set out in English and Welsh in the National

Assembly for Wales (Representation of the People) Order 2007, SI 2007/236, Sch 10 Appendix of Forms (Form CP: Form of directions for guidance of the voters in voting) (see Sch 5 para 37(14)).

In the case of a poll on a question of appointment to an office, see the Parish and Community Meetings (Polls) Rules 1987, SI 1987/1, Schedule Appendix of Forms (Form of directions for the guidance of the voters in voting where the poll is on a question of appointment to an office) (amended by SI 1987/262).

Where elections take place in Wales see also the forms issued partly in English and partly in Welsh in:

(i)   the Parliamentary Elections (Welsh Forms) Order 2007, SI 2007/1014, art 6(b), (d), Sch 2 (Form 2 (Ffurflen 2): Form of Directions for the Guidance of the Voters in Voting; Ffurf Cyfarwyddiadau i Gynorthwyo'r Pleidleiswyr Wrth Iddynt Bleidleisio; Form 4 (Ffurflen 4): Form of Directions for the Guidance of the Voters in Voting; Ffurf Cyfarwyddiadau i Gynorthwyo'r Pleidleiswyr Wrth Iddynt Bleidleisio (combined polls));

(ii)   the Local Elections (Principal Areas) (Welsh Forms) Order 2007, SI 2007/1015, arts 6(d), 8(d), Sch 2 (Form 4 (Ffurflen 4): Form of Directions for the Guidance of the Voters in Voting; Ffurf Cyfarwyddiadau i Gynorthwyo'r Pleidleiswyr Wrth Iddynt Bleidleisio), Sch 4 (Form 4 (Ffurflen 4): Form of Directions for the Guidance of the Voters in Voting; Ffurf Cyfarwyddiadau i Gynorthwyo'r Pleidleiswyr Wrth Iddynt Bleidleisio (combined polls));

(iii) the Local Elections (Communities) (Welsh Forms) Order 2007, SI 2007/1013, arts 6(d), 8(d), Sch 2 (Form 4 (Ffurflen 4): Form of Directions for the Guidance of the Voters in Voting; Ffurf Cyfarwyddiadau i Gynorthwyo'r Pleidleiswyr Wrth Iddynt Bleidleisio), Sch 4 (Form 4 (Ffurflen 4): Form of Directions for the Guidance of the Voters in Voting; Ffurf Cyfarwyddiadau i Gynorthwyo'r Pleidleiswyr Wrth Iddynt Bleidleisio (combined polls)); and

(iv) the European Parliamentary Elections (Welsh Forms) Order 2009, SI 2009/781, art 6(1)(j), Sch 2 (Form 10 (Ffurflen 10): Guidance for Voters; Cyfarwyddiadau i Bleidleisio).

18 Representation of the People Act 1983 Sch 1 r 29(4); Parish and Community Meetings (Polls) Rules 1987, SI 1987/1, Schedule r 11(4); European Parliamentary Elections Regulations 2004, SI 2004/293, Sch 1 para 32(6) (as substituted: see note 3); Local Elections (Principal Areas) (England and Wales) Rules 2006, SI 2006/3304, Sch 2 r 26(6); Local Elections (Parishes and Communities) (England and Wales) Rules 2006, SI 2006/3305, Sch 2 r 26(6); National Assembly for Wales (Representation of the People) Order 2007, SI 2007/236, Sch 5 para 37(14); Local Authorities (Mayoral Elections) (England and Wales) Regulations 2007, SI 2007/1024, Sch 1 r 28(6); Greater London Authority Elections Rules 2007, SI 2007/3541, Sch 1 r 28(8), Sch 2 r 29(8), Sch 3 r 28(8). As to the grounds on which a ballot paper may be rejected during the count see PARA 427 et seq; and as to the treatment of rejected votes see PARA 431 et seq.

The person who is required or authorised to give or display any document, which under or by virtue of the Representation of the People Act 1983 is required or authorised to be given to voters or displayed in any place for the purposes of a parliamentary or local government election, must, as he thinks appropriate, give or display or otherwise make available in such form as he thinks appropriate the document in Braille or in languages other than English, graphical representations of the information contained in the document and other means of making the information contained in the document accessible to persons who might not otherwise have reasonable access to the information: s 199B(1), (2) (s 199B added by the Electoral Administration Act 2006 s 36). Such a person must also, as he thinks appropriate, make available the information contained in the document in such audible form as he thinks appropriate: Representation of the People Act 1983 s 199B(3) (as so added). Although these provisions do not apply to either the nomination paper or the ballot paper (see PARAS 260, 386) (see s 199B(4) (as so added)), the returning officer at a parliamentary election or a local government election may cause to be displayed at every polling station in the election an enlarged sample copy of the ballot paper (see s 199B(5) (as so added)); and he must provide at every polling station in the election an enlarged handheld sample copy of the ballot paper for the assistance of voters who are partially sighted (s 199B(7) (as so added)). As to the form of the sample copies see s 199B(6), (8) (as so added); and see also head (c) in the text. The Representation of the People Act 1983 s 199B is applied and modified for the purpose of local authority mayoral elections in England and Wales by the Local Authorities (Mayoral Elections) (England and Wales) Regulations 2007, SI 2007/1024, reg 3(2)–(5), Sch 2 Table 1 (see PARA 11 note 14); and the Representation of the People Act 1983 s 199B has effect also for the purposes of local authority referendums, subject to the modifications specified, in relation to Wales, by the Local Authorities (Conduct of Referendums) (Wales) Regulations 2008, SI 2008/1848, reg 8(2), Sch 4 Table 1, and, in relation to England, by the Local Authorities (Conduct of Referendums) (England) Regulations 2012, SI 2012/323, regs 8(2), 11–13, Sch 4 Table 1 (see PARA 15 note 2). It is specifically provided that the returning officer at a local government election (except at a London Authority election) may provide copies of the notice mentioned in head (a) in the text in Braille or translated into languages other than English as he considers appropriate, provided that these notices are accurate reproductions, in Braille or that other language, of that notice: Local Elections (Principal Areas) (England and Wales) Rules 2006, SI 2006/3304, Sch 2 r 26(7); Local Elections (Parishes and Communities) (England and Wales) Rules 2006, SI 2006/3305, Sch 2 r 26(7); Local Authorities (Mayoral Elections) (England and Wales) Regulations 2007, SI 2007/1024, Sch 1 r 28(7). See also the National Assembly for Wales (Representation of the People) Order 2007, SI 2007/236, art 141, which makes similar provision, except that the languages specified are languages other than English and Welsh.

The notice to be exhibited pursuant to head (a) in the text for the purposes of an Authority election must be exhibited outside the polling station and/or inside the polling station (in the communal areas, and in every voting compartment): see the Greater London Authority Elections Rules 2007, SI 2007/3541, Sch 1 r 28(8), Sch 2 r 29(8), Sch 3 r 28(8). The GLRO must prepare and provide each CRO with the notices to be exhibited under Sch 1 r 28(8), Sch 2 r 29(8), Sch 3 r 28(8), except that the CRO must prepare the notices to be exhibited under Sch 1 r 28(8) at a constituency members election that is not an ordinary election: see Sch 1 r 29(1), Sch 2 r 30(1), Sch 3 r 29(1). At an ordinary election, the GLRO must prepare the notices and versions of notices to be exhibited under Sch 1 r 28(8) and supply them to the CRO in the appropriate form, and they may include such alternative information relating to Authority elections as meets with the requirements of r 8, Sch 9 ('the Notices Schedule': see r 2(1)), and as the GLRO may decide: see Sch 1 r 29(3), (5). The CRO may also prepare, and the GLRO may prepare and provide each CRO with, as the case may be, versions of the notices in such other form as he thinks appropriate, in accordance with the Representation of the People Act 1983 s 199B: see the Greater London Authority Elections Rules 2007, SI 2007/3541, Sch 1 r 29(2), Sch 2 r 30(2), Sch 3 r 29(2). The enlarged sample copies of the ballot paper that the CRO or GLRO is required to provide, or cause to be displayed at every polling station, in accordance with the Representation of the People Act 1983 s 199B(5), (7), must be printed on paper of the same colour as the ballot paper at the election (and they must be provided to the CRO by the GLRO, where the CRO is not required to provide them): Greater London Authority Elections Rules 2007, SI 2007/3541, Sch 1 r 28(7), Sch 2 r 29(7), Sch 3 r 28(7). Notices for the guidance of voters exhibited under Sch 1 r 28(8), Sch 2 r 29(8), Sch 3 r 28(8), or under Sch 1 r 29(2), Sch 2 r 30(2), Sch 3 r 29(2), must be in the appropriate form, but they may include such alternative information relating to Authority elections as meets with the requirements of the Notices Schedule, and as the CRO may decide for a London constituency members election, or as the GLRO may decide otherwise: see Sch 1 r 29(3), Sch 2 r 30(3), Sch 3 r 29(3). Notices provided under Sch 1 r 29(2), Sch 2 r 30(2), or Sch 3 r 29(2) may, if the CRO agrees, be exhibited at any polling station outside the polling station and/or inside the polling station (in the communal areas, and in every voting compartment): see Sch 1 r 29(4), Sch 2 r 30(4), Sch 3 r 29(4). In accordance with the Notices Schedule, notices must be provided by the GLRO for the guidance of voters in accordance with the constituency members election rules, the London members election rules, or the mayoral election rules: Sch 9 paras 1, 2. All notices provided must be of the same description and appearance or in a form to the like effect for use at all polling stations in all Assembly constituencies (Sch 9 para 4); and they may contain any information providing guidance to voters as to how to exercise their vote in a manner that will ensure that it is regarded as validly cast and can be efficiently processed by the electronic counting system (if one is in use), but they must not contain any material referring to or promoting any candidate or party at the election (other than such name and particulars of such candidate or registered party as may appear on a ballot paper at the election), or any example or illustration referring to a candidate or a registered party that does not equally refer to all candidates and registered parties (as the case may be) at the election (Sch 9 para 5). Notices for the guidance of voters to be exhibited outside the polling station, or inside the polling station (in the communal areas, and in a voting compartment), may differ depending on where they are to be displayed: Sch 9 para 3. Notices for display inside a polling station must contain information explaining which election each ballot paper is for, how many votes a voter has in each election, the marks to be used, and the manner in which they should be used, in order to ensure that a vote is counted for any candidate or party (as the case may be), whether or not the voter should fold the ballot paper in two before showing the presiding officer the number and the other unique identifying mark on the back and putting it in the ballot box, which ballot box the voter is to put their ballot paper into after recording their vote, and what to do if the voter spoils a ballot paper (Sch 9 para 6);

and notices for display inside a polling station may also contain information giving examples or illustrating of any of the kinds of information in Sch 9 para 5 (Sch 9 para 7). Notices for display inside a voting compartment must contain information explaining which election each ballot paper is for, and how many votes a voter has in each election: Sch 9 para 8. Notices for display inside a polling booth may also contain information explaining the marks to be used, and the manner in which they should be used, in order to ensure that a vote is counted for any candidate or party (as the case may be), whether or not the voter should fold the ballot paper in two before showing the presiding officer the number and the other unique identifying mark on the back and putting it in the ballot box, which ballot box the voter is to put their ballot paper into after recording their vote, and what to do if the voter spoils a ballot paper; and such notices may also contain information giving examples or illustration of any of the information mentioned in Sch 9 para 6: see Sch 9 para 9. All notices for display must be easily legible: Sch 9 para 10. As to the meaning of 'electronic counting system' see PARA 443 note 18. As to the constituency members election rules, the London members election rules and the mayoral election rules see PARA 383 note 10.

Where any document which by virtue of the European Parliamentary Elections Regulations 2004, SI 2004/293, is required or authorised to be given to voters or displayed in any place for the purposes of a European Parliamentary election, the person who is required or authorised to give or display the document must, as he thinks appropriate (see reg 122A(1), (2), (3) (reg 122A added by SI 2009/186)):

(1)   give or display or otherwise make available, in such form as he thinks appropriate, the document in Braille, the document in languages other than English, graphical representations of the information contained in the document, and other means of making the information contained in the document accessible to persons who might not otherwise have reasonable access to the information (see the European Parliamentary Elections Regulations 2004, SI 2004/293, reg 122A(2) (as so added)); and also

(2)   make available the information contained in the document in such audible form as he thinks appropriate (see reg 122A(3) (as so added)).

Specifically, the local returning officer at a European Parliamentary election:

(a)   must cause to be displayed at every polling station in the election an enlarged sample copy of the ballot paper in accordance with the European Parliamentary Elections Regulations 2004, SI 2004/293, Sch 1 r 32(5)(a) (see head (c) in the text), which must have printed the words 'Vote once (X) in one blank box' at the top, and may include a translation of those words into such other languages as the local returning officer thinks appropriate (see reg 122A(5), (6) (as so added)); and

(b)   must provide at every polling station in the election an enlarged hand-held sample copy of the ballot paper for the assistance of voters who are partially sighted, which must be clearly marked as a specimen provided only for the guidance of voters (see reg 122A(7), (8) (as so added)).

Heads (1) and (2) above do not apply to the nomination paper and the ballot paper (see PARAS 260, 386): see reg 122A(4); and PARAS 260 note 60, 386 note 3.

19   As to the provision of compartments in polling stations see PARA 390.

20   Representation of the People Act 1983 Sch 1 r 29(5) (amended by the Representation of the People Act 1985 s 24, Sch 4 para 79); Parish and Community Meetings (Polls) Rules 1987, SI 1987/1, Schedule r 11(5); European Parliamentary Elections Regulations 2004, SI 2004/293, Sch 1 para 32(7) (as substituted: see note 3); Local Elections (Principal Areas) (England and Wales) Rules 2006, SI 2006/3304, Sch 2 r 26(8); Local Elections (Parishes and Communities) (England and Wales) Rules 2006, SI 2006/3305, Sch 2 r 26(8); National Assembly for Wales (Representation of the People) Order 2007, SI 2007/236, Sch 5 para 37(15), (16); Greater London Authority Elections Rules 2007, SI 2007/3541, Sch 9 paras 8, 9. Although a notice complying with head (b) in the text is specified in the local authority mayoral election (combination of polls) rules (see the Local Authorities (Mayoral Elections) (England and Wales) Regulations 2007, SI 2007/1024, Sch 3 r 28(10)), no such provision is made in Sch 1 r 28 for the purposes of a local authority mayoral election taken alone, although the predecessor rules of conduct for local authority mayoral elections did make such provision (see the Local Authorities (Mayoral Elections) (England and Wales) Regulations 2002, SI 2002/185, Sch 1 r 28(6), Appendix of Forms (Form 9: notices for display in polling booths (Notice A—for use where there are only two mayoral candidates, Notice B—for use where there are three or more candidates)) (revoked)).

The statutory notice:

(1)   must read, in the case of a parliamentary election: 'Vote for one candidate only. Put no other mark on the ballot paper, or your vote may not be counted' (see the Representation of the People Act 1983 Sch 1 r 29(5) (as so amended));

(2)   must read, in the case of a European parliamentary election: 'Put only one cross on the
        ballot paper. Put no other mark on the ballot paper, or your vote may not count' (see
        the European Parliamentary Elections Regulations 2004, SI 2004/293, Sch 1 para 32(7)
        (as so substituted));

(3)   must read, in the case of a local government election for a principal area, parish or
        community: 'Vote for no more than [..] candidates [Vote for ONE candidate only]. Put
        no other mark on the ballot paper, or your vote may not be counted' (see the Local
        Elections (Principal Areas) (England and Wales) Rules 2006, SI 2006/3304, Sch 2
        r 26(8); and the Local Elections (Parishes and Communities) (England and Wales)
        Rules 2006, SI 2006/3305, Sch 2 r 26(8));

(4)   must comply, in the case of a London Authority election, with the requirements of the
        Greater London Authority Elections Rules 2007, SI 2007/3541, Sch 9 paras 8, 9 (see
        note 18);

(5)   must read:
        (a)   in the case of a contested Welsh Assembly constituency election where votes are
                also given at the polling station in respect of a contested regional election: 'Vote
                for one candidate only on the constituency ballot paper coloured [*colour of ballot
                paper*]. Put no other mark on the ballot paper or your vote may not be
                counted/Pleidleisiwch dros un ymgeisydd yn unig ar y papur pleidleisio etholaeth
                lliw [*lliw'r papur pleidleisio*]. Peidiwch â rhoi unrhyw farc arall ar y papur
                pleidleisio, neu fe all na chaiff eich pleidlais ei chyfrif.'; or, in any other case at a
                constituency election: 'Vote for one candidate only on the ballot paper. Put no
                other mark on the ballot paper or your vote may not be counted/Pleidleisiwch
                dros un ymgeisydd yn unig ar y papur pleidleisio. Peidiwch â rhoi unrhyw farc
                arall ar y papur pleidleisio, neu fe all na chaiff eich pleidlais ei chyfrif' (National
                Assembly for Wales (Representation of the People) Order 2007, SI 2007/236,
                Sch 5 para 37(15)); and
        (b)   in the case of a contested Welsh Assembly regional election where votes are also
                given at the polling station in respect of a contested constituency election: 'Vote
                once only on the regional ballot paper coloured [*colour of ballot paper*]. Put no
                other mark on the ballot paper or your vote may not be counted/Pleidleisiwch
                unwaith yn unig ar y papur pleidleisio rhanbarthol lliw [*lliw'r papur pleidleisio*].
                Peidiwch â rhoi unrhyw farc arall ar y papur pleidleisio, neu fe all na chaiff eich
                pleidlais ei chyfrif.'; or, in any other case at a regional election: 'Vote once only on
                the ballot paper. Put no other mark on the ballot paper or your vote may not be
                counted/Pleidleisiwch unwaith yn unig ar y papur pleidleisio. Peidiwch â rhoi
                unrhyw farc arall ar y papur pleidleisio, neu fe all na chaiff eich pleidlais ei
                chyfrif' (Sch 5 para 37(16));

(6)   must read, in the case of a poll taken consequent on a parish meeting on a question
        which involves appointment to office: 'Vote for [..] candidates only as [*name of office*].
        Put no other mark on the ballot paper, or your vote may not be counted' (see the Parish
        and Community Meetings (Polls) Rules 1987, SI 1987/1, Schedule r 11(5)).

Where elections take place in Wales see also the forms issued partly in English and partly in
Welsh in the Parliamentary Elections (Welsh Forms) Order 2007, SI 2007/1014, art 6(c), Sch 2
(Form 3 (Ffurflen 3): the notice prescribed by rule 29(5); Yr hysbysiad a ragnodwyd gan Roel
29(5)); the Local Elections (Principal Areas) (Welsh Forms) Order 2007, SI 2007/1015, art 7(2),
Sch 3 (Form 9 (Ffurflen 9): the notice prescribed by rule 26(8); hysbysiad a ragnodwyd gan Roel
26(8)); the Local Elections (Communities) (Welsh Forms) Order 2007, SI 2007/1013, art 7(2),
Sch 3 (Form 9 (Ffurflen 9): the notice prescribed by rule 26(8); hysbysiad a ragnodwyd gan Roel
26(8)); and the European Parliamentary Elections (Welsh Forms) Order 2009, SI 2009/781,
art 6(1)(k), Sch 2 (Form 11 (Ffurflen 11)).

21 Representation of the People Act 1983 Sch 1 r 29(3A)(a) (as added: see note 6); European
    Parliamentary Elections Regulations 2004, SI 2004/293, Sch 1 para 32(5)(a) (as substituted: see
    note 3); Local Elections (Principal Areas) (England and Wales) Rules 2006, SI 2006/3304, Sch 2
    r 26(5)(a); Local Elections (Parishes and Communities) (England and Wales) Rules 2006,
    SI 2006/3305, Sch 2 r 26(5)(a); National Assembly for Wales (Representation of the People)
    Order 2007, SI 2007/236, Sch 5 para 37(7)(a); Local Authorities (Mayoral Elections) (England
    and Wales) Regulations 2007, SI 2007/1024, Sch 1 r 28(5)(a). See also the Representation of the
    People Act 1983 s 199B(5); the National Assembly for Wales (Representation of the People)
    Order 2007, SI 2007/236, Sch 5 para 37(7)(b); the Greater London Authority Elections
    Rules 2007, SI 2007/3541, Sch 1 r 28(7), Sch 2 r 29(7), Sch 3 r 28(7); and note 18.

22 National Assembly for Wales (Representation of the People) Order 2007, SI 2007/236, Sch 5
    para 37(17). As to the statement of persons nominated see PARA 267.

23 At a London members election, the CRO must provide each polling station with a notice of the death of any person (ie an individual candidate who is named (or is to be named) in the ballot papers, or a candidate whose name appears on a party list), which information has been passed on to him by the GLRO in accordance with the Greater London Authority Elections Rules 2007, SI 2007/3541, Sch 2 r 15(4) (see PARA 262 notes 9, 15): Sch 2 r 29(3)(d). As to references to party lists in elections for the return of London members of the London Assembly see PARA 255 note 23.

In the case of a European parliamentary election, where proof has been given to the returning officer's satisfaction of the death of an individual candidate or a candidate named on a registered party's list or, he must request each local returning officer to provide each presiding officer with a sufficient number of notices to this effect for display in every compartment of every polling station: European Parliamentary Elections Regulations 2004, SI 2004/293, Sch 1 para 32(9) (as substituted: see note 3). As to the meaning of 'list' for these purposes see PARA 230 note 29. As to the system of candidature whereby registered parties submit lists of candidates see PARA 340.

24 As to the equipment of polling stations to be used where polls at elections or referendums are taken together see PARA 19.

392. Loan of equipment provided for elections. Any ballot boxes, fittings and compartments provided for parliamentary elections[1] out of money provided by Parliament may, on request, be lent to:

(1)   the returning officer at a local government election[2];

(2)   the returning officer at a poll consequent on a parish meeting on a question involving an appointment to office[3]; or

(3)   a constituency returning officer at a Welsh Assembly election[4],

on such terms and conditions as:

(a)   pursuant to head (1) above, the Secretary of State[5]; or

(b)   pursuant to head (2) above, the Treasury[6]; or

(c)   pursuant to head (3) above, the Electoral Commission[7],

may determine[8].

Any ballot boxes, fittings and compartments provided by, or belonging to, a local authority[9], must, on request, and if not required for immediate use by that authority, be lent to the officer listed under head (1), head (2) or head (3) above for the purposes of such an election or poll, on such terms and conditions as may be agreed[10].

1   As to the provision and allotment of polling stations see PARA 390; and as to the equipment of polling stations see PARA 391. As to the meaning of 'parliamentary election' see PARA 9.

2   See the Representation of the People Act 1983 s 47(1) (amended by SI 1991/1728). As to the meaning of 'local government election' see PARA 11. As to returning officers for local government elections see PARA 354 et seq.

The Representation of the People Act 1983 s 47 is applied and modified for the purpose of local authority mayoral elections in England and Wales by the Local Authorities (Mayoral Elections) (England and Wales) Regulations 2007, SI 2007/1024, reg 3(2)–(5), Sch 2 Table 1 (see PARA 11 note 14); and the Representation of the People Act 1983 s 47 has effect also for the purposes of local authority referendums, subject to the modifications specified, in relation to Wales, by the Local Authorities (Conduct of Referendums) (Wales) Regulations 2008, SI 2008/1848, reg 8(2), Sch 4 Table 1, and, in relation to England, by the Local Authorities (Conduct of Referendums) (England) Regulations 2012, SI 2012/323, regs 8(2), 11–13, Sch 4 Table 1 (see PARA 15 note 2).

3   See the Local Government Act 1972 s 99, Sch 12 para 21(1). As to polls consequent on a parish meeting on a question involving appointment to office see PARA 200 et seq; and as to the returning officer at such a poll see PARA 356.

4   See the National Assembly for Wales (Representation of the People) Order 2007, SI 2007/236, art 25(1). As to the meaning of 'Assembly election' see PARA 3 note 2; and as to the meaning of 'constituency returning officer' at such an election see PARA 18 note 2.

5   See the Representation of the People Act 1983 s 47(1) (as amended: see note 2). As from a day to be appointed under the Political Parties, Elections and Referendums Act 2000 s 163(2), the reference in the Representation of the People Act 1983 s 47(1) to the Secretary of State is

repealed and a reference to the Electoral Commission added in its place: see s 47(1) (as so amended; prospectively further amended by the Political Parties, Elections and Referendums Act 2000 s 158(1), Sch 21 para 6(1), (4)). At the date at which this volume states the law, no such day had been appointed. As to the Secretary of State see PARA 2. As to the Electoral Commission see PARA 34 et seq.

6   See the Local Government Act 1972 Sch 12 para 21(1). As to the Treasury see CONSTITUTIONAL LAW AND HUMAN RIGHTS vol 8(2) (Reissue) PARAS 512–517.

7   See the National Assembly for Wales (Representation of the People) Order 2007, SI 2007/236, art 25(1).

8   Representation of the People Act 1983 s 47(1) (as amended: see note 2); Local Government Act 1972 Sch 12 para 21(1); National Assembly for Wales (Representation of the People) Order 2007, SI 2007/236, art 25(1).

9   Ie within the meaning of the Local Government Act 1972: see LOCAL GOVERNMENT vol 69 (2009) PARA 23.

10 Representation of the People Act 1983 s 47(2) (amended by the Education Reform Act 1988 s 237, Sch 13 Pt I); Local Government Act 1972 Sch 12 para 21(2); National Assembly for Wales (Representation of the People) Order 2007, SI 2007/236, art 25(2).

393.   Appointment of presiding officers and their clerks by returning officer. At an election[1], or at a poll taken consequent on a parish meeting on a question which involves appointment to office[2], the returning officer[3] must appoint and pay a presiding officer[4] to attend at each polling station[5]. The returning officer must also appoint and pay such clerks as may be necessary[6] for the purposes of the election or poll[7]. However, the returning officer must not appoint for these purposes any person who has been employed by, or on behalf of, a candidate in or about the election or poll[8]. The returning officer may, if he thinks fit, preside at a polling station[9].

A presiding officer may do, by the clerks appointed to assist him, any act (including the asking of questions) which he is required or authorised to do at a polling station except order the arrest, exclusion or removal of any person from the polling station[10].

Where the poll at an election is taken together with the poll at another election or referendum, special provision is made for the appointment of presiding officers and their clerks[11].

1   Ie a parliamentary election, a local government election (which includes any London Authority election and a local authority mayoral election), a Welsh Assembly constituency or regional election or a European parliamentary election. As to the meanings of 'Assembly election', 'constituency election' and 'regional election' see PARA 3 note 2. As to the meaning of 'parliamentary election' see PARA 9. As to the meanings of 'Authority election' and 'local government election' see PARA 11. As to elections in the City of London see PARA 33. As to elections for the return of a local authority mayor see PARA 198; and as to European parliamentary elections see PARA 217 et seq.

2   As to polls consequent on a parish meeting on a question involving appointment to office see PARA 200 et seq.

3   As to returning officers generally see PARA 350 et seq. At any London Authority election, the duties mentioned in the text are undertaken by the constituency returning officer ('CRO'): see the Greater London Authority Elections Rules 2007, SI 2007/3541, Sch 1 r 25(1), (2), Sch 2 r 26(1), (2), Sch 3 r 25(1), (2). As to the meaning of the 'constituency returning officer' ('CRO') see PARA 211 note 9. At a European parliamentary election, the reference is to a local returning officer (see PARA 360 et seq): see the European Parliamentary Elections Regulations 2004, SI 2004/293, Sch 1 para 30 (Sch 1 substituted by SI 2009/186). The reference is to a constituency returning officer at a Welsh Assembly election (see the National Assembly for Wales (Representation of the People) Order 2007, SI 2007/236, Sch 5 para 35(1), (3)), except that a regional returning officer may appoint and pay clerks for the purposes of a regional election (see Sch 5 para 35(2); and notes 5–7). As to the meanings of 'constituency returning officer' and 'regional returning officer' for the purposes of Welsh Assembly elections see PARA 18 note 2.

4   An oral appointment of a presiding officer is apparently sufficient: see *R v Garvey* (1887) 16 Cox CC 252. At a poll consequent on a parish meeting, although the returning officer may appoint a presiding officer and such clerks as may be necessary (see also the text and notes 6–7), their remuneration is discretionary: see the Parish and Community Meetings (Polls) Rules 1987, SI 1987/1, Schedule r 10(1).

5   Representation of the People Act 1983 Sch 1 r 26(1); Parish and Community Meetings (Polls) Rules 1987, SI 1987/1, Schedule r 10(1); European Parliamentary Elections Regulations 2004, SI 2004/293, Sch 1 para 30(1) (as substituted: see note 3); Local Elections (Principal Areas) (England and Wales) Rules 2006, SI 2006/3304, Sch 2 r 24(1); Local Elections (Parishes and Communities) (England and Wales) Rules 2006, SI 2006/3305, Sch 2 r 24(1); National Assembly for Wales (Representation of the People) Order 2007, SI 2007/236, Sch 5 para 35(1); Local Authorities (Mayoral Elections) (England and Wales) Regulations 2007, SI 2007/1024, Sch 1 r 26(1); Greater London Authority Elections Rules 2007, SI 2007/3541, Sch 1 r 25(1), Sch 2 r 26(1), Sch 3 r 25(1). As to the provision and allotment of polling stations see PARA 390.

     A presiding officer is not appointed to attend at each polling station for the purposes of a Welsh Assembly regional election, because votes at such an election are cast at the same time and place as at a constituency election; however, clerks may be appointed to assist the regional returning officer in his duties: see the National Assembly for Wales (Representation of the People) Order 2007, SI 2007/236, Sch 5 para 35(2); and see the text and notes 6–7.

6   Appointments are made of clerks as mentioned in the text to assist the presiding officer and to assist in counting the votes. Because non-manual counting methods may be employed at London Authority elections, the CRO may also appoint and pay such technical assistants as may be necessary for the purposes of such an election: see the Greater London Authority Elections Rules 2007, SI 2007/3541, Sch 1 r 25(1), Sch 2 r 26(1), Sch 3 r 25(1). In practice, the limits set of maximum charges, to which a returning officer is subject in claiming his expenses, restrict the number of clerks who are appointed: see PARA 352 et seq. See also note 4.

7   Representation of the People Act 1983 Sch 1 r 26(1); Parish and Community Meetings (Polls) Rules 1987, SI 1987/1, Schedule r 10(1); European Parliamentary Elections Regulations 2004, SI 2004/293, Sch 1 para 30(1) (as substituted: see note 3); Local Elections (Principal Areas) (England and Wales) Rules 2006, SI 2006/3304, Sch 2 r 24(1); Local Elections (Parishes and Communities) (England and Wales) Rules 2006, SI 2006/3305, Sch 2 r 24(1); National Assembly for Wales (Representation of the People) Order 2007, SI 2007/236, Sch 5 para 35(1), (2); Local Authorities (Mayoral Elections) (England and Wales) Regulations 2007, SI 2007/1024, Sch 1 r 26(1); Greater London Authority Elections Rules 2007, SI 2007/3541, Sch 1 r 25(1), Sch 2 r 26(1), Sch 3 r 25(1). At a Welsh Assembly regional election, the regional returning officer (ie as well as the constituency returning officer) must appoint and pay such clerks as may be necessary for the purposes of such an election: see the National Assembly for Wales (Representation of the People) Order 2007, SI 2007/236, Sch 5 para 35(2); and see note 5.

8   Representation of the People Act 1983 Sch 1 r 26(1); Parish and Community Meetings (Polls) Rules 1987, SI 1987/1, Schedule r 10(1); European Parliamentary Elections Regulations 2004, SI 2004/293, Sch 1 para 30(1) (as substituted: see note 3); Local Elections (Principal Areas) (England and Wales) Rules 2006, SI 2006/3304, Sch 2 r 24(1); Local Elections (Parishes and Communities) (England and Wales) Rules 2006, SI 2006/3305, Sch 2 r 24(1); National Assembly for Wales (Representation of the People) Order 2007, SI 2007/236, Sch 5 para 35(1), (2); Local Authorities (Mayoral Elections) (England and Wales) Regulations 2007, SI 2007/1024, Sch 1 r 26(1); Greater London Authority Elections Rules 2007, SI 2007/3541, Sch 1 r 25(1), Sch 2 r 26(1), Sch 3 r 25(1).

     The restriction mentioned in the text applies to any person who has been employed in or about a London members election, either by or on behalf of a candidate or a registered party which has been nominated: see the Greater London Authority Elections Rules 2007, SI 2007/3541, Sch 2 r 26(1). As to the meaning of 'registered political party' for these purposes see PARA 256 note 27.

     In the case of a European parliamentary election, the restriction applies to any person who has been employed by or on behalf of a registered party or individual candidate in or about the election: see the European Parliamentary Elections Regulations 2004, SI 2004/293, Sch 1 para 30(1) (as so substituted). As to the meaning of 'registered party' for the purposes of a European parliamentary election see PARA 230 note 29; and as to the meaning of 'individual candidate' at a European parliamentary election see PARA 230 note 32.

     In the case of a Welsh Assembly constituency or regional election, the restriction applies to any person who has been employed either by, or on behalf of, a candidate, or a registered political party, in or about the election: see the National Assembly for Wales (Representation of the People) Order 2007, SI 2007/236, Sch 5 para 35(1), (2). As to the meaning of 'registered political party' see PARA 215 note 19; and as to the meaning of 'candidate' for these purposes see PARA 230 note 19.

9   Representation of the People Act 1983 Sch 1 r 26(2); Parish and Community Meetings (Polls) Rules 1987, SI 1987/1, Schedule r 10(2); European Parliamentary Elections Regulations 2004, SI 2004/293, Sch 1 para 30(2) (as substituted: see note 3); Local Elections (Principal Areas) (England and Wales) Rules 2006, SI 2006/3304, Sch 2 r 24(2); Local Elections (Parishes and Communities) (England and Wales) Rules 2006, SI 2006/3305, Sch 2 r 24(2); National Assembly for Wales (Representation of the People) Order 2007, SI 2007/236, Sch 5 para 35(3); Local Authorities (Mayoral Elections) (England and Wales) Regulations 2007, SI 2007/1024, Sch 1 r 26(2); Greater London Authority Elections Rules 2007, SI 2007/3541, Sch 1 r 25(2), Sch 2 r 26(2), Sch 3 r 25(2). Where a returning officer presides as mentioned in the text, the provisions in the rules that relate to a presiding officer apply to him, with the necessary modifications as to things to be done by the returning officer to the presiding officer, or by the presiding officer to the returning officer: Representation of the People Act 1983 Sch 1 r 26(2); Parish and Community Meetings (Polls) Rules 1987, SI 1987/1, Schedule r 10(2); European Parliamentary Elections Regulations 2004, SI 2004/293, Sch 1 para 30(2) (as so substituted); Local Elections (Principal Areas) (England and Wales) Rules 2006, SI 2006/3304, Sch 2 r 24(2); Local Elections (Parishes and Communities) (England and Wales) Rules 2006, SI 2006/3305, Sch 2 r 24(2); National Assembly for Wales (Representation of the People) Order 2007, SI 2007/236, Sch 5 para 35(3); Local Authorities (Mayoral Elections) (England and Wales) Regulations 2007, SI 2007/1024, Sch 1 r 26(2); Greater London Authority Elections Rules 2007, SI 2007/3541, Sch 1 r 25(2), Sch 2 r 26(2), Sch 3 r 25(2).

10 Representation of the People Act 1983 Sch 1 r 26(3); Parish and Community Meetings (Polls) Rules 1987, SI 1987/1, Schedule r 10(3); European Parliamentary Elections Regulations 2004, SI 2004/293, Sch 1 para 30(3) (as substituted: see note 3); Local Elections (Principal Areas) (England and Wales) Rules 2006, SI 2006/3304, Sch 2 r 24(3); Local Elections (Parishes and Communities) (England and Wales) Rules 2006, SI 2006/3305, Sch 2 r 24(3); National Assembly for Wales (Representation of the People) Order 2007, SI 2007/236, Sch 5 para 35(4); Local Authorities (Mayoral Elections) (England and Wales) Regulations 2007, SI 2007/1024, Sch 1 r 26(3); Greater London Authority Elections Rules 2007, SI 2007/3541, Sch 1 r 25(3), Sch 2 r 26(3), Sch 3 r 25(3). As to the presiding officer's duty to keep order in a polling station see PARA 396.

11 As to polls at elections or referendums which are taken together see PARA 16 et seq.

394. Appointment of polling and counting agents. Before the commencement of the poll at an election[1], or of a poll taken consequent on a parish meeting on a question which involves appointment to office[2], each candidate[3] (or, in certain cases, his election agent)[4] may appoint[5]:

(1)   polling agents to attend at polling stations for the purpose of detecting personation[6]; and

(2)   counting agents to attend at the counting of the votes (or, in the case of a European parliamentary election, to attend at the verification of the ballot paper accounts and the counting of the votes)[7].

However, the number of counting agents to attend at the counting of the votes for an election may be limited by the returning officer so that the number is the same in the case of each candidate, and so that the number allowed to a candidate is not (except in special circumstances) less than the number obtained by dividing the number of clerks employed on the counting by the number of candidates[8].

Written notice of the appointment of polling or counting agents, stating the names and addresses of the persons appointed, must be given by the candidate (or, as the case may be, by the person authorised to make the appointments) to the returning officer[9]:

(a)   in the case of a parliamentary or Welsh Assembly election, not later than the second day before the day of the poll[10];

(b)   in the case of a local government, or European parliamentary, election, not later than the fifth day before the day of the poll[11]; or

(c)   in the case of a poll consequent on a parish meeting on a question involving appointment to office, not later than the third day before the day of the poll[12].

If an agent appointed under head (1) or head (2) above dies, or becomes incapable of acting, the candidate (or, as the case may be, the person authorised to make the appointments) may appoint another such agent in his place, and must forthwith give to the returning officer written notice of the name and address of the agent so appointed[13].

A candidate may himself do any act or thing which any polling or counting agent of his, if appointed, would have been authorised to do or may assist any such agent in doing any such act or thing[14]; and, at elections where election agents may be appointed, a candidate's election agent may do or assist in doing anything which a polling or counting agent of his is authorised to do, and anything required or authorised to be done in the presence of the polling or counting agents may be done in the presence of any candidate's election agent instead of the polling agent or counting agents[15].

Where any act or thing is required or authorised to be done, by the rules governing the conduct of elections or polls, in the presence of the polling or counting agents, the non-attendance of any agent or agents at the time and place appointed for the purpose does not, if the act or thing is otherwise duly done, invalidate the act or thing done[16].

Any notice required to be given to a counting agent by the returning officer may be delivered at, or sent by post to, the address stated in the notice of appointment[17].

Where the poll at an election is taken together with the poll at another election or referendum, special provision is made for the appointment of polling and counting agents[18].

1   Ie a parliamentary election, a local government election (which includes any London Authority election and a local authority mayoral election), a Welsh Assembly constituency or regional election or a European parliamentary election. As to the meanings of 'Assembly election', 'constituency election' and 'regional election' see PARA 3 note 2. As to the meaning of 'parliamentary election' see PARA 9. As to the meanings of 'Authority election' and 'local government election' see PARA 11. As to elections in the City of London see PARA 33. As to elections for the return of a local authority mayor see PARA 198; and as to European parliamentary elections see PARA 217 et seq.

2   As to polls consequent on a parish meeting on a question involving appointment to office see PARA 200 et seq.

3   As to the meaning of 'candidate' generally see PARA 230. In the case of a London members election, the reference is to each individual candidate (but not a list candidate: see note 4): see the Greater London Authority Elections Rules 2007, SI 2007/3541, Sch 2 r 31(1)(a). As to individual candidates to be London members see LONDON GOVERNMENT vol 71 (2013) PARA 81. At a Welsh Assembly election, the reference is to each constituency candidate at a constituency election (see the National Assembly for Wales (Representation of the People) Order 2007, SI 2007/236, Sch 5 para 38(1)), and to each individual candidate at a regional election (see Sch 5 para 38(3)(a)). As to the meanings of 'candidate', 'constituency candidate' and 'individual candidate' for these purposes see PARA 230 note 19.

4   As to the appointment of election agents see PARA 231 et seq. In the case of a London members election, the reference in the text to an election agent is to the election agent of each list candidate: Greater London Authority Elections Rules 2007, SI 2007/3541, Sch 2 r 31(1)(b). As to references to party lists in elections for the return of London members of the London Assembly see PARA 255 note 23. In the case of a Welsh Assembly regional election, the reference in the text is to each election agent for a registered political party standing nominated: see the National Assembly for Wales (Representation of the People) Order 2007, SI 2007/236, Sch 5

para 38(3)(b). As to the meaning of 'registered political party' for these purposes see PARA 215 note 19. Individual candidates at a London members, or Welsh Assembly regional, election can appoint agents personally: see note 3.

At a European parliamentary election, only the election agent (or sub-agent) of a registered party standing nominated, or the election agent (or sub-agent) of an individual candidate, or any person authorised in writing by such an agent or candidate, may appoint agents under head (1) or head (2) in the text: see the European Parliamentary Elections Regulations 2004, SI 2004/293, Sch 1 para 33(1) (Sch 1 substituted by SI 2009/186). As to the meaning of 'registered party' for these purposes see PARA 230 note 29; and as to the meaning of 'individual candidate' see PARA 230 note 32. At any other election where election agents may be appointed (excepting from that group, a local government election for a principal area), any appointment under head (1) or head (2) in the text authorised by the rule set out in the text may be made, and the notice of appointment given to the returning officer, by the candidate's election agent, instead of by the candidate: Representation of the People Act 1983 Sch 1 r 30(5); National Assembly for Wales (Representation of the People) Order 2007, SI 2007/236, Sch 5 para 38(7); Local Authorities (Mayoral Elections) (England and Wales) Regulations 2007, SI 2007/1024, Sch 1 r 29(9); Greater London Authority Elections Rules 2007, SI 2007/3541, Sch 1 r 30(10), Sch 2 r 31(10), Sch 3 r 30(10). As to returning officers generally see PARA 350 et seq. At any London Authority election, the duties mentioned in the text are undertaken by the constituency returning officer ('CRO'): see the Greater London Authority Elections Rules 2007, SI 2007/3541, Sch 1 r 30(4)–(6), (8)–(10), (12), Sch 2 r 31(4)–(6), (8)–(10), (12), Sch 3 r 30(4)–(6), (8)–(10), (12). As to the meaning of the 'constituency returning officer' ('CRO') see PARA 211 note 9. At a European parliamentary election, the reference is to a local returning officer (see PARA 360 et seq): see the European Parliamentary Elections Regulations 2004, SI 2004/293, Sch 1 para 33(3)–(5), (7) (as so substituted). At a Welsh Assembly election, the reference is to a constituency returning officer, regardless of whether a constituency or regional election is in question: see the National Assembly for Wales (Representation of the People) Order 2007, SI 2007/236, Sch 5 para 38(2), (4)–(7), (9). As to the meaning of 'constituency returning officer' for these purposes see PARA 18 note 2.

5   Representation of the People Act 1983 Sch 1 r 30(1); Parish and Community Meetings (Polls) Rules 1987, SI 1987/1, Schedule r 12(1); European Parliamentary Elections Regulations 2004, SI 2004/293, Sch 1 para 33(1) (as substituted: see note 4); Local Elections (Principal Areas) (England and Wales) Rules 2006, SI 2006/3304, Sch 2 r 27(1); Local Elections (Parishes and Communities) (England and Wales) Rules 2006, SI 2006/3305, Sch 2 r 27(1); National Assembly for Wales (Representation of the People) Order 2007, SI 2007/236, Sch 5 para 38(1), (3); Local Authorities (Mayoral Elections) (England and Wales) Regulations 2007, SI 2007/1024, Sch 1 r 29(1); Greater London Authority Elections Rules 2007, SI 2007/3541, Sch 1 r 30(1), Sch 2 r 31(1), Sch 3 r 30(1). At a Welsh Assembly regional election, any appointment under head (1) or head (2) in the text may be made in relation to each Assembly constituency in the Assembly electoral region: see the National Assembly for Wales (Representation of the People) Order 2007, SI 2007/236, Sch 5 para 38(3). As to the meanings of 'Assembly constituency' and 'Assembly electoral region' see PARA 3 note 2.

6   Representation of the People Act 1983 Sch 1 r 30(1)(a); Parish and Community Meetings (Polls) Rules 1987, SI 1987/1, Schedule r 12(1)(a); European Parliamentary Elections Regulations 2004, SI 2004/293, Sch 1 para 33(1)(a) (as substituted: see note 4); Local Elections (Principal Areas) (England and Wales) Rules 2006, SI 2006/3304, Sch 2 r 27(1)(a); Local Elections (Parishes and Communities) (England and Wales) Rules 2006, SI 2006/3305, Sch 2 r 27(1)(a); National Assembly for Wales (Representation of the People) Order 2007, SI 2007/236, Sch 5 para 38(1)(a), (3)(i); Local Authorities (Mayoral Elections) (England and Wales) Regulations 2007, SI 2007/1024, Sch 1 r 29(1)(a); Greater London Authority Elections Rules 2007, SI 2007/3541, Sch 1 r 30(1)(a), Sch 2 r 31(1)(i), Sch 3 r 30(1)(a). As to the provision and allotment of polling stations see PARA 390. As to personation (which is both an offence and a corrupt practice) see PARA 730.

At a local government election, the same person may be appointed as a polling agent by more than one candidate: Local Elections (Principal Areas) (England and Wales) Rules 2006, SI 2006/3304, Sch 2 r 27(2); Local Elections (Parishes and Communities) (England and Wales) Rules 2006, SI 2006/3305, Sch 2 r 27(2); Local Authorities (Mayoral Elections) (England and Wales) Regulations 2007, SI 2007/1024, Sch 1 r 29(2); Greater London Authority Elections Rules 2007, SI 2007/3541, Sch 1 r 30(2), Sch 2 r 31(2), Sch 3 r 30(2).

At a poll consequent on a parish meeting on a question involving appointment to office, each candidate may appoint only one polling agent to attend at each polling station under head (1) in the text: see the Parish and Community Meetings (Polls) Rules 1987, SI 1987/1, Schedule r 12(1)(a).

7   Representation of the People Act 1983 Sch 1 r 30(1)(b); Parish and Community Meetings (Polls) Rules 1987, SI 1987/1, Schedule r 12(1)(b); European Parliamentary Elections Regulations 2004, SI 2004/293, Sch 1 para 33(1)(b) (as substituted: see note 4); Local Elections (Principal Areas) (England and Wales) Rules 2006, SI 2006/3304, Sch 2 r 27(1)(b); Local Elections (Parishes and Communities) (England and Wales) Rules 2006, SI 2006/3305, Sch 2 r 27(1)(b); National Assembly for Wales (Representation of the People) Order 2007, SI 2007/236, Sch 5 para 38(1)(b), (3)(ii); Local Authorities (Mayoral Elections) (England and Wales) Regulations 2007, SI 2007/1024, Sch 1 r 29(1)(b); Greater London Authority Elections Rules 2007, SI 2007/3541, Sch 1 r 30(1)(b), Sch 2 r 31(1)(ii), Sch 3 r 30(1)(b). As to the counting of votes at a local government election (except a London Authority election) see PARA 425; in relation to a local authority mayoral election see PARA 436; in relation to a London Authority election see PARA 444; in relation to a London mayoral election see PARA 451; in relation to a Welsh Assembly election see PARA 458; and as to the counting of votes at a European parliamentary election see PARA 466 et seq.

      At a poll consequent on a parish meeting on a question involving appointment to office, each candidate may appoint only one counting agent at the counting of the votes: see the Parish and Community Meetings (Polls) Rules 1987, SI 1987/1, Schedule r 12(1)(b). At a local government election, the same person may be appointed as a counting agent by more than one candidate: Local Elections (Principal Areas) (England and Wales) Rules 2006, SI 2006/3304, Sch 2 r 27(2); Local Elections (Parishes and Communities) (England and Wales) Rules 2006, SI 2006/3305, Sch 2 r 27(2); Local Authorities (Mayoral Elections) (England and Wales) Regulations 2007, SI 2007/1024, Sch 1 r 29(2); Greater London Authority Elections Rules 2007, SI 2007/3541, Sch 1 r 30(2), Sch 2 r 31(2), Sch 3 r 30(2). For the count at a London Authority constituency members election, or for each local count at a London members, London Mayoral, or European parliamentary election, one (but no more than one) counting agent of each candidate (ie, at a London members or European parliamentary election, each registered party standing nominated or each individual candidate) may be authorised by the terms of his appointment to require a recount at that count: European Parliamentary Elections Regulations 2004, SI 2004/293, Sch 1 para 33(2) (as so substituted); Greater London Authority Elections Rules 2007, SI 2007/3541, Sch 1 r 30(3), Sch 2 r 31(3), Sch 3 r 30(3). See also PARA 471.

      Where no candidate or election agent is present on the completion of the counting, or any recount, of electoral region votes in a Welsh Assembly constituency, the right conferred on that person (if he had been present) to request a recount under the National Assembly for Wales (Representation of the People) Order 2007, SI 2007/236, Sch 5 para 57 (see PARA 462) may be exercised by a counting agent for an individual candidate, or for a registered party standing nominated, who is present provided that, in his terms of appointment as a counting agent, he is authorised to exercise the right conferred by Sch 5 para 57; but not more than one such counting agent for the same individual candidate or registered party standing nominated may be appointed for these purposes in relation to the same Assembly constituency: see Sch 5 para 57(3); and PARA 462 note 14.

8   Representation of the People Act 1983 Sch 1 r 30(2); European Parliamentary Elections Regulations 2004, SI 2004/293, Sch 1 para 33(3) (as substituted: see note 4); Local Elections (Principal Areas) (England and Wales) Rules 2006, SI 2006/3304, Sch 2 r 27(4); Local Elections (Parishes and Communities) (England and Wales) Rules 2006, SI 2006/3305, Sch 2 r 27(4); National Assembly for Wales (Representation of the People) Order 2007, SI 2007/236, Sch 5 para 38(2), (4); Local Authorities (Mayoral Elections) (England and Wales) Regulations 2007, SI 2007/1024, Sch 1 r 29(5); Greater London Authority Elections Rules 2007, SI 2007/3541, Sch 1 r 30(6), Sch 2 r 31(6), Sch 3 r 30(6). For the purposes of the calculation required as mentioned in the text, a counting agent who has been appointed for more than one candidate at a local government election (see note 6), other than a list candidate at a London members election, is a separate agent for each of the candidates by whom he has been appointed: Local Elections (Principal Areas) (England and Wales) Rules 2006, SI 2006/3304, Sch 2 r 27(4); Local Elections (Parishes and Communities) (England and Wales) Rules 2006, SI 2006/3305, Sch 2 r 27(4); Local Authorities (Mayoral Elections) (England and Wales) Regulations 2007, SI 2007/1024, Sch 1 r 29(6); Greater London Authority Elections Rules 2007, SI 2007/3541, Sch 1 r 30(7), Sch 2 r 31(7)(b), Sch 3 r 30(7). For the purposes of a London members election, the calculation must take into account a counting agent appointed for more than one list candidate who must be deemed for these purposes to be appointed for all the candidates on the list: Sch 2 r 31(7)(a). For the purposes of PARA 397 et seq, references to polling and counting agents must be taken as references to agents whose appointments have been duly made and notified and (where the number of agents is restricted) who are within the permitted number: Representation of the People Act 1983 Sch 1 r 30(6); Parish and Community Meetings (Polls) Rules 1987, SI 1987/1, Schedule r 12(4); European Parliamentary Elections Regulations 2004,

SI 2004/293, Sch 1 para 33(6) (as so substituted); Local Elections (Principal Areas) (England and Wales) Rules 2006, SI 2006/3304, Sch 2 r 27(7); Local Elections (Parishes and Communities) (England and Wales) Rules 2006, SI 2006/3305, Sch 2 r 27(7); National Assembly for Wales (Representation of the People) Order 2007, SI 2007/236, Sch 5 para 38(8); Local Authorities (Mayoral Elections) (England and Wales) Regulations 2007, SI 2007/1024, Sch 1 r 29(10); Greater London Authority Elections Rules 2007, SI 2007/3541, Sch 1 r 30(11), Sch 2 r 31(11), Sch 3 r 30(11).

At a poll consequent on a parish meeting on a question involving appointment to office, each candidate may appoint only one agent for each purpose: see notes 6–7.

At a local government election, not more than four polling agents may be appointed to attend at any particular polling station unless the returning officer by notice allows otherwise: Local Elections (Principal Areas) (England and Wales) Rules 2006, SI 2006/3304, Sch 2 r 27(3); Local Elections (Parishes and Communities) (England and Wales) Rules 2006, SI 2006/3305, Sch 2 r 27(3); Local Authorities (Mayoral Elections) (England and Wales) Regulations 2007, SI 2007/1024, Sch 1 r 29(3); Greater London Authority Elections Rules 2007, SI 2007/3541, Sch 1 r 30(4), Sch 2 r 31(4), Sch 3 r 30(4). If, at such an election, the number of polling agents appointed to attend at a polling station exceeds the permitted number, the returning officer must determine which agents are permitted to attend by lot and only the agents on whom the lot falls are deemed to be duly appointed: Local Elections (Principal Areas) (England and Wales) Rules 2006, SI 2006/3304, Sch 2 r 27(3); Local Elections (Parishes and Communities) (England and Wales) Rules 2006, SI 2006/3305, Sch 2 r 27(3); Local Authorities (Mayoral Elections) (England and Wales) Regulations 2007, SI 2007/1024, Sch 1 r 29(4); Greater London Authority Elections Rules 2007, SI 2007/3541, Sch 1 r 30(5), Sch 2 r 31(5), Sch 3 r 30(5).

At a European parliamentary election, in particular, the local returning officer may limit the number of counting agents, so that the number is the same in the case of each registered party standing nominated or each individual candidate, and the number allowed to such an individual candidate or such a registered party must not (except in special circumstances) be less than the number obtained by dividing the number of clerks employed on the verification of the ballot paper accounts, or on the counting of the votes, by the number obtained by adding together the number of registered parties which stand nominated and the number of individual candidates: see the European Parliamentary Elections Regulations 2004, SI 2004/293, Sch 1 para 33(3) (as so substituted).

In relation to the Welsh Assembly constituency for which he is the returning officer, the constituency returning officer may limit the number of counting agents that may be appointed for the purposes of a regional election under the National Assembly for Wales (Representation of the People) Order 2007, SI 2007/236, Sch 5 para 38(3) (see the text and notes 1–7) so that the number is the same in the case of each individual candidate or registered political party, and so that the number allowed to an individual candidate or registered political party may not (except in special circumstances) be less than the number obtained by dividing the number of clerks employed on the counting by the total of the number of individual candidates and registered political parties standing nominated: see Sch 5 para 38(4).

9   Representation of the People Act 1983 Sch 1 r 30(3); Parish and Community Meetings (Polls) Rules 1987, SI 1987/1, Schedule r 12(2); European Parliamentary Elections Regulations 2004, SI 2004/293, Sch 1 para 33(4) (as substituted: see note 4); Local Elections (Principal Areas) (England and Wales) Rules 2006, SI 2006/3304, Sch 2 r 27(5); Local Elections (Parishes and Communities) (England and Wales) Rules 2006, SI 2006/3305, Sch 2 r 27(5); National Assembly for Wales (Representation of the People) Order 2007, SI 2007/236, Sch 5 para 38(5); Local Authorities (Mayoral Elections) (England and Wales) Regulations 2007, SI 2007/1024, Sch 1 r 29(7); Greater London Authority Elections Rules 2007, SI 2007/3541, Sch 1 r 30(8), Sch 2 r 31(8), Sch 3 r 30(8).

10   See the Representation of the People Act 1983 Sch 1 r 30(3); and the National Assembly for Wales (Representation of the People) Order 2007, SI 2007/236, Sch 5 para 38(5). As to the date of the poll at a parliamentary general election or by-election see PARA 195; and as to the date of the poll at Welsh Assembly elections (including elections to fill vacancies in an Assembly constituency) see PARAS 213–214. As to the computation of time for the purposes of a parliamentary election see PARA 195 note 27; and for the purposes of a Welsh Assembly election see PARA 213 note 5.

As from a day to be appointed under the Electoral Registration and Administration Act 2013 s 27(1), the Representation of the People Act 1983 Sch 1 r 30(3) is amended so that the reference in the text to 'the second day' becomes a reference to 'the fifth day': see Sch 1 r 30(3) (prospectively amended by the Electoral Registration and Administration Act 2013 s 14(2), (4)). However, at the date at which this volume states the law, no such day had been appointed.

11 See the European Parliamentary Elections Regulations 2004, SI 2004/293, Sch 1 para 33(4) (as substituted: see note 4); the Local Elections (Principal Areas) (England and Wales) Rules 2006, SI 2006/3304, Sch 2 r 27(5); the Local Elections (Parishes and Communities) (England and Wales) Rules 2006, SI 2006/3305, Sch 2 r 27(5); the Local Authorities (Mayoral Elections) (England and Wales) Regulations 2007, SI 2007/1024, Sch 1 r 29(7); and the Greater London Authority Elections Rules 2007, SI 2007/3541, Sch 1 r 30(8), Sch 2 r 31(8), Sch 3 r 30(8). As to the date of the poll at local government elections (including elections to fill vacancies) see PARAS 206–209; as to date of elections for the return of a local authority mayor see PARA 198; and as to the date of the poll at a European parliamentary election see PARA 222. As to the computation of time for the purposes of a local government election see PARA 211 notes 1, 4; and for the purposes of a European parliamentary election see PARA 223 note 1.

12 See the Parish and Community Meetings (Polls) Rules 1987, SI 1987/1, Schedule r 12(2). As to the date of the poll consequent on a parish meeting on a question involving appointment to office see PARA 207. As to the computation of time for the purpose of such a poll see PARA 212 note 5.

13 Representation of the People Act 1983 Sch 1 r 30(4); Parish and Community Meetings (Polls) Rules 1987, SI 1987/1, Schedule r 12(3); European Parliamentary Elections Regulations 2004, SI 2004/293, Sch 1 para 33(5) (as substituted: see note 4); Local Elections (Principal Areas) (England and Wales) Rules 2006, SI 2006/3304, Sch 2 r 27(6); Local Elections (Parishes and Communities) (England and Wales) Rules 2006, SI 2006/3305, Sch 2 r 27(6); National Assembly for Wales (Representation of the People) Order 2007, SI 2007/236, Sch 5 para 38(6); Local Authorities (Mayoral Elections) (England and Wales) Regulations 2007, SI 2007/1024, Sch 1 r 29(8); Greater London Authority Elections Rules 2007, SI 2007/3541, Sch 1 r 30(9), Sch 2 r 31(9), Sch 3 r 30(9).

14 Representation of the People Act 1983 Sch 1 r 30(8); Parish and Community Meetings (Polls) Rules 1987, SI 1987/1, Schedule r 12(6); European Parliamentary Elections Regulations 2004, SI 2004/293, Sch 1 para 33(8) (as substituted: see note 4); Local Elections (Principal Areas) (England and Wales) Rules 2006, SI 2006/3304, Sch 2 r 27(9); Local Elections (Parishes and Communities) (England and Wales) Rules 2006, SI 2006/3305, Sch 2 r 27(9); National Assembly for Wales (Representation of the People) Order 2007, SI 2007/236, Sch 5 para 38(10); Local Authorities (Mayoral Elections) (England and Wales) Regulations 2007, SI 2007/1024, Sch 1 r 29(12); Greater London Authority Elections Rules 2007, SI 2007/3541, Sch 1 r 30(13), Sch 2 r 31(13), Sch 3 r 30(13).

15 Representation of the People Act 1983 Sch 1 r 30(9); European Parliamentary Elections Regulations 2004, SI 2004/293, Sch 1 para 33(9) (as substituted: see note 4); Local Elections (Principal Areas) (England and Wales) Rules 2006, SI 2006/3304, Sch 2 r 27(10); National Assembly for Wales (Representation of the People) Order 2007, SI 2007/236, Sch 5 para 38(11); Local Authorities (Mayoral Elections) (England and Wales) Regulations 2007, SI 2007/1024, Sch 1 r 29(13); Greater London Authority Elections Rules 2007, SI 2007/3541, Sch 1 r 30(14), Sch 2 r 31(14), Sch 3 r 30(14). In the case of a Welsh Assembly election, the reference in the text to an election agent is to an election agent for a constituency candidate, an individual candidate or for a registered political party standing nominated: see the National Assembly for Wales (Representation of the People) Order 2007, SI 2007/236, Sch 5 para 38(11). For the purposes of a European parliamentary election, the reference in the text is to 'a polling or counting agent of his' includes a reference to a polling or counting agent of the candidate's registered party, if appointed: see the European Parliamentary Elections Regulations 2004, SI 2004/293, Sch 1 para 33(9) (as so substituted). Equally, an election agent or sub-agent of a registered party standing nominated or the election agent or sub-agent of an individual candidate may do or assist in doing anything which a polling or counting agent of that party or candidate is authorised to do; and anything required or authorised by the European Parliamentary Elections Regulations 2004, SI 2004/293, Sch 1, to be done in the presence of the polling or counting agents may be done in the presence of an election agent or sub-agent of a registered party standing nominated or the election agent or sub-agent of an individual candidate instead of that party's or candidate's polling agent or counting agents: Sch 1 para 33(10) (as so substituted).

16 Representation of the People Act 1983 Sch 1 r 30(10); Parish and Community Meetings (Polls) Rules 1987, SI 1987/1, Schedule r 12(7); European Parliamentary Elections Regulations 2004, SI 2004/293, Sch 1 para 33(11) (as substituted: see note 4); Local Elections (Principal Areas) (England and Wales) Rules 2006, SI 2006/3304, Sch 2 r 27(11); Local Elections (Parishes and Communities) (England and Wales) Rules 2006, SI 2006/3305, Sch 2 r 27(10); National Assembly for Wales (Representation of the People) Order 2007, SI 2007/236, Sch 5 para 38(12); Local Authorities (Mayoral Elections) (England and Wales) Regulations 2007, SI 2007/1024, Sch 1 r 29(14); Greater London Authority Elections Rules 2007, SI 2007/3541, Sch 1 r 30(15), Sch 2 r 31(15), Sch 3 r 30(15).

17 Representation of the People Act 1983 Sch 1 r 30(7); Parish and Community Meetings (Polls) Rules 1987, SI 1987/1, Schedule r 12(5); European Parliamentary Elections Regulations 2004, SI 2004/293, Sch 1 para 33(7) (as substituted: see note 4); Local Elections (Principal Areas) (England and Wales) Rules 2006, SI 2006/3304, Sch 2 r 27(8); Local Elections (Parishes and Communities) (England and Wales) Rules 2006, SI 2006/3305, Sch 2 r 27(8); National Assembly for Wales (Representation of the People) Order 2007, SI 2007/236, Sch 5 para 38(9); Local Authorities (Mayoral Elections) (England and Wales) Regulations 2007, SI 2007/1024, Sch 1 r 29(11); Greater London Authority Elections Rules 2007, SI 2007/3541, Sch 1 r 30(12), Sch 2 r 31(12), Sch 3 r 30(12).

18 As to polls at elections or referendums which are taken together see PARA 16 et seq.

395. Attendance at polling station. The presiding officer[1] must regulate the number of voters[2] to be admitted to the polling station at the same time[3]. He must exclude all other persons[4], except:

(1) voters at elections[5];

(2) persons under the age of 18 who accompany voters at elections to the polling station[6];

(3) the candidates (and, at elections where election agents are appointed, their election agents)[7];

(4) the polling agents appointed to attend at the polling station[8];

(5) the clerks appointed to attend the polling station[9];

(6) the constables on duty[10];

(7) the companions of voters with disabilities[11]; and

(8) representatives of the Electoral Commission who are entitled by virtue of the Political Parties, Elections and Referendums Act 2000[12] to attend electoral proceedings and observe working practices[13].

Each voter must vote at the polling station allotted to him[14] with the exception of constables on duty and persons employed by the returning officer[15] in connection with the election, who may be admitted to vote in person elsewhere than at his own polling station, but only on production and surrender of a certificate as to his employment which must be in the prescribed form[16], or a form to like effect[17]. The certificate must be signed, in the case of a constable, by an officer of a police force of or above the rank of inspector or, otherwise, by the returning officer, as the case may be[18]. The certificate when surrendered must forthwith be cancelled[19].

The returning officer must make such arrangements as he thinks fit to ensure that every person attending at a polling station (otherwise than for the purpose of voting or assisting a voter who has an incapacity or as a constable on duty there) has been given a copy in writing of the statutory provisions relating to the requirement of secrecy that apply to such attendance[20].

1 As to the presiding officer see PARA 393.

2 Ie, in the case of an election, but not at a poll, the total number of voters and persons under the age of 18 who accompany them: see the Representation of the People Act 1983 Sch 1 r 32(1A) (r 32(1) substituted, r 32(1A) added, by the Electoral Administration Act 2006 s 47, Sch 1 paras 69, 84); the European Parliamentary Elections Regulations 2004, SI 2004/293, Sch 1 para 36(2) (Sch 1 substituted by SI 2009/186); the Local Elections (Principal Areas) (England and Wales) Rules 2006, SI 2006/3304, Sch 2 r 30(2); the Local Elections (Parishes and Communities) (England and Wales) Rules 2006, SI 2006/3305, Sch 2 r 30(2); the National Assembly for Wales (Representation of the People) Order 2007, SI 2007/236, Sch 5 para 41(2); the Local Authorities (Mayoral Elections) (England and Wales) Regulations 2007, SI 2007/1024, Sch 1 r 32(2); and the Greater London Authority Elections Rules 2007, SI 2007/3541, Sch 1 r 33(2), Sch 2 r 34(2), Sch 3 r 33(2). As to the meanings of 'Assembly election', 'constituency election' and 'regional election' see PARA 3 note 2. As to the meaning of 'parliamentary election' see PARA 9. As to the meanings of 'Authority election' and 'local government election' see

PARA 11. As to European parliamentary elections see PARA 217 et seq. As to polls consequent on a parish meeting on a question involving appointment to office see PARA 200 et seq.

3   Representation of the People Act 1983 Sch 1 r 32(1A) (as added: see note 2); Parish and Community Meetings (Polls) Rules 1987, SI 1987/1, Schedule r 14; European Parliamentary Elections Regulations 2004, SI 2004/293, Sch 1 para 36(2) (as substituted: see note 2); Local Elections (Principal Areas) (England and Wales) Rules 2006, SI 2006/3304, Sch 2 r 30(2); Local Elections (Parishes and Communities) (England and Wales) Rules 2006, SI 2006/3305, Sch 2 r 30(2); National Assembly for Wales (Representation of the People) Order 2007, SI 2007/236, Sch 5 para 41(2); Local Authorities (Mayoral Elections) (England and Wales) Regulations 2007, SI 2007/1024, Sch 1 r 32(2); Greater London Authority Elections Rules 2007, SI 2007/3541, Sch 1 r 33(2), Sch 2 r 34(2), Sch 3 r 33(2). As to the provision and allotment of polling stations see PARA 390.

4   Representation of the People Act 1983 Sch 1 r 32(1) (as substituted: see note 2); Parish and Community Meetings (Polls) Rules 1987, SI 1987/1, Schedule r 14; European Parliamentary Elections Regulations 2004, SI 2004/293, Sch 1 para 36(1) (as substituted: see note 2); Local Elections (Principal Areas) (England and Wales) Rules 2006, SI 2006/3304, Sch 2 r 30(1); Local Elections (Parishes and Communities) (England and Wales) Rules 2006, SI 2006/3305, Sch 2 r 30(1); National Assembly for Wales (Representation of the People) Order 2007, SI 2007/236, Sch 5 para 41(1); Local Authorities (Mayoral Elections) (England and Wales) Regulations 2007, SI 2007/1024, Sch 1 r 32(1); Greater London Authority Elections Rules 2007, SI 2007/3541, Sch 1 r 33(1), Sch 2 r 34(1), Sch 3 r 33(1). The power of arrest, exclusion or removal of any person from the polling station may be exercised only by the presiding officer and not by one of the clerks appointed to assist him: see PARA 393.

5   Representation of the People Act 1983 Sch 1 r 32(1)(a) (as substituted: see note 2); European Parliamentary Elections Regulations 2004, SI 2004/293, Sch 1 para 36(1)(a) (as substituted: see note 2); Local Elections (Principal Areas) (England and Wales) Rules 2006, SI 2006/3304, Sch 2 r 30(1)(a); Local Elections (Parishes and Communities) (England and Wales) Rules 2006, SI 2006/3305, Sch 2 r 30(1)(a); National Assembly for Wales (Representation of the People) Order 2007, SI 2007/236, Sch 5 para 41(1)(a); Local Authorities (Mayoral Elections) (England and Wales) Regulations 2007, SI 2007/1024, Sch 1 r 32(1)(a); Greater London Authority Elections Rules 2007, SI 2007/3541, Sch 1 r 33(1)(a), Sch 2 r 34(1)(a), Sch 3 r 33(1)(a).

6   Representation of the People Act 1983 Sch 1 r 32(1)(b) (as substituted: see note 2); European Parliamentary Elections Regulations 2004, SI 2004/293, Sch 1 para 36(1)(b) (as substituted: see note 2); Local Elections (Principal Areas) (England and Wales) Rules 2006, SI 2006/3304, Sch 2 r 30(1)(b); Local Elections (Parishes and Communities) (England and Wales) Rules 2006, SI 2006/3305, Sch 2 r 30(1)(b); National Assembly for Wales (Representation of the People) Order 2007, SI 2007/236, Sch 5 para 41(1)(b); Local Authorities (Mayoral Elections) (England and Wales) Regulations 2007, SI 2007/1024, Sch 1 r 32(1)(b); Greater London Authority Elections Rules 2007, SI 2007/3541, Sch 1 r 33(1)(b), Sch 2 r 34(1)(b), Sch 3 r 33(1)(b).

7   Representation of the People Act 1983 Sch 1 r 32(1)(c) (as substituted: see note 2); Parish and Community Meetings (Polls) Rules 1987, SI 1987/1, Schedule r 14(a) (amended by SI 2005/2114); European Parliamentary Elections Regulations 2004, SI 2004/293, Sch 1 para 36(1)(c) (as substituted: see note 2); Local Elections (Principal Areas) (England and Wales) Rules 2006, SI 2006/3304, Sch 2 r 30(1)(c); Local Elections (Parishes and Communities) (England and Wales) Rules 2006, SI 2006/3305, Sch 2 r 30(1)(c); National Assembly for Wales (Representation of the People) Order 2007, SI 2007/236, Sch 5 para 41(1)(c); Local Authorities (Mayoral Elections) (England and Wales) Regulations 2007, SI 2007/1024, Sch 1 r 32(1)(c); Greater London Authority Elections Rules 2007, SI 2007/3541, Sch 1 r 33(1)(c), Sch 2 r 34(1)(c), Sch 3 r 33(1)(c). Head (3) in the text refers:

    (1)   at a European parliamentary election, to the candidates and the election agents of any registered party standing nominated and any individual candidate and their election agents (see the European Parliamentary Elections Regulations 2004, SI 2004/293, Sch 1 para 36(1)(c)(as so substituted)); and

    (2)   at a Welsh Assembly election, to the candidates and the election agents of any constituency or individual candidates or in relation to any registered political party standing nominated, the election agent of such party in respect of the list it has submitted (see the National Assembly for Wales (Representation of the People) Order 2007, SI 2007/236, Sch 5 para 41(1)(c)).

Not more than one party list candidate from the same party list submitted by a registered political party is to be admitted at the same time to a polling station: Sch 5 para 41(3). As to the meaning of 'registered political party' for these purposes see PARA 215 note 19. As to the meaning of 'candidate' generally see PARA 230; as to the meanings of 'candidate', 'constituency candidate' and 'individual candidate' for the purposes of a Welsh Assembly election see

PARA 230 note 19; and as to the meanings of 'party list' and 'party list candidate' see PARA 230 note 23. As to the meaning of 'registered party' for the purposes of a European parliamentary election see PARA 230 note 29; and as to the meaning of 'individual candidate' for the purposes of a European parliamentary election see PARA 230 note 32. As to the appointment of election agents see PARA 231 et seq. There is no provision for election agents at a poll consequent on a parish meeting on a question involving appointment to office but, where a poll is taken on such a question, it is provided specifically that the candidates may be accompanied by their spouses or civil partners: see the Parish and Community Meetings (Polls) Rules 1987, SI 1987/1, Schedule r 14(a) (as so amended).

8   Representation of the People Act 1983 Sch 1 r 32(1)(d) (as substituted: see note 2); Parish and Community Meetings (Polls) Rules 1987, SI 1987/1, Schedule r 14(b); European Parliamentary Elections Regulations 2004, SI 2004/293, Sch 1 para 36(1)(d) (as substituted: see note 2); Local Elections (Principal Areas) (England and Wales) Rules 2006, SI 2006/3304, Sch 2 r 30(1)(d); Local Elections (Parishes and Communities) (England and Wales) Rules 2006, SI 2006/3305, Sch 2 r 30(1)(d); National Assembly for Wales (Representation of the People) Order 2007, SI 2007/236, Sch 5 para 41(1)(d); Local Authorities (Mayoral Elections) (England and Wales) Regulations 2007, SI 2007/1024, Sch 1 r 32(1)(d); Greater London Authority Elections Rules 2007, SI 2007/3541, Sch 1 r 33(1)(d), Sch 2 r 34(1)(d), Sch 3 r 33(1)(d). As to the appointment of polling agents see PARA 394.

   Not more than one polling agent may be admitted at the same time to a polling station on behalf of the same candidate (Representation of the People Act 1983 Sch 1 r 32(2); Local Elections (Principal Areas) (England and Wales) Rules 2006, SI 2006/3304, Sch 2 r 30(3); Local Elections (Parishes and Communities) (England and Wales) Rules 2006, SI 2006/3305, Sch 2 r 30(3); Local Authorities (Mayoral Elections) (England and Wales) Regulations 2007, SI 2007/1024, Sch 1 r 32(3); Greater London Authority Elections Rules 2007, SI 2007/3541, Sch 1 r 33(3), Sch 3 r 33(3)), except that:

   (1)   at a London members election, not more than one polling agent may be admitted at the same time to a polling station on behalf of the same party or individual candidate (Sch 2 r 34(3));

   (2)   at a European parliamentary election, not more than one polling agent may be admitted at the same time to a polling station on behalf of the same registered party standing nominated and any individual candidate (European Parliamentary Elections Regulations 2004, SI 2004/293, Sch 1 para 36(3) (as so substituted));

   (3)   at a Welsh Assembly election, not more than one polling agent is to be admitted at the same time to a polling station on behalf of the same constituency or individual candidate or on behalf of the same registered political party (see the National Assembly for Wales (Representation of the People) Order 2007, SI 2007/236, Sch 5 para 41(4)).

   As to individual candidates to be London members see LONDON GOVERNMENT vol 71 (2013) PARA 81. As to the meaning of 'registered political party' for the purposes of a London members election see PARA 256 note 27. At a poll consequent on a parish or community meeting, a candidate may appoint only one polling agent: see PARA 394 note 6.

9   Representation of the People Act 1983 Sch 1 r 32(1)(e) (as substituted: see note 2); Parish and Community Meetings (Polls) Rules 1987, SI 1987/1, Schedule r 14(d); European Parliamentary Elections Regulations 2004, SI 2004/293, Sch 1 para 36(1)(e) (as substituted: see note 2); Local Elections (Principal Areas) (England and Wales) Rules 2006, SI 2006/3304, Sch 2 r 30(1)(e); Local Elections (Parishes and Communities) (England and Wales) Rules 2006, SI 2006/3305, Sch 2 r 30(1)(e); National Assembly for Wales (Representation of the People) Order 2007, SI 2007/236, Sch 5 para 41(1)(e); Local Authorities (Mayoral Elections) (England and Wales) Regulations 2007, SI 2007/1024, Sch 1 r 32(1)(e); Greater London Authority Elections Rules 2007, SI 2007/3541, Sch 1 r 33(1)(e), Sch 2 r 34(1)(e), Sch 3 r 33(1)(e). As to the appointment of presiding officers and their clerks by the returning officer see PARA 393. Because non-manual counting methods may be employed at London Authority elections, the CRO may also appoint and pay such technical assistants as may be necessary for the purposes of such an election (see PARA 393 note 6), although no explicit provision is made for them to attend under head (5) in the text.

10   Representation of the People Act 1983 Sch 1 r 32(1)(g) (as substituted: see note 2); Parish and Community Meetings (Polls) Rules 1987, SI 1987/1, Schedule r 14(e); European Parliamentary Elections Regulations 2004, SI 2004/293, Sch 1 para 36(1)(g) (as substituted: see note 2); Local Elections (Principal Areas) (England and Wales) Rules 2006, SI 2006/3304, Sch 2 r 30(1)(g); Local Elections (Parishes and Communities) (England and Wales) Rules 2006, SI 2006/3305, Sch 2 r 30(1)(g); National Assembly for Wales (Representation of the People) Order 2007, SI 2007/236, Sch 5 para 41(1)(g); Local Authorities (Mayoral Elections) (England and Wales)

Regulations 2007, SI 2007/1024, Sch 1 r 32(1)(g); Greater London Authority Elections Rules 2007, SI 2007/3541, Sch 1 r 33(1)(g), Sch 2 r 34(1)(g), Sch 3 r 33(1)(g).

As from a day to be appointed under the Electoral Registration and Administration Act 2013 s 27(1), in the application of the Representation of the People Act 1983 Sch 1 r 32 to an election in England or Wales, a reference to a constable includes a person designated as a community support officer under the Police Reform Act 2002 s 38 (police powers for employees: see POLICE AND INVESTIGATORY POWERS vol 84 (2013) PARA 366): see the Representation of the People Act 1983 Sch 1 r 32(5) (prospectively added by the Electoral Registration and Administration Act 2013 s 21(2)). However, at the date at which this volume states the law, no such day had been appointed.

11   Representation of the People Act 1983 Sch 1 r 32(1)(h) (as substituted: see note 2); Parish and Community Meetings (Polls) Rules 1987, SI 1987/1, Schedule r 14(f); European Parliamentary Elections Regulations 2004, SI 2004/293, Sch 1 para 36(1)(h) (as substituted: see note 2); Local Elections (Principal Areas) (England and Wales) Rules 2006, SI 2006/3304, Sch 2 r 30(1)(h); Local Elections (Parishes and Communities) (England and Wales) Rules 2006, SI 2006/3305, Sch 2 r 30(1)(h); National Assembly for Wales (Representation of the People) Order 2007, SI 2007/236, Sch 5 para 41(1)(h); Local Authorities (Mayoral Elections) (England and Wales) Regulations 2007, SI 2007/1024, Sch 1 r 32(1)(h); Greater London Authority Elections Rules 2007, SI 2007/3541, Sch 1 r 33(1)(h), Sch 2 r 34(1)(h), Sch 3 r 33(1)(h). As to companions assisting voters with incapacities see PARA 402.

12   Ie by virtue of any of the Political Parties, Elections and Referendums Act 2000 ss 6A–6D (see PARA 53): see the Representation of the People Act 1983 Sch 1 r 32(1)(f) (as substituted: see note 2); the European Parliamentary Elections Regulations 2004, SI 2004/293, Sch 1 para 36(1)(f) (as substituted: see note 2); the Local Elections (Principal Areas) (England and Wales) Rules 2006, SI 2006/3304, Sch 2 r 30(1)(f); the Local Elections (Parishes and Communities) (England and Wales) Rules 2006, SI 2006/3305, Sch 2 r 30(1)(f); the National Assembly for Wales (Representation of the People) Order 2007, SI 2007/236, Sch 5 para 41(1)(f); the Local Authorities (Mayoral Elections) (England and Wales) Regulations 2007, SI 2007/1024, Sch 1 r 32(1)(f); and the Greater London Authority Elections Rules 2007, SI 2007/3541, Sch 1 r 33(1)(f), Sch 2 r 34(1)(f), Sch 3 r 33(1)(f).

13   Representation of the People Act 1983 Sch 1 r 32(1)(f) (as substituted: see note 2); European Parliamentary Elections Regulations 2004, SI 2004/293, Sch 1 para 36(1)(f) (as substituted: see note 2); Local Elections (Principal Areas) (England and Wales) Rules 2006, SI 2006/3304, Sch 2 r 30(1)(f); Local Elections (Parishes and Communities) (England and Wales) Rules 2006, SI 2006/3305, Sch 2 r 30(1)(f); National Assembly for Wales (Representation of the People) Order 2007, SI 2007/236, Sch 5 para 41(1)(f); Local Authorities (Mayoral Elections) (England and Wales) Regulations 2007, SI 2007/1024, Sch 1 r 32(1)(f); Greater London Authority Elections Rules 2007, SI 2007/3541, Sch 1 r 33(1)(f), Sch 2 r 34(1)(f), Sch 3 r 33(1)(f). As to the Electoral Commission see PARA 34 et seq.

14   As to the manner of voting at elections see PARA 363.

15   As to returning officers generally see PARA 350 et seq. At any London Authority election, the reference is to the constituency returning officer ('CRO'): see the Greater London Authority Elections Rules 2007, SI 2007/3541, Sch 1 r 33(4), Sch 2 r 34(4), Sch 3 r 33(4). As to the meaning of the 'constituency returning officer' ('CRO') see PARA 211 note 9. At a European parliamentary election, the reference is to a local returning officer (see PARA 360 et seq): see the European Parliamentary Elections Regulations 2004, SI 2004/293, Sch 1 para 30(4) (as substituted: see note 2). The reference is to a constituency or regional returning officer at a Welsh Assembly election, according to context: see the National Assembly for Wales (Representation of the People) Order 2007, SI 2007/236, Sch 5 para 41(5). As to the meanings of 'constituency returning officer' and 'regional returning officer' for the purposes of Welsh Assembly elections see PARA 18 note 2.

16   For the purposes of the Representation of the People Act 1983, 'prescribed' means prescribed by regulations: s 202(1). As to the making of regulations under the Representation of the People Act 1983 generally see PARA 28 note 16. As to the regulations made see the Representation of the People (England and Wales) Regulations 2001, SI 2001/341; and see note 17. In all other cases, the form must be in the appropriate form that is set out in the rules: see note 17.

17   Representation of the People Act 1983 Sch 1 r 32(3); European Parliamentary Elections Regulations 2004, SI 2004/293, Sch 1 para 36(4) (as substituted: see note 2); Local Elections (Principal Areas) (England and Wales) Rules 2006, SI 2006/3304, Sch 2 r 30(4); Local Elections (Parishes and Communities) (England and Wales) Rules 2006, SI 2006/3305, Sch 2 r 30(4); National Assembly for Wales (Representation of the People) Order 2007, SI 2007/236, Sch 1 para 16, Sch 5 para 41(5); Local Authorities (Mayoral Elections) (England and Wales)

Regulations 2007, SI 2007/1024, Sch 1 r 32(4); Greater London Authority Elections Rules 2007, SI 2007/3541, Sch 1 r 33(4), Sch 2 r 34(4), Sch 3 r 33(4). As to the form of the certificate of employment see:

(1)   in the case of a parliamentary election, the Representation of the People (England and Wales) Regulations 2001, SI 2001/341, reg 63(1), Sch 3 (Form F: certificate of employment);

(2)   at a European parliamentary election, the European Parliamentary Elections Regulations 2004, SI 2004/293, Sch 1 Appendix of Forms (Form L: certificate of employment) (as so substituted);

(3)   in the case of a local government election:

    (a)   the Local Elections (Principal Areas) (England and Wales) Rules 2006, SI 2006/3304, Sch 2 Appendix of Forms (Form of certificate of employment); and Sch 3 Appendix of Forms (Form of certificate of employment) (where such a poll is taken together with another relevant election or referendum);

    (b)   the Local Elections (Parishes and Communities) (England and Wales) Rules 2006, SI 2006/3305, Sch 2 Appendix of Forms (Form of certificate of employment); and Sch 3 Appendix of Forms (Form of certificate of employment) (where such a poll is taken together with another relevant election or referendum);

    (c)   the Local Authorities (Mayoral Elections) (England and Wales) Regulations 2007, SI 2007/1024, Sch 1 Appendix of Forms (Form 13: certificate of employment) (Form 13 substituted by SI 2012/2059);

    (d)   the Greater London Authority Elections Rules 2007, SI 2007/3541, Sch 10 r 2 (Form 18: certificate of employment);

(4)   at a Welsh Assembly election, the form set out in English and Welsh in the National Assembly for Wales (Representation of the People) Order 2007, SI 2007/236, Sch 10 Appendix of Forms (Form CB: Form of certificate of employment) (see Sch 1 para 16, Sch 5 para 41(5)).

There is no provision for a certificate of employment to be issued in the case of a poll on a question of appointment to an office.

Where elections take place in Wales see also the forms issued partly in English and partly in Welsh in:

(i)   the Parliamentary Elections (Welsh Forms) Order 2007, SI 2007/1014, art 5(a), Sch 1 (Form 1 (Ffurflen 1): Form F: CERTIFICATE OF EMPLOYMENT/Ffurflen F: TYSTYSGRIF CYFLOGAETH);

(ii)   the Local Elections (Principal Areas) (Welsh Forms) Order 2007, SI 2007/1015, arts 7(1)(h), 9(1)(i), Sch 3 (Form 8 (Ffurflen 8): Form of Certificate of Employment/ Ffurf ar Dystysgrif Cyflogaeth), Sch 5 (Form 9 (Ffurflen 9): Form of Certificate of Employment/Ffurf ar Dystysgrif Cyflogaeth (combined polls));

(iii)   the Local Elections (Communities) (Welsh Forms) Order 2007, SI 2007/1013, arts 7(1)(h), 9(1)(i), Sch 3 (Form 8 (Ffurflen 8): Form of Certificate of Employment/ Ffurf ar Dystysgrif Cyflogaeth), Sch 5 (Form 9 (Ffurflen 9): Form of Certificate of Employment/Ffurf ar Dystysgrif Cyflogaeth (combined polls)); and

(iv)   the European Parliamentary Elections (Welsh Forms) Order 2009, SI 2009/781, art 5(1), (2)(a), Sch 1 (Form 1 (Ffurflen 1): Certificate of Employment; Tystysgrif Cyflogaeth).

18   Representation of the People Act 1983 Sch 1 r 32(3); Representation of the People (England and Wales) Regulations 2001, SI 2001/341, reg 63(2); European Parliamentary Elections Regulations 2004, SI 2004/293, Sch 1 para 36(4) (as substituted: see note 2); Local Elections (Principal Areas) (England and Wales) Rules 2006, SI 2006/3304, Sch 2 r 30(4); Local Elections (Parishes and Communities) (England and Wales) Rules 2006, SI 2006/3305, Sch 2 r 30(4); National Assembly for Wales (Representation of the People) Order 2007, SI 2007/236, Sch 1 para 16, Sch 5 para 41(5); Local Authorities (Mayoral Elections) (England and Wales) Regulations 2007, SI 2007/1024, Sch 1 r 32(4); Greater London Authority Elections Rules 2007, SI 2007/3541, Sch 1 r 33(4), Sch 2 r 34(4), Sch 3 r 33(4).

19   Representation of the People Act 1983 Sch 1 r 32(4); European Parliamentary Elections Regulations 2004, SI 2004/293, Sch 1 para 36(5) (as substituted: see note 2); Local Elections (Principal Areas) (England and Wales) Rules 2006, SI 2006/3304, Sch 2 r 30(5); Local Elections (Parishes and Communities) (England and Wales) Rules 2006, SI 2006/3305, Sch 2 r 30(5); National Assembly for Wales (Representation of the People) Order 2007, SI 2007/236, Sch 5 para 41(6); Local Authorities (Mayoral Elections) (England and Wales) Regulations 2007, SI 2007/1024, Sch 1 r 32(5); Greater London Authority Elections Rules 2007, SI 2007/3541, Sch 1 r 33(5), Sch 2 r 34(5), Sch 3 r 33(5).

20   See PARAS 385, 739–741.

396. Keeping of order in polling station; adjournment in case of riot. It is the duty of the presiding officer[1] to keep order at his polling station[2]. If a person misconducts himself in the polling station, or fails to obey the lawful orders of the presiding officer, he may immediately, by order of the presiding officer, be removed from the polling station[3]:

(1)   by a constable in or near that station[4]; or

(2)   by any other person authorised in writing by the returning officer to remove him[5].

The person so removed may not, without the permission of the presiding officer, again enter the polling station during the day[6]; and any person so removed, may, if charged with the commission in the polling station of an offence, be dealt with as a person taken into custody by a constable for an offence without a warrant[7]. However, the powers so conferred to keep order are not to be exercised so as to prevent a voter who is otherwise entitled to vote at a polling station from having an opportunity of voting at that station[8].

Where the proceedings at any polling station are interrupted or obstructed by riot or open violence, the presiding officer must adjourn the proceedings until the following working day[9]; and he must forthwith give notice to the returning officer[10]. The hours of the poll on the day to which it is adjourned are the same as for the original day, and references to the close of the poll are to be construed accordingly[11].

1   As to the presiding officer see PARA 393.
2   Representation of the People Act 1983 Sch 1 r 33(1); Parish and Community Meetings (Polls) Rules 1987, SI 1987/1, Schedule r 15(1); European Parliamentary Elections Regulations 2004, SI 2004/293, Sch 1 para 37(1) (Sch 1 substituted by SI 2009/186); Local Elections (Principal Areas) (England and Wales) Rules 2006, SI 2006/3304, Sch 2 r 31(1); Local Elections (Parishes and Communities) (England and Wales) Rules 2006, SI 2006/3305, Sch 2 r 31(1); National Assembly for Wales (Representation of the People) Order 2007, SI 2007/236, Sch 5 para 42(1); Local Authorities (Mayoral Elections) (England and Wales) Regulations 2007, SI 2007/1024, Sch 1 r 33(1); Greater London Authority Elections Rules 2007, SI 2007/3541, Sch 1 r 34(1), Sch 2 r 35(1), Sch 3 r 34(1). As to polling stations see PARA 343 et seq.
3   Representation of the People Act 1983 Sch 1 r 33(2); Parish and Community Meetings (Polls) Rules 1987, SI 1987/1, Schedule r 15(2); European Parliamentary Elections Regulations 2004, SI 2004/293, Sch 1 para 37(2) (as substituted: see note 2); Local Elections (Principal Areas) (England and Wales) Rules 2006, SI 2006/3304, Sch 2 r 31(2); Local Elections (Parishes and Communities) (England and Wales) Rules 2006, SI 2006/3305, Sch 2 r 31(2); National Assembly for Wales (Representation of the People) Order 2007, SI 2007/236, Sch 5 para 42(2); Local Authorities (Mayoral Elections) (England and Wales) Regulations 2007, SI 2007/1024, Sch 1 r 33(2); Greater London Authority Elections Rules 2007, SI 2007/3541, Sch 1 r 34(2), Sch 2 r 35(2), Sch 3 r 34(2). The power to order the removal of any person may be exercised only by the presiding officer and not by one of the clerks appointed to assist him: see PARA 393.
4   Representation of the People Act 1983 Sch 1 r 33(2)(a); Parish and Community Meetings (Polls) Rules 1987, SI 1987/1, Schedule r 15(2)(a); European Parliamentary Elections Regulations 2004, SI 2004/293, Sch 1 para 37(2)(a) (as substituted: see note 2); Local Elections (Principal Areas) (England and Wales) Rules 2006, SI 2006/3304, Sch 2 r 31(2)(a); Local Elections (Parishes and Communities) (England and Wales) Rules 2006, SI 2006/3305, Sch 2 r 31(2)(a); National Assembly for Wales (Representation of the People) Order 2007, SI 2007/236, Sch 5 para 42(2)(a); Local Authorities (Mayoral Elections) (England and Wales) Regulations 2007, SI 2007/1024, Sch 1 r 33(2)(a); Greater London Authority Elections Rules 2007, SI 2007/3541, Sch 1 r 34(2)(a), Sch 2 r 35(2)(a), Sch 3 r 34(2)(a).
5   Representation of the People Act 1983 Sch 1 r 33(2)(b); Parish and Community Meetings (Polls) Rules 1987, SI 1987/1, Schedule r 15(2)(b); European Parliamentary Elections Regulations 2004, SI 2004/293, Sch 1 para 37(2)(b) (as substituted: see note 2); Local Elections (Principal Areas) (England and Wales) Rules 2006, SI 2006/3304, Sch 2 r 31(2)(b); Local Elections (Parishes and Communities) (England and Wales) Rules 2006, SI 2006/3305, Sch 2 r 31(2)(b); National Assembly for Wales (Representation of the People) Order 2007, SI 2007/236, Sch 5 para 42(2)(b); Local Authorities (Mayoral Elections) (England and Wales)

Regulations 2007, SI 2007/1024, Sch 1 r 33(2)(b); Greater London Authority Elections Rules 2007, SI 2007/3541, Sch 1 r 34(2)(b), Sch 2 r 35(2)(b), Sch 3 r 34(2)(b). The provision made by head (2) in the text obviates the need for amendment allowing for references to a constable to include a person designated as a community support officer under the Police Reform Act 2002 s 38 (police powers for employees: see POLICE AND INVESTIGATORY POWERS vol 84 (2013) PARA 366): see eg the Representation of the People Act 1983 Sch 1 r 31(2) (prospectively added) (cited in PARA 385); and the Representation of the People Act 1983 Sch 1 r 32(5) (prospectively added) (cited in PARA 395 note 10).

As to returning officers generally see PARA 350 et seq. At any London Authority election, the duties mentioned in the text are undertaken by the constituency returning officer ('CRO'): see the Greater London Authority Elections Rules 2007, SI 2007/3541, Sch 1 rr 34(2)(b), 45(1), (3), Sch 2 rr 35(2)(b), 45(1), (3), Sch 3 rr 34(2)(b), 45(1), (3). As to the meaning of the 'constituency returning officer' ('CRO') see PARA 211 note 9. At a European parliamentary election, the reference is to a local returning officer (see PARA 360 et seq): see the European Parliamentary Elections Regulations 2004, SI 2004/293, Sch 1 paras 37(2)(b), 48(1). The reference is to a constituency returning officer at a Welsh Assembly election: see the National Assembly for Wales (Representation of the People) Order 2007, SI 2007/236, Sch 5 para 42(2); but see note 10. As to the meaning of 'Assembly election' see PARA 3 note 2. As to the meaning of 'constituency returning officer' for the purposes of Welsh Assembly elections see PARA 18 note 2.

6   Representation of the People Act 1983 Sch 1 r 33(2); Parish and Community Meetings (Polls) Rules 1987, SI 1987/1, Schedule r 15(2); European Parliamentary Elections Regulations 2004, SI 2004/293, Sch 1 para 37(2) (as substituted: see note 2); Local Elections (Principal Areas) (England and Wales) Rules 2006, SI 2006/3304, Sch 2 r 31(2); Local Elections (Parishes and Communities) (England and Wales) Rules 2006, SI 2006/3305, Sch 2 r 31(2); National Assembly for Wales (Representation of the People) Order 2007, SI 2007/236, Sch 5 para 42(2); Local Authorities (Mayoral Elections) (England and Wales) Regulations 2007, SI 2007/1024, Sch 1 r 33(2); Greater London Authority Elections Rules 2007, SI 2007/3541, Sch 1 r 34(2), Sch 2 r 35(2), Sch 3 r 34(2).

7   Representation of the People Act 1983 Sch 1 r 33(3); Parish and Community Meetings (Polls) Rules 1987, SI 1987/1, Schedule r 15(3); European Parliamentary Elections Regulations 2004, SI 2004/293, Sch 1 para 37(3) (as substituted: see note 2); Local Elections (Principal Areas) (England and Wales) Rules 2006, SI 2006/3304, Sch 2 r 31(3); Local Elections (Parishes and Communities) (England and Wales) Rules 2006, SI 2006/3305, Sch 2 r 31(3); National Assembly for Wales (Representation of the People) Order 2007, SI 2007/236, Sch 5 para 42(3); Local Authorities (Mayoral Elections) (England and Wales) Regulations 2007, SI 2007/1024, Sch 1 r 33(3); Greater London Authority Elections Rules 2007, SI 2007/3541, Sch 1 r 34(3), Sch 2 r 35(3), Sch 3 r 34(3).

8   Representation of the People Act 1983 Sch 1 r 33(4); Parish and Community Meetings (Polls) Rules 1987, SI 1987/1, Schedule r 15(4); European Parliamentary Elections Regulations 2004, SI 2004/293, Sch 1 para 37(4) (as substituted: see note 2); Local Elections (Principal Areas) (England and Wales) Rules 2006, SI 2006/3304, Sch 2 r 31(4); Local Elections (Parishes and Communities) (England and Wales) Rules 2006, SI 2006/3305, Sch 2 r 31(4); National Assembly for Wales (Representation of the People) Order 2007, SI 2007/236, Sch 5 para 42(4); Local Authorities (Mayoral Elections) (England and Wales) Regulations 2007, SI 2007/1024, Sch 1 r 33(4); Greater London Authority Elections Rules 2007, SI 2007/3541, Sch 1 r 34(4), Sch 2 r 35(4), Sch 3 r 34(4).

9   As to the computation of time for the purposes of a parliamentary election see PARA 195 note 27; for the purposes of a local government election see PARA 211 notes 1, 4; for the purposes of a poll consequent on a parish or community meeting see PARA 212 note 5; for the purposes of a Welsh Assembly election see PARA 213 note 5; and for the purposes of a European parliamentary election see PARA 223 note 1.

10   Representation of the People Act 1983 Sch 1 r 42(1); Parish and Community Meetings (Polls) Rules 1987, SI 1987/1, Schedule r 24(1); European Parliamentary Elections Regulations 2004, SI 2004/293, Sch 1 para 48(1) (as substituted: see note 2); Local Elections (Principal Areas) (England and Wales) Rules 2006, SI 2006/3304, Sch 2 r 42(1); Local Elections (Parishes and Communities) (England and Wales) Rules 2006, SI 2006/3305, Sch 2 r 42(1); National Assembly for Wales (Representation of the People) Order 2007, SI 2007/236, Sch 5 para 52(1); Local Authorities (Mayoral Elections) (England and Wales) Regulations 2007, SI 2007/1024, Sch 1 r 44(1); Greater London Authority Elections Rules 2007, SI 2007/3541, Sch 1 r 45(1), Sch 2 r 46(1), Sch 3 r 45(1). At a Welsh Assembly election, notice must be given as mentioned in the text:

(1)   in the case where the polls at a constituency election and at a regional election are taken

together, to the constituency and to the regional returning officer (National Assembly for Wales (Representation of the People) Order 2007, SI 2007/236, Sch 5 para 52(1)(a)); but otherwise

(2)　in the case of a constituency election, to the constituency returning officer (Sch 5 para 52(1)(b)); or

(3)　in the case of a regional election, to the constituency returning officer for the Assembly constituency in which the polling station is situated and to the regional returning officer (Sch 5 para 52(1)(c)).

As to the meanings of 'Assembly constituency', 'constituency election' and 'regional election' for these purposes see PARA 3 note 2; and as to the meaning of 'regional returning officer' see PARA 18 note 2. See also note 3.

11　Representation of the People Act 1983 Sch 1 r 42(2); Parish and Community Meetings (Polls) Rules 1987, SI 1987/1, Schedule r 24(2); European Parliamentary Elections Regulations 2004, SI 2004/293, Sch 1 para 48(2) (as substituted: see note 2); Local Elections (Principal Areas) (England and Wales) Rules 2006, SI 2006/3304, Sch 2 r 42(2); Local Elections (Parishes and Communities) (England and Wales) Rules 2006, SI 2006/3305, Sch 2 r 42(2); National Assembly for Wales (Representation of the People) Order 2007, SI 2007/236, Sch 5 para 52(2); Local Authorities (Mayoral Elections) (England and Wales) Regulations 2007, SI 2007/1024, Sch 1 r 44(2); Greater London Authority Elections Rules 2007, SI 2007/3541, Sch 1 r 45(2), Sch 2 r 46(2), Sch 3 r 45(2). As to the normal procedure on close of poll see PARA 405.

　　As soon as practicable after being informed of the adjournment of a poll at a London Authority election, the CRO must inform the Greater London returning officer ('GLRO') of that fact, and of the cause of its adjournment: Sch 1 r 45(3), Sch 2 r 46(3), Sch 3 r 45(3). As to the meaning of 'Greater London returning officer' ('GLRO') see PARA 211 note 8.

397.　Sealing, locking of ballot boxes.　Immediately before the commencement of the poll at an election[1], or of a poll taken consequent on a parish meeting on a question which involves appointment to office[2], the presiding officer must[3]:

(1)　show the ballot box, empty, to such persons, if any, as are present in the polling station, so that they may see that it is empty[4]; and then

(2)　lock up the ballot box (if it has a lock)[5]; and

(3)　(in any case) place his seal on the ballot box, in such a manner as to prevent its being opened without breaking the seal[6]; and

(4)　place the ballot box in his view for the receipt of ballot papers[7]; and

(5)　keep the ballot box so sealed (or both sealed and locked, as the case may be, if it has a lock)[8].

1　Ie a parliamentary election, a local government election (which includes any London Authority election and a local authority mayoral election), a Welsh Assembly constituency or regional election or a European parliamentary election. As to the meanings of 'Assembly election', 'constituency election' and 'regional election' see PARA 3 note 2. As to the meaning of 'parliamentary election' see PARA 9. As to the meanings of 'Authority election' and 'local government election' see PARA 11. As to elections in the City of London see PARA 33. As to elections for the return of a local authority mayor see PARA 198; and as to European parliamentary elections see PARA 217 et seq.

2　As to polls consequent on a parish meeting on a question involving appointment to office see PARA 200 et seq.

3　Representation of the People Act 1983 Sch 1 r 34; Parish and Community Meetings (Polls) Rules 1987, SI 1987/1, Schedule r 16; European Parliamentary Elections Regulations 2004, SI 2004/293, Sch 1 para 38 (Sch 1 substituted by SI 2009/186); Local Elections (Principal Areas) (England and Wales) Rules 2006, SI 2006/3304, Sch 2 r 32; Local Elections (Parishes and Communities) (England and Wales) Rules 2006, SI 2006/3305, Sch 2 r 32; National Assembly for Wales (Representation of the People) Order 2007, SI 2007/236, Sch 5 para 43; Local Authorities (Mayoral Elections) (England and Wales) Regulations 2007, SI 2007/1024, Sch 1 r 34; Greater London Authority Elections Rules 2007, SI 2007/3541, Sch 1 r 35, Sch 2 r 36, Sch 3 r 35. As to the presiding officer see PARA 393.

4　Representation of the People Act 1983 Sch 1 r 34; Parish and Community Meetings (Polls) Rules 1987, SI 1987/1, Schedule r 16; European Parliamentary Elections Regulations 2004, SI 2004/293, Sch 1 para 38(a) (as substituted: see note 3); Local Elections (Principal Areas) (England and Wales) Rules 2006, SI 2006/3304, Sch 2 r 32; Local Elections (Parishes and

Communities) (England and Wales) Rules 2006, SI 2006/3305, Sch 2 r 32; National Assembly for Wales (Representation of the People) Order 2007, SI 2007/236, Sch 5 para 43(a); Local Authorities (Mayoral Elections) (England and Wales) Regulations 2007, SI 2007/1024, Sch 1 r 34(a); Greater London Authority Elections Rules 2007, SI 2007/3541, Sch 1 r 35(a), Sch 2 r 36(a), Sch 3 r 35(a). At a London Authority or Welsh Assembly election, where candidates may have more than one vote to cast (see PARAS 363–364), heads (1)–(5) in the text apply to each ballot box proposed to be used for the purposes of the poll: see the National Assembly for Wales (Representation of the People) Order 2007, SI 2007/236, Sch 5 para 43(a); and the Greater London Authority Elections Rules 2007, SI 2007/3541, Sch 1 r 35(a), Sch 2 r 36(a), Sch 3 r 35(a).

5   Representation of the People Act 1983 Sch 1 r 34; Parish and Community Meetings (Polls) Rules 1987, SI 1987/1, Schedule r 16; European Parliamentary Elections Regulations 2004, SI 2004/293, Sch 1 para 38(b) (as substituted: see note 3); Local Elections (Principal Areas) (England and Wales) Rules 2006, SI 2006/3304, Sch 2 r 32; Local Elections (Parishes and Communities) (England and Wales) Rules 2006, SI 2006/3305, Sch 2 r 32; Local Authorities (Mayoral Elections) (England and Wales) Regulations 2007, SI 2007/1024, Sch 1 r 34(b); Greater London Authority Elections Rules 2007, SI 2007/3541, Sch 1 r 35(b), Sch 2 r 36(b), Sch 3 r 35(b). See note 4. Head (2) in the text does not apply at a Welsh Assembly election, whose governing rules make no mention of a ballot box with a lock: see note 6.

6   Representation of the People Act 1983 Sch 1 r 34; Parish and Community Meetings (Polls) Rules 1987, SI 1987/1, Schedule r 16; European Parliamentary Elections Regulations 2004, SI 2004/293, Sch 1 para 38(c) (as substituted: see note 3); Local Elections (Principal Areas) (England and Wales) Rules 2006, SI 2006/3304, Sch 2 r 32; Local Elections (Parishes and Communities) (England and Wales) Rules 2006, SI 2006/3305, Sch 2 r 32; National Assembly for Wales (Representation of the People) Order 2007, SI 2007/236, Sch 5 para 43(b); Local Authorities (Mayoral Elections) (England and Wales) Regulations 2007, SI 2007/1024, Sch 1 r 34(c); Greater London Authority Elections Rules 2007, SI 2007/3541, Sch 1 r 35(c), Sch 2 r 36(c), Sch 3 r 35(c). See note 4. The rules that apply at a London Authority or local authority mayoral election specify that the seal must be placed on each lock or, where the ballot box has no lock, on the ballot box itself: see the Local Authorities (Mayoral Elections) (England and Wales) Regulations 2007, SI 2007/1024, Sch 1 r 34(c); and the Greater London Authority Elections Rules 2007, SI 2007/3541, Sch 1 r 35(c), Sch 2 r 36(c), Sch 3 r 35(c). Only the rules that apply at a local government or European parliamentary election include specific additional wording that provides for a ballot box, where the box has no lock, to be so constructed that the ballot papers can be put in it, but cannot be withdrawn from it, without the seal being broken; and the rules that apply at a Welsh Assembly election make no mention of a ballot box with a lock, the wording providing only for a ballot box to have a seal: see PARA 391.

7   Representation of the People Act 1983 Sch 1 r 34; Parish and Community Meetings (Polls) Rules 1987, SI 1987/1, Schedule r 16; European Parliamentary Elections Regulations 2004, SI 2004/293, Sch 1 para 38(d) (as substituted: see note 3); Local Elections (Principal Areas) (England and Wales) Rules 2006, SI 2006/3304, Sch 2 r 32; Local Elections (Parishes and Communities) (England and Wales) Rules 2006, SI 2006/3305, Sch 2 r 32; National Assembly for Wales (Representation of the People) Order 2007, SI 2007/236, Sch 5 para 43(c); Local Authorities (Mayoral Elections) (England and Wales) Regulations 2007, SI 2007/1024, Sch 1 r 34(d); Greater London Authority Elections Rules 2007, SI 2007/3541, Sch 1 r 35(d), Sch 2 r 36(d), Sch 3 r 35(d). See note 4.

8   Representation of the People Act 1983 Sch 1 r 34; Parish and Community Meetings (Polls) Rules 1987, SI 1987/1, Schedule r 16; European Parliamentary Elections Regulations 2004, SI 2004/293, Sch 1 para 38(e) (as substituted: see note 3); Local Elections (Principal Areas) (England and Wales) Rules 2006, SI 2006/3304, Sch 2 r 32; Local Elections (Parishes and Communities) (England and Wales) Rules 2006, SI 2006/3305, Sch 2 r 32; National Assembly for Wales (Representation of the People) Order 2007, SI 2007/236, Sch 5 para 43(d); Local Authorities (Mayoral Elections) (England and Wales) Regulations 2007, SI 2007/1024, Sch 1 r 34(e); Greater London Authority Elections Rules 2007, SI 2007/3541, Sch 1 r 35(e), Sch 2 r 36(e), Sch 3 r 35(e). See note 4.

398.   Questions to be put to person applying for ballot paper at a polling station. When any person applies for a ballot paper at a polling station[1], either as an elector[2] or as proxy[3], at the time of his application (but not afterwards), certain specified questions[4]:

(1)   may be put by the presiding officer[5] to that elector or proxy[6]; and

(2)   must be put if the candidate[7], or his polling agent[8], or (at elections where election agents are appointed) his election agent[9], requires the allowed question to be put[10].

A ballot paper must not be delivered to any person required to answer any of the questions unless he has answered each question satisfactorily[11]. No other inquiry is permitted as to the right of any person to vote[12].

Where the poll at an election is taken together with the poll at another election or referendum, special provision is made for the questions that may be put to a person applying for a ballot paper[13].

If any person knowingly and wilfully makes a false answer to any of the questions so prescribed, he is guilty of an indictable offence and may be punished accordingly[14].

1   As to the provision and allotment of polling stations see PARA 390.
2   As to the meaning of 'elector', in relation to a parliamentary or local government election, see PARA 95 note 2; in relation to a Welsh Assembly election, see PARA 110 note 6; and, in relation to European parliamentary election, see PARA 111 note 4.
3   As to voting by proxy see PARA 366 et seq. There is no provision for voting by proxy at a poll consequent on a parish meeting on a question involving appointment to office (see PARA 200 et seq).
4   The prescribed questions are set out:
     (1)   for the purposes of a parliamentary election, in the Representation of the People Act 1983 Sch 1 r 35(1) Table (Sch 1 r 35 substituted by the Electoral Administration Act 2006 s 47, Sch 1 paras 69, 74);
     (2)   for the purposes of a European parliamentary election, in the European Parliamentary Elections Regulations 2004, SI 2004/293, Sch 1 para 39(1) Table (Sch 1 substituted by SI 2009/186);
     (3)   for the purposes of the case of a local government election:
            (a)   in the Local Elections (Principal Areas) (England and Wales) Rules 2006, SI 2006/3304, Sch 2 r 33(1) Table;
            (b)   in the Local Elections (Parishes and Communities) (England and Wales) Rules 2006, SI 2006/3305, Sch 2 r 33(1) Table;
            (c)   in the Local Authorities (Mayoral Elections) (England and Wales) Regulations 2007, SI 2007/1024, Sch 1 r 35(1) Table;
            (d)   in the Greater London Authority Elections Rules 2007, SI 2007/3541, Sch 1 r 36(1) Table, Sch 2 r 37(1) Table, Sch 3 r 36(1) Table;
     (4)   for the purposes of a Welsh Assembly election, in English and Welsh in the National Assembly for Wales (Representation of the People) Order 2007, SI 2007/236, Sch 5 para 44(1)–(3) Table.
     Certain questions specified under head (4) above may be asked only where the polls at an Assembly constituency election and regional election are taken together: see Sch 5 para 44(3). As to the meanings of 'Assembly election', 'constituency election' and 'regional election' for these purposes see PARA 3 note 2. As to the meaning of 'parliamentary election' see PARA 9. As to the meanings of 'Authority election' and 'local government election' see PARA 11. As to European parliamentary elections see PARA 217 et seq. Where elections take place in Wales see also the forms issued partly in English and partly in Welsh in:
            (i)   the Parliamentary Elections (Welsh Forms) Order 2007, SI 2007/1014, art 5(b), Sch 1 (Form 2 (Ffurflen 2));
            (ii)   the Local Elections (Principal Areas) (Welsh Forms) Order 2007, SI 2007/1015, arts 6(a), 8(a), Sch 2 (Form 1 (Ffurflen 1)), Sch 4 (Form 1 (Ffurflen 1) (combined polls));
            (iii)   the Local Elections (Communities) (Welsh Forms) Order 2007, SI 2007/1013, arts 6(a), 8(a), Sch 2 (Form 1 (Ffurflen 1)), Sch 4 (Form 1 (Ffurflen 1) (combined polls)); and
            (iv)   the European Parliamentary Elections (Welsh Forms) Order 2009, SI 2009/781, art 5(1), (2)(b), Sch 1 (Form 2 (Ffurflen 2): Questions to be put to voters; Cwestiynau i'w gofyn i bleideiswyr).
     In the case of an elector who is added to the register in pursuance of a notice issued under the Representation of the People Act 1983 s 13B(3B) or s 13B(3D) (see PARA 168), the references in the questions that require the presiding officer to read from the register must be taken as references to reading from the notice: Representation of the People Act 1983 Sch 1 r 35(2) (as so

substituted); European Parliamentary Elections Regulations 2004, SI 2004/293, Sch 1 para 39(2) (as so substituted); Local Elections (Principal Areas) (England and Wales) Rules 2006, SI 2006/3304, Sch 2 r 33(2); Local Elections (Parishes and Communities) (England and Wales) Rules 2006, SI 2006/3305, Sch 2 r 33(2); National Assembly for Wales (Representation of the People) Order 2007, SI 2007/236, Sch 5 para 44(5); Local Authorities (Mayoral Elections) (England and Wales) Regulations 2007, SI 2007/1024, Sch 1 r 35(2); Greater London Authority Elections Rules 2007, SI 2007/3541, Sch 1 r 36(2), Sch 2 r 37(2), Sch 3 r 36(2). As to the appointment of presiding officers see PARA 393.

In relation to a poll consequent on a parish meeting where the poll is on a question of appointment to an office see the questions set out in Parish and Community Meetings (Polls) Rules 1987, SI 1987/1, Schedule r 17(1)(i), (ii).

5 Ie or a clerk appointed to assist the presiding officer: see PARA 393.
6 Representation of the People Act 1983 Sch 1 r 35(1)(a) (as substituted: see note 4); Parish and Community Meetings (Polls) Rules 1987, SI 1987/1, Schedule r 17(1); European Parliamentary Elections Regulations 2004, SI 2004/293, Sch 1 para 39(1)(a) (as substituted: see note 4); Local Elections (Principal Areas) (England and Wales) Rules 2006, SI 2006/3304, Sch 2 r 33(1)(a); Local Elections (Parishes and Communities) (England and Wales) Rules 2006, SI 2006/3305, Sch 2 r 33(1)(a); National Assembly for Wales (Representation of the People) Order 2007, SI 2007/236, Sch 5 para 44(1)–(3); Local Authorities (Mayoral Elections) (England and Wales) Regulations 2007, SI 2007/1024, Sch 1 r 35(1)(a); Greater London Authority Elections Rules 2007, SI 2007/3541, Sch 1 r 36(1)(a), Sch 2 r 37(1)(a), Sch 3 r 36(1)(a).
7 As to the meaning of 'candidate' generally see PARA 230; but see note 10.
8 As to polling agents see PARA 394.
9 As to the appointment of election agents see PARA 231 et seq. There is no requirement for election agents to be appointed at parish or community council elections (see PARA 231 note 3), and no such provision is made in relation to a poll consequent on a parish meeting on a question involving appointment to office.
10 Representation of the People Act 1983 Sch 1 r 35(1)(b) (as substituted: see note 4); Parish and Community Meetings (Polls) Rules 1987, SI 1987/1, Schedule r 17(1); European Parliamentary Elections Regulations 2004, SI 2004/293, Sch 1 para 39(1)(b) (as substituted: see note 4); Local Elections (Principal Areas) (England and Wales) Rules 2006, SI 2006/3304, Sch 2 r 33(1)(b); Local Elections (Parishes and Communities) (England and Wales) Rules 2006, SI 2006/3305, Sch 2 r 33(1)(b); National Assembly for Wales (Representation of the People) Order 2007, SI 2007/236, Sch 5 para 44(4); Local Authorities (Mayoral Elections) (England and Wales) Regulations 2007, SI 2007/1024, Sch 1 r 35(1)(b); Greater London Authority Elections Rules 2007, SI 2007/3541, Sch 1 r 36(1)(b), Sch 2 r 37(1)(b), Sch 3 r 36(1)(b). The questions that must be put by the presiding officer if the candidate or his election or polling agent so requires are marked in the Tables mentioned in note 4 by a letter 'R': Representation of the People Act 1983 Sch 1 r 35(1)(b) (as so substituted); European Parliamentary Elections Regulations 2004, SI 2004/293, Sch 1 para 39(1)(b) (as so substituted); Local Elections (Principal Areas) (England and Wales) Rules 2006, SI 2006/3304, Sch 2 r 33(1)(b); Local Elections (Parishes and Communities) (England and Wales) Rules 2006, SI 2006/3305, Sch 2 r 33(1)(b); National Assembly for Wales (Representation of the People) Order 2007, SI 2007/236, Sch 5 para 44(4); Local Authorities (Mayoral Elections) (England and Wales) Regulations 2007, SI 2007/1024, Sch 1 r 35(1)(b); Greater London Authority Elections Rules 2007, SI 2007/3541, Sch 1 r 36(1)(b), Sch 2 r 37(1)(b), Sch 3 r 36(1)(b). Head (2) in the text applies:

(1) in the case of a European parliamentary election, to: (a) a candidate or the election agent or polling agent of a registered party standing nominated; (b) an individual candidate or the election agent or polling agent of an individual candidate (see the European Parliamentary Elections Regulations 2004, SI 2004/293, Sch 1 para 39(1)(b) (as so substituted));

(2) in the case of a Welsh Assembly election, to a candidate or his election agent or polling agent (including such an agent of a registered party standing nominated) (see the National Assembly for Wales (Representation of the People) Order 2007, SI 2007/236, Sch 5 para 44(4)).

As to the meaning of 'registered political party' for the purposes of a Welsh Assembly election see PARA 215 note 19; and as to the meaning of candidate' 'for those purposes see PARA 230 note 19. As to the meaning of 'registered party' for the purposes of a European parliamentary election see PARA 230 note 29; and as to the meaning of 'individual candidate' for those purposes see PARA 230 note 32.

11 Representation of the People Act 1983 Sch 1 r 35(3) (as substituted: see note 4); Parish and Community Meetings (Polls) Rules 1987, SI 1987/1, Schedule r 17(2); European Parliamentary

Elections Regulations 2004, SI 2004/293, Sch 1 para 39(3) (as substituted: see note 4); Local Elections (Principal Areas) (England and Wales) Rules 2006, SI 2006/3304, Sch 2 r 33(3); Local Elections (Parishes and Communities) (England and Wales) Rules 2006, SI 2006/3305, Sch 2 r 33(3); National Assembly for Wales (Representation of the People) Order 2007, SI 2007/236, Sch 5 para 44(6); Local Authorities (Mayoral Elections) (England and Wales) Regulations 2007, SI 2007/1024, Sch 1 r 35(3); Greater London Authority Elections Rules 2007, SI 2007/3541, Sch 1 r 36(3), Sch 2 r 37(3), Sch 3 r 36(3). It would appear that the application is not complete until the questions have been answered and that the onus is on the applicant to demand that they be put: *Lyons v Cunningham* (1920) 55 ILT 35 at 38. As to the names under which persons are registered and may vote (and whether any difference between them is allowed) see *R v Thwaites* (1853) 1 E & B 704 at 711 per Crompton J.

12 Representation of the People Act 1983 Sch 1 r 35(4) (as substituted: see note 4); Parish and Community Meetings (Polls) Rules 1987, SI 1987/1, Schedule r 17(3); European Parliamentary Elections Regulations 2004, SI 2004/293, Sch 1 para 39(4) (as substituted: see note 4); Local Elections (Principal Areas) (England and Wales) Rules 2006, SI 2006/3304, Sch 2 r 33(4); Local Elections (Parishes and Communities) (England and Wales) Rules 2006, SI 2006/3305, Sch 2 r 33(4); National Assembly for Wales (Representation of the People) Order 2007, SI 2007/236, Sch 5 para 44(7); Local Authorities (Mayoral Elections) (England and Wales) Regulations 2007, SI 2007/1024, Sch 1 r 35(4); Greater London Authority Elections Rules 2007, SI 2007/3541, Sch 1 r 36(3), Sch 2 r 37(4), Sch 3 r 36(4).

13 As to polls at elections or referendums which are taken together see PARA 16 et seq.

14 See the Perjury Act 1911 s 5 (false statutory declarations and other false statements without oath); and CRIMINAL LAW vol 26 (2010) PARA 673.

399. Voting procedure. A ballot paper must be delivered to a voter[1] who applies for one at an election[2]; and, immediately before delivery[3]:

(1)   the number and name of the elector[4] as stated in the copy of the register of electors must be called out[5], unless the elector in question has an anonymous entry in the register[6], in which case he must first show the presiding officer his official poll card and then only his number will be called out[7];

(2)   the number of the elector must be marked, on the version of the corresponding number list supplied to the polling station[8], beside the number of the ballot paper to be issued to him[9];

(3)   a mark must be placed in the register of electors supplied to the polling station against the number of the elector to note that a ballot paper has been received but without showing the particular ballot paper which has been received[10];

(4)   as from a day to be appointed in relation to a parliamentary election[11], the voter must sign the corresponding number list mentioned in head (2) above beside the number of the elector marked on the list in accordance with head (2) above[12]; and

(5)   in the case of a person applying for a ballot paper as proxy, a mark must also be placed against his name in the list of proxies[13].

At a poll consequent on a parish meeting on a question involving appointment to office[14], a ballot paper must be delivered to a voter who applies for one and, immediately before delivery[15]:

(a)   the ballot paper must be stamped with the official mark[16];

(b)   the number and name of the elector as stated in the copy of the register of electors must be called out[17];

(c)   the number of the elector must be marked on the counterfoil[18]; and

(d)   a mark must be placed in the register of electors against the number of the elector to denote that a ballot paper has been received but without showing the particular ballot paper which has been received[19].

At any such election or poll, the voter, on receiving the ballot paper, must forthwith proceed into one of the compartments in the polling station and there secretly mark his paper[20]. The voter must then fold his paper up in such a way as to conceal his vote and he must then show to the presiding officer the back of the paper, so as to disclose, at an election, the number and other unique identifying mark (or so as to disclose, at a poll, the official mark), and put the ballot paper so folded up in the ballot box in the presence of the presiding officer[21]. The voter must vote without undue delay and must leave the polling station as soon as he has put his ballot paper into the ballot box[22].

It is an offence to interfere or attempt to interfere with a voter when he is recording his vote[23].

1   For the purposes of the statutory provisions governing elections, a voter is defined as a person voting at an election and includes a person voting as proxy (but not necessarily a person voting by proxy): see PARA 95 note 2. As to voting by proxy see PARA 366 et seq. To indicate that an elector or his proxy is entitled to vote by post (and is for that reason not entitled to vote in person), the letter 'A' is placed against the name of that elector in any copy of the register, or part of it, provided for a polling station: see PARA 377.

2   Ie a parliamentary election, a local government election (which includes any London Authority election and a local authority mayoral election), a Welsh Assembly constituency or regional election or a European parliamentary election. As to the meanings of 'Assembly election', 'constituency election' and 'regional election' see PARA 3 note 2. As to the meaning of 'parliamentary election' see PARA 9. As to the meanings of 'Authority election' and 'local government election' see PARA 11. As to elections in the City of London see PARA 33. As to elections for the return of a local authority mayor see PARA 198; and as to European parliamentary elections see PARA 217 et seq. As to the questions that may be put to a person applying for a ballot paper at a polling station at the time of his application see PARA 398.

As from a day to be appointed under the Electoral Registration and Administration Act 2013 s 27(1), a voter who at the close of the poll is in the polling station, or in a queue outside the polling station, for the purpose of voting is (despite the close of the poll) entitled to apply for a ballot paper under the Representation of the People Act 1983 Sch 1 r 37(1); and Sch 1 r 37 applies in relation to such a voter accordingly: Sch 1 r 37(7) (prospectively added by the Electoral Registration and Administration Act 2013 s 19(1), (2)). However, at the date at which this volume states the law, no such day had been appointed.

3   Representation of the People Act 1983 Sch 1 r 37(1) (Sch 1 r 37(1)–(3) substituted, Sch 1 r 37(4)–(6) added, by the Electoral Administration Act 2006 s 47, Sch 1 paras 69, 75); European Parliamentary Elections Regulations 2004, SI 2004/293, Sch 1 para 41(1) (Sch 1 substituted by SI 2009/186); Local Elections (Principal Areas) (England and Wales) Rules 2006, SI 2006/3304, Sch 2 r 35(1); Local Elections (Parishes and Communities) (England and Wales) Rules 2006, SI 2006/3305, Sch 2 r 35(1); National Assembly for Wales (Representation of the People) Order 2007, SI 2007/236, Sch 5 para 46(1); Local Authorities (Mayoral Elections) (England and Wales) Regulations 2007, SI 2007/1024, Sch 1 r 37(1); Greater London Authority Elections Rules 2007, SI 2007/3541, Sch 1 r 38(1), Sch 2 r 39(1), Sch 3 r 38(1). As to the commencement of amendments effected by the Electoral Administration Act 2006 Sch 1 para 75 see note 11.

4   As to the meaning of 'elector' see PARA 95 note 2. As to the number of an elector see PARA 145.

5   Representation of the People Act 1983 Sch 1 r 37(1)(a) (as substituted: see note 3); European Parliamentary Elections Regulations 2004, SI 2004/293, Sch 1 para 41(1)(a) (as substituted: see note 3); Local Elections (Principal Areas) (England and Wales) Rules 2006, SI 2006/3304, Sch 2 r 35(1)(a); Local Elections (Parishes and Communities) (England and Wales) Rules 2006, SI 2006/3305, Sch 2 r 35(1)(a); National Assembly for Wales (Representation of the People) Order 2007, SI 2007/236, Sch 5 para 46(1)(a); Local Authorities (Mayoral Elections) (England and Wales) Regulations 2007, SI 2007/1024, Sch 1 r 37(1)(a); Greater London Authority Elections Rules 2007, SI 2007/3541, Sch 1 r 38(1)(a), Sch 2 r 39(1)(a), Sch 3 r 38(1)(a). As to the registers of electors see PARA 145 et seq.

In the case of an elector who is added to the register in pursuance of a notice issued under the Representation of the People Act 1983 s 13B(3B) or s 13B(3D) (see PARA 168), the reference in head (1) in the text to the copy of the register of electors is to be read as a reference to the copy of the notice issued under s 13B(3B) or s 13B(3D): see Sch 1 r 37(3)(a) (as so substituted); European Parliamentary Elections Regulations 2004, SI 2004/293, Sch 1 para 41(3)(a) (as so substituted); Local Elections (Principal Areas) (England and Wales) Rules 2006, SI 2006/3304, Sch 2 r 35(3)(a); Local Elections (Parishes and Communities) (England and Wales) Rules 2006,

SI 2006/3305, Sch 2 r 35(3)(a); National Assembly for Wales (Representation of the People) Order 2007, SI 2007/236, Sch 5 para 46(3)(a); Local Authorities (Mayoral Elections) (England and Wales) Regulations 2007, SI 2007/1024, Sch 1 r 37(3)(a); Greater London Authority Elections Rules 2007, SI 2007/3541, Sch 1 r 38(3)(a), Sch 2 r 39(3)(a), Sch 3 r 38(3)(a). The presiding officer at an election must keep a list of persons to whom ballot papers are delivered in consequence of an alteration to the register made by virtue of the Representation of the People Act 1983 s 13B(3B) or s 13B(3D) which takes effect on the day of the poll: Representation of the People Act 1983 Sch 1 r 41A (added by the Electoral Administration Act 2006 s 11(6), Sch 1 Pt 2 paras 31, 33, 38); European Parliamentary Elections Regulations 2004, SI 2004/293, Sch 1 para 47(1) (as so substituted); Local Elections (Principal Areas) (England and Wales) Rules 2006, SI 2006/3304, Sch 2 r 41; Local Elections (Parishes and Communities) (England and Wales) Rules 2006, SI 2006/3305, Sch 2 r 41; National Assembly for Wales (Representation of the People) Order 2007, SI 2007/236, Sch 5 para 51; Local Authorities (Mayoral Elections) (England and Wales) Regulations 2007, SI 2007/1024, Sch 1 r 43; Greater London Authority Elections Rules 2007, SI 2007/3541, Sch 1 r 44(1), Sch 2 r 45(1), Sch 3 r 44(1). At an ordinary London Authority election, where any other ordinary Authority election in the Assembly constituency is contested, the same list may be used for each Authority election, and where it is so used, an entry in that list must be taken to mean that ballot papers were delivered in respect of each Authority election, unless the list identifies the election for which a tendered ballot paper was delivered (see PARA 403): see Sch 1 r 44(2), Sch 2 r 45(2), Sch 3 r 44(2). As to the meaning of 'Assembly constituency', in relation to the London Assembly, see PARA 11 note 6. As to the appointment of presiding officers see PARA 393.

6   As to the meaning of 'anonymous entry' in relation to a register of electors see PARA 148.

7   Representation of the People Act 1983 Sch 1 r 37(2) (as substituted: see note 3); European Parliamentary Elections Regulations 2004, SI 2004/293, Sch 1 para 41(2) (as substituted: see note 3); Local Elections (Principal Areas) (England and Wales) Rules 2006, SI 2006/3304, Sch 2 r 35(2); Local Elections (Parishes and Communities) (England and Wales) Rules 2006, SI 2006/3305, Sch 2 r 35(2); National Assembly for Wales (Representation of the People) Order 2007, SI 2007/236, Sch 5 para 46(2); Local Authorities (Mayoral Elections) (England and Wales) Regulations 2007, SI 2007/1024, Sch 1 r 37(2); Greater London Authority Elections Rules 2007, SI 2007/3541, Sch 1 r 38(2), Sch 2 r 39(2), Sch 3 r 38(2). As to the issue of official poll cards at elections see PARA 389.

8   Ie the list prepared, in relation to a parliamentary election, under the Representation of the People Act 1983 Sch 1 r 19A, or, in relation to a local government election, under the Local Elections (Principal Areas) (England and Wales) Rules 2006, SI 2006/3304, Sch 2 r 17, the Local Elections (Parishes and Communities) (England and Wales) Rules 2006, SI 2006/3305, Sch 2 r 17, the Local Authorities (Mayoral Elections) (England and Wales) Regulations 2007, SI 2007/1024, Sch 1 r 19, or the Greater London Authority Elections Rules 2007, SI 2007/3541, Sch 1 r 18, Sch 2 r 19, Sch 3 r 18, or, in relation to a European parliamentary election, under the European Parliamentary Elections Regulations 2004, SI 2004/293, Sch 1 para 23, or, in relation to a Welsh Assembly election, under the National Assembly for Wales (Representation of the People) Order 2007, SI 2007/236, Sch 5 para 27 (see PARA 387): see the Representation of the People Act 1983 Sch 1 r 29(3)(e); the European Parliamentary Elections Regulations 2004, SI 2004/293, Sch 1 para 32(3)(d); the Local Elections (Principal Areas) (England and Wales) Rules 2006, SI 2006/3304, Sch 2 r 26(3)(d); the Local Elections (Parishes and Communities) (England and Wales) Rules 2006, SI 2006/3305, Sch 2 r 26(3)(d); the National Assembly for Wales (Representation of the People) Order 2007, SI 2007/236, Sch 5 para 37(5)(d); the Local Authorities (Mayoral Elections) (England and Wales) Regulations 2007, SI 2007/1024, Sch 1 r 28(3)(d); the Greater London Authority Elections Rules 2007, SI 2007/3541, Sch 1 r 28(3)(d), Sch 2 r 29(3)(e), Sch 3 r 28(3)(d); and PARA 391. As to the form of corresponding number list to be prepared by a returning officer for these purposes see PARA 391 note 14.

At an ordinary London Authority election, where any other ordinary Authority election in the Assembly constituency is contested, the same copy of the list mentioned in the Greater London Authority Elections Rules 2007, SI 2007/3541, Sch 1 r 28(3)(d), Sch 2 r 29(3)(e), Sch 3 r 28(3)(d), may be used for each Authority election and one mark may be placed in the list to denote that a ballot paper has been delivered in respect of each Authority election; except that, where a ballot paper has not been issued in respect of any Authority election, a different mark must be placed in the list so as to identify the elections in respect of which a ballot paper was issued: see Sch 1 r 38(7)(b), Sch 2 r 39(7)(b), Sch 3 r 38(7)(b).

9   Representation of the People Act 1983 Sch 1 r 37(1)(b) (as substituted: see note 3); European Parliamentary Elections Regulations 2004, SI 2004/293, Sch 1 para 41(1)(b) (as substituted: see note 3); Local Elections (Principal Areas) (England and Wales) Rules 2006, SI 2006/3304, Sch 2 r 35(1)(b); Local Elections (Parishes and Communities) (England and Wales) Rules 2006,

SI 2006/3305, Sch 2 r 35(1)(b); National Assembly for Wales (Representation of the People) Order 2007, SI 2007/236, Sch 5 para 46(1)(b); Local Authorities (Mayoral Elections) (England and Wales) Regulations 2007, SI 2007/1024, Sch 1 r 37(1)(b); Greater London Authority Elections Rules 2007, SI 2007/3541, Sch 1 r 38(1)(b), Sch 2 r 39(1)(b), Sch 3 r 38(1)(b). Where a voter at a Welsh Assembly election is entitled to two votes, then, subject to the National Assembly for Wales (Representation of the People) Order 2007, SI 2007/236, Sch 5 para 50(4) (one spoilt and one unspoilt ballot paper: see PARA 404), the constituency ballot paper and the regional ballot paper delivered to the voter must bear the same number: Sch 5 para 46(7).

10 Representation of the People Act 1983 Sch 1 r 37(1)(c) (as substituted: see note 3); European Parliamentary Elections Regulations 2004, SI 2004/293, Sch 1 para 41(1)(c) (as substituted: see note 3); Local Elections (Principal Areas) (England and Wales) Rules 2006, SI 2006/3304, Sch 2 r 35(1)(c); Local Elections (Parishes and Communities) (England and Wales) Rules 2006, SI 2006/3305, Sch 2 r 35(1)(c); National Assembly for Wales (Representation of the People) Order 2007, SI 2007/236, Sch 5 para 46(1)(c); Local Authorities (Mayoral Elections) (England and Wales) Regulations 2007, SI 2007/1024, Sch 1 r 37(1)(c); Greater London Authority Elections Rules 2007, SI 2007/3541, Sch 1 r 38(1)(c), Sch 2 r 39(1)(c), Sch 3 r 38(1)(c). At a London Authority election, the wording of head (3) in the text refers to a ballot paper that 'has been applied for' and 'which may be delivered' (ie rather than 'has been received' in both instances): see Sch 1 r 38(1)(c), Sch 2 r 39(1)(c), Sch 3 r 38(1)(c). In the case of an elector who is added to the register in pursuance of a notice issued under the Representation of the People Act 1983 s 13B(3B) or s 13B(3D) (see PARA 168), the reference in head (3) in the text to placing a mark in the register of electors is to be read as a reference to placing a mark on the copy of the notice issued under s 13B(3B) or s 13B(3D): see Sch 1 r 37(3)(b) (as so substituted); European Parliamentary Elections Regulations 2004, SI 2004/293, Sch 1 para 41(3)(b) (as so substituted); Local Elections (Principal Areas) (England and Wales) Rules 2006, SI 2006/3304, Sch 2 r 35(3)(b); Local Elections (Parishes and Communities) (England and Wales) Rules 2006, SI 2006/3305, Sch 2 r 35(3)(b); National Assembly for Wales (Representation of the People) Order 2007, SI 2007/236, Sch 5 para 46(3)(b); Local Authorities (Mayoral Elections) (England and Wales) Regulations 2007, SI 2007/1024, Sch 1 r 37(3)(b); Greater London Authority Elections Rules 2007, SI 2007/3541, Sch 1 r 38(3)(b), Sch 2 r 39(3)(b), Sch 3 r 38(3)(b). See note 5.

At an ordinary London Authority election, where any other ordinary Authority election in the Assembly constituency is contested, the same copy of the register of electors, and of any notice issued under the Representation of the People Act 1983 s 13B(3B) or s 13B(3D) (marked in the case of an elector who is added to the register in pursuance of such a notice), may be used for each Authority election and one mark may be placed in the register or notice (as the case may be) under head (3) in the text to denote that a ballot paper has been delivered in respect of each Authority election; except that, where a ballot paper has not been issued in respect of any Authority election, a different mark must be placed in the register or notice so as to identify the elections in respect of which a ballot paper was issued: see Sch 1 r 38(7)(c), (d), Sch 2 r 39(7)(c), (d), Sch 3 r 38(7)(c), (d). Where the polls at a Welsh Assembly constituency or regional election are to be taken together, the same copy of the register of electors (or copy of the notice) may be used for a constituency election and a regional election; and one mark may be placed in that register or on that copy under head (3) in the text to denote that a ballot paper has been received in respect of each election except that, where a ballot paper has been issued in respect of one election only, a different mark must be placed in the register (or copy of the notice) so as to identify the election in respect of which the ballot paper was issued: National Assembly for Wales (Representation of the People) Order 2007, SI 2007/236, Sch 5 para 46(6).

11 Until a day to be appointed under the Electoral Administration Act 2006 s 77(2), any amendment effected by Sch 1 para 75 (see note 3) has no effect in so far as it relates to the substitution of the Representation of the People Act 1983 Sch 1 r 37(1)(d) and the addition of Sch 1 r 37(4): see the Electoral Administration Act 2006 (Commencement No 2, Transitional and Savings Provisions) Order 2006, SI 2006/3412, arts 3, 6, Sch 1 para 12(d), Sch 2 para 1. At the date at which this volume states the law, no such day had been appointed.

12 Representation of the People Act 1983 Sch 1 r 37(1)(d) (prospectively substituted: see note 3). The provision set out in Sch 1 r 37(1)(d) does not apply to a voter to whom Sch 1 r 38 applies (ie a voter with an incapacity who votes with the assistance of the presiding officer: see PARA 401) or to a voter to whom Sch 1 r 39 applies (ie a voter with an incapacity who votes with the assistance of a companion: see PARA 402): Sch 1 r 37(4) (prospectively added: see note 3). See also note 11.

13 Representation of the People Act 1983 Sch 1 r 37(1)(e) (as substituted: see note 3); European Parliamentary Elections Regulations 2004, SI 2004/293, Sch 1 para 41(1)(d) (as substituted: see note 3); Local Elections (Principal Areas) (England and Wales) Rules 2006, SI 2006/3304, Sch 2

r 35(1)(d); Local Elections (Parishes and Communities) (England and Wales) Rules 2006, SI 2006/3305, Sch 2 r 35(1)(d); National Assembly for Wales (Representation of the People) Order 2007, SI 2007/236, Sch 5 para 46(1)(d); Local Authorities (Mayoral Elections) (England and Wales) Regulations 2007, SI 2007/1024, Sch 1 r 37(1)(d); Greater London Authority Elections Rules 2007, SI 2007/3541, Sch 1 r 38(1)(d), Sch 2 r 39(1)(d), Sch 3 r 38(1)(d). As to the meaning of 'list of proxies' see PARA 373 note 14.

At an ordinary London Authority election, where any other ordinary Authority election in the Assembly constituency is contested, the same copy of the list of proxies may be used for each Authority election and one mark may be placed in the list under head (5) in the text to denote that a ballot paper has been delivered in respect of each Authority election; except that, where a ballot paper has not been issued in respect of any Authority election, a different mark must be placed in the list so as to identify the elections in respect of which a ballot paper was issued: see Sch 1 r 38(7)(a), Sch 2 r 39(7)(a), Sch 3 r 38(7)(a). Where the polls at a Welsh Assembly constituency or regional election are to be taken together, one mark may be placed in the list of proxies under head (5) in the text to denote that a ballot paper has been received in respect of each election except that, where a ballot paper has been issued in respect of one election only, a different mark must be placed in the register (or copy of the notice) so as to identify the election in respect of which the ballot paper was issued: see the National Assembly for Wales (Representation of the People) Order 2007, SI 2007/236, Sch 5 para 46(6).

14 As to polls consequent on a parish meeting on a question involving appointment to office see PARA 200 et seq.

15 See the Parish and Community Meetings (Polls) Rules 1987, SI 1987/1, Schedule r 19(1).

16 Parish and Community Meetings (Polls) Rules 1987, SI 1987/1, Schedule r 19(1)(a). As to the official mark see PARA 387.

17 Parish and Community Meetings (Polls) Rules 1987, SI 1987/1, Schedule r 19(1)(b).

18 Parish and Community Meetings (Polls) Rules 1987, SI 1987/1, Schedule r 19(1)(c).

19 Parish and Community Meetings (Polls) Rules 1987, SI 1987/1, Schedule r 19(1)(d).

20 Representation of the People Act 1983 Sch 1 r 37(5) (as added: see note 3); Parish and Community Meetings (Polls) Rules 1987, SI 1987/1, Schedule r 19(2); European Parliamentary Elections Regulations 2004, SI 2004/293, Sch 1 para 41(4) (as substituted: see note 3); Local Elections (Principal Areas) (England and Wales) Rules 2006, SI 2006/3304, Sch 2 r 35(4); Local Elections (Parishes and Communities) (England and Wales) Rules 2006, SI 2006/3305, Sch 2 r 35(4); National Assembly for Wales (Representation of the People) Order 2007, SI 2007/236, Sch 5 para 46(4); Local Authorities (Mayoral Elections) (England and Wales) Regulations 2007, SI 2007/1024, Sch 1 r 37(4); Greater London Authority Elections Rules 2007, SI 2007/3541, Sch 1 r 38(4), Sch 2 r 39(4), Sch 3 r 38(4). As to the mark (or, as the case may be, marks) to be made on a ballot paper see the directions for the guidance of the voters in voting; and PARA 391 note 17. As to the grounds on which a ballot paper may be rejected during the count see PARA 427 et seq; and as to the treatment of rejected votes see PARA 431 et seq.

A voter who has had a ballot paper delivered to him under the Greater London Authority Elections Rules 2007, SI 2007/3541, Sch 1 r 38(1), Sch 2 r 39(1), or Sch 3 r 38(1) (see the text and notes 1–13), but has decided not to mark it, may return it to the presiding officer and, where the voter does so, the presiding officer must immediately cancel the ballot paper and, for the purposes of the Greater London Authority Elections Rules 2007, SI 2007/3541, treat it as a spoilt ballot paper, and he must place a mark beside the number of that ballot paper on the corresponding number list to show that the ballot paper has been cancelled: Sch 1 r 38(6), Sch 2 r 39(6), Sch 3 r 38(6). If a voter decides, after he has returned his ballot paper and it has been cancelled in accordance with Sch 1 r 38(6), Sch 2 r 39(6), Sch 3 r 38(6), but before the close of the poll, that he wishes to vote in the election, he may obtain a replacement for the returned ballot paper: Sch 1 r 43(2), Sch 2 r 44(2), Sch 3 r 43(2). As to spoilt and replacement ballot papers see PARA 404.

21 Representation of the People Act 1983 Sch 1 r 37(5) (as added: see note 3); Parish and Community Meetings (Polls) Rules 1987, SI 1987/1, Schedule r 19(2); European Parliamentary Elections Regulations 2004, SI 2004/293, Sch 1 para 41(4) (as substituted: see note 3); Local Elections (Principal Areas) (England and Wales) Rules 2006, SI 2006/3304, Sch 2 r 35(4); Local Elections (Parishes and Communities) (England and Wales) Rules 2006, SI 2006/3305, Sch 2 r 35(4); National Assembly for Wales (Representation of the People) Order 2007, SI 2007/236, Sch 5 para 46(4); Local Authorities (Mayoral Elections) (England and Wales) Regulations 2007, SI 2007/1024, Sch 1 r 37(4); Greater London Authority Elections Rules 2007, SI 2007/3541, Sch 1 r 38(4), Sch 2 r 39(4), Sch 3 r 38(4). *Quare* whether the ballot paper can be placed validly in a ballot box notwithstanding the absence of the presiding officer (see PARA 393). As to security measures associated with the ballot paper see PARA 387.

22 Representation of the People Act 1983 Sch 1 r 37(6) (as added: see note 3); Parish and Community Meetings (Polls) Rules 1987, SI 1987/1, Schedule r 19(3); European Parliamentary Elections Regulations 2004, SI 2004/293, Sch 1 para 41(5) (as substituted: see note 3); Local Elections (Principal Areas) (England and Wales) Rules 2006, SI 2006/3304, Sch 2 r 35(5); Local Elections (Parishes and Communities) (England and Wales) Rules 2006, SI 2006/3305, Sch 2 r 35(5); National Assembly for Wales (Representation of the People) Order 2007, SI 2007/236, Sch 5 para 46(5); Local Authorities (Mayoral Elections) (England and Wales) Regulations 2007, SI 2007/1024, Sch 1 r 37(5); Greater London Authority Elections Rules 2007, SI 2007/3541, Sch 1 r 38(5), Sch 2 r 39(5), Sch 3 r 38(5). As to the keeping of order in a polling station, and the presiding officer's powers to remove persons who are misconducting themselves, see PARA 396.

23 See PARA 741.

400. Effect of voter being challenged on suspicion of personation. A person is not to be prevented from voting at an election[1] by reason only that[2]:

(1) a candidate[3], or his polling agent[4], or (at elections where election agents are appointed) his election agent[5], declares that he has reasonable cause to believe that the person has committed an offence of personation[6]; or

(2) the person is arrested on the grounds that he is suspected of committing or of being about to commit such an offence[7].

If, at the time a person applies for a ballot paper at a poll consequent on a parish meeting on a question involving appointment to office[8], for the purpose of voting in person, or after he has applied for a ballot paper for that purpose and before he has left the polling station[9], a candidate or his polling agent[10]:

(a) declares to the presiding officer[11] that he has reasonable cause to believe that the applicant has committed an offence of personation[12]; and

(b) undertakes to substantiate the charge in a court of law[13],

the presiding officer may order a constable to arrest the applicant[14], and the order of the presiding officer is sufficient authority for the constable so to do[15]. The person who has been challenged in this way must not by reason of it be prevented from voting[16].

1 Ie a parliamentary election, a local government election (which includes any London Authority election and a local authority mayoral election), a Welsh Assembly constituency or regional election or a European parliamentary election. As to the meanings of 'Assembly election', 'constituency election' and 'regional election' see PARA 3 note 2. As to the meaning of 'parliamentary election' see PARA 9. As to the meanings of 'Authority election' and 'local government election' see PARA 11. As to elections in the City of London see PARA 33. As to European parliamentary elections see PARA 217 et seq. As to the questions that may be put to a person applying for a ballot paper at a polling station at the time of his application see PARA 398.

2 Representation of the People Act 1983 Sch 1 r 36 (substituted by the Electoral Administration Act 2006 s 74(1), Sch 1 paras 104, 132); European Parliamentary Elections Regulations 2004, SI 2004/293, Sch 1 para 40 (Sch 1 substituted by SI 2009/186); Local Elections (Principal Areas) (England and Wales) Rules 2006, SI 2006/3304, Sch 2 r 34; Local Elections (Parishes and Communities) (England and Wales) Rules 2006, SI 2006/3305, Sch 2 r 34; National Assembly for Wales (Representation of the People) Order 2007, SI 2007/236, Sch 5 para 45; Local Authorities (Mayoral Elections) (England and Wales) Regulations 2007, SI 2007/1024, Sch 1 r 36; Greater London Authority Elections Rules 2007, SI 2007/3541, Sch 1 r 37, Sch 2 r 38, Sch 3 r 37.

3 As to the meaning of 'candidate' generally see PARA 230. See also note 6.

4 As to polling agents see PARA 394.

5 As to the appointment of election agents see PARA 231 et seq. There is no requirement for election agents to be appointed at parish or community council elections: see PARA 231 note 3.

6 Representation of the People Act 1983 Sch 1 r 36(a) (as substituted: see note 2); European Parliamentary Elections Regulations 2004, SI 2004/293, Sch 1 para 40(a) (as substituted: see note 2); Local Elections (Principal Areas) (England and Wales) Rules 2006, SI 2006/3304, Sch 2 r 34(a); Local Elections (Parishes and Communities) (England and Wales) Rules 2006, SI 2006/3305, Sch 2 r 34(a); National Assembly for Wales (Representation of the People)

Order 2007, SI 2007/236, Sch 5 para 45(a); Local Authorities (Mayoral Elections) (England and Wales) Regulations 2007, SI 2007/1024, Sch 1 r 36(a); Greater London Authority Elections Rules 2007, SI 2007/3541, Sch 1 r 37(a), Sch 2 r 38(a), Sch 3 r 37(a). As to the offence of personation see PARA 730. Head (1) in the text applies, in the case of a European parliamentary election, to: (1) a candidate or the election agent or polling agent of a registered party standing nominated; or (2) an individual candidate or the election agent or polling agent of an individual candidate: see the European Parliamentary Elections Regulations 2004, SI 2004/293, Sch 1 para 40(a) (as so substituted). As to the meaning of 'registered party' for the purposes of a European parliamentary election see PARA 230 note 29; and as to the meaning of 'individual candidate' for those purposes see PARA 230 note 32.

7   Representation of the People Act 1983 Sch 1 r 36(b) (as substituted: see note 2); European Parliamentary Elections Regulations 2004, SI 2004/293, Sch 1 para 40(b) (as substituted: see note 2); Local Elections (Principal Areas) (England and Wales) Rules 2006, SI 2006/3304, Sch 2 r 34(b); Local Elections (Parishes and Communities) (England and Wales) Rules 2006, SI 2006/3305, Sch 2 r 34(b); National Assembly for Wales (Representation of the People) Order 2007, SI 2007/236, Sch 5 para 45(b); Local Authorities (Mayoral Elections) (England and Wales) Regulations 2007, SI 2007/1024, Sch 1 r 36(b); Greater London Authority Elections Rules 2007, SI 2007/3541, Sch 1 r 37(b), Sch 2 r 38(b), Sch 3 r 37(b).

The Police and Criminal Evidence Act 1984 s 24A (arrest without warrant: other persons) does not permit a person other than a constable to arrest a person inside a polling station who commits or is suspected of committing an offence of personation (see PARA 730); and although s 26 (repeal of statutory powers of arrest: see POLICE AND INVESTIGATORY POWERS vol 84A (2013) PARA 490) does not apply to the power of arrest in the Representation of the People Act 1983 Sch 1 r 36 (see the Representation of the People Act 1985 s 25(1)), the wording of the Representation of the People Act 1983 Sch 1 r 36 (as so substituted) no longer embodies the power of arrest upon which the Representation of the People Act 1985 s 25(1) purports to bite. As from a day to be appointed under the Electoral Administration Act 2006 s 77(2), the Representation of the People Act 1985 s 25(1) is repealed by the Electoral Administration Act 2006 s 74(2), Sch 2. However, at the date at which this volume states the law, no such day had been appointed.

8   As to polls consequent on a parish meeting on a question involving appointment to office see PARA 200 et seq.

9   As to voting procedure see PARA 399.

10   See the Parish and Community Meetings (Polls) Rules 1987, SI 1987/1, Schedule r 18(1).

11   As to the presiding officer see PARA 393.

12   Parish and Community Meetings (Polls) Rules 1987, SI 1987/1, Schedule r 18(1)(a).

13   Parish and Community Meetings (Polls) Rules 1987, SI 1987/1, Schedule r 18(1)(b).

14   A person arrested under the Parish and Community Meetings (Polls) Rules 1987, SI 1987/1, Schedule r 18 is to be dealt with as a person taken into custody by a constable for an offence without a warrant: Schedule r 18(3). See also note 7.

15   See the Parish and Community Meetings (Polls) Rules 1987, SI 1987/1, Schedule r 18(1). The power to order the arrest, exclusion or removal of any person from a polling station may be exercised only by the presiding officer and not by one of the clerks appointed to assist him: see PARA 393.

16   Parish and Community Meetings (Polls) Rules 1987, SI 1987/1, Schedule r 18(2).

401. Votes marked by presiding officer on application of voter with incapacities. On the application of a voter[1]:

(1)   who is incapacitated by blindness or other disability[2] from voting in the manner directed by the rules[3]; or

(2)   who declares orally that he is unable to read[4],

the presiding officer[5] must, in the presence of the polling agents[6], cause the voter's vote to be marked on a ballot paper in the manner directed by the voter, and the ballot paper to be placed in the ballot box[7].

The name and number on the register of electors[8] of every voter whose vote is marked by the presiding officer in this way, and the reason why it is so marked, must be entered on a list which is called the 'list of votes marked by the presiding officer'[9]. For these purposes, in the case of a person voting at an election as proxy for an elector, the number to be entered together with the voter's name is the elector's number[10].

Where the poll at an election is taken together with the poll at another election or referendum, special provision is made for voting with the assistance of the presiding officer[11].

1   Ie at a parliamentary election, a local government election (which includes any London Authority election and a local authority mayoral election), a Welsh Assembly constituency or regional election or a European parliamentary election. As to the meanings of 'Assembly election', 'constituency election' and 'regional election' see PARA 3 note 2. As to the meaning of 'parliamentary election' see PARA 9. As to the meanings of 'Authority election' and 'local government election' see PARA 11. As to elections in the City of London see PARA 33. As to European parliamentary elections see PARA 217 et seq. For the purposes of the statutory provisions governing elections, a voter is defined as a person voting at an election and includes a person voting as proxy (but not necessarily a person voting by proxy): in relation to parliamentary and local government elections see PARA 95 note 2; in relation to Welsh Assembly elections see PARA 110 note 7; and in relation to European parliamentary elections see PARA 111 note 5.

2   As to the meaning of 'disability' see PARA 367 note 8. At a poll consequent on a parish meeting where the poll is on a question of appointment to an office, the reference is to blindness or other physical cause: see the Parish and Community Meetings (Polls) Rules 1987, SI 1987/1, Schedule r 20(1)(a).

3   Representation of the People Act 1983 Sch 1 r 38(1)(a) (amended by the Electoral Administration Act 2006 s 47, Sch 1 paras 69, 77); Parish and Community Meetings (Polls) Rules 1987, SI 1987/1, Schedule r 20(1)(a); European Parliamentary Elections Regulations 2004, SI 2004/293, Sch 1 para 42(1)(a) (Sch 1 substituted by SI 2009/186); Local Elections (Principal Areas) (England and Wales) Rules 2006, SI 2006/3304, Sch 2 r 36(1)(a); Local Elections (Parishes and Communities) (England and Wales) Rules 2006, SI 2006/3305, Sch 2 r 36(1)(a); National Assembly for Wales (Representation of the People) Order 2007, SI 2007/236, Sch 5 para 47(1)(a); Local Authorities (Mayoral Elections) (England and Wales) Regulations 2007, SI 2007/1024, Sch 1 r 38(1)(a); Greater London Authority Elections Rules 2007, SI 2007/3541, Sch 1 r 39(1)(a), Sch 2 r 40(1)(a), Sch 3 r 39(1)(a). As to companions assisting voters with incapacities to vote see PARA 402.

4   Representation of the People Act 1983 Sch 1 r 38(1)(b); Parish and Community Meetings (Polls) Rules 1987, SI 1987/1, Schedule r 20(1)(b); European Parliamentary Elections Regulations 2004, SI 2004/293, Sch 1 para 42(1)(b) (as substituted: see note 3); Local Elections (Principal Areas) (England and Wales) Rules 2006, SI 2006/3304, Sch 2 r 36(1)(b); Local Elections (Parishes and Communities) (England and Wales) Rules 2006, SI 2006/3305, Sch 2 r 36(1)(b); National Assembly for Wales (Representation of the People) Order 2007, SI 2007/236, Sch 5 para 47(1)(b); Local Authorities (Mayoral Elections) (England and Wales) Regulations 2007, SI 2007/1024, Sch 1 r 38(1)(b); Greater London Authority Elections Rules 2007, SI 2007/3541, Sch 1 r 39(1)(b), Sch 2 r 40(1)(b), Sch 3 r 39(1)(b).

5   As to the presiding officer see PARA 393. This function of the presiding officer may be discharged by one of the clerks appointed to assist him: see PARA 393.

6   As to polling agents see PARA 394. The non-attendance of the polling agents does not invalidate any act or thing done, if the act or thing is otherwise duly done: see PARA 394.

7   Representation of the People Act 1983 Sch 1 r 38(1); Parish and Community Meetings (Polls) Rules 1987, SI 1987/1, Schedule r 20(1); European Parliamentary Elections Regulations 2004, SI 2004/293, Sch 1 para 42(1) (as substituted: see note 3); Local Elections (Principal Areas) (England and Wales) Rules 2006, SI 2006/3304, Sch 2 r 36(1); Local Elections (Parishes and Communities) (England and Wales) Rules 2006, SI 2006/3305, Sch 2 r 36(1); National Assembly for Wales (Representation of the People) Order 2007, SI 2007/236, Sch 5 para 47(1); Local Authorities (Mayoral Elections) (England and Wales) Regulations 2007, SI 2007/1024, Sch 1 r 38(1); Greater London Authority Elections Rules 2007, SI 2007/3541, Sch 1 r 39(1), Sch 2 r 40(1), Sch 3 r 39(1).

8   As to the number of an elector see PARA 145; and as to the registers of electors see PARA 145 et seq.

9   Representation of the People Act 1983 Sch 1 r 38(2); Parish and Community Meetings (Polls) Rules 1987, SI 1987/1, Schedule r 20(2); European Parliamentary Elections Regulations 2004, SI 2004/293, Sch 1 para 42(2) (as substituted: see note 3); Local Elections (Principal Areas) (England and Wales) Rules 2006, SI 2006/3304, Sch 2 r 36(2); Local Elections (Parishes and Communities) (England and Wales) Rules 2006, SI 2006/3305, Sch 2 r 36(2); National Assembly for Wales (Representation of the People) Order 2007, SI 2007/236, Sch 5 para 47(2); Local Authorities (Mayoral Elections) (England and Wales) Regulations 2007, SI 2007/1024,

Sch 1 r 38(2); Greater London Authority Elections Rules 2007, SI 2007/3541, Sch 1 r 39(2), Sch 2 r 40(2), Sch 3 r 39(2). A statement of the number of voters whose votes are so marked by the presiding officer under the heads 'disability' and 'unable to read' must be delivered to the returning officer on the close of a poll: see PARA 405.

In the case of a person in respect of whom a notice has been issued under the Representation of the People Act 1983 s 13B(3B) or s 13B(3D) (see PARA 168), the provision set out in the text applies as if, instead of referring to the name and number of every voter on the register of electors, it referred to the name and number relating to every voter in respect of whom a notice under s 13B(3B) or s 13B(3D) has been issued: Sch 1 r 38(3) (added by the Electoral Administration Act 2006 s 11(6), Sch 1 paras 31, 33, 35); European Parliamentary Elections Regulations 2004, SI 2004/293, Sch 1 para 42(4) (as so substituted); Local Elections (Principal Areas) (England and Wales) Rules 2006, SI 2006/3304, Sch 2 r 36(3); Local Elections (Parishes and Communities) (England and Wales) Rules 2006, SI 2006/3305, Sch 2 r 36(3); National Assembly for Wales (Representation of the People) Order 2007, SI 2007/236, Sch 5 para 47(4); Local Authorities (Mayoral Elections) (England and Wales) Regulations 2007, SI 2007/1024, Sch 1 r 38(4); Greater London Authority Elections Rules 2007, SI 2007/3541, Sch 1 r 39(3), Sch 2 r 40(3), Sch 3 r 39(3).

At an ordinary London Authority constituency members or London Mayoral election, or at any London members election, the same list of votes marked by the presiding officer may be used for each Authority election and, where it is so used, an entry in that list must be taken to mean that the ballot papers were so marked in respect of each Authority election, unless the list identifies the election at which the ballot paper was so marked: Greater London Authority Elections Rules 2007, SI 2007/3541, Sch 1 r 39(4), Sch 2 r 40(4), Sch 3 r 39(4). Where the polls at a Welsh Assembly constituency election and a regional election are to be taken together, the same list of votes marked by the presiding officer may be used for the constituency and regional elections at which the voters are entitled to vote and, where it is so used, an entry in that list must be taken to mean that the ballot papers were so marked in respect of each election, unless the list identifies the election at which the ballot paper was so marked: National Assembly for Wales (Representation of the People) Order 2007, SI 2007/236, Sch 5 para 47(5). As to the meanings of 'constituency election' and 'regional election' in the context of Welsh Assembly elections see PARA 3 note 2. As to the meaning of 'Authority election' see PARA 11.

10 Representation of the People Act 1983 Sch 1 r 38(2); European Parliamentary Elections Regulations 2004, SI 2004/293, Sch 1 para 42(3) (as substituted: see note 3); Local Elections (Principal Areas) (England and Wales) Rules 2006, SI 2006/3304, Sch 2 r 36(2); Local Elections (Parishes and Communities) (England and Wales) Rules 2006, SI 2006/3305, Sch 2 r 36(2); National Assembly for Wales (Representation of the People) Order 2007, SI 2007/236, Sch 5 para 47(3); Local Authorities (Mayoral Elections) (England and Wales) Regulations 2007, SI 2007/1024, Sch 1 r 38(3); Greater London Authority Elections Rules 2007, SI 2007/3541, Sch 1 r 39(2), Sch 2 r 40(2), Sch 3 r 39(2). There is no provision for voting by proxy at a poll consequent on a parish meeting on a question involving appointment to office and accordingly the provision that is set out in the text does not apply in that case. As to voting by proxy see PARA 366 et seq.

11 As to polls at elections or referendums which are taken together see PARA 16 et seq.

402.   Votes given by voters with disabilities assisted by companions. If a voter at an election[1], or at a poll consequent on a parish meeting on a question involving appointment to office[2], makes an application to the presiding officer[3] to be allowed, on the ground of[4]:

(1)   blindness or other disability[5]; or

(2)   inability to read[6],

to vote with the assistance of another person by whom he is accompanied (the 'companion'), the presiding officer must require the voter to declare, orally or in writing, whether he is so incapacitated by his blindness or other disability, or by his inability to read, as to be unable to vote without assistance[7].

If the presiding officer:

(a)   is satisfied that the voter is so incapacitated[8]; and

(b)   is also satisfied by a written declaration made by the companion (called the 'declaration made by the companion of a voter with disabilities')[9] that the companion is a qualified person[10], and has not previously assisted more than one voter with disabilities to vote at the election[11], he must grant the application, and then anything required to be done to or by the voter in connection with the giving of his vote may be done to, or with the assistance of, the companion[12]. The declaration made by the companion: (i) must be in the prescribed form[13]; (ii) must be made before the presiding officer at the time when the voter applies to vote with the assistance of a companion[14]; and (iii) must forthwith be given to the presiding officer who must attest and retain it[15]. No fee or other payment is to be charged in respect of the declaration[16].

The name and number in the register of electors of every voter[17] whose vote is given by a companion in this way, together with the name and address of the companion, must be entered on a list (called, at an election, the 'list of voters with disabilities assisted by companions')[18]. For these purposes, in the case of a person voting at an election as proxy for an elector, the number to be entered together with the voter's name is the elector's number[19].

Where the poll at an election is taken together with the poll at another election or referendum, special provision is made for voting with the assistance of a companion[20].

1 Ie at a parliamentary election, a local government election (which includes any London Authority election and a local authority mayoral election), a Welsh Assembly constituency or regional election or a European parliamentary election. As to the meanings of 'Assembly election', 'constituency election' and 'regional election' see PARA 3 note 2. As to the meaning of 'parliamentary election' see PARA 9. As to the meanings of 'Authority election' and 'local government election' see PARA 11. As to elections in the City of London see PARA 33. As to European parliamentary elections see PARA 217 et seq. For the purposes of the statutory provisions governing elections, a voter is defined as a person voting at an election and includes a person voting as proxy (but not necessarily a person voting by proxy): in relation to parliamentary and local government elections see PARA 95 note 2; in relation to Welsh Assembly elections see PARA 110 note 7; and in relation to European parliamentary elections see PARA 111 note 5.

2 As to polls consequent on a parish meeting on a question involving appointment to office see PARA 200 et seq.

3 As to the presiding officer see PARA 393. This function of the presiding officer may be discharged by one of the clerks appointed to assist him: see PARA 393.

4 Representation of the People Act 1983 Sch 1 r 39(1) (Sch 1 r 39 substituted by the Representation of the People Act 2000 s 13(1), (3); Representation of the People Act 1983 Sch 1 r 39(1), (1)(a) amended by the Electoral Administration Act 2006 s 47, Sch 1 paras 69, 78); Parish and Community Meetings (Polls) Rules 1987, SI 1987/1, Schedule r 21(1); European Parliamentary Elections Regulations 2004, SI 2004/293, Sch 1 para 43(1) (Sch 1 substituted by SI 2009/186); Local Elections (Principal Areas) (England and Wales) Rules 2006, SI 2006/3304, Sch 2 r 37(1); Local Elections (Parishes and Communities) (England and Wales) Rules 2006, SI 2006/3305, Sch 2 r 37(1); National Assembly for Wales (Representation of the People) Order 2007, SI 2007/236, Sch 5 para 48(1); Local Authorities (Mayoral Elections) (England and Wales) Regulations 2007, SI 2007/1024, Sch 1 r 39(1); Greater London Authority Elections Rules 2007, SI 2007/3541, Sch 1 r 40(1), Sch 2 r 41(1), Sch 3 r 40(1).

5 Representation of the People Act 1983 Sch 1 r 39(1)(a) (Sch 1 r 39(1) as substituted, Sch 1 r 39(1)(a) as amended: see note 4); Parish and Community Meetings (Polls) Rules 1987, SI 1987/1, Schedule r 21(1); European Parliamentary Elections Regulations 2004, SI 2004/293, Sch 1 para 43(1)(a) (as substituted: see note 4); Local Elections (Principal Areas) (England and Wales) Rules 2006, SI 2006/3304, Sch 2 r 37(1)(a); Local Elections (Parishes and Communities) (England and Wales) Rules 2006, SI 2006/3305, Sch 2 r 37(1)(a); National Assembly for Wales (Representation of the People) Order 2007, SI 2007/236, Sch 5 para 48(1)(a); Local Authorities (Mayoral Elections) (England and Wales) Regulations 2007, SI 2007/1024, Sch 1 r 39(1)(a); Greater London Authority Elections Rules 2007, SI 2007/3541, Sch 1 r 40(1)(a), Sch 2 r 41(1)(a), Sch 3 r 40(1)(a). As to the meaning of 'disability' see PARA 367 note 8. At a poll consequent on a parish meeting where the poll is on a question of appointment to an office, the reference is to blindness only: see the Parish and Community Meetings (Polls) Rules 1987, SI 1987/1, Schedule r 21(1).

6   Representation of the People Act 1983 Sch 1 r 39(1)(b) (as substituted: see note 4); Parish and Community Meetings (Polls) Rules 1987, SI 1987/1, Schedule r 21(1); European Parliamentary Elections Regulations 2004, SI 2004/293, Sch 1 para 43(1)(b) (as substituted: see note 4); Local Elections (Principal Areas) (England and Wales) Rules 2006, SI 2006/3304, Sch 2 r 37(1)(b); Local Elections (Parishes and Communities) (England and Wales) Rules 2006, SI 2006/3305, Sch 2 r 37(1)(b); National Assembly for Wales (Representation of the People) Order 2007, SI 2007/236, Sch 5 para 48(1)(b); Local Authorities (Mayoral Elections) (England and Wales) Regulations 2007, SI 2007/1024, Sch 1 r 39(1)(b); Greater London Authority Elections Rules 2007, SI 2007/3541, Sch 1 r 40(1)(b), Sch 2 r 41(1)(b), Sch 3 r 40(1)(b). Head (2) in the text does not apply at a poll consequent on a parish meeting where the poll is on a question of appointment to an office: see the Parish and Community Meetings (Polls) Rules 1987, SI 1987/1, Schedule r 21(1); and see note 5.

7   Representation of the People Act 1983 Sch 1 r 39(1) (as substituted and amended: see note 4); Parish and Community Meetings (Polls) Rules 1987, SI 1987/1, Schedule r 21(1); European Parliamentary Elections Regulations 2004, SI 2004/293, Sch 1 para 43(1) (as substituted: see note 4); Local Elections (Principal Areas) (England and Wales) Rules 2006, SI 2006/3304, Sch 2 r 37(1); Local Elections (Parishes and Communities) (England and Wales) Rules 2006, SI 2006/3305, Sch 2 r 37(1); National Assembly for Wales (Representation of the People) Order 2007, SI 2007/236, Sch 5 para 48(1); Local Authorities (Mayoral Elections) (England and Wales) Regulations 2007, SI 2007/1024, Sch 1 r 39(1); Greater London Authority Elections Rules 2007, SI 2007/3541, Sch 1 r 40(1), Sch 2 r 41(1), Sch 3 r 40(1). At a poll consequent on a parish meeting on a question of appointment to an office, there is no mention of making the required declaration orally or in writing: see the Parish and Community Meetings (Polls) Rules 1987, SI 1987/1, Schedule r 21(1), Voters with incapacities who are without companions may apply to the presiding officer to assist them in voting: see PARA 401.

8   Representation of the People Act 1983 Sch 1 r 39(2)(a) (as substituted: see note 4); Parish and Community Meetings (Polls) Rules 1987, SI 1987/1, Schedule r 21(2)(a); European Parliamentary Elections Regulations 2004, SI 2004/293, Sch 1 para 43(2)(a) (as substituted: see note 4); Local Elections (Principal Areas) (England and Wales) Rules 2006, SI 2006/3304, Sch 2 r 37(2)(a); Local Elections (Parishes and Communities) (England and Wales) Rules 2006, SI 2006/3305, Sch 2 r 37(2)(a); National Assembly for Wales (Representation of the People) Order 2007, SI 2007/236, Sch 5 para 48(2)(a); Local Authorities (Mayoral Elections) (England and Wales) Regulations 2007, SI 2007/1024, Sch 1 r 39(2)(a); Greater London Authority Elections Rules 2007, SI 2007/3541, Sch 1 r 40(2)(a), Sch 2 r 41(2)(a), Sch 3 r 40(2)(a).

9   Representation of the People Act 1983 Sch 1 r 39(2)(b) (as substituted: see note 4); Parish and Community Meetings (Polls) Rules 1987, SI 1987/1, Schedule r 21(2)(b); European Parliamentary Elections Regulations 2004, SI 2004/293, Sch 1 para 43(2)(b) (as substituted: see note 4); Local Elections (Principal Areas) (England and Wales) Rules 2006, SI 2006/3304, Sch 2 r 37(2)(b); Local Elections (Parishes and Communities) (England and Wales) Rules 2006, SI 2006/3305, Sch 2 r 37(2)(b); National Assembly for Wales (Representation of the People) Order 2007, SI 2007/236, Sch 5 para 48(2)(b); Local Authorities (Mayoral Elections) (England and Wales) Regulations 2007, SI 2007/1024, Sch 1 r 39(2)(b); Greater London Authority Elections Rules 2007, SI 2007/3541, Sch 1 r 40(2)(b), Sch 2 r 41(2)(b), Sch 3 r 40(2)(b).

For the purposes of an election, a person is a voter with disabilities if he has made such a declaration as is mentioned in the text: Representation of the People Act 1983 Sch 1 r 39(3) (Sch 1 r 39 as substituted (see note 4); Sch 1 r 39(3) amended by the Civil Partnership Act 2004 s 261(1), Sch 27 para 85(1), (4)); European Parliamentary Elections Regulations 2004, SI 2004/293, Sch 1 para 43(3) (as so substituted); Local Elections (Principal Areas) (England and Wales) Rules 2006, SI 2006/3304, Sch 2 r 37(3); Local Elections (Parishes and Communities) (England and Wales) Rules 2006, SI 2006/3305, Sch 2 r 37(3); National Assembly for Wales (Representation of the People) Order 2007, SI 2007/236, Sch 5 para 48(3); Local Authorities (Mayoral Elections) (England and Wales) Regulations 2007, SI 2007/1024, Sch 1 r 39(3)(a); Greater London Authority Elections Rules 2007, SI 2007/3541, Sch 1 r 40(3), Sch 2 r 41(3), Sch 3 r 40(3). The written declaration made by the companion at a poll consequent on a parish meeting on a question involving appointment to office is known as the 'declaration made by the companion of a blind voter': see the Parish and Community Meetings (Polls) Rules 1987, SI 1987/1, Schedule r 21(2); and see note 5.

10   Representation of the People Act 1983 Sch 1 r 39(2)(b)(i) (as substituted: see note 4); Parish and Community Meetings (Polls) Rules 1987, SI 1987/1, Schedule r 21(2)(b)(i); European Parliamentary Elections Regulations 2004, SI 2004/293, Sch 1 para 43(2)(b)(i) (as substituted: see note 4); Local Elections (Principal Areas) (England and Wales) Rules 2006, SI 2006/3304, Sch 2 r 37(2)(b)(i); Local Elections (Parishes and Communities) (England and Wales) Rules 2006, SI 2006/3305, Sch 2 r 37(2)(b)(i); National Assembly for Wales (Representation of

the People) Order 2007, SI 2007/236, Sch 5 para 48(2)(b)(i); Local Authorities (Mayoral Elections) (England and Wales) Regulations 2007, SI 2007/1024, Sch 1 r 39(2)(b)(i); Greater London Authority Elections Rules 2007, SI 2007/3541, Sch 1 r 40(2)(b)(i), Sch 2 r 41(2)(b)(i), Sch 3 r 40(2)(b)(i).

For the purposes of an election or poll, a person is qualified to assist a voter with disabilities (or, at a poll, a blind voter) to vote if that person either is a person who is entitled to vote as an elector at the election or poll in question, or is the father, mother, brother, sister, spouse, civil partner, son or daughter of the voter and has attained the age of 18 years: Representation of the People Act 1983 Sch 1 r 39(3) (as substituted and amended: see note 9); Parish and Community Meetings (Polls) Rules 1987, SI 1987/1, Schedule r 21(3) (amended by SI 2005/2114); European Parliamentary Elections Regulations 2004, SI 2004/293, Sch 1 para 43(3) (as so substituted); Local Elections (Principal Areas) (England and Wales) Rules 2006, SI 2006/3304, Sch 2 r 37(3); Local Elections (Parishes and Communities) (England and Wales) Rules 2006, SI 2006/3305, Sch 2 r 37(3); National Assembly for Wales (Representation of the People) Order 2007, SI 2007/236, Sch 5 para 48(3); Local Authorities (Mayoral Elections) (England and Wales) Regulations 2007, SI 2007/1024, Sch 1 r 39(3)(b); Greater London Authority Elections Rules 2007, SI 2007/3541, Sch 1 r 40(3), Sch 2 r 41(3), Sch 3 r 40(3). As to the meaning of 'elector', in relation to a parliamentary or local government election, see PARA 95 note 2; in relation to a Welsh Assembly election, see PARA 110 note 6; and in relation to European parliamentary elections see PARA 111 note 4.

11 Representation of the People Act 1983 Sch 1 r 39(2)(b)(ii) (as substituted: see note 4); Parish and Community Meetings (Polls) Rules 1987, SI 1987/1, Schedule r 21(2)(b)(ii); European Parliamentary Elections Regulations 2004, SI 2004/293, Sch 1 para 43(2)(b)(ii) (as substituted: see note 4); Local Elections (Principal Areas) (England and Wales) Rules 2006, SI 2006/3304, Sch 2 r 37(2)(b)(ii); Local Elections (Parishes and Communities) (England and Wales) Rules 2006, SI 2006/3305, Sch 2 r 37(2)(b)(ii); National Assembly for Wales (Representation of the People) Order 2007, SI 2007/236, Sch 5 para 48(2)(b)(ii); Local Authorities (Mayoral Elections) (England and Wales) Regulations 2007, SI 2007/1024, Sch 1 r 39(2)(b)(ii); Greater London Authority Elections Rules 2007, SI 2007/3541, Sch 1 r 40(2)(b)(ii), Sch 2 r 41(2)(b)(ii), Sch 3 r 40(2)(b)(ii). For the purposes of a poll consequent on a parish meeting on a question involving appointment to office, the reference is to assisting 'more than one blind person to vote': see the Parish and Community Meetings (Polls) Rules 1987, SI 1987/1, Schedule r 21(2)(b)(ii).

12 Representation of the People Act 1983 Sch 1 r 39(2) (as substituted: see note 4); Parish and Community Meetings (Polls) Rules 1987, SI 1987/1, Schedule r 21(2); European Parliamentary Elections Regulations 2004, SI 2004/293, Sch 1 para 43(2) (as substituted: see note 4); Local Elections (Principal Areas) (England and Wales) Rules 2006, SI 2006/3304, Sch 2 r 37(2); Local Elections (Parishes and Communities) (England and Wales) Rules 2006, SI 2006/3305, Sch 2 r 37(2); National Assembly for Wales (Representation of the People) Order 2007, SI 2007/236, Sch 5 para 48(2); Local Authorities (Mayoral Elections) (England and Wales) Regulations 2007, SI 2007/1024, Sch 1 r 39(2); Greater London Authority Elections Rules 2007, SI 2007/3541, Sch 1 r 40(2), Sch 2 r 41(2), Sch 3 r 40(2).

13 Representation of the People Act 1983 Sch 1 r 39(5)(a) (as substituted: see note 4); Parish and Community Meetings (Polls) Rules 1987, SI 1987/1, Schedule r 21(5)(a); European Parliamentary Elections Regulations 2004, SI 2004/293, Sch 1 para 43(7)(a) (as substituted: see note 4); Local Elections (Principal Areas) (England and Wales) Rules 2006, SI 2006/3304, Sch 2 r 37(6)(a); Local Elections (Parishes and Communities) (England and Wales) Rules 2006, SI 2006/3305, Sch 2 r 37(6)(a); National Assembly for Wales (Representation of the People) Order 2007, SI 2007/236, Sch 5 para 48(7)(a); Local Authorities (Mayoral Elections) (England and Wales) Regulations 2007, SI 2007/1024, Sch 1 r 39(7)(a); Greater London Authority Elections Rules 2007, SI 2007/3541, Sch 1 r 40(6)(a), Sch 2 r 41(6)(a), Sch 3 r 40(6)(a). The declaration made by the companion must be in the form:

(1) in the case of a parliamentary election, in the Representation of the People Act 1983 Sch 1 Appendix of Forms (Form of declaration to be made by the companion of a voter with disabilities) (amended by the Representation of the People Act 2000 s 13(1), (5)(a), (b); and the Electoral Administration Act 2006 Sch 1 paras 69, 80);

(2) at a European parliamentary election, in the European Parliamentary Elections Regulations 2004, SI 2004/293, Sch 1 Appendix of Forms (Form M: Form of declaration to be made by the companion of a voter with disabilities) (as so substituted);

(3) in the case of a local government election:

(a) in the Local Elections (Principal Areas) (England and Wales) Rules 2006, SI 2006/3304, Sch 2 Appendix of Forms (Form of declaration to be made by the companion of a voter with disabilities); and Sch 3 Appendix of Forms (Form of declaration to be made by the companion of a voter with disabilities) (where such a poll is taken together with another relevant election or referendum);

(b)   in the Local Elections (Parishes and Communities) (England and Wales) Rules 2006, SI 2006/3305, Sch 2 Appendix of Forms (Form of declaration to be made by the companion of a voter with disabilities); and Sch 3 Appendix of Forms (Form of declaration to be made by the companion of a voter with disabilities) (where such a poll is taken together with another relevant election or referendum);

(c)   in the Local Authorities (Mayoral Elections) (England and Wales) Regulations 2007, SI 2007/1024, Sch 1 Appendix of Forms (Form 14: declaration to be made by the companion of a voter with disabilities) (Form 14 substituted by SI 2012/2059);

(d)   in the Greater London Authority Elections Rules 2007, SI 2007/3541, Sch 10 r 2 (Form 19: declaration to be made by the companion of a voter with disabilities);

(4)   at a Welsh Assembly election, set out in English and Welsh in the National Assembly for Wales (Representation of the People) Order 2007, SI 2007/236, Sch 10 Appendix of Forms (Form CQ: Form of declaration to be made by the companion of a voter with disabilities).

In relation to a poll consequent on a parish meeting on a question involving appointment to office see the Parish and Community Meetings (Polls) Rules 1987, SI 1987/1, Schedule Appendix of Forms (Form of declaration to be made by the companion of a blind voter).

Where elections take place in Wales see also the forms issued partly in English and partly in Welsh in:

(i)   the Parliamentary Elections (Welsh Forms) Order 2007, SI 2007/1014, art 5(d), Sch 1 (Form 4 (Ffurflen 4): Form of declaration to be made by the companion of a voter with disabilities/ffurf ar ddatganiad sydd i'w wneud gan gydymaith pleidleisiwr/wraig gydag anableddau);

(ii)   the Local Elections (Principal Areas) (Welsh Forms) Order 2007, SI 2007/1015, arts 6(e), 8(e), Sch 2 (Form 5 (Ffurflen 5): Form of declaration to be made by the companion of a voter with disabilities/ffurf ar ddatganiad sydd i'w wneud gan gydymaith pleidleisiwr gydag anableddau), Sch 4 (Form 5 (Ffurflen 5): Form of declaration to be made by the companion of a voter with disabilities/ffurf ar ddatganiad sydd i'w wneud gan gydymaith pleidleisiwr gydag anableddau (combined polls));

(iii)   the Local Elections (Communities) (Welsh Forms) Order 2007, SI 2007/1013, arts 6(e), 8(e), Sch 2 (Form 5 (Ffurflen 5): Form of declaration to be made by the companion of a voter with disabilities/ffurf ar ddatganiad sydd i'w wneud gan gydymaith pleidleisiwr gydag anableddau), Sch 4 (Form 5 (Ffurflen 5): Form of declaration to be made by the companion of a voter with disabilities/ffurf ar ddatganiad sydd i'w wneud gan gydymaith pleidleisiwr gydag anableddau (combined polls)); and

(iv)   the European Parliamentary Elections (Welsh Forms) Order 2009, SI 2009/781, art 5(1), (2)(c), Sch 1 (Form 3 (Ffurflen 3): Form of declaration to be made by the companion of a voter with disabilities/ffurf ar ddatganiad i'w lenwi gan gydymaith pleidleisiwr anabl).

14 Representation of the People Act 1983 Sch 1 r 39(5)(b) (as substituted: see note 4); Parish and Community Meetings (Polls) Rules 1987, SI 1987/1, Schedule r 21(5)(b); European Parliamentary Elections Regulations 2004, SI 2004/293, Sch 1 para 43(7)(b) (as substituted: see note 4); Local Elections (Principal Areas) (England and Wales) Rules 2006, SI 2006/3304, Sch 2 r 37(6)(b); Local Elections (Parishes and Communities) (England and Wales) Rules 2006, SI 2006/3305, Sch 2 r 37(6)(b); National Assembly for Wales (Representation of the People) Order 2007, SI 2007/236, Sch 5 para 48(7)(b); Local Authorities (Mayoral Elections) (England and Wales) Regulations 2007, SI 2007/1024, Sch 1 r 39(7)(b); Greater London Authority Elections Rules 2007, SI 2007/3541, Sch 1 r 40(6)(b), Sch 2 r 41(6)(b), Sch 3 r 40(6)(b).

15 Representation of the People Act 1983 Sch 1 r 39(5)(b) (as substituted: see note 4); Parish and Community Meetings (Polls) Rules 1987, SI 1987/1, Schedule r 21(5)(b); European Parliamentary Elections Regulations 2004, SI 2004/293, Sch 1 para 43(7)(b) (as substituted: see note 4); Local Elections (Principal Areas) (England and Wales) Rules 2006, SI 2006/3304, Sch 2 r 37(6)(c); Local Elections (Parishes and Communities) (England and Wales) Rules 2006, SI 2006/3305, Sch 2 r 37(6)(c); National Assembly for Wales (Representation of the People) Order 2007, SI 2007/236, Sch 5 para 48(7)(b); Local Authorities (Mayoral Elections) (England and Wales) Regulations 2007, SI 2007/1024, Sch 1 r 39(7)(c); Greater London Authority Elections Rules 2007, SI 2007/3541, Sch 1 r 40(6)(c), Sch 2 r 41(6)(c), Sch 3 r 40(6)(c).

16 Representation of the People Act 1983 Sch 1 r 39(6) (as substituted: see note 4); Parish and Community Meetings (Polls) Rules 1987, SI 1987/1, Schedule r 21(6); European Parliamentary Elections Regulations 2004, SI 2004/293, Sch 1 para 43(8) (as substituted: see note 4); Local Elections (Principal Areas) (England and Wales) Rules 2006, SI 2006/3304, Sch 2 r 37(7); Local Elections (Parishes and Communities) (England and Wales) Rules 2006, SI 2006/3305, Sch 2 r 37(7); National Assembly for Wales (Representation of the People) Order 2007, SI 2007/236, Sch 5 para 48(8); Local Authorities (Mayoral Elections) (England and Wales) Regulations 2007, SI 2007/1024, Sch 1 r 39(8); Greater London Authority Elections Rules 2007, SI 2007/3541, Sch 1 r 40(7), Sch 2 r 41(7), Sch 3 r 40(7).

17 As to the number of an elector and the form and content of registers of electors see PARA 145. In the case of a person in respect of whom a notice has been issued under the Representation of the People Act 1983 s 13B(3B) or s 13B(3D) (see PARA 168), the provision set out in the text applies as if, instead of referring to the name and number of every voter on the register of electors, it referred to the name and number relating to every voter in respect of whom a notice under s 13B(3B) or s 13B(3D) has been issued: Sch 1 r 39(4A) (Sch 1 r 39 as substituted (see note 4); Sch 1 r 39(4A) added by the Electoral Administration Act 2006 s 11(6), Sch 1 paras 31, 33, 36); European Parliamentary Elections Regulations 2004, SI 2004/293, Sch 1 para 43(6) (as substituted: see note 4); Local Elections (Principal Areas) (England and Wales) Rules 2006, SI 2006/3304, Sch 2 r 37(5); Local Elections (Parishes and Communities) (England and Wales) Rules 2006, SI 2006/3305, Sch 2 r 37(5); National Assembly for Wales (Representation of the People) Order 2007, SI 2007/236, Sch 5 para 48(6); Local Authorities (Mayoral Elections) (England and Wales) Regulations 2007, SI 2007/1024, Sch 1 r 39(6); Greater London Authority Elections Rules 2007, SI 2007/3541, Sch 1 r 40(5), Sch 2 r 41(5), Sch 3 r 40(5).

18 Representation of the People Act 1983 Sch 1 r 39(4) (as substituted: see note 4); Parish and Community Meetings (Polls) Rules 1987, SI 1987/1, Schedule r 21(4); European Parliamentary Elections Regulations 2004, SI 2004/293, Sch 1 para 43(4) (as substituted: see note 4); Local Elections (Principal Areas) (England and Wales) Rules 2006, SI 2006/3304, Sch 2 r 37(4); Local Elections (Parishes and Communities) (England and Wales) Rules 2006, SI 2006/3305, Sch 2 r 37(4); National Assembly for Wales (Representation of the People) Order 2007, SI 2007/236, Sch 5 para 48(4); Local Authorities (Mayoral Elections) (England and Wales) Regulations 2007, SI 2007/1024, Sch 1 r 39(4); Greater London Authority Elections Rules 2007, SI 2007/3541, Sch 1 r 40(4), Sch 2 r 41(4), Sch 3 r 40(4). At a poll consequent on a parish meeting on a question involving appointment to office, the list referred to in the text is known as the 'list of blind voters assisted by companions': see the Parish and Community Meetings (Polls) Rules 1987, SI 1987/1, Schedule r 21(4); and see note 5.

Where any other ordinary London Authority election in the Assembly constituency is contested, the same list of voters with disabilities assisted by companions may be used for each Authority election and, where it is so used, an entry in that list must be taken to mean that the votes were so given in respect of each Authority election, unless the list identifies the election at which the vote was so given: Greater London Authority Elections Rules 2007, SI 2007/3541, Sch 1 r 40(8), Sch 2 r 41(8), Sch 3 r 40(8). Where the polls at a Welsh Assembly constituency election and a regional election are to be taken together, the same list of voters with disabilities assisted by companions may be used for the constituency and regional elections at which the voters are entitled to vote and, where it is so used, an entry in that list must be taken to mean that the votes were so given in respect of each election, unless the list identifies the election at which a vote was so given: National Assembly for Wales (Representation of the People) Order 2007, SI 2007/236, Sch 5 para 48(9). As to the meaning of 'Assembly constituency', in relation to a London Authority election, see PARA 11 note 6.

19 Representation of the People Act 1983 Sch 1 r 39(4) (as substituted: see note 4); European Parliamentary Elections Regulations 2004, SI 2004/293, Sch 1 para 43(5) (as substituted: see note 4); Local Elections (Principal Areas) (England and Wales) Rules 2006, SI 2006/3304, Sch 2 r 37(4); Local Elections (Parishes and Communities) (England and Wales) Rules 2006, SI 2006/3305, Sch 2 r 37(4); National Assembly for Wales (Representation of the People) Order 2007, SI 2007/236, Sch 5 para 48(5); Local Authorities (Mayoral Elections) (England and Wales) Regulations 2007, SI 2007/1024, Sch 1 r 39(5); Greater London Authority Elections Rules 2007, SI 2007/3541, Sch 1 r 40(4), Sch 2 r 41(4), Sch 3 r 40(4). There is no provision for voting by proxy at a poll consequent on a parish meeting on a question involving appointment to office and accordingly the provision that is set out in the text does not apply in that case. As to voting by proxy see PARA 366 et seq.

20 As to polls at elections or referendums which are taken together see PARA 16 et seq.

403. Tendered ballot papers. If a person, representing himself to be:

(1)   a particular elector named on the register[1] (and not named in the postal voters list)[2]; or

(2)   a particular person named in the list of proxies as proxy for an elector (and not entitled to vote by post as proxy)[3],

applies for a ballot paper after another person has voted in person either as the elector or his proxy, as the case may be, the applicant, on satisfactorily answering the questions permitted by law to be asked at the poll[4], is entitled to mark a ballot paper (called a 'tendered ballot paper') in the same manner as any other voter[5].

Additionally, if a person:

(a)   applies for a ballot paper representing himself to be: (i) a particular elector named on the register[6]; or (ii) (alternatively) a particular person named as a proxy in the list of proxies[7]; and

(b)   he is also named: (i) in the postal voters list[8]; or (ii) (alternatively) in the proxy postal voters list[9]; and

(c)   that person claims: (i) that he did not make an application to vote by post at the election[10]; or (ii) (alternatively) that he did not make an application to vote by post as proxy[11],

then that person, on satisfactorily answering the questions permitted by law to be asked at the poll, is entitled to mark a ballot paper (a 'tendered ballot paper') in the same manner as any other voter[12].

Also, if, before the close of the poll but after the last time at which a person may apply for a replacement postal ballot paper, a person represents himself to be:

(A)   a particular elector named on the register[13] (and who is also named in the postal voters list)[14]; or

(B)   a particular person named as a proxy in the list of proxies (and who is also named in the proxy postal voters list)[15],

and claims that he has lost or has not received his postal ballot paper[16], then that person, on satisfactorily answering the questions permitted by law to be asked at the poll, is entitled to mark a ballot paper (a 'tendered ballot paper') in the same manner as any other voter[17].

Any such tendered ballot paper:

(aa)   must be of a colour differing from the other ballot papers[18]; and

(bb)   instead of being put into the ballot box, must be given to the presiding officer[19] and endorsed by him[20] with the name of the voter and his number in the register of electors[21], and set aside in a separate packet[22].

The name of the voter and his number on the register of electors[23] must be entered on a list (called the 'tendered votes list')[24]. For these purposes, in the case of a person voting at an election as proxy for an elector, the number to be endorsed or entered together with the voter's name is the elector's number[25].

---

1   As to the registers of electors see PARA 143 et seq. Where an elector has an anonymous entry in the register of electors, references in the text to a person named on a register or list must be construed as a reference to a person whose number appears on the register or list (as the case may be): Representation of the People Act 1983 Sch 1 r 40(4A)(b) (Sch 1 r 40(4A) added by the Electoral Administration Act 2006 s 10(2), Sch 1 paras 2, 14(1), (5)); European Parliamentary Elections Regulations 2004, SI 2004/293, Sch 1 para 45(4)(b) (Sch 1 substituted by SI 2009/186); Local Elections (Principal Areas) (England and Wales) Rules 2006, SI 2006/3304, Sch 2 r 39(4)(b); Local Elections (Parishes and Communities) (England and Wales) Rules 2006, SI 2006/3305, Sch 2 r 39(4)(b); National Assembly for Wales (Representation of the People) Order 2007, SI 2007/236, Sch 5 para 49(10)(b); Local Authorities (Mayoral Elections) (England and Wales) Regulations 2007, SI 2007/1024, Sch 1 r 41(4)(b); Greater London Authority Elections Rules 2007, SI 2007/3541, Sch 1 r 42(4)(b), Sch 2 r 43(4)(b), Sch 3 r 42(4)(b). This

does not apply to the provisions set out in the text and notes 19–24, however: see notes 21, 23. As to the meaning of 'anonymous entry' in relation to a register of electors see PARA 148. In the case of a person in respect of whom a notice has been issued under the Representation of the People Act 1983 s 13B(3B) or s 13B(3D) (see PARA 168), references to an elector named on the register must be read as references to an elector in respect of whom a notice under s 13B(3B) or s 13B(3D) has been issued: Sch 1 r 40(4B)(a) (Sch 1 r 40(4B) added by the Electoral Administration Act 2006 s 11(6), Sch 1 paras 31, 33, 37); European Parliamentary Elections Regulations 2004, SI 2004/293, Sch 1 para 45(5)(a) (as so substituted); Local Elections (Principal Areas) (England and Wales) Rules 2006, SI 2006/3304, Sch 2 r 39(5)(a); Local Elections (Parishes and Communities) (England and Wales) Rules 2006, SI 2006/3305, Sch 2 r 39(5)(a); National Assembly for Wales (Representation of the People) Order 2007, SI 2007/236, Sch 5 para 49(11)(a); Local Authorities (Mayoral Elections) (England and Wales) Regulations 2007, SI 2007/1024, Sch 1 r 41(5)(a); Greater London Authority Elections Rules 2007, SI 2007/3541, Sch 1 r 42(5)(a), Sch 2 r 43(5)(a), Sch 3 r 42(5)(a). As to the meaning of 'elector', in relation to a parliamentary or local government election, see PARA 95 note 2; in relation to a Welsh Assembly election, see PARA 110 note 6; and in relation to European parliamentary elections see PARA 111 note 4. As to the meanings of 'Assembly election', 'constituency election' and 'regional election' see PARA 3 note 2. As to the meaning of 'parliamentary election' see PARA 9. As to the meaning of 'local government election' see PARA 11. As to European parliamentary elections see PARA 217 et seq.

2 Representation of the People Act 1983 Sch 1 r 40(1)(a); European Parliamentary Elections Regulations 2004, SI 2004/293, Sch 1 para 44(1)(a) (as substituted: see note 1); Local Elections (Principal Areas) (England and Wales) Rules 2006, SI 2006/3304, Sch 2 r 38(1)(a); Local Elections (Parishes and Communities) (England and Wales) Rules 2006, SI 2006/3305, Sch 2 r 38(1)(a); National Assembly for Wales (Representation of the People) Order 2007, SI 2007/236, Sch 5 para 49(1)(a); Local Authorities (Mayoral Elections) (England and Wales) Regulations 2007, SI 2007/1024, Sch 1 r 40(1)(a); Greater London Authority Elections Rules 2007, SI 2007/3541, Sch 1 r 41(1)(a), Sch 2 r 42(1)(a), Sch 3 r 41(1)(a). The definition of 'absent voters list' that used to be given in electoral law has not been used as a term of art since the Electoral Administration Act 2006 introduced reforms which required two special lists to be kept in respect of absent voters (the 'postal voters list' and the 'list of proxies'): see PARA 373. However, at the date at which this volume states the law, the correct term ('postal voters list'), as it appears in head (1) in the text, is cited only by the European Parliamentary Elections Regulations 2004, SI 2004/293, Sch 1 para 44(1)(a) (as so substituted), and by the National Assembly for Wales (Representation of the People) Order 2007, SI 2007/236 (see Sch 5 para 49(1)(a)), while the parliamentary and local government provisions continue to cite the repealed term ('absent voters list'). All provisions use the correct term as shown in head (b) and in head (A) in the text and it is submitted that it is correct for that term to be applied for the purposes of parliamentary and local government elections to head (1) in the text also.

There is no provision for absent voting at a poll consequent on a parish meeting on a question involving appointment to office and, accordingly at such a poll, head (1) in the text must be read simply as applying to a person representing himself to be a particular elector named on the register, and head (2) in the text does not apply: see the Parish and Community Meetings (Polls) Rules 1987, SI 1987/1, Schedule r 22(1). As to polls consequent on a parish meeting on a question involving appointment to office see PARA 200 et seq.

3 Representation of the People Act 1983 Sch 1 r 40(1)(b) (amended by the Representation of the People Act 1985 ss 11, 28, Sch 2 para 7, Sch 5); European Parliamentary Elections Regulations 2004, SI 2004/293, Sch 1 para 44(1)(b) (as substituted: see note 1); Local Elections (Principal Areas) (England and Wales) Rules 2006, SI 2006/3304, Sch 2 r 38(1)(b); Local Elections (Parishes and Communities) (England and Wales) Rules 2006, SI 2006/3305, Sch 2 r 38(1)(b); National Assembly for Wales (Representation of the People) Order 2007, SI 2007/236, Sch 5 para 49(1)(b); Local Authorities (Mayoral Elections) (England and Wales) Regulations 2007, SI 2007/1024, Sch 1 r 40(1)(b); Greater London Authority Elections Rules 2007, SI 2007/3541, Sch 1 r 41(1)(b), Sch 2 r 42(1)(b), Sch 3 r 41(1)(b). As to references to a person named on a list where an elector has an anonymous entry in the register of electors see note 1. As to the 'list of proxies' see note 2. As to voting by proxy see PARA 366 et seq; and as to the entitlement to vote by post as proxy see PARAS 377, 382. To indicate that an elector or his proxy is entitled to vote by post and is for that reason not entitled to vote in person, the letter 'A' is placed against the name of that elector in any copy of the register, or part of it, provided for a polling station: see PARA 377.

Head (2) in the text does not apply to a poll consequent on a parish meeting on a question involving appointment to office (where is no provision for absent voting): see note 2.

4 As to the questions that may be put to person applying for a ballot paper see PARA 398.

5 Representation of the People Act 1983 Sch 1 r 40(1); Parish and Community Meetings (Polls) Rules 1987, SI 1987/1, Schedule r 22(1); European Parliamentary Elections Regulations 2004, SI 2004/293, Sch 1 para 44(1) (as substituted: see note 1); Local Elections (Principal Areas) (England and Wales) Rules 2006, SI 2006/3304, Sch 2 r 38(1); Local Elections (Parishes and Communities) (England and Wales) Rules 2006, SI 2006/3305, Sch 2 r 38(1); National Assembly for Wales (Representation of the People) Order 2007, SI 2007/236, Sch 5 para 49(1); Local Authorities (Mayoral Elections) (England and Wales) Regulations 2007, SI 2007/1024, Sch 1 r 40(1); Greater London Authority Elections Rules 2007, SI 2007/3541, Sch 1 r 41(1), Sch 2 r 42(1), Sch 3 r 41(1).

6 Representation of the People Act 1983 Sch 1 r 40(1ZA)(a) (Sch 1 r 40(1ZA)–(1ZE) added by the Electoral Administration Act 2006 s 38(1), (2)); European Parliamentary Elections Regulations 2004, SI 2004/293, Sch 1 para 44(2)(a) (as substituted: see note 1); Local Elections (Principal Areas) (England and Wales) Rules 2006, SI 2006/3304, Sch 2 r 38(2)(a); Local Elections (Parishes and Communities) (England and Wales) Rules 2006, SI 2006/3305, Sch 2 r 38(2)(a); National Assembly for Wales (Representation of the People) Order 2007, SI 2007/236, Sch 5 para 49(2)(a); Local Authorities (Mayoral Elections) (England and Wales) Regulations 2007, SI 2007/1024, Sch 1 r 40(2)(a); Greater London Authority Elections Rules 2007, SI 2007/3541, Sch 1 r 41(2)(a), Sch 2 r 42(2)(a), Sch 3 r 41(2)(a). In the case of a person in respect of whom a notice has been issued under the Representation of the People Act 1983 s 13B(3B) or s 13B(3D) (see PARA 168), references to an elector named on the register must be read as references to an elector in respect of whom a notice under s 13B(3B) or s 13B(3D) has been issued: Sch 1 r 40(4B)(a) (as added: see note 1); European Parliamentary Elections Regulations 2004, SI 2004/293, Sch 1 para 45(5)(a) (as so substituted); Local Elections (Principal Areas) (England and Wales) Rules 2006, SI 2006/3304, Sch 2 r 39(5)(a); Local Elections (Parishes and Communities) (England and Wales) Rules 2006, SI 2006/3305, Sch 2 r 39(5)(a); National Assembly for Wales (Representation of the People) Order 2007, SI 2007/236, Sch 5 para 49(11)(a); Local Authorities (Mayoral Elections) (England and Wales) Regulations 2007, SI 2007/1024, Sch 1 r 41(5)(a); Greater London Authority Elections Rules 2007, SI 2007/3541, Sch 1 r 42(5)(a), Sch 2 r 43(5)(a), Sch 3 r 42(5)(a). As to references to a person named on a register where an elector has an anonymous entry in the register of electors see note 1.

7 Representation of the People Act 1983 Sch 1 r 40((1ZB)(a) (as added: see note 6); European Parliamentary Elections Regulations 2004, SI 2004/293, Sch 1 para 44(3)(a) (as substituted: see note 1); Local Elections (Principal Areas) (England and Wales) Rules 2006, SI 2006/3304, Sch 2 r 38(3)(a); Local Elections (Parishes and Communities) (England and Wales) Rules 2006, SI 2006/3305, Sch 2 r 38(3)(a); National Assembly for Wales (Representation of the People) Order 2007, SI 2007/236, Sch 5 para 49(3)(a); Local Authorities (Mayoral Elections) (England and Wales) Regulations 2007, SI 2007/1024, Sch 1 r 40(3)(a); Greater London Authority Elections Rules 2007, SI 2007/3541, Sch 1 r 41(3)(a), Sch 2 r 42(3)(a), Sch 3 r 41(3)(a). As to references to a person named on a list where an elector has an anonymous entry in the register of electors see note 1.

8 Representation of the People Act 1983 Sch 1 r 40(1ZA)(b) (as added: see note 6); European Parliamentary Elections Regulations 2004, SI 2004/293, Sch 1 para 44(2)(b) (as substituted: see note 1); Local Elections (Principal Areas) (England and Wales) Rules 2006, SI 2006/3304, Sch 2 r 38(2)(b); Local Elections (Parishes and Communities) (England and Wales) Rules 2006, SI 2006/3305, Sch 2 r 38(2)(b); National Assembly for Wales (Representation of the People) Order 2007, SI 2007/236, Sch 5 para 49(2)(b); Local Authorities (Mayoral Elections) (England and Wales) Regulations 2007, SI 2007/1024, Sch 1 r 40(2)(b); Greater London Authority Elections Rules 2007, SI 2007/3541, Sch 1 r 41(2)(b), Sch 2 r 42(2)(b), Sch 3 r 41(2)(b). As to references to a person named on a list where an elector has an anonymous entry in the register of electors see note 1.

9 Representation of the People Act 1983 Sch 1 r 40(1ZB)(b) (as added: see note 6); European Parliamentary Elections Regulations 2004, SI 2004/293, Sch 1 para 44(3)(b) (as substituted: see note 1); Local Elections (Principal Areas) (England and Wales) Rules 2006, SI 2006/3304, Sch 2 r 38(3)(b); Local Elections (Parishes and Communities) (England and Wales) Rules 2006, SI 2006/3305, Sch 2 r 38(3)(b); National Assembly for Wales (Representation of the People) Order 2007, SI 2007/236, Sch 5 para 49(3)(b); Local Authorities (Mayoral Elections) (England and Wales) Regulations 2007, SI 2007/1024, Sch 1 r 40(3)(b); Greater London Authority Elections Rules 2007, SI 2007/3541, Sch 1 r 41(3)(b), Sch 2 r 42(3)(b), Sch 3 r 41(3)(b). As to references to a person named on a list where an elector has an anonymous entry in the register of electors see note 1.

10 Representation of the People Act 1983 Sch 1 r 40(1ZA)(c) (as added: see note 6); European Parliamentary Elections Regulations 2004, SI 2004/293, Sch 1 para 44(2)(c) (as substituted: see

note 1); Local Elections (Principal Areas) (England and Wales) Rules 2006, SI 2006/3304, Sch 2 r 38(2)(c); Local Elections (Parishes and Communities) (England and Wales) Rules 2006, SI 2006/3305, Sch 2 r 38(2)(c); National Assembly for Wales (Representation of the People) Order 2007, SI 2007/236, Sch 5 para 49(2)(c); Local Authorities (Mayoral Elections) (England and Wales) Regulations 2007, SI 2007/1024, Sch 1 r 40(2)(c); Greater London Authority Elections Rules 2007, SI 2007/3541, Sch 1 r 41(2)(c), Sch 2 r 42(2)(c), Sch 3 r 41(2)(c).

11 Representation of the People Act 1983 Sch 1 r 40(1ZB)(c) (as added: see note 6); European Parliamentary Elections Regulations 2004, SI 2004/293, Sch 1 para 44(3)(c) (as substituted: see note 1); Local Elections (Principal Areas) (England and Wales) Rules 2006, SI 2006/3304, Sch 2 r 38(3)(c); Local Elections (Parishes and Communities) (England and Wales) Rules 2006, SI 2006/3305, Sch 2 r 38(3)(c); National Assembly for Wales (Representation of the People) Order 2007, SI 2007/236, Sch 5 para 49(3)(c); Local Authorities (Mayoral Elections) (England and Wales) Regulations 2007, SI 2007/1024, Sch 1 r 40(3)(c); Greater London Authority Elections Rules 2007, SI 2007/3541, Sch 1 r 41(3)(c), Sch 2 r 42(3)(c), Sch 3 r 41(3)(c).

12 Representation of the People Act 1983 Sch 1 r 40(1ZC) (as added: see note 6); European Parliamentary Elections Regulations 2004, SI 2004/293, Sch 1 para 44(4) (as substituted: see note 1); Local Elections (Principal Areas) (England and Wales) Rules 2006, SI 2006/3304, Sch 2 r 38(4); Local Elections (Parishes and Communities) (England and Wales) Rules 2006, SI 2006/3305, Sch 2 r 38(4); National Assembly for Wales (Representation of the People) Order 2007, SI 2007/236, Sch 5 para 49(4); Local Authorities (Mayoral Elections) (England and Wales) Regulations 2007, SI 2007/1024, Sch 1 r 40(4); Greater London Authority Elections Rules 2007, SI 2007/3541, Sch 1 r 41(4), Sch 2 r 42(4), Sch 3 r 41(4).

13 In the case of a person in respect of whom a notice has been issued under the Representation of the People Act 1983 s 13B(3B) or s 13B(3D) (see PARA 168), references to an elector named on the register must be read as references to an elector in respect of whom a notice under s 13B(3B) or s 13B(3D) has been issued: Sch 1 r 40(4B)(a) (as added: see note 1); European Parliamentary Elections Regulations 2004, SI 2004/293, Sch 1 para 45(5)(a) (as substituted: see note 1); Local Elections (Principal Areas) (England and Wales) Rules 2006, SI 2006/3304, Sch 2 r 39(5)(a); Local Elections (Parishes and Communities) (England and Wales) Rules 2006, SI 2006/3305, Sch 2 r 39(5)(a); National Assembly for Wales (Representation of the People) Order 2007, SI 2007/236, Sch 5 para 49(11)(a); Local Authorities (Mayoral Elections) (England and Wales) Regulations 2007, SI 2007/1024, Sch 1 r 41(5)(a); Greater London Authority Elections Rules 2007, SI 2007/3541, Sch 1 r 42(5)(a), Sch 2 r 43(5)(a), Sch 3 r 42(5)(a). As to references to a person named on a register where an elector has an anonymous entry in the register of electors see note 1.

14 Representation of the People Act 1983 Sch 1 r 40(1ZD)(a) (as added: see note 6); European Parliamentary Elections Regulations 2004, SI 2004/293, Sch 1 para 44(5)(a) (as substituted: see note 1); Local Elections (Principal Areas) (England and Wales) Rules 2006, SI 2006/3304, Sch 2 r 38(5)(a); Local Elections (Parishes and Communities) (England and Wales) Rules 2006, SI 2006/3305, Sch 2 r 38(5)(a); National Assembly for Wales (Representation of the People) Order 2007, SI 2007/236, Sch 5 para 49(5)(a); Local Authorities (Mayoral Elections) (England and Wales) Regulations 2007, SI 2007/1024, Sch 1 r 40(5)(a); Greater London Authority Elections Rules 2007, SI 2007/3541, Sch 1 r 41(5)(a), Sch 2 r 42(5)(a), Sch 3 r 41(5)(a). As to references to a person named on a list where an elector has an anonymous entry in the register of electors see note 1.

15 Representation of the People Act 1983 Sch 1 r 40(1ZD)(b) (as added: see note 6); European Parliamentary Elections Regulations 2004, SI 2004/293, Sch 1 para 44(5)(b) (as substituted: see note 1); Local Elections (Principal Areas) (England and Wales) Rules 2006, SI 2006/3304, Sch 2 r 38(5)(b); Local Elections (Parishes and Communities) (England and Wales) Rules 2006, SI 2006/3305, Sch 2 r 38(5)(b); National Assembly for Wales (Representation of the People) Order 2007, SI 2007/236, Sch 5 para 49(5)(b); Local Authorities (Mayoral Elections) (England and Wales) Regulations 2007, SI 2007/1024, Sch 1 r 40(5)(b); Greater London Authority Elections Rules 2007, SI 2007/3541, Sch 1 r 41(5)(b), Sch 2 r 42(5)(b), Sch 3 r 41(5)(b). As to references to a person named on a list where an elector has an anonymous entry in the register of electors see note 1.

16 Representation of the People Act 1983 Sch 1 r 40(1ZD) (as added: see note 6); European Parliamentary Elections Regulations 2004, SI 2004/293, Sch 1 para 44(5) (as substituted: see note 1); Local Elections (Principal Areas) (England and Wales) Rules 2006, SI 2006/3304, Sch 2 r 38(5); Local Elections (Parishes and Communities) (England and Wales) Rules 2006, SI 2006/3305, Sch 2 r 38(5); National Assembly for Wales (Representation of the People) Order 2007, SI 2007/236, Sch 5 para 49(5); Local Authorities (Mayoral Elections) (England and Wales) Regulations 2007, SI 2007/1024, Sch 1 r 40(5); Greater London Authority Elections Rules 2007, SI 2007/3541, Sch 1 r 41(5), Sch 2 r 42(5), Sch 3 r 41(5).

17   Representation of the People Act 1983 Sch 1 r 40(1ZE) (as added: see note 6); European Parliamentary Elections Regulations 2004, SI 2004/293, Sch 1 para 44(6) (as substituted: see note 1); Local Elections (Principal Areas) (England and Wales) Rules 2006, SI 2006/3304, Sch 2 r 38(6); Local Elections (Parishes and Communities) (England and Wales) Rules 2006, SI 2006/3305, Sch 2 r 38(6); National Assembly for Wales (Representation of the People) Order 2007, SI 2007/236, Sch 5 para 49(6); Local Authorities (Mayoral Elections) (England and Wales) Regulations 2007, SI 2007/1024, Sch 1 r 40(6); Greater London Authority Elections Rules 2007, SI 2007/3541, Sch 1 r 41(6), Sch 2 r 42(6), Sch 3 r 41(6).

18   Representation of the People Act 1983 Sch 1 r 40(2)(a); Parish and Community Meetings (Polls) Rules 1987, SI 1987/1, Schedule r 22(2)(a); European Parliamentary Elections Regulations 2004, SI 2004/293, Sch 1 para 45(1)(a) (as substituted: see note 1); Local Elections (Principal Areas) (England and Wales) Rules 2006, SI 2006/3304, Sch 2 r 39(1)(a); Local Elections (Parishes and Communities) (England and Wales) Rules 2006, SI 2006/3305, Sch 2 r 39(1)(a); National Assembly for Wales (Representation of the People) Order 2007, SI 2007/236, Sch 5 para 49(7)(a); Local Authorities (Mayoral Elections) (England and Wales) Regulations 2007, SI 2007/1024, Sch 1 r 41(1)(a); Greater London Authority Elections Rules 2007, SI 2007/3541, Sch 1 r 42(1)(a), Sch 2 r 43(1)(a), Sch 3 r 42(1)(a).

19   As to the presiding officer see PARA 393. This function of the presiding officer may be discharged by one of the clerks appointed to assist him: see PARA 393. If the applicant puts his vote in the ballot box instead of giving it to the presiding officer the vote is bad: *York County East Riding, Buckrose Division, Case* (1886) 4 O'M & H 110 at 115.

20   The omission to make the endorsement is not a fatal objection to the vote: *Stepney Division, Tower Hamlets Case* (1886) 4 O'M & H 34 at 43.

21   As to the number of an elector and the form and content of registers of electors see PARA 145. In the case of a person in respect of whom a notice has been issued under the Representation of the People Act 1983 s 13B(3B) or s 13B(3D) (see PARA 168), the reference in the text to an elector's number in the register of electors must be read as a reference to the number relating to him on a notice issued under s 13B(3B) or s 13B(3D): Sch 1 r 40(4B)(b) (as added: see note 1); European Parliamentary Elections Regulations 2004, SI 2004/293, Sch 1 para 45(5)(b) (as substituted: see note 1); Local Elections (Principal Areas) (England and Wales) Rules 2006, SI 2006/3304, Sch 2 r 39(5)(b); Local Elections (Parishes and Communities) (England and Wales) Rules 2006, SI 2006/3305, Sch 2 r 39(5)(b); National Assembly for Wales (Representation of the People) Order 2007, SI 2007/236, Sch 5 para 49(11)(b); Local Authorities (Mayoral Elections) (England and Wales) Regulations 2007, SI 2007/1024, Sch 1 r 41(5)(b); Greater London Authority Elections Rules 2007, SI 2007/3541, Sch 1 r 42(5)(b), Sch 2 r 43(5)(b), Sch 3 r 42(5)(b).

     Where an elector has an anonymous entry in the register of electors, the reference in the text to the name of the voter must be ignored: Representation of the People Act 1983 Sch 1 r 40(4A)(a) (as added: see note 1); European Parliamentary Elections Regulations 2004, SI 2004/293, Sch 1 para 45(4)(a) (as so substituted); Local Elections (Principal Areas) (England and Wales) Rules 2006, SI 2006/3304, Sch 2 r 39(4)(a); Local Elections (Parishes and Communities) (England and Wales) Rules 2006, SI 2006/3305, Sch 2 r 39(4)(a); National Assembly for Wales (Representation of the People) Order 2007, SI 2007/236, Sch 5 para 49(10)(a); Local Authorities (Mayoral Elections) (England and Wales) Regulations 2007, SI 2007/1024, Sch 1 r 41(4)(a); Greater London Authority Elections Rules 2007, SI 2007/3541, Sch 1 r 42(4)(a), Sch 2 r 43(4)(a), Sch 3 r 42(4)(a). See note 1.

22   Representation of the People Act 1983 Sch 1 r 40(2)(b); Parish and Community Meetings (Polls) Rules 1987, SI 1987/1, Schedule r 22(2)(b); European Parliamentary Elections Regulations 2004, SI 2004/293, Sch 1 para 45(1)(b) (as substituted: see note 1); Local Elections (Principal Areas) (England and Wales) Rules 2006, SI 2006/3304, Sch 2 r 39(1)(b); Local Elections (Parishes and Communities) (England and Wales) Rules 2006, SI 2006/3305, Sch 2 r 39(1)(b); National Assembly for Wales (Representation of the People) Order 2007, SI 2007/236, Sch 5 para 49(7)(b); Local Authorities (Mayoral Elections) (England and Wales) Regulations 2007, SI 2007/1024, Sch 1 r 41(1)(b); Greater London Authority Elections Rules 2007, SI 2007/3541, Sch 1 r 42(1)(b), Sch 2 r 43(1)(b), Sch 3 r 42(1)(b). A tendered vote is not counted by the returning officer: in relation to a local government election (except a London Authority election) see PARA 425; in relation to a local authority mayoral election see PARA 436; in relation to a London Authority election see PARA 444; in relation to a London mayoral election see PARA 451; in relation to a Welsh Assembly election see PARA 458; and in relation to a European parliamentary election see PARA 468. As to the adding of the vote on a scrutiny see PARA 839 et seq.

23   In the case of a person in respect of whom a notice has been issued under the Representation of the People Act 1983 s 13B(3B) or s 13B(3D) (see PARA 168), the reference in the text to an elector's number in the register of electors must be read as a reference to the number relating to

him on a notice issued under s 13B(3B) or s 13B(3D): Sch 1 r 40(4B)(c) (as added: see note 1); European Parliamentary Elections Regulations 2004, SI 2004/293, Sch 1 para 45(5)(c) (as substituted: see note 1); Local Elections (Principal Areas) (England and Wales) Rules 2006, SI 2006/3304, Sch 2 r 39(5)(c); Local Elections (Parishes and Communities) (England and Wales) Rules 2006, SI 2006/3305, Sch 2 r 39(5)(c); National Assembly for Wales (Representation of the People) Order 2007, SI 2007/236, Sch 5 para 49(11)(b); Local Authorities (Mayoral Elections) (England and Wales) Regulations 2007, SI 2007/1024, Sch 1 r 41(5)(c); Greater London Authority Elections Rules 2007, SI 2007/3541, Sch 1 r 42(5)(c), Sch 2 r 43(5)(c), Sch 3 r 42(5)(c). The reference in the text to the name of the voter must be ignored in the case of an elector who has an anonymous entry in the register of electors: Representation of the People Act 1983 Sch 1 r 40(4A)(a) (as added: see note 1); European Parliamentary Elections Regulations 2004, SI 2004/293, Sch 1 para 45(4)(a) (as so substituted); Local Elections (Principal Areas) (England and Wales) Rules 2006, SI 2006/3304, Sch 2 r 39(4)(a); Local Elections (Parishes and Communities) (England and Wales) Rules 2006, SI 2006/3305, Sch 2 r 39(4)(a); National Assembly for Wales (Representation of the People) Order 2007, SI 2007/236, Sch 5 para 49(10)(a); Local Authorities (Mayoral Elections) (England and Wales) Regulations 2007, SI 2007/1024, Sch 1 r 41(4)(a); Greater London Authority Elections Rules 2007, SI 2007/3541, Sch 1 r 42(4)(a), Sch 2 r 43(4)(a), Sch 3 r 42(4)(a). See note 1.

24 Representation of the People Act 1983 Sch 1 r 40(3) (amended by the Electoral Administration Act 2006 s 47, Sch 1 paras 69, 81(1), (3)); Parish and Community Meetings (Polls) Rules 1987, SI 1987/1, Schedule r 22(3); European Parliamentary Elections Regulations 2004, SI 2004/293, Sch 1 para 45(2) (as substituted: see note 1); Local Elections (Principal Areas) (England and Wales) Rules 2006, SI 2006/3304, Sch 2 r 39(2); Local Elections (Parishes and Communities) (England and Wales) Rules 2006, SI 2006/3305, Sch 2 r 39(2); National Assembly for Wales (Representation of the People) Order 2007, SI 2007/236, Sch 5 para 49(8); Local Authorities (Mayoral Elections) (England and Wales) Regulations 2007, SI 2007/1024, Sch 1 r 41(2); Greater London Authority Elections Rules 2007, SI 2007/3541, Sch 1 r 42(2), Sch 2 r 43(2), Sch 3 r 42(2). In the case of a parliamentary election, the voter must also sign the tendered votes list opposite the entry relating to him: see the Representation of the People Act 1983 Sch 1 r 40(3) (as so amended).

Where any other ordinary London Authority election in the Assembly constituency is contested, the same tendered votes list may be used for each Authority election and, where it is so used, an entry in that list must be taken to mean that tendered ballot papers were marked in respect of each Authority election, unless the list identifies the election for which a tendered ballot paper was delivered: Greater London Authority Elections Rules 2007, SI 2007/3541, Sch 1 r 42(6), Sch 2 r 43(6), Sch 3 r 42(6). Where the polls at a Welsh Assembly constituency election and a regional election are to be taken together, the same tendered votes list for the constituency and regional elections at which the voters are entitled to vote may be used and, where it is so used, an entry in that list must be taken to mean that tendered ballot papers were so marked in respect of each election, unless the list identifies the election at which a tendered ballot paper was so marked: National Assembly for Wales (Representation of the People) Order 2007, SI 2007/236, Sch 5 para 49(12). As to the meaning of 'Assembly constituency', in relation to a London Authority election, see PARA 11 note 6.

25 Representation of the People Act 1983 Sch 1 r 40(4); European Parliamentary Elections Regulations 2004, SI 2004/293, Sch 1 para 45(3) (as substituted: see note 1); Local Elections (Principal Areas) (England and Wales) Rules 2006, SI 2006/3304, Sch 2 r 39(3); Local Elections (Parishes and Communities) (England and Wales) Rules 2006, SI 2006/3305, Sch 2 r 39(3); National Assembly for Wales (Representation of the People) Order 2007, SI 2007/236, Sch 5 para 49(9); Local Authorities (Mayoral Elections) (England and Wales) Regulations 2007, SI 2007/1024, Sch 1 r 41(3); Greater London Authority Elections Rules 2007, SI 2007/3541, Sch 1 r 42(3), Sch 2 r 43(3), Sch 3 r 42(3). See also note 23. There is no provision for voting by proxy at a poll consequent on a parish meeting on a question involving appointment to office and accordingly the provision that is set out in the text does not apply in that case.

404. Spoilt and replacement ballot papers. A voter at an election[1], or at a poll consequent on a parish meeting on a question involving appointment to office[2], who has inadvertently dealt with his ballot paper[3] in such manner that it cannot be conveniently used as a ballot paper may, on delivering it to the presiding officer[4] and proving to his satisfaction the fact of the inadvertence, obtain another ballot paper (a 'replacement ballot paper') in place of the ballot paper so delivered (called a 'spoilt ballot paper')[5]. The spoilt ballot paper must be immediately cancelled[6]. Where a voter at a Welsh Assembly election is entitled to give two votes at a polling station[7]:

(1)   if the voter proves to the satisfaction of the presiding officer that only one ballot paper is spoilt inadvertently[8]: (a) the voter must nevertheless deliver both ballot papers (the 'surrendered ballot papers') to the presiding officer[9]; (b) the presiding officer must deliver to the voter two replacement ballot papers[10]; and (c) the presiding officer must treat both of the surrendered ballot papers as spoilt ballot papers and must immediately cancel them[11]; or

(2)   if a voter proves to the satisfaction of the presiding officer that one ballot paper is spoilt inadvertently and that the other ballot paper (the 'used ballot paper') has been placed in the ballot box[12]: (a) the voter must deliver the spoilt ballot paper (the 'returned ballot paper') to the presiding officer[13]; (b) the presiding officer must deliver to the voter a replacement ballot paper in place of the returned ballot paper (notwithstanding that the number on the replacement ballot paper is not the same as the number on the used ballot paper previously delivered to the voter)[14]; and (c) the presiding officer, in addition to cancelling the returned ballot paper, must treat the constituency or, as the case may be, regional ballot paper that has the same number as the replacement ballot paper delivered to the voter as a spoilt ballot paper, and he must also immediately cancel it[15].

Before a replacement ballot paper may be obtained at a London Authority election, the presiding officer must mark the corresponding number list that was marked[16] before delivery of the original ballot paper[17]:

(i)   beside the number of the replacement ballot paper obtained to show the number of the elector, and the number of the ballot paper which is being replaced[18]; or

(ii)   beside the number of the spoilt ballot paper to show that the ballot paper was replaced[19].

At an ordinary London constituency members or Mayoral election, or at a London members election held at the same time as another contested Authority election, the voter must only receive a replacement for a spoilt or returned ballot paper[20].

1   Ie at a parliamentary election, a local government election (which includes any London Authority election and a local authority mayoral election), a Welsh Assembly constituency or regional election or a European parliamentary election. As to the meanings of 'Assembly election', 'constituency election' and 'regional election' see PARA 3 note 2. As to the meaning of 'parliamentary election' see PARA 9. As to the meanings of 'Authority election' and 'local government election' see PARA 11. As to elections in the City of London see PARA 33. As to European parliamentary elections see PARA 217 et seq. For the purposes of the statutory provisions governing elections, a voter is defined as a person voting at an election and includes a person voting as proxy (but not necessarily a person voting by proxy): in relation to parliamentary and local government elections see PARA 95 note 2; in relation to Welsh Assembly elections see PARA 110 note 7; and in relation to European parliamentary elections see PARA 111 note 5.

2   As to polls consequent on a parish meeting on a question involving appointment to office see PARA 200 et seq.

3   As to the provisions relating to ballot papers generally see PARA 386 et seq.

4   As to the presiding officer see PARA 393. This function of the presiding officer may be discharged by one of the clerks appointed to assist him: see PARA 393.

5   Representation of the People Act 1983 Sch 1 r 41; Parish and Community Meetings (Polls) Rules 1987, SI 1987/1, Schedule r 23; European Parliamentary Elections Regulations 2004,

SI 2004/293, Sch 1 para 46 (Sch 1 substituted by SI 2009/186); Local Elections (Principal Areas) (England and Wales) Rules 2006, SI 2006/3304, Sch 2 r 40; Local Elections (Parishes and Communities) (England and Wales) Rules 2006, SI 2006/3305, Sch 2 r 40; National Assembly for Wales (Representation of the People) Order 2007, SI 2007/236, Sch 5 para 50(1); Local Authorities (Mayoral Elections) (England and Wales) Regulations 2007, SI 2007/1024, Sch 1 r 42; Greater London Authority Elections Rules 2007, SI 2007/3541, Sch 1 r 43(1), Sch 2 r 44(1), Sch 3 r 43(1).

6	Representation of the People Act 1983 Sch 1 r 41; Parish and Community Meetings (Polls) Rules 1987, SI 1987/1, Schedule r 23; European Parliamentary Elections Regulations 2004, SI 2004/293, Sch 1 para 46 (as substituted: see note 5); Local Elections (Principal Areas) (England and Wales) Rules 2006, SI 2006/3304, Sch 2 r 40; Local Elections (Parishes and Communities) (England and Wales) Rules 2006, SI 2006/3305, Sch 2 r 40; National Assembly for Wales (Representation of the People) Order 2007, SI 2007/236, Sch 5 para 50(1); Local Authorities (Mayoral Elections) (England and Wales) Regulations 2007, SI 2007/1024, Sch 1 r 42; Greater London Authority Elections Rules 2007, SI 2007/3541, Sch 1 r 43(1), Sch 2 r 44(1), Sch 3 r 43(1).

7	See the National Assembly for Wales (Representation of the People) Order 2007, SI 2007/236, Sch 5 para 50(2). Each person entitled to vote at a general election in an Assembly constituency has two votes: (1) a 'constituency vote' (ie a vote which may be given for a candidate to be the Assembly constituency member for the Assembly constituency); and (2) an 'electoral region vote' (ie a vote which may be given for either: (a) a registered political party which has submitted a list of candidates to be Assembly regional members for the Assembly electoral region in which the Assembly constituency is included; or (b) an individual who is a candidate to be an Assembly regional member for that Assembly electoral region): see the Government of Wales Act 2006 s 6; and PARA 364.

8	See the National Assembly for Wales (Representation of the People) Order 2007, SI 2007/236, Sch 5 para 50(3).

9	National Assembly for Wales (Representation of the People) Order 2007, SI 2007/236, Sch 5 para 50(3)(a).

10	National Assembly for Wales (Representation of the People) Order 2007, SI 2007/236, Sch 5 para 50(3)(b).

11	National Assembly for Wales (Representation of the People) Order 2007, SI 2007/236, Sch 5 para 50(3)(c).

12	See the National Assembly for Wales (Representation of the People) Order 2007, SI 2007/236, Sch 5 para 50(4).

13	National Assembly for Wales (Representation of the People) Order 2007, SI 2007/236, Sch 5 para 50(4)(a).

14	National Assembly for Wales (Representation of the People) Order 2007, SI 2007/236, Sch 5 para 50(4)(b).

15	National Assembly for Wales (Representation of the People) Order 2007, SI 2007/236, Sch 5 para 50(4)(c).

16	Ie under the Greater London Authority Elections Rules 2007, SI 2007/3541, Sch 1 r 38(1), Sch 2 r 39(1), Sch 3 r 38(1) (see PARA 399): see Sch 1 r 43(3), Sch 2 r 44(3), Sch 3 r 43(3). The Queen's Printers' copy of Sch 1 r 43(3) refers to the corresponding number list that was marked under Sch 1 r 39(1) (votes marked by presiding officer on application of voter with incapacities: see PARA 401), although no reference to the corresponding number list appears there. It is submitted that a reference to Sch 1 r 38(1) is to be preferred.

17	Greater London Authority Elections Rules 2007, SI 2007/3541, Sch 1 r 43(3), Sch 2 r 44(3), Sch 3 r 43(3). If the same corresponding number list is used for more than one Authority election in accordance with Sch 1 r 38(7), Sch 2 r 39(7), Sch 3 r 38(7) (see PARA 399 note 8), the marks made under Sch 1 r 43(3), Sch 2 r 44(3), Sch 3 r 43(3) must identify the election for which a ballot paper has been replaced, and any ballot paper which the voter has not applied for or obtained as a replacement, but which bears the same ballot paper number as a ballot paper delivered under Sch 1 r 38(1), Sch 2 r 39(1), Sch 3 r 38(1), or obtained under either Sch 1 r 43(1), Sch 2 r 44(1), Sch 3 r 43(1) (see the text and notes 1–6) or Sch 1 r 43(2), Sch 2 r 44(2), Sch 3 r 43(2) (see PARA 399 note 20), must not be delivered to the voter, must be cancelled, and must be treated as a spoilt ballot paper: see Sch 1 r 43(5), Sch 2 r 44(5), Sch 3 r 43(5).

18	Greater London Authority Elections Rules 2007, SI 2007/3541, Sch 1 r 43(3)(a), Sch 2 r 44(3)(a), Sch 3 r 43(3)(a). Head (i) in the text applies to a ballot paper that is being replaced under either Sch 1 r 43(1), Sch 2 r 44(1), Sch 3 r 43(1) (see the text and notes 1–6) or Sch 1 r 43(2), Sch 2 r 44(2), Sch 3 r 43(2) (see PARA 399 note 20): see Sch 1 r 43(3)(a), Sch 2 r 44(3)(a), Sch 3 r 43(3)(a). As to the number of an elector and the form and content of registers of electors see PARA 145.

19   Greater London Authority Elections Rules 2007, SI 2007/3541, Sch 1 r 43(3)(b), Sch 2 r 44(3)(b), Sch 3 r 43(3)(b). Head (ii) in the text applies to a ballot paper that is being replaced under either Sch 1 r 43(1), Sch 2 r 44(1), Sch 3 r 43(1) (see the text and notes 1–6) only: see Sch 1 r 43(3)(b), Sch 2 r 44(3)(b), Sch 3 r 43(3)(b).
20   Greater London Authority Elections Rules 2007, SI 2007/3541, Sch 1 r 43(4), Sch 2 r 44(4), Sch 3 r 43(4).

405. Procedure on close of poll at a polling station. As soon as practicable after the close of the poll at an election[1], or of a poll consequent on a parish meeting on a question involving appointment to office[2], the presiding officer[3] must, in the presence of the polling agents[4], make up into separate packets, sealed with his own seal, and the seals of such polling agents as desire to affix their seals[5]:

(1)   each ballot box in use at his station, sealed so as to prevent the introduction of additional ballot papers, and unopened (but, if the boxes are capable of being locked, with the key attached)[6];

(2)   the unused and spoilt ballot papers, placed together[7];

(3)   the tendered ballot papers[8];

(4)   the marked copies of the register of electors[9] and of the list of proxies[10];

(5)   the completed corresponding number lists for any election[11] (or, in the case of a poll consequent on a parish meeting on a question involving appointment to office, the counterfoils of the used ballot papers)[12];

(6)   the certificates as to employment on duty on the day of the poll at an election[13]; and

(7)   the tendered votes list[14], the list of voters with disabilities assisted by companions[15], the list of votes marked by the presiding officer on the application of a voter with incapacities[16], a statement of the number of voters whose votes are so marked by the presiding officer under the heads 'disability' and 'unable to read'[17], the declarations made by the companions of voters with disabilities[18], and the list maintained by the presiding officer[19] of persons to whom ballot papers were delivered at an election in consequence of an alteration to the register which took effect on the day of the poll[20].

The materials mentioned in head (4) above must be in one packet but must not be in the same packet as the materials mentioned in heads (5) and (6) above[21].

The presiding officer must deliver the packets or cause them to be delivered to the returning officer[22] to be taken charge of by him; but if the packets are not delivered by the presiding officer personally to the returning officer, the arrangements for their delivery require the approval of the returning officer[23]. The packets must be accompanied by a statement (the 'ballot paper account') made by the presiding officer showing the number of ballot papers entrusted to him[24], and accounting for them under the heads of:

(a)   'ballot papers issued and not otherwise accounted for'[25];

(b)   'unused ballot papers'[26];

(c)   'spoilt ballot papers'[27]; and

(d)   'tendered ballot papers'[28].

Where the poll at an election is taken together with the poll at another election or referendum, special provision is made for the procedure on the close of a poll[29].

1   Ie at a parliamentary election, a local government election (which includes any London Authority election and a local authority mayoral election), a Welsh Assembly constituency or regional election (whether the polls are taken separately or together) or a European parliamentary election. As to the meanings of 'Assembly election', 'constituency election' and

'regional election' see PARA 3 note 2. As to the meaning of 'parliamentary election' see PARA 9. As to the meanings of 'Authority election' and 'local government election' see PARA 11. As to elections in the City of London see PARA 33. As to European parliamentary elections see PARA 217 et seq.

2   As to polls consequent on a parish meeting on a question involving appointment to office see PARA 200 et seq.

3   As to the presiding officer see PARA 393. This function of the presiding officer may be discharged by one of the clerks appointed to assist him: see PARA 393.

4   As to the appointment of polling agents to attend at polling stations for the purpose of detecting personation, and the effect of their non-attendance, see PARA 394.

5   Representation of the People Act 1983 Sch 1 r 43(1); Parish and Community Meetings (Polls) Rules 1987, SI 1987/1, Schedule r 25(1); European Parliamentary Elections Regulations 2004, SI 2004/293, Sch 1 para 49(1) (Sch 1 substituted by SI 2009/186); Local Elections (Principal Areas) (England and Wales) Rules 2006, SI 2006/3304, Sch 2 r 43(1); Local Elections (Parishes and Communities) (England and Wales) Rules 2006, SI 2006/3305, Sch 2 r 43(1); National Assembly for Wales (Representation of the People) Order 2007, SI 2007/236, Sch 5 para 53(1), (2); Local Authorities (Mayoral Elections) (England and Wales) Regulations 2007, SI 2007/1024, Sch 1 r 45(1); Greater London Authority Elections Rules 2007, SI 2007/3541, Sch 1 r 46(1), Sch 2 r 47(1), Sch 3 r 46(1). Where electors at a Welsh Assembly election are entitled to give two votes at the polling station (ie where the polls at a constituency election and at a regional election have been taken together), minor modifications are made to the provisions to ensure that the documents relating to the two elections are kept separate: see the National Assembly for Wales (Representation of the People) Order 2007, SI 2007/236, Sch 5 para 53(1); and notes 7, 8.

6   Representation of the People Act 1983 Sch 1 r 43(1)(a); Parish and Community Meetings (Polls) Rules 1987, SI 1987/1, Schedule r 25(1)(a); European Parliamentary Elections Regulations 2004, SI 2004/293, Sch 1 para 49(1)(a) (as substituted: see note 5); Local Elections (Principal Areas) (England and Wales) Rules 2006, SI 2006/3304, Sch 2 r 43(1)(a); Local Elections (Parishes and Communities) (England and Wales) Rules 2006, SI 2006/3305, Sch 2 r 43(1)(a); National Assembly for Wales (Representation of the People) Order 2007, SI 2007/236, Sch 5 para 53(1)(a), (2)(a); Local Authorities (Mayoral Elections) (England and Wales) Regulations 2007, SI 2007/1024, Sch 1 r 45(1)(a); Greater London Authority Elections Rules 2007, SI 2007/3541, Sch 1 r 46(1)(a), Sch 2 r 47(1)(a), Sch 3 r 46(1)(a). As to the equipment of polling stations with sufficient ballot boxes, ballot papers etc see PARA 391.

7   Representation of the People Act 1983 Sch 1 r 43(1)(b); Parish and Community Meetings (Polls) Rules 1987, SI 1987/1, Schedule r 25(1)(b); European Parliamentary Elections Regulations 2004, SI 2004/293, Sch 1 para 49(1)(b) (as substituted: see note 5); Local Elections (Principal Areas) (England and Wales) Rules 2006, SI 2006/3304, Sch 2 r 43(1)(b); Local Elections (Parishes and Communities) (England and Wales) Rules 2006, SI 2006/3305, Sch 2 r 43(1)(b); National Assembly for Wales (Representation of the People) Order 2007, SI 2007/236, Sch 5 para 53(1)(b), (c), (2)(b); Local Authorities (Mayoral Elections) (England and Wales) Regulations 2007, SI 2007/1024, Sch 1 r 45(1)(b); Greater London Authority Elections Rules 2007, SI 2007/3541, Sch 1 r 46(1)(b), Sch 2 r 47(1)(b), Sch 3 r 46(1)(b). See note 21. Where the polls at a Welsh Assembly constituency election and at a Welsh Assembly regional election have been taken together, separate packets must be made up and sealed for:

(1)   the unused and spoilt ballot papers, placed together, relating to the constituency election (see the National Assembly for Wales (Representation of the People) Order 2007, SI 2007/236, Sch 5 para 53(1)(b)); and

(2)   the unused and spoilt ballot papers, placed together, relating to the regional election (see Sch 5 para 53(1)(c)).

As to spoilt ballot papers see PARA 404.

8   Representation of the People Act 1983 Sch 1 r 43(1)(c); Parish and Community Meetings (Polls) Rules 1987, SI 1987/1, Schedule r 25(1)(c); European Parliamentary Elections Regulations 2004, SI 2004/293, Sch 1 para 49(1)(c) (as substituted: see note 5); Local Elections (Principal Areas) (England and Wales) Rules 2006, SI 2006/3304, Sch 2 r 43(1)(c); Local Elections (Parishes and Communities) (England and Wales) Rules 2006, SI 2006/3305, Sch 2 r 43(1)(c); National Assembly for Wales (Representation of the People) Order 2007, SI 2007/236, Sch 5 para 53(1)(d), (e), (2)(c); Local Authorities (Mayoral Elections) (England and Wales) Regulations 2007, SI 2007/1024, Sch 1 r 45(1)(c); Greater London Authority Elections Rules 2007, SI 2007/3541, Sch 1 r 46(1)(c), Sch 2 r 47(1)(c), Sch 3 r 46(1)(c). See note 21. Where the polls at a Welsh Assembly constituency election and at a Welsh Assembly regional election have been taken together, separate packets must be made up and sealed for:

(1) the tendered ballot papers relating to the constituency election (see the National Assembly for Wales (Representation of the People) Order 2007, SI 2007/236, Sch 5 para 53(1)(d)); and

(2) the tendered ballot papers relating to the regional election (see Sch 5 para 53(1)(e)).
As to tendered ballot papers see PARA 403.

9 Ie including any marked copy notices of alteration to the register issued under the Representation of the People Act 1983 s 13B(3B) or s 13B(3D) (see PARA 168): Sch 1 r 43(1)(d) (amended by the Electoral Administration Act 2006 s 11(6), Sch 1 paras 31, 33, 39(a)); European Parliamentary Elections Regulations 2004, SI 2004/293, Sch 1 para 49(1)(d) (as substituted: see note 5); Local Elections (Principal Areas) (England and Wales) Rules 2006, SI 2006/3304, Sch 2 r 43(1)(d); Local Elections (Parishes and Communities) (England and Wales) Rules 2006, SI 2006/3305, Sch 2 r 43(1)(d); National Assembly for Wales (Representation of the People) Order 2007, SI 2007/236, Sch 5 para 52(1)(f), (2)(d); Local Authorities (Mayoral Elections) (England and Wales) Regulations 2007, SI 2007/1024, Sch 1 r 45(1)(d); Greater London Authority Elections Rules 2007, SI 2007/3541, Sch 1 r 46(1)(d), Sch 2 r 47(1)(d), Sch 3 r 46(1)(d).

10 Representation of the People Act 1983 Sch 1 r 43(1)(d) (as amended: see note 9); Parish and Community Meetings (Polls) Rules 1987, SI 1987/1, Schedule r 25(1)(d); European Parliamentary Elections Regulations 2004, SI 2004/293, Sch 1 para 49(1)(d) (as substituted: see note 5); Local Elections (Principal Areas) (England and Wales) Rules 2006, SI 2006/3304, Sch 2 r 43(1)(d); Local Elections (Parishes and Communities) (England and Wales) Rules 2006, SI 2006/3305, Sch 2 r 43(1)(d); National Assembly for Wales (Representation of the People) Order 2007, SI 2007/236, Sch 5 para 52(1)(f), (2)(d); Local Authorities (Mayoral Elections) (England and Wales) Regulations 2007, SI 2007/1024, Sch 1 r 45(1)(d); Greater London Authority Elections Rules 2007, SI 2007/3541, Sch 1 r 46(1)(d), Sch 2 r 47(1)(d), Sch 3 r 46(1)(d). There is no provision for voting by proxy at a poll consequent on a parish meeting on a question involving appointment to office and accordingly the reference to the list of proxies in head (4) in the text does not apply in that case. As to the list of proxies see PARA 373.

11 Representation of the People Act 1983 Sch 1 r 43(1)(da) (added by the Electoral Administration Act 2006 s 31(1), (4)(a)); European Parliamentary Elections Regulations 2004, SI 2004/293, Sch 1 para 49(1)(e) (as substituted: see note 5); Local Elections (Principal Areas) (England and Wales) Rules 2006, SI 2006/3304, Sch 2 r 43(1)(e); Local Elections (Parishes and Communities) (England and Wales) Rules 2006, SI 2006/3305, Sch 2 r 43(1)(e); National Assembly for Wales (Representation of the People) Order 2007, SI 2007/236, Sch 5 para 53(1)(g), (2)(e); Local Authorities (Mayoral Elections) (England and Wales) Regulations 2007, SI 2007/1024, Sch 1 r 45(1)(e); Greater London Authority Elections Rules 2007, SI 2007/3541, Sch 1 r 46(1)(e), Sch 2 r 47(1)(e), Sch 3 r 46(1)(e).

The text refers to the lists prepared, in relation to a parliamentary election, under the Representation of the People Act 1983 Sch 1 r 19A, or, in relation to a European parliamentary election, under the European Parliamentary Elections Regulations 2004, SI 2004/293, Sch 1 para 23, or, in relation to a local government election, under the Local Elections (Principal Areas) (England and Wales) Rules 2006, SI 2006/3304, Sch 2 r 17, the Local Elections (Parishes and Communities) (England and Wales) Rules 2006, SI 2006/3305, Sch 2 r 17, the Local Authorities (Mayoral Elections) (England and Wales) Regulations 2007, SI 2007/1024, Sch 1 r 19, or the Greater London Authority Elections Rules 2007, SI 2007/3541, Sch 1 r 18, Sch 2 r 19, Sch 3 r 18, or, in relation to a Welsh Assembly election, under the National Assembly for Wales (Representation of the People) Order 2007, SI 2007/236, Sch 5 para 27 (corresponding number list: see PARA 387), including the parts which were completed in accordance with, respectively, the Representation of the People Act 1983 Sch 1 r 37(1)(b), (d), the European Parliamentary Elections Regulations 2004, SI 2004/293, Sch 1 para 41(1)(b), the Local Elections (Principal Areas) (England and Wales) Rules 2006, SI 2006/3304, Sch 2 r 35(1)(b), the Local Elections (Parishes and Communities) (England and Wales) Rules 2006, SI 2006/3305, Sch 2 r 35(1)(b), the Local Authorities (Mayoral Elections) (England and Wales) Regulations 2007, SI 2007/1024, Sch 1 r 37(1)(b), the Greater London Authority Elections Rules 2007, SI 2007/3541, Sch 1 r 38(1)(b), Sch 2 r 39(1)(b), Sch 3 r 38(1)(b), and the National Assembly for Wales (Representation of the People) Order 2007, SI 2007/236, Sch 5 para 46(1)(b) (see PARA 399), which are together referred to in the elections rules as the 'completed corresponding number lists': Representation of the People Act 1983 Sch 1 r 43(1)(da) (as so added); European Parliamentary Elections Regulations 2004, SI 2004/293, Sch 1 para 49(1)(e) (as so substituted); Local Elections (Principal Areas) (England and Wales) Rules 2006, SI 2006/3304, Sch 2 r 43(1)(e); Local Elections (Parishes and Communities) (England and Wales) Rules 2006, SI 2006/3305, Sch 2 r 43(1)(e); National Assembly for Wales (Representation of the People) Order 2007, SI 2007/236, Sch 5 para 53(1)(g), (2)(e); Local Authorities (Mayoral Elections)

(England and Wales) Regulations 2007, SI 2007/1024, Sch 1 r 45(1)(e); Greater London Authority Elections Rules 2007, SI 2007/3541, Sch 1 r 46(1)(e), Sch 2 r 47(1)(e), Sch 3 r 46(1)(e). As to the elections rules see PARA 383. As to the form of corresponding number list to be prepared by a returning officer see PARA 391 note 14.

12 Parish and Community Meetings (Polls) Rules 1987, SI 1987/1, Schedule r 25(1)(e).

13 Representation of the People Act 1983 Sch 1 r 43(1)(e) (amended by the Electoral Administration Act 2006 ss 31(1), (4)(b), 74(2), Sch 2); European Parliamentary Elections Regulations 2004, SI 2004/293, Sch 1 para 49(1)(f) (as substituted: see note 5); Local Elections (Principal Areas) (England and Wales) Rules 2006, SI 2006/3304, Sch 2 r 43(1)(f); Local Elections (Parishes and Communities) (England and Wales) Rules 2006, SI 2006/3305, Sch 2 r 43(1)(f); National Assembly for Wales (Representation of the People) Order 2007, SI 2007/236, Sch 5 para 53(1)(h), (2)(f); Local Authorities (Mayoral Elections) (England and Wales) Regulations 2007, SI 2007/1024, Sch 1 r 45(1)(f); Greater London Authority Elections Rules 2007, SI 2007/3541, Sch 1 r 46(1)(f), Sch 2 r 47(1)(f), Sch 3 r 46(1)(f). See note 21. There is no provision for certificates as to employment on duty at a poll consequent on a parish meeting on a question involving appointment to office and accordingly head (6) in the text does not apply in that case. As to certificates of employment on duty on the day of the poll see PARA 395.

14 As to the tendered votes list see PARA 403.

15 As to the list of voters with disabilities assisted by companions see PARA 402. At a poll consequent on a parish meeting on a question involving appointment to office, only voters with blindness are provided for and, accordingly, all references to other physical incapacities must be ignored in that case, albeit that the statement of the number of voters whose votes are marked by the presiding officer contains the head 'physical incapacity' rather than 'blindness' (see note 17): see the Parish and Community Meetings (Polls) Rules 1987, SI 1987/1, Schedule r 25(1)(f).

16 Ie the 'list of votes marked by the presiding officer': see PARA 401.

17 See PARA 401. At a poll consequent on a parish meeting on a question involving appointment to office, the statement of the number of voters whose votes are marked by the presiding officer contains the head 'physical incapacity' rather than 'disability' (or 'blindness': see note 15): see the Parish and Community Meetings (Polls) Rules 1987, SI 1987/1, Schedule r 25(1)(f)

18 As to declarations made by the companion of a voter with disabilities see PARA 402.

19 Ie the list maintained, in relation to a parliamentary election, under the Representation of the People Act 1983 Sch 1 r 41A, or, in relation to a European parliamentary election, under the European Parliamentary Elections Regulations 2004, SI 2004/293, Sch 1 para 47(1), or, in relation to a local government election, under the Local Elections (Principal Areas) (England and Wales) Rules 2006, SI 2006/3304, Sch 2 r 41, the Local Elections (Parishes and Communities) (England and Wales) Rules 2006, SI 2006/3305, Sch 2 r 41, the Local Authorities (Mayoral Elections) (England and Wales) Regulations 2007, SI 2007/1024, Sch 1 r 43, or the Greater London Authority Elections Rules 2007, SI 2007/3541, Sch 1 r 44(1), Sch 2 r 45(1), Sch 3 r 44(1), or, in relation to a Welsh Assembly election, under the National Assembly for Wales (Representation of the People) Order 2007, SI 2007/236, Sch 5 para 51 (correction of errors on day of poll: see PARA 399 note 5): Representation of the People Act 1983 Sch 1 r 43(1)(f) (amended by the Representation of the People Act 2000 s 13(1), (4); and the Electoral Administration Act 2006 s 47, Sch 1 paras 31, 33, 39(b), 69, 79); Parish and Community Meetings (Polls) Rules 1987, SI 1987/1, Schedule r 25(1)(f); European Parliamentary Elections Regulations 2004, SI 2004/293, Sch 1 para 49(1)(g) (as substituted: see note 5); Local Elections (Principal Areas) (England and Wales) Rules 2006, SI 2006/3304, Sch 2 r 43(1)(g); Local Elections (Parishes and Communities) (England and Wales) Rules 2006, SI 2006/3305, Sch 2 r 43(1)(g); National Assembly for Wales (Representation of the People) Order 2007, SI 2007/236, Sch 5 para 53(1)(i), (2)(g); Local Authorities (Mayoral Elections) (England and Wales) Regulations 2007, SI 2007/1024, Sch 1 r 45(1)(g); Greater London Authority Elections Rules 2007, SI 2007/3541, Sch 1 r 46(1)(g), Sch 2 r 47(1)(g), Sch 3 r 46(1)(g).

20 Representation of the People Act 1983 Sch 1 r 43(1)(f) (as amended: see note 19); Parish and Community Meetings (Polls) Rules 1987, SI 1987/1, Schedule r 25(1)(f); European Parliamentary Elections Regulations 2004, SI 2004/293, Sch 1 para 49(1)(g) (as substituted: see note 5); Local Elections (Principal Areas) (England and Wales) Rules 2006, SI 2006/3304, Sch 2 r 43(1)(g); Local Elections (Parishes and Communities) (England and Wales) Rules 2006, SI 2006/3305, Sch 2 r 43(1)(g); National Assembly for Wales (Representation of the People) Order 2007, SI 2007/236, Sch 5 para 53(1)(i), (2)(g); Local Authorities (Mayoral Elections) (England and Wales) Regulations 2007, SI 2007/1024, Sch 1 r 45(1)(g); Greater London Authority Elections Rules 2007, SI 2007/3541, Sch 1 r 46(1)(g), Sch 2 r 47(1)(g), Sch 3 r 46(1)(g).

21 Representation of the People Act 1983 Sch 1 r 43(2) (amended by the Electoral Administration
    Act 2006 s 31(1), (4)(c)); Parish and Community Meetings (Polls) Rules 1987, SI 1987/1,
    Schedule r 25(2); European Parliamentary Elections Regulations 2004, SI 2004/293, Sch 1
    para 49(2) (as substituted: see note 5); Local Elections (Principal Areas) (England and Wales)
    Rules 2006, SI 2006/3304, Sch 2 r 43(2); Local Elections (Parishes and Communities) (England
    and Wales) Rules 2006, SI 2006/3305, Sch 2 r 43(2); Local Authorities (Mayoral Elections)
    (England and Wales) Regulations 2007, SI 2007/1024, Sch 1 r 45(2); Greater London Authority
    Elections Rules 2007, SI 2007/3541, Sch 1 r 46(3), Sch 2 r 47(3), Sch 3 r 46(3). The provision
    set out in the text does not apply at a Welsh Assembly election because special provision is made
    for the number and contents of the packets: see the National Assembly for Wales
    (Representation of the People) Order 2007, SI 2007/236, Sch 5 para 53(1), (2); and notes 7, 8.
    At a London Authority election, the contents of the packets of:
    (1)   the unused and spoilt ballot papers (placed together) (see head (2) in the text);
    (2)   the tendered ballot papers (see head (3) in the text); and
    (3)   the certificates as to employment on duty on the day of the poll (see head (6) in the
          text),
    must not be combined with the contents of the packets made under the corresponding rule that
    applies at other Assembly elections: Greater London Authority Elections Rules 2007,
    SI 2007/3541, Sch 1 r 46(2), Sch 2 r 47(2), Sch 3 r 46(2).
        At a poll consequent on a parish meeting on a question involving appointment to office,
    there is no provision either for voting by proxy (see note 10) or for certificates as to employment
    on duty (see note 13) and accordingly the provision referred to in the text is limited in such a
    case to requiring that the marked copy of the register of electors (see head (4) in the text) must
    not be in the same packet as the counterfoils of the used ballot papers (see head (5) in the text):
    see the Parish and Community Meetings (Polls) Rules 1987, SI 1987/1, Schedule r 25(2).

22 As to returning officers generally see PARA 350 et seq. For the purposes of any London Authority
    election, the reference is to the constituency returning officer ('CRO'): see the Greater London
    Authority Elections Rules 2007, SI 2007/3541, Sch 1 r 46(1), Sch 2 r 47(1), Sch 3 r 46(1). As to
    the meaning of the 'constituency returning officer' in this context see PARA 211 note 9. At a
    European parliamentary election, the returning officer referred to in the text is the local
    returning officer (see PARA 360): see the European Parliamentary Elections Regulations 2004,
    SI 2004/293, Sch 1 para 49(1) (as substituted: see note 5). At a Welsh Assembly election, the
    constituency returning officer is the returning officer referred to in the text: see the National
    Assembly for Wales (Representation of the People) Order 2007, SI 2007/236, Sch 5 para 53(3).
    As to the meaning of 'constituency returning officer' for the purposes of Welsh Assembly
    elections see PARA 18 note 2.

23 Representation of the People Act 1983 Sch 1 r 43(1); Parish and Community Meetings (Polls)
    Rules 1987, SI 1987/1, Schedule r 25(1); European Parliamentary Elections Regulations 2004,
    SI 2004/293, Sch 1 para 49(1) (as substituted: see note 5); Local Elections (Principal Areas)
    (England and Wales) Rules 2006, SI 2006/3304, Sch 2 r 43(1); Local Elections (Parishes and
    Communities) (England and Wales) Rules 2006, SI 2006/3305, Sch 2 r 43(1); National
    Assembly for Wales (Representation of the People) Order 2007, SI 2007/236, Sch 5 para 53(3);
    Local Authorities (Mayoral Elections) (England and Wales) Regulations 2007, SI 2007/1024,
    Sch 1 r 45(1); Greater London Authority Elections Rules 2007, SI 2007/3541, Sch 1 r 46(1),
    Sch 2 r 47(1), Sch 3 r 46(1).

24 Representation of the People Act 1983 Sch 1 r 43(3); Parish and Community Meetings (Polls)
    Rules 1987, SI 1987/1, Schedule r 25(3); European Parliamentary Elections Regulations 2004,
    SI 2004/293, Sch 1 para 49(3) (as substituted: see note 5); Local Elections (Principal Areas)
    (England and Wales) Rules 2006, SI 2006/3304, Sch 2 r 43(3); Local Elections (Parishes and
    Communities) (England and Wales) Rules 2006, SI 2006/3305, Sch 2 r 43(3); National
    Assembly for Wales (Representation of the People) Order 2007, SI 2007/236, Sch 5 para 53(4);
    Local Authorities (Mayoral Elections) (England and Wales) Regulations 2007, SI 2007/1024,
    Sch 1 r 45(3); Greater London Authority Elections Rules 2007, SI 2007/3541, Sch 1 r 46(4),
    Sch 2 r 47(4), Sch 3 r 46(4). The packets at a Welsh Assembly election must be accompanied:
    (1)   by a separate statement relating to each Assembly election, where the polls at a Welsh
          Assembly constituency election and at a Welsh Assembly regional election have been
          taken together (see the National Assembly for Wales (Representation of the People)
          Order 2007, SI 2007/236, Sch 5 para 53(4)(a)); or
    (2)   otherwise, by a statement relating to the Assembly election (see Sch 5 para 53(4)(b)).
    At an ordinary London Authority constituency members or London Mayoral election, and at
    any London members election, ballot paper accounts may be combined with the statements
    produced in relation to other Authority elections, but the combined statement must be arranged

in such manner as the Greater London returning officer ('GLRO') may direct: Sch 1 r 46(5), Sch 2 r 47(5), Sch 3 r 46(5). As to the meaning of 'Greater London returning officer' see PARA 211 note 8.

25 Representation of the People Act 1983 Sch 1 r 43(3); Parish and Community Meetings (Polls) Rules 1987, SI 1987/1, Schedule r 25(3); European Parliamentary Elections Regulations 2004, SI 2004/293, Sch 1 para 49(3) (as substituted: see note 5); Local Elections (Principal Areas) (England and Wales) Rules 2006, SI 2006/3304, Sch 2 r 43(3); Local Elections (Parishes and Communities) (England and Wales) Rules 2006, SI 2006/3305, Sch 2 r 43(3); National Assembly for Wales (Representation of the People) Order 2007, SI 2007/236, Sch 5 para 53(4); Local Authorities (Mayoral Elections) (England and Wales) Regulations 2007, SI 2007/1024, Sch 1 r 45(3)(a); Greater London Authority Elections Rules 2007, SI 2007/3541, Sch 1 r 46(4)(a), Sch 2 r 47(4)(a), Sch 3 r 46(4)(a).

26 Representation of the People Act 1983 Sch 1 r 43(3); Parish and Community Meetings (Polls) Rules 1987, SI 1987/1, Schedule r 25(3); European Parliamentary Elections Regulations 2004, SI 2004/293, Sch 1 para 49(3) (as substituted: see note 5); Local Elections (Principal Areas) (England and Wales) Rules 2006, SI 2006/3304, Sch 2 r 43(3); Local Elections (Parishes and Communities) (England and Wales) Rules 2006, SI 2006/3305, Sch 2 r 43(3); National Assembly for Wales (Representation of the People) Order 2007, SI 2007/236, Sch 5 para 53(4); Local Authorities (Mayoral Elections) (England and Wales) Regulations 2007, SI 2007/1024, Sch 1 r 45(3)(b); Greater London Authority Elections Rules 2007, SI 2007/3541, Sch 1 r 46(4)(b), Sch 2 r 47(4)(b), Sch 3 r 46(4)(b).

27 Representation of the People Act 1983 Sch 1 r 43(3); Parish and Community Meetings (Polls) Rules 1987, SI 1987/1, Schedule r 25(3); European Parliamentary Elections Regulations 2004, SI 2004/293, Sch 1 para 49(3) (as substituted: see note 5); Local Elections (Principal Areas) (England and Wales) Rules 2006, SI 2006/3304, Sch 2 r 43(3); Local Elections (Parishes and Communities) (England and Wales) Rules 2006, SI 2006/3305, Sch 2 r 43(3); National Assembly for Wales (Representation of the People) Order 2007, SI 2007/236, Sch 5 para 53(4); Local Authorities (Mayoral Elections) (England and Wales) Regulations 2007, SI 2007/1024, Sch 1 r 45(3)(c); Greater London Authority Elections Rules 2007, SI 2007/3541, Sch 1 r 46(4)(c), Sch 2 r 47(4)(c), Sch 3 r 46(4)(c).

28 Representation of the People Act 1983 Sch 1 r 43(3); Parish and Community Meetings (Polls) Rules 1987, SI 1987/1, Schedule r 25(3); European Parliamentary Elections Regulations 2004, SI 2004/293, Sch 1 para 49(3) (as substituted: see note 5); Local Elections (Principal Areas) (England and Wales) Rules 2006, SI 2006/3304, Sch 2 r 43(3); Local Elections (Parishes and Communities) (England and Wales) Rules 2006, SI 2006/3305, Sch 2 r 43(3); National Assembly for Wales (Representation of the People) Order 2007, SI 2007/236, Sch 5 para 53(4); Local Authorities (Mayoral Elections) (England and Wales) Regulations 2007, SI 2007/1024, Sch 1 r 45(3)(d); Greater London Authority Elections Rules 2007, SI 2007/3541, Sch 1 r 46(4)(d), Sch 2 r 47(4)(d), Sch 3 r 46(4)(d).

29 As to polls at elections or referendums which are taken together see PARA 16 et seq.

C. VOTES GIVEN BY POSTAL BALLOT

(A) Issue of Postal Ballot Papers

406. Returning officer's duty to issue postal ballot papers, etc. The returning officer at an election[1] must, in accordance with the electoral rules[2], issue to those entitled to vote by post[3]:

(1) a ballot paper[4]; and

(2) a postal voting statement in the prescribed form[5],

together with such envelopes for their return as may be so prescribed[6]. The returning officer must also issue to those entitled to vote by post such information as he thinks appropriate about how to obtain[7]:

(a) translations into languages other than English of any directions to or guidance for voters sent with the ballot paper[8];

(b) a translation into Braille of such directions or guidance[9];

(c) graphical representations of such directions or guidance[10];

(d) the directions or guidance in any other form (including any audible form)[11].

In the case of a ballot paper issued to a person resident at an address in the United Kingdom[12], the returning officer must ensure that the return of the ballot paper and postal voting statement is free of charge to the voter[13].

Where the polls at elections are taken together, the proceedings on the issue and receipt of postal ballot papers in respect of each election may, if the returning officers agree, be taken together[14].

1　Ie at a parliamentary election, a local government election (which includes any London Authority election and a local authority mayoral election), a Welsh Assembly constituency or regional election (whether the polls are taken separately or together) or a European parliamentary election. As to the meanings of 'Assembly election', 'constituency election' and 'regional election' see PARA 3 note 2. As to the meaning of 'parliamentary election' see PARA 9. As to the meanings of 'Authority election' and 'local government election' see PARA 11. As to elections in the City of London see PARA 33. As to European parliamentary elections see PARA 217 et seq. There is no provision for absent voting at a poll consequent on a parish meeting on a question involving appointment to office: see PARA 200 et seq.

　　As to returning officers generally see PARA 350 et seq. For the purposes of any London Authority election, the reference is to the constituency returning officer ('CRO'): see the Greater London Authority Elections Rules 2007, SI 2007/3541, Sch 1 r 23(1), (4), (5), Sch 2 r 24(1), (4), (5), Sch 3 r 23(1), (4), (5). As to the meaning of the 'constituency returning officer' in this context see PARA 211 note 9. At a European parliamentary election, the returning officer referred to in the text is the local returning officer (see PARA 360): see the European Parliamentary Elections Regulations 2004, SI 2004/293, Sch 1 para 28(1)–(3) (Sch 1 substituted by SI 2009/186). At a Welsh Assembly election, the constituency returning officer is the returning officer referred to in the text: see the National Assembly for Wales (Representation of the People) Order 2007, SI 2007/236, Sch 5 para 33(1), (3), (4). At a Welsh Assembly regional election, the functions connected with the issue and receipt of postal ballot papers are to be exercised in relation to each Assembly constituency in an Assembly electoral region by the returning officer for such a constituency: Sch 3 para 4. As to the meanings of 'Assembly constituency' and 'Assembly electoral region' see PARA 3 note 2. As to the meaning of 'constituency returning officer' for the purposes of Welsh Assembly elections see PARA 18 note 2.

2　Ie in accordance with regulations made under the Representation of the People Act 1983, for the purpose of a parliamentary of local government election, or in accordance with the European Parliamentary Elections Regulations 2004, SI 2004/293, Sch 2, in the case of a European parliamentary election, or, in accordance with the National Assembly for Wales (Representation of the People) Order 2007, SI 2007/236, Sch 3, in the case of a Welsh Assembly election: see the Representation of the People Act 1983 Sch 1 r 24(1) (Sch 1 r 24(1), (2) substituted, Sch 1 para 24(3)–(5) added, by the Electoral Administration Act 2006 s 37); the European Parliamentary Elections Regulations 2004, SI 2004/293, Sch 1 para 28(1) (as substituted: see note 1); the Local Elections (Principal Areas) (England and Wales) Rules 2006, SI 2006/3304, Sch 2 r 22(1); the Local Elections (Parishes and Communities) (England and Wales) Rules 2006, SI 2006/3305, Sch 2 r 22(1); the National Assembly for Wales (Representation of the People) Order 2007, SI 2007/236, Sch 5 para 33(1); Local Authorities (Mayoral Elections) (England and Wales) Regulations 2007, SI 2007/1024, Sch 1 r 24(1); and the Greater London Authority Elections Rules 2007, SI 2007/3541, Sch 1 r 23(1), Sch 2 r 24(1), Sch 3 r 23(1). As to the making of regulations under the Representation of the People Act 1983 generally see PARA 28 note 16.

3　Representation of the People Act 1983 Sch 1 r 24(1) (as substituted: see note 2); European Parliamentary Elections Regulations 2004, SI 2004/293, Sch 1 para 28(1) (as substituted: see note 1); Local Elections (Principal Areas) (England and Wales) Rules 2006, SI 2006/3304, Sch 2 r 22(1); Local Elections (Parishes and Communities) (England and Wales) Rules 2006, SI 2006/3305, Sch 2 r 22(1); National Assembly for Wales (Representation of the People) Order 2007, SI 2007/236, Sch 5 para 33(1); Local Authorities (Mayoral Elections) (England and Wales) Regulations 2007, SI 2007/1024, Sch 1 r 24(1); Greater London Authority Elections Rules 2007, SI 2007/3541, Sch 1 r 23(1), Sch 2 r 24(1), Sch 3 r 23(1). As to applications made for absent voting see PARA 367 et seq.

　　The requirement is only for the returning officer to issue the ballot papers in accordance with the statutory scheme and his responsibilities do not go beyond that: *Knight v Nicholls* [2004] EWCA Civ 68, [2004] 1 WLR 1653, [2004] LGR 524 (considering what is now the Local Elections (Principal Areas) (England and Wales) Rules 2006, SI 2006/3304, Sch 2 r 22). As to delivery see further PARA 411.

4   Representation of the People Act 1983 Sch 1 r 24(1)(a) (as substituted: see note 2); European
Parliamentary Elections Regulations 2004, SI 2004/293, Sch 1 para 28(1) (as substituted: see
note 1); Local Elections (Principal Areas) (England and Wales) Rules 2006, SI 2006/3304, Sch 2
r 22(1); Local Elections (Parishes and Communities) (England and Wales) Rules 2006,
SI 2006/3305, Sch 2 r 22(1); National Assembly for Wales (Representation of the People)
Order 2007, SI 2007/236, Sch 5 para 33(1)(a); Local Authorities (Mayoral Elections) (England
and Wales) Regulations 2007, SI 2007/1024, Sch 1 r 24(1); Greater London Authority Elections
Rules 2007, SI 2007/3541, Sch 1 r 23(1), Sch 2 r 24(1), Sch 3 r 23(1).
In the case of a person who is entitled to give a Welsh Assembly constituency vote and an
electoral region vote by post, the provisions of the National Assembly for Wales (Representation
of the People) Order 2007, SI 2007/236, Sch 5 para 33(1) apply, except that the reference in
head (1) in the text to 'a ballot paper' must be construed as a reference to a constituency ballot
paper and a regional ballot paper, and subsequent references in Sch 5 para 33 to 'ballot paper'
must be construed accordingly: Sch 5 para 33(2). Each person entitled to vote at a general
election in an Assembly constituency has two votes: (1) a 'constituency vote' (ie a vote which
may be given for a candidate to be the Assembly constituency member for the Assembly
constituency); and (2) an 'electoral region vote' (ie a vote which may be given for either: (a) a
registered political party which has submitted a list of candidates to be Assembly regional
members for the Assembly electoral region in which the Assembly constituency is included; or
(b) an individual who is a candidate to be an Assembly regional member for that Assembly
electoral region): see the Government of Wales Act 2006 s 6; and PARA 364.

5   Representation of the People Act 1983 Sch 1 r 24(1)(b) (as substituted: see note 2); European
Parliamentary Elections Regulations 2004, SI 2004/293, Sch 1 para 28(1) (as substituted: see
note 1); Local Elections (Principal Areas) (England and Wales) Rules 2006, SI 2006/3304, Sch 2
r 22(1); Local Elections (Parishes and Communities) (England and Wales) Rules 2006,
SI 2006/3305, Sch 2 r 22(1); National Assembly for Wales (Representation of the People)
Order 2007, SI 2007/236, Sch 5 para 33(1)(b); Local Authorities (Mayoral Elections) (England
and Wales) Regulations 2007, SI 2007/1024, Sch 1 r 24(1); Greater London Authority Elections
Rules 2007, SI 2007/3541, Sch 1 r 23(1), (2), Sch 2 r 24(1), (2), Sch 3 r 23(1), (2). The
prescribed form of the postal voting statement (except the forms specified under head (2) and
head (4) below) must include provision for the form to be signed and for stating the date of birth
of the elector or proxy, as the case may be: Representation of the People Act 1983 Sch 1 r 24(3)
(as added: see note 2); Local Elections (Principal Areas) (England and Wales) Rules 2006,
SI 2006/3304, Sch 2 r 22(3); Local Elections (Parishes and Communities) (England and Wales)
Rules 2006, SI 2006/3305, Sch 2 r 22(3); Local Authorities (Mayoral Elections) (England and
Wales) Regulations 2007, SI 2007/1024, Sch 1 r 24(3); Greater London Authority Elections
Rules 2007, SI 2007/3541, Sch 1 r 23(3), Sch 2 r 24(3), Sch 3 r 23(3). As to the meaning of
'elector' see PARA 95 note 2. The prescribed form of the postal voting statement to be used:

(1)   in the case of a parliamentary election, is set out in the Representation of the People
(England and Wales) Regulations 2001, SI 2001/341, reg 66(a), Sch 3 (Form G: form of
postal voting statement (for use at parliamentary elections)) (reg 66 amended, and
Forms G–J substituted, by SI 2006/2910); the Representation of the People (England
and Wales) Regulations 2001, SI 2001/341, reg 66(b), Sch 3 (Form H: form of postal
voting statement (for use where there is a joint issue and receipt of postal ballot
papers)) (reg 66 as so amended, Form H as so substituted); and reg 66(c), Sch 3
(Form J: form of postal voting statement) (for use when a parliamentary poll is
combined with another poll but the postal ballot papers are not combined) (reg 66 as so
amended, Form J as so substituted);

(2)   at a European parliamentary election, is set out in the European Parliamentary
Elections Regulations 2004, SI 2004/293, Sch 2 para 42(a), Appendix of Forms (Form
O: Form of postal voting statement to be used at a European Parliamentary election
taken alone), Sch 2 para 42(b), Appendix of Forms (Form P: Form of postal voting
statement to be used at a European Parliamentary election where the proceedings on the
issue and receipt of postal ballot papers are taken together with those proceedings at a
relevant election or referendum), Sch 2 para 42(c), Appendix of Forms (Form Q: Form
of postal voting statement to be used at a European Parliamentary election where the
poll is taken together with the poll at a relevant election or referendum, but where the
proceedings on the issue and receipt of postal ballot papers are not) (Sch 2 substituted
by SI 2009/186);

(3)   at a local government election:
(a)   is set out in the Local Elections (Principal Areas) (England and Wales)
Rules 2006, SI 2006/3304, Sch 2 Appendix of Forms (Form of postal voting
statement (for use at local government elections)); Sch 3 Appendix of Forms

(Form of postal voting statement (for use where there is a joint issue and receipt of postal ballot papers); Form of postal voting statement (for use when a local government poll is combined with another poll but the postal ballot papers are not combined)); or

(b)　is set out in the Local Elections (Parishes and Communities) (England and Wales) Rules 2006, SI 2006/3305, Sch 2 Appendix of Forms (Form of postal voting statement (for use at a Parish or Community election)); Sch 3 Appendix of Forms (Form of postal voting statement (for use where there is a joint issue and receipt of postal ballot papers); Form of postal voting statement (for use when a parish or community poll is combined with another poll but the postal ballot papers are not combined)); or

(c)　is set out in the Local Authorities (Mayoral Elections) (England and Wales) Regulations 2007, SI 2007/1024, Sch 1 Appendix of Forms (Form 7: postal voting statement) (Form 7 substituted by SI 2012/2059); or

(d)　is set out in the Greater London Authority Elections Rules 2007, SI 2007/3541, Sch 10 r 2 (Form 10: postal voting statement (constituency member or mayoral by-election); Form 11: postal voting statement (ordinary election));

(4)　at a Welsh Assembly election, is set out in English and Welsh in the National Assembly for Wales (Representation of the People) Order 2007, SI 2007/236, Sch 3 para 3(a), Sch 10 Appendix of Forms (Form CC1: Form of postal voting statement (at an Assembly election the poll at which is not taken together with another election)), Sch 3 para 3(b), Sch 10 Appendix of Forms (Form CC2: Form of postal voting statement (at an Assembly election where the proceedings on the issue and receipt of postal ballot papers are taken together under Sch 3 para 2 with those proceedings at another election)), Sch 3 para 3(c), Sch 10 Appendix of Forms (Form CC3: Form of postal voting statement (at an Assembly election, the polls at which are taken together with the poll at another election in any part of an Assembly constituency, but where the proceedings on the issue and receipt of postal ballot papers are not taken together under Sch 3 para 2, for use in that part of the constituency in which polls at more than one election are taken together)).

Where the proceedings on the issue and receipt of postal ballot papers at any particular Authority election are taken together with any other Authority election, the appropriate form of postal voting statement under head (3)(d) above may be the joint postal voting statement which must be in the appropriate form or form to like effect: Greater London Authority Elections Rules 2007, SI 2007/3541, Sch 1 r 23(6), Sch 2 r 24(6), Sch 3 r 23(6).

Where elections take place in Wales see also the forms issued partly in English and partly in Welsh in:

(i)　the Parliamentary Elections (Welsh Forms) Order 2007, SI 2007/1014, art 6(l)–(m), Sch 2 (Form 12 (Ffurflen 12): Form G: Postal Voting Statement (for use at parliamentary elections)/Ffurflen G: Datganiad Pleidleisio drwy'r post (i'w ddefnyddio mewn etholiadau seneddol); Form 13 (Ffurflen 13): Form H: Postal Voting Statement (for use where there is a joint issue and receipt of postal ballot papers)/Ffurflen H: Ffurf ar ddatganiad pleidleisio drwy'r post (i'w ddefnyddio pan fydd pleidleisiau post yn cael eu darparu a'u derbyn ar y cyd); Form 14 (Ffurflen 14): Form J: Postal Voting Statement (for use when a local government poll is combined with another poll but the postal ballot papers are not combined)/Ffurflen J: Datganiad Pleidleisio drwy'r post (i'w ddefnyddio pan fydd etholiad Llywodraeth Leol yn cael ei gyfuno gydag etholiad arall ond nad yw'r pleidleisiau post wedi'u cyfuno);

(ii)　the Local Elections (Principal Areas) (Welsh Forms) Order 2007, SI 2007/1015, arts 7(1)(c), 9(1)(c), (d), Sch 3 (Form 3: Form of Postal Voting Statement (for use at local government elections)), Sch 5 (Form 3: Form of postal voting statement (for use where there is a joint issue and receipt of postal ballot papers); (Form 4: Form of postal voting statement (for use when a local government poll is combined with another poll but the postal ballot papers are not combined));

(iii)　the Local Elections (Communities) (Welsh Forms) Order 2007, SI 2007/1013, arts 7(1)(c), 9(1), (c), (d), Sch 3 (Form 3: Form of Postal Voting Statement (for use at local government elections)), Sch 5 (Form 3: Form of postal voting statement (for use where there is a joint issue and receipt of postal ballot papers); (Form 4: Form of postal voting statement (for use when a local government poll is combined with another poll but the postal ballot papers are not combined)); and

(iv)　the European Parliamentary Elections (Welsh Forms) Order 2009, SI 2009/781, art 6(1)(m)–(o), Sch 2 (Form 13 (Ffurflen 13): Form of Postal Voting Statement (for use at European parliamentary elections)/ffurf datganiad pleidleisio drwy'r post (i'w ddefnyddio yn etholiadau senedd Ewrop); Form 14 (Ffurflen 14): Form of Postal Voting Statement (for use where there is a joint issue and receipt of postal ballot papers)/Ffurf datganiad pleidleisio drwy'r post (i'w ddefnyddio pan fydd pleidleisiau post yn cael eu darparu a'u derbyn ar y cyd); Form 15 (Ffurflen 15): Form of Postal Voting Statement (for use when a European Parliamentary poll is combined with another poll but the postal ballot papers are not combined)/Ffurf datganiad pleidleisio drwy'r post (i'w ddefnyddio pan fydd etholiadau senedd Ewrop yn cael ei gyfuno a phleidlais arall ond nid yw'r papurau drwy'r post yn cael eu cyfuno)).

The Representation of the People (England and Wales) Regulations 2001, SI 2001/341, reg 66, has effect for the purposes of local authority referendums, subject to the modifications specified, in relation to Wales, by the Local Authorities (Conduct of Referendums) (Wales) Regulations 2008, SI 2008/1848, reg 8(2), Sch 4 Table 5, and, in relation to England, by the Local Authorities (Conduct of Referendums) (England) Regulations 2012, SI 2012/323, regs 8(2), 11–13, Sch 4 Table 6 (see PARA 15 note 2).

6   Representation of the People Act 1983 Sch 1 r 24(1) (as substituted: see note 2); European Parliamentary Elections Regulations 2004, SI 2004/293, Sch 1 para 28(1) (as substituted: see note 1); Local Elections (Principal Areas) (England and Wales) Rules 2006, SI 2006/3304, Sch 2 r 22(1); Local Elections (Parishes and Communities) (England and Wales) Rules 2006, SI 2006/3305, Sch 2 r 22(1); National Assembly for Wales (Representation of the People) Order 2007, SI 2007/236, Sch 5 para 33(1); Local Authorities (Mayoral Elections) (England and Wales) Regulations 2007, SI 2007/1024, Sch 1 r 24(1); Greater London Authority Elections Rules 2007, SI 2007/3541, Sch 1 r 23(1), Sch 2 r 24(1), Sch 3 r 23(1). As to the return of postal ballot papers see PARA 418.

7   Representation of the People Act 1983 Sch 1 r 24(2) (as substituted: see note 2); European Parliamentary Elections Regulations 2004, SI 2004/293, Sch 1 para 28(2) (as substituted: see note 1); Local Elections (Principal Areas) (England and Wales) Rules 2006, SI 2006/3304, Sch 2 r 22(2); Local Elections (Parishes and Communities) (England and Wales) Rules 2006, SI 2006/3305, Sch 2 r 22(2); National Assembly for Wales (Representation of the People) Order 2007, SI 2007/236, Sch 5 para 33(4); Local Authorities (Mayoral Elections) (England and Wales) Regulations 2007, SI 2007/1024, Sch 1 r 24(2); Greater London Authority Elections Rules 2007, SI 2007/3541, Sch 1 r 23(4), Sch 2 r 24(4), Sch 3 r 23(4).

8   Representation of the People Act 1983 Sch 1 r 24(2)(a) (as substituted: see note 2); European Parliamentary Elections Regulations 2004, SI 2004/293, Sch 1 para 28(2)(a) (as substituted: see note 1); Local Elections (Principal Areas) (England and Wales) Rules 2006, SI 2006/3304, Sch 2 r 22(2)(a); Local Elections (Parishes and Communities) (England and Wales) Rules 2006, SI 2006/3305, Sch 2 r 22(2)(a); National Assembly for Wales (Representation of the People) Order 2007, SI 2007/236, Sch 5 para 33(4)(a); Local Authorities (Mayoral Elections) (England and Wales) Regulations 2007, SI 2007/1024, Sch 1 r 24(2)(a); Greater London Authority Elections Rules 2007, SI 2007/3541, Sch 1 r 23(4)(a), Sch 2 r 24(4)(a), Sch 3 r 23(4)(a).

9   Representation of the People Act 1983 Sch 1 r 24(2)(b) (as substituted: see note 2); European Parliamentary Elections Regulations 2004, SI 2004/293, Sch 1 para 28(2)(b) (as substituted: see note 1); Local Elections (Principal Areas) (England and Wales) Rules 2006, SI 2006/3304, Sch 2 r 22(2)(b); Local Elections (Parishes and Communities) (England and Wales) Rules 2006, SI 2006/3305, Sch 2 r 22(2)(b); National Assembly for Wales (Representation of the People) Order 2007, SI 2007/236, Sch 5 para 33(4)(b); Local Authorities (Mayoral Elections) (England and Wales) Regulations 2007, SI 2007/1024, Sch 1 r 24(2)(b); Greater London Authority Elections Rules 2007, SI 2007/3541, Sch 1 r 23(4)(b), Sch 2 r 24(4)(b), Sch 3 r 23(4)(b).

10 Representation of the People Act 1983 Sch 1 r 24(2)(c) (as substituted: see note 2); European Parliamentary Elections Regulations 2004, SI 2004/293, Sch 1 para 28(2)(c) (as substituted: see note 1); Local Elections (Principal Areas) (England and Wales) Rules 2006, SI 2006/3304, Sch 2 r 22(2)(c); Local Elections (Parishes and Communities) (England and Wales) Rules 2006, SI 2006/3305, Sch 2 r 22(2)(c); National Assembly for Wales (Representation of the People) Order 2007, SI 2007/236, Sch 5 para 33(4)(c); Local Authorities (Mayoral Elections) (England and Wales) Regulations 2007, SI 2007/1024, Sch 1 r 24(2)(c); Greater London Authority Elections Rules 2007, SI 2007/3541, Sch 1 r 23(4)(c), Sch 2 r 24(4)(c), Sch 3 r 23(4)(c).

11 Representation of the People Act 1983 Sch 1 r 24(2)(d) (as substituted: see note 2); European Parliamentary Elections Regulations 2004, SI 2004/293, Sch 1 para 28(2)(d) (as substituted: see note 1); Local Elections (Principal Areas) (England and Wales) Rules 2006, SI 2006/3304, Sch 2 r 22(2)(d); Local Elections (Parishes and Communities) (England and Wales) Rules 2006, SI 2006/3305, Sch 2 r 22(2)(d); National Assembly for Wales (Representation of the People) Order 2007, SI 2007/236, Sch 5 para 33(4)(d); Local Authorities (Mayoral Elections) (England and Wales) Regulations 2007, SI 2007/1024, Sch 1 r 24(2)(d); Greater London Authority Elections Rules 2007, SI 2007/3541, Sch 1 r 23(4)(d), Sch 2 r 24(4)(d), Sch 3 r 23(4)(d).

12   As to the meaning of 'United Kingdom' see PARA 1 note 1. For the purposes of European parliamentary elections held in the combined region (as to which see PARA 77), an address in Gibraltar may be specified: see the European Parliamentary Elections Regulations 2004, SI 2004/293, Sch 1 para 28(3) (as substituted: see note 1). As to the marking of the envelopes and the addresses to be used see PARA 410.

13   Representation of the People Act 1983 Sch 1 r 24(4) (as added: see note 2); European Parliamentary Elections Regulations 2004, SI 2004/293, Sch 1 para 28(3) (as substituted: see note 1); Local Elections (Principal Areas) (England and Wales) Rules 2006, SI 2006/3304, Sch 2 r 22(4); Local Elections (Parishes and Communities) (England and Wales) Rules 2006, SI 2006/3305, Sch 2 r 22(4); National Assembly for Wales (Representation of the People) Order 2007, SI 2007/236, Sch 5 para 33(3); Local Authorities (Mayoral Elections) (England and Wales) Regulations 2007, SI 2007/1024, Sch 1 r 24(4); Greater London Authority Elections Rules 2007, SI 2007/3541, Sch 1 r 23(5), Sch 2 r 24(5), Sch 3 r 23(5). In relation to a parliamentary election only, regulations may provide that the returning officer must so ensure that certain requirements in any other case are free of charge to the voter: Representation of the People Act 1983 Sch 1 r 24(5) (as so added).

14   As to the issue and receipt of postal ballot papers when polls are combined see PARA 20.

407. Time of issue of postal ballot papers, etc. The postal ballot paper[1] and postal voting statement[2] must be issued by the returning officer[3] as soon as practicable after the registration officer[4] has granted the application to vote by post[5]. However, where a person is shown in the records kept of:

(1)   those entitled (for a defined period or for an indefinite period) to an absent vote at elections[6]; or

(2)   those entitled to vote by post as proxy at elections[7],

no postal ballot paper and no postal voting statement may be issued until after 5 pm on the eleventh day before the date of the poll[8].

An elector or a proxy voter who is shown in the postal voters list[9] or proxy postal voters list[10] may make a request, at any time between the first issue of postal ballots[11] and the close of the poll, that the returning officer confirm[12]:

(a)   whether a mark is shown in the marked copy of the postal voters list or proxy postal voters list in a place corresponding to the number of the elector to denote that a postal vote has been returned[13]; and

(b)   whether the number of the ballot paper issued to the elector or his proxy has been recorded on either of the lists of provisionally rejected votes kept by the returning officer[14].

Such a request must be made by any method specified by[15], and must include any evidence of the voter's identity requested by[16], the returning officer[17]. Where a request is duly received in this way, the returning officer must satisfy himself that the request has been made by the elector or his proxy and, where he is so satisfied, provide confirmation of the matters under heads (a) and (b) above[18].

1   For these purposes, 'postal ballot paper' means a ballot paper issued to a postal voter; and 'postal voter' means an elector or proxy who is entitled to vote by post: Representation of the People (England and Wales) Regulations 2001, SI 2001/341, reg 64; European Parliamentary Elections Regulations 2004, SI 2004/293, Sch 2 para 40(1) (Sch 2 substituted by SI 2009/186); National Assembly for Wales (Representation of the People) Order 2007, SI 2007/236, art 2(1). For the purposes of a Welsh Assembly election, 'issue' includes the original and any subsequent issue: see Sch 3 para 1. As to the meaning of 'Assembly election' for these purposes see PARA 3 note 2. As to procedure on the issue of postal ballot papers, etc see PARA 406.

2   As to the postal voting statement see PARA 406.

3   As to returning officers generally see PARA 350 et seq. At a European parliamentary election, the returning officer referred to in the text is the local returning officer (see PARA 360): see the European Parliamentary Elections Regulations 2004, SI 2004/293, Sch 2 para 47(2) (as substituted: see note 1). At a Welsh Assembly election, the constituency returning officer exercises functions connected with the issue and receipt of postal ballot papers: see the National Assembly for Wales (Representation of the People) Order 2007, SI 2007/236, Sch 3 para 8(2); but see also PARA 406 note 1. As to the meaning of 'constituency returning officer' for these

purposes see PARA 18 note 2. As to the returning officer's duty to issue postal ballot papers, etc see PARA 406. As to the marking of the envelopes and the addresses to be used see PARA 410.

4   As to electoral registration officers and the areas for which they act see PARA 139 et seq.

5   Representation of the People (England and Wales) Regulations 2001, SI 2001/341, reg 71(2) (reg 71(1), (2) amended, reg 84A added, by SI 2006/2910); European Parliamentary Elections Regulations 2004, SI 2004/293, Sch 2 para 47(2) (as substituted: see note 1); National Assembly for Wales (Representation of the People) Order 2007, SI 2007/236, Sch 3 para 8(2). As to applications to vote by post see PARA 367 et seq.

For the purposes of extending the rights of citizens and nationals of accession states who (subject to the requirement of registration) may vote at local government and European parliamentary elections, the Representation of the People (England and Wales) Regulations 2001, SI 2001/341, reg 71 applies with modifications: see the Local and European Parliamentary Elections (Registration of Citizens of Accession States) Regulations 2003, SI 2003/1557, reg 7, Sch 2 para 1(1), (5).

6   Ie the record kept, for the purposes of a parliamentary or local government election, under the Representation of the People Act 2000 Sch 4 para 3(4), for the purposes of a European parliamentary election, under the European Parliamentary Elections Regulations 2004, SI 2004/293, Sch 2 para 3(4), or, for the purposes of a Welsh Assembly election, under the National Assembly for Wales (Representation of the People) Order 2007, SI 2007/236, art 8(3), as the case may be (see PARA 370): see the Representation of the People (England and Wales) Regulations 2001, SI 2001/341, reg 71(1)(a) (as amended: see note 5); the European Parliamentary Elections Regulations 2004, SI 2004/293, Sch 2 para 47(1)(a) (as substituted: see note 1); and the National Assembly for Wales (Representation of the People) Order 2007, SI 2007/236, Sch 3 para 8(1)(a).

7   Ie the record kept, for the purposes of a parliamentary or local government election, under the Representation of the People Act 2000 Sch 4 para 7(6), for the purposes of a European parliamentary election, under the European Parliamentary Elections Regulations 2004, SI 2004/293, Sch 2 para 7(6), or, for the purposes of a Welsh Assembly election, under the National Assembly for Wales (Representation of the People) Order 2007, SI 2007/236, art 12(6), as the case may be (see PARA 379): see the Representation of the People (England and Wales) Regulations 2001, SI 2001/341, reg 71(1)(b) (as amended: see note 5); the European Parliamentary Elections Regulations 2004, SI 2004/293, Sch 2 para 47(1)(b) (as substituted: see note 1); and the National Assembly for Wales (Representation of the People) Order 2007, SI 2007/236, Sch 3 para 8(1)(b).

8   Representation of the People (England and Wales) Regulations 2001, SI 2001/341, reg 71(1) (as amended: see note 5); European Parliamentary Elections Regulations 2004, SI 2004/293, Sch 2 para 47(1) (as substituted: see note 1); National Assembly for Wales (Representation of the People) Order 2007, SI 2007/236, Sch 3 para 8(1). See note 5. As to the computation of time for these purposes see PARA 367 note 6. As to the date of the poll at a parliamentary general election or by-election see PARA 195; as to the date of the poll at local government elections (including elections to fill vacancies) see PARAS 206–209; as to the date of the poll at Welsh Assembly elections (including elections to fill vacancies in an Assembly constituency) see PARAS 213–214; and as to the date of the poll at a European parliamentary election see PARA 222.

The Representation of the People (England and Wales) Regulations 2001, SI 2001/341, regs 71, 84A have effect for the purposes of local authority referendums, subject to the modifications specified, in relation to Wales, by the Local Authorities (Conduct of Referendums) (Wales) Regulations 2008, SI 2008/1848, reg 8(2), Sch 4 Table 5, and, in relation to England, by the Local Authorities (Conduct of Referendums) (England) Regulations 2012, SI 2012/323, regs 8(2), 11–13, Sch 4 Table 6 (see PARA 15 note 2).

9   As to the postal voters list see PARA 373.

10   As to the record of persons entitled to vote by post as proxy see PARA 379.

11   Ie under the Representation of the People (England and Wales) Regulations 2001, SI 2001/341, reg 71, the European Parliamentary Elections Regulations 2004, SI 2004/293, Sch 2 para 47, or the National Assembly for Wales (Representation of the People) Order 2007, SI 2007/236, Sch 3 para 8, as the case may be (see the text and notes 1–8): see the Representation of the People (England and Wales) Regulations 2001, SI 2001/341, reg 84A(1) (as added: see note 5); the European Parliamentary Elections Regulations 2004, SI 2004/293, Sch 2 para 61(1) (as substituted: see note 1); and the National Assembly for Wales (Representation of the People) Order 2007, SI 2007/236, Sch 3 para 21(1).

12   Representation of the People (England and Wales) Regulations 2001, SI 2001/341, reg 84A(1) (as added: see note 5); European Parliamentary Elections Regulations 2004, SI 2004/293, Sch 2 para 61(1) (as substituted: see note 1); National Assembly for Wales (Representation of the People) Order 2007, SI 2007/236, Sch 3 para 21(1). In carrying out the procedure mentioned in

the text, the returning officer must keep the ballot papers face downwards, he must take proper precautions for preventing any person from seeing the votes made on the ballot papers, and he is not permitted to view the corresponding number list used at the issue of postal ballot papers: see the Representation of the People (England and Wales) Regulations 2001, SI 2001/341, reg 84(6); the European Parliamentary Elections Regulations 2004, SI 2004/293, Sch 2 para 60(8); the National Assembly for Wales (Representation of the People) Order 2007, SI 2007/236, Sch 3 para 20(8); and PARA 421. As to the corresponding number list used at the issue of postal ballot papers see PARA 408.

13 Representation of the People (England and Wales) Regulations 2001, SI 2001/341, reg 84A(1)(a) (as added: see note 5); European Parliamentary Elections Regulations 2004, SI 2004/293, Sch 2 para 61(1)(a) (as substituted: see note 1); National Assembly for Wales (Representation of the People) Order 2007, SI 2007/236, Sch 3 para 21(1)(a). As to the returning officer's duty to mark the postal voters list where a postal vote has been returned and the proxy postal voters list where a proxy postal vote has been returned see PARA 418.

14 Representation of the People (England and Wales) Regulations 2001, SI 2001/341, reg 84A(1)(b) (as added: see note 5); European Parliamentary Elections Regulations 2004, SI 2004/293, Sch 2 para 61(1)(b) (as substituted: see note 1); National Assembly for Wales (Representation of the People) Order 2007, SI 2007/236, Sch 3 para 21(1)(b). The text refers to the lists of provisionally rejected votes kept by the returning officer under the Representation of the People (England and Wales) Regulations 2001, SI 2001/341, reg 87(2), (3) or the European Parliamentary Elections Regulations 2004, SI 2004/293, Sch 2 para 67(2), (3) (see PARA 423): see the Representation of the People (England and Wales) Regulations 2001, SI 2001/341, reg 84A(1)(b) (as so added); the European Parliamentary Elections Regulations 2004, SI 2004/293, Sch 2 para 61(1)(b) (as so substituted); and the National Assembly for Wales (Representation of the People) Order 2007, SI 2007/236, Sch 3 para 21(1)(b).

15 Representation of the People (England and Wales) Regulations 2001, SI 2001/341, reg 84A(2)(a) (as added: see note 5); European Parliamentary Elections Regulations 2004, SI 2004/293, Sch 2 para 61(2)(a) (as substituted: see note 1); National Assembly for Wales (Representation of the People) Order 2007, SI 2007/236, Sch 3 para 21(2)(a).

16 Representation of the People (England and Wales) Regulations 2001, SI 2001/341, reg 84A(2)(b) (as added: see note 5); European Parliamentary Elections Regulations 2004, SI 2004/293, Sch 2 para 61(2)(b) (as substituted: see note 1); National Assembly for Wales (Representation of the People) Order 2007, SI 2007/236, Sch 3 para 21(2)(b).

17 Representation of the People (England and Wales) Regulations 2001, SI 2001/341, reg 84A(2) (as added: see note 5); European Parliamentary Elections Regulations 2004, SI 2004/293, Sch 2 para 61(2) (as substituted: see note 1); National Assembly for Wales (Representation of the People) Order 2007, SI 2007/236, Sch 3 para 21(2).

18 Representation of the People (England and Wales) Regulations 2001, SI 2001/341, reg 84A(3) (as added: see note 5); European Parliamentary Elections Regulations 2004, SI 2004/293, Sch 2 para 61(3) (as substituted: see note 1); National Assembly for Wales (Representation of the People) Order 2007, SI 2007/236, Sch 3 para 21(3).

408. Procedure on the issue of postal ballot papers. Without prejudice to the provisions of the Political Parties, Elections and Referendums Act 2000 that allow for Electoral Commission representatives and accredited observers to attend electoral proceedings and observe working practices[1], no person may be present at the proceedings on the issue of postal ballot papers at an election[2] other than the returning officer and his clerks[3]. The following procedure must be followed:

(1)   the number of the elector[4] as stated in the register (or in the copy of the register that is supplied)[5] must be marked on the corresponding number list[6], next to the number and unique identifying mark of the ballot paper issued to that elector[7];

(2)   a mark must be placed in the postal voters list[8] or proxy postal voters list[9] against the number of the elector to denote that a ballot paper has been issued to the elector or his proxy, but without showing the particular ballot paper issued[10]; and

(3)   the number of a postal ballot paper must be marked on the postal voting statement sent with that paper[11].

Where the poll at one election is taken with the poll at another election, special provision is made for procedure on the issue of postal ballot papers[12].

The returning officer must make such arrangements as he thinks fit to ensure that every person attending the proceedings in connection with the issue of postal ballot papers has been given a copy in writing of the statutory provisions that require such persons to maintain the secrecy of the voting[13].

1 Ie without prejudice to the provisions of the Political Parties, Elections and Referendums Act 2000 ss 6A–6E (see PARA 53): see the Representation of the People (England and Wales) Regulations 2001, SI 2001/341, reg 67 (amended by SI 2006/2910); the European Parliamentary Elections Regulations 2004, SI 2004/293, Sch 2 para 43 (Sch 2 substituted by SI 2009/186); and the National Assembly for Wales (Representation of the People) Order 2007, SI 2007/236, Sch 3 para 5. As to the establishment and constitution of the Electoral Commission see PARA 34 et seq.

   The Representation of the People (England and Wales) Regulations 2001, SI 2001/341, regs 67, 70, 72 have effect for the purposes of local authority referendums, subject to the modifications specified, in relation to Wales, by the Local Authorities (Conduct of Referendums) (Wales) Regulations 2008, SI 2008/1848, reg 8(2), Sch 4 Table 5, and, in relation to England, by the Local Authorities (Conduct of Referendums) (England) Regulations 2012, SI 2012/323, regs 8(2), 11–13, Sch 4 Table 6 (see PARA 15 note 2).

2 Ie at a parliamentary election, a local government election (which includes any London Authority election and a local authority mayoral election), a Welsh Assembly constituency or regional election (whether the polls are taken separately or together) or a European parliamentary election. As to the meanings of 'Assembly election', 'constituency election' and 'regional election' see PARA 3 note 2. As to the meaning of 'parliamentary election' see PARA 9. As to the meanings of 'Authority election' and 'local government election' see PARA 11. As to elections in the City of London see PARA 33. As to European parliamentary elections see PARA 217 et seq. There is no provision for absent voting at a poll consequent on a parish meeting on a question involving appointment to office: see PARA 200 et seq. As to the meaning of 'postal ballot paper' see PARA 407 note 1.

3 Representation of the People (England and Wales) Regulations 2001, SI 2001/341, reg 67 (as amended: see note 1); European Parliamentary Elections Regulations 2004, SI 2004/293, Sch 2 para 43 (as substituted: see note 1); National Assembly for Wales (Representation of the People) Order 2007, SI 2007/236, Sch 3 para 5. As to returning officers and their clerks generally see PARA 350 et seq. At a European parliamentary election, the returning officer referred to in the text is the local returning officer (see PARA 360): see the European Parliamentary Elections Regulations 2004, SI 2004/293, Sch 2 paras 43, 46 (as so substituted). At a Welsh Assembly election, the constituency returning officer exercises functions connected with the issue and receipt of postal ballot papers: see the National Assembly for Wales (Representation of the People) Order 2007, SI 2007/236, Sch 3 paras 4, 7; but see also PARA 406 note 1. As to the meaning of 'constituency returning officer' see PARA 18 note 2. As to the returning officer's duty to issue postal ballot papers, etc see PARA 406. As to the marking of the envelopes and the addresses to be used see PARA 410.

4 As to the meaning of 'elector', in relation to a parliamentary or local government election, see PARA 95 note 2; in relation to a Welsh Assembly election, see PARA 110 note 6; and in relation to European parliamentary elections see PARA 111 note 4. As to the number of an elector see PARA 145.

5 As to the registers of electors see PARA 143 et seq.

6 As to the corresponding number list see PARA 387.

7 Representation of the People (England and Wales) Regulations 2001, SI 2001/341, reg 72(2) (reg 72(2)–(6) amended by SI 2006/2910); European Parliamentary Elections Regulations 2004, SI 2004/293, Sch 2 para 48(1) (as substituted: see note 1); National Assembly for Wales (Representation of the People) Order 2007, SI 2007/236, Sch 3 para 9(1). At a Welsh Assembly election where an elector is entitled to give two votes, the constituency ballot paper and the regional ballot paper must have the same number: Sch 3 para 9(2). As to the number and unique identifying mark of the ballot paper referred to in the text see PARA 387. As to persons entitled to give two votes at a general election in an Assembly constituency see PARA 406 note 4.

8 As to the postal voters list see PARA 373.

9 As to the record of persons entitled to vote by post as proxy see PARA 379.

10 Representation of the People (England and Wales) Regulations 2001, SI 2001/341, reg 72(3) (as amended: see note 7); European Parliamentary Elections Regulations 2004, SI 2004/293, Sch 2 para 48(2) (as substituted: see note 1); National Assembly for Wales (Representation of the People) Order 2007, SI 2007/236, Sch 3 para 9(3).

11 Representation of the People (England and Wales) Regulations 2001, SI 2001/341, reg 72(4) (as amended: see note 7); European Parliamentary Elections Regulations 2004, SI 2004/293, Sch 2 para 48(3) (as substituted: see note 1); National Assembly for Wales (Representation of the People) Order 2007, SI 2007/236, Sch 3 para 9(4). As to the postal voting statement see PARA 406.

12 See the Representation of the People (England and Wales) Regulations 2001, SI 2001/341, reg 72(5), (6) (as amended: see note 7); the European Parliamentary Elections Regulations 2004, SI 2004/293, Sch 2 para 48(4), (5) (as substituted: see note 1); and the National Assembly for Wales (Representation of the People) Order 2007, SI 2007/236, Sch 3 para 9(5), (6). As to the issue and receipt of postal ballot papers when polls are combined see PARA 20.

13 Representation of the People (England and Wales) Regulations 2001, SI 2001/341, reg 70; European Parliamentary Elections Regulations 2004, SI 2004/293, Sch 2 para 46 (as substituted: see note 1); National Assembly for Wales (Representation of the People) Order 2007, SI 2007/236, Sch 3 para 7. The text refers to the requirement of secrecy set out in the Representation of the People Act 1983 s 66(4), (6), in relation to a parliamentary election, or, in relation to European parliamentary elections, in the European Parliamentary Elections Regulations 2004, SI 2004/293, reg 29(5), (7). or, in relation to Welsh Assembly elections, in the National Assembly for Wales (Representation of the People) Order 2007, SI 2007/236, art 35(4), (6) (see PARA 742): see the Representation of the People (England and Wales) Regulations 2001, SI 2001/341, reg 70; the European Parliamentary Elections Regulations 2004, SI 2004/293, Sch 2 para 46 (as so substituted); and the National Assembly for Wales (Representation of the People) Order 2007, SI 2007/236, Sch 3 para 7.

409.   Refusal to issue more than one postal ballot paper to each elector.
Where the returning officer at an election[1] is satisfied that two or more entries in the postal voters list[2], or in the proxy postal voters list[3], or in each of those lists, relate to the same elector[4], he must not issue more than one ballot paper[5] in respect of the same elector in respect of any one election[6].

1   Ie at a parliamentary election, a local government election (which includes any London Authority election and a local authority mayoral election), a Welsh Assembly constituency or regional election (whether the polls are taken separately or together) or a European parliamentary election. As to the meanings of 'Assembly election', 'constituency election' and 'regional election' see PARA 3 note 2. As to the meaning of 'parliamentary election' see PARA 9. As to the meanings of 'Authority election' and 'local government election' see PARA 11. As to elections in the City of London see PARA 33. As to European parliamentary elections see PARA 217 et seq. There is no provision for absent voting at a poll consequent on a parish meeting on a question involving appointment to office: see PARA 200 et seq.
    As to returning officers generally see PARA 350 et seq. At a European parliamentary election, the returning officer referred to in the text is the local returning officer (see PARA 360): see the European Parliamentary Elections Regulations 2004, SI 2004/293, Sch 2 para 49 (Sch 2 substituted by SI 2009/186). At a Welsh Assembly election, the constituency returning officer is the returning officer referred to in the text: see the National Assembly for Wales (Representation of the People) Order 2007, SI 2007/236, Sch 3 para 10; but see also PARA 406 note 1. As to the meaning of 'constituency returning officer' for the purposes of Welsh Assembly elections see PARA 18 note 2.

2   As to the postal voters list see PARA 373.

3   As to the record of persons entitled to vote by post as proxy see PARA 379.

4   As to the meaning of 'elector', in relation to a parliamentary or local government election, see PARA 95 note 2; in relation to a Welsh Assembly election, see PARA 110 note 6; and in relation to European parliamentary elections see PARA 111 note 4.

5   As to the meaning of 'postal ballot paper' see PARA 407 note 1. As to the returning officer's duty to issue postal ballot papers, etc see PARA 406; as to the time of issue of postal ballot papers, etc see PARA 407; and as to the marking of the envelopes and the addresses to be used see PARA 410.

6   Representation of the People (England and Wales) Regulations 2001, SI 2001/341, reg 73 (amended by SI 2006/2910); European Parliamentary Elections Regulations 2004, SI 2004/293, Sch 2 para 49 (as substituted: see note 1); National Assembly for Wales (Representation of the People) Order 2007, SI 2007/236, Sch 3 para 10.
    The Representation of the People (England and Wales) Regulations 2001, SI 2001/341, reg 73 has effect for the purposes of local authority referendums, subject to the modifications specified, in relation to Wales, by the Local Authorities (Conduct of Referendums) (Wales) Regulations 2008, SI 2008/1848, reg 8(2), Sch 4 Table 5, and, in relation to England, by the

Local Authorities (Conduct of Referendums) (England) Regulations 2012, SI 2012/323, regs 8(2), 11–13, Sch 4 Table 6 (see PARA 15 note 2).

410. Envelopes to be issued to postal voter. The following envelopes must be issued to a postal voter[1] at an election[2], in addition to the postal ballot paper[3] (and the postal voting statement[4] that must be sent with that paper)[5]:

(1)   an envelope marked with the letter 'B' (a 'covering envelope'[6]) must be issued for the return of the postal ballot paper (or postal ballot papers, as the case may be) and the postal voting statement[7]; and

(2)   a smaller envelope (a 'ballot paper envelope'[8]) also must be issued which must be marked with[9]:

    (a)   the letter 'A'[10];

    (b)   the words 'ballot paper envelope' (and, at a Welsh Assembly election, the words 'amlen papur pleidleisio')[11]; and

    (c)   unless the envelope has a window through which the number on the ballot paper (or ballot papers) can be displayed, the number of the ballot paper (or, as the case may be, ballot papers)[12].

The address to which the postal ballot paper, postal voting statement and the envelopes referred to in heads (1) and (2) above are to be sent is[13]:

(i)   in the case of an elector[14], the address shown in the postal voters list[15];

(ii)   in the case of a proxy[16], the address shown in the proxy postal voters list[17].

Where the poll at one election is taken with the poll at another election, special provision is made for the marking of the envelopes so issued[18].

1   As to the meaning of 'postal voter' see PARA 407 note 1.
2   Ie at a parliamentary election, a local government election (which includes any London Authority election and a local authority mayoral election), a Welsh Assembly constituency or regional election (whether the polls are taken separately or together) or a European parliamentary election. As to the meanings of 'Assembly election', 'constituency election' and 'regional election' see PARA 3 note 2. As to the meaning of 'parliamentary election' see PARA 9. As to the meanings of 'Authority election' and 'local government election' see PARA 11. As to elections in the City of London see PARA 33. As to European parliamentary elections see PARA 217 et seq. There is no provision for absent voting at a poll consequent on a parish meeting on a question involving appointment to office: see PARA 200 et seq.
3   As to the meaning of 'postal ballot paper' see PARA 407 note 1.
4   As to the postal voting statement see PARA 406.
5   Representation of the People (England and Wales) Regulations 2001, SI 2001/341, reg 74(1) (reg 74(1), (2), (3)(c) amended by SI 2006/2910); European Parliamentary Elections Regulations 2004, SI 2004/293, Sch 2 para 50(1) (Sch 2 substituted by SI 2009/186); National Assembly for Wales (Representation of the People) Order 2007, SI 2007/236, Sch 3 para 11(1). The text refers to the ballot paper and postal voting statement which are issued to a postal voter, in the case of a parliamentary election, under the Representation of the People Act 1983 Sch 1 r 24, or, in the case of a local government election, under the Local Elections (Principal Areas) (England and Wales) Rules 2006, SI 2006/3304, Sch 2 r 22, the Local Elections (Parishes and Communities) (England and Wales) Rules 2006, SI 2006/3305, Sch 2 r 22, the Local Authorities (Mayoral Elections) (England and Wales) Regulations 2007, SI 2007/1024, Sch 1 r 24, or the Greater London Authority Elections Rules 2007, SI 2007/3541, Sch 1 r 23, Sch 2 r 24, Sch 3 r 23, or, in the case of a European parliamentary election, under the European Parliamentary Elections Regulations 2004, SI 2004/293, Sch 1 para 28, or, a at a Welsh Assembly election, under the National Assembly for Wales (Representation of the People) Order 2007, SI 2007/236, Sch 5 para 33 (see PARA 406): see the Representation of the People (England and Wales) Regulations 2001, SI 2001/341, reg 74(1) (as so amended); the European Parliamentary Elections Regulations 2004, SI 2004/293, Sch 2 para 50(1) (as so substituted); and the National Assembly for Wales (Representation of the People) Order 2007, SI 2007/236, Sch 3 para 11(1). As to the time of issue of postal ballot papers, etc see PARA 407.
    The Representation of the People (England and Wales) Regulations 2001, SI 2001/341, regs 72, 74 have effect for the purposes of local authority referendums, subject to the

modifications specified, in relation to Wales, by the Local Authorities (Conduct of Referendums) (Wales) Regulations 2008, SI 2008/1848, reg 8(2), Sch 4 Table 5, and, in relation to England, by the Local Authorities (Conduct of Referendums) (England) Regulations 2012, SI 2012/323, regs 8(2), 11–13, Sch 4 Table 6 (see PARA 15 note 2).

6 'Covering envelope' means the envelope referred to, in relation to a parliamentary election, in the Representation of the People (England and Wales) Regulations 2001, SI 2001/341, reg 74, or, in relation to a European parliamentary election, in the European Parliamentary Elections Regulations 2004, SI 2004/293, Sch 2 para 50, or, in relation to a Welsh Assembly election, in the National Assembly for Wales (Representation of the People) Order 2007, SI 2007/236, Sch 3 para 11, as the case may be: Representation of the People (England and Wales) Regulations 2001, SI 2001/341, reg 64; European Parliamentary Elections Regulations 2004, SI 2004/293, Sch 2 para 40(1) (as substituted: see note 5); National Assembly for Wales (Representation of the People) Order 2007, SI 2007/236, Sch 3 para 1.

7 Representation of the People (England and Wales) Regulations 2001, SI 2001/341, reg 74(2) (as amended: see note 5); European Parliamentary Elections Regulations 2004, SI 2004/293, Sch 2 para 50(2) (as substituted: see note 5); National Assembly for Wales (Representation of the People) Order 2007, SI 2007/236, Sch 3 para 11(1).

8 'Ballot paper envelope' means the referred to, in relation to a parliamentary election, in the Representation of the People (England and Wales) Regulations 2001, SI 2001/341, reg 74, or, in relation to a European parliamentary election, in the European Parliamentary Elections Regulations 2004, SI 2004/293, Sch 2 para 50, or, in relation to a Welsh Assembly election, in the National Assembly for Wales (Representation of the People) Order 2007, SI 2007/236, Sch 3 para 11, as the case may be: Representation of the People (England and Wales) Regulations 2001, SI 2001/341, reg 64; European Parliamentary Elections Regulations 2004, SI 2004/293, Sch 2 para 40(1) (as substituted: see note 5); National Assembly for Wales (Representation of the People) Order 2007, SI 2007/236, Sch 3 para 1.

9 Representation of the People (England and Wales) Regulations 2001, SI 2001/341, reg 74(3); European Parliamentary Elections Regulations 2004, SI 2004/293, Sch 2 para 50(3) (as substituted: see note 5); National Assembly for Wales (Representation of the People) Order 2007, SI 2007/236, Sch 3 para 11(2).

10 Representation of the People (England and Wales) Regulations 2001, SI 2001/341, reg 74(3)(a); European Parliamentary Elections Regulations 2004, SI 2004/293, Sch 2 para 50(3)(a) (as substituted: see note 5); National Assembly for Wales (Representation of the People) Order 2007, SI 2007/236, Sch 3 para 11(2)(a).

11 Representation of the People (England and Wales) Regulations 2001, SI 2001/341, reg 74(3)(b); European Parliamentary Elections Regulations 2004, SI 2004/293, Sch 2 para 50(3)(b) (as substituted: see note 5); National Assembly for Wales (Representation of the People) Order 2007, SI 2007/236, Sch 3 para 11(2)(b).

12 Representation of the People (England and Wales) Regulations 2001, SI 2001/341, reg 74(3)(c) (as amended: see note 5); European Parliamentary Elections Regulations 2004, SI 2004/293, Sch 2 para 50(3)(c) (as substituted: see note 5); National Assembly for Wales (Representation of the People) Order 2007, SI 2007/236, Sch 3 para 11(2)(c). At a Welsh Assembly election, the proviso that qualifies head (2)(c) in the text is absent so that, at such an election, the number of the ballot paper (or, as the case may be, ballot papers) must always be marked on the ballot paper envelope: see Sch 3 para 11(2)(c).

13 Representation of the People (England and Wales) Regulations 2001, SI 2001/341, reg 72(7) (reg 72(7) added by SI 2002/1871; reg 72(7) amended, reg 72(8) added, by SI 2006/2910); European Parliamentary Elections Regulations 2004, SI 2004/293, Sch 2 para 48(6) (as substituted: see note 5); National Assembly for Wales (Representation of the People) Order 2007, SI 2007/236, Sch 3 para 9(7).

Where a person has an anonymous entry in the register, the items specified in the Representation of the People (England and Wales) Regulations 2001, SI 2001/341, reg 72(7), or the European Parliamentary Elections Regulations 2004, SI 2004/293, Sch 2 para 48(6), or the National Assembly for Wales (Representation of the People) Order 2007, SI 2007/236, Sch 3 para 9(7), as, the case may be, must be sent, as the case may be, to the address to which postal ballot papers should be sent:

(1) as shown in the record kept, for the purposes of a parliamentary or local government election, under the Representation of the People Act 2000 Sch 4 para 3(4), or in the record kept, for the purposes of a European parliamentary election, under the European Parliamentary Elections Regulations 2004, SI 2004/293, Sch 2 para 3(4), or in the record kept, for the purposes of a Welsh Assembly election, under the National Assembly for Wales (Representation of the People) Order 2007, SI 2007/236, art 8(3) (record of those entitled to an absent vote at elections for a definite period or for an

indefinite period see PARA 370) or in the records kept under the Representation of the People Act 2000 Sch 4 para 7(6), or under the European Parliamentary Elections Regulations 2004, SI 2004/293, Sch 2 para 7(6), or under the National Assembly for Wales (Representation of the People) Order 2007, SI 2007/236, art 12(6) (record of persons entitled to vote by post as proxy see PARA 379) (Representation of the People (England and Wales) Regulations 2001, SI 2001/341, reg 72(8)(a) (as so added); European Parliamentary Elections Regulations 2004, SI 2004/293, Sch 2 para 48(7)(a) (as so substituted)); National Assembly for Wales (Representation of the People) Order 2007, SI 2007/236, Sch 3 para 9(8)(a)); or

(2) as given in pursuance of an application made, in relation to a particular parliamentary or local government election, under the Representation of the People Act 2000 Sch 4 para 4(1), or, in relation to a particular European parliamentary election, under the European Parliamentary Elections Regulations 2004, SI 2004/293, Sch 2 para 4(1), or, in relation to a particular Welsh Assembly election, under the National Assembly for Wales (Representation of the People) Order 2007, SI 2007/236, art 9(1) (absent vote at particular election: see PARA 371), or in pursuance of an application made under the Representation of the People Act 2000 Sch 4 para 7(4)(b), or the European Parliamentary Elections Regulations 2004, SI 2004/293, Sch 2 para 7(4)(b), or the National Assembly for Wales (Representation of the People) Order 2007, SI 2007/236, art 12(4)(b) (voting as proxy for an indefinite period or for a particular period or at a particular election: see PARA 378), as the case may be (Representation of the People (England and Wales) Regulations 2001, SI 2001/341, reg 72(8)(b) (as so added); European Parliamentary Elections Regulations 2004, SI 2004/293, Sch 2 para 48(7)(b) (as so substituted)); National Assembly for Wales (Representation of the People) Order 2007, SI 2007/236, Sch 3 para 9(8)(b)).

As to the meaning of 'anonymous entry', in relation to a register of electors, see PARA 148.

14 As to the meaning of 'elector', in relation to a parliamentary or local government election, see PARA 95 note 2; in relation to a Welsh Assembly election, see PARA 110 note 6; and in relation to European parliamentary elections see PARA 111 note 4.

15 Representation of the People (England and Wales) Regulations 2001, SI 2001/341, reg 72(7)(a) (reg 72(7) as added (see note 13); reg 72(7)(a), (b) amended by SI 2006/2910); European Parliamentary Elections Regulations 2004, SI 2004/293, Sch 2 para 48(6)(a) (as substituted: see note 5); National Assembly for Wales (Representation of the People) Order 2007, SI 2007/236, Sch 3 para 9(7)(a). As to the postal voters list see PARA 373.

16 As to voting by proxy see PARA 366 et seq; and as to the entitlement to vote by post as proxy see PARAS 377, 382.

17 Representation of the People (England and Wales) Regulations 2001, SI 2001/341, reg 72(7)(b) (as added and amended: see note 15); European Parliamentary Elections Regulations 2004, SI 2004/293, Sch 2 para 48(6)(b) (as substituted: see note 5); National Assembly for Wales (Representation of the People) Order 2007, SI 2007/236, Sch 3 para 9(7)(b). As to the record of persons entitled to vote by post as proxy see PARA 379.

18 See the Representation of the People (England and Wales) Regulations 2001, SI 2001/341, reg 74(4); the European Parliamentary Elections Regulations 2004, SI 2004/293, Sch 2 para 50(4) (as substituted: see note 5); and the National Assembly for Wales (Representation of the People) Order 2007, SI 2007/236, Sch 3 para 11(3). As to the issue and receipt of postal ballot papers when polls are combined see PARA 20.

411. Delivery of postal ballot papers by returning officer. For the purposes of delivering postal ballot papers[1], the returning officer at an election[2] may use[3]:

(1) a universal postal service provider[4];

(2) a commercial delivery firm[5]; or

(3) clerks appointed by a returning officer to aid a presiding officer[6].

Except where head (3) above applies, postage must be pre-paid on the envelopes addressed to the postal voters[7]; and, where the address provided by the postal voter for the receipt of the postal ballot paper is within the United Kingdom[8], return postage must be pre-paid on all covering envelopes also[9]. Where the services of a universal postal service provider (see head (1) above) or a commercial delivery firm (see head (2) above) are to be used, envelopes addressed to postal voters must be counted and delivered by the returning officer with such form of receipt to be endorsed by that provider or firm as may be arranged[10].

The returning officer is required only to deliver the postal ballot papers in accordance with this statutory scheme and he is not required to deliver the postal ballot papers into the hands of the electors[11].

1   As to the meaning of 'postal ballot paper' see PARA 407 note 1. As to the issue of postal ballot papers, etc see PARA 406 et seq. As to the marking of the envelopes and the addresses to be used see PARA 410.

2   Ie at a parliamentary election, a local government election (which includes any London Authority election and a local authority mayoral election), a Welsh Assembly constituency or regional election (whether the polls are taken separately or together) or a European parliamentary election. As to the meanings of 'Assembly election', 'constituency election' and 'regional election' see PARA 3 note 2. As to the meaning of 'parliamentary election' see PARA 9. As to the meanings of 'Authority election' and 'local government election' see PARA 11. As to elections in the City of London see PARA 33. As to European parliamentary elections see PARA 217 et seq. There is no provision for absent voting at a poll consequent on a parish meeting on a question involving appointment to office: see PARA 200 et seq.

     As to returning officers generally see PARA 350 et seq. At a European parliamentary election, the returning officer referred to in the text is the local returning officer (see PARA 360): see the European Parliamentary Elections Regulations 2004, SI 2004/293, Sch 2 para 52(1), (2) (Sch 2 substituted by SI 2009/186). At a Welsh Assembly election, the constituency returning officer is the returning officer referred to in the text: see the National Assembly for Wales (Representation of the People) Order 2007, SI 2007/236, Sch 3 para 13(1), (2); but see also PARA 406 note 1. As to the meaning of 'constituency returning officer' for the purposes of Welsh Assembly elections see PARA 18 note 2.

3   Representation of the People (England and Wales) Regulations 2001, SI 2001/341, reg 76(1); European Parliamentary Elections Regulations 2004, SI 2004/293, Sch 2 para 52(1) (as substituted: see note 2); National Assembly for Wales (Representation of the People) Order 2007, SI 2007/236, Sch 3 para 13(1).

     The Representation of the People (England and Wales) Regulations 2001, SI 2001/341, reg 76 has effect for the purposes of local authority referendums, subject to the modifications specified, in relation to Wales, by the Local Authorities (Conduct of Referendums) (Wales) Regulations 2008, SI 2008/1848, reg 8(2), Sch 4 Table 5, and, in relation to England, by the Local Authorities (Conduct of Referendums) (England) Regulations 2012, SI 2012/323, regs 8(2), 11–13, Sch 4 Table 6 (see PARA 15 note 2).

4   Representation of the People (England and Wales) Regulations 2001, SI 2001/341, reg 76(1)(a); European Parliamentary Elections Regulations 2004, SI 2004/293, Sch 2 para 52(1)(a) (as substituted: see note 2); National Assembly for Wales (Representation of the People) Order 2007, SI 2007/236, Sch 3 para 13(1)(a). For the purposes of the Representation of the People (England and Wales) Regulations 2001, SI 2001/341, Pt V (regs 64–91) (issue and receipt of postal ballot papers), 'universal postal service provider' has the meaning given in the Postal Services Act 2011 Pt 3 (ss 27–67) to 'universal service provider' (see POSTAL SERVICES vol 85 (2012) PARA 252): Representation of the People (England and Wales) Regulations 2001, SI 2001/341, reg 64 (definition of 'universal postal service provider' amended by SI 2011/2085). As to the meaning of 'universal postal service provider' for the purposes of a European parliamentary election see PARA 366 note 16; and for the purposes of a Welsh Assembly election see PARA 330 note 1.

5   Representation of the People (England and Wales) Regulations 2001, SI 2001/341, reg 76(1)(b); European Parliamentary Elections Regulations 2004, SI 2004/293, Sch 2 para 52(1)(b) (as substituted: see note 2); National Assembly for Wales (Representation of the People) Order 2007, SI 2007/236, Sch 3 para 13(1)(b).

6   Representation of the People (England and Wales) Regulations 2001, SI 2001/341, reg 76(1)(c); European Parliamentary Elections Regulations 2004, SI 2004/293, Sch 2 para 52(1)(c) (as substituted: see note 2); National Assembly for Wales (Representation of the People) Order 2007, SI 2007/236, Sch 3 para 13(1)(c). As to the appointment of presiding officers and their clerks see PARA 393.

7   Representation of the People (England and Wales) Regulations 2001, SI 2001/341, reg 76(3); European Parliamentary Elections Regulations 2004, SI 2004/293, Sch 2 para 52(3) (as

substituted: see note 2); National Assembly for Wales (Representation of the People) Order 2007, SI 2007/236, Sch 3 para 13(3). As to the meaning of 'postal voter' see PARA 407 note 1.

8 As to the meaning of 'United Kingdom' see PARA 1 note 1. For the purposes of a European parliamentary election taking place in the combined region, the European Parliamentary Elections Regulations 2004, SI 2004/293, Sch 2 para 52(4) applies to an address within Gibraltar also: see Sch 2 para 52(4) (as substituted: see note 2). As to the establishment of electoral regions (including the 'combined region') for the purpose of elections to the European Parliament see PARA 77.

9 Representation of the People (England and Wales) Regulations 2001, SI 2001/341, reg 76(4); European Parliamentary Elections Regulations 2004, SI 2004/293, Sch 2 para 52(4) (as substituted: see note 2); National Assembly for Wales (Representation of the People) Order 2007, SI 2007/236, Sch 3 para 13(4).

10 Representation of the People (England and Wales) Regulations 2001, SI 2001/341, reg 76(2); European Parliamentary Elections Regulations 2004, SI 2004/293, Sch 2 para 52(2) (as substituted: see note 2); National Assembly for Wales (Representation of the People) Order 2007, SI 2007/236, Sch 3 para 13(2).

11 *Knight v Nicholls* [2004] EWCA Civ 68, [2004] 1 WLR 1653, [2004] LGR 524 (election not void due to undelivered postal ballot papers; duty of returning officer satisfied by delivery to mail provider). On its true construction, the statutory scheme (as to which see PARA 406) requires the returning officer only to deliver the postal ballot papers to an authorised carrier in accordance with the Representation of the People (England and Wales) Regulations 2001, SI 2001/341; because the regulations intend the voter to take the risk of non-delivery, a 'safety-net' is provided in the form of the provisions relating to lost postal ballot papers (as to which see PARA 415): *Knight v Nicholls*.

412. Sealing up of completed corresponding number lists for issued postal ballot papers and security of special lists. As soon as practicable after the issue of each batch of postal ballot papers[1], the returning officer at an election[2] must make up into a packet the completed corresponding number lists[3] of those ballot papers which have been issued and he must seal such a packet[4].

Until the last covering envelope has been opened[5], the returning officer must take proper precautions for the security of the marked copy of the postal voters list and the proxy postal voters list[6].

1 As to the meaning of 'postal ballot paper' see PARA 407 note 1. As to the issue of postal ballot papers see PARA 406 et seq.

2 Ie at a parliamentary election, a local government election (which includes any London Authority election and a local authority mayoral election), a Welsh Assembly constituency or regional election (whether the polls are taken separately or together) or a European parliamentary election. As to the meanings of 'Assembly election', 'constituency election' and 'regional election' see PARA 3 note 2. As to the meaning of 'parliamentary election' see PARA 9. As to the meanings of 'Authority election' and 'local government election' see PARA 11. As to elections in the City of London see PARA 33. As to European parliamentary elections see PARA 217 et seq. There is no provision for absent voting at a poll consequent on a parish meeting on a question involving appointment to office: see PARA 200 et seq.

As to returning officers generally see PARA 350 et seq. At a European parliamentary election, the returning officer referred to in the text is the local returning officer (see PARA 360): see the European Parliamentary Elections Regulations 2004, SI 2004/293, Sch 2 para 51(1), (2) (Sch 2 substituted by SI 2009/186). At a Welsh Assembly election, the constituency returning officer is the returning officer referred to in the text: see the National Assembly for Wales (Representation of the People) Order 2007, SI 2007/236, Sch 3 para 12(1), (2); but see also PARA 406 note 1. As to the meaning of 'constituency returning officer' for the purposes of Welsh Assembly elections see PARA 18 note 2.

3 As to the completed corresponding number lists see PARA 405 note 11.

4 Representation of the People (England and Wales) Regulations 2001, SI 2001/341, reg 75(1) (reg 75(1) amended, reg 75(2) substituted, by SI 2006/2910); European Parliamentary Elections Regulations 2004, SI 2004/293, Sch 2 para 51(1) (as substituted: see note 2); National Assembly for Wales (Representation of the People) Order 2007, SI 2007/236, Sch 3 para 12(1).

The Representation of the People (England and Wales) Regulations 2001, SI 2001/341, reg 75 has effect for the purposes of local authority referendums, subject to the modifications specified, in relation to Wales, by the Local Authorities (Conduct of Referendums) (Wales) Regulations 2008, SI 2008/1848, reg 8(2), Sch 4 Table 5, and, in relation to England, by the Local Authorities (Conduct of Referendums) (England) Regulations 2012, SI 2012/323, regs 8(2), 11–13, Sch 4 Table 6 (see PARA 15 note 2).

5   Ie until the time referred to, in relation to a parliamentary or local government election, in the Representation of the People (England and Wales) Regulations 2001, SI 2001/341, reg 84(9), or, in relation to a European parliamentary election, in the European Parliamentary Elections Regulations 2004, SI 2004/293, Sch 2 para 60(11), or, in relation to a particular Welsh Assembly election, in the National Assembly for Wales (Representation of the People) Order 2007, SI 2007/236, Sch 3 para 20(11) (see PARA 421): see the Representation of the People (England and Wales) Regulations 2001, SI 2001/341, reg 75(2) (as substituted: see note 4); the European Parliamentary Elections Regulations 2004, SI 2004/293, Sch 2 para 51(2) (as substituted: see note 2); and the National Assembly for Wales (Representation of the People) Order 2007, SI 2007/236, Sch 3 para 12(2). As to the meaning of 'covering envelope' see PARA 410.

6   Representation of the People (England and Wales) Regulations 2001, SI 2001/341, reg 75(2) (as substituted: see note 4); European Parliamentary Elections Regulations 2004, SI 2004/293, Sch 2 para 51(2) (as substituted: see note 2); National Assembly for Wales (Representation of the People) Order 2007, SI 2007/236, Sch 3 para 12(2). As to the postal voters list see PARA 373; and as to the record of persons entitled to vote by post as proxy see PARA 379. As to the marking of special lists in the course of issuing postal ballot papers see PARA 408.

413.   Instructions for voting by post. In order to vote, a postal voter[1] is instructed to[2]:

(1)   record his vote on the ballot paper[3], according to the instructions given;

(2)   put the ballot paper (or papers) in the small envelope[4] marked 'A' and seal it;

(3)   validate the postal voting statement in the prescribed manner;

(4)   put the envelope marked 'A', together with the postal voting statement, in the larger envelope marked 'B' and return it without delay, so that it is received by the returning officer not later than the close of the poll[5].

The voter is reminded that, at the election in question and otherwise than as a proxy, he cannot vote in person at a polling station after receiving a postal vote, nor can he vote using a ballot paper that is not addressed to him personally or interfere with another voter's ballot paper, and that it is illegal to vote more than once at the same election[6].

Instructions are also given in the event of a postal voter inadvertently spoiling the ballot paper[7].

1   As to the meaning of 'postal voter' see PARA 407 note 1.
2   These instructions appear on the form of the postal voting statement (as to which see PARA 406 note 5). The precise wording may vary according to the election in question.
3   As to the issue of postal ballot papers see PARA 406 et seq.
4   As to the envelopes used for postal voting see PARA 410.
5   See note 2.
6   See note 2.
7   See note 2.

414.   Spoilt postal ballot papers and spoilt postal voting statements. If a postal voter[1] has inadvertently dealt with his postal ballot paper[2] in such a manner that it cannot conveniently be used as a ballot paper (a 'spoilt postal ballot paper'[3]), or if he has inadvertently dealt with his postal voting statement[4] in such a manner that it cannot be conveniently used as a postal voting statement (a 'spoilt postal voting statement'), he may return the spoilt ballot paper or the spoilt postal voting statement, as the case may be, either by hand or by post to the returning officer[5]. Where a postal voter exercises this entitlement to return spoilt papers, he must also return[6]:

(1) the postal ballot paper (or, as the case may be, the postal voting statement), whether spoilt or not[7];

(2) where postal ballot papers for more than one election have been issued together, all other postal ballot papers so issued, whether spoilt or not[8];

(3) the envelopes supplied for the return of postal ballot papers and postal voting statements in normal circumstances[9].

On receipt of any such documents, the returning officer must issue another postal ballot paper (or, as the case may be, ballot papers) except where those documents are received after 5 pm on the day of the poll[10]. Where the returning officer receives any such documents after 5pm on the day before the day of the poll, however, he may only issue another postal ballot paper (or, as the case may be, ballot papers) if the postal voter has returned the documents by hand[11].

Any such postal ballot paper or postal voting statement, whether spoilt or not, which has been returned must be immediately cancelled[12]; and, as soon as practicable after cancelling those documents, the returning officer must make up those documents in a separate packet and he must seal the packet[13]. If, on any subsequent occasion, documents are cancelled in this way, the sealed packet must be opened and the additional cancelled documents included in it, and the packet must be again made up and sealed[14].

The returning officer must enter in a list kept for the purpose (the 'list of spoilt postal ballot papers')[15]:

(a) the name and number of the elector as stated in the register[16] (or, in the case of an elector who has an anonymous entry, his electoral number alone)[17];

(b) the number of the replacement postal ballot paper (or papers) so issued[18]; and

(c) where the postal voter whose ballot paper is spoilt is a proxy[19], his name and address[20].

1 As to the meaning of 'postal voter' see PARA 407 note 1.
2 As to the meaning of 'postal ballot paper' see PARA 407 note 1.
3 'Spoilt postal ballot paper' means a ballot paper referred to, in relation to a parliamentary or local government election, in the Representation of the People (England and Wales) Regulations 2001, SI 2001/341, reg 77(1), or, in relation to a European parliamentary election, in the European Parliamentary Elections Regulations 2004, SI 2004/293, Sch 2 para 53(1), or, in relation to a particular Welsh Assembly election, in the National Assembly for Wales (Representation of the People) Order 2007, SI 2007/236, Sch 3 para 14(1): Representation of the People (England and Wales) Regulations 2001, SI 2001/341, reg 64; European Parliamentary Elections Regulations 2004, SI 2004/293, Sch 2 para 40(1) (Sch 2 substituted by SI 2009/186); National Assembly for Wales (Representation of the People) Order 2007, SI 2007/236, Sch 3 para 1. Although the Representation of the People (England and Wales) Regulations 2001, SI 2001/341, reg 64 defines 'spoilt postal ballot paper' for the purposes of Pt V (regs 64–91) (issue and receipt of postal ballot papers), reg 77(1) itself refers simply to a 'spoilt ballot paper' but it is submitted that the former usage is to be preferred in this context in order to prevent confusion with the latter term as it is used in the Representation of the People Act 1983 Sch 1 r 41 (see PARA 404). As to instructions for voting by post see PARA 413.
4 As to the postal voting statement see PARA 406.
5 Representation of the People (England and Wales) Regulations 2001, SI 2001/341, reg 77(1) (reg 77(1), (2) substituted by SI 2006/752, amended by SI 2006/2910); European Parliamentary Elections Regulations 2004, SI 2004/293, Sch 2 para 53(1) (as substituted: see note 3); National Assembly for Wales (Representation of the People) Order 2007, SI 2007/236, Sch 3 para 14(1). As to returning officers generally see PARA 350 et seq. At a European parliamentary election, the returning officer referred to in the text is the local returning officer (see PARA 360): see the European Parliamentary Elections Regulations 2004, SI 2004/293, Sch 2 para 53(1), (3), (4), (7)–(9) (as so substituted). At a Welsh Assembly election, the constituency returning officer is the returning officer referred to in the text: see the National Assembly for Wales (Representation of the People) Order 2007, SI 2007/236, Sch 3 para 14(1), (3), (4), (7)–(9); but

see also PARA 406 note 1. As to the meaning of 'constituency returning officer' for the purposes of Welsh Assembly elections see PARA 18 note 2.

The Representation of the People (England and Wales) Regulations 2001, SI 2001/341, reg 77 has effect for the purposes of local authority referendums, subject to the modifications specified, in relation to Wales, by the Local Authorities (Conduct of Referendums) (Wales) Regulations 2008, SI 2008/1848, reg 8(2), Sch 4 Table 5, and, in relation to England, by the Local Authorities (Conduct of Referendums) (England) Regulations 2012, SI 2012/323, regs 8(2), 11–13, Sch 4 Table 6 (see PARA 15 note 2).

6 Representation of the People (England and Wales) Regulations 2001, SI 2001/341, reg 77(2) (as substituted and amended: see note 5); European Parliamentary Elections Regulations 2004, SI 2004/293, Sch 2 para 53(2) (as substituted: see note 3); National Assembly for Wales (Representation of the People) Order 2007, SI 2007/236, Sch 3 para 14(2).

7 Representation of the People (England and Wales) Regulations 2001, SI 2001/341, reg 77(2)(a) (as substituted and amended: see note 5); European Parliamentary Elections Regulations 2004, SI 2004/293, Sch 2 para 53(2)(a) (as substituted: see note 3); National Assembly for Wales (Representation of the People) Order 2007, SI 2007/236, Sch 3 para 14(2)(a).

8 Representation of the People (England and Wales) Regulations 2001, SI 2001/341, reg 77(2)(b) (as substituted and amended: see note 5); European Parliamentary Elections Regulations 2004, SI 2004/293, Sch 2 para 53(2)(b) (as substituted: see note 3); National Assembly for Wales (Representation of the People) Order 2007, SI 2007/236, Sch 3 para 14(2)(b). As to proceedings on the issue and receipt of postal ballot papers where more than one election or referendum are taken together see PARA 20.

9 Representation of the People (England and Wales) Regulations 2001, SI 2001/341, reg 77(2)(c) (as substituted and amended: see note 5); European Parliamentary Elections Regulations 2004, SI 2004/293, Sch 2 para 53(2)(c) (as substituted: see note 3); National Assembly for Wales (Representation of the People) Order 2007, SI 2007/236, Sch 3 para 14(2)(c). As to the ballot paper envelope and the covering envelope see PARA 410.

10 Representation of the People (England and Wales) Regulations 2001, SI 2001/341, reg 77(3) (reg 77(3) amended, reg 77(3A) added, by SI 2006/752); European Parliamentary Elections Regulations 2004, SI 2004/293, Sch 2 para 53(3) (as substituted: see note 3); National Assembly for Wales (Representation of the People) Order 2007, SI 2007/236, Sch 3 para 14(3).

Specified provisions relating to the issue of postal ballot papers apply to the issue of replacement postal ballot papers, namely, in relation to a parliamentary or local government election, the Representation of the People (England and Wales) Regulations 2001, SI 2001/341, reg 72 (except reg 72(3)) and, subject to reg 77(7) (see note 11), regs 74–76, in relation to a European parliamentary election, the European Parliamentary Elections Regulations 2004, SI 2004/293, Sch 2 para 48 (except Sch 2 para 48(2)) and, subject to Sch 2 para 53(8) (see note 11), Sch 2 paras 50–52, and, in relation to a Welsh Assembly election, the National Assembly for Wales (Representation of the People) Order 2007, SI 2007/236, Sch 3 paras 9–12 (except Sch 3 para 9(3)) and, subject to Sch 3 para 14(8) (see note 11), Sch 3 para 13 (see PARA 411): see the Representation of the People (England and Wales) Regulations 2001, SI 2001/341, reg 77(4); the European Parliamentary Elections Regulations 2004, SI 2004/293, Sch 2 para 53(5) (as so substituted); and the National Assembly for Wales (Representation of the People) Order 2007, SI 2007/236, Sch 3 para 14(5).

11 Representation of the People (England and Wales) Regulations 2001, SI 2001/341, reg 77(3A) (as added: see note 10); European Parliamentary Elections Regulations 2004, SI 2004/293, Sch 2 para 53(4) (as substituted: see note 3); National Assembly for Wales (Representation of the People) Order 2007, SI 2007/236, Sch 3 para 14(4).

Instead of delivering a replacement postal ballot paper in accordance with, in relation to a parliamentary or local government election, the Representation of the People (England and Wales) Regulations 2001, SI 2001/341, reg 76, or, in relation to a European parliamentary election, the European Parliamentary Elections Regulations 2004, SI 2004/293, Sch 2 para 52, or, in relation to a Welsh Assembly election, the National Assembly for Wales (Representation of the People) Order 2007, SI 2007/236, Sch 3 para 13, as the case may be (see PARA 411), the returning officer may hand a replacement postal ballot paper to a postal voter who applies in person by 5 pm on the day before the day of the poll (and he may only hand a replacement postal ballot paper to a postal voter who applies in person after 5 pm on the day before the day of the poll): Representation of the People (England and Wales) Regulations 2001, SI 2001/341, reg 77(7) (substituted by SI 2006/752); European Parliamentary Elections Regulations 2004, SI 2004/293, Sch 2 para 53(8) (as substituted: see note 3); National Assembly for Wales (Representation of the People) Order 2007, SI 2007/236, Sch 3 para 14(8).

12 Representation of the People (England and Wales) Regulations 2001, SI 2001/341, reg 77(5) (substituted by SI 2006/752, amended by SI 2006/2910); European Parliamentary Elections

Regulations 2004, SI 2004/293, Sch 2 para 53(6) (as substituted: see note 3); National Assembly for Wales (Representation of the People) Order 2007, SI 2007/236, Sch 3 para 14(6).

13 Representation of the People (England and Wales) Regulations 2001, SI 2001/341, reg 77(6); European Parliamentary Elections Regulations 2004, SI 2004/293, Sch 2 para 53(7) (as substituted: see note 3); National Assembly for Wales (Representation of the People) Order 2007, SI 2007/236, Sch 3 para 14(7).

14 Representation of the People (England and Wales) Regulations 2001, SI 2001/341, reg 77(6); European Parliamentary Elections Regulations 2004, SI 2004/293, Sch 2 para 53(7) (as substituted: see note 3); National Assembly for Wales (Representation of the People) Order 2007, SI 2007/236, Sch 3 para 14(7).

15 Representation of the People (England and Wales) Regulations 2001, SI 2001/341, reg 77(8); European Parliamentary Elections Regulations 2004, SI 2004/293, Sch 2 para 53(9) (as substituted: see note 3); National Assembly for Wales (Representation of the People) Order 2007, SI 2007/236, Sch 3 para 14(9).

16 As to the meaning of 'elector', in relation to a parliamentary or local government election, see PARA 95 note 2; in relation to a Welsh Assembly election, see PARA 110 note 6; and in relation to European parliamentary elections see PARA 111 note 4. As to the registers of electors see PARA 143 et seq. As to the number of an elector see PARA 145.

17 Representation of the People (England and Wales) Regulations 2001, SI 2001/341, reg 77(8)(a) (amended by SI 2006/2910); European Parliamentary Elections Regulations 2004, SI 2004/293, Sch 2 para 53(9)(a) (as substituted: see note 3); National Assembly for Wales (Representation of the People) Order 2007, SI 2007/236, Sch 3 para 14(9)(a). As to the meaning of 'anonymous entry', in relation to a register of electors, see PARA 148.

18 Representation of the People (England and Wales) Regulations 2001, SI 2001/341, reg 77(8)(b); European Parliamentary Elections Regulations 2004, SI 2004/293, Sch 2 para 53(9)(b) (as substituted: see note 3); National Assembly for Wales (Representation of the People) Order 2007, SI 2007/236, Sch 3 para 14(9)(b).

19 As to applications to vote by post or by proxy (or both) see PARA 367 et seq.

20 Representation of the People (England and Wales) Regulations 2001, SI 2001/341, reg 77(8)(c); European Parliamentary Elections Regulations 2004, SI 2004/293, Sch 2 para 53(9)(c) (as substituted: see note 3); National Assembly for Wales (Representation of the People) Order 2007, SI 2007/236, Sch 3 para 14(9)(c).

415. Lost postal ballot papers. If, by the fourth day before the day of the poll at an election[1], a postal voter[2] claims either to have lost or not to have received[3]:

(1) his postal ballot paper[4]; or

(2) the postal voting statement[5]; or

(3) one or more of the envelopes supplied for their return[6],

he may apply (whether or not in person) to the returning officer[7] for a replacement ballot paper[8]. The voter must include evidence of his identity with any such application[9].

Where a postal voter exercises his entitlement to a replacement for a lost ballot paper, he must return the other documents which he has received and which have not been lost[10]. Any such postal ballot paper or postal voting statement which has been returned in this way must be immediately cancelled[11]; and, as soon as practicable after cancelling those documents, the returning officer must make up those documents in a separate packet and he must seal the packet[12]. If, on any subsequent occasion, documents are cancelled in this way, the sealed packet must be opened and the additional cancelled documents included in it and the packet must be again made up and sealed[13].

Where the application for a replacement ballot paper is received by the returning officer before 5 pm on the day of the poll, and where the returning officer is satisfied as to the voter's identity, and where he has no reason to doubt that the postal voter has either lost or has not received the original postal ballot paper or the postal voting statement, or one or more of the envelopes provided for their return, he must issue another postal ballot paper (or, as the case may be, postal ballot papers)[14]. Where the application is received by the returning officer after 5 pm on the day before the day of the poll, however, he must only issue another postal ballot paper (or, as the case may be, other ballot papers) if the postal voter applies in person[15].

The returning officer must enter in a list kept for the purpose (the 'list of lost postal ballot papers')[16]:

(a)   the name and number of the elector as stated in the register[17] (or, in the case of an elector who has an anonymous entry, his electoral number alone)[18];

(b)   the number of the replacement postal ballot paper (or papers) so issued[19]; and

(c)   where the postal voter whose ballot paper is lost is a proxy[20], his name and address[21].

1   Ie at a parliamentary election, a local government election (which includes any London Authority election and a local authority mayoral election), a Welsh Assembly constituency or regional election (whether the polls are taken separately or together) or a European parliamentary election. As to the meanings of 'Assembly election', 'constituency election' and 'regional election' see PARA 3 note 2. As to the meaning of 'parliamentary election' see PARA 9. As to the meanings of 'Authority election' and 'local government election' see PARA 11. As to elections in the City of London see PARA 33. As to European parliamentary elections see PARA 217 et seq. There is no provision for absent voting at a poll consequent on a parish meeting on a question involving appointment to office: see PARA 200 et seq.

2   As to the meaning of 'postal voter' see PARA 407 note 1.

3   Representation of the People (England and Wales) Regulations 2001, SI 2001/341, reg 78(1) (reg 78(1) substituted by SI 2006/752); European Parliamentary Elections Regulations 2004, SI 2004/293, Sch 2 para 54(1) (Sch 2 substituted by SI 2009/186); National Assembly for Wales (Representation of the People) Order 2007, SI 2007/236, Sch 3 para 15(1).
    The Representation of the People (England and Wales) Regulations 2001, SI 2001/341, reg 78 has effect for the purposes of local authority referendums, subject to the modifications specified, in relation to Wales, by the Local Authorities (Conduct of Referendums) (Wales) Regulations 2008, SI 2008/1848, reg 8(2), Sch 4 Table 5, and, in relation to England, by the Local Authorities (Conduct of Referendums) (England) Regulations 2012, SI 2012/323, regs 8(2), 11–13, Sch 4 Table 6 (see PARA 15 note 2).

4   Representation of the People (England and Wales) Regulations 2001, SI 2001/341, reg 78(1)(a) (as substituted: see note 3); European Parliamentary Elections Regulations 2004, SI 2004/293, Sch 2 para 54(1)(a) (as substituted: see note 3); National Assembly for Wales (Representation of the People) Order 2007, SI 2007/236, Sch 3 para 15(1)(a). As to the meaning of 'postal ballot paper' see PARA 407 note 1. As to the issue of postal ballot papers see PARA 406 et seq.

5   Representation of the People (England and Wales) Regulations 2001, SI 2001/341, reg 78(1)(b) (reg 78(1) as substituted (see note 3); reg 78(1)(b) amended by SI 2006/2910); European Parliamentary Elections Regulations 2004, SI 2004/293, Sch 2 para 54(1)(b) (as substituted: see note 3); National Assembly for Wales (Representation of the People) Order 2007, SI 2007/236, Sch 3 para 15(1)(b). As to the postal voting statement see PARA 406.

6   Representation of the People (England and Wales) Regulations 2001, SI 2001/341, reg 78(1)(c) (as substituted: see note 3); European Parliamentary Elections Regulations 2004, SI 2004/293, Sch 2 para 54(1)(c) (as substituted: see note 3); National Assembly for Wales (Representation of the People) Order 2007, SI 2007/236, Sch 3 para 15(1)(c). As to the ballot paper envelope and the covering envelope see PARA 410.

7   As to returning officers generally see PARA 350 et seq. At a European parliamentary election, the returning officer referred to in the text is the local returning officer (see PARA 360): see the European Parliamentary Elections Regulations 2004, SI 2004/293, Sch 2 para 54(1), (4)–(8) (as substituted: see note 3). At a Welsh Assembly election, the constituency returning officer is the returning officer referred to in the text: see the National Assembly for Wales (Representation of the People) Order 2007, SI 2007/236, Sch 3 para 15(1), (5)–(8), (10), (11); but see also PARA 406 note 1. As to the meaning of 'constituency returning officer' for the purposes of Welsh Assembly elections see PARA 18 note 2.

8   Representation of the People (England and Wales) Regulations 2001, SI 2001/341, reg 78(1) (as substituted: see note 3); European Parliamentary Elections Regulations 2004, SI 2004/293, Sch 2 para 54(1) (as substituted: see note 3); National Assembly for Wales (Representation of the People) Order 2007, SI 2007/236, Sch 3 para 15(1). The scheme set out in the text provides

a 'safety-net' for the voter, who necessarily takes the risk of non-delivery of his postal ballot paper: *Knight v Nicholls* [2004] EWCA Civ 68, [2004] 1 WLR 1653, [2004] LGR 524.

9   Representation of the People (England and Wales) Regulations 2001, SI 2001/341, reg 78(2); European Parliamentary Elections Regulations 2004, SI 2004/293, Sch 2 para 54(2) (as substituted: see note 3); National Assembly for Wales (Representation of the People) Order 2007, SI 2007/236, Sch 3 para 15(2).

10   Representation of the People (England and Wales) Regulations 2001, SI 2001/341, reg 78(2A) (reg 78(2A)–(2C), (3A) added by SI 2006/752); European Parliamentary Elections Regulations 2004, SI 2004/293, Sch 2 para 54(3) (as substituted: see note 3); National Assembly for Wales (Representation of the People) Order 2007, SI 2007/236, Sch 3 para 15(3). The text refers to the documents referred to in heads (1) to (3) in the text and, where postal ballot papers for more than one election have been issued together (see PARA 20), all other postal ballot papers so issued, which the postal voter has received but which have not been lost: see the Representation of the People (England and Wales) Regulations 2001, SI 2001/341, reg 78(2A) (as so added); the European Parliamentary Elections Regulations 2004, SI 2004/293, Sch 2 para 54(3) (as so substituted); and the National Assembly for Wales (Representation of the People) Order 2007, SI 2007/236, Sch 3 para 15(3).

11   Representation of the People (England and Wales) Regulations 2001, SI 2001/341, reg 78(2B) (reg 78(2B) as added (see note 10); amended by SI 2006/2910); European Parliamentary Elections Regulations 2004, SI 2004/293, Sch 2 para 54(4) (as substituted: see note 3); National Assembly for Wales (Representation of the People) Order 2007, SI 2007/236, Sch 3 para 15(4).

12   Representation of the People (England and Wales) Regulations 2001, SI 2001/341, reg 78(2C) (as added: see note 10); European Parliamentary Elections Regulations 2004, SI 2004/293, Sch 2 para 54(5) (as substituted: see note 3); National Assembly for Wales (Representation of the People) Order 2007, SI 2007/236, Sch 3 para 15(5).

13   Representation of the People (England and Wales) Regulations 2001, SI 2001/341, reg 78(2C) (as added: see note 10); European Parliamentary Elections Regulations 2004, SI 2004/293, Sch 2 para 54(5) (as substituted: see note 3); National Assembly for Wales (Representation of the People) Order 2007, SI 2007/236, Sch 3 para 15(5).

14   Representation of the People (England and Wales) Regulations 2001, SI 2001/341, reg 78(3) (amended by SI 2006/752; SI 2006/2910); European Parliamentary Elections Regulations 2004, SI 2004/293, Sch 2 para 54(6) (as substituted: see note 3); National Assembly for Wales (Representation of the People) Order 2007, SI 2007/236, Sch 3 para 15(6). Where the constituency returning officer at a Welsh Assembly election issues another postal ballot paper (or, as the case may be, postal ballot papers) under Sch 3 para 15(6), the postal ballot paper which has been lost or not received must be cancelled and is of no effect: Sch 3 para 15(11).

     Specified provisions relating to the issue of postal ballot papers apply to the issue of replacement postal ballot papers, namely, in relation to a parliamentary or local government election, the Representation of the People (England and Wales) Regulations 2001, SI 2001/341, reg 72 (except reg 72(3)) and, subject to reg 78(6) (see note 15), regs 74–76, in relation to a European parliamentary election, the European Parliamentary Elections Regulations 2004, SI 2004/293, Sch 2 para 48 (except Sch 2 para 48(2)) and, subject to Sch 2 para 54(10) (see note 15), Sch 2 paras 50–52, and, in relation to a Welsh Assembly election, the National Assembly for Wales (Representation of the People) Order 2007, SI 2007/236, Sch 3 paras 9–12 (except Sch 3 para 9(3)) and, subject to Sch 3 para 15(10) (see note 15), Sch 3 para 13 (see PARA 411): see the Representation of the People (England and Wales) Regulations 2001, SI 2001/341, reg 78(5); the European Parliamentary Elections Regulations 2004, SI 2004/293, Sch 2 para 54(9) (as so substituted); and the National Assembly for Wales (Representation of the People) Order 2007, SI 2007/236, Sch 3 para 15(9).

15   Representation of the People (England and Wales) Regulations 2001, SI 2001/341, reg 78(3A) (as added: see note 10); European Parliamentary Elections Regulations 2004, SI 2004/293, Sch 2 para 54(7) (as substituted: see note 3); National Assembly for Wales (Representation of the People) Order 2007, SI 2007/236, Sch 3 para 15(7).

     Instead of delivering a replacement postal ballot paper in accordance with, in relation to a parliamentary or local government election, the Representation of the People (England and Wales) Regulations 2001, SI 2001/341, reg 76, or, in relation to a European parliamentary election, the European Parliamentary Elections Regulations 2004, SI 2004/293, Sch 2 para 52, or, in relation to a Welsh Assembly election, the National Assembly for Wales (Representation of the People) Order 2007, SI 2007/236, Sch 3 para 13, as the case may be (see PARA 411), the returning officer may hand a replacement postal ballot paper to a postal voter who applies in person by 5 pm on the day before the day of the poll (and he may only hand a replacement postal ballot paper to a postal voter who applies in person after 5 pm on the day before the day of the poll): Representation of the People (England and Wales) Regulations 2001, SI 2001/341, reg 78(6) (substituted by SI 2006/752); European Parliamentary Elections Regulations 2004, SI 2004/293, Sch 2 para 54(10) (Sch 2 as substituted (see note 3); Sch 2 para 54(10) amended by SI 2009/848); National Assembly for Wales (Representation of the People) Order 2007, SI 2007/236, Sch 3 para 15(10).

16   Representation of the People (England and Wales) Regulations 2001, SI 2001/341, reg 78(4); European Parliamentary Elections Regulations 2004, SI 2004/293, Sch 2 para 54(8) (as substituted: see note 3); National Assembly for Wales (Representation of the People) Order 2007, SI 2007/236, Sch 3 para 15(8).

17   As to the meaning of 'elector', in relation to a parliamentary or local government election, see PARA 95 note 2; in relation to a Welsh Assembly election, see PARA 110 note 6; and in relation to European parliamentary elections see PARA 111 note 4. As to the registers of electors see PARA 143 et seq. As to the number of an elector see PARA 145.

18   Representation of the People (England and Wales) Regulations 2001, SI 2001/341, reg 78(4)(a) (amended by SI 2006/2910); European Parliamentary Elections Regulations 2004, SI 2004/293, Sch 2 para 54(8)(a) (as substituted: see note 3); National Assembly for Wales (Representation of the People) Order 2007, SI 2007/236, Sch 3 para 15(8)(a). As to the meaning of 'anonymous entry', in relation to a register of electors, see PARA 148.

19   Representation of the People (England and Wales) Regulations 2001, SI 2001/341, reg 78(4)(b); European Parliamentary Elections Regulations 2004, SI 2004/293, Sch 2 para 54(8)(b) (as substituted: see note 3); National Assembly for Wales (Representation of the People) Order 2007, SI 2007/236, Sch 3 para 15(8)(b). In the case of a Welsh Assembly election, the number of the postal ballot paper which has been lost or not received must also be entered on the list: see Sch 3 para 15(8)(b).

20   As to applications to vote by post or by proxy (or both) see PARA 367 et seq.

21   Representation of the People (England and Wales) Regulations 2001, SI 2001/341, reg 78(4)(c) (substituted by SI 2006/752); European Parliamentary Elections Regulations 2004, SI 2004/293, Sch 2 para 54(8)(c) (as substituted: see note 3); National Assembly for Wales (Representation of the People) Order 2007, SI 2007/236, Sch 3 para 15(8)(c).

(B) Receipt of Postal Ballot Papers

416.   Persons entitled to be present at receipt of postal ballot papers. Without prejudice to the provisions of the Political Parties, Elections and Referendums Act 2000 that allow for Electoral Commission representatives and accredited observers to attend electoral proceedings and observe working practices[1], no person may be present at the proceedings on the receipt of postal ballot papers at an election[2] other than[3]:

(1)   the returning officer and his clerks[4];

(2)   a candidate[5];

(3)   an election agent[6] or any person appointed to attend in his place[7] (or, at a parish or community council election[8], any person appointed by the candidate to attend at those proceedings)[9]; and

(4)   any agents who have been duly appointed[10].

For the purposes of head (4) above, each candidate[11] (or each election agent[12], as the case may be) may appoint one or more agents to attend the proceedings on the receipt of postal ballot papers up to the number he may be authorised by the returning officer to appoint[13]. The number authorised, however, must be the same for each person standing nominated[14]. Written notice of the appointment stating the names and addresses of the persons appointed must be given to the returning officer by the person with the power of appointment[15] before the time fixed for the opening of the postal voters' ballot box[16].

If an agent dies or becomes incapable of acting, the candidate (or election agent, as the case may be)[17] may appoint another agent in his place and must forthwith give to the returning officer written notice of the name and address of the agent appointed[18]. Except in relation to a European parliamentary election, agents may be appointed and notice of appointment given to the returning officer by the candidate's election agent instead of by the candidate (that is, where candidates have the power of appointment)[19]. In relation to the receipt of postal ballot papers, references to agents are to be taken as references to agents whose appointments have been duly made and notified and, where a restriction on the number of appointees applies[20], who are within the number authorised by the returning officer[21].

A candidate[22] may himself do any act or thing which any agent, if appointed, would have been authorised to do, or may assist his agent in doing any such act or thing[23]. Where, in relation to the receipt of postal ballot papers, any act or thing is required or authorised to be done in the presence of the candidates or their agents, the non-attendance of any such persons or person at the time and place appointed for the purpose will not, if the act or thing is otherwise duly done, invalidate the act or thing done[24].

1　Ie without prejudice to the provisions of the Political Parties, Elections and Referendums Act 2000 ss 6A–6E (see PARA 53): see the Representation of the People (England and Wales) Regulations 2001, SI 2001/341, reg 68 (amended by SI 2006/2910); the European Parliamentary Elections Regulations 2004, SI 2004/293, Sch 2 para 44 (Sch 2 substituted by SI 2009/186); and the National Assembly for Wales (Representation of the People) Order 2007, SI 2007/236, Sch 3 para 6. As to the establishment and constitution of the Electoral Commission see PARA 34 et seq.

　　The Representation of the People (England and Wales) Regulations 2001, SI 2001/341, regs 68, 69 have effect for the purposes of local authority referendums, subject to the modifications specified, in relation to Wales, by the Local Authorities (Conduct of Referendums) (Wales) Regulations 2008, SI 2008/1848, reg 8(2), Sch 4 Table 5, and, in relation to England, by the Local Authorities (Conduct of Referendums) (England) Regulations 2012, SI 2012/323, regs 8(2), 11–13, Sch 4 Table 6 (see PARA 15 note 2).

2　Ie at a parliamentary election, a local government election (which includes any London Authority election and a local authority mayoral election), a Welsh Assembly constituency or regional election (whether the polls are taken separately or together) or a European parliamentary election. As to the meanings of 'Assembly election', 'constituency election' and 'regional election' see PARA 3 note 2. As to the meaning of 'parliamentary election' see PARA 9. As to the meanings of 'Authority election' and 'local government election' see PARA 11. As to elections in the City of London see PARA 33. As to European parliamentary elections see PARA 217 et seq. There is no provision for absent voting at a poll consequent on a parish meeting on a question involving appointment to office: see PARA 200 et seq. As to the meaning of 'postal ballot paper' see PARA 407 note 1.

　　Where the proceedings on the receipt of postal ballot papers at a European parliamentary election are taken together with the proceedings for a relevant election or referendum, persons entitled to be present at the proceedings for the relevant election or referendum may be present at the proceedings on the receipt of postal ballot papers at a European parliamentary election: European Parliamentary Elections Regulations 2004, SI 2004/293, Sch 2 para 44(f) (as substituted: see note 1). For these purposes, 'relevant election or referendum' means a parliamentary election, a local government election (including a mayoral election), an election of a police and crime commissioner under the Police Reform and Social Responsibility Act 2011 Pt 1 Ch 6 (ss 50–76, Schs 9, 10) (Police and Crime Commissioners: elections and vacancies: see POLICE AND INVESTIGATORY POWERS vol 84 (2013) PARA 62 et seq) or a referendum, in relation to England, conducted under the Local Authorities (Conduct of Referendums) (England) Regulations 2012, SI 2012/323 (see PARA 15), the poll at which is taken together with the poll at a European parliamentary election: see the European Parliamentary Elections Regulations 2004, SI 2004/293, Sch 2 para 40(1) (Sch 2 as so substituted; definition of 'relevant election or referendum' in Sch 2 para 40(1) amended by SI 2012/1917); Interpretation Act 1978 s 17(2).

3　Representation of the People (England and Wales) Regulations 2001, SI 2001/341, reg 68 (as amended: see note 1); European Parliamentary Elections Regulations 2004, SI 2004/293, Sch 2 para 44 (as substituted: see note 1); National Assembly for Wales (Representation of the People) Order 2007, SI 2007/236, Sch 3 para 6.

4　Representation of the People (England and Wales) Regulations 2001, SI 2001/341, reg 68(a); European Parliamentary Elections Regulations 2004, SI 2004/293, Sch 2 para 44(a) (as substituted: see note 1); National Assembly for Wales (Representation of the People) Order 2007, SI 2007/236, Sch 3 para 6(1)(a). As to returning officers generally see PARA 350 et seq. At a European parliamentary election, the returning officer referred to in the text is the local returning officer (see PARA 360): see the European Parliamentary Elections Regulations 2004,

SI 2004/293, Sch 2 paras 44(a), 45(1), (2), (4), (5) (as so substituted). At a Welsh Assembly election, the constituency returning officer is the returning officer referred to in the text for most purposes: see the National Assembly for Wales (Representation of the People) Order 2007, SI 2007/236, Sch 3 para 6(1)–(6); but see also PARA 406 note 1. However, the regional returning officer may be present at the proceedings on the receipt of postal ballot papers in the case of a regional election: Sch 3 para 6(1)(b). See also PARA 406 note 1. As to the meanings of 'constituency returning officer' and 'regional returning officer' see PARA 18 note 2.

5   Representation of the People (England and Wales) Regulations 2001, SI 2001/341, reg 68(b); European Parliamentary Elections Regulations 2004, SI 2004/293, Sch 2 para 44(b) (as substituted: see note 1); National Assembly for Wales (Representation of the People) Order 2007, SI 2007/236, Sch 3 para 6(1)(c). As to the meaning of 'candidate' generally see PARA 230.

6   As to the appointment of election agents see PARA 231 et seq. At a European parliamentary election, a sub-agent also may be present at proceedings on the receipt of postal ballot papers: European Parliamentary Elections Regulations 2004, SI 2004/293, Sch 2 para 44(d) (as substituted: see note 1). As to the nomination of sub-agents for European parliamentary elections see PARA 241.

7   Representation of the People (England and Wales) Regulations 2001, SI 2001/341, reg 68(c); European Parliamentary Elections Regulations 2004, SI 2004/293, Sch 2 para 44(c) (as substituted: see note 1); National Assembly for Wales (Representation of the People) Order 2007, SI 2007/236, Sch 3 para 6(1)(d). At a European parliamentary election, the appointment is made by the election agent (see the European Parliamentary Elections Regulations 2004, SI 2004/293, Sch 2 para 44(c) (as so substituted)); but at a parliamentary election the candidate makes this appointment (see the Representation of the People (England and Wales) Regulations 2001, SI 2001/341, reg 68(c)). At a Welsh Assembly election, the appointment is made by a candidate, in the case of a constituency election (see the National Assembly for Wales (Representation of the People) Order 2007, SI 2007/236, Sch 3 para 6(1)(d)(i)), but, in the case of a regional election, it is made by an individual candidate (see Sch 3 para 6(1)(d)(ii)) or by the election agent of a registered political party standing nominated (or by the registered nominating officer of that party) (see Sch 3 para 6(1)(d)(iii)). As to the meanings of 'candidate' and 'individual candidate' at a Welsh Assembly election see PARA 230 note 19; and as to the meaning of 'registered political party' in this context see PARA 230 note 23. As to the registered nominating officer of a party see PARA 253.

In relation to the receipt of postal ballot papers, the expression 'agent' includes the election agent and a person appointed to attend in the election agent's place: Representation of the People (England and Wales) Regulations 2001, SI 2001/341, reg 64; European Parliamentary Elections Regulations 2004, SI 2004/293, Sch 2 para 40(1) (as so substituted); National Assembly for Wales (Representation of the People) Order 2007, SI 2007/236, Sch 3 para 1.

8   There is no requirement for election agents to be appointed for the purposes of parish or community council elections: see PARa 231 note 3. As to the election of councillors for parish or community councils see PARA 200 et seq.

9   See the Representation of the People (England and Wales) Regulations 2001, SI 2001/341, reg 68(c).

10 Representation of the People (England and Wales) Regulations 2001, SI 2001/341, reg 68(d); European Parliamentary Elections Regulations 2004, SI 2004/293, Sch 2 para 44(e) (as substituted: see note 1); National Assembly for Wales (Representation of the People) Order 2007, SI 2007/236, Sch 3 para 6(1)(e). As to the appointment of such agents see the text and notes 11–24.

11 At a European parliamentary election, only agents or sub-agents of candidates may appoint: see notes 7, 12. At a Welsh Assembly election, the reference in the text is to each candidate in the case of a constituency election (see the National Assembly for Wales (Representation of the People) Order 2007, SI 2007/236, Sch 3 para 6(2)(a)), and to each individual candidate in the case of a regional election (see Sch 3 para 6(2)(b)).

12 At a European parliamentary election, the election agent (or sub-agent) of each registered party standing nominated, or the election agent (or sub-agent) of each individual candidate may make the appointment: see the European Parliamentary Elections Regulations 2004, SI 2004/293, Sch 2 para 45(1) (as substituted: see note 1). As to the meaning of 'registered party' in the context of a European parliamentary election see PARA 230 note 29; and as to the meaning of 'individual candidate' see PARA 230 note 32. In the case of a Welsh Assembly regional election, each election agent for a registered political party standing nominated may make the appointment: see the National Assembly for Wales (Representation of the People) Order 2007, SI 2007/236, Sch 3 para 6(2)(b).

13 Representation of the People (England and Wales) Regulations 2001, SI 2001/341, reg 69(1); European Parliamentary Elections Regulations 2004, SI 2004/293, Sch 2 para 45(1) (as substituted: see note 1); National Assembly for Wales (Representation of the People) Order 2007, SI 2007/236, Sch 3 para 6(2).

14 Representation of the People (England and Wales) Regulations 2001, SI 2001/341, reg 69(1); European Parliamentary Elections Regulations 2004, SI 2004/293, Sch 2 para 45(1) (as substituted: see note 1); National Assembly for Wales (Representation of the People) Order 2007, SI 2007/236, Sch 3 para 6(2). At a European parliamentary election, the number authorised as mentioned in the text must the same for each individual candidate or for each registered party standing nominated: see the European Parliamentary Elections Regulations 2004, SI 2004/293, Sch 2 para 45(1) (as so substituted). At a Welsh Assembly regional election, the number authorised must the same in the case of each individual candidate and in the case of each election agent for a registered political party standing nominated: see the National Assembly for Wales (Representation of the People) Order 2007, SI 2007/236, Sch 3 para 6(2).

15 Ie the candidate (see note 11) or the election agent (see note 12) or, in the case of a European parliamentary election only, the sub-agent (see note 12): see the Representation of the People (England and Wales) Regulations 2001, SI 2001/341, reg 69(2); the European Parliamentary Elections Regulations 2004, SI 2004/293, Sch 2 para 45(2) (as substituted: see note 1); and the National Assembly for Wales (Representation of the People) Order 2007, SI 2007/236, Sch 3 para 6(3).

16 Representation of the People (England and Wales) Regulations 2001, SI 2001/341, reg 69(2); European Parliamentary Elections Regulations 2004, SI 2004/293, Sch 2 para 45(2) (as substituted: see note 1); National Assembly for Wales (Representation of the People) Order 2007, SI 2007/236, Sch 3 para 6(3). Where postal ballot papers for more than one election are issued together (see PARA 20), the returning officer to whom notice must be given as mentioned in the text is the returning officer who issues the postal ballot papers: see the Representation of the People (England and Wales) Regulations 2001, SI 2001/341, reg 69(3); the European Parliamentary Elections Regulations 2004, SI 2004/293, Sch 2 para 45(3) (as so substituted); and the National Assembly for Wales (Representation of the People) Order 2007, SI 2007/236, Sch 3 para 6(4). 'Postal voters' ballot box' means the ballot box referred to, in relation to a parliamentary or local government election, in the Representation of the People (England and Wales) Regulations 2001, SI 2001/341, reg 81(1)(a), or, in relation to a European parliamentary election, the European Parliamentary Elections Regulations 2004, SI 2004/293, Sch 2 para 57(1)(a), or, in relation to a Welsh Assembly election, the National Assembly for Wales (Representation of the People) Order 2007, SI 2007/236, Sch 3 para 17(1)(a), as the case may be (see PARA 417): Representation of the People (England and Wales) Regulations 2001, SI 2001/341, reg 64; European Parliamentary Elections Regulations 2004, SI 2004/293, Sch 2 para 40(1) (as so substituted); National Assembly for Wales (Representation of the People) Order 2007, SI 2007/236, Sch 3 para 1. As to the opening of the postal voters' ballot boxes see PARA 420.

17 At a Welsh Assembly or European parliamentary election, the reference is to the candidate or election agent of a registered party: see the European Parliamentary Elections Regulations 2004, SI 2004/293, Sch 2 para 45(4) (as substituted: see note 1); and the National Assembly for Wales (Representation of the People) Order 2007, SI 2007/236, Sch 3 para 6(5).

18 Representation of the People (England and Wales) Regulations 2001, SI 2001/341, reg 69(4); European Parliamentary Elections Regulations 2004, SI 2004/293, Sch 2 para 45(4) (as substituted: see note 1); National Assembly for Wales (Representation of the People) Order 2007, SI 2007/236, Sch 3 para 6(5). Where postal ballot papers for more than one election are issued together (see PARA 20), the returning officer to whom notice must be given as mentioned in the text is the returning officer who issues the postal ballot papers: see the Representation of the People (England and Wales) Regulations 2001, SI 2001/341, reg 69(3); the European Parliamentary Elections Regulations 2004, SI 2004/293, Sch 2 para 45(3) (as so substituted); and the National Assembly for Wales (Representation of the People) Order 2007, SI 2007/236, Sch 3 para 6(4).

19 Representation of the People (England and Wales) Regulations 2001, SI 2001/341, reg 69(5); National Assembly for Wales (Representation of the People) Order 2007, SI 2007/236, Sch 3 para 6(6). Where postal ballot papers for more than one election are issued together (see PARA 20), the returning officer to whom notice must be given as mentioned in the text is the returning officer who issues the postal ballot papers: see the Representation of the People (England and Wales) Regulations 2001, SI 2001/341, reg 69(3); and the National Assembly for Wales (Representation of the People) Order 2007, SI 2007/236, Sch 3 para 6(4).

20 See the text and notes 11–14.

21 Representation of the People (England and Wales) Regulations 2001, SI 2001/341, reg 69(6); European Parliamentary Elections Regulations 2004, SI 2004/293, Sch 2 para 45(5) (as substituted: see note 1); National Assembly for Wales (Representation of the People) Order 2007, SI 2007/236, Sch 3 para 6(7).

22 Ie, in the case of a Welsh Assembly election, any of the following persons:
    (1)   a candidate in a constituency election (National Assembly for Wales (Representation of the People) Order 2007, SI 2007/236, Sch 3 para 6(8)(a));
    (2)   an individual candidate in a regional election (Sch 3 para 6(8)(b)); or
    (3)   the election agent of a registered political party standing nominated (Sch 3 para 6(8)(c)).

23 Representation of the People (England and Wales) Regulations 2001, SI 2001/341, reg 69(7); European Parliamentary Elections Regulations 2004, SI 2004/293, Sch 2 para 45(6) (as substituted: see note 1); National Assembly for Wales (Representation of the People) Order 2007, SI 2007/236, Sch 3 para 6(8). At a European parliamentary election, the reference is to any agent of a candidate or his party: see the European Parliamentary Elections Regulations 2004, SI 2004/293, Sch 2 para 45(6) (as so substituted). At a Welsh Assembly election, the reference is to any agent of a candidate or of the registered political party on whose list he is a candidate: see the National Assembly for Wales (Representation of the People) Order 2007, SI 2007/236, Sch 3 para 6(8). As to the meanings of 'party list' and 'party list candidate' in this context see PARA 230 note 23.

24 Representation of the People (England and Wales) Regulations 2001, SI 2001/341, reg 69(8); European Parliamentary Elections Regulations 2004, SI 2004/293, Sch 2 para 45(7) (as substituted: see note 1); National Assembly for Wales (Representation of the People) Order 2007, SI 2007/236, Sch 3 para 6(9).

417. Returning officer's duty to provide postal ballot boxes, receptacles, and to ensure security and secrecy. The returning officer at an election[1] must provide a separate ballot box for the reception of:
    (1)   the covering envelopes[2] when returned by the postal voters[3] (the 'postal voters' ballot box')[4]; and
    (2)   postal ballot papers[5] (the 'postal ballot box')[6].

Each such ballot box must be marked 'postal voters' ballot box' or 'postal ballot box', as the case may be, and with the name of the constituency[7], or electoral area (or areas)[8], or local counting area[9], for which the election (or elections) are held[10]. The postal ballot box must be shown to the agents present on the occasion of opening the first postal voters' ballot box[11] as being empty[12], and it must then be locked by the returning officer (if it has a lock) and sealed with his seal, and then with the seals of such of the agents present who wish to affix their seals, in such manner as to prevent the box being opened without breaking the seal[13].

The returning officer also must provide the following receptacles[14]:
    (a)   the receptacle for rejected votes[15];
    (b)   the receptacle for postal voting statements[16];
    (c)   the receptacle for ballot paper envelopes[17];
    (d)   the receptacle for rejected ballot paper envelopes[18];
    (e)   the receptacle for rejected votes (verification procedure)[19]; and
    (f)   the receptacle for postal voting statements (verification procedure)[20].

The returning officer must take proper precautions for the safe custody of every such ballot box and receptacle[21]; and he must make such arrangements as he thinks fit to ensure that every person attending the proceedings in connection with the receipt of postal ballot papers[22] has been given a copy in writing of the statutory provisions relating to the requirement of secrecy that apply to those proceedings[23].

1 Ie at a parliamentary election, a local government election (which includes any London Authority election and a local authority mayoral election), a Welsh Assembly constituency or regional election (whether the polls are taken separately or together) or a European

parliamentary election. As to the meanings of 'Assembly election', 'constituency election' and 'regional election' see PARA 3 note 2. As to the meaning of 'parliamentary election' see PARA 9. As to the meanings of 'Authority election' and 'local government election' see PARA 11. As to elections in the City of London see PARA 33. As to European parliamentary elections see PARA 217 et seq. There is no provision for absent voting at a poll consequent on a parish meeting on a question involving appointment to office: see PARA 200 et seq.

As to returning officers generally see PARA 350 et seq. At a European parliamentary election, the returning officer referred to in the text is the local returning officer (see PARA 360): see the European Parliamentary Elections Regulations 2004, SI 2004/293, Sch 2 para 57(1), (4)–(6) (Sch 2 substituted by SI 2009/186). At a Welsh Assembly election, the constituency returning officer is the returning officer referred to in the text: see the National Assembly for Wales (Representation of the People) Order 2007, SI 2007/236, Sch 3 para 17(1), (4)–(6); but see also PARA 406 note 1. As to the meaning of 'constituency returning officer' for the purposes of Welsh Assembly elections see PARA 18 note 2.

2   As to the meaning of 'covering envelope' see PARA 410.

3   As to the meaning of 'postal voter' see PARA 407 note 1.

4   Representation of the People (England and Wales) Regulations 2001, SI 2001/341, reg 81(1)(a); European Parliamentary Elections Regulations 2004, SI 2004/293, Sch 2 para 57(1)(a) (as substituted: see note 1); National Assembly for Wales (Representation of the People) Order 2007, SI 2007/236, Sch 3 para 17(1)(a). As to the meaning of 'postal voters' ballot box' see PARA 416 note 16.

    The Representation of the People (England and Wales) Regulations 2001, SI 2001/341, regs 70, 81 have effect for the purposes of local authority referendums, subject to the modifications specified, in relation to Wales, by the Local Authorities (Conduct of Referendums) (Wales) Regulations 2008, SI 2008/1848, reg 8(2), Sch 4 Table 5, and, in relation to England, by the Local Authorities (Conduct of Referendums) (England) Regulations 2012, SI 2012/323, regs 8(2), 11–13, Sch 4 Table 6 (see PARA 15 note 2).

5   As to the meaning of 'postal ballot paper' see PARA 407 note 1. As to the issue of postal ballot papers see PARA 406 et seq.

6   Representation of the People (England and Wales) Regulations 2001, SI 2001/341, reg 81(1)(b); European Parliamentary Elections Regulations 2004, SI 2004/293, Sch 2 para 57(1)(b) (as substituted: see note 1); National Assembly for Wales (Representation of the People) Order 2007, SI 2007/236, Sch 3 para 17(1)(b).

7   As to the meaning of 'Assembly constituency' in relation to a Welsh Assembly election see PARA 3 note 2; and as to the meaning of 'constituency' in relation to a parliamentary election see PARA 9.

8   As to the meaning of 'electoral area' see PARA 11. Where a poll at an election is combined with a referendum (see PARA 31), the ballot box may be marked with the name of the voting area (meaning the area in which a referendum is held: see PARA 580 note 2). At a Welsh Assembly election, the name of the electoral region may be used: see the National Assembly for Wales (Representation of the People) Order 2007, SI 2007/236, Sch 3 para 17(2). As to the meaning of 'Assembly electoral region' see PARA 3 note 2.

9   As to the meaning of 'local counting area' see PARA 139 note 1.

10   Representation of the People (England and Wales) Regulations 2001, SI 2001/341, reg 81(2); European Parliamentary Elections Regulations 2004, SI 2004/293, Sch 2 para 57(2) (as substituted: see note 1); National Assembly for Wales (Representation of the People) Order 2007, SI 2007/236, Sch 3 para 17(2).

11   As to the appointment of agents to be present at the receipt of postal ballot papers see PARA 416.

12   Representation of the People (England and Wales) Regulations 2001, SI 2001/341, reg 81(3); European Parliamentary Elections Regulations 2004, SI 2004/293, Sch 2 para 57(3) (as substituted: see note 1); National Assembly for Wales (Representation of the People) Order 2007, SI 2007/236, Sch 3 para 17(3).

13   Representation of the People (England and Wales) Regulations 2001, SI 2001/341, reg 81(4); European Parliamentary Elections Regulations 2004, SI 2004/293, Sch 2 para 57(4) (as substituted: see note 1); National Assembly for Wales (Representation of the People) Order 2007, SI 2007/236, Sch 3 para 17(4). *Quaere* whether the breaking of any agent's seal affects the integrity of the box in any way if the returning officer's seal remains intact.

14   Representation of the People (England and Wales) Regulations 2001, SI 2001/341, reg 81(5); European Parliamentary Elections Regulations 2004, SI 2004/293, Sch 2 para 57(5) (as substituted: see note 1); National Assembly for Wales (Representation of the People) Order 2007, SI 2007/236, Sch 3 para 17(5). The 'receptacle for ballot paper envelopes' (see head (c) in the text), and other references to specified receptacles, means the receptacles referred to in heads (a) to (f) in the text: Representation of the People (England and Wales)

Regulations 2001, SI 2001/341, reg 64; European Parliamentary Elections Regulations 2004, SI 2004/293, Sch 2 para 40(1) (as so substituted); National Assembly for Wales (Representation of the People) Order 2007, SI 2007/236, Sch 3 para 1.

15 Representation of the People (England and Wales) Regulations 2001, SI 2001/341, reg 81(5)(a); European Parliamentary Elections Regulations 2004, SI 2004/293, Sch 2 para 57(5)(a) (as substituted: see note 1); National Assembly for Wales (Representation of the People) Order 2007, SI 2007/236, Sch 3 para 17(5)(a). As to the procedure in relation to postal voting see PARA 421.

16 Representation of the People (England and Wales) Regulations 2001, SI 2001/341, reg 81(5)(b) (reg 81(5)(b), (c) amended, reg 81(5)(e), (f) added, by SI 2006/2910); European Parliamentary Elections Regulations 2004, SI 2004/293, Sch 2 para 57(5)(b) (as substituted: see note 1); National Assembly for Wales (Representation of the People) Order 2007, SI 2007/236, Sch 3 para 17(5)(b). As to the postal voting statement see PARA 406.

17 Representation of the People (England and Wales) Regulations 2001, SI 2001/341, reg 81(5)(c) (as amended: see note 16); European Parliamentary Elections Regulations 2004, SI 2004/293, Sch 2 para 57(5)(c) (as substituted: see note 1); National Assembly for Wales (Representation of the People) Order 2007, SI 2007/236, Sch 3 para 17(5)(c). As to the ballot paper envelope and the covering envelope see PARA 410.

18 Representation of the People (England and Wales) Regulations 2001, SI 2001/341, reg 81(5)(d); European Parliamentary Elections Regulations 2004, SI 2004/293, Sch 2 para 57(5)(d) (as substituted: see note 1); National Assembly for Wales (Representation of the People) Order 2007, SI 2007/236, Sch 3 para 17(5)(d).

19 Representation of the People (England and Wales) Regulations 2001, SI 2001/341, reg 81(5)(e) (as added: see note 16); European Parliamentary Elections Regulations 2004, SI 2004/293, Sch 2 para 57(5)(e) (as substituted: see note 1); National Assembly for Wales (Representation of the People) Order 2007, SI 2007/236, Sch 3 para 17(5)(e). As to the verification procedure see PARA 421.

20 Representation of the People (England and Wales) Regulations 2001, SI 2001/341, reg 81(5)(f) (as added: see note 16); European Parliamentary Elections Regulations 2004, SI 2004/293, Sch 2 para 57(5)(f) (as substituted: see note 1); National Assembly for Wales (Representation of the People) Order 2007, SI 2007/236, Sch 3 para 17(5)(f).

21 Representation of the People (England and Wales) Regulations 2001, SI 2001/341, reg 81(6); European Parliamentary Elections Regulations 2004, SI 2004/293, Sch 2 para 57(6) (as substituted: see note 1); National Assembly for Wales (Representation of the People) Order 2007, SI 2007/236, Sch 3 para 17(6).

22 As to the persons entitled to be present at the receipt of postal ballot papers see PARA 416.

23 Representation of the People (England and Wales) Regulations 2001, SI 2001/341, reg 70; European Parliamentary Elections Regulations 2004, SI 2004/293, Sch 2 para 46 (as substituted: see note 1); National Assembly for Wales (Representation of the People) Order 2007, SI 2007/236, Sch 3 para 7. The text refers to the requirement of secrecy set out in the Representation of the People Act 1983 s 66(4), (6), in relation to a parliamentary election, or, in relation to European parliamentary elections, in the European Parliamentary Elections Regulations 2004, SI 2004/293, reg 29(5), (7). or, in relation to Welsh Assembly elections, in the National Assembly for Wales (Representation of the People) Order 2007, SI 2007/236, art 35(4), (6) (see PARA 742): see the Representation of the People (England and Wales) Regulations 2001, SI 2001/341, reg 70; the European Parliamentary Elections Regulations 2004, SI 2004/293, Sch 2 para 46 (as so substituted); and the National Assembly for Wales (Representation of the People) Order 2007, SI 2007/236, Sch 3 para 7.

418. Return of postal ballot papers, etc to returning officer. A postal ballot paper or postal voting statement[1] is not taken to be duly returned at an election[2] unless it is returned in the prescribed manner and reaches either the returning officer[3] or a polling station in the constituency[4] or electoral area or areas[5] or local counting area[6] in question (as the case may be) before the close of the poll[7].

Where a covering envelope[8] (or an envelope which is stated to include a postal vote) is received by a returning officer (whether by hand or by post) before the close of the poll, he must, immediately on receipt, place it unopened in a postal voters' ballot box[9]. Where an envelope, other than a covering envelope issued by the returning officer, has been opened, and where it contains a ballot paper envelope[10], postal voting statement, or ballot paper, the first-mentioned envelope, together with its contents, also must be placed in a postal voters' ballot box[11].

Where any postal ballot paper or postal voting statement has been returned to a polling station, the presiding officer[12] of that station must deliver it, or cause it to be delivered, to the returning officer in the same manner and at the same time as he delivers, or causes to be delivered, the packets of ballot papers and other documents which he is required to prepare on the close of poll at his polling station[13]. However, the returning officer himself may collect, or cause to be collected, any such postal ballot paper or postal voting statement which has been returned to a polling station (and which the presiding officer of a polling station would otherwise be required to deliver or cause to be delivered to him)[14]; and, where the returning officer collects, or causes to be collected, any such postal ballot paper or postal voting statement in this way, the presiding officer must first make it (or them) up into a packet (or packets) sealed with his own seal, and the seals of such polling agents[15] as are present and desire to affix their seals[16].

Where a postal vote has been returned in respect of a person who is entered on the postal voters list[17], or where a proxy postal vote[18] has been returned in respect of a proxy who is entered on the proxy postal voters list[19], the returning officer must mark the list in the prescribed manner[20].

1　As to the meaning of 'postal ballot paper' see PARA 407 note 1. As to the issue of postal ballot papers and as to the postal voting statement see PARA 406 et seq.

2　Ie at a parliamentary election, a local government election (which includes any London Authority election and a local authority mayoral election), a Welsh Assembly constituency or regional election (whether the polls are taken separately or together) or a European parliamentary election. As to the meanings of 'Assembly election', 'constituency election' and 'regional election' see PARA 3 note 2. As to the meaning of 'parliamentary election' see PARA 9. As to the meanings of 'Authority election' and 'local government election' see PARA 11. As to elections in the City of London see PARA 33. As to European parliamentary elections see PARA 217 et seq. There is no provision for absent voting at a poll consequent on a parish meeting on a question involving appointment to office: see PARA 200 et seq.

3　As to returning officers generally see PARA 350 et seq. At a European parliamentary election, the returning officer referred to in the text is the local returning officer (see PARA 360): see the European Parliamentary Elections Regulations 2004, SI 2004/293, Sch 1 para 35(1), Sch 2 paras 55(2)–(4), 58(1), (2) (Sch 2 substituted by SI 2009/186). At a Welsh Assembly election, the constituency returning officer is the returning officer referred to in the text: see the National Assembly for Wales (Representation of the People) Order 2007, SI 2007/236, Sch 3 para 18(1), (2)–(6), Sch 5 para 55(7)–(9); but see also PARA 406 note 1. As to the meaning of 'constituency returning officer' for the purposes of Welsh Assembly elections see PARA 18 note 2.

4　As to the meaning of 'Assembly constituency' in relation to a Welsh Assembly election see PARA 3 note 2; and as to the meaning of 'constituency' in relation to a parliamentary election see PARA 9. As to the provision and allotment of polling stations see PARA 390.

5　As to the meaning of 'electoral area' see PARA 11.

6　As to the meaning of 'local counting area' see PARA 139 note 1.

7　See PARA 424 et seq.

8　As to the meaning of 'covering envelope' see PARA 410.

9　Representation of the People (England and Wales) Regulations 2001, SI 2001/341, reg 82(1); European Parliamentary Elections Regulations 2004, SI 2004/293, Sch 2 para 58(1) (as substituted: see note 3); National Assembly for Wales (Representation of the People) Order 2007, SI 2007/236, Sch 3 para 18(1). As to the meaning of 'postal voters' ballot box' see PARA 416 note 16.

　　The Representation of the People (England and Wales) Regulations 2001, SI 2001/341, regs 79, 82, have effect for the purposes of local authority referendums, subject to the modifications specified, in relation to Wales, by the Local Authorities (Conduct of Referendums) (Wales) Regulations 2008, SI 2008/1848, reg 8(2), Sch 4 Table 5, and, in relation to England, by the Local Authorities (Conduct of Referendums) (England) Regulations 2012, SI 2012/323, regs 8(2), 11–13, Sch 4 Table 6 (see PARA 15 note 2).

10　As to the meaning of 'ballot paper envelope' see PARA 410.

11 Representation of the People (England and Wales) Regulations 2001, SI 2001/341, reg 82(2) (amended by SI 2006/2910); European Parliamentary Elections Regulations 2004, SI 2004/293, Sch 2 para 58(2) (as substituted: see note 3); National Assembly for Wales (Representation of the People) Order 2007, SI 2007/236, Sch 3 para 18(2).

12 As to the appointment of presiding officers and their clerks see PARA 393.

13 Representation of the People (England and Wales) Regulations 2001, SI 2001/341, reg 79(3) (amended by SI 2006/752; SI 2006/2910); European Parliamentary Elections Regulations 2004, SI 2004/293, Sch 2 para 55(2) (as substituted: see note 3); National Assembly for Wales (Representation of the People) Order 2007, SI 2007/236, Sch 5 para 55(7). As to the procedure on the close of poll at a polling station see PARA 405.

14 Representation of the People (England and Wales) Regulations 2001, SI 2001/341, reg 79(4) (reg 79(4), (5) added by SI 2006/752, amended by SI 2006/2910); European Parliamentary Elections Regulations 2004, SI 2004/293, Sch 2 para 55(3) (as substituted: see note 3); National Assembly for Wales (Representation of the People) Order 2003, Sch 5 para 55(8).

15 As to the appointment of polling agents to attend at polling stations for the purpose of detecting personation see PARA 394.

16 Representation of the People (England and Wales) Regulations 2001, SI 2001/341, reg 79(5) (as added and amended: see note 14); European Parliamentary Elections Regulations 2004, SI 2004/293, Sch 2 para 55(4) (as substituted: see note 3); National Assembly for Wales (Representation of the People) Order 2007, SI 2007/236, Sch 5 para 55(9).

17 Representation of the People Act 1983 Sch 1 r 31A(1)(a) (Sch 1 r 31A added by the Electoral Administration Act 2006 s 45(1), (2)); European Parliamentary Elections Regulations 2004, SI 2004/293, Sch 1 para 35(1)(a) (as substituted: see note 3); Local Elections (Principal Areas) (England and Wales) Rules 2006, SI 2006/3304, Sch 2 r 29(1)(a); Local Elections (Parishes and Communities) (England and Wales) Rules 2006, SI 2006/3305, Sch 2 r 29(1)(a); National Assembly for Wales (Representation of the People) Order 2007, SI 2007/236, Sch 5 para 40(1)(a); Local Authorities (Mayoral Elections) (England and Wales) Regulations 2007, SI 2007/1024, Sch 1 r 31(1)(a); Greater London Authority Elections Rules 2007, SI 2007/3541, Sch 1 r 32(1)(a), Sch 2 r 33(1)(a), Sch 3 r 32(1)(a). As to the postal voters list see PARA 373.

The Representation of the People Act 1983 Sch 1 r 45(1B), in relation to a parliamentary election, the Local Elections (Principal Areas) (England and Wales) Rules 2006, SI 2006/3304, Sch 2 r 45(3), the Local Elections (Parishes and Communities) (England and Wales) Rules 2006, SI 2006/3305, Sch 2 r 45(3), the Local Authorities (Mayoral Elections) (England and Wales) Regulations 2007, SI 2007/1024, Sch 1 r 47(4), and the Greater London Authority Elections Rules 2007, SI 2007/3541, Sch 1 r 49(2), Sch 2 r 50(2), Sch 3 r 49(2), in relation to a local government election (see PARAS 425, 436, 444, 451), the European Parliamentary Elections Regulations 2004, SI 2004/293, Sch 1 para 51(2), in relation to a European parliamentary election (see PARA 466), and the National Assembly for Wales (Representation of the People) Order 2007, SI 2007/236, Sch 5 para 55(6), in relation to a Welsh Assembly election (see PARA 459 note 12), do not apply for the purpose of determining whether, for these purposes, a postal vote or a proxy postal vote is returned: Representation of the People Act 1983 Sch 1 r 31A(3) (as so added); European Parliamentary Elections Regulations 2004, SI 2004/293, Sch 1 para 35(2) (as so substituted); Local Elections (Principal Areas) (England and Wales) Rules 2006, SI 2006/3304, Sch 2 r 29(2); Local Elections (Parishes and Communities) (England and Wales) Rules 2006, SI 2006/3305, Sch 2 r 29(2); National Assembly for Wales (Representation of the People) Order 2007, SI 2007/236, Sch 5 para 40(2); Local Authorities (Mayoral Elections) (England and Wales) Regulations 2007, SI 2007/1024, Sch 1 r 31(2); Greater London Authority Elections Rules 2007, SI 2007/3541, Sch 1 r 32(2), Sch 2 r 33(2), Sch 3 r 32(2). However, regulations made under the Representation of the People Act 1983 may prescribe the circumstances in which a postal vote is or is not to be treated as having been returned, in the case of a parliamentary or local government election: Sch 1 r 31A(2) (as so added). As to the making of regulations under the Representation of the People Act 1983 generally see PARA 28 note 16. As to the regulations so prescribed see the Representation of the People (England and Wales) Regulations 2001, SI 2001/341, reg 79(1), (2); and PARA 425 note 8.

18 As to applications to vote by proxy see PARA 367 et seq.

19 Representation of the People Act 1983 Sch 1 r 31A(1)(b) (as added: see note 17); European Parliamentary Elections Regulations 2004, SI 2004/293, Sch 1 para 35(1)(b) (as substituted: see note 3); Local Elections (Principal Areas) (England and Wales) Rules 2006, SI 2006/3304, Sch 2 r 29(1)(b); Local Elections (Parishes and Communities) (England and Wales) Rules 2006, SI 2006/3305, Sch 2 r 29(1)(b); National Assembly for Wales (Representation of the People) Order 2007, SI 2007/236, Sch 5 para 40(1)(b); Local Authorities (Mayoral Elections) (England and Wales) Regulations 2007, SI 2007/1024, Sch 1 r 31(1)(b); Greater London Authority

Elections Rules 2007, SI 2007/3541, Sch 1 r 32(1)(b), Sch 2 r 33(1)(b), Sch 3 r 32(1)(b). For the purposes of a parliamentary election, regulations may prescribe the circumstances in which a proxy postal vote is or is not to be treated as having been returned: see the Representation of the People Act 1983 Sch 1 r 31A(2) (as so added); and see note 17. As to the proxy postal voters list see PARA 381.

20 Representation of the People Act 1983 Sch 1 r 31A(1) (as added: see note 17); European Parliamentary Elections Regulations 2004, SI 2004/293, Sch 1 para 35(1) (as substituted: see note 3); Local Elections (Principal Areas) (England and Wales) Rules 2006, SI 2006/3304, Sch 2 r 29(1); Local Elections (Parishes and Communities) (England and Wales) Rules 2006, SI 2006/3305, Sch 2 r 29(1); National Assembly for Wales (Representation of the People) Order 2007, SI 2007/236, Sch 5 para 40(1); Local Authorities (Mayoral Elections) (England and Wales) Regulations 2007, SI 2007/1024, Sch 1 r 31(1); Greater London Authority Elections Rules 2007, SI 2007/3541, Sch 1 r 32(1), Sch 2 r 33(1), Sch 3 r 32(1). The returning officer referred to in the text is, for the purposes of any London Authority election, the constituency returning officer: see Sch 1 r 32(1), Sch 2 r 33(1), Sch 3 r 32(1). As to the meaning of the 'constituency returning officer' in this context see PARA 211 note 9. For the purposes of a parliamentary or local government election, 'prescribed' means prescribed by regulations made under the Representation of the People Act 1983: see s 202(1); the Local Elections (Principal Areas) (England and Wales) Rules 2006, SI 2006/3304, Sch 2 r 29(1); the Local Elections (Parishes and Communities) (England and Wales) Rules 2006, SI 2006/3305, Sch 2 r 29(1); the Local Authorities (Mayoral Elections) (England and Wales) Regulations 2007, SI 2007/1024, Sch 1 r 31(1); and the Greater London Authority Elections Rules 2007, SI 2007/3541, Sch 1 r 32(1), Sch 2 r 33(1), Sch 3 r 32(1). The list referred to in the text must be marked in the manner prescribed:

(1)   in the case of a parliamentary or local government election, by the Representation of the People (England and Wales) Regulations 2001, SI 2001/341, reg 84 (see PARA 421);

(2)   in the case of a European parliamentary election, by the European Parliamentary Elections Regulations 2004, SI 2004/293, Sch 2 para 60 (see PARA 421) (see Sch 1 para 35(1) (as so substituted).

In relation to a Welsh Assembly election, it is specified merely that the constituency returning officer must mark the appropriate list accordingly: see Sch 5 para 40(1).

419.   Notice of opening of postal voters' ballot box and covering envelopes.
The returning officer at an election[1] must give to each candidate[2] (or to each election agent[3], as the case may be) not less than 48 hours' notice in writing of each occasion on which a postal voters' ballot box[4] (and the envelopes contained in it) is to be opened[5]. Such a notice must specify: (1) the time and place at which such an opening is to take place[6]; and (2) the number of agents who may be appointed[7] to attend each opening[8].

1   Ie at a parliamentary election, a local government election (which includes any London Authority election and a local authority mayoral election), a Welsh Assembly constituency or regional election (whether the polls are taken separately or together) or a European parliamentary election. As to the meanings of 'Assembly election', 'constituency election' and 'regional election' see PARA 3 note 2. As to the meaning of 'parliamentary election' see PARA 9. As to the meanings of 'Authority election' and 'local government election' see PARA 11. As to elections in the City of London see PARA 33. As to European parliamentary elections see PARA 217 et seq. There is no provision for absent voting at a poll consequent on a parish meeting on a question involving appointment to office: see PARA 200 et seq.

As to returning officers generally see PARA 350 et seq. At a European parliamentary election, the returning officer referred to in the text is the local returning officer (see PARA 360): see the European Parliamentary Elections Regulations 2004, SI 2004/293, Sch 2 para 56(1) (Sch 2 substituted by SI 2009/186). At a Welsh Assembly election, the constituency returning officer is the returning officer referred to in the text: see the National Assembly for Wales (Representation of the People) Order 2007, SI 2007/236, Sch 3 para 16(1); but see also PARA 406 note 1. As to the meaning of 'constituency returning officer' for the purposes of Welsh Assembly elections see PARA 18 note 2.

2   As to the meaning of 'candidate' generally see PARA 230. The notice is not given to a candidate in the case of a European parliamentary election, but only to each election agent or sub-agent: see note 3. At a Welsh Assembly election, the notice given to a candidate as mentioned in the text must be given to each candidate in a constituency election (see the National Assembly for Wales

(Representation of the People) Order 2007, SI 2007/236, Sch 3 para 16(1)(a)), and to each individual candidate in an election for any Assembly electoral region (Sch 3 para 16(1)(b)). As to the meaning of 'Assembly electoral region' see PARA 3 note 2. As to the meanings of 'candidate' and 'individual candidate' at a Welsh Assembly election see PARA 230 note 19.

3　　At a European parliamentary election, the notice mentioned in the text is given only to each election agent, or where sub-agents have been appointed, to each sub-agent: see the European Parliamentary Elections Regulations 2004, SI 2004/293, Sch 2 para 56(1) (as substituted: see note 1). For the purposes of a Welsh Assembly election, the notice mentioned in the text may be given to the election agent for each registered party standing nominated at a Welsh Assembly regional election: see the National Assembly for Wales (Representation of the People) Order 2007, SI 2007/236, Sch 3 para 16(1)(b). As to the meaning of 'registered political party' in this context see PARA 230 note 23.

4　　As to the meaning of 'postal voters' ballot box' see PARA 416 note 16.

5　　Representation of the People (England and Wales) Regulations 2001, SI 2001/341, reg 80(1); European Parliamentary Elections Regulations 2004, SI 2004/293, Sch 2 para 56(1) (as substituted: see note 1); National Assembly for Wales (Representation of the People) Order 2007, SI 2007/236, Sch 3 para 16(1).

　　　　The Representation of the People (England and Wales) Regulations 2001, SI 2001/341, reg 80 has effect for the purposes of local authority referendums, subject to the modifications specified, in relation to Wales, by the Local Authorities (Conduct of Referendums) (Wales) Regulations 2008, SI 2008/1848, reg 8(2), Sch 4 Table 5, and, in relation to England, by the Local Authorities (Conduct of Referendums) (England) Regulations 2012, SI 2012/323, regs 8(2), 11–13, Sch 4 Table 6 (see PARA 15 note 2).

6　　Representation of the People (England and Wales) Regulations 2001, SI 2001/341, reg 80(2)(a); European Parliamentary Elections Regulations 2004, SI 2004/293, Sch 2 para 56(2)(a) (as substituted: see note 1); National Assembly for Wales (Representation of the People) Order 2007, SI 2007/236, Sch 3 para 16(2)(a).

7　　As to the appointment of agents to be present at the receipt of postal ballot papers see PARA 416.

8　　Representation of the People (England and Wales) Regulations 2001, SI 2001/341, reg 80(2)(b); European Parliamentary Elections Regulations 2004, SI 2004/293, Sch 2 para 56(2)(b) (as substituted: see note 1); National Assembly for Wales (Representation of the People) Order 2007, SI 2007/236, Sch 3 para 16(2)(b).

420.　　Opening of postal voters' ballot box; additional verification of personal identifiers; retrieval of cancelled papers. Each postal voters' ballot box[1] at an election[2] must be opened by the returning officer[3] in the presence of the agents[4] (if, indeed, any are in attendance)[5]. So long as the returning officer ensures that there is at least one sealed postal voters' ballot box for the reception of covering envelopes[6] up to the time of the close of the poll, the other postal voters' ballot boxes may previously be opened by him[7]. The last postal voters' ballot box and the postal ballot box[8] must be opened:

(1)　　at the verification of the ballot paper accounts, in the case of a European parliamentary election[9]; or

(2)　　otherwise, at the counting of the votes[10].

A returning officer may on any occasion at which a postal voters' ballot box is opened[11] undertake verification of the personal identifiers[12] on any postal voting statement[13] that has on a prior occasion been placed in the receptacle for postal voting statements[14]. Where a returning officer undertakes additional verification of personal identifiers[15], he must[16]:

(a)　　remove as many postal voting statements from the receptacle for postal voting statements as he wishes to subject to additional verification[17]; and

(b)　　compare the date of birth and the signature on each such postal voting statement against the date of birth and signature contained in the personal identifiers record relating to the person to whom the postal ballot paper was addressed[18].

Where the returning officer is no longer satisfied that the postal voting statement has been duly completed, he must mark the statement 'rejected'[19]; and, before placing the postal voting statement in the receptacle for rejected votes (verification procedure)[20], he must:

(i) show it to the agents, and he must permit them to view the entries in the personal identifiers record which relate to the person to whom the postal ballot paper was addressed, and if any of them object to his decision, he must add the words 'rejection objected to'[21];

(ii) open any postal ballot box and retrieve the ballot paper corresponding to the ballot paper number on the postal voting statement[22];

(iii) show the ballot paper number on the retrieved ballot paper to the agents[23]; and

(iv) attach the ballot paper to the postal voting statement[24].

Whilst retrieving a ballot paper in this way, the returning officer and his staff must keep the ballot papers face downwards and must take proper precautions for preventing any person seeing the votes made on the ballot papers[25], and they must not be permitted to view the corresponding number list used at the issue of postal ballot papers[26]. Following the removal of a postal ballot paper from a postal ballot box, the returning officer must lock and reseal the postal ballot box in the presence of the agents[27].

Where it appears to the returning officer that a cancelled postal ballot paper[28] has been placed in a postal voters' ballot box, or in the receptacle for ballot paper envelopes[29] or in a postal ballot box[30], he must, on at least one occasion on which a postal voters ballot box is opened[31], also open any postal ballot box and the receptacle for ballot paper envelopes[32], and:

(A) retrieve the cancelled ballot paper[33];

(B) show the ballot paper number on the cancelled ballot paper to the agents[34];

(C) retrieve the postal voting statement that relates to a cancelled ballot paper from the receptacle for postal voting statements[35];

(D) attach any cancelled postal ballot paper to the postal voting statement to which it relates[36];

(E) place the cancelled documents in a separate packet and deal with that packet in the manner provided for[37] in relation to spoilt postal ballot papers[38]; and

(F) unless the postal ballot box has been opened for the purposes of the counting of votes[39], re-lock the postal ballot box (if it has a lock), and reseal it in the presence of the agents[40].

Whilst retrieving a cancelled ballot paper in this way, the returning officer and his staff must keep the ballot papers face downwards, they must take proper precautions for preventing any person seeing the votes made on the ballot papers[41], and they are not permitted to view the corresponding number list used at the issue of postal ballot papers[42].

1   As to the meaning of 'postal voters' ballot box' see PARA 416 note 16.

2   Ie at a parliamentary election, a local government election (which includes any London Authority election and a local authority mayoral election), a Welsh Assembly constituency or regional election (whether the polls are taken separately or together) or a European parliamentary election. As to the meanings of 'Assembly election', 'constituency election' and 'regional election' see PARA 3 note 2. As to the meaning of 'parliamentary election' see PARA 9. As to the meanings of 'Authority election' and 'local government election' see PARA 11. As to elections in the City of London see PARA 33. As to European parliamentary elections see

PARA 217 et seq. There is no provision for absent voting at a poll consequent on a parish meeting on a question involving appointment to office: see PARA 200 et seq.

3   As to returning officers generally see PARA 350 et seq. At a European parliamentary election, the returning officer referred to in the text is the local returning officer (see PARA 360): see the European Parliamentary Elections Regulations 2004, SI 2004/293, Sch 2 paras 59(1), (2), 64(1)–(5), 66(1)–(3) (Sch 2 substituted by SI 2009/186). At a Welsh Assembly election, the constituency returning officer is the returning officer referred to in the text: see the National Assembly for Wales (Representation of the People) Order 2007, SI 2007/236, Sch 3 paras 19(1), (2), 24(1)–(4), 26(1), (2); but see also PARA 406 note 1. As to the meaning of 'constituency returning officer' for the purposes of Welsh Assembly elections see PARA 18 note 2.

4   As to the appointment of agents to be present at the receipt of postal ballot papers see PARA 416.

5   Representation of the People (England and Wales) Regulations 2001, SI 2001/341, reg 83(1); European Parliamentary Elections Regulations 2004, SI 2004/293, Sch 2 para 59(1) (as substituted: see note 3); National Assembly for Wales (Representation of the People) Order 2007, SI 2007/236, Sch 3 para 19(1).

   The Representation of the People (England and Wales) Regulations 2001, SI 2001/341, regs 83, 85B, 86A, have effect for the purposes of local authority referendums, subject to the modifications specified, in relation to Wales, by the Local Authorities (Conduct of Referendums) (Wales) Regulations 2008, SI 2008/1848, reg 8(2), Sch 4 Table 5, and, in relation to England, by the Local Authorities (Conduct of Referendums) (England) Regulations 2012, SI 2012/323, regs 8(2), 11–13, Sch 4 Table 6 (see PARA 15 note 2).

6   As to the meaning of 'covering envelope' see PARA 410.

7   Representation of the People (England and Wales) Regulations 2001, SI 2001/341, reg 83(2); European Parliamentary Elections Regulations 2004, SI 2004/293, Sch 2 para 59(2) (as substituted: see note 3); National Assembly for Wales (Representation of the People) Order 2007, SI 2007/236, Sch 3 para 19(2).

8   As to the meaning of 'postal ballot box' see PARA 417.

9   European Parliamentary Elections Regulations 2004, SI 2004/293, Sch 2 para 59(3) (as substituted: see note 3). As to the verification of the ballot paper accounts at a European parliamentary election see PARA 466.

10 Representation of the People (England and Wales) Regulations 2001, SI 2001/341, reg 83(3); National Assembly for Wales (Representation of the People) Order 2007, SI 2007/236, Sch 3 para 19(3). As to the counting of votes at a local government election (except a London Authority election) see PARA 425; in relation to a local authority mayoral election see PARA 436; in relation to a London Authority election see PARA 444; in relation to a London mayoral election see PARA 451; in relation to a Welsh Assembly election see PARA 458.

11 Ie opened in accordance with the Representation of the People (England and Wales) Regulations 2001, SI 2001/341, reg 83, in the case of a parliamentary or local government election, or in accordance with the European Parliamentary Elections Regulations 2004, SI 2004/293, Sch 2 para 59, in the case of a European parliamentary election, or in accordance with the National Assembly for Wales (Representation of the People) Order 2007, SI 2007/236, Sch 3 para 19, at a Welsh Assembly election (see the text and notes 1–10): Representation of the People (England and Wales) Regulations 2001, SI 2001/341, reg 85B(1) (regs 85B, 86A added by SI 2006/2910); European Parliamentary Elections Regulations 2004, SI 2004/293, Sch 2 para 64(1) (as substituted: see note 3); National Assembly for Wales (Representation of the People) Order 2007, SI 2007/236, Sch 3 para 24(1).

12 As to personal identifiers see PARA 366.

13 As to the postal voting statement see PARA 406.

14 Representation of the People (England and Wales) Regulations 2001, SI 2001/341, reg 85B(1) (as added: see note 11); European Parliamentary Elections Regulations 2004, SI 2004/293, Sch 2 para 64(1) (as substituted: see note 3); National Assembly for Wales (Representation of the People) Order 2007, SI 2007/236, Sch 3 para 24(1). As to the receptacle for postal voting statements see PARA 417.

15 Ie additional to the mandatory procedure according to which a percentage (not less than 20%) of the covering envelopes recorded by the returning officer (ie when a postal voters' ballot box is opened at an election) is set aside for personal identifier verification: see PARA 421.

16 Representation of the People (England and Wales) Regulations 2001, SI 2001/341, reg 85B(2) (as added: see note 11); European Parliamentary Elections Regulations 2004, SI 2004/293, Sch 2 para 64(2) (as substituted: see note 3); National Assembly for Wales (Representation of the People) Order 2007, SI 2007/236, Sch 3 para 24(2).

17 Representation of the People (England and Wales) Regulations 2001, SI 2001/341, reg 85B(2)(a) (as added: see note 11); European Parliamentary Elections Regulations 2004, SI 2004/293, Sch 2

para 64(2)(a) (as substituted: see note 3); National Assembly for Wales (Representation of the People) Order 2007, SI 2007/236, Sch 3 para 24(2)(a).

18   Representation of the People (England and Wales) Regulations 2001, SI 2001/341, reg 85B(2)(b) (as added: see note 11); European Parliamentary Elections Regulations 2004, SI 2004/293, Sch 2 para 64(2)(b) (as substituted: see note 3); National Assembly for Wales (Representation of the People) Order 2007, SI 2007/236, Sch 3 para 24(2)(b). As to the meaning of 'postal ballot paper' see PARA 407 note 1. As to the personal identifiers record see PARA 366.

19   Representation of the People (England and Wales) Regulations 2001, SI 2001/341, reg 85B(3) (as added: see note 11); European Parliamentary Elections Regulations 2004, SI 2004/293, Sch 2 para 64(3) (as substituted: see note 3); National Assembly for Wales (Representation of the People) Order 2007, SI 2007/236, Sch 3 para 24(3).

20   As to the receptacle for rejected votes (verification procedure) see PARA 417.

21   Representation of the People (England and Wales) Regulations 2001, SI 2001/341, reg 85B(3)(a) (as added: see note 11); European Parliamentary Elections Regulations 2004, SI 2004/293, Sch 2 para 64(3)(a) (as substituted: see note 3); National Assembly for Wales (Representation of the People) Order 2007, SI 2007/236, Sch 3 para 24(3)(a).

22   Representation of the People (England and Wales) Regulations 2001, SI 2001/341, reg 85B(3)(b) (as added: see note 11); European Parliamentary Elections Regulations 2004, SI 2004/293, Sch 2 para 64(3)(b) (as substituted: see note 3); National Assembly for Wales (Representation of the People) Order 2007, SI 2007/236, Sch 3 para 24(3)(b). As to the issue of postal voting statements see PARA 406.

23   Representation of the People (England and Wales) Regulations 2001, SI 2001/341, reg 85B(3)(c) (as added: see note 11); European Parliamentary Elections Regulations 2004, SI 2004/293, Sch 2 para 64(3)(c) (as substituted: see note 3); National Assembly for Wales (Representation of the People) Order 2007, SI 2007/236, Sch 3 para 24(3)(c).

24   Representation of the People (England and Wales) Regulations 2001, SI 2001/341, reg 85B(3)(d) (as added: see note 11); European Parliamentary Elections Regulations 2004, SI 2004/293, Sch 2 para 64(3)(d) (as substituted: see note 3); National Assembly for Wales (Representation of the People) Order 2007, SI 2007/236, Sch 3 para 24(3)(d).

25   Representation of the People (England and Wales) Regulations 2001, SI 2001/341, reg 85B(5)(a) (as added: see note 11); European Parliamentary Elections Regulations 2004, SI 2004/293, Sch 2 para 64(5)(a) (as substituted: see note 3). No specific instruction as described in the text is set down for the purposes of retrieving ballot papers at a Welsh Assembly election; however, the instructions described in the text are reiterated by the Representation of the People (England and Wales) Regulations 2001, SI 2001/341, reg 84(6), the European Parliamentary Elections Regulations 2004, SI 2004/293, Sch 2 para 60(8), and the National Assembly for Wales (Representation of the People) Order 2007, SI 2007/236, Sch 3 para 20(8), which also apply (see PARA 421).

26   Representation of the People (England and Wales) Regulations 2001, SI 2001/341, reg 85B(5)(b) (as added: see note 11); European Parliamentary Elections Regulations 2004, SI 2004/293, Sch 2 para 64(5)(b) (as substituted: see note 3). As to Welsh Assembly elections see note 25. As to the corresponding number list used at the issue of postal ballot papers see PARA 408.

27   Representation of the People (England and Wales) Regulations 2001, SI 2001/341, reg 85B(4) (as added: see note 11); European Parliamentary Elections Regulations 2004, SI 2004/293, Sch 2 para 64(4) (as substituted: see note 3); National Assembly for Wales (Representation of the People) Order 2007, SI 2007/236, Sch 3 para 24(4).

28   Ie a postal ballot paper that has been cancelled on grounds of it being either spoilt or lost: see PARAS 414, 415.

29   As to the provision of a receptacle for ballot paper envelopes see PARA 417.

30   See the Representation of the People (England and Wales) Regulations 2001, SI 2001/341, reg 86A(1) (as added: see note 11); European Parliamentary Elections Regulations 2004, SI 2004/293, Sch 2 para 66(1) (as substituted: see note 3); National Assembly for Wales (Representation of the People) Order 2007, SI 2007/236, Sch 3 para 26(1).

31   Ie opened in accordance with the Representation of the People (England and Wales) Regulations 2001, SI 2001/341, reg 83, in the case of a parliamentary or local government election, or in accordance with the European Parliamentary Elections Regulations 2004, SI 2004/293, Sch 2 para 59, in the case of a European parliamentary election, or in accordance with the National Assembly for Wales (Representation of the People) Order 2007, SI 2007/236, Sch 3 para 19, at a Welsh Assembly election (see the text and notes 1–10): Representation of the People (England and Wales) Regulations 2001, SI 2001/341, reg 86A(2) (as added: see note 11); European Parliamentary Elections Regulations 2004, SI 2004/293, Sch 2 para 66(2) (as substituted: see note 3); National Assembly for Wales (Representation of the People) Order 2007, SI 2007/236, Sch 3 para 26(2).

32 Representation of the People (England and Wales) Regulations 2001, SI 2001/341, reg 86A(2) (as added: see note 11); European Parliamentary Elections Regulations 2004, SI 2004/293, Sch 2 para 66(2) (as substituted: see note 3); National Assembly for Wales (Representation of the People) Order 2007, SI 2007/236, Sch 3 para 26(2).

33 Representation of the People (England and Wales) Regulations 2001, SI 2001/341, reg 86A(2)(a) (as added: see note 11); European Parliamentary Elections Regulations 2004, SI 2004/293, Sch 2 para 66(2)(a) (as substituted: see note 3); National Assembly for Wales (Representation of the People) Order 2007, SI 2007/236, Sch 3 para 26(2)(a).

34 Representation of the People (England and Wales) Regulations 2001, SI 2001/341, reg 86A(2)(b) (as added: see note 11); European Parliamentary Elections Regulations 2004, SI 2004/293, Sch 2 para 66(2)(b) (as substituted: see note 3); National Assembly for Wales (Representation of the People) Order 2007, SI 2007/236, Sch 3 para 26(2)(b).

35 Representation of the People (England and Wales) Regulations 2001, SI 2001/341, reg 86A(2)(c) (as added: see note 11); European Parliamentary Elections Regulations 2004, SI 2004/293, Sch 2 para 66(2)(c) (as substituted: see note 3); National Assembly for Wales (Representation of the People) Order 2007, SI 2007/236, Sch 3 para 26(2)(c).

36 Representation of the People (England and Wales) Regulations 2001, SI 2001/341, reg 86A(2)(d) (as added: see note 11); European Parliamentary Elections Regulations 2004, SI 2004/293, Sch 2 para 66(2)(d) (as substituted: see note 3); National Assembly for Wales (Representation of the People) Order 2007, SI 2007/236, Sch 3 para 26(2)(d).

37 Ie in accordance with the Representation of the People (England and Wales) Regulations 2001, SI 2001/341, reg 77(6), in the case of a parliamentary or local government election, or in accordance with the European Parliamentary Elections Regulations 2004, SI 2004/293, Sch 2 para 53(7), in the case of a European parliamentary election, or in accordance with the National Assembly for Wales (Representation of the People) Order 2007, SI 2007/236, Sch 3 para 14(7), at a Welsh Assembly election (see PARA 414): Representation of the People (England and Wales) Regulations 2001, SI 2001/341, reg 86A(2)(e) (as added: see note 11); European Parliamentary Elections Regulations 2004, SI 2004/293, Sch 2 para 66(2)(e) (as substituted: see note 3); National Assembly for Wales (Representation of the People) Order 2007, SI 2007/236, Sch 3 para 26(2)(e).

38 Representation of the People (England and Wales) Regulations 2001, SI 2001/341, reg 86A(2)(e) (as added: see note 11); European Parliamentary Elections Regulations 2004, SI 2004/293, Sch 2 para 66(2)(e) (as substituted: see note 3); National Assembly for Wales (Representation of the People) Order 2007, SI 2007/236, Sch 3 para 26(2)(e).

39 Ie under the Representation of the People Act 1983 Sch 1 r 45, in the case of a parliamentary or local government election (see PARA 425 et seq), or under the European Parliamentary Elections Regulations 2004, SI 2004/293, Sch 1 para 53, in the case of a European parliamentary election (see PARA 468 et seq), or under the National Assembly for Wales (Representation of the People) Order 2007, SI 2007/236, Sch 5 para 55, at a Welsh Assembly election (see PARA 458 et seq).

40 Representation of the People (England and Wales) Regulations 2001, SI 2001/341, reg 86A(2)(f) (as added: see note 11); European Parliamentary Elections Regulations 2004, SI 2004/293, Sch 2 para 66(2)(f) (as substituted: see note 3); National Assembly for Wales (Representation of the People) Order 2007, SI 2007/236, Sch 3 para 26(2)(f).

41 Representation of the People (England and Wales) Regulations 2001, SI 2001/341, reg 86A(3)(a) (as added: see note 11); European Parliamentary Elections Regulations 2004, SI 2004/293, Sch 2 para 66(3)(a) (as substituted: see note 3). As to Welsh Assembly elections see note 25.

42 Representation of the People (England and Wales) Regulations 2001, SI 2001/341, reg 86A(3)(b) (as added: see note 11); European Parliamentary Elections Regulations 2004, SI 2004/293, Sch 2 para 66(3)(b) (as substituted: see note 3). As to Welsh Assembly elections see note 25.

421.   Opening of postal voters' ballot box and procedures applying to covering envelopes and postal voting statements.   When a postal voters' ballot box is opened[1] at an election[2], the returning officer[3] must count and record the number of covering envelopes[4], including: (1) any envelope received by him (whether by hand or by post) which is stated to include a postal vote; and (2) any other envelope[5] which has been placed in a postal voters' ballot box having been opened and found to contain voting documents[6]. From the envelopes recorded on that occasion, the returning officer must set aside a percentage of them, being not less than 20 per cent, for personal identifier verification[7]. In carrying out the procedures that follow on from the opening of a postal voters' ballot box[8], the returning officer must keep the ballot papers face downwards and must take proper precautions for preventing any person from seeing the votes made on the ballot papers[9]; and he is not permitted to view the corresponding number list used at the issue of postal ballot papers[10].

The returning officer must open separately each covering envelope (including any envelope that falls within head (2) above)[11]; and where the covering envelope:

(a) does not contain the postal voting statement separately, the returning officer must open the ballot paper envelope[12] to ascertain whether the postal voting statement is inside[13];

(b) does not contain both a postal voting statement (whether separately or not), and a ballot paper envelope (or, if there is no ballot paper envelope, a ballot paper or ballot papers), the returning officer must mark the covering envelope 'provisionally rejected', attach its contents (if any), and place it in the receptacle for rejected votes[14];

(c) contains the postal voting statement of an elector with an anonymous entry[15] (and where head (b) above does not apply[16]), the returning officer must set aside that envelope and its contents for personal identifier verification[17].

As soon as practicable after the last covering envelope has been opened, the returning officer must make up into a packet the copy of the marked postal voters list and proxy postal voters list[18], and he must seal the packet[19].

Where a covering envelope (including any envelope that falls within head (2) above) contains both a postal voting statement and a ballot paper envelope (or, if there is no ballot paper envelope, a ballot paper or ballot papers), the returning officer must:

(i) satisfy himself that every postal voting statement contained in it is duly completed[20]; and

(ii) also conduct personal identifier verification on any postal voting statement contained in any such envelope that has been set aside for this purpose[21].

Accordingly, for the purposes of head (i) above, the returning officer must satisfy himself that the postal voting statement is duly completed[22]; and, as part of that process, but only for the purposes of head (ii) above, he must also compare the date of birth and the signature on the postal voting statement against the date of birth and signature contained in the personal identifier record[23] relating to the person to whom the postal ballot paper was addressed[24]. Where the returning officer is not so satisfied (for either purpose), he must mark the statement 'rejected', attach to it the ballot paper envelope (or, if there is no such envelope, to the ballot paper or ballot papers), and place the statement in the receptacle for rejected votes, or, where the statement has been subjected to personal identifier verification, in the receptacle for rejected votes (verification procedure)[25]. Before so placing a postal voting statement in either such receptacle, however, the returning officer must show it to the agents[26] (and, for the purposes of personal identifier verification, he must permit them to view the entries in the personal identifiers record which relate to the person to whom the postal ballot paper was addressed), and, if any of the agents objects to the returning officer's decision to reject a postal voting statement, he must add the words 'rejection objected to'[27]. The returning officer must then examine the number (or numbers) on the postal voting statement against the number (or numbers) on the ballot paper envelope and, where they are the same, he must place the statement in the receptacle for postal voting statements (or, where the statement has been subjected to personal identifier verification, in the receptacle for postal voting statements (verification procedure)), and he must place the ballot paper envelope in the receptacle for ballot paper envelopes[28]. Where the number (or numbers) on a valid postal voting statement is (or are) not the same as the number (or numbers) on the ballot paper envelope, or where that envelope has no number on it (or only one number when the postal voting statement has more than one), the returning officer must open the envelope[29].

Where a ballot paper envelope has been opened either because there is such a mis-match between numbers[30], or under head (a) above[31], or where there is a valid postal voting statement but no ballot paper envelope[32], the returning officer must place:

(A) in the postal ballot box[33], any ballot paper the number on which is the same as the number (or one of the numbers) on the valid postal voting statement[34];

(B) in the appropriate receptacle for rejected votes[35], any other ballot paper, with the valid postal voting statement attached and marked 'provisionally rejected'[36];

(C) in the appropriate receptacle for rejected votes[37], any valid postal voting statement marked 'provisionally rejected' either where there is no ballot paper or where, in the case of a statement on which the number of more than one ballot paper appears, there is not a sufficient number of ballot papers (and, in such a case, he must mark the statement to indicate which ballot paper is missing)[38];

(D) in the appropriate receptacle for postal voting statements[39], any valid statement not disposed of under head (B) or head (C) above[40].

1   As to the meaning of 'postal voters' ballot box' see PARA 416 note 16. As to the opening of postal voters' ballot boxes see PARA 420.

2   Ie at a parliamentary election, a local government election (which includes any London Authority election and a local authority mayoral election), a Welsh Assembly constituency or regional election (whether the polls are taken separately or together) or a European parliamentary election. As to the meanings of 'Assembly election', 'constituency election' and 'regional election' see PARA 3 note 2. As to the meaning of 'parliamentary election' see PARA 9. As to the meanings of 'Authority election' and 'local government election' see PARA 11. As to elections in the City of London see PARA 33. As to European parliamentary elections see PARA 217 et seq. There is no provision for absent voting at a poll consequent on a parish meeting on a question involving appointment to office: see PARA 200 et seq.

3   As to returning officers generally see PARA 350 et seq. At a European parliamentary election, the returning officer referred to in the text is the local returning officer (see PARA 360): see the European Parliamentary Elections Regulations 2004, SI 2004/293, Sch 2 paras 60(1)–(3), (5)–(9), (11), 62(2)–(6), (8), 63(2)–(6), (8) (Sch 2 substituted by SI 2009/186). At a Welsh Assembly election, the constituency returning officer is the returning officer referred to in the text: see the National Assembly for Wales (Representation of the People) Order 2007, SI 2007/236, Sch 3 paras 20(1)–(3), (5)–(9), (11), 22(2)–(5), (7), 23(2)–(6), (8); but see also PARA 406 note 1. As to the meaning of 'constituency returning officer' for the purposes of Welsh Assembly elections see PARA 18 note 2.

4   As to the meaning of 'covering envelope' see PARA 410.

5   Ie as described in the Representation of the People (England and Wales) Regulations 2001, SI 2001/341, reg 82(2), the European Parliamentary Elections Regulations 2004, SI 2004/293, Sch 2 para 58(2), or the National Assembly for Wales (Representation of the People) Order 2007, SI 2007/236, Sch 3 para 18(2), as the case may be (see PARA 418).

6   Representation of the People (England and Wales) Regulations 2001, SI 2001/341, reg 84(1) (reg 84(1) substituted, reg 84(1A), (1B), (5)–(9) added, by SI 2006/2910); European

Parliamentary Elections Regulations 2004, SI 2004/293, Sch 2 para 60(1) (as substituted: see note 3); National Assembly for Wales (Representation of the People) Order 2007, SI 2007/236, Sch 3 para 20(1).

The Representation of the People (England and Wales) Regulations 2001, SI 2001/341, regs 84, 85, 85A, have effect for the purposes of local authority referendums, subject to the modifications specified, in relation to Wales, by the Local Authorities (Conduct of Referendums) (Wales) Regulations 2008, SI 2008/1848, reg 8(2), Sch 4 Table 5, and, in relation to England, by the Local Authorities (Conduct of Referendums) (England) Regulations 2012, SI 2012/323, regs 8(2), 11–13, Sch 4 Table 6 (see PARA 15 note 2).

7 Representation of the People (England and Wales) Regulations 2001, SI 2001/341, reg 84(1A) (as added: see note 6); European Parliamentary Elections Regulations 2004, SI 2004/293, Sch 2 para 60(2) (as substituted: see note 3); National Assembly for Wales (Representation of the People) Order 2007, SI 2007/236, Sch 3 para 20(2). As to personal identifier verification see the text and notes 20–40. Additional personal identifier verification may be performed on any other occasion at which a postal voters' ballot box is opened: see PARA 420.

8 Ie in carrying out the procedures, for the purposes of a parliamentary or local government election, in the Representation of the People (England and Wales) Regulations 2001, SI 2001/341, regs 84–88, or, for the purposes of a European parliamentary election, in the European Parliamentary Elections Regulations 2004, SI 2004/293, Sch 2 paras 60–68, or, for the purposes of a Welsh Assembly election, in the National Assembly for Wales (Representation of the People) Order 2007, SI 2007/236, Sch 3 paras 20, 22–28 (see also PARAS 407, 420, 422–423): see the Representation of the People (England and Wales) Regulations 2001, SI 2001/341, reg 84(6) (as added: see note 6); the European Parliamentary Elections Regulations 2004, SI 2004/293, Sch 2 para 60(8) (as substituted: see note 3); and the National Assembly for Wales (Representation of the People) Order 2007, SI 2007/236, Sch 3 para 20(8).

9 Representation of the People (England and Wales) Regulations 2001, SI 2001/341, reg 84(6)(a) (as added: see note 6); European Parliamentary Elections Regulations 2004, SI 2004/293, Sch 2 para 60(8)(a) (as substituted: see note 3); National Assembly for Wales (Representation of the People) Order 2007, SI 2007/236, Sch 3 para 20(8)(a).

10 Representation of the People (England and Wales) Regulations 2001, SI 2001/341, reg 84(6)(b) (as added: see note 6); European Parliamentary Elections Regulations 2004, SI 2004/293, Sch 2 para 60(8)(b) (as substituted: see note 3); National Assembly for Wales (Representation of the People) Order 2007, SI 2007/236, Sch 3 para 20(8)(b). As to the meaning of 'postal ballot paper' see PARA 407 note 1. As to the corresponding number list used at the issue of postal ballot papers see PARA 408.

11 Representation of the People (England and Wales) Regulations 2001, SI 2001/341, reg 84(1B) (as added: see note 6); European Parliamentary Elections Regulations 2004, SI 2004/293, Sch 2 para 60(3) (as substituted: see note 3); National Assembly for Wales (Representation of the People) Order 2007, SI 2007/236, Sch 3 para 20(3). Where an envelope opened as described in the text contains a postal voting statement, the returning officer must place a mark in the marked copy of the postal voters list or proxy postal voters list in a place corresponding to the number of the elector to denote that a postal vote has been returned (see PARA 418): Representation of the People (England and Wales) Regulations 2001, SI 2001/341, reg 84(7) (as so added); European Parliamentary Elections Regulations 2004, SI 2004/293, Sch 2 para 60(9) (as so substituted); National Assembly for Wales (Representation of the People) Order 2007, SI 2007/236, Sch 3 para 20(9). A mark so made must be distinguishable from and must not obscure the mark made, for the purposes of a parliamentary or local government election, under the Representation of the People (England and Wales) Regulations 2001, SI 2001/341, reg 72(3), or, for the purposes of a European parliamentary election, under the European Parliamentary Elections Regulations 2004, SI 2004/293, Sch 2 para 48(2), or, for the purposes of a Welsh Assembly election, under the National Assembly for Wales (Representation of the People) Order 2007, SI 2007/236, Sch 3 para 9 (mark placed in the absent voters list or the list of postal proxies to denote that a ballot paper has been issued to the elector or his proxy: see PARA 408): Representation of the People (England and Wales) Regulations 2001, SI 2001/341, reg 84(8) (as so added); European Parliamentary Elections Regulations 2004, SI 2004/293, Sch 2 para 60(10) (as so substituted); National Assembly for Wales (Representation of the People) Order 2007, SI 2007/236, Sch 3 para 20(10). As to the meaning of 'elector', in relation to a parliamentary or local government election, see PARA 95 note 2; in relation to a Welsh Assembly election, see PARA 110 note 6; and in relation to European parliamentary elections see PARA 111 note 4. As to the registers of electors see PARA 143 et seq; and as to the number of an elector see PARA 145. As to the meaning of 'postal voters list' see PARA 373 note 7; and as to the meaning of 'proxy postal voters list' see PARA 381 note 6. As to the postal voting statement see PARA 406.

12 As to the meaning of 'ballot paper envelope' see PARA 410.

13 Representation of the People (England and Wales) Regulations 2001, SI 2001/341, reg 84(3) (reg 84(2)–(4) amended by SI 2006/2910); European Parliamentary Elections Regulations 2004, SI 2004/293, Sch 2 para 60(5) (as substituted: see note 3); National Assembly for Wales (Representation of the People) Order 2007, SI 2007/236, Sch 3 para 20(5).

14 Representation of the People (England and Wales) Regulations 2001, SI 2001/341, reg 84(4) (as amended: see note 13); European Parliamentary Elections Regulations 2004, SI 2004/293, Sch 2 para 60(6) (as substituted: see note 3); National Assembly for Wales (Representation of the People) Order 2007, SI 2007/236, Sch 3 para 20(6). As to the provision of a receptacle for rejected votes see PARA 417.

15 Representation of the People (England and Wales) Regulations 2001, SI 2001/341, reg 84(5)(a) (as added: see note 6); European Parliamentary Elections Regulations 2004, SI 2004/293, Sch 2 para 60(7)(a) (as substituted: see note 3); National Assembly for Wales (Representation of the People) Order 2007, SI 2007/236, Sch 3 para 20(7)(a). As to the meaning of 'anonymous entry' in relation to a register of electors see PARA 148.

16 Representation of the People (England and Wales) Regulations 2001, SI 2001/341, reg 84(5)(b) (as added: see note 6); European Parliamentary Elections Regulations 2004, SI 2004/293, Sch 2 para 60(7)(b) (as substituted: see note 3); National Assembly for Wales (Representation of the People) Order 2007, SI 2007/236, Sch 3 para 20(7)(b).

17 Representation of the People (England and Wales) Regulations 2001, SI 2001/341, reg 84(5) (as added: see note 6); European Parliamentary Elections Regulations 2004, SI 2004/293, Sch 2 para 60(7) (as substituted: see note 3); National Assembly for Wales (Representation of the People) Order 2007, SI 2007/236, Sch 3 para 20(7). As to personal identifier verification see the text and notes 20–40.

18 Ie marked, for the purposes of a parliamentary or local government election, in accordance with the Representation of the People (England and Wales) Regulations 2001, SI 2001/341, reg 84(7), or, for the purposes of a European parliamentary election, in accordance with the European Parliamentary Elections Regulations 2004, SI 2004/293, Sch 2 para 60(9), or, for the purposes of a Welsh Assembly election, under the National Assembly for Wales (Representation of the People) Order 2007, SI 2007/236, Sch 3 para 20(9) (see note 11).

19 Representation of the People (England and Wales) Regulations 2001, SI 2001/341, reg 84(9) (as added: see note 6); European Parliamentary Elections Regulations 2004, SI 2004/293, Sch 2 para 60(11) (as substituted: see note 3); National Assembly for Wales (Representation of the People) Order 2007, SI 2007/236, Sch 3 para 20(11).

20 Ie the procedures in the Representation of the People (England and Wales) Regulations 2001, SI 2001/341, regs 85, 85A apply, for the purposes of a parliamentary or local government election, the procedures in the European Parliamentary Elections Regulations 2004, SI 2004/293, Sch 2 paras 62, 63 apply, for the purposes of a European parliamentary election, and the National Assembly for Wales (Representation of the People) Order 2007, SI 2007/236, Sch 3 paras 22, 23 apply, for the purposes of a Welsh Assembly election: see the Representation of the People (England and Wales) Regulations 2001, SI 2001/341, reg 84(2) (as amended: see note 13); European Parliamentary Elections Regulations 2004, SI 2004/293, Sch 2 para 60(4) (as substituted: see note 3); National Assembly for Wales (Representation of the People) Order 2007, SI 2007/236, Sch 3 para 20(4).

The Representation of the People (England and Wales) Regulations 2001, SI 2001/341, reg 85 applies, in relation to a parliamentary or local government election, the European Parliamentary Elections Regulations 2004, SI 2004/293, Sch 2 para 62 applies, in relation to a European parliamentary election, and the National Assembly for Wales (Representation of the People) Order 2007, SI 2007/236, Sch 3 para 22 applies, for the purposes of a Welsh Assembly election, to any postal voting statement contained in an envelope that has not been set aside for personal identifier verification in accordance with the Representation of the People (England and Wales) Regulations 2001, SI 2001/341, reg 84(1A) (see the text and note 7) or reg 84(5) (see the text and notes 15–17), the European Parliamentary Elections Regulations 2004, SI 2004/293, Sch 2 para 60(2) (see the text and note 7) or Sch 2 para 60(7) (see the text and notes 15–17), or the National Assembly for Wales (Representation of the People) Order 2007, SI 2007/236, Sch 3 para 20(2) (see the text and note 7) or Sch 3 para 20(7) (see the text and notes 15–17): Representation of the People (England and Wales) Regulations 2001, SI 2001/341, reg 85(1) (reg 85(1) substituted, reg 85(1A) added, by SI 2006/2910); European Parliamentary Elections Regulations 2004, SI 2004/293, Sch 2 para 62(1) (as so substituted); National Assembly for Wales (Representation of the People) Order 2007, SI 2007/236, Sch 3 para 22(1).

The Representation of the People (England and Wales) Regulations 2001, SI 2001/341, reg 85A applies, in relation to a parliamentary or local government election, and the European Parliamentary Elections Regulations 2004, SI 2004/293, Sch 2 para 63 applies, in relation to a

European parliamentary election, and the National Assembly for Wales (Representation of the People) Order 2007, SI 2007/236, Sch 3 para 23 applies, for the purposes of a Welsh Assembly election, to any postal voting statement contained in an envelope that is set aside for personal identifier verification in accordance with the Representation of the People (England and Wales) Regulations 2001, SI 2001/341, reg 84(1A) or reg 84(5), or the European Parliamentary Elections Regulations 2004, SI 2004/293, Sch 2 para 60(2) or Sch 2 para 60(7), or the National Assembly for Wales (Representation of the People) Order 2007, SI 2007/236, Sch 3 para 20(2) or Sch 3 para 20(7), as the case may be: Representation of the People (England and Wales) Regulations 2001, SI 2001/341, reg 85A(1) (reg 85A added by SI 2006/2910); European Parliamentary Elections Regulations 2004, SI 2004/293, Sch 2 para 63(1) (as so substituted); National Assembly for Wales (Representation of the People) Order 2007, SI 2007/236, Sch 3 para 23(1).

21 Ie the additional requirements of the procedure in the Representation of the People (England and Wales) Regulations 2001, SI 2001/341, reg 85A apply, for the purposes of a parliamentary or local government election, the additional requirements of the procedure in the European Parliamentary Elections Regulations 2004, SI 2004/293, Sch 2 para 63 apply, for the purposes of a European parliamentary election, and the additional requirements of the procedure in the National Assembly for Wales (Representation of the People) Order 2007, SI 2007/236, Sch 3 para 23 apply, for the purposes of a Welsh Assembly election (see note 20): see the Representation of the People (England and Wales) Regulations 2001, SI 2001/341, reg 84(2) (as amended: see note 13); European Parliamentary Elections Regulations 2004, SI 2004/293, Sch 2 para 60(4) (as substituted: see note 3); National Assembly for Wales (Representation of the People) Order 2007, SI 2007/236, Sch 3 para 20(4).

22 Representation of the People (England and Wales) Regulations 2001, SI 2001/341, reg 85(1A) (as added: see note 20), reg 85A(2) (as added: see note 20); European Parliamentary Elections Regulations 2004, SI 2004/293, Sch 2 paras 62(2), 63(2) (as substituted: see note 3); National Assembly for Wales (Representation of the People) Order 2007, SI 2007/236, Sch 3 paras 22(2), 23(2).

For the purposes of the Representation of the People (England and Wales) Regulations 2001, SI 2001/341, 'valid postal voting statement' means a postal voting statement which, in accordance with reg 85 or reg 85A, the returning officer is satisfied has been duly completed: reg 64 (definition added by SI 2006/2910).

23 As to the personal identifier record see PARA 366.

24 See the Representation of the People (England and Wales) Regulations 2001, SI 2001/341, reg 85A(2) (as added: see note 20); the European Parliamentary Elections Regulations 2004, SI 2004/293, Sch 2 para 63(2) (as substituted: see note 3); and the National Assembly for Wales (Representation of the People) Order 2007, SI 2007/236, Sch 3 para 23(2).

25 Representation of the People (England and Wales) Regulations 2001, SI 2001/341, reg 85(2) (reg 85(2)–(4) amended by SI 2006/2910), reg 85A(3) (as added: see note 20); European Parliamentary Elections Regulations 2004, SI 2004/293, Sch 2 paras 62(3), 63(3) (as substituted: see note 3); National Assembly for Wales (Representation of the People) Order 2007, SI 2007/236, Sch 3 paras 22(3), 23(3). As to the provision of the receptacle for rejected votes and the receptacle for rejected votes (verification procedure) see PARA 417. As to the separate lists that the returning officer must keep of rejected postal ballot papers see PARA 423.

26 Ie but only, at a Welsh Assembly election, when conducting personal identifier verification: see the National Assembly for Wales (Representation of the People) Order 2007, SI 2007/236, Sch 3 para 23(4). As to the appointment of agents to be present at the receipt of postal ballot papers see PARA 416.

27 Representation of the People (England and Wales) Regulations 2001, SI 2001/341, reg 85(3) (as amended: see note 25), reg 85A(4) (as added: see note 20); European Parliamentary Elections Regulations 2004, SI 2004/293, Sch 2 paras 62(4), 63(4) (as substituted: see note 3); National Assembly for Wales (Representation of the People) Order 2007, SI 2007/236, Sch 3 para 23(4).

28 Representation of the People (England and Wales) Regulations 2001, SI 2001/341, reg 85(4) (as amended: see note 25), reg 85A(5) (as added: see note 20); European Parliamentary Elections Regulations 2004, SI 2004/293, Sch 2 paras 62(5), 63(5) (as substituted: see note 3); National Assembly for Wales (Representation of the People) Order 2007, SI 2007/236, Sch 3 paras 22(4), 23(5). As to the provision of the receptacle for ballot paper envelopes see PARA 417.

29 Representation of the People (England and Wales) Regulations 2001, SI 2001/341, reg 85(5) (reg 85(5)–(7) substituted by SI 2002/1871; and amended by SI 2006/2910), reg 85A(6) (as added: see note 20); European Parliamentary Elections Regulations 2004, SI 2004/293, Sch 2 paras 62(6), 63(6) (as substituted: see note 3); National Assembly for Wales (Representation of the People) Order 2007, SI 2007/236, Sch 3 paras 22(5), 23(6).

30 Ie under the Representation of the People (England and Wales) Regulations 2001, SI 2001/341, regs 85(5), 85A(6), in the case of a parliamentary or local government election, or, in relation to a European parliamentary election, under the European Parliamentary Elections Regulations 2004, SI 2004/293, Sch 2 paras 62(6), 63(6), or, in relation to a Welsh Assembly election, under the National Assembly for Wales (Representation of the People) Order 2007, SI 2007/236, Sch 3 paras 22(5), 23(6) (see the text and note 29). The Queen's Printers' copy of the National Assembly for Wales (Representation of the People) Order 2007, SI 2007/236, Sch 3 para 22(6) refers to Sch 3 para 22(7) but it is submitted that a reference to Sch 3 para 22(5) is intended.

31 Ie under the Representation of the People (England and Wales) Regulations 2001, SI 2001/341, reg 84(3) in the case of a parliamentary or local government election, or, in relation to a European parliamentary election, under the European Parliamentary Elections Regulations 2004, SI 2004/293, Sch 2 para 60(5), or, in relation to a Welsh Assembly election, under the National Assembly for Wales (Representation of the People) Order 2007, SI 2007/236, Sch 3 para 20(5) (see head (a) in the text).

32 Representation of the People (England and Wales) Regulations 2001, SI 2001/341, reg 85(6) (as substituted and amended: see note 29), reg 85A(7) (as added: see note 20); European Parliamentary Elections Regulations 2004, SI 2004/293, Sch 2 paras 62(7), 63(7) (as substituted: see note 3); National Assembly for Wales (Representation of the People) Order 2007, SI 2007/236, Sch 3 paras 22(6), 23(7) (Sch 3 para 22(6) amended by SI 2010/2931). As to the opening of ballot paper envelopes placed in the receptacle for ballot paper envelopes see PARA 422.

33 As to the meaning of 'postal ballot box' see PARA 417.

34 Representation of the People (England and Wales) Regulations 2001, SI 2001/341, reg 85(7)(a) (as substituted and amended: see note 29), reg 85A(8)(a) (as added: see note 20); European Parliamentary Elections Regulations 2004, SI 2004/293, Sch 2 paras 62(8)(a), 63(8)(a) (as substituted: see note 3); National Assembly for Wales (Representation of the People) Order 2007, SI 2007/236, Sch 3 paras 22(7)(a), 23(8)(a).

35 Ie in the receptacle for rejected votes, or, where the postal voting statement has been subjected to personal identifier verification, in the receptacle for rejected votes (verification procedure).

36 Representation of the People (England and Wales) Regulations 2001, SI 2001/341, reg 85(7)(b) (as substituted and amended: see note 29), reg 85A(8)(b) (as added: see note 20); European Parliamentary Elections Regulations 2004, SI 2004/293, Sch 2 paras 62(8)(b), 63(8)(b) (as substituted: see note 3); National Assembly for Wales (Representation of the People) Order 2007, SI 2007/236, Sch 3 paras 22(7)(b), 23(8)(b).

37 See note 35.

38 Representation of the People (England and Wales) Regulations 2001, SI 2001/341, reg 85(7)(c) (as substituted and amended: see note 29), reg 85A(8)(c) (as added: see note 20); European Parliamentary Elections Regulations 2004, SI 2004/293, Sch 2 paras 62(8)(c), 63(8)(c) (as substituted: see note 3); National Assembly for Wales (Representation of the People) Order 2007, SI 2007/236, Sch 3 paras 22(7)(c), 23(8)(c).

39 Ie in the receptacle for postal voting statements, or, where the statement has been subjected to personal identifier verification, in the receptacle for postal voting statements (verification procedure).

40 Representation of the People (England and Wales) Regulations 2001, SI 2001/341, reg 85(7)(d) (as substituted and amended: see note 29), reg 85A(8)(d) (as added: see note 20); European Parliamentary Elections Regulations 2004, SI 2004/293, Sch 2 paras 62(8)(d), 63(8)(d) (as substituted: see note 3); National Assembly for Wales (Representation of the People) Order 2007, SI 2007/236, Sch 3 paras 22(7)(d), 23(8)(d).

422. Opening of ballot paper envelopes placed in the receptacle for ballot paper envelopes. The returning officer at an election[1] must open separately each ballot paper envelope[2] placed in the receptacle for ballot paper envelopes[3]. He must place:

(1)   in the postal ballot box[4], any ballot paper the number on which is the same as the number (or one of the numbers) on the ballot paper envelope[5];

(2)   in the receptacle for rejected votes[6], any other ballot paper which is marked 'provisionally rejected' and must have the ballot paper envelope attached[7]; and

(3)   in the receptacle for rejected ballot paper envelopes[8], any ballot paper envelope which is marked 'provisionally rejected' because it does not contain either a ballot paper or, where more than one number appears on the ballot paper envelope, a sufficient number of ballot papers (and indicating, in such a case, the missing ballot paper)[9].

1   Ie at a parliamentary election, a local government election (which includes any London Authority election and a local authority mayoral election), a Welsh Assembly constituency or regional election (whether the polls are taken separately or together) or a European parliamentary election. As to the meanings of 'Assembly election', 'constituency election' and 'regional election' see PARA 3 note 2. As to the meaning of 'parliamentary election' see PARA 9. As to the meanings of 'Authority election' and 'local government election' see PARA 11. As to elections in the City of London see PARA 33. As to European parliamentary elections see PARA 217 et seq. There is no provision for absent voting at a poll consequent on a parish meeting on a question involving appointment to office: see PARA 200 et seq.
        As to returning officers generally see PARA 350 et seq. At a European parliamentary election, the returning officer referred to in the text is the local returning officer (see PARA 360): see the European Parliamentary Elections Regulations 2004, SI 2004/293, Sch 2 para 65(1), (2) (Sch 2 substituted by SI 2009/186). At a Welsh Assembly election, the constituency returning officer is the returning officer referred to in the text: see the National Assembly for Wales (Representation of the People) Order 2007, SI 2007/236, Sch 3 para 25(1), (2); but see also PARA 406 note 1. As to the meaning of 'constituency returning officer' for the purposes of Welsh Assembly elections see PARA 18 note 2.
2   As to the meaning of 'ballot paper envelope' see PARA 410.
3   Representation of the People (England and Wales) Regulations 2001, SI 2001/341, reg 86(1); European Parliamentary Elections Regulations 2004, SI 2004/293, Sch 2 para 65(1) (as substituted: see note 1); National Assembly for Wales (Representation of the People) Order 2007, SI 2007/236, Sch 3 para 25(1). As to the provision of a receptacle for ballot paper envelopes see PARA 417. As to the opening of a ballot paper envelope either because there is a mis-match between numbers on the voting documents or because the returning officer receives a covering envelope that does not contain the postal voting statement separately (and he has to open the ballot paper envelope to ascertain whether the postal voting statement is inside) see PARA 421.
        The Representation of the People (England and Wales) Regulations 2001, SI 2001/341, reg 86 has effect for the purposes of local authority referendums, subject to the modifications specified, in relation to Wales, by the Local Authorities (Conduct of Referendums) (Wales) Regulations 2008, SI 2008/1848, reg 8(2), Sch 4 Table 5, and, in relation to England, by the Local Authorities (Conduct of Referendums) (England) Regulations 2012, SI 2012/323, regs 8(2), 11–13, Sch 4 Table 6 (see PARA 15 note 2).
4   As to the meaning of 'postal ballot box' see PARA 417.
5   Representation of the People (England and Wales) Regulations 2001, SI 2001/341, reg 86(2)(a); European Parliamentary Elections Regulations 2004, SI 2004/293, Sch 2 para 65(2)(a) (as substituted: see note 1); National Assembly for Wales (Representation of the People) Order 2007, SI 2007/236, Sch 3 para 25(2)(a).
6   As to the provision of a receptacle for rejected votes see PARA 417.
7   Representation of the People (England and Wales) Regulations 2001, SI 2001/341, reg 86(2)(b); European Parliamentary Elections Regulations 2004, SI 2004/293, Sch 2 para 65(2)(b) (as substituted: see note 1); National Assembly for Wales (Representation of the People) Order 2007, SI 2007/236, Sch 3 para 25(2)(b).
8   As to the provision of a receptacle for rejected ballot paper envelopes see PARA 417.
9   Representation of the People (England and Wales) Regulations 2001, SI 2001/341, reg 86(2)(c); European Parliamentary Elections Regulations 2004, SI 2004/293, Sch 2 para 65(2)(c) (as substituted: see note 1); National Assembly for Wales (Representation of the People) Order 2007, SI 2007/236, Sch 3 para 25(2)(c).

423.   Conclusion of postal ballot procedure.   In respect of any election[1], the returning officer[2] must keep two separate lists of rejected postal ballot papers[3]:
(1)   in the first list, he must record the ballot paper number of any postal ballot paper for which no valid postal voting statement was received with it[4];
(2)   in the second list, he must record the ballot paper number of any postal

ballot paper which is entered on a valid postal voting statement where that ballot paper is not received with the postal voting statement[5].

Where the returning officer receives:

(a) a valid postal voting statement without the postal ballot paper (or papers or, as the case may be, all of the papers) to which it relates, he may, at any time prior to the close of the poll, check the list kept under head (1) above to see whether the number (or numbers) of a postal ballot paper to which the statement relates is entered in that list[6];

(b) a postal ballot paper without the postal voting statement to which it relates, he may, at any time prior to the close of the poll, check the list kept under head (2) above to see whether the number of that ballot paper is entered in that list[7].

The returning officer must conduct the checks required by heads (a) and (b) above as soon as practicable after the receipt of packets from every polling station in the constituency[8] or electoral area (or areas)[9] or local counting area[10] in question (as the case may be) following the close of poll[11]. Where the ballot paper number in the list matches that number on a valid postal voting statement or, as the case may be, the postal ballot paper, the returning officer must retrieve that statement or that paper[12]. As soon as practicable after the completion of this procedure, the returning officer must make up into separate packets the contents of:

(i) the receptacle of rejected votes[13];

(ii) the receptacle for postal voting statements[14];

(iii) the receptacle of rejected ballot paper envelopes[15];

(iv) the lists of spoilt and lost postal ballot papers[16];

(v) the receptacle of rejected votes (verification procedure)[17]; and

(vi) the receptacle of postal voting statements (verification procedure)[18],

and he must seal up the packets[19]. Any document in those packets marked 'provisionally rejected' must be deemed to be marked 'rejected'[20].

The returning officer must then take the appropriate steps under the provisions governing the receipt of postal ballot papers[21] as though any document earlier marked 'provisionally rejected' had not been so marked and he must amend the document accordingly[22].

1　Ie in respect of any parliamentary election or local government election (which includes any London Authority election and a local authority mayoral election), any Welsh Assembly constituency or regional election (whether the polls are taken separately or together) or any European parliamentary election. As to the meanings of 'Assembly election', 'constituency election' and 'regional election' see PARA 3 note 2. As to the meaning of 'parliamentary election' see PARA 9. As to the meanings of 'Authority election' and 'local government election' see PARA 11. As to elections in the City of London see PARA 33. As to European parliamentary elections see PARA 217 et seq. There is no provision for absent voting at a poll consequent on a parish meeting on a question involving appointment to office: see PARA 200 et seq.

2　As to returning officers generally see PARA 350 et seq. At a European parliamentary election, the returning officer referred to in the text is the local returning officer (see PARA 360): see the European Parliamentary Elections Regulations 2004, SI 2004/293, Sch 2 paras 67(1)–(3), 68(1)–(5), 69(1) (Sch 2 substituted by SI 2009/186). At a Welsh Assembly election, the constituency returning officer is the returning officer referred to in the text: see the National Assembly for Wales (Representation of the People) Order 2007, SI 2007/236, Sch 3 paras 27(1)–(3), 28(1)–(5), 29(1); but see also PARA 406 note 1. As to the meaning of 'constituency returning officer' for the purposes of Welsh Assembly elections see PARA 18 note 2.

3　Representation of the People (England and Wales) Regulations 2001, SI 2001/341, reg 87(1); European Parliamentary Elections Regulations 2004, SI 2004/293, Sch 2 para 67(1) (as substituted: see note 2); National Assembly for Wales (Representation of the People) Order 2007, SI 2007/236, Sch 3 para 27(1). As to the meaning of 'postal ballot paper' see PARA 407 note 1. As to the issue of postal ballot papers see PARA 406 et seq; and as to the rejection of postal ballot papers see also PARAS 420, 421. As to circumstances in which, following the close of the poll at a parliamentary or local government election, a registration officer must notify a person that his postal ballot paper has been rejected see PARA 426.

The Representation of the People (England and Wales) Regulations 2001, SI 2001/341, regs 87, 88, 89, have effect for the purposes of local authority referendums, subject to the modifications specified, in relation to Wales, by the Local Authorities (Conduct of Referendums) (Wales) Regulations 2008, SI 2008/1848, reg 8(2), Sch 4 Table 5, and, in relation to England, by the Local Authorities (Conduct of Referendums) (England) Regulations 2012, SI 2012/323, regs 8(2), 11–13, Sch 4 Table 6 (see PARA 15 note 2).

4   Representation of the People (England and Wales) Regulations 2001, SI 2001/341, reg 87(2) (regs 87(2), (3), 88(1), (2), (4) amended by SI 2006/2910); European Parliamentary Elections Regulations 2004, SI 2004/293, Sch 2 para 67(2) (as substituted: see note 2); National Assembly for Wales (Representation of the People) Order 2007, SI 2007/236, Sch 3 para 27(2). As to the postal voting statement see PARA 406. As to the meaning of 'valid postal voting statement', defined for the purposes of the Representation of the People (England and Wales) Regulations 2001, SI 2001/341, see PARA 421 note 22.

5   Representation of the People (England and Wales) Regulations 2001, SI 2001/341, reg 87(3) (as amended: see note 4); European Parliamentary Elections Regulations 2004, SI 2004/293, Sch 2 para 67(3) (as substituted: see note 2); National Assembly for Wales (Representation of the People) Order 2007, SI 2007/236, Sch 3 para 27(3).

6   Representation of the People (England and Wales) Regulations 2001, SI 2001/341, reg 88(1) (as amended: see note 4); European Parliamentary Elections Regulations 2004, SI 2004/293, Sch 2 para 68(1) (as substituted: see note 2); National Assembly for Wales (Representation of the People) Order 2007, SI 2007/236, Sch 3 para 28(1).

7   Representation of the People (England and Wales) Regulations 2001, SI 2001/341, reg 88(2) (as amended: see note 4); European Parliamentary Elections Regulations 2004, SI 2004/293, Sch 2 para 68(2) (as substituted: see note 2); National Assembly for Wales (Representation of the People) Order 2007, SI 2007/236, Sch 3 para 28(2).

8   As to the meaning of 'Assembly constituency' in relation to a Welsh Assembly election see PARA 3 note 2; as to the meaning of 'constituency' in relation to a parliamentary election see PARA 9; and as to the meaning of 'Assembly constituency' in the context of elections to the London Assembly see PARA 11.

9   As to the meaning of 'electoral area' for the purposes of local government elections see PARA 11. The National Assembly for Wales (Representation of the People) Order 2007, SI 2007/236, Sch 3 para 28(3) uses the term electoral area also but it is more usual to refer to an 'Assembly electoral region' (ie in contradistinction to an 'Assembly constituency': see note 8) (see PARA 3 note 2).

10   As to the meaning of 'local counting area' see PARA 139 note 1.

11   Representation of the People (England and Wales) Regulations 2001, SI 2001/341, reg 88(3); European Parliamentary Elections Regulations 2004, SI 2004/293, Sch 2 para 68(3) (as substituted: see note 2); National Assembly for Wales (Representation of the People) Order 2007, SI 2007/236, Sch 3 para 28(3). The text refers to the receipt of packets of ballot papers and other documents which the presiding officer is required to prepare on the close of poll at a polling station: see PARA 405. Where a poll at an election is combined with a referendum (see PARA 31), a polling station referred to in the text may be located in a voting area (meaning the area in which a referendum is held: see PARA 580 note 2).

12   Representation of the People (England and Wales) Regulations 2001, SI 2001/341, reg 88(4) (as amended: see note 4); European Parliamentary Elections Regulations 2004, SI 2004/293, Sch 2 para 68(4) (as substituted: see note 2); National Assembly for Wales (Representation of the People) Order 2007, SI 2007/236, Sch 3 para 28(4).

13   Representation of the People (England and Wales) Regulations 2001, SI 2001/341, reg 89(1)(a); European Parliamentary Elections Regulations 2004, SI 2004/293, Sch 2 para 69(1)(a) (as substituted: see note 2); National Assembly for Wales (Representation of the People) Order 2007, SI 2007/236, Sch 3 para 29(1)(a). As to the provision of a receptacle for rejected votes see PARA 417.

14   Representation of the People (England and Wales) Regulations 2001, SI 2001/341, reg 89(1)(b) (reg 89(1)(b), (c) amended, reg 89(1)(e), (f) added, by SI 2006/2910); European Parliamentary Elections Regulations 2004, SI 2004/293, Sch 2 para 69(1)(b) (as substituted: see note 2); National Assembly for Wales (Representation of the People) Order 2007, SI 2007/236, Sch 3 para 29(1)(b). As to the provision of a receptacle for postal voting statements see PARA 417.

15   Representation of the People (England and Wales) Regulations 2001, SI 2001/341, reg 89(1)(c) (as amended: see note 14); European Parliamentary Elections Regulations 2004, SI 2004/293,

Sch 2 para 69(1)(c) (as substituted: see note 2); National Assembly for Wales (Representation of the People) Order 2007, SI 2007/236, Sch 3 para 29(1)(c). As to the provision of a receptacle for rejected ballot paper envelopes see PARA 417.

16 Representation of the People (England and Wales) Regulations 2001, SI 2001/341, reg 89(1)(d); European Parliamentary Elections Regulations 2004, SI 2004/293, Sch 2 para 69(1)(d) (as substituted: see note 2); National Assembly for Wales (Representation of the People) Order 2007, SI 2007/236, Sch 3 para 29(1)(d). As to the lists of spoilt and lost postal ballot papers see PARAS 414, 415.

17 Representation of the People (England and Wales) Regulations 2001, SI 2001/341, reg 89(1)(e) (as added: see note 14); European Parliamentary Elections Regulations 2004, SI 2004/293, Sch 2 para 69(1)(e) (as substituted: see note 2); National Assembly for Wales (Representation of the People) Order 2007, SI 2007/236, Sch 3 para 29(1)(e). As to the provision of a receptacle for rejected votes (verification procedure) see PARA 417.

18 Representation of the People (England and Wales) Regulations 2001, SI 2001/341, reg 89(1)(f) (as added: see note 14); European Parliamentary Elections Regulations 2004, SI 2004/293, Sch 2 para 69(1)(f) (as substituted: see note 2); National Assembly for Wales (Representation of the People) Order 2007, SI 2007/236, Sch 3 para 29(1)(f). As to the provision of a receptacle for postal voting statements (verification procedure) see PARA 417.

19 Representation of the People (England and Wales) Regulations 2001, SI 2001/341, reg 89(1); European Parliamentary Elections Regulations 2004, SI 2004/293, Sch 2 para 69(1) (as substituted: see note 2); National Assembly for Wales (Representation of the People) Order 2007, SI 2007/236, Sch 3 para 29(1).

20 Representation of the People (England and Wales) Regulations 2001, SI 2001/341, reg 89(2); European Parliamentary Elections Regulations 2004, SI 2004/293, Sch 2 para 69(2) (as substituted: see note 2); National Assembly for Wales (Representation of the People) Order 2007, SI 2007/236, Sch 3 para 29(2).

21 Ie under the Representation of the People (England and Wales) Regulations 2001, SI 2001/341, Pt V (regs 64–91), or under the European Parliamentary Elections Regulations 2004, SI 2004/293, Sch 2 Pt 4 (Sch 2 paras 40–70), or under the National Assembly for Wales (Representation of the People) Order 2007, SI 2007/236, Sch 3 (see PARA 416 et seq): see the Representation of the People (England and Wales) Regulations 2001, SI 2001/341, reg 88(5); the European Parliamentary Elections Regulations 2004, SI 2004/293, Sch 2 para 68(5) (as substituted: see note 2); and the National Assembly for Wales (Representation of the People) Order 2007, SI 2007/236, Sch 3 para 28(5).

22 Representation of the People (England and Wales) Regulations 2001, SI 2001/341, reg 88(5); European Parliamentary Elections Regulations 2004, SI 2004/293, Sch 2 para 68(5) (as substituted: see note 2); National Assembly for Wales (Representation of the People) Order 2007, SI 2007/236, Sch 3 para 28(5).

(vii) Counting of the Votes

A.   PARLIAMENTARY AND LOCAL GOVERNMENT ELECTIONS (EXCEPT LOCAL AUTHORITY MAYORAL OR LONDON AUTHORITY ELECTION)

424. Arrangements for counting the votes at parliamentary and certain local elections. As soon as practicable after the close of the poll at a parliamentary or local government election (except an Authority or mayoral election)[1], or at a poll consequent on a parish meeting taken on the question of appointment to any office[2], the returning officer[3] must make arrangements for counting the votes in the presence of the counting agents[4]; and he must give to them notice in writing of the time and place at which he will begin to count the votes[5]. No person other than:

(1)   the returning officer and his clerks[6];

(2)   the candidates and one other person chosen by each of them (or, in the case of such a poll consequent on a parish meeting, the candidates and their spouses or civil partners)[7];

(3)   the election agents (at elections where election agents are appointed)[8];

(4)   the counting agents[9]; and

(5)   persons who are entitled to attend at such an election (but not at such a
        poll consequent on a parish meeting) by virtue of any of the provisions
        of the Political Parties, Elections and Referendums Act 2000[10] which
        allow Electoral Commission representatives and accredited observers to
        attend electoral proceedings and observe working practices[11],

may be present at the counting of the votes, unless permitted by the returning
officer to attend[12]. A person not entitled to attend at the counting of the votes
may not be permitted to do so by the returning officer, however, unless:

(a)   he is satisfied that the efficient counting of the votes will not be
        impeded[13]; and

(b)   he has either consulted the election agents (if appointed) or thought it
        impracticable to do so[14].

The returning officer must make such arrangements as he thinks fit to ensure
that every person attending at the counting of the votes (other than any constable
on duty at the counting) has been given a copy in writing of the statutory
provisions relating to the requirement of secrecy that apply to such attendance[15].

The returning officer must give the counting agents all such reasonable
facilities for overseeing the proceedings, and all such information with respect to
them, as he can give them consistently with the orderly conduct of the
proceedings and the discharge of his duties in connection with them[16]. In
particular, where the votes are counted by sorting the ballot papers according to
the candidate for whom the vote is given, and then counting the number of ballot
papers for each candidate, the counting agents are entitled to satisfy themselves
that the ballot papers are correctly sorted[17].

Where the poll at an election is taken together with the poll at another
election or referendum, special provision is made for counting the votes[18].

1   As to the meaning of 'parliamentary election' see PARA 9; and as to the meanings of 'Authority
    election' and 'local government election' see PARA 11. As to elections in the City of London see
    PARA 33. As to the count at a London Authority election (except for London Mayor) see
    PARA 443 et seq; and as to the counting at elections for a local authority or London Mayor see
    PARAS 435 et seq, 451 et seq.

2   As to polls consequent on a parish meeting on a question involving appointment to office see
    PARA 200 et seq.

3   As to returning officers for parliamentary elections see PARA 350 et seq; as to returning officers
    for local government elections see PARA 354 et seq; and as to the returning officer at a poll
    consequent on parish meeting taken on the question of appointment to any office see PARA 356.
    As to the functions of returning officers where the poll at an election is taken together with the
    poll at another election or referendum see PARA 18.

4   As to the appointment of counting agents by a candidate, and as to the effect of their
    non-attendance, see PARA 394. In making such arrangements in relation to a parliamentary
    election, the returning officer must have regard to the duty imposed on him, to start counting
    within four hours starting with the close of the poll, by the Representation of the People
    Act 1983 Sch 1 r 45(3A) (see PARA 425): Sch 1 r 44(6) (added by the Constitutional Reform and
    Governance Act 2010 s 48(1), (2)).

5   Representation of the People Act 1983 Sch 1 r 44(1); Parish and Community Meetings (Polls)
    Rules 1987, SI 1987/1, Schedule r 26(1); Local Elections (Principal Areas) (England and Wales)
    Rules 2006, SI 2006/3304, Sch 2 r 44(1); Local Elections (Parishes and Communities) (England
    and Wales) Rules 2006, SI 2006/3305, Sch 2 r 44(1).

6   Representation of the People Act 1983 Sch 1 r 44(2)(a); Parish and Community Meetings (Polls)
    Rules 1987, SI 1987/1, Schedule r 26(2)(a); Local Elections (Principal Areas) (England and
    Wales) Rules 2006, SI 2006/3304, Sch 2 r 44(2)(a); Local Elections (Parishes and Communities)
    (England and Wales) Rules 2006, SI 2006/3305, Sch 2 r 44(2)(a).

7   Representation of the People Act 1983 Sch 1 r 44(2)(b) (amended by the Electoral
    Administration Act 2006 s 47, Sch 1 paras 69, 85(1), (2)); Parish and Community Meetings
    (Polls) Rules 1987, SI 1987/1, Schedule r 26(2)(b) (amended by SI 2005/2114); Local Elections

(Principal Areas) (England and Wales) Rules 2006, SI 2006/3304, Sch 2 r 44(2)(b); Local Elections (Parishes and Communities) (England and Wales) Rules 2006, SI 2006/3305, Sch 2 r 44(2)(b).

8 Representation of the People Act 1983 Sch 1 r 44(2)(c); Local Elections (Principal Areas) (England and Wales) Rules 2006, SI 2006/3304, Sch 2 r 44(2)(c); Local Elections (Parishes and Communities) (England and Wales) Rules 2006, SI 2006/3305, Sch 2 r 44(2)(c). As to the appointment of election agents for parliamentary or local government elections see PARA 231 et seq. A candidate at a local government election for a parish or community council need not have an election agent (see PARA 231 note 3) and no provision is made at all for election agents to be appointed at a poll consequent on a parish meeting on a question involving appointment to office. Accordingly, the provision set out in head (3) in the text is omitted in the latter case and may be redundant in the first case.

9 Representation of the People Act 1983 Sch 1 r 44(2)(d); Parish and Community Meetings (Polls) Rules 1987, SI 1987/1, Schedule r 26(2)(d); Local Elections (Principal Areas) (England and Wales) Rules 2006, SI 2006/3304, Sch 2 r 44(2)(d); Local Elections (Parishes and Communities) (England and Wales) Rules 2006, SI 2006/3305, Sch 2 r 44(2)(d).

10 Ie by virtue of any of the provisions of the Political Parties, Elections and Referendums Act 2000 ss 6A–6D (see PARA 53): see the Representation of the People Act 1983 Sch 1 r 44(2)(e) (added by the Electoral Administration Act 2006 Sch 1 paras 69, 85(1), (3)); the Local Elections (Principal Areas) (England and Wales) Rules 2006, SI 2006/3304, Sch 2 r 44(2)(e); and the Local Elections (Parishes and Communities) (England and Wales) Rules 2006, SI 2006/3305, Sch 2 r 44(2)(e).

11 Representation of the People Act 1983 Sch 1 r 44(2)(e) (as added: see note 10); Local Elections (Principal Areas) (England and Wales) Rules 2006, SI 2006/3304, Sch 2 r 44(2)(e); Local Elections (Parishes and Communities) (England and Wales) Rules 2006, SI 2006/3305, Sch 2 r 44(2)(e).

12 Representation of the People Act 1983 Sch 1 r 44(2); Parish and Community Meetings (Polls) Rules 1987, SI 1987/1, Schedule r 26(2); Local Elections (Principal Areas) (England and Wales) Rules 2006, SI 2006/3304, Sch 2 r 44(2); Local Elections (Parishes and Communities) (England and Wales) Rules 2006, SI 2006/3305, Sch 2 r 44(2).

13 Representation of the People Act 1983 Sch 1 r 44(3)(a); Parish and Community Meetings (Polls) Rules 1987, SI 1987/1, Schedule r 26(3); Local Elections (Principal Areas) (England and Wales) Rules 2006, SI 2006/3304, Sch 2 r 44(3)(a); Local Elections (Parishes and Communities) (England and Wales) Rules 2006, SI 2006/3305, Sch 2 r 44(3)(a).

14 Representation of the People Act 1983 Sch 1 r 44(3)(b); Local Elections (Principal Areas) (England and Wales) Rules 2006, SI 2006/3304, Sch 2 r 44(3)(b); Local Elections (Parishes and Communities) (England and Wales) Rules 2006, SI 2006/3305, Sch 2 r 44(3)(b). At parish or community council elections, where there is no requirement for election agents to be appointed (see note 8), the reference in the text to election agents should be read as a reference to the candidates: see Sch 2 r 44(3)(b). At a poll consequent on a parish meeting on a question involving appointment to office, where there is no provision at all for election agents to be appointed (see note 8), head (b) in the text does not apply at all.

15 See PARAS 385, 739–741.

16 Representation of the People Act 1983 Sch 1 r 44(4); Parish and Community Meetings (Polls) Rules 1987, SI 1987/1, Schedule r 26(4); Local Elections (Principal Areas) (England and Wales) Rules 2006, SI 2006/3304, Sch 2 r 44(4); Local Elections (Parishes and Communities) (England and Wales) Rules 2006, SI 2006/3305, Sch 2 r 44(4).

17 Representation of the People Act 1983 Sch 1 r 44(5); Parish and Community Meetings (Polls) Rules 1987, SI 1987/1, Schedule r 26(5)(a); Local Elections (Principal Areas) (England and Wales) Rules 2006, SI 2006/3304, Sch 2 r 44(5); Local Elections (Parishes and Communities) (England and Wales) Rules 2006, SI 2006/3305, Sch 2 r 44(5).

18 As to polls at elections or referendums which are taken together see PARA 16 et seq.

425. Verification of ballot paper accounts and counting of ballot papers at parliamentary and certain local elections. The returning officer at a parliamentary or local government election (except an Authority or mayoral election)[1], or at a poll consequent on a parish meeting taken on the question of appointment to any office[2], must:

(1)   in the presence of the counting agents[3], open each ballot box and count and record the number of ballot papers in it[4];

(2) in the presence of the election agents (or, where such agents are not appointed, the counting agents[5]), verify each ballot paper account[6]; and

(3) count such of the postal ballot papers as have been duly returned and record the number counted[7].

A postal ballot paper must not be taken to be duly returned at an election unless:

(a) it is returned in the prescribed manner[8] and reaches the returning officer or a polling station in the constituency or electoral area in question (as the case may be) before the close of the poll[9];

(b) the postal voting statement, duly signed, is also returned in the prescribed manner[10], and reaches him or such a polling station before that time[11];

(c) the postal voting statement also states the date of birth of the elector or proxy, as the case may be[12]; and

(d) in a case where steps for verifying the date of birth and signature of an elector or proxy have been prescribed[13], the returning officer (having taken such steps) has verified the date of birth and signature of the elector or proxy, as the case may be[14].

The returning officer at a parliamentary election must take reasonable steps to begin counting the votes given on the ballot papers as soon as practicable within the period of four hours starting with the close of the poll[15]; but the returning officer at any election must not count the votes given on any ballot papers until:

(i) in the case of postal ballot papers, they have been mixed with the ballot papers from at least one ballot box[16]; and

(ii) in the case of ballot papers from a ballot box, they have been mixed with the ballot papers from at least one other ballot box[17].

The returning officer must not count any tendered ballot paper[18]. While counting and recording the number of ballot papers and counting the votes, the returning officer must keep the ballot papers with their faces upwards, and he must take all proper precautions for preventing any person from seeing the numbers and other unique identifying marks (where these apply) printed on the back of the papers[19].

The returning officer must verify each ballot paper account by comparing it with the number of ballot papers recorded by him, and the unused and spoilt ballot papers[20] in his possession, and the tendered votes list[21] (opening and resealing the packets containing the unused and spoilt ballot papers, and the tendered votes list)[22]. He must draw up a statement as to the result of the verification, which any election agent (or any counting agent, as the case may be[23]) may copy[24].

The returning officer must, so far as practicable, proceed continuously with counting the votes, allowing only time for refreshment, except that he may[25] exclude the hours between seven in the evening and nine on the following morning[26]. During the time so excluded, the returning officer must:

(A) place the ballot papers and other documents relating to the election under his own seal, and the seals of such of the counting agents as desire to affix their seals[27]; and

(B) otherwise take proper precautions for the security of the papers and documents[28].

Where the poll at an election is taken together with the poll at another election or referendum, special provision is made for counting the votes[29].

1 As to the meaning of 'parliamentary election' see PARA 9; and as to the meanings of 'Authority election' and 'local government election' see PARA 11. As to elections in the City of London see

PARA 33. As to the count at a London Authority election (except for London Mayor) see PARA 443 et seq; and as to the counting at elections for a local authority or London Mayor see PARAS 435 et seq, 451 et seq. As to returning officers for parliamentary elections see PARA 350 et seq; and as to returning officers for local government elections see PARA 354 et seq. As to the functions of returning officers where the poll at an election is taken together with the poll at another election or referendum see PARA 18.

2   As to polls consequent on a parish meeting on a question involving appointment to office see PARA 200 et seq. As to the returning officer at a poll consequent on parish meeting taken on the question of appointment to any office see PARA 356.

3   As to the appointment of counting agents by a candidate, and as to the effect of their non-attendance, see PARA 394.

4   Representation of the People Act 1983 Sch 1 r 45(1)(a) (Sch 1 r 45(1) substituted, Sch 1 r 45(1A) added, by the Representation of the People Act 1985 s 24, Sch 4 para 82); Parish and Community Meetings (Polls) Rules 1987, SI 1987/1, Schedule r 27(1)(a); Local Elections (Principal Areas) (England and Wales) Rules 2006, SI 2006/3304, Sch 2 r 45(1)(a); Local Elections (Parishes and Communities) (England and Wales) Rules 2006, SI 2006/3305, Sch 2 r 45(1)(a).

5   As to the appointment of election agents at parliamentary or local government elections see PARA 231 et seq. A candidate at a local government election for a parish or community council need not have an election agent (see PARA 231 note 3), and no provision is made at all for election agents to be appointed at a poll consequent on a parish meeting on a question involving appointment to office, so verification can only take place in those cases in the presence of counting agents.

6   Representation of the People Act 1983 Sch 1 r 45(1)(b) (as substituted: see note 4); Parish and Community Meetings (Polls) Rules 1987, SI 1987/1, Schedule r 27(1)(a); Local Elections (Principal Areas) (England and Wales) Rules 2006, SI 2006/3304, Sch 2 r 45(1)(b); Local Elections (Parishes and Communities) (England and Wales) Rules 2006, SI 2006/3305, Sch 2 r 45(1)(b). As to the ballot paper account see PARA 405.

7   Representation of the People Act 1983 Sch 1 r 45(1)(c) (as substituted: see note 4); Local Elections (Principal Areas) (England and Wales) Rules 2006, SI 2006/3304, Sch 2 r 45(1)(c); Local Elections (Parishes and Communities) (England and Wales) Rules 2006, SI 2006/3305, Sch 2 r 45(1)(c). There is no provision for voting by post or by proxy at a poll consequent on a parish meeting on a question involving appointment to office, and accordingly the provisions set out in head (2), heads (a)–(d), and head (i) in the text do not apply in that case. As to the returning officer's duty to record the return of a postal vote in respect of a person who is entered on the postal voters list, or a proxy postal vote in respect of a proxy who is entered on the proxy postal voters list, see PARA 418.

8   For the purposes of the Representation of the People Act 1983, 'prescribed' means prescribed by regulations: see s 202(1). As to the making of regulations under the Representation of the People Act 1983 generally see PARA 28 note 16. Accordingly, for the purposes of a parliamentary election, the manner in which a postal ballot paper or postal voting statement (as to which see head (b) in the text) may be returned to a polling station is by hand only (Representation of the People (England and Wales) Regulations 2001, SI 2001/341, reg 79(1) (reg 79(1), (2) amended by SI 2006/2910)); and the manner in which such a paper or statement may be returned to the returning officer is either by hand or by post (Representation of the People (England and Wales) Regulations 2001, SI 2001/341, reg 79(2) (as so amended). As to the meaning of 'postal ballot paper' see PARA 407 note 1. As to the postal voting statement see PARA 406. The provision made by reg 79 has effect for the purposes of local authority referendums, subject to the modifications specified, in relation to Wales, by the Local Authorities (Conduct of Referendums) (Wales) Regulations 2008, SI 2008/1848, reg 8(2), Sch 4 Table 5, and, in relation to England, by the Local Authorities (Conduct of Referendums) (England) Regulations 2012, SI 2012/323, regs 8(2), 11–13, Sch 4 Table 6 (see para 15 note 2).

For the purposes of a local government election for a principal area, parish or community council, the manner in which any postal ballot paper or postal voting statement may be returned is set out as follows, i e either by hand or by post, if returned to the returning officer, or by hand only, if returned to a polling station: Local Elections (Principal Areas) (England and Wales) Rules 2006, SI 2006/3304, Sch 2 r 45(4); Local Elections (Parishes and Communities) (England and Wales) Rules 2006, SI 2006/3305, Sch 2 r 45(4). As to a poll consequent on a parish meeting on a question involving appointment to office see note 5.

As to the provision that may be made regarding the circumstances in which, following the close of the poll at a parliamentary or local government election, a registration officer must notify a person that the person's postal ballot paper has been rejected see PARA 426.

9   Representation of the People Act 1983 Sch 1 r 45(1B)(a) (Sch 1 r 45(1B) added by the
    Representation of the People Act 2000 s 15(1), Sch 6 paras 3, 10(1), (4)(a)); Local Elections
    (Principal Areas) (England and Wales) Rules 2006, SI 2006/3304, Sch 2 r 45(3)(a); Local
    Elections (Parishes and Communities) (England and Wales) Rules 2006, SI 2006/3305, Sch 2
    r 45(3)(a). As to a poll consequent on a parish meeting on a question involving appointment to
    office see note 7.

10 See note 8.

11 Representation of the People Act 1983 Sch 1 r 45(1B)(b) (Sch 1 r 45(1B) as added (see note 9);
    Sch 1 r 45(1B)(b) amended, Sch 1 r 45(1B)(c), (d) added, by the Electoral Administration
    Act 2006 ss 47, 74(2), Sch 1 paras 69, 73(1), (2), (3), Sch 2); Local Elections (Principal Areas)
    (England and Wales) Rules 2006, SI 2006/3304, Sch 2 r 45(3)(b); Local Elections (Parishes and
    Communities) (England and Wales) Rules 2006, SI 2006/3305, Sch 2 r 45(3)(b). As to a poll
    consequent on a parish meeting on a question involving appointment to office see note 7. As to
    the means by which a postal voter may validly make the returns mentioned in the text see
    further PARA 418.

12 Representation of the People Act 1983 Sch 1 r 45(1B)(c) (as added: see note 9); Local Elections
    (Principal Areas) (England and Wales) Rules 2006, SI 2006/3304, Sch 2 r 45(3)(c); Local
    Elections (Parishes and Communities) (England and Wales) Rules 2006, SI 2006/3305, Sch 2
    r 45(3)(c). As to a poll consequent on a parish meeting on a question involving appointment to
    office see note 7.

13 Ie prescribed by regulations made under the Representation of the People Act 1983: see
    s 202(1); the Local Elections (Principal Areas) (England and Wales) Rules 2006, SI 2006/3304,
    Sch 2 r 45(3)(d); and the Local Elections (Parishes and Communities) (England and Wales)
    Rules 2006, SI 2006/3305, Sch 2 r 45(3)(d). As to the regulations so prescribed see the
    Representation of the People (England and Wales) Regulations 2001, SI 2001/341, regs 85, 85A;
    and PARA 421.

14 Representation of the People Act 1983 Sch 1 r 45(1B)(d) (as added: see note 9); Local Elections
    (Principal Areas) (England and Wales) Rules 2006, SI 2006/3304, Sch 2 r 45(3)(d); Local
    Elections (Parishes and Communities) (England and Wales) Rules 2006, SI 2006/3305, Sch 2
    r 45(3)(d). As to a poll consequent on a parish meeting on a question involving appointment to
    office see note 7.

15 Representation of the People Act 1983 Sch 1 r 45(3A) (Sch 1 r 45(3A), (8) added by the
    Constitutional Reform and Governance Act 2010 s 48(1), (3)). The Electoral Commission must
    issue guidance to returning officer on the duty imposed by the Representation of the People
    Act 1983 Sch 1 r 45(3A): see Sch 1 r 45(8) (as so added). The returning officer, in making
    arrangements for counting the votes in the presence of counting agents at a parliamentary
    election, must have regard to the duty imposed on him by Sch 1 r 45(3A): see Sch 1 r 44(6); and
    PARA 424 note 4. In a contested parliamentary election, if the counting of the votes given on the
    ballot papers did not begin within the period specified in Sch 1 r 45(3A), the returning officer
    must, before the expiry of the period of 30 days starting with the day on which the poll closed
    prepare and publish a statement, which must (see Sch 1 r 53ZA(1)(a), (2) (Sch 1 r 53ZA added
    by the Constitutional Reform and Governance Act 2010 s 48(1), (4))):
    (1)   specify the time at which the counting of the votes given on the ballot papers began
          (Representation of the People Act 1983 Sch 1 r 53ZA(2)(a) (as so added));
    (2)   describe the steps taken under Sch 1 r 45(3A) (see Sch 1 r 53ZA(2)(b) (as so added));
          and
    (3)   explain why the counting of the votes given on the ballot papers did not start within the
          period specified in Sch 1 r 45(3A) (see Sch 1 r 53ZA(2)(c) (as so added)),
    and he must deliver it to the Electoral Commission (Sch 1 r 53ZA(1)(b) (as so added)). Where a
    statement is so delivered to the Electoral Commission, the Commission must specify in any
    election report they produce that a statement has been delivered to them under Sch 1
    r 53ZA(1)(b) in respect of the constituency to which the statement relates: Sch 1 r 53ZA(3) (as
    so added). For these purposes, 'election report' means a report under the Political Parties,
    Elections and Referendums Act 2000 s 5(1) or s 5(2A) (see PARA 51) in relation to the
    parliamentary election in question: Representation of the People Act 1983 Sch 1 r 53ZA(4) (as
    so added). As to the establishment and constitution of the Electoral Commission see PARA 34 et
    seq.

16 Representation of the People Act 1983 Sch 1 r 45(1A)(a) (as added see note 4); Local Elections
    (Principal Areas) (England and Wales) Rules 2006, SI 2006/3304, Sch 2 r 45(2)(a); Local
    Elections (Parishes and Communities) (England and Wales) Rules 2006, SI 2006/3305, Sch 2
    r 45(2)(a). There is no provision for voting by post or by proxy at a poll consequent on a parish
    meeting on a question involving appointment to office; but see note 17.

17 Representation of the People Act 1983 Sch 1 r 45(1A)(b) (as added see note 4); Local Elections (Principal Areas) (England and Wales) Rules 2006, SI 2006/3304, Sch 2 r 45(2)(b); Local Elections (Parishes and Communities) (England and Wales) Rules 2006, SI 2006/3305, Sch 2 r 45(2)(b). The procedure set out in the text does not apply at a poll consequent on a parish meeting on a question involving appointment to office. However, where two such polls have been taken together, the returning officer must separate the ballot papers relating to each poll and count and record the number of ballot papers relating to each poll (Parish and Community Meetings (Polls) Rules 1987, SI 1987/1, Schedule r 27(1)(b)), and he must then mix together the whole of the ballot papers relating to the poll or each poll, as the case may be, which were contained in the ballot boxes (Schedule r 27(1)(c)).

18 Representation of the People Act 1983 Sch 1 r 45(3); Parish and Community Meetings (Polls) Rules 1987, SI 1987/1, Schedule r 27(2); Local Elections (Principal Areas) (England and Wales) Rules 2006, SI 2006/3304, Sch 2 r 45(5); Local Elections (Parishes and Communities) (England and Wales) Rules 2006, SI 2006/3305, Sch 2 r 45(5). As to tendered ballot papers see PARA 403; and as to adding votes on a scrutiny see PARA 839 et seq.

19 Representation of the People Act 1983 Sch 1 r 45(4) (amended by the Electoral Administration Act 2006 Sch 1 paras 69, 91); Parish and Community Meetings (Polls) Rules 1987, SI 1987/1, Schedule r 27(3); Local Elections (Principal Areas) (England and Wales) Rules 2006, SI 2006/3304, Sch 2 r 45(6); Local Elections (Parishes and Communities) (England and Wales) Rules 2006, SI 2006/3305, Sch 2 r 45(6). At a poll consequent on a parish meeting on a question involving appointment to office, the returning officer must keep the ballot papers with their faces upwards and take all proper precautions for preventing any person from seeing the numbers printed on the back of the papers also while separating the ballot papers (see note 17): see the Parish and Community Meetings (Polls) Rules 1987, SI 1987/1, Schedule r 27(3). As to the number and other security marks which must be printed on the back of every ballot paper see PARA 387.

20 As to spoilt ballot papers see PARA 404.

21 As to the tendered votes list see PARA 403.

22 Representation of the People Act 1983 Sch 1 r 45(5); Parish and Community Meetings (Polls) Rules 1987, SI 1987/1, Schedule r 27(4); Local Elections (Principal Areas) (England and Wales) Rules 2006, SI 2006/3304, Sch 2 r 45(7); Local Elections (Parishes and Communities) (England and Wales) Rules 2006, SI 2006/3305, Sch 2 r 45(7).

23 See note 5.

24 Representation of the People Act 1983 Sch 1 r 45(5); Parish and Community Meetings (Polls) Rules 1987, SI 1987/1, Schedule r 27(4); Local Elections (Principal Areas) (England and Wales) Rules 2006, SI 2006/3304, Sch 2 r 45(7); Local Elections (Parishes and Communities) (England and Wales) Rules 2006, SI 2006/3305, Sch 2 r 45(7).

25 This exception applies at a parliamentary election only in so far as the returning officer and the counting agents agree, although the agreement of a candidate or his election agent is as effective as the agreement of his counting agents: see the Representation of the People Act 1983 Sch 1 r 45(6). At a poll consequent on a parish meeting on a question involving appointment to office, the exception applies only in so far as the returning officer thinks necessary: see the Parish and Community Meetings (Polls) Rules 1987, SI 1987/1, Schedule r 27(5).

26 Representation of the People Act 1983 Sch 1 r 45(6); Parish and Community Meetings (Polls) Rules 1987, SI 1987/1, Schedule r 27(5); Local Elections (Principal Areas) (England and Wales) Rules 2006, SI 2006/3304, Sch 2 r 45(8); Local Elections (Parishes and Communities) (England and Wales) Rules 2006, SI 2006/3305, Sch 2 r 45(8).

27 Representation of the People Act 1983 Sch 1 r 45(7)(a); Parish and Community Meetings (Polls) Rules 1987, SI 1987/1, Schedule r 27(6)(a); Local Elections (Principal Areas) (England and Wales) Rules 2006, SI 2006/3304, Sch 2 r 45(9)(a); Local Elections (Parishes and Communities) (England and Wales) Rules 2006, SI 2006/3305, Sch 2 r 45(9)(a).

28 Representation of the People Act 1983 Sch 1 r 45(7)(b); Parish and Community Meetings (Polls) Rules 1987, SI 1987/1, Schedule r 27(6)(b); Local Elections (Principal Areas) (England and Wales) Rules 2006, SI 2006/3304, Sch 2 r 45(9)(b); Local Elections (Parishes and Communities) (England and Wales) Rules 2006, SI 2006/3305, Sch 2 r 45(9)(b).

29 As to polls at elections or referendums which are taken together see PARA 16 et seq.

426.   Notification of rejected postal vote following close of poll at parliamentary or local government election. Regulations may make provision as to circumstances in which, following the close of the poll at a parliamentary or local government election[1], a registration officer[2] must[3]:

(1)   notify a person that the person's postal ballot paper has been rejected[4]; and

(2)   where such notification is required to be given to a person appointed as proxy to vote for another ('the elector')[5] in respect of a proxy postal ballot paper, notify the elector that the ballot paper has been rejected[6].

Such regulations may include provision as to: (a) the information to be notified (which may include information as to the respect in which the postal voting statement was not duly completed)[7]; (b) the time within which the notification is to be given[8]; and (c) the way in which it is to be given[9].

1   As to the meaning of 'parliamentary election' see PARA 9; and as to the meaning of 'local government election' see PARA 11.
2   As to registration officers see PARA 139 et seq.
3   See the Representation of the People Act 2000 s 12, Sch 4 para 7E(1) (Sch 4 para 7E added by the Electoral Registration and Administration Act 2013 s 22(1)). At the date at which this volume states the law, no such regulations had been made.
     The Representation of the People Act 2000 s 12, Sch 4 are applied and modified for the purpose of local authority mayoral elections in England and Wales by the Local Authorities (Mayoral Elections) (England and Wales) Regulations 2007, SI 2007/1024, reg 3(2)–(5), Sch 2 Table 3 (see PARA 11 note 14); and they have effect for the purposes of local authority referendums, subject to the modifications specified, in relation to Wales, by the Local Authorities (Conduct of Referendums) (Wales) Regulations 2008, SI 2008/1848, reg 8(2), Sch 4 Table 2, and, in relation to England, by the Local Authorities (Conduct of Referendums) (England) Regulations 2012, SI 2012/323, regs 8(2), 11–13, Sch 4 Table 3 (see PARA 15 note 2).
4   Representation of the People Act 2000 Sch 4 para 7E(1)(a) (as added: see note 3). For these purposes, a postal ballot paper is 'rejected' if it was not taken to have been duly returned in accordance with the appropriate rules because the returned postal voting statement was not duly completed: Sch 4 para 7E(2) (as so added). For these purposes, the 'appropriate rules' means, in the case of a parliamentary election, the parliamentary elections rules, and, in the case of a local government election, rules made (or having effect as if made) under the Representation of the People Act 1983 s 36 (see PARA 383): see the Representation of the People Act 2000 Sch 4 para 1(1). As to the meaning of 'parliamentary elections rules' see PARA 383 note 2; definition applied by virtue of Sch 4 para 1(2). As to the issue of postal ballot papers and postal voting statements see PARA 406 et seq; as to their return see PARA 416 et seq; and as to the rejection of postal ballot papers see PARAS 420–423, 425.
5   As to the meaning of 'elector', in relation to a parliamentary or local government election generally, see PARA 95 note 2. As to persons appointed to vote as proxy for an elector see PARA 374 et seq.
6   Representation of the People Act 2000 Sch 4 para 7E(1)(b) (as added: see note 3).
7   Representation of the People Act 2000 Sch 4 para 7E(3)(a) (as added: see note 3).
8   Representation of the People Act 2000 Sch 4 para 7E(3)(b) (as added: see note 3).
9   Representation of the People Act 2000 Sch 4 para 7E(3)(c) (as added: see note 3).

427. Ballot papers rejected for want of official mark at parliamentary and certain local elections.   Any ballot paper which has been given at a parliamentary or local government election (except an Authority or mayoral election)[1], or at a poll consequent on a parish meeting taken on the question of appointment to any office[2], and which does not bear the official mark[3], is void and must not be counted[4]. However, where not all of the holes which should have been made by the official mark perforate the ballot paper, but the marks which do appear indicate the intention to apply the official mark, the ballot paper should not be rejected[5].

1   As to the meaning of 'parliamentary election' see PARA 9; and as to the meanings of 'Authority election' and 'local government election' see PARA 11. As to elections in the City of London see PARA 33. As to the count at a London Authority election (except for London Mayor) see PARA 443 et seq; and as to the counting at elections for a local authority or London Mayor see PARAS 435 et seq, 451 et seq.

2 As to polls consequent on a parish meeting on a question involving appointment to office see PARA 200 et seq.

3 Representation of the People Act 1983 Sch 1 r 47(1)(a); Parish and Community Meetings (Polls) Rules 1987, SI 1987/1, Schedule r 29(1)(a); Local Elections (Principal Areas) (England and Wales) Rules 2006, SI 2006/3304, Sch 2 r 47(1)(a); Local Elections (Parishes and Communities) (England and Wales) Rules 2006, SI 2006/3305, Sch 2 r 47(1)(a). As to the official mark in use at each election see PARA 387.

4 See the Representation of the People Act 1983 Sch 1 r 47(1); the Parish and Community Meetings (Polls) Rules 1987, SI 1987/1, Schedule r 29(1); the Local Elections (Principal Areas) (England and Wales) Rules 2006, SI 2006/3304, Sch 2 r 47(1); and the Local Elections (Parishes and Communities) (England and Wales) Rules 2006, SI 2006/3305, Sch 2 r 47(1). As to the treatment of rejected votes see PARA 431 et seq; and as to scrutiny, which may look at ballot papers and investigate how votes have been recorded, see PARA 839 et seq.

5 _Re South Newington (Kingston-upon-Hull) Municipal Election Petition, Lewis v Shepperdson_ [1948] 2 All ER 503 at 507 per Birkett J (applying the reasoning in _Gloucester County, Cirencester Division, Case_ (1893) 4 O'M & H 194).

428. Ballot papers rejected for voter exceeding the number of votes he is entitled to give at parliamentary and certain local elections. Any ballot paper which has been given at a parliamentary or local government election (except an Authority or mayoral election)[1], or at a poll consequent on a parish meeting taken on the question of appointment to any office[2], and on which votes are given:

(1)   for more than one candidate at a parliamentary election[3]; or
(2)   (otherwise) for more candidates than the voter is entitled to vote for[4],

is void and must not be counted[5].

1 As to the meaning of 'parliamentary election' see PARA 9; and as to the meanings of 'Authority election' and 'local government election' see PARA 11. As to elections in the City of London see PARA 33. As to the count at a London Authority election (except for London Mayor) see PARA 443 et seq; and as to the counting at elections for a local authority or London Mayor see PARAS 435 et seq, 451 et seq.

2 As to polls consequent on a parish meeting on a question involving appointment to office see PARA 200 et seq.

3 Representation of the People Act 1983 Sch 1 r 47(1)(b).

4 Parish and Community Meetings (Polls) Rules 1987, SI 1987/1, Schedule r 29(1)(b); Local Elections (Principal Areas) (England and Wales) Rules 2006, SI 2006/3304, Sch 2 r 47(1)(b); Local Elections (Parishes and Communities) (England and Wales) Rules 2006, SI 2006/3305, Sch 2 r 47(1)(b). As to the number of votes permitted at a local government election see PARA 384.

5 See the Representation of the People Act 1983 Sch 1 r 47(1); the Parish and Community Meetings (Polls) Rules 1987, SI 1987/1, Schedule r 29(1); the Local Elections (Principal Areas) (England and Wales) Rules 2006, SI 2006/3304, Sch 2 r 47(1); and the Local Elections (Parishes and Communities) (England and Wales) Rules 2006, SI 2006/3305, Sch 2 r 47(1). As to the treatment of rejected votes see PARA 431 et seq. As to scrutiny, which may look at ballot papers and investigate how votes have been recorded, see PARA 839 et seq. Whether a mark on a ballot paper amounts to a vote for a particular candidate is a matter of fact: see PARA 856 note 4.

429. Ballot papers rejected for marks identifying the voter at parliamentary and certain local elections. Any ballot paper which has been given at a parliamentary or local government election (except an Authority or mayoral election)[1], or at a poll consequent on a parish meeting taken on the question of appointment to any office[2], and on which anything is written or marked by which the voter can be identified (except the printed number or other unique identifying mark on the back) is void and must not be counted[3]. The writing or mark must be such that the voter can be, and not merely might be, identified[4]. Ballot papers have been rejected because they were marked upon their faces by the presiding officer with the number on the register of the voter[5]. A ballot paper on which the vote is marked:

(1)   elsewhere than in the proper place[6];

(2)   otherwise than by means of a cross[7]; or

(3)   by more than one mark[8],

must not for such reason be deemed to be void[9] if an intention that the vote is for one or other of the candidates clearly appears, and the way the paper is marked does not of itself identify the voter and it is not shown that he can be identified by it[10]. The mere fact that it is in handwriting does not of itself show the voter can be identified[11].

The returning officer is not obliged to hold an inquiry to enable him to decide whether the voter can be identified by the mark[12], but he should receive evidence which is offered to him[13].

1   As to the meaning of 'parliamentary election' see PARA 9; and as to the meanings of 'Authority election' and 'local government election' see PARA 11. As to elections in the City of London see PARA 33. As to the count at a London Authority election (except for London Mayor) see PARA 443 et seq; and as to the counting at elections for a local authority or London Mayor see PARAS 435 et seq, 451 et seq.

2   As to polls consequent on a parish meeting on a question involving appointment to office see PARA 200 et seq.

3   Representation of the People Act 1983 Sch 1 r 47(1)(c) (amended by the Electoral Administration Act 2006 s 47, Sch 1 paras 69, 92); Parish and Community Meetings (Polls) Rules 1987, SI 1987/1, Schedule r 29(1)(c); Local Elections (Principal Areas) (England and Wales) Rules 2006, SI 2006/3304, Sch 2 r 47(1)(c); Local Elections (Parishes and Communities) (England and Wales) Rules 2006, SI 2006/3305, Sch 2 r 47(1)(c). As to the number and other security marks which must be printed on the back of every ballot paper see PARA 387. As to the treatment of rejected votes see PARA 431 et seq; and as to scrutiny, which may look at ballot papers and investigate how votes have been recorded, see PARA 839 et seq.

4   *Gloucester County, Cirencester Division Case* (1893) 4 O'M & H 194; *Ruffle v Rogers* [1982] QB 1220 at 1231, [1982] 3 All ER 157 at 161, CA, per Eveleigh LJ; and see Lord Denning MR at 1230 and 160. A voter can presumably be identified by his initials, at least in relatively small electoral areas: see the decision in *Re South Newington (Kingston-upon-Hull) Municipal Election Petition, Lewis v Shepperdson* [1948] 2 All ER 503 at 507 per Birkett J.

5   *Woodward v Sarsons* (1875) LR 10 CP 733. In *Clare, Eastern Division, Case* (1892) 4 O'M & H 162, the returning officer had rejected ballot papers from which the counterfoil had not been detached; but quaere whether the provision set out in the text supports rejection on grounds that the identification of the voter is on the counterfoil (rather than the ballot paper).

6   Representation of the People Act 1983 Sch 1 r 47(2)(a); Parish and Community Meetings (Polls) Rules 1987, SI 1987/1, Schedule r 29(3)(a); Local Elections (Principal Areas) (England and Wales) Rules 2006, SI 2006/3304, Sch 2 r 47(3)(a); Local Elections (Parishes and Communities) (England and Wales) Rules 2006, SI 2006/3305, Sch 2 r 47(3)(a). See *Pontardawe Rural Council Election Petition* [1907] 2 KB 313, DC. As to the layout of the ballot paper see PARA 386.

7   Representation of the People Act 1983 Sch 1 r 47(2)(b); Parish and Community Meetings (Polls) Rules 1987, SI 1987/1, Schedule r 29(3)(b); Local Elections (Principal Areas) (England and Wales) Rules 2006, SI 2006/3304, Sch 2 r 47(3)(b); Local Elections (Parishes and Communities) (England and Wales) Rules 2006, SI 2006/3305, Sch 2 r 47(3)(b). See *Ruffle v Rogers* [1982] QB 1220, [1982] 3 All ER 157, CA (vote marked by candidate's name being written in place of cross); *West Bromwich Case* (1911) 6 O'M & H 256 at 257; *Phillips v Goff* (1886) 17 QBD 805, DC; *York County East Riding, Buckrose Division, Case* (1886) 4 O'M & H 110.

8   Representation of the People Act 1983 Sch 1 r 47(2)(c); Parish and Community Meetings (Polls) Rules 1987, SI 1987/1, Schedule r 29(3)(c); Local Elections (Principal Areas) (England and Wales) Rules 2006, SI 2006/3304, Sch 2 r 47(3)(c); Local Elections (Parishes and Communities) (England and Wales) Rules 2006, SI 2006/3305, Sch 2 r 47(3)(c).

9   Ie, in the case of a local government election for a principal area, parish or community council, and at polls consequent on a parish meeting on a question of appointment to office, either wholly or as respects that vote: see the Parish and Community Meetings (Polls) Rules 1987, SI 1987/1, Schedule r 29(3); the Local Elections (Principal Areas) (England and Wales) Rules 2006, SI 2006/3304, Sch 2 r 47(3); and the Local Elections (Parishes and Communities) (England and Wales) Rules 2006, SI 2006/3305, Sch 2 r 47(3).

10   Representation of the People Act 1983 Sch 1 r 47(2); Parish and Community Meetings (Polls) Rules 1987, SI 1987/1, Schedule r 29(3); Local Elections (Principal Areas) (England and Wales)

Rules 2006, SI 2006/3304, Sch 2 r 47(3); Local Elections (Parishes and Communities) (England and Wales) Rules 2006, SI 2006/3305, Sch 2 r 47(3). These provisions derive from one first enacted in the Representation of the People Act 1948 (repealed) and have the effect of overruling some of the earlier case law. They do not, however, constitute additional tests for validity: see *Pilling v Reynolds* [2008] EWHC 316 (QB), [2009] 1 All ER 163, DC; and PARA 430. Whether a mark on a ballot paper amounts to a vote for a particular candidate is a matter of fact: see PARA 856 note 4.

11 *Ruffle v Rogers* [1982] QB 1220 at 1231, [1982] 3 All ER 157 at 161, CA, per Eveleigh LJ; and see per Lord Denning MR at 1229 and 160.

12 *Wigtown District Burgh Case* (1874) 2 O'M & H 215 at 225. As to returning officers for parliamentary elections see PARA 350 et seq; and as to returning officers for local government elections see PARA 354 et seq. As to the functions of returning officers where the poll at an election is taken together with the poll at another election or referendum see PARA 18.

13 This is implicit from the closing words of the provisions quoted in the text to note 10 ('it is not shown that [the voter] can be identified by it'). See also *Woodward v Sarsons* (1875) LR 10 CP 733 at 749 per Lord Coleridge CJ ('If there were evidence of an arrangement that the voter would place two marks, so as to indicate that it was he, that voter, who had used that ballot paper, then, by reason of such evidence, such double mark would be a mark by which the voter could be identified, and then the paper, upon such proof being made, should be rejected').

430. Ballot papers rejected for being unmarked or void for uncertainty at parliamentary and certain local elections. A ballot paper which has been given at a parliamentary or local government election (except an Authority or mayoral election)[1], or at a poll consequent on a parish meeting taken on the question of appointment to any office[2], and which is unmarked or void for uncertainty[3], is void and must not be counted[4]; but where at a local government election for a principal area, parish or community council, or at a poll consequent on a parish meeting, the voter is entitled to vote for more than one candidate, a ballot paper is not to be deemed to be void for uncertainty in respect of any vote in relation to which no uncertainty arises and that vote is to be counted[5]. A ballot paper on which the vote is marked:

(1) elsewhere than in the proper place[6];
(2) otherwise than by means of a cross[7]; or
(3) by more than one mark[8],

must not for such reason be deemed to be void[9] if an intention that the vote is for one or other of the candidates clearly appears, and the way the paper is marked does not of itself identify the voter and it is not shown that he can be identified by it[10]. These provisions do not, however, constitute additional tests for validity: the legislative purpose is to save votes where the intention of the voter clearly appears, and the legislation is to be read so that it provides only guidance, not a prescriptive set of rules as to how a voter has to mark a ballot paper[11]. The following examples provide further guidance and illustration.

A ballot paper may be well marked although the mark does not discolour the paper if from any circumstances the court can infer that the marks were intentionally made by the voter[12]. Where, at an election at which the voter may vote for one candidate only, a ballot paper carries a cross opposite the name of one candidate and a smudge which appears to have been caused by rubbing out a mark opposite the name of another candidate, this has been held to be a good vote for the former candidate[13]. A ballot paper may be well marked for one candidate although a great portion of the cross is opposite the name of another candidate if the point of intersection of the crossing lines is in the space appropriate to the former[14]. A ballot paper may be well marked also where the point of intersection of the cross is outside any of the compartments reserved to indicate a vote for a candidate but where the trailing ends of the cross extend into one only of those compartments[15].

A ballot paper may be well marked even though it carries more than the minimum number of marks necessary to indicate a vote. For example, where there was a cross opposite the name of a candidate and other crosses which had the effect of obscuring that candidate's name altogether, this was held to be a good vote for that candidate[16]; but where the only mark upon the paper was a cross immediately upon the name of one of the candidates in such a way as to make it possible that the voter intended to strike that name out, the vote was disallowed[17]. At an election at which the voter could vote for one candidate only, where the names of two candidates had been struck out and no mark had been placed against the name of the remaining candidate, the ballot paper was held to be a valid vote for the last-mentioned candidate[18]. In an election where there were six candidates, and two were to be elected, the voter had placed a cross by the names of four candidates, and a tick by two; the paper was held to be valid, with the ticks being counted[19]. However, where a voter who was entitled to vote for five candidates had placed a distinct cross against each of five names and an encircled cross against a sixth name, the ballot paper was held to be invalid for showing six votes instead of the permitted five[20].

Tearing the ballot paper is not of itself a fatal defect[21], but a ballot paper of which half had been torn away so that only one candidate's name remained has been held to be bad although there was a cross opposite that candidate's name[22].

1   As to the meaning of 'parliamentary election' see PARA 9; and as to the meanings of 'Authority election' and 'local government election' see PARA 11. As to elections in the City of London see PARA 33. As to the count at a London Authority election (except for London Mayor) see PARA 443 et seq; and as to the counting at elections for a local authority or London Mayor see PARAS 435 et seq, 451 et seq.

2   As to polls consequent on a parish meeting on a question involving appointment to office see PARA 200 et seq.

3   Representation of the People Act 1983 Sch 1 r 47(1)(d); Parish and Community Meetings (Polls) Rules 1987, SI 1987/1, Schedule r 29(1)(d); Local Elections (Principal Areas) (England and Wales) Rules 2006, SI 2006/3304, Sch 2 r 47(1)(d); Local Elections (Parishes and Communities) (England and Wales) Rules 2006, SI 2006/3305, Sch 2 r 47(1)(d). A vote is bad for uncertainty where it is upon the face of the ballot paper doubtful whether the voter intended to vote for one candidate or the other: *Gloucester County, Cirencester Division Case* (1893) 4 O'M & H 194 at 197. See further the text and notes 12–22.

4   See the Representation of the People Act 1983 Sch 1 r 47(1); the Parish and Community Meetings (Polls) Rules 1987, SI 1987/1, Schedule r 29(1); the Local Elections (Principal Areas) (England and Wales) Rules 2006, SI 2006/3304, Sch 2 r 47(1); and the Local Elections (Parishes and Communities) (England and Wales) Rules 2006, SI 2006/3305, Sch 2 r 47(1). As to the treatment of rejected votes see PARA 431 et seq; and as to scrutiny, which may look at ballot papers and investigate how votes have been recorded, see PARA 839 et seq.

5   Parish and Community Meetings (Polls) Rules 1987, SI 1987/1, Schedule r 29(2); Local Elections (Principal Areas) (England and Wales) Rules 2006, SI 2006/3304, Sch 2 r 47(2); Local Elections (Parishes and Communities) (England and Wales) Rules 2006, SI 2006/3305, Sch 2 r 47(2). Where a ballot paper is void in part but on which any vote is counted, the returning officer must endorse the words 'rejected in part' on the ballot paper and indicate which vote or votes have been counted: see the Parish and Community Meetings (Polls) Rules 1987, SI 1987/1, Schedule r 29(4)(b); the Local Elections (Principal Areas) (England and Wales) Rules 2006, SI 2006/3304, Sch 2 r 47(4)(b); the Local Elections (Parishes and Communities) (England and Wales) Rules 2006, SI 2006/3305, Sch 2 r 47(4)(b); and PARA 431.

6   Representation of the People Act 1983 Sch 1 r 47(2)(a); Parish and Community Meetings (Polls) Rules 1987, SI 1987/1, Schedule r 29(3)(a); Local Elections (Principal Areas) (England and Wales) Rules 2006, SI 2006/3304, Sch 2 r 47(3)(a); Local Elections (Parishes and Communities) (England and Wales) Rules 2006, SI 2006/3305, Sch 2 r 47(3)(a). See *Pontardawe Rural Council Election Petition* [1907] 2 KB 313, DC. A ballot paper marked only with a cross on the back of the paper has been rejected for endangering the secrecy of the vote, even though it was contended that the voter had misinterpreted the instruction to mark the paper opposite the candidate's name (ie by positioning his mark purposely over the blind printed impression of the

candidate's name which was evident to the rear face of the paper): *Berwick Case, McLaren v Home* (1880) 44 LT 289, 3 O'M & H 178. As to the prescribed layout of the ballot paper see PARA 386.

7   Representation of the People Act 1983 Sch 1 r 47(2)(b); Parish and Community Meetings (Polls) Rules 1987, SI 1987/1, Schedule r 29(3)(b); Local Elections (Principal Areas) (England and Wales) Rules 2006, SI 2006/3304, Sch 2 r 47(3)(b); Local Elections (Parishes and Communities) (England and Wales) Rules 2006, SI 2006/3305, Sch 2 r 47(3)(b). See *Ruffle v Rogers* [1982] QB 1220, [1982] 3 All ER 157, CA (vote marked by candidate's name being written in place of cross); *West Bromwich Case* (1911) 6 O'M & H 256 at 257; *Phillips v Goff* (1886) 17 QBD 805, DC; *York County East Riding, Buckrose Division, Case* (1886) 4 O'M & H 110; *Pilling v Reynolds* [2008] EWHC 316 (QB), [2009] 1 All ER 163, DC (ballot paper marked by an oblique line rather than by a cross not void for uncertainty).

8   Representation of the People Act 1983 Sch 1 r 47(2)(c); Parish and Community Meetings (Polls) Rules 1987, SI 1987/1, Schedule r 29(3)(c); Local Elections (Principal Areas) (England and Wales) Rules 2006, SI 2006/3304, Sch 2 r 47(3)(c); Local Elections (Parishes and Communities) (England and Wales) Rules 2006, SI 2006/3305, Sch 2 r 47(3)(c).

9   Ie, in the case of a local government election for a principal area, parish or community council, and at polls consequent on a parish meeting on a question of appointment to office, either wholly or as respects that vote: see the Parish and Community Meetings (Polls) Rules 1987, SI 1987/1, Schedule r 29(3); the Local Elections (Principal Areas) (England and Wales) Rules 2006, SI 2006/3304, Sch 2 r 47(3); and the Local Elections (Parishes and Communities) (England and Wales) Rules 2006, SI 2006/3305, Sch 2 r 47(3).

10 Representation of the People Act 1983 Sch 1 r 47(2); Parish and Community Meetings (Polls) Rules 1987, SI 1987/1, Schedule r 29(3); Local Elections (Principal Areas) (England and Wales) Rules 2006, SI 2006/3304, Sch 2 r 47(3); Local Elections (Parishes and Communities) (England and Wales) Rules 2006, SI 2006/3305, Sch 2 r 47(3). These provisions derive from one first enacted in the Representation of the People Act 1948 (repealed) and have the effect of overruling some of the earlier case law. Whether a mark on a ballot paper amounts to a vote for a particular candidate is a matter of fact: see PARA 856 note 4.

11 *Pilling v Reynolds* [2008] EWHC 316 (QB), [2009] 1 All ER 163, DC (voter had gone so far as to attend the polling station, had intended to vote, and his intention as to whom to vote for was clear).

12 *Berwick Case, McLaren v Home* (1880) 44 LT 289, 3 O'M & H 178; *Gloucester County, Cirencester Division Case* (1893) 4 O'M & H 194. The mark need not appear to have been made with a pencil; a scratch with a finger nail is sufficient: *Berwick Case, McLaren v Home*; *Gloucester County, Cirencester Division Case*. A ballot paper marked with a dot caused by the breaking of the pencil point has been held good: *Cooper v Ogden, Re Oldham Case* (1908) 72 JP 115.

13 *Gloucester County, Cirencester Division Case* (1893) 4 O'M & H 194. Where a paper contained an ink mark of uncertain character at its bottom below a candidate's name the paper was disallowed for uncertainty: *Berwick Case, McLaren v Home* (1880) 44 LT 289, 3 O'M & H 178.

14 *Berwick Case, McLaren v Home* (1880) 44 LT 289, 3 O'M & H 178; *Gloucester County, Cirencester Division Case* (1893) 4 O'M & H 194.

15 *Cooper v Ogden, Re Oldham Case* (1908) 72 JP 115. A cross or mark that is completely outside any of the compartments on the ballot paper is not a valid mark: *Berwick Case, McLaren v Home* (1880) 44 LT 289, 3 O'M & H 178; *Stepney Division, Tower Hamlets Case* (1886) 4 O'M & H 34, 37; *York County, East Riding, Buckrose Division Case* (1886) 4 O'M & H 110.

16 *Gloucester County, Cirencester Division Case* (1893) 4 O'M & H 194 (the crosses other than the cross appearing opposite the name of the candidate were assumed to be added for emphasis).

17 *York County, East Riding, Buckrose Division Case* (1886) 4 O'M & H 110 at 112. In *Levers v Morris* [1972] 1 QB 221, [1971] 3 All ER 1300, DC, regarding an election where three candidates stood for only one office, a ballot paper on which the only mark was a cross appearing over the name of one candidate was held to be a good vote for that candidate.

18 *Levers v Morris* [1972] 1 QB 221, [1971] 3 All ER 1300, DC.

19 *Three Rivers District Council Election Petition* (26 July 1991, unreported), DC. In *Cooper v Ogden, Re Oldham Case* (1908) 72 JP 115, ballot papers which contained a cross in one candidate's compartment as well as another type of mark in the other candidate's compartment were held to be good votes for the candidate against whose name the cross appeared, on the grounds that a cross was the valid mark used to indicate a vote and the other marks were thought to indicate merely that the voter had not forgotten the other candidate.

20 *Pontardawe Rural Council Election Petition* [1907] 2 KB 313, DC.

21 *Woodward v Sarsons* (1875) LR 10 CP 733 (ballot paper which had been torn through its centre longitudinally was counted and the vote on it held to be valid).
22 *West Bromwich Case* (1911) 6 O'M & H 256 at 257.

431.   Treatment of rejected ballot papers at parliamentary and certain local elections.   The returning officer at a parliamentary or local government election (except an Authority or mayoral election)[1], or at a poll consequent on a parish meeting taken on the question of appointment to any office[2], must endorse the word 'rejected' on any ballot paper which is not to be counted[3], and he must add to the endorsement the words 'rejection objected to' if an objection is made by a counting agent[4] to his decision[5]. The returning officer must draw up a statement showing the number of ballot papers rejected under the several heads of:

(1)   want of official mark[6];
(2)   voting for more than one candidate (or, as the case may be, for more candidates than the voter is entitled to)[7];
(3)   writing or mark by which a voter could be identified[8];
(4)   unmarked or void for uncertainty[9].

In the case of a local government election for a principal area, parish or community council, or at a poll consequent on a parish meeting, such a statement must record also the number of ballot papers rejected in part and show them under the several heads (1) to (4) mentioned above[10].

1   As to the meaning of 'parliamentary election' see PARA 9; and as to the meanings of 'Authority election' and 'local government election' see PARA 11. As to elections in the City of London see PARA 33. As to the count at a London Authority election (except for London Mayor) see PARA 443 et seq; and as to the counting at elections for a local authority or London Mayor see PARAS 435 et seq, 451 et seq. As to returning officers for parliamentary elections see PARA 350 et seq; and as to returning officers for local government elections see PARA 354 et seq. As to the functions of returning officers where the poll at an election is taken together with the poll at another election or referendum see PARA 18.
2   As to polls consequent on a parish meeting on a question involving appointment to office see PARA 200 et seq. As to the returning officer at a poll consequent on parish meeting taken on the question of appointment to any office see PARA 356.
3   Representation of the People Act 1983 Sch 1 r 47(3); Parish and Community Meetings (Polls) Rules 1987, SI 1987/1, Schedule r 29(4)(a); Local Elections (Principal Areas) (England and Wales) Rules 2006, SI 2006/3304, Sch 2 r 47(4)(a); Local Elections (Parishes and Communities) (England and Wales) Rules 2006, SI 2006/3305, Sch 2 r 47(4)(a). In the case of a local government election for a principal area, parish or community council, or at a poll consequent on a parish meeting on a question of appointment to office, where a ballot paper is void in part but on which any vote is counted (see PARA 430), the returning officer must endorse the words 'rejected in part' on the ballot paper and indicate which vote or votes have been counted: Parish and Community Meetings (Polls) Rules 1987, SI 1987/1, Schedule r 29(4)(b); Local Elections (Principal Areas) (England and Wales) Rules 2006, SI 2006/3304, Sch 2 r 47(4)(b); Local Elections (Parishes and Communities) (England and Wales) Rules 2006, SI 2006/3305, Sch 2 r 47(4)(b). As to the grounds on which a ballot paper may be rejected see PARAS 427–430.
4   As to the discharge of this function by the candidate or (where there is such an agent) his election agent see PARA 394.
5   Representation of the People Act 1983 Sch 1 r 47(3); Parish and Community Meetings (Polls) Rules 1987, SI 1987/1, Schedule r 29(4); Local Elections (Principal Areas) (England and Wales) Rules 2006, SI 2006/3304, Sch 2 r 47(4); Local Elections (Parishes and Communities) (England and Wales) Rules 2006, SI 2006/3305, Sch 2 r 47(4).
6   Representation of the People Act 1983 Sch 1 r 47(4)(a); Parish and Community Meetings (Polls) Rules 1987, SI 1987/1, Schedule r 29(5)(a); Local Elections (Principal Areas) (England and Wales) Rules 2006, SI 2006/3304, Sch 2 r 47(5)(a); Local Elections (Parishes and Communities) (England and Wales) Rules 2006, SI 2006/3305, Sch 2 r 47(5)(a).
7   Representation of the People Act 1983 Sch 1 r 47(4)(b); Parish and Community Meetings (Polls) Rules 1987, SI 1987/1, Schedule r 29(5)(b); Local Elections (Principal Areas) (England and Wales) Rules 2006, SI 2006/3304, Sch 2 r 47(5)(b); Local Elections (Parishes and Communities) (England and Wales) Rules 2006, SI 2006/3305, Sch 2 r 47(5)(b).

8   Representation of the People Act 1983 Sch 1 r 47(4)(c); Parish and Community Meetings (Polls) Rules 1987, SI 1987/1, Schedule r 29(5)(c); Local Elections (Principal Areas) (England and Wales) Rules 2006, SI 2006/3304, Sch 2 r 47(5)(c); Local Elections (Parishes and Communities) (England and Wales) Rules 2006, SI 2006/3305, Sch 2 r 47(5)(c).

9   Representation of the People Act 1983 Sch 1 r 47(4)(d); Parish and Community Meetings (Polls) Rules 1987, SI 1987/1, Schedule r 29(5)(d); Local Elections (Principal Areas) (England and Wales) Rules 2006, SI 2006/3304, Sch 2 r 47(5)(d); Local Elections (Parishes and Communities) (England and Wales) Rules 2006, SI 2006/3305, Sch 2 r 47(5)(d).

10   See the Parish and Community Meetings (Polls) Rules 1987, SI 1987/1, Schedule r 29(5); the Local Elections (Principal Areas) (England and Wales) Rules 2006, SI 2006/3304, Sch 2 r 47(5); and the Local Elections (Parishes and Communities) (England and Wales) Rules 2006, SI 2006/3305, Sch 2 r 47(5).

432. Conclusiveness of returning officer's decision on any question arising as to ballot papers at parliamentary and certain local elections. The decision of the returning officer at a parliamentary or local government election (except an Authority or mayoral election)[1], or at a poll consequent on a parish meeting taken on the question of appointment to any office[2], on any question arising in respect of a ballot paper is final, but is subject to review on an election petition[3].

1   As to the meaning of 'parliamentary election' see PARA 9; and as to the meanings of 'Authority election' and 'local government election' see PARA 11. As to elections in the City of London see PARA 33. As to the count at a London Authority election (except for London Mayor) see PARA 443 et seq; and as to the counting at elections for a local authority or London Mayor see PARAS 435 et seq, 451 et seq. As to returning officers for parliamentary elections see PARA 350 et seq; and as to returning officers for local government elections see PARA 354 et seq. As to the functions of returning officers where the poll at an election is taken together with the poll at another election or referendum see PARA 18.

2   As to polls consequent on a parish meeting on a question involving appointment to office see PARA 200 et seq. As to the returning officer at a poll consequent on parish meeting taken on the question of appointment to any office see PARA 356.

3   Representation of the People Act 1983 Sch 1 r 48; Parish and Community Meetings (Polls) Rules 1987, SI 1987/1, Schedule r 30; Local Elections (Principal Areas) (England and Wales) Rules 2006, SI 2006/3304, Sch 2 r 48; Local Elections (Parishes and Communities) (England and Wales) Rules 2006, SI 2006/3305, Sch 2 r 48. As to election petitions at parliamentary elections see PARA 761 et seq; and as to election petitions at local government elections see PARA 762 et seq.

433. Recounts at parliamentary and certain local elections. A candidate, or (if appointed) his election agent, at a parliamentary or local government election (except an Authority or mayoral election)[1], or at a poll consequent on a parish meeting taken on the question of appointment to any office[2], may, if present when the counting or any recount of the votes is completed[3], require the returning officer[4] to have the votes recounted (or again recounted), but the returning officer may refuse to do so if in his opinion the request is unreasonable[5]. No step may be taken on the completion of the counting, or any recount, of votes until the candidates (or election agents, as, the case may be[6]) present at its completion have been given reasonable opportunity to exercise the right to demand a recount[7].

1   As to the meaning of 'parliamentary election' see PARA 9; and as to the meanings of 'Authority election' and 'local government election' see PARA 11. As to elections in the City of London see PARA 33. As to the meaning of 'candidate' generally see PARA 230. A candidate at a local government election for a parish or community council need not have an election agent (see PARA 231 note 3) and, accordingly, the right set out in the text is exercised by a candidate in those circumstances: see the Local Elections (Parishes and Communities) (England and Wales) Rules 2006, SI 2006/3305, Sch 2 r 46(1), (2). As to the appointment of election agents at parliamentary and local government elections see PARA 231 et seq.

2   As to polls consequent on a parish meeting on a question involving appointment to office see
    PARA 200 et seq. There is no provision for election agents to be appointed at such a poll and,
    accordingly, in relation to such a poll, only a candidate may exercise the right set out in the text:
    see the Parish and Community Meetings (Polls) Rules 1987, SI 1987/1, Schedule r 28.
3   As to the counting of votes at a parliamentary or local government election (except a London
    Authority or mayoral election) see PARA 425. As to the count at a London Authority election
    (except for London Mayor) see PARA 443 et seq; and as to the counting at elections for a local
    authority or London Mayor see PARAS 435 et seq, 451 et seq.
4   As to returning officers for parliamentary elections see PARA 350 et seq; as to returning officers
    for local government elections (including local authority mayoral elections) see PARA 354 et seq;
    and as to the returning officer at a poll consequent on parish meeting see PARA 356. As to the
    functions of returning officers where the poll at an election is taken together with the poll at
    another election or referendum see PARA 18.
5   Representation of the People Act 1983 Sch 1 r 46(1); Parish and Community Meetings (Polls)
    Rules 1987, SI 1987/1, Schedule r 28(1); Local Elections (Principal Areas) (England and Wales)
    Rules 2006, SI 2006/3304, Sch 2 r 46(1); Local Elections (Parishes and Communities) (England
    and Wales) Rules 2006, SI 2006/3305, Sch 2 r 46(1).
6   See note 2.
7   Representation of the People Act 1983 Sch 1 r 46(2); Parish and Community Meetings (Polls)
    Rules 1987, SI 1987/1, Schedule r 28(2); Local Elections (Principal Areas) (England and Wales)
    Rules 2006, SI 2006/3304, Sch 2 r 46(2); Local Elections (Parishes and Communities) (England
    and Wales) Rules 2006, SI 2006/3305, Sch 2 r 46(2).
    Non-observance of this rule does not necessarily invalidate the election: *Levers v Morris*
    [1972] 1 QB 221, [1971] 3 All ER 1300, DC (a case in which a candidate's request for a recount
    was not heard by the returning officer). As to the procedure to be followed when, the result of
    an election having been declared by the returning officer, a parcel of ballot papers is discovered
    uncounted see PARA 856 note 3.

**434.   Casting of lots in case of equality of votes at parliamentary and certain
local elections.**   After the counting of the votes (including any recount) is
completed at a parliamentary or local government election (except an Authority
or mayoral election)[1], or at a poll consequent on a parish meeting taken on the
question of appointment to any office[2], where an equality of votes is found to
exist between any candidates, and the addition of a vote would entitle any of
those candidates to be declared elected, the returning officer[3] must forthwith
decide between those candidates by lot, and proceed as if the candidate on whom
the lot falls had received an additional vote[4].

1   As to the meaning of 'parliamentary election' see PARA 9; and as to the meanings of 'Authority
    election' and 'local government election' see PARA 11. As to elections in the City of London see
    PARA 33. As to the count at a London Authority election (except for London Mayor) see
    PARA 443 et seq; and as to the counting at elections for a local authority or London Mayor see
    PARAS 435 et seq, 451 et seq.
2   As to polls consequent on a parish meeting on a question involving appointment to office see
    PARA 200 et seq. As to the returning officer at a poll consequent on parish meeting taken on the
    question of appointment to any office see PARA 356.
3   As to returning officers for parliamentary elections see PARA 350 et seq; and as to returning
    officers for local government elections (including local authority mayoral elections) see
    PARA 354 et seq. As to the functions of returning officers where the poll at an election is taken
    together with the poll at another election or referendum see PARA 18.
4   Representation of the People Act 1983 Sch 1 r 49; Parish and Community Meetings (Polls)
    Rules 1987, SI 1987/1, Schedule r 31; Local Elections (Principal Areas) (England and Wales)
    Rules 2006, SI 2006/3304, Sch 2 r 49; Local Elections (Parishes and Communities) (England
    and Wales) Rules 2006, SI 2006/3305, Sch 2 r 49.
    For a case where, apart from a disputed vote, the votes were equally divided between two
    candidates and the returning officer spun a coin to decide between them, but the disputed vote
    was on an election petition held good see *Fryer v Harris* (1955) Times, 30 July. See also *Lever v
    Morris* [1972] 1 QB 221, [1971] 3 All ER 1300, DC (whether incorrectly marked ballot papers
    void; equality of votes cast and decision taken by lot); *Ruffle v Rogers* [1982] QB 1220, [1982]
    3 All ER 157, CA (where the inclusion of a wrongly rejected vote would have resulted in an

equality of votes which is a 'result' for the purposes of the provision re-enacted as the Representation of the People Act 1983 s 48(1) (see PARA 354)).

B. LOCAL GOVERNMENT ELECTION FOR RETURN OF LOCAL AUTHORITY MAYOR

(A) Attendance at Proceedings

435.   Attendance at count of ballot papers at elections for the return of local authority mayor. As soon as practicable after the close of the poll for the return of an elected local authority mayor[1], the returning officer[2] must make arrangements for counting the votes, in the presence of the counting agents appointed for the purposes of the election[3]. The returning officer must give to the counting agents notice in writing of the time and place at which he will begin to count the votes[4], and at which he will begin any count of the second preference votes[5]. No person other than:

(1)   the returning officer and his clerks[6];
(2)   the candidates and one other person chosen by each of them[7];
(3)   the election agents[8];
(4)   the counting agents[9]; and
(5)   persons who are entitled to attend at such an election by virtue of any of the provisions of the Political Parties, Elections and Referendums Act 2000[10] which allow Electoral Commission representatives and accredited observers to attend electoral proceedings and observe working practices[11],

may be present at the counting of the votes, unless permitted by the returning officer to attend[12]. A person not entitled to attend at the counting of the votes must not be permitted to do so by the returning officer, however, unless:

(a)   the returning officer is satisfied that the efficient counting of the votes will not be impeded[13]; and
(b)   he has either consulted the election agents or thought it impracticable to do so[14].

The returning officer must make such arrangements as he thinks fit to ensure that every person attending at the counting of the votes (other than any constable on duty at the counting) has been given a copy in writing of the statutory provisions relating to the requirement of secrecy that apply to such attendance[15].

The returning officer also must give the counting agents all such reasonable facilities for overseeing the proceedings, and all such information with respect to them, as he can give them consistently with the orderly conduct of the proceedings and the discharge of his duties in connection with them[16]. In particular, where the votes are counted by sorting the ballot papers according to the candidate for whom the vote is given, and then counting the number of ballot papers for each candidate, the counting agents must be entitled to satisfy themselves that the ballot papers are correctly sorted[17].

Where the poll at an election is taken together with the poll at another election or referendum, special provision is made for counting the votes[18].

1   As to local government elections for the return of an elected mayor see PARA 198. As to the meaning of 'local government election' see PARA 11.
2   As to returning officers for local government elections see PARA 354 et seq.
3   Local Authorities (Mayoral Elections) (England and Wales) Regulations 2007, SI 2007/1024, Sch 1 r 46(1). As to the appointment of counting agents by a candidate, and as to the effect of their non-attendance, see PARA 394.

4   Local Authorities (Mayoral Elections) (England and Wales) Regulations 2007, SI 2007/1024,
    Sch 1 r 46(1)(a). The initial stage of the count at a local authority mayoral election is known as
    the 'first count'.
5   Local Authorities (Mayoral Elections) (England and Wales) Regulations 2007, SI 2007/1024,
    Sch 1 r 46(1)(b). As to elections at which second preference votes are cast see PARA 341; and as
    to the counting of second preference votes at a local authority mayoral election see PARA 441.
6   Local Authorities (Mayoral Elections) (England and Wales) Regulations 2007, SI 2007/1024,
    Sch 1 r 46(2)(a). As to persons appointed as clerks by a returning officer see PARA 393.
7   Local Authorities (Mayoral Elections) (England and Wales) Regulations 2007, SI 2007/1024,
    Sch 1 r 46(2)(b). As to the meaning of 'candidate' generally see PARA 230.
8   Local Authorities (Mayoral Elections) (England and Wales) Regulations 2007, SI 2007/1024,
    Sch 1 r 46(2)(c). As to the appointment of election agents at local authority mayoral elections
    see PARA 231 et seq.
9   Local Authorities (Mayoral Elections) (England and Wales) Regulations 2007, SI 2007/1024,
    Sch 1 r 46(2)(d).
10 Ie by virtue of any of the provisions of the Political Parties, Elections and Referendums Act 2000
    ss 6A–6D (see PARA 53): see the Local Authorities (Mayoral Elections) (England and Wales)
    Regulations 2007, SI 2007/1024, Sch 1 r 46(2)(e).
11 Local Authorities (Mayoral Elections) (England and Wales) Regulations 2007, SI 2007/1024,
    Sch 1 r 46(2)(e). As to the Electoral Commission see PARA 34 et seq; and as to authorised
    representatives of the Electoral Commission attending electoral proceedings see PARA 53.
12 Local Authorities (Mayoral Elections) (England and Wales) Regulations 2007, SI 2007/1024,
    Sch 1 r 46(2).
13 Local Authorities (Mayoral Elections) (England and Wales) Regulations 2007, SI 2007/1024,
    Sch 1 r 46(3)(a).
14 Local Authorities (Mayoral Elections) (England and Wales) Regulations 2007, SI 2007/1024,
    Sch 1 r 46(3)(b).
15 See PARAS 385, 739–741.
16 Local Authorities (Mayoral Elections) (England and Wales) Regulations 2007, SI 2007/1024,
    Sch 1 r 46(4).
17 Local Authorities (Mayoral Elections) (England and Wales) Regulations 2007, SI 2007/1024,
    Sch 1 r 46(5).
18 As to polls at elections or referendums which are taken together see PARA 16 et seq.

(B) First Count

436. Verification of ballot paper accounts and the first count of votes at an election for the return of a local authority mayor. At the first count of a local government election for the return of an elected mayor[1], the returning officer[2] must:

(1)   in the presence of the counting agents[3], open each ballot box and count and record the number of ballot papers in it[4];

(2)   in the presence of the election agents[5], verify each ballot paper account[6]; and

(3)   count such of the postal ballot papers as have been duly returned[7] and record the number counted[8].

The returning officer must not count the votes given on any such ballot papers, however, until:

(a)   in the case of postal ballot papers, they have been mixed with the ballot papers from at least one ballot box[9]; and

(b)   in the case of ballot papers from a ballot box, they have been mixed with the ballot papers from at least one other ballot box[10].

The returning officer must then:

(i)   where the election is contested by more than two candidates, count the first preference votes given on them[11]; and

(ii)   where the election is contested by only two candidates, count the votes given on them[12].

The returning officer must not count any tendered ballot paper[13]. While counting and recording the number of ballot papers and counting the votes, the returning officer must keep the ballot papers with their faces upwards and take all proper precautions for preventing any person from seeing the numbers or other unique identifying marks printed on the back of the papers[14].

The returning officer must verify each ballot paper account by comparing it with the number of ballot papers recorded by him, and the unused and spoilt ballot papers[15] in his possession and the tendered votes list[16] (opening and resealing the packets containing the unused and spoilt ballot papers and the tendered votes list)[17]. He must draw up a statement as to the result of the verification, which any election agent may copy[18].

The returning officer must, so far as practicable, proceed continuously with counting the votes, allowing only time for refreshment, except that he may exclude the hours between seven in the evening and nine on the following morning[19]. During the time so excluded, the returning officer must: (A) place the ballot papers and other documents relating to the election under his own seal and the seals of such of the counting agents as desire to affix their seals[20]; and (B) otherwise take proper precautions for the security of the papers and documents[21].

Where the poll at an election is taken together with the poll at another election or referendum, special provision is made for counting the votes[22].

1   As to local government elections for the return of an elected mayor see PARA 198. As to the meaning of 'local government election' see PARA 11. As to use of the term 'first count' see PARA 435 note 4.
2   As to returning officers for local government elections (including local authority mayoral elections) see PARA 354 et seq.
3   As to the appointment of counting agents by a candidate, and as to the effect of their non-attendance, see PARA 394.
4   Local Authorities (Mayoral Elections) (England and Wales) Regulations 2007, SI 2007/1024, Sch 1 r 47(1)(a).
5   As to the appointment of election agents at local authority elections see PARA 231 et seq.
6   Local Authorities (Mayoral Elections) (England and Wales) Regulations 2007, SI 2007/1024, Sch 1 r 47(1)(b). As to the ballot paper account see PARA 405.
7   A postal ballot paper must not be taken to be duly returned unless:
    (1)   it is returned in the prescribed manner (ie either by hand or by post to the returning officer, or by hand only to a polling station), and reaches the returning officer or any polling station in the electoral area in question before the close of the poll (Local Authorities (Mayoral Elections) (England and Wales) Regulations 2007, SI 2007/1024, Sch 1 r 47(4)(a), (5));
    (2)   the postal voting statement, duly signed, is also returned in the prescribed manner (ie either by hand or by post to the returning officer, or by hand only to a polling station), and reaches him or such a polling station before that time (Sch 1 r 47(4)(b), (5));
    (3)   the postal voting statement also states the date of birth of the elector or proxy (as the case may be) (Sch 1 r 47(4)(c)); and
    (4)   in a case where the steps for verifying the date of birth and signature of an elector or proxy have been prescribed by regulations made under the Representation of the People Act 1983, the returning officer (having taken such steps) verifies the date of birth and signature of the elector or proxy (as the case may be) (Local Authorities (Mayoral Elections) (England and Wales) Regulations 2007, SI 2007/1024, Sch 1 r 47(4)(d)).
    As to the regulations that have been prescribed for the purposes of head (4) above see the Representation of the People (England and Wales) Regulations 2001, SI 2001/341, regs 85, 85A; and PARA 421. As to the meaning of 'electoral area' for the purposes of local government elections see PARA 11. As to the meaning of 'elector', in relation to a local government election, see PARA 95 note 2. As to the meaning of 'postal ballot paper' see PARA 407 note 1. As to voting by proxy see PARA 366 et seq; and as to the entitlement to vote by post as proxy see PARAS 377, 382. As to the postal voting statement see PARA 406. As to the means by which a postal voter

may validly return a postal ballot paper see also PARA 418. As to the provision that may be made regarding the circumstances in which, following the close of the poll at a parliamentary or local government election, a registration officer must notify a person that the person's postal ballot paper has been rejected see PARA 426.

8   Local Authorities (Mayoral Elections) (England and Wales) Regulations 2007, SI 2007/1024, Sch 1 r 47(1)(c).
9   Local Authorities (Mayoral Elections) (England and Wales) Regulations 2007, SI 2007/1024, Sch 1 r 47(2)(a).
10 Local Authorities (Mayoral Elections) (England and Wales) Regulations 2007, SI 2007/1024, Sch 1 r 47(2)(b).
11 Local Authorities (Mayoral Elections) (England and Wales) Regulations 2007, SI 2007/1024, Sch 1 r 47(3)(a). As to elections at which first and second preference votes are cast (the 'supplementary vote system') see PARA 341; and as to the counting of second preference votes at a local authority mayoral election see PARA 441.
12 Local Authorities (Mayoral Elections) (England and Wales) Regulations 2007, SI 2007/1024, Sch 1 r 47(3)(b).
13 Local Authorities (Mayoral Elections) (England and Wales) Regulations 2007, SI 2007/1024, Sch 1 r 47(6). As to tendered ballot papers see PARA 403. As to scrutiny, which may look at ballot papers and investigate how votes have been recorded, see PARA 839 et seq.
14 Local Authorities (Mayoral Elections) (England and Wales) Regulations 2007, SI 2007/1024, Sch 1 r 47(7). As to the numbers and other unique identifying marks which must be printed on the back of every ballot paper see PARA 387.
15 As to spoilt ballot papers see PARA 404.
16 As to the tendered votes list see PARA 403.
17 Local Authorities (Mayoral Elections) (England and Wales) Regulations 2007, SI 2007/1024, Sch 1 r 47(8).
18 Local Authorities (Mayoral Elections) (England and Wales) Regulations 2007, SI 2007/1024, Sch 1 r 47(8).
19 Local Authorities (Mayoral Elections) (England and Wales) Regulations 2007, SI 2007/1024, Sch 1 r 47(9).
20 Local Authorities (Mayoral Elections) (England and Wales) Regulations 2007, SI 2007/1024, Sch 1 r 47(10)(a).
21 Local Authorities (Mayoral Elections) (England and Wales) Regulations 2007, SI 2007/1024, Sch 1 r 47(10)(b).
22 As to polls at elections or referendums which are taken together see PARA 16 et seq.

437. Rejected ballot papers at elections for the return of local authority mayor. At the first count of a local government election for the return of an elected mayor[1], any ballot paper:

(1)   which does not bear the official mark[2];
(2)   on which more than one first preference vote is given[3];
(3)   on which anything is written or marked by which the voter can be identified (except the printed number and other unique identifying mark on the back)[4];
(4)   which is unmarked or void for uncertainty as to the first preference vote[5],

is void and must not be counted[6]. However, a ballot paper on which a vote is marked:

(a)   elsewhere than in the proper place[7]; or
(b)   otherwise than by means of a cross[8]; or
(c)   by more than one mark[9],

is not for such reason void if:

(i)   at an election at which more than two candidates remain validly nominated, an intention that a vote is to be given, by way of a first preference vote, for not more than one of the candidates clearly appears[10]; or
(ii) at any other election, an intention that a vote is to be for one only of the candidates clearly appears[11],

and (in the case of either head (i) or head (ii) above) the way the paper is marked does not itself identify the voter and it is not shown that he can be identified by it[12]. A ballot paper which is not otherwise void and on which not more than one first preference vote is marked (whether or not a second preference vote is marked) is valid as respects that vote, and must be counted accordingly[13].

The returning officer[14] must endorse the word 'rejected' on any ballot paper which is not to be counted, and he must add to the endorsement the words 'rejection objected to' if an objection is made by a counting agent[15] to his decision[16]. The returning officer must draw up a statement showing the number of ballot papers rejected under the several heads of:

(A)　　want of official mark[17];
(B)　　voting for more than one candidate as to the first preference vote[18];
(C)　　writing or mark by which the voter could be identified[19]; and
(D)　　unmarked or void for uncertainty as to the first preference vote[20].

1　As to local government elections for the return of an elected mayor see PARA 198. As to the meaning of 'local government election' see PARA 11. As to use of the term 'first count' see PARA 435 note 4.

2　Local Authorities (Mayoral Elections) (England and Wales) Regulations 2007, SI 2007/1024, Sch 1 r 48(1)(a). As to the official mark see PARA 387. As to ballot papers rejected for want of official mark at parliamentary and other local elections see PARA 427.

3　Local Authorities (Mayoral Elections) (England and Wales) Regulations 2007, SI 2007/1024, Sch 1 r 48(1)(b). In the case of an election where only two candidates remain validly nominated, head (2) in the text is modified to read: 'on which more than one vote is given': see Sch 1 r 48(1)(b); modified by Sch 1 r 48(6)(a). As to elections at which first and second preference votes are cast (the 'supplementary vote system') see PARA 341; and as to the counting of second preference votes at a local authority mayoral election see PARA 441. Whether a mark on a ballot paper amounts to a vote for a particular candidate is a matter of fact: see PARA 856 note 4.

4　Local Authorities (Mayoral Elections) (England and Wales) Regulations 2007, SI 2007/1024, Sch 1 r 48(1)(c). As to the number and other unique identifying marks which must be printed on the back of every ballot paper see PARA 387. As to ballot papers rejected for marks identifying the voter at parliamentary and other local elections see PARA 429.

5　Local Authorities (Mayoral Elections) (England and Wales) Regulations 2007, SI 2007/1024, Sch 1 r 48(1)(d). In the case of an election where only two candidates remain validly nominated, head (4) in the text is modified to read simply: 'which is unmarked or void for uncertainty': see Sch 1 r 48(1)(d); modified by Sch 1 r 48(6)(b). As to ballot papers rejected for being unmarked or void for uncertainty at parliamentary and other local elections see PARA 430.

6　Local Authorities (Mayoral Elections) (England and Wales) Regulations 2007, SI 2007/1024, Sch 1 r 48(1). As to scrutiny, which may look at ballot papers and investigate how votes have been recorded, see PARA 839 et seq.

7　Local Authorities (Mayoral Elections) (England and Wales) Regulations 2007, SI 2007/1024, Sch 1 r 48(2)(a). As to the prescribed layout of the ballot paper see PARA 386. As to ballot papers rejected at parliamentary and other local elections on the grounds set out in heads (a) to (c) in the text see PARA 430.

8　Local Authorities (Mayoral Elections) (England and Wales) Regulations 2007, SI 2007/1024, Sch 1 r 48(2)(b). See note 7.

9　Local Authorities (Mayoral Elections) (England and Wales) Regulations 2007, SI 2007/1024, Sch 1 r 48(2)(c). See note 7.

10　Local Authorities (Mayoral Elections) (England and Wales) Regulations 2007, SI 2007/1024, Sch 1 r 48(2)(i).

11　Local Authorities (Mayoral Elections) (England and Wales) Regulations 2007, SI 2007/1024, Sch 1 r 48(2)(ii).

12　Local Authorities (Mayoral Elections) (England and Wales) Regulations 2007, SI 2007/1024, Sch 1 r 48(2).

13　Local Authorities (Mayoral Elections) (England and Wales) Regulations 2007, SI 2007/1024, Sch 1 r 48(3). This provision does not apply in the case of an election where only two candidates remain validly nominated and must be omitted in such a case: Sch 1 r 48(6)(c).

14　As to returning officers for local government elections (including local authority mayoral elections) see PARA 354 et seq.

15 As to the appointment of counting agents by a candidate, and as to the discharge of this function by the candidate or (where there is such an agent) his election agent, see PARA 394.
16 Local Authorities (Mayoral Elections) (England and Wales) Regulations 2007, SI 2007/1024, Sch 1 r 48(4).
17 Local Authorities (Mayoral Elections) (England and Wales) Regulations 2007, SI 2007/1024, Sch 1 r 48(5)(a).
18 Local Authorities (Mayoral Elections) (England and Wales) Regulations 2007, SI 2007/1024, Sch 1 r 48(5)(b). In the case of an election where only two candidates remain validly nominated, head (B) in the text is modified to read simply: 'voting for more than one candidate': see Sch 1 r 48(5)(b); modified by Sch 1 r 48(6)(b).
19 Local Authorities (Mayoral Elections) (England and Wales) Regulations 2007, SI 2007/1024, Sch 1 r 48(5)(c).
20 Local Authorities (Mayoral Elections) (England and Wales) Regulations 2007, SI 2007/1024, Sch 1 r 48(5)(d). In the case of an election where only two candidates remain validly nominated, head (D) in the text is modified to read simply: 'unmarked or void for uncertainty': see Sch 1 r 48(5)(d); modified by Sch 1 r 48(6)(b).

438. Conclusiveness of returning officer's decision as to ballot papers at elections for the return of local authority mayor. At the first count of a local government election for the return of an elected mayor[1], the decision of the returning officer[2] on any question arising in respect of a ballot paper is final[3], but is subject to review on an election petition[4].

1   As to local government elections for the return of an elected mayor see PARA 198. As to the meaning of 'local government election' see PARA 11. As to use of the term 'first count' see PARA 435 note 4.
2   As to returning officers for local government elections (including local authority mayoral elections) see PARA 354 et seq.
3   As to decisions made on ballot papers at elections for the return of a local authority mayor see PARA 437.
4   Local Authorities (Mayoral Elections) (England and Wales) Regulations 2007, SI 2007/1024, Sch 1 r 49. As to petitions questioning such elections see PARA 762 et seq.

439. Recount at elections for the return of local authority mayor. A candidate at a local government election for the return of an elected mayor[1] (or his election agent[2]) may, if present when the counting or any recount of the votes (or as the case may be, the first preference votes) is completed[3], require the returning officer[4] to have the votes recounted or again recounted[5]. However, the returning officer may refuse to do so if in his opinion the request is unreasonable[6]. No step may be taken on the completion of the counting or any recount of the votes (or as the case may be, the first preference votes) until the candidates and election agents who are present at its completion have been given reasonable opportunity to exercise the right of demanding a recount[7].

1   As to the meaning of 'local government election' see PARA 11. As to the meaning of 'candidate' generally see PARA 230. As to local government elections for the return of an elected mayor see PARA 198.
2   As to the appointment of election agents for local government elections see PARA 231 et seq.
3   As to elections at which first and second preference votes are cast (the 'supplementary vote system') see PARA 341; as to the first count at an election for the return of a local authority mayor see PARA 436; and as to the counting of second preference votes at a local authority mayoral election see PARA 441.
4   As to returning officers for local government elections (including local authority mayoral elections) see PARA 354 et seq.
5   Local Authorities (Mayoral Elections) (England and Wales) Regulations 2007, SI 2007/1024, Sch 1 r 50(1).
6   Local Authorities (Mayoral Elections) (England and Wales) Regulations 2007, SI 2007/1024, Sch 1 r 50(1).
7   Local Authorities (Mayoral Elections) (England and Wales) Regulations 2007, SI 2007/1024, Sch 1 r 50(2).

440.   Procedure at conclusion of first count at an election for the return of a local authority mayor. As soon as practicable after the conclusion of the first count of a local government election for the return of an elected mayor[1] (including any recount)[2], the returning officer[3] must draw up a statement showing:

(1)   the total number of ballot papers used[4];

(2)   the total number of rejected ballot papers[5];

(3)   at an election contested by more than two candidates[6]:
    (a)   the number of first preference votes given for each candidate[7]; and
    (b)   the total number of first preference votes given[8]; and

(4)   at an election contested by only two candidates, the number of votes given for each candidate[9].

As soon as practicable after completion of the statement, the returning officer must inform such of the candidates and their election agents[10] as are then present of its contents and of the contents of the statement previously prepared showing the number of ballot papers rejected under the various heads[11], and he must give public notice of the contents of those statements[12].

Where an election is contested by only two candidates[13], and:

(i)   where the total number of votes given for each of them is unequal[14], the person to be returned as the elected mayor is the candidate to whom the majority of the votes is given[15]; but

(ii)   where the total number of votes given for each of them is equal[16], the returning officer must decide by lot which of them is to be returned as the elected mayor[17].

In the case of either head (i) or head (ii) above, the declaration of the person to be returned as the elected mayor must then be made[18].

Where an election is contested by more than two candidates, the returning officer must:

(A)   if one of the candidates to be the elected mayor receives more than half of all the first preference votes given in the election[19], make the required declaration of the result that the candidate is to be returned as the elected mayor[20]; or

(B)   if none of the candidates to be the elected mayor receives more than half of all the first preference votes given in the election[21], count the second preference votes at the time and place previously notified in writing to the counting agents[22].

1   As to local government elections for the return of an elected mayor see PARA 198. As to the meaning of 'local government election' see PARA 11. As to use of the term 'first count' see PARA 435 note 4.

2   As to recounts at elections for the return of a local authority mayor see PARA 439.

3   As to returning officers for local government elections (including local authority mayoral elections) see PARA 354 et seq.

4   Local Authorities (Mayoral Elections) (England and Wales) Regulations 2007, SI 2007/1024, Sch 1 r 51(1)(a).

5   Local Authorities (Mayoral Elections) (England and Wales) Regulations 2007, SI 2007/1024, Sch 1 r 51(1)(b). As to the rejection of ballot papers at the election of a local authority mayor see PARA 437.

6   Local Authorities (Mayoral Elections) (England and Wales) Regulations 2007, SI 2007/1024, Sch 1 r 51(1)(c). As to the meaning of 'candidate' generally see PARA 230.

7   Local Authorities (Mayoral Elections) (England and Wales) Regulations 2007, SI 2007/1024, Sch 1 r 51(1)(c)(i). As to elections at which first and second preference votes are cast (the 'supplementary vote system') see PARA 341; and as to the counting of second preference votes at a local authority mayoral election see PARA 441.

8   Local Authorities (Mayoral Elections) (England and Wales) Regulations 2007, SI 2007/1024,
    Sch 1 r 51(1)(c)(ii).
9   Local Authorities (Mayoral Elections) (England and Wales) Regulations 2007, SI 2007/1024,
    Sch 1 r 51(1)(d).
10 As to the appointment of election agents at local authority mayoral elections see PARA 231 et
    seq.
11 Local Authorities (Mayoral Elections) (England and Wales) Regulations 2007, SI 2007/1024,
    Sch 1 r 51(2)(a). The text refers to the contents of the statement prepared in accordance with
    Sch 1 r 48(5) (see PARA 437): see Sch 1 r 51(2)(a).
12 Local Authorities (Mayoral Elections) (England and Wales) Regulations 2007, SI 2007/1024,
    Sch 1 r 51(2)(b).
13 See the Local Authorities (Mayoral Elections) (England and Wales) Regulations 2007,
    SI 2007/1024, Sch 1 r 51(4)(a), (5)(a).
14 Local Authorities (Mayoral Elections) (England and Wales) Regulations 2007, SI 2007/1024,
    Sch 1 r 51(4)(b).
15 Local Authorities (Mayoral Elections) (England and Wales) Regulations 2007, SI 2007/1024,
    Sch 1 r 51(4).
16 Local Authorities (Mayoral Elections) (England and Wales) Regulations 2007, SI 2007/1024,
    Sch 1 r 51(5)(b).
17 Local Authorities (Mayoral Elections) (England and Wales) Regulations 2007, SI 2007/1024,
    Sch 1 r 51(5).
18 Local Authorities (Mayoral Elections) (England and Wales) Regulations 2007, SI 2007/1024,
    Sch 1 r 51(6). The text refers to the declaration required by Sch 1 r 54 (see PARA 484): see Sch 1
    r 51(6).
19 Ie if the Local Government Act 2000 s 42(3), Sch 2 para 2 applies (candidate with overall
    majority of first preference votes to be returned as the elected mayor: see PARA 341): see the
    Local Authorities (Mayoral Elections) (England and Wales) Regulations 2007, SI 2007/1024,
    Sch 1 r 51(3)(a).
20 Local Authorities (Mayoral Elections) (England and Wales) Regulations 2007, SI 2007/1024,
    Sch 1 r 51(3)(a). The text refers to the declaration required by Sch 1 r 54(1) (see PARA 484): see
    Sch 1 r 51(3)(a).
21 Ie if the Local Government Act 2000 Sch 2 para 3 applies (two candidates who received the
    greatest number of first preference votes given in the election must remain in the contest: see
    PARA 341): see the Local Authorities (Mayoral Elections) (England and Wales)
    Regulations 2007, SI 2007/1024, Sch 1 r 51(3)(b).
22 Local Authorities (Mayoral Elections) (England and Wales) Regulations 2007, SI 2007/1024,
    Sch 1 r 51(3)(b). The text refers to counting the second preference votes at the time and place
    notified in accordance with Sch 1 r 46(1)(b) (see PARA 435): see Sch 1 r 51(3)(b).

(C) Count of Second Preference Votes

**441. The count of second preference votes at election for the return of a local
authority mayor.** The returning officer at a local government election for the
return of an elected mayor[1] must count the number of second preference votes
for each of the candidates remaining in the contest[2], given by voters who did not
give their first preference vote to any of those candidates[3]. A ballot paper which
is not otherwise void[4], and on which not more than one second preference vote is
marked, is valid as respects that vote and must be counted accordingly if, but
only if, a valid first preference vote has also been marked[5]. The provisions which
govern the first count at a local authority mayoral election in respect of:

(1)   the returning officer' s powers to regulate attendance at the count[6];
(2)   the restriction imposed on the returning officer not to count any
      tendered ballot papers[7];
(3)   duties imposed on the returning officer during the counting procedure[8];
(4)   the rejection of ballot papers[9]; and
(5)   the power available to a candidate (or election agent) to request a
      recount[10],

are applied with modifications for the purposes of counting the second preference votes[11].

The returning officer is not required to re-examine any decision taken in respect of a rejected ballot paper[12].

1 As to the meaning of 'local government election' see PARA 11. As to local government elections for the return of an elected mayor see PARA 198. As to returning officers for local government elections (including local authority mayoral elections) see PARA 354 et seq.

2 Ie where none of the candidates to be the elected mayor receives more than half of all the first preference votes given in the election, and the two candidates who received the greatest number of first preference votes given in the election remain in the contest: see the Local Government Act 2000 Sch 2 para 3; and PARA 341. As to the first count at an election for the return of a local authority mayor see PARA 436. As to the meaning of 'candidate' generally see PARA 230.

3 Local Authorities (Mayoral Elections) (England and Wales) Regulations 2007, SI 2007/1024, Sch 1 r 52(1).

4 As to the rejection of ballot papers at a local authority mayoral election see PARA 437.

5 Local Authorities (Mayoral Elections) (England and Wales) Regulations 2007, SI 2007/1024, Sch 1 r 52(2). As to the treatment of ballot papers at local authority mayoral elections on which more than one first preference vote is given, or which are unmarked or void for uncertainty as to the first preference vote, see PARA 437.

6 Ie the Local Authorities (Mayoral Elections) (England and Wales) Regulations 2007, SI 2007/1024, Sch 1 r 46(2)–(5) (see PARA 435): see Sch 1 r 52(3).

7 Ie the Local Authorities (Mayoral Elections) (England and Wales) Regulations 2007, SI 2007/1024, Sch 1 r 47(6) (see PARA 436): see Sch 1 r 52(3).

8 Ie the Local Authorities (Mayoral Elections) (England and Wales) Regulations 2007, SI 2007/1024, Sch 1 r 47(7), (9), (10) (see PARA 436): see Sch 1 r 52(3).

9 Ie the Local Authorities (Mayoral Elections) (England and Wales) Regulations 2007, SI 2007/1024, Sch 1 r 48(1), (2), (4), (5) (see PARA 437): see Sch 1 r 52(3).

10 Ie the Local Authorities (Mayoral Elections) (England and Wales) Regulations 2007, SI 2007/1024, Sch 1 r 50(1), (2) (see PARA 439): see Sch 1 r 52(3).

11 Local Authorities (Mayoral Elections) (England and Wales) Regulations 2007, SI 2007/1024, Sch 1 r 52(3). The modifications are that:
   (1) references to first preference votes should be taken as references to second preference votes (see Sch 1 r 52(3)); and
   (2) the words 'the votes or, as the case may be' should be omitted from Sch 1 r 50(1), (2) (see PARA 439) (see Sch 1 r 52(3)).

12 Local Authorities (Mayoral Elections) (England and Wales) Regulations 2007, SI 2007/1024, Sch 1 r 52(4). The text refers to any decision taken under Sch 1 r 49 (see PARA 438): see Sch 1 r 52(4).

442. Procedure at conclusion of count of second preference votes at election for the return of a local authority mayor. The returning officer at a local government election for the return of an elected mayor[1] must add the number of second preference votes given in the election for each of the candidates remaining in the contest by voters who did not give their first preference vote to any of those candidates to the number of first preference votes given for that candidate, to give his total number of preference votes (the 'second calculation')[2].

The returning officer must then draw up a statement showing:

(1) the total number of first preference votes given for each candidate[3];

(2) the total number of second preference votes given for each of the candidates remaining in the contest after the count of the first preference votes[4];

(3) the total number of votes given for each of those candidates[5]; and

(4) the number of ballot papers that were: (a) valid as respects a first preference vote given for a candidate who did not remain in the contest after the count of the first preference votes[6]; and (b) rejected for the

purposes of the count of second preference votes on the ground that they were unmarked or void for uncertainty as to the second preference vote[7].

As soon as practicable after the completion of this statement, the returning officer must provide such of the election agents for those candidates[8] who remain in the contest, as are then present, with a copy of the statement, and he must give them a reasonable opportunity to satisfy themselves as to the accuracy of the second calculation[9]. If, after the second preference votes have been counted, the total number of votes given for two or more candidates remaining in the contest is equal, the person to be returned as the elected mayor is the person whom the returning officer decides by lot[10] is to be returned as the elected mayor[11].

1   As to the meaning of 'local government election' see PARA 11. As to local government elections for the return of an elected mayor see PARA 198. As to returning officers for local government elections (including local authority mayoral elections) see PARA 354 et seq.
2   Local Authorities (Mayoral Elections) (England and Wales) Regulations 2007, SI 2007/1024, Sch 1 r 53(1). The text refers to the requirement placed on the returning officer to comply with the Local Government Act 2000 s 42(3), Sch 2 para 3(6) (see PARA 341): see the Local Authorities (Mayoral Elections) (England and Wales) Regulations 2007, SI 2007/1024, r 53(1). As to the meaning of 'candidate' generally see PARA 230. As to elections at which first and second preference votes are cast (the 'supplementary vote system') see PARA 341; as to the first count at an election for the return of a local authority mayor see PARA 436; and as to the counting of second preference votes at a local authority mayoral election see PARA 441.
3   Local Authorities (Mayoral Elections) (England and Wales) Regulations 2007, SI 2007/1024, Sch 1 r 53(2)(a).
4   Local Authorities (Mayoral Elections) (England and Wales) Regulations 2007, SI 2007/1024, Sch 1 r 53(2)(b).
5   Local Authorities (Mayoral Elections) (England and Wales) Regulations 2007, SI 2007/1024, Sch 1 r 53(2)(c).
6   Local Authorities (Mayoral Elections) (England and Wales) Regulations 2007, SI 2007/1024, Sch 1 r 53(2)(d)(i). As to the rejection of ballot papers at local authority mayoral elections see PARA 437.
7   Local Authorities (Mayoral Elections) (England and Wales) Regulations 2007, SI 2007/1024, Sch 1 r 53(2)(d)(ii).
8   As to the appointment of election agents at local authority mayoral elections see PARA 231 et seq.
9   Local Authorities (Mayoral Elections) (England and Wales) Regulations 2007, SI 2007/1024, Sch 1 r 53(3).
10 Ie in accordance with the Local Government Act 2000 Sch 2 para 3(8) (see PARA 341): see the Local Authorities (Mayoral Elections) (England and Wales) Regulations 2007, SI 2007/1024, Sch 1 r 53(4).
11 Local Authorities (Mayoral Elections) (England and Wales) Regulations 2007, SI 2007/1024, Sch 1 r 53(4).

C. LONDON AUTHORITY ELECTION

(A) General Arrangements for verifying and counting Votes at London Authority Elections

443. Arrangements for verifying and counting votes at Authority elections; the electronic counting system. As soon as practicable after the close of the poll at an Authority election[1], the constituency returning officer[2] must make arrangements for carrying out, in the presence of the counting agents[3], the verification and counting of votes[4]. The constituency returning officer must give to the counting agents notice in writing of the time and place at which he will begin to verify and count the votes[5]. No person other than:

(1) the constituency returning officer ('CRO') and his clerks and technical assistants[6];

(2)   the Greater London returning officer ('GLRO')[7];

(3)   the candidates and one other person chosen by each of them[8];

(4)   the election agents[9];

(5)   the counting agents[10]; and

(6)   persons who are entitled to attend by virtue of any of the provisions of the Political Parties, Elections and Referendums Act 2000[11] which allow Electoral Commission representatives and accredited observers to attend electoral proceedings and observe working practices[12],

may be present at the verification and counting of the votes, unless permitted by the CRO to attend[13]. A person not entitled to attend at the verification and counting of votes must not be permitted to do so by the CRO, however, unless:

(a)   the CRO is satisfied that the efficient conduct of those proceedings will not be impeded[14]; and

(b)   the CRO has either consulted the candidates (at a constituency members election) or the elections agents (at a London members or London Mayoral election), or he has thought it impracticable to do so[15].

The returning officer must make such arrangements as he thinks fit to ensure that every person attending at the counting of the votes (other than any constable on duty at the counting) has been given a copy in writing of the statutory provisions relating to the requirement of secrecy that apply to such attendance[16].

The CRO must give the counting agents all such reasonable facilities for overseeing the proceedings, and all such information with respect to them, as he can give them consistently with the orderly conduct of the proceedings and the discharge of his duties in connection with them[17].

The GLRO may provide the CRO with an electronic counting system consisting of computer hardware, software and other equipment or services[18], for the purpose of counting the number of ballot papers, to verify the ballot paper accounts, and to count the votes cast on them at an Authority election[19]. If the GLRO has provided the CRO with such a system for use at the election, the CRO must obtain the prior written consent of the GLRO before he may conduct the verification of ballot paper accounts or count the votes manually[20], although, where the count or a recount has been conducted using the electronic counting system, the CRO may, if he considers it appropriate, conduct any recount without using that system[21].

Where the poll at an election is taken together with the poll at another election or referendum, special provision is made for counting the votes[22].

1   As to the meaning of 'Authority election' see PARA 11. As to elections in the City of London see PARA 33.

2   As to the meaning of 'constituency returning officer' for these purposes see PARA 211 note 9.

3   As to the appointment of counting agents by a candidate, and as to the effect of their non-attendance, see PARA 394.

4   Greater London Authority Elections Rules 2007, SI 2007/3541, Sch 1 r 47(1), Sch 2 r 48(1), Sch 3 r 47(1). The arrangements mentioned in the text that are made for a London members or London Mayoral election are known as the 'local count': see Sch 2 r 48(1), Sch 3 r 47(1). As to the count at Authority elections for the return of constituency or London members see PARA 444 et seq; and as to the count at an Authority election for the return of London Mayor see PARA 451 et seq.

5   Greater London Authority Elections Rules 2007, SI 2007/3541, Sch 1 r 47(1), Sch 2 r 48(1), Sch 3 r 47(1).

6   Greater London Authority Elections Rules 2007, SI 2007/3541, Sch 1 r 47(2)(a), Sch 2 r 48(2)(a), Sch 3 r 47(2)(a). As to persons appointed as clerks by a returning officer see PARA 393. Because non-manual counting methods may be employed at London Authority elections (see the text and notes 18–21), the CRO may appoint and pay such technical assistants as may be necessary for the purposes of such an election: see PARA 393 note 6.

7   Greater London Authority Elections Rules 2007, SI 2007/3541, Sch 1 r 47(2)(b), Sch 2
     r 48(2)(b), Sch 3 r 47(2)(b). As to the meaning of 'Greater London returning officer' see
     PARA 211 note 8.

8   Greater London Authority Elections Rules 2007, SI 2007/3541, Sch 1 r 47(2)(c), Sch 2
     r 48(2)(c), Sch 3 r 47(2)(c).

9   Greater London Authority Elections Rules 2007, SI 2007/3541, Sch 1 r 47(2)(d), Sch 2
     r 48(2)(d), Sch 3 r 47(2)(d). As to the appointment of election agents at Authority elections see
     PARA 231 et seq.

10   Greater London Authority Elections Rules 2007, SI 2007/3541, Sch 1 r 47(2)(e), Sch 2
     r 48(2)(e), Sch 3 r 47(2)(e).

11   Ie by virtue of any of the provisions of the Political Parties, Elections and Referendums Act 2000
     ss 6A–6D (see PARA 53): see the Greater London Authority Elections Rules 2007, SI 2007/3541,
     Sch 1 r 47(2)(f), Sch 2 r 48(2)(f), Sch 3 r 47(2)(f).

12   Greater London Authority Elections Rules 2007, SI 2007/3541, Sch 1 r 47(2)(f), Sch 2
     r 48(2)(f), Sch 3 r 47(2)(f). As to the Electoral Commission see PARA 34 et seq; and as to
     authorised representatives of the Electoral Commission attending electoral proceedings see
     PARA 53.

13   Greater London Authority Elections Rules 2007, SI 2007/3541, Sch 1 r 47(2), Sch 2 r 48(2),
     Sch 3 r 47(2).

14   Greater London Authority Elections Rules 2007, SI 2007/3541, Sch 1 r 47(3)(a), Sch 2
     r 48(3)(a), Sch 3 r 47(3)(a).

15   Greater London Authority Elections Rules 2007, SI 2007/3541, Sch 1 r 47(3)(b), Sch 2
     r 48(3)(b), Sch 3 r 47(3)(b).

16   See PARAS 385, 739–741.

17   Greater London Authority Elections Rules 2007, SI 2007/3541, Sch 1 r 47(4), Sch 2 r 48(4),
     Sch 3 r 47(4).

18   Accordingly, 'electronic counting system' means such computer hardware, software and other
     equipment or services as may be provided by the GLRO to the CRO in accordance with the
     rules applying at the Authority election (ie the constituency members election rules, the london
     members election rules, or the London mayoral elections rules, as the case may be: see PARA 383
     note 10) for the purpose of counting the number of ballot papers to verify the ballot paper
     accounts and to count the votes cast on them: see the Greater London Authority Elections
     Rules 2007, SI 2007/3541, r 2(1). Where some or all of the votes cast at any such Authority
     election are to be counted without the use of an electronic counting system, the constituency
     members election rules, the London members election rules and the mayoral election rules have
     effect, in respect of those votes counted manually, subject to the modifications set out in the
     manual counts rules in r 4, Sch 4: see rr 2(1), 4; and see PARA 383 note 10. As to the
     modification of the combined poll rules contained in Schs 5–7 where votes are counted without
     the use of an electronic counting system see r 6, Sch 8 (the 'combined manual count rules': see
     r 2(1)); and PARA 22 note 11.

19   Greater London Authority Elections Rules 2007, SI 2007/3541, Sch 1 r 48(1), Sch 2 r 49(1),
     Sch 3 r 48(1). Any verification of ballot paper accounts, count or recount at the election
     conducted using the electronic counting system must be conducted in accordance with Sch 1
     r 49, Sch 2 r 50, Sch 3 r 49 (see PARAS 444, 451): Sch 1 r 48(2), Sch 2 r 49(2), Sch 3 r 48(2).
     Where verification or any count or recount is conducted using the electronic counting system,
     any of the steps referred to in Sch 1 r 49, Sch 2 r 50, Sch 3 r 49, in so far as practicable, may be
     undertaken concurrently with any other of those steps, or in a different order: see Sch 1 r 48(6),
     Sch 2 r 49(6), Sch 3 r 48(6). If the verification of ballot paper accounts, count or recount has
     commenced using the electronic counting system but has not been completed, the CRO may, if
     he considers it appropriate, discontinue the count and instead count the votes manually: Sch 1
     r 48(4), Sch 2 r 49(4), Sch 3 r 48(4). As to the ballot paper account see PARA 405. As to recounts
     at an Authority election for the return of constituency or London members see PARA 447. As to
     verification of the ballot paper account at London mayoral elections see PARA 451.

20   Greater London Authority Elections Rules 2007, SI 2007/3541, Sch 1 r 48(3), Sch 2 r 49(3),
     Sch 3 r 48(3). As to the rules that apply at manual counts see note 18.

21   Greater London Authority Elections Rules 2007, SI 2007/3541, Sch 1 r 48(5), Sch 2 r 49(5),
     Sch 3 r 48(5).

22   As to polls at elections or referendums which are taken together see PARA 16 et seq.

(B) London Authority Election (except Election for London Mayor)

444.   Verification of ballot paper accounts and the count at Authority elections for return of constituency or London members. The constituency returning officer ('CRO') at an Authority election[1] for the return of constituency or London members[2] must[3]:

(1)   open the ballot boxes from each polling station[4] together, in the presence of the counting agents[5] appointed for the purposes of the election and any other Authority election with which is its combined[6];

(2)   cause the electronic counting system[7] to count such of the postal ballot papers as have been duly returned[8], and record separately the number counted[9];

(3)   not mix the contents of any ballot box with the contents of any other ballot box during the conduct of any count or recount[10].

After completing the proceedings under heads (1) to (3) above, the CRO must cause the electronic counting system to process the ballot papers so as to count[11]:

(a)   the number of ballot papers[12]; and

(b)   votes given on the ballot papers[13].

The CRO must not cause the electronic counting system to count any tendered ballot paper[14].

The CRO must verify each ballot paper account by comparing it with the number of ballot papers processed by the electronic counting system, and the unused and spoilt ballot papers[15] in his possession and the tendered votes list[16] (opening and resealing the packets containing the unused and spoilt ballot papers and the tendered votes list), and he must draw up a statement as to the result of the verification, which any election agent may copy[17]. While verifying the ballot paper accounts and counting the votes, the CRO must take all proper precautions for preventing any person from seeing the numbers printed on the back of the papers[18]. The CRO also must, so far as practicable, proceed continuously with counting the votes, allowing only time for refreshment, except that the hours between five in the afternoon and ten on the following morning may be excluded[19]. During the time so excluded, the CRO must:

(i)   place the ballot papers and other documents relating to the election under his own seal and the seals of such of the counting agents as desire to affix their seals[20]; and

(ii)   otherwise take proper precautions for the security of the papers and documents[21].

Where the poll at an election is taken together with the poll at another election or referendum, special provision is made for counting the votes[22].

1   As to the meaning of 'Authority election' see PARA 11. As to the meaning of 'constituency returning officer' for these purposes see PARA 211 note 9.

2   As to the meaning of 'constituency member', in relation to the London Assembly, see PARA 11 note 6; definition applied by virtue of the Greater London Authority Elections Rules 2007, SI 2007/3541, r 2(2). As to the meaning of 'London member', in relation to the London Assembly, see PARA 11 note 5; definition applied by virtue of r 2(2). As to elections for the return of constituency or London members of the London Assembly see PARA 199 et seq. As to elections in the City of London see PARA 33.

3   Greater London Authority Elections Rules 2007, SI 2007/3541, Sch 1 r 49(1), Sch 2 r 50(1).

4   As to the provision and allotment of polling stations see PARA 390.

5   As to the appointment of counting agents by a candidate, and as to the effect of their non-attendance, see PARA 394.

6   Greater London Authority Elections Rules 2007, SI 2007/3541, Sch 1 r 49(1)(a), Sch 2 r 50(1)(a). As to polls at elections or referendums which are taken together see the text and note 22. As to the counting of votes at a London mayoral election see PARA 451.

7   As to the meaning of 'electronic counting system' see PARA 443 note 18.
8   Ie returned in accordance with the Greater London Authority Elections Rules 2007, SI 2007/3541, Sch 1 r 49(2), (3), Sch 2 r 50(2), (3): see Sch 1 r 49(1)(b), Sch 2 r 50(1)(b). Accordingly, a postal ballot paper must not be taken to be duly returned unless:

(1)   it is returned in the prescribed manner (ie either by hand or by post to the CRO, or by hand only to a polling station in the Assembly constituency), and reaches the CRO or any polling station in the Assembly constituency that includes the electoral area for which the elector is registered as a local government elector, before the close of the poll (Sch 1 r 49(2)(a), (3), Sch 2 r 50(2)(a), (3));

(2)   the postal voting statement, duly signed, is also returned in the prescribed manner (ie either by hand or by post to the CRO, or by hand only to a polling station in the Assembly constituency), and reaches him or such a polling station before that time (Sch 1 r 49(2)(b), (3), Sch 2 r 50(2)(b), (3));

(3)   the postal voting statement also states the date of birth of the elector or proxy (as the case may be) (Sch 1 r 49(2)(c), Sch 2 r 50(2)(c)); and

(4)   in a case where the steps for verifying the date of birth and signature of an elector or proxy have been prescribed by regulations made under the Representation of the People Act 1983, the CRO (having taken such steps) verifies the date of birth and signature of the elector or proxy (as the case may be) (Greater London Authority Elections Rules 2007, SI 2007/3541, Sch 1 r 49(2)(d), Sch 2 r 50(2)(d)).

As to the regulations that have been prescribed for the purposes of head (4) above see the Representation of the People (England and Wales) Regulations 2001, SI 2001/341, regs 85, 85A; and PARA 421. As to the meaning of 'electoral area' for the purposes of local government elections see PARA 11; and as to the meaning of 'Assembly constituency', in relation to the London Assembly, see PARA 11 note 6. As to the meaning of 'elector', in relation to a local government election, see PARA 95 note 2. As to the meaning of 'postal ballot paper' see PARA 407 note 1. As to voting by proxy see PARA 366 et seq; and as to the entitlement to vote by post as proxy see PARAS 377, 382. As to the postal voting statement see PARA 406. As to the means by which a postal voter may validly return a postal ballot paper see also PARA 418. As to the provision that may be made regarding the circumstances in which, following the close of the poll at a parliamentary or local government election, a registration officer must notify a person that the person's postal ballot paper has been rejected see PARA 426.

9   Greater London Authority Elections Rules 2007, SI 2007/3541, Sch 1 r 49(1)(b), Sch 2 r 50(1)(b).
10   Greater London Authority Elections Rules 2007, SI 2007/3541, Sch 1 r 49(1)(c), Sch 2 r 50(1)(c).
11   Greater London Authority Elections Rules 2007, SI 2007/3541, Sch 1 r 49(4), Sch 2 r 50(4).
12   Greater London Authority Elections Rules 2007, SI 2007/3541, Sch 1 r 49(4)(a), Sch 2 r 50(4)(a).
13   Greater London Authority Elections Rules 2007, SI 2007/3541, Sch 1 r 49(4)(b), Sch 2 r 50(4)(b).
14   Greater London Authority Elections Rules 2007, SI 2007/3541, Sch 1 r 49(5), Sch 2 r 50(5). As to tendered ballot papers see PARA 403; and as to adding votes on a scrutiny see PARA 839 et seq.
15   As to spoilt ballot papers see PARA 404.
16   As to the tendered votes list see PARA 403.
17   Greater London Authority Elections Rules 2007, SI 2007/3541, Sch 1 r 49(6), Sch 2 r 50(6). As to the appointment of election agents at Authority elections see PARA 231 et seq.
18   Greater London Authority Elections Rules 2007, SI 2007/3541, Sch 1 r 49(7), Sch 2 r 50(7). As to the number which must be printed on the back of every ballot paper see PARA 387.
19   Greater London Authority Elections Rules 2007, SI 2007/3541, Sch 1 r 49(8), Sch 2 r 50(8). At an ordinary election of constituency members, and at any London members election, the hours between five in the afternoon and ten on the following morning may only be excluded with the prior consent of the GLRO, however: Sch 1 r 49(9), Sch 2 r 50(8).
20   Greater London Authority Elections Rules 2007, SI 2007/3541, Sch 1 r 49(10)(a), Sch 2 r 50(9)(a).
21   Greater London Authority Elections Rules 2007, SI 2007/3541, Sch 1 r 49(10)(b), Sch 2 r 50(9)(b).
22   As to polls at elections or referendums which are taken together see PARA 16 et seq.

445.   Ballot papers rejected at Authority elections for return of constituency or London members. At a Authority election[1] for the return of constituency or London members[2], any ballot paper:

(1)   which does not bear the official mark[3];
(2)   on which votes are given for more than one candidate[4];
(3)   on which anything is written or marked by which the voter can be identified (except the printed number or other unique identifying mark on the back)[5];
(4)   which is unmarked[6]; or
(5)   which is void for uncertainty[7],

is void and must not be counted[8]. However, a ballot paper on which a vote is marked:

(a)   elsewhere than in the proper place[9]; or
(b)   otherwise than by means of a cross[10]; or
(c)   by more than one mark[11],

must not for such reason be void if an intention that the vote to be given for one only of the candidates clearly appears[12], and the way the paper is marked does not itself identify the voter, and it is not shown that he can be identified by it[13]. Where the electronic counting system[14] identifies a ballot paper that has been marked, but which appears for whatever reason to be void, it must be examined by a clerk appointed by the constituency returning officer ('CRO')[15], achieved by the clerk examining an image of the ballot paper which is shown on a screen so as to be visible to those attending the count[16]. If the clerk, having examined the ballot, considers that the vote is void, then the CRO also must examine[17] the image of the ballot paper which is shown on a screen so as to be visible to those attending the count[18]. After the CRO examines the ballot paper, he must give his decision as to the validity of the vote[19]. If a counting agent[20] objects to the CRO's decision, the CRO must record on the electronic counting system that the decision was objected to[21].

The CRO must draw up a statement showing the number of ballot papers rejected under the several heads of:

(i)   want of official mark[22];
(ii)   voting for more than one candidate[23];
(iii)   writing or mark by which a voter could be identified[24];
(iv)   unmarked ballot paper[25]; or
(v)   void for uncertainty[26].

As soon as practicable after the completion of such a statement, the CRO must inform such candidates, election agents[27], and counting agents, as are present at the count[28], and the Greater London returning officer ('GLRO')[29], of its contents[30].

1   As to the meaning of 'Authority election' see PARA 11.
2   As to the meaning of 'constituency member', in relation to the London Assembly, see PARA 11 note 6; definition applied by virtue of the Greater London Authority Elections Rules 2007, SI 2007/3541, r 2(2). As to the meaning of 'London member', in relation to the London Assembly, see PARA 11 note 5; definition applied by virtue of r 2(2). As to elections for the return of constituency or London members of the London Assembly see PARA 199 et seq. As to the count at a London mayoral election see PARA 451.
3   Greater London Authority Elections Rules 2007, SI 2007/3541, Sch 1 r 50(1)(a), Sch 2 r 51(1)(a). As to the official mark see PARA 387. As to ballot papers rejected for want of official mark at parliamentary and other local elections see PARA 427.
4   Greater London Authority Elections Rules 2007, SI 2007/3541, Sch 1 r 50(1)(b), Sch 2 r 51(1)(b). In the case of a London members election, head (2) in the text refers to any ballot paper on which votes are given for more than one party or individual candidate: see Sch 2 r 51(1)(b). As to the meaning of 'individual candidate' in this context see PARA 255 note 9; and as to the meaning of 'registered political party' for these purposes see PARA 255 note 18. Whether a mark on a ballot paper amounts to a vote for a particular candidate is a matter of fact: see PARA 856 note 4.

5 Greater London Authority Elections Rules 2007, SI 2007/3541, Sch 1 r 50(1)(c), Sch 2 r 51(1)(c). As to the number and other unique identifying marks which must be printed on the back of every ballot paper see PARA 387. As to ballot papers rejected for marks identifying the voter at parliamentary and other local elections see PARA 429.

6 Greater London Authority Elections Rules 2007, SI 2007/3541, Sch 1 r 50(1)(d), Sch 2 r 51(1)(d). As to ballot papers rejected for being unmarked at parliamentary and other local elections see PARA 430.

7 Greater London Authority Elections Rules 2007, SI 2007/3541, Sch 1 r 50(1)(e), Sch 2 r 51(1)(e). As to ballot papers rejected for being void for uncertainty at parliamentary and other local elections see PARA 430.

8 Greater London Authority Elections Rules 2007, SI 2007/3541, Sch 1 r 50(1), Sch 2 r 51(1). As to scrutiny, which may look at ballot papers and investigate how votes have been recorded, see PARA 839 et seq.

9 Greater London Authority Elections Rules 2007, SI 2007/3541, Sch 1 r 50(2)(a), Sch 2 r 51(2)(a). As to the prescribed layout of the ballot paper see PARA 386. As to ballot papers rejected at parliamentary and other local elections on the grounds set out in heads (a) to (c) in the text see PARA 430.

10 Greater London Authority Elections Rules 2007, SI 2007/3541, Sch 1 r 50(2)(b), Sch 2 r 51(2)(b). See note 9.

11 Greater London Authority Elections Rules 2007, SI 2007/3541, Sch 1 r 50(2)(c), Sch 2 r 51(2)(c). See note 9.

12 In the case of a London members election, the text refers to an intention that the vote to be given for one only of the party or individual candidates: see the Greater London Authority Elections Rules 2007, SI 2007/3541, Sch 2 r 51(2).

13 Greater London Authority Elections Rules 2007, SI 2007/3541, Sch 1 r 50(2), Sch 2 r 51(2). As to the purposive interpretation that is required of this kind of provision see PARA 430.

14 As to the meaning of 'electronic counting system' see PARA 443 note 18.

15 See the Greater London Authority Elections Rules 2007, SI 2007/3541, Sch 1 r 50(3), Sch 2 r 51(3). As to the meaning of 'constituency returning officer' ('CRO') for these purposes see PARA 211 note 9.

16 See the Greater London Authority Elections Rules 2007, SI 2007/3541, Sch 1 r 50(6), Sch 2 r 51(6).

17 See the Greater London Authority Elections Rules 2007, SI 2007/3541, Sch 1 r 50(4), Sch 2 r 51(4). See also note 19.

18 See the Greater London Authority Elections Rules 2007, SI 2007/3541, Sch 1 r 50(6), Sch 2 r 51(6).

19 Greater London Authority Elections Rules 2007, SI 2007/3541, Sch 1 r 50(5), Sch 2 r 51(5). A record of the CRO's decision must be retained in the electronic counting system together with, in the case of a decision that the ballot paper is void, his reasons by reference to heads (1) to (5) in the text: Sch 1 r 50(9), Sch 2 r 51(9).

The CRO may examine any ballot paper that he is not required to examine in accordance with, Sch 1 r 50(4), Sch 2 r 51(4) (see the text and notes 17–18), either by examining an image of the ballot paper which is shown on a screen so as to be visible to those attending the count, or by examining a paper copy: see Sch 1 r 50(6), (7), Sch 2 r 51(6), (7). Where the CRO does so, he must give a decision on that paper in accordance with Sch 1 r 50(5), Sch 2 r 51(5): see Sch 1 r 50(7), Sch 2 r 51(7). No person attending the count is to be entitled to require the clerk or CRO to examine a ballot paper or to provide a paper copy for inspection, however: Sch 1 r 50(8), Sch 2 r 51(8).

20 As to the appointment of counting agents by a candidate, as to the effect of their non-attendance, see PARA 394.

21 Greater London Authority Elections Rules 2007, SI 2007/3541, Sch 1 r 50(10), Sch 2 r 51(10).

22 Greater London Authority Elections Rules 2007, SI 2007/3541, Sch 1 r 50(11)(a), Sch 2 r 51(11)(a).

23 Greater London Authority Elections Rules 2007, SI 2007/3541, Sch 1 r 50(11)(b), Sch 2 r 51(11)(b). In the case of a London members election, head (ii) in the text refers to voting for more than one party or individual candidate: see Sch 2 r 51(11)(b).

24 Greater London Authority Elections Rules 2007, SI 2007/3541, Sch 1 r 50(11)(c), Sch 2 r 51(11)(c).

25 Greater London Authority Elections Rules 2007, SI 2007/3541, Sch 1 r 50(11)(d), Sch 2 r 51(11)(d).

26 Greater London Authority Elections Rules 2007, SI 2007/3541, Sch 1 r 50(11)(e), Sch 2 r 51(11)(e).

27 As to the appointment of election agents at Authority elections see PARA 231 et seq.

28　Greater London Authority Elections Rules 2007, SI 2007/3541, Sch 1 r 50(12)(a), Sch 2 r 51(12)(a).
29　Greater London Authority Elections Rules 2007, SI 2007/3541, Sch 1 r 50(12)(b), Sch 2 r 51(12)(b). As to the meaning of 'Greater London returning officer' ('GLRO') see PARA 211 note 8.
30　Greater London Authority Elections Rules 2007, SI 2007/3541, Sch 1 r 50(12), Sch 2 r 51(12).

446.　Conclusiveness of returning officer's decision as to ballot papers at Authority elections for return of constituency or London members. The decision of the constituency returning officer[1], at a London Authority election[2] for the return of constituency or London members[3], on any question arising in respect of a ballot paper[4] is final, but is subject to review on an election petition[5].

1　As to the meaning of 'constituency returning officer' ('CRO') for these purposes see PARA 211 note 9.
2　As to the meaning of 'Authority election' see PARA 11.
3　As to the meaning of 'constituency member', in relation to the London Assembly, see PARA 11 note 6; definition applied by virtue of the Greater London Authority Elections Rules 2007, SI 2007/3541, r 2(2). As to the meaning of 'London member', in relation to the London Assembly, see PARA 11 note 5; definition applied by virtue of r 2(2). As to elections for the return of constituency or London members of the London Assembly see PARA 199 et seq.
4　As to decisions made on ballot papers rejected at Authority elections for the return of constituency or London members see PARA 445. As to the count at a London mayoral election see PARA 451.
5　Greater London Authority Elections Rules 2007, SI 2007/3541, Sch 1 r 51, Sch 2 r 52. As to petitions questioning a local government election see PARA 762 et seq.

447.　Recount at Authority elections for return of constituency or London members. A candidate at a London Authority election[1] for the return of constituency or London members[2] (or his election agent[3], or any counting agent duly authorised[4]) may, if present when the counting, or any recount, of the votes is completed[5], require the constituency returning officer ('CRO')[6] to have the votes recounted or again recounted[7]. However, the CRO may refuse to do so if in his opinion the request is unreasonable[8].

No step may be taken on the completion of the counting, or any recount, of the votes until the candidates and election agents (and counting agents duly authorised, in the case of a London members election) who are present at its completion have been given reasonable opportunity to exercise the right of demanding a recount[9]. The CRO may determine the extent to which any recount involves the electronic counting of votes[10]; but, when the returning officer uses the electronic counting system[11] for the recounting of votes, he must not reconsider any decision made previously on a ballot paper[12].

1　As to the meaning of 'Authority election' see PARA 11; and as to the meaning of 'candidate' generally see PARA 230.
2　As to the meaning of 'constituency member', in relation to the London Assembly, see PARA 11 note 6; definition applied by virtue of the Greater London Authority Elections Rules 2007, SI 2007/3541, r 2(2). As to the meaning of 'London member', in relation to the London Assembly, see PARA 11 note 5; definition applied by virtue of r 2(2). As to elections for the return of constituency or London members of the London Assembly see PARA 199 et seq.
3　As to the appointment of election agents at Authority elections see PARA 231 et seq. In the case of a list candidate at a London members election, the reference to an election agent includes a reference to the election agent for that list: see the Greater London Authority Elections Rules 2007, SI 2007/3541, Sch 2 r 53(1). As to references to party lists in elections for the return of London members of the London Assembly see PARA 255 note 23.
4　Ie any counting agent authorised under the Greater London Authority Elections Rules 2007, SI 2007/3541, Sch 1 r 30(3) or Sch 2 r 31(3), as the case may be (see PARA 394): see Sch 1 r 52(1), Sch 2 r 53(1).

5 As to the counting of votes at Authority elections for the return of constituency or London members see PARA 444 et seq.
6 As to the meaning of 'constituency returning officer' ('CRO') for these purposes see PARA 211 note 9.
7 Greater London Authority Elections Rules 2007, SI 2007/3541, Sch 1 r 52(1), Sch 2 r 53(1).
8 Greater London Authority Elections Rules 2007, SI 2007/3541, Sch 1 r 52(1), Sch 2 r 53(1).
9 Greater London Authority Elections Rules 2007, SI 2007/3541, Sch 1 r 52(2), Sch 2 r 53(2).
10 Greater London Authority Elections Rules 2007, SI 2007/3541, Sch 1 r 52(3), Sch 2 r 53(3). As to the electronic counting of votes see PARA 443 note 18.
11 As to the meaning of 'electronic counting system' see PARA 443 note 18.
12 Greater London Authority Elections Rules 2007, SI 2007/3541, Sch 1 r 52(4), Sch 2 r 53(4). The text refers to any decision made on any ballot paper under Sch 1 r 50(5) or Sch 2 r 51(5), as the case may be (see PARA 445): see Sch 1 r 52(4), Sch 2 r 53(4).

448. Procedure at conclusion of count at Authority elections for return of constituency members. After the counting of the votes (including any recount) is completed at a London Authority election[1] for the return of constituency members[2], where an equality of votes is found to exist between any candidates[3], and the addition of a vote would entitle any of those candidates to be declared elected, the constituency returning officer[4] must forthwith decide between those candidates by lot, and proceed as if the candidate on whom the lot falls had received an additional vote[5].

1 As to the meaning of 'Authority election' see PARA 11.
2 As to the meaning of 'constituency member', in relation to the London Assembly, see PARA 11 note 6; definition applied by virtue of the Greater London Authority Elections Rules 2007, SI 2007/3541, r 2(2). As to elections for the return of constituency members of the London Assembly see PARA 199 et seq; and as to the counting of votes at such an election see PARA 444 et seq.
3 As to the meaning of 'candidate' generally see PARA 230.
4 As to the meaning of 'constituency returning officer' ('CRO') for these purposes see PARA 211 note 9.
5 Greater London Authority Elections Rules 2007, SI 2007/3541, Sch 1 r 53.

449. Procedure at conclusion of count at Authority elections for return of London members. As soon as practicable after the conclusion of the local count[1] at a London Authority election[2] for the return of London members[3], including any recount[4], the constituency returning officer ('CRO')[5] must draw up a statement showing[6]:

(1)   the total number of votes cast[7];
(2)   the total number of votes rejected[8];
(3)   the number of votes given for each registered party[9]; and
(4)   the number of votes cast for each individual candidate[10].

As soon as practicable after such a statement is drawn up, the CRO must inform the Greater London returning officer ('GLRO')[11] of its contents, and if it is practicable to do so, must also provide that information so as to show the total number of votes under each of those heads in each ward[12].

As soon as practicable after the GLRO has authorised him to do so, the CRO must: (a) inform such of the candidates and their election agents[13] as are then present of the content of the statement prepared showing the information under heads (1) to (4) above, as well as the content of the statement showing the number of ballot papers rejected under the various heads[14]; and (b) give public notice of the contents of those statements[15].

1 As to the local count see PARA 443 note 4.
2 As to the meaning of 'Authority election' see PARA 11.

3   As to the meaning of 'London member', in relation to the London Assembly, see PARA 11 note 5; definition applied by virtue of r 2(2). As to the counting of votes at a London Authority election for the return of London members see PARA 444 et seq.

4   As to recounts of votes at a London Authority election for the return of London members see PARA 447.

5   As to the meaning of 'constituency returning officer' ('CRO') for these purposes see PARA 211 note 9.

6   Greater London Authority Elections Rules 2007, SI 2007/3541, Sch 2 r 54(1).

7   Greater London Authority Elections Rules 2007, SI 2007/3541, Sch 2 r 54(1)(a).

8   Greater London Authority Elections Rules 2007, SI 2007/3541, Sch 2 r 54(1)(b). Head (2) in the text refers to the total number of votes rejected under Sch 2 r 51 (see PARA 445): see Sch 2 r 54(1)(b).

9   Greater London Authority Elections Rules 2007, SI 2007/3541, Sch 2 r 54(1)(c). As to the meaning of 'registered political party' for these purposes see PARA 255 note 18.

10   Greater London Authority Elections Rules 2007, SI 2007/3541, Sch 2 r 54(1)(d). As to the meaning of 'individual candidate' at an election for London members see PARA 255 note 9.

11   As to the meaning of 'Greater London returning officer' ('GLRO') see PARA 211 note 8.

12   Greater London Authority Elections Rules 2007, SI 2007/3541, Sch 2 r 54(2). As soon as the GLRO has received from every CRO the contents of the statement required under heads (1) to (4) in the text, the GLRO must calculate the figure (the 'London figure') for each registered party and for each individual candidate: see Sch 2 r 56; and PARA 450. As to the establishment of electoral areas for the purpose of local government elections in England see PARA 74.

13   As to the appointment of election agents at Authority elections see PARA 231 et seq.

14   Greater London Authority Elections Rules 2007, SI 2007/3541, Sch 2 r 54(3)(a). The text refers to the statement prepared under Sch 2 r 51 showing the number of ballot papers rejected under the several heads of want of official mark, voting for more than one candidate, writing or mark by which a voter could be identified, unmarked ballot paper, or void for uncertainty (see PARA 445): see Sch 2 r 54(3)(a).

15   Greater London Authority Elections Rules 2007, SI 2007/3541, Sch 2 r 54(3)(b). As to the giving of public notices by a returning officer generally see PARA 350 et seq.

450. The calculation of the London figure for the allocation of seats at Authority elections for return of London members. The Greater London returning officer ('GLRO')[1] must make arrangements for making the allocation of seats at a London Authority election[2] for the return of London members[3], in the presence of the election agents of the individual candidates[4] (including, in respect of any list candidate, the election agent for that party list)[5]; and the GLRO must give to those agents notice in writing of the time and place at which he will begin the allocation[6]. No person other than:

(1)   the GLRO and his clerks[7];

(2)   the constituency returning officers ('CROs') and a clerk or technical assistant chosen by each of them[8];

(3)   the individual candidates, and one other person chosen by each of them[9];

(4)   candidates included on a party list, and one other person chosen by each of them[10];

(5)   the election agents[11];

(6)   the nominating officers for those registered political parties standing nominated at the election[12];

(7)   persons who are entitled to attend by virtue of any of the provisions of the Political Parties, Elections and Referendums Act 2000[13] which allow Electoral Commission representatives and accredited observers to attend electoral proceedings and observe working practices[14]; and

(8)   persons permitted to be present at the central calculation at the election of the Mayor of London[15],

may be present at an allocation, unless permitted by the GLRO to attend[16]. A person not entitled to attend an allocation must not be permitted to do so by the GLRO, however, unless the GLRO[17]:

(a)   is satisfied that the efficiency of the allocation will not be impeded[18]; and

(b)   has either consulted the election agents or thought it impracticable to do so[19].

As soon as the GLRO has received from every CRO the contents of the statement showing the total number of votes under various headings of votes cast and rejected, votes given for each registered party, and votes given for each individual candidate[20], he must calculate the figure (the 'London figure') for each registered party and for each individual candidate[21]. The seats are then allocated in accordance with the rules[22]. As soon as the GLRO has ascertained the result of the calculation, he must inform such of the election agents for the candidates as are then present of the relevant figures[23], and he must give them a reasonable opportunity to satisfy themselves as to the accuracy of the calculation[24].

1   As to the meaning of 'Greater London returning officer' ('GLRO') see PARA 211 note 8.
2   As to the meaning of 'Authority election' see PARA 11.
3   As to the meaning of 'London member', in relation to the London Assembly, see PARA 11 note 5; definition applied by virtue of the Greater London Authority Elections Rules 2007, SI 2007/3541, r 2(2). As to the counting of votes at a London Authority election for the return of London members see PARA 444 et seq.
4   As to the meaning of 'candidate' generally see PARA 230. As to the meaning of 'individual candidate' at an election for London members see PARA 255 note 9. As to the appointment of election agents at Authority elections see PARA 231 et seq.
5   See the Greater London Authority Elections Rules 2007, SI 2007/3541, Sch 2 r 55(1). As to references to party lists in elections for the return of London members of the London Assembly see PARA 255 note 23.
6   Greater London Authority Elections Rules 2007, SI 2007/3541, Sch 2 r 55(1).
7   Greater London Authority Elections Rules 2007, SI 2007/3541, Sch 2 r 55(2)(a). As to persons appointed as clerks by a returning officer see PARA 393.
8   Greater London Authority Elections Rules 2007, SI 2007/3541, Sch 2 r 55(2)(b). As to the meaning of 'constituency returning officer' for these purposes see PARA 211 note 9. Because non-manual counting methods may be employed at London Authority elections, the CRO may appoint and pay such technical assistants as may be necessary for the purposes of such an election: see PARA 393 note 6. As to the electronic counting of votes see PARA 443 note 18.
9   Greater London Authority Elections Rules 2007, SI 2007/3541, Sch 2 r 55(2)(c).
10   Greater London Authority Elections Rules 2007, SI 2007/3541, Sch 2 r 55(2)(d).
11   Greater London Authority Elections Rules 2007, SI 2007/3541, Sch 2 r 55(2)(e).
12   Greater London Authority Elections Rules 2007, SI 2007/3541, Sch 2 r 55(2)(f). As to the meaning of 'registered political party' for these purposes see PARA 255 note 18. As to nominating officers for registered political parties standing nominated see PARA 253.
13   Ie by virtue of any of the provisions of the Political Parties, Elections and Referendums Act 2000 ss 6A–6D (see PARA 53): see the Greater London Authority Elections Rules 2007, SI 2007/3541, Sch 2 r 55(2)(g).
14   Greater London Authority Elections Rules 2007, SI 2007/3541, Sch 2 r 55(2)(g). As to the Electoral Commission see PARA 34 et seq; and as to authorised representatives of the Electoral Commission attending electoral proceedings see PARA 53.
15   Greater London Authority Elections Rules 2007, SI 2007/3541, Sch 2 r 55(2)(h). As to the central calculation at the election of the Mayor of London see PARA 457.
16   See the Greater London Authority Elections Rules 2007, SI 2007/3541, Sch 2 r 55(2).
17   See the Greater London Authority Elections Rules 2007, SI 2007/3541, Sch 2 r 55(3).
18   Greater London Authority Elections Rules 2007, SI 2007/3541, Sch 2 r 55(3)(a).
19   Greater London Authority Elections Rules 2007, SI 2007/3541, Sch 2 r 55(3)(b).
20   Ie the information required to be submitted under the Greater London Authority Elections Rules 2007, SI 2007/3541, Sch 2 r 54 (see PARA 449): see Sch 2 r 56(1).

21 Greater London Authority Elections Rules 2007, SI 2007/3541, Sch 2 r 56(1). Where proof is given to the GLRO's satisfaction that a person whose name is for the time being included in a party list has died, then the GLRO must remove that person's name from that list: see Sch 2 r 64(3); and PARA 204 note 30.

Where the GLRO is notified under Sch 1 r 54(5) (see PARA 486) that a candidate who is returned as a constituency member is the candidate with a description authorised under Sch 1 r 6(7)(a) (candidate unduly associated with one or more registered political parties: see PARA 256), the GLRO must, in calculating the London figure of each registered party whose nominating officer issued a certificate to which Sch 1 r 6(7)(a) refers, include that candidate as a candidate of that party; and in doing so must disregard the fact that for the purposes of calculating the London figure of another registered party, the candidate is also included as the candidate of that other registered party: see Sch 2 r 56(5), (6).

22 As to the allocation of London Assembly seats to the London members, and as to the significance of the London figure in that process, see PARA 340.

23 For these purposes, the 'relevant figures' means:
    (1)   the number of London votes given in the Assembly constituencies for each registered party and for each individual candidate at that election (Greater London Authority Elections Rules 2007, SI 2007/3541, Sch 2 r 56(4)(a));
    (2)   in respect of each party, the number of successful candidates to be constituency members who were the subject of that party's authorisation under Sch 1 r 6(5) or Sch 1 r 6(7) (authorised description: see PARA 256) (Sch 2 r 56(4)(b) (amended by SI 2012/198));
    (3)   the calculation of the London figure (Greater London Authority Elections Rules 2007, SI 2007/3541, Sch 2 r 56(4)(c));
    (4)   any recalculation required by the Greater London Authority Act 1999 s 4(6), Sch 2 para 8(3) (allocation of second and subsequent seats: see PARA 340), or carried out in the circumstances mentioned in Sch 2 para 8(8) (two or more registered parties or individual candidates having an equal number of votes in the case of the last seat to be allocated: see PARA 340) (Greater London Authority Elections Rules 2007, SI 2007/3541, Sch 2 r 56(4)(d)); and
    (5)   the number of persons whose names have been omitted from a party list, or who, pursuant to the Greater London Authority Act 1999 s 4, Sch 2 para 8(10) (person included on a list submitted by a registered political party returned as the Mayor of London or as a London Assembly member: see PARA 340), are to be treated as ceasing to be on a party list (Greater London Authority Elections Rules 2007, SI 2007/3541, Sch 2 r 56(4)(e)).

Where information of the description mentioned in head (5) is so given, the GLRO must provide the persons to whom it was given with a statement containing the names of the persons concerned and, with respect to each such person, the name of the party from whose list his name has been omitted or treated as omitted, and the reason therefor: Sch 2 r 56(3). As to the meaning of 'constituency', in relation to the London Assembly, see PARA 11 note 6. As to the meaning of 'London votes' see PARA 340 note 9.

24 Greater London Authority Elections Rules 2007, SI 2007/3541, Sch 2 r 56(2).

(C) London Authority Election for London Mayor

(a) Local Count

451. Verification of ballot paper accounts and the local count at an election for the return of London Mayor. The constituency returning officer ('CRO') at an Authority election[1] for the return of London Mayor[2] must[3]:
    (1)   open the ballot boxes from each polling station[4] together, in the presence of the counting agents[5] appointed for the purposes of the election and any other Authority election with which is its combined[6];
    (2)   cause the electronic counting system[7] to count such of the postal ballot papers as have been duly returned[8], and record separately the number counted[9];
    (3)   not mix the contents of any ballot box with the contents of any other ballot box during the conduct of any count or recount[10].

After completing the proceedings under heads (1) to (3) above, the CRO must cause the electronic counting system to process the ballot papers so as to:

(a)   count the number of ballot papers[11];

(b)   count the number of first preference votes given for each candidate[12]; and

(c)   record the way that second preference votes have been given on the ballot papers[13].

The CRO must not cause the electronic counting system to count any tendered ballot paper, however[14].

The CRO must verify each ballot paper account by comparing it with the number of ballot papers processed by the electronic counting system, and the unused and spoilt ballot papers[15] in his possession and the tendered votes list[16] (opening and resealing the packets containing the unused and spoilt ballot papers and the tendered votes list), and he must draw up a statement as to the result of the verification, which any election agent may copy[17]. While verifying the ballot paper accounts and counting the votes, the CRO must take all proper precautions for preventing any person from seeing the numbers printed on the back of the papers[18]. The CRO also must, so far as practicable, proceed continuously with counting the votes, allowing only time for refreshment, except that the hours between five in the afternoon and ten on the following morning may be excluded with the prior consent of the Greater London returning officer ('GLRO')[19]. During the time so excluded, the CRO must:

(i)   place the ballot papers and other documents relating to the election under his own seal and the seals of such of the counting agents as desire to affix their seals[20]; and

(ii)   otherwise take proper precautions for the security of the papers and documents[21].

Where the poll at an election is taken together with the poll at another election or referendum, special provision is made for counting the votes[22].

1   As to the meaning of 'Authority election' see PARA 11. As to the meaning of 'constituency returning officer' for these purposes see PARA 211 note 9.

2   As to London Authority elections for the return of London Mayor see PARA 199. As to elections in the City of London see PARA 33.

3   Greater London Authority Elections Rules 2007, SI 2007/3541, Sch 3 r 49(1).

4   As to the provision and allotment of polling stations see PARA 390.

5   As to the appointment of counting agents by a candidate, and as to the effect of their non-attendance, see PARA 394.

6   Greater London Authority Elections Rules 2007, SI 2007/3541, Sch 3 r 49(1)(a). As to polls at elections or referendums which are taken together see the text and note 22. As to the counting of votes at Authority elections for the return of constituency or London members see PARA 444.

7   As to the meaning of 'electronic counting system' see PARA 443 note 18.

8   Ie returned in accordance with the Greater London Authority Elections Rules 2007, SI 2007/3541, Sch 3 r 49(2), (3): see Sch 3 r 49(1)(b). Accordingly, a postal ballot paper must not be taken to be duly returned unless:

(1)   it is returned in the prescribed manner (ie either by hand or by post to the CRO, or by hand only to a polling station in the Assembly constituency), and reaches the CRO or any polling station in the Assembly constituency that includes the electoral area for which the elector is registered as a local government elector, before the close of the poll (Sch 3 r 49(2)(a), (3));

(2)   the postal voting statement, duly signed, is also returned in the prescribed manner (ie either by hand or by post to the CRO, or by hand only to a polling station in the Assembly constituency), and reaches him or such a polling station before that time (Sch 3 r 49(2)(b), (3));

(3)   the postal voting statement also states the date of birth of the elector or proxy (as the case may be) (Sch 3 r 49(2)(c)); and

(4)   in a case where the steps for verifying the date of birth and signature of an elector or

proxy have been prescribed by regulations made under the Representation of the People Act 1983, the CRO (having taken such steps) verifies the date of birth and signature of the elector or proxy (as the case may be) (Greater London Authority Elections Rules 2007, SI 2007/3541, Sch 3 r 49(2)(d)).

As to the regulations that have been prescribed for the purposes of head (4) above see the Representation of the People (England and Wales) Regulations 2001, SI 2001/341, regs 85, 85A; and PARA 421. As to the meaning of 'electoral area' for the purposes of local government elections see PARA 11; and as to the meaning of 'Assembly constituency', in relation to the London Assembly, see PARA 11 note 6. As to the meaning of 'elector', in relation to a local government election, see PARA 95 note 2. As to the meaning of 'postal ballot paper' see PARA 407 note 1. As to voting by proxy see PARA 366 et seq; and as to the entitlement to vote by post as proxy see PARAS 377, 382. As to the postal voting statement see PARA 406. As to the means by which a postal voter may validly return a postal ballot paper see also PARA 418. As to the provision that may be made regarding the circumstances in which, following the close of the poll at a parliamentary or local government election, a registration officer must notify a person that the person's postal ballot paper has been rejected see PARA 426.

9   Greater London Authority Elections Rules 2007, SI 2007/3541, Sch 3 r 49(1)(b).
10   Greater London Authority Elections Rules 2007, SI 2007/3541, Sch 3 r 49(1)(c).
11   Greater London Authority Elections Rules 2007, SI 2007/3541, Sch 3 r 49(4)(a).
12   Greater London Authority Elections Rules 2007, SI 2007/3541, Sch 3 r 49(4)(b). As to elections at which first and second preference votes are cast (the 'supplementary vote system') see PARA 341; and as to the counting of second preference votes at a London Mayoral election see PARA 457.
13   Greater London Authority Elections Rules 2007, SI 2007/3541, Sch 3 r 49(4)(c).
14   Greater London Authority Elections Rules 2007, SI 2007/3541, Sch 3 r 49(5). As to tendered ballot papers see PARA 403; and as to adding votes on a scrutiny see PARA 839 et seq.
15   As to spoilt ballot papers see PARA 404.
16   As to the tendered votes list see PARA 403.
17   Greater London Authority Elections Rules 2007, SI 2007/3541, Sch 3 r 49(6). As to the appointment of election agents at Authority elections see PARA 231 et seq.
18   Greater London Authority Elections Rules 2007, SI 2007/3541, Sch 3 r 49(7). As to the numbers which must be printed on the back of every ballot paper see PARA 387.
19   Greater London Authority Elections Rules 2007, SI 2007/3541, Sch 3 r 49(8). As to the meaning of 'Greater London returning officer' ('GLRO') see PARA 211 note 8.
20   Greater London Authority Elections Rules 2007, SI 2007/3541, Sch 3 r 49(9)(a).
21   Greater London Authority Elections Rules 2007, SI 2007/3541, Sch 3 r 49(9)(b).
22   As to polls at elections or referendums which are taken together see PARA 16 et seq.

452.   Rejected ballot papers at elections for the return of London Mayor. At the local count for an Authority election[1] for the return of London Mayor[2], any ballot paper:

(1)   which does not bear the official mark[3];
(2)   on which anything is written or marked by which the voter can be identified (except the printed number or other unique identifying mark on the back)[4];
(3)   which is unmarked[5]; or
(4)   which is void for uncertainty[6],

is void and must not be counted[7]. However, a ballot paper on which a vote is marked:

(a)   elsewhere than in the proper place[8]; or
(b)   otherwise than by means of a cross[9]; or
(c)   by more than one mark[10],

is not for such reason void if:

(i)   at an election at which more than two candidates remain validly nominated, an intention that a first preference vote be given for not more than one of the candidates clearly appears[11]; or
(ii)   at any other election, an intention that a vote is for one only of the candidates clearly appears[12].

A ballot paper which is not void, and on which an intention that a second preference vote be given for not more than one of the candidates clearly appears, is valid as respects that second preference vote, and it must be counted accordingly[13]. Where the electronic counting system[14] identifies a ballot paper that has been marked, but which appears to be void, or which appears to contain a first preference vote that can be counted and another mark that cannot be counted as a second preference vote, it must be examined by a clerk appointed by the constituency returning officer ('CRO')[15], achieved by the clerk examining an image of the ballot paper which is shown on a screen so as to be visible to those attending the count[16]. If the clerk, having examined the ballot, considers either that it is void, or that it is marked with a first preference vote that can be counted but that it is not marked with a second preference vote that can be counted, then the CRO also must examine[17] the image of the ballot paper which is shown on a screen so as to be visible to those attending the count[18]. After the CRO examines the ballot paper, he must give his decision as to whether or not it is void, or as to whether or not it is marked with a second preference vote that can be counted[19]. If a counting agent[20] objects to the CRO's decision that the ballot paper is void, or that it is marked with a second preference vote that cannot be counted, the CRO must record on the electronic counting system that the decision was objected to[21].

The CRO must draw up a statement showing the number of ballot papers rejected under the several heads of:

(A)   want of official mark[22];

(B)   voting for more than one candidate as to first preference vote[23];

(C)   writing or mark by which a voter could be identified[24];

(D)   unmarked as to first preference vote[25]; or

(E)   void for uncertainty[26].

As soon as practicable after the completion of such a statement, the CRO must inform such candidates, election agents[27], and counting agents, as are present at the count[28], and the Greater London returning officer ('GLRO')[29], of its contents[30].

1   As to the meaning of 'Authority election' see PARA 11. As to use of the term 'local count' see PARA 443 note 4.

2   As to London Authority elections for the return of London Mayor see PARA 199. As to elections in the City of London see PARA 33.

3   Greater London Authority Elections Rules 2007, SI 2007/3541, Sch 3 r 50(1)(a). As to the official mark see PARA 387. As to ballot papers rejected for want of official mark at parliamentary and other local elections see PARA 427.

4   Greater London Authority Elections Rules 2007, SI 2007/3541, Sch 3 r 50(1)(b). As to the number and other unique identifying marks which must be printed on the back of every ballot paper see PARA 387. As to ballot papers rejected for marks identifying the voter at parliamentary and other local elections see PARA 429.

5   Greater London Authority Elections Rules 2007, SI 2007/3541, Sch 3 r 50(1)(c). As to ballot papers rejected for being unmarked at parliamentary and other local elections see PARA 430.

6   Greater London Authority Elections Rules 2007, SI 2007/3541, Sch 3 r 50(1)(d). As to ballot papers rejected for being void for uncertainty at parliamentary and other local elections see PARA 430.

7   Greater London Authority Elections Rules 2007, SI 2007/3541, Sch 3 r 50(1). As to scrutiny, which may look at ballot papers and investigate how votes have been recorded, see PARA 839 et seq.

8   Greater London Authority Elections Rules 2007, SI 2007/3541, Sch 3 r 50(2)(a). As to the prescribed layout of the ballot paper see PARA 386. As to ballot papers rejected at parliamentary and other local elections on the grounds set out in heads (a) to (c) in the text see PARA 430.

9   Greater London Authority Elections Rules 2007, SI 2007/3541, Sch 3 r 50(2)(b). See note 8.

10   Greater London Authority Elections Rules 2007, SI 2007/3541, Sch 3 r 50(2)(c). See note 8.

11 Greater London Authority Elections Rules 2007, SI 2007/3541, Sch 3 r 50(2)(i). As to the purposive interpretation that is required of this kind of provision see PARA 430. As to elections at which first and second preference votes are cast (the 'supplementary vote system') see PARA 341; and as to the counting of second preference votes at a London Mayoral election see PARA 457.

12 Greater London Authority Elections Rules 2007, SI 2007/3541, Sch 3 r 50(2)(ii). See note 11.

13 See the Greater London Authority Elections Rules 2007, SI 2007/3541, Sch 3 r 50(3).

14 As to the meaning of 'electronic counting system' see PARA 443 note 18.

15 See the Greater London Authority Elections Rules 2007, SI 2007/3541, Sch 3 r 50(4). As to the meaning of 'constituency returning officer' ('CRO') for these purposes see PARA 211 note 9.

16 See the Greater London Authority Elections Rules 2007, SI 2007/3541, Sch 3 r 50(7).

17 See the Greater London Authority Elections Rules 2007, SI 2007/3541, Sch 3 r 50(5). See also note 19.

18 See the Greater London Authority Elections Rules 2007, SI 2007/3541, Sch 3 r 50(7).

19 Greater London Authority Elections Rules 2007, SI 2007/3541, Sch 3 r 50(6). A record of the CRO's decision must be retained in the electronic counting system together with, in the case of a decision that the ballot paper is void, his reasons by reference to heads (1) to (4) in the text: Sch 3 r 50(10). A record also must be retained in the electronic counting system of the number of ballot papers which are not void, but on which a second preference vote has not been counted because: (1) a vote has not been marked (Sch 3 r 50(12)(a)); (2) a vote has been given for more than one candidate (Sch 3 r 50(12)(b)); or (3) there is uncertainty as to for whom a vote was given (Sch 3 r 50(12)(c)). See also note 23.

     The CRO may examine any ballot paper that he is not required to examine in accordance with, Sch 3 r 50(5) (see the text and notes 17–18), either by examining an image of the ballot paper which is shown on a screen so as to be visible to those attending the count, or by examining a paper copy: see Sch 3 r 50(7), (8). Where the CRO does so, he must give a decision on that paper in accordance with Sch 3 r 50(6): see Sch 3 r 50(8). No person attending the count is to be entitled to require the clerk or CRO to examine a ballot paper or to provide a paper copy for inspection, however: Sch 3 r 50(9).

20 As to the appointment of counting agents by a candidate, as to the effect of their non-attendance, see PARA 394.

21 Greater London Authority Elections Rules 2007, SI 2007/3541, Sch 3 r 50(11).

22 Greater London Authority Elections Rules 2007, SI 2007/3541, Sch 3 r 50(13)(a).

23 Greater London Authority Elections Rules 2007, SI 2007/3541, Sch 3 r 50(13)(b). The CRO must also include in the statement, the numbers of second preference votes for which a record has been retained, set out under the several heads in Sch 3 r 50(12)(a)–(c) (see note 19): Sch 3 r 50(15).

24 Greater London Authority Elections Rules 2007, SI 2007/3541, Sch 3 r 50(13)(c).

25 Greater London Authority Elections Rules 2007, SI 2007/3541, Sch 3 r 50(13)(d).

26 Greater London Authority Elections Rules 2007, SI 2007/3541, Sch 3 r 50(13)(e).

27 As to the appointment of election agents at Authority elections see PARA 231 et seq.

28 Greater London Authority Elections Rules 2007, SI 2007/3541, Sch 3 r 50(14)(a).

29 Greater London Authority Elections Rules 2007, SI 2007/3541, Sch 3 r 50(14)(b). As to the meaning of 'Greater London returning officer' ('GLRO') see PARA 211 note 8.

30 Greater London Authority Elections Rules 2007, SI 2007/3541, Sch 3 r 50(14).

453. Conclusiveness of returning officer's decision as to ballot papers at elections for the return of London Mayor. At the local count for an Authority election[1] for the return of London Mayor[2], the decision of the constituency returning officer ('CRO')[3] on any question arising in respect of a ballot paper is final[4], but may be subject to review on an election petition[5].

1 As to the meaning of 'Authority election' see PARA 11. As to use of the term 'local count' see PARA 443 note 4.

2 As to London Authority elections for the return of London Mayor see PARA 199. As to elections in the City of London see PARA 33.

3 As to the meaning of 'constituency returning officer' ('CRO') for these purposes see PARA 211 note 9.

4 As to the rejection of ballot papers at London mayoral elections see PARA 452.

5 Greater London Authority Elections Rules 2007, SI 2007/3541, Sch 3 r 51. As to petitions questioning such elections see PARA 762 et seq.

454. Recount at elections for the return of London Mayor. A candidate at an Authority election[1] for the return of London Mayor[2] (or his election agent[3], or any counting agent duly authorised for the purpose[4]) may, if present when the counting, or any recount, of the votes is completed[5], require the constituency returning officer ('CRO')[6] to have the votes recounted or again recounted[7]. However, the CRO may refuse to do so if in his opinion the request is unreasonable[8].

No step may be taken on the completion of the counting, or any recount, of the votes until the candidates and election agents (and counting agents duly authorised for the purpose[9]) who are present at its completion have been given reasonable opportunity to exercise the right of demanding a recount[10]. The CRO may determine the extent to which any recount involves the electronic counting of votes[11]; but, when the returning officer uses the electronic counting system[12] for the recounting of votes, he must not reconsider any decision made previously on a ballot paper[13].

1 As to the meaning of 'Authority election' see PARA 11; and as to the meaning of 'candidate' generally see PARA 230.
2 As to London Authority elections for the return of London Mayor see PARA 199. As to elections in the City of London see PARA 33.
3 As to the appointment of election agents at Authority elections see PARA 231 et seq.
4 Ie any counting agent authorised under the Greater London Authority Elections Rules 2007, SI 2007/3541, Sch 3 r 30(3) (see PARA 394): see Sch 3 r 52(1).
5 As to the counting of votes at Authority elections for the return of London Mayor see PARA 451 et seq.
6 As to the meaning of 'constituency returning officer' ('CRO') for these purposes see PARA 211 note 9.
7 Greater London Authority Elections Rules 2007, SI 2007/3541, Sch 3 r 52(1).
8 Greater London Authority Elections Rules 2007, SI 2007/3541, Sch 3 r 52(1).
9 Ie authorised under the Greater London Authority Elections Rules 2007, SI 2007/3541, Sch 3 r 30(1) (see PARA 394): see Sch 3 r 52(2).
10 Greater London Authority Elections Rules 2007, SI 2007/3541, Sch 3 r 52(2).
11 Greater London Authority Elections Rules 2007, SI 2007/3541, Sch 3 r 52(3). As to the electronic counting of votes see PARA 443 note 18.
12 As to the meaning of 'electronic counting system' see PARA 443 note 18.
13 Greater London Authority Elections Rules 2007, SI 2007/3541, Sch 3 r 52(4). The text refers to any decision made on any ballot paper under Sch 3 r 50(6) (see PARA 452): see Sch 3 r 52(4).

455. Procedure at conclusion of local count at an election for the return of London Mayor. As soon as practicable after the conclusion of the local count at an Authority election[1] for the return of London Mayor[2] (including any recount)[3], the constituency returning officer ('CRO')[4] must draw up a statement showing[5]:

(1) the total number of ballot papers used[6];
(2) the total number of rejected ballot papers[7];
(3) at an election contested by more than two candidates[8]:
    (a) the total number of first preference votes given[9];
    (b) the number of first preference votes given for each candidate[10]; and
    (c) the total number of second preference votes given for each candidate, correlated with the way the first preference votes have been cast[11].
(4) at an election contested by only two candidates, the number of votes given for each candidate[12].

As soon as practicable after such a statement is drawn up, the CRO must inform the Greater London returning officer ('GLRO')[13] of its contents, and if it is practicable to do so, must also provide that information so as to show the total number of votes under each of those heads in each ward[14].

As soon as practicable after the GLRO has authorised him to do so, the CRO must: (i) inform such of the candidates and their election agents[15] as are then present of the content of the statement prepared showing the information under heads (1) to (4) above, as well as the content of the statement showing the number of ballot papers rejected under the various heads[16]; and (ii) give public notice of the contents of those statements[17].

1   As to the meaning of 'Authority election' see PARA 11. As to use of the term 'local count' see PARA 443 note 4.
2   As to London Authority elections for the return of London Mayor see PARA 199. As to elections in the City of London see PARA 33.
3   As to recounts of votes at an Authority election for the return of London Mayor see PARA 454.
4   As to the meaning of 'constituency returning officer' ('CRO') for these purposes see PARA 211 note 9.
5   Greater London Authority Elections Rules 2007, SI 2007/3541, Sch 3 r 53(1).
6   Greater London Authority Elections Rules 2007, SI 2007/3541, Sch 3 r 53(1)(a).
7   Greater London Authority Elections Rules 2007, SI 2007/3541, Sch 3 r 53(1)(b). As to rejected ballot papers at elections for the return of London Mayor see PARA 452.
8   Greater London Authority Elections Rules 2007, SI 2007/3541, Sch 3 r 53(1)(c). As to the meaning of 'candidate' generally see PARA 230.
9   Greater London Authority Elections Rules 2007, SI 2007/3541, Sch 3 r 53(1)(c)(i). As to elections at which first and second preference votes are cast (the 'supplementary vote system') see PARA 341; and as to the counting of second preference votes at a London mayoral election see PARA 457.
10 Greater London Authority Elections Rules 2007, SI 2007/3541, Sch 3 r 53(1)(c)(ii).
11 Greater London Authority Elections Rules 2007, SI 2007/3541, Sch 3 r 53(1)(c)(iii).
12 Greater London Authority Elections Rules 2007, SI 2007/3541, Sch 3 r 53(1)(d).
13 As to the meaning of 'Greater London returning officer' ('GLRO') see PARA 211 note 8.
14 Greater London Authority Elections Rules 2007, SI 2007/3541, Sch 3 r 53(2) (amended by SI 2012/198). As soon as the GLRO has received from every CRO the contents of the statement required under heads (1) to (4) in the text, the GLRO must make the central calculation that is required to be made based on the votes cast: see the Greater London Authority Elections Rules 2007, SI 2007/3541, Sch 3 rr 55, 56; and PARAS 456, 457. As to the establishment of electoral areas for the purpose of local government elections in England see PARA 74.
15 As to the appointment of election agents at Authority elections see PARA 231 et seq.
16 Greater London Authority Elections Rules 2007, SI 2007/3541, Sch 3 r 53(3)(a). The text refers to the statement prepared under Sch 3 r 50 showing the number of ballot papers rejected under the several heads of want of official mark, voting for more than one candidate as to first preference vote, writing or mark by which a voter could be identified, unmarked as to first preference vote, or void for uncertainty (see PARA 452): see Sch 3 r 53(3)(a).
17 Greater London Authority Elections Rules 2007, SI 2007/3541, Sch 3 r 53(3)(b). As to the giving of public notices by a returning officer generally see PARA 350 et seq.

456.   The first calculation. The Greater London returning officer ('GLRO')[1] must make arrangements for making the central calculation that is required to be made based on the votes cast at a London Authority election[2] for the return of London Mayor[3], in the presence of the election agents[4]; and the GLRO must give to those agents notice in writing of the time and place at which he will begin the calculation[5]. No person other than:

(1)   the GLRO and his clerks[6];
(2)   the constituency returning officers ('CROs') and a clerk or technical assistant chosen by each of them[7];
(3)   the candidates, and one other person chosen by each of them[8];
(4)   the election agents[9];
(5)   persons who are entitled to attend by virtue of any of the provisions of the Political Parties, Elections and Referendums Act 2000[10] which allow

Electoral Commission representatives and accredited observers to attend electoral proceedings and observe working practices[11]; and

(6)	at an ordinary election[12], the persons permitted to be present at the allocation of seats at the election of London members of the London Assembly[13],

may be present at a calculation, unless permitted by the GLRO to attend[14]. A person not entitled to attend a calculation must not be permitted to do so by the GLRO, however, unless the GLRO[15]:

(a)	is satisfied that the efficiency of the calculation will not be impeded[16]; and

(b)	has either consulted the election agents or thought it impracticable to do so[17].

As soon as the GLRO has received from every CRO the contents of the statement showing the total number of votes under various headings of ballot papers used, and those rejected, and the votes given for each candidate[18], he must[19]:

(i)	in relation to an election contested by more than two candidates, ascertain the total of the first preference votes given in the Assembly constituencies to each candidate[20]; and

(ii)	in relation to an election contested by only two candidates, ascertain the total number of votes given in the Assembly constituencies to each candidate[21].

As soon as the GLRO has ascertained the result of the calculation, he must inform such of the election agents as are then present of the relevant figures[22], and he must give them a reasonable opportunity to satisfy themselves as to the accuracy of the calculation[23].

Where an election is contested by only two candidates[24], and:

(A)	where the total number of votes given for each of them is unequal, the person to be returned as the elected Mayor is the candidate to whom the majority of the votes is given[25]; but

(B)	where the total number of votes given for each of them is equal, the returning officer must decide by lot[26] which of them is to be returned as the elected Mayor[27].

In the case of either head (A) or head (B) above, the declaration of the person to be returned as the elected Mayor must then be made[28].

Where an election is contested by more than two candidates:

(aa)	if one of the candidates to be the elected Mayor receives more than half of all the first preference votes given in the election[29], the returning officer must make the required declaration of the result that that candidate is to be returned as the elected Mayor[30]; or

(bb)	if none of the candidates to be the Mayor receives more than half of all the first preference votes given in the Assembly constituencies[31], the GLRO must proceed with the second calculation[32].

1	As to the meaning of 'Greater London returning officer' ('GLRO') see PARA 211 note 8.
2	Ie the calculations made under the Greater London Authority Elections Rules 2007, SI 2007/3541, Sch 3 r 55 (see the text and notes 18–32): see Sch 3 r 54(1). As to the meaning of 'Authority election' see PARA 11.
3	As to London Authority elections for the return of London Mayor see PARA 199. As to the counting of votes at Authority elections for the return of London Mayor see PARA 451 et seq. As to elections in the City of London see PARA 33.
4	See the Greater London Authority Elections Rules 2007, SI 2007/3541, Sch 3 r 54(1). As to the appointment of election agents at Authority elections see PARA 231 et seq.

5   Greater London Authority Elections Rules 2007, SI 2007/3541, Sch 3 r 54(1).
6   Greater London Authority Elections Rules 2007, SI 2007/3541, Sch 3 r 54(2)(a). As to persons appointed as clerks by a returning officer see PARA 393.
7   Greater London Authority Elections Rules 2007, SI 2007/3541, Sch 3 r 54(2)(b). As to the meaning of 'constituency returning officer' for these purposes see PARA 211 note 9. Because non-manual counting methods may be employed at London Authority elections, the CRO may appoint and pay such technical assistants as may be necessary for the purposes of such an election: see PARA 393 note 6. As to the electronic counting of votes see PARA 443 note 18.
8   Greater London Authority Elections Rules 2007, SI 2007/3541, Sch 3 r 54(2)(c). As to the meaning of 'candidate' generally see PARA 230.
9   Greater London Authority Elections Rules 2007, SI 2007/3541, Sch 3 r 54(2)(d).
10   Ie by virtue of any of the provisions of the Political Parties, Elections and Referendums Act 2000 ss 6A–6D (see PARA 53): see the Greater London Authority Elections Rules 2007, SI 2007/3541, Sch 3 r 54(2)(e).
11   Greater London Authority Elections Rules 2007, SI 2007/3541, Sch 3 r 54(2)(e). As to the Electoral Commission see PARA 34 et seq; and as to authorised representatives of the Electoral Commission attending electoral proceedings see PARA 53.
12   As to London Assembly or London Mayoral ordinary elections see PARA 199.
13   Greater London Authority Elections Rules 2007, SI 2007/3541, Sch 3 r 54(2)(f). As to the meaning of 'London member', in relation to the London Assembly, see PARA 11 note 5; definition applied by virtue of r 2(2). As to the counting of votes at a London Authority election for the return of London members see PARA 444 et seq; and as to calculation of the London figure for the allocation of seats at Authority elections for return of London members see PARA 450.
14   See the Greater London Authority Elections Rules 2007, SI 2007/3541, Sch 3 r 54(2).
15   See the Greater London Authority Elections Rules 2007, SI 2007/3541, Sch 3 r 54(3).
16   Greater London Authority Elections Rules 2007, SI 2007/3541, Sch 3 r 54(3)(a).
17   Greater London Authority Elections Rules 2007, SI 2007/3541, Sch 3 r 54(3)(b).
18   Ie the information required to be submitted under the Greater London Authority Elections Rules 2007, SI 2007/3541, Sch 3 r 53 (see PARA 455): see Sch 3 r 55(1).
19   Greater London Authority Elections Rules 2007, SI 2007/3541, Sch 3 r 55(1).
20   Greater London Authority Elections Rules 2007, SI 2007/3541, Sch 3 r 55(1)(a). As to the meaning of 'Assembly constituency', in relation to the London Assembly, see PARA 11 note 6. As to elections at which first and second preference votes are cast (the 'supplementary vote system') see PARA 341.
21   Greater London Authority Elections Rules 2007, SI 2007/3541, Sch 3 r 55(1)(b).
22   For these purposes, the 'relevant figures' means:
     (1)   in the case of an election contested by more than two candidates, the number of first preference votes given in each of the Assembly constituencies for each candidate and the calculation undertaken by the GLRO for the purposes of ascertaining whether a candidate is to be returned in accordance with the Greater London Authority Act 1999 s 4, Sch 2 para 3 (ie where one of the candidates to be the Mayor receives more than half of all the first preference votes given in the Assembly constituencies: see PARA 341) (Greater London Authority Elections Rules 2007, SI 2007/3541, Sch 3 r 55(3)(a));
     (2)   in the case of an election contested by only two candidates, the number of votes given in each Assembly constituency for each candidate and the total number of votes given for each candidate (Sch 3 r 55(3)(b)).
23   Greater London Authority Elections Rules 2007, SI 2007/3541, Sch 3 r 55(2).
24   See the Greater London Authority Elections Rules 2007, SI 2007/3541, Sch 3 r 55(5), (6).
25   See the Greater London Authority Elections Rules 2007, SI 2007/3541, Sch 3 r 55(5).
26   Ie in accordance with the Greater London Authority Act 1999 Sch 2 para 4(8) (see PARA 341): see the Greater London Authority Elections Rules 2007, SI 2007/3541, Sch 3 r 55(6).
27   See the Greater London Authority Elections Rules 2007, SI 2007/3541, Sch 3 r 55(6).
28   Greater London Authority Elections Rules 2007, SI 2007/3541, Sch 3 r 55(7). As to the declaration of the result that is required to be made see PARA 488.
29   Ie if the Greater London Authority Act 1999 Sch 2 para 3 applies (ie candidate receiving more than half of all the first preference votes given in the Assembly constituencies returned as the Mayor: see PARA 341): see the Greater London Authority Elections Rules 2007, SI 2007/3541, Sch 3 r 55(4)(a).
30   Greater London Authority Elections Rules 2007, SI 2007/3541, Sch 3 r 55(4)(a). The text refers to the declaration required to be made in accordance with Sch 3 r 57 (see PARA 488): see Sch 3 r 55(4)(a).

31 Ie if the Greater London Authority Act 1999 Sch 2 para 4(1) applies (see PARA 341): see the Greater London Authority Elections Rules 2007, SI 2007/3541, Sch 3 r 55(4)(b).
32 Greater London Authority Elections Rules 2007, SI 2007/3541, Sch 3 r 55(4)(b). The text refers to the second calculation to be made in accordance with Sch 3 Pt 5 (r 56) (see PARA 457): see Sch 3 r 55(4)(b).

(b) Count of Second Preference Votes ('the Second Calculation')

457. The second calculation and resolution. The Greater London returning officer ('GLRO')[1] must make arrangements for making the central calculation that is required to be made based on the votes cast at a London Authority election[2] for the return of London Mayor[3], in the presence of the election agents[4]; and the GLRO must give to those agents notice in writing of the time and place at which he will begin the calculation[5]. No person other than:

(1)   the GLRO and his clerks[6];

(2)   the constituency returning officers ('CROs') and a clerk or technical assistant chosen by each of them[7];

(3)   the candidates, and one other person chosen by each of them[8];

(4)   the election agents[9];

(5)   persons who are entitled to attend by virtue of any of the provisions of the Political Parties, Elections and Referendums Act 2000[10] which allow Electoral Commission representatives and accredited observers to attend electoral proceedings and observe working practices[11]; and

(6)   at an ordinary election[12], the persons permitted to be present at the allocation of seats at the election of London members of the London Assembly[13],

may be present at a calculation, unless permitted by the GLRO to attend[14]. A person not entitled to attend a calculation must not be permitted to do so by the GLRO, however, unless the GLRO[15]:

(a)   is satisfied that the efficiency of the calculation will not be impeded[16]; and

(b)   has either consulted the election agents or thought it impracticable to do so[17].

As soon as the GLRO has determined that a second calculation is required in an election for London Mayor that is contested by more than two candidates[18], he must[19]:

(i)   ascertain the number of second preference votes given in the Assembly constituencies[20] for each of the candidates remaining in the contest, by voters who did not give their first preference vote to any of those candidates[21]; and

(ii)   add that number to the number of first preference votes given for that candidate, to give his total number of preference votes[22].

As soon as the GLRO has ascertained the result of the second calculation, he must provide such of the election agents for those candidates who remain in the contest as are then present with a copy of the relevant figures[23], and he must give them a reasonable opportunity to satisfy themselves as to the accuracy of the calculation[24].

If, after the second calculation, the total number of votes given for two or more candidates remaining in the contest is equal, the person to be returned as the elected mayor is the person whom the GLRO decides by lot[25] is to be returned as the elected Mayor[26].

A declaration of the result of the election for the return of London Mayor must then be made[27].

1 As to the meaning of 'Greater London returning officer' ('GLRO') see PARA 211 note 8.
2 Ie the calculations made under the Greater London Authority Elections Rules 2007, SI 2007/3541, Sch 3 r 56 (see the text and notes 18–26): see Sch 3 r 54(1). As to the meaning of 'Authority election' see PARA 11.
3 As to London Authority elections for the return of London Mayor see PARA 199. As to the counting of votes at Authority elections for the return of London Mayor see PARA 451 et seq. As to elections in the City of London see PARA 33.
4 See the Greater London Authority Elections Rules 2007, SI 2007/3541, Sch 3 r 54(1). As to the appointment of election agents at Authority elections see PARA 231 et seq.
5 Greater London Authority Elections Rules 2007, SI 2007/3541, Sch 3 r 54(1).
6 Greater London Authority Elections Rules 2007, SI 2007/3541, Sch 3 r 54(2)(a). As to persons appointed as clerks by a returning officer see PARA 393.
7 Greater London Authority Elections Rules 2007, SI 2007/3541, Sch 3 r 54(2)(b). As to the meaning of 'constituency returning officer' for these purposes see PARA 211 note 9. Because non-manual counting methods may be employed at London Authority elections, the CRO may appoint and pay such technical assistants as may be necessary for the purposes of such an election: see PARA 393 note 6. As to the electronic counting of votes see PARA 443 note 18.
8 Greater London Authority Elections Rules 2007, SI 2007/3541, Sch 3 r 54(2)(c). As to the meaning of 'candidate' generally see PARA 230.
9 Greater London Authority Elections Rules 2007, SI 2007/3541, Sch 3 r 54(2)(d).
10 Ie by virtue of any of the provisions of the Political Parties, Elections and Referendums Act 2000 ss 6A–6D (see PARA 53): see the Greater London Authority Elections Rules 2007, SI 2007/3541, Sch 3 r 54(2)(e).
11 Greater London Authority Elections Rules 2007, SI 2007/3541, Sch 3 r 54(2)(e). As to the Electoral Commission see PARA 34 et seq; and as to authorised representatives of the Electoral Commission attending electoral proceedings see PARA 53.
12 As to London Assembly or London Mayoral ordinary elections see PARA 199.
13 Greater London Authority Elections Rules 2007, SI 2007/3541, Sch 3 r 54(2)(f). As to the meaning of 'London member', in relation to the London Assembly, see PARA 11 note 5; definition applied by virtue of r 2(2). As to the counting of votes at a London Authority election for the return of London members see PARA 444 et seq; and as to calculation of the London figure for the allocation of seats at Authority elections for return of London members see PARA 450.
14 See the Greater London Authority Elections Rules 2007, SI 2007/3541, Sch 3 r 54(2).
15 See the Greater London Authority Elections Rules 2007, SI 2007/3541, Sch 3 r 54(3).
16 Greater London Authority Elections Rules 2007, SI 2007/3541, Sch 3 r 54(3)(a).
17 Greater London Authority Elections Rules 2007, SI 2007/3541, Sch 3 r 54(3)(b).
18 Ie the GLRO has determined that the Greater London Authority Act 1999 s 4, Sch 2 para 4(1) applies (see PARA 341): see the Greater London Authority Elections Rules 2007, SI 2007/3541, Sch 3 r 56(1).
19 Greater London Authority Elections Rules 2007, SI 2007/3541, Sch 3 r 56(1).
20 As to the meaning of 'Assembly constituency', in relation to the London Assembly, see PARA 11 note 6. As to elections at which first and second preference votes are cast (the 'supplementary vote system') see PARA 341.
21 Ie the GLRO must comply with the Greater London Authority Act 1999 Sch 2 para 4(5) (see PARA 341): see the Greater London Authority Elections Rules 2007, SI 2007/3541, Sch 3 r 56(1).
22 Ie the GLRO must comply with the Greater London Authority Act 1999 Sch 2 para 4(6) (see PARA 341): see the Greater London Authority Elections Rules 2007, SI 2007/3541, Sch 3 r 56(1).
23 For these purposes, the 'relevant figures' means:
    (1) the number of second preference votes given in each of the Assembly constituencies for each of the candidates remaining in the contest (Greater London Authority Elections Rules 2007, SI 2007/3541, Sch 3 r 56(3)(a)); and
    (2) the calculation undertaken by the GLRO for the purpose of ascertaining the total number of first and second preference votes given to each of those candidates (Sch 3 r 56(3)(b)).
24 Greater London Authority Elections Rules 2007, SI 2007/3541, Sch 3 r 56(2).

25 Ie in accordance with the Greater London Authority Act 1999 Sch 2 para 4(8) (see PARA 341): see the Greater London Authority Elections Rules 2007, SI 2007/3541, Sch 3 r 56(4).
26 Greater London Authority Elections Rules 2007, SI 2007/3541, Sch 3 r 56(4).
27 See the Greater London Authority Elections Rules 2007, SI 2007/3541, Sch 3 r 57; and PARA 488.

D.   WELSH ASSEMBLY ELECTIONS

458.   Time of count and verification at a Welsh Assembly election; attendance at count. At a Welsh Assembly election[1], the constituency returning officer[2] must[3]:

(1)   as soon as practicable after the close of the poll, make arrangements for counting the votes in the presence of the counting agents appointed for the purposes of the election[4]; and

(2)   give to the counting agents (as well as to the regional returning officer[5] at an Assembly regional election[6]) notice in writing[7] of the time and place at which the constituency returning officer will:

(a)   begin to verify the ballot paper account, and count, record, and separate the ballot papers[8]; and

(b)   following completion of the proceedings mentioned in head (a) above, count the votes (that is, where the place used for the count differs from the place notified under head (a) above)[9].

At an Assembly general election[10], where there are polls at a regional election[11], and where there are polls at constituency elections[12] in the Assembly electoral region[13] for which the regional election is held[14], the Secretary of State[15] may direct each constituency returning officer for any Assembly constituency[16] within that Assembly electoral region that the counting of votes[17], in respect of the regional and each constituency election, must not begin before such time between the hours of nine in the morning and noon on the day following the close of polls for those elections[18] as is specified in the direction[19].

No person other than:

(i)   the constituency returning officer and his clerks[20];

(ii)   the candidates, and one other person chosen by each of them[21];

(iii)   the election agents[22];

(iv)   the counting agents[23];

(v)   persons who are entitled to attend by virtue of any of the provisions of the Political Parties, Elections and Referendums Act 2000[24] which allow Electoral Commission representatives and accredited observers to attend electoral proceedings and observe working practices[25]; and

(vi)   in the case of an Assembly regional election, the regional returning officer[26],

may be present at the arrangements made for counting the votes[27], or at the counting of the votes itself, unless permitted by the constituency returning officer to attend[28]. A person not entitled to attend at the arrangements made for counting the votes[29], or at the counting of the votes itself, may not be permitted to do so by the constituency returning officer, however, unless[30]:

(A)   he is satisfied that the efficient counting of the votes will not be impeded[31]; and

(B)   he has either consulted the election agents or thought it impracticable to do so[32].

The returning officer must make such arrangements as he thinks fit to ensure that every person attending at the counting of the votes (other than any constable on duty at the counting) has been given a copy in writing of the statutory provisions relating to the requirement of secrecy that apply to such attendance[33].

The constituency returning officer must give the counting agents all such reasonable facilities for overseeing the proceedings, and all such information with respect to them, as he can give them consistently with the orderly conduct of the proceedings and the discharge of his duties in connection with them[34]. In particular, where the votes are counted by sorting the ballot papers according to the candidate for whom a vote is given (in the case of a constituency election)[35], or according to the individual candidate[36] or registered political party[37] for which a vote is given (in the case of a regional election)[38], and then counting the number of ballot papers for each such candidate or party, the counting agents are entitled to satisfy themselves that the ballot papers are correctly sorted[39].

Where the poll at an election is taken together with the poll at another election or referendum, special provision is made for counting the votes[40].

1 As to the meaning of 'Assembly election' see PARA 3 note 2.
2 As to the meaning of 'constituency returning officer' for these purposes see PARA 18 note 2.
3 See the National Assembly for Wales (Representation of the People) Order 2007, SI 2007/236, Sch 5 para 54(1).
4 National Assembly for Wales (Representation of the People) Order 2007, SI 2007/236, Sch 5 para 54(1)(a). Head (1) in the text is subject to Sch 5 para 54(2) (see the text and notes 10–19): see Sch 5 para 54(1)(a). As to the appointment of counting agents by a candidate, and as to the effect of their non-attendance, see PARA 394.
5 As to the meaning of 'regional returning officer' see PARA 18 note 2.
6 As to the meaning of 'Assembly regional election' see PARA 3 note 2.
7 See the National Assembly for Wales (Representation of the People) Order 2007, SI 2007/236, Sch 5 para 54(1)(b). A notice under Sch 5 para 54(1) may be combined with another such notice: see Sch 5 para 54(1).
8 National Assembly for Wales (Representation of the People) Order 2007, SI 2007/236, Sch 5 para 54(1)(b)(i). Head (2)(a) in the text refers to notice in writing of the time and place at which the proceedings described in Sch 5 para 55(1) (see PARA 459) will begin: see Sch 5 para 54(1)(b)(i).
9 See the National Assembly for Wales (Representation of the People) Order 2007, SI 2007/236, Sch 5 para 54(1)(b)(ii), (iii). Head (2)(b) in the text refers to notice in writing:
    (1) in the case where the power conferred by Sch 5 para 55(3) is exercised (ie the constituency returning officer's power to undertake proceedings described in Sch 5 para 55(1) at a place different from where votes are counted: see PARA 459), of the time and the place at which the constituency returning officer will count the votes following completion of the proceedings described in Sch 5 para 55(1) (see PARA 459) (see Sch 5 para 54(1)(b)(ii)); and
    (2) in the case of a direction given under Sch 5 para 54(2) (Secretary of State's power to specify time for start of count: see the text and notes 10–19), of the time and the place at which he will count the votes following completion of the proceedings described in Sch 5 para 55(1) (see PARA 459) (see Sch 5 para 54(1)(b)(iii)).
    In relation to an Assembly election to which Sch 5 para 55(1) does not apply see PARA 459 note 6.
10 As to Welsh Assembly general elections see PARA 12 et seq.
11 National Assembly for Wales (Representation of the People) Order 2007, SI 2007/236, Sch 5 para 54(2)(a).
12 As to the meaning of 'constituency election' see PARA 3 note 2.
13 As to the meaning of 'Assembly electoral region' see PARA 3 note 2.
14 National Assembly for Wales (Representation of the People) Order 2007, SI 2007/236, Sch 5 para 54(2)(b).
15 As to the Secretary of State see PARA 2.
16 As to the meaning of 'Assembly constituency' see PARA 3 note 2.
17 Ie the counting of votes as provided for in the National Assembly for Wales (Representation of the People) Order 2007, SI 2007/236, Sch 5 para 55(5) (ballot papers used for each type of election mixed together, followed by counting of votes: see PARA 459): see Sch 5 para 54(2).
18 Ie disregarding any day mentioned in the National Assembly for Wales (Representation of the People) Order 2007, SI 2007/236, Sch 5 para 2 (see PARA 213 note 5): see Sch 5 para 54(2).

19 National Assembly for Wales (Representation of the People) Order 2007, SI 2007/236, Sch 5 para 54(2). Any such direction must be given not later than 28 days before the date of the poll at the Assembly general election in question: Sch 5 para 54(3). Where such a direction is given, then, during the period beginning with the conclusion of the proceedings described in Sch 5 para 55(1) (see PARA 459) and ending with the time specified in the direction, the constituency returning officer must:

  (1) place the ballot papers and other documents relating to each election under his own seal, and the seals of such of the counting agents as desire to affix their seals (Sch 5 para 54(4)(a)); and

  (2) otherwise take proper precautions for the security of the papers and documents (Sch 5 para 54(4)(b)).

As to the computation of time for these purposes see PARA 213 note 5.

20 National Assembly for Wales (Representation of the People) Order 2007, SI 2007/236, Sch 5 para 54(5)(a). As to persons appointed as clerks by a returning officer see PARA 393.

21 National Assembly for Wales (Representation of the People) Order 2007, SI 2007/236, Sch 5 para 54(5)(b). As to the meaning of 'candidate', in the context of a Welsh Assembly election, see PARA 230 note 19.

22 National Assembly for Wales (Representation of the People) Order 2007, SI 2007/236, Sch 5 para 54(5)(c). As to the appointment of election agents at Welsh Assembly elections see PARA 235 et seq.

23 National Assembly for Wales (Representation of the People) Order 2007, SI 2007/236, Sch 5 para 54(5)(d).

24 Ie by virtue of any of the provisions of the Political Parties, Elections and Referendums Act 2000 ss 6A–6D (see PARA 53): see the National Assembly for Wales (Representation of the People) Order 2007, SI 2007/236, Sch 5 para 54(5)(e).

25 National Assembly for Wales (Representation of the People) Order 2007, SI 2007/236, Sch 5 para 54(5)(e). As to the Electoral Commission see PARA 34 et seq; and as to authorised representatives of the Electoral Commission attending electoral proceedings see PARA 53.

26 National Assembly for Wales (Representation of the People) Order 2007, SI 2007/236, Sch 5 para 54(5)(f).

27 Ie the arrangements for counting the votes made under the National Assembly for Wales (Representation of the People) Order 2007, SI 2007/236, Sch 5 para 55(1) (see PARA 459): see Sch 5 para 54(5). In relation to an Assembly election to which Sch 5 para 55(1) does not apply see PARA 459 note 6.

28 National Assembly for Wales (Representation of the People) Order 2007, SI 2007/236, Sch 5 para 54(5).

29 Ie the arrangements for counting the votes made under the National Assembly for Wales (Representation of the People) Order 2007, SI 2007/236, Sch 5 para 55(1) (see PARA 459): see Sch 5 para 54(6). In relation to an Assembly election to which Sch 5 para 55(1) does not apply see PARA 459 note 6.

30 See the National Assembly for Wales (Representation of the People) Order 2007, SI 2007/236, Sch 5 para 54(6).

31 National Assembly for Wales (Representation of the People) Order 2007, SI 2007/236, Sch 5 para 54(6)(a).

32 National Assembly for Wales (Representation of the People) Order 2007, SI 2007/236, Sch 5 para 54(6)(b).

33 See PARAS 385, 739–741.

34 National Assembly for Wales (Representation of the People) Order 2007, SI 2007/236, Sch 5 para 54(7).

35 National Assembly for Wales (Representation of the People) Order 2007, SI 2007/236, Sch 5 para 54(8)(a).

36 As to the meaning of 'individual candidate', in the context of a Welsh Assembly regional election, see PARA 230 note 19.

37 As to the meaning of 'registered political party', in the context of a Welsh Assembly regional election, see PARA 230 note 23.

38 National Assembly for Wales (Representation of the People) Order 2007, SI 2007/236, Sch 5 para 54(8)(b).

39 See the National Assembly for Wales (Representation of the People) Order 2007, SI 2007/236, Sch 5 para 54(8).

40 As to polls at elections or referendums which are taken together see PARA 16 et seq.

459. Verification of ballot paper accounts and counting of ballot papers at a Welsh Assembly election. Where the polls at a Welsh Assembly regional election[1], and the polls at a Welsh Assembly constituency election[2] for a constituency situated in the same electoral region[3], are held on the same day[4], the constituency returning officer[5] must[6]:

(1) in the presence of the counting agents appointed for the purposes of each election[7], open each ballot box and count and record separately the number of ballot papers in each box for each election[8];

(2) in the presence of the election agents appointed for the purposes of each election[9], verify each ballot paper account[10];

(3) count such of the postal ballot papers[11] as have been duly returned[12], and record separately the number counted for each election[13]; and

(4) separate the ballot papers relating to the constituency election from those relating to the Assembly regional election[14].

Following completion of the proceedings described in heads (1) to (4) above, which may be undertaken at a different place (or at different places) than a place at which the votes given on ballot papers are counted[15], the constituency returning officer must in respect of the ballot papers relating to each election mix together all the ballot papers used at that election and count the votes given on them[16]. The constituency returning officer must not count any tendered ballot paper[17]. While counting and recording the number of ballot papers and counting the votes, the constituency returning officer must keep the ballot papers with their faces upwards, and he must take all proper precautions for preventing any person from seeing the numbers or other unique identifying marks printed on the back of the papers[18].

The constituency returning officer must verify the ballot paper account by comparing it with the number of ballot papers recorded by him, and the unused and spoilt ballot papers[19] in his possession, and the tendered votes list[20] (opening and resealing the packets containing the unused and spoilt ballot papers and the tendered votes list)[21]. He must draw up a statement as to the result of the verification, which any election agent appointed for the purposes of that election may copy[22]. Such a statement must be drawn up in respect of each place in cases where the proceedings described in heads (1) to (4) above are undertaken at a different place (or at different places) than a place at which the votes given on ballot papers are counted[23].

The constituency returning officer must, so far as practicable, proceed continuously with the votes, allowing only time for refreshment, except that he may, in so far as he and the counting agents appointed for the purpose of the election in question agree[24], exclude the hours between seven in the evening and nine on the following morning[25]. During the time so excluded, the constituency returning officer must:

(a) place the ballot papers and other documents relating to the election under his own seal, and the seals of such of the counting agents as desire to affix their seals[26]; and

(b) otherwise take proper precautions for the security of the papers and documents[27].

Where the poll at an election is taken together with the poll at another election or referendum, special provision is made for counting the votes[28].

1　As to the meaning of 'Assembly regional election' see PARA 3 note 2.
2　As to the meaning of 'constituency election' see PARA 3 note 2.

3   As to the meanings of 'Assembly constituency' and 'Assembly electoral region' see PARA 3 note 2.

4   In relation to an Assembly election to which this provision does not apply see note 6.

5   As to the meaning of 'constituency returning officer' for these purposes see PARA 18 note 2.

6   See the National Assembly for Wales (Representation of the People) Order 2007, SI 2007/236, Sch 5 para 55(1). The provision made by Sch 5 para 55(1) is expressed to be subject to Sch 5 para 55(8) (ie the returning officer himself may collect, or cause to be collected, any postal ballot paper or postal voting statement which has been returned to a polling station): see PARA 418): see Sch 5 para 55(1). In relation to an Assembly election to which Sch 5 para 55(1) does not apply:

   (1)   Sch 5 para 55(17) (see heads (a)–(c) below) applies in place of Sch 5 para 55(1) (Sch 5 para 55(16)(a));

   (2)   the references to Sch 5 para 55(1) in Sch 5 para 54(1), (5) and (6) (see PARA 458), and in Sch 5 para 55(3), (4) (see the text and note 15), must be construed as references to Sch 5 para 55(17) (Sch 5 para 55(16)(b));

   (3)   the reference to 'each election' in Sch 5 para 55(4)(a) (see note 15) must be construed as a reference to 'the election' (Sch 5 para 55(16)(c)); and

   (4)   Sch 5 para 55(18) applies in place of Sch 5 para 55(5) (see note 16), and the reference to Sch 5 para 55(5) in Sch 5 para 55(4) must be construed as a reference to Sch 5 para 55(18) (Sch 5 para 55(16)(d)).

   Pursuant to head (1) above, the constituency returning officer must:

   (a)   in the presence of the counting agents open each ballot box and count and record the number of ballot papers in those boxes (Sch 5 para 55(17)(a));

   (b)   in the presence of the election agents verify each ballot paper account (Sch 5 para 55(17)(b)); and

   (c)   count such of the postal ballot papers as have been duly returned and record the number counted (Sch 5 para 55(17)(c)).

   As to the procedure that applies where polls are taken on the same day see heads (1) to (4) in the text.

7   As to the appointment of counting agents by a candidate, and as to the effect of their non-attendance, see PARA 394.

8   National Assembly for Wales (Representation of the People) Order 2007, SI 2007/236, Sch 5 para 55(1)(a). Where separate ballot boxes are used at polls in respect of a regional election and a constituency election for a constituency situated within that region, no vote is to be rendered invalid solely by the ballot paper being placed in the wrong ballot box: Sch 5 para 55(2). As to the provision of ballot boxes and ballot papers see PARA 391. In relation to an Assembly election to which Sch 5 para 55(1) does not apply see note 6.

9   As to the appointment of election agents at Welsh Assembly elections see PARA 235 et seq.

10 National Assembly for Wales (Representation of the People) Order 2007, SI 2007/236, Sch 5 para 55(1)(b). In relation to an Assembly election to which Sch 5 para 55(1) does not apply see note 6.

11 As to the meaning of 'postal ballot paper' see PARA 407 note 1. As to the issue and return of postal ballot papers see PARA 406 et seq.

12 A postal ballot paper must not be taken to be duly returned unless:

   (1)   before the close of the poll, either: (a) it is returned, by hand or by post, so that it reaches the constituency returning officer before that time (National Assembly for Wales (Representation of the People) Order 2007, SI 2007/236, Sch 5 para 55(6)(a)(i)); or (b) it is returned, by hand only, to a polling station in the same Assembly constituency as that for which the constituency returning officer is appointed (Sch 5 para 55(6)(a)(ii));

   (2)   the postal voting statement, duly signed, is, before the close of the poll, also returned either by hand or by post, so that it reaches the constituency returning officer before that time (Sch 5 para 55(6)(b)(i)); or it is returned, by hand only, so that it reaches a polling station in the same Assembly constituency as that for which the constituency returning officer is appointed before that time (Sch 5 para 55(6)(b)(ii));

   (3)   the postal voting statement also states the date of birth of the elector or proxy (as the case may be) (Sch 5 para 55(6)(c)); and

   (4)   in a case where the constituency returning officer takes steps to verify the date of birth and signature of an elector or proxy (as the case may be) in accordance with Sch 3 para 23 or, as the case may be, Sch 3 para 24 (ie when a postal voters' ballot box is opened: see PARA 421), he so verifies the date of birth and signature of that elector or proxy (as the case may be) (Sch 5 para 55(6)(d)).

In relation to an Assembly election to which Sch 5 para 55(1) does not apply see note 6. As to the meaning of 'elector', in relation to an Assembly election, see PARA 110 note 6. As to voting by proxy see PARA 366 et seq; and as to the entitlement to vote by post as proxy see PARAS 377, 382. As to the postal voting statement see PARA 406. As to the means by which a postal voter may validly return a postal ballot paper see also PARA 418.

13 National Assembly for Wales (Representation of the People) Order 2007, SI 2007/236, Sch 5 para 55(1)(c). In relation to an Assembly election to which Sch 5 para 55(1) does not apply see note 6.

14 National Assembly for Wales (Representation of the People) Order 2007, SI 2007/236, Sch 5 para 55(1)(d). In relation to an Assembly election to which Sch 5 para 55(1) does not apply see note 6.

15 See the National Assembly for Wales (Representation of the People) Order 2007, SI 2007/236, Sch 5 para 55(3). If the power in Sch 5 para 55(3) is exercised, however, during the period beginning with the conclusion of the proceedings described in Sch 5 para 55(1) (see heads (1) to (4) in the text), and ending with the commencement of proceedings described in Sch 5 para 55(5) (see the text and note 16), the constituency returning officer must:

(1) place the ballot papers and other documents relating to each election under his own seal and the seals of such of the counting agents as desire to affix their seals (Sch 5 para 55(4)(a)); and

(2) otherwise take proper precautions for the security of the papers and documents (Sch 5 para 55(4)(b)).

In relation to an Assembly election to which Sch 5 para 55(1) does not apply see note 6.

16 See the National Assembly for Wales (Representation of the People) Order 2007, SI 2007/236, Sch 5 para 55(5). This provision is subject to Sch 5 para 55(3), (4) (see the text and note 15), and also subject to any direction made by the Secretary of State under Sch 5 para 54(2) (see PARA 458): see Sch 5 para 55(5). In relation to an Assembly election to which Sch 5 para 55(1) does not apply (see the text and notes 1–6), Sch 5 para 55(18) applies in place of Sch 5 para 55(5) (see Sch 5 para 55(16)(d); and note 6) and, accordingly, subject to Sch 5 para 55(3), (4), following completion of the proceedings described in Sch 5 para 55(17) (see note 6), the constituency returning officer must count the votes given on the ballot papers after:

(1) in the case of postal ballot papers, they have been mixed with the ballot papers from at least one ballot box (Sch 5 para 55(18)(a)); and

(2) in the case of ballot papers from a ballot box, they have been mixed with the ballot papers from at least one other ballot box (Sch 5 para 55(18)(b)).

17 National Assembly for Wales (Representation of the People) Order 2007, SI 2007/236, Sch 5 para 55(10). As to tendered ballot papers see PARA 403. As to scrutiny, which may look at ballot papers and investigate how votes have been recorded, see PARA 839 et seq.

18 National Assembly for Wales (Representation of the People) Order 2007, SI 2007/236, Sch 5 para 55(11). As to the number and other unique identifying marks which must be printed on the back of every ballot paper see PARA 387.

19 As to spoilt ballot papers see PARA 404.

20 As to the tendered votes list see PARA 403.

21 National Assembly for Wales (Representation of the People) Order 2007, SI 2007/236, Sch 5 para 55(12).

22 National Assembly for Wales (Representation of the People) Order 2007, SI 2007/236, Sch 5 para 55(12).

23 National Assembly for Wales (Representation of the People) Order 2007, SI 2007/236, Sch 5 para 55(12). The text refers to cases where the power conferred by Sch 5 para 55(3) is exercised in relation to proceedings described in Sch 5 para 55(1) in respect of more than one place (see the text and note 15): see Sch 5 para 55(12).

24 For the purposes of this exception, the agreement of:

(1) a candidate or his election agent, in the case of a constituency election (National Assembly for Wales (Representation of the People) Order 2007, SI 2007/236, Sch 5 para 55(14)(a)); or

(2) in the case of a regional election, an individual candidate (or his election agent), or the election agent for a registered party (Sch 5 para 55(14)(b)),

is as effective as the agreement of his (or of its) counting agents (Sch 5 para 55(14)). As to the meanings of 'candidate' and 'individual candidate', in the context of a Welsh Assembly regional election, see PARA 230 note 19. As to the meaning of 'registered political party' for those purposes see PARA 230 note 23.

25 National Assembly for Wales (Representation of the People) Order 2007, SI 2007/236, Sch 5 para 55(13).

26 National Assembly for Wales (Representation of the People) Order 2007, SI 2007/236, Sch 5 para 55(15)(a).

27 National Assembly for Wales (Representation of the People) Order 2007, SI 2007/236, Sch 5 para 55(15)(b).

28 As to polls at elections or referendums which are taken together see PARA 16 et seq.

460. Rejected ballot papers at a Welsh Assembly election. Any ballot paper given at a Welsh Assembly election[1]:

(1) which does not bear the official mark[2];

(2) on which more than one vote is given[3];

(3) on which anything is written or marked by which the voter can be identified (except the printed number or other unique identifying mark on the back)[4]; or

(4) which is unmarked, or void for uncertainty[5],

is void and must not be counted[6]. However, a ballot paper on which a vote is marked:

(a) elsewhere than in the proper place[7]; or

(b) otherwise than by means of a cross[8]; or

(c) by more than one mark[9],

must not for such reason be deemed to be void if an intention as to how the vote is to be given clearly appears, and the way the paper is marked does not of itself identify the voter, and it is not shown that he can be identified by it[10]. At an Assembly regional election[11], a ballot paper on which a vote is marked for a particular party list candidate on the party list of a registered political party[12] must, if otherwise valid, be treated as a vote for that party, whether or not there is also a vote marked for that party[13]. The constituency returning officer[14] must endorse the word 'rejected' on any ballot paper which is not to be so counted, and he must add to the endorsement the words 'rejection objected to' if an objection is made by a counting agent[15] to his decision[16].

The constituency returning officer must draw up a statement showing the number of ballot papers rejected under the several heads of:

(i) want of official mark[17];

(ii) giving more than one vote[18];

(iii) writing or mark by which voter could be identified[19]; and

(iv) unmarked or void for uncertainty[20].

1 See the National Assembly for Wales (Representation of the People) Order 2007, SI 2007/236, Sch 5 para 58(1). As to the meaning of 'Assembly election' see PARA 3 note 2.

2 National Assembly for Wales (Representation of the People) Order 2007, SI 2007/236, Sch 5 para 58(1)(a). As to the official mark see PARA 387. As to ballot papers rejected for want of official mark at parliamentary and other local elections see PARA 427.

3 National Assembly for Wales (Representation of the People) Order 2007, SI 2007/236, Sch 5 para 58(1)(b). Whether a mark on a ballot paper amounts to a vote for a particular candidate is a matter of fact: see PARA 856 note 4.

4 National Assembly for Wales (Representation of the People) Order 2007, SI 2007/236, Sch 5 para 58(1)(c). As to the number and other unique identifying marks which must be printed on the back of every ballot paper see PARA 387. As to ballot papers rejected for marks identifying the voter at parliamentary and other local elections see PARA 429.

5 National Assembly for Wales (Representation of the People) Order 2007, SI 2007/236, Sch 5 para 58(1)(d). As to ballot papers rejected for being unmarked or void for uncertainty at parliamentary and other local elections see PARA 430.

6 See the National Assembly for Wales (Representation of the People) Order 2007, SI 2007/236, Sch 5 para 58(1). As to scrutiny, which may look at ballot papers and investigate how votes have been recorded, see PARA 839 et seq.

7   National Assembly for Wales (Representation of the People) Order 2007, SI 2007/236, Sch 5 para 58(2)(a). As to the prescribed layout of the ballot paper see PARA 386. As to ballot papers rejected at parliamentary and other local elections on the grounds set out in heads (a) to (c) in the text see PARA 430.

8   National Assembly for Wales (Representation of the People) Order 2007, SI 2007/236, Sch 5 para 58(2)(b). See note 7.

9   National Assembly for Wales (Representation of the People) Order 2007, SI 2007/236, Sch 5 para 58(2)(c). See note 7.

10 National Assembly for Wales (Representation of the People) Order 2007, SI 2007/236, Sch 5 para 58(2). As to the purposive interpretation that is required of this kind of provision see PARA 430.

11 As to the meaning of 'Assembly regional election' see PARA 3 note 2.

12 As to the meanings of 'party list', 'party list candidate' and 'registered political party', in the context of Welsh Assembly regional elections, see PARA 230 note 23.

13 National Assembly for Wales (Representation of the People) Order 2007, SI 2007/236, Sch 5 para 58(3).

14 As to the meaning of 'constituency returning officer', in the context of Welsh Assembly elections, see PARA 18 note 2.

15 As to the appointment of counting agents, and as to the discharge of the function mentioned in the text by the candidate or (where there is such an agent) his election agent, see PARA 394.

16 National Assembly for Wales (Representation of the People) Order 2007, SI 2007/236, Sch 5 para 58(4).

17 National Assembly for Wales (Representation of the People) Order 2007, SI 2007/236, Sch 5 para 58(5)(a).

18 National Assembly for Wales (Representation of the People) Order 2007, SI 2007/236, Sch 5 para 58(5)(b).

19 National Assembly for Wales (Representation of the People) Order 2007, SI 2007/236, Sch 5 para 58(5)(c).

20 National Assembly for Wales (Representation of the People) Order 2007, SI 2007/236, Sch 5 para 58(5)(d).

461.   Conclusiveness of returning officer's decision as to ballot papers at a Welsh Assembly election. The decision of the constituency returning officer at a Welsh Assembly election[1] on any question arising in respect of a ballot paper is final[2], but is subject to review on an Assembly election petition[3].

1   As to the meaning of 'Assembly election' see PARA 3 note 2; and as to the meaning of 'constituency returning officer' for these purposes see PARA 18 note 2.

2   As to the rejection of ballot papers at a Welsh Assembly election see PARA 460.

3   National Assembly for Wales (Representation of the People) Order 2007, SI 2007/236, Sch 5 para 59. As to petitions questioning an Assembly election see PARA 764 et seq.

462.   Recount at a Welsh Assembly election. At a Welsh Assembly constituency election[1], a candidate[2] or his election agent[3] may, if present when the counting or any recount of the votes is completed[4], require the constituency returning officer[5] to have the votes recounted, or again recounted[6]. However, the constituency returning officer may refuse to do so if in his opinion the request is unreasonable[7].

At a Welsh Assembly regional election[8], and prior to certification[9] of the results to the count[10]:

(1)   an individual candidate, or his election agent[11];

(2)   a party list candidate[12], or an election agent for a registered political party standing nominated[13]; or

(3)   a counting agent for an individual candidate, or for a registered political party standing nominated, who is duly authorised for the purpose[14],

may, if present when the counting or any recount of the votes is completed in a constituency, require the constituency returning officer to have the votes recounted, or again recounted[15]. However, the constituency returning officer may refuse to do so if in his opinion the request is unreasonable[16].

No step may be taken on the completion of the counting, or any recount, of votes until the candidates and election agents (and, in the case of a regional election, any counting agents) who are present at its completion have been given a reasonable opportunity to exercise the right to request a recount[17].

1   As to the meanings of 'Assembly election' and 'Assembly constituency election' see PARA 3 note 2.
2   As to the meaning of 'candidate', in the context of a Welsh Assembly election, see PARA 230 note 19.
3   As to the appointment of election agents at Welsh Assembly elections see PARA 235 et seq.
4   As to attendance at the counting of votes at a Welsh Assembly election see PARA 458; and as to the count itself see PARA 459.
5   As to the meaning of 'constituency returning officer' for these purposes see PARA 18 note 2.
6   See the National Assembly for Wales (Representation of the People) Order 2007, SI 2007/236, Sch 5 para 56(1).
7   See the National Assembly for Wales (Representation of the People) Order 2007, SI 2007/236, Sch 5 para 56(1).
8   As to the meaning of 'Assembly regional election' see PARA 3 note 2.
9   Ie under the National Assembly for Wales (Representation of the People) Order 2007, SI 2007/236, Sch 5 para 61(1) (see PARA 463): see Sch 5 para 57(1).
10 See the National Assembly for Wales (Representation of the People) Order 2007, SI 2007/236, Sch 5 para 57(1).
11 National Assembly for Wales (Representation of the People) Order 2007, SI 2007/236, Sch 5 para 57(1)(a). As to the meaning of 'individual candidate', in the context of a Welsh Assembly regional election, see PARA 230 note 19.
12 As to the meanings of 'party list' and 'party list candidate', in the context of Welsh Assembly regional elections, see PARA 230 note 23.
13 National Assembly for Wales (Representation of the People) Order 2007, SI 2007/236, Sch 5 para 57(1)(b). As to the meaning of 'registered political party', in the context of Welsh Assembly regional elections, see PARA 230 note 23.
14 National Assembly for Wales (Representation of the People) Order 2007, SI 2007/236, Sch 5 para 57(1)(c). Head (3) in the text is subject to Sch 5 para 57(3): see Sch 5 para 57(1)(c). Accordingly, where no candidate or election agent is present on the completion of the counting, or any recount, of electoral region votes in a Welsh Assembly constituency, the right conferred on that person (if he had been present) to request a recount under head (3) in the text may be exercised by a counting agent for an individual candidate, or for a registered party standing nominated, who is present provided that, in his terms of appointment as a counting agent, he is authorised to exercise the right conferred by Sch 5 para 57 (see PARA 394 note 7); but not more than one such counting agent for the same individual candidate or registered party standing nominated may be appointed for these purposes in relation to the same Assembly constituency: Sch 5 para 57(3). As to the meaning of 'Assembly constituency', in the context of Welsh Assembly elections, see PARA 3 note 2.
15 See the National Assembly for Wales (Representation of the People) Order 2007, SI 2007/236, Sch 5 para 57(1).
16 See the National Assembly for Wales (Representation of the People) Order 2007, SI 2007/236, Sch 5 para 57(1).
17 See the National Assembly for Wales (Representation of the People) Order 2007, SI 2007/236, Sch 5 paras 56(2), 57(2).

463.   Procedure at conclusion of count at a Welsh Assembly election; resolution of constituency election in case of equality of votes between candidates.   At a Welsh Assembly constituency election[1], where, after the counting of the votes (including any recount) is completed[2], an equality of votes is found to exist between any candidates[3], and the addition of a vote would entitle any of those candidates to be declared elected, the constituency returning officer[4] must forthwith decide between those candidates by lot, and proceed as if the candidate on whom the lot falls had received an additional vote[5].

At the conclusion of the count of ballot papers in an Assembly constituency[6] at a regional election[7], the constituency returning officer must, in accordance with any directions given by the regional returning officer[8], certify[9]:

(1)   the number of ballot papers counted by him, and the total number of votes given for each individual candidate or registered political party[10]; and

(2)   the number of rejected ballot papers under each head shown in the statement of rejected ballot papers[11], namely: (a) want of official mark; (b) giving more than one vote; (c) writing or mark by which voter could be identified; and (d) unmarked or void for uncertainty[12].

The constituency returning officer must forthwith convey that information to the regional returning officer[13]. Where the regional returning officer has received the information so required to be conveyed to him from each constituency returning officer for an Assembly constituency in the Assembly electoral region[14], he must certify the totals of the numbers referred to in heads (1) and (2) above for the electoral region[15]. A constituency returning officer, after he has conveyed to the regional returning officer the information required to be conveyed under heads (1) and (2) above, may give public notice of the information so conveyed (in such manner as he considers appropriate)[16], unless the regional returning officer directs that the constituency returning officer may only give such notice after the regional returning officer himself has given the notice that he is required to give in declaring the results at a regional election[17].

1   As to the meanings of 'Assembly election' and 'Assembly constituency election' see PARA 3 note 2.
2   As to the counting of votes at a Welsh Assembly election see PARA 458 et seq. As to the recount at such an election see PARA 462.
3   As to the meaning of 'candidate', in the context of a Welsh Assembly election, see PARA 230 note 19.
4   As to the meaning of 'constituency returning officer' for these purposes see PARA 18 note 2.
5   National Assembly for Wales (Representation of the People) Order 2007, SI 2007/236, Sch 5 para 60.
6   As to the meaning of 'Assembly constituency', in the context of Welsh Assembly elections, see PARA 3 note 2.
7   As to the meaning of 'Assembly regional election' see PARA 3 note 2.
8   As to the meaning of 'regional returning officer' for these purposes see PARA 18 note 2.
9   See the National Assembly for Wales (Representation of the People) Order 2007, SI 2007/236, Sch 5 para 61(1).
10   National Assembly for Wales (Representation of the People) Order 2007, SI 2007/236, Sch 5 para 61(1)(a). As to the meaning of 'individual candidate', in the context of a Welsh Assembly regional election, see PARA 230 note 19. As to the meaning of 'registered political party' for those purposes see PARA 230 note 23.
11   National Assembly for Wales (Representation of the People) Order 2007, SI 2007/236, Sch 5 para 61(1)(b). Head (2) in the text refers to each head shown in the statement under Sch 5 para 58(5) (ie namely: (1) want of official mark; (2) giving more than one vote; (3) writing or mark by which voter could be identified; and (4) unmarked or void for uncertainty: see PARA 460): see Sch 5 para 61(1)(b).
12   See note 11.
13   See the National Assembly for Wales (Representation of the People) Order 2007, SI 2007/236, Sch 5 para 61(1).
14   As to the meaning of 'Assembly electoral region' see PARA 3 note 2.
15   National Assembly for Wales (Representation of the People) Order 2007, SI 2007/236, Sch 5 para 61(2).
16   See the National Assembly for Wales (Representation of the People) Order 2007, SI 2007/236, Sch 5 para 61(3).
17   See the National Assembly for Wales (Representation of the People) Order 2007, SI 2007/236, Sch 5 para 61(4). The text refers to the public notice that the regional returning officer is required to give under Sch 5 para 64(1)(d) (see PARA 491): see Sch 5 para 61(4).

464.   Ascertainment of results at a contested Welsh Assembly regional election.   At a contested Welsh Assembly regional election[1], the regional returning officer[2] must make arrangements for ascertaining the results of the poll[3] as soon as practicable after he has[4]:

(1)   given the certification that is required[5] of the numbers of ballot papers counted and rejected and of votes given in total for the electoral region[6]; and

(2)   received the notification that is required[7], from each constituency returning officer[8] for an Assembly constituency in the Assembly electoral region[9], of any candidate returned as the Assembly member for a constituency and whether he is the candidate of more than one registered political party[10].

At such an election, the regional returning officer also must give notice in writing to the election agents[11], and to each constituency returning officer for an Assembly constituency in the Assembly electoral region for which the election is held, of the place at which he will begin to ascertain the results of the poll (together with such other information as he considers appropriate)[12].

No person other than:

(a)   the regional returning officer and his clerks[13];

(b)   the individual and party list candidates[14], and one other person chosen by each of them[15];

(c)   the election agents[16];

(d)   persons who are entitled to attend by virtue of any of the provisions of the Political Parties, Elections and Referendums Act 2000[17] which allow Electoral Commission representatives and accredited observers to attend electoral proceedings and observe working practices[18]; and

(e)   the constituency returning officer for any Assembly constituency in the Assembly electoral region for which the election is held[19],

may be present at the proceedings on the ascertainment of the results, unless permitted by the regional returning officer to attend[20]. A person not entitled to attend at the proceedings must not be permitted to do so by the regional returning officer, however, unless[21]:

(i)   he is satisfied that the efficient ascertainment of the results will not be impeded[22]; and

(ii)   he has either consulted the election agents or thought it impracticable to do so[23].

The returning officer must make such arrangements as he thinks fit to ensure that every person attending at the counting of the votes (other than any constable on duty at the counting) has been given a copy in writing of the statutory provisions relating to the requirement of secrecy that apply to such attendance[24]. The regional returning officer must give the election agents and candidates all such reasonable facilities for overseeing the proceedings, and all such information with respect to them (including for satisfying themselves that the ascertainment of the result that he is required to make is accurate), as he can give them consistently with the orderly conduct of the proceedings and the discharge of his duties in connection with them[25].

The regional returning officer must provisionally ascertain the results of the poll[26], and he must notify that provisional ascertainment to such of the following persons as are present, namely[27]:

(A)   an individual candidate or his election agent[28]; and

(B)   the election agent for a registered political party standing nominated or (in his absence) one of the candidates on the list submitted by that party[29].

Where notification has been given to a person under head (A) or head (B) above, he may require the regional returning officer to ascertain provisionally those results again[30]. However, the regional returning officer may refuse to do so if in his opinion the request is unreasonable[31]. The regional returning officer completes ascertaining the results of the poll when, following a provisional ascertainment[32]:

(aa)   there is no request for him to make a further provisional ascertainment[33]; or

(bb)   if there is such a request, the regional returning officer refuses to make a further provisional ascertainment[34].

If, in ascertaining the results of the poll, the regional returning officer is required to draws lots[35], he must allocate the seat to the individual candidate or party on whom the lot falls[36].

1   As to the meanings of 'Assembly election' and 'Assembly regional election' see PARA 3 note 2.

2   As to the meaning of 'regional returning officer' for these purposes see PARA 18 note 2.

3   As to the 'additional member' system of proportional representation that is used for ascertaining the results of the poll at an election of Welsh Assembly regional members see the Government of Wales Act 2006 ss 6(5), 8, 9; and PARA 340.

4   See the National Assembly for Wales (Representation of the People) Order 2007, SI 2007/236, Sch 5 para 63(1).

5   Ie under the National Assembly for Wales (Representation of the People) Order 2007, SI 2007/236, Sch 5 para 61(2) (see PARA 463): see Sch 5 para 63(1)(a).

6   National Assembly for Wales (Representation of the People) Order 2007, SI 2007/236, Sch 5 para 63(1)(a).

7   Ie by the National Assembly for Wales (Representation of the People) Order 2007, SI 2007/236, Sch 5 para 62(3) (see PARA 490), but subject to Sch 5 para 74(1) (effect of countermand or abandonment of constituency poll: see PARA 516 note 7): see Sch 5 para 63(1)(b).

8   As to the meaning of 'constituency returning officer', in the context of Welsh Assembly elections, see PARA 18 note 2.

9   As to the meanings of 'Assembly constituency' and 'Assembly electoral region' see PARA 3 note 2.

10   National Assembly for Wales (Representation of the People) Order 2007, SI 2007/236, Sch 5 para 63(1)(b). See also note 26. As to the meaning of 'candidate' see PARA 230 note 19; and as to the meaning of 'registered political party' for these purposes see PARA 230 note 23.

11   As to the appointment of election agents at Welsh Assembly elections see PARA 235 et seq.

12   National Assembly for Wales (Representation of the People) Order 2007, SI 2007/236, Sch 5 para 63(2).

13   National Assembly for Wales (Representation of the People) Order 2007, SI 2007/236, Sch 5 para 63(3)(a). As to persons appointed as clerks by a returning officer see PARA 393.

14   As to the meaning of 'individual candidate' for these purposes see PARA 230 note 19; and as to the meanings of 'party list' and 'party list candidate' see PARA 230 note 23.

15   National Assembly for Wales (Representation of the People) Order 2007, SI 2007/236, Sch 5 para 63(3)(b).

16   National Assembly for Wales (Representation of the People) Order 2007, SI 2007/236, Sch 5 para 63(3)(c).

17   Ie by virtue of any of the provisions of the Political Parties, Elections and Referendums Act 2000 ss 6A–6D (see PARA 53): see the National Assembly for Wales (Representation of the People) Order 2007, SI 2007/236, Sch 5 para 63(3)(d).

18   National Assembly for Wales (Representation of the People) Order 2007, SI 2007/236, Sch 5 para 63(3)(d). As to the Electoral Commission see PARA 34 et seq; and as to authorised representatives of the Electoral Commission attending electoral proceedings see PARA 53.

19   National Assembly for Wales (Representation of the People) Order 2007, SI 2007/236, Sch 5 para 63(3)(e).

20   National Assembly for Wales (Representation of the People) Order 2007, SI 2007/236, Sch 5 para 63(3).

21 See the National Assembly for Wales (Representation of the People) Order 2007, SI 2007/236, Sch 5 para 63(4).

22 National Assembly for Wales (Representation of the People) Order 2007, SI 2007/236, Sch 5 para 63(4)(a).

23 National Assembly for Wales (Representation of the People) Order 2007, SI 2007/236, Sch 5 para 63(4)(b).

24 See PARAS 385, 739–741.

25 National Assembly for Wales (Representation of the People) Order 2007, SI 2007/236, Sch 5 para 63(5).

26 Ie in accordance with the Government of Wales Act 2006 ss 8, 9: see PARA 340. Where the regional returning officer is notified under the National Assembly for Wales (Representation of the People) Order 2007, SI 2007/236, Sch 5 para 62(3) (see PARA 490) that a candidate who is returned as the Assembly member for a constituency is the candidate of more than one registered political party (Sch 5 para 63(12)), the regional returning officer must, in calculating the electoral region figure of a registered political party named in the notification (see PARA 340), include that candidate as a candidate of that party; and in doing so he must disregard the fact that, for the purposes of calculating the electoral region figure of another registered political party named in that notification, the candidate is also included as the candidate of that other registered political party (Sch 5 para 63(13)).

27 See the National Assembly for Wales (Representation of the People) Order 2007, SI 2007/236, Sch 5 para 63(6).

28 National Assembly for Wales (Representation of the People) Order 2007, SI 2007/236, Sch 5 para 63(6)(a).

29 National Assembly for Wales (Representation of the People) Order 2007, SI 2007/236, Sch 5 para 63(6)(b).

30 See the National Assembly for Wales (Representation of the People) Order 2007, SI 2007/236, Sch 5 para 63(7). No step may be taken to complete the ascertainment of the result until the persons notified under head (A) or head (B) in the text have been given a reasonable opportunity to exercise the right conferred under Sch 5 para 63(7): see Sch 5 para 63(8). Where the regional returning officer has provisionally ascertained the results again under Sch 5 para 63(7), the provisions of Sch 5 para 63(6) (see the text and notes 26–29), and of Sch 5 para 63(7)–(9), apply to the further provisional ascertainment: Sch 5 para 63(9).

31 See the National Assembly for Wales (Representation of the People) Order 2007, SI 2007/236, Sch 5 para 63(7).

32 See the National Assembly for Wales (Representation of the People) Order 2007, SI 2007/236, Sch 5 para 63(11).

33 National Assembly for Wales (Representation of the People) Order 2007, SI 2007/236, Sch 5 para 63(11)(a). Head (aa) in the text refers to there being no request under Sch 5 para 63(7) (see the text and notes 30–31) for the regional returning officer to make a further provisional ascertainment: see Sch 5 para 63(11)(a).

34 National Assembly for Wales (Representation of the People) Order 2007, SI 2007/236, Sch 5 para 63(11)(b).

35 Ie in the circumstances referred to in the Government of Wales Act 2006 s 9(9) (ie, if the highest electoral region figure is still the electoral region figure of two or more parties or individual candidates): see PARA 340.

36 National Assembly for Wales (Representation of the People) Order 2007, SI 2007/236, Sch 5 para 63(10).

E. EUROPEAN PARLIAMENTARY ELECTIONS

465. Attendance at verification of ballot paper accounts at a European parliamentary election. As soon as practicable after the close of the poll at a European parliamentary election[1], the local returning officer[2] must make arrangements for the verification of the ballot paper accounts[3] in the presence of the counting agents[4]; and he must give to the returning officer[5] and the counting agents notice in writing of the time and place at which he will begin such verification[6].

No person other than:

(1) the returning officer, the local returning officer and his clerks[7];

(2) the candidates, and one other person chosen by each of them[8];

(3)   the election agents[9];
(4)   the counting agents[10]; and
(5)   persons who are entitled to attend by virtue of any of the provisions of
       the Political Parties, Elections and Referendums Act 2000[11] which allow
       Electoral Commission representatives and accredited observers to attend
       electoral proceedings and observe working practices[12],

may attend the verification of the ballot paper accounts, unless permitted by the
local returning officer to attend[13]. A person not entitled to attend at the
verification of the ballot paper accounts may not be permitted to do so by the
local returning officer, however, unless he is satisfied that the efficient verification
of the ballot paper accounts will not be impeded[14]. The local returning officer
must make such arrangements as he thinks fit to ensure that every person
attending at the verification of the ballot paper accounts (other than any
constable on duty at the counting) has been given a copy in writing of the
statutory provisions relating to the requirement of secrecy that apply to such
attendance[15].

The local returning officer must give the counting agents all such reasonable
facilities for observing the proceedings, and all such information with respect to
them, as he can give them, consistent with the orderly conduct of the
proceedings, and the discharge of his duties in connection with them[16].

Where the poll at an election is taken together with the poll at another
election or referendum, special provision is made for the verification of the ballot
paper accounts[17].

1   As to European parliamentary elections see PARA 217 et seq.
2   As to local returning officers appointed for the purposes of elections to the European Parliament
     see PARA 360.
3   As to the ballot paper account see PARA 405.
4   See the European Parliamentary Elections Regulations 2004, SI 2004/293, Sch 1 para 50(1)
     (Sch 1 substituted by SI 2009/186). As to the appointment of counting agents by a candidate,
     and as to the effect of their non-attendance, see PARA 394.
5   As to returning officers appointed for the purposes of elections to the European Parliament see
     PARA 360.
6   See the European Parliamentary Elections Regulations 2004, SI 2004/293, Sch 1 para 50(1) (as
     substituted: see note 4).
7   European Parliamentary Elections Regulations 2004, SI 2004/293, Sch 1 para 50(2)(a) (as
     substituted: see note 4). As to persons appointed as clerks by a returning officer see PARA 393.
8   European Parliamentary Elections Regulations 2004, SI 2004/293, Sch 1 para 50(2)(b) (as
     substituted: see note 4). As to the meaning of 'candidate' generally see PARA 230.
9   European Parliamentary Elections Regulations 2004, SI 2004/293, Sch 1 para 50(2)(c) (as
     substituted: see note 4). As to the appointment of election agents at a European parliamentary
     election see PARA 239 et seq.
10   European Parliamentary Elections Regulations 2004, SI 2004/293, Sch 1 para 50(2)(d) (as
     substituted: see note 4).
11   Ie by virtue of any of the provisions of the Political Parties, Elections and Referendums Act 2000
     ss 6A–6D (see PARA 53): see the European Parliamentary Elections Regulations 2004,
     SI 2004/293, Sch 1 para 50(2)(e) (as substituted: see note 4).
12   European Parliamentary Elections Regulations 2004, SI 2004/293, Sch 1 para 50(2)(e) (as
     substituted: see note 4). As to the Electoral Commission see PARA 34 et seq; and as to authorised
     representatives of the Electoral Commission attending electoral proceedings see PARA 53.
13   European Parliamentary Elections Regulations 2004, SI 2004/293, Sch 1 para 50(2) (as
     substituted: see note 4).
14   European Parliamentary Elections Regulations 2004, SI 2004/293, Sch 1 para 50(3) (as
     substituted: see note 4).
15   See PARAS 385, 739–741.
16   European Parliamentary Elections Regulations 2004, SI 2004/293, Sch 1 para 50(4) (as
     substituted: see note 4).
17   As to polls at elections or referendums which are taken together see PARA 16 et seq.

466. Verification of ballot paper accounts and counting of ballot papers at a European parliamentary election. At a European parliamentary election[1], the local returning officer[2] must, in the presence of the counting agents[3]:

(1) open each ballot box, and count and record the number of ballot papers in it, and verify each ballot paper account[4]; and

(2) count such of the postal ballot papers as have been duly returned[5], and record the number counted[6].

While counting and recording the number of ballot papers, the local returning officer must keep the ballot papers with their faces downwards[7]; and he must not count any tendered ballot paper[8]. The local returning officer must verify each ballot paper account by comparing it with the number of ballot papers recorded by him, the unused and spoilt ballot papers[9] in his possession and the tendered votes list[10] (opening and resealing the packets containing the unused and spoilt ballot papers and the tendered votes list) and he must draw up a statement as to the result of the verification, which any counting agent may copy[11]. The hours during which the procedure of verification of ballot paper accounts and the counting of ballot papers is to be proceeded with must be determined by the local returning officer[12], who must take proper precautions for the security of the ballot papers and documents[13]. On completion of these procedures, he must[14]:

(a) place the ballot papers and other documents relating to the election in packets under his own seal and the seals of such counting agents as desire to affix their seals (unless he proceeds immediately to the counting of the votes)[15];

(b) otherwise take proper precautions for the security of the papers and documents[16]; and

(c) inform the returning officer of the total number of ballot papers counted[17].

Where the poll at an election is taken together with the poll at another election or referendum, special provision is made for the verification of the ballot paper accounts[18].

1 As to European parliamentary elections see PARA 217 et seq.
2 As to local returning officers appointed for the purposes of elections to the European Parliament see PARA 360.
3 See the European Parliamentary Elections Regulations 2004, SI 2004/293, Sch 1 para 51(1) (Schs 1, 2 substituted by SI 2009/186). As to the appointment of counting agents, and as to the effect of their non-attendance, see PARA 394.
4 European Parliamentary Elections Regulations 2004, SI 2004/293, Sch 1 para 51(1)(a) (as substituted: see note 3). As to the ballot paper account see PARA 405.
5 A postal ballot paper must not be deemed to be duly returned unless:
    (1) it is returned in the prescribed manner (ie either by post or by hand to the local returning officer, or by hand only to a polling station), so as to reach the local returning officer, or any polling station in the local counting area in question, before the close of the poll (European Parliamentary Elections Regulations 2004, SI 2004/293, Sch 1 para 51(2)(a), Sch 2 para 55(1) (as substituted: see note 3));
    (2) the postal voting statement, duly signed, is also returned in the prescribed manner (ie either by post or by hand to the local returning officer, or by hand only to a polling station), so as to reach him, or such a polling station, before that time (Sch 1 para 51(2)(b), Sch 2 para 55(1) (as so substituted));
    (3) the postal voting statement also states the date of birth of the elector or proxy (as the case may be) (Sch 1 para 51(2)(c) (as so substituted)); and
    (4) in a case where steps for verifying the date of birth and signature of an elector or proxy have taken under Sch 2 para 63 or, as the case may be, Sch 2 para 64 (ie when a postal voters' ballot box is opened: see PARA 421), the local returning officer (having taken such steps) verifies the date of birth and signature of the elector or proxy (as the case may be) (Sch 1 para 51(2)(d) (as so substituted)).

As to the meaning of 'elector', in relation to a European parliamentary election, see PARA 111 note 4. As to the meaning of 'local counting area' see PARA 139 note 1. As to voting by proxy see PARA 366 et seq; and as to the entitlement to vote by post as proxy see PARAS 377, 382. As to the postal voting statement see PARA 406. As to the means by which a postal voter may validly return a postal ballot paper see also PARA 418.

6   European Parliamentary Elections Regulations 2004, SI 2004/293, Sch 1 para 51(1)(b) (as substituted: see note 3).

7   European Parliamentary Elections Regulations 2004, SI 2004/293, Sch 1 para 51(4) (as substituted: see note 3).

8   European Parliamentary Elections Regulations 2004, SI 2004/293, Sch 1 para 51(3) (as substituted: see note 3). As to tendered ballot papers see PARA 403. As to scrutiny, which may look at ballot papers and investigate how votes have been recorded, see PARA 839 et seq.

9   As to spoilt ballot papers see PARA 404.

10   As to the tendered votes list see PARA 403.

11   European Parliamentary Elections Regulations 2004, SI 2004/293, Sch 1 para 51(5) (as substituted: see note 3).

12   See the European Parliamentary Elections Regulations 2004, SI 2004/293, Sch 1 para 51(6) (as substituted: see note 3).

13   See the European Parliamentary Elections Regulations 2004, SI 2004/293, Sch 1 para 51(7) (as substituted: see note 3).

14   See the European Parliamentary Elections Regulations 2004, SI 2004/293, Sch 1 para 51(8) (as substituted: see note 3).

15   European Parliamentary Elections Regulations 2004, SI 2004/293, Sch 1 para 51(8)(a) (as substituted: see note 3). The text refers to the provision that may be made for the counting of votes to take place at the same time as verification (see Sch 1 para 53; and PARA 468): see Sch 1 para 51(8)(a) (as so substituted).

16   European Parliamentary Elections Regulations 2004, SI 2004/293, Sch 1 para 51(8)(b) (as substituted: see note 3).

17   European Parliamentary Elections Regulations 2004, SI 2004/293, Sch 1 para 51(8)(c) (as substituted: see note 3).

18   As to polls at elections or referendums which are taken together see PARA 16 et seq.

467.   Attendance at counting of votes at a European parliamentary election.
At a European parliamentary election[1], the local returning officer[2] must make arrangements for counting the votes in the presence of the counting agents[3]:

(1)   in the case of a general election of members of the European Parliament[4], before or after the material time[5] (and, in either case, so that the requirement to notify the returning officer of the local result[6] is satisfied as soon as practicable after the material time)[7]; and

(2)   in the case of a by-election[8], as soon as practicable after the close of the poll[9]; and

the local returning officer must give to the counting agents, and to the returning officer, notice in writing of the time and place at which he will begin to count the votes[10]. No person other than:

(a)   the returning officer, the local returning officer and his clerks[11];

(b)   the candidates, and one other person chosen by each of them[12];

(c)   the election agents[13];

(d)   the counting agents[14]; and

(e)   persons who are entitled to attend by virtue of any of the provisions of the Political Parties, Elections and Referendums Act 2000[15] which allow Electoral Commission representatives and accredited observers to attend electoral proceedings and observe working practices[16],

may be present at the counting of the votes, unless permitted by the local returning officer to attend[17]. A person not entitled to attend at the counting of the votes must not be permitted to do so by the local returning officer, however, unless[18]:

(i)   he is satisfied that the efficient counting of the votes will not be impeded[19]; and

(ii)   he has either consulted the election agents or thought it impracticable to do so[20].

The local returning officer must make such arrangements as he thinks fit to ensure that every person attending at the counting of the votes (other than any constable on duty at the counting) has been given a copy in writing of the statutory provisions relating to the requirement of secrecy that apply to such attendance[21].

The local returning officer must give the counting agents all such reasonable facilities for overseeing the proceedings, and all such information with respect to them, as he can give them consistently with the orderly conduct of the proceedings, and the discharge of his duties in connection with them[22]. In particular, where the votes are counted by sorting the ballot papers according to the registered party[23] or individual candidate[24] for whom the vote is given, and then counting the number of ballot papers for each registered party or individual candidate, the counting agents must be allowed to satisfy themselves that the ballot papers are correctly sorted[25].

Where the poll at an election is taken together with the poll at another election or referendum, special provision is made for the counting of votes at the European parliamentary election[26].

1   As to European parliamentary elections see PARA 217 et seq.
2   As to local returning officers appointed for the purposes of elections to the European Parliament see PARA 360.
3   See the European Parliamentary Elections Regulations 2004, SI 2004/293, Sch 1 para 52(1) (Sch 1 substituted by SI 2009/186). As to the appointment of counting agents by a candidate, and as to the effect of their non-attendance, see PARA 394. As to the verification of ballot paper accounts and the counting of ballot papers at a European parliamentary election see PARA 466.
4   As to European parliamentary general elections see PARA 217.
5   For these purposes, the 'material time' means, in relation to a general election of MEPs, the close of the polling in the member state whose electors are the last to vote in the election: European Parliamentary Elections Regulations 2004, SI 2004/293, Sch 1 para 52(2) (as substituted: see note 3). Under European Union legislation, elections to the European Parliament are held on the date and at the times fixed by each member state but for all member states this date must fall within the same period starting on a Thursday morning and ending on the following Sunday: see PARA 222.
6   Ie the requirement of the European Parliamentary Elections Regulations 2004, SI 2004/293, Sch 1 para 57(1) (see PARA 472): see Sch 1 para 52(1)(a) (as substituted: see note 3). As to returning officers appointed for the purposes of elections to the European Parliament see PARA 360.
7   European Parliamentary Elections Regulations 2004, SI 2004/293, Sch 1 para 52(1)(a) (as substituted: see note 3).
8   As to European by-elections and the filling of vacancies see PARA 218 et seq.
9   European Parliamentary Elections Regulations 2004, SI 2004/293, Sch 1 para 52(1)(b) (as substituted: see note 3).
10 See the European Parliamentary Elections Regulations 2004, SI 2004/293, Sch 1 para 52(1) (as substituted: see note 3).
11 European Parliamentary Elections Regulations 2004, SI 2004/293, Sch 1 para 52(3)(a) (as substituted: see note 3). As to persons appointed as clerks by a returning officer see PARA 393.
12 European Parliamentary Elections Regulations 2004, SI 2004/293, Sch 1 para 52(3)(b) (as substituted: see note 3). As to the meaning of 'candidate' generally see PARA 230.
13 European Parliamentary Elections Regulations 2004, SI 2004/293, Sch 1 para 52(3)(c) (as substituted: see note 3). As to the appointment of election agents at a European parliamentary election see PARA 239 et seq.
14 European Parliamentary Elections Regulations 2004, SI 2004/293, Sch 1 para 52(3)(d) (as substituted: see note 3).

15 Ie by virtue of any of the provisions of the Political Parties, Elections and Referendums Act 2000 ss 6A–6D (see PARA 53): see the European Parliamentary Elections Regulations 2004, SI 2004/293, Sch 1 para 52(3)(e) (as substituted: see note 3).
16 European Parliamentary Elections Regulations 2004, SI 2004/293, Sch 1 para 52(3)(e) (as substituted: see note 3). As to the Electoral Commission see PARA 34 et seq; and as to authorised representatives of the Electoral Commission attending electoral proceedings see PARA 53.
17 See the European Parliamentary Elections Regulations 2004, SI 2004/293, Sch 1 para 52(3) (as substituted: see note 3).
18 See the European Parliamentary Elections Regulations 2004, SI 2004/293, Sch 1 para 52(4) (as substituted: see note 3).
19 European Parliamentary Elections Regulations 2004, SI 2004/293, Sch 1 para 52(4)(a) (as substituted: see note 3).
20 European Parliamentary Elections Regulations 2004, SI 2004/293, Sch 1 para 52(4)(b) (as substituted: see note 3).
21 See PARAS 385, 739–741.
22 European Parliamentary Elections Regulations 2004, SI 2004/293, Sch 1 para 52(5) (as substituted: see note 3).
23 As to the meaning of 'registered political party' for the purposes of a European parliamentary election see PARA 230 note 29.
24 As to the meaning of 'individual candidate' for the purposes of a European parliamentary election see PARA 230 note 32.
25 European Parliamentary Elections Regulations 2004, SI 2004/293, Sch 1 para 52(6) (as substituted: see note 3).
26 As to polls at elections or referendums which are taken together see PARA 16 et seq.

468.   The count at a European parliamentary election.   The local returning officer at a European parliamentary election must[1]:

(1)   where the ballot papers and other documents have been placed in packets following completion of the procedure to verify the ballot paper accounts and count the number of ballot papers[2], open the packets of ballot papers other than unused, spoilt[3] and tendered ballot papers[4]; and

(2)   mix together the ballot papers (with the exception of unused, spoilt and tendered ballot papers)[5].

While counting the votes, the local returning officer must keep the ballot papers with their faces upwards, and he must take all proper precautions for preventing any person from seeing the numbers or other unique identifying marks printed on the back of the papers[6]. He must not count any tendered ballot paper[7]. The local returning officer must so far as practicable proceed continuously with counting the votes, allowing only time for refreshment, except that he may, in so far as he and the counting agents[8] agree, exclude the hours between seven in the evening and nine on the following morning[9]. For the purposes of this exception, the agreement of an individual candidate[10], or of the election agent of a registered party[11], is as effective as the agreement of the counting agents of that individual candidate or party[12]. During the time so excluded, the local returning officer must:

(a)   place the ballot papers and other documents relating to the election under his own seal, and the seals of such of the counting agents as desire to affix their seals[13]; and

(b)   otherwise take proper precautions for the security of the papers and documents[14].

In the case of a general election of members of the European Parliament[15], if the counting of the votes has commenced before the close of the polling in the member state whose electors are the last to vote in the election[16], the local returning officer or his clerks must not disclose the number of votes given for each registered party and individual candidate to anyone other than the returning officer or his clerks until after that time, and the counting of the votes is deemed not to have been completed until after that time[17].

Where the poll at an election is taken together with the poll at another election or referendum, special provision is made for the counting of votes at the European parliamentary election[18].

1 See the European Parliamentary Elections Regulations 2004, SI 2004/293, Sch 1 para 53(1) (Sch 1 substituted by SI 2009/186). As to European parliamentary elections see PARA 217 et seq; and as to local returning officers appointed for the purposes of elections to the European Parliament see PARA 360.
2 Ie placed in packets under the European Parliamentary Elections Regulations 2004, SI 2004/293, Sch 1 para 51(8) (see PARA 466): see Sch 1 para 53(1)(a) (as substituted: see note 1).
3 As to spoilt ballot papers see PARA 404.
4 European Parliamentary Elections Regulations 2004, SI 2004/293, Sch 1 para 53(1)(a) (as substituted: see note 1). As to tendered ballot papers see PARA 403.
5 European Parliamentary Elections Regulations 2004, SI 2004/293, Sch 1 para 53(1)(b) (as substituted: see note 1).
6 European Parliamentary Elections Regulations 2004, SI 2004/293, Sch 1 para 53(3) (Sch 1 as substituted (see note 1); Sch 1 para 53(3) amended by SI 2009/848). As to the number and other unique identifying marks which must be printed on the back of every ballot paper see PARA 387.
7 European Parliamentary Elections Regulations 2004, SI 2004/293, Sch 1 para 53(2) (as substituted: see note 1). As to scrutiny, which may look at ballot papers and investigate how votes have been recorded, see PARA 839 et seq.
8 As to the appointment of counting agents by a candidate, and as to the effect of their non-attendance, see PARA 394.
9 European Parliamentary Elections Regulations 2004, SI 2004/293, Sch 1 para 53(4) (as substituted: see note 1).
10 As to the meaning of 'individual candidate' for the purposes of a European parliamentary election see PARA 230 note 32.
11 As to the meaning of 'registered political party' for the purposes of a European parliamentary election see PARA 230 note 29. As to the appointment of election agents at a European parliamentary election see PARA 239 et seq.
12 European Parliamentary Elections Regulations 2004, SI 2004/293, Sch 1 para 53(5) (as substituted: see note 1).
13 European Parliamentary Elections Regulations 2004, SI 2004/293, Sch 1 para 53(6)(a) (as substituted: see note 1).
14 European Parliamentary Elections Regulations 2004, SI 2004/293, Sch 1 para 53(6)(b) (as substituted: see note 1).
15 As to European parliamentary general elections see PARA 217.
16 Ie before the 'material time' within the meaning of the European Parliamentary Elections Regulations 2004, SI 2004/293, Sch 1 para 52(1) (see PARA 467 note 5): see Sch 1 para 53(7) (as substituted: see note 1).
17 European Parliamentary Elections Regulations 2004, SI 2004/293, Sch 1 para 53(7) (as substituted: see note 1).
18 As to polls at elections or referendums which are taken together see PARA 16 et seq.

469. Rejected ballot papers at a European parliamentary election. Any ballot paper given at a European parliamentary election[1]:

(1) which does not bear the official mark[2];

(2) on which votes are given for more than one registered party[3] or individual candidate[4] (or for both a registered party and an individual candidate)[5];

(3) on which anything is written or marked by which the voter can be identified (except the printed number or other unique identifying mark on the back)[6]; or

(4) which is unmarked, or void for uncertainty[7],

is void and must not be counted[8]. However, a ballot paper on which the vote is marked:

(a)   elsewhere than in the proper place[9]; or
(b)   otherwise than by means of a cross[10]; or
(c)   by more than one mark[11],

must not for such reason be deemed to be void if an intention that the vote is to be for one or other of the registered parties or individual candidates clearly appears, and the way the paper is marked does not of itself identify the voter, and it is not shown that he can be identified by it[12]. A ballot paper on which a vote is marked for a particular candidate on a party's list[13] of candidates must, if otherwise valid, be treated as a vote for that party, whether or not there is also a vote marked for that party[14]. The local returning officer[15] must endorse the word 'rejected' on any ballot paper which is not to be so counted, and he must add to the endorsement the words 'rejection objected to' if an objection is made by a counting agent[16] to his decision[17].

The local returning officer must draw up a statement showing the number of ballot papers rejected under the several heads of:

(i)   want of official mark[18];
(ii)   voting for more than one registered party or individual candidate[19];
(iii) writing or mark by which voter could be identified[20]; and
(iv)   unmarked or void for uncertainty[21].

1   See the European Parliamentary Elections Regulations 2004, SI 2004/293, Sch 1 para 55(1) (Sch 1 substituted by SI 2009/186). As to European parliamentary elections see PARA 217 et seq.
2   European Parliamentary Elections Regulations 2004, SI 2004/293, Sch 1 para 55(1)(a) (as substituted: see note 1). As to the official mark see PARA 387. As to ballot papers rejected for want of official mark at parliamentary and other local elections see PARA 427.
3   As to the meaning of 'registered political party' for the purposes of a European parliamentary election see PARA 230 note 29.
4   As to the meaning of 'individual candidate' for the purposes of a European parliamentary election see PARA 230 note 32.
5   European Parliamentary Elections Regulations 2004, SI 2004/293, Sch 1 para 55(1)(b) (as substituted: see note 1). Whether a mark on a ballot paper amounts to a vote for a particular candidate is a matter of fact: see PARA 856 note 4.
6   European Parliamentary Elections Regulations 2004, SI 2004/293, Sch 1 para 55(1)(c) (as substituted: see note 1). As to the number and other unique identifying marks which must be printed on the back of every ballot paper see PARA 387. As to ballot papers rejected for marks identifying the voter at parliamentary and other local elections see PARA 429.
7   European Parliamentary Elections Regulations 2004, SI 2004/293, Sch 1 para 55(1)(d) (as substituted: see note 1). As to ballot papers rejected for being unmarked or void for uncertainty at parliamentary and other local elections see PARA 430.
8   See the European Parliamentary Elections Regulations 2004, SI 2004/293, Sch 1 para 55(1) (as substituted: see note 1). As to scrutiny, which may look at ballot papers and investigate how votes have been recorded, see PARA 839 et seq.
9   European Parliamentary Elections Regulations 2004, SI 2004/293, Sch 1 para 55(2)(a) (as substituted: see note 1). As to the prescribed layout of the ballot paper see PARA 386. As to ballot papers rejected at parliamentary and other local elections on the grounds set out in heads (a) to (c) in the text see PARA 430.
10 European Parliamentary Elections Regulations 2004, SI 2004/293, Sch 1 para 55(2)(b) (as substituted: see note 1). See note 9.
11 European Parliamentary Elections Regulations 2004, SI 2004/293, Sch 1 para 55(2)(c) (as substituted: see note 1). See note 9.
12 See the European Parliamentary Elections Regulations 2004, SI 2004/293, Sch 1 para 55(2) (as substituted: see note 1). As to the purposive interpretation that is required of this kind of provision see PARA 430.
13 As to the meaning of 'list' for these purposes see PARA 230 note 29.
14 European Parliamentary Elections Regulations 2004, SI 2004/293, Sch 1 para 55(3) (as substituted: see note 1).
15 As to local returning officers appointed for the purposes of elections to the European Parliament see PARA 360.

16 As to the appointment of counting agents, and as to the discharge of the function mentioned in the text by the candidate or (where there is such an agent) his election agent, see PARA 394.

17 European Parliamentary Elections Regulations 2004, SI 2004/293, Sch 1 para 55(4) (as substituted: see note 1).

18 European Parliamentary Elections Regulations 2004, SI 2004/293, Sch 1 para 55(5)(a) (as substituted: see note 1).

19 European Parliamentary Elections Regulations 2004, SI 2004/293, Sch 1 para 55(5)(b) (as substituted: see note 1).

20 European Parliamentary Elections Regulations 2004, SI 2004/293, Sch 1 para 55(5)(c) (as substituted: see note 1).

21 European Parliamentary Elections Regulations 2004, SI 2004/293, Sch 1 para 55(5)(d) (as substituted: see note 1).

470. Conclusiveness of returning officer's decision as to ballot papers at a European parliamentary election. The decision of the local returning officer at a European parliamentary election[1] on any question arising in respect of a ballot paper is final[2], but may be subject to review on an election petition[3].

1 As to European parliamentary elections see PARA 217 et seq; and as to local returning officers appointed for the purposes of elections to the European Parliament see PARA 360.

2 As to the rejection of ballot papers at a European parliamentary election see PARA 469.

3 European Parliamentary Elections Regulations 2004, SI 2004/293, Sch 1 para 56 (Sch 1 substituted by SI 2009/186). As to petitions questioning a European parliamentary election see PARA 765 et seq.

471. Recount at a European parliamentary election. If any of the following persons[1], namely:

(1) a candidate at a European parliamentary election[2];

(2) the election agent of a registered party[3];

(3) the election agent of an individual candidate[4]; or

(4) a counting agent who is duly authorised for the purpose[5],

are present when the counting of the votes is completed (or, if later, when it is deemed to be completed)[6], or when any recount of the votes is completed, he or she may require the local returning officer[7] to have the votes recounted (or again recounted)[8]. However, the local returning officer may refuse to do so if in his opinion the request is unreasonable[9].

No step may be taken on the completion of the counting (or, if later, its deemed completion), or any recount of votes, until any of the persons mentioned in heads (1) to (4) above, and who are present at its completion (or, if later, its deemed completion), have been given a reasonable opportunity to exercise this right to request a recount[10].

1 See the European Parliamentary Elections Regulations 2004, SI 2004/293, Sch 1 para 54(1) (Sch 1 substituted by SI 2009/186).

2 European Parliamentary Elections Regulations 2004, SI 2004/293, Sch 1 para 54(2)(a) (as substituted: see note 1). As to the meaning of 'candidate' generally see PARA 230. As to European parliamentary elections see PARA 217 et seq.

3 European Parliamentary Elections Regulations 2004, SI 2004/293, Sch 1 para 54(2)(b) (as substituted: see note 1). As to the meaning of 'registered political party' for the purposes of a European parliamentary election see PARA 230 note 29. As to the appointment of election agents at a European parliamentary election see PARA 239 et seq.

4 European Parliamentary Elections Regulations 2004, SI 2004/293, Sch 1 para 54(2)(c) (as substituted: see note 1). As to the meaning of 'individual candidate' for the purposes of a European parliamentary election see PARA 230 note 32.

5 European Parliamentary Elections Regulations 2004, SI 2004/293, Sch 1 para 54(2)(d) (as substituted: see note 1). Head (4) in the text refers to a counting agent authorised under Sch 1 para 33(2) (ie authorised by the terms of his appointment to require a recount at that count: see PARA 394 note 7): see Sch 1 para 54(2)(d) (as so substituted). As to the appointment of counting agents generally see PARA 394.

6   As to the count at European parliamentary elections see PARA 468. As to the deemed completion of the counting of the votes in cases where the count has commenced before the close of the polling in the member state whose electors are the last to vote in the election see the European Parliamentary Elections Regulations 2004, SI 2004/293, Sch 1 para 53(7); and PARA 468.

7   As to local returning officers appointed for the purposes of elections to the European Parliament see PARA 360.

8   See the European Parliamentary Elections Regulations 2004, SI 2004/293, Sch 1 para 54(1) (as substituted: see note 1).

9   See the European Parliamentary Elections Regulations 2004, SI 2004/293, Sch 1 para 54(1) (as substituted: see note 1).

10   European Parliamentary Elections Regulations 2004, SI 2004/293, Sch 1 para 54(3) (as substituted: see note 1).

472. Procedure at conclusion of count at a European parliamentary election. As soon as practicable after the completion of the count at a European parliamentary election[1] (or, if later, its deemed completion[2]), the local returning officer[3] must draw up a statement showing the number of votes given for each registered party[4] and individual candidate[5], excluding any votes given on ballot papers which have been rejected[6]. The local returning officer must forthwith inform the returning officer[7] of the contents of that statement[8]; and he must give public notice of the statement so prepared, together with the statement showing the number of ballot papers rejected under the various heads[9], as soon as practicable after the returning officer has agreed that he should do so[10].

1   As to European parliamentary elections see PARA 217 et seq; and as to the count at such elections see PARA 468.

2   Ie the deemed completion of the counting of the votes in cases where the count has commenced before the close of the polling in the member state whose electors are the last to vote in the election (see the European Parliamentary Elections Regulations 2004, SI 2004/293, Sch 1 para 53(7); and PARA 468): see Sch 1 para 57(1) (Sch 1 substituted by SI 2009/186).

3   As to local returning officers appointed for the purposes of elections to the European Parliament see PARA 360.

4   As to the meaning of 'registered political party' for the purposes of a European parliamentary election see PARA 230 note 29.

5   As to the meaning of 'individual candidate' for the purposes of a European parliamentary election see PARA 230 note 32.

6   European Parliamentary Elections Regulations 2004, SI 2004/293, Sch 1 para 57(1) (as substituted: see note 2). The text refers to ballot papers rejected under Sch 1 para 55 (see PARA 469): see Sch 1 para 57(1) (as so substituted).

7   As to returning officers appointed for the purposes of elections to the European Parliament see PARA 360.

8   European Parliamentary Elections Regulations 2004, SI 2004/293, Sch 1 para 57(2) (as substituted: see note 2).

9   Ie the statement prepared under the European Parliamentary Elections Regulations 2004, SI 2004/293, Sch 1 para 55 showing the number of ballot papers rejected under the several heads of: (1) want of official mark; (2) voting for more than one registered party or individual candidate; (3) writing or mark by which voter could be identified; and (4) unmarked or void for uncertainty (see PARA 469): see Sch 1 para 57(3) (as substituted: see note 2).

10   European Parliamentary Elections Regulations 2004, SI 2004/293, Sch 1 para 57(3) (as substituted: see note 2). As to public notice by a returning officer for a European Parliamentary election that is required to be given by or under the European Parliamentary Elections Regulations 2004, SI 2004/293, see PARA 239 note 23.

473. The calculation and the allocation of seats at a European parliamentary election. The returning officer at a European parliamentary election[1] must make arrangements for making the required allocation of seats in the European Parliament, based on calculations as to how the total number of votes given have been distributed[2]. No person other than[3]:

(1)   the returning officer and his clerks[4];

(2)   the election agent of each registered party standing at the election[5], or a person acting on his behalf[6];

(3)   each candidate on the list[7] of such a party, and one other person chosen by each of them[8];

(4)   each individual candidate[9], and one person chosen by each of them[10];

(5)   the election agent of each individual candidate, or a person acting on his behalf[11];

(6)   the nominating officer of each registered party[12] which is contesting the election to the European Parliament in the electoral region[13];

(7)   persons who are entitled to attend by virtue of any of the provisions of the Political Parties, Elections and Referendums Act 2000[14] which allow Electoral Commission representatives and accredited observers to attend electoral proceedings and observe working practices[15],

may be present at that calculation and allocation, unless permitted by the returning officer to attend[16]. The returning officer must give to:

(a)   the election agent of each registered party standing at the election[17]; and

(b)   each individual candidate[18],

notice in writing of the place at which he will conduct the calculation and allocation of seats[19], and of the time after which he will begin those proceedings[20].

As soon as practicable after the returning officer has been informed of the contents of the statements showing the number of votes given for each registered party and individual candidate prepared by local returning officers in his region[21], the returning officer must calculate the total number of votes given to each registered party and individual candidate in all of the local counting areas[22] within the electoral region, as shown in those statements[23].

The returning officer must then allocate the seats in accordance with the European Parliamentary Elections Act 2002[24]. The returning officer must give the persons entitled to be present reasonable facilities for satisfying themselves that the results of the calculation and allocation which he is required to make are accurate; and, in particular, a person entitled to be present may require the returning officer to make a calculation or allocation again[25]. However, the returning officer may refuse to do so if in his opinion the request is unreasonable[26].

Where, in the case of the last seat to be allocated, two or more registered parties or individual candidates have an equal number of votes, and that number is greater than the number of votes of any other party or candidate, one vote must be added to the votes of each party or individual candidate having such an equal number, and the allocation procedure[27] must be applied again[28]. If, after that, two or more parties or individual candidates still have an equal number of votes, and that number is greater than the number of votes of any other party or candidate, the returning officer must forthwith decide between the parties and individual candidates having such an equal number by lot, and allocate the seat to the party or candidate on whom the lot falls[29].

1   As to European parliamentary elections see PARA 217 et seq; and as to returning officers appointed for the purposes of elections to the European Parliament see PARA 360.

2   European Parliamentary Elections Regulations 2004, SI 2004/293, Sch 1 para 58(1) (Sch 1 substituted by SI 2009/186). The text refers to the calculation and allocation that is required by the European Parliamentary Elections Regulations 2004, SI 2004/293, Sch 1 para 59 (see the text and notes 21–26): see Sch 1 para 58(1) (as so substituted).

3   See the European Parliamentary Elections Regulations 2004, SI 2004/293, Sch 1 para 58(2) (as substituted: see note 2).

4   European Parliamentary Elections Regulations 2004, SI 2004/293, Sch 1 para 58(2)(a) (as substituted: see note 2). As to persons appointed as clerks by a returning officer see PARA 393.

5   As to the meaning of 'registered political party' for the purposes of a European parliamentary election see PARA 230 note 29. As to the appointment of election agents at such an election see PARA 239 et seq.

6   European Parliamentary Elections Regulations 2004, SI 2004/293, Sch 1 para 58(2)(b) (as substituted: see note 2).

7   As to the meaning of 'candidate' generally see PARA 230. As to the meaning of 'list' for the purposes of elections to the European Parliament see PARA 230 note 29.

8   European Parliamentary Elections Regulations 2004, SI 2004/293, Sch 1 para 58(2)(c) (as substituted: see note 2).

9   As to the meaning of 'individual candidate' for the purposes of a European parliamentary election see PARA 230 note 32.

10   European Parliamentary Elections Regulations 2004, SI 2004/293, Sch 1 para 58(2)(d) (as substituted: see note 2).

11   European Parliamentary Elections Regulations 2004, SI 2004/293, Sch 1 para 58(2)(e) (as substituted: see note 2).

12   As to nominating officers for registered political parties standing nominated see PARA 253.

13   European Parliamentary Elections Regulations 2004, SI 2004/293, Sch 1 para 58(2)(f) (as substituted: see note 2). As to the establishment of electoral regions (including the combined region) for the purpose of elections to the European Parliament see PARA 77.

14   Ie by virtue of any of the provisions of the Political Parties, Elections and Referendums Act 2000 ss 6A–6D (see PARA 53): see the European Parliamentary Elections Regulations 2004, SI 2004/293, Sch 1 para 58(2)(g) (as substituted: see note 2).

15   European Parliamentary Elections Regulations 2004, SI 2004/293, Sch 1 para 58(2)(g) (as substituted: see note 2). As to the Electoral Commission see PARA 34 et seq; and as to authorised representatives of the Electoral Commission attending electoral proceedings see PARA 53.

16   See the European Parliamentary Elections Regulations 2004, SI 2004/293, Sch 1 para 58(2) (as substituted: see note 2).

17   European Parliamentary Elections Regulations 2004, SI 2004/293, Sch 1 para 58(3)(a) (as substituted: see note 2).

18   European Parliamentary Elections Regulations 2004, SI 2004/293, Sch 1 para 58(3)(b) (as substituted: see note 2).

19   Ie the place at which he will conduct the proceedings under the European Parliamentary Elections Regulations 2004, SI 2004/293, Sch 1 para 59 (see the text and notes 21–26): see Sch 1 para 58(3) (as substituted: see note 2).

20   See the European Parliamentary Elections Regulations 2004, SI 2004/293, Sch 1 para 58(3) (as substituted: see note 2).

21   Ie the statements prepared under the European Parliamentary Elections Regulations 2004, SI 2004/293, Sch 1 para 57(1) (see PARA 472): see Sch 1 para 59(1) (as substituted: see note 2). As to local returning officers appointed for the purposes of elections to the European Parliament see PARA 360.

22   As to the meaning of 'local counting area' see PARA 139 note 1.

23   European Parliamentary Elections Regulations 2004, SI 2004/293, Sch 1 para 59(1) (as substituted: see note 2).

24   European Parliamentary Elections Regulations 2004, SI 2004/293, Sch 1 para 59(2) (as substituted: see note 2). The text refers to the allocation of seats in accordance with the European Parliamentary Elections Act 2002 s 2(5)–(9) (see PARA 340), subject to the European Parliamentary Elections Regulations 2004, SI 2004/293, Sch 1 para 59(4) and Sch 1 para 60 (equality of seats: see the text and notes 27–29): see Sch 1 para 59(2) (as so substituted). At a by-election at which there is only one vacancy, the European Parliamentary Elections Act 2002 s 2(5)–(9) has effect as though it provided that the party or individual candidate to whom the majority of the votes has been given must be declared to be elected: European Parliamentary Elections Regulations 2004, SI 2004/293, Sch 1 para 59(4) (as so substituted). As to European by-elections and the filling of vacancies see PARA 218 et seq.

25   See the European Parliamentary Elections Regulations 2004, SI 2004/293, Sch 1 para 59(3) (as substituted: see note 2).

26   See the European Parliamentary Elections Regulations 2004, SI 2004/293, Sch 1 para 59(3) (as substituted: see note 2).

27   Ie the rules in the European Parliamentary Elections Act 2002 s 2(5)–(9) (see PARA 340): see the European Parliamentary Elections Regulations 2004, SI 2004/293, Sch 1 para 60(1) (as substituted: see note 2); and PARA 340.

28 See the European Parliamentary Elections Regulations 2004, SI 2004/293, Sch 1 para 60(1) (as substituted: see note 2); and PARA 340.

29 See the European Parliamentary Elections Regulations 2004, SI 2004/293, Sch 1 para 60(2) (as substituted: see note 2); and PARA 340. Where the lot falls on a party, the returning officer must allocate the seat according to the order in which the persons named on the party's list of candidates appear on that list: see the European Parliamentary Elections Act 2002 s 2(8); the European Parliamentary Elections Regulations 2004, SI 2004/293, Sch 1 para 60(3) (as so substituted); and PARA 340.

(viii) Uncontested Elections

474. The procedure at uncontested parliamentary elections. If the statement of persons nominated at a parliamentary election[1], shows only one person standing nominated[2], that person is declared to be elected in accordance with those provisions of the parliamentary election rules[3] that govern final proceedings in both contested and uncontested elections[4].

1 As to the meaning of 'parliamentary election' see PARA 9. As to the statement of persons nominated see PARA 267.

2 As to the withdrawal of candidates see PARA 266.

3 Ie in accordance with the Representation of the People Act 1983 Sch 1 Pt IV (rr 50–53A) (see PARAS 479–481, 503): see Sch 1 r 17(2). As to the meaning of 'parliamentary election rules' see PARA 383 note 2.

4 Representation of the People Act 1983 Sch 1 r 17(2). As to contested elections see PARA 339 et seq.

475. The procedure at uncontested local government elections. At a local government election employing a simple majority system of polling[1], if, after any withdrawals duly made[2]:

(1) the number of persons remaining validly nominated for the electoral area[3] does not exceed the number of councillors to be elected to a principal area, parish or community council (as the case may be)[4]; or

(2) only one person remains validly nominated for the London Assembly constituency[5]; or

(3) only one candidate remains validly nominated for the office of a local authority mayor or London Mayor[6],

such person or persons must be declared to be elected in accordance with those provisions of the applicable elections rules[7] that govern final proceedings in both contested and uncontested elections[8].

If the number of persons remaining validly nominated at an election for the return of London members of the London Assembly[9], after any withdrawals duly made[10], does not exceed the number of seats available for allocation to London members[11], or if all of those persons who remain nominated are named on the same party list[12], the seats are allocated in accordance with the method that is set out in the Greater London Authority Act 1999[13].

1 As to the meaning of 'local government election' see PARA 11. The elections mentioned in the text that employ a simple majority ('first past the post') system of polling (see PARA 339) are a local government election for: (1) a principal area (see PARA 197 et seq); (2) a parish and community council (see PARA 200 et seq); (3) a local authority elected mayor (two candidates) (see PARA 198 et seq); (4) constituency members of the London Assembly (a London Authority election) (see PARA 199 et seq); and (5) London Mayor (two candidates) (a London Authority election) (see PARA 199 et seq). A local authority mayor or London Mayor is returned under the simple majority system only where there are two candidates; where three or more candidates contest the election, it is held under a supplementary vote system: see PARAS 198, 199 et seq, 341. As to the meaning of 'Authority election' see PARA 11.

2 Ie made, in relation to a local government election for a principal area, in accordance with the Local Elections (Principal Areas) (England and Wales) Rules 2006, SI 2006/3304, Sch 2 r 13, or,

in relation to a local government election for a parish and community council, in accordance with the Local Elections (Parishes and Communities) (England and Wales) Rules 2006, SI 2006/3305, Sch 2 r 13, or, in relation to a local authority mayoral election, in accordance with the Local Authorities (Mayoral Elections) (England and Wales) Regulations 2007, SI 2007/1024, Sch 1 r 15, or, in relation to a London Authority constituency members election, in accordance with the Greater London Authority Elections Rules 2007, SI 2007/3541, Sch 1 r 14, or, in relation to a London Mayoral election, in accordance with Sch 3 r 14 (see PARA 266): see the Local Elections (Principal Areas) (England and Wales) Rules 2006, SI 2006/3304, Sch 2 r 14(2); the Local Elections (Parishes and Communities) (England and Wales) Rules 2006, SI 2006/3305, Sch 2 r 14(2); the Local Authorities (Mayoral Elections) (England and Wales) Regulations 2007, SI 2007/1024, Sch 1 r 16; and the Greater London Authority Elections Rules 2007, SI 2007/3541, Sch 1 r 15, Sch 3 r 15.

3   As to the meaning of 'electoral area' see PARA 11.
4   See the Local Elections (Principal Areas) (England and Wales) Rules 2006, SI 2006/3304, Sch 2 r 14(2); and the Local Elections (Parishes and Communities) (England and Wales) Rules 2006, SI 2006/3305, Sch 2 r 14(2).
5   See the Greater London Authority Elections Rules 2007, SI 2007/3541, Sch 1 r 15(2). As to the meaning of 'Assembly constituency' for these purposes see PARA 11 note 6.
6   See the Local Authorities (Mayoral Elections) (England and Wales) Regulations 2007, SI 2007/1024, Sch 1 r 16(c); and the Greater London Authority Elections Rules 2007, SI 2007/3541, Sch 3 r 15(c).
7   Ie, for the purposes of a local government election for a principal area, in accordance with the Local Elections (Principal Areas) (England and Wales) Rules 2006, SI 2006/3304, Sch 2 Pt IV (r 50) (see PARA 482), for the purposes of a local government election for a parish and community council, in accordance with the Local Elections (Parishes and Communities) (England and Wales) Rules 2006, SI 2006/3305, Sch 2 Pt IV (r 50) (see PARA 482), or, for the purposes of a local authority mayoral election, in accordance with the Local Authorities (Mayoral Elections) (England and Wales) Regulations 2007, SI 2007/1024, Sch 1 Pt 6 (rr 54–55) (see PARAS 484, 485), or, for the purposes of a London Authority constituency members election, in accordance with the Greater London Authority Elections Rules 2007, SI 2007/3541 Sch 1 Pt 5 (rr 54–55) (see PARAS 486, 489), or, for the purposes of a London Mayoral election, in accordance with Sch 3 Pt 6 (rr 57–58) (see PARAS 488, 489): see the Local Elections (Principal Areas) (England and Wales) Rules 2006, SI 2006/3304, Sch 2 r 14(2); the Local Elections (Parishes and Communities) (England and Wales) Rules 2006, SI 2006/3305, Sch 2 r 14(2); the Local Authorities (Mayoral Elections) (England and Wales) Regulations 2007, SI 2007/1024, Sch 1 r 16(c); and the Greater London Authority Elections Rules 2007, SI 2007/3541, Sch 1 r 15(2), Sch 3 r 15(c).
8   Local Elections (Principal Areas) (England and Wales) Rules 2006, SI 2006/3304, Sch 2 r 14(2); Local Elections (Parishes and Communities) (England and Wales) Rules 2006, SI 2006/3305, Sch 2 r 14(2); Local Authorities (Mayoral Elections) (England and Wales) Regulations 2007, SI 2007/1024, Sch 1 r 16(c); Greater London Authority Elections Rules 2007, SI 2007/3541, Sch 1 r 15(2), Sch 3 r 15(c). As to contested elections see PARA 339 et seq.
9   As to elections for the return of London members of the London Assembly see PARA 199 et seq.
10 Ie made in accordance with the Greater London Authority Elections Rules 2007, SI 2007/3541, Sch 2 r 15 (see PARA 266): see Sch 2 r 16.
12 As to the system of calculation and allocation by which London members are returned for the London Assembly (the 'additional member' system) see PARA 340.
13 As to references to party lists in elections for the return of London members of the London Assembly see PARA 255 note 23.
14 See the Greater London Authority Elections Rules 2007, SI 2007/3541, Sch 2 r 16. As to the rules of allocation that are set out in the Greater London Authority Act 1999 see PARA 450; and see further PARA 487 et seq.

476.   The procedure at uncontested Welsh Assembly elections.   At a Welsh Assembly constituency election[1], if the statement of persons nominated[2] shows only one person standing nominated[3], that person is declared to be elected in accordance with those provisions of the Welsh Assembly electoral rules[4] that govern final proceedings in both contested and uncontested elections[5].

If the statement of persons standing nominated at an Assembly regional election[6]:

(1)   shows more persons standing nominated (whether as party list

candidates or as individual candidates[7]) than the number of seats for that Assembly electoral region[8], and where each person is included on the same party list[9]; or

(2) shows the number of persons standing nominated (whether as party list candidates or as individual candidates) is the same as, or fewer than, the number of seats for the Assembly electoral region[10],

those persons standing nominated are declared to be elected in accordance with those provisions of the Welsh Assembly electoral rules[11] that govern final proceedings in both contested and uncontested elections[12].

1 As to the meanings of 'Assembly election' and 'constituency election' see PARA 3 note 2.
2 As to the statement of persons nominated see PARA 267.
3 As to the withdrawal of candidates see PARA 266.
4 Ie in accordance with the National Assembly for Wales (Representation of the People) Order 2007, SI 2007/236, Sch 5 Pt 4 (paras 62–65) (see PARAS 490–492): see Sch 5 para 21(b). As to the Welsh Assembly electoral rules see PARA 383.
5 National Assembly for Wales (Representation of the People) Order 2007, SI 2007/236, Sch 5 para 21(b). As to contested elections see PARA 339 et seq.
6 As to the meaning of 'regional election' in relation to a Welsh Assembly election see PARA 3 note 2.
7 As to the meaning of 'individual candidate' for these purposes see PARA 230 note 19; and as to the meanings of 'party list' and 'party list candidate' see PARA 230 note 23.
8 See the National Assembly for Wales (Representation of the People) Order 2007, SI 2007/236, Sch 5 para 22(1). As to the meaning of 'Assembly electoral region' in relation to a Welsh Assembly election see PARA 3 note 2.
9 See the National Assembly for Wales (Representation of the People) Order 2007, SI 2007/236, Sch 5 para 22(2). As to the meaning of 'party list' in relation to a Welsh Assembly regional election see PARA 230 note 23.
10 See the National Assembly for Wales (Representation of the People) Order 2007, SI 2007/236, Sch 5 para 22(3).
11 Ie in accordance with the National Assembly for Wales (Representation of the People) Order 2007, SI 2007/236, Sch 5 Pt 4 (see PARAS 490–492): see Sch 5 para 22(2), (3).
12 See the National Assembly for Wales (Representation of the People) Order 2007, SI 2007/236, Sch 5 para 22(2), (3). Where head (1) in the text applies, the persons shown standing nominated are declared to be elected in the order that they are included on the party list (starting with the highest) up to the number of seats to be filled for that Assembly electoral region: see Sch 5 para 22(2). The provision made by Sch 5 para 22(2) or, as the case may be, Sch 5 para 22(3) also applies where notice of a poll at a regional election is countermanded, or where the poll is abandoned under Sch 5 para 75(1) (election uncontested through death of candidate: see PARA 516): Sch 5 para 22(4).

477. The procedure at uncontested European parliamentary elections.

At a European parliamentary election[1], if the statement of parties and individual candidates nominated[2] shows a number of candidates (whether on a registered party's list[3] or individual candidates) which is the same as, or less than, the number of seats to be filled, those candidates must be declared to be elected in accordance with those provisions of the European parliamentary electoral rules[4] that govern final proceedings in both contested and uncontested elections[5].

1 As to European parliamentary elections see PARA 217 et seq.
2 As to the meaning of 'statement of parties and individual candidates nominated' see PARA 267 note 3. As to the meaning of 'individual candidate' at a European parliamentary election see PARA 230 note 32.
3 As to the meanings of 'list' and 'registered political party' for the purposes of a European parliamentary election see PARA 230 note 29.
4 Ie in accordance with the European Parliamentary Elections Regulations 2004, SI 2004/293, Sch 1 Pt 4 (paras 61–62) (see PARAS 493–494): see Sch 1 para 20(2) (Sch 1 substituted by SI 2009/186). As to the European parliamentary election rules see PARA 383.
5 European Parliamentary Elections Regulations 2004, SI 2004/293, Sch 1 para 20(2) (as substituted: see note 4). As to contested elections see PARA 339 et seq.

478.   The procedure at uncontested poll consequent on a parish meeting on a question involving appointment to office.   If the number of candidates remaining at a poll consequent on a parish meeting on a question involving appointment to office[1], after any withdrawals made under the rules that govern such a poll[2], does not exceed the number of persons to be elected, such candidates are deemed to be elected, and the returning officer[3] must as soon as possible give public notice of the abandonment of the poll[4]. Such a notice must:

(1)   refer to the meeting at which the poll was demanded and the offices in respect which the poll was demanded[5];

(2)   set out the full names, home addresses and (if required) descriptions of the candidates[6];

(3)   indicate which of those candidates has withdrawn[7];

(4)   state that no poll will be taken[8]; and

(5)   list the candidates deemed to be elected[9].

The returning officer must send a copy of that notice to each of the candidates, and to the chairman of the meeting at which the poll was demanded[10].

1   As to polls consequent on a parish meeting on a question involving appointment to office see PARA 200 et seq. As to the meaning of 'candidate' generally see PARA 230.
2   Ie after any withdrawals under the Parish and Community Meetings (Polls) Rules 1987, SI 1987/1, Schedule r 3(1) (see PARA 266): see Schedule r 3(2).
3   As to the returning officer at a poll consequent on parish meeting taken on the question of appointment to any office see PARA 356.
4   See the Parish and Community Meetings (Polls) Rules 1987, Schedule r 3(2). As to contested polls see PARA 339 et seq.
5   Parish and Community Meetings (Polls) Rules 1987, Schedule r 3(2)(a).
6   Parish and Community Meetings (Polls) Rules 1987, Schedule r 3(2)(b).
7   Parish and Community Meetings (Polls) Rules 1987, Schedule r 3(2)(c).
8   Parish and Community Meetings (Polls) Rules 1987, Schedule r 3(2)(d).
9   Parish and Community Meetings (Polls) Rules 1987, Schedule r 3(2)(e).
10   See the Parish and Community Meetings (Polls) Rules 1987, Schedule r 3(2).

(ix)   Final Proceedings

A.   PARLIAMENTARY ELECTIONS

479.   Declaration of result at parliamentary election.   In a contested parliamentary election[1], when the result of the poll has been ascertained[2], the returning officer[3] must forthwith[4]:

(1)   declare to be elected the candidate[5] to whom the majority of votes has been given[6];

(2)   return his name to the Clerk of the Crown[7]; and

(3)   give public notice[8] of his name and of the total number of votes given for each candidate together with the number of rejected ballot papers under each head shown in the statement of rejected ballot papers[9].

In an uncontested parliamentary election[10], the statement of persons nominated[11], in addition to showing the person standing nominated, must also declare that person to be elected, and the returning officer must forthwith return his name to the Clerk of the Crown[12].

1   As to the meaning of 'parliamentary election' see PARA 9. As to contested parliamentary elections see PARA 189 et seq.
2   As to the method of election at a parliamentary election see PARA 384 et seq.
3   As to returning officers for parliamentary elections see PARA 350 et seq.
4   See the Representation of the People Act 1983 Sch 1 r 50(1).
5   As to the meaning of 'candidate' generally see PARA 230.

6   Representation of the People Act 1983 Sch 1 r 50(1)(a). The returning officer is not a judge of
     the qualifications of the successful candidate: *Pritchard v Bangor Corpn* (1888) 13 App Cas
     241, HL.
7   Representation of the People Act 1983 Sch 1 r 50(1)(b). As to the meaning of 'Clerk of the
     Crown' see PARA 192 note 1.
8   As to the giving of public notice by returning officers for parliamentary elections see PARA 350.
9   Representation of the People Act 1983 Sch 1 r 50(1)(c). As to the statement of rejected ballot
     papers see PARA 431.
10   As to the procedure at uncontested elections see PARA 474.
11   As to the statement of persons nominated see PARA 267.
12   Representation of the People Act 1983 Sch 1 r 50(2). See also *R v Soothill, ex p Ashdown*
     (1955) Times, 21 April (cited in PARA 262 note 31).

480.   Return to the writ and record of returns in parliamentary elections.   The
returning officer[1] must return the name of the member elected at a parliamentary
election by endorsing on the writ a certificate in the proper form[2]. Any rule of
law or enactment as to the effect of, or manner of dealing with, the return of a
member to serve in Parliament applies to the certificate[3].

The returning officer may, on receiving a receipt, deliver the writ with the
certificate endorsed on it to an official designated for that purpose by a universal
postal service provider who is providing a universal postal service[4] for the area in
which the election is being held, or to his deputy, provided that the official or
deputy is at that time within the area concerned[5]. The designated official,or his
deputy, must send the writ so endorsed by the first post, free of charge, under
cover to the Clerk of the Crown[6] with the words 'Election Writ and Return'
endorsed on it[7].

From the certificate on each writ returned to him, the Clerk of the Crown
must enter the name of the member returned in a book to be kept by him at the
Crown Office[8] (known as the 'return book'). The return is not completed until it
reaches his hands so that he can act upon it; he transmits what is in substance a
copy of the return book to the Clerk of the House of Commons[9]. The Clerk of
the Crown must also enter in the return book any alteration or amendment made
by him in the certificate endorsed on any writ[10]. The return book kept by the
Clerk of the Crown is open to public inspection at reasonable times, and any
person may, on payment of a reasonable fee, take copies from the book[11].

1   As to returning officers for parliamentary elections see PARA 350 et seq. As to the meaning of
     'parliamentary election' see PARA 9.
2   Representation of the People Act 1983 Sch 1 r 51(1). As to the proper form of the certificate
     referred to in the text see Sch 1 Appendix of Forms (Certificate endorsed on writ) (amended by
     the Local Government (Wales) Act 1994 s 1(3), Sch 2 para 12(2)). Where the returning officer
     lost the writ and was therefore unable to endorse on the writ the certificate in the prescribed
     form, the returning officer sent to the Speaker of the House of Commons a statutory declaration
     as to the person elected and the House of Commons then instructed the Clerk of the Crown to
     receive the names: see *Portsmouth Election Case* (1910) 21 HC Deb 22. As to cases where a
     special return was made see *Hackney Case* (1874) 2 O'M & H 77; *Knaresborough Case* (1805)
     2 Peck 382. As to the issue and conveyance of writs for parliamentary elections see PARA 192 et
     seq.
3   Representation of the People Act 1983 Sch 1 r 51(2). As to the effect of a defective return see
     Pontefract Case (1623) Glanv El Cas 133.
4   Ie within the meaning of the Postal Services Act 2011 Pt 3 (ss 27–67) (regulation of postal
     services) (see POSTAL SERVICES vol 85 (2012) PARA 252): see the Representation of the People
     Act 1983 Sch 1 r 51(3) (amended by the Postal Services Act 2011 s 91(1), (2), Sch 12 paras 116,
     121; and by SI 2001/1149).
5   Representation of the People Act 1983 Sch 1 r 51(3) (as amended: see note 4).
6   As to the meaning of 'Clerk of the Crown' see PARA 192 note 1.
7   Representation of the People Act 1983 Sch 1 r 51(4) (amended by SI 2001/1149).
8   Representation of the People Act 1983 Sch 1 r 52(1).

9   *Poole Case, Hurdle v Waring* (1874) LR 9 CP 435.

10   Representation of the People Act 1983 Sch 1 r 52(2).

11   Representation of the People Act 1983 Sch 1 r 52(3).

481.   Return or forfeiture of candidate's deposit at parliamentary election. At a parliamentary election[1], a candidate's deposit[2] is forfeited to the Crown if a poll is taken and, after the counting of the votes by the returning officer[3] (including any recount) is completed, the candidate is found not to have polled more than one-twentieth of the total number of votes polled by all the candidates[4].

Otherwise, the deposit must be returned, not later than the next day after that on which the result of the election is declared[5], either to the person making it or to his personal representatives[6]. For these purposes, a deposit is to be treated as being returned on a day if a cheque for the amount of the deposit is posted on that day[7]. However, if the candidate is not shown as standing nominated in the statement of persons nominated[8], or if the poll is countermanded or abandoned by reason of his death[9], the deposit must be returned[10] as soon as practicable after the publication of the statement, or after his death, as the case may be[11]. If, at a general election, a candidate is shown as standing nominated in more than one constituency[12] in the statements of persons nominated, not more than one of the deposits is to be returned and, if necessary, the Treasury must direct which it is to be[13].

1   As to the meaning of 'parliamentary election' see PARA 9. As to parliamentary elections see PARA 189 et seq.

2   Ie the deposit required by the Representation of the People Act 1983 Sch 1 r 9 (see PARA 259): see Sch 1 r 53(1). As to the meaning of 'candidate' generally see PARA 230.

3   As to the returning officers appointed for parliamentary elections see PARA 350 et seq; and as to the count at parliamentary elections see PARA 425 et seq.

4   See the Representation of the People Act 1983 Sch 1 r 53(1), (4) (Sch 1 r 53(2), (4) amended, Sch 1 r 53(2A) added, by the Representation of the People Act 1985 ss 13, 24, Sch 4 para 83). Votes rejected by the returning officer are not included in the number of votes polled: see PARA 431.

5   For these purposes, a day is to be disregarded if it would be disregarded under the Representation of the People Act 1983 Sch 1 r 2 (see PARA 195 note 27) in computing any period of time for the purposes of the timetable for an election of the kind in question: Sch 1 r 53(2A)(a) (as added: see note 4). As to the declaration of the result at a parliamentary election see PARA 479.

6   See the Representation of the People Act 1983 Sch 1 r 53(1), (2) (Sch 1 r 53(2) as amended: see note 4). As to the meaning of 'personal representative' see WILLS AND INTESTACY vol 103 (2010) PARA 608.

7   Representation of the People Act 1983 Sch 1 r 53(2A)(b) (as added: see note 4).

8   As to the statement of persons nominated see PARA 267.

9   As to countermand on the death of the candidate at a parliamentary election see PARA 513.

10   Ie, by virtue of the Representation of the People Act 1983 Sch 1 r 53(1), to the person making the deposit or his personal representatives, as the case may be: see the text and note 6.

11   Representation of the People Act 1983 Sch 1 r 53(3).

12   As to the meaning of 'constituency' in relation to a parliamentary election see PARA 9.

13   Representation of the People Act 1983 Sch 1 r 53(5). As to the Treasury see CONSTITUTIONAL LAW AND HUMAN RIGHTS vol 8(2) (Reissue) PARAS 512–517.

B. LOCAL GOVERNMENT ELECTIONS

(A) Local Government Election (except London Authority Election or Local Authority Mayoral Election) and Poll consequent on a Parish Meeting

482.   Declaration of result at local government election for a principal area, parish or community council.   In a contested local government election for a principal area, parish or community[1], when the result of the poll has been ascertained[2], the returning officer must forthwith[3]:

(1)   declare to be elected the candidate or candidates to whom more votes have been given than to the other candidates[4], up to the number of councillors to be elected[5];

(2)   give notice of the name of each candidate to whom head (1) above applies, to the proper officer of the council for which the election is held[6]; and

(3)   give public notice[7] of the name of each candidate elected, and of the total number of votes given for each candidate (whether elected or not), together with the number of rejected ballot papers under each head shown in the statement of rejected ballot papers[8].

In an uncontested local government election for a principal area, parish or community[9], the returning officer must, as soon as practicable after the latest time for the delivery of notices of withdrawals of candidature[10]:

(a)   declare to be elected the person (or persons, as the case may be) remaining validly nominated[11];

(b)   give notice of the name of each person to whom head (a) above applies, to the proper officer of the council for which the election is held[12]; and

(c)   give public notice of the name of each such person[13].

1   As to the meaning of 'local government election' see PARA 11. As to local government elections for a principal area see PARA 197 et seq; and as to local government elections for a parish and community council see PARA 200 et seq. As to contested local government elections see PARA 384 et seq; and as to uncontested elections see the text and notes 9–13.

2   As to the counting of the votes at a local government election see PARA 424 et seq.

3   See the Local Elections (Principal Areas) (England and Wales) Rules 2006, SI 2006/3304, Sch 2 r 50(1); and the Local Elections (Parishes and Communities) (England and Wales) Rules 2006, SI 2006/3305, Sch 2 r 50(1). As to returning officers at local government elections see PARA 354 et seq.

4   As to the meaning of 'candidate' generally see PARA 230.

5   Local Elections (Principal Areas) (England and Wales) Rules 2006, SI 2006/3304, Sch 2 r 50(1)(a); Local Elections (Parishes and Communities) (England and Wales) Rules 2006, SI 2006/3305, Sch 2 r 50(1)(a).

6   Local Elections (Principal Areas) (England and Wales) Rules 2006, SI 2006/3304, Sch 2 r 50(1)(b); Local Elections (Parishes and Communities) (England and Wales) Rules 2006, SI 2006/3305, Sch 2 r 50(1)(b)(i). At a parish or community council election, notice must be given also to the proper officer of the council of the district in which the parish is situate, or to the proper officer of the county or county borough in which the community is situate, as, the case may be: Sch 2 r 50(1)(b)(ii). As to the meaning of 'proper officer' see PARA 140 note 2. As to the council of a district in England see LOCAL GOVERNMENT vol 69 (2009) PARA 24 et seq; and as to parishes and their councillors generally see LOCAL GOVERNMENT vol 69 (2009) PARA 27 et seq. As to the council of a county or county borough in Wales see LOCAL GOVERNMENT vol 69 (2009) PARA 37 et seq; and as to communities and their councillors generally see LOCAL GOVERNMENT vol 69 (2009) PARA 41 et seq. As to the formal declaration of acceptance of office that must be made, and delivered to the proper officer of the council, within the prescribed time see the Local Government Act 1972 s 83; and LOCAL GOVERNMENT vol 69 (2009) PARA 143.

7   As to the giving of public notice by a returning officer at a local government election see PARA 354.

8   Local Elections (Principal Areas) (England and Wales) Rules 2006, SI 2006/3304, Sch 2 r 50(1)(c); Local Elections (Parishes and Communities) (England and Wales) Rules 2006,

SI 2006/3305, Sch 2 r 50(1)(c). As to the statement of rejected ballot papers at a contested local government election, showing the number of ballot papers rejected under the several heads of: (1) want of official mark; (2) voting for more candidates than the voter is entitled to; (3) writing or mark by which voter could be identified; and (4) unmarked or void for uncertainty, see PARA 431.

    The Local Government (Wales) Measure 2011 s 1 imposes a duty on a local authority (a county council or a county borough council), in accordance with regulations, to conduct a survey after each ordinary election to the council of the county or county borough and to each community council (normally held concurrently every four years) in the local authority's area, by asking prescribed questions of councillors and unsuccessful candidates who have stood for election as councillors in the local authority's area: see LOCAL GOVERNMENT.

9   As to the procedure at uncontested local government elections see PARA 475.

10 See the Local Elections (Principal Areas) (England and Wales) Rules 2006, SI 2006/3304, Sch 2 r 50(2); and the Local Elections (Parishes and Communities) (England and Wales) Rules 2006, SI 2006/3305, Sch 2 r 50(2). As to the time for the delivery of notices of withdrawals of candidature see PARA 266.

11 Local Elections (Principal Areas) (England and Wales) Rules 2006, SI 2006/3304, Sch 2 r 50(2)(a); Local Elections (Parishes and Communities) (England and Wales) Rules 2006, SI 2006/3305, Sch 2 r 50(2)(a). See *R v Soothill, ex p Ashdown* (1955) Times, 21 April (cited in PARA 262 note 31).

12 Local Elections (Principal Areas) (England and Wales) Rules 2006, SI 2006/3304, Sch 2 r 50(2)(b); Local Elections (Parishes and Communities) (England and Wales) Rules 2006, SI 2006/3305, Sch 2 r 50(2)(b)(i). At a parish or community council election, notice must be given also to the proper officer of the council of the district in which the parish is situate, or to the proper officer of the county or county borough in which the community is situate, as, the case may be: Sch 2 r 50(2)(b)(ii).

13 Local Elections (Principal Areas) (England and Wales) Rules 2006, SI 2006/3304, Sch 2 r 50(2)(c); Local Elections (Parishes and Communities) (England and Wales) Rules 2006, SI 2006/3305, Sch 2 r 50(2)(c).

483. Declaration of result at a poll consequent on a parish meeting. At a poll consequent on a parish meeting taken on a question of appointment to any office[1], when the result of the poll has been ascertained[2], the returning officer must forthwith[3]:

(1)   declare to be elected the candidate or candidates to whom more votes have been given than to the other candidates[4], up to the number of appointments to be made[5];

(2)   give notice of the name of each person elected to the chairman of the meeting at which the poll was demanded[6];

(3)   give public notice[7] of the name of each candidate elected, and of the total number of votes given for each candidate (whether elected or not), together with the number of rejected ballot papers under each head shown in the statement of rejected ballot papers[8].

1 See the Parish and Community Meetings (Polls) Rules 1987, SI 1987/1, Schedule r 32(a). As to polls consequent on a parish meeting on a question involving appointment to office see PARA 200 et seq.

2 As to the counting of the votes at a poll consequent on parish meeting see PARA 424 et seq.

3 See the Parish and Community Meetings (Polls) Rules 1987, SI 1987/1, Schedule r 32. As to the returning officer at a poll consequent on parish meeting see PARA 356.

4 As to the meaning of 'candidate' generally see PARA 230.

5 Parish and Community Meetings (Polls) Rules 1987, SI 1987/1, Schedule r 32(a)(i). As to the procedure at uncontested elections see PARA 478.

6 Parish and Community Meetings (Polls) Rules 1987, SI 1987/1, Schedule r 32(a)(ii).

7 As to public notice required to be given by a returning officer for the purposes of a poll consequent on a parish meeting see PARA 356.

8 Parish and Community Meetings (Polls) Rules 1987, SI 1987/1, Schedule r 32(a)(iii). As to the statement of rejected ballot papers at a poll consequent on a parish meeting, showing the number of ballot papers rejected under the several heads of: (1) want of official mark; (2) voting

for more candidates than the voter is entitled to; (3) writing or mark by which voter could be identified; and (4) unmarked or void for uncertainty, see PARA 431.

(B) Local Government Election for return of a Local Authority Mayor

484. Declaration of result at local authority mayoral election. The returning officer at a contested local government election for the return of a local authority mayor[1] must declare the elected mayor to be the candidate who[2]:

(1)   under the simple majority system[3]; or

(2)   where there are three or more candidates, under the supplementary vote system[4],

is to be returned as the elected mayor at that election[5]. The returning officer must give public notice of[6]:

(a)   the name of the successful candidate[7];

(b)   the total number of first preference votes given for each candidate[8];

(c)   the number of rejected ballot papers at the election under each head shown in the statement of rejected ballot papers[9]; and

(d)   if second preference votes were counted[10]: (i) the total number of second preference votes given for each of the candidates remaining in the contest after the count of the first preference votes[11]; and (ii) the number of ballot papers rejected for the purposes of the count of second preference votes, on the ground that they were unmarked or void for uncertainty as to the second preference vote[12].

In an uncontested election[13], the returning officer must, as soon as practicable after the latest time for the delivery of notices of withdrawals of candidature[14]:

(A)   declare to be elected the person remaining validly nominated[15]; and

(B)   give public notice of the name of the person declared to be elected[16].

In either case, the returning officer must inform the proper officer[17] of the local authority concerned[18] of the result of the election[19].

1   As to the meaning of 'local government election' see PARA 11. As to elections for the return of an elected local authority mayor see PARA 198 et seq; and as to returning officers at local government elections (which include elections for the return of an elected local authority mayor) see PARA 354 et seq. As to contested local government elections see PARA 384 et seq; and as to uncontested elections see the text and notes 13–16.

2   See the Local Authorities (Mayoral Elections) (England and Wales) Regulations 2007, SI 2007/1024, Sch 1 r 54(1). As to the meaning of 'candidate' generally see PARA 230.

3   Ie in accordance with the Local Government Act 2000 ss 9HC(2), 42(2) (see PARA 341): see the Local Authorities (Mayoral Elections) (England and Wales) Regulations 2007, SI 2007/1024, Sch 1 r 54(1); Interpretation Act 1978 s 17(2).

4   Ie in accordance with the Local Government Act 2000 ss 9HC(3), 42(3), Sch 2 (see PARA 341): see the Local Authorities (Mayoral Elections) (England and Wales) Regulations 2007, SI 2007/1024, Sch 1 r 54(1); Interpretation Act 1978 s 17(2).

5   See the Local Authorities (Mayoral Elections) (England and Wales) Regulations 2007, SI 2007/1024, Sch 1 r 54(1).

6   See the Local Authorities (Mayoral Elections) (England and Wales) Regulations 2007, SI 2007/1024, Sch 1 r 54(2). As to the giving of public notice by the returning officer at an election for the return of an elected local authority mayor see PARA 354.

7   Local Authorities (Mayoral Elections) (England and Wales) Regulations 2007, SI 2007/1024, Sch 1 r 54(2)(a).

8   Local Authorities (Mayoral Elections) (England and Wales) Regulations 2007, SI 2007/1024, Sch 1 r 54(2)(b). As to elections at which first and second preference votes are cast (the 'supplementary vote system') see PARA 341. As to the count of first preference votes at an election for local authority mayor see PARA 436 et seq.

9   Local Authorities (Mayoral Elections) (England and Wales) Regulations 2007, SI 2007/1024, Sch 1 r 54(2)(c). As to the statement of rejected ballot papers at a contested local government election for the return of a local authority mayor, showing the number of ballot papers rejected

under the several heads of: (1) want of official mark; (2) voting for more than one candidate as to the first preference vote; (3) writing or mark by which the voter could be identified; and (4) unmarked or void for uncertainty as to the first preference vote, see Sch 1 r 48(5); and PARA 437.

10 See the Local Authorities (Mayoral Elections) (England and Wales) Regulations 2007, SI 2007/1024, Sch 1 r 54(2)(d). As to the count of second preference votes at an election for local authority mayor see PARAS 441, 442.

11 Local Authorities (Mayoral Elections) (England and Wales) Regulations 2007, SI 2007/1024, Sch 1 r 54(2)(d)(i).

12 Local Authorities (Mayoral Elections) (England and Wales) Regulations 2007, SI 2007/1024, Sch 1 r 54(2)(d)(ii).

13 As to the procedure at uncontested local government elections see PARA 475.

14 See the Local Authorities (Mayoral Elections) (England and Wales) Regulations 2007, SI 2007/1024, Sch 1 r 54(3). As to the time for the delivery of notices of withdrawals of candidature see PARA 266.

15 Local Authorities (Mayoral Elections) (England and Wales) Regulations 2007, SI 2007/1024, Sch 1 r 54(3)(a).

16 Local Authorities (Mayoral Elections) (England and Wales) Regulations 2007, SI 2007/1024, Sch 1 r 54(3)(b).

17 As to the meaning of 'proper officer' see PARA 140 note 2.

18 As to the meaning of 'local authority' for these purposes see LOCAL GOVERNMENT vol 69 (2009) PARA 23.

19 Local Authorities (Mayoral Elections) (England and Wales) Regulations 2007, SI 2007/1024, Sch 1 r 54(4). As to the declaration of acceptance of office that must be made within the prescribed time see the Local Government Act 1972 s 83; and LOCAL GOVERNMENT vol 69 (2009) PARA 143.

485. Return or forfeiture of candidate's deposit at local authority mayoral election. A candidate's deposit at an election for the return of an elected local authority mayor[1] is forfeited to the local authority of the electoral areas concerned[2], if:

(1)   a poll is taken[3]; and

(2)   after the conclusion of the first count[4], the candidate is found not to have polled more than one-twentieth of the total number of first preference votes polled by all the candidates[5].

Otherwise, the deposit must be returned, not later than the next day[6] after that on which the result of the election is declared[7], to the person making it or to his personal representative[8]. For these purposes, a deposit is to be treated as being returned on a day if a cheque for the amount of the deposit is posted on that day[9]. However, if the candidate is not shown as standing nominated in the statement of persons nominated[10], or if proof of his death has been given to the returning officer before the conclusion of the first count[11], the deposit must be returned[12] as soon as practicable after the publication of the statement, or after his death, as the case may be[13].

1   Ie the deposit made under the Local Authorities (Mayoral Elections) (England and Wales) Regulations 2007, SI 2007/1024, Sch 1 r 10 (see PARA 259): see Sch 1 r 55(1). As to the meaning of 'candidate' generally see PARA 230. As to elections for the return of an elected local authority mayor see PARA 198 et seq.

2   See the Local Authorities (Mayoral Elections) (England and Wales) Regulations 2007, SI 2007/1024, Sch 1 r 55(5). As to the meaning of 'electoral area' see PARA 11. As to the meaning of 'local authority' for these purposes see LOCAL GOVERNMENT vol 69 (2009) PARA 23.

3   See the Local Authorities (Mayoral Elections) (England and Wales) Regulations 2007, SI 2007/1024, Sch 1 r 55(5). As to contested local government elections see PARA 384 et seq.

4   As to the first count at an election for the return of an elected local authority mayor see PARA 436.

5   See the Local Authorities (Mayoral Elections) (England and Wales) Regulations 2007, SI 2007/1024, Sch 1 r 55(5). As to elections at which first and second preference votes are cast (the 'supplementary vote system') see PARA 341.

6 For these purposes, a day is to be disregarded if it would be disregarded under the Local Authorities (Mayoral Elections) (England and Wales) Regulations 2007, SI 2007/1024, Sch 1 r 4 (see PARA 211 note 1) in computing any period of time for the purposes of the timetable for a mayoral election: Sch 1 r 55(3)(a). Accordingly, as to the computation of time for these purposes see PARA 211 notes 1, 4.

7 See the Local Authorities (Mayoral Elections) (England and Wales) Regulations 2007, SI 2007/1024, Sch 1 r 55(2). As to the declaration of result at a local authority mayoral election see PARA 484.

8 See the Local Authorities (Mayoral Elections) (England and Wales) Regulations 2007, SI 2007/1024, Sch 1 r 55(1). As to the meaning of 'personal representative' see WILLS AND INTESTACY vol 103 (2010) PARA 608.

9 Local Authorities (Mayoral Elections) (England and Wales) Regulations 2007, SI 2007/1024, Sch 1 r 55(3)(b).

10 As to the statement of persons nominated see PARA 267.

11 As to returning officers at local government elections (which include elections for the return of an elected local authority mayor) see PARA 354 et seq. As to countermand on the death of the candidate at a local government election see PARA 516.

12 Ie, by virtue of the Local Authorities (Mayoral Elections) (England and Wales) Regulations 2007, SI 2007/1024, Sch 1 r 55(1), to the person making the deposit or his personal representative, as the case may be: see the text and note 8.

13 Local Authorities (Mayoral Elections) (England and Wales) Regulations 2007, SI 2007/1024, Sch 1 r 55(4).

(C) London Authority Elections

486. Declaration of result at London Authority election for the return of constituency members. In a contested Authority election for the return of constituency members of the London Assembly[1], when the result of the poll has been ascertained[2], the constituency returning officer ('CRO') must forthwith[3]:

(1) declare to be elected the candidate to whom the majority of votes has been given[4];

(2) give public notice of[5]: (a) the name of the person declared to be elected[6]; (b) the person's authorised description (if any)[7]; and (c) the total number of votes given for each candidate, together with the number of rejected ballot papers under each head shown in the statement of rejected ballot papers[8].

After the CRO has complied with his duties under heads (1) and (2) above, he may give public notice of the information referred to under head (2)(c) above, so as to set out the number of votes falling under each of the heads shown in the statement of rejected ballot papers, in respect of each ward[9].

In an uncontested London Authority constituency members election[10], the CRO must, as soon as practicable after the latest time for the delivery of notices of withdrawals of candidature[11]:

(i) declare to be elected the candidate remaining validly nominated[12];

(ii) give public notice of[13]: (A) the name of the person declared to be elected[14]; and (B) the person's authorised description (if any)[15].

In either case, the CRO must, as soon as practicable, inform the Greater London returning officer[16], and the proper officer of the London Authority[17], of the information in the public notice given under head (2) above[18].

1 As to the meaning of 'Authority election' see PARA 11. As to the meaning of 'constituency member', in relation to the London Assembly, see PARA 11 note 6; definition applied by virtue of the Greater London Authority Elections Rules 2007, SI 2007/3541, r 2(2). As to ordinary elections of constituency members of the London Assembly see PARA 199 et seq. As to contested local government elections (which include an Authority election) see PARA 384 et seq. As to the London Assembly see LONDON GOVERNMENT vol 71 (2013) PARA 70.

2   As to the count at Authority elections for the return of constituency members see PARA 444 et seq.

3   See the Greater London Authority Elections Rules 2007, SI 2007/3541, Sch 1 r 54(1). As to the meaning of 'constituency returning officer' ('CRO') see PARA 211 note 9.

4   Greater London Authority Elections Rules 2007, SI 2007/3541, Sch 1 r 54(1)(a). As to the meaning of 'candidate' generally see PARA 230.

5   See the Greater London Authority Elections Rules 2007, SI 2007/3541, Sch 1 r 54(1)(b). As to the giving of public notice by a returning officer at a local government election see PARA 354.

6   Greater London Authority Elections Rules 2007, SI 2007/3541, Sch 1 r 54(1)(b)(i).

7   Greater London Authority Elections Rules 2007, SI 2007/3541, Sch 1 r 54(1)(b)(ii). Head (2)(b) in the text refers to the person's authorised description (if any) within the meaning of Sch 1 r 6(5) or Sch 1 r 6(7) (see PARA 256): see Sch 1 r 54(1)(b)(ii).

8   Greater London Authority Elections Rules 2007, SI 2007/3541, Sch 1 r 54(1)(b)(iii). As to the statement of rejected ballot papers at a contested Authority election for the return of constituency members, showing the number of ballot papers rejected under the several heads of: (1) want of an official mark; (2) voting for more than one candidate; (3) writing or mark by which the voter could be identified; (4) unmarked ballot paper; and (5) void for uncertainty, see PARA 445.

9   Greater London Authority Elections Rules 2007, SI 2007/3541, Sch 1 r 54(2). Where the sum of votes given for all candidates in any ward does not exceed 500, however, the returning officer must not give notice under Sch 1 r 54(2) in respect of that ward alone, but must amalgamate the figures for that ward with those for any other ward in which more than 500 votes have been given, in the same Assembly constituency: Sch 1 r 54(3) (amended by SI 2012/198). The Greater London Authority Elections Rules 2007, SI 2007/3541, Sch 1 r 54(3) specifies the Greater London returning officer (see note 16) as the returning officer in question, although it is the CRO who gives notice under Sch 1 r 54(2). (The GLRO must give similar notice that is required under Sch 2 r 57(3) (see PARA 487), and under Sch 3 r 57(4) (see PARA 488), but he does not give the notice that is required under Sch 1 r 54(2)). As to the meaning of 'Assembly constituency' for these purposes see PARA 11 note 6. As to the establishment of electoral areas for the purpose of local government elections in England see PARA 74.

10   As to the procedure at uncontested local government elections see PARA 475.

11   See the Greater London Authority Elections Rules 2007, SI 2007/3541, Sch 1 r 54(4). As to the time for the delivery of notices of withdrawals of candidature see PARA 266.

12   Greater London Authority Elections Rules 2007, SI 2007/3541, Sch 1 r 54(4)(a). See *R v Soothill, ex p Ashdown* (1955) Times, 21 April (cited in PARA 262 note 31).

13   See the Greater London Authority Elections Rules 2007, SI 2007/3541, Sch 1 r 54(4)(b).

14   Greater London Authority Elections Rules 2007, SI 2007/3541, Sch 1 r 54(4)(b)(i).

15   Greater London Authority Elections Rules 2007, SI 2007/3541, Sch 1 r 54(4)(b)(ii). Head (ii)(B) in the text refers to the person's authorised description (if any) within the meaning of Sch 1 r 6(5) or Sch 1 r 6(7) (see PARA 256): see Sch 1 r 54(4)(b)(ii).

16   As to the meaning of 'Greater London returning officer' ('GLRO') see PARA 211 note 8.

17   As to the meaning of 'proper officer' see LONDON GOVERNMENT vol 29(2) (Reissue) PARA 83.

18   Greater London Authority Elections Rules 2007, SI 2007/3541, Sch 1 r 54(5).

487. Declaration of result at London Authority election for the return of the London members. At a contested Authority election for the return of London members of the London Assembly[1], the Greater London returning officer ('GLRO')[2] must declare the allocation of the seats for London members[3] and, where seats are allocated to a registered party[4], the names of the persons on the party list[5] who are to fill those seats[6]. The GLRO must give public notice of[7]:

(1)   the registered parties to which seats for London members have been allocated, and the names of the list candidates by whom those seats are to be filled[8];

(2)   the names of the successful individual candidates[9];

(3)   the total number of London votes[10] given for each registered party, and each individual candidate[11];

(4)   the total number of candidates of registered parties returned as constituency members[12];

(5)　　the number of rejected ballot papers under each head shown in the statement of rejected ballot papers[13];

(6)　　the name of every person included on a party list who has been omitted from, or is to be treated[14] as ceasing to be on, that list, together with the reason for the omission or cessation, as the case may be[15].

After the GLRO has duly made such a declaration, and given the required public notice under heads (1) to (6) above, he may give public notice of the information referred to under head (3) and head (5) above, so as to set out the number of votes falling under each of those heads, in respect of each ward[16].

1　As to the meaning of 'Authority election' see PARA 11. As to the meaning of 'London member', in relation to the London Assembly, see PARA 11 note 5; definition applied by virtue of the Greater London Authority Elections Rules 2007, SI 2007/3541, r 2(2). As to ordinary elections of London members of the London Assembly see PARA 199 et seq. As to contested local government elections (which include an Authority election) see PARA 384 et seq; and as to the count at Authority elections for the return of London members see PARA 444 et seq. As to the London Assembly see LONDON GOVERNMENT vol 71 (2013) PARA 70.

2　As to the meaning of 'Greater London returning officer' ('GLRO') see PARA 211 note 8.

3　As to the allocation of seats at a London members election see PARA 450.

4　As to the meaning of 'registered political party' for these purposes see PARA 256 note 27.

5　As to the meaning of 'party list' for these purposes see PARA 230 note 23.

6　Greater London Authority Elections Rules 2007, SI 2007/3541, Sch 2 r 57(1). The text refers to the names of the persons on the party list who are to fill seats for London members in accordance with the Greater London Authority Act 1999 s 4, Sch 2 para 8(5) (seats for London members which are allocated to a party must be filled by the persons on the party's list in the order in which they appear on the list: see PARA 340): see the Greater London Authority Elections Rules 2007, SI 2007/3541, Sch 2 r 57(1).

7　See the Greater London Authority Elections Rules 2007, SI 2007/3541, Sch 2 r 57(2). As to the giving of public notice by the GLRO see PARA 354.

8　Greater London Authority Elections Rules 2007, SI 2007/3541, Sch 2 r 57(2)(a). As to the meaning of 'candidate' generally see PARA 230. As to the meaning of references to a registered political party submitting a list of candidates to be London members of the London Assembly see PARA 230 note 14.

9　Greater London Authority Elections Rules 2007, SI 2007/3541, Sch 2 r 57(2)(b). As to the meaning of 'individual candidate' at an election for London members see PARA 255 note 9.

10　As to the meaning of 'London votes' see PARA 340 note 9.

11　Greater London Authority Elections Rules 2007, SI 2007/3541, Sch 2 r 57(2)(c).

12　Greater London Authority Elections Rules 2007, SI 2007/3541, Sch 2 r 57(2)(d).

13　Greater London Authority Elections Rules 2007, SI 2007/3541, Sch 2 r 57(2)(e). As to the statement of rejected ballot papers at a contested Authority election for the return of London members, showing the number of ballot papers rejected under the several heads of: (1) want of an official mark; (2) voting for more than one party or individual candidate; (3) writing or mark by which the voter could be identified; (4) unmarked ballot paper; and (5) void for uncertainty, see PARA 445.

14　Ie pursuant to the Greater London Authority Act 1999 Sch 2 para 8(10) (person included on a list submitted by a registered political party returned as the Mayor of London or as a London Assembly member: see PARA 340): see the Greater London Authority Elections Rules 2007, SI 2007/3541, Sch 2 r 57(2)(f).

15　Greater London Authority Elections Rules 2007, SI 2007/3541, Sch 2 r 57(2)(f).

16　Greater London Authority Elections Rules 2007, SI 2007/3541, Sch 2 r 57(3). Where the sum of votes given for all registered parties and individual candidates in any ward does not exceed 500, however, the GLRO must not give notice under Sch 2 r 57(3) in respect of that ward alone, but must amalgamate the figures for that ward with those for any other ward in which more than 500 votes have been given, in the same Assembly constituency: Sch 2 r 57(4) (amended by SI 2012/198). As to the meaning of 'Assembly constituency' for these purposes see PARA 11 note 6. As to the establishment of electoral areas for the purpose of local government elections in England see PARA 74.

488. Declaration of result at London Authority election for the return of London Mayor. At a contested Authority election for the return of London Mayor[1], the Greater London returning officer ('GLRO')[2] must declare to be elected as the Mayor of London the candidate who[3]:

(1)   under the simple majority system[4]; or

(2)   where there are three or more candidates, under the supplementary vote system[5],

is to be returned as the Mayor at that election[6]. The GLRO must give public notice of[7]:

(a)   the name of the person declared to be elected, and his authorised description (if any)[8];

(b)   the total number of first preference votes given for each candidate[9];

(c)   the total number of second preference votes given for each of the candidates remaining in the contest after the count of the first preference votes[10];

(d)   the number of rejected ballot papers at the election, under each head shown in the statement of rejected ballot papers[11]; and

(e)   the number of ballot papers on which no second preference vote was counted, under each head shown in the statement of rejected ballot papers[12].

In an uncontested Authority election for the return of London Mayor[13], the GLRO must, as soon as practicable after the latest time for the delivery of notices of withdrawals of candidature[14]:

(i)   declare to be elected the candidate remaining validly nominated[15]; and

(ii)   give public notice of the name of the person declared to be elected, and his authorised description (if any)[16].

After the GLRO has duly made such a declaration, and given the required public notice under heads (a) to (e) above, he may, in so far as is practicable, give public notice of the information referred to under heads (b) to (e) above, so as to set out the number of votes falling under each of those heads, in respect of each ward[17].

1   As to the meaning of 'Authority election' see PARA 11. As to elections for the return of London Mayor see PARA 199 et seq. As to contested local government elections (which include an Authority election) see PARA 384 et seq.

2   As to the meaning of 'Greater London returning officer' ('GLRO') see PARA 211 note 8.

3   See the Greater London Authority Elections Rules 2007, SI 2007/3541, Sch 3 r 57(1). As to the meaning of 'candidate' generally see PARA 230.

4   Ie in accordance with the Greater London Authority Act 1999 s 4(2) (ie the Mayor must be returned under the simple majority system, unless there are three or more candidates: see PARA 341): see the Greater London Authority Elections Rules 2007, SI 2007/3541, Sch 3 r 57(1). The Greater London Authority Act 1999 s 4(2) applies where a vacancy occurs in the office of London Mayor (see PARA 204), as it applies in relation to the election of London Mayor at an ordinary election: see s 16(4); and LONDON GOVERNMENT vol 71 (2013) PARA 99. Accordingly, head (1) in the text applies also where a vacancy occurs in the office of London Mayor: see the Greater London Authority Elections Rules 2007, SI 2007/3541, Sch 3 r 57(1).

5   Ie in accordance with the Greater London Authority Act 1999 s 4(6), Sch 2 Pt I (paras 1–4) (see PARA 341): see the Greater London Authority Elections Rules 2007, SI 2007/3541, Sch 3 r 57(1). The Greater London Authority Act 1999 Sch 2 Pt I applies where a vacancy occurs in the office of London Mayor (see PARA 204), as it applies in relation to the election of London Mayor at an ordinary election: see s 16(4); and LONDON GOVERNMENT vol 71 (2013) PARA 99. Accordingly, head (2) in the text applies also where a vacancy occurs in the office of London Mayor: see the Greater London Authority Elections Rules 2007, SI 2007/3541, Sch 3 r 57(1).

6   See the Greater London Authority Elections Rules 2007, SI 2007/3541, Sch 3 r 57(1).

7   See the Greater London Authority Elections Rules 2007, SI 2007/3541, Sch 3 r 57(2). As to the giving of public notice by the GLRO see PARA 354.

8 Greater London Authority Elections Rules 2007, SI 2007/3541, Sch 3 r 57(2)(a). Head (a) in the text refers to the person's authorised description (if any) within the meaning of Sch 3 r 6(5) or Sch 3 r 6(7) (see PARA 256): see Sch 3 r 57(2)(a).

9 Greater London Authority Elections Rules 2007, SI 2007/3541, Sch 3 r 57(2)(b). As to elections at which first and second preference votes are cast (the 'supplementary vote system') see PARA 341. As to the count of first preference votes at an election for London Mayor see PARA 436 et seq.

10 Greater London Authority Elections Rules 2007, SI 2007/3541, Sch 3 r 57(2)(c). As to the count of second preference votes at an election for London Mayor see PARA 457.

11 Greater London Authority Elections Rules 2007, SI 2007/3541, Sch 3 r 57(2)(d). As to the statement of rejected ballot papers at elections for the return of London Mayor, showing the number of ballot papers rejected under the several heads of: (1) want of an official mark; (2) voting for more than one candidate as to first preference vote; (3) writing or mark by which the voter could be identified; (4) unmarked as to the first preference vote; and (5) void for uncertainty, see PARA 452.

12 Greater London Authority Elections Rules 2007, SI 2007/3541, Sch 3 r 57(2)(e). See note 11.

13 As to the procedure at an uncontested Authority election for the return of London Mayor see PARA 475.

14 See the Greater London Authority Elections Rules 2007, SI 2007/3541, Sch 3 r 57(3). As to the time for the delivery of notices of withdrawals of candidature see PARA 266.

15 Greater London Authority Elections Rules 2007, SI 2007/3541, Sch 3 r 57(3)(a).

16 Greater London Authority Elections Rules 2007, SI 2007/3541, Sch 3 r 57(3)(b). Head (ii) in the text refers to the person's authorised description (if any) within the meaning of Sch 3 r 6(5) or Sch 3 r 6(7) (see PARA 256): see Sch 3 r 57(3)(b).

17 Greater London Authority Elections Rules 2007, SI 2007/3541, Sch 3 r 57(4). Where the sum of first preference votes given for all candidates in any ward does not exceed 500, however, the GLRO must not give notice under Sch 3 r 57(4) in respect of that ward alone, but must amalgamate the figures for that ward with those for any other ward in which more than 500 votes have been given, in the same Assembly constituency: Sch 3 r 57(5). As to the meaning of 'Assembly constituency' for these purposes see PARA 11 note 6. As to the establishment of electoral areas for the purpose of local government elections in England see PARA 74.

489. Return or forfeiture of candidate's deposit at London Authority election.
The deposit that is required to be made by a candidate at a London Authority election[1] is forfeited to the Greater London Authority[2], if a poll is taken, and if:

(1) in the case of a constituency members election[3], after the counting of the votes by the constituency returning officer ('CRO')[4] (including any recount) is completed[5], the candidate is found not to have polled more than one-twentieth of the total number of votes polled by all the candidates[6]; or

(2) in the case of a London members election[7], after the declaration of the result[8], a candidate or registered party[9] is found not to have polled more than one-fortieth of the total number of votes polled by all the candidates and registered parties[10]; or

(3) in the case of an Authority election for the return of London Mayor[11], after the first calculation is completed[12], the candidate is found not to have polled more than one-twentieth of the total number of first preference votes polled by all the candidates[13].

Otherwise, the deposit must be returned, not later than the next day[14] after that on which the result of the election is declared[15], to the person making it, or to his personal representative[16]. For these purposes, a deposit is to be treated as being returned on a day if a cheque for the amount of the deposit is posted on that day[17]. However, if the candidate is not shown as standing nominated in the statement of persons nominated[18], or if:

(a) in the case of a constituency members election, the poll is countermanded or abandoned by reason of his death[19]; or

(b) in the case of a London members election, proof has been given to the

Greater London returning officer ('GLRO')[20], before the allocation of seats[21], of the death of an individual candidate[22]; or

(c) in the case of an Authority election for the return of London Mayor, proof of his death has been given to the GLRO before the first calculation[23],

the deposit must be returned[24] as soon as practicable after the publication of the statement, or after the candidate's death, as the case may be[25].

1 Ie the deposit made under the Greater London Authority Elections Rules 2007, SI 2007/3541, Sch 1 r 8, or Sch 2 r 10, or Sch 3 r 9, as the case may be (see PARA 259): see Sch 1 r 55(1), Sch 2 r 58(1), Sch 3 r 58(1). As to the meaning of 'Authority election' see PARA 11. As to the meaning of 'candidate' generally see PARA 230. As to contested local government elections (which include an Authority election) see PARA 384 et seq.

2 As to the Greater London Authority see LONDON GOVERNMENT vol 71 (2013) PARA 67 et seq.

3 As to the meaning of 'constituency member', in relation to the London Assembly, see PARA 11 note 6; definition applied by virtue of the Greater London Authority Elections Rules 2007, SI 2007/3541, r 2(2). As to ordinary elections of constituency members of the London Assembly see PARA 199 et seq.

4 As to the meaning of 'constituency returning officer' ('CRO') see PARA 211 note 9.

5 As to the count at Authority elections for the return of constituency members see PARA 444 et seq.

6 See the Greater London Authority Elections Rules 2007, SI 2007/3541, Sch 1 r 55(5).

7 As to the meaning of 'London member', in relation to the London Assembly, see PARA 11 note 5; definition applied by virtue of the Greater London Authority Elections Rules 2007, SI 2007/3541, r 2(2). As to ordinary elections of London members of the London Assembly see PARA 199 et seq.

8 Ie under the Greater London Authority Elections Rules 2007, SI 2007/3541, Sch 2 r 57 (see PARA 487): see Sch 2 r 58(5).

9 As to the meaning of 'registered political party' for these purposes see PARA 256 note 27.

10 See the Greater London Authority Elections Rules 2007, SI 2007/3541, Sch 2 r 58(5).

11 As to ordinary elections for the return of London Mayor see PARA 199 et seq.

12 Ie under the Greater London Authority Elections Rules 2007, SI 2007/3541, Sch 3 r 55 (see PARA 456): see Sch 3 r 58(5).

13 See the Greater London Authority Elections Rules 2007, SI 2007/3541, Sch 3 r 58(5). As to elections at which first and second preference votes are cast (the 'supplementary vote system') see PARA 341. As to the count of first preference votes at an election for London Mayor see PARA 436 et seq.

14 For these purposes, a day is to be disregarded if, in accordance with the Greater London Authority Elections Rules 2007, SI 2007/3541, Sch 1 r 4, or Sch 2 r 4, or Sch 3 r 4, as the case may be (see PARA 211 note 4), it would be disregarded in computing any period of time for the purposes of the timetable for the election in question: Sch 1 r 55(3)(a), Sch 2 r 58(3)(a), Sch 3 r 58(3)(a). Accordingly, as to the computation of time for these purposes see PARA 211 note 4.

15 See the Greater London Authority Elections Rules 2007, SI 2007/3541, Sch 1 r 55(2), Sch 2 r 58(2), Sch 3 r 58(2). As to the declaration of the result at a London Authority election for the return of constituency members see PARA 486; for the return of London members see PARA 487; and for the return of London Mayor see PARA 488.

16 See the Greater London Authority Elections Rules 2007, SI 2007/3541, Sch 1 r 55(1), Sch 2 r 58(1), Sch 3 r 58(1). As to the meaning of 'personal representative' see WILLS AND INTESTACY vol 103 (2010) PARA 608.

17 Greater London Authority Elections Rules 2007, SI 2007/3541, Sch 1 r 55(3)(b), Sch 2 r 58(3)(b), Sch 3 r 58(3)(b).

18 See the Greater London Authority Elections Rules 2007, SI 2007/3541, Sch 1 r 55(4), Sch 2 r 58(4), Sch 3 r 58(4). In the case of a London members election, the reference to a candidate is to either an individual candidate or registered party: see Sch 2 r 58(4). As to the meaning of 'individual candidate' at an election for London members see PARA 255 note 9. As to the statement of persons nominated at an election see PARA 267.

19 See the Greater London Authority Elections Rules 2007, SI 2007/3541, Sch 1 r 55(4). As to countermand on the death of the candidate at a London Authority election see PARA 516.

20 As to the meaning of 'Greater London returning officer' ('GLRO') see PARA 211 note 8.

21 As to the allocation of seats at a London members election see PARA 450.

22 See the Greater London Authority Elections Rules 2007, SI 2007/3541, Sch 2 r 58(4).

23 See the Greater London Authority Elections Rules 2007, SI 2007/3541, Sch 3 r 58(4). The text refers to the first calculation under Sch 3 r 55 (see PARA 456): see Sch 3 r 58(4).

24 Ie, by virtue of the Greater London Authority Elections Rules 2007, SI 2007/3541, Sch 1 r 55(1), Sch 2 r 58(1), Sch 3 r 58(1), either to the person making it or to his personal representative: see the text and note 16.

25 See the Greater London Authority Elections Rules 2007, SI 2007/3541, Sch 1 r 55(4), Sch 2 r 58(4), Sch 3 r 58(4).

C. WELSH ASSEMBLY ELECTIONS

490. Declaration of result at Welsh Assembly constituency election. At a contested Welsh Assembly constituency election[1], when the result of the poll has been ascertained[2], the constituency returning officer[3] must forthwith[4]:

(1) declare to be elected the candidate to whom the majority of votes has been given[5];

(2) return his name, and, if a certificate has been received by the constituency returning officer issued by the registered nominating officer of one or more registered political parties[6] in respect of the candidate, the name of the party (or parties, as the case may be), to the Clerk of the Assembly[7];

(3) give public notice of[8]: (a) his name and, if applicable, the name of any registered political party referred to under head (2) above[9]; and (b) the total number of votes given for each candidate, together with the number of rejected ballot papers under each head shown in the statement of rejected ballot papers[10].

At an uncontested constituency election[11], the statement of persons nominated[12], in addition to showing the person standing nominated, must also declare that person elected, and the constituency returning officer must forthwith return his name and, if a certificate has been received by the constituency returning officer issued by the registered nominating officer of a registered political party[13] in respect of the candidate, the name of the party (or parties, as the case may be), to the Clerk of the Assembly[14].

At an Assembly general election[15], the constituency returning officer must, in either case, forthwith also notify the regional returning officer[16] for the Assembly electoral region[17] in which the Assembly constituency[18] is situated as to[19]: (i) the name of the candidate who has been returned[20];and (ii) if applicable, the name of the registered political party or parties[21], and for which party or parties the candidate is, for the purposes of ascertaining the result at that regional election[22], returned as the Assembly member for that constituency[23].

1 As to the meanings of 'Assembly election' and 'Assembly constituency election' see PARA 3 note 2. As to contested elections see PARA 384 et seq.

2 As to conclusion of the count at a Welsh Assembly constituency election see PARA 463.

3 As to the meaning of 'constituency returning officer' in the context of Welsh Assembly elections see PARA 18 note 2.

4 See the National Assembly for Wales (Representation of the People) Order 2007, SI 2007/236, Sch 5 para 62(1).

5 National Assembly for Wales (Representation of the People) Order 2007, SI 2007/236, Sch 5 para 62(1)(a). As to the meaning of 'candidate' for these purposes see PARA 230 note 19.

6 Ie under the National Assembly for Wales (Representation of the People) Order 2007, SI 2007/236, Sch 5 para 5(1) or Sch 5 para 5(3) (see PARA 256): see Sch 5 para 62(1)(b). As to the meaning of 'registered political party' for these purposes see PARA 230 note 23. As to the registered nominating officer of a registered political party see PARA 253.

7 National Assembly for Wales (Representation of the People) Order 2007, SI 2007/236, Sch 5 para 62(1)(b). The returns referred to in the text must be made in accordance with Sch 5

para 62(4): see Sch 5 para 62(1)(b). Accordingly. for these purposes, the constituency returning officer must return those names required to be returned, by:

(1) completing a certificate in the form set out in English and Welsh in Sch 10 (Form CR: Form of certificate declaring candidate to be returned at a constituency election) declaring the candidate to be returned (Sch 5 para 62(4)(a)); and

(2) delivering it, or causing it to be delivered, to the Clerk of the Assembly (Sch 5 para 62(4)(b)).

On receipt of a certificate delivered under Sch 5 para 62(4), the Clerk must enter the information contained in the certificate in a book kept for that purpose at the Assembly (the 'returns book'): Sch 5 para 79(1). The returns book must be open to public inspection at reasonable times and any person may, on payment of a reasonable fee, obtain copies from the book: Sch 5 para 79(6). The 'Clerk' must be construed in accordance with the Government of Wales Act 2006 s 26 (ie the Clerk of the Assembly: see CONSTITUTIONAL LAW AND HUMAN RIGHTS): see the National Assembly for Wales (Representation of the People) Order 2007, SI 2007/236, art 2(1).

8 National Assembly for Wales (Representation of the People) Order 2007, SI 2007/236, Sch 5 para 62(1)(c). As to the manner in which public notice is to be given see PARA 235 note 27.

9 National Assembly for Wales (Representation of the People) Order 2007, SI 2007/236, Sch 5 para 62(1)(c)(i).

10 National Assembly for Wales (Representation of the People) Order 2007, SI 2007/236, Sch 5 para 62(1)(c)(ii). Head (3)(b) in the text refers to each head shown in the statement of rejected ballot papers under Sch 5 para 58(5) (ie namely: (1) want of official mark; (2) giving more than one vote; (3) writing or mark by which voter could be identified; and (4) unmarked or void for uncertainty: see PARA 460): see Sch 5 para 62(1)(c)(ii).

11 As to the procedure at uncontested Welsh Assembly elections see PARA 476.

12 As to the statement of persons nominated see PARA 267.

13 Ie under the National Assembly for Wales (Representation of the People) Order 2007, SI 2007/236, Sch 5 para 5(1) or Sch 5 para 5(3) (see PARA 256): see Sch 5 para 62(2).

14 National Assembly for Wales (Representation of the People) Order 2007, SI 2007/236, Sch 5 para 62(2). The returns referred to in the text must be made in accordance with Sch 5 para 62(4) (see note 7): see Sch 5 para 62(2).

15 As to Welsh Assembly general elections see PARA 12 et seq.

16 As to the meaning of 'regional returning officer' see PARA 18 note 2.

17 As to the meaning of 'Assembly regional election' see PARA 3 note 2.

18 As to the meaning of 'Assembly constituency' in the context of Welsh Assembly elections see PARA 3 note 2.

19 See the National Assembly for Wales (Representation of the People) Order 2007, SI 2007/236, Sch 5 para 62(3).

20 National Assembly for Wales (Representation of the People) Order 2007, SI 2007/236, Sch 5 para 62(3)(a).

21 Ie the name of the registered political party or parties referred to in the National Assembly for Wales (Representation of the People) Order 2007, SI 2007/236, Sch 5 para 62(1)(b) (see head (2) in the text) or in Sch 5 para 62(2) (see the text and notes 11–14): see Sch 5 para 62(3)(b).

22 For these purposes, references to 'ascertaining the result', in relation to a contested regional election, mean:

(1) calculating the electoral region figure of each individual candidate, and of each registered political party standing nominated at that election (National Assembly for Wales (Representation of the People) Order 2007, SI 2007/236, Sch 5 para 62(6)(a)); and

(2) allocating the seats to the electoral region members for that region (Sch 5 para 62(6)(b)).

Like terms must be construed accordingly: see Sch 5 para 62(6). As to the meaning of 'individual candidate' for these purposes see PARA 230 note 19. As to calculating the electoral region figure see PARA 340.

23 National Assembly for Wales (Representation of the People) Order 2007, SI 2007/236, Sch 5 para 62(3)(b).

491. Declaration of result at Welsh Assembly regional election. After the regional returning officer[1] at a Welsh Assembly regional election[2] has ascertained the results of the poll[3], he must forthwith[4]:

(1) announce the individual candidates[5], or the registered political parties[6],

to whom seats have been allocated (together with the names of the party list candidates[7] who are to fill such seats)[8];

(2)	declare those individual candidates or party list candidates to have been elected[9];

(3)	return the names of those persons to the Clerk of the Assembly[10] (and, in respect of any party list candidate, the name of the registered political party for which he was such a candidate)[11];

(4)	give public notice of[12]: (a) the name of any individual candidate elected[13]; (b) the name of any party list candidate elected (and the name of the registered political party for which he was such a candidate)[14]; (c) the total number of votes given for each individual candidate or registered political party, together with the number of rejected ballot papers under each head shown in the statement of rejected ballot papers[15]; and (d) in respect of the number of votes referred to under head (c) above, a breakdown of the number of votes given for each such candidate or party in each Assembly constituency in the Assembly electoral region[16].

At an uncontested Assembly regional election[17], the statement of persons nominated[18], in addition to showing the registered political parties and other person standing nominated, must also[19]:

(i)	set out the individual candidates, or the registered political parties, to whom seats have been allocated (together with the names of the party list candidates who are to fill such seats)[20]; and

(ii)	declare those individual or party list candidates to have been elected and returned[21]; and

the regional returning officer must forthwith return the names of those persons to the Clerk of the Assembly (and, in respect of any party list candidate, the name of the registered political party for which he was such a candidate)[22].

1	As to the meaning of 'regional returning officer' see PARA 18 note 2.
2	As to the meanings of 'Assembly election' and 'Assembly regional election' see PARA 3 note 2. As to contested elections see PARA 384 et seq.
3	As to ascertainment of results at a contested Welsh Assembly regional election see PARA 464.
4	See the National Assembly for Wales (Representation of the People) Order 2007, SI 2007/236, Sch 5 para 64(1).
5	As to the meanings of 'candidate' and 'individual candidate' for these purposes see PARA 230 note 19.
6	As to the meaning of 'registered political party' for these purposes see PARA 230 note 23.
7	As to the meanings of 'party list' and 'party list candidate', in the context of Welsh Assembly regional elections, see PARA 230 note 23.
8	National Assembly for Wales (Representation of the People) Order 2007, SI 2007/236, Sch 5 para 64(1)(a). As to the allocation of seats at a Welsh Assembly regional election see PARA 464.
9	National Assembly for Wales (Representation of the People) Order 2007, SI 2007/236, Sch 5 para 64(1)(b).
10	As to the Clerk of the Assembly see note 11.
11	National Assembly for Wales (Representation of the People) Order 2007, SI 2007/236, Sch 5 para 64(1)(c). The returns referred to in the text must be made in accordance with Sch 5 para 64(3): see Sch 5 para 64(1)(c). Accordingly. for these purposes, the regional returning officer must return those names required to be returned, by:
	(1)	completing a certificate in the form set out in English and Welsh in Sch 10 (Form CS: Form of certificate declaring candidates to be returned at a regional election) declaring the candidates to be returned (Sch 5 para 64(3)(a)); and
	(2)	delivering it, or causing it to be delivered, to the Clerk of the Assembly (Sch 5 para 64(3)(b)).
On receipt of a certificate delivered under Sch 5 para 64(3), the Clerk must enter the information contained in the certificate in a book kept for that purpose at the Assembly (the 'returns book'): Sch 5 para 79(1). The returns book must be open to public inspection at

reasonable times and any person may, on payment of a reasonable fee, obtain copies from the book: Sch 5 para 79(6). The 'Clerk' must be construed in accordance with the Government of Wales Act 2006 s 26 (ie the Clerk of the Assembly: see CONSTITUTIONAL LAW AND HUMAN RIGHTS): see the National Assembly for Wales (Representation of the People) Order 2007, SI 2007/236, art 2(1).

12 See the National Assembly for Wales (Representation of the People) Order 2007, SI 2007/236, Sch 5 para 64(1)(d). As to the manner in which public notice is to be given see PARA 235 note 27.

13 National Assembly for Wales (Representation of the People) Order 2007, SI 2007/236, Sch 5 para 64(1)(d)(i).

14 National Assembly for Wales (Representation of the People) Order 2007, SI 2007/236, Sch 5 para 64(1)(d)(ii).

15 National Assembly for Wales (Representation of the People) Order 2007, SI 2007/236, Sch 5 para 64(1)(d)(iii). Head (4)(c) in the text refers to each head shown in the statement of rejected ballot papers under Sch 5 para 58(5), namely: (1) want of official mark; (2) giving more than one vote; (3) writing or mark by which voter could be identified; and (4) unmarked or void for uncertainty (see PARA 460).

16 National Assembly for Wales (Representation of the People) Order 2007, SI 2007/236, Sch 5 para 64(1)(d)(iv). As to the meanings of 'Assembly constituency' and 'Assembly electoral region' in the context of Welsh Assembly elections see PARA 3 note 2.

17 As to the procedure at uncontested Welsh Assembly elections see PARA 476.

18 As to the statement of persons nominated see PARA 267.

19 See the National Assembly for Wales (Representation of the People) Order 2007, SI 2007/236, Sch 5 para 64(2).

20 National Assembly for Wales (Representation of the People) Order 2007, SI 2007/236, Sch 5 para 64(2)(a).

21 National Assembly for Wales (Representation of the People) Order 2007, SI 2007/236, Sch 5 para 64(2)(b).

22 See the National Assembly for Wales (Representation of the People) Order 2007, SI 2007/236, Sch 5 para 64(2). The returns referred to in the text must be made in accordance with Sch 5 para 64(3) (see note 11): see Sch 5 para 64(2).

492. Return or forfeiture of candidate's deposit at Welsh Assembly election. The deposit made at an Assembly election[1] must be[2]:

    (1)   returned to the person making it, or his personal representative[3], in the case of either a candidate[4] at a constituency election[5] or an individual candidate[6] at a regional election[7];

    (2)   returned to the registered nominating officer of a registered political party[8] which has submitted a party list[9], in the case of a regional election[10]; or

    (3)   forfeited to the Secretary of State[11].

A deposit must be returned not later than the next day after that on which the result or results of the election are declared[12], except in the following cases[13]:

    (a)   if a candidate at a constituency election is not shown as standing nominated in the statement of persons nominated[14], or if the poll is countermanded or abandoned by reason of the candidate's death[15], his deposit must be returned[16] as soon as practicable after the publication of the statement, or after his death, as the case may be[17]; and, if an individual candidate, or a registered political party, at a regional election is not shown as standing nominated in the statement of persons nominated, his (or its) deposit must be returned[18] as soon as practicable after the publication of the statement[19];

    (b)   if a poll is taken, the deposit must be forfeited in any case where, after the counting of the votes (including any recount) is completed, a candidate for return as a constituency member (in the case of a constituency election)[20], or a registered political party standing nominated or an individual candidate for return as a regional member (in the case of a regional election)[21], is found not to have polled more than one-twentieth of the total number of votes polled by all candidates in the constituency or, as the case may be, by all registered political parties and individual candidates in the electoral region[22];

(c)   if, at an Assembly election, a person is shown as standing nominated as a candidate at a constituency election[23], or as an individual or party list candidate at a regional election[24], and, by virtue of such nomination, he is in breach of the provisions that restrict candidacy at a constituency election[25], or he is in breach of the provisions that restrict individual candidacy or inclusion in a party list at a regional election[26], then not more than one of the deposits must be returned and, if necessary, the Secretary of State must determine which it is to be[27].

1 Ie the deposit made under the National Assembly for Wales (Representation of the People) Order 2007, SI 2007/236, Sch 5 para 10 (see PARA 259): see Sch 5 para 65(1). As to the meaning of 'Assembly election' see PARA 3 note 2.

2 See the National Assembly for Wales (Representation of the People) Order 2007, SI 2007/236, Sch 5 para 65(1).

3 As to the meaning of 'personal representative' see WILLS AND INTESTACY vol 103 (2010) PARA 608.

4 As to the meaning of 'candidate' for these purposes see PARA 230 note 19.

5 As to the meaning of 'constituency election' for these purposes see PARA 3 note 2.

6 As to the meaning of 'individual candidate' for these purposes see PARA 230 note 19.

7 National Assembly for Wales (Representation of the People) Order 2007, SI 2007/236, Sch 5 para 65(1)(a). As to the meaning of 'Assembly regional election' see PARA 3 note 2.

8 As to the meaning of 'registered political party' for these purposes see PARA 230 note 23. As to the registered nominating officer of a registered political party see PARA 253.

9 As to the meaning of 'party list', in the context of Welsh Assembly regional elections, see PARA 230 note 23.

10 National Assembly for Wales (Representation of the People) Order 2007, SI 2007/236, Sch 5 para 65(1)(b).

11 National Assembly for Wales (Representation of the People) Order 2007, SI 2007/236, Sch 5 para 65(1)(c). As to the Secretary of State see PARA 2.

12 For these purposes:
    (1)   a day is to be disregarded if it would be disregarded under the National Assembly for Wales (Representation of the People) Order 2007, SI 2007/236, Sch 5 para 2 (see PARA 213 note 5) in computing any period of time for the purposes of the timetable for the election (Sch 5 para 65(3)(a)); and
    (2)   the deposit must be treated as being returned on a day if a cheque for the amount of the deposit is posted on that day (Sch 5 para 65(3)(b)).
  Accordingly, pursuant to head (1) above, as to the computation of time for these purposes see PARA 213 note 5. As to the declaration of result at a Welsh Assembly constituency election see PARA 490; and as to the declaration of result at Welsh Assembly regional election see PARA 491.

13 See the National Assembly for Wales (Representation of the People) Order 2007, SI 2007/236, Sch 5 para 65(2).

14 As to the statement of persons nominated at an election see PARA 267.

15 As to countermand on the death of the candidate at a Welsh Assembly election see PARA 516.

16 Ie, by virtue of head (1) in the text, either to the person making it or his personal representative.

17 See the National Assembly for Wales (Representation of the People) Order 2007, SI 2007/236, Sch 5 para 65(4).

18 Ie, by virtue of head (1) in the text, to the person making it or his personal representative (in the case of an individual candidate), or, by virtue of head (2) in the text, to the registered nominating officer of a registered political party (in the case of a registered political party which has submitted a party list).

19 See the National Assembly for Wales (Representation of the People) Order 2007, SI 2007/236, Sch 5 para 65(5).

20 See the National Assembly for Wales (Representation of the People) Order 2007, SI 2007/236, Sch 5 para 65(6).

21 See the National Assembly for Wales (Representation of the People) Order 2007, SI 2007/236, Sch 5 para 65(7).

22 See the National Assembly for Wales (Representation of the People) Order 2007, SI 2007/236, Sch 5 para 65(6), (7).

23 National Assembly for Wales (Representation of the People) Order 2007, SI 2007/236, Sch 5 para 65(8)(a).

24 National Assembly for Wales (Representation of the People) Order 2007, SI 2007/236, Sch 5 para 65(8)(b).

25 Ie he is in breach of the Government of Wales Act 2006 s 7(1) (a person may not be a candidate at a general election to be the Assembly constituency member for more than one Assembly constituency: see PARA 227) or s 10(9) (ie a person may not be a candidate in an election to fill a constituency vacancy if the person is an Assembly member, or a candidate in another such election: see PARA 214): see the National Assembly for Wales (Representation of the People) Order 2007, SI 2007/236, Sch 5 para 65(8)(i), (9)(a).

26 Ie he is in breach of the Government of Wales Act 2006 s 7(5) (persons denied from inclusion on a party list: see PARA 227) or s 7(6) (persons denied from being an individual candidate to be an Assembly regional member for the Assembly electoral region: see PARA 227): see the National Assembly for Wales (Representation of the People) Order 2007, SI 2007/236, Sch 5 para 65(8)(ii), (9)(b).

27 National Assembly for Wales (Representation of the People) Order 2007, SI 2007/236, Sch 5 para 65(8).

D. EUROPEAN PARLIAMENTARY ELECTIONS

493. Declaration of result at a European parliamentary election. In a contested European parliamentary election[1], when the result of the allocation and the filling of seats has been ascertained[2], the returning officer[3] must[4]:

(1)   forthwith declare to be elected those candidates on a registered party's list[5] by whom seats are filled, and those individual candidates[6] to whom seats are allocated[7];

(2)   prepare a statement setting out: (a) the total number of valid votes (as notified to him) given to each registered party and individual candidate[8]; (b) the number of votes which such a party or candidate had[9] at any stage when a seat was allocated to that party or candidate[10]; (c) the names in full and home address in full of each candidate who fills a seat, or to whom a seat has been allocated[11]; and (d) whether, in the case of a party, there are remaining candidates on that party's list who have not been declared to be elected[12]; and

(3)   give public notice[13] of that statement, and send a copy to the Secretary of State[14].

In the case of an uncontested election[15], the statement of parties and individual candidates nominated[16], in addition to showing the registered parties, the candidates on the list of those parties, and individual candidates standing nominated, must also declare to be elected any candidate so shown[17]. The returning officer must send a copy of that statement and declaration also to the Secretary of State[18].

1   As to European parliamentary elections see PARA 217 et seq; and as to contested elections generally see PARA 384 et seq.

2   As to the allocation of seats at a European parliamentary election see PARA 473.

3   As to returning officers appointed for the purposes of elections to the European Parliament see PARA 360.

4   See the European Parliamentary Elections Regulations 2004, SI 2004/293, Sch 1 para 61(1) (Sch 1 substituted by SI 2009/186).

5   As to the meanings of 'list' and 'registered political party' for the purposes of a European parliamentary election see PARA 230 note 29.

6   As to the meaning of 'individual candidate' at a European parliamentary election see PARA 230 note 32.

7   European Parliamentary Elections Regulations 2004, SI 2004/293, Sch 1 para 61(1)(a) (as substituted: see note 4). The text refers to those candidates on a registered party's list by whom seats are filled and those individual candidates to whom seats are allocated under Sch 1 para 59 (ie by the calculation and allocation of seats: see PARA 473) and Sch 1 para 60 (ie by drawing lots where there is an equality of seats: see PARA 340): see Sch 1 para 61(1)(a) (as so substituted).

8   European Parliamentary Elections Regulations 2004, SI 2004/293, Sch 1 para 61(1)(b)(i) (as substituted: see note 4). As to the statement that must be drawn up by the local returning officer as soon as practicable after the completion of the count at a European parliamentary election, and made known to the returning officer, showing the number of votes given for each registered party and individual candidate, excluding any votes given on ballot papers which have been rejected, see PARA 472.

9   Ie after the application of the European Parliamentary Elections Act 2002 s 2(5)–(9) (see PARA 340): see the European Parliamentary Elections Regulations 2004, SI 2004/293, Sch 1 para 61(1)(b)(ii) (as substituted: see note 4).

10 European Parliamentary Elections Regulations 2004, SI 2004/293, Sch 1 para 61(1)(b)(ii) (as substituted: see note 4).

11 European Parliamentary Elections Regulations 2004, SI 2004/293, Sch 1 para 61(1)(b)(iii) (as substituted: see note 4).

12 European Parliamentary Elections Regulations 2004, SI 2004/293, Sch 1 para 61(1)(b)(iv) (as substituted: see note 4).

13 As to the giving of public notice by the returning officer or local returning officer for a European parliamentary election see PARA 239 note 23.

14 European Parliamentary Elections Regulations 2004, SI 2004/293, Sch 1 para 61(1)(b)(v) (as substituted: see note 4). The returning officer for the combined region must also send a copy of the statement mentioned in head (2) in the text to the Chief Secretary of the Government of Gibraltar: see Sch 1 para 61(3) (as so substituted). As to the Secretary of State see PARA 2. As to the establishment of electoral regions (including the combined region) for the purpose of elections to the European Parliament see PARA 77.

15 As to the procedure at uncontested European parliamentary elections see PARA 477.

16 As to the meaning of 'statement of parties and individual candidates nominated' see PARA 267 note 3.

17 See the European Parliamentary Elections Regulations 2004, SI 2004/293, Sch 1 para 61(2) (as substituted: see note 4).

18 See the European Parliamentary Elections Regulations 2004, SI 2004/293, Sch 1 para 61(2) (as substituted: see note 4). The returning officer for the combined region must also send a copy of the statement mentioned in the text to the Chief Secretary of the Government of Gibraltar: see Sch 1 para 61(3) (as so substituted).

494.   Return or forfeiture of candidate's deposit.   The deposit made at a European parliamentary election[1] is forfeited to the Crown if a poll is taken and if, after the total number of valid votes for each registered party[2] and individual candidate[3] has been ascertained[4], the party or candidate is found not to have polled more than one-fortieth of the total number of votes polled by all the parties and candidates[5].

Otherwise, a deposit must be returned, not later than the next day[6] after that on which the result of the election is declared[7], either to the person making it or to his personal representatives, as the case may be[8]. For these purposes, a deposit is to be treated as being returned on a day if a cheque for the amount of the deposit is posted on that day[9]. However, where a registered party or an individual candidate is not shown as standing nominated in the statement of parties and individual candidates nominated[10], or where, in the case of an individual candidate, the candidate has died[11], the deposit must be returned[12] as soon as practicable after the publication of that statement, or the time when the returning officer is satisfied of the candidate's death, as the case may be[13].

1   Ie the deposit made under the European Parliamentary Elections Regulations 2004, SI 2004/293, Sch 1 para 10 (see PARA 259): see Sch 1 para 62(1) (Sch 1 substituted by SI 2009/186). As to European parliamentary elections see PARA 217 et seq.

2   As to the meaning of 'registered political party' for the purposes of a European parliamentary election see PARA 230 note 29.

3   As to the meaning of 'individual candidate' at a European parliamentary election see PARA 230 note 32.

4   Ie ascertained under the European Parliamentary Elections Regulations 2004, SI 2004/293, Sch 1 para 59(1) (see PARA 473): see Sch 1 para 62(5) (as substituted: see note 1).

5   See the European Parliamentary Elections Regulations 2004, SI 2004/293, Sch 1 para 62(1), (5) (as substituted: see note 1).

6   For these purposes, a day must be disregarded if it would be disregarded under the European Parliamentary Elections Regulations 2004, SI 2004/293, Sch 1 para 2(1) (see PARA 223 note 1) in computing any period of time for the purposes of the timetable in Sch 1 para 1 for an election of the kind in question: Sch 1 para 62(3)(a) (as substituted: see note 1). Accordingly, as to the computation of time for these purposes see PARA 223 note 1.

7   See the European Parliamentary Elections Regulations 2004, SI 2004/293, Sch 1 para 62(2) (as substituted: see note 1). As to the declaration of the result at a European parliamentary election see PARA 493.

8   See the European Parliamentary Elections Regulations 2004, SI 2004/293, Sch 1 para 62(1) (as substituted: see note 1). As to the meaning of 'personal representative' see WILLS AND INTESTACY vol 103 (2010) PARA 608.

9   European Parliamentary Elections Regulations 2004, SI 2004/293, Sch 1 para 62(3)(b) (as substituted: see note 1).

10   European Parliamentary Elections Regulations 2004, SI 2004/293, Sch 1 para 62(4)(a) (as substituted: see note 1). As to the meaning of 'statement of parties and individual candidates nominated' see PARA 267 note 3.

11   European Parliamentary Elections Regulations 2004, SI 2004/293, Sch 1 para 62(4)(b) (as substituted: see note 1). There is no further provision as to countermand on the death of the candidate at a European parliamentary election: see PARA 513 et seq.

12   Ie, by virtue of the European Parliamentary Elections Regulations 2004, SI 2004/293, Sch 1 para 62(1), to the person making the deposit or his personal representative, as the case may be: see the text and note 8.

13   European Parliamentary Elections Regulations 2004, SI 2004/293, Sch 1 para 62(4) (as substituted: see note 1).

(x) Disposal of Documents

A. SEALING OF BALLOT PAPERS

495. Sealing up of ballot papers. On the completion of the counting at a contested election[1], or at a poll consequent on a parish meeting involving an appointment to office[2], the returning officer[3] must seal up in separate packets the counted and rejected ballot papers[4]. The returning officer must not open the sealed packets of:

    (1)   tendered ballot papers[5];

    (2)   the completed corresponding number lists[6] (or counterfoils, in the case of a poll consequent on a parish meeting)[7];

    (3)   certificates as to employment on duty on the day of the poll[8]; or

    (4)   marked copies of the register of electors[9] and lists of proxies[10].

1   Ie at a contested parliamentary election, a local government election (which includes any London Authority election and a local authority mayoral election), a Welsh Assembly constituency or regional election (whether the polls are taken separately or together) or a European parliamentary election. As to the meanings of 'Assembly election', 'constituency election' and 'regional election' see PARA 3 note 2. As to the meaning of 'parliamentary election' see PARA 9. As to the meanings of 'Authority election' and 'local government election' see PARA 11. As to elections in the City of London see PARA 33. As to European parliamentary elections see PARA 217 et seq. As to contested elections see PARA 384 et seq.

    The provision that is set out in the text applies after completion of the counting of the votes at a contested European parliamentary election, where such completion is deemed to occur (i e in cases where the count has commenced before the close of the polling in the member state whose electors are the last to vote in the election: see the European Parliamentary Elections Regulations 2004, SI 2004/293, Sch 1 para 53(7); and PARA 468): see Sch 1 para 63(1) (Sch 1 substituted by SI 2009/186).

2   As to polls consequent on a parish meeting on a question involving appointment to office see PARA 200 et seq. As to contested polls consequent on a parish or community meeting involving an appointment to office see PARA 384 note 11.

3   As to returning officers generally see PARA 350 et seq. In the case of a London Authority election, the constituency returning officer (see PARA 211 note 9) is specified: see the Greater London Authority Elections Rules 2007, SI 2007/3541, Sch 1 r 56(1)–(4), Sch 2 r 59(1)–(4), Sch 3 r 59(1)–(4). At a European parliamentary election, the returning officer referred to in the text is the local returning officer (see PARA 360): see the European Parliamentary Elections Regulations 2004, SI 2004/293, Sch 1 para 63(1), (2) (as substituted: see note 1). At a Welsh Assembly election, the constituency returning officer is the returning officer referred to in the text: see the National Assembly for Wales (Representation of the People) Order 2007, SI 2007/236, Sch 5 para 66(1)–(3); but see also PARA 406 note 1. As to the meaning of 'constituency returning officer' for the purposes of Welsh Assembly elections see PARA 18 note 2.

4   Representation of the People Act 1983 Sch 1 r 54(1); Parish and Community Meetings (Polls) Rules 1987, SI 1987/1, Schedule r 33(1); European Parliamentary Elections Regulations 2004, SI 2004/293, Sch 1 para 63(1) (as substituted: see note 1); Local Elections (Principal Areas) (England and Wales) Rules 2006, SI 2006/3304, Sch 2 r 51(1); Local Elections (Parishes and Communities) (England and Wales) Rules 2006, SI 2006/3305, Sch 2 r 51(1); National Assembly for Wales (Representation of the People) Order 2007, SI 2007/236, Sch 5 para 66(1); Local Authorities (Mayoral Elections) (England and Wales) Regulations 2007, SI 2007/1024, Sch 1 r 56(1); Greater London Authority Elections Rules 2007, SI 2007/3541, Sch 1 r 56(1), Sch 2 r 59(1), Sch 3 r 59(1). As to the procedure to be followed when, the result of an election having been declared by the returning officer, a parcel of ballot papers is discovered uncounted see PARA 856 note 3.

In the case of a local government election which is not an Authority election, and a poll consequent on a parish meeting involving an appointment to office, it is specified that the packet of rejected ballot papers must include those rejected in part also: see the Parish and Community Meetings (Polls) Rules 1987, SI 1987/1, Schedule r 33(1); the Local Elections (Principal Areas) (England and Wales) Rules 2006, SI 2006/3304, Sch 2 r 51(1); the Local Elections (Parishes and Communities) (England and Wales) Rules 2006, SI 2006/3305, Sch 2 r 51(1); and the Local Authorities (Mayoral Elections) (England and Wales) Regulations 2007, SI 2007/1024, Sch 1 r 56(1).

At an Authority election where some or all of the votes have been counted using the electronic counting system, the CRO must also seal up in a separate packet a complete electronic record (the 'electronic record') of the information stored in the electronic counting system, held in such device as may be suitable for the purpose of its storage: Sch 1 r 56(2), Sch 2 r 59(2), Sch 3 r 59(2). After making the electronic record, the CRO must arrange for the original records in the electronic counting system to be removed from it and destroyed in a manner that ensures that the secrecy of those records is preserved: Sch 1 r 56(3), Sch 2 r 59(3), Sch 3 r 59(3). As to the meaning of 'electronic counting system' see PARA 443 note 18.

Where the polls at a Welsh Assembly constituency election and a regional election are taken together, the packets sealed up as mentioned in the text must not contain ballot papers relating to different elections: National Assembly for Wales (Representation of the People) Order 2007, SI 2007/236, Sch 5 para 66(2).

5   Representation of the People Act 1983 Sch 1 r 54(2)(a) (Sch 1 r 54(2) substituted by the Electoral Administration Act 2006 s 31(1), (5)); Parish and Community Meetings (Polls) Rules 1987, SI 1987/1, Schedule r 33(2); European Parliamentary Elections Regulations 2004, SI 2004/293, Sch 1 para 63(2)(a) (as substituted: see note 1); Local Elections (Principal Areas) (England and Wales) Rules 2006, SI 2006/3304, Sch 2 r 51(2)(a); Local Elections (Parishes and Communities) (England and Wales) Rules 2006, SI 2006/3305, Sch 2 r 51(2)(a); National Assembly for Wales (Representation of the People) Order 2007, SI 2007/236, Sch 5 para 66(3)(a); Local Authorities (Mayoral Elections) (England and Wales) Regulations 2007, SI 2007/1024, Sch 1 r 56(2)(a); Greater London Authority Elections Rules 2007, SI 2007/3541, Sch 1 r 56(4)(a), Sch 2 r 59(4)(a), Sch 3 r 59(4)(a). As to tendered ballot papers see PARA 403.

6   Representation of the People Act 1983 Sch 1 r 54(2)(b) (as substituted: see note 5); European Parliamentary Elections Regulations 2004, SI 2004/293, Sch 1 para 63(2)(b) (as substituted: see note 1); Local Elections (Principal Areas) (England and Wales) Rules 2006, SI 2006/3304, Sch 2 r 51(2)(b); Local Elections (Parishes and Communities) (England and Wales) Rules 2006, SI 2006/3305, Sch 2 r 51(2)(b); National Assembly for Wales (Representation of the People) Order 2007, SI 2007/236, Sch 5 para 66(3)(b); Local Authorities (Mayoral Elections) (England

and Wales) Regulations 2007, SI 2007/1024, Sch 1 r 56(2)(b); Greater London Authority Elections Rules 2007, SI 2007/3541, Sch 1 r 56(4)(c), Sch 2 r 59(4)(c), Sch 3 r 59(4)(c). As to the completed corresponding number lists see PARA 405 note 11.

7   See the Parish and Community Meetings (Polls) Rules 1987, SI 1987/1, Schedule r 33(2). As to the retention of counterfoils see PARA 405.

8   Representation of the People Act 1983 Sch 1 r 54(2)(c) (as substituted: see note 5); European Parliamentary Elections Regulations 2004, SI 2004/293, Sch 1 para 63(2)(c) (as substituted: see note 1); Local Elections (Principal Areas) (England and Wales) Rules 2006, SI 2006/3304, Sch 2 r 51(2)(c); Local Elections (Parishes and Communities) (England and Wales) Rules 2006, SI 2006/3305, Sch 2 r 51(2)(c); National Assembly for Wales (Representation of the People) Order 2007, SI 2007/236, Sch 5 para 66(3)(c); Local Authorities (Mayoral Elections) (England and Wales) Regulations 2007, SI 2007/1024, Sch 1 r 56(2)(c); Greater London Authority Elections Rules 2007, SI 2007/3541, Sch 1 r 56(4)(b), Sch 2 r 59(4)(b), Sch 3 r 59(4)(b). There is no provision for certificates as to employment on duty at a poll consequent on a parish meeting on a question involving appointment to office and accordingly head (3) in the text does not apply in that case: see the Parish and Community Meetings (Polls) Rules 1987, SI 1987/1, Schedule r 33(2). As to certificates of employment on duty on the day of the poll see PARA 395.

9   Ie, at any election (but not at a poll consequent on a parish meeting), including any marked copy notices issued under the Representation of the People Act 1983 s 13B(3B) or s 13B(3D) (notices specifying appropriate alterations to the register: see PARA 168): see Sch 1 r 54(2)(d) (as substituted: see note 5); the European Parliamentary Elections Regulations 2004, SI 2004/293, Sch 1 para 63(2)(d) (as substituted: see note 1); the Local Elections (Principal Areas) (England and Wales) Rules 2006, SI 2006/3304, Sch 2 r 51(2)(d); the Local Elections (Parishes and Communities) (England and Wales) Rules 2006, SI 2006/3305, Sch 2 r 51(2)(d); the National Assembly for Wales (Representation of the People) Order 2007, SI 2007/236, Sch 5 para 66(3)(d); the Local Authorities (Mayoral Elections) (England and Wales) Regulations 2007, SI 2007/1024, Sch 1 r 56(2)(d); and the Greater London Authority Elections Rules 2007, SI 2007/3541, Sch 1 r 56(4)(d), Sch 2 r 59(4)(d), Sch 3 r 59(4)(d).

10 Representation of the People Act 1983 Sch 1 r 54(2)(d) (as substituted: see note 5); Parish and Community Meetings (Polls) Rules 1987, SI 1987/1, Schedule r 33(2); European Parliamentary Elections Regulations 2004, SI 2004/293, Sch 1 para 63(2)(d) (as substituted: see note 1); Local Elections (Principal Areas) (England and Wales) Rules 2006, SI 2006/3304, Sch 2 r 51(2)(d); Local Elections (Parishes and Communities) (England and Wales) Rules 2006, SI 2006/3305, Sch 2 r 51(2)(d); National Assembly for Wales (Representation of the People) Order 2007, SI 2007/236, Sch 5 para 66(3)(d); Local Authorities (Mayoral Elections) (England and Wales) Regulations 2007, SI 2007/1024, Sch 1 r 56(2)(d); Greater London Authority Elections Rules 2007, SI 2007/3541, Sch 1 r 56(4)(d), Sch 2 r 59(4)(d), Sch 3 r 59(4)(d). There is no provision for voting by proxy at a poll consequent on a parish meeting on a question involving appointment to office and accordingly the reference to the list of proxies is omitted in that case: see the Parish and Community Meetings (Polls) Rules 1987, SI 1987/1, Schedule r 33(2). As to the list of proxies see PARA 373.

B. CONTROL OF ELECTION DOCUMENTS

496.   Transfer of documents relating to parliamentary elections. The returning officer at a parliamentary election[1] must, after sealing up the ballot papers[2], forward to the relevant registration officer[3]:

(1)   the packets of ballot papers in his possession[4];

(2)   the ballot paper accounts, the statement of rejected ballot papers, and the statement of the result of the verification of the ballot paper accounts[5];

(3)   the tendered votes lists[6], the lists of voters with disabilities assisted by companions[7], the lists of votes marked by the presiding officers, and the statements relating to them[8], the lists maintained of persons to whom ballot papers are delivered in consequence of an alteration to the register which takes effect on the day of the poll[9], and the declarations made by the companions of voters with disabilities[10];

(4)   the packets of the completed corresponding number lists[11];

(5)　　the packets of certificates as to employment on duty on the day of the poll[12];

(6)　　the packets containing marked copies of the registers of electors[13] and marked copies of the postal voters list[14], of lists of proxies[15] and of the proxy postal voters list[16]; and

(7)　　such other documents relating to elections as are prescribed[17],

endorsing on each packet a description of its contents, the date of the election to which they relate, and the name of the constituency for which the election was held[18].

1　As to the meaning of 'parliamentary election' see PARA 9. As to returning officers for parliamentary elections see PARA 350 et seq.

2·　As to the sealing up of ballot papers see PARA 495.

3　See the Representation of the People Act 1983 Sch 1 r 55(1) (Sch 1 r 55(1) amended, Sch 1 r 55(1A) added, by the Electoral Administration Act 2006 s 41(1), (3)). For the purposes of the Representation of the People Act 1983 Sch 1 rr 55–57 (see also PARAS 503, 836, 851), references to the relevant registration officer are to the registration officer of the local authority in whose area the constituency is situated or, if the constituency comprises any part of the area of more than one local authority, to the registration officer of the local authority in whose area the greater or greatest (as the case may be) number of electors is registered: see Sch 1 r 55(1A) (as so added). As to the meaning of 'constituency' for these purposes see PARA 9. As to registration officers and the areas for which they act see PARA 139.

4　Representation of the People Act 1983 Sch 1 r 55(1)(a).

5　Representation of the People Act 1983 Sch 1 r 55(1)(b). As to the verification of the ballot paper account at a parliamentary election see PARA 425; and as to the statement of rejected ballot papers see PARA 431.

6　As to the tendered votes list see PARA 403.

7　As to the list of voters with disabilities assisted by companions see PARA 402.

8　As to the list of votes marked by the presiding officer see PARA 401.

9　Ie the lists maintained under the Representation of the People Act 1983 Sch 1 r 41A (see PARA 399 note 5): see Sch 1 r 55(1)(c) (amended by the Representation of the People Act 2000 s 13(1), (4); and the Electoral Administration Act 2006 s 11(6), Sch 1 paras 31, 33, 40(a)).

10　Representation of the People Act 1983 Sch 1 r 55(1)(c) (as amended: see note 9). As to declarations made by the companions of voters with disabilities see PARA 402.

11　Representation of the People Act 1983 Sch 1 r 55(1)(ca) (added by the Electoral Administration Act 2006 s 31(1), (6)(a)). As to the completed corresponding number lists see PARA 405 note 11.

12　Representation of the People Act 1983 Sch 1 r 55(1)(d) (amended by the Electoral Administration Act 2006 ss 31(1), (6)(b), 74(2), Sch 2. As to certificates of employment on duty on the day of the poll see PARA 395.

13　Ie including any marked copy notices issued under the Representation of the People Act 1983 s 13B(3B) or s 13B(3D) (notices specifying appropriate alterations to the register: see PARA 168): see Sch 1 r 55(1)(e) (amended by the Electoral Administration Act 2006 s 45(1), (3)(a), Sch 1 paras 31, 33, 40(b)).

14　As to the postal voters list see PARA 373.

15　As to the list of proxies see PARA 373.

16　Representation of the People Act 1983 Sch 1 r 55(1)(e) (as amended: see note 13). As to the proxy postal voters list see PARA 381. As to regulations that govern the supply and inspection of these documents see PARA 504.

17　Representation of the People Act 1983 Sch 1 r 55(1)(f) (added by the Electoral Administration Act 2006 s 45(1), (3)(b)). 'Prescribed' means prescribed by regulations: see the Representation of the People Act 1983 s 202(1). As to the making of regulations under the Representation of the People Act 1983 generally see PARA 28 note 16. At the date at which this volume states the law, no such regulations had been made.

18　See the Representation of the People Act 1983 Sch 1 r 55(1). As to the meaning of 'constituency' in relation to a parliamentary election see PARA 9. As to provisions which govern the retention and public inspection of election documents see PARA 503.

497.　Forwarding of documents after postal voting at a parliamentary election. The returning officer at a parliamentary election[1], at the same time as he forwards the election documents collated from polling stations[2], must forward to the relevant registration officer[3] certain specified packets[4] containing documents relating to postal voting[5]. He must endorse on each such packet a description of its contents, the date of the election to which it relates, and the name of the constituency for which the election was held[6]. He must also forward to the relevant registration officer a completed statement in the prescribed form[7] of the number of postal ballot papers issued[8] at a parliamentary election[9], a copy of which must be provided to the Secretary of State[10], and to the Electoral Commission[11], by the returning officer, in the period which starts ten days after the day of the poll and ends 15 days after that day[12].

Where any covering envelopes[13] are received by the returning officer after the close of the poll[14], where any envelopes addressed to postal voters[15] are returned as undelivered too late to be re-addressed, or where any spoilt postal ballot papers[16] are returned too late to enable other postal ballot papers to be issued, the returning officer must put them unopened into a separate packet, seal up the packet and endorse and forward it at a subsequent date in the same manner as the postal voting packets previously forwarded[17].

Any such packet or statement that is forwarded in this way is deemed to have been forwarded in pursuance of the parliamentary elections rules[18] and is subject to the usual provisions which govern orders for the production of election documents[19] and the retention and public inspection of election documents[20].

1   As to the meaning of 'parliamentary election' see PARA 9. As to returning officers for parliamentary elections see PARA 350 et seq.
2   Ie the documents referred to in the Representation of the People Act 1983 Sch 1 r 55 (see PARA 496): see the Representation of the People (England and Wales) Regulations 2001, SI 2001/341, reg 91(1) (amended by SI 2006/2910).
3   See the Representation of the People (England and Wales) Regulations 2001, SI 2001/341, reg 91(1) (as amended: see note 2). The text refers to the relevant registration officer determined in accordance with the Representation of the People Act 1983 Sch 1 r 55(1A) (see PARA 496 note 3): see the Representation of the People (England and Wales) Regulations 2001, SI 2001/341, reg 91(1) (as so amended).
4   Ie any packets referred to in the Representation of the People (England and Wales) Regulations 2001, SI 2001/341, reg 75 (corresponding number lists and special lists: see PARA 412), reg 77(6) (spoilt postal ballot papers: see PARA 414), reg 78(2C) (cancelled postal ballot papers: see PARA 415), reg 84(9) (copy of the marked postal voters list and proxy postal voters list: see PARA 421) and reg 89 (contents of receptacles: see PARA 423): see reg 91(1)(a) (amended by SI 2006/752; SI 2006/2910).
5   See the Representation of the People (England and Wales) Regulations 2001, SI 2001/341, reg 91(1)(a) (as amended: see note 4). This provision is subject to reg 90 (countermand or abandonment of poll after postal ballot papers have been issued: see PARA 514); see reg 91(1)(a) (as so amended).
6   See the Representation of the People (England and Wales) Regulations 2001, SI 2001/341, reg 91(1)(a) (as amended: see note 4). As to the meaning of 'constituency' in relation to a parliamentary election see PARA 9.
7   The prescribed form is set out for the purposes of a parliamentary election in the Representation of the People (England and Wales) Regulations 2001, SI 2001/341, reg 91(1)(b), Sch 3 Forms (Form K: statement as to postal ballot papers) (substituted by SI 2006/2910). The version partly in Welsh and partly in English must be used at a parliamentary election in Wales as set out in the Parliamentary Elections (Welsh Forms) Order 2007, SI 2007/1014, art 6(1)(o), Sch 2 (Form 15 (Ffurflen 15): Form K: STATEMENT AS TO POSTAL BALLOT PAPERS/Ffurflen K: DATGANIAD YNGHYLCH PAPURAU PLEIDLEISIO DRWY'R POST).
8   As to the meaning of 'postal ballot paper' see PARA 407 note 1. As to the issue of postal ballot papers see PARA 406 et seq.
9   Representation of the People (England and Wales) Regulations 2001, SI 2001/341, reg 91(1)(b) (reg 91(1)(b), (5) amended by SI 2006/752).
10 As to the Secretary of State see PARA 2.
11 As to the Electoral Commission see PARA 34 et seq.
12 Representation of the People (England and Wales) Regulations 2001, SI 2001/341, reg 91(5) (as amended: see note 9).

13 As to the meaning of 'covering envelope' see PARA 410.

14 Ie apart from those delivered by the presiding officer in accordance with the provisions of the Representation of the People (England and Wales) Regulations 2001, SI 2001/341, reg 79(3) (see PARA 418): see reg 91(3).

15 As to the meaning of 'postal voter' see PARA 407 note 1.

16 As to spoilt postal ballot papers see PARA 414.

17 Representation of the People (England and Wales) Regulations 2001, SI 2001/341, reg 91(3). The text refers to forwarding the packet mentioned in the text at a subsequent date in the manner described in reg 91(1) (see the text and notes 1–9): see reg 91(3).

18 As to the meaning of 'parliamentary elections rules' see PARA 383 note 2.

19 Ie is subject to the Representation of the People Act 1983 Sch 1 r 56 (see PARAS 836, 851): see reg 91(4).

20 Representation of the People (England and Wales) Regulations 2001, SI 2001/341, reg 91(4). The text refers to the packets or documents forwarded as mentioned in the text being subject also to the provisions set out in the Representation of the People Act 1983 Sch 1 r 57 (see PARA 503): see the Representation of the People (England and Wales) Regulations 2001, SI 2001/341, reg 91(4).

498.   Transfer of documents relating to local government elections or a poll consequent on a parish meeting. The returning officer at a local government election[1], or at a poll consequent on a parish meeting involving an appointment to office[2], must, after sealing up the ballot papers[3], forward to the appropriate officer[4]:

(1)   the packets of ballot papers in his possession[5];

(2)   the ballot paper accounts, the statements of rejected ballot papers, and the statement of the result of the verification of the ballot paper accounts[6];

(3)   the tendered votes lists[7], the lists of voters with disabilities assisted by companions[8], the lists of votes marked by the presiding officers and the statements relating to them[9], the declarations made by the companions of voters with disabilities[10], and (except at a poll consequent on a parish meeting) the list of persons to whom ballot papers were delivered in consequence of an alteration to the register which took effect on the day of the poll[11];

(4)   the packets of the completed corresponding number lists[12] (or, in the case of a poll consequent on a parish meeting, the packets of counterfoils)[13];

(5)   the packets of certificates as to employment on duty on the day of the poll[14]; and

(6)   the packets containing marked copies of the registers of electors[15], and of the postal voters' list, of the lists of proxies and of the proxy postal voters' list[16].

At an Authority election, as well as forwarding the documents listed under heads (1) to (6) above, the CRO also must forward to the relevant registration officer the packet containing the electronic record (if any)[17]; and he must endorse on each packet a description of its contents, the date of election to which they relate, and the name of the Assembly constituency for which the election was held[18]. The returning officer for a local authority mayoral election also must endorse on each packet a description of its contents, the date of election to which they relate, and the name of the electoral area for which the election was held[19]; and, at a poll consequent on a parish meeting, the returning officer must endorse on each packet a description of its contents, the date of the poll to which they relate, and the name of the parish for which the poll was held[20].

1   As to the meaning of 'local government election' see PARA 11. As to elections in the City of London see PARA 33. As to returning officers for local government elections (which include local authority mayoral elections) see PARA 354 et seq. In the case of a London Authority election, the constituency returning officer (see PARA 211 note 9) is specified: see the Greater London Authority Elections Rules 2007, SI 2007/3541, Sch 1 r 57(1), Sch 2 r 60(1), Sch 3 r 60(1).

2   As to polls consequent on a parish meeting on a question involving appointment to office see PARA 200 et seq. As to the returning officer at a poll consequent on parish meeting see PARA 356.

3   As to the sealing up of ballot papers see PARA 495.

4   Ie:

    (1)   in the case of a local government election, the relevant registration officer (see the Local Elections (Principal Areas) (England and Wales) Rules 2006, SI 2006/3304, Sch 2 r 52(1); the Local Elections (Parishes and Communities) (England and Wales) Rules 2006, SI 2006/3305, Sch 2 r 52(1); the Local Authorities (Mayoral Elections) (England and Wales) Regulations 2007, SI 2007/1024, Sch 1 r 57; and the Greater London Authority Elections Rules 2007, SI 2007/3541, Sch 1 r 57(1), Sch 2 r 60(1), Sch 3 r 60(1));

    (2)   at a poll consequent on a parish meeting involving an appointment to office, the proper officer of the council of the district in which the parish is situate (see the Parish and Community Meetings (Polls) Rules 1987, SI 1987/1, Schedule r 34).

For the purposes of head (1) above, except in relation to an Authority election, references to the relevant registration officer are to the registration officer of the local authority in whose area the election is held (and, in the case of a parish or community election, in which the parish or community is situate): see the Local Elections (Principal Areas) (England and Wales) Rules 2006, SI 2006/3304, Sch 2 r 52(2); the Local Elections (Parishes and Communities) (England and Wales) Rules 2006, SI 2006/3305, Sch 2 r 52(2); and the Local Authorities (Mayoral Elections) (England and Wales) Regulations 2007, SI 2007/1024, Sch 1 r 57. As to registration officers see PARA 139 et seq. For the purposes of an Authority election, 'relevant registration officer' means the registration officer within the meaning of the Electoral Administration Act 2006 s 44(3)(a), or appointed by an order made under s 44(3)(b) (retention and inspection of documents relating to Authority elections: see PARA 508 note 5): see the Greater London Authority Elections Rules 2007, SI 2007/3541, r 2(1). As to the meaning of 'Authority election' see PARA 11. Any references in the Parish and Community Meetings (Polls) Rules 1987, SI 1987/1, to a proper officer of a council means any officer appointed for the purpose by that council: see Schedule r 38(3). As to the meaning of 'proper officer' generally see PARA 140 note 2.

5   Parish and Community Meetings (Polls) Rules 1987, SI 1987/1, Schedule r 34(a); Local Elections (Principal Areas) (England and Wales) Rules 2006, SI 2006/3304, Sch 2 r 52(1)(a); Local Elections (Parishes and Communities) (England and Wales) Rules 2006, SI 2006/3305, Sch 2 r 52(1)(a); Local Authorities (Mayoral Elections) (England and Wales) Regulations 2007, SI 2007/1024, Sch 1 r 57(a); Greater London Authority Elections Rules 2007, SI 2007/3541, Sch 1 r 57(1)(a), Sch 2 r 60(1)(a), Sch 3 r 60(1)(a).

6   Parish and Community Meetings (Polls) Rules 1987, SI 1987/1, Schedule r 34(b); Local Elections (Principal Areas) (England and Wales) Rules 2006, SI 2006/3304, Sch 2 r 52(1)(b); Local Elections (Parishes and Communities) (England and Wales) Rules 2006, SI 2006/3305, Sch 2 r 52(1)(b); Local Authorities (Mayoral Elections) (England and Wales) Regulations 2007, SI 2007/1024, Sch 1 r 57(b); Greater London Authority Elections Rules 2007, SI 2007/3541, Sch 1 r 57(1)(c), Sch 2 r 60(1)(c), Sch 3 r 60(1)(c).

7   As to the tendered votes list see PARA 403.

8   As to the list of voters with disabilities assisted by companions see PARA 402. At a poll consequent on a parish meeting involving an appointment to office, the reference is to the lists of blind voters assisted by companions: see the Parish and Community Meetings (Polls) Rules 1987, SI 1987/1, Schedule r 34 (c).

9   As to the list of votes marked by the presiding officer see PARA 401.

10 As to declarations made by the companions of voters with disabilities see PARA 402. At a poll consequent on a parish meeting involving an appointment to office, the reference is to the declarations made by the companions of blind voters: see the Parish and Community Meetings (Polls) Rules 1987, SI 1987/1, Schedule r 34 (c).

11 Parish and Community Meetings (Polls) Rules 1987, SI 1987/1, Schedule r 34(c); Local Elections (Principal Areas) (England and Wales) Rules 2006, SI 2006/3304, Sch 2 r 52(1)(c); Local Elections (Parishes and Communities) (England and Wales) Rules 2006, SI 2006/3305, Sch 2 r 52(1)(c); Local Authorities (Mayoral Elections) (England and Wales) Regulations 2007, SI 2007/1024, Sch 1 r 57(c); Greater London Authority Elections Rules 2007, SI 2007/3541, Sch 1 r 57(1)(d), Sch 2 r 60(1)(d), Sch 3 r 60(1)(d). Head (3) in the text refers to the list of persons maintained by the presiding officer, in relation to a local government election for a

principal area, under the Local Elections (Principal Areas) (England and Wales) Rules 2006, SI 2006/3304, Sch 2 r 41, or, in relation to a local government election for a parish and community council, under the Local Elections (Parishes and Communities) (England and Wales) Rules 2006, SI 2006/3305, Sch 2 r 41, or, in relation to a local authority mayoral election, under the Local Authorities (Mayoral Elections) (England and Wales) Regulations 2007, SI 2007/1024, Sch 1 r 43, or, in relation to an Authority election, under the Greater London Authority Elections Rules 2007, SI 2007/3541, Sch 1 r 44, Sch 2 r 45, Sch 3 r 44 (see PARA 399 note 5): see the Local Elections (Principal Areas) (England and Wales) Rules 2006, SI 2006/3304, Sch 2 r 52(1)(c); the Local Elections (Parishes and Communities) (England and Wales) Rules 2006, SI 2006/3305, Sch 2 r 52(1)(c); the Local Authorities (Mayoral Elections) (England and Wales) Regulations 2007, SI 2007/1024, Sch 1 r 57(c); and the Greater London Authority Elections Rules 2007, SI 2007/3541, Sch 1 r 57(1)(d), Sch 2 r 60(1)(d), Sch 3 r 60(1)(d).

12 Local Elections (Principal Areas) (England and Wales) Rules 2006, SI 2006/3304, Sch 2 r 52(1)(d); Local Elections (Parishes and Communities) (England and Wales) Rules 2006, SI 2006/3305, Sch 2 r 52(1)(d); Local Authorities (Mayoral Elections) (England and Wales) Regulations 2007, SI 2007/1024, Sch 1 r 57(d); Greater London Authority Elections Rules 2007, SI 2007/3541, Sch 1 r 57(1)(e), Sch 2 r 60(1)(e), Sch 3 r 60(1)(e). As to the completed corresponding number lists see PARA 405 note 11.

13 Parish and Community Meetings (Polls) Rules 1987, SI 1987/1, Schedule r 34(d).

14 Local Elections (Principal Areas) (England and Wales) Rules 2006, SI 2006/3304, Sch 2 r 52(1)(e); Local Elections (Parishes and Communities) (England and Wales) Rules 2006, SI 2006/3305, Sch 2 r 52(1)(e); Local Authorities (Mayoral Elections) (England and Wales) Regulations 2007, SI 2007/1024, Sch 1 r 57(e); Greater London Authority Elections Rules 2007, SI 2007/3541, Sch 1 r 57(1)(f), Sch 2 r 60(1)(f), Sch 3 r 60(1)(f). There is no provision for certificates as to employment on duty at a poll consequent on a parish meeting on a question involving appointment to office, and accordingly the reference to such certificates in head (5) in the text is omitted in that case. As to certificates of employment on duty on the day of the poll see PARA 395.

15 Ie including, in the case of a local government election, any marked copy notices of alteration to the register issued under the Representation of the People Act 1983 s 13B(3B) or s 13B(3D) (see PARA 168): see the Local Elections (Principal Areas) (England and Wales) Rules 2006, SI 2006/3304, Sch 2 r 52(1)(f); the Local Elections (Parishes and Communities) (England and Wales) Rules 2006, SI 2006/3305, Sch 2 r 52(1)(f); the Local Authorities (Mayoral Elections) (England and Wales) Regulations 2007, SI 2007/1024, Sch 1 r 57(f); and the Greater London Authority Elections Rules 2007, SI 2007/3541, Sch 1 r 57(1)(g), Sch 2 r 60(1)(g), Sch 3 r 60(1)(g).

16 Parish and Community Meetings (Polls) Rules 1987, SI 1987/1, Schedule r 34(e); Local Elections (Principal Areas) (England and Wales) Rules 2006, SI 2006/3304, Sch 2 r 52(1)(f); Local Elections (Parishes and Communities) (England and Wales) Rules 2006, SI 2006/3305, Sch 2 r 52(1)(f); Local Authorities (Mayoral Elections) (England and Wales) Regulations 2007, SI 2007/1024, Sch 1 r 57(f); Greater London Authority Elections Rules 2007, SI 2007/3541, Sch 1 r 57(1)(g), Sch 2 r 60(1)(g), Sch 3 r 60(1)(g). There is no provision for voting by proxy at a poll consequent on a parish meeting on a question involving appointment to office, and accordingly the references in head (6) in the text to the postal voters' list, the lists of proxies and the proxy postal voters' list are omitted in that case. As to the postal voters list and the list of proxies see PARA 373; and as to the proxy postal voters list see PARA 381.

17 Greater London Authority Elections Rules 2007, SI 2007/3541, Sch 1 r 57(1)(b), Sch 2 r 60(1)(b), Sch 3 r 60(1)(b). As to the electronic record see PARA 495 note 4.

18 See the Greater London Authority Elections Rules 2007, SI 2007/3541, Sch 1 r 57(1), Sch 2 r 60(1), Sch 3 r 60(1). As to the meaning of 'Assembly constituency' for these purposes see PARA 11 note 6.

19 See the Local Authorities (Mayoral Elections) (England and Wales) Regulations 2007, SI 2007/1024, Sch 1 r 57. As to the meaning of 'electoral area' see PARA 11.

20 See the Parish and Community Meetings (Polls) Rules 1987, SI 1987/1, Schedule r 34. As to parishes see LOCAL GOVERNMENT vol 69 (2009) PARA 27 et seq.

499. Transfer of documents relating to Welsh Assembly elections. Where an Assembly constituency returning officer[1] has conducted a count where the poll at a constituency election[2] and a regional election[3] have been taken together[4], he must then forward to the relevant registration officer[5]:

(1)   the packets of ballot papers in his possession relating to a constituency election[6];

(2)   the packets of ballot papers in his possession relating to a regional election[7];

(3)   the ballot paper accounts, the statement of rejected ballot papers, and the statement of the result of the verification of the ballot paper accounts, relating to a constituency election[8];

(4)   the ballot paper accounts, the statement of rejected ballot papers, and the statement of the result of the verification of the ballot paper accounts, relating to a regional election[9];

(5)   the tendered votes lists[10], the lists of voters with disabilities assisted by companions[11], the lists of votes marked by the presiding officer and the related statements[12], the list of persons to whom ballot papers were delivered in consequence of an alteration to the register which took effect on the day of the poll[13], and the declarations made by the companions of voters with disabilities[14], relating to the election (or, as the case may be, elections)[15];

(6)   the packets of the completed corresponding number lists[16];

(7)   the packets of the certificates as to employment on duty on the day of the poll, relating to the election (or, as the case may be, elections)[17]; and

(8)   the packets containing marked copies of the registers of electors[18], and of the postal voters' list, of the lists of proxies and of the proxy postal voters' list, relating to the election (or, as the case may be, elections)[19],

endorsing on each packet: (a) a description of its contents[20]; (b) the date of the election or elections to which they relate[21]; (c) where the packet relates to the constituency election, the name of the Assembly constituency[22] for which the election was held[23]; (d) where the packet relates to a regional election, the name of the Assembly electoral region[24] for which the election was held, and the name of the Assembly constituency in which the electoral region votes were given[25]; and (e) where the packet relates to both a constituency election and a regional election, the name of the Assembly constituency and electoral region for which the elections were held[26].

Where a constituency returning officer has conducted a count at an Assembly election other than one at which the polls for a constituency and a regional election were combined, he must forward to the relevant registration officer:

(i)   the packets of ballot papers in his possession[27];

(ii)   the ballot paper accounts, the statement of rejected ballot papers, and the statement of the result of the verification of the ballot paper accounts[28];

(iii)   the tendered votes lists, the lists of voters with disabilities assisted by companions, the lists of votes marked by the presiding officer and the related statements, the list of persons to whom ballot papers were delivered in consequence of an alteration to the register which took effect on the day of the poll[29], and the declarations made by the companions of voters with disabilities[30];

(iv)   the packets of the completed corresponding number lists[31];

(v)   the packets of the certificates as to employment on duty on the day of the poll[32]; and

(vi)   the packets containing marked copies of the registers of electors[33], and of the postal voters' list, of the lists of proxies and of the proxy postal voters' list[34], endorsing on each packet: (A) a description of its contents[35]; (B) the date of the election to which they relate[36]; (C) the name of the Assembly constituency or electoral region for which the election was held[37]; and (D) in the case of a regional election, the name of the Assembly constituency in which the electoral region votes were given[38].

1	As to the meaning of 'constituency returning officer' for these purposes see PARA 18 note 2.
2	As to the meanings of 'Assembly election' and 'constituency election' see PARA 3 note 2.
3	As to the meaning of 'Assembly regional election' see PARA 3 note 2.
4	As to counts made at Assembly elections see PARA 458 et seq.
5	See the National Assembly for Wales (Representation of the People) Order 2007, SI 2007/236, Sch 5 para 67(1). As to the meaning of 'relevant registration officer' see PARA 139 note 1.
6	National Assembly for Wales (Representation of the People) Order 2007, SI 2007/236, Sch 5 para 67(1)(a).
7	National Assembly for Wales (Representation of the People) Order 2007, SI 2007/236, Sch 5 para 67(1)(b).
8	National Assembly for Wales (Representation of the People) Order 2007, SI 2007/236, Sch 5 para 67(1)(c). As to the verification of the ballot paper account at a parliamentary election see PARA 425; and as to the statement of rejected ballot papers see PARA 460.
9	National Assembly for Wales (Representation of the People) Order 2007, SI 2007/236, Sch 5 para 67(1)(d).
10	As to the tendered votes list see PARA 403.
11	As to the list of voters with disabilities assisted by companions see PARA 402.
12	As to the list of votes marked by the presiding officer see PARA 401.
13	Ie the list of persons maintained by the presiding officer under the National Assembly for Wales (Representation of the People) Order 2007, SI 2007/236, Sch 5 para 51 (see PARA 399 note 5): see Sch 5 r 67(1)(e).
14	As to declarations made by the companions of voters with disabilities see PARA 402.
15	National Assembly for Wales (Representation of the People) Order 2007, SI 2007/236, Sch 5 para 67(1)(e).
16	National Assembly for Wales (Representation of the People) Order 2007, SI 2007/236, Sch 5 para 67(1)(f). As to the completed corresponding number lists see PARA 405 note 11.
17	National Assembly for Wales (Representation of the People) Order 2007, SI 2007/236, Sch 5 para 67(1)(g). As to certificates of employment on duty on the day of the poll see PARA 395.
18	Ie including any marked copy notices of alteration to the register issued under the Representation of the People Act 1983 s 13B(3B) or s 13B(3D) (see PARA 168): see the National Assembly for Wales (Representation of the People) Order 2007, SI 2007/236, Sch 5 para 67(1)(h).
19	National Assembly for Wales (Representation of the People) Order 2007, SI 2007/236, Sch 5 para 67(1)(h). As to the postal voters list and the list of proxies see PARA 373; and as to the proxy postal voters list see PARA 381.
20	National Assembly for Wales (Representation of the People) Order 2007, SI 2007/236, Sch 5 para 67(1)(i).
21	National Assembly for Wales (Representation of the People) Order 2007, SI 2007/236, Sch 5 para 67(1)(ii).
22	As to the meaning of 'Assembly constituency' for these purposes see PARA 3 note 2.
23	National Assembly for Wales (Representation of the People) Order 2007, SI 2007/236, Sch 5 para 67(1)(iii).
24	As to the meaning of 'electoral region' for these purposes see PARA 3 note 2.
25	National Assembly for Wales (Representation of the People) Order 2007, SI 2007/236, Sch 5 para 67(1)(iv).
26	National Assembly for Wales (Representation of the People) Order 2007, SI 2007/236, Sch 5 para 67(1)(v).
27	National Assembly for Wales (Representation of the People) Order 2007, SI 2007/236, Sch 5 para 67(2)(a).
28	National Assembly for Wales (Representation of the People) Order 2007, SI 2007/236, Sch 5 para 67(2)(b).
29	Ie the list of persons maintained by the presiding officer under the National Assembly for Wales (Representation of the People) Order 2007, SI 2007/236, Sch 5 para 51 (see PARA 399 note 5): see Sch 5 r 67(2)(c).
30	National Assembly for Wales (Representation of the People) Order 2007, SI 2007/236, Sch 5 para 67(2)(c).

31 National Assembly for Wales (Representation of the People) Order 2007, SI 2007/236, Sch 5 para 67(2)(d).

32 National Assembly for Wales (Representation of the People) Order 2007, SI 2007/236, Sch 5 para 67(2)(e).

33 Ie including any marked copy notices of alteration to the register issued under the Representation of the People Act 1983 s 13B(3B) or s 13B(3D) (see PARA 168): see the National Assembly for Wales (Representation of the People) Order 2007, SI 2007/236, Sch 5 para 67(2)(f).

34 National Assembly for Wales (Representation of the People) Order 2007, SI 2007/236, Sch 5 para 67(2)(f).

35 National Assembly for Wales (Representation of the People) Order 2007, SI 2007/236, Sch 5 para 67(2)(i).

36 National Assembly for Wales (Representation of the People) Order 2007, SI 2007/236, Sch 5 para 67(2)(ii).

37 National Assembly for Wales (Representation of the People) Order 2007, SI 2007/236, Sch 5 para 67(2)(iii).

38 National Assembly for Wales (Representation of the People) Order 2007, SI 2007/236, Sch 5 para 67(2)(iv).

500. Forwarding of documents after postal voting at Welsh Assembly election. The constituency returning officer at a Welsh Assembly election[1], at the same time as he forwards the election documents collated from polling stations[2], must forward to the relevant registration officer[3] certain specified packets[4] containing documents relating to postal voting[5]. He must endorse on each packet a description of its contents, the date of the election to which it relates, and the name of the Assembly constituency[6] or electoral area[7] for which the election was held (or for which the elections were held)[8]. He also must forward to the relevant registration officer a completed 'statement as to postal ballot papers' in the prescribed form[9], stating the number of postal ballot papers issued[10] at the election[11]. A copy of that statement must be provided by the constituency returning officer to the Electoral Commission[12] in the period which starts ten days after the day of the poll and ends 15 days after that day[13].

Where:

(1)   any covering envelopes[14] are received by the constituency returning officer[15] after the close of the poll[16];

(2)   any envelopes addressed to postal voters[17] are returned as undelivered too late to be re-addressed[18]; or

(3)   any spoilt postal ballot papers[19] are returned too late to enable other postal ballot papers to be issued[20],

the constituency returning officer must put them unopened into a separate packet, seal up the packet and endorse and forward it at a subsequent date in the same manner as the postal voting packets previously forwarded[21].

Any such packet or statement forwarded in this way is deemed to have been forwarded in pursuance of the elections rules[22] and is subject to the usual provisions that govern orders for the production of election documents, and their retention and public inspection[23].

1 As to the meaning of 'Assembly election' see PARA 3 note 2; and as to the meaning of 'constituency returning officer' for these purposes see PARA 18 note 2.

2 Ie at the same time as he forwards the documents mentioned in the National Assembly for Wales (Representation of the People) Order 2007, SI 2007/236, Sch 5 para 67 (delivery of documents to relevant registration officer: see PARA 499): see Sch 3 para 31(1).

3 As to the meaning of 'relevant registration officer' see PARA 139 note 1.

4 Ie any packets referred to in the National Assembly for Wales (Representation of the People) Order 2007, SI 2007/236, Sch 3 para 12 (corresponding number lists and special lists: see PARA 412), Sch 3 para 14(7) (spoilt postal ballot papers: see PARA 414), Sch 3 para 15(5)

(cancelled postal ballot papers: see PARA 415), Sch 3 para 20(11) (copy of the marked postal voters list and proxy postal voters list: see PARA 421) and Sch 3 para 29 (contents of receptacles: see PARA 423): see Sch 3 para 31(1)(a).

5   See the National Assembly for Wales (Representation of the People) Order 2007, SI 2007/236, Sch 3 para 31(1)(a). This provision is subject to Sch 3 para 30 (countermand or abandonment of poll after postal ballot papers have been issued: see PARA 517): see Sch 3 para 31(1)(a).

6   As to the meaning of 'Assembly constituency' for these purposes see PARA 3 note 2.

7   Ie in the case of combined polls (see PARA 20). As to the meaning of 'electoral area' see PARA 11.

8   See the National Assembly for Wales (Representation of the People) Order 2007, SI 2007/236, Sch 3 para 31(1)(a).

9   Ie a completed statement in the form set out in English and Welsh in the National Assembly for Wales (Representation of the People) Order 2007, SI 2007/236, Sch 10 (Form CD: Statement as to postal ballot papers): see Sch 3 para 31(1)(b).

10   As to the meaning of 'postal ballot paper' see PARA 407 note 1. As to the issue of postal ballot papers see PARA 406 et seq.

11   National Assembly for Wales (Representation of the People) Order 2007, SI 2007/236, Sch 3 para 31(1)(b).

12   As to the Electoral Commission see PARA 34 et seq.

13   National Assembly for Wales (Representation of the People) Order 2007, SI 2007/236, Sch 3 para 31(4).

14   As to the meaning of 'covering envelope' see PARA 410.

15   Ie apart from those delivered by the presiding officer in accordance with the National Assembly for Wales (Representation of the People) Order 2007, SI 2007/236, Sch 5 para 55(7) (see PARA 418): see Sch 3 para 31(2)(a).

16   National Assembly for Wales (Representation of the People) Order 2007, SI 2007/236, Sch 3 para 31(2)(a).

17   As to the meaning of 'postal voter' see PARA 407 note 1.

18   National Assembly for Wales (Representation of the People) Order 2007, SI 2007/236, Sch 3 para 31(2)(b).

19   As to spoilt postal ballot papers see PARA 414.

20   National Assembly for Wales (Representation of the People) Order 2007, SI 2007/236, Sch 3 para 31(2)(c).

21   See the National Assembly for Wales (Representation of the People) Order 2007, SI 2007/236, Sch 3 para 31(2). The text refers to forwarding the packet mentioned in the text at a subsequent date in the manner described in Sch 3 para 31(1) (see the text and notes 1–11): see Sch 3 para 31(2).

22   Ie the rules contained in the National Assembly for Wales (Representation of the People) Order 2007, SI 2007/236 (see PARA 383).

23   National Assembly for Wales (Representation of the People) Order 2007, SI 2007/236, Sch 3 para 31(3). This provision applies Sch 5 para 68 (order for production of documents: see PARAS 836, 851, 852) and Sch 5 para 69 (retention and public inspection of documents: see PARA 508) to any packet or document forwarded under Sch 3 para 31: see Sch 3 para 31(3).

501.   Transfer of documents relating to European parliamentary elections.
The local returning officer at a European parliamentary election[1] must, after sealing up the ballot papers[2], forward to the relevant registration officer[3]:

(1)   the packets of ballot papers in his possession[4];

(2)   the ballot paper accounts, the statements of rejected ballot papers, and the statement of the result of the verification of the ballot paper accounts[5];

(3)   the tendered votes lists[6], the lists of voters with disabilities assisted by companions[7], the lists of votes marked by the presiding officers and the statements relating to them[8], the list of persons to whom ballot papers were delivered in consequence of an alteration to the register which took effect on the day of the poll[9], and the declarations made by the companions of voters with disabilities[10];

(4)   the packets of the completed corresponding number lists[11];

(5)   the packets of certificates as to employment on duty on the day of the poll[12]; and

(6)   the packets containing marked copies of the registers of electors[13], and
of the postal voters' list, of the lists of proxies and of the proxy postal
voters' list[14].

endorsing on each packet a description of its contents[15].

1   As to European parliamentary elections see PARA 217 et seq; and as to local returning officers
appointed for the purposes of European parliamentary elections see PARA 360 et seq.
2   As to the sealing up of ballot papers see PARA 495.
3   See the European Parliamentary Elections Regulations 2004, SI 2004/293, Sch 1 para 64(1)
(Sch 1 substituted by SI 2009/186). As to the meaning of 'relevant registration officer' see PARA
139 note 1. For the purposes of European Parliamentary elections taking place in the combined
region see the European Parliamentary Elections Regulations 2004, SI 2004/293, Sch 1
para 64(3) (as so substituted). As to the establishment of electoral regions (including the
combined region) for the purpose of elections to the European Parliament see PARA 77.
4   European Parliamentary Elections Regulations 2004, SI 2004/293, Sch 1 para 64(1)(a) (as
substituted: see note 3).
5   European Parliamentary Elections Regulations 2004, SI 2004/293, Sch 1 para 64(1)(b) (as
substituted: see note 3). As to the verification of the ballot paper account at a parliamentary
election see PARA 425; and as to the statement of rejected ballot papers see PARA 469.
6   As to the tendered votes list see PARA 403.
7   As to the list of voters with disabilities assisted by companions see PARA 402.
8   As to the list of votes marked by the presiding officer see PARA 401.
9   Ie the list of persons maintained by the presiding officer under the European Parliamentary
Elections Regulations 2004, SI 2004/293, Sch 1 para 47 (see PARA 399 note 5): see Sch 1
para 64(1)(c) (as substituted: see note 3).
10   European Parliamentary Elections Regulations 2004, SI 2004/293, Sch 1 para 64(1)(c) (as
substituted: see note 3). As to declarations made by the companions of voters with disabilities
see PARA 402.
11   European Parliamentary Elections Regulations 2004, SI 2004/293, Sch 1 para 64(1)(d) (as
substituted: see note 3). As to the completed corresponding number lists see PARA 405 note 11.
12   European Parliamentary Elections Regulations 2004, SI 2004/293, Sch 1 para 64(1)(e) (as
substituted: see note 3). As to certificates of employment on duty on the day of the poll see
PARA 395.
13   Ie including any marked copy notices of alteration to the register issued under the
Representation of the People Act 1983 s 13B(3B) or s 13B(3D) (see PARA 168): see the European
Parliamentary Elections Regulations 2004, SI 2004/293, Sch 1 para 64(1)(f) (as substituted: see
note 3).
14   European Parliamentary Elections Regulations 2004, SI 2004/293, Sch 1 para 64(1)(f) (as
substituted: see note 3). As to the postal voters list and the list of proxies see PARA 373; and as
to the proxy postal voters list see PARA 381.
15   See the European Parliamentary Elections Regulations 2004, SI 2004/293, Sch 1 para 64(1) (as
substituted: see note 3).

**502.   Forwarding of documents after postal voting at a European
parliamentary election.** The local returning officer at a European parliamentary
election[1], at the same time as he forwards the election documents collated from
polling stations[2], must forward to the relevant registration officer[3] certain
specified packets[4] containing documents relating to postal voting[5]. He must
endorse on each packet a description of its contents[6]. Where the proceedings on
the issue and receipt of postal ballot papers are taken together[7], the returning
officer[8], or local returning officer discharging those functions, must forward the
packets containing[9]:

(1)   the marked copies of the postal voters list and proxy postal voters list[10];
and
(2)   the postal voting statements[11],

to the same person, and at the same time and in the same manner, as he is
required to forward those documents as respects the election or referendum for
which he is the returning officer[12].

The local returning officer also must provide a completed 'statement as to postal ballot papers' in the prescribed form[13] to the Secretary of State[14], and to the Electoral Commission[15], in the period which starts ten days after the day of the poll and ends 15 days after that day[16].

Where:

(a)   any covering envelopes[17] are received by the local returning officer[18] after the close of the poll[19];

(b)   any envelopes addressed to postal voters[20] are returned as undelivered too late to be re-addressed[21]; or

(c)   any spoilt postal ballot papers[22] are returned too late to enable other postal ballot papers to be issued[23],

the local returning officer must put them unopened into a separate packet, seal up the packet and endorse and retain it, and subsequently deal with it in the same manner as the postal voting packets previously forwarded[24].

Any such packet or statement forwarded in this way is deemed to have been forwarded in pursuance of the European parliamentary elections rules[25] and is subject to the provisions of those rules that govern orders for the production of election documents, and their retention and public inspection[26].

1   As to European parliamentary elections see PARA 217 et seq; and as to local returning officers appointed for the purposes of European parliamentary elections see PARA 360 et seq.

2   Ie at the same time as he forwards the documents mentioned in the European Parliamentary Elections Regulations 2004, SI 2004/293, Sch 1 para 64 (forwarding of documents by local returning officer at a European parliamentary election to relevant registration officer: see PARA 501): see Sch 2 para 70(1) (Sch 2 substituted by SI 2009/186; European Parliamentary Elections Regulations 2004, SI 2004/293, Sch 2 para 70(1) amended by SI 2009/848).

3   As to the meaning of 'relevant registration officer' see PARA 139 note 1.

4   Ie the packets referred to in the European Parliamentary Elections Regulations 2004, SI 2004/293, Sch 2 para 51(1) (corresponding number lists and special lists: see PARA 412), Sch 2 para 53(7) (spoilt postal ballot papers: see PARA 414), Sch 2 para 54(5) (cancelled postal ballot papers: see PARA 415), Sch 2 para 60(11) (copy of the marked postal voters list and proxy postal voters list: see PARA 421) and Sch 2 para 69 (contents of receptacles: see PARA 423): see Sch 2 para 70(1) (as substituted and amended: see note 2).

5   See the European Parliamentary Elections Regulations 2004, SI 2004/293, Sch 2 para 70(1) (as substituted and amended: see note 2).

6   See the European Parliamentary Elections Regulations 2004, SI 2004/293, Sch 2 para 70(1) (as substituted and amended: see note 2).

7   Ie under the European Parliamentary Elections Regulations 2004, SI 2004/293, Sch 2 para 41 (proceedings on issue and receipt of postal ballot papers where polls are combined: see PARA 20): see Sch 2 para 70(2) (as substituted: see note 2). As to the meaning of 'postal ballot paper' see PARA 407 note 1. As to the issue of postal ballot papers generally see PARA 406 et seq.

8   As to returning officers appointed for the purposes of European parliamentary elections see PARA 360 et seq.

9   See the European Parliamentary Elections Regulations 2004, SI 2004/293, Sch 2 para 70(2) (as substituted: see note 2).

10   European Parliamentary Elections Regulations 2004, SI 2004/293, Sch 2 para 70(2)(a) (as substituted: see note 2). As to the postal voters list see PARA 373; and as to the proxy postal voters list see PARA 381.

11   European Parliamentary Elections Regulations 2004, SI 2004/293, Sch 2 para 70(2)(b) (as substituted: see note 2). As to the postal voters statements see PARA 406.

12   See the European Parliamentary Elections Regulations 2004, SI 2004/293, Sch 2 para 70(2) (as substituted: see note 2).

13   Ie a completed statement in the form set out in the European Parliamentary Elections Regulations 2004, SI 2004/293, Sch 2 Appendix of Forms (Form R: statement as to postal ballot papers): see Sch 2 para 70(5) (as substituted: see note 2). Such a statement must identify the local counting areas within the electoral region for which it is prepared: see Sch 2 para 70(6) (as so substituted). As to the meaning of 'local counting area' see PARA 139 note 1. As to the electoral areas established for the purposes of European parliamentary elections see PARA 77.

    The version of the form partly in Welsh and partly in English which must be used at a European parliamentary election in Wales is set out in the European Parliamentary Elections (Welsh Forms) Order 2009, SI 2009/781, art 6(1)(p), Sch 2 (Form 16 (Ffurflen 16): statement as to postal ballot papers, datganiad ynghylch papurau pleidleisio drwy'r post).

14 As to the Secretary of State see PARA 2.

15 As to the Electoral Commission see PARA 34 et seq.

16 See the European Parliamentary Elections Regulations 2004, SI 2004/293, Sch 2 para 70(5) (as substituted: see note 2).

17 As to the meaning of 'covering envelope' see PARA 410.

18 Ie apart from those delivered by the presiding officer in accordance with the European Parliamentary Elections Regulations 2004, SI 2004/293, Sch 2 para 55(2) (see PARA 418): see Sch 2 para 70(3)(a) (as substituted: see note 2).

19 European Parliamentary Elections Regulations 2004, SI 2004/293, Sch 2 para 70(3)(a) (as substituted: see note 2).

20 As to the meaning of 'postal voter' see PARA 407 note 1.

21 European Parliamentary Elections Regulations 2004, SI 2004/293, Sch 2 para 70(3)(b) (as substituted: see note 2).

22 As to spoilt postal ballot papers see PARA 414.

23 European Parliamentary Elections Regulations 2004, SI 2004/293, Sch 2 para 70(3)(c) (as substituted: see note 2).

24 See the European Parliamentary Elections Regulations 2004, SI 2004/293, Sch 2 para 70(3) (as substituted: see note 2). The text refers to subsequently dealing with any such packet mentioned in the text in the manner described in Sch 2 para 70(1) (see the text and notes 1–6): see Sch 2 para 70(3) (as so substituted).

25 Ie the rules contained in the European Parliamentary Elections Regulations 2004, SI 2004/293 (the 'European parliamentary elections rules': see PARA 383 note 16).

26 European Parliamentary Elections Regulations 2004, SI 2004/293, Sch 2 para 70(4) (as substituted: see note 2). This provision applies Sch 1 para 65 (order for production of documents: see PARAS 836, 851, 852) and Sch 1 para 66 (supply to relevant registration officer, and retention by him of, documents relating to European parliamentary elections: see PARA 510) to any packet or document forwarded under Sch 2 para 70: see Sch 2 para 70(4) (as so substituted).

C. RETENTION, INSPECTION AND SUPPLY OF ELECTION DOCUMENTS

(A) Documents relating to Parliamentary Elections

503. Requirement to retain and supply documents relating to parliamentary elections. The relevant registration officer[1] must retain for a year all documents relating to a parliamentary election[2] forwarded to him by a returning officer[3]; and then, unless otherwise directed by an order of the House of Commons or the High Court, the Crown Court or a magistrates' court[4], he must cause them to be destroyed[5]. All documents so retained, except:

(1)   ballot papers[6];

(2)   the completed corresponding number lists[7]; and

(3)   certificates as to employment on the day of the poll[8],

must be open to public inspection[9].

    The relevant registration officer must, on request, supply to any person copies of or extracts from such description of the documents open to public inspection as is prescribed by regulations[10]; and a copy of the marked copies of the register, the postal voters list[11], the list of proxies[12] and the proxy postal voters list[13] must, on request, be supplied to[14]: (a) a registered party[15]; or (b) a person who was a candidate at the election, in relation to the constituency for which he was a candidate[16].

1 As to the meaning of references to the relevant registration officer for these purposes see PARA 496 note 3.

2 Ie except each candidate's home address form, which the returning officer must destroy: (1) on the next working day following the twenty-first day after the officer has returned the name of the member elected (Representation of the People Act 1983 Sch 1 r 53A(a) (Sch 1 r 53A added by the Political Parties and Elections Act 2009 s 24(1), (7))); or (2) if an election petition questioning the election or return is presented before that day, on the next working day following the conclusion of proceedings on the petition or on appeal from such proceedings (Representation of the People Act 1983 Sch 1 r 53A(b) (as so added)). As to the meaning of 'parliamentary election' see PARA 9. As to the meaning of 'candidate' see PARA 230. As to the requirement for a nomination paper at a parliamentary election to be accompanied by a home address form see PARA 256. As to returning officers for parliamentary elections see PARA 350 et seq. As to return to the writ and record of returns in parliamentary elections see PARA 480. As to election petitions at parliamentary elections see PARA 761 et seq.

3 Ie forwarded to the relevant registration officer in pursuance of the parliamentary elections rules by a returning officer: see the Representation of the People Act 1983 Sch 1 r 57(1) (amended by the Electoral Administration Act 2006 ss 41(1), (5)(a), 70(2), 78(3)). As to the meaning of 'parliamentary elections rules' see PARA 383 note 2. As to the transfer of documents relating to parliamentary elections see PARA 496. As to the penalty for breach of duty by persons responsible for used ballot papers and other documents see PARA 737; and as to offences which relate to persons who interfere with access to or the control of election documents see PARA 745.

4 As to the production and inspection of documents by order of the House of Commons or the court see PARAS 836, 851, 852.

5 Representation of the People Act 1983 Sch 1 r 57(1) (as amended: see note 3). For the purposes of prosecuting an offence under the Representation of the People Act 1983, an application may be made for an order to extend the period of time for which election documents are required to be retained under Sch 1 r 57(1): see PARA 883.

6 Representation of the People Act 1983 Sch 1 r 57(2)(a) (Sch 1 r 57(2) substituted by the Electoral Administration Act 2006 s 31(1), (8)). As to the sealing up of ballot papers see PARA 495.

7 Representation of the People Act 1983 Sch 1 r 57(2)(b) (as substituted: see note 6). As to the completed corresponding number lists see PARA 405 note 11.

8 Representation of the People Act 1983 Sch 1 r 57(2)(c) (as substituted: see note 6). As to certificates of employment on duty on the day of the poll see PARA 395.

9 See the Representation of the People Act 1983 Sch 1 r 57(2) (as substituted: see note 6). Regulations may impose conditions in relation to the inspection of any document in pursuance of Sch 1 r 57(2): see Sch 1 r 57(5)(a) (Sch 1 r 57(3) substituted, Sch 1 r 57(4)–(9) added, by the Electoral Administration Act 2006 s 41(1), (5)(b), (c)). Conditions which may be imposed for these purposes include conditions as to:
    (1) whether a person may take any copy of a document he is permitted to inspect (Representation of the People Act 1983 Sch 1 r 57(7)(a) (as so added));
    (2) the manner in which any such copy is to be taken (Sch 1 r 57(7)(b) (as so added)); and
    (3) the purposes for which information contained in any document or part of a document which is inspected in pursuance of Sch 1 r 57(2) may be used (Sch 1 r 57(7)(c) (as so added)).
   As to the making of regulations under the Representation of the People Act 1983 generally see PARA 28 note 16. As to the regulations so made see PARA 504.

10 Representation of the People Act 1983 Sch 1 r 57(3) (as substituted: see note 9). Regulations may impose conditions in relation to the supply of any document or part of a document in pursuance of Sch 1 r 57(3): see Sch 1 r 57(5)(b) (Sch 1 r 57(5), (7) as added: see note 9). Conditions which may be imposed for these purposes include conditions as to:
    (1) the purposes for which information contained in any document or part of a document which is supplied in pursuance of Sch 1 r 57(3) may be used (Sch 1 r 57(7)(c) (as so added)); and
    (2) conditions as to the extent to which a person to whom a document or part of a document has been supplied may: (a) supply that document or part to any other person (Sch 1 r 57(8)(a) (as so added)); (b) disclose to any other person any information contained in the document or part (Sch 1 r 57(8)(b) (as so added)); and (c) use any such information for a purpose other than that for which the document or part was supplied to him (Sch 1 r 57(8)(c) (as so added)).
   Regulations may also make provision as to the form in which any such document or part is supplied and for the payment of a fee in respect of the supply of a document or part: Sch 1 r 57(6) (as so added). As to the regulations so made see PARA 504.

11 As to the postal voters list see PARA 373.

12 As to the list of proxies see PARA 373.

13 As to the proxy postal voters list see PARA 381.
14 See the Representation of the People Act 1983 Sch 1 r 57(4) (Sch 1 r 57(4)–(6), (8), (9) as added: see note 9). Regulations may impose conditions in relation to the supply of any document or part of a document in pursuance of Sch 1 r 57(4): see Sch 1 r 57(5)(c) (as so added). Conditions which may be imposed for these purposes include conditions as to the extent to which a person to whom a document or part of a document has been supplied may:
   (1)   supply that document or part to any other person (Sch 1 r 57(8)(a) (as so added));
   (2)   disclose to any other person any information contained in the document or part (Sch 1 r 57(8)(b) (as so added)); and
   (3)   use any such information for a purpose other than that for which the document or part was supplied to him (Sch 1 r 57(8)(c) (as so added)).
   Regulations may also: (a) make provision as to the form in which any such document or part is supplied and for the payment of a fee in respect of the supply of a document or part (see Sch 1 r 57(6) (as so added)); and (b) impose conditions corresponding to those mentioned in Sch 1 r 57(8) (see heads (1) to (3) above) in respect of persons who have obtained a document or part of a document mentioned in Sch 1 r 57(4) which was supplied to another person in pursuance of Sch 1 r 57(4) or otherwise than in accordance with regulations made under Sch 1 r 57 (see Sch 1 r 57(9) (as so added)). As to the regulations so made see PARA 504.
15 Representation of the People Act 1983 Sch 1 r 57(4)(a) (as added: see note 9). Head (a) in the text refers to a registered party within the meaning of the Political Parties, Elections and Referendums Act 2000 Pt II (ss 22–40) (see PARA 253): see the Representation of the People Act 1983 Sch 1 r 57(4)(a) (as so added).
16 Representation of the People Act 1983 Sch 1 r 57(4)(b) (as added: see note 9). As to the meaning of 'constituency' for these purposes see PARA 9.

504.   Supply and inspection of documents relating to parliamentary elections.
Any person entitled to be supplied[1] with copies of the full register[2] at a particular parliamentary election is also a person entitled[3] to request[4] that a relevant registration officer supply copies of the relevant part[5] of the marked register or lists he is required to keep[6]. The relevant registration officer must supply a copy of the relevant part of the marked register or lists where a request is duly made[7], and where:
   (1)   he is satisfied that the requestor needs to see the marks on the marked register or lists in order to achieve the purpose for which it is requested[8]; and
   (2)   he has received payment of a fee[9].
If the relevant registration officer is not satisfied in accordance with head (1) above, he may treat the request for a marked register or list as a request for information in unmarked lists[10], or as a request for the published copy of the full register[11], or both[12].
   Any person is entitled to request that the relevant registration officer make available for inspection a copy of any of the following documents ('the documents open to public inspection')[13]:
   (a)   the marked register or lists[14];
   (b)   such other documents relating to an election as the relevant registration officer is required by or under any enactment to retain for any period[15], except: (i) ballot papers[16]; (ii) completed corresponding number lists[17]; and (iii) certificates as to employment on the day of the election[18].
The relevant registration officer must make the documents open to public inspection available for inspection under supervision not later than ten days[19] after the date of receipt of a request that has been duly made[20]. However, where a request has been made to inspect copies of the marked register or lists[21], and where the relevant registration officer is not satisfied that the purposes of the requestor cannot be met by inspection of the full register, he must inform the requestor of his decision to this effect, and he must provide the requestor with information concerning the availability for inspection of the published full

register[22]. The relevant registration officer must, on request, supply free of charge copies of any documents open to public inspection to each of the Security Service[23], the Government Communications Headquarters[24], and the Secret Intelligence Service[25], and to a person who has inspected those documents and who is entitled to be supplied with a copy of the marked register or lists[26].

1   Ie in accordance with the Representation of the People (England and Wales) Regulations 2001, SI 2001/341, reg 100 (supply of full register to Electoral Commission: see PARA 183), reg 103 (supply of full register to elected representatives for electoral purposes: see PARA 185), reg 105 (supply of full register to local constituency parties: see PARA 185), reg 106 (supply of full register to registered political parties: see PARA 185), reg 108 (supply of full register to certain candidates: see PARA 185), reg 109 (supply of full register to police forces and other agencies: see PARA 186) or reg 113 (sale of full register to certain government departments and other bodies: see PARA 188): see reg 117(1) (regs 116–120 added by SI 2006/2910).
2   As to the meaning of 'full register' see PARA 167 note 2.
3   Ie subject to the Representation of the People (England and Wales) Regulations 2001, SI 2001/341, reg 117 (see also the text and notes 1–2, 4–12) and reg 119 (see notes 6, 13, 26): see reg 117(1) (as added: see note 1).
4   A person whose entitlement to request copies of the marked register or lists under the Representation of the People (England and Wales) Regulations 2001, SI 2001/341, reg 117(1) arises from being in a category of persons covered by reg 103 (supply of full register to elected representatives for electoral purposes: see PARA 185), reg 105 (supply of full register to local constituency parties: see PARA 185), reg 106 (supply of full register to registered political parties: see PARA 185) or reg 108 (supply of full register to certain candidates: see PARA 185) before a particular election, is entitled to request those documents regardless of whether he remains in an entitled category after that election for which the marked register or list was prepared: reg 117(2) (as added: see note 1). In Pt 7 (regs 116–120), references to the 'marked register or lists' means any part of the marked copies of:
     (1)   the full register (reg 116(1)(a) (as so added));
     (2)   the notices of alteration amending the full register issued under the Representation of the People Act 1983 s 13B(3B) or s 13B(3D) (see PARA 168) (Representation of the People (England and Wales) Regulations 2001, SI 2001/341, reg 116(1)(aa) (reg 116 as so added; reg 116(1)(aa) added by SI 2008/1901));
     (3)   the postal voters list (Representation of the People (England and Wales) Regulations 2001, SI 2001/341, reg 116(1)(b) (as so added));
     (4)   the list of proxies (reg 116(1)(c) (as so added)); and
     (5)   the proxy postal voters list (reg 116(1)(d) (as so added)),
     forwarded to the relevant registration officer either under the Representation of the People Act 1983 Sch 1 r 55(1)(e) (see PARA 496) or under the Representation of the People (England and Wales) Regulations 2001, SI 2001/341, reg 91 (see PARA 497) (see reg 116(1) (reg 116 as so added; reg 116(1) amended by SI 2007/1025). As to the meaning of references to the relevant registration officer for these purposes see PARA 496 note 3. As to the postal voters list and the list of proxies see PARA 373; and as to the proxy postal voters list see PARA 381.
          The Representation of the People (England and Wales) Regulations 2001, SI 2001/341, Pt 7, applies, subject to modifications, in respect of the marked Assembly register or lists and the other relevant Assembly election documents as it applies in respect of the marked register or lists and other documents open to inspection: see regs 121–126; and PARA 509. Regulations 116, 118, and 119 also have effect for the purposes of local authority referendums, subject to the modifications specified, in relation to Wales, by the Local Authorities (Conduct of Referendums) (Wales) Regulations 2008, SI 2008/1848, reg 8(2), Sch 4 Table 5, and, in relation to England, by the Local Authorities (Conduct of Referendums) (England) Regulations 2012, SI 2012/323, regs 8(2), 11–13, Sch 4 Table 6 (see PARA 15 note 2).
5   Ie within the meaning of the Representation of the People (England and Wales) Regulations 2001, SI 2001/341, reg 100 (supply of full register to Electoral Commission: see PARA 183), reg 103 (supply of full register to elected representatives for electoral purposes: see PARA 185), reg 105 (supply of full register to local constituency parties: see PARA 185), reg 106 (supply of full register to registered political parties: see PARA 185), reg 108 (supply of full register to certain candidates: see PARA 185), reg 109 (supply of full register to police forces and other agencies: see PARA 186) or reg 113 (sale of full register to government departments and other bodies: see PARA 188): see reg 117(1) (as added: see note 1).
6   Representation of the People (England and Wales) Regulations 2001, SI 2001/341, reg 117(1) (as added: see note 1). A request under reg 117(1) must be made in writing; and it must:

(1)   specify which of the marked register or lists (or the relevant part of the register or lists) are requested (reg 117(3)(a) (as so added));

(2)   state whether a printed copy of the records or lists is requested or a copy in data form (reg 117(3)(b) (as so added)); and

(3)   state the purposes for which the marked register or lists will be used and why the supply or purchase of a copy of the full register or unmarked lists would not be sufficient to achieve that purpose (reg 117(3)(c) (as so added)).

Subject to any direction by the Secretary of State under the Representation of the People Act 1983 s 52(1) (discharge of registration duties: see PARA 141), any duty on a relevant registration officer to supply records or lists under the Representation of the People (England and Wales) Regulations 2001, SI 2001/341, Pt 7 imposes only a duty to provide that information in the form in which he holds it, however: see reg 116(4) (as so added). As to the meaning of 'data form' see PARA 180 note 11. As to the Secretary of State see PARA 2.

A person who obtains a copy of any part of a marked register or list under reg 117 may use it only for the permitted purposes specified in reg 119(2), and any conditions specified in reg 119(2) (or any conditions which would apply to the use of the full register under whichever of reg 100 (supply of full register to Electoral Commission: see PARA 183), reg 103 (supply of full register to elected representatives for electoral purposes: see PARA 185), reg 105 (supply of full register to local constituency parties: see PARA 185), reg 106 (supply of full register to registered political parties: see PARA 185), reg 108 (supply of full register to certain candidates: see PARA 185), reg 109 (supply of full register to police forces and other agencies: see PARA 186) or reg 113 (sale of full register to government departments and other bodies: see PARA 188), entitled that person to obtain that document) apply to such use: see reg 117(6) (as so added). The conditions in reg 100(3) (see PARA 183), reg 103(3) (see PARA 185), reg 105(4) (see PARA 185), reg 106(3) (see PARA 185), reg 108(5) (see PARA 185), and reg 109(3) (see PARA 186), apply to a person to whom a marked register or list, or any information contained in it (that is not contained in the edited register), has been so supplied or disclosed as they apply to the person to whom those regulations apply: reg 117(7) (reg 117 as so added; reg 117(7) amended by SI 2007/1025). As to the meaning of 'edited register' see PARA 167 note 4.

Any person who has obtained or is entitled to obtain a copy of the marked register or lists under the Representation of the People (England and Wales) Regulations 2001, SI 2001/341, reg 117 may:

(a)   supply a copy of the marked register or lists to a processor for the purpose of processing the information contained therein (reg 117(8)(a) (as so added)); or

(b)   procure that a processor processes and supplies to him any copy of the information in the marked register or lists which the processor has obtained under reg 117 (reg 117(8)(b) (as so added)),

for use in respect of the purposes for which that person is entitled to obtain any such copy or information (as the case may be) (reg 117(8) (as so added)). The processor may not disclose the information so supplied except to the person who supplied it to the processor or an employee of that person or a person who is entitled to obtain a copy of the full register under the Representation of the People (England and Wales) Regulations 2001, SI 2001/341 or any employee of such a person: reg 92(9) (reg 92 added by SI 2002/1871); applied by the Representation of the People (England and Wales) Regulations 2001, SI 2001/341, reg 116(3) (as so added). Where a person obtains copies of the information in the marked register or lists in accordance with reg 117(1), the permitted purpose (see PARA 179 note 18) means either research purposes within the meaning of that term in the Data Protection Act 1998 s 33 (see CONFIDENCE AND INFORMATIONAL PRIVACY vol 19 (2011) PARA 144) or electoral purposes: Representation of the People (England and Wales) Regulations 2001, SI 2001/341, reg 119(2) (as so added). As to references to an employee of any person who has access to a copy of the full register see PARA 180 note 6 (applied by virtue of reg 116(3) (as so added)). As to the meaning of 'processor' see PARA 180 note 11 (applied by virtue of reg 116(3) (as so added)).

7   Representation of the People (England and Wales) Regulations 2001, SI 2001/341, reg 117(4) (as added: see note 1).

8   Representation of the People (England and Wales) Regulations 2001, SI 2001/341, reg 117(4)(a) (as added: see note 1).

9   Representation of the People (England and Wales) Regulations 2001, SI 2001/341, reg 117(4)(b) (as added: see note 1). The fee mentioned in head (2) in the text must be calculated in accordance with reg 120: see reg 117(4)(b) (as so added). Accordingly, the fee to be paid in accordance with reg 117(4)(b) by a person making a request for a copy of the whole or of any part of the marked register or lists must be the sum of £10 (see reg 120(1), (2) (reg 120 as so added; substituted by SI 2008/1901)), plus:

(1)   for a copy in printed form, £2 for each 1,000 entries (or remaining part of 1,000 entries) covered by the request (reg 120(2)(a) (as so added and substituted)); and

(2)   for a copy in data form, £1 for each 1,000 entries (or remaining part of 1,000 entries) covered by the request (reg 120(2)(b) (as so added and substituted)).

For these purposes, a request for a copy of the whole or the same part of the marked register or lists in both a printed and data form may be treated as two separate requests: see reg 120(3) (as so substituted).

10 Ie under the Representation of the People (England and Wales) Regulations 2001, SI 2001/341, reg 61 (see PARA 185 note 11): see reg 117(5) (as added: see note 1).

11 Ie in accordance with the Representation of the People (England and Wales) Regulations 2001, SI 2001/341, reg 102 (see PARA 185): see reg 117(5) (as added: see note 1).

12 Representation of the People (England and Wales) Regulations 2001, SI 2001/341, reg 117(5) (as added: see note 1).

13 See the Representation of the People (England and Wales) Regulations 2001, SI 2001/341, reg 118(1) (as added: see note 1). A request under reg 118(1) must be made in writing; and it must specify:

(1)   which documents are requested (reg 118(2)(a) (as so added));

(2)   the purposes for which the information in any document will be used (reg 118(2)(b) (as so added));

(3)   any reason why inspecting the full register or unmarked lists would not be sufficient to achieve that purpose (ie where the request is to inspect the marked register or lists) (reg 118(2)(c) (as so added));

(4)   who will inspect the documents (reg 118(2)(d) (as so added));

(5)   the date on which they wish to inspect the documents (reg 118(2)(e) (as so added)); and

(6)   whether they would prefer to inspect the documents in a printed or data form (reg 118(2)(f) (as so added)).

Subject to any direction by the Secretary of State under the Representation of the People Act 1983 s 52(1) (discharge of registration duties: see PARA 141), any duty on a registration officer to make records or lists available for inspection under the Representation of the People (England and Wales) Regulations 2001, SI 2001/341, Pt 7 imposes only a duty to provide that information in the form in which he holds it, however: see reg 116(4) (as so added).

A person who obtains a copy of or information in any document open to public inspection under reg 118 may use it only for the permitted purposes specified in reg 119; and any conditions:

(a)   specified in reg 119 (see reg 118(5)(a) (as so added));

(b)   specified in reg 118(7) (see reg 118(5)(b) (as so added)); or

(c)   which would apply to the use of the full register under reg 109 (supply of full register to police forces and other agencies: see PARA 186) where such a person has obtained a copy of that document under reg 118(8) (see the text and notes 23–26) (see reg 118(5)(c) (as so added)),

apply to such use (see reg 118(5) (as so added)). The restrictions on the supply, disclosure and use of the full register in reg 94 (restrictions on supply of full register and disclosure of information from it by the registration officer and his staff: see PARA 179) and reg 96 (restrictions on use of full register or information contained in it: see PARA 179) apply to documents open to public inspection, as they apply to the full register (reg 119(1) (as so added)), except that, where a person inspects information in accordance with reg 118(1), the permitted purpose (see PARA 179 note 18) means either research purposes within the meaning of that term in the Data Protection Act 1998 s 33 (see CONFIDENCE AND INFORMATIONAL PRIVACY vol 19 (2011) PARA 144) or electoral purposes (Representation of the People (England and Wales) Regulations 2001, SI 2001/341, reg 119(2) (as so added)).

14 Representation of the People (England and Wales) Regulations 2001, SI 2001/341, reg 118(1)(a) (as added: see note 1).

15 Representation of the People (England and Wales) Regulations 2001, SI 2001/341, reg 118(1)(b) (as added: see note 1). As to the meaning of 'enactment' see PARA 179 note 8 (applied by virtue of reg 116(3) (as so added)).

16 Representation of the People (England and Wales) Regulations 2001, SI 2001/341, reg 118(1)(b)(i) (as added: see note 1). As to the sealing up of ballot papers see PARA 495.

17 Representation of the People (England and Wales) Regulations 2001, SI 2001/341, reg 118(1)(b)(ii) (as added: see note 1). As to the completed corresponding number lists see PARA 405 note 11.

18 Representation of the People (England and Wales) Regulations 2001, SI 2001/341, reg 118(1)(b)(iii) (as added: see note 1). As to certificates of employment on duty on the day of the poll see PARA 395.

19 For these purposes, any period of days must be calculated in accordance with the Representation of the People (England and Wales) Regulations 2001, SI 2001/341, reg 56(6) and reg 56(7) (see PARA 367 note 6): see reg 116(2) (as added: see note 1).

20 Representation of the People (England and Wales) Regulations 2001, SI 2001/341, reg 118(3) (reg 118 as added: see note 1). Where inspection takes place by providing a copy of the records or lists on a computer screen or otherwise in data form, the relevant registration officer must ensure that the manner in, and equipment on, which that copy is provided do not permit any person consulting that copy to search it by electronic means by reference to the name of any person or to copy or transmit any part of that copy by electronic or any other means: see reg 118(6) (as so added). Subject to reg 118(8) (see the text and notes 23–26), a person who inspects a copy of a document open to public inspection, whether a printed copy or in data form, may not make copies of any part of it, or record any particulars in it, except that a person who inspects a copy of the marked register or lists may make handwritten notes: reg 118(7) (as so added). The provision allowing copying that usually applies where a document is made available for inspection under the Representation of the People (England and Wales) Regulations 2001, SI 2001/341, (i e reg 7(1): see PARA 142 note 18), does not apply to any of the documents open to public inspection under reg 118: see reg 7(6) (added by SI 2006/2910).

21 Ie under the Representation of the People (England and Wales) Regulations 2001, SI 2001/341, reg 118(2) (see note 13): see reg 118(4) (as added: see note 1).

22 See the Representation of the People (England and Wales) Regulations 2001, SI 2001/341, reg 118(4) (as added: see note 1). The text refers to the availability of the published full register for inspection in accordance with reg 43 (publication of register: see PARA 165 note 3): see reg 118(4) (as so added).

23 As to the Security Service see CONSTITUTIONAL LAW AND HUMAN RIGHTS vol 8(2) (Reissue) PARA 471.

24 As to the Government Communications Headquarters see CONSTITUTIONAL LAW AND HUMAN RIGHTS vol 8(2) (Reissue) PARA 473.

25 Ie to each of the departments mentioned in the Representation of the People (England and Wales) Regulations 2001, SI 2001/341, reg 108A (see PARA 186): see reg 118(8)(a) (reg 118 (as added: see note 1); reg 118(8) substituted by the Counter-Terrorism Act 2008 s 20(4), Sch 1 para 2(1), (8)). As to the Secret Intelligence Service see CONSTITUTIONAL LAW AND HUMAN RIGHTS vol 8(2) (Reissue) PARA 472.

26 Representation of the People (England and Wales) Regulations 2001, SI 2001/341, reg 118(8)(b) (as added and substituted: see note 25). The text refers to entitlement to be supplied with a copy of the marked register or lists by virtue of being a person to whom reg 109 (supply of full register to police forces and other agencies: see PARA 186) applies: see reg 118(8)(b) (as so added and substituted). Where a copy of any information was supplied in the circumstances to which reg 118(8)(b) applies, the permitted purpose means the purposes set out in reg 109(4) (see PARA 186): reg 119(3) (reg 119 (as added: see note 1); reg 119(3) amended by the Counter-Terrorism Act 2008 Sch 1 para 2(1), (9)). As to further conditions imposed regarding the use of information so obtained see note 13.

(B) Documents relating to Local Government Elections

505. Requirement to retain and supply documents relating to local government elections. Following a local government election[1], the relevant registration officer[2] must retain for one year all documents relating to such an election[3] forwarded to him by a returning officer[4] and then, unless otherwise directed by an order of a county court, Crown court, or magistrates' court or an election court[5], must cause them to be destroyed[6].

The relevant registration officer[7] must:

(1) make available for inspection by members of the public such documents ('relevant election documents') relating to an election other than a parliamentary election, except ballot papers[8], completed corresponding number lists[9] and certificates as to employment on the day of the poll[10], as he is required by or under any enactment to retain for any period[11]; and

(2) supply, on request, copies of or extracts from such description of relevant election documents as is prescribed by regulations[12].

A copy of the marked copies of the register[13], the postal voters list[14], the list of proxies[15] and the proxy postal voters list[16] must, on request, be supplied to[17]:

(a)   a registered party[18];

(b)   a person who was a candidate at the election (in relation to the electoral area for which he was a candidate)[19];

(c)   at an election where a registered party submits a list of candidates[20], a person who was appointed as an agent for the candidates on the party's list[21].

1   As to the meaning of 'local government election' see PARA 11.

2   As to the meaning of references to the relevant registration officer for these purposes see PARA 498 note 4.

3   Ie including, at an Authority election, the electronic record (where applicable): see the Greater London Authority Elections Rules 2007, SI 2007/3541, Sch 1 r 59, Sch 2 r 62, Sch 3 r 62. As to the electronic record see PARA 495 note 4. As to the meaning of 'Authority election' see PARA 11.

4   Ie forwarded to him, in relation to a local government election for a principal area, in pursuance of the Local Elections (Principal Areas) (England and Wales) Rules 2006, SI 2006/3304, Sch 2 in relation to a local government election for a parish and community council, in pursuance of the Local Elections (Parishes and Communities) (England and Wales) Rules 2006, SI 2006/3305, Sch 2 or, in relation to a local authority mayoral election, in pursuance of the Local Authorities (Mayoral Elections) (England and Wales) Regulations 2007, SI 2007/1024, Sch 1, or, in relation to an Authority election, in pursuance of the Greater London Authority Elections Rules 2007, SI 2007/3541, Sch 1, Sch 2, Sch 3 (see PARA 498); see the Local Elections (Principal Areas) (England and Wales) Rules 2006, SI 2006/3304, Sch 2 r 54; the Local Elections (Parishes and Communities) (England and Wales) Rules 2006, SI 2006/3305, Sch 2 r 54; the Local Authorities (Mayoral Elections) (England and Wales) Regulations 2007, SI 2007/1024, Sch 1 r 59; and the Greater London Authority Elections Rules 2007, SI 2007/3541, Sch 1 r 59, Sch 2 r 62, Sch 3 r 62. In the case of a London Authority election, the constituency returning officer is specified as the returning officer in question (see PARA 211 note 9): see Sch 1 r 59, Sch 2 r 62, Sch 3 r 62. As to returning officers for local government elections generally see PARA 354 et seq.

5   As to the production and inspection of documents by order of the court see PARAS 836, 851, 852.

6   Local Elections (Principal Areas) (England and Wales) Rules 2006, SI 2006/3304, Sch 2 r 54; Local Elections (Parishes and Communities) (England and Wales) Rules 2006, SI 2006/3305, Sch 2 r 54; Local Authorities (Mayoral Elections) (England and Wales) Regulations 2007, SI 2007/1024, Sch 1 r 59; Greater London Authority Elections Rules 2007, SI 2007/3541, Sch 1 r 59, Sch 2 r 62, Sch 3 r 62. As to the penalty for breach of duty by persons responsible for used ballot papers and other documents see PARA 737; and as to offences which relate to persons who interfere with access to or the control of election documents see PARA 745.

7   For these purposes, the relevant registration officer is the registration officer of the local authority in whose area the election is held (or, if the election is held in respect of an electoral area which comprises any part of the area of more than one local authority, such registration officer as the Secretary of State by order appoints): see the Electoral Administration Act 2006 s 44(1), (2)(a), (3). An electoral area is, in relation to a local government election, an electoral area within the meaning of the Representation of the People Act 1983 s 203(1) (see PARA 11): see the Electoral Administration Act 2006 s 44(1), (7)(a). As to the Secretary of State see PARA 2.
     The provision made by ss 42, 44 is applied and modified for the purpose of local authority mayoral elections in England and Wales by the Local Authorities (Mayoral Elections) (England and Wales) Regulations 2007, SI 2007/1024, reg 3(2)–(5), Sch 2 Table 5 (see PARA 11 note 14); and for the purposes of local authority referendums, in relation to Wales, by the Local Authorities (Conduct of Referendums) (Wales) Regulations 2008, SI 2008/1848, reg 8(2), Sch 4 Table 4; and, in relation to England, by the Local Authorities (Conduct of Referendums) (England) Regulations 2012, SI 2012/323, regs 8(2), 11–13, Sch 4 Table 5 (see PARA 15).

8   As to the sealing up of ballot papers see PARA 495.

9   For these purposes, a completed corresponding number list is a list prepared under provision corresponding to the Representation of the People Act 1983 Sch 1 r 19A (see PARA 387), which is completed in accordance with provision corresponding to Sch 1 r 37(1)(b) and Sch 1 r 37(1)(d) (see PARA 399): see the Electoral Administration Act 2006 s 44(1), (11).

10   As to certificates of employment on the day of the poll see PARA 395.

11 See the Electoral Administration Act 2006 ss 42(1)(a), 44(1), (2)(a), (5). The Secretary of State may by regulations impose conditions in relation to the inspection of any document in pursuance of s 42(1)(a): s 42(3)(a). Conditions which may be imposed for these purposes include conditions as to:

    (1)   whether a person may take any copy of a document he is permitted to inspect (s 42(5)(a));

    (2)   the manner in which any such copy is to be taken (s 42(5)(b)); and

    (3)   the purposes for which information contained in any document or part of a document which is inspected in pursuance of s 42(1)(a) may be used (s 42(5)(c)).

The power to make regulations under s 42 is exercisable by the Secretary of State by statutory instrument and includes power to make different provision for different purposes: s 42(8). However, the Secretary of State must not make such regulations unless he first consults the Electoral Commission (s 42(9)); and no such regulations may be made unless a draft of the statutory instrument containing the regulations has been laid before, and approved by resolution of, each House of Parliament (s 42(10)). As to the Electoral Commission see PARA 34 et seq. As to the regulations so made see PARA 506.

12 Electoral Administration Act 2006 s 42(1)(b). The Secretary of State may by regulations impose conditions in relation to the supply of any document or part of a document in pursuance of s 42(1)(b): s 42(3)(b). Conditions which may be imposed for these purposes include conditions as to:

    (1)   the purposes for which information contained in any document or part of a document which is supplied in pursuance of s 42(1)(b) may be used (s 42(5)(c)); and

    (2)   the extent to which a person to whom a document or part of a document has been supplied may: (a) supply that document or part to any other person (s 42(6)(a)); (b) disclose to any other person any information contained in the document or part (s 42(6)(b)); and (c) use any such information for a purpose other than that for which the document or part was supplied to him (s 42(6)(c)).

Regulations may also make provision as to the form in which any such document or part is supplied and for the payment of a fee in respect of the supply of a document or part: s 42(4). As to the regulations so made see PARA 506.

13 For these purposes, the marked register is the copy of the register of electors marked in accordance with provision corresponding to the Representation of the People Act 1983 Sch 1 r 37(1)(c) (see PARA 399): see the Electoral Administration Act 2006 s 44(1), (8).

14 For these purposes, a marked copy of the postal voters list is the copy of that list marked in accordance with provision corresponding to the Representation of the People Act 1983 Sch 1 r 31A(1) (see PARA 418): see the Electoral Administration Act 2006 s 44(1), (10).

15 For these purposes, a marked copy of the list of proxies is the copy of that list marked in accordance with provision corresponding to the Representation of the People Act 1983 Sch 1 r 37(1)(e) (see PARA 399): see the Electoral Administration Act 2006 s 44(1), (9).

16 For these purposes, a marked copy of the proxy postal voters list is the copy of that list marked in accordance with provision corresponding to the Representation of the People Act 1983 Sch 1 r 31A(1) (see PARA 418): see the Electoral Administration Act 2006 s 44(1), (10).

17 See the Electoral Administration Act 2006 s 42(2). The Secretary of State may by regulations impose conditions in relation to the supply of any document or part of a document in pursuance of s 42(2): s 42(3)(c). Conditions which may be imposed for these purposes include conditions as to the extent to which a person to whom a document or part of a document has been supplied may:

    (1)   supply that document or part to any other person (s 42(6)(a));

    (2)   disclose to any other person any information contained in the document or part (s 42(6)(b)); and

    (3)   use any such information for a purpose other than that for which the document or part was supplied to him (s 42(6)(c)).

Regulations may also make provision as to the form in which any such document or part is supplied and for the payment of a fee in respect of the supply of a document or part: see s 42(4). Regulations may also impose conditions corresponding to those mentioned in 42(6) in respect of persons who have obtained a document or part of a document mentioned in s 42(2): (a) which was supplied to another person in pursuance of s 42(2) (s 42(7)(a)); or (b) otherwise than in accordance with regulations under s 42 (s 42(7)(b)). As to the regulations so made see PARA 506.

18 Electoral Administration Act 2006 s 42(2)(a). For these purposes, a party is a registered party if it is registered for the purposes of the Political Parties, Elections and Referendums Act 2000 Pt II (ss 22–40) (see PARA 253): see the Electoral Administration Act 2006 s 44(1), (6).

19 Electoral Administration Act 2006 s 42(2)(b). As to the meaning of 'candidate' see PARA 230.

20 A London Authority London Members election is an election at which a registered party may submit a list of candidates: see PARA 340.
21 Electoral Administration Act 2006 s 42(2)(c).

506. Supply and inspection of documents relating to local government elections. Any person entitled to be supplied[1] with copies of the full register[2] at a particular local government election is also a person entitled[3] to request[4] that a relevant registration officer supply copies of the relevant part[5] of the marked register or lists he is required to keep[6]. The relevant registration officer must supply a copy of the relevant part of the marked register or lists where a request is duly made[7], and where:

(1)   he is satisfied that the requestor needs to see the marks on the marked register or lists in order to achieve the purpose for which it is requested[8]; and

(2)   he has received payment of a fee[9].

If the relevant registration officer is not satisfied in accordance with head (1) above, he may treat the request for a marked register or list as a request for information in unmarked lists[10], or as a request for the published copy of the full register[11], or both[12].

Any person is entitled to request that the relevant registration officer make available for inspection a copy of any of the following documents ('the documents open to public inspection')[13]:

(a)   the marked register or lists[14];

(b)   such other documents relating to an election as the relevant registration officer is required by or under any enactment to retain for any period[15], except: (i) ballot papers[16]; (ii) completed corresponding number lists[17]; and (iii) certificates as to employment on the day of the election[18].

The relevant registration officer must make the documents open to public inspection available for inspection under supervision not later than ten days[19] after the date of receipt of a request that has been duly made[20]. However, where a request has been made to inspect copies of the marked register or lists[21], and where the relevant registration officer is not satisfied that the purposes of the requestor cannot be met by inspection of the full register, he must inform the requestor of his decision to this effect, and he must provide the requestor with information concerning the availability for inspection of the published full register[22]. The relevant registration officer must, on request, supply free of charge copies of any documents open to public inspection to each of the Security Service[23], the Government Communications Headquarters[24], and the Secret Intelligence Service[25], and to a person who has inspected those documents and who is entitled to be supplied with a copy of the marked register or lists[26].

1   Ie in accordance with the Representation of the People (England and Wales) Regulations 2001, SI 2001/341, reg 100 (supply of full register to Electoral Commission: see PARA 183), reg 103 (supply of full register to elected representatives for electoral purposes: see PARA 185), reg 105 (supply of full register to local constituency parties: see PARA 185), reg 106 (supply of full register to registered political parties: see PARA 185), reg 108 (supply of full register to certain candidates: see PARA 185), reg 109 (supply of full register to police forces and other agencies: see PARA 186) or reg 113 (sale of full register to certain government departments and other bodies: see PARA 188): see reg 117(1) (regs 116–120 added by SI 2006/2910).
2   As to the meaning of 'full register' see PARA 167 note 2.
3   Ie subject to the Representation of the People (England and Wales) Regulations 2001, SI 2001/341, reg 117 (see also the text and notes 1–2, 4–12) and reg 119 (see notes 6, 13, 26): see reg 117(1) (as added: see note 1).
4   A person whose entitlement to request copies of the marked register or lists under the Representation of the People (England and Wales) Regulations 2001, SI 2001/341, reg 117(1)

arises from being in a category of persons covered by reg 103 (supply of full register to elected representatives for electoral purposes: see PARA 185), reg 105 (supply of full register to local constituency parties: see PARA 185), reg 106 (supply of full register to registered political parties: see PARA 185) or reg 108 (supply of full register to certain candidates: see PARA 185) before a particular election, is entitled to request those documents regardless of whether he remains in an entitled category after that election for which the marked register or list was prepared: reg 117(2) (as added: see note 1). In Pt 7 (regs 116–120), references to the 'marked register or lists' means any part of the marked copies of:

(1)   the full register (reg 116(1)(a) (as so added));

(2)   the notices of alteration amending the full register issued under the Representation of the People Act 1983 s 13B(3B) or s 13B(3D) (see PARA 168) (Representation of the People (England and Wales) Regulations 2001, SI 2001/341, reg 116(1)(aa) (reg 116 as so added; reg 116(1)(aa) added by SI 2008/1901));

(3)   the postal voters list (Representation of the People (England and Wales) Regulations 2001, SI 2001/341, reg 116(1)(b) (as so added));

(4)   the list of proxies (reg 116(1)(c) (as so added)); and

(5)   the proxy postal voters list (reg 116(1)(d) (as so added)),

forwarded to the relevant registration officer either under the Representation of the People Act 1983 Sch 1 r 55(1)(e) (see PARA 496) or under the Representation of the People (England and Wales) Regulations 2001, SI 2001/341, reg 91 (see PARA 497) (see reg 116(1) (reg 116 as so added; reg 116(1) amended by SI 2007/1025). As to the meaning of references to the relevant registration officer for these purposes see PARA 496 note 3. As to the postal voters list and the list of proxies see PARA 373; and as to the proxy postal voters list see PARA 381.

The Representation of the People (England and Wales) Regulations 2001, SI 2001/341, Pt 7, applies, subject to modifications, in respect of the marked Assembly register or lists and the other relevant Assembly election documents as it applies in respect of the marked register or lists and other documents open to inspection: see regs 121–126; and PARA 509. Regulations 116, 118, and 119 also have effect for the purposes of local authority referendums, subject to the modifications specified, in relation to Wales, by the Local Authorities (Conduct of Referendums) (Wales) Regulations 2008, SI 2008/1848, reg 8(2), Sch 4 Table 5, and, in relation to England, by the Local Authorities (Conduct of Referendums) (England) Regulations 2012, SI 2012/323, regs 8(2), 11–13, Sch 4 Table 6 (see PARA 15 note 2).

5   Ie within the meaning of the Representation of the People (England and Wales) Regulations 2001, SI 2001/341, reg 100 (supply of full register to Electoral Commission: see PARA 183), reg 103 (supply of full register to elected representatives for electoral purposes: see PARA 185), reg 105 (supply of full register to local constituency parties: see PARA 185), reg 106 (supply of full register to registered political parties: see PARA 185), reg 108 (supply of full register to certain candidates: see PARA 185), reg 109 (supply of full register to police forces and other agencies: see PARA 186) or reg 113 (sale of full register to government departments and other bodies: see PARA 188): see reg 117(1) (as added: see note 1).

6   Representation of the People (England and Wales) Regulations 2001, SI 2001/341, reg 117(1) (as added: see note 1). A request under reg 117(1) must be made in writing; and it must:

(1)   specify which of the marked register or lists (or the relevant part of the register or lists) are requested (reg 117(3)(a) (as so added));

(2)   state whether a printed copy of the records or lists is requested or a copy in data form (reg 117(3)(b) (as so added)); and

(3)   state the purposes for which the marked register or lists will be used and why the supply or purchase of a copy of the full register or unmarked lists would not be sufficient to achieve that purpose (reg 117(3)(c) (as so added)).

Subject to any direction by the Secretary of State under the Representation of the People Act 1983 s 52(1) (discharge of registration duties: see PARA 141), any duty on a relevant registration officer to supply records or lists under the Representation of the People (England and Wales) Regulations 2001, SI 2001/341, Pt 7 imposes only a duty to provide that information in the form in which he holds it, however: see reg 116(4) (as so added). As to the meaning of 'data form' see PARA 180 note 11. As to the Secretary of State see PARA 2.

A person who obtains a copy of any part of a marked register or list under reg 117 may use it only for the permitted purposes specified in reg 119(2), and any conditions specified in reg 119(2) (or any conditions which would apply to the use of the full register under whichever of reg 100 (supply of full register to Electoral Commission: see PARA 183), reg 103 (supply of full register to elected representatives for electoral purposes: see PARA 185), reg 105 (supply of full register to local constituency parties: see PARA 185), reg 106 (supply of full register to registered political parties: see PARA 185), reg 108 (supply of full register to certain candidates: see PARA 185), reg 109 (supply of full register to police forces and other agencies: see PARA 186) or reg 113 (sale of full register to government departments and other bodies: see PARA 188), entitled that person to obtain that document) apply to such use: see reg 117(6) (as so added). The conditions in reg 100(3) (see PARA 183), reg 103(3) (see PARA 185), reg 105(4) (see PARA 185), reg 106(3) (see PARA 185), reg 108(5) (see PARA 185), and reg 109(3) (see PARA 186), apply to a person to whom a marked register or list, or any information contained in it (that is not contained in the edited register), has been so supplied or disclosed as they apply to the person to whom those regulations apply: reg 117(7) (reg 117 as so added; reg 117(7) amended by SI 2007/1025). As to the meaning of 'edited register' see PARA 167 note 4.

Any person who has obtained or is entitled to obtain a copy of the marked register or lists under the Representation of the People (England and Wales) Regulations 2001, SI 2001/341, reg 117 may:

(a)   supply a copy of the marked register or lists to a processor for the purpose of processing the information contained therein (reg 117(8)(a) (as so added)); or

(b)   procure that a processor processes and supplies to him any copy of the information in the marked register or lists which the processor has obtained under reg 117 (reg 117(8)(b) (as so added)),

for use in respect of the purposes for which that person is entitled to obtain any such copy or information (as the case may be) (reg 117(8) (as so added)). The processor may not disclose the information so supplied except to the person who supplied it to the processor or an employee of that person or a person who is entitled to obtain a copy of the full register under the Representation of the People (England and Wales) Regulations 2001, SI 2001/341 or any employee of such a person: reg 92(9) (reg 92 added by SI 2002/1871); applied by the Representation of the People (England and Wales) Regulations 2001, SI 2001/341, reg 116(3) (as so added). Where a person obtains copies of the information in the marked register or lists in accordance with reg 117(1), the permitted purpose (see PARA 179 note 18) means either research purposes within the meaning of that term in the Data Protection Act 1998 s 33 (see CONFIDENCE AND INFORMATIONAL PRIVACY vol 19 (2011) PARA 144) or electoral purposes: Representation of the People (England and Wales) Regulations 2001, SI 2001/341, reg 119(2) (as so added). As to references to an employee of any person who has access to a copy of the full register see PARA 180 note 6 (applied by virtue of reg 116(3) (as so added)). As to the meaning of 'processor' see PARA 180 note 11 (applied by virtue of reg 116(3) (as so added)).

7   Representation of the People (England and Wales) Regulations 2001, SI 2001/341, reg 117(4) (as added: see note 1).

8   Representation of the People (England and Wales) Regulations 2001, SI 2001/341, reg 117(4)(a) (as added: see note 1).

9   Representation of the People (England and Wales) Regulations 2001, SI 2001/341, reg 117(4)(b) (as added: see note 1). The fee mentioned in head (2) in the text must be calculated in accordance with reg 120: see reg 117(4)(b) (as so added). Accordingly, the fee to be paid in accordance with reg 117(4)(b) by a person making a request for a copy of the whole or of any part of the marked register or lists must be the sum of £10 (see reg 120(1), (2) (reg 120 as so added; substituted by SI 2008/1901)), plus:

(1)   for a copy in printed form, £2 for each 1,000 entries (or remaining part of 1,000 entries) covered by the request (reg 120(2)(a) (as so added and substituted)); and

(2)   for a copy in data form, £1 for each 1,000 entries (or remaining part of 1,000 entries) covered by the request (reg 120(2)(b) (as so added and substituted)).

For these purposes, a request for a copy of the whole or the same part of the marked register or lists in both a printed and data form may be treated as two separate requests: see reg 120(3) (as so substituted).

10   Ie under the Representation of the People (England and Wales) Regulations 2001, SI 2001/341, reg 61 (see PARA 185 note 11): see reg 117(5) (as added: see note 1).

11   Ie in accordance with the Representation of the People (England and Wales) Regulations 2001, SI 2001/341, reg 102 (see PARA 185): see reg 117(5) (as added: see note 1).

12   Representation of the People (England and Wales) Regulations 2001, SI 2001/341, reg 117(5) (as added: see note 1).

13   See the Representation of the People (England and Wales) Regulations 2001, SI 2001/341, reg 118(1) (as added: see note 1). A request under reg 118(1) must be made in writing; and it must specify:

(1)   which documents are requested (reg 118(2)(a) (as so added));

(2)   the purposes for which the information in any document will be used (reg 118(2)(b) (as so added));

(3)   any reason why inspecting the full register or unmarked lists would not be sufficient to achieve that purpose (ie where the request is to inspect the marked register or lists) (reg 118(2)(c) (as so added));

(4)   who will inspect the documents (reg 118(2)(d) (as so added));

(5)   the date on which they wish to inspect the documents (reg 118(2)(e) (as so added)); and

(6)   whether they would prefer to inspect the documents in a printed or data form (reg 118(2)(f) (as so added)).

Subject to any direction by the Secretary of State under the Representation of the People Act 1983 s 52(1) (discharge of registration duties: see PARA 141), any duty on a registration officer to make records or lists available for inspection under the Representation of the People (England and Wales) Regulations 2001, SI 2001/341, Pt 7 imposes only a duty to provide that information in the form in which he holds it, however: see reg 116(4) (as so added).

A person who obtains a copy of or information in any document open to public inspection under reg 118 may use it only for the permitted purposes specified in reg 119; and any conditions:

(a)   specified in reg 119 (see reg 118(5)(a) (as so added));

(b)   specified in reg 118(7) (see note 20) (see reg 118(5)(b) (as so added)); or

(c)   which would apply to the use of the full register under reg 109 (supply of full register to police forces and other agencies: see PARA 186) where such a person has obtained a copy of that document under reg 118(8) (see the text and notes 23–26) (see reg 118(5)(c) (as so added)),

apply to such use (see reg 118(5) (as so added)). The restrictions on the supply, disclosure and use of the full register in reg 94 (restrictions on supply of full register and disclosure of information from it by the registration officer and his staff: see PARA 179) and reg 96 (restrictions on use of full register or information contained in it: see PARA 179) apply to documents open to public inspection, as they apply to the full register (reg 119(1) (as so added)), except that, where a person inspects information in accordance with reg 118(1), the permitted purpose (see PARA 179 note 18) means either research purposes within the meaning of that term in the Data Protection Act 1998 s 33 (see CONFIDENCE AND INFORMATIONAL PRIVACY vol 19 (2011) PARA 144) or electoral purposes (Representation of the People (England and Wales) Regulations 2001, SI 2001/341, reg 119(2) (as so added)).

14   Representation of the People (England and Wales) Regulations 2001, SI 2001/341, reg 118(1)(a) (as added: see note 1).

15   Representation of the People (England and Wales) Regulations 2001, SI 2001/341, reg 118(1)(b) (as added: see note 1). As to the meaning of 'enactment' see PARA 179 note 8 (applied by virtue of reg 116(3) (as so added)).

16   Representation of the People (England and Wales) Regulations 2001, SI 2001/341, reg 118(1)(b)(i) (as added: see note 1). As to the sealing up of ballot papers see PARA 495.

17   Representation of the People (England and Wales) Regulations 2001, SI 2001/341, reg 118(1)(b)(ii) (as added: see note 1). As to the completed corresponding number lists see PARA 405 note 11.

18   Representation of the People (England and Wales) Regulations 2001, SI 2001/341, reg 118(1)(b)(iii) (as added: see note 1). As to certificates of employment on duty on the day of the poll see PARA 395.

19   For these purposes, any period of days must be calculated in accordance with the Representation of the People (England and Wales) Regulations 2001, SI 2001/341, reg 56(6) and reg 56(7) (see PARA 367 note 6): see reg 116(2) (as added: see note 1).

20   Representation of the People (England and Wales) Regulations 2001, SI 2001/341, reg 118(3) (reg 118 as added: see note 1). Where inspection takes place by providing a copy of the records or lists on a computer screen or otherwise in data form, the relevant registration officer must ensure that the manner in, and equipment on, which that copy is provided do not permit any person consulting that copy to search it by electronic means by reference to the name of any person or to copy or transmit any part of that copy by electronic or any other means: see reg 118(6) (as so added). Subject to reg 118(8) (see the text and notes 23–26), a person who inspects a copy of a document open to public inspection, whether a printed copy or in data form, may not make copies of any part of it, or record any particulars in it, except that a person who inspects a copy of the marked register or lists may make handwritten notes: reg 118(7) (as so added). The provision allowing copying that usually applies where a document is made available for inspection under the Representation of the People (England and Wales) Regulations 2001, SI 2001/341, (i e reg 7(1): see PARA 142 note 18), does not apply to any of the documents open to public inspection under reg 118: see reg 7(6) (added by SI 2006/2910).

21   Ie under the Representation of the People (England and Wales) Regulations 2001, SI 2001/341, reg 118(2) (see note 13): see reg 118(4) (as added: see note 1).

22 See the Representation of the People (England and Wales) Regulations 2001, SI 2001/341, reg 118(4) (as added: see note 1). The text refers to the availability of the published full register for inspection in accordance with reg 43 (publication of register: see PARA 165 note 3): see reg 118(4) (as so added).

23 As to the Security Service see CONSTITUTIONAL LAW AND HUMAN RIGHTS vol 8(2) (Reissue) PARA 471.

24 As to the Government Communications Headquarters see CONSTITUTIONAL LAW AND HUMAN RIGHTS vol 8(2) (Reissue) PARA 473.

25 Ie to each of the departments mentioned in the Representation of the People (England and Wales) Regulations 2001, SI 2001/341, reg 108A (see PARA 186): see reg 118(8)(a) (reg 118 (as added: see note 1); reg 118(8) substituted by the Counter-Terrorism Act 2008 s 20(4), Sch 1 para 2(1), (8)). As to the Secret Intelligence Service see CONSTITUTIONAL LAW AND HUMAN RIGHTS vol 8(2) (Reissue) PARA 472.

26 Representation of the People (England and Wales) Regulations 2001, SI 2001/341, reg 118(8)(b) (as added and substituted: see note 25). The text refers to entitlement to be supplied with a copy of the marked register or lists by virtue of being a person to whom reg 109 (supply of full register to police forces and other agencies: see PARA 186) applies: see reg 118(8)(b) (as so added and substituted). Where a copy of any information was supplied in the circumstances to which reg 118(8)(b) applies, the permitted purpose means the purposes set out in reg 109(4) (see PARA 186): reg 119(3) (reg 119 (as added: see note 1); reg 119(3) amended by the Counter-Terrorism Act 2008 Sch 1 para 2(1), (9)). As to further conditions imposed regarding the use of information so obtained see note 13.

507.   Requirement to retain and supply documents relating to a poll consequent on a parish meeting.   Following a poll consequent on a parish meeting on a question involving appointment to office[1], the proper officer of the council of the district in which the parish is situate[2] must retain for six months among the records of the council all documents relating to such a poll forwarded to him by a returning officer[3]; and then, unless otherwise directed by an order of a county court or an election court, he must cause them to be destroyed[4]. The documents relating to such a poll, except ballot papers and counterfoils[5], must be open to public inspection ('the documents open to public inspection') at such time and in such manner as the district council may determine[6]. The proper officer must, on request, supply copies of, or extracts from, the documents open to public inspection on payment of such fees, and subject to such conditions, as may be determined by the district council[7].

1 As to polls consequent on a parish meeting on a question involving appointment to office see PARA 200 et seq.

2 For the purposes of a poll consequent on a parish meeting, any references to a proper officer of a council means any officer appointed for the purpose by that council: Parish and Community Meetings (Polls) Rules 1987, SI 1987/1, Schedule r 38(3). As to the meaning of 'proper officer' see PARA 140 note 2. As to the council of a district in England see LOCAL GOVERNMENT vol 69 (2009) PARA 24 et seq; and as to parishes and their councillors generally see LOCAL GOVERNMENT vol 69 (2009) PARA 27 et seq.

3 Ie forwarded to him in pursuance of the Parish and Community Meetings (Polls) Rules 1987, SI 1987/1, Schedule, by a returning officer: see Schedule r 36(1). As to returning officers for a poll consequent on a parish meeting see PARA 356. As to the transfer of documents relating to a poll consequent on a parish meeting see PARA 498.

4 Parish and Community Meetings (Polls) Rules 1987, SI 1987/1, Schedule r 36(1). As to the production and inspection of documents by order of the court see PARAS 836, 851, 852.

5 As to the sealing up of ballot papers and counterfoils see PARA 495.

6 Parish and Community Meetings (Polls) Rules 1987, SI 1987/1, Schedule r 36(2).

7 Parish and Community Meetings (Polls) Rules 1987, SI 1987/1, Schedule r 36(3).

(C) Documents relating to Welsh Assembly Elections

508.   Requirement to retain and supply documents relating to Welsh Assembly elections.   The relevant registration officer[1] must retain for a year all documents relating to a Welsh Assembly election[2] forwarded to him by a constituency returning officer[3]; and then, unless otherwise directed by order of the High Court, the Crown Court or a magistrates' court, he must cause them to be destroyed[4].

The relevant registration officer[5] must:

(1)   make available for inspection by members of the public such documents ('relevant election documents') relating to an election other than a parliamentary election, except ballot papers[6], completed corresponding number lists[7] and certificates as to employment on the day of the poll[8], as he is required by or under any enactment to retain for any period[9]; and

(2)   supply, on request, copies of or extracts from such description of relevant election documents as is prescribed by regulations[10].

A copy of the marked copies of the register[11], the postal voters list[12], the list of proxies[13] and the proxy postal voters list[14] must, on request, be supplied to[15]:

(a)   a registered party[16];

(b)   a person who was a candidate at the election (in relation to the electoral area for which he was a candidate)[17];

(c)   at an election where a registered party submits a list of candidates[18], a person who was appointed as an agent for the candidates on the party's list[19].

1   As to the meaning of 'relevant registration officer' see PARA 139 note 1.
2   As to the meaning of 'Assembly election' see PARA 3 note 2.
3   Ie forwarded in pursuance of the National Assembly for Wales (Representation of the People) Order 2007, SI 2007/236, Sch 5 (including postal voting documents deemed to 'be so forwarded): see Sch 5 para 69(1). As to the meaning of 'constituency returning officer' in this context see PARA 18 note 2. As to the transfer of documents relating to Welsh Assembly elections to the relevant registration officer see PARA 499.
4   National Assembly for Wales (Representation of the People) Order 2007, SI 2007/236, Sch 5 para 69(1). As to the production and inspection of documents by order of the court see PARAS 836, 851, 852. As to the penalty for breach of duty by persons responsible for used ballot papers and other documents see PARA 737; and as to offences which relate to persons who interfere with access to or the control of election documents see PARA 745.
5   For these purposes, the relevant registration officer is:
        (1)   the registration officer of the local authority in whose area the election is held (see the Electoral Administration Act 2006 s 44(1), (2)(a), (3)(a)); or
        (2)   if the election is held in respect of an electoral area which comprises any part of the area of more than one local authority, such registration officer as the Secretary of State by order appoints (see s 44(1), (2)(a), (3)(b)).
    In relation to a Welsh Assembly election, an electoral area is an Assembly constituency or an Assembly electoral region within the meaning of the Government of Wales Act 2006 s 2 (see PARA 76): see the Electoral Administration Act 2006 s 44(1), (7)(b) (s 44(7)(b) amended by SI 2007/1388). As to the Secretary of State see PARA 2. In exercise of the powers conferred by the Electoral Administration Act 2006 s 44(3), the Secretary of State has made the Representation of the People (National Assembly for Wales) (Relevant Registration Officer) Order 2007, SI 2007/1372, which provides that, where a Welsh Assembly election is held in respect of an electoral area comprising any part of the area of more than one local authority, the relevant registration officer is to be the office holder designated in art 2, Schedule, and he must carry out this function in relation to the electoral area also shown therein: art 2.
6   As to the sealing up of ballot papers see PARA 495.
7   For these purposes, a completed corresponding number list is a list prepared under provision corresponding to the Representation of the People Act 1983 Sch 1 r 19A (see PARA 387), which is completed in accordance with provision corresponding to Sch 1 r 37(1)(b) and Sch 1 r 37(1)(d) (see PARA 399): see the Electoral Administration Act 2006 s 44(1), (11).
8   As to certificates of employment on the day of the poll see PARA 395.
9   See the Electoral Administration Act 2006 ss 42(1)(a), 44(1), (2)(a), (5). The Secretary of State may by regulations impose conditions in relation to the inspection of any document in pursuance of s 42(1)(a): s 42(3)(a). Conditions which may be imposed for these purposes include conditions as to:

(1) whether a person may take any copy of a document he is permitted to inspect (s 42(5)(a));

(2) the manner in which any such copy is to be taken (s 42(5)(b)); and

(3) the purposes for which information contained in any document or part of a document which is inspected in pursuance of s 42(1)(a) may be used (s 42(5)(c)).

The power to make regulations under s 42 is exercisable by the Secretary of State by statutory instrument and includes power to make different provision for different purposes: s 42(8). However, the Secretary of State must not make such regulations unless he first consults the Electoral Commission (s 42(9)); and no such regulations may be made unless a draft of the statutory instrument containing the regulations has been laid before, and approved by resolution of, each House of Parliament (s 42(10)). As to the Electoral Commission see PARA 34 et seq. As to the regulations so made see PARA 509.

10 Electoral Administration Act 2006 s 42(1)(b). The Secretary of State may by regulations impose conditions in relation to the supply of any document or part of a document in pursuance of s 42(1)(b): s 42(3)(b). Conditions which may be imposed for these purposes include conditions as to:

(1) the purposes for which information contained in any document or part of a document which is supplied in pursuance of s 42(1)(b) may be used (s 42(5)(c)); and

(2) the extent to which a person to whom a document or part of a document has been supplied may: (a) supply that document or part to any other person (s 42(6)(a)); (b) disclose to any other person any information contained in the document or part (s 42(6)(b)); and (c) use any such information for a purpose other than that for which the document or part was supplied to him (s 42(6)(c)).

Regulations may also make provision as to the form in which any such document or part is supplied and for the payment of a fee in respect of the supply of a document or part: s 42(4). As to the regulations so made see PARA 509.

11 For these purposes, the marked register is the copy of the register of electors marked in accordance with provision corresponding to the Representation of the People Act 1983 Sch 1 r 37(1)(c) (see PARA 399): see the Electoral Administration Act 2006 s 44(1), (8).

12 For these purposes, a marked copy of the postal voters list is the copy of that list marked in accordance with provision corresponding to the Representation of the People Act 1983 Sch 1 r 31A(1) (see PARA 418): see the Electoral Administration Act 2006 s 44(1), (10).

13 For these purposes, a marked copy of the list of proxies is the copy of that list marked in accordance with provision corresponding to the Representation of the People Act 1983 Sch 1 r 37(1)(e) (see PARA 399): see the Electoral Administration Act 2006 s 44(1), (9).

14 For these purposes, a marked copy of the proxy postal voters list is the copy of that list marked in accordance with provision corresponding to the Representation of the People Act 1983 Sch 1 r 31A(1) (see PARA 418): see the Electoral Administration Act 2006 s 44(1), (10).

15 See the Electoral Administration Act 2006 s 42(2). The Secretary of State may by regulations impose conditions in relation to the supply of any document or part of a document in pursuance of s 42(2): s 42(3)(c). Conditions which may be imposed for these purposes include conditions as to the extent to which a person to whom a document or part of a document has been supplied may:

(1) supply that document or part to any other person (s 42(6)(a));

(2) disclose to any other person any information contained in the document or part (s 42(6)(b)); and

(3) use any such information for a purpose other than that for which the document or part was supplied to him (s 42(6)(c)).

Regulations may also make provision as to the form in which any such document or part is supplied and for the payment of a fee in respect of the supply of a document or part: see s 42(4). Regulations may also impose conditions corresponding to those mentioned in 42(6) in respect of persons who have obtained a document or part of a document mentioned in s 42(2): (a) which was supplied to another person in pursuance of s 42(2) (s 42(7)(a)); or (b) otherwise than in accordance with regulations under s 42 (s 42(7)(b)). As to the regulations so made see PARA 509.

16 Electoral Administration Act 2006 s 42(2)(a). For these purposes, a party is a registered party if it is registered for the purposes of the Political Parties, Elections and Referendums Act 2000 Pt II (ss 22–40) (see PARA 253): see the Electoral Administration Act 2006 s 44(1), (6).

17 Electoral Administration Act 2006 s 42(2)(b). As to the meaning of 'candidate' see PARA 230.

18 A Welsh Assembly regional election is an election at which a registered party may submit a list of candidates: see PARA 340.

19 Electoral Administration Act 2006 s 42(2)(c).

509.   Supply and inspection of documents relating to Welsh Assembly elections.   Provision is made for access to, and public inspection of, such documents relating to a Welsh Assembly election as the relevant registration officer is required to retain ('relevant Assembly election documents')[1] for county and county borough councils[2]. The provision so made applies, with modifications, the provision that is made for equivalent purposes in relation to a particular parliamentary and local government election[3].

1   Ie such documents relating to an Assembly election as the relevant registration officer is required to retain by the National Assembly for Wales (Representation of the People) Order 2007, SI 2007/236, Sch 5 para 69(1) (see PARA 508): see the Representation of the People (England and Wales) Regulations 2001, SI 2001/341, reg 121(1) (regs 121–126 added by SI 2007/1368). For these purposes, 'Assembly election' means an election to the National Assembly for Wales under the Government of Wales Act 2006 Pt 1 (ss 1–43) (see PARA 3 et seq): see the Representation of the People (England and Wales) Regulations 2001, SI 2001/341, reg 121(1) (as so added). As to the meaning of 'relevant registration officer' see PARA 139 note 1.

2   See the Representation of the People (National Assembly for Wales) (Access to Election Documents) Regulations 2007, SI 2007/1368 (made by the Secretary of State in exercise of the powers conferred by the Electoral Administration Act 2006 s 42 (see PARA 508)), which adds the Representation of the People (England and Wales) Regulations 2001, SI 2001/341, Pt 8 (regs 121–126) (see note 1). As to the council of a county or county borough in Wales see LOCAL GOVERNMENT vol 69 (2009) PARA 37 et seq.

3   Accordingly, the Representation of the People (England and Wales) Regulations 2001, SI 2001/341, Pt 7 (regs 116–120) (cited in PARAS 504, 506), subject to the modifications in regs 123–128, applies in respect of the marked Assembly register or lists and the other relevant Assembly election documents as it applies in respect of the marked register or lists and other documents open to inspection under Pt 7: see reg 122 (as added: see note 1). For these purposes, 'the marked Assembly register or lists' means any part of the marked copies, forwarded to the relevant registration officer under the National Assembly for Wales (Representation of the People) Order 2007, SI 2007/236, Sch 3 para 31 (see PARA 500), or Sch 5 r 67(1)(h), (2)(f) (see PARA 499), of: (1) the full register (see PARA 167 note 2); (2) the list kept under art 10(1), (2) ('the Assembly postal voters list': see PARA 373); (3) the list kept under art 10(1), (3) ('the Assembly list of proxies': see PARA 373); and (4) the list kept under art 12(8) ('the Assembly proxy postal voters list': see PARA 381): see the Representation of the People (England and Wales) Regulations 2001, SI 2001/341, reg 121(1), (2) (as so added).

(D) Documents relating to European Parliamentary Elections

510.   Requirement to retain and supply documents relating to European parliamentary elections.   The relevant registration officer[1] must retain, or cause to be retained, for one year all documents relating to a European Parliamentary election[2] forwarded to him by a local returning officer[3]; and then, unless otherwise directed by order of the High Court, the Crown Court or a magistrates' court, he must cause them to be destroyed[4]. All such documents, except:

(1)   ballot papers[5];
(2)   completed corresponding number lists[6]; and
(3)   certificates as to employment on the day of the election[7],

must be open to public inspection[8].

The relevant registration officer[9] must:

(a)   make available for inspection by members of the public such documents ('relevant election documents') relating to an election other than a parliamentary election, except ballot papers[10], completed corresponding number lists[11] and certificates as to employment on the day of the poll[12], as he is required by or under any enactment to retain for any period[13]; and (b)　　supply, on request, copies of or extracts from such description of relevant election documents as is prescribed by regulations[14].

A copy of the marked copies of the register[15], the postal voters list[16], the list of proxies[17] and the proxy postal voters list[18] must, on request, be supplied to[19]:

(i)　　a registered party[20];

(ii)　　a person who was a candidate at the election (in relation to the electoral area for which he was a candidate)[21];

(iii)　　at an election where a registered party submits a list of candidates[22], a person who was appointed as an agent for the candidates on the party's list[23].

1　As to the meaning of 'relevant registration officer' see PARA 139 note 1.

2　As to European parliamentary elections see PARA 217 et seq.

3　Ie all documents relating to an election forwarded to him in accordance with the European Parliamentary Elections Regulations 2004, SI 2004/293, Sch 1 (see PARA 501): see Sch 1 para 66(1) (Sch 1 substituted by SI 2009/186). As to local returning officers appointed for the purposes of European parliamentary elections see PARA 360 et seq.

4　European Parliamentary Elections Regulations 2004, SI 2004/293, Sch 1 para 66(1) (as substituted: see note 3). For the purposes of the combined region, an order of the Supreme Court or Court of Appeal in Gibraltar is also specified: see Sch 1 para 66(1) (as so substituted). As to the electoral areas established for the purposes of European parliamentary elections (including the 'combined region' which incorporates Gibraltar) see PARA 77. As to the production and inspection of documents by order of the court see PARAS 836, 851, 852. As to the penalty for breach of duty by persons responsible for used ballot papers and other documents see PARA 737; and as to offences which relate to persons who interfere with access to or the control of election documents see PARA 745.

5　European Parliamentary Elections Regulations 2004, SI 2004/293, Sch 1 para 66(2)(a) (as substituted: see note 3).

6　European Parliamentary Elections Regulations 2004, SI 2004/293, Sch 1 para 66(2)(b) (as substituted: see note 3). As to the completed corresponding number lists see PARA 405 note 11.

7　European Parliamentary Elections Regulations 2004, SI 2004/293, Sch 1 para 66(2)(c) (as substituted: see note 3). As to certificates of employment on duty on the day of the poll see PARA 395.

8　See the European Parliamentary Elections Regulations 2004, SI 2004/293, Sch 1 para 66(2) (as substituted: see note 3).

9　For these purposes, the relevant registration officer is the registration officer of the local authority in whose area the election is held or, if the election is held in respect of an electoral area which comprises any part of the area of more than one local authority, such registration officer as the Secretary of State by order appoints: Electoral Administration Act 2006 s 44(1), (3). An electoral area is, in relation to an election to the European Parliament, an electoral region within the meaning of the European Parliamentary Elections Act 2002 s 1 (electoral regions and number of MEPs: see PARA 77): Electoral Administration Act 2006 s 44(1), (7)(e). As to the Secretary of State see PARA 2.

10　As to the sealing up of ballot papers see PARA 495.

11　For these purposes, a completed corresponding number list is a list prepared under provision corresponding to the Representation of the People Act 1983 Sch 1 r 19A (see PARA 387), which is completed in accordance with provision corresponding to Sch 1 r 37(1)(b) and Sch 1 r 37(1)(d) (see PARA 399): see the Electoral Administration Act 2006 s 44(1), (11).

12　See note 7.

13　See the Electoral Administration Act 2006 ss 42(1)(a), 44(1), (2)(a), (5). The Secretary of State may by regulations impose conditions in relation to the inspection of any document in pursuance of s 42(1)(a): s 42(3)(a). Conditions which may be imposed for these purposes include conditions as to:

(1)　　whether a person may take any copy of a document he is permitted to inspect (s 42(5)(a));

(2)　　the manner in which any such copy is to be taken (s 42(5)(b)); and

(3)　　the purposes for which information contained in any document or part of a document which is inspected in pursuance of s 42(1)(a) may be used (s 42(5)(c)).

The power to make regulations under s 42 is exercisable by the Secretary of State by statutory instrument and includes power to make different provision for different purposes: s 42(8). However, the Secretary of State must not make such regulations unless he first consults the

Electoral Commission (s 42(9)); and no such regulations may be made unless a draft of the statutory instrument containing the regulations has been laid before, and approved by resolution of, each House of Parliament (s 42(10)). As to the Electoral Commission see PARA 34 et seq. As to the regulations so made see PARA 511.

14   Electoral Administration Act 2006 s 42(1)(b). The Secretary of State may by regulations impose conditions in relation to the supply of any document or part of a document in pursuance of s 42(1)(b): s 42(3)(b). Conditions which may be imposed for these purposes include conditions as to:
- (1)   the purposes for which information contained in any document or part of a document which is supplied in pursuance of s 42(1)(b) may be used (s 42(5)(c)); and
- (2)   the extent to which a person to whom a document or part of a document has been supplied may: (a) supply that document or part to any other person (s 42(6)(a)); (b) disclose to any other person any information contained in the document or part (s 42(6)(b)); and (c) use any such information for a purpose other than that for which the document or part was supplied to him (s 42(6)(c)).

Regulations may also make provision as to the form in which any such document or part is supplied and for the payment of a fee in respect of the supply of a document or part: s 42(4). As to the regulations so made see PARA 511.

15   For these purposes, the marked register is the copy of the register of electors marked in accordance with provision corresponding to the Representation of the People Act 1983 Sch 1 r 37(1)(c) (see PARA 399): see the Electoral Administration Act 2006 s 44(1), (8).

16   For these purposes, a marked copy of the postal voters list is the copy of that list marked in accordance with provision corresponding to the Representation of the People Act 1983 Sch 1 r 31A(1) (see PARA 418): see the Electoral Administration Act 2006 s 44(1), (10).

17   For these purposes, a marked copy of the list of proxies is the copy of that list marked in accordance with provision corresponding to the Representation of the People Act 1983 Sch 1 r 37(1)(e) (see PARA 399): see the Electoral Administration Act 2006 s 44(1), (9).

18   For these purposes, a marked copy of the proxy postal voters list is the copy of that list marked in accordance with provision corresponding to the Representation of the People Act 1983 Sch 1 r 31A(1) (see PARA 418): see the Electoral Administration Act 2006 s 44(1), (10).

19   See the Electoral Administration Act 2006 s 42(2). The Secretary of State may by regulations impose conditions in relation to the supply of any document or part of a document in pursuance of s 42(2): s 42(3)(c). Conditions which may be imposed for these purposes include conditions as to the extent to which a person to whom a document or part of a document has been supplied may:
- (1)   supply that document or part to any other person (s 42(6)(a));
- (2)   disclose to any other person any information contained in the document or part (s 42(6)(b)); and
- (3)   use any such information for a purpose other than that for which the document or part was supplied to him (s 42(6)(c)).

Regulations may also make provision as to the form in which any such document or part is supplied and for the payment of a fee in respect of the supply of a document or part: see s 42(4). Regulations may also impose conditions corresponding to those mentioned in 42(6) in respect of persons who have obtained a document or part of a document mentioned in s 42(2): (a) which was supplied to another person in pursuance of s 42(2) (s 42(7)(a)); or (b) otherwise than in accordance with regulations under s 42 (s 42(7)(b)). As to the regulations so made see PARA 511.

20   Electoral Administration Act 2006 s 42(2)(a). For these purposes, a party is a registered party if it is registered for the purposes of the Political Parties, Elections and Referendums Act 2000 Pt II (ss 22–40) (see PARA 253): see the Electoral Administration Act 2006 s 44(1), (6).

21   Electoral Administration Act 2006 s 42(2)(b). As to the meaning of 'candidate' see PARA 230.

22   A European parliamentary election is an election at which a registered party submits a list of candidates for the purposes of allocating seats in the European Parliament: see PARA 340.

23   Electoral Administration Act 2006 s 42(2)(c).

511.   Supply and inspection of documents relating to European parliamentary elections.   Any person entitled to be supplied[1] with copies of the full register[2] at a European parliamentary election is also a person entitled[3] to request[4] that a relevant registration officer supply copies of the relevant part[5] of the marked register or lists he is required to keep[6]. The relevant registration officer must supply a copy of the relevant part of the marked register or lists where a request is duly made[7], and where:

(1)　　he is satisfied that the requestor needs to see the marks on the marked register or lists in order to achieve the purpose for which it is requested[8]; and

(2)　　he has received payment of a fee[9].

If the relevant registration officer is not satisfied in accordance with head (1) above, he may treat the request for a marked register or list as a request for information in unmarked lists[10], or as a request for the published copy of the full register[11], or both[12].

Any person is entitled to request that the relevant registration officer make available for inspection a copy of any of the following documents ('the documents open to public inspection')[13]:

(a)　　the marked register or lists[14];

(b)　　such other documents relating to an election as the relevant registration officer is required by or under any enactment to retain for any period[15], except: (i) ballot papers[16]; (ii) completed corresponding number lists[17]; and (iii) certificates as to employment on duty on the day of the election[18].

The relevant registration officer must make the documents open to public inspection available for inspection under supervision not later than ten days[19] after the date of receipt of a request that has been duly made[20]. However, where a request has been made to inspect copies of the marked register or lists[21], and where the relevant registration officer is not satisfied that the purposes of the requestor cannot be met by inspection of the full register, he must inform the requestor of his decision to this effect, and he must provide the requestor with information concerning the availability for inspection of the published full register[22]. The relevant registration officer must, on request, supply free of charge copies of any documents open to public inspection to a person who has inspected those documents and who is entitled to be supplied with a copy of the marked register or lists[23].

1　Ie in accordance with the Representation of the People (England and Wales) Regulations 2001, SI 2001/341, reg 100 (supply of full register to Electoral Commission: see PARA 183), reg 103 (supply of full register to elected representatives for electoral purposes: see PARA 185), reg 105 (supply of full register to local constituency parties: see PARA 185), reg 106 (supply of full register to registered political parties: see PARA 185), reg 108 (supply of full register to certain candidates: see PARA 185), reg 109 (supply of full register to police forces and other agencies: see PARA 186) or reg 113 (sale of full register to certain government departments and other bodies: see PARA 188): see the European Parliamentary Elections Regulations 2004, SI 2004/293, Sch 1 para 68(1)(a) (Sch 1 substituted by SI 2009/186). As to the equivalent provisions that apply for Gibraltar see the European Parliamentary Elections Regulations 2004, SI 2004/293, Sch 1 para 68(1)(c) (as so substituted). As to the electoral areas established for the purposes of European parliamentary elections (including the 'combined region' which incorporates Gibraltar) see PARA 77.

2　For these purposes, 'full register' means the version of the register published under the Representation of the People Act 1983 s 13(1) or (3) (see PARA 165), or under equivalent provisions that apply for Gibraltar: see the European Parliamentary Elections Regulations 2004, SI 2004/293, Sch 1 para 67(1) (as substituted: see note 1).

3　Ie subject to the European Parliamentary Elections Regulations 2004, SI 2004/293, Sch 1 para 68 (see also the text and notes 1–2, 4–12) and Sch 1 para 70 (see notes 6, 13, 23): see Sch 1 para 68(1) (as substituted: see note 1).

4　A person whose entitlement to request copies of the marked register or lists under the European Parliamentary Elections Regulations 2004, SI 2004/293, Sch 1 para 68(1) arises from being in a category of persons covered by the Representation of the People (England and Wales) Regulations 2001, SI 2001/341, reg 103 (supply of full register to elected representatives for electoral purposes: see PARA 185), reg 105 (supply of full register to local constituency parties: see PARA 185), reg 106 (supply of full register to registered political parties: see PARA 185) or reg 108 (supply of full register to certain candidates: see PARA 185), or under equivalent provisions that apply for Gibraltar, before a particular European Parliamentary election, is entitled to request those documents regardless of whether after that election he remains in a category of persons so entitled: European Parliamentary Elections Regulations 2004, SI 2004/293, Sch 1 para 68(2) (as substituted: see note 1). In Pt 6 (Sch 1 paras 67–72), 'marked register or lists' means any part of the marked copies of the full register, the list of proxies, the postal voters list, and the proxy postal voters list forwarded to the relevant registration officer Sch 1 para 64 (forwarding of documents to relevant registration officer: see PARA 501): see Sch 1 para 67(1) (as so substituted). As to the meaning of references to the relevant registration officer for these purposes see PARA 496 note 3. As to the postal voters list and the list of proxies see PARA 373; and as to the proxy postal voters list see PARA 381.

5   Ie within the meaning of the Representation of the People (England and Wales) Regulations 2001, SI 2001/341, reg 100 (supply of full register to Electoral Commission: see PARA 183), reg 103 (supply of full register to elected representatives for electoral purposes: see PARA 185), reg 105 (supply of full register to local constituency parties: see PARA 185), reg 106 (supply of full register to registered political parties: see PARA 185), reg 108 (supply of full register to certain candidates: see PARA 185), reg 109 (supply of full register to police forces and other agencies: see PARA 186) or reg 113 (sale of full register to government departments and other bodies: see PARA 188), or under equivalent provisions that apply for Gibraltar: see the European Parliamentary Elections Regulations 2004, SI 2004/293, Sch 1 para 68(1) (as substituted: see note 1).

6   European Parliamentary Elections Regulations 2004, SI 2004/293, Sch 1 para 68(1) (as substituted: see note 1). A request under Sch 1 para 68(1) must be made in writing; and it must:
    (1)   specify which of the marked register or lists (or the relevant part of the register or lists) are requested (Sch 1 para 68(3)(a) (as so substituted));
    (2)   state whether a printed copy of the records or lists or a copy in data form is requested (Sch 1 para 68(3)(b) (as so substituted)); and
    (3)   state the purposes for which the marked register or lists will be used and why the supply or purchase of a copy of the full register or unmarked lists would not be sufficient to achieve those purposes (Sch 1 para 68(3)(c) (as so substituted)).
Subject to any direction by the Secretary of State under the Representation of the People Act 1983 s 52(1) (discharge of registration duties: see PARA 141), or under the equivalent provision that applies for Gibraltar, any duty on a relevant registration officer to supply records or lists under the European Parliamentary Elections Regulations 2004, SI 2004/293, Pt 6, imposes only a duty to provide that information in the form in which he holds it, however: see Sch 1 para 67(5) (as so substituted). As to the meaning of 'data form' see PARA 180 note 11. As to the Secretary of State see PARA 2.

A person who obtains a copy of any part of a marked register or list under Sch 1 para 68(1)(a) (see note 1) may use it only for the permitted purposes specified in Sch 1 para 70(2) (see note 13), and any conditions specified in Sch 1 para 70(2) (or any conditions which would apply to the use of the full register under whichever of the Representation of the People (England and Wales) Regulations 2001, SI 2001/341, reg 100 (supply of full register to Electoral Commission: see PARA 183), reg 103 (supply of full register to elected representatives for electoral purposes: see PARA 185), reg 105 (supply of full register to local constituency parties: see PARA 185), reg 106 (supply of full register to registered political parties: see PARA 185), reg 108 (supply of full register to certain candidates: see PARA 185), reg 109 (supply of full register to police forces and other agencies: see PARA 186) or reg 113 (sale of full register to government departments and other bodies: see PARA 188), entitled that person to obtain that document) apply to such use: see the European Parliamentary Elections Regulations 2004, SI 2004/293, Sch 1 para 68(6) (as so substituted). As to an entitlement arising under Sch 1 para 68(1)(c) (see note 1), see Sch 1 para 68(8) (as so substituted). The conditions which would thus apply, apply to a person to whom a copy of a marked register or list, or any information contained in it (that is not contained in the edited register), has been so supplied or disclosed, as they apply to the person to whom those regulations apply: Sch 1 para 68(9) (as so substituted). As to the meaning of 'edited register' see PARA 167 note 4.

Any person who has obtained or is entitled to obtain a copy of the marked register or lists under the European Parliamentary Elections Regulations 2004, SI 2004/293, Sch 1 para 68 may:
    (a)   supply a copy of the marked register or lists to a processor for the purpose of processing the information contained therein (Sch 1 para 68(10)(a) (as so substituted)); or
    (b)   procure that a processor processes and supplies to him any copy of the information in the marked register or lists which the processor has obtained under Sch 1 para 68 (Sch 1 para 68(10)(b) (as so substituted)),

for use in respect of the purposes for which that person is entitled to obtain any such copy or information (as the case may be) (Sch 1 para 68(10) (as so substituted)). The processor of the register may not disclose the full register, or the information contained in it, except to the person who supplied the information to the processor or an employee of that person or a person who is entitled to obtain a copy of the full register under the Representation of the People (England and Wales) Regulations 2001, SI 2001/341 (or under the equivalent provisions that apply for Gibraltar), or any employee of such a person: European Parliamentary Elections Regulations 2004, SI 2004/293, Sch 1 para 67(2) (as so substituted). Where a person obtains copies of the information in the marked register or lists in accordance with Sch 1 para 68(1), the permitted purpose (see PARA 179 note 18) means either research purposes or electoral purposes: Sch 1 para 70(2) (as so substituted). For these purposes, any reference to an employee of any person who has access to a copy of the full register must be deemed to include a person working or providing services for the purposes of that person or employed by or on behalf of, or working for, any person who is so working or who is supplying such a service: Sch 1 para 67(3) (as so substituted). 'Processor' means any person who provides a service which consists of putting information into data form or processing information in data form and any reference to a processor includes a reference to his employees; and 'research purposes' includes statistical or historical purposes: Sch 1 para 67(1) (as so substituted).

7 European Parliamentary Elections Regulations 2004, SI 2004/293, Sch 1 para 68(4) (as substituted: see note 1).

8 European Parliamentary Elections Regulations 2004, SI 2004/293, Sch 1 para 68(4)(a) (as substituted: see note 1).

9 European Parliamentary Elections Regulations 2004, SI 2004/293, Sch 1 para 68(4)(b) (as substituted: see note 1). The fee mentioned in head (2) in the text must be calculated in accordance with Sch 1 para 71: see Sch 1 para 68(4)(b) (as so substituted). Accordingly, the fee to be paid in accordance with Sch 1 para 68(4)(b) by a person making a request for a copy of the whole or of any part of the marked register or lists must be the sum of £10 (see Sch 1 para 71(1), (2) (as so substituted)), plus:

(1) for a copy in printed form, £2 for each 1,000 entries (or remaining part of 1,000 entries) covered by the request (Sch 1 para 71(2)(a) (as so substituted and substituted)); and

(2) for a copy in data form, £1 for each 1,000 entries (or remaining part of 1,000 entries) covered by the request (Sch 1 para 71(2)(b) (as so substituted and substituted)).

For these purposes, a request for a copy of the whole or the same part of the marked register or lists in both a printed and data form may be treated as two separate requests: see Sch 1 para 71(3) (as so substituted).

10 Ie under the European Parliamentary Elections Regulations 2004, SI 2004/293, Sch 2 para 32 (see PARA 185 note 12): see Sch 1 para 68(5) (as substituted: see note 1).

11 Ie in accordance with the Representation of the People (England and Wales) Regulations 2001, SI 2001/341, reg 102 (see PARA 185): see the European Parliamentary Elections Regulations 2004, SI 2004/293, Sch 1 para 68(5) (as substituted: see note 1).

12 European Parliamentary Elections Regulations 2004, SI 2004/293, Sch 1 para 68(5) (as substituted: see note 1). The relevant registration officer must provide the requestor with information concerning the availability of the unmarked lists, full register, or both, as the case may be, accordingly: see Sch 1 para 68(5) (as so substituted).

13 See the European Parliamentary Elections Regulations 2004, SI 2004/293, Sch 1 para 69(1) (as substituted: see note 1). A request under Sch 1 para 69(1) must be made in writing; and it must specify:

(1) which documents are requested (Sch 1 para 69(2)(a) (as so substituted));

(2) the purposes for which the information in any document will be used (Sch 1 para 69(2)(b) (as so substituted));

(3) any reason why inspecting the full register or unmarked lists would not be sufficient to achieve that purpose (ie where the request is to inspect the marked register or lists) (Sch 1 para 69(2)(c) (as so substituted));

(4) who will inspect the documents (Sch 1 para 69(2)(d) (as so substituted));

(5) the date on which they wish to inspect the documents (Sch 1 para 69(2)(e) (as so substituted)); and

(6) whether they would prefer to inspect the documents in printed or data form (Sch 1 para 69(2)(f) (as so substituted)).

Subject to any direction by the Secretary of State under the Representation of the People Act 1983 s 52(1) (discharge of registration duties: see PARA 141), or under the equivalent provision that applies for Gibraltar, any duty on a registration officer to make records or lists available for inspection under the European Parliamentary Elections Regulations 2004,

SI 2004/293, Pt 6, imposes only a duty to provide that information in the form in which he holds it, however: see Sch 1 para 67(5) (as so substituted).

A person who obtains a copy of or information in any document open to public inspection under Sch 1 para 69 may use it only for the permitted purposes specified in Sch 1 para 70; and any conditions:

(a)   specified in Sch 1 para 70 (see Sch 1 para 69(5)(a) (as so substituted));

(b)   specified in Sch 1 para 69(7) (see note 20) (see Sch 1 para 69(5)(b) (as so substituted)); or

(c)   which would apply to the use of the full register under the Representation of the People (England and Wales) Regulations 2001, SI 2001/341, reg 109 (supply of full register to police forces and other agencies: see PARA 186), or under the equivalent provision that applies for Gibraltar, where such a person has obtained a copy of that document under the European Parliamentary Elections Regulations 2004, SI 2004/293, Sch 1 para 69(8) (see the text and note 23) (see Sch 1 para 69(5)(c) (as so substituted)),

apply to such use (see Sch 1 para 69(5) (as so substituted)). The restrictions on the supply, disclosure and use of information in the Representation of the People (England and Wales) Regulations 2001, SI 2001/341, reg 94 (restrictions on supply of full register and disclosure of information from it by the registration officer and his staff: see PARA 179) and reg 96 (restrictions on use of full register or information contained in it: see PARA 179), or under the equivalent provisions that apply for Gibraltar, apply to documents open to public inspection, as they apply to the full register (European Parliamentary Elections Regulations 2004, SI 2004/293, Sch 1 para 70(1) (as so substituted)), except that, where a person inspects information in accordance with Sch 1 para 69(1), the permitted purpose (see PARA 179 note 18) means either research purposes or electoral purposes (Sch 1 para 70(2) (as so substituted)).

14 European Parliamentary Elections Regulations 2004, SI 2004/293, Sch 1 para 69(1)(a) (as substituted: see note 1).

15 European Parliamentary Elections Regulations 2004, SI 2004/293, Sch 1 para 69(1)(b) (as substituted: see note 1). For these purposes, 'enactment' includes any provision of an Act, including any provision of an Act of the Gibraltar Parliament, any provision of, or of any instrument made under, an Act of the Scottish Parliament, any provision of, or of any instrument made under, Northern Ireland legislation, and any provision of subordinate legislation (within the meaning of the Interpretation Act 1978: see STATUTES AND LEGISLATIVE PROCESS vol 96 (2012) PARA 609): see the European Parliamentary Elections Regulations 2004, SI 2004/293, Sch 1 para 67(1) (as so substituted).

16 European Parliamentary Elections Regulations 2004, SI 2004/293, Sch 1 para 69(1)(b)(i) (as substituted: see note 1). As to the sealing up of ballot papers see PARA 495.

17 European Parliamentary Elections Regulations 2004, SI 2004/293, Sch 1 para 69(1)(b)(ii) (as substituted: see note 1). As to the completed corresponding number lists see PARA 405 note 11.

18 European Parliamentary Elections Regulations 2004, SI 2004/293, Sch 1 para 69(1)(b)(iii) (as substituted: see note 1). As to certificates of employment on duty on the day of the poll see PARA 395.

19 For these purposes, any period of days must be calculated in accordance with the European Parliamentary Elections Regulations 2004, SI 2004/293, Sch 1 para 2(1) (see PARA 223 note 1): see Sch 1 para 67(4) (as substituted: see note 1).

20 European Parliamentary Elections Regulations 2004, SI 2004/293, Sch 1 para 69(3) (as substituted: see note 1). Where inspection takes place by providing the records or lists on a computer screen or otherwise in data form, the relevant registration officer must ensure that the manner in, and equipment on, which that copy is provided do not permit any person consulting that copy to search it by electronic means by reference to the name of any person or to copy or transmit any part of that copy by electronic or any other means: see Sch 1 para 69(6) (as so substituted). Subject to Sch 1 para 69(8) (see the text and note 23), a person who inspects a copy of a document open to public inspection, whether in printed copy or in data form, may not make copies of any part of it, or record any particulars in it, except that a person who inspects a copy of the marked register or lists may make handwritten notes: Sch 1 para 69(7) (as so substituted).

21 Ie under the European Parliamentary Elections Regulations 2004, SI 2004/293, Sch 1 para 69(1) (see the text and notes 13–18): see Sch 1 para 69(4) (as substituted: see note 1).

22 See the European Parliamentary Elections Regulations 2004, SI 2004/293, Sch 1 para 69(4) (as substituted: see note 1). The text refers to the availability of the published full register for inspection in accordance with the Representation of the People (England and Wales) Regulations 2001, SI 2001/341, reg 43 (publication of register: see PARA 165 note 3), or under the equivalent provisions that apply for Gibraltar: see the European Parliamentary Elections Regulations 2004, SI 2004/293, Sch 1 para 69(4) (as so substituted).

23 European Parliamentary Elections Regulations 2004, SI 2004/293, Sch 1 para 69(8) (as substituted: see note 1). The text refers to entitlement to be supplied with a copy of the marked register or lists by virtue of being a person to whom with the Representation of the People (England and Wales) Regulations 2001, SI 2001/341, reg 109 (supply of full register to police forces and other agencies: see PARA 186) applies: see European Parliamentary Elections Regulations 2004, SI 2004/293, Sch 1 para 69(8) (as so substituted). Where a copy of any information was supplied in the circumstances to which Sch 1 para 69(8) applies, the permitted purpose means the purposes set out in the Representation of the People (England and Wales) Regulations 2001, SI 2001/341, reg 109(4) (see PARA 186), or under the equivalent provisions that apply for Gibraltar: European Parliamentary Elections Regulations 2004, SI 2004/293, Sch 1 para 70(3) (as so substituted). As to further conditions imposed regarding the use of information so obtained see note 13.

D. ORDERS FOR PRODUCTION OR INSPECTION OF ELECTION DOCUMENTS

512. Orders for production or inspection of documents. Documents relating to elections which have been retained may be produced or inspected by order of the House of Commons or by order of the election court[1].

1 See PARAS 836, 851, 852.

(xi) Countermand or Abandonment of Poll on Death of Candidate

A. PARLIAMENTARY ELECTIONS

513. Countermand or abandonment of poll at a parliamentary election on the death of independent or party candidate or Speaker of House of Commons seeking re-election. If, at a contested parliamentary election[1], proof is given to the satisfaction of the returning officer[2], before the result of the election is declared[3], that one of the persons named or to be named in the ballot papers as an independent candidate has died[4], then the parliamentary election rules apply to the election as if the candidate had not died[5], but subject to the following provisions[6]. Accordingly, if only two persons are shown as standing nominated in the statement of persons nominated[7], the returning officer must:

(1) if polling has not begun, countermand the notice of poll[8];
(2) if polling has begun, direct that the poll is abandoned[9]; or
(3) treat the election as an uncontested election[10].

However, if, at such an election where an independent candidate has died, the majority of votes is given to the deceased independent candidate himself[11], the declaration of the result must be achieved[12] by the returning officer:

(a) declaring that the majority of votes has been given to the deceased candidate[13];
(b) declaring that no member is returned[14]; and
(c) giving public notice[15] of the total number of votes given for each candidate, together with the number of rejected ballot papers under each head shown in the statement of rejected ballot papers[16].

If, after the counting of the votes (including any recount) is completed at an election where an independent candidate has died, an equality of votes is found to exist between any candidates[17], and if any of those candidates is a deceased candidate, the deceased candidate must be ignored for those purposes[18]. If, at a contested parliamentary election, proof is given to the satisfaction of the returning officer before the result of the election is declared that one of the persons named or to be named as a candidate in the ballot paper has died[19], and if that person is standing in the name of a registered political party[20], the returning officer must countermand notice of the poll[21] (or, if polling has begun, direct that the poll be abandoned)[22]. If, at a contested parliamentary election, one of the candidates is the Speaker of the House of Commons seeking re-election[23], and if proof is given to the returning officer's satisfaction before the result of the election is declared that that candidate has died[24], the returning officer must countermand notice of the poll[25] (or, if polling has begun, direct that the poll be abandoned)[26].

Where a poll is abandoned:

(i)   by reason of an independent candidate's death[27]; or

(ii)   by reason of the death of a party candidate[28]; or

(iii)   following the death of the speaker of House of Commons seeking re-election[29],

the presiding officer[30] at a polling station must take the like steps (so far as not already taken) for the delivery to the returning officer of ballot boxes and other documents as he is required to take on the close of the poll[31]. The returning officer must dispose of ballot papers and other documents in his possession as he is required to do on the completion in due course of the counting of the votes[32]. However, it is not necessary for any ballot paper account to be prepared or verified[33]; and the returning officer, without taking any step or further step for the counting of the ballot papers or of the votes[34], must seal up all the ballot papers, whether the votes on them have been counted or not[35]. The provisions of the parliamentary election rules as to the inspection, production, retention and destruction of ballot papers and other documents relating to a poll at an election apply to any such documents relating to a poll abandoned by reason of the death of a candidate[36], except that: (A) ballot papers on which the votes were neither counted nor rejected must be treated as counted ballot papers[37]; and (B) no order is to be made for the production or inspection of any ballot papers[38], or for the opening of a sealed packet of the completed corresponding number lists[39] or of certificates as to employment on duty on the day of the poll[40], unless the order is made by a court with reference to a prosecution[41].

Where the poll at an election is taken together with the poll at another election, special provision is made and neither the countermand of the poll at one election nor the direction that polling be abandoned at that election is to affect the poll at the other election[42].

1   As to the meaning of 'parliamentary election' see PARA 9. As to contested elections see PARA 384 et seq.

2   As to returning officers for parliamentary elections see PARA 350 et seq.

3   As to the declaration of result at a parliamentary election see PARA 479.

4   See the Representation of the People Act 1983 Sch 1 r 60(1) (Sch 1 r 60 substituted, Sch 1 rr 61–65 added, by the Electoral Administration Act 2006 s 24). For these purposes, a person is named or to be named on the ballot papers as an independent candidate if the description (if any) on his nomination paper is not authorised as mentioned in the Representation of the People Act 1983 Sch 1 r 6A(1) (see PARA 256) or Sch 1 r 6A(1B) (see PARA 256): see Sch 1 r 60(1), (5) (as so substituted). As to the time at which the returning officer can be satisfied that a candidate satisfies the test set out in the text see PARA 262.

5   Ie except the Representation of the People Act 1983 Sch 1 r 32(1)(c), (d) (admission of candidates and their agents to polling station: see PARA 395), Sch 1 r 44(2)(b)–(d) (attendance of candidates and their agents at count: see PARA 424) and Sch 1 r 53(4) (forfeiture of deposit based on percentage of votes cast for candidate: see PARA 481), which do not apply to the deceased candidate: see Sch 1 r 60(1), (3) (as substituted: see note 4). As to the meaning of the 'parliamentary election rules' see PARA 383 note 2.

6   See the Representation of the People Act 1983 Sch 1 r 60(1), (2) (as substituted: see note 4). The parliamentary election rules apply as mentioned in the text subject to Sch 1 r 60 and Sch 1 rr 61–62 (see the text and notes 7–18): see Sch 1 r 60(2) (as so substituted).

7   As to the statement of persons nominated see PARA 267.
8   Representation of the People Act 1983 Sch 1 r 60(1), (4)(a) (as substituted: see note 4). As to the notice of poll see PARA 388. As to a fresh election following the countermand or abandonment of the poll on the death of an independent candidate see PARA 515.
9   Representation of the People Act 1983 Sch 1 r 60(1), (4)(b) (as substituted: see note 4). See note 8.
10 Representation of the People Act 1983 Sch 1 r 60(1), (4)(c) (as substituted: see note 4). Head (3) in the text is subject to Sch 1 r 65 (see the text and notes 27–41): see Sch 1 r 60(4)(c) (as so substituted). As to the procedure at uncontested parliamentary elections see PARA 474.
11 See the Representation of the People Act 1983 Sch 1 r 61(1) (as added: see note 4).
12 Ie the Representation of the People Act 1983 Sch 1 r 50 (procedure as to declaration of result in contested and uncontested elections: see PARA 479) does not apply: see Sch 1 r 61(2) (as added: see note 4).
13 Representation of the People Act 1983 Sch 1 r 61(1), (2)(a) (as added: see note 4).
14 Representation of the People Act 1983 Sch 1 r 61(1), (2)(b) (as added: see note 4). The rule regarding forfeiture of deposit (ie Sch 1 r 53(4): see PARA 481) does not apply in relation to the remaining candidates either: Sch 1 r 61(1), (3) (as so added).
15 As to the giving of public notice by returning officers for parliamentary elections see PARA 350.
16 Representation of the People Act 1983 Sch 1 r 61(1), (2)(c) (as added: see note 4). As to the statement of rejected ballot papers at a parliamentary election see PARA 431.
17 Ie if the Representation of the People Act 1983 Sch 1 r 49 applies (see PARA 434): see Sch 1 r 62 (as added: see note 4).
18 See the Representation of the People Act 1983 Sch 1 r 62 (as added: see note 4).
19 Representation of the People Act 1983 Sch 1 r 63(1)(a) (as added: see note 4).
20 Representation of the People Act 1983 Sch 1 r 63(1)(b) (as added: see note 4). For these purposes, a person stands in the name of a registered political party if his nomination paper contains a description which is authorised as mentioned in Sch 1 r 6A(1) or Sch 1 r 6A(1B) (see PARA 256) (Sch 1 r 63(10)(a) (as so added)); and a registered political party is a party which is registered under the Political Parties, Elections and Referendums Act 2000 Pt II (ss 22–40) (see PARA 253) (Representation of the People Act 1983 Sch 1 r 63(10)(b) (as so added)).
21 Representation of the People Act 1983 Sch 1 r 63(2)(a) (as added: see note 4). As to a fresh election following the countermand or abandonment of the poll on the death of a party candidate see PARA 515.
22 Representation of the People Act 1983 Sch 1 r 63(2)(b) (as added: see note 4). See note 21.
23 Representation of the People Act 1983 Sch 1 r 64(1)(a) (as added: see note 4).
24 Representation of the People Act 1983 Sch 1 r 64(1)(b) (as added: see note 4).
25 Representation of the People Act 1983 Sch 1 r 64(2)(a) (as added: see note 4). As to a fresh election following the countermand or abandonment of the poll on the death of the Speaker of the House of Commons seeking re-election see PARA 515.
26 Representation of the People Act 1983 Sch 1 r 64(2)(b) (as added: see note 4). See note 25.
27 Ie in pursuance of the Representation of the People Act 1983 Sch 1 r 60(4)(b) (see the text and note 9): see Sch 1 r 65(1)(a) (as added: see note 4).
28 Ie in pursuance of the Representation of the People Act 1983 Sch 1 r 63(2)(b) (see the text and note 22): see Sch 1 r 65(1)(b) (as added: see note 4).
29 Ie in pursuance of the Representation of the People Act 1983 Sch 1 r 64(2)(b) (see the text and note 26): see Sch 1 r 65(1)(b) (as added: see note 4).
30 As to the appointment of presiding officers and their clerks see PARA 393.
31 See the Representation of the People Act 1983 Sch 1 r 65(2) (as added: see note 4). As to the usual procedure on the close of poll see PARA 405.
32 Representation of the People Act 1983 Sch 1 r 65(3) (as added: see note 4).
33 Representation of the People Act 1983 Sch 1 r 65(4) (as added: see note 4). As to the preparation and verification of the ballot paper accounts see PARA 405 et seq.
34 See the Representation of the People Act 1983 Sch 1 r 65(5) (as added: see note 4).
35 See the Representation of the People Act 1983 Sch 1 r 65(6) (as added: see note 4). In such circumstances, it is not necessary to seal up counted and rejected ballot papers in separate packets, as the normal close of poll procedure requires (see PARA 405): see Sch 1 r 65(6) (as so added).
36 Representation of the People Act 1983 Sch 1 r 65(7) (as added: see note 4).
37 Representation of the People Act 1983 Sch 1 r 65(8) (as added: see note 4).
38 Representation of the People Act 1983 Sch 1 r 65(9)(a) (as added: see note 4). As to documents relating to elections which have been retained and may be produced or inspected by order of the House of Commons or by order of the election court see PARAS 836, 851, 852.
39 As to completed corresponding number lists see PARA 405 note 11.

40　Representation of the People Act 1983 Sch 1 r 65(9)(b) (as added: see note 4). As to certificates of employment on duty on the day of the poll see PARA 395.
41　See the Representation of the People Act 1983 Sch 1 r 65(9) (as added: see note 4).
42　See PARA 16 et seq.

514.　Poll abandoned or countermanded after postal ballot papers have been issued at a parliamentary election.　Where, after postal ballot papers have been issued[1], a poll at a parliamentary election is abandoned or countermanded by reason of the death of a candidate[2], the returning officer[3]:

(1)　must not take any step or further step to open covering envelopes[4] or deal with their contents[5]; and

(2)　must[6] treat all unopened covering envelopes and the contents of those which have been opened as if they were counted ballot papers[7].

These provisions do not apply where postal ballot papers for more than one election have been issued together[8].

1　As to the issue of postal ballot papers see PARA 406 et seq.
2　As to the countermand or abandonment of the poll at a parliamentary election on the death of an independent or party candidate or of the Speaker of House of Commons seeking re-election see PARA 513.
3　See the Representation of the People (England and Wales) Regulations 2001, SI 2001/341, reg 90(1). As to returning officers for parliamentary elections see PARA 350 et seq.
4　As to the meaning of 'covering envelope' see PARA 410.
5　Representation of the People (England and Wales) Regulations 2001, SI 2001/341, reg 90(1)(a). Head (1) in the text refers to any step or further step that would otherwise be taken normally in accordance with Pt V (regs 64–91) (issue and receipt of postal ballot papers): see reg 90(1)(a).
6　Ie notwithstanding the Representation of the People (England and Wales) Regulations 2001, SI 2001/341, regs 84–86 (procedure following on from opening covering envelopes: see PARAS 421–422): see reg 90(1)(b).
7　Representation of the People (England and Wales) Regulations 2001, SI 2001/341, reg 90(1)(b).
8　Representation of the People (England and Wales) Regulations 2001, SI 2001/341, reg 90(2). As to the issue and receipt of postal ballot papers when polls are combined see PARA 20.

515.　Fresh election following countermand or abandonment of poll on death of candidate at a parliamentary election.　Where the poll at a parliamentary election[1] is countermanded or abandoned by reason of the death of an independent candidate who has polled a majority of the votes[2], the returning officer[3] must not return the writ[4]. Instead, the proceedings with reference to the election must be commenced afresh[5], with the writ for the election taken to have been received on the first working day[6] after the end of the period of seven days starting on the day of the original election[7]. No fresh nomination is necessary in the case of a person shown in the statement of persons nominated as standing nominated[8], and no other nomination may be made[9]. The requirement to validate the nomination by the making of a deposit does not apply in this case[10].

Where the poll at a parliamentary election is countermanded or abandoned by reason of the death of a party candidate[11], the proceedings with reference to the election must be commenced afresh[12], with the writ for the election taken to have been received on the first working day[13] after the end of the period of seven days starting on the day the proof of death is given to the returning officer[14]. No fresh nomination is necessary in the case of a person shown in the statement of persons nominated as standing nominated[15]; and no other nomination may be made except for a person standing in the name of the same registered political party in whose name the deceased candidate was standing[16].

Where the poll at a parliamentary election is countermanded or abandoned by reason of the death of the Speaker of the House of Commons seeking re-election[17], the proceedings with reference to the election must be commenced afresh[18], with the writ for the election taken to have been received on the first working day[19] after the end of the period of seven days starting on the day the proof of death is given to the returning officer[20].

In all cases where a fresh election is commenced following the death of an independent or party candidate or following the death of the speaker of House of Commons seeking re-election, the poll must be held on a day in the period which starts 15 working days after the day on which the writ is taken to have been received and ends 19 working days after that day[21].

Where the poll at an election is taken together with the poll at another election, special provision is made and neither the countermand of the poll at one election nor the direction that polling be abandoned at that election is to affect the poll at the other election[22].

1   As to the meaning of 'parliamentary election' see PARA 9.
2   See PARA 513.
3   As to returning officers for parliamentary elections see PARA 350 et seq.
4   See the Representation of the People Act 1983 Sch 1 r 61(1), (4) (Sch 1 rr 61, 63–64 added by the Electoral Administration Act 2006 s 24). As to the issue and return of the writ at a parliamentary election see PARA 192 et seq.
5   Ie subject to the Representation of the People Act 1983 Sch 1 r 61(1), (5)–(10) (see the text and notes 6–10, 21): see Sch 1 r 61(4) (as added: see note 4).
6   For these purposes, a working day is a day which is not a day specified in the Representation of the People Act 1983 Sch 1 r 2(1)(a)–(c) (see PARA 195 note 27): Sch 1 r 61(1), (10) (as added: see note 4).
7   Representation of the People Act 1983 Sch 1 r 61(1), (5) (as added: see note 4). The text refers to the day of the election mentioned in Sch 1 r 60(1) (see PARA 513): see Sch 1 r 61(5) (as so added).
8   As to the statement of persons nominated see PARA 267.
9   Representation of the People Act 1983 Sch 1 r 61(1), (6) (as added: see note 4). The last day on which a notice of withdrawal of candidature by a person who stands nominated by virtue of Sch 1 r 61(6) may be delivered is the seventh working day after the day on which the writ is taken to be received: Sch 1 r 61(1), (7) (as so added).
10 Representation of the People Act 1983 Sch 1 r 61(1), (8) (as added: see note 4). The text refers to the rule in Sch 1 r 9 (deposit: see PARA 259): see Sch 1 r 61(8) (as so added).
11 See PARA 513.
12 See the Representation of the People Act 1983 Sch 1 r 63(1), (3) (as added: see note 4). The commencement of such proceedings is subject to Sch 1 r 63(1), (4)–(10) (see the text and notes 13–16, 21): see Sch 1 r 63(3) (as so added).
13 For these purposes, a working day is a day which is not a day specified in the Representation of the People Act 1983 Sch 1 r 2(1)(a)–(c) (see PARA 195 note 27): Sch 1 r 63(1), (10)(c) (as added: see note 4).
14 Representation of the People Act 1983 Sch 1 r 63(1), (4) (as added: see note 4).
15 Representation of the People Act 1983 Sch 1 r 63(1), (5) (as added: see note 4). The last day on which a notice of withdrawal of candidature by a person who stands nominated by virtue of Sch 1 r 63(5) may be delivered is the seventh working day after the day on which the writ is taken to be received: see Sch 1 r 63(1), (8) (as so added).
16 Representation of the People Act 1983 Sch 1 r 63(1), (6) (as added: see note 4). The last day on which a nomination mentioned in Sch 1 r 63(6) may be delivered, or on which a notice of withdrawal of candidature by a person who stands nominated in pursuance of Sch 1 r 63(6) may be delivered, is the seventh working day after the day on which the writ is taken to be received: see Sch 1 r 63(7), (8) (as so added).
17 See PARA 513.
18 Representation of the People Act 1983 Sch 1 r 64(1), (3) (as added: see note 4). The commencement of proceedings as mentioned in the text is subject to Sch 1 r 64(1), (4)–(7) (see the text and notes 19–21): see Sch 1 r 64(3) (as so added).
19 For these purposes, a working day is a day which is not a day specified in the Representation of the People Act 1983 Sch 1 r 2(1)(a)–(c) (see PARA 195 note 27): Sch 1 r 64(1), (7) (as added: see note 4).

20 Representation of the People Act 1983 Sch 1 r 64(1), (4) (as added: see note 4). The last day on which either nominations,or notice of withdrawal of candidature, may be delivered is the seventh working day after the day on which the writ is taken to be received: see Sch 1 r 64(1), (5) (as so added).

21 See the Representation of the People Act 1983 Sch 1 rr 61(1), (9), 63(1), (9), 64(1), (6) (as added: see note 4).

    As from a day to be appointed under the Electoral Registration and Administration Act 2013 s 27(1), the Representation of the People Act 1983 Sch 1 rr 61(9), 63(9), 64(6) are amended so that the poll must be held on a day in the period which starts 21 working days after the day on which the writ is taken to have been received and ends 27 working days after that day: see Sch 1 rr 61(9), 63(9), 64(6) (Sch 1 rr 61(9), 63(9), 64(6) as so added; prospectively amended by the Electoral Registration and Administration Act 2013 s 14(2), (5)). However, at the date at which this volume states the law, no such day had been appointed.

22 See PARA 16 et seq.

B. ELECTIONS OTHER THAN A PARLIAMENTARY ELECTION

516. Countermand or abandonment of poll on death of candidate at poll consequent on a parish meeting or election which is not a parliamentary election. If, at a contested election which is not a parliamentary election[1], or at a poll consequent on a parish meeting on a question involving appointment to office[2], proof is given to the satisfaction of the returning officer[3] before the result is declared[4] that one of the persons named or to be named as a candidate in the ballot papers[5] has died[6], then the returning officer must countermand notice of the poll or, if polling has begun, he must direct that the poll be abandoned[7].

Where such a poll is abandoned by reason of a candidate's death, no further ballot papers are to be issued, and the presiding officer[8] at any polling station must take the like steps (so far as not already taken) for the delivery to the returning officer[9] of ballot boxes and other documents as he is required to take on the close of the poll in due course[10]. The returning officer must dispose of ballot papers and other documents in his possession as he is required to do on the completion in due course of the counting of the votes[11]. However, it is not necessary for any ballot paper account to be prepared or verified[12]; and the returning officer, without taking any step or further step for the counting of the ballot papers or of the votes, must seal up all the ballot papers, whether the votes on them have been counted or not, although counted and rejected ballot papers need not be sealed up in separate packets[13]. The provisions as to the inspection, production, retention and destruction of ballot papers and other documents relating to a poll at such an election (or at such a poll consequent on a parish meeting)[14] apply to any such documents relating to a poll abandoned by reason of the death of a candidate[15]. Ballot papers on which the votes were neither counted nor rejected must, however, be treated as counted ballot papers[16]; and no order may be made for the production or inspection of any ballot papers, or for the opening of a sealed packet of the completed corresponding number lists (or counterfoils, in the case of a poll consequent on a parish meeting) or certificates as to employment on duty on the day of the poll[17], unless the order is made by a court with reference to a prosecution[18].

Where the poll at such an election is taken together with the poll at another election, special provision is made and neither the countermand of the poll at one election nor the direction that polling be abandoned at that election is to affect the poll at the other election[19].

1 Ie at a contested local government election (which includes an Authority election and a local authority mayoral election), or a Welsh Assembly constituency or regional election (whether the polls are taken separately or together), except that no provision is made for the countermand or

abandonment of the poll on the death of a candidate at a European parliamentary election (although provision is made for the return of a deceased candidate's deposit in such a case: see PARA 494); and as to London members' elections see note 7. As to the meanings of 'Assembly election', 'constituency election' and 'regional election' see PARA 3 note 2. As to the meaning of 'parliamentary election' see PARA 9. As to the meanings of 'Authority election' and 'local government election' see PARA 11. As to elections in the City of London see PARA 33. As to contested elections generally see PARA 384 et seq. As to the provision made for the countermand or abandonment of the poll at a parliamentary election see PARA 513. As to vacancies arising in the seats of London members of the London Assembly see PARA 204 et seq; and as to vacancies arising in the office of member of the European Parliament ('MEP') see PARA 218 et seq.

2   As to polls consequent on a parish meeting on a question involving appointment to office see PARA 200 et seq.

3   As to returning officers for local government elections see PARA 354 et seq; and as to the returning officer at a poll consequent on a parish meeting on a question involving appointment to office see PARA 356. In the case of an Authority election for London constituency members, or for the return of a London Mayor, the appropriate returning officer in most circumstances is the constituency returning officer (see PARA 211 note 9): see the Greater London Authority Elections Rules 2007, SI 2007/3541, Sch 1 r 60(1)–(4), (6), Sch 3 r 66(2)–(6). However, the Greater London returning officer (see PARA 211 note 8) deals with the early stages of the procedure where a candidate dies at a London Members' or London Mayoral election: see Sch 2 r 15(4), Sch 3 rr 63, 64, 65(1), (2); and see further notes 5, 7. As to the meanings of 'constituency member' and 'London Member' see PARA 11 notes 5, 6. For the purposes of Welsh Assembly elections, the appropriate returning officer is, in relation to an Assembly constituency election, the constituency returning officer and, in relation to an Assembly regional election, it is the regional returning officer: see the National Assembly for Wales (Representation of the People) Order 2007, SI 2007/236, Sch 5 paras 70–76. As to the meanings of 'constituency returning officer' and 'regional returning officer' see PARA 18 note 2.

4   As to declaration of the result at a local government election for a principal area, parish or community council see PARA 482; as to declaration of the result at a poll consequent on a parish meeting see PARA 483; as to declaration of the result at a local authority mayoral election see PARA 484; as to declaration of the result at a London Authority election see PARA 486 et seq; and as to declaration of the result at a Welsh Assembly election see PARAS 490, 491.

5   At a poll consequent on a parish meeting on a question involving appointment to office, the reference is simply to a candidate who has not withdrawn: see the Parish and Community Meetings (Polls) Rules 1987, SI 1987/1, Schedule r 37(1).

      For the purposes of an election for the return of the Mayor of London, the reference is to a person who is standing in the name of registered party (a 'deceased party candidate'): see the Greater London Authority Elections Rules 2007, SI 2007/3541, Sch 3 r 65(1)(b). For these purposes, a person stands in the name of a registered political party if his nomination paper contains a description which is authorised as mentioned in Sch 3 r 6(5) or Sch 3 r 6(7) (see PARA 256) (Sch 3 r 65(3)(a)); and a registered political party is a party which is registered under the Political Parties, Elections and Referendums Act 2000 Pt II (ss 22–40) (see PARA 253) (Greater London Authority Elections Rules 2007, SI 2007/3541, Sch 3 r 65(3)(b)). As to the provisions that apply specifically to a deceased independent candidate at such an election (which are similar to those that apply at a Parliamentary election: see PARA 513) see Sch 3 rr 63, 64(1)–(4), 66(1)(a), (2)–(9).

      Similarly, the reference at a Welsh Assembly constituency election is to a person who is standing in the name of registered party ('death of a party candidate'): see the National Assembly for Wales (Representation of the People) Order 2007, SI 2007/236, Sch 5 para 73(1)(b). For these purposes, a person stands in the name of a registered political party if his nomination paper contains a description which is authorised as mentioned in Sch 5 para 5(1) or Sch 5 para 5(3), and, where Sch 5 para 5(3) applies, references to 'party' refer to each party that has authorised use of that description (see PARA 256): see Sch 5 para 73(13)(a). As to the provisions that apply specifically to a deceased independent candidate at a Welsh Assembly constituency election (which are similar to those that apply at a Parliamentary election) see Sch 5 paras 70, 71(1)–(3), 72, 76(1)(a). As to the meaning of 'registered political party' for these purposes see PARA 230 note 23. At a Welsh Assembly regional election, the candidate referred to in the text may be either an individual candidate or a party list candidate: see Sch 5 para 75(1)–(4). As to the meanings of 'candidate' and individual candidate' for these purposes see PARA 230 note 19; and as to the meaning of 'party list candidate' see PARA 230 note 23.

6   As to the time at which the returning officer can be satisfied that a candidate satisfies this test see PARA 262. At a Welsh Assembly regional election, the provision set out in the text applies only if the election becomes uncontested as a result of the death: see the National Assembly for

Wales (Representation of the People) Order 2007, SI 2007/236, Sch 5 para 75(1). Where such an election remains contested see Sch 5 para 75(2), (3); and note 7.

7   Parish and Community Meetings (Polls) Rules 1987, SI 1987/1, Schedule r 37(1); Local Elections (Principal Areas) (England and Wales) Rules 2006, SI 2006/3304, Sch 2 r 55(1); Local Elections (Parishes and Communities) (England and Wales) Rules 2006, SI 2006/3305, Sch 2 r 55(1); National Assembly for Wales (Representation of the People) Order 2007, SI 2007/236, Sch 5 paras 73(1)(a), (2), 75(1)(a), (b); Local Authorities (Mayoral Elections) (England and Wales) Regulations 2007, SI 2007/1024, Sch 1 r 60(1); Greater London Authority Elections Rules 2007, SI 2007/3541, Sch 1 r 60(1)(a), Sch 3 r 65(1)(b), (2). At a London constituency members' election, the CRO must inform the GLRO of the countermand or abandonment of the poll and of the name of the candidate who has died: Sch 1 r 60(1)(b). Where, before the result of a London members' election is declared, proof is given, to the GLRO's satisfaction, that a candidate whose name appears on a party list has died, then, in addition to complying with any other requirement of the Greater London Authority Elections Rules 2007, SI 2007/3541, relevant to that event, the GLRO must remove that person's name from that list: see Sch 2 r 15(4); and PARA 262 notes 9, 15. As to the notice of poll see PARA 388. As to the ordering of a fresh election following the countermand or abandonment of a poll on the death of a candidate see PARA 515.

At a Welsh Assembly general election, the constituency returning officer must forthwith notify the regional returning officer for the Assembly electoral region in which the Assembly constituency is situated that he has countermanded notice of the poll at that constituency election or, if polling had begun, that he has directed the poll to be abandoned, and that no member is returned for that constituency: National Assembly for Wales (Representation of the People) Order 2007, SI 2007/236, Sch 5 para 73(3). Similarly, where a contested regional election has been countermanded or abandoned, the regional returning officer must forthwith notify each constituency returning officer in the Assembly electoral region of the action that he has taken: Sch 5 para 75(1)(c). Where at an Assembly general election, there is a contested regional election and the poll or declaration of result at a constituency election for an Assembly constituency in the Assembly electoral region is postponed in accordance with Sch 5 para 71 (see note 5) or Sch 5 para 73, then Sch 5 para 63(1)(b) (ascertainment of results at a contested Welsh Assembly regional election: see PARA 464) is satisfied when the regional returning officer has received the notification required by Sch 5 para 62(3) (declaration of result: see PARA 490) in respect of each of the other Assembly constituencies in the Assembly electoral region (other than in respect of an Assembly constituency to which Sch 5 para 74(1) also applies): Sch 5 para 74(1). In such circumstances, the subsequent election of a candidate for the Assembly constituency has no effect upon the validity of the election and return of any candidate at the regional election: Sch 5 para 74(2). As to the meanings of 'Assembly constituency' and 'Assembly electoral region' for these purposes see PARA 3 note 2.

If, at a contested Welsh Assembly regional election, proof is given to the regional returning officer's satisfaction before the results of the election are declared that one of the persons named or to be named as a candidate on the ballot paper (whether as an individual or party list candidate) has died, but, notwithstanding that death, the election continues to be contested, the notice of poll is not to be countermanded nor the poll abandoned, and such a death has no effect upon the validity of the election and return of any other candidate at the regional election: Sch 5 para 75(2). However, in these circumstances, the regional returning officer must take such steps as he considers reasonable to publicise, in the Assembly electoral region for which the election is held, the name of that candidate and the fact of his death, whether that candidate was an individual or party list candidate (and, if he was a party list candidate, the name of the registered political party for which that person was such a candidate): Sch 5 para 75(3). The regional returning officer must, in particular, consider whether he should take the required steps to publicise by causing notices to be placed outside polling stations: see Sch 5 para 75(3). In respect of an election to which Sch 5 para 75(1), (2) applies, Sch 5 para 41(1)(c), (d) (admission of candidates and their agents to polling station: see PARA 395), Sch 5 para 54(5)(b)–(d) (attendance of candidates and their agents at count: see PARA 458) do not apply to the deceased candidate, and Sch 5 para 65(6) (forfeiture of deposit based on percentage of votes cast for candidate: see PARA 492) does not apply where the deceased was an individual candidate: Sch 5 para 75(4).

8   As to the appointment of presiding officers and their clerks see PARA 393.

9   In the case of an election for the return of the Mayor of London and in the case of a Welsh Assembly regional election, the items referred to in the text are to be delivered to the appropriate constituency returning officer (see PARA 405; cf note 3).

10 Parish and Community Meetings (Polls) Rules 1987, SI 1987/1, Schedule r 37(2); Local Elections (Principal Areas) (England and Wales) Rules 2006, SI 2006/3304, Sch 2 r 55(2); Local

Elections (Parishes and Communities) (England and Wales) Rules 2006, SI 2006/3305, Sch 2 r 55(2); National Assembly for Wales (Representation of the People) Order 2007, SI 2007/236, Sch 5 para 76(1)(a), (b), (2); Local Authorities (Mayoral Elections) (England and Wales) Regulations 2007, SI 2007/1024, Sch 1 r 60(2);. Greater London Authority Elections Rules 2007, SI 2007/3541, Sch 1 r 60(3), Sch 3 r 66(1)(b), (2).

Where the polls at an Assembly regional election and at an Assembly constituency election for a constituency within that region are held on the same day but the poll at one election is abandoned in any of the circumstances mentioned in the National Assembly for Wales (Representation of the People) Order 2007, SI 2007/236, Sch 5 para 76(1)(a), (b), the steps which the presiding officer is required to take at such a polling station by Sch 5 para 76(2) must take place at the close of the poll at the other election; and Sch 5 para 76(4)–(9) (see the text and notes 12–18) applies only to the abandoned poll: Sch 5 para 76(10)(a).

11 Parish and Community Meetings (Polls) Rules 1987, SI 1987/1, Schedule r 37(2); Local Elections (Principal Areas) (England and Wales) Rules 2006, SI 2006/3304, Sch 2 r 55(3); Local Elections (Parishes and Communities) (England and Wales) Rules 2006, SI 2006/3305, Sch 2 r 55(3); National Assembly for Wales (Representation of the People) Order 2007, SI 2007/236, Sch 5 para 76(3); Local Authorities (Mayoral Elections) (England and Wales) Regulations 2007, SI 2007/1024, Sch 1 r 60(3); Greater London Authority Elections Rules 2007, SI 2007/3541, Sch 1 r 60(4), Sch 3 r 66(3).

Where the polls at an Assembly regional election and at an Assembly constituency election for a constituency within that region are held on the same day but the poll at one election is abandoned in any of the circumstances mentioned in the National Assembly for Wales (Representation of the People) Order 2007, SI 2007/236, Sch 5 para 76(1)(a), (b) (see the text and notes 8–10), the constituency returning officer must first separate out the ballot papers relating to the other Assembly election before sealing up the ballot papers; and Sch 5 para 76(4)–(9) (see the text and notes 12–18) applies only to the abandoned poll: Sch 5 para 76(10)(b).

12 Parish and Community Meetings (Polls) Rules 1987, SI 1987/1, Schedule r 37(2)(a); Local Elections (Principal Areas) (England and Wales) Rules 2006, SI 2006/3304, Sch 2 r 55(4); Local Elections (Parishes and Communities) (England and Wales) Rules 2006, SI 2006/3305, Sch 2 r 55(4); National Assembly for Wales (Representation of the People) Order 2007, SI 2007/236, Sch 5 para 76(4); Local Authorities (Mayoral Elections) (England and Wales) Regulations 2007, SI 2007/1024, Sch 1 r 60(4); Greater London Authority Elections Rules 2007, SI 2007/3541, Sch 1 r 60(5), Sch 3 r 66(4). As to the preparation and verification of the ballot paper accounts see PARA 405 et seq.

13 Parish and Community Meetings (Polls) Rules 1987, SI 1987/1, Schedule r 37(2)(b); Local Elections (Principal Areas) (England and Wales) Rules 2006, SI 2006/3304, Sch 2 r 55(5); Local Elections (Parishes and Communities) (England and Wales) Rules 2006, SI 2006/3305, Sch 2 r 55(5); National Assembly for Wales (Representation of the People) Order 2007, SI 2007/236, Sch 5 para 76(5), (6); Local Authorities (Mayoral Elections) (England and Wales) Regulations 2007, SI 2007/1024, Sch 1 r 60(5); Greater London Authority Elections Rules 2007, SI 2007/3541, Sch 1 r 60(6), Sch 3 r 66(5), (6).

14 See PARAS 503 et seq, 836, 851.

15 Parish and Community Meetings (Polls) Rules 1987, SI 1987/1, Schedule r 37(3); Local Elections (Principal Areas) (England and Wales) Rules 2006, SI 2006/3304, Sch 2 r 55(6); Local Elections (Parishes and Communities) (England and Wales) Rules 2006, SI 2006/3305, Sch 2 r 55(6); National Assembly for Wales (Representation of the People) Order 2007, SI 2007/236, Sch 5 para 76(7); Local Authorities (Mayoral Elections) (England and Wales) Regulations 2007, SI 2007/1024, Sch 1 r 60(6); Greater London Authority Elections Rules 2007, SI 2007/3541, Sch 1 r 60(7), Sch 3 r 66(7).

16 Parish and Community Meetings (Polls) Rules 1987, SI 1987/1, Schedule r 37(3)(a); Local Elections (Principal Areas) (England and Wales) Rules 2006, SI 2006/3304, Sch 2 r 55(7); Local Elections (Parishes and Communities) (England and Wales) Rules 2006, SI 2006/3305, Sch 2 r 55(7); National Assembly for Wales (Representation of the People) Order 2007, SI 2007/236, Sch 5 para 76(8); Local Authorities (Mayoral Elections) (England and Wales) Regulations 2007, SI 2007/1024, Sch 1 r 60(7); Greater London Authority Elections Rules 2007, SI 2007/3541, Sch 1 r 60(8), Sch 3 r 66(8).

17 As to certificates of employment on duty on the day of the poll see PARA 395. There are no certificates as to employment on duty on the day of the poll at a poll consequent on a parish meeting on a question involving appointment to office and accordingly no reference is made to them in the Parish and Community Meetings (Polls) Rules 1987, SI 1987/1: see Schedule r 37(3).

18 Parish and Community Meetings (Polls) Rules 1987, SI 1987/1, Schedule r 37(3)(b); Local Elections (Principal Areas) (England and Wales) Rules 2006, SI 2006/3304, Sch 2 r 55(8); Local

Elections (Parishes and Communities) (England and Wales) Rules 2006, SI 2006/3305, Sch 2 r 55(8); National Assembly for Wales (Representation of the People) Order 2007, SI 2007/236, Sch 5 para 76(9); Local Authorities (Mayoral Elections) (England and Wales) Regulations 2007, SI 2007/1024, Sch 1 r 60(8); Greater London Authority Elections Rules 2007, SI 2007/3541, Sch 1 r 60(9), Sch 3 r 66(9).
19 See PARA 16 et seq.

517. Poll abandoned or countermanded after postal ballot papers have been issued at local government or Welsh Assembly election. Where, after postal ballot papers have been issued[1], a poll at a local government or Welsh Assembly election is abandoned or countermanded by reason of the death of a candidate[2], the returning officer[3]:

(1) must not take any step or further step to open covering envelopes[4] or deal with their contents[5]; and

(2) must[6] treat all unopened covering envelopes and the contents of those which have been opened as if they were counted ballot papers[7].

Heads (1) and (2) above do not apply, however, where postal ballot papers for more than one election have been issued together[8].

1 As to the issue of postal ballot papers see PARA 406 et seq.
2 As to the countermand or abandonment of the poll other than at a parliamentary election see PARA 516. There is no provision for the poll at a European parliamentary election to be abandoned or countermanded (although provision is made for the return of a deceased candidate's deposit in such a case: see PARA 494).
3 See the Representation of the People (England and Wales) Regulations 2001, SI 2001/341, reg 90(1); and the National Assembly for Wales (Representation of the People) Order 2007, SI 2007/236, Sch 3 para 30(1). As to the returning officers and elections referred to in the text see PARA 406 note 1; and see also PARA 409 note 1.
4 As to the meaning of 'covering envelope' see PARA 410.
5 Representation of the People (England and Wales) Regulations 2001, SI 2001/341, reg 90(1)(a); National Assembly for Wales (Representation of the People) Order 2007, SI 2007/236, Sch 3 para 30(1)(a). Head (1) in the text refers to any step or further step that would otherwise be taken normally in accordance with the Representation of the People (England and Wales) Regulations 2001, SI 2001/341, Pt V (regs 64–91), or, in relation to a Welsh Assembly election, the National Assembly for Wales (Representation of the People) Order 2007, SI 2007/236, Sch 3 (issue and receipt of postal ballot papers: see PARA 406 et seq): see the Representation of the People (England and Wales) Regulations 2001, SI 2001/341, reg 90(1)(a); and the National Assembly for Wales (Representation of the People) Order 2007, SI 2007/236, Sch 3 para 30(1)(a).
6 Ie notwithstanding the Representation of the People (England and Wales) Regulations 2001, SI 2001/341, regs 84–86, or, in relation to a Welsh Assembly election, the National Assembly for Wales (Representation of the People) Order 2007, SI 2007/236, Sch 3 paras 20–26 (procedure following on from opening covering envelopes: see PARAS 421–422): see the Representation of the People (England and Wales) Regulations 2001, SI 2001/341, reg 90(1)(b); and the National Assembly for Wales (Representation of the People) Order 2007, SI 2007/236, Sch 3 para 30(1)(b).
7 Representation of the People (England and Wales) Regulations 2001, SI 2001/341, reg 90(1)(b); National Assembly for Wales (Representation of the People) Order 2007, SI 2007/236, Sch 3 para 30(1)(b).
8 Representation of the People (England and Wales) Regulations 2001, SI 2001/341, reg 90(2); National Assembly for Wales (Representation of the People) Order 2007, SI 2007/236, Sch 3 para 30(2). As to the issue and receipt of postal ballot papers when polls are combined see PARA 20.

518. Fresh local government election following countermand or abandonment of poll on death of candidate. If, at a local government election in England and Wales[1], other than an election for the return of the London members of the London Assembly[2]:

(1) the poll is abandoned or countermanded for any reason[3]; or

(2)   no person is or remains, or an insufficient number of persons are or remain, validly nominated to fill the vacancy or vacancies in respect of which the election is held[4],

the returning officer[5] must order an election to fill any vacancy which remains unfilled to be held on a day appointed by him[6]. That day must be within the period of 35 days beginning with the day fixed as the day of election for the first-mentioned election[7]. Where an election is ordered to be held in this way[8]:

(a)   the relevant elections rules[9] relating to the notice to be given of an election and the manner in which an election is to be conducted apply in relation to the election so ordered to be held as they applied or would have applied in relation to the election which had not been duly held or has failed or become void[10]; and

(b)   no fresh nomination is necessary in the case of a candidate who remains validly nominated for the election[11].

Where the poll at an election is taken together with the poll at another election, special provision is made and neither the countermand of the poll at one election nor the direction that polling be abandoned at that election is to affect the poll at the other election[12].

1   As to the meanings of 'England' and 'Wales' see PARA 1 note 1. As to the meaning of 'local government election' see PARA 11.

2   See the Representation of the People Act 1983 s 39(1) (amended by the Greater London Authority Act 1999 s 17, Sch 3 paras 1, 6(1), (2)). As to the meaning of 'London member', in relation to the London Assembly, see PARA 11 note 5. Where, before the result of a London members' election is declared, proof is given, to the Greater London returning officer's (GLRO's) satisfaction, that a candidate whose name appears on a party list has died, then, in addition to complying with any other requirement of the Greater London Authority Elections Rules 2007, SI 2007/3541, relevant to that event, the GLRO must remove that person's name from that list: see Sch 2 r 15(4); and PARA 262 notes 9, 15. As to the filling of vacancies arising in the seats of London members of the London Assembly see PARA 204 et seq.

The Representation of the People Act 1983 s 39(1), (5) is applied, in respect of vacancies that remain unfilled when a poll is countermanded or abandoned on the death of a candidate, by the Local Elections (Principal Areas) (England and Wales) Rules 2006, SI 2006/3304, Sch 2 r 55(1); the Local Elections (Parishes and Communities) (England and Wales) Rules 2006, SI 2006/3305, Sch 2 r 55(1); the Local Authorities (Mayoral Elections) (England and Wales) Regulations 2007, SI 2007/1024, Sch 1 r 60(1); and the Greater London Authority Elections Rules 2007, SI 2007/3541, Sch 1 r 60(2), Sch 3 r 65(2). As to the provisions that apply specifically to a deceased independent candidate at a London Mayoral election (which are similar to those that apply at a Parliamentary election: see PARA 515) see Sch 3 rr 63(1), (4), 64(1), (5)–(9). As to the countermand or abandonment of the poll at a local government election by reason of the death of a candidate see PARA 516.

3   Representation of the People Act 1983 s 39(1)(a); as applied (see note 2).

It is for the returning officer and not for the court to countermand a poll when appropriate: *R (on the application of Begum) v Tower Hamlets London Borough Council* [2006] EWCA Civ 733 at [12], [2006] LGR 674 at [12] per Sir Anthony Clarke MR (obiter) (the returning officer will countermand a poll in the case of the death of a candidate and it is something of a puzzle why the Representation of the People Act 1983 s 39(1) uses the words 'for any reason').

4   Representation of the People Act 1983 s 39(1)(b); as applied (see note 2). As to the nomination of candidates and their validity generally see PARA 253 et seq.

5   As to returning officers for local government elections generally see PARA 354 et seq. For the purposes of elections for the return of constituency members of the London Assembly, the Representation of the People Act 1983 s 39(1) applies in respect of any vacancy which remains unfilled as if for the reference to the returning officer there were substituted a reference to the constituency returning officer (see PARA 211 note 9): see the Greater London Authority Elections Rules 2007, SI 2007/3541, Sch 1 r 60(2).

6   See the Representation of the People Act 1983 s 39(1) (amended by the Local Government Act 1985 s 102(2), Sch 17); as applied (see note 2).

7   See the Representation of the People Act 1983 s 39(1) (amended by the Representation of the People Act 1985 s 19(2)); as applied (see note 2). The period mentioned in the text must be

computed according to the Representation of the People Act 1983 s 40 (see PARA 209 note 7): see s 39(1) (as so amended and as so applied). As to the giving of notice of a local government election see PARA 211.

8 Ie under the Representation of the People Act 1983 s 39: see s 39(5); as applied (see note 2).

9 Ie the relevant rules made under the Representation of the People Act 1983 s 36 (see PARA 383): see s 39(5)(a); as applied (see note 2).

10 Representation of the People Act 1983 s 39(5)(a); as applied (see note 2).

11 Representation of the People Act 1983 s 39(5)(b); as applied (see note 2).

12 See PARA 16 et seq.

519. Fresh Welsh Assembly constituency election following countermand or abandonment of poll on death of candidate. Where the poll at a contested Welsh Assembly constituency election is countermanded or abandoned by reason of the death of a party candidate[1], the proceedings with reference to the election must be commenced afresh[2]. A new notice of election (the 'new notice') must be published on the first working day after the end of the period of seven days[3] starting on the day the proof of death is given to the constituency returning officer[4]. No fresh nomination is necessary in the case of a person shown in the previous statement of persons nominated as standing nominated[5]; and no other nomination may be made except for a person standing in the name of the same registered political party in whose name the deceased candidate was standing[6]. The poll must be held on a day in the period ('the first period')[7] which starts 15 working days after the day on which the new notice is published and ends 19 working days after that day[8].

Where the poll at an election is taken together with the poll at another election, special provision is made and neither the countermand of the poll at one election nor the direction that polling be abandoned at that election is to affect the poll at the other election[9].

1 See PARA 516. As to the meanings of 'Assembly election' and 'constituency election' see PARA 3 note 2. As to the provisions that apply specifically to a deceased independent candidate at a Welsh Assembly constituency election (which are similar to those that apply at a Parliamentary election: see PARA 515) see the National Assembly for Wales (Representation of the People) Order 2007, SI 2007/236, Sch 5 paras 70(1), (4), 71(1), (4)–(12).

2 See the National Assembly for Wales (Representation of the People) Order 2007, SI 2007/236, Sch 5 para 73(1), (4). The commencement of such proceedings is subject to Sch 5 para 73(1), (5)–(13) (see the text and notes 3–8): see Sch 5 para 73(4).

3 For these purposes, a working day is a day which is not a day specified in the National Assembly for Wales (Representation of the People) Order 2007, SI 2007/236, Sch 5 para 2(a)–(d) (see PARA 213 note 5): see Sch 5 para 73(1), (13)(b); and see also Sch 5 para 73(11), (12).

4 National Assembly for Wales (Representation of the People) Order 2007, SI 2007/236, Sch 5 para 73(1), (5). As to the meaning of 'constituency returning officer' see PARA 18 note 2.

5 National Assembly for Wales (Representation of the People) Order 2007, SI 2007/236, Sch 5 para 73(1), (6). 'Previous statement of person nominated' means the statement of persons nominated in operation at the time of the death of the person standing in the name of the registered political party: see Sch 5 para 73(1), (13)(c). The last day on which a notice of withdrawal of candidature by a person who stands nominated by virtue of Sch 5 para 73(6) may be delivered is the seventh working day after the day on which the new notice of election is published: see Sch 5 para 73(1), (9). As to the meaning of 'registered political party' see PARA 230 note 23; and as to the meaning of 'person standing in the name of the registered political party' for these purposes see PARA 516 note 5.

6 National Assembly for Wales (Representation of the People) Order 2007, SI 2007/236, Sch 5 para 73(1), (7). The last day on which a nomination mentioned in Sch 5 para 73(7) may be delivered, or on which a notice of withdrawal of candidature by a person who stands nominated in pursuance of Sch 5 para 73(7) may be delivered, is the seventh working day after the day on which the new notice of election is published: see Sch 5 para 73(8), (9).

7 Ie subject to the National Assembly for Wales (Representation of the People) Order 2007, SI 2007/236, Sch 5 para 73(1), (11), (12) (first period: excluded days): see Sch 5 para 73(10).

8　See the National Assembly for Wales (Representation of the People) Order 2007, SI 2007/236, Sch 5 para 73(1), (10).
9　See PARA 16 et seq.

520. Action following countermand or abandonment of poll consequent on a parish meeting on a question involving appointment to office. Where a poll consequent on a parish meeting on a question involving appointment to office[1] is countermanded or abandoned by reason of the death of a candidate[2], the district council in which the parish is situate[3] may by order make any appointment or make provision for the holding of a parish meeting or do such other thing as appears to it to be expedient in the circumstances[4].

1　As to polls consequent on a parish meeting on a question involving appointment to office see PARA 200 et seq.
2　See PARA 516.
3　As to the council of a district in England see LOCAL GOVERNMENT vol 69 (2009) PARA 24 et seq; and as to parishes and their councillors generally see LOCAL GOVERNMENT vol 69 (2009) PARA 27 et seq.
4　Parish and Community Meetings (Polls) Rules 1987, SI 1987/1, Schedule r 37(4).

(5) PILOT SCHEMES MODIFYING THE CONDUCT OF ELECTIONS

(i) Pilot Schemes regarding Voting and Campaigning at Local Government Elections

521. Pilot orders relating to schemes for voting and campaigning at local government elections. Where:

(1)　a relevant local authority[1] submits to the Secretary of State[2] proposals for a pilot scheme to apply to particular local government elections[3] held in the authority's area[4]; and

(2)　those proposals are approved by the Secretary of State (either without modification[5], or with such modifications as, after consulting the authority, he considers appropriate)[6],

the Secretary of State must by order[7] make such provision for and in connection with the implementation of the scheme in relation to those elections as he considers appropriate (which may include provision modifying or disapplying any enactment)[8]. Such a scheme may make, in relation to local government elections in the area of a relevant local authority[9], provision differing in any respect from that made under or by virtue of the Representation of the People Acts[10] as regards one or more of the following, namely:

(a)　when, where and how voting at the elections is to take place[11];

(b)　how the votes cast at the elections are to be counted[12];

(c)　the sending by candidates of election communications free of charge for postage[13].

Without prejudice to the generality of these provisions, such a scheme may make provision: (i) for voting to take place on more than one day (whether each of those days is designated as a day of the poll or otherwise) and at places other than polling stations[14]; or (ii) for postal charges incurred in respect of the sending of candidates' election communications as mentioned in head (c) above to be paid by the authority concerned[15].

1　For these purposes, 'relevant local authority' means, as respects England, a county council, a district council, a London borough council or the Greater London Authority, and, as respects

Wales, a county council or a county borough council: see the Representation of the People Act 2000 s 10(11). As to the meanings of 'England' and 'Wales' see PARA 1 note 1. As to counties and districts in England, and their councils, see LOCAL GOVERNMENT vol 69 (2009) PARA 24 et seq; as to counties and county boroughs in Wales, and their councils, see LOCAL GOVERNMENT vol 69 (2009) PARA 37 et seq; as to London boroughs and their councils see LOCAL GOVERNMENT vol 69 (2009) PARA 35; LONDON GOVERNMENT vol 71 (2013) PARA 15 et seq; and as to the Greater London Authority see LONDON GOVERNMENT vol 71 (2013) PARA 67 et seq. A county council, a district council or a London borough council in England, and a county council or a county borough council in Wales, is referred to as a 'principal council': see LOCAL GOVERNMENT vol 69 (2009) PARA 23.

The Representation of the People Act 2000 s 10 has effect for the purposes of local authority referendums, subject to the modifications specified, in relation to Wales, by the Local Authorities (Conduct of Referendums) (Wales) Regulations 2008, SI 2008/1848, reg 8(2), Sch 4 Table 2, and, in relation to England, by the Local Authorities (Conduct of Referendums) (England) Regulations 2012, SI 2012/323, regs 8(2), 11–13, Sch 4 Table 3 (see PARA 15 note 2).

2 As to the Secretary of State see PARA 2.

3 Ie including any such proposals which are submitted by a relevant local authority jointly with the Electoral Commission, in which case references to the authority must be read as references to the authority and the Commission: see the Representation of the People Act 2000 s 10(1A) (added by the Political Parties, Elections and Referendums Act 2000 s 158(1), Sch 21 para 16(1), (2)). As to the Electoral Commission see PARA 34 et seq; and as to the involvement of the Commission in changes in electoral procedures see PARA 55. See also the European Parliamentary and Local Elections (Pilots) Act 2004, which disapplied the Representation of the People Act 2000 s 10 for the purposes of making provision for the piloting of all-postal voting (or any other innovative voting method) in relation to European parliamentary elections for the 2004 elections only: see s 3.

4 Representation of the People Act 2000 s 10(1)(a). As to the meaning of 'local government election' see PARA 11; definition applied by s 17(2). As to the meaning of 'local government area' see PARA 33 note 7; definition applied by s 17(2).

5 For these purposes, 'modifications' includes additions, omissions and amendments (and 'modify' has a corresponding meaning): see the Representation of the People Act 2000 s 17(2).

6 Representation of the People Act 2000 s 10(1)(b).

7 Where the Secretary of State makes any such order he must send a copy of the order to the authority concerned and to the Electoral Commission, and that authority must publish the order in its area in such manner as it thinks fit: Representation of the People Act 2000 s 10(5) (amended by the Political Parties, Elections and Referendums Act 2000 Sch 21 para 16(1), (3)). In a case where any proposals are not jointly submitted under the Representation of the People Act 2000 s 10(1A) (see note 3), the Secretary of State must consult the Electoral Commission before making any such order: see s 10(1A) (as added: see note 3). At the date at which this volume states the law, no such order had been made.

8 Representation of the People Act 2000 s 10(1). For these purposes, 'enactment' includes any provision of an Act (including the Representation of the People Act 2000) and any provision of subordinate legislation (within the meaning of the Interpretation Act 1978: see STATUTES AND LEGISLATIVE PROCESS vol 96 (2012) PARA 609): see the Representation of the People Act 2000 s 17(2).

9 For this purpose, the reference to local government elections in the area of a relevant local authority is a reference to such elections, either throughout that area, or in any particular part or parts of it. as the scheme may provide: see the Representation of the People Act 2000 s 10(4).

10 As to the meaning of 'the Representation of the People Acts' see PARA 3 note 1.

11 Representation of the People Act 2000 s 10(2)(a).

12 Representation of the People Act 2000 s 10(2)(b).

13 Representation of the People Act 2000 s 10(2)(c).

14 Representation of the People Act 2000 s 10(3)(a).

15 Representation of the People Act 2000 s 10(3)(b). Where a scheme makes provision for postal charges incurred in respect of the sending of candidates' election communications to be paid as mentioned in head (ii) in the text, the Secretary of State's order under s 10(1) (see the text and notes 1–8) may make provision for disapplying the Representation of the People Act 1983 s 75(1) (restriction on third party election expenditure: see PARA 272), in relation to the payment of such charges by the authority: see the Representation of the People Act 2000 s 10(3).

522. Evaluation by the Electoral Commission of pilot schemes relating to voting and campaigning at local government elections. Once any local government elections[1] have taken place in relation to which a pilot scheme order under the Representation of the People Act 2000 applied[2], the Electoral Commission[3] must prepare a report on the scheme[4]. Such a report must be prepared in consultation with the local authority concerned[5]; and that authority must provide the Commission with such assistance as it may reasonably require in connection with the preparation of the report (and such assistance may, in particular, include the making by the authority of arrangements for ascertaining the views of voters about the operation of the scheme)[6]. The report must, in particular, contain[7]:

(1) a description of the scheme and of the respects in which the provision made by it differed from that made by or under the Representation of the People Acts[8];

(2) a copy of the Secretary of State's pilot scheme order[9]; and

(3) an assessment of the scheme's success or otherwise in facilitating: (a) voting at the elections in question[10]; and (b) if it made provision as respects the counting of votes cast at those elections, the counting of votes[11]; or in encouraging voting at the elections in question or enabling voters to make informed decisions at those elections[12].

If the Secretary of State so requests in writing, the report must also contain an assessment of such other matters relating to the scheme as are specified in his request[13]. Once the Electoral Commission has prepared the report, it must send a copy of it to the Secretary of State, and to the authority concerned, and that authority must publish the report in its area, in such manner as it thinks fit, by the end of the period of three months beginning with the date of the declaration of the result of the elections in question[14].

1 As to the meaning of 'local government election' see PARA 11; definition applied by the Representation of the People Act 2000 s 17(2).

2 Ie in relation to which a scheme under the Representation of the People Act 2000 s 10(1) applied (see PARA 521): see s 10(6) (amended by the Political Parties, Elections and Referendums Act 2000 s 158(1), Sch 21 para 16(1), (4)).

The Representation of the People Act 2000 s 10 has effect for the purposes of local authority referendums, subject to the modifications specified, in relation to Wales, by the Local Authorities (Conduct of Referendums) (Wales) Regulations 2008, SI 2008/1848, reg 8(2), Sch 4 Table 2, and, in relation to England, by the Local Authorities (Conduct of Referendums) (England) Regulations 2012, SI 2012/323, regs 8(2), 11–13, Sch 4 Table 3 (see PARA 15 note 2).

3 As to the Electoral Commission see PARA 34 et seq; and as to the involvement of the Commission in changes in electoral procedures see PARA 55.

4 Representation of the People Act 2000 s 10(6) (as amended: see note 2).

5 As to the local authorities which may propose such a scheme see PARA 521 note 1.

6 Representation of the People Act 2000 s 10(6A) (added by the Political Parties, Elections and Referendums Act 2000 Sch 21 para 16(1), (5)).

7 Representation of the People Act 2000 s 10(7) (amended by the Political Parties, Elections and Referendums Act 2000 Sch 21 para 16(1), (6)).

8 Representation of the People Act 2000 s 10(7)(a). As to the meaning of 'the Representation of the People Acts' see PARA 3 note 1.

9 Representation of the People Act 2000 s 10(7)(b). The text refers to the order of the Secretary of State made under s 10(1) (see PARA 521): see s 10(7)(b). As to the Secretary of State see PARA 2.

10 Representation of the People Act 2000 s 10(7)(c)(i). An assessment of the scheme's success under head (3)(a) in the text must include a statement by the authority concerned as to whether, in its opinion:

(1) the turnout of voters was higher than it would have been if the scheme had not applied (s 10(8)(a));

(2) voters found the procedures provided for their assistance by the scheme easy to use (s 10(8)(b));

(3)   the procedures provided for by the scheme led to any increase in personation or other electoral offences or in any other malpractice in connection with elections (s 10(8)(c));

(4)   those procedures led to any increase in expenditure, or to any savings, by the authority (s 10(8)(d)).

11 Representation of the People Act 2000 s 10(7)(c)(ii).

12 Representation of the People Act 2000 s 10(7)(c).

13 Representation of the People Act 2000 s 10(9).

14 Representation of the People Act 2000 s 10(10) (substituted by the Political Parties, Elections and Referendums Act 2000 Sch 21 para 16(1), (7)). As to the declaration of the result at a local government election see PARA 482.

523.   Revision of procedures following report on pilot schemes relating to voting and campaigning at local government elections.   If it appears to the Secretary of State[1], in the light of any report on a pilot scheme made under the Representation of the People Act 2000 regarding voting and campaigning at local government elections[2], that it would be desirable for provision similar to that made by the scheme to apply generally, and on a permanent basis, in relation to[3]:

(1)   local government elections in England and Wales[4]; or

(2)   any particular description of such elections[5],

he may by order[6] make such provision for and in connection with achieving that result as he considers appropriate[7]. However, the power of the Secretary of State to make such an order is exercisable only on a recommendation of the Electoral Commission[8]. Such an order: (a) may except from the operation of any of its provisions any local government area[9] specified in the order[10]; but (b) subject to that, must make the same provision in relation to local government elections (or, if it applies only to a particular description of such elections, in relation to elections of that description)[11] throughout England and Wales[12].

1   As to the Secretary of State see PARA 2.

2   Ie in the light of any report made under the Representation of the People Act 2000 s 10 (see PARA 522): see s 11(1). As to the meaning of 'local government election' see PARA 11; definition applied by s 17(2).

3   See the Representation of the People Act 2000 s 11(1).

4   Representation of the People Act 2000 s 11(1)(a). As to the meanings of 'England' and 'Wales' see PARA 1 note 1.

5   Representation of the People Act 2000 s 11(1)(b).

6   Such an order must be made by statutory instrument; and no such order may be made unless a draft of the statutory instrument containing the order has been laid before, and approved by a resolution of, each House of Parliament: Representation of the People Act 2000 s 11(3). When laying such a draft before either House of Parliament the Secretary of State must also lay before that House a copy of every report under s 10 (see PARA 522) which relates to a scheme making provision similar to that made by the order: s 11(4) (amended by the Political Parties, Elections and Referendums Act 2000 s 158(1), Sch 21 para 17(1), (3)). At the date at which this volume states the law, no such order had been made. Rules made under the Representation of the People Act 1983 s 36 (local elections in England and Wales: see PARA 383) may make such provision as the Secretary of State considers appropriate in connection with any provision made by such an order: Representation of the People Act 2000 s 11(6). However, nothing in s 11 is to be taken as prejudicing the generality of any power contained in any other Act to make subordinate legislation (within the meaning of the Interpretation Act 1978: see STATUTES AND LEGISLATIVE PROCESS vol 96 (2012) PARA 608) with respect to elections of any description: Representation of the People Act 2000 s 11(7).

7   See the Representation of the People Act 2000 s 11(1). Such provision may include provision modifying or disapplying any provision of an Act, including the Representation of the People Act 2000: see s 11(1). As to the meaning of 'modify' for these purposes see PARA 521 note 5.

8   See the Representation of the People Act 2000 s 11(1) (amended by the Political Parties, Elections and Referendums Act 2000 Sch 21 para 17(1), (2)). As to the Electoral Commission see PARA 34 et seq; and as to the involvement of the Commission in changes in electoral procedures see PARA 55.

9　As to the meaning of 'local government area' see PARA 33 note 7; definition applied by the
　　Representation of the People Act 2000 s 17(2).
10　Representation of the People Act 2000 s 11(2)(a). An order which excepts any local government
　　area as mentioned in head (a) in the text must, if it would otherwise be treated for the purposes
　　of the standing orders of either House of Parliament as a hybrid instrument, proceed in that
　　House as if it were not such an instrument: s 11(5).
11　Representation of the People Act 2000 s 11(2)(b).
12　Representation of the People Act 2000 s 11(2).

(ii)　Pilot Schemes relating to Ballot Papers at Local Government Elections

**524.　Pilot orders relating to schemes for modifying ballot papers used at local
government elections.**　A local authority[1] may make a proposal that a pilot order
be made applying to particular local government elections[2] held in its area[3]; and
the Secretary of State[4] may by order (a 'pilot order') make provision for the
purposes of enabling ballot papers[5] issued at such local government elections as
are specified in the order to contain photographs of the candidates[6]. A pilot
order may include such provision modifying or disapplying any enactment as the
Secretary of State thinks is necessary or expedient for the purposes of the order[7];
but the Secretary of State must not make a pilot order unless he first consults the
Electoral Commission[8]. A pilot order may make provision implementing the
local authority's proposal either without modification, or with such
modifications as the Secretary of State and the local authority agree between
them[9]. If the Secretary of State makes a pilot order, he must send a copy of it to
the local authority and to the Electoral Commission[10]; and the local authority
must publish the order in its area in such manner as it thinks fit[11].

1　Ie in England, a county council, a district council, a London borough council or the Greater
　　London Authority and, in Wales, a county council or a county borough council: see the Electoral
　　Administration Act 2006 s 32(9). As to the meanings of 'England' and 'Wales' see PARA 1 note
　　1. As to counties and districts in England, and their councils, see LOCAL GOVERNMENT vol 69
　　(2009) PARA 24 et seq; as to counties and county boroughs in Wales, and their councils, see
　　LOCAL GOVERNMENT vol 69 (2009) PARA 37 et seq; as to London boroughs and their councils
　　see LOCAL GOVERNMENT vol 69 (2009) PARA 35; LONDON GOVERNMENT vol 71 (2013) PARA
　　15 et seq; and as to the Greater London Authority see LONDON GOVERNMENT vol 71 (2013)
　　PARA 67 et seq. A county council, a district council or a London borough council in England and
　　a county council or a county borough council in Wales is referred to as a 'principal council': see
　　LOCAL GOVERNMENT vol 69 (2009) PARA 23.
　　　　The Electoral Administration Act 2006 s 32 is applied and modified for the purpose of local
　　authority mayoral elections in England and Wales by the Local Authorities (Mayoral Elections)
　　(England and Wales) Regulations 2007, SI 2007/1024, reg 3(2)–(5), Sch 2 Table 5: see PARA 11
　　note 14,
2　For these purposes, 'local government election' must be construed in accordance with the
　　definition in the Representation of the People Act 1983 s 203(1) (see PARA 11); and any
　　reference to the area of a local authority must be construed in accordance with that definition:
　　Electoral Administration Act 2006 s 32(10).
3　See the Electoral Administration Act 2006 s 32(1).
4　As to the Secretary of State see PARA 2.
5　As to the form and printing of ballot papers see PARA 386 et seq.
6　Electoral Administration Act 2006 s 32(2). A pilot order may be amended or revoked by a
　　further order: s 32(7). The Secretary of State may reimburse a returning officer for any
　　expenditure necessarily incurred by him in consequence of the making of a pilot order: s 32(8).
　　At the date at which this volume states the law, no such order had been made. As to returning
　　officers for local government elections see PARA 354 et seq.
7　Electoral Administration Act 2006 s 32(3).
8　Electoral Administration Act 2006 s 32(4). As to the Electoral Commission see PARA 34 et seq.
9　Electoral Administration Act 2006 s 32(5).
10　Electoral Administration Act 2006 s 32(6)(a).
11　Electoral Administration Act 2006 s 32(6)(b).

525.   Evaluation by the Electoral Commission of pilot schemes for modifying ballot papers used at local government elections.   After any elections have taken place which were specified in a pilot order[1] enabling ballot papers to contain photographs of the candidates, the Electoral Commission[2] must prepare a report on the operation of the order[3], which must contain, in particular:

(1)   a description of the way in which the provision made by the order differed from the provisions which would otherwise have applied to the election or elections[4];

(2)   a copy of the order[5];

(3)   an assessment of the success or otherwise of the order in assisting voters to make informed decisions at the election or elections in question[6];

(4)   an assessment of the success or otherwise of the order in encouraging voting at the election or elections in question[7];

(5)   an assessment of whether the procedures provided for in the order operated satisfactorily[8].

The local authority concerned[9] must give the Commission such assistance as the Commission may reasonably require in connection with the preparation of the report[10]. The assistance may include: (a) making arrangements for ascertaining the views of electors about the operation of the provisions of the order[11]; or (b) reporting to the Commission allegations of electoral offences or other malpractice[12]. The Commission must, before the end of the period of three months beginning with the date of the declaration of the result of the election or elections in question[13], send a copy of the report to the Secretary of State[14], and to the local authority[15]; and the local authority must publish the report in its area in such manner as it thinks fit[16].

1   As to the meaning of 'pilot order' for these purposes see PARA 524; definition applied by the Representation of the People Act 2000 s 33(11).
2   As to the Electoral Commission see PARA 34 et seq.
3   Electoral Administration Act 2006 s 33(1).
4   Electoral Administration Act 2006 s 33(2)(a).
5   Electoral Administration Act 2006 s 33(2)(b).
6   Electoral Administration Act 2006 s 33(2)(c). An assessment under head (3) in the text must include a statement of whether, in the opinion of the Commission, the inclusion of photographs on the ballot paper:
    (1)   assisted voters in marking their papers with a vote for a candidate (or with votes for candidates) for whom they had decided to vote on grounds other than the candidates' appearance (s 33(3)(a)); or
    (2)   resulted in voters being influenced (or more influenced) by the appearance of candidates in deciding for whom to vote (s 33(3)(b)).
    In making such an assessment, the Commission must also apply such other criteria as are specified in the order in relation to that assessment: see s 33(6).
7   Electoral Administration Act 2006 s 33(2)(d). An assessment under head (4) in the text must include a statement of whether, in the opinion of the Commission, the turnout of voters was higher than it would have been if the order had not applied (s 33(4)); and, in making such an assessment, the Commission must also apply such other criteria as are specified in the order in relation to that assessment (see s 33(6)).
8   Electoral Administration Act 2006 s 33(2)(e). An assessment under head (5) in the text must include a statement of:
    (1)   whether the candidates and their agents found the procedures provided for in the order easy to use (s 33(5)(a));
    (2)   whether the returning officer found those procedures easy to administer (s 33(5)(b));
    (3)   whether those procedures had any effect on the incidence of malpractice (whether or not amounting to an offence) in connection with elections (s 33(5)(c));
    (4)   the amount of any increase attributable to those procedures in the resources applied by the authority concerned to the election or elections (s 33(5)(d)).

In making such an assessment, the Commission must also apply such other criteria as are specified in the order in relation to that assessment: see s 33(6). As to returning officers for local government elections see PARA 354 et seq.

9   As to the meaning of 'local authority' for these purposes see PARA 524 note 1; definition applied by the Representation of the People Act 2000 s 33(11).

10 Electoral Administration Act 2006 s 33(7).

11 Electoral Administration Act 2006 s 33(8)(a).

12 Electoral Administration Act 2006 s 33(8)(b).

13 As to the declaration of the result at a local government election see PARA 482.

14 As to the Secretary of State see PARA 2.

15 See the Electoral Administration Act 2006 s 33(9).

16 Electoral Administration Act 2006 s 33(10).

526. Revision of procedures following report on pilot schemes for modifying ballot papers used at local government elections. If the Secretary of State[1] thinks, in the light of a report made[2] on the operation of a pilot order[3] which enabled ballot papers at a local government election[4] to contain photographs of the candidates, that it would be desirable for provision similar to that made by the order to apply generally, and on a permanent basis, in relation to:

(1)   parliamentary elections[5];

(2)   local government elections in England and Wales[6]; or

(3)   any description of election falling within head (1) or head (2) above[7],

the Secretary of State may by order[8] make provision for the purposes of enabling ballot papers issued at such elections as are specified in the order to contain photographs of the candidates[9]. However, the Secretary of State must not make such an order unless he first consults the Electoral Commission[10].

1   As to the Secretary of State see PARA 2.

2   Ie a report made under the Electoral Administration Act 2006 s 33 (see PARA 525): see s 34(1).

3   Ie a pilot order made under the Representation of the People Act 2000 s 32 (see PARA 524): s 34(1).

4   As to the meaning of 'local government election' see PARA 524 note 2; definition applied by the Representation of the People Act 2000 s 34(7).

5   Electoral Administration Act 2006 s 34(1)(a). As to the meaning of 'parliamentary election' see PARA 9.

6   Electoral Administration Act 2006 s 34(1)(b). As to the meanings of 'England' and 'Wales' see PARA 1 note 1.

7   Electoral Administration Act 2006 s 34(1)(c).

8   The power to make such an order is exercisable by statutory instrument, but no such order may be made unless a draft of the instrument containing the order has been laid before and approved by a resolution of each House of Parliament: Representation of the People Act 2000 s 34(6). At the date at which this volume states the law, no such order had been made.

9   Electoral Administration Act 2006 s 34(2). Such an order may include such provision modifying or disapplying any enactment as the Secretary of State thinks is necessary or expedient for the purposes of the order, and may create or extend the application of an offence: see s 34(4). However, such an order must not create an offence punishable (on conviction on indictment) with imprisonment for a term exceeding one year, or (on summary conviction) with imprisonment for a term exceeding 51 weeks or with a fine exceeding the statutory maximum: see s 34(5). If such an order is made before the date of commencement of the Criminal Justice Act 2003 s 281(5) (not yet in force) (alteration of penalties for summary offences: see SENTENCING AND DISPOSITION OF OFFENDERS vol 92 (2010) PARA 374), then in relation to any offence committed before that date the reference in the Electoral Administration Act 2006 s 34(5) to 51 weeks must be taken to be a reference to six months: s 34(8). As to the statutory maximum see SENTENCING AND DISPOSITION OF OFFENDERS vol 92 (2010) PARA 140.

10 Electoral Administration Act 2006 s 34(3). As to the Electoral Commission see PARA 34 et seq.

INDEX

Elections and Referendums

CANDIDATE (ELECTION)—*continued*
Mayor of London. *See under* MAYOR OF
    LONDON (election)
nomination—
    consent to, 258
    deposit, requirement for, 259
    party's nominating officer's
        functions, 253
    person not representing any party,
        where, 253n[9]
    proceedings, 261
    publication of statement of persons
        nominated, 267
    registration of party and officials as
        condition precedent, 253
    selection of candidate by political
        party, 254
    validity, 262
    wrongful rejection, effect on election,
        667
    See also NOMINATION PAPER
party list candidate, 230n[23]
polling agent, right to appoint, 394
supply of electoral records to, 185
time at which one becomes, 230
Welsh Assembly election—
    by-election, inclusion on political
        party's list, 215n[10]
    generally, 227
    time at which one becomes
        candidate, 230
withdrawal—
    corrupt inducement of, 266, 683
    false statement withdrawal, 266
    procedure, 266
    returning officer's duty on, 262
CANVASSER
    meaning, 247
    candidate's agent, as, 247
    police officer, by, 252, 747
CHARITABLE GIFT
    bribe, as, 714
CLERK OF THE CROWN
    breach of duty at parliamentary
        election, penalty for, 737
CODE OF PRACTICE
    campaign broadcasting, 332
    campaign expenditure, 299
    election expenses, as to, 269
    Electoral Commission's power to
        prepare, 53, 269
COMMUNITY COUNCIL ELECTION.
    See also LOCAL GOVERNMENT
    ELECTION
    abortive election, 210
    combined poll, where not permitted, 25

COMMUNITY COUNCIL
    ELECTION—*continued*
    declaration of result, 482
    election agent, 231n[3]
    electoral areas—
        establishment, 74
        review of electoral arrangements, 88,
            89
    election expenses—
        claim as to expenses, 294
        declaration as to, failure to make,
            676
        disapplication of statutory
            provisions, 293
        financial return as to, failure to
            make, 676
        illegal payment, 675
        public inspection of returns and
            declarations, 296
        return and declaration as to—
            duty to make, 295
            relief in respect of, 689
            time for making, 294
    frequency and term of office, 200
    notice of, 211
    official poll cards, prescribed form,
        389n[7]
    ordinary election—
        generally, 200
        insufficient nominations, 201
    questioning, 763
    vacancy in office, 205
COMMUNITY MEETING
    poll consequent on. *See* POLL
        CONSEQUENT ON PARISH ETC
        MEETING
CONSTITUENCY
    meaning, 9
    Boundary Commission. *See* BOUNDARY
        COMMISSION
    county and borough, 73
    establishment, for purpose of
        parliamentary elections, 73
    London Assembly. *See under* LONDON
        ASSEMBLY
    numbers in UK, 79
    parliamentary, division into districts,
        343
    reduction, plans for, 79
    Welsh Assembly, 76
CONTROLLED EXPENDITURE
    (NATIONAL ELECTION)
    meaning, 313
    application for leave to pay claim, 318
    appropriate amount, determining, 313
    authorisation, need for, 315

CONTROLLED EXPENDITURE
(NATIONAL
ELECTION)—*continued*
claim against third party, 317
declaration by responsible person, 323
disputed claim, 317
election material: meaning, 313n[4]
excluded amounts, 313
false declaration, 323
leave to pay claim, 318
limitation—
　combined polls, 320
　European parliamentary election, 319
　generally, 319
　parliamentary general election, 319
　Welsh Assembly election, 319
notification by third party, 314
recognised third party—
　meaning, 313n[15]
　generally, 314
restrictions—
　financial limits, 319, 320
　payments, as to, 316
　statute-barred claim, 317
　unauthorised expenditure, 315
returns—
　auditor's report, 321
　contents, 321
　declaration to accompany, 323
　delivery to Electoral Commission,
　　322
　documents to accompany, 321
　failure to comply with requirements,
　　civil liability, 755
　generally, 321
　public inspection, 324
　responsible person's duty to prepare,
　　321
　safe-keeping and destruction, 324
third party: meaning, 313n[1]

CORRUPT PRACTICES. *See also* ILLEGAL
　PRACTICES
meaning, 704
association or body, by, 891
avoidance of election. *See under*
　ELECTION
bribery. *See* BRIBERY
costs on trial of election petition, 875
drafting of charges, 890
election expenses—
　false declaration, 707, 708
　outsider's expenses, 272
　unauthorised expenses, 707
electoral fraud, 754
evidence by certificate, 886
examples, 704

CORRUPT PRACTICES—*continued*
false certificate authorising description
　to be used by candidate, 706
false statement supporting candidate's
　nomination, 705
incapacity imposed for—
　European parliamentary election,
　　111, 909
　licence or certificate under Licensing
　　Act 2003, person holding, 908
　local authority referendum, 905
　mitigation and remission, 910
　parliamentary or local government
　　election, 109, 905
　Welsh Assembly election, 907
offences also constituting—
　examples, 729
　personation, 730
　postal or proxy voting, offences
　　associated with, 729, 731
penalties, 887
practices constituting, 704
report by election court—
　barrister, solicitor etc found guilty,
　　903
　candidate or agent found personally
　　guilty, 901
　justice of the peace found guilty, 902
striking off of vote on scrutiny, 843
treating. *See* TREATING
undue influence. *See* UNDUE INFLUENCE
　(VOTING)

COSTS
election court. *See* ELECTION COURT
　(costs)
electoral registration appeal, 175
illegal practice, application for relief,
　698

COUNCILLOR
election. *See* LOCAL GOVERNMENT
　ELECTION

COUNTING OFFICER
meaning, 179n[20]
local authority referendum. *See under*
　LOCAL AUTHORITY REFERENDUM
performance standards, 57
referendum. *See under* REFERENDUM
working practices, observation by
　Electoral Commission, 53

COUNTY COUNCIL
councillors, term of office, 197n[2]
election. *See* LOCAL GOVERNMENT
　ELECTION

COURT
election court. *See* ELECTION COURT

References are to paragraph numbers; superior figures refer to notes

References are to paragraph numbers; superior figures refer to notes

ELECTION—*continued*
  financial controls—
    candidate's election expenses. *See*
      ELECTION EXPENSES
    contravention, offence, 751
    donations. *See* CAMPAIGN DONATION
    recognised third parties, on. *See*
      CONTROLLED EXPENDITURE
      (NATIONAL ELECTION)
    registered party's campaign
      expenditure. *See* CAMPAIGN
      EXPENDITURE
    regulated transactions involving
      registered party, 312
    third party expenditure in national
      parliamentary campaign. *See*
      CONTROLLED EXPENDITURE
      (NATIONAL ELECTION)
  freedom of expression, right to, 7
  generally, 1
  holding of, evidence by certificate, 886
  human rights—
    European Convention, 7
    international conventions, 8
  illegal practices. *See* ILLEGAL PRACTICES
  legislation—
    European elections, $3n^3$
    generally, 3
    local government elections, $3n^1$
    parliamentary elections, $3n^1$
    purpose, 3
    Representation of the People Acts,
      $3n^1$
    Welsh Assembly elections, as to, $3n^2$
  local government election. *See* LOCAL
    GOVERNMENT ELECTION
  London Assembly election. *See* LONDON
    ASSEMBLY ELECTION
  mayoral election. *See* MAYORAL
    ELECTION
  meeting. *See* ELECTION MEETING
  offences. *See* ELECTION OFFENCES
  parish council election. *See* PARISH
    COUNCIL ELECTION
  parliamentary election. *See*
    PARLIAMENTARY ELECTION
  petition. *See* ELECTION PETITION
  poll. *See* POLLING; POLLING DISTRICT;
    POLLING PLACE; POLLING STATION
  postal vote. *See* POSTAL VOTE
  principal area election. *See* PRINCIPAL
    AREA ELECTION
  proxy vote. *See* PROXY VOTE
  publicity at—
    advertisements, control of, 333

ELECTION—*continued*
  publicity at—*continued*
    broadcasting. *See* CAMPAIGN
      BROADCASTING
    defamatory statement, $330n^{18}$
    election booklet, $330n^{15}$
    free postal communications,
      candidate's right to, 330
  questioning—
    application of provisions to other
      polls, 763
    election court. *See* ELECTION COURT
    election petition. *See* ELECTION
      PETITION
    European parliamentary election, 765
    local election, 762
    parliamentary election, 761
    time limits, 768
    Welsh Assembly elections, 764
  recount following application, 900
  registration of electors. *See* ELECTORAL
    REGISTER; REGISTRATION OF
    ELECTORS
  returning officer. *See* RETURNING
    OFFICER
  right to vote. *See* RIGHT TO VOTE
  rules for conduct, 383, 556
  scrutiny. *See* SCRUTINY
  secret ballot—
    poll to be taken by, 385
    right to, 7
  supply of electoral records. *See under*
    ELECTORAL REGISTER
  uncontested—
    European parliamentary election, at,
      477
    local government election, at, 475
    parliamentary election, at, 474
    poll consequent on parish meeting
      etc, 478
    Welsh Assembly election, at, 476
  undue influence. *See* UNDUE INFLUENCE
    (VOTING)
  void, following breach of rules, 667
  voting. *See* VOTING
  Welsh Assembly election. *See* WELSH
    ASSEMBLY ELECTION

ELECTION AGENCY. *See also* ELECTION
  AGENT
  candidate's liability for corrupt or illegal
    practices, 244
  canvasser as agent, 247
  corrupt or illegal practice, court's duty
    to report where agent guilty of,
    901

ELECTION AGENCY—*continued*
  election committee member as agent,
    248
  election official forbidden to act as
    agent, 252
  employment or authorisation test, 245
  evidence of, 245, 832
  examples of agents, 250
  official acting as, prohibition, 746
  one act of corruption only, where, 246
  police officer prohibited from
    canvassing, 252
  political association as agent, 249
  proof of, 245, 832
  statutory prohibition, 252
  termination, 251

ELECTION AGENT. *See also* ELECTION
    AGENCY
  appointment—
    European parliamentary elections,
      239
    local government election, 231
    parliamentary election, 231
    Welsh Assembly elections, 235
  attendance at receipt of postal ballot
    papers, 416
  candidate as—
    European parliamentary elections,
      239
    parliamentary and local government
      elections, $231n^8$
    Welsh Assembly elections, 235
  candidate's liability for corrupt or illegal
    practices, 244
  community council election, $231n^3$
  corrupt, avoidance of election for
    employment of, 896
  counting agent, appointment of, 394
  death of—
    European parliamentary elections,
      239, 240
    parliamentary or local election, 231,
      232
    Welsh Assembly election, 235, 236
  default in appointment, effect—
    European parliamentary elections,
      240
    parliamentary and local government
      elections, 232
    Welsh Assembly elections, 236
  duties, 243
  election expenses, payment of—
    declaration accompanying return, 279
    generally, 270
    illegal practice, 675
    return as to, 279

ELECTION AGENT—*continued*
  election expenses, payment
    of—*continued*
    statutory bar on claims against, 276
  illegal payment or employment by, 682
  local government election. *See under*
    LOCAL GOVERNMENT ELECTION
  name and address, public notice of—
    European parliamentary elections,
      $239n^{23}$
    parliamentary or local elections,
      $231n^{12}$
    Welsh Assembly elections, $235n^{27}$
  office of—
    European parliamentary elections,
      242
    parliamentary and local elections,
      234
    Welsh Assembly elections, 238
  parish council election, $231n^3$
  parliamentary election. *See under*
    PARLIAMENTARY ELECTION
  polling agent, appointment of, 394
  sub-agent—
    nomination—
      European parliamentary elections,
        241
      parliamentary or local elections,
        233
      Welsh Assembly elections, 237
    office, 234, 238, 242
  transfer of donation to, 290
  Welsh Assembly election. *See under*
    WELSH ASSEMBLY ELECTION

ELECTION COURT
  adjournment of trial, 819
  amendment of parliamentary election
    petition, 772
  constitution—
    European parliamentary election
      petition, 769
    local election or referendum, 775
    parliamentary election petition, 769
    Welsh Assembly election petition, 769
  continuation of trial despite occurrence
    of certain events, 814
  costs—
    corrupt practices, where, 875
    Director of Public Prosecution's
      expenses, 877
    disagreement between judges, 874
    general rule, 872
    High Court principles, application
      of, 870
    manner of defrayal, 871
    publication costs, 871

References are to paragraph numbers; superior figures refer to notes

References are to paragraph numbers; superior figures refer to notes

References are to paragraph numbers; superior figures refer to notes

ELECTORAL COMMISSION—*continued*
report on elections and referendums, 51
representatives' power to attend
    electoral proceedings and observe
    working practices, 53
returns and declarations delivered to,
    285, 308, 309, 322
review of electoral and political
    matters, 52
review of polling districts and places,
    representations to Commission,
    346
staff—
    appointment etc, 38
    delegation to, 42
    disqualification from membership of
      House of Commons, 38n[4]
    political restrictions on, 39
stop notice, power to impose, 759
transfer of property, rights and
    liabilities—
    from, to Local Government Boundary
      Commission for England, 67
    to, from Secretary of State, 34n[2]
views expressed on broadcasts, 59

ELECTORAL FRAUD
meaning, 754
corrupt or illegal practice, 754
effect, 754
generally, 754
postal voting, 754
scope of term, 754

ELECTORAL REGIONS
European parliamentary electoral
    regions—
    generally, 13, 77
    review—
      implementation of recommendation
        following periodic review, 93
      order giving effect to change in
        number of UK MEPs to be
        elected, 94
      periodic review of the distribution
        of MEPs between electoral
        regions, 92
      recommendations as to distribution
        of UK MEPs, 91
Welsh Assembly election—
    establishment, 76
    review, 90

ELECTORAL REGISTER
alterations—
    annual canvass, following, 151
    appeal, following, 178

ELECTORAL REGISTER—*continued*
alterations—*continued*
    notice of—
      address in relevant election area,
        168n[31]
      appropriate publication date,
        168n[28, 55]
      clerical error, register containing,
        168n[11]
      determination of right to
        registration, where, 168n[5, 6]
      duty to issue, 168
      effective date of, 168
      interim publication dates, 168n[55]
      prescribed manner for issue,
        168n[12]
      prescribed time on day of poll,
        168n[36]
      removal from register, 168n[8]
      representation, person making,
        168n[47]
      time for issue, calculating, 168n[14,
        15]
anonymous entry—
    meaning, 145
    application for, 147
    certificate of anonymous registration,
      145n[12]
    declaration, offence, 735
    omission from edited register, 167
    police etc, supply to, 186
    procedure for determining
      application, 148
    record of, 145n[12], 148n[12]
    restriction on supply of record, 179
    safety test, 147, 148
    termination of entitlement to, 171
application for entry derived from
    annual canvass—
    determination of applications for
      registration and alteration, 157
    European parliamentary elector, EU
      citizen's application for
      registration, 159
    form of objection to registration, 161
    local government elector, form of
      application for registration as,
      158
    objections to registration,
      determining, 160, 162
    parliamentary elector, form of
      application for registration as,
      158
    procedural requirements, 162
    registration, procedure for
      determining applications for, 162

ELECTORAL REGISTRATION
OFFICER. *See* REGISTRATION OFFICER

ENFORCEMENT UNDERTAKING
meaning, 760n[5]
certificate—
appeal against decision not to issue,
760n[18]
application, 760n[18]
revocation, 760n[18]
cessation, 760n[18]
compliance with, 760
Electoral Commission's power to
impose, 760
reasons for imposing, 760

ENVIRONMENT AGENCY
sale of electoral records to, 188

EUROPEAN PARLIAMENT
election to. *See* EUROPEAN
PARLIAMENTARY ELECTION
seats allocated to member states, limits
on, 6n[2]
total number of representatives, 6n[2]

EUROPEAN PARLIAMENTARY
ELECTION
meaning, 1n[4], 21n[2]
ballot paper. *See* BALLOT PAPER
by-election—
day of, 218
general election intervening, 221
generally, 13, 221
maximum delay in holding, 219n[11]
nominating officer: meaning, 220n[6]
See also vacancy, filling *below*
candidacy—
competent administrative authorities,
certificate made by, 228n[8]
court's power to make declaration,
228
disqualification for office of MEP,
228
generally, 228
House of Commons, member of,
228n[5]
nomination paper. *See* NOMINATION
PAPER
regulations, power to make, 228
relevant citizen of the Union, 229
time at which one becomes
candidate, 230
citizen of the European Union, 92n[6]
combined polls—
generally, 13
local government election, 16
parliamentary general election, 16
See also POLLING (combined polls)

EUROPEAN PARLIAMENTARY
ELECTION—*continued*
combined region, Gibraltar as part of,
13n[3, 12], 77n[4]
conduct of, rules for, 383
consent to nomination, 258
contested election. *See* ELECTION
(contested)
date for holding, 6n[5], 222
declaration of result at, 493
deposit—
requirement for, 259
return or forfeiture, 494
See also CANDIDATE (ELECTION)
deposit)
documents—
access to or control of, offence and
penalty, 745
order for production or inspection,
512
retention after postal voting, 502
retention and supply, 510
supply and inspection, 511
transfer after sealing up of ballot
papers, 501
election agent—
appointment, 239
candidate as, 239
death of, 239, 240
default in appointment, 240
name and address—
provided to appropriate officer,
239n[16]
public notice of, 239n[23]
national election agent—
meaning, 239n[5]
nominating officer deemed to be,
240
office, 242
revocation of appointment, 239
sub-agent—
illegal practice and offence, 241n[26]
nomination of, 241
office, 242
See also ELECTION AGENT
election expenses. *See* ELECTION
EXPENSES
election meeting. *See* ELECTION MEETING
elector—
meaning, 92n[6]
calculating number for electoral
region, 92n[6]
electoral regions—
generally, 13, 77
review. *See under* ELECTORAL
BOUNDARIES (review)

GREATER LONDON AUTHORITY
ELECTION—*continued*
ballot paper—
supply of, 387n[10]
See also BALLOT PAPER
conduct of, rules for, 383
death of candidate, effect, 516
deposit—
requirement for, 259
return or forfeiture, 489
election expenses, limits on, 273n[12]
Greater London returning officer,
211n[8]
London Assembly members. *See*
LONDON ASSEMBLY ELECTION
Mayor of London. *See* MAYOR OF
LONDON (election)
notice of poll, 388
vote counting. *See* VOTE COUNTING
(London Authority election)

HIGH COURT OF JUSTICE
injunction, power to grant, 665

HOMELESSNESS
voter registration, declaration of local
connection, 121

HOUSE OF COMMONS
disqualification for membership of—
Electoral Commission staff, 38n[4]
European Parliament, effect on
candidacy for, 228n[5]
generally, 224
person elected despite being
disqualified, 224n[8]
statutory penalty, imposition of,
224n[13]
membership, qualifying Commonwealth
citizen, 224n[5]

HUMAN RIGHTS
electoral rights and freedoms, 7, 8

ILLEGAL PRACTICES. *See also* CORRUPT
PRACTICES
meaning, 671
association or body, by, 891
avoidance of election. *See under*
ELECTION
broadcasting from outside UK with
intention to influence election, 701
canvasser, illegal employment of, 685
disturbing election or referendum
meeting, 679
drafting of charges, 890
election expenses—
acceptance of prohibited donations,
672
declaration as to, failure to make,
676

ILLEGAL PRACTICES—*continued*
election expenses—*continued*
failure to deliver or send returns or
declarations authorised by
election agent, 677
financial return as to, failure to
make, 676
knowingly incurred in excess of
financial limits, 673
out-of-time claims, payment of, 675
paying or incurring expenses at
election under statute where
election agent not required, 678
statute-barred claims, payment of,
675
election publication, failure to comply
with requirements as to, 703
electoral fraud, 754
European parliamentary election,
multiple nominations, 681
evidence by certificate, 886
examples, 671
false statement as to candidate's
character or conduct, 680
illegal payment, employment or hiring—
association or body, by, 891
candidate or election agent, by, 682
corrupt withdrawal of candidate, to
induce or procure, 683
drafting of charges, 890
evidence by certificate, 886
exhibition of election notices, for,
684
generally, 671
paid canvasser, illegal employment,
685
penalties, 889
providing money for prohibited
payment or expenses incurred in
excess of maximum amount, 686
relief, 690
imitation poll card, issue of, 702
incapacity imposed for—
European parliamentary election,
111, 909
licence or certificate under Licensing
Act 2003, person holding, 908
local authority referendum, 905
mitigation and remission, 910
parliamentary or local government
election, 109, 905
Welsh Assembly election, 907
offences also constituting—
broadcasting from outside UK with
intention to influence election,
701

ILLEGAL PRACTICES—*continued*
  offences also constituting—*continued*
    examples, 699
    election publication, failure to comply
        with requirements as to, 703
    generally, 699
    issue of imitation poll card, 702
    summary offences, 671, 699
    voting offences, 700
  penalties, 888
  relief—
    affidavit supporting application, 697
    contravention of statutory
        requirements as to election
        expense returns or declarations,
        688
    costs of application, 698
    examples, 693
    failure to deliver or send returns or
        declarations of expenses
        authorised by election agent, 687
    grant of, 693
    illegal practice, payment, employment
        or hiring, 690
    inadvertence as ground for, 691
    notice of application, 696
    other reasonable cause as ground
        for, 692
    parish or community council election
        expense returns or declarations,
        689
    parties to proceedings, 698
    refusal, 694
    supporting affidavit, 697
    time of application, 695
  report by election court, 901
  striking off on vote on scrutiny, 843
  voting offences, 700

INJUNCTION
  court's power to grant, 665
  false statement about candidate,
      restraining, 665, 666

INTIMIDATION
  avoidance of election, 895
  local authority referendum, avoidance
      of, 897

JURISDICTION
  election court, 771

JURY
  electoral register as basis of selection,
      142n^2

JUSTICE OF THE PEACE
  corrupt or illegal practice, court's duty
      to report where guilty of, 902

JUSTICE OF THE PEACE—*continued*
  inspection warrant on behalf of
      Electoral Commission, power to
      issue, 64

LOCAL AUTHORITY
  archives service, supply of electoral
      records to, 181
  elections. *See* LOCAL GOVERNMENT
      ELECTION
  poll, power to conduct, 15, 557
  referendum. *See* LOCAL AUTHORITY
      REFERENDUM

LOCAL AUTHORITY REFERENDUM
  absent voter—
    absent voters list, 596
    application for absent vote—
      indefinite period, for, 592
      particular period, for, 592
      particular referendum, at, 594–596
    different address, ballot paper sent
        to, 594
    postal vote. *See* postal vote *below*
    proxy vote. *See* proxy vote *below*
    record of entitlement, 593
    removal from record, 593
  advertisements, control of, 580
  approval of proposals, 654
  avoidance by reason of corruption,
      bribery, treating or intimidation,
      897
  ballot paper—
    false answers to questions put,
        offence, 619
    form of, 607
    inadvertently spoilt, 625
    marked by presiding officer, 622
    official mark, 607
    postal ballot paper. *See* postal ballot
        paper *below*
    procedure after receiving, 620
    questions to be put to voters, 619
    sealing up of papers, 656
    stamping of, 620
    tendered ballot paper, 624
  campaigning etc, pilot schemes. *See* pilot
      scheme *below*
  challenging voter, on suspicion of
      personation, 621
  close of poll, procedure on, 626
  conduct—
    pilot schemes. *See* pilot scheme *below*
    relevant legislation, 555
  counting of votes—
    appointment of persons for, 614
    arrangements for, 646
    attendance at, 646

References are to paragraph numbers; superior figures refer to notes

PEER
  right to vote—
    European parliamentary election,
      where resident outside UK, 101,
      115
    parliamentary election, 95n[8]
    registration provisions, 112
PERJURY
  election petition proceedings, 826
PERSONATION
  corrupt practice, as, 729, 730
  striking off on vote on scrutiny, 844
  voter challenged on suspicion of, 400
POLICE
  canvassing by officer, 252, 747
  electoral records, right to be supplied
    with, 185
  police area: meaning, 18n[2]
POLITICAL ASSOCIATION
  candidate's agent, as, 249
POLITICAL PARTY
  accounting requirements—
    financial year: meaning, 298n[3]
    generally, 298
    qualified auditor: meaning, 298n[5]
  campaign expenditure. See CAMPAIGN
    EXPENDITURE
  candidate—
    selection of, 254
    See also CANDIDATE (ELECTION)
  donation to—
    recognised third party. See under
      CAMPAIGN DONATION
    registered party—
      acceptance or return, 289
      exemption declaration, 311
      weekly reporting during election
        period. See weekly reporting
        during election period below
  electoral records, right to be supplied
    with, 185
  financial year: meaning, 298n[3]
  funding, report on, 3n[6]
  registered political party: meaning,
    215n[19]
  registration as condition precedent to
    participation in election, 253
  regulated transactions, weekly reporting
    during election period—
    anonymous participant in
      transaction, 312n[17]
    contents of report, 312
    generally, 312
    reporting period: meaning, 312
    Secretary of State's powers, 312
    weekly report: meaning, 312

POLITICAL PARTY—*continued*
  weekly reporting during election
    period—
    anonymous donation, 311n[15]
    content of weekly report, 311
    declaration signed by responsible
      officers, 311n[26]
    donations, 311
    exemption from requirement, 311
    regulated transactions. See regulated
      transactions, weekly reporting
      during election period *above*
    reporting period: meaning, 311
    Secretary of State's powers, 311
    specified election period: meaning,
      311n[44]
    weekly report: meaning, 311
POLL
  parish or community meeting,
    consequent on. See POLL
    CONSEQUENT ON PARISH OR
    COMMUNITY MEETING
  right to vote in—
    parish or community meeting,
      consequent on, 106
    Welsh Ministers' function, as to
      exercise of, 105
  Welsh Ministers, as to functions. See
    WELSH MINISTERS (poll as to
    functions)
POLL CONSEQUENT ON PARISH OR
  COMMUNITY MEETING
  meaning, 581
  appointment to office, on question of—
    public notice, duty to give, 212
    uncontested poll, procedure at, 478
  ballot paper—
    false answers to questions put,
      offence, 619
    form of, 607n[3]
    inadvertently spoilt, 625
    marked by presiding officer, 622
    official mark, 607
    procedure after receiving, 620
    questions to be put to voters, 619
    sealing up of papers, 656
    stamping of, 620
    tendered ballot paper, 624
    See also BALLOT PAPER
  candidate's withdrawal, 265
  challenging voter, on suspicion of
    personation, 400, 621
  circumstances for, 581
  close of poll—
    procedure on, 405, 626
    sealing up of ballot papers, 495, 626

POLL CONSEQUENT ON PARISH OR
    COMMUNITY
    MEETING—*continued*
conduct of, rules for, 383n[6], 556
counting agent, 394n[7]
counting of votes—
    appointment of persons for, 614
    arrangements for, 424, 646
    attendance at, 646
    ballot paper void for uncertainty, 430
    casting of lots in event of tie, 434
    conclusiveness of counting officer's
        decision, 649
    conclusiveness of returning officer's
        decision, 432, 649
    counting and recording number of
        ballot papers, 647
    counting observer, 614
    duly returned postal ballot paper,
        647n[10]
    equality of votes, 651
    facilities for overseeing proceedings,
        provision of, 646
    generally, 425
    recount, 433, 650
    refreshments etc during, 647
    rejected ballot papers, grounds for—
        generally, 648
        lack of official mark, 427
        mark identifying voter, 429
        uncertainty, paper void for, 430
        unmarked paper, 430
        voting for too many candidates,
            428
    time provisions, 647
    verification of ballot paper accounts,
        425, 647, 740
day of—
    abortive poll, where, 210
    power to fix, 582
    timing, 582
death of candidate, effect, 210, 516,
    520
declaration of result, 483, 655
disabled voter, assistance from
    companion, 402, 623
documents relating to—
    delivery of documents to registration
        officer, 657
    order for production or inspection,
        512, 659
    retention and public inspection, 659
    retention and supply, 507
    transfer, 498
expenses incurred, 589
extent of, 585

POLL CONSEQUENT ON PARISH OR
    COMMUNITY
    MEETING—*continued*
hours of polling, 615
illiterate voter, assistance from
    companion, 402
interfering with voter, offence, 620
keeping of order at, 617
manner of voting at, 591
notice of, 212, 388, 583, 608
personation, offence, 621
polling agent, 394n[8]
polling station—
    admission to, 618
    allotment of electors to, 610
    counting observers, appointment, 614
    equipment, 611, 612
    exclusion of persons from, 618
    hours of polling, 615
    keeping of order at, 617
    loan of equipment, 612
    misconduct in, 617
    notice for guidance of voters, 611
    polling observers, appointment, 614
    presiding officers, appointment of,
        613
    provision of sufficient numbers, 610
    removal of person from, 617
    rooms, use of, 610
    See also POLLING STATION
power to demand, 15
proxy voter, requiring assistance due to
    incapacity, 623
questioning, 763
returning officer—
    appointment, 356, 588
    duty to deliver documents, 657
    notice given by, 356, 588
right to demand, 581
right to vote in, 106
sealing of ballot boxes, 616, 626
secret ballot, 606
transfer of documents relating to, 498
vote counting. *See* counting of votes
    above
voting procedure, 620
voting system, 342

POLLING
combined polls—
    costs, apportionment of, 17
    counting agent, 394
    elections and local authority
        referendum in England, 31
    elections for related areas, 30
    examples, 16
    expenses at, 17

POLLING—*continued*
　combined polls—*continued*
　　general provision, 16
　　incapacitated person, marking or
　　　paper, 401
　　local authority referendum and
　　　election in England, 27
　　local authority referendums in
　　　England, 32
　　local authority mayoral election and
　　　elections for related electoral
　　　areas, 29
　　local government election and
　　　European parliamentary general
　　　election, 24
　　mayoral, European, parliamentary
　　　and local government elections,
　　　26
　　not permitted, where, 25
　　official poll cards, 389
　　parish or community council elections
　　　not to be combined with certain
　　　other elections,25
　　parliamentary and European
　　　parliamentary general elections,
　　　21
　　parliamentary general election and
　　　local government election, 22
　　permissible combinations, 16
　　polling agent, 394
　　polling stations, 19
　　postal ballots, proceedings on issue
　　　and receipt of, 20, 408
　　presiding officers and clerks at polling
　　　station, 393
　　related areas, elections for, 16, 28
　　transfer of returning officer's
　　　functions, 18
　　vote counting at—
　　　European parliamentary election,
　　　　465–468
　　　local authority mayor, 435
　　　London Authority election, 443
　　　London Mayor, 451
　　　parliamentary or local government
　　　　election, 425
　　　Welsh Assembly election, 458
　　Welsh Assembly general election and
　　　local government election, 23
　hours of, 385
　official poll cards, issue, 389
　polling agent, appointment, 394
　polling district. *See* POLLING DISTRICT
　polling place. *See* POLLING PLACE
　polling station. *See* POLLING STATION

POLLING DISTRICT
　European parliamentary election, for,
　　349
　local government election, at, 347
　parliamentary election, at—
　　alteration, 343
　　division of constituency into
　　　districts, 343
　　generally, 343
　　polling place, as, 344
　　relevant authority: meaning, 343n[3]
　　review, 345, 346
　Welsh Assembly election, at, 348
POLLING PLACE
　European parliamentary election, for,
　　349
　parliamentary election, at—
　　designation of polling place, 344
　　review, 345, 346
　Welsh Assembly election, at, 348
POLLING STATION
　adjournment of proceedings, 396
　allotment of electors to, 390
　attendance at, 395
　ballot box. *See* BALLOT BOX
　clerks at, 393
　close of poll at, procedure on, 405
　equipment at—
　　loan of, 392
　　provision of, 391
　exclusion of persons at, 395
　local authority referendum. *See* LOCAL
　　AUTHORITY REFERENDUM
　local government election, at, 347
　misconduct at, 396
　notices at, 391
　order at, duty to keep, 396
　poll consequent on parish or community
　　meeting. *See* POLL CONSEQUENT ON
　　PARISH OR COMMUNITY MEETING
　　(polling station)
　polling agent, 394
　presiding officer at, 393
　provision of, 390
　questions to be put to person applying
　　for ballot paper at, 398
　removal of persons from, 396
　riot etc at, 396
　voters at, regulation of numbers, 395
　voting procedure, 399
POSTAL BALLOT PAPER
　meaning, 407n[1]
　ballot box. *See under* POSTAL VOTE
　ballot paper envelope, 410n[8]
　cancelled paper, retrieval, 420
　combined poll, 20, 406, 408

References are to paragraph numbers; superior figures refer to notes

References are to paragraph numbers; superior figures refer to notes

REGISTRATION OF
    ELECTORS—*continued*
service declaration—
    appropriate registration officer,
        transmission to, 128n[2]
    cancellation, 126
    conditions, power to prescribe, 126n[3]
    effect, 130
    entitlement to make, 126
    formalities associated with, 127
    guidance for service voters, 131
    invalid declaration, 129
    offence as to, 138, 735
    service voter: meaning, 126n[4]
    transmission, 128
service qualification, 125
termination of entitlement to be
    registered—
    anonymous entry, 171
    determining non-residence, 169n[5]
    information-seeking powers, 169n[13]
    local government elector, 169
    notional residence or voter's
        declaration, 170
    parliamentary elector, 169
    prescribed requirements for removal,
        169n[15]
voter declaration—
    offences associated with, 138
    overseas elector's declaration. *See*
        overseas elector's declaration
        above
    service declaration. *See* service
        declaration *above*
    termination of entitlement to be
        registered, 170

REGISTRATION OFFICER
    meaning, 139n[1]
    absent voter—
        lists, duty to keep, 373
        notice in writing to, 141n[17], 366
        records, duty to keep, 370
        removal of persons from register, 370
    advance on account of expenses, request
        for, 144
    annual canvass—
        duty to conduct, 151, 154
        See further under REGISTRATION OF
            ELECTORS
    anonymous entries, duty to keep record
        of, 143
    appeal against decision. *See*
        REGISTRATION OF ELECTORS
        (appeals)
    appointment, 139
    assistants, 140

REGISTRATION OFFICER—*continued*
    breach of official duty, penalty for, 737
    data protection duties, 141n[4]
    deputies, 140
    duties, 141, 143
    electoral participation, encouragement
        of—
        generally, 141
        reimbursement of expenditure
            incurred, 144n[10]
    expenses, payment of, 144
    fees paid to, duty to account for, 144
    generally, 139
    individual electoral registration duties.
        See REGISTRATION OF ELECTORS
    information-gathering powers, 142
    inspection powers, 142
    interference with duties, as election
        offence, 733
    list of overseas electors, preparation and
        publication, 143
    local counting area, 139n[1]
    maintenance of registers, 142, 143
    objectives, duty to secure, 141
    peers entitled to vote, preparation etc
        of, 143
    performance standards, 57
    proxy voters, duty to keep record of,
        379
    publication duties. *See* ELECTORAL
        REGISTER (publication)
    records, right to inspect, 142
    register of electors. *See* ELECTORAL
        REGISTER
    registration area, 139n[1]
    registration of electors, duties as to. *See*
        generally under REGISTRATION OF
        ELECTORS
    supply of electoral records. *See under*
        ELECTORAL REGISTER
    vacancy in office, acts performed
        where, 140
    working practices, observation by
        Electoral Commission, 53

REMUNERATION
    Electoral Commissioner, 37

RETURNING OFFICER
    act or omission by, effect on election,
        667
    attendance at receipt of postal ballot
        papers, 416
    breach of election rules by, effect, 667
    breach of official duty, penalty for, 737
    combined polls, transfer of functions,
        18

RETURNING OFFICER—*continued*
conduct of election, duty to ensure
compliance with rules, 383
constituency returning officer—
European parliamentary election,
18n^2
London Assembly elections, 211n^9
costs, 878
counting of votes. *See* VOTE COUNTING
declaration of election result. *See* VOTE
COUNTING (declaration of result)
defect in title, 668
electoral records, right to, 182
European parliamentary election, for—
deputies, appointment, 360
designation, 360
detailed assessment of account at,
362
duties, 360
encouragement of electoral
participation, 360, 361
expenses, recovery, 361n$^{5, 18}$
functions, 360
local returning officer, designation,
360
payments by and to, 361
list of lost postal ballot papers, duty to
keep, 415
list of spoilt postal ballot papers, duty
to keep, 414
local government election, for—
designation of, 354
discharge of functions, 354
encouragement of electoral
participation, 354, 355
expenses incurred by, reimbursement
etc, 355
voting by, 354
Wales, in, 354
nomination paper—
decisions as to validity of, 264
duties generally, 255
errors, correction of, 265
grounds for holding paper invalid,
263
See also NOMINATION PAPER
notice of election, duty to publish—
European parliamentary election, 223
local government election, 211
parliamentary election, 196
notice of poll, duties, 388
official poll cards, issue of, 389
parliamentary election, for—
meaning, 350
act or omission by, effect on election,
350

RETURNING OFFICER—*continued*
parliamentary election, for—*continued*
advance on account of charges, 352
detailed assessment etc of account,
353
discharge of functions, 351
duties, 350
encouragement of electoral
participation, 350, 352
execution of writ for, 350
expenses, recovery of, 352n^9
payments by and to, 352
persons who can be, 350
recovery of charges, 352
sheriff as, death of, 350n^5
performance standards, 57
poll consequent on parish etc meeting,
356
polling stations—
duty to provide, 390
presiding at, 393
presiding officer and clerk at, duty to
appoint, 393
See also POLLING STATION
postal voting—
ballot boxes etc, duty to provide, 417
postal ballot paper, duty to issue, 406
receptacles, duty to provide, 417
security and secrecy, duty to ensure,
417
secret ballot, duty to ensure, 385, 395
statement of persons nominated, duty to
publish, 267
Welsh Assembly election, for—
designation, 357
detailed assessment etc of account,
359
duties, 357
encouragement of electoral
participation, 357, 358
expenses, recovery of, 358n$^{5, 6, 19}$
payments by and to, 358
working practices, observation by
Electoral Commission, 53

RIGHT TO VOTE
British citizens overseas, extension of
franchise to, 96
elector: meaning, 95n^2
European parliamentary election. *See
under* EUROPEAN PARLIAMENTARY
ELECTION
generally, 385
legal incapacity, person subject to, 95n^8
local government election, 97
mayoral election, 98
parliamentary election, at, 95, 96

References are to paragraph numbers; superior figures refer to notes

STOP NOTICE
meaning, 759n[2]
cessation, 759n[12]
completion certificate, application for,
759n[12]

SUMMARY PROCEEDINGS
Electoral Commission's power to
impose, 759
Political Parties, Elections and
Referendums Act 200, offence
under, 892

THIRD PARTY
expenditure during national
parliamentary election. *See*
CONTROLLED EXPENDITURE
(NATIONAL ELECTION)

TREATING
meaning, 721
avoidance of election, 895
bribery distinguished, 710
corruption as essence of, 722
custom, whether relevant, 722
dissolution of Parliament, prior to, 722
examples, 721
local authority referendum, avoidance
of, 897
persons guilty of corrupt practice, 724
refreshments, provision of, 722
striking off on vote on scrutiny, 842
time of, 722

UNDUE INFLUENCE (VOTING)
meaning, 723
acquiescence by official, 728
examples, 723
force, violence or restraint, 724
fraudulent device or contrivance, 727
persons guilty of corrupt practice, 723
spiritual influence, 726
striking off on vote on scrutiny, 842
temporal influence, 725
threat of violence etc, 724

UNIVERSAL POSTAL SERVICE
parliamentary writs list, duties in respect
of, 193

VOTE COUNTING
counting agent, appointment of, 394
declaration of result—
community council election, 482
European parliamentary election, 493
local authority referendum, 652
local government election, 482
London Authority election, 486, 487
Mayor of London, 488
mayoral election, 484
parliamentary election, 479

VOTE COUNTING—*continued*
declaration of result—*continued*
poll consequent on parish meeting,
483
Welsh assembly election—
constituency election, 490
regional election, 491
European parliamentary election—
arrangements for counting, 467
attendance at count, 467
by-election, 467
calculation and allocation of seats,
473
combined poll, 467, 468
conclusiveness of returning officer's
decision, 470
counting procedure, 468
duly returned postal ballot paper,
466n[5]
facilities for overseeing proceedings,
provision of, 467
notification provisions, 467
procedure at conclusion of count,
472
public statement of votes given etc,
472
recount, 471
refreshments etc at count, 468
rejected ballot papers, 469
verification of paper ballot accounts—
arrangements for, 465
attendance at, 465
combined poll, 465, 466
offence, 740
procedure, 466
local authority referendum. *See* LOCAL
AUTHORITY REFERENDUM (counting
of votes)
local government election. *See*
parliamentary or local government
election *below*
London Authority election—
arrangements for count, 443
attendance at verification and
counting of votes, 443
calculation of figure for allocation of
London member seats, 450
combined poll, 443
conclusion of count, procedure at—
constituency members, return of,
448
London members, return of, 449
constituency or London members,
return of—
conclusiveness of returning officer's
decision, 446

WELSH ASSEMBLY
ELECTION—*continued*
election agent—*continued*
sub-agent, nomination, 237
election expenses. *See* ELECTION
EXPENSES
election meeting. *See* ELECTION MEETING
electoral regions—
establishment, 76
review, 90
extraordinary general election, 214
financial controls. *See* ELECTION
(financial controls)
first meeting of new Assembly, 213n[6]
generally, 12
legal incapacity, person subject to, 95n[8], 110
legislation, 3n[2]
manner of voting at, 364
meeting. *See* ELECTION MEETING
nomination—
nomination paper. *See* NOMINATION
PAPER
proceedings, 261
validity, 262, 263
See also under CANDIDATE (ELECTION)
notice of election, 216
notice of poll, 388
official poll cards, 389
ordinary general election, 12, 213
petition questioning. *See* ELECTION
PETITION (Welsh Assembly election
petition)
polling district at, 348
polling place at, 348
polling station. *See* POLLING STATION
procedure, 12
questioning—
grounds for, 764
petition. *See* ELECTION PETITION
(Welsh Assembly election
petition)
time limits, 768

WELSH ASSEMBLY
ELECTION—*continued*
registration officer. *See* REGISTRATION
OFFICER
returning officer. *See under* RETURNING
OFFICER
right to vote—
generally, 99
See also RIGHT TO VOTE
uncontested, procedure at, 476
vacancy, filling—
constituency seats, 214
electoral region seats, 215
person filling vacancy, notification of
name to Presiding Officer,
215n[36]
vote counting. *See under* VOTE
COUNTING
voting system—
additional member system, 340
corrective system of calculation, 340
generally, 339, 340
WELSH MINISTERS
Boundary Commission, power to make
appointments, 72
mayoral election—
power to make regulations as to, 198
vacancy in office, 203
poll as to functions—
conduct of poll, provision as to, 664
how functions should be exercised,
662
persons entitled to vote, 663
whether functions should be
exercised, 662
review of electoral arrangements,
statutory rules to be observed, 89
WITNESS
election court, at. *See* ELECTION COURT
(witness)
WRIT
parliamentary election. *See under*
PARLIAMENTARY ELECTION

Words and Phrases

Words in parentheses indicate the context in which the word or phrase is used

material time (vote counting at European parliamentary election), 467n[5]

mayoral election, 383n[14]

mayoral elections rules, 383n[14]

meeting room (for use during elections), 334n[15], 337n[15]

MEP, 91n[5]

minor party, 253n[8]

moratorium period—
(local authority referendum held in England), 560n[5]
(local authority referendum held in Wales), 560n[18]

municipal election in the City of London, 33n[6]

national election agent, 239n[5]

new application for registration, 156n[5]

nominating officer, 204n[30]

nominating party, 35n[16]

notice period (local authority referendum), 564n[9]

notification date (local authority referendum held in Wales), 574

objection (electoral registration), 161n[1]

official duty (officers at election), 737

ordinary council-election day, 80n[13]

ordinary day of election, 198n[9]

ordinary general election to the National Assembly for Wales, 319n[9]

outcome (referendum), 529n[13]

outline fall-back proposals (local authority referendum), 568n[15], 574n[16]

overseas elector, 100n[12]

overseas elector's declaration, 100n[12]

parish or community election, 253n[3]

parliamentary election, 9

parliamentary writs list, 193

party list candidate, 230n[23]

penal institution, 107n[2]

pending boundary report, 78n[9]

permitted participant (referendum), 529

person standing for election in name of registered party, 253n[8]

personal expenses, 271n[3]

personal identifiers record, 366

petition date (local authority referendum), 563n[11]

petition organiser (local authority referendum), 561n[6], 614n[5]

petition period (local authority referendum held in Wales), 560n[18]

policy development grant, 60n[3]

poll, 3n[4]

poll consequent on parish or community meeting, 581

polling, 3n[4]

polling day, 3n[4]

polling observers, 614

postal ballot box, 417

postal ballot paper, 407n[1], 628n[4]

postal voters' ballot box, 417

postal voters list, 373n[7]

post-announcement petition, 561n[7]

pre-election year, 92n[1]

principal area council election, 18n[2]

principal or only place of work, 225n[12]

procuring an office (bribery), 709n[6]

promoter (election publication), 748n[7]

property (donation to candidate), 286n[3]

proposals date (local authority referendum), 574n[13]

proxy postal voters list, 381n[6]

publication—
(election material), 287n[20], 325n[20]
(referendum material), 546n[25]

publish—
(election material), 749n[2]
(exit poll), 744n[1]
(referendum promotional material), 579n[5], 750n[3]

qualifying registered party, 253n[8]

recognised third party (in relation to national election), 313n[15], 314

recommendations as to single-member electoral areas, 83n[40]

record of anonymous entries, 148n[12]

recordable donation (weekly report), 311n[14]

recriminatory case, 837

recriminatory evidence, 837

referendum—
(Local Authorities (Elected Mayors) (Elections, Terms of Office and Casual Vacancies) (England) Regulations 2012), 198n[16]
(Local Government Act 2000), 574n[2, 13]
(Political Parties, Elections and Referendums Act 2000), 527
(Representation of the People (Combination of Polls) (England and Wales) Regulations 2004), 18n[1]

referendum area, 533n[6]

referendum campaign, 535n[4]

referendum campaign broadcast, 552

referendum expenses, 535, 577

referendum period (local authority referendum), 574n[11]

referendum petition, 766

referendum question, 528n[3]